W9-BBD-521

THE HORIZON HISTORY OF AFRICA

PUBLISHED BY AMERICAN HERITAGE PUBLISHING CO. INC., NEW YORK

A. ADU BOAHEN
J. DESMOND CLARK
JOHN HENRIK CLARKE
PHILIP D. CURTIN
BASIL DAVIDSON
STANLAKE SAMKANGE
STUART SCHAAR
GEORGE SHEPPERSON
MARGARET SHINNIE
JAN VANSINA
IMMANUEL WALLERSTEIN
JOHN RALPH WILLIS
JOHN HENRIK CLARKE, CONSULTANT
ELLIOTT P. SKINNER, CONSULTANT
ALVIN M. JOSEPHY, JR., EDITOR IN CHARGE
WENDY BUEHR, MANAGING EDITOR

THE HORIZON HISTORY OF AFRICA

RAPHO-GUILLUMETTE—SABINE WEISS

ABOVE: *Berbers, harried by a sandstorm, scurry for cover at an oasis in Tunisia's hinterland.*

TITLE PAGE: *A Uganda shepherd guides his Ankoli cattle, still legal currency in his country.*
PHOTO RESEARCHERS—ARTHUR GRIFFIN

Library of Congress Catalog Card Number: 75-149732
ISBN: Regular Edition 07-030342-8; Deluxe Edition (2 volumes, slipcased) 07-030343-6

Contents

THE EMERGENCE OF AFRICAN HISTORY

By Philip D. Curtin

HISTORY HAS ALL TOO OFTEN been an ethnocentric subject written (often intentionally) to foster patriotism by emphasizing the deeds of ancestors. In Europe and North America this tendency has led historians to concentrate on national history, looking only secondly at the broader developments of Western civilization. Cultures beyond the West were either left out altogether or relegated to a minor place. The crucial and organizing question was "How do we come to be as we are?"—not "How did the modern world come to be as it is?" or "How do human societies change through time?"

African history fell under this blight, as did the histories of pre-Columbian America and of Asia. For Americans, "ancestors" include Africans as well as Europeans, but there has been a tendency to sweep the African heritage under the rug in a general pattern of Jim Crow history, negating the role of black Americans in the national life. Africa crept into the ken of European national interest during the colonial period, when Britain, France, Belgium, Portugal, and other nations had political commitments that seemed to call for a knowledge of the African past. But the African history these outsiders wrote tended to be colonial history, emphasizing the role of missionaries, merchants, administrators, explorers, and settlers.

Then, in the aftermath of World War II, people woke to the fact that relations between the Western and the non-Western world were rapidly changing. In Africa the drive for independence swept from North Africa to the south and east, where it stabilized in the early 1960's. Historians in and out of Africa began to take another look. Most had assumed that African history could not be investigated beyond the colonial fringe because it had to do with preliterate societies. In this they were three-times wrong. Most Africans before the colonial period lived in societies that were literate, at least to the extent of having a literate class of scribes or clerics. Even societies that were nonliterate often had a retrievable oral history. Finally, a good deal of African history had been written.

The "discovery" of African history after 1950 can be likened to the discovery of Victoria Falls or Mount Kenya by a European "explorer": its existence was suddenly publicized abroad, but the Africans knew it was there all along. Many African societies had institutions for preserving and transmitting oral traditions, but, even beyond that, Western-educated Africans had long been recording, gathering, and translating key works in Arabic by native writers on both sides of the Sahara. A small number of anthropologists, colonial administrators, and amateur historians also became fascinated by the depth and breadth of the subject. Working often in isolation, these people mapped the main lines of African history as it is still understood.

This is not to underplay the contribution of the last two decades. Intensive research has multiplied our knowledge of the African past many times over. And the new African history is not simply a matter of unearthing more data. Modern historians have new questions and new attitudes. Some are Africans seeking to integrate the modernizing present with its roots in the past. Others are non-Africans who have found that Africa's recent strides require new explanations, raising issues no one thought to consider at the high noon of colonialism.

Equally important, the study of history itself is changing. The ethnocentric bias is weakening, which means that historians—both African and non-African—have begun trying to see African history in the perspective of human history as a whole. The first step is to take an Africa-centered view of African history, and this adjustment is more difficult and more dramatic than one might suppose. It is not enough to turn colonial heroes into villains and resistance leaders into heroes. Instead, historians often have to go back to the original sources with new questions about the dynamics of African societies: "What recurrent patterns of change existed there that may have been different from those of the West?" "Why did various African societies react differently to the Western challenge?"

Much of the new, Afro-centric history could be written using European works, colonial records, travelers' accounts, and the like. It is simply a matter of taking a new point of departure. For example, instead of asking why the British took a certain line of policy in Uganda, the contemporary historian asks why the Ganda people reacted a certain way to conquest by Britain. Both questions are important to an understanding of the colonial period, but both had been seldom asked by the same analyst.

Along with the new attitudes have come new techniques. Before 1950 very little archeological work had been done in tropical Africa, but then the newly established governments and their universities began to sponsor research. With techniques like radiocarbon dating to place basic changes in material culture, such critical revolutions as the beginning of the iron age could be traced.

The new research techniques soon began to interact with a broadening field of historiography. Botanical history, for example, has a special importance in Africa, which was poor in indigenous, cultivable plants. The introduction of plants from southeast Asia and, much later, the Americas, brought to the African regions greater mastery of the environment and a food surplus over the needs of the farmers, leading to denser populations and the possibility of urban life, with its more complex civilization. Botanical history, therefore, becomes an important part of general history. In addition, historians came to realize that disease environments have differed throughout the world and that these differences influenced the way people moved about. As a result, disease was linked to migration, and Africa's demographic history could be explained by findings of epidemiologists. And much of the best evidence used so far to determine the movements of peoples within Africa has been provided by still another discipline: the study of languages.

Even more than new attitudes and new techniques, the new African history continues to explore the great riches of oral tradition. Most African societies have a sense of history and often a professional class of minstrels who remember and recite their communal past; but even where no professional class exists, many people are still alive who can remember the early years of the colonial period. And where Islamic civilization is found, African societies also have a literate tradition. This means documents written in Arabic (or in other African languages using Arabic characters) have often survived and are now beginning to be collected systematically. When these sources are used in combination with the reports of Europeans (who have, after all, been frequenting all the coasts of Africa since the beginning of the sixteenth century), it is possible to reconstruct far more of African history than anyone imagined only a few decades ago.

This work of recovery is far from complete, but the pages that follow will demonstrate its new depth. Africa no longer appears as a changeless continent lost in "barbarism"; rather, the reader will find that Africa has experienced a pace and quality of change similar to the pace and quality of change in human history as a whole. Nor is it split across the middle of the Sahara, divided into a White Africa to the north and a Black Africa to the south. Neither history nor color lent itself to such strict demarcations. North African history is, indeed, crucial to understanding the past of sub-Saharan Africa, for it forms a key link between Black Africa and the great bloc of intercommunicating civilizations stretching from the Mediterranean to China; Africa's relationship to this bloc of civilizations is often the key to understanding Africa's place in the history of mankind.

WHERE THERE ARE PEOPLE, THERE IS HISTORY

"Africa is no vast island. . . . She has been closely connected, both as source and nourisher, with some of the most potent influences which have affected for good the history of the world." So wrote Edward Blyden, a prominent black nationalist of the nineteenth century. The world's second largest continent was probably the birthplace of man. From its tropical rain forests, silvery velds, undulating savannas, and parched deserts have sprung hundreds of societies whose traditions and histories have been handed down from generation to generation. In ancient times Africa was the "granary" of the Roman empire—a number of whose officials, including an emperor, were Africans. Monasticism, a vital Christian institution, was born on African soil. And out of Africa came the spectacular civilization of Moorish Spain. From Africa, also, came the inspiration for both jazz and cubism. In many ways, then, Africa's history is mankind's history, of import to all. It is the brilliant past of over 237,000,000 people that forms the story of this book.

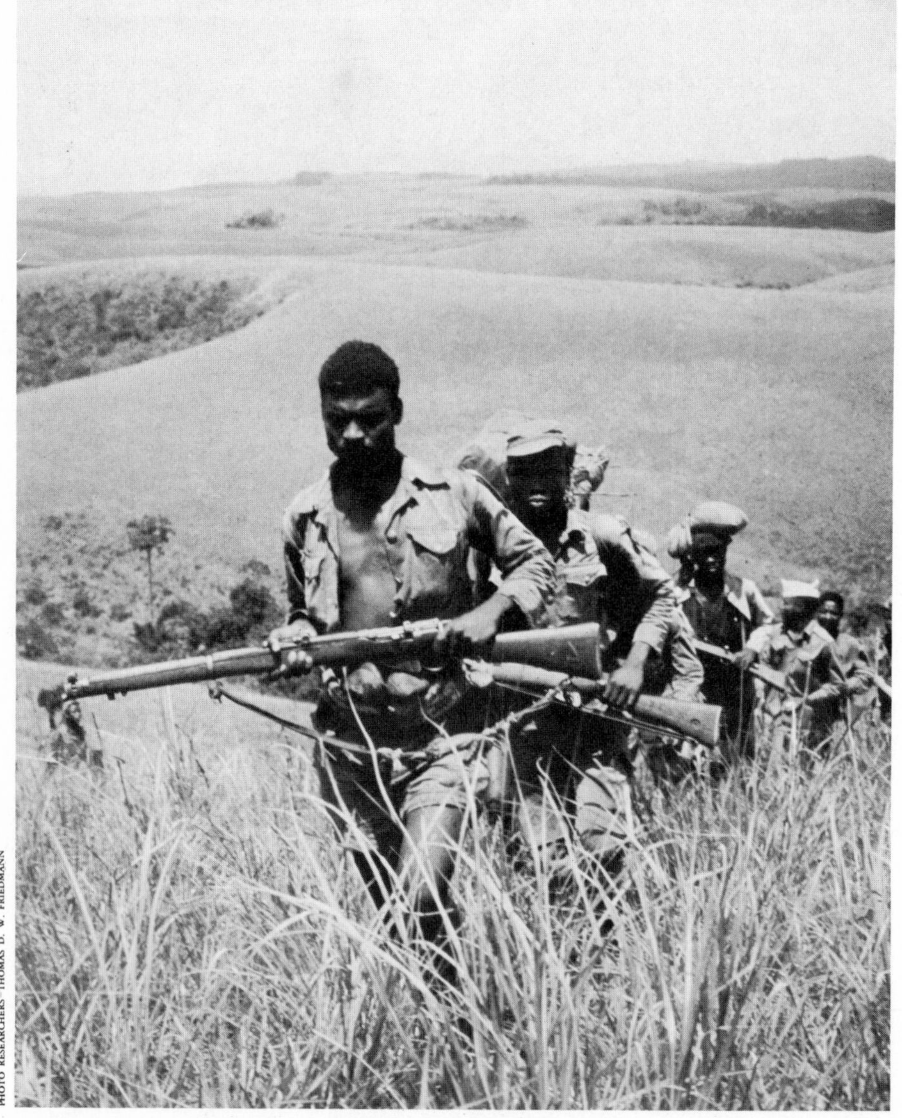

PHOTO RESEARCHERS–THOMAS D. W. FRIEDMANN

Today's Africans, like those pictured in this portfolio, are maintaining many ancient traditions, but are also taking on the challenge of modernization and self-rule. Left, rebels of the 1960's patrol in northern Angola, where their forefathers resisted the Portuguese for five hundred years; opposite, children play below the guardian angel of a seventeenth-century Coptic church at Gondar, one of the pillars of Ethiopia's Christian heritage; page 10 *education reaches Kenya youth via a rural school;* 11 *Congolese copper miners end their shift;* 12 *the emir of Kano, the ruler of over two million Nigerians, exits from his one hundred-fifty year old palace;* 13 *South African gold miners perform an age-old dance;* 14–15 *a Mauritanian nomad, the descendant of men who controlled the rich trans-Saharan trade, confronts the endless desert.*

9 RAPHO-GUILLUMETTE–MARC AND EVELYNE BERNHEIM; 10 MAGNUM–GEORGE RODGER; 11 *Life* MAGAZINE © TIME INC.–DMITRI KESSEL; 12 MAGNUM–GEORGE RODGER; 13, 14–15 BOTH: RAPHO-GUILLUMETTE–MARC AND EVELYNE BERNHEIM.

Tiki nan buk.
Bole kume ilot.
Möji Pioŋ

Chapter One

AFRICAN BEGINNINGS

by

J. Desmond Clark

FOR CENTURIES MAN'S IMAGINATION has been captured by attempts, usually fanciful, to establish the exact locality of the place of origin of the human race—the paradise of ancient mythology. Scientific research of the last few decades, carried out by archeologists, paleontologists, and workers in allied disciplines, is making it increasingly likely that the legendary birthplace was somewhere on the African continent, probably south of the Sahara.

Today Africa is the home of many human cultural traditions, ranging from simple hunting societies to elaborate urban civilizations—a result of interaction over many millenniums and the selective use of the potentialities of the different environments. Indeed, the single most powerful influence on the lives of men, as of other creatures, is the environment in which they live. Temperature, rainfall and its distribution throughout the year—in short, climate—together with the kind of plant communities, the associated animal life, the availability of surface water sources or of economically important minerals not only shape the tenor of man's daily life but have been significant influences on his biological evolution.

Animals and plants are adapted to living in a particular habitat through natural selection and competition. Some creatures have succeeded in adapting to several different ecological niches, but by reason of man's culture and technology, only he and some life forms dependent upon him have been able to make adjustments that permit him to live anywhere he wants to in the world.

Man's emancipation from environmental controls has been a comparatively gradual process, though one of steadily quickening tempo. For nine tenths or so of human history, however, the rate of biological and cultural progress was extremely slow, almost imperceptible; only in the past

Mankind's birthplace; lowering skies over an African savanna

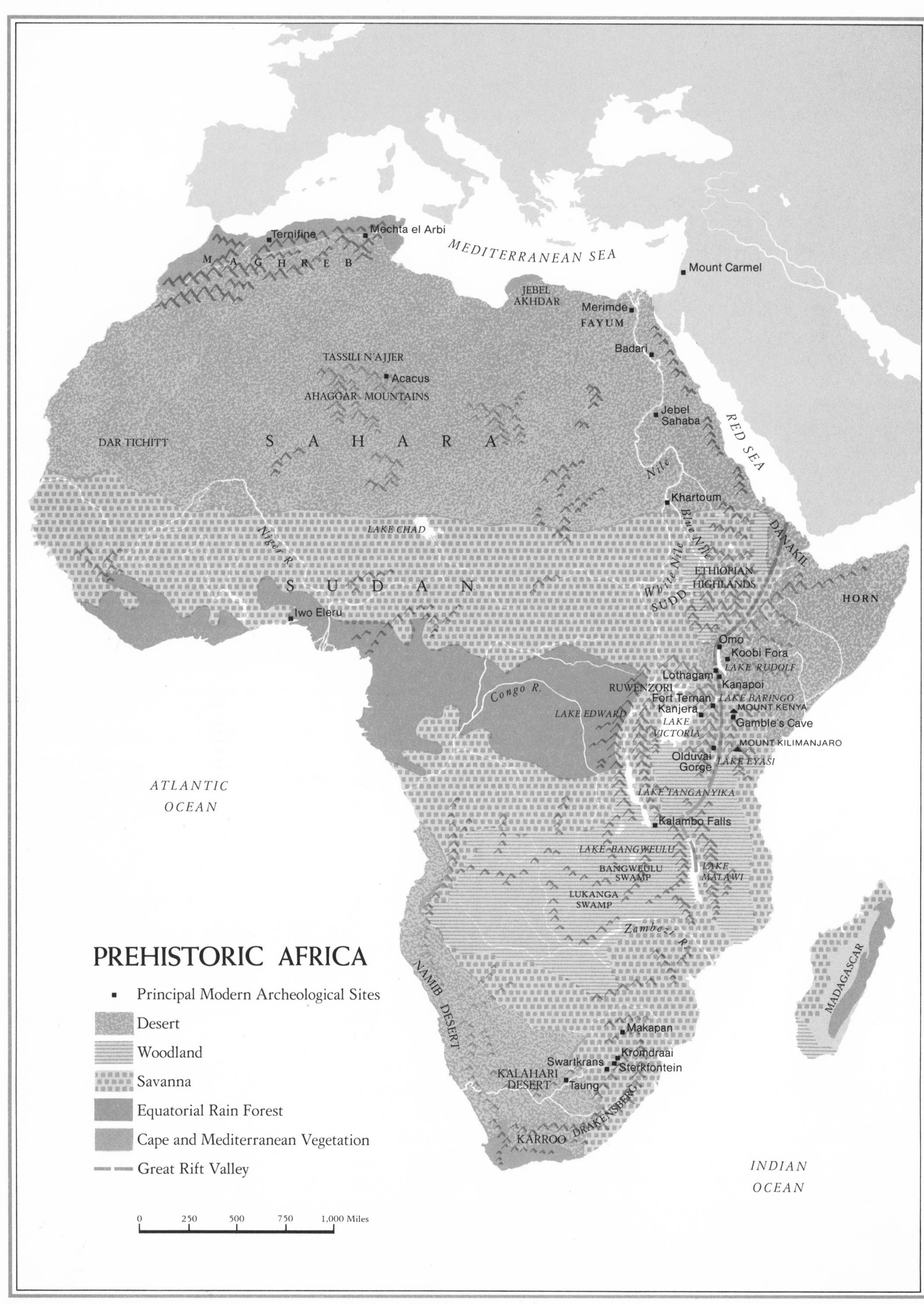

PREHISTORIC AFRICA
Principal Modern Archeological Sites
Desert
Woodland
Savanna
Equatorial Rain Forest
Cape and Mediterranean Vegetation
Great Rift Valley
0 250 500 750 1,000 Miles
MEDITERRANEAN SEA
ATLANTIC OCEAN
INDIAN OCEAN
RED SEA
Ternifine
Mechta el Arbi
M A G H R E B
Mount Carmel
JEBEL AKHDAR
Merimde
FAYUM
Badari
TASSILI N'AJJER
Acacus
AHAGGAR MOUNTAINS
Jebel Sahaba
DAR TICHITT
S A H A R A
Nile
Khartoum
LAKE CHAD
Niger R.
Blue Nile
DANAKIL
White Nile
ETHIOPIAN HIGHLANDS
S U D A N
SUDD
HORN
Iwo Eleru
Omo
Koobi Fora
LAKE RUDOLF
Lothagam
Kanapoi
RUWENZORI
Fort Ternan
LAKE BARINGO
Congo R.
Kanjera
MOUNT KENYA
Gamble's Cave
LAKE EDWARD
LAKE VICTORIA
MOUNT KILIMANJARO
Olduvai Gorge
LAKE EYASI
LAKE TANGANYIKA
Kalambo Falls
LAKE BANGWEULU
BANGWEULU SWAMP
LAKE MALAWI
LUKANGA SWAMP
Zambezi R.
MADAGASCAR
NAMIB DESERT
Makapan
Kromdraai
Swartkrans
Sterkfontein
KALAHARI DESERT
Taung
DRAKENSBERG
KARROO

few thousand years has man developed the abilities that make possible today's sophisticated urban civilizations. Nonetheless, man remains an integral part, though by far the most influential part, of the many different eco-systems in which he lives, and he now has it in his power to destroy or to conserve and improve them. Moreover, from the beginning man's relationship with his environment was one in which he always had the freedom to choose how he could make best use of the natural resources and which of them he should select.

It is the possession of a rational intellect and of culture—the ability to manufacture artifacts and the skill to use them—that gives man the opportunity to exploit the resources offered by the different habitats, and this finds expression in the patterns of behavior that control the lives of every human community. Depending on social, legal, and religious sanctions, all of which affect the way a population reacts to innovations and the pressures of external influences, a culture may be sympathetic or conservative in its acceptance and modification of new beliefs, tastes, or technologies.

In any community the cultural tradition is made up of the social structure, the economic pattern, the learned ways of behavior, and the influence on these of technology and material culture—all of which are handed down from one generation to the next. For example, in Africa the peoples south of the Sahara may be separated generally into two geographical culture areas: those in the south and east, where hunting, wild food gathering, and the herding of livestock determine the culture; those in West Africa and Equatoria, where the economy is based upon cultivation by sedentary populations. The ways of life of the peoples in each of these main culture areas are broadly similar except where historical interaction has brought about some modification or displacement.

The concept of culture areas is of great value for the study of cultural evolution. Except in the latest, prehistoric periods, however, little evidence, other than the less perishable parts of the material culture, has survived. But as research becomes more advanced, archeology—the science that seeks to interpret these material remains—is able to provide a time perspective for some of the culture areas. An understanding of the main geographical regions of the continent is not only essential to an explanation of the varied ways of life of the African peoples today but is even more important for understanding the evolution of man and his culture in prehistoric times and his preference for and selection of some habitats rather than others.

Geographically, Africa can be divided roughly into a highland and a lowland zone by drawing a line from the mouth of the Congo river in the west to the Ethiopia-Sudan border in the east. South of this line, High Africa comprises mainly an interior plateau, most of it between 3,000 and 5,000 feet above sea level, but with higher ridges and mountains. The bedrock is formed of pre-Cambrian crystalline metamorphic rocks that also commonly obtrude, and some of them provide important sources of mineral wealth. North of our imaginary line, Low Africa composed largely of plains and basins of sedimentation in which are found the younger sedimentary rocks of Cretaceous and early Tertiary periods, is generally between 500 and 2,000 feet above sea level.

In the depressions on the plateau are large, relatively shallow lakes and swamps containing a seemingly inexhaustible supply of fish and, formerly, large numbers of hippopotamuses. The major rivers have their sources in the higher mountain ranges, from which they descend to undulating savanna, meandering in broad, deep valleys until they reach the escarpments, where they fall in a series of rapids and waterfalls, often through narrow gorges, to the coastal plains. Thus, the rivers are never navigable for any great distance from their mouths. This feature was directly responsible for the general failure of alien peoples—travelers, traders, soldiers, and geographers—from classical times into the nineteenth century to penetrate the interior and relay knowledge concerning the country and its inhabitants to the outside world.

The eastern part of Africa is split by a huge trough, or fault, that runs nearly the whole length of the continent. This is the Great Rift Valley, which starts in Asia, in Syria, and continues southward down the Red Sea, through Ethiopia into Kenya, Uganda, and Tanzania, and finally loses itself beneath the alluvial sediments in the lower Zambezi valley in Mozambique. In Kenya and Uganda the trough splits into the Eastern Rift and the Western Rift; in a shallow basin on the plateau between the two branches lies Lake Victoria, Africa's greatest lake.

The bottom of the Great Rift lies at extremely variable elevations. In the Danakil section of the Ethiopian Rift the bottom drops in places to nearly 400 feet below sea level, but southward the floor rises in a series of steps until in Kenya, in the Eastern Rift, the elevation is over 5,000 feet. The volcanic rocks and sediments of the area support short grasses and thorn bushes, which are highly favorable to wild game and the pastoralist way of life.

The Great Rift is a tectonically unstable zone where compression and tension of the earth's crust have pushed

Elephants, once distributed more widely in Africa than now, provided food for hunters over thousands of years. They were used in warfare long before Hannibal's day, and their tusks have been the basis of the continent's important, lucrative ivory trade.

RAPHO-GUILLUMETTE—YLLA

up the land bordering the trough into high ridges and mountains. The deeper portions of the trough are filled by great lakes, some of which, such as Lakes Tanganyika and Malawi, are among the deepest and longest in the world.

Although there exists now only one active volcano in the rift zone (Ol Doingo Lengai in Tanzania), there are numerous dormant and extinct ones, two of which—Mount Kilimanjaro (19,565 feet) and Mount Kenya (17,040 feet)—are perpetually snowcapped. Another huge snow-covered mass—this one a crystalline rock thrust of nonvolcanic origin—is the Ruwenzori range. Its highest peak, Mount Stanley, rises to 16,795 feet. The vegetation zones of the rift run in belts around the mountains, changing with altitude from rain forest at the foot to alpine tundra near the top, and the scenery is some of the most beautiful and varied in the world. The very rich fossil record preserved in the Great Rift Valley is due to the accumulation of deep sediments in the bottom of the trough and to the rapid burial of land surfaces by ash and dust from the volcanoes.

Elsewhere in Africa the climate and vegetation zones generally fall in a similar system to the north and south of a central, equatorial region of high rainfall and evergreen forest, though altitude, monsoons, and other factors have modified this pattern, especially in the eastern and southeastern parts of the continent. Africa is not the all-over forest-covered steaming jungle that popular belief often assumes it to be, and the zone of rain forest is now greatly restricted as a result of some two to three thousand years of cutting and burning by man. Most of the continent is covered by a wooded savanna where deciduous trees predominate. The further removed from the equator, the longer the winter, or dry season, lasting up to six months or more. The ubiquitous green cover, stretching over mile upon mile of undulating plateau, varies in the thickness of its tree communities from a nearly continuous canopy with only sparse grass beneath, or the gallery forest, to park land, where the grasses predominate over scattered bush.

The savanna zone north of the equatorial forest is known as the Sudan belt, and that to the south as *miombo* woodland. These savanna lands are the home of a mammalian fauna uniquely rich not only in the great variety of its species but in the size of the herds of its gregarious animals: antelopes, buffaloes, horses, elephants, and many others. The variety of this "Ethiopian fauna," as it is called, indicates the continuing favorability of the habitats in which the animals evolved over many millenniums and which we now think were also the original home of man himself.

To the north and south of the savanna belts the climate becomes drier, supporting only sparse grass and low bushes—steppelands. In turn, these give way to true desert, the Sahel grading to the Sahara in the north and the Karroo to the Namib and Kalahari deserts in the southwest.

All these tropical and subtropical regions of Africa enjoy a summer rainfall system; but in the north, along the coast of the Mediterranean, and at the southern end of the continent south of the Great Escarpment, or Drakensberg range, the country is fed by winter rains and experiences a much more temperate climate.

There is evidence for considerable past fluctuation in these vegetation zones, with their closely adapted animal communities, in response to changes in rainfall, temperature, and the intensity of winds and ocean currents. Plant and animal species and even communities, now isolated sometimes by hundreds of miles from the main center of distribution, are evidence for a previously more extended and continuous spread of these forms at a time when the climatic conditions favored this. Such changes in the habitat of prehistoric man were of considerable importance in influencing his biological and cultural evolution and thus inducing variations in the pattern of his behavior. It becomes of great importance, therefore, to be able to reconstruct past habitats in order to understand the way of life of the human populations.

There are many ways in which it is now proving possible to reconstruct Africa's past habitats, and these involve scientists in a number of different disciplines. The sedimentary history of a lake basin, a river valley, or a cave is interpreted by geologists and soil chemists. Botanists identify the microscopic pollen grains of plants, sometimes preserved in muds and silts recovered from the basins of existing and former lakes and rivers. Zoologists and paleontologists examine the assemblages of animal bones to determine to which point in the time scale these belong. By comparison with the general habitats and behavior of similar species and communities today, they can deduce what type of faunal community might have existed at that time.

It is essential to be able to arrange all these data into a logical, historical sequence within an established chronological framework. Since 1950 several methods have been developed by physicists and chemists to provide a radiometric time scale of the greatest significance. Two methods are of particular importance for African prehistory. The first is that of potassium-argon; it is based upon the measurable amount of argon in rocks rich in radioactive potassium (K40), which, over time, decays at a regular rate into the isotopes of calcium (Ca40) and argon (A40). This method is valuable for measuring the age of rocks and of formations of volcanic origin, both those that are geologically very old and quite young—as recent as a quarter of a million years or less.

Of more universal use, but more limited in time range, is the radiocarbon method, based upon the measurement of the radioactive isotope of carbon (C14), which remains in a plant or animal organism after death. Animal bone, or shell, or charcoals from hearths are, in varying degrees, suitable substances whose age can be determined, back sometimes to a maximum of sixty thousand years. The time scale thus achieved provides the basis for understanding the rate at which man's biological and cultural evolution took place.

The prehistorian is in much the same position as a man trying to reconstruct the picture of a jigsaw puzzle of which half the pieces are missing. It is both challenging and exciting, and the degree of success is determined by recognition of the pattern and the significance of the missing pieces. For the more recent periods the record is obviously much more complete than it is for the beginning, where little evidence of man, other than stone and bone, is preserved. However, much can be learned from the tools and waste material at the sites where they were manufactured, the dispersal of dwellings, the disposition of bone fragments from meals, and from the other kinds of artifacts.

It is also fortunate for the prehistorian that Africa has preserved in contemporary society a number of different ways of life, techniques, and tools, the origins of which lie deeply buried in the past. Of course, the present way of life of all these economically simpler societies, such as the hunting-and-gathering Bushmen of the Kalahari Desert or the Pygmy peoples of the Ituri forests, has been affected by contact with peoples of more complex institutions and technologies so that no *direct* comparisons between ancient and modern societies are possible. But, through analogies, archeologists can construct models that make it possible to surmise how prehistoric man behaved.

Another means to rediscover the past, though of more limited extent both in space and time, is the interpretation of the rock art of the Late Stone Age, some of which is incomparable for the liveliness of its styles and its portrayal of events and customs. Later in time other sources, such as historical traditions passed on by word of mouth, the evidence of linguistics by which the history of a language can be deduced, and, finally, written documents, all combine to create a better understanding of the past.

When it is assembled, all this evidence provides a record of man's activities that covers some four to five million years. It shows that Charles Darwin was right when he suggested in his *Descent of Man* that it was somewhere in the tropics, perhaps in Africa, that man the toolmaker first evolved, and leaves no doubt that man shares a common ancestor with the great apes, or Pongidae.

This ancestor, who lived at some distant time as yet not precisely identified, must have been a small, unspecialized apelike animal, probably similar to the subfamily of fossil apes known as *Dryopithecus*, a term meaning "tree ape." The earliest of these dryopithecines was found in sediments of the Oligocene epoch of the Tertiary period (about twenty-eight or thirty million years ago) in the Fayum depression not far from Cairo in the Nile Valley. This fossil, named *Aegyptopithecus zeuxis*, is a quadrupedal ape with a tail and an apelike tooth pattern. *Aegyptopithecus* was an arboreal ape, as were later forms found in East Africa, and dates from the Miocene epoch (about twenty million years ago); the Miocene apes, however, show some modification of the hand

and forelimb, suggesting that they may have been partly terrestrial. A smaller species, known as *Dryopithecus africanus* (sometimes less formally referred to as Proconsul), appears to have been adapted to living in gallery forest along the streams and in the savanna, while a larger form, *Dryopithecus major*, occupied the forests on the slopes of volcanoes.

In 1961 the Kenya-born British prehistorian Dr. Louis Leakey found pieces of an upper jaw and two isolated teeth in late Miocene deposits at Fort Ternan in western Kenya that have since been dated to fourteen million years old. This fossil, which he named *Kenyapithecus wickeri*, showed unmistakable human characteristics of the hominid branch of the Hominoidea family, from which man and apes are descended. Later it was demonstrated by Dr. Elwyn Simons of Yale University that Leakey's discovery differed in no essential respect from *Ramapithecus punjabicus*, a form discovered earlier in India. Although the India fossil is unfortunately known only from fragments of the upper and lower jaw, the modifications of the face and the tooth pattern that these exhibit have given rise to the suggestion that *Ramapithecus* (to which species the East African find was subsequently assigned) was not only a hominid but a tool user. A further indication was the discovery at the same site of a long bone that had been fractured in a manner suggesting crushing; close by lay a piece of lava with a battered ridge on one side. Proof of man's tool-using ability, however, must rest upon the discovery of limb bones showing whether *Ramapithecus* was a quadruped or a biped.

Professor Sherwood L. Washburn of the University of California has recently postulated the likelihood that the earlier hominids were knuckle-walkers like the apes. This would not only allow for more specialized use of the forelimbs for manipulating objects but would suggest, as does the estimated size range, that *Ramapithecus* lived mostly on the ground.

The place of both the dryopithecine apes and the more advanced *Ramapithecus* is yet to be conclusively determined. Some physical anthropologists consider the dryopithecine apes to be ancestral to the chimpanzee and gorilla. If so, they probably lie close in time and not far removed biologically from the common ancestor of apes and man. However, certain recent biochemical studies have cast doubt on this theory. These studies, based upon the analysis of blood serum proteins and on the chromosome composition of the higher primates, suggest that species have evolved at a constant rate and that man and the African apes split off from a common ancestor as recently as the Pliocene epoch (some five million years ago). If this were the case, then *Ramapithecus*, a savanna dweller, would be an aberrant ape that left no descendants. It is to be hoped that the search of newly discovered Pliocene formations in East Africa will provide evidence to show whether the long chronology for the time of separation of the hominid and pongid lines, suggested by the earlier fossil finds, or the short one based upon the biochemical studies is likely to be the correct evaluation.

By the beginning of the Pleistocene epoch (some three and a half million years ago) there were present in the savanna land of East Africa, and probably also of South Africa, hominid forms known as australopithecines, or man-apes. There can be no doubt that through natural and social selection processes, which bred out the less desirable genetic characteristics and encouraged the increase of those more highly favored, the man-apes became ecologically well adapted to life in the open savannas. They were possessed of an upright carriage, using the forelimbs for tool manipulation and the hindlimbs for bipedal locomotion. It can be inferred that these fundamental changes were brought about by the greater potential of the woodland and grassland environments, with their wider opportunities to experiment and the greater excitement of a life in the open over one in the forests.

These hominids are the best known of any of the fossil ancestors of modern man, being represented today by several hundred specimens. The first of these fossils was found in 1924 at Taung in the northern part of the Cape Province in South Africa in brecciated cave deposits that were being exploited for limestone. Here, uncovered by a blast, was found the cast of the greater part of a juvenile skull; it showed characteristics that, in the opinion of its discoverer, Dr. Raymond Dart of South Africa, placed it midway morphologically between the apes and the oldest definitely identifiable human fossils.

Some believed Dart was wrong and considered the skull to be that of a fossil ape. Others, including Dr. Robert Broom, also of South Africa, thought that "In *Australopithecus* we have a being also with a chimpanzeelike jaw but a subhuman brain. We seem justified in concluding that in this new form discovered by Professor Dart, we have a connecting link between the higher apes and one of the lowest human types."

A few years later Dart was proved correct when Broom discovered the first adult australopithecine fossil at the cave of Sterkfontein in the Transvaal. Systematic investigation of similar limestone caves at other sites in the Sterkfontein area and in the Makapan Valley in the northern Transvaal

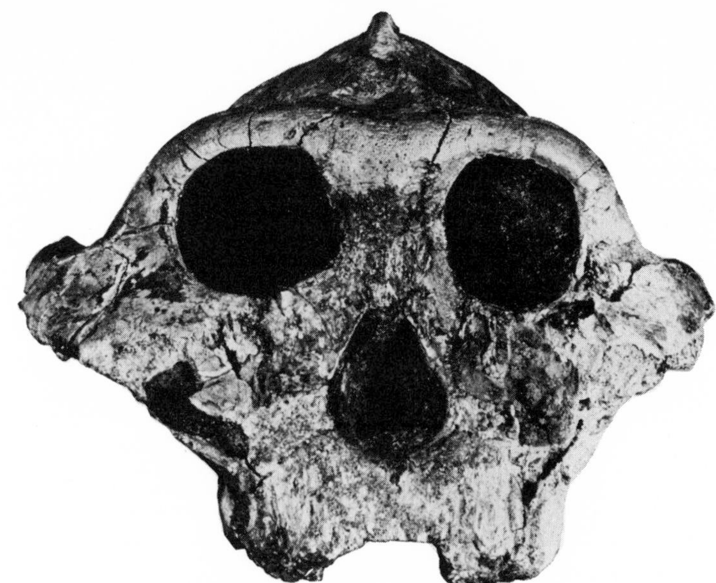

This ancient skull of Australopithecus boisei, *or man-ape, found in June,* 1969, *by Richard Leakey on the eastern side of Lake Rudolf in Kenya, is slightly older than* 2.6 *million years. An ancestor of modern man, this East African type of the robust hominid walked upright and manipulated stone tools with his forearms.*

NATIONAL MUSEUM, NAIROBI–RICHARD LEAKEY

produced a number of other man-ape fossils in association with many bones of animals.

On the basis of the fossil fauna, the earlier South African deposits could be no younger than the Lower Pleistocene and might be as old as two million years or more. The later deposits appear to belong in the Middle Pleistocene and could be half as young again. The earlier sites—Sterkfontein, Makapan limeworks, and Taung—contained the remains of a small, slender form, *Australopithecus africanus*, whereas at the later sites—Swartkrans and Kromdraai—only a robust form was present. At Swartkrans were also found the remains of a more advanced hominid, which has now been shown to represent an early form of *Homo* species. It is this form that is believed to have been the maker of the stone tools found in these breccias. No implements of flaked stone have yet been discovered with the gracile form (*Australopithecus africanus*), but what are claimed to be clubs and cutting, piercing, and chopping tools have been found among the many thousands of bones of other creatures in these deposits.

The australopithecines were small-brained hominids with cranial capacities of between about 435 and 530 cubic centimeters—around the average for the gorilla and about one third the size of modern man. Their rather muzzlelike face shows a number of apelike features, but the tooth pattern is essentially human, as are many features of the brain case. The head was centrally placed on the spinal column. The pelvic girdle and bones of the lower limbs show that the man-apes walked upright on two feet, and the arms and hands show that they were capable of simple toolmaking. *Australopithecus africanus* measured an average 4 feet 6 inches tall and weighed about 60 to 70 pounds; *Australopithecus robustus* was taller, about 5 feet in height, and weighed about 130 pounds.

It appears now most likely that the Transvaal caves were not the dwelling places of the man-apes but rather the sites where carnivores, possibly leopards, brought their victims. In this case the australopithecines were not the aggressive hunters that some have claimed them to be.

East African discoveries that have been underway since 1959 have greatly enhanced our knowledge of these earliest hominids. There, australopithecine fossils are known from a number of different localities in the Lake Rudolf section of the Rift Valley (Omo, Lothagam, Kanapoi, and sites on the east side of the lake), from Lake Baringo (Chemeron) in Kenya, and from the Olduvai Gorge and Garusi in northern Tanzania. The oldest of these fossils dates from about five million years ago, and by the beginning of the Pleistocene both a slender and a robust form were living in the Lake Rudolf rift. The oldest stone tools, made some 2.6 million years ago, are from Koobi Fora on the east side of Lake Rudolf. At a nearby site have been found one well-preserved skull of the robust australopithecine and parts of another representing a more gracile form. Stone tools are also present at one layer in the Omo beds, about 1.8 million years old, and in the bottom of the 350-foot sequence of Pleistocene lake sediments at Olduvai Gorge.

Olduvai is unique for what it can tell us about early man. Here, since 1931, Drs. Louis and Mary Leakey have recovered the remains of a number of hominids associated with concentrations of animal bones and stone implements. These lay on land surfaces that had been rapidly covered either by ash and dust from periodic eruptions of the nearby volcanoes or by the rising waters of the lake, thus sealing

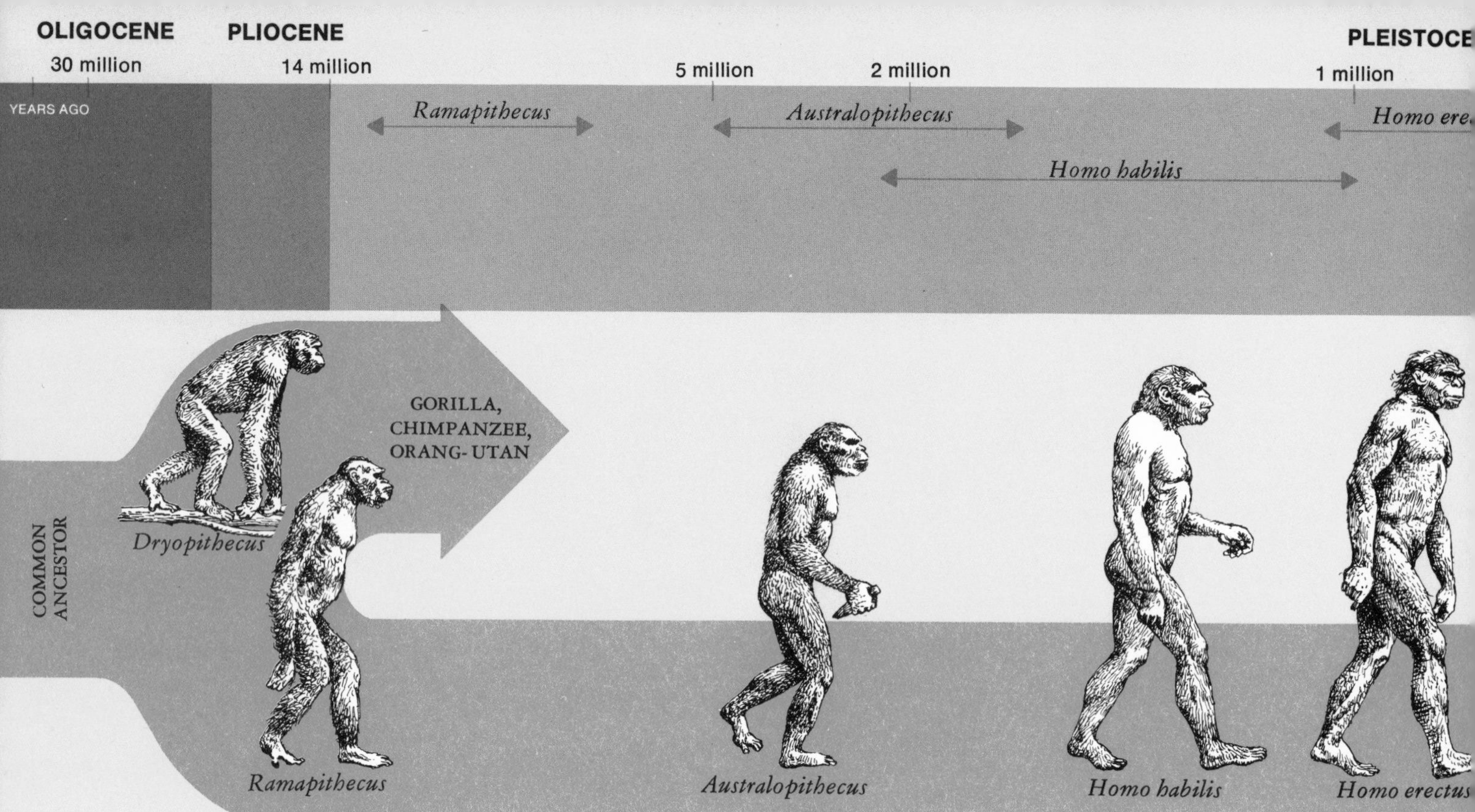

THE EMERGENCE OF MAN IN AFRICA *(conjectural)*

the remains in a remarkably fine state of preservation.

The base of the Olduvai sequence begins about 1.9 million years ago, and in the lowest level (Bed I) *Australopithecus robustus* was found together with a more advanced form named *Homo habilis*. The name implies the ability to make tools, and it is the association of this form with evidence of stone toolmaking that has justified including it with *Homo* rather than with *Australopithecus*. His remains are known from six sites and include three fairly complete craniums and lower jaws, together with bones of the lower leg, a nearly complete foot, and a number of the bones of the hand as well as isolated finds of teeth.

Homo habilis was possessed of a larger brain (640–650 cubic centimeters) than either of the australopithecines. However, in the remainder of the skeleton, so far as can be observed, the differences are not very great. *Homo habilis* resembles *Australopithecus africanus* in its slender build, and since it is of a later date, it could have evolved from the latter form; as yet, no certain identification of a slender australopithecine has been made at Olduvai. Alternatively, the evidence can be interpreted as showing three distinct and evolving hominid lines of which only the third, *Homo habilis*, survived to become a competent toolmaker and to be the ancestor of modern man.

The remains that are found at Olduvai provide almost the only evidence for the technological capabilities and activities of the Lower Pleistocene hominids. Concentrations of animal bones, split to extract the marrow, and numbers of stone tools, together with the waste resulting from their manufacture, can be seen as their living places or home bases, to which were brought back the results of hunting, scavenging, and other gathering activities to be shared among the members of the group. Some time in a previous epoch, therefore, most likely in the Pliocene, which immediately preceded the Pleistocene, some of the ancestral hominids turned from a largely vegetarian to an omnivorous diet in which the hunting of animals became the most significant activity. In fact, it is likely that the need for sharp cutting implements to skin and dismember a carcass was the factor that made these groups take the momentous step involved in working stone to make tools.

The home bases were more than the transitory sleeping places of the hominids. The numbers of individual animals and species represented there suggest that the sites were occupied for several days at least. They were also the places where the juveniles were taught the skills and behavior that made for the successful perpetuation of the species, and it is now apparent from a study of the age when the young's permanent teeth erupted that they were dependent upon their parents for about the same time as those in simpler societies are today. The nature of the learned behavior can be gauged from several different lines of evidence—from the morphology of the fossils themselves, from artifacts, and from what is now known of the behavior of the gorilla

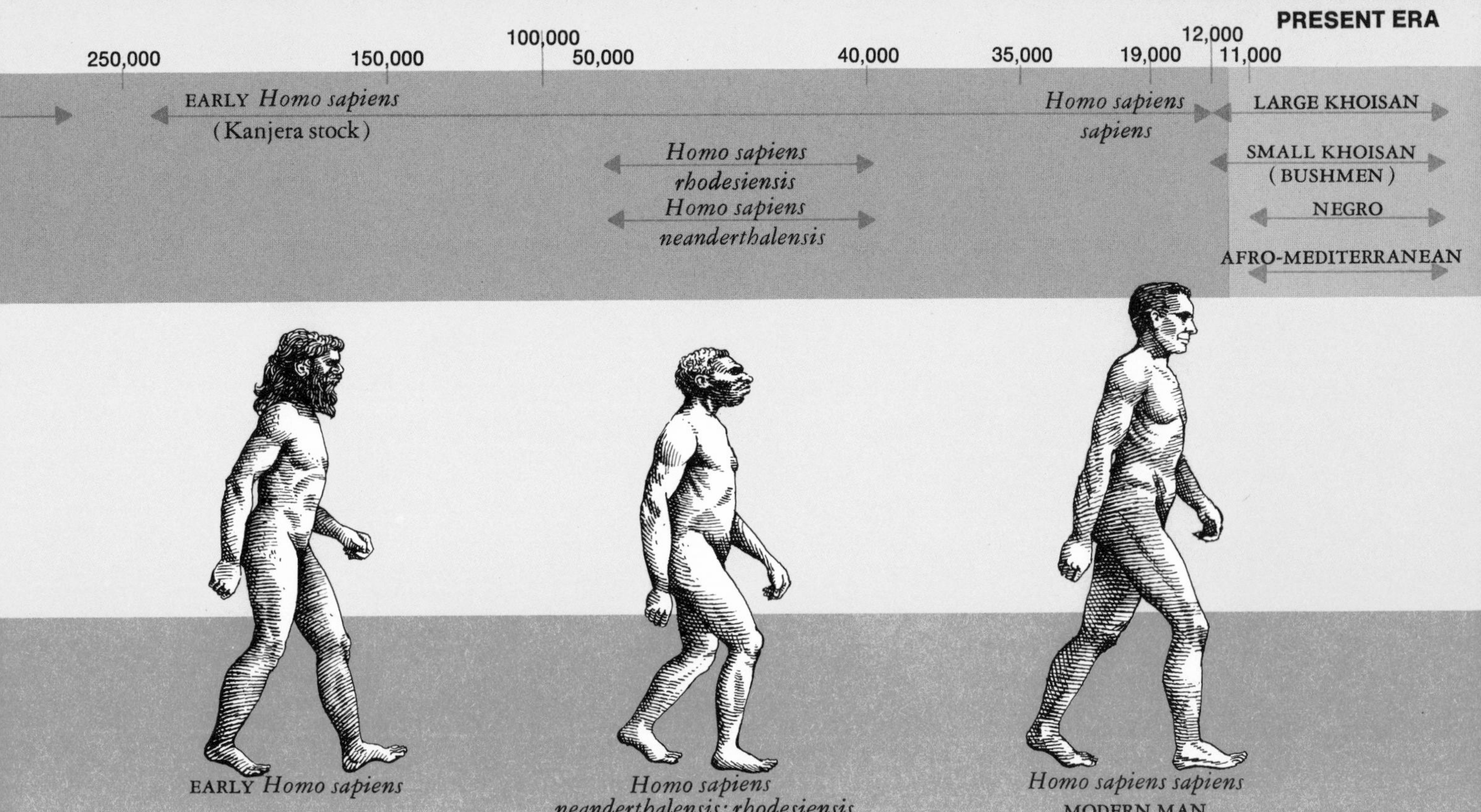

and chimpanzee, the latter in particular.

Studies of free-ranging groups of chimpanzees in wooded savanna (by the English ethologist Jane van Lawick-Goodall in the Gombe Stream Reserve in western Tanzania) and in forest (by English zoologist Vernon Reynolds in Uganda's Budongo forest and by others in West Africa) show that these animals live in highly sociable groups that are continually changing in composition. They do not indulge in any regular defense of territory, and they use some twenty-three different calls, together with facial expressions and gestures, for communication. They manufacture and use simple tools—peeled sticks and grasses for extracting termites from their nests, sponges for sucking water contained in hollow trees, sticks for breaking open the nests of tree ants or for defense; they also throw stones and regularly weave sleeping platforms. These observations, in combination with the fossil evidence, provide a basis for assessing the capabilities of *Australopithecus* and other early hominids, since what the chimpanzees are capable of doing, the australopithecines were biologically equipped to do appreciably better, and much else besides. Already it is probable that we can differentiate between the activities of the males and females, the males engaging in hunting and the females and young gathering wild plant foods.

It is, however, man's toolmaking ability that places him above all other forms of life, and his first great step in the manufacture of simple stone tools required a mind capable of inventing and transmitting a rudimentary knowledge of how stone is fractured so as to produce sharp fragments, or flakes, from the parent lump, or core, and a hand that could do the work. Such tools belong to what is called the Oldowan industry (after the site at Olduvai), and they consist of choppers, flakes for cutting, and rounded, many-faceted lumps for pounding or breaking bone to extract the marrow. Sometimes a flake will show a small amount of fashioning to form a scraper, or more rarely, a bone fragment may show signs of having been employed as a tool. These represent domestic equipment used at the home base, and there has been little, if anything, found to support the view that man was from his earliest beginnings the armed aggressor he has become today. Stones and sticks for throwing at game are likely to have been the only weapons, if such they can be called.

Fossils of early hominids in South and East Africa, and another in the basin of Lake Chad, show them to have been widely spread over the savanna and drier regions of the continent by the beginning of the Middle Pleistocene (about a million or more years ago), about the time that the australopithecine forms had given place to the biologically more evolved *Homo erectus*. So far, australopithecine fossils have not been found outside the continent of Africa; however, *Homo erectus* forms, with their toolmaking skills, were widely distributed throughout all the inhabited regions of the Old World.

Two fossils from Olduvai (classified by archeologists as Hominids 13 and 16), the one from the upper and the other from the lower part of Bed II, were originally grouped with *Homo habilis;* but they have more recently been shown to have more evolved features, indicating that they could be forms intermediate to *Homo erectus.* As known from sites in China and Java and from a third example found in the middle of Bed II at Olduvai (Hominid 9), the skull of *Homo erectus* shows quite a variation in cranial capacity (therefore in brain size), ranging from about 750 to over 1,000 cubic centimeters, with a longer, broader, and thicker skull, a larger palate, a low vault, and projecting brow ridges. *Homo erectus* was taller and had larger bones; indeed, there appears to be little difference between the rest of the skeleton and our own. This Olduvai specimen is probably about half a million years old, though the earliest of the *Homo erectus* fossils probably is as old as a million years or more.

At a site on the edge of what was once a small lake at Ternifine on the Algerian plateau, *Homo erectus* is represented by three lower jaws and one of the side bones of a skull. These jaws are massive and lack a developed mental eminence, or chin, but the pattern of the teeth is not markedly different from that of modern man. Biological changes of the magnitude that occured between the australopithecines and *Homo erectus* typically take about eight million years to effect in other animal species, but in the case of these ancestral human fossils, they seem to have transpired in not more than one million years. There is small doubt that the reason for the evolutionary speedup lies in man's cultural abilities and the attendant potential for improving his way of life. Once the great initial step had been taken—and it is likely to have been a comparatively sudden invention whereby the finished stone tool was envisaged in the rude block or cobble from which it was to be manufactured—it was inevitable that the innovator's descendants would dominate the less gifted species and that genetic changes would be further accelerated.

At much the same time as *Homo erectus* appears on the African scene there also appears a new bifacial technique for making stone tools, and we find the first characteristic tools of the Middle Pleistocene: the hand axe and cleaver. They were made from boulders fractured into large flakes; the pieces were then retouched and shaped on both sides with a hammer stone or by striking them on a stone anvil. This Acheulian industrial complex (named after a site in France) lasted for more than 750,000 years. Sites are found throughout Africa, southern Europe, and Asia. The bifacial tools often show considerable skill in manufacture, and the degree of symmetry and finish of some of the later ones reveals the beginnings of an aesthetic appreciation among the makers.

Camping and flaking sites of Acheulian man are known in almost all parts of the continent with the exception of the primary rain forest, showing that by this time the hominid populations were able to live in a number of different ecological niches. The sites are nearly all in the open, close to water, and cover larger areas than do those of the makers of the Oldowan industry. Many hundreds of hand axes and cleavers may be found on the living sites, along with a range of other tools, and it would seem that the number of individuals making up the social group had by now increased and that some of the camps were revisited seasonally.

The stone tools still appear to be domestic equipment rather than weapons. We know from sites in Europe that simple pointed wooden spears were in use by this time, and a site at the Kalambo Falls in Zambia has produced a wooden club as well as primitive digging sticks.

The makers of Acheulian tools were more competent hunters, if the increased variety of species of animals and greater number of carcasses represented by the bones found at the dwelling places are acceptable as evidence. Improved methods of communication (signs and grunts), and so, more efficient group hunting techniques, were probably the chief factors behind the extended "awareness" of *Homo erectus.* At Ternifine many large and medium-sized animals had been dismembered and eaten, and their bones thrown into the water from the lakeside camp. At Olduvai and other East African sites there seems to have been some definite selection of the animals that were hunted, and at one of these, near the top of Bed II, herds of sheeplike and giraffelike creatures (both now extinct) were apparently driven into a muddy stream and there killed and butchered. At another of these artifact concentrations in Kenya the remains of some eighty giant baboons have been found among the food waste.

The different tool kits and the activities they represent suggest that individuals were now beginning to communicate with each other by means of some form of language. This protolanguage was, no doubt, essentially connected with staying alive and securing the immediate necessities of the moment, but, nonetheless, it provided the foundation on which language as we know it developed in the Middle Pleistocene. However, the fact that at this time one cannot see any regional specialization suggests that man continued to make only rather limited exploitation of the resources of his habitat. Very similar living patterns existed wherever the

Acheulian, or hand-axe, industry is found.

Homo sapiens makes his first appearance at about much the same time in Europe and Africa, about 150,000 to 200,000 years ago. European forerunners of modern man (*Homo sapiens sapiens*) are associated with Acheulian hand axes at Swanscombe in the Thames valley in England, and it seems likely that the fragmentary skulls and tools found at Kanjera on Lake Victoria were also those of *Homo sapiens*. Most of the other fossils are unassociated finds. Recently two almost complete craniums have been found from late Middle or early Upper Pleistocene sediments in the Omo valley in northern Kenya and probably date to about 200,000 years old. Though they represent the oldest *Homo sapiens* fossils from Africa, they do not look alike. Clearly, there was considerable genetic variability within a single population at this time.

A similar situation is exhibited by the later (about 50,000 years old) human fossils from the Mount Carmel caves in Israel, where both modern and primitive *sapiens* features are present in the same population. However, wherever it was that modern man originated, perhaps in southwest Asia or perhaps distributed over a wider area, it would seem that his intellectual and cultural abilities were such that the *Homo erectus* form was replaced with remarkable rapidity. By 50,000 or 40,000 B.C. Neanderthalers (*Homo sapiens neanderthalensis*) were present in North Africa, and a closely connected race of Rhodesioids (*Homo sapiens rhodesiensis*) in the southern part of the continent.

We can now see clearly for the first time the beginnings of a broad, regional specialization in stone tool manufacture. The cultural pattern of the North African population was not unlike that of the other contemporary peoples in Europe and Asia in that they made much use of light cutting and scraping equipment, such as has been associated with hunting camps and the working and flensing of skins. South of the Sudan modifications of the old Acheulian bifacial technique continued in use, together with a quantity of light wood-working equipment. In the open grasslands of the Horn and the South African Highveld an evolved expression of the Acheulian tradition (the Fauresmith) is found, while in the forests and woodland savannas of Equatoria and West Africa, now occupied permanently for the first time, many heavy-duty and denticulated (toothed) flake tools (the Sangoan tradition) are found. It has been suggested that the Sangoan tools may be those of a carpenter, reflecting a growing use of wood and such byproducts as bark and resin. The working of wood with stone tools is made appreciably easier by the discovery of a technique of controlled charring with fire and scraping. Utensils can be hollowed out by this method, and weapons and tools made with comparative ease.

Firemaking also has important implications for codifying the social behavior of the groups. Evidence from sites in the Far East and western Europe shows that fire was definitely used by *Homo erectus* in the colder regions close to the ice sheets during the Middle Pleistocene. None of the Acheulian sites in Africa shows indisputable use of man-made fire before the Upper Pleistocene (about 70,000 years ago). It is from the end of the Acheulian also that we begin to find many occupation sites in caves and rock shelters, and although weathering will have destroyed much of the older evidence for cave occupation, these kinds of sites appear to have been more frequently sought from this time onward.

About 40,000 to 50,000 years ago, therefore, three "races," or subspecific forms, of man were present on the continent: Neanderthalers in North Africa; Rhodesioids in southern Africa; and a stock tentatively identified as the ancestors of modern man to be seen in the Kanjera and Omo fossils from East Africa. However, by about 35,000 years ago the Neanderthaloid and Rhodesioid populations had been largely replaced, it would seem, by modern man (*Homo sapiens sapiens*). The disappearance of these Neanderthaloid populations is most likely to have come about, not as a result of wholesale replacement, but through long-term natural and social selection.

The tool kits are now more complex and exhibit a diversity of regional variations within several more general patterns, but it must be in the greatly stimulated intellectual life that the superiority of these Upper Pleistocene races lay. Whereas in the time of Neanderthal and Rhodesian man it is possible to see the beginnings of a concern with abstract beliefs, ritual, and a superior technology, these find full expression only with the coming of modern man.

It seems probable, though as yet the evidence is insubstantial, that the distinctive success of *Homo sapiens sapiens* lay in his possession of language, in the true sense of the word, without which man's life could never be complete. After 35,000 B.C. we have evidence of consciousness in art, music, ritual, as well as care for the dead and a counting system. More sophisticated tool kits speak of more efficient and extensive exploitation of the natural resources of the habitat, and the increased number of sites that are known to belong to this time suggests an overall increase in population density.

The fossil record for the Upper Pleistocene in Africa is not a particularly complete one; though a number of fossils are known, mostly from the drier parts of the continent, their precise age is often a matter for dispute. However, by about 10,000 B.C. the relatively unspecialized ancestral stock of modern man in Africa, which is generally identified with the Kanjera type, had undergone genetic changes, resulting in the appearance of the large and small Khoisan, or Bushman, types, the robust and gracile Negro stocks, and perhaps also the tall, long-headed Afro-Mediterranean stock.

The large Khoisan type was probably the oldest, dating to about 17,000 B.C., and the most unspecialized. It had evolved in the more open savanna and grasslands of southern and East Africa, even as far north as Khartoum. The small Khoisan—the Bushman proper—appears to have evolved out of the larger type in the southwestern parts of the continent only some 11,000 years ago.

The earliest remains that show Negro characteristics come from the West African forest country and the western branch of the Great Rift Valley. The first of these, from a burial site in a rock shelter at Iwo Eleru, near Benin in Nigeria, dates to about 9000 B.C. The second, at a site on the shore of Lake Edward, discloses skull fragments that are more robust, but with limb bones that show the slenderness of the West African Negro; these date to about 6500 to 6000 B.C. Unfortunately, the rain forest is not favorable to the preservation of bone, so the ancestry of the Negro is very imperfectly known as yet.

The Afro-Mediterranean type appears at about the same time in the Eastern Rift at Gamble's Cave, and both Negro and Afro-Mediterranean are present in the Sahara after 5000 B.C., being known from a number of burials and settlement finds.

In North Africa the population of the Maghreb, during the closing stages of the Upper Pleistocene and later, is known from many remains found buried in settlement middens and in caves. The physical type was tall and robust, and is known as the Mechta el Arbi stock—from the name of the shell midden in eastern Algeria where some of the first remains were found. These people show a general likeness to the type of man from the Cro-Magnon shelter in southwest France (of a much earlier date), but the associated cultural remains are very different. The oldest Mechta el Arbi skeletons date from about 10,000 B.C., but there was also present in northwest Africa by about 6000 B.C. a more slenderly built type representing an early Afro-Mediterranean stock that would ultimately dominate the area.

Both of these local races were associated with stone tools known as microliths, made by using parallel-sided flakes, or blades. These microliths included various kinds of scraping, grooving, and cutting tools, many of the last devices having the back blunted so that they could be held in the hand or, since many of the blades are quite small, mounted in a series. An ingenious notching technique was used to reduce long blades to sections of the required length. The sections were trimmed to various shapes to form the barbs of spears and arrows, the blades of sickles, and so on. Several sickle handles of bone have been found in the Maghreb, one with the microliths still in position, though the tree gum, or mastic, with which they had been held firm had long since disappeared. Microliths became considerably more common after about 15,000 B.C. They are indicative of fundamental changes in the technology, and it is hardly surprising that their use spread rapidly.

It has been suggested that technical innovation of this kind must have been accompanied by population migration, but this is not necessarily the case. Since hunting-and-gathering populations maintain regular contact between their various component groups, an innovation, if it is a sufficient improvement on the existing system, is likely to spread and be quickly adopted. Its progress is especially rapid if it concerns more efficient ways of food getting, for this allows more leisure to devote to intellectual pursuits. In this case it was a change to lighter equipment: microliths were very easy to make, they could be quickly hafted, or mounted, in the most effective manner. The bow and arrow was invented somewhere about 9000 to 8000 B.C., and because of its greater efficiency in some types of country (for example, low grass savanna), it was widely, though not universally, adopted.

From the beginning of the Upper Pleistocene epoch, the coastal regions of North Africa were the home of cultural traditions that differed from those found south of the Sahara. The North African Neanderthalers were associated with industries known as Mousterian, in the pattern of those found in the Levant and in Europe. It is as yet unknown whether Mousterian technology (successor to the Acheulian tool culture and also named after its earliest discovery site in France) developed independently in each area or whether some population movement was involved. By about 40,000 years ago, however, we find present in northeastern Libya a blade industry typologically in the Upper Pleistocene tradition of the north side of the Mediterranean basin. This would seem to have been an introduction from outside the continent, but, since it is known from only two caves in the Jebel Akhdar, it is unlikely that it was widely distributed, nor can it be seen to have had any profound influence on the essentially local traditions of the African

Middle Stone Age or on the contemporary North African industrial complex. This last culture—known as Aterian—developed out of the Mousterian and spread throughout the Sahara; it is distinguished by the use of different kinds of tanged, or stemmed, points, suitable for inserting into handles or attaching as heads of spears, and similar projectiles.

Several local industries based on blades, sometimes employing microliths, have been recently found in the Nile Valley north of Aswan, and it seems probable that there was not a little interaction between Egypt and the Levant from about 15,000 B.C. onward, and possibly earlier. The effect of this is also manifest far to the west throughout most of northwestern Africa. The similarities between the two regions, however, remain at the general level rather than the specific. As in the Mousterian, it was more probably the knowledge and innovative behavior that spread, rather than any significant group movement. Some of these blade industries are found south of the Sahara: one site on Somalia's northern coast; another in the East African Rift, where it is associated with a fishing as well as a hunting economy about 7000 to 6000 B.C.; and others, though as yet scarcely explored, in Ethiopia.

It is from the desert-confined Nile Valley at this time that there comes the earliest evidence of intergroup warfare. Two cemeteries in the Jebel Sahaba area of the Upper Nile contained a number of burials that had microliths associated with skeletons in such a way as to suggest death as a result of injury. Some even had broken microliths sticking in the skull, pelvis, and thigh bone. It was probably economic pressure on an increasing population of culturally distinct units that brought about the need for each group to seek to preserve its own territory intact and steal some of its neighbors'. Since groups could exploit, but not move permanently into, the desert, it would seem that defense of the more desirable flood plain by force of arms was necessary. Another outcome of this economic pressure was the much greater use of wild cereal grasses, as seen in the large numbers of grindstones in the equipment inventory of some of the hunting camps. Large quantities of wild grain could be harvested by means of primitive sickles, and when stored, could serve as a main food source for several months.

The savanna and forest lands south of the Sahara do not appear to have experienced similar economic pressure, and, indeed, these have always been among the richest natural environments in the world. Most of the Bushmanoid and early Negro populations that exploited the unlimited plant and animal foods of these habitats would have had little cause to encroach on each other's territory. Those occupying the West African savanna and forest were also hunters, made microlithic tools, mostly from quartz, and had both axes and adzes. They experimented more specifically with wild plant foods, so that by perhaps about 3000 B.C., if not earlier, selective genetic processes had resulted in the development of early forms of African domestic cereals.

In the Congo Basin the characteristic stone implement was a trapezoidal piece of stone that could be used in several different ways. It could be fashioned into the head of an arrow to cut the hide of prey, leaving a blood spoor; it could also be used as sickle or knife, as a chisel for hollowing or a drawknife for smoothing wood.

In East Africa and the southern African savanna and steppe the population was mostly of Bushman, or Khoisan, stock. Here also many of them used microlithic stone tools, including scrapers and hand adzes—tools of the woodworker. They made arrow points, linkshafts, and ornaments of bone; ivory and shell were commonly used for beads and pendants. Among other regional groups larger scraping tools and pounding and grinding equipment were common, and the microlith rare or absent. In Zambia and Malawi, for example, there was an emphasis on grinding equipment, presumably because of the greater reliance on plant foods; in the Highveld of South Africa the emphasis was more on cutting and flensing equipment and on bone arrow points, showing the greater importance of game herds to the hunting groups there.

The rock art of Africa gives us a very good indication of the activities and beliefs of these hunting-and-gathering peoples. The pictures are engraved on rocks in the open or painted in caves or rock shelters. Women are shown gathering wild plant foods, sometimes with the aid of a digging stick on which was occasionally set a stone with a hole pierced through the center for weight. The all important occupation of the men was hunting, and many paintings are scenes of stalking with animal-head disguises or the killing of antelopes, elephants, giraffes, and hippopotamuses with bows and arrows, and less frequently, with spears. Honey gathering was another male occupation. Dancing and social get-togethers also played a part in the way of life that one authority has called the "master behavior pattern of the human species."

Still more complete information of the prehistoric life patterns can be collected from the example of modern survivals of primitive hunters, though their continued existence has often depended upon accommodation to more advanced neighbors. The later Bushmen of the Drakensburg range in southeast Africa persisted, a dwindling population until the

1870's, when they finally succumbed to the pressures of Bantu and European farmers who had taken over their hunting lands. On the other hand, the Bushmen of the central and northern Kalahari demonstrate successfully how hunting groups can make a living out of dry, near-waterless country. The relatively unattractive character of their environment to other, economically more advanced peoples has saved them. So, too, the Hadza people demonstrate how much leisure the rich, though dry and tsetse-ridden, game country of the Lake Eyasi Rift in Tanzania permits to those hunters with six-foot bows. The Pygmies of the Ituri forests, and to a lesser extent the Nderobo of the montane forests of Kenya, show how hunting peoples can adopt and develop a system of exchange relationships with their Bantu agricultural neighbors.

A rare instance of peoples who have made few apparent modifications of the hunting and gathering way of life are two communities of OvaTjimba people, who were recently discovered in the Baynes Mountains in the extreme north of South West Africa. Their only contact has been with pastoral Hottentots, and they still make and use stone tools—the only people in contemporary Africa known to do so. What a wealth of information exists here for the archeologist and ethnographer to link directly the past and the present.

Elsewhere in Africa, in the region of the many lakes that existed in early post-Pleistocene times in the southern Sahara, as also along the seacoasts, man turned from strict hunting and gathering to exploiting the food resources offered by the water. Special equipment was developed at the close of the Pleistocene, and we find spearheads, barbed harpoons of bone, and fishhooks and gorges of bone and shell. Abundant fish and shellfish could be caught in tidal weirs, and stranded sea mammals supplied quantities of meat, as on the South African south coast. In the lakes and rivers fish and shellfish were taken, and the hippopotamus and other water mammals were hunted with spears and harpoons. Some of the waterside camps, such as those just mentioned and others on the Upper Nile at Khartoum or on Lake Edward must have been near-permanent settlements. Today some of the Batwa peoples of central Africa (for example, those living in Zambia's Bangweulu and Lukanga swamps) persist in a way of life that can give an idea of what some of these late prehistoric fishing camps were like.

There would have been small reason for the sub-Saharan peoples to exchange the hunter's way of life for that of the cultivator, especially if the farming tools were not very effective ones for dealing with the tropical woodlands and forests. How strong is the excitement of the hunt can be seen the world over by the amount of hunting that is still done today even in the most sophisticated societies. This is primarily the reason why farming came to sub-Saharan Africa fairly late in time.

As yet, no evidence has been found of food producers anywhere on the continent before about 5000 B.C., several millenniums later than their first appearance in southwest Asia. Whether domestication of plants and animals is, in fact, later in Africa will not be known until further work on settlement sites of this time has been carried out, especially the Nile Valley, where circumstances were most favorable.

The Nile Delta is only some three hundred miles from southern Palestine, where the incipient stages of domestication go back to 7500 B.C. and further, and it is difficult to understand what barrier could have prevented the spread of the experimental techniques that were already widely dispersed in the Near East. Was it the abundance of natural food supply? Perhaps so along the Nile, but this cannot have been the case in other parts of North Africa. Was it the fact that the Nile was then flowing in a channel now covered by many feet of alluvial sediment and that these earlier stages are buried and have escaped detection? Or is it that the evidence is already present in the archeological record but has not yet been recognized as such? The initial steps toward domestication form the substratum of urban civilization and have manifested themselves very differently in the New World from the way they have in the Old. So, too, the first advances may have been different in Africa from the now well-known pattern of southwest Asia's agricultural revolution; remembering the trend in the use of wild grains after 15,000 B.C. in the Nile, it seems not unlikely that earlier farming settlements, making use of local grains, may eventually be found there.

The settlements at Merimde in the Delta (dating to about 3600 B.C.), at Badari in Upper Egypt (about 4000 B.C.) in the Fayum depression (about 4500 B.C.) are of groups of farmers cultivating emmer wheat, barley, and flax. Flint-bladed sickles in wooden handles were used for harvesting the grain, which was then stored in basketwork silos. These people made pottery and lived in permanent and semi-permanent villages. Bones of cattle, sheep, and goats, probably domesticated, have also been found. At Badari careful burial of animals suggests the emergence of animal cults, which later became such a feature of the religion of dynastic Egypt.

Whether the first farmers in the Nile were migrants from Asia or of indigenous African stock has been much debated.

A group of Bushmen, living much as their ancestors did 10,000 years ago, are pictured in the Kalahari Desert of Botswana. Nomadic hunters and gatherers of wild food, they possess only what they can carry, using poisoned arrowheads to fell game and transporting their water in huge ostrich eggshells from one water hole to another.

BLACK STAR–CONSTANCE STUART

There are a few cultural traits that suggest connections with Asia (for example, some of the pottery, a type of barbed harpoon, and notched arrowheads), but most of the material culture exhibits a characteristically African tradition of bifacial stone flaking, as in the axes and adzes, the sickle blades, knife blades, and scrapers. Sheep and goats as well as cereals, however, must have been introduced from elsewhere since there are no wild forms known in Africa from which they could have come. This is not the case for the cattle, for two wild species were present in northern Africa; cattle bones, said to date to 5400 B.C., have been found in the Sahara. The bas-reliefs in the tombs of the Old Kingdom in Egypt (3200–2900 B.C.) show what appear to be experiments in domesticating native species of gazelle, hyena, ass, and various birds. How far back this goes is not known; with the exception of the ass, these experiments came to nothing, presumably because of the greater potential of the Asian domesticates.

By 5000 B.C. there were certainly domesticated sheep or goats, though not cattle, in eastern Libya, but we have as yet no means of knowing whether the people also cultivated grain crops. It is interesting that, except for the introduction of pottery and a more refined manner of making flint tools, the material culture of these early farmers shows very little change from that of the immediately preceding hunting population. It is likely that the new economy resulted from the diffusion of outside ideas, rather than from a substantial change of population. In the same way northwest Africa probably acquired domestic animals, wheat, and barley about the same time that the Sahara was also populated by nomadic pastoralists with herds of sheep and cattle.

All these peoples have been described as being in possession of a Neolithic economy: they owned livestock and sometimes cultivated plants, made pottery, and ground and polished their stone axes and other implements to produce tougher cutting edges. There is little or no substantial evidence of cultivation by the Saharan pastoralists before about 1100 B.C., when bullrush millet was being grown by the Neolithic peoples living in defended villages at the western edge of the Sahara along Mauritania's Dar Tichitt escarpment.

The Sahara at this time, as during most of the Upper Pleistocene, was a much more favorable place to live than this arid desert landscape is today. Up to about 2000 B.C. the large Ethiopian game animals abounded and were regularly hunted, as is evidenced by the many different forms of arrowheads that occur in large numbers at desert sites. The grazing by lakes and swamps and in the wadis supported not only wild game but large herds of cattle besides. Cattle bones have been found dating from the middle of the sixth millennium B.C. in the Acacus caves in the Saharan desert of southern Libya and from 2000 B.C. in the Dar Tichitt. The people were mostly nomadic, living in easily transportable dwellings, probably made of mats or skins laid over a bent wood framework. Sometimes, as in the Tassili caves of Algeria—among the greatest storehouses of art in the world—these pastoral peoples are portrayed as Negroes, at other times they are shown as Afro-Mediterraneans.

These Neolithic pastoralists spread throughout the Sahara, and it can be expected that they made contact with the hunting communities living in the savanna belt to the south, where much of the country was unsuitable for livestock because of the tsetse fly. Intradesert movement, evidenced by the wide distribution of certain traditions (for example, that of the dotted wavy line pottery motif), would also have led to the spread of knowledge of domestication. Since, however, the wheats and barleys are winter rainfall crops and do not do well in the tropics (other than on the high plateau of Ethiopia) except under irrigation, local cultigens had to be developed.

Although the evidence for the stages of incipient agriculture south of the Sahara still has to be found and documented, it is clear from the stone tools that have been uncovered that there must have been from about 3000 B.C. onward considerable experimentation. At first this was random, but later it was planned. Eventually, by hybridization and selection, indigenous wild prototypes were converted into staple West African and Ethiopian food crops. How long this took is unknown, but it was the essential basis for all large-scale settlement.

Dry rice in Guinea, sorghum and bullrush millet in the Sudan savanna belt, yams in the forests of West Africa, and the indigenous teff (a grain) and ensete (African banana) were cultivated similarly in the highlands of Ethiopia, as were also emmer wheat and barley, which presumably spread from the Upper Nile. Sites in northern Ethiopia and rock art depicting long-horned cattle suggest the likelihood that food production had spread to Ethiopia by at least the beginning of the second millennium B.C., if not appreciably earlier.

In the first millennium B.C., perhaps due ultimately to the desiccation of the Sahara and the consequent exodus of peoples, pastoralists appear in the Eastern African Rift with herds of sheep and cattle, introduced probably from the southern Sudan and Ethiopia. These herdsmen were long-headed Afro-Mediterraneans who buried their dead in communal graves under stone cairns or sometimes cremated them in caves. They had ground stone axes, made several different kinds of pottery, and used pestles and curious thick platters and bowls made of lava, probably for cooking food. They made a range of implements from obsidian, the black volcanic glass.

As their handiwork shows no obvious break with local tradition, nor do the physical remains of the people themselves suggest a new physical type, it seems likely that it was the economy rather than the population that changed, as in Libya and West Africa. Some of these early peoples may even have penetrated into the southwestern parts of the continent, where they introduced cattle and sheep. Some of the large Bushmanoid peoples, including ancestors of the Hottentots now living there, were not slow to become pastoralists themselves.

The bushlands are yielding up a unique record for the understanding of our human origins. The seemingly unchanging and limitless expanse of Africa's savanna lands would appear to have been the cradle of mankind, and it was here about two million years ago that the first technological advances were made that led to the complex civilizations of the twentieth century.

By 8000 B.C. the ethnic and linguistic maps of the continent as we know it began to take shape. Berbers occupied North Africa and the Sahara, and Ancient Egyptians the Nile Valley. Sudanese Negroes lived in Nubia. Other Negro types lived in the West African savanna, the Sahara, and the rain forests. Long-headed proto-Nilotes and proto-Kushites inhabited the drier parts of East Africa and the Horn. To the south in the savanna grasslands were the Bushman races, who spoke Bush and Hottentot languages; and small-statured Negroid peoples occupied the equatorial forests.

Each had its individual cultural tradition and developed those skills and patterns of social and economic behavior that were dictated by the record of the past and the exigencies of the surroundings. So there emerged the naturalistic art of the Bushman hunters; the plastic art of the West African potter; the simplistic, but highly symbolic, skills and craftsmanship of the artists in wood carving in the equatorial and West African forests; the self-sufficiency and knowledge of animal husbandry of the Berber peoples. Each was in turn affected by contact with peoples of different races and different traditions in other culture areas, and so the way was paved for the appearance of more complex civilizations in the more strategically situated and economically richer parts of the continent. These new civilizations and cultures were also influenced by external factors, but they were, nonetheless, essentially African, with their roots buried deep in the land of Africa.

TONGUE, *Bushman Painting*

STONE AGE ARTISTS

Some of the world's oldest and most wondrous art exists in various parts of Africa. Painted or engraved by Stone Age peoples on rock surfaces, including the walls of caves and rock shelters, it was done over many millenniums, from approximately 6000 B.C. to perhaps as recently as the eighteenth or nineteenth centuries. Thousands of paintings and petroglyphs record with vigor and beauty the activities of primitive societies of hunters and gatherers and of early pastoralists and farmers. In South Africa prehistoric rock art of Bushmen, and possibly other groups, has been known to the world for two hundred fifty years. Scenes like the one above, of Bushmen trapping a hippopotamus (shown in a copy made early in this century by M. Helen Tongue from a wall painting in the district of Molteno), range in age from at least two thousand years old to comparatively recent work. Similar paintings, skillfully executed by Bushmen and other Stone Age artists, have also been found in many parts of eastern Africa, from Transvaal and Rhodesia to the Upper Nile. In North Africa in Algeria's Tassili plateau, rock art is the work of ancient peoples who occupied the Sahara before its desiccation forced them to migrate elsewhere. Their work was revealed only in the late 1950's, following the expeditions of the French explorer-ethnologist Dr. Henri Lhote. At Tassili and at other sites in the Sahara vast numbers of paintings and engravings, like those reproduced on the next two pages, provide a vivid and surprising picture of that now arid region at a time when it abounded with human and animal life. The polychrome paintings were done with pigments extracted from ocherous earths, mineral oxides, and powdered schists found locally. Representations of hunters, dancers, symbolic figures, wild animals, and cattle herds often overlap, the different subjects and styles revealing a steady development of these people toward more complex societies.

The powerful, charging rhinoceros at right was painted by an artist at the Tassili's Ozaneare site at a time in the past when a wetter Sahara was the habitation of big game animals and cattle.

JEAN-DOMINIQUE LAJOUX, *Merveilles du Tassili N'Ajjer*

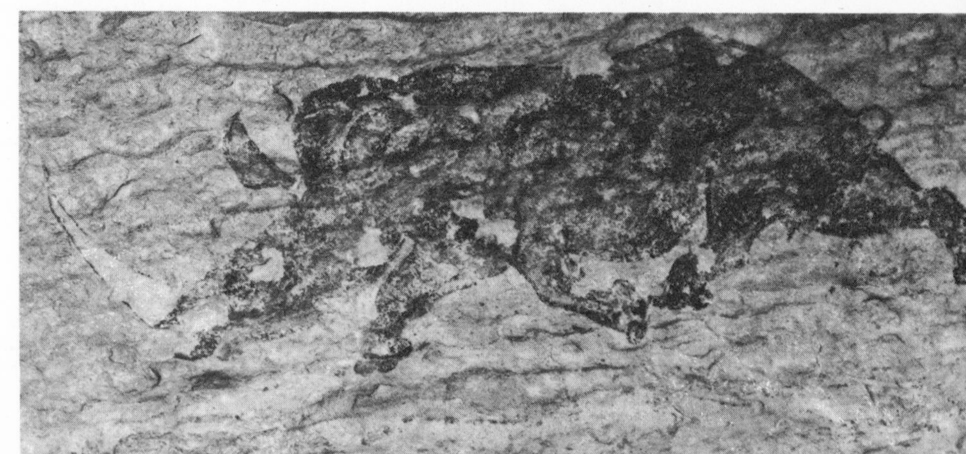

Prehistoric Saharan bowmen (left) race across a rock wall at Sefar in the Tassili region. The rhythm and excitement of the mural are heightened by the running archers' greatly exaggerated stride.

JEAN-DOMINIQUE LAJOUX, *Merveilles du Tassili N'Ajjer*

The graceful dancers below, evidently in ritual dress, were painted on cliffs in the Libyan Sahara. Their discoverer, Fabrizio Mori, places them before 2000 B.C.

DR. FABRIZIO MORI—NANNINI, ROME

A hunter stalks a giraffe in the copy at right of another painting from the Libyan Sahara. Killed for their hides and meat, giraffes probably vanished from the arid wasteland in the first century A.D.

DR. FABRIZIO MORI—NANNINI, ROME

SEEKING MAN'S ORIGINS

BLACK STAR–CONSTANCE STUART

THE TWO GUELAS

The creation of the world and of human life is one of the most popular subjects of the myths and legends handed down from generation to generation by the various peoples of Africa. The following tale is from the Ivory Coast.

There lived, before all things were on the earth and in the sky,

Two very powerful creators.

There was the Guela on High!

And there was the Guela Below.

One day the wind did not blow.

The Guela Below became bored; he began to yawn—

And some clay issued from his mouth. He said:

"I will make some men, women, fish, animals, and plants with the clay."

And with the clay he made some men, women, fish, animals, and plants. He said:

"I will put blood into the bodies of the men, women, fish, animals, and plants that I made in clay so that they can live by my doing."

The Guela Below poured blood into the bodies of the men, women, fish, and animals, but they did not come to life! The Guela Below became angry; and he left the clay men, women, fish, animals, and plants outside.

He grew impatient. He went away. He left all the clay statues outside.

One day the rain fell. Many of the clay men melted in the rain. The Guela saw what had happened to many of the men, women, fish, animals, and plants that were of clay. The Guela said:

"They melted in the rain because they are clay."

Sadness grew in the heart of the Guela Below. He took the clay men, women, fish, animals, and plants that were still in one piece. He took them and put them in a cave.

At that time the night was always on the earth.

At that time the earth was always in the night.

The Guela Below had only fire by which to see.

At that time the day was always in the sky.

At that time the sky was the day. The Guela on High had the sun to light his way.

The Guela on High saw that the Guela Below had some fine playthings. He said:

"Give me some of your clay men, women, fish, animals. I will give them life, and to you I will give the light of my sun."

The Guela Below said:

"I will give you only the clay fish, animals, and plants. I will not give you clay men and women." The Guela on High said:

"I also want the men and the women—"

The Guela Below said:

"So be it. You will have them, but first you must give them life."

Then the Guela on High brought life to the bodies of the men, women, fish, animals, and plants.

Then the men and the women arose and began to walk, the fish arose and began to swim, the animals arose and began to leap, the plants arose and began to grow.

The Guela on High said:

"Now, Guela Below, keep your promise. I gave life to the men, women, fish, animals, and plants that are of clay; I gave you sunlight; now keep your promise!"

But the Guela Below did not wish to hear of it. Then the two Guelas argued. Both of them became angry for all the time to come until the end of time.

Since that time the Guela on High tries to take back the life he gave to the clay men, women, fish, animals, and plants shaped by the Guela Below.

Each time the Guela on High appears to take back the life that he gave to the men, women, fish, and animals, and plants, a man, a woman, a fish, or a plant dies.

But since the Guela Below contests the life the Guela on High gave to the clay men, women, fish, animals, and plants, the time of their quarrels is the time when the men, women, fish, and animals, and plants are sick.

It is also the time of the sirocco.

It is also the time of war.

Ceremonial mask from the Ivory Coast

ABIJAN MUSEUM; RAPHO-GUILLUMETTE–MARC AND EVELYNE BERNHEIM

It is also the time of storms—

The stars are precious stones that the Guela on High makes shine to attract women to him.

The moon is the eye of the Guela on High.

With its eye open or half-open, the Guela on High watches the Guela Below, his enemy—even in the night, when he takes away the sun from the Guela Below, the sun he gave him along with life to the men, women, fish, animals, and plants of clay.

This was before all things were on the earth and in the sky.

THE REVOLT AGAINST GOD

This vivid creation myth, related by the Fang people of Gabon in West Africa, tells of a being whose ambition causes his fall from grace.

At the beginning of Things, when there was nothing, neither man, nor animals, nor plants, nor heaven, nor earth, nothing, nothing, God *was* and he was called Nzame. The three who are Nzame, we call them Nzame, Mebere, and Nkwa. At the beginning Nzame made the heaven and the earth and he reserved the heaven for himself. Then he blew onto the earth and earth and water were created, each on its side.

Nzame made everything: heaven, earth, sun, moon, stars, animals, plants; everything. When he had finished everything that we see today, he called Mebere and Nkwa and showed them his work.

"This is my work. Is it good?"

They replied, "Yes, you have done well."

"Does anything remain to be done?"

Mebere and Nkwa answered him, "We see many animals, but we do not see their chief; we see many plants, but we do not see their master."

As masters for all these things, they appointed the elephant, because he had wisdom; the leopard, because he had power and cunning; and the monkey, because he had malice and suppleness.

But Nzame wanted to do even better; and between them he, Mebere, and Nkwa created a being almost like themselves. One gave him force, the second sway, and the third beauty. Then the three of them said:

"Take the earth. You are henceforth the master of all that exists. Like us you have life, all things belong to you, you are the master."

Nzame, Mebere, and Nkwa returned to the heights to their dwelling place, and the new creature remained below alone, and everything obeyed him. But among all the animals the elephant remained the first, the leopard the second, and the monkey the third, because it was they whom Mebere and Nkwa had first chosen.

Nzame, Mebere, and Nkwa called the first man *Fam*—which means power.

Proud of his sway, his power, and his beauty, because he surpassed in these three qualities the elephant, the leopard, and the monkey, proud of being able to defeat all the animals, this first man grew wicked; he became arrogant, and did not want to worship Nzame again: and he scorned him:

> Yeye, o, layeye,
> God on high, man on the earth,
> Yeye, o, layeye,
> God is God,
> Man is man,
> Everyone in his house, everyone
> for himself!

God heard the song. "Who sings?" he asked.

"Look for him," cried Fam.

"Who sings?"

"Yeye, o, layeye!"

"Who sings?"

"Eh! it is me!" cried Fam.

Furious, God called Nzalan, the thunder. "Nzalan, come!" Nzalan came running with great noise: *boom, boom, boom!* The fire of heaven fell on the forest. The plantations burnt like vast torches. *Foo, foo, foo!*—everything in flames. The earth was then, as today, covered with forests. The trees burnt; the plants, the bananas, the cassava, even the pistachio nuts, everything dried up; animals, birds, fishes, all were destroyed, everything was dead. But when God had created the first man, he had told him, "You will never die." And what God gives he does not take away. The first man was burnt, but none knows what became of him. He is alive, yes, but where?

But God looked at the earth, all black, without anything, and idle; he felt ashamed and wanted to do better. Nzame, Mebere, and Nkwa took counsel and they did as follows: over the black earth covered with coal they put a new layer of earth; a tree grew, grew bigger and bigger and when one of its seeds fell down, a new tree was born, when a leaf severed itself it grew and grew and began to walk. It was an animal, an elephant, a leopard, an antelope, a tortoise—all of them. When a leaf fell into the water it swam, it was a fish, a sardine, a crab, an oyster—all of them. The earth became again what it had been, and what it still is today. The proof that this is the truth is this: when one digs up the earth in certain places, one finds a hard black stone which breaks; throw it in the fire and it burns.

But Nzame, Mebere, and Nkwa took counsel again; they needed a chief to command all the animals. "We shall make a man like Fam," said Nzame, "the same legs and arms, but we shall turn his head and he shall see death."

Ancestor head of Gabon's Fang people

GIRAUDON

This was the second man and the father of all. Nzame called him *Sekume*, but did not want to leave him alone, and said, "Make yourself a woman from a tree."

Sekume made himself a woman and she walked and he called her *Mbongwe*.

When Nzame made Sekume and Mbongwe he made them in two parts, an outer part called Gnoul, the body, and the other which lives in the body, called Nsissim.

Nsissim is that which produces the shadow, Nsissim is the shadow—it is the same thing. It is Nsissim who makes Gnoul live. Nsissim goes away when man dies, but Nsissim does not die. Do you know where he lives? He lives in the eye. The little shining point you see in the middle, that is Nsissim.

> Stars above
> Fire below
> Coal in the hearth
> The soul in the eye
> Cloud smoke and death.

Sekume and Mbongwe lived happily on earth and had many children. But Fam, the first man, was imprisoned by God under the earth. With a large stone he blocked the entrance. But the malicious Fam tunneled at the earth for a long time, and one day, at last, he was outside! Who had taken his place? The new man. Fam was furious with him. Now he hides in the forest to kill them, under the water to capsize their boats.

> Remain silent,
> Fam is listening,
> To bring misfortune;
> Remain silent.

MAN'S NOBLE PEDIGREE

The great nineteenth-century English naturalist Charles Darwin shocked the world and revolutionized science by proposing that all life can be traced to a common ancestry. His two most famous works are The Origin of Species (1859), *in which he outlines the theory of natural selection, and* The Descent of Man (1871), *from which these passages are taken. Darwin was accused of denigrating man by relating him to apes and of having underminded the credibility of science through "flimsy speculation." However, as is shown here, the scientist was a profound admirer of all life, especially his human brethren.*

The most ancient progenitors in the kingdom of the Vertebrata, at which we are able to obtain an obscure glance, apparently consisted of a group of marine animals. . . . These animals probably gave rise to a group of fishes, as lowly organized as the lancelet; and from these the Ganoids, and other fishes like the Lepidosiren, must have been developed. From such fish a very small advance would carry us on to the Amphibians. We have seen that birds and reptiles were once intimately connected together; and the Monotremata [egg-laying mammals such as the platypus] now connect mammals with reptiles in a slight degree. But no one can at present say by what line of descent the three higher and related classes, namely, mammals, birds, and reptiles, were derived from the two lower vertebrate classes, namely, amphibians and fishes. In the class of mammals the steps are not difficult to conceive which led from the ancient Monotremata to the ancient Marsupials; and from these to the early progenitors of the placental mammals. We may thus ascend to the Lemuridae; and the interval is not very wide from these to the Simiadae. The Simiadae then branched off into two great stems, the New World and Old World monkeys; and from the latter, at a remote period, Man, the wonder and glory of the Universe, proceeded.

We are naturally led to enquire, where was the birthplace of man at that stage of descent when our progenitors diverged from the Catarhine stock? The fact that they belonged to this stock clearly shows that they inhabited the Old World; but not Australia nor any oceanic island, as we may infer from the laws of geographical distribution. In each great region of the world the living mammals are closely related to the extinct species of the same region. It is therefore probable that Africa was formerly inhabited by extinct apes closely allied to the gorilla and chimpanzee; and as these two species are now man's nearest allies, it is somewhat more probable that our early progenitors lived on the African continent than elsewhere. But it is useless to speculate on this subject. . . .

Thus we have given to man a pedigree of prodigious length, but not, it may be said, of noble quality. The world, it has often been remarked, appears as if it had long been preparing for the advent of man: and this, in one sense is strictly true, for he owes his birth to a long line of progenitors. If any single link in this chain had never existed, man would not have been exactly what he now is. Unless we willfully close our eyes, we may, with our present knowledge, approximately recognize our parentage; nor need we feel ashamed of it. The most humble organism is something much higher then the inorganic dust under our feet; and no one with an unbiased mind can study any living creature, however humble, without being struck with enthusiasm at its marvelous structure and properties.

EMERGING MAN

In the century that has elapsed since Darwin published his studies of evolution, dramatic progress has been made in anthropology and related disciplines. Although much data is still conjectural and controversial, scholars can now piece together, with a fair degree of accuracy, the fascinating story of man's African beginnings. The following essay, recently written by Dr. C. Loring Brace, curator of physical anthropology at the University of Michigan's museum, is a lucid survey of what has been learned to date. It suggests how man originated in Africa; why all his forebears were black; and why some, through adaptation, have what we call white skins.

Central to any definition of man, and the key to his evolutionary success, is a phenomenon not immediately visible when specimens of the creature are scrutinized. This phenomenon is what the anthropologist calls culture. It includes not only the high points of art, music, and literature, but also all those things that result from the cumulative efforts of other people and previous generations. Tools, the traditions regulating their use, vital information, and language itself—all are included in the concept culture. Man is not just an animal that possesses culture, but an animal that cannot survive without it. Men could not exist if each had to discover anew the control of fire, the manufacture of clothing and shelter, the sources of edible sustenance, and the guidelines for workable interpersonal relationships, to say nothing of the mechanics, electronics, chemistry, and physics on which human life depends today. These elements of culture are a cumulative continuation of simpler counterparts in the past.

In the beginning our ancestors, like other animals, must have been faced with the problem of surviving without the aid of culture. So much of culture is perishable or intangible that there is no way to determine when culture as a cumulative phenomenon began. Nonperishable cultural elements have an antiquity of about two million years in Africa. The cultural tradition of which they are a part continues without break, expanding to occupy the tropical and temperate parts of the Old World around 800,000 years ago, and ultimately developing into all the cultures in the world today.

From this we postulate an African origin for all mankind. The existence of crude stone tools in Africa a million and a half to two million years ago allows us to suppose the existence of culture at that time. Our guess suggests that the possessor of this culture could not have survived without it; therefore, he deserves the designation *man*—however primitive and crude he might have been.

We further postulate that culture existed a long time before the initial appearance of recognizable stone tools. This is speculation, but not idle specula-

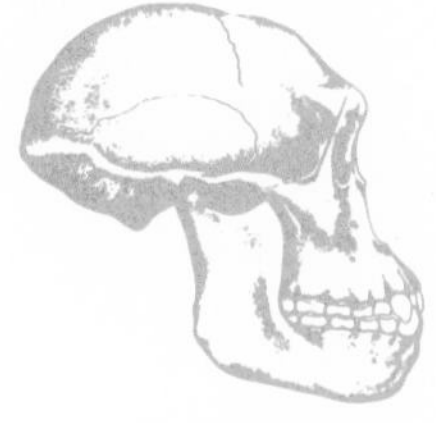

These skulls represent, in descending order, three critical stages in evolution: Australopithecus, *Neanderthal man, and Cro-Magnon man, an early* Homo sapiens.
ROMER, *Vertebrate Paleontology*, SMITHSONIAN INSTITUTION

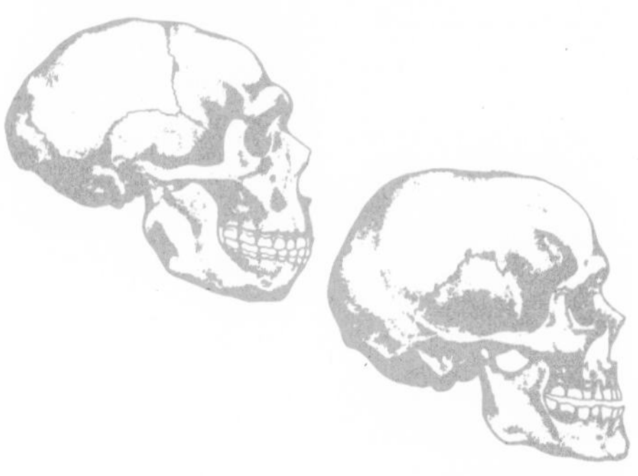

tion, because we could not otherwise account for the transformation of ape to man. Although small in quantity, supporting evidence exists in the form of skeletal material. Fossilized remains, including skulls, jaws, teeth, and a few other skeletal pieces have been found in association with the oldest known stone tools both in Olduvai Gorge in East Africa and in the Transvaal of South Africa. Since the discovery of these fossils in 1924, argument has continued over their status—ape? man? human ancestor? extinct side line? Brain size was within the range of that for the large modern anthropoid apes, but these early hominids walked erect on two feet as does modern man. Molar teeth were of gorilloid size, but the canines did not project beyond the level of the other teeth.

Despite continuing arguments over whether the balance of traits was on the human or simian side, it is apparent that the survival of these early hominids depended on a distinctly non-apelike adaptation. Bipedal locomotion did not enable hominids to escape predators by rapid flight. Neither could these hominids seriously threaten to bite a potential predator. Contrast this with such modern ground-dwelling primates as baboon and gorillas where the enlarged canine teeth of the males represent formidable defense weapons. We can guess that these early hominids depended for survival on something not visible in their anatomy, and our guess is that they used hand-held tools.

Possibly they defended themselves with the crude hunks of worked stone found at the sites where their skeletal remains have been discovered, but more likely they relied on pointed sticks. To use a rock as a defensive weapon requires close contact with the attacking creature, while the defender probably preferred to face his tormentor from the far end of a pointed stick. Not only is the pointed stick a simple and effective weapon—devisable with a minimum of manufacturing effort—but it can also double as a digging tool. Edible roots and bulbs are a substantial part of the diet of baboons that live today in the savanna, an environment typical of the areas inhabited by the earliest hominids. The addition of a simple digging stick of the kind used by the surviving hunting and gathering human groups—and probably by the early hominids—could easily double the baboons' food supply.

The huge, worn molars of the early hominids indicate that they relied on gritty, uncooked vegetables for subsistence. Unlike any other primates, their canine teeth are functionally indistinguishable from their small incisors. Assuming that the remote hominid ancestor had enlarged canine teeth like all other primates, then the creatures associated with the stone tools in East and South Africa two million years ago belonged to a line in which the selective pressures needed to maintain large canines had been suspended for a long time. Cultural means of defense must have existed long before the earliest stone tools.

Within the last three years jaws and teeth have been found in southwestern Ethiopia that are so like the Olduvai and Transvaal finds that they must be related. Their antiquity, however, extends back nearly four million years, and no stone tools are associated with them. The canine teeth in the fragmentary remains are not enlarged, leaving us to infer that defensive weapons must have been used some four million years ago—two million years before the earliest stone tools existed. Reliance on hand-held weapons for defense (and perhaps also for food getting) did not automatically convert apes into men, but it altered the forces of selection so that evolution in the human direction was a consequence. For one thing, occupation with tool wielding reduced the locomotor role of hands. Legs and feet, as a result of natural selection, assumed the entire burden of locomotion. Tools usurped the defensive role of canine teeth, and, with an accumulation of mutations, these teeth were reduced. The vast majority of mutations interfere with the development of the structures that depend on their control, but usually these "deleterious mutations" are eliminated by selection. When selection is reduced or suspended—as when tools reduced the defensive role of teeth—the reductive mutations simply accumulate in the ongoing gene pool of the population. The structure controlled by the genes—the canine teeth, for example—eventually fails to achieve the full development once characteristic of the remote ancestral population. . . .

The evidence from Olduvai Gorge in East Africa shows that crude stone tools were added to the limited cultural repertoire toward the end of this long early hominid phase—a period I prefer to call the australopithecine stage. These tools belong to the incipient part of a tradition of butchering large animals in the Middle Pleistocene. At the end of the Lower Pleistocene, however, they occur mainly with the fossilized remains of immature animals. We can guess that this records the beginning of the adaptive shift that was largely responsible for the development of *Homo sapiens*, a shift related to the development of hunting as a major subsistence activity.

In the Middle Pleistocene, somewhat less than a million years ago, man emerges as a major predator. This adaptation is unique among the primates, and it is not surprising that many of the physical, behavioral, and physiological characteristics that distinguish man from his closest animal relatives are related to this adaptation. While we cannot make direct behavioral or physiological tests on fossils, we can make inferences based on their anatomy, on their apparent ecological adaptation, and on conditions observable in their modern descendants.

Anthropologists generally agree that the men of the Middle Pleistocene are properly classified as *Homo erectus*. The first specimen to be discovered was classified in the genus *Pithecanthropus* at the end of the nineteenth century. While we no longer accept this generic designation, pithecanthropine remains a convenient, nontechnical term for Middle Pleistocene hominids.

Brain size was twice that of the preceding australopithecines and two-thirds that of the average modern man. With the absence of a specialized predatory physique, natural selection probably encouraged the evolution of intelligence. While brain size had increased, the size of the molar teeth had reduced, although they were still quite large by modern standards. This reduction may have been related to the shift from a rough vegetable diet to one with a large proportion of meat. Meat, needing only to be reduced to swallowable pieces, requires far less mastication than starches, which begin the process of conversion to simple sugars by mixing with salivary enzymes through extensive chewing.

Evidence, although fragmentary, also suggests that bipedal locomotion in its modern form was perfected at this time, the Middle Pleistocene. While man's mode of locomotion may not be speedy, it requires an expenditure of relatively little energy. To this day, primitive hunters employ the technique of trotting persistently on the trail of an herbivore until it is brought to bay, often many days later.

Several correlates of this hunting life are suggested. Man, reflecting his primate heritage, is relatively night-blind and must, therefore, confine his hunting activities to the daytime. A tropical mammal (and physiologically man is still a tropical mammal) pursuing strenuous activities in broad daylight is faced with the problem of dissipating metabolically generated heat. The hairless human skin, richly endowed with sweat glands, is unique among terrestrial mammals of much less than elephantine size, and I suggest that this developed under the selective pressures of regular big game hunting early in the pithecanthropine stage.

The elimination of the hairy coat by natural selection left the skin exposed to the potentially damaging effect of the ultraviolet component of tropical sunlight. The obvious response was the development of the protective pigment melanin. Consequently the Middle Pleistocene ancestors of all modern men were probably what in America today is called black.

The conversion of this being into what is technically known as *Homo sapiens* requires only the further expansion of the brain from the pithecanthropine average of 1,000 cubic centimeters (actually well within the range of modern variation) to the average today of 1,400 cubic centimeters. Fragmentary fossil evidence suggests that this transition had taken place by the beginning of the Upper Pleistocene, about 120,000 years ago. Men at that time—referred to as Neanderthals—still had an archaic appearance. In general these early representatives of *Homo sapiens* were more muscular and robust than their modern descendants—particularly the males. Jaws and teeth were large, especially the front teeth, which, from their wear patterns, evidently served as all-purpose tools.

Since the first appearance of *Homo sapiens* in his Neanderthal form, human evolution has been characterized by a series of reductions. Whenever human ingenuity made life easier, there was a relaxation of the forces of selection, and these reductions followed. More effective hunting techniques lessened the burden on the hunter's physique, and an eventual reduction in muscularity was the result. Manipulating tools lessened the stress on the anterior teeth, and the consequent reduction of these and their supporting bony architecture converted the Neanderthal face into modern form. In parts of the world where manipulative technology is a late phenomenon, such as aboriginal Australia, faces and teeth have remained large. Where clothing was developed for survival in northern climes, the significance of protective skin pigment was lessened, and the consequent reduction produced the phenomenon that is euphemistically called white.

The only thing that has not been reduced is the number of human beings. We cannot even guess at the population density of the australopithecines. Throughout the Middle Pleistocene, the archeological record suggests a fairly constant population for the hunting pithecanthropines. Evidently the population increased dramatically with the Neanderthal form of *Homo sapiens*. The diversification of food resources and the increase in cultural complexity that accompanied the first appearance of modern *Homo sapiens* just under 35,000 years ago also signaled another sharp jump in population. This set the stage for the tremendous population growth made possible by the development of agriculture after the end of the Pleistocene 10,000 years ago.

Thus did *Homo sapiens* emerge—a manifestation of ecological imbalance, literally shaped by the consequences of his own impact upon the world. His fate, too, will be shaped by his future impact on the world—the result of his numbers and his actions. Malthus sounded the alarm nearly two centuries ago, but few listened to his warning. One who did was Ambrose Bierce, who added to his definition of man that "his chief occupation is extermination of other animals and his own species, which, however, multiplies with such insistent rapidity as to infest the whole habitable earth. . . ."

"THE MISSING LINK"

Misreadings of Darwin and other evolutionists led many people to the erroneous conclusion that man is directly descended from the gorilla and chimpanzee. This idea provoked a world-wide search for the fossil of a creature that stood halfway between ape and man. Even after it was known that man and the great apes (Pongidae) are descended from a common hominoid ancestor and stand in a cousin to cousin, rather than grandfather to grandchild, relationship, people continued to seek "the missing link." In 1938 the late Dr. Robert Broom, a physician and paleontologist who excavated extensively in the Transvaal, unearthed an ape-man fossil that seemed to confirm earlier suspicions. In this excerpt, from a 1950 report, he describes his discovery of the "Kromdraai ape-man," which he called Paranthropus robustus, *recently reclassified as* Australopithecus.

On the forenoon of Wednesday, June 8, 1938, when I met Barlow, he said, "I've something nice for you this morning"; and he held out part of a fine palate with the first molar-tooth in position. I said, "Yes, it's quite nice. I'll give you a couple of pounds for it." He was delighted; so I wrote out a cheque, and put the specimen in my pocket. He did not seem quite willing to say where or how he had obtained it; and I did not press the matter. The specimen clearly belonged to a large ape-man, and was apparently different from the Sterkfontein being [an *Australopithecus africanus*].

I was again at Sterkfontein on Saturday, when I knew Barlow would be away. I showed the specimen to the native boys in the quarry; but none of them had ever seen it before. I felt sure it had not come from the quarry, as the matrix was different. On Tuesday forenoon I was again at Sterkfontein, when I insisted on Barlow telling me how he had got the specimen. I pointed out that two teeth had been freshly broken off, and that they might be lying where the specimen had been obtained. He apologized for having misled me; and told me it was a school-boy, Gert Terblanche, who acted as guide in the caves on Sundays, who had picked it up and given it to him. I found where Gert lived, about two miles away; but Barlow said he was sure to be away at school. . . .

The road to the school was a very bad one, and we had to leave the car, and walk about a mile over rough ground. When we got there, it was about half-past twelve, and it was play time. I found the headmaster, and told him that I wanted to see Gert Terblanche in connection with some teeth he had picked up. Gert was soon found, and drew from the pocket of his trousers four of the most wonderful teeth ever seen in the world's history. These I promptly purchased from Gert, and transferred to my pocket. I had the palate with me, and I found that two of the teeth were the second pre-molar and second molar, and that they fitted on to the palate. The two others were teeth of the other side. Gert told me about the piece he had hidden away. As the school did not break up till two o'clock, I suggested to the principal that I should give a lecture to the teachers and children about caves, how they were formed, and how bones got into them. He was delighted. So it was arranged; and I lectured to four teachers and about 120 children for over an hour, with blackboard illustrations, till it was nearly two o'clock. When I had finished, the principal broke up the school, and Gert came home with me. He took us up to the hill, and brought out from his hiding place a beautiful lower jaw with two teeth in position. . . .

The spot where the skull had been found was much more carefully examined within a few days. All the ground in the neighborhood was carefully worked over with a sieve, and every fragmentary bone or tooth collected. . . .

When the skull was restored, it was seen to be larger than that of the Sterkfontein ape-man, and to differ in a number of respects. The face is flatter, and the jaw more powerful. The teeth are larger, and in a number of characters different. I therefore made this Kromdraai skull the type of a new genus and species, *Paranthropus robustus.* A preliminary account of the discovery appeared in *The Illustrated London News* of August 20, 1938, under the heading "The Missing Link No Longer Missing"; for which title I think I was not responsible.

There are a number of characters in which this new skull is more human than the Sterkfontein. In the Sterkfontein ape-man we know that the lower canine, at least in the male, is rather large and with a well-marked posterior cusp. In the Kromdraai jaw, though the canine has lost the crown, we have the impression of it on the matrix, and it is about as small as in man, with apparently no posterior cusp. . . .

The teeth of Paranthropus are almost fully known. The incisors and canines are relatively small, but the pre-molars are very large . . . and the molars are also very large, and a little different in details of structure. . . .

In February, 1941, I sent a new assistant with a couple of boys to clean out a little pocket of bone breccia near the spot where the Kromdraai skull had been found. They brought the breccia back to the Museum, and when this was broken up and examined we found a badly preserved lower jaw, but with perfect teeth. Except for the first incisor the whole milk set is preserved and the first true molar crown is shown, but it had probably not yet cut the gum. The milkteeth are practically unworn, and the little being who had them was certainly a little younger than the Taungs child—perhaps three years old.

We do not, of course, know for certain whether this is the jaw of a Paranthropus. As we get the specimens, they are not labeled. But, as it is certainly the jaw of an ape-man child found within two yards of the spot where the adult skull of Paranthropus was discovered, we can refer it with much confidence to the same species. It is most unlikely that two species of ape-men were contemporaries in the same locality. . . .

In the block of matrix in which the Paranthropus skull lay, I was able to find a number of important post-cranial bones. I got the distal end of the right humerus and much of the proximal end of the right ulna. These are so very human that had they been found isolated probably every anatomist in the world would say that they were undoubtedly human. Yet they were found in the matrix only a matter of inches from this remarkably man-like skull; and no trace of any human teeth or implements have been found.

Further, against the maxilla lay a second metacarpal bone with a number of phalanges. These show that the hand was so slender that it could not possibly have been used for walking on.

In the same block of matrix I found an ankle bone—the astragalus, or talus. This bone differs markedly from that of the chimpanzee, and is nearly human, but not quite. It confirms the view that Paranthropus walked on his hand-legs, and used his hands for the manipulation of tools and weapons.

CAVE-KEEPING 20,000 B.C.

Years of research in East Africa have enabled Dr. Louis Leakey to produce the following reconstruction of the life of a caveman.

A Stone Age hunter is wandering down the valley in search of game when he espies a rock-shelter in the side of the rocky cliff above him. Carefully, and with the utmost caution, he climbs up to it, fearful lest he may find that it is occupied by the members of some other Stone Age family who will resent his intrusion, or possibly even that it is the lair of a lion or a cave bear. At last he is close enough, and he sees that it is quite unoccupied, and so he enters and makes a thorough examination. He decides that it is a much more suitable habitation than the little shelter where he and his family are living at present, and he goes off to fetch them.

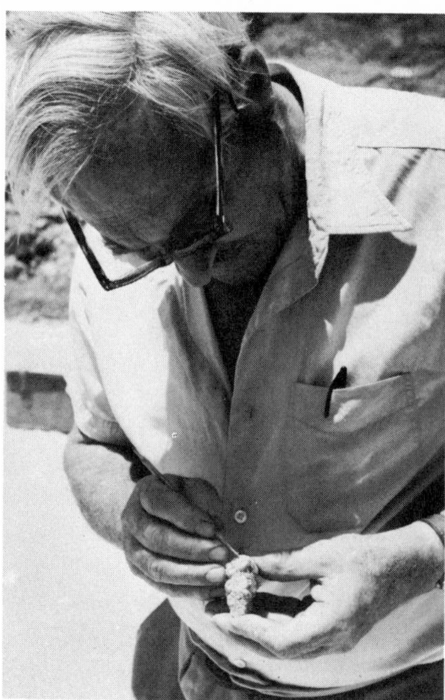

Dr. Louis Leakey examines a fossilized specimen on one of the sites at Olduvai.
RAPHO-GUILLUMETTE; CAMERAPIX, DAR ES SALAAM

Next we see the family arriving and settling into their new home. A fire is lit either from some embers carefully nursed and brought from the old home, or else by means of a simple, wooden fire drill. (We cannot say for certain what methods Stone Age man used for obtaining fire, but we do know that from a very early period he did make use of fire, for hearths are a common feature in almost any occupation level in caves and rock-shelters.)

Probably some of the family then go off to collect grass or bracken to make rough beds upon which they will sleep, while others break branches from bushes and trees in the near-by thicket and construct a rude wall across the front of the shelter. The skins of various wild animals are then unrolled and deposited in the new home, together with such household goods as they possess.

And now the family is fully settled in,

and the day-to-day routine is resumed once more. The men hunt and trap animals for food, the women probably help in this and also collect edible fruits and nuts and roots. Gradually, rubbish starts to accumulate on the floor; decaying vegetation mingles with wood ash scraped from the hearth, and mixed with all this are the bones and teeth of the animals that have served for food. The stone and bone tools, which comprise the weapons and domestic implements of the family, break or become blunt through use, and they are discarded and new ones made. Blocks of suitable material collected during hunting expeditions have been brought to the new home, and from these flakes are knocked off to make new tools. This process involves the scattering of many waste flakes and chips over the floor, and these soon become incorporated in the debris in the same way as the tools that have become too blunt for further use. When the weather is fine a great deal of the work is done on the platform outside the shelter, so that deposits accumulate there too.

Years pass, the older members of the family die and—according to custom—are buried in the floor of the shelter; the younger members of the family grow up and marry, and all the time the home continues to be used, so that more and more debris accumulates on the floor. A large part of this debris is perishable material which by the process of decay turns into soil, throughout which imperishable objects of stone and bone are scattered.

Naturally enough, the deposits so formed do not accumulate evenly over the whole floor, and although the floor may have been level to start with (and even this is seldom the case) it very soon ceases to be so.

And so generations pass and a considerable depth of deposit is formed representing an occupation level, and then something happens which results in the shelter being vacated. When this occurs the shelter may perhaps be taken over almost immediately by some other Stone Age family—possibly of a different tribe and with a somewhat different culture—in which case we shall get a somewhat different occupation level superimposed upon the first one. On the other hand, the shelter may remain untenanted for a considerable period of time, in which case dust and leaves and other purely natural material will collect and gradually build up a sterile layer covering the occupation level, until the place is once more selected as a living site.

THE ART OF THE BUSHMEN

The naturalistic rock paintings and engravings of South Africa are among the richest and best preserved in the world; they provide invaluable information regarding the Bushmen and their ancestors. The surviving paintings and carvings were probably executed no earlier than 2,000 *years ago; however, they are based on traditions that date back to the beginning of the Late Stone Age, about* 11,000 *years ago. The following description of the life of the Bushmen and Late Stone Age hunters was written in* 1963 *by Alex Willcox, a noted interpreter of South African rock art.*

"Bushmanoid" peoples occupied most of Southern Africa, except the heavily forested areas, for many centuries before the pastoral Hottentots and the Bantu arrived.

Their culture, it has already been said, was non-pastoral and non-agricultural, the natural resources of the veld alone providing their food and their whole equipment. Hunting and fishing secured their protein requirements, but their very varied diet included innumerable varieties of berries and other fruits, bulbs, roots and nuts, seeds, insects, ant and termite eggs, birds' eggs, shell-fish, honey, etc. Some of these were sources of liquid also (or at least they are now), e.g. the body fluids and stomach contents of animals and the juices of fruits such as the tsamma melon. Although a hard struggle in their latter days and now, their life must have been easy enough before being disrupted by newcomers, for the earliest travelers found immense herds of game roaming the still unravished veld in the Bushmen territories.

Their habitations were natural rock shelters where these were found and small crude shelters of branches elsewhere; their clothing, loin cloths, aprons and cloaks (karosses) of animal skins, their ornaments, beads made from ostrich eggshell, bands of leather or rings of ivory about their limbs, or simply body paint. Having to trek whenever, because of local drought or over-hunting, the game became scarce, the Bushmen kept their equipment to a minimum in quantity and weight. A typical camp would have, in addition to clothes and ornaments, only the women's digging sticks and the spheroidal bored stones which weighted them, leather bags to contain the collected foods, calabashes, ostrich eggshells or the sewn-up skins of small animals as water containers, probably an upper and nether grindstone for crushing seeds, melon pips, etc. and perhaps a crude pot or two. There would also be the men's bows and arrows, quivers, knob-kerries, fire-sticks and painting equipment. Stone implements for cutting up and skinning their kills, for scraping the skins and for wood working (e.g. making bows and arrows and knob-kerries) would lie about but would not be transported when trekking, others being made in a few seconds when required.

The short weak Bushman bow with its bow-string of twisted sinew, the quiver made of leather or by hollowing out a section of a branch of Aloe Dichotoma, and the reed arrows, are too well known to need further description here. The arrow heads were most commonly of bone and latterly formed by a small triangle of iron beaten flat, but a few perfect tanged and barbed stone points have been found and there is good historical evidence that arrow heads were also made of laurel-leaf shaped points and by a pair of *crescents* placed together and cemented to the foreshaft with vegetable mastic. These were barbed with quills, thorns or small splinters of stone. The minutest crescents might have been used thus. It is difficult to see any other use for them. The poison spread behind the point was from many sources including snake venom, spiders, grubs of a certain insect and the juices of various plants.

The curious implement often seen in the rock paintings made by fixing a jackal's tail to the end of a short stick, which served various purposes from wiping perspiration from the brow, to swatting flies and signaling, was commonly used also by Hottentots and Bantu.

Naturalists to a man the Bushmen had names for the flora and fauna of their environment and knew well the habits of the animals, birds, and insects, and the properties as food, medicine, poison and perhaps as paint media, of the plants. They had even discovered a plant which by its smell would keep lions away. They were geologists enough to know where to find the minerals from which they made pigments and the best stones for making implements; and they were astronomers enough to name the principal stars and planets and know their peculiarities. As meteorologists they became renowned rain-doctors. In short they had an impressive body of practical knowledge and knew their environment better than most civilized men know theirs.

Their amusements were dancing, mime, music, storytelling and the graphic arts. Rhythmic clapping accompanied the dances which often took the form of one or a few dancers dressed in the skins of animals miming their actions, sometimes solely for entertainment, but sometimes no doubt, also for ritual and magical purposes, as in the case of the eland bull dance of the Naron.

STONE AGE SURVIVORS

Ethnographical studies are often valuable supplements to paleontological and artistic materials. The following excerpt is from a 1965 report by H. R. MacCalman and B. J. Grobbelaar describing two stone-working OvaTjimba groups that still exist in the Kaokoveld mountain range of South West Africa. Despite long contacts with the pastoral Hottentots, they remain hunters and gatherers.

Living with these OvaHimba was a group of fourteen people who, it was immediately apparent, did not correspond to them either physically or culturally. They spoke Herero like the OvaHimba but in a dialect form, and said that they were of the Tjimba tribe. The group consisted of three men with their wives, three adult daughters, three small children and two babies. On questioning we learned that they normally lived in the heights of the Baynes Mountains, but had come down because of a sick child and were now living with the OvaHimba, helping in the village and herding goats in return for medicine and food. They informed us that they owned no cattle but lived by hunting and gathering. On being asked to show their hunting weapons they produced bows and arrows with crude iron arrowheads and demonstrated that for other activities they used stone tools. . . .

The most important aspect of the Okombambi group technology, however, is the use of stone as an habitual and integral part of their material culture. On being asked what implements they used they replied that they made knives and choppers from stone, and voluntarily demonstrated their manufacture. . . .

Kaupatana regarded his stay at Otjinungua as merely a temporary move.

This Bushman woman transports her youngest—and probably all her household belongings—in a pair of leather slings. Typically, her people own no domesticated animals, and the task of providing sustenance is sharply divided between the hunters (male) and the gatherers (female). The life of Bushmen is one of mobility; they travel in small, semiautonomous groups under the leadership of a headman and come together in larger assemblies only during the melon season, the occasion for joyous celebration.

BLACK STAR—CONSTANCE STUART

When the rains came, he told us, he would take his family back up the Baynes Mountains and they would continue to live, as before, by hunting and gathering.

Kaupatana does the hunting using a bow and poisoned arrow, and the same range of animals are hunted and trapped as by the Okombambi group. He is also responsible for the collection of wild honey. The two women collect *veldkos* [vegetable foods] and this also comprises the same species as the Okombambi group collects.

When a big animal is killed it is first skinned and then the meat is cut off and the carcase dismembered, in all cases using stone flakes. As Kaupatana's bow needed restringing, a springbok was shot by the stock inspector and given to Kaupatana so that he could demonstrate how he would skin and butcher the animal while living in the mountains.

First, Kaupatana selected a suitable pebble from the river bed and struck some twenty flakes from it using the block-on-block method. These he examined very carefully and selected four flakes, all between two and three inches in length, which had a suitable shape and sharp edge. No further sharpening or shaping of these flakes was done.

Using one of the flakes Kaupatana slit the skin of the belly of the springbok from throat to tail and proceeded to cut the skin, which he held in his right hand, from the carcase. The flake was held between the thumb and first two fingers of the left hand, Kaupatana being left-handed, with the forefinger resting along the top and was used with short slashing strokes. In this way he skinned one half of the springbok, the skin on the legs being slit and taken off up to the hoof. The other half of the springbok was then skinned and the animal was turned over so that the complete skin could be detached along the back. Finally, Kaupatana cut off one shoulder, still using a stone flake, in order to demonstrate how the carcase is dismembered. The carcase was then carried back to the camp place . . .

BUSHMAN'S PRAYER

This prayer reflects the Bushman's age-old activity: hunting. These hardy peoples still live in the Kalahari, which covers large areas of Botswana and South West Africa.

I do not know
What will happen to me
Regarding food.
I do not know
What I shall do
To get something to eat.
Let us eat and become big.

HUNTERS OF MODERN AFRICA

When the first Europeans arrived in South Africa in the fifteenth century, they found groups of hunters who had not yet entered the Iron Age. Indeed, some hunters, having retreated into the Kalahari under Bantu and European pressure, have even today continued to perpetuate ancient modes, barely altered by outside influences. The following excerpt by Monica Wilson, professor of social anthropology at the University of Cape Town, describes the present economy and social structure of southern Africa's hunters and collectors, notably the Kung, the San, and G/wi peoples. It is based in part on reports of colonists and travelers up through the 1800's, but it also draws on contemporary scholarship, such as L. Marshall's studies of the Kung Bushmen.

The hunters and collectors described by the early travelers and settlers inhabited the mountains and the sea-shore. They had no domestic animals except the dog and lived off game, of which there were enormous herds in southern Africa; wild roots and berries, commonly called veldkos; caterpillars, termites, and locusts; wild honey; and fish. . . . Recent studies in the Kalahari show that, even in the desert, vegetable foods play a major part in the diet of hunters, and this is likely to have been the case when they occupied better-watered country. A digging stick, tipped with bone and weighted with a bored stone, and a skin cloak which also served as a bag, were the women's equipment among the mountain people, and these are still used in the desert, though the stick is not always tipped and weighted; in the desert ostrich eggshells, used for storing water, are a housekeeper's essential utensils.

Honey was so important that wild hives were marked as private property and a thief who stole from one might be killed by the owner. . . . The hunters of the mountains fished in the rivers with harpoons made of bone, and trapped eels, when opportunity offered, and the Strandlopers [hunters and collectors on the shore] lived off shellfish and other fish caught on lines, and in the fishgarths which are still visible along the Cape coast. All the hunters used bows and poisoned arrows. The effective range was small—twenty-five yards among the G/wi—and hunters crept up on herds, sometimes disguising themselves in buck-skins or ostrich feathers. Then they followed the wounded animal until the poison took effect; they were highly skilled in tracing a spoor. They dug traps for large game, and built stone or brushwood fences, or posts or cairns, the height of a hunter, and surmounted by feathers, to form converging lanes through which game was driven. This suggests co-operation between a considerable number of men. . . .

The hunters also burnt the grass during winter to attract game to the fresh pasture and to make them more visible, and to encourage the growth of spring bulbs. This firing of the grass was a common cause of friction with the herders, who likewise burnt for fresh pasture, but who needed to preserve some areas of long grass to maintain their cattle. The hunters were fair-weather men, because their bows were not serviceable in the rain—the gut string snapped—and they always lay up in their caves during rain in the mountains and, where they had the choice, selected drier rather than wetter country.

The hunt supplied not only food but clothing, which was made of skins, and the furs and feathers which were, and still are, traded to other peoples for iron and tobacco. Even the every-day utensils of ostrich-eggshell and tortoise carapace were hunters' trophies.

The hunters lived and still live in bands, each independent of the next, and their characteristic is isolation. . . . In the Queenstown district in the nineteenth century every band used a cave as its headquarters, and in each of these there was a painting which was sacred and from which a band took its name. One painting was of a python, another of springbok, another of eland, and so forth. The desert bands, on which we have evidence, have no headquarters, but each has a name, which continues through time, and each moves within a defined area. All the hunting groups have, and had, territories over which their prior rights are recognized. . . . Mrs. Marshall's statement fits very closely with that of Kolb who reported in 1707 that "Hottentots of every kraal and nation have the liberty of hunting throughout all the Hottentot countries."

However, neither isolation nor the recognition of territory precluded movement over a hundred miles or perhaps much further. San living in the Drakensberg [Mountains] painted boats which could only have been seen near the coast, a hundred miles away, and mounds of shells from shellfish have been found on middens fifty miles inland. Hunting expeditions typically lure men far afield, and in the traditional histories of Africa it is most often the hunter who explores and settles in a new territory. The San were surely no exception. Interaction with only a small number of people is not to be confused with confinements to a limited area.

Among the !Kung, marriage between neighboring bands is approved, and movement of families of parents and children from one band to another occurs, but only within the area recognizing some common unity. This includes thirty-six or thirty-seven bands and a thousand persons. The diversity in language among the hunters, even neighboring bands sometimes not understanding one another . . . is surely a reflection of long isolation.

Control over rights in water and vegetable foods is vested in a custodian among the !Kung. The office is hereditary, passing from father to son (or failing a son to a daughter and through her to her son), but there is no chief with power to adjudicate in disputes and enforce judgments. The custodian's precedence is recognized by his taking the head of the line when the band moves, and making the first fire in a new camp, from which others take brands, but he does not necessarily organize hunting parties or trading trips, and when theft or adultery occurs the wronged person will kill the one who has injured him, or they fight until both are killed. The whole band, however, is concerned to reconcile quarrelling members, for the loss of a hunter means a serious loss in food and, if weapons are used, the smallest scratch may mean death, since the poison with which arrows are smeared is deadly. Mrs. Marshall describes very vividly how men and women gather quickly, seeking to compose any quarrel that arises. A fight once begun is feared almost like atomic warfare. Taking fire from the custodian is a recognition of his leadership among the !Kung, as among so many peoples in Africa. He himself starts the first fire at each camp with firesticks, and even where hunters are clients of herders there is no fiction of inability to ignite a fire as among the pygmies.

No matter how wide the territory they occupy, or how much individual families may have to scatter during drought to find food, when a band moves as a group the members camp and build their shelters close together—so close that sisters in different households can hand things to each other. . . . One of the jibes of the Sotho against the San was that all slept together without regard for decency, but eyewitness evidence shows that the !Kung camp in a regular order, each married couple establishing their shelter, or a symbol of it, beside their fire, and people sitting in their set order, men to the right of the fire facing the entrance to the shelter, women to the left. Boys from about the age of puberty sleep by their own fire with other boys of the band, and girls of the same age with some single woman, unless they themselves are already married. Each person may indeed hollow out a sleeping place to escape the biting night wind. The shelters and fires are huddled together in the wide expanse of the desert, and it might be that a stranger, coming on a deserted camp, would suppose that the whole band slept promiscuously. He would be mistaken, but relationships in an isolated band are necessarily intimate. . . .

Among the !Kung each woman cooked the veldkos she had collected for her own husband and young children, but the meat of any animal shot was distributed, the man whose arrow had first struck the animal allocating portions, according to set rule, to individuals in the band, for no one eats alone "like a lion."

The family of parents and children held together until a son married, when he went to live with his wife's band, and to hunt for his parents-in-law. Only after the birth of several children was he free to rejoin his own band, but he did not always do so, and no large descent groups, such as are common among the herders and cultivators, developed. . . .

At her first menstruation a girl, even though already married, was secluded and observed various taboos, and a great dance miming the courtship of the eland bull was performed in her honor. Circumcision was not a general practice among the hunters (though the Sotho claim to have learned it from the San), but a ritual which marked the attainment of adult status was celebrated for groups of boys. The elements emphasized by various writers are the testing of a boy's ability as a hunter; treatment with medicines to give him skill in hunting; and the performance of certain dances. The boy's rite preceded marriage, and among the !Kung it was a condition of marriage, for he must have proved himself as a hunter before he could marry, and bring to his bride's parents a large animal he, himself, had killed. . . .

Property that could be inherited did not exist—except for certain rights over the water and veldkos in a given area—and kinship bonds in time, which are so closely tied to the inheritance of wealth, were not treated as important. Nor was there a veneration of the ancestors comparable to that general among the Bantu-speaking peoples. . . .

The gods spoken of by the San of the Cape were Kaggen (Cagn, Qhang, 'Kaang) who made all things, and the mantis which was his embodiment. To J. M. Orpen's query: "Where is !Kaang?" a hunter replied: "We don't know, but the elands do. Have you not hunted and heard his cry, when the elands suddenly started and ran to his call? Where he is the elands are in droves like cattle." It is as though Pan and the mantis held the poetic imagination in the south of Africa as on the Mediterranean shore. The hunters danced at the new moon and full moon, and prayed for good hunting. . . . But these ideas were not held by all the hunters, and from the scanty material it is not possible to formulate any general beliefs which have continued through time. . . .

For all that their food supply was precarious and search for food occupied most of their time, San hunters were prolific artists. They painted or engraved on stone and ostrich eggs; they made thousands of ostrich eggshell beads to adorn themselves; they told myths; and above all, they danced. The myths and paintings were connected and so, perhaps, were the dances, for they painted dances as well as animals and hunting scenes. . . .

Men and women, daily engaged in the strenuous search for food, nevertheless found strength at night to dance. . . . In the dances the hunters regularly mimed animals: the courtship of the eland bull; the kudu; a gemsbok hunt; a hyena feeding off a carcass and keeping jackals at bay; vultures at the carcass of a zebra; ostriches. It seems as if the acute observation of animals, necessary to a hunter, had to find some expression in artistic form, whether it be painting, or dancing, or myth. The Naron say "in olden times the trees were people, and the animals were people . . .", and the world view of all the hunters depicted a time when animals spoke like men, and there was friendship between them.

TRACKING FATHER ELEPHANT

The spirit and drama of the chase is expressed in numerous tribal poems. This one, chanted by the Gabon Pygmies, evokes the mystery and stillness of the black forest night.

Elephant hunter, take your bow!
Elephant hunter, take your bow!

In the weeping forest, under the wing of the evening
the night all black has gone to rest happy:
in the sky the stars have fled trembling,
fireflies shine vaguely and put out their lights:
above us the moon is dark, its white light is put out.
The spirits are wandering.

Elephant hunter, take your bow!
Elephant hunter, take your bow!

In the frightened forest the tree sleeps, the leaves are dead,
the monkeys have closed their eyes, hanging from the branches above us:
the antelope slip past with silent steps,
eat the fresh grass, prick their ears,
lift their heads and listen frightened:
the cicada is silent, stops his grinding song.

Elephant hunter, take your bow!
Elephant hunter, take your bow!

In the forest lashed by the great rain
Father elephant walks heavily, *baou, baou,*
careless, without fear, sure of his strength,
Father elephant, whom no one can vanquish:
among the trees which he breaks he stops and starts again:
he eats, roars, overturns trees and seeks his mate:
Father elephant, you have been heard from far.

Elephant hunter, take your bow!
Elephant hunter, take your bow!

In the forest where no one passes but you,
hunter, lift up your heart, leap and walk:
meat in front of you, the huge piece of meat,
the meat that walks like a hill,
the meat that makes the heart glad,
the meat that we'll roast on our coals,
the meat into which our teeth sink,
the fine red meat and the blood we drink smoking.

Elephant hunter, take your bow!
Elephant hunter, take your bow!

DEATH OF THE HUNTER

This poem, also included in the repertoire of the Gabon Pygmies, is called "Death Rites." It implies belief in the ascendance of the soul.

The animal runs, it passes, it dies. And it is the great cold.
It is the great cold of the night, it is the dark.
The bird flies, it passes, it dies. And it is the great cold.
It is the great cold of the night, it is the dark.
The fish flees, it passes, it dies. And it is the great cold.
It is the great cold of the night, it is the dark.
Man eats and sleeps. He dies. And it is the great cold.
It is the great cold of night, it is the dark.
There is light in the sky, the eyes are extinguished, the star shines.
The cold is below, the light is on high.
The man has passed, the shade has vanished, the prisoner is free!
Khvum, Khvum, come in answer to our call!

Chapter Two

CIVILIZATIONS OF THE NILE

(c. 4500 B.C.-A.D. 350)

by

Margaret Shinnie

THE ADVANCE FROM A LIFE OF FOOD GATHERING and hunting to one of agriculture brought far-reaching changes to the people. Nomadic life, with its urgent search for food, was replaced by permanent agricultural communities and a greater sense of security. Villages gradually gave rise to towns and the organization of forms of government, and the reliability of seasonal crops and animal herding provided leisure time in which to practice all the arts and crafts, a noticeable feature of this stage of man's development.

Agriculture probably came to Egypt from western Asia, where it had been practiced since about 6000 B.C. or possibly earlier. Although the Nile Valley is particularly well suited to agricultural pursuits, the earliest known farming settlements there date from as late as about 4500 B.C. By about the middle of the fourth century B.C., however, the Egyptians had become dependent on agriculture.

Once this advanced stage of life had been established in Egypt, more sophisticated social and cultural achievements rapidly followed, partly because farming was so unusually easy in the Nile Valley: grain scattered on the silt deposited by the river's annual flood grew of its own accord and had only to be harvested. It has been calculated that by sensible exploitation of his land an Egyptian farmer could produce three times as much grain as was needed for his domestic purposes. As a result, society could support craftsmen, officials, priests, and landowners. Another reason for Egypt's progress was that the Nile Valley, enclosed by infertile land, was slightly remote and easy to defend except in times of internal weakness. Lastly, because of its location, Egypt could share in the advances of the countries of the Levant, whose perpetual struggles with one another may well have given rise to technical achievements that they, involuntarily perhaps, placed at Egypt's disposal.

'he mortuary temple of Ramses II *at Luxor, with a statue of the great ruler*

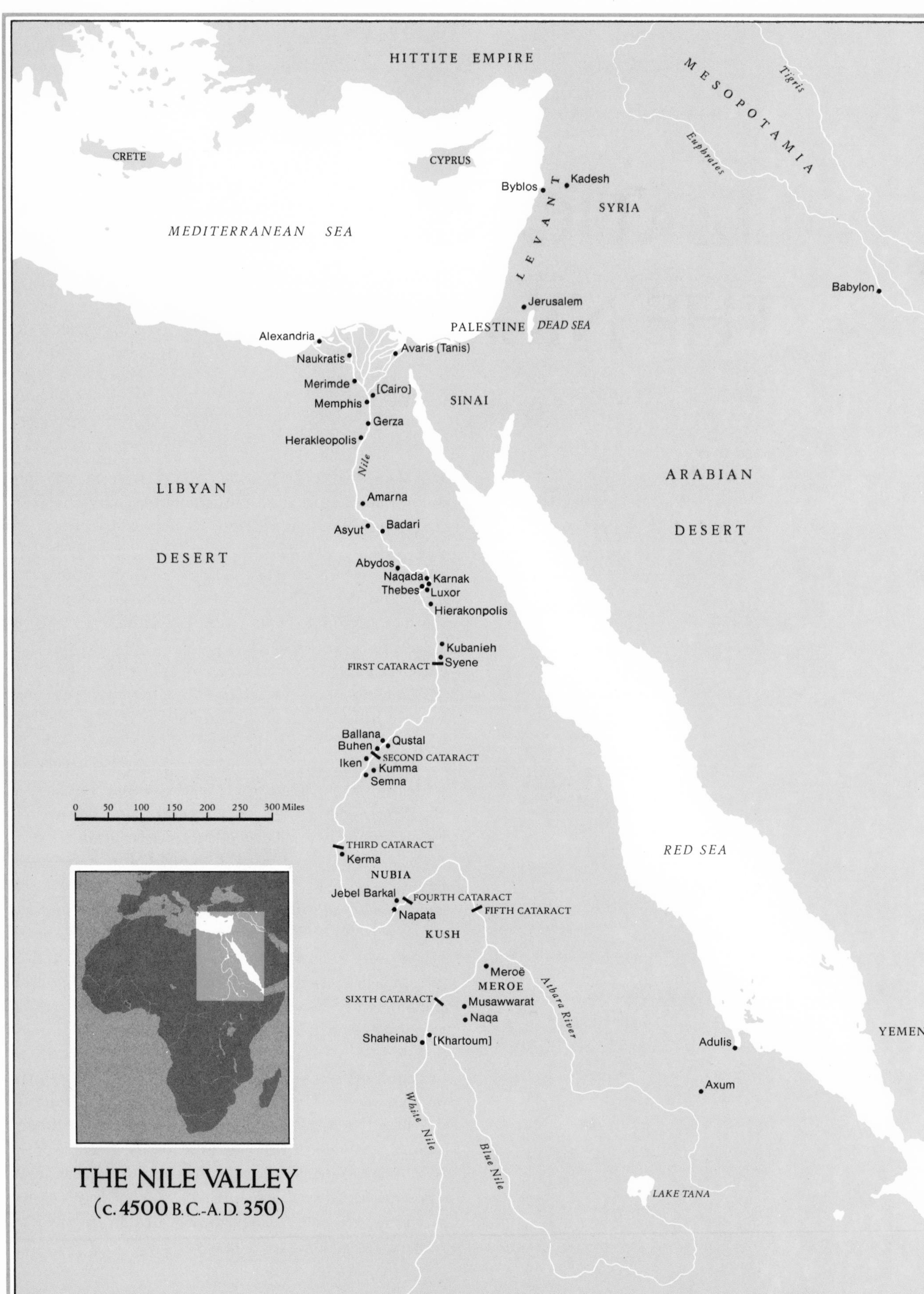
HITTITE EMPIRE
MESOPOTAMIA
Tigris
Euphrates
CRETE
CYPRUS
Byblos
Kadesh
LEVANT
SYRIA
MEDITERRANEAN SEA
Babylon
Jerusalem
PALESTINE
DEAD SEA
Alexandria
Naukratis
Avaris (Tanis)
Merimde
[Cairo]
Memphis
SINAI
Gerza
Herakleopolis
Nile
LIBYAN
DESERT
ARABIAN
DESERT
Amarna
Asyut
Badari
Abydos
Naqada
Karnak
Thebes
Luxor
Hierakonpolis
Kubanieh
Syene
FIRST CATARACT
Ballana
Qustal
Buhen
SECOND CATARACT
Iken
Kumma
Semna
0 50 100 150 200 250 300 Miles
THIRD CATARACT
Kerma
NUBIA
RED SEA
Jebel Barkal
FOURTH CATARACT
Napata
FIFTH CATARACT
KUSH
Meroë
MEROE
Atbara River
SIXTH CATARACT
Musawwarat
Naqa
Shaheinab
[Khartoum]
Adulis
YEMEN
Axum
White Nile
Blue Nile
LAKE TANA

THE NILE VALLEY
(c. 4500 B.C.–A.D. 350)

Although ancient Egypt seems separate from the rest of Africa, isolated in the narrow valley of the Nile and unique in its culture and achievements, there was nevertheless contact with other African peoples—with Libyans to the west and with Kushites and the inhabitants of Punt to the south and southeast. In the earliest days of Egyptian agriculture the neighboring Sahara was not the arid expanse of desert that it later became. Climatically, there was a wet phase. The Saharan rock drawings make this clear, for the many animals portrayed, including cattle, would not be able to exist in the current environment. The people of the Sahara were not only pastoralists but also hunters, who must have hunted over land that was savanna. About 3000 B.C. the wet phase came to an end, and desiccation set in, accelerated perhaps by overgrazing as the aridity increased. It is not unlikely that the Saharan people learned the practice of animal herding and domestication from Egypt, and as the encroaching desert forced them to search farther and farther for better grazing lands, this knowledge was carried slowly to other areas by peoples whose identity is still something of a mystery. (In 1907 the remains of three previously unknown cultures were discovered in the region of Aswan; they were designated as A-, B-, and C-Group people.) The C-Group people, who moved into Nubia from the western desert about 2300 B.C., may have been one of the tribes who were forced southward; others may have gone toward the fertile banks of other great rivers. At Ntereso in northern (modern) Ghana arrowheads of a type common among the Saharan people were found, very much farther south than had been earlier supposed.

Traces of the various peoples who lived in the Nile Valley are prolific, and it is hardly possible to walk along the banks of the river without treading on antiquities—almost every part of the river's bank was inhabited at some time or other. For most of its course the Nile flows through a valley made cultivable by the deposit of silt that the flood brings down from the Ethiopian highlands following the summer monsoon rains. In a year of heavy flood, enriched soil extends some way up the wadis, thus providing further areas for cultivation. Back of the valley lies the desert sand, and at various places, particularly in Upper Egypt and the northern Sudan, a barrier of rocky cliffs separates the flood plain and the desert. Proceeding south into the area of annual rains, the desert lands and the scrub and seasonal grazing lands of the central Sudan give way to wide savannas, and even farther south, near the headwaters, to tropical forest. There is a barrier to river travel in the south in the shape of a tangled mass of floating papyrus and aquatic grass, known as the sudd (meaning in Arabic "obstruction" or "dam"), which even today must be cleared if boats are to pass. It has always been possible to travel overland, however, though the terrain might seem uninviting for such a trek.

Although the Nile would appear to be a natural link between the lands and peoples along its banks, river travel south of Aswan is made difficult by a series of cataracts or, more properly, rapids. The First Cataract at Aswan and the five more cataracts in the Sudan are all unnavigable; even small boats have frequently met with disaster in their attempts to negotiate the currents. All these natural barriers probably impeded the Egyptians from penetrating as far south as they might otherwise have done; but they did have constant contact with Nubia (the lands along the Nile south of the First Cataract) and are known to have traveled as far as the Fifth Cataract.

The earliest agricultural settlements in the Nile Valley are those discovered in the Fayum in Middle Egypt. Here, on the edge of a lake, were village communities that grew wheat and barley—staples of their diet—and possibly herded livestock. Tools and weapons of stone and spear points of bone indicate that they engaged in hunting, which must have played a large part in their lives. They made simple, rough pottery for cooking and storage—useful rather than beautiful—the shapes patterned on leather bags and baskets familiar from times when there was no pottery. If there was a more rudimentary agriculture at an earlier time, evidence of it has either been buried deep in the Nile silt or eroded away by subsequent exploitation of the land for farming and grazing.

Later settlements, whose inhabitants had more sophisticated skills such as carving bone and ivory into spoons and combs, decorating pottery with painted designs, and grinding jars out of alabaster and basalt, have been discovered at various places, the best known being Merimde, Badari, and Naqada. Much of this work reveals a growing appreciation of artistic design and expression, and there must have been craftsmen with tools adequate to practice it. There is also evidence that trade with outside peoples was beginning, for copper objects and fragments of cedar and juniper wood (materials not indigenous to Egypt) suggest contact with other lands, probably by an overland route that presumably crossed Palestine to Syria and the more advanced cultures of western Asia. Arrowheads of a type found widely in the Sahara were also found at Merimde, so there must have been contacts with people to the west of Egypt as well. Malachite, used in the preparation of eye paint, may have come from Nubia or Sinai.

METROPOLITAN MUSEUM OF ART, ROGERS FUND, 1920

METROPOLITAN MUSEUM OF ART

GIRAUDON

BOTH: METROPOLITAN MUSEUM OF ART

Much farther upstream, in and around Khartoum, hunting and fishing and food-gathering communities lived on the riverbank. Two sites that date from fourth century B.C. have been identified, similar in many ways to those of Egypt, but later by a thousand years. Neither crop growing nor animal herding was practiced, though there is a possibility that at the later site, Shaheinab, the domestication of animals had just begun, as evidenced by the discovery of bones identified as those of a domesticated goat. Similarities in the stone tools of this village with some of those of the Fayum villages suggest contact between them, even though the Egyptian influence would have taken about a thousand years to take hold in the Sudan.

Up till this point in time, 3500 B.C. in Egypt and a little later in the Sudan, these small farming communities grew and developed their skills without much contact with the civilizations around them (particularly the more advanced cultures of Mesopotamia). Although agriculture presumably came to Egypt from western Asia, further influences are not apparent at this stage, despite some evidence that small trading activities were beginning. Another factor limiting the development of Egyptian technology was that many of the raw materials, such as hardwoods and metals, essential to the more advanced techniques of Mesopotamia, were not available in Egypt. Vague references in the later literature of early dynastic Egypt allow the inference that these small settlements were products of a social system essentially African in character, with a rainmaking god-king as leader. It was probably very similar to practices that still survive in parts of southern Sudan, where the leader is invested with the power of bringing rain and is ritually killed when his powers begin to wane. (In Egypt it was not so much the bringing of rain that was desired as the control of the Nile flood, which itself is dependent on rain far upstream.)

Physically, the Egyptians at this time were typical North Africans, lightly built brown-skinned people. They were predominately of Afro-Mediterranean type, though in Upper Egypt skeletons of Negroid type have been found. (By pharaonic times a mixing of peoples would take place, and the careful depiction in the tomb paintings of skin color, facial features, and kinds of hair make it clear that there were Afro-Mediterranean, Southwest Asian, and Negroid types among them.) The people of early Khartoum were Negroid, and they shared a distinctive custom of the modern southern Sudanese, that of extracting two incisor teeth. The custom is still observed today to signify manhood.

The next period, starting about 3400 B.C., was one of great development in Egypt; it contained all the fundamental advances that would lead to the brilliance of the Old Kingdom. The most impressive features almost certainly arose out of contacts with Mesopotamia and are well seen at the Nile settlements of Hierakonpolis, Naqada, and Gerza. While it had been possible earlier to make trading ventures by overland routes, the development of a seagoing ship was vital in encouraging and widening the scope of such activities. It was at this time that seaworthy ships capable of sailing the tideless Mediterranean Sea were probably first used; they were most likely built in a well-wooded

The clay models at right, of what may have been fertility figures, were fashioned in the fifth and fourth millenniums B.C. *by predynastic Egyptians. They were principally hunters and fishermen, but also primitive stockbreeders and farmers, and their small, agricultural villages were scattered throughout the Nile Valley before the formation of states and the rise of the great dynastic kingdoms. Also found at ancient sites were the objects on the opposite page: a pottery jar decorated with drawings of human figures, boats, and ostriches; and an assortment of flint knives, including one whose carved handle depicts warriors and boats engaged in a fierce river battle.*

METROPOLITAN MUSEUM OF ART, ROGERS FUND, 1907

area such as the Lebanon. Other innovations found at prehistoric sites included a distinctive wavy-handled pottery, which is related to similar ware from Palestine. Still other innovations came seemingly from Mesopotamian sources: for example, building with sun-dried mud bricks, thus making possible more substantial houses than the earlier light reed or matting huts; using cylinder seals as amulets to protect personal belongings; and, most important of all, developing a pictographic form of writing. Though Egyptian writing was entirely different from that of Mesopotamia, it may well have been inspired by the concept of literacy derived from that culture. Trade, however, was not all in one direction, and Egyptian wares found in Palestine testify to the passage of their goods into wider areas.

During this period the first small states probably emerged in the Nile Valley (on the evidence of ruins found, it looks as though they fell into conflict.) Towns grew up and some of them were apparently fortified. Excavations at Naqada have revealed part of a town wall standing below the enveloping sand, and a little clay model found in a tomb shows a similar wall being guarded by soldiers. Rectangular-shaped townhouses were built of mud brick, though no doubt in the countryside the traditional reed or matting huts, usually approximately circular, persisted, as they still do today. Technological skills increased, and the working of flint reached a standard of perfection that has never been surpassed; the thinnest of knife blades were finished with regular ripple flaking, showing a mastery over material that is truly astonishing.

Toward the end of this period, about 3100 B.C., the coalescing of small towns gave rise to two main states: Lower Egypt, from the Mediterranean to the apex of the Delta; and Upper Egypt, from the south to the First Cataract. These became unified under the first pharaoh, Narmer, but the duality of two states continued down through Egyptian history. In times of internal dissension the rivalry between Lower and Upper Egypt asserted itself until a powerful leader came to the fore with the ability to reunite the country. The pharaoh was known as Lord of the Two Lands, and his two-tiered crown expressed this duality, the white mitre of Upper Egypt being superimposed on the red crown of Lower Egypt. Our conventional division of Egyptian history into dynasties is that given by the third-century B.C. Greek historian Manetho, who also gives the names of royalty and some account of events occurring in the various reigns. The dynasties in turn are conveniently grouped into kingdoms: the Old Kingdom (2664–2155 B.C.); the Middle Kingdom (2052–1786 B.C.); and the New Kingdom (1570–1075 B.C.). The periods between the kingdoms, called Intermediate Periods, were times of confusion and dissent, and it is in the three kingdoms that the mainstream of Egyptian history and culture developed.

Preceding the Old Kingdom was a time known as the Archaic Period, which was one of great development in many fields, and Narmer was the first known king of this period. His monuments have been found at Hierakonpolis, Abydos, and in the robbed tombs at Saqqara near Memphis. He also built a city called White Walls (later Memphis) as his residence; it was to become one of the great cities of ancient Egypt. Throughout the Archaic Period trade with the

Life MAGAZINE © TIME INC.—ELIOT ELISOFON

Osiris, seen at left in a wall painting at the tomb of the Nineteenth Dynasty queen Nefertari, was the chief god of the dead. He carries his traditional emblems—the flail and crook—traceable perhaps to the Egyptians' nomad origins. Anubis, guardian-god of the necropolis, appears below on a chest from Tutankhamon's tomb.

EGYPTIAN MUSEUM, CAIRO

Levant increased. Wood in particular was imported and employed in building. Another major import was copper, turned to new uses for making tools, vessels, and even statues. Expeditions penetrated far south, and a rock-cut inscription of the First Dynasty pharaoh Djer near the Second Cataract in Nubia records an invasion and conquest of local tribes, though it may be a rather boastful description of a successful raid. Technical skills increased, and building became more magnificent, large stone blocks being hewn for funerary monuments and temples. In the making of smaller scaled artifacts craftsmen became more competent, not only at making jars and ornaments but also statues from various kinds of stone. The potter's wheel was introduced and ceramic styles became more varied. Most important of all, however, was the use of writing and the manufacture of a kind of paper from the papyrus reed, so that records could be kept, instructions sent, and all the business of state noted down.

During this time foundations were laid for the role of the king, the pharaoh of Egypt, as a divine god-king who embodied the spirit of ancient Egypt. Originally, simply the most powerful among regional leaders, he became associated with divine functions, in particular the control of the Nile flood, which meant life to the country. (The powers of the Nineteenth Dynasty pharaoh Ramses II were thought to be so great in this respect that he was credited with the ability to affect rainfall in the far country of the Hittites.) A well-known stone plaque, the Palette of Narmer, found at Hierakonpolis, shows the contemporary view of the pharaoh: the typical stance, huge in proportion to the other figures in the picture, smiting his enemy before the hawk-god Horus, and treading on two captives beneath his feet. Even at this early time the extraordinary power of the pharaoh was evident.

The seeds sown during the Archaic Period came into full flower in the Old Kingdom. An impression of peaceful development, together with a broadening of trading activity, is conveyed. Royal burial customs became elaborate, as illustrated by the Great Pyramids of Giza (about 2600 B.C.). Organizing a sufficient labor force, and conceiving and carrying out the architectural plans, testify to the prosperity and order of the country and to the divine omnipotence of the pharaoh, who could command such resources for his personal use.

From the pyramids and from temple reliefs and wall paintings much can be inferred of religious beliefs. For example, the tomb structure—be it pyramid for the royal or rich, or brick-lined grave for the poor—was seen as a house to live in forever, where objects serviceable or precious in life were placed with the dead for use in the afterlife. Gods other than the pharaoh appear in the reliefs, most commonly Hathor, protectress of the City of the Dead, and Osiris, god of the dead, and the pantheon became established. Much of the artistic endeavor of the time must have been devoted to funerary building, and wall paintings and reliefs on tombs and temples show aspects of daily life, of the running of the country estate and country crafts, amusements, and even the arrival of the tax collector. Statues were also placed in tombs; they were carved of wood or limestone and often painted, and many appear to be realistic portraits, for physical defects are not disguised and there is little suggestion of flattery.

Trading activities were more venturesome, and expeditions were sent to Kush (the Egyptian name for Nubia), to Punt, probably along the coast of the Gulf of Aden, and into the Levant. Egyptian penetration into Palestine is revealed in tomb reliefs, which show Asian fortresses being stormed. At Byblos in the Lebanon a temple was built by the Egyptians as early as the Fourth Dynasty, about 2600 B.C., perhaps for a local community of their people, implying peaceful contact with this great trading center.

Nubia was invaded on several occasions, and early in the Fourth Dynasty the Pharaoh Snefru launched an invasion that cost the Nubians 7,000 prisoners and 200,000 head of cattle. It subdued the local population for some time to come. The wealth of the country was exploited, particularly gold, and at Buhen, near the Second Cataract, an Egyptian settlement was established that was in effect a trading post, and at which copper smelting was carried on. Nubia had been settled by a population archeologists call the A-Group people for lack of more information. Such evidence as there is suggests an appreciable increase in the population of Nubia in the third century B.C. due to settlement by the A-Group people, who may have drifted in from Egypt or from Saharan areas. Physically they were similar to Egyptians, and their culture was much like that of predynastic Egypt, based on small agricultural communities. They were probably not subject to a central authority, though each community would have had its leader.

The basis of Egyptian interest in this land was trade, and Mernera, a pharaoh of the Sixth Dynasty, sent four peaceful expeditions into Nubia, led by a nobleman named Harkhuf, that were of a more ambitious nature than before. The purpose was to open up communications with a country called Yam, whose exact geographical location is uncertain, though it must have been south of the Second Cataract. Harkhuf's fourth journey took place in the time of Pepi II, then a young ruler, who was delighted with the offer of a Pygmy. He wrote to Harkhuf, giving instructions for the care of the Pgymy on the journey northward and adding: "My Majesty desires to see this Pgymy more than all the gifts of Sinai and Punt." All control of Kush was lost, however, during the period of anarchy that followed the Old Kingdom, and the Egyptians withdrew into their homeland.

Up till the Fourth Dynasty power and government had been centralized in the pharaoh, aided by officials whom he chose and to whom he delegated various responsibilities. During the Fourth Dynasty the post of provincial governor and some local offices came to be accepted as hereditary, and the holders of these positions were very conscious of their power. It needed only an old or a weak pharaoh for the whole structure of government to collapse under the jealous ambitions of an anarchic elite. This very situation caused the downfall of the Old Kingdom. At the death of Pepi II, an old man, reputedly a centenarian, who had ruled for many decades, a formidable blow was dealt to the achievements of the Old Kingdom. A vivid account is given in *The Admonitions of the Prophet Ipuwer:* "Behold, they that had clothes are now in rags. . . . Squalor is throughout the land: no clothes are white these days. . . . The Nile is in flood yet no one has the heart to plow. . . . Corn has perished everywhere. . . . Men do not sail to Byblos today: What shall we do for fine wood. . . . Laughter has perished. Grief walks the land, mingled with lamentation."

All the artistic achievement of the Old Kingdom withered, and much of the work of craftsmen ceased to be practiced except in poor and debased forms. Various leaders made unsuccessful attempts to restore peace and order. Finally, a powerful family from Herakleopolis managed to unite Middle Egypt and also bring the Delta under its control. However, Upper Egypt seems to have maintained virtual independence, ruled by the Theban princes. (Thebes was the most important city in that area and the capital of Upper Egypt in times of disunity.) The Herakleopolitans (Ninth and Tenth Dynasties) made an impressive attempt to restore order out of chaos, expelling numbers of Asian and Libyan settlers from the land around the Delta, fortifying their northeastern frontier, reopening trade with Byblos, and re-establishing Memphis as the capital city. Nevertheless, there was sporadic warfare with the Thebans throughout this time, fortune favoring first one side and then the

LOUVRE; PHOTO BULLOZ

The Egyptian artists and craftsmen were often organized like common workmen, laboring in gangs under the direction of a foreman. They produced one of the world's richest art legacies, ranging from tiny jewel masterpieces to works of monumental grandeur. The head at left, which once adorned a harp, was probably carved during the New Kingdom. Opposite, a copy of a wall painting in the Eighteenth Dynasty tomb of a Theban prime minister and governor, named Rekmire, shows artisans chiseling and polishing royal statues with tools made of dolorite, a hard stone.

other. After a decisive battle in about 2061 B.C., the Thebans defeated the people of Herakleopolis, and Mentuhotep I became pharaoh of a reunited Egypt. This marks the birth of the Middle Kingdom.

During the time of conflict a secular literature grew, in which appeals were made to the peoples' feelings by means of artistic expression. At a time when the divine guidance of the pharaoh was lacking, this had a particular relevance. Elegant and poetic as it was, much of the writing was inspired by a deep pessimism, an expression of the tremendous misfortune that had befallen a land bereft of its god-king. Titles such as "An Argument between a Man Contemplating Suicide and his Soul" or "The Complaints of the Peasant" give a hint of the sense of depression experienced. "The Instructions for His Son, Mery-ka-re," thought to have been written by one of the Herakleopolitan kings, is concerned with promoting a code of conduct based on moral principles. "Do right," he says, "as long as you are on earth. Calm the afflicted, oppress no widow. . . . Do not kill; but punish with beatings and imprisonment. . . . Leave vengeance to God. . . . More acceptable to Him is the virtue of one who is upright of heart than the ox of the wrongdoer. . . ." Yet another piece of advice praises the art of speaking, "for power is in the tongue, and speech is mightier than fighting."

The Middle Kingdom was a period of further expansion and development in all fields of activity. It was not entirely peaceful, for a bout of anarchy intervened before long and abated only when Amenemhet, who had been a governor of the South, claimed the throne as first pharaoh of the powerful Twelfth Dynasty. A prophecy attributed to the time of Pharaoh Snefru had forewarned that a period of disaster in Egypt would come to an end only "when a king shall come from the South called Ameny"—but this prediction was contained in a papyrus of Twelfth Dynasty date and is more likely to be a piece of royal propaganda aimed at supporting Amenemhet's ambitions.

About this time a determined effort was made to subdue Kush. A series of remarkable forts was built to control the river passage and quell any insurrection by the local population. The southernmost of these was at Semna, above the Second Cataract; some were built on the eminences along the banks of the river and some on islands in it. The fortifications were strategically placed so that should any be attacked, it could call for help by signaling with a beacon to its neighbors. They served as trading posts as well as military garrisons, for the purpose of Egyptian excursions into Kush was as much for trade as to secure the southern frontier of Egypt. An inscription of a governor of Middle Egypt says that he followed his lord when he sailed south to overthrow his enemies: "I passed through Kush in sailing southward and reached the borders of the earth. I brought back tribute. . . . Then His Majesty returned in safety having overthrown his enemies in Kush, the vile." Efforts to subdue Kush reached their peak in the time of Sesostris III (1878–1843 B.C.), who rebuilt where necessary and consolidated the line of forts, and whose connection with the area was so close that he was later worshiped as a local god.

LEPSIUS, *Denkmäler . . .*, 1860

The people of Kush at this time were the earlier mentioned C-Group people, a cattle-owning people living in small communities. Although their culture was dissimilar from that of contemporary Egypt, it had, nevertheless, affinities with the pastoral civilizations of late predynastic Egypt, including a distinctive pottery, much of it black with incised geometric designs, by which their settlements are easily recognized. Their animals were of such importance to them that they sometimes buried the skulls of cattle around their own graves and scratched pictures of them on pots. The C-Group were a non-Negroid people, and their settlements and cemeteries have been found from Kubanieh near the First Cataract to as far south as the area of the Third Cataract. One concludes from the number of fortresses built that they were extremely troublesome to the Egyptian forces occupying their land. In an inscription at the fortress of Semna, Sesostris III instructed his men "to prevent any Nubian from passing downstream or overland or by boat, [also] any herds of Nubians, apart from any Nubian who shall come to trade at Iken or upon any good business that may be done with them." (Iken was the name of the fortress at the Second Cataract.) Even their most trivial movements were reported back to Egypt, and the almost daily accounts end with, "All the affairs of the king's domain are safe and sound."

At about the same time, around 1900 B.C., a trading post was set up at Kerma in the neighborhood of the Third Cataract, but whether by the Egyptians or by the local people is not known, though it was certainly a native entrepôt. The remains of the material culture found there are entirely different from that of the contemporary C-Group people. A spectacular burial mound revealed the interment of an important chief with the accompanying sacrifice of over three hundred others, mostly women and children. The pottery of Kerma, a very fine, highly polished, black-topped red ware, was unique, as were the little ivory and mica figures of birds and animals, which seem to have been used decoratively, the former as inlay for furniture, and the latter attached to leather caps. In the rooms around the trading post were found a variety of raw materials together with manufactured objects, including fragments of Sixth Dynasty alabaster jars, which had no doubt gone out of fashion in Egypt and were foisted off on the natives of Kush in trade. Various Egyptian statues, including one of the Lady Senuwy, wife of Hepzefa, a governor-general of Kush and prince of Asyut, and a fragment of a statue of Hepzefa himself, were discovered; these had probably also been passed in trade.

While the southern border of Egypt had been secured to some extent by deliberate expansion and subjugation of the native population, the northeastern border, which was frequently crossed by Asians, had still to be strengthened. To this end a series of fortified positions, named the Walls of the Prince, was set up along the frontier; but there was no attempt to conquer land or peoples, merely to define the frontier and protect it. Egypt's main interest in Palestine and Syria was undoubtedly a commercial one, though there are evidences of occasional wars; there was, however, much interchange of products of countries in the eastern Mediterranean, including Crete, most of which was conducted through an entrepôt city, such as Byblos.

After the death in 1797 B.C. of Amenemhet III, the last great ruler of the Middle Kingdom, the strength and prosperity of Egypt declined. After about 1785 B.C. a number of Asian names appear in the king lists, and evidently by about 1750 B.C. an Asian people, the Hyksos, had established a principality at Avaris in the eastern Delta. Hyksos control spread over Egypt, and Memphis, the capital city, was seized. Egyptians continued to rule Upper Egypt from Thebes, paying tribute to the Hyksos and holding an uneasy independence only as far north as Asyut. The Theban rulers had apparently also lost their hegemony to the south of Aswan, the land being ruled by a prince of Kush, probably from Kerma. His people had stormed and destroyed that great system of fortresses guarding the First and Second Cataracts, and had evidently made an alliance with the Hyksos. Kamose, "a mighty king in Thebes," writes: "I should like to know what serves this strength of mine, when a chieftain is in Avaris, and another in Kush, and I sit united with an Asiatic and a Nubian each man in possession of his slice of this Egypt, and I cannot pass by him as far as Memphis."

Kamose decided to deliver Egypt from Asian power and set out to crush the Hyksos, along the way meting out ruthless destruction to the towns that had "forsaken Egypt, their mistress." He also captured a messenger traveling southward to the chieftain of Kush. The letter he was carrying from Apopi, the chieftain of Avaris, makes clear the alliance between the two: "Why have you arisen as chieftain without letting me know? Have you [not] beheld what Egypt has done against me, the Chieftain who is in it, Kamose the Mighty, ousting me from my soil . . . come, fare north at once, do not be timid. . . . Then will we divide the towns of this Egypt between us."

Kamose did not live to see the final destruction of Hyksos' rule. His younger brother, Ahmose, carried on the war, eventually bringing about the fall of Avaris and the expulsion of the Asian invaders. He also killed the king of Kush, thereby regaining control of Upper Egypt. By about 1570 B.C., through these successes, Egypt had regained its strength and Ahmose I became the founder of the Eighteenth Dynasty and the New Kingdom—in many ways the most glorious period of Egyptian history. The result of the Hyksos invasion was not a total loss to Egypt in that new ideas and techniques had come with it, among the most important of which was the horse-drawn chariot. The Thebans adopted not only the chariot but the Hyksos designs in armor and weapons in clashes with the enemy.

Ahmose I set to work to re-establish his kingdom and secure it from further invasion. The subduing of the states of the Levant as far as the Euphrates was to continue under his successors. The states of Palestine and Syria were formed into dependencies through treaties with the rulers, whose sons were removed to Egypt as hostages for guarantee of good behavior. On the whole, this was a policy of indirect rule rather than one of colonization, and it was quite different from the treatment meted out to Kush.

Once again in power, the pharaohs waxed supreme and complacent. By 1370 B.C., however, the Hittites of the Anatolian plateau had become strong enough to present a direct challenge to Egypt. No effective answer was given, and Akhenaten, a somewhat eccentric pharaoh who was on the throne at the time, was entirely abstracted by his new religious ideas, which were apparently monotheistic. As a result, Egyptian influence in Syria waned.

Early in the twelfth century B.C. masses of peoples, known in Egyptian texts as the Peoples of the Sea, migrated through the Levant in search of land; they spread destruction wherever they passed, causing further loss of Egyptian power and prestige. Though Egypt did manage to protect its own borders, all its possessions to the northeast had to be sacrificed. Egypt remained a conservative element in the fast-developing world of the Mediterranean. Throughout the New Kingdom the power of the pharaoh was identified with military conquest and the preservation of Egypt's borders, a concept that could not be satisfied once strong enemies and new iron weapons successfully challenged its supremacy.

On the western borders of Egypt the Libyans became troublesome, and on more than one occasion attempted to settle on the rich Delta lands. Driven out of their territory by the incursions of Sea Peoples, and possibly also by increasing aridity of their own lands, the Libyans were so harried that they were difficult to repel. Even after Pharaoh Ramses III of the Twentieth Dynasty crushed them finally, parties of Libyans still infiltrated Egypt. Many became mercenaries in the army, later forming a special military caste that grew strong enough to provide two dynasties among the rulers of Egypt.

The abundance of archeological discoveries from the New Kingdom makes its civilization seem very real—even the shrunken forms of dead kings can be seen, their names known, their possessions studied. The splendor of the tomb of Tutankhamon—rich in alabaster, gold, and pre-

The ceremonial axehead below, found at Thebes and showing Pharaoh Ahmose smiting a foe, celebrates the Eighteenth Dynasty ruler who, after 1570 B.C., completed the expulsion of the Hyksos.

EGYPTIAN MUSEUM, CAIRO

The Eighteenth Dynasty "Heretic King," Akhenaten, worshiped only the sun god, Aten. In the relief above, he is seen at left, seated with Nefertiti and their daughters under the sun disc.

STATE MUSEUM, BERLIN–F. L. KENETT

cious ornaments—gives an idea of the luxury and art of the period, as do the fine temples and sculpture. This was a time of massive architecture and colossal statues, much of which still stand as testimony to the power of the pharaoh. But the basic wealth of Egypt was in agriculture, and the tomb paintings frequently depict agricultural pursuits. The wealthy occupant of the tomb is shown inspecting his fields, vineyards, and gardens. But there were also fishing trips and wild fowl hunts or picnics and entertainments in his house, accompanied by his servants and slaves or on appropriate occasions by his family. The gulf that separated the rich from the poor, the landlord from the peasant, is very clear.

After the Twentieth Dynasty, about 1075 B.C., Egypt again fell into lawlessness and decay. Over the centuries Libyans, Kushites, Persians, Greeks, and Romans dominated, each group holding power for as long as it could. The Libyans form the Twenty-second and the Twenty-third Dynasties. Having been soldiers in the army, they set up a form of military dictatorship; but it ended in dissension and instability, to be succeeded in time by a line of Kushite kings.

The pharaohs of the New Kingdom had brought Kush under direct government control. The territory was put into the charge of a governor, "King's Son of Kush," residing probably at modern Amarna, a town on the east bank of the Nile well above the Second Cataract. He was appointed by the pharaoh and was directly responsible to him. The frontier was extended beyond the area of the Middle Kingdom forts to a point south of the Fourth Cataract. Towns and temples and military garrisons were established, and the names of many of the rulers are to be found carved on temple walls and columns in the land of Kush. Frequent raids by Egyptian forces were needed to keep the population under control, both the riverain people, with whom they were mainly in contact, and the desert tribesmen, who never became imbued with Egyptian influences. In time the riverain Kushites became completely Egyptianized, adopting Egyptian religious practices and becoming part of the land of the pharaohs. Kush supplied many products that added greatly to the wealth and luxury of Egypt, in particular gold, ebony, ivory, cattle, and slaves.

Under the New Kingdom Kush prospered and became culturally and economically part of Egypt, their people serving in the army and government. Many Egyptian priests, traders, and officials settled in Kush and gave the Kushites a lasting flavor of their culture. At Jebel Barkal a religious center devoted to Egyptian theological beliefs was probably controlled by an Egyptian priesthood.

But by the end of the Twenty-second Dynasty, profiting

Though King Tutankhamon was a man of peace, Egyptian custom dictated that a pharaoh be shown also as a brave and mighty warrior. This feather holder depicts him as an archer in a chariot drawn by caparisoned horses.
EGYPTIAN MUSEUM, CAIRO

from the weakness that had overcome Egypt, Kush became effectively independent, although maintaining its traditions and orthodoxy. Napata, on the east bank of the Nile just downstream from the Fourth Cataract, was the great city of Kushite-Egyptian culture and became the capital of the independent state of Kush. About 750 B.C. a Kushite king, Kashta, felt himself powerful enough to gain control of Upper Egypt, and his son Piankhi (751–716 B.C.) completed the conquest of the country, though this was not accomplished lightly and the Kushite armies had to penetrate Egypt on more than one occasion to achieve their objective. Piankhi made the mistake of withdrawing to Napata, having, as he thought, subdued the Egyptian princes. As a result, it was left to his brother and successor, Shabako (707–696 B.C.), to establish power over the whole of Egypt and assert Kushite administration. Shabako became known throughout the ancient world as King of Kush and Misr (Egypt), and he and his successors form the Twenty-fifth Dynasty.

The Kushite kings, imbued with an orthodox, slightly old-fashioned view of Egyptian life, a reflection of their remoteness from the sources of their adopted culture, were probably welcomed by some in Egypt: by the Theban priests, who saw the possibility of re-establishing their own power under the piety of the conquerors; by those who foresaw a return to the good old days of law and order under the traditionalist usurpers. Indeed, the Kushite kings proved themselves to be pharaohs in the old manner, larger-than-life majesties who left a fine record, both in Egypt and in Kush. They, too, were responsible for temples, colossal statues, inscriptions in Egyptian hieroglyphs—extremely valuable in relating the events of the period—and they were able to establish a measure of law and order that gained them the respect of other rulers.

In time the Assyrians replaced the Hittites as the dominant power in western Asia. In the reign of Pharaoh Taharqa, in 671 B.C., the Assyrians descended on Egypt. The king was forced to retreat to Thebes from the residence he had established at Tanis (Avaris) in the Delta. A second invasion in the reign of Taharqa's successor, Tanwetamani (664–653 B.C.), drove the pharaoh out of Egypt and back to his own domains. The descendants of these Kushite kings were to rule in their own land for nearly a thousand years, maintaining a state with its own complex culture.

The Kushite capital was moved from Napata to Meroë, located above the Atbara River, probably in the sixth century B.C., perhaps because of the sack in 591 B.C. of Napata by the Greek mercenaries of an Egyptian pharaoh, Psammetik II. An equally likely reason for the move was the fact that Meroë lies in an area of annual rainfall (approximately 4 inches), and grazing for the huge herds of Kushite cattle was more certain.

The Greeks called the Kushites "Ethiopians," which means "burnt faces," implying a darker skin color than that to which they were accustomed. The term does not denote any connection with the modern state of Ethiopia. The Kushites were probably much like modern Sudanese, a varying mixture of the light brown-skinned people of North Africa and the more Negroid people from farther south. In Egyptian tomb paintings they are always shown as darker than the Egyptians themselves. Kushite art, too, makes it clear that there was a difference; the royal ladies of Kush are shown as markedly plump women, and both male and female portrait subjects often are characterized by tightly curled Negroid hair. The culture of Kush, though always overlaid with characteristic Egyptian influences, became more individual after the removal of the capital to Meroë, partly because links with Egypt were more tenuous and partly because lively and more essentially African influences were at work. At one time the Kushites were literate to some extent in Egyptian language and hieroglyphs (though this may have been the prerogative of the priesthood only), but lack of close contact with Egypt caused this skill to decline. The shapes of signs were altered and sometimes given different phonetic values, and finally a new script was developed. While the phonetic values of the new signs are known, they express a language that cannot as yet be interpreted. Except when Meroë is mentioned in the writings of other peoples, knowledge of its culture has to be inferred from material remains.

Many standing monuments of the Kushites can be seen today: the ruins of the city of Meroë; the pyramids where members of the royal family were buried both near Napata and near Meroë; temples; reservoirs for catching water during the rainy season. The greatest concentration of monuments is in the "Island of Meroë," not actually an island but the stretch of country between the Nile and Atbara rivers that was the heartland of the state. Southwest of Meroë is the famous site at Musawwarat-es-Sufra—a complex of temples built, altered, and rebuilt over a period of a thousand years. It is a most spectacular place, where temples, once plastered with sparkling white gypsum, were set in a small plain surrounded by black hills, and it is thought to have been a place of pilgrimage, for there are no dwellings other than a single house, presumably that of a priest.

Objects found in Meroitic pyramid tombs show the influences of pharaonic and Hellenistic Egypt, but also, especially in the pottery, the spirit of Africa. In the Egyptian fashion, objects both precious and useful were placed in the graves: gold and enameled jewelry, beads of all kinds, glass, silver and bronze vessels, bells that were buckled to the necks of cattle, both decorated and plain pottery, quiv-

ARCHIVES PHOTOGRAPHIQUES, PARIS

Wooden models of a pharaoh's army include ranks of Nubians.

ers, arrowheads, spears, bronze and silver lamps, wooden and ivory boxes, furniture, wrappings of cotton cloth, and scatters of animal bones indicating the sacrifice of cattle and horses. The royal pyramid tombs, the majority looted before archeological excavation, must have been very rich in these objects. The mound graves of the common people, with a burial chamber cut deep into the ground, offered up pottery, beads of stone and glass, traces of basketware and fragments of cloth, a hunter's favorite weapon, or a child's toy. In the royal tombs many of the objects were ones that had been imported from Egypt and are some indication of the wealth of the royal personages and of the continuing trade with Hellenistic and Roman Egypt. But the presence of local ware also expresses their appreciation of their own, less sophisticated products, including their beautiful decorated pottery, both that showing Mediterranean influences and that more typically African—such as can be found in many parts of the continent still today.

Little is known of the social organization of Kush in Meroitic times. However, it is clear that royalty was revered, probably as divine beings as in Egypt. Also, there was possibly an elite priesthood, again in the tradition of Egypt. The importance of the royal ladies, as evidenced by temple reliefs and by reference to Candace, queen of the Ethiopians, in the Acts of the Apostles ("Candace" is a Meroitic word meaning "queen" or "queen mother"), suggests that it may have been a matrilineal society; in that case succession to the throne would have been through the female line, a not uncommon African practice. As in Egypt, there may also have been brother-sister marriages, though it is more likely that they were marriages of cousins, an arrangement still considered desirable in many parts of Africa today. Indeed, cousins are referred to and thought of as brothers and sisters in some African societies. Religion was obviously an important part of life, as shown by the devoted work, both architectural and artistic, in temples; they were all built of hewn sandstone blocks in contrast to the sun-dried brick dwellings, royal or common.

The greatest achievement of Meroë, however, was the practice of ironworking. Iron was first introduced into Egypt perhaps by Greeks who had settled there or perhaps by the Assyrians, who used iron weapons in war. As far as is at present known, the Kushites seem to be the first people of sub-Saharan Africa to have used iron, starting perhaps about 500 B.C., though this may be due simply to the accident of where excavation and study have taken place. The Kushites were fortunate in having iron-bearing sandstone in their hills and the wood for charcoal with which to smelt it. So precious was this metal reckoned that an iron spearhead, wrapped in gold foil, was buried in the tomb of King Taharqa. Mounds of iron slag abound at Meroë, and smelting as well as forging were practiced on a fairly large scale. Whether this knowledge passed from Meroë to other parts of Africa, as has often been argued, cannot yet be established.

Apart from raiding bands of desert dwellers, Kush was left largely alone and grew into a state that stretched from the borders of Egypt between the First and Second Cataracts to at least as far south as Sennar in the modern Sudan. Meanwhile, Egypt had fallen prey to yet another invader. The Persian conquest of Egypt in 525 B.C., when Cambyses defeated Psammetik III, hardly affected Kush, though the Persians made an unsuccessful attempt to invade the country.

Subsequently, the Greeks, led by Alexander the Great, occupied Egypt in 332 B.C. The Greeks were not strangers in Egypt, their forebears having lived and worked there for some centuries as merchants and soldiers, and having been allowed to establish a trading center of their own at Naukratis in the Delta. Ptolemy, one of their victorious generals, was left in charge of Egypt. When the Greek empire broke up at Alexander's death, Ptolemy became the ruler of an independent kingdom. Attempts at peaceful integration were made: the Greeks worshiped Egyptian gods, and upper-class Egyptians learned Greek. But the peasant

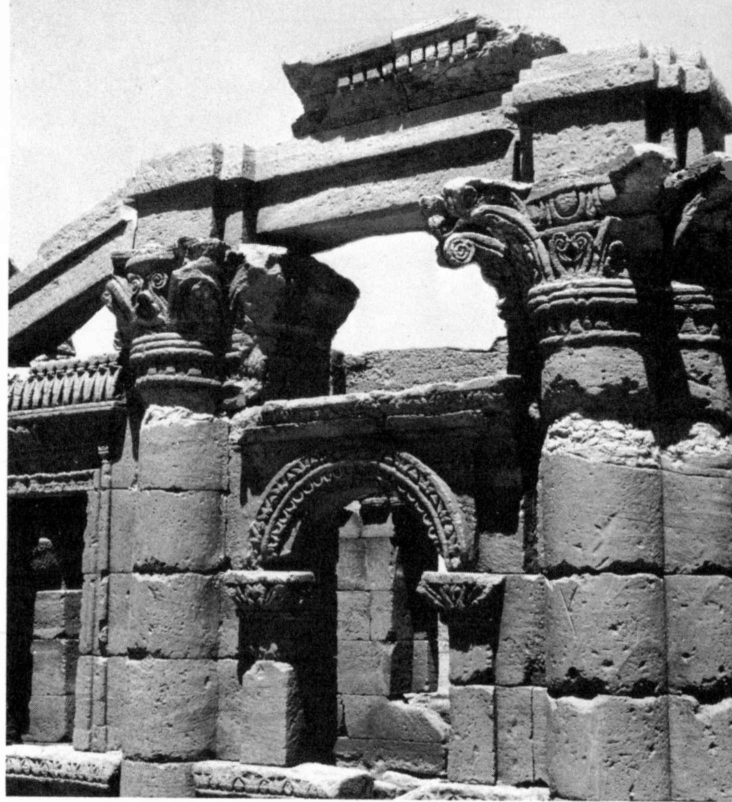

population was oppressed and resentful at having to hand over to the foreign ruler half their produce as rent for their land. The ruling dynasty of the Ptolemies encouraged trading ventures, setting up new ports on the Red Sea coast and extending trade toward the east. (Ptolemy II completed the last link in a series of canals reaching from the Nile to the Red Sea.) They introduced currency into Egypt, where barter had been the common practice, and Alexandria, said to have been planned and laid out by Alexander himself, became a center of learning and crafts, among the greatest in the ancient world.

During the period of Hellenistic power in Egypt, Kush appears to have enjoyed particular prosperity. The Kushites maintained friendly relations with the Greeks, and one of the Kushite kings, Arkamani (about 218–200 B.C.), called Ergamenes by the Greeks, is said to have acquired a smattering of Greek learning. He is known to have joined Ptolemy IV in some temple building; and the number of buildings erected in Kush and the luxury of the objects found in the royal tombs illustrate the degree of security known. Somewhat later Netekamani and his queen, Amantari, also built extensively, including two temples at Naqa, a town some distance from the Nile. The first structure, the Lion Temple, shows Apedemek, an indigenous lion god or god of war, who, on this occasion at least, had three heads and four arms, causing speculation about possible contacts with India. (A number of local gods had been added to the Egyptian pantheon some time after the capital was moved to Meroë. Whether they were of long standing or not is unknown.) By contrast, the second temple, known as the

The Kushite kingdom of Meroë in northern Sudan was forgotten by the world for centuries until travelers and archeologists in recent times began to reveal evidences of its ancient glories. The Kiosk (opposite), a temple with both Egyptian and Roman influences, was built at Naqa, a Meroitic center, by Netekamani and his queen, Amantari, about the first century B.C. *The colossal statue at right, several centuries older, was found on the site of the Temple of Isis at Meroë itself.*

NY CARLSBERG GLYPTOTEK, COPENHAGEN

Kiosk, is strikingly Roman in style, and though decorated with Egyptian symbols, it seems very strange so far south in Africa.

Roman occupation at the death of Cleopatra in 30 B.C. brought no relief to the discontented peasantry of Egypt. Their country became merely a province of the Roman empire, exploited for its grain supplies and paying taxes to the colonial governors. The middle classes became poor, and the poor, destitute. It was not surprising that Alexandria's intellectuals and malcontents began to look at the teachings of a new religion. By A.D. 330, when Christianity was the religion of the Roman empire and the Christian capital was Constantinople, not Rome, most of Egypt had already been converted, and Alexandria had already been a great center of Eastern Christianity for almost two hundred years. Later, at the Council of Chalcedon in A.D. 451, the patriarch of Alexandria declined to subscribe to the orthodox doctrine. As will be explained more fully in Chapter Three, the Church was divided over doctrinal issues, and Egypt became more secluded from its neighbors, its indigenous Coptic Church no longer a participant in the mainstream of the Christian world. Kush, too, became more remote as its contacts with the northern neighbors declined. Further, it was harried by desert tribesmen and by a new power to the southeast, Axum, whose strength was already being felt.

To explain the rise of Axum, one must go back to 700 B.C., when bands of immigrants from the Yemen began to cross the Red Sea and settle among the people of the Ethiopian highlands. They mixed with the local population, and there is no evidence that they did so violently; their impact seems to have been cultural. They were sophisticated farmers who understood terracing and the intricacies of irrigation, and employed such tools as the plow. They spoke a Semitic language, Sabean, and inscriptions in Sabean characters have been found, though there are enough departures from the language used in Saba (Sheba), to show its local development. The earliest inscriptions and monuments so far discovered date from about 500 B.C. By the third or second century B.C., one group of them, the Habashat (from which came the later name Abyssinia), established a strong kingdom with its capital at Axum and developed their own language, Ge'ez. This was one of the Ethiopian kingdoms that grew out of the synthesis of Yemenite and local endeavor. There is not much information about its early days, yet we know that their religion was analagous with that of southern Arabia: worship of the divinities Astar, Mahrem, and Beher, the divine symbol being a disc resting on a crescent, the Sabean moon god's symbol.

When the Ptolemies began to extend their trade empire, the Axumite state became of immediate importance, being well placed to take advantage of the new commercial development. Its main port was Adulis. The Ptolemies wanted to acquire elephants for war purposes, and among other trade goods were rhinoceros horn, tortoise shell, and the various perfumes, incense, and spices for which this area had been famous as the probable Land of Punt to which Hatshepsut sent ships. Much of this trading activity was in the hands of Greeks, and Greek became the language of commerce and diplomacy in Axum. Greek and Jewish traders from the Levant settled there from about the first century A.D., and, later, inscriptions on coins and monuments were in Greek. By the fifth century A.D. the state of Axum had probably become the main trading center for the Mediterranean-Indian Ocean routes. It may have been the Greeks who first brought Christianity to Axum; sometime in the fourth century it had become the official religion of the country, as it still is, being retained with great tenacity in the fastnesses of Ethiopia.

The culture of Axum was largely south Arabian in character, modified by local tradition, but uninfluenced by contacts with Egypt or Meroë. The buildings of Axum, of which there are remnants visible today, were characterized by stepped walls. Stone thrones or their pedestals, column bases and capitals, and fragments of columns, all testify to architectural achievement. Most impressive of all are the tall steles, some sixty feet high, which recreate in stone many-storied wooden buildings typical of Axumite architecture; these were probably funerary monuments.

The mountainous highlands of central Ethiopia, over which Axumite rulers once held sway, and where Greek merchants had come to trade, offer some of the most challenging terrain in Africa, with many stony peaks rising more than 12,000 feet. This engraving, which suggests the mystery of that impenetrable land, was made in London in 1813, when the region was known to the world as Abyssinia.

AMERICAN HERITAGE COLLECTION

Ambition led the rulers of Axum to extend the boundaries of their new kingdom and to regain the land of their ancestors. About the first century B.C. their agents are found in the Yemen, making alliances with various tribes in an attempt to regain control in southern Arabia, though it is not clear whether they achieved a position of direct rule there. At later times invasions were made culminating in that of King Afilas toward the end of the third century A.D. (see Chapter Four). The Axumites also sought to subdue their immediate neighbors and claimed to have taken their power to the borders of Egypt by the third century A.D.

An inscription found on a stele of one Axumite king, Ezana, relates that about A.D. 350 he and his army invaded the kingdom of Kush, which had been a source of perpetual annoyance to him. He burned and destroyed their cities, "both those built of bricks and those built of reeds," causing as much devastation as possible and chasing the Kushites for twenty-three days. The nomads, called the Red and the Black Noba according to Ezana, had been particularly troublesome, interfering with his officials and messengers and fighting among themselves, which they had promised not to do. "Twice and thrice they had broken their solemn oaths," Ezana says. So, he claims, he attacked and scattered them also. This may be an overboastful account of the event, especially as recent excavations at Meroë show no sign, so far, of sudden destruction or burning; but, equally, there is no doubt that the power of Kush waned at about this time, and it was no longer a viable kingdom.

Once Meroë had ceased to be a power, wandering bands of tribesmen, the Noba and the Blemmyes, both from the desert areas beyond the Nile, mingled with the Kushites and assimilated their culture. From Roman accounts they seem to have been a rather intractable people, and at a time when Egypt was already virtually a Christian country, they won special dispensation from the Romans to worship the Egyptian goddess Isis at the temple at Philae, the last remnant of pharaonic religion in the Nile Valley.

Rich tombs of their rulers at Ballana and Qustul in Egyptian Nubia were filled with amazing objects showing a strong flavor of pharaonic culture allied to Byzantine splendor: jewel-studded crowns of Byzantine style, decorated with pharaonic religious symbols such as the uraeus, or sacred serpent, the ram's head and plumes of Amon, the eye of Horus; iron furniture and inlaid wooden boxes, bronze vessels and hanging lamps, vessels of silver and glass, elaborate and beautiful horse trappings, pottery, linen shrouds, and fragments of rugs on which the dead had rested. Many were luxury imports from Egypt; indeed, the decoration of a cross on some of them implies their manufacture at Byzantine hands. To accompany him in death, the king's retinue, his queen, slaves, and guards, his dogs and horses, were sacrificed with him. This was not an Egyptian or Meroitic custom in which the necessity of providing servants for the afterlife had been circumvented by placing in the tomb little figures called *shawabtis*, which were thought to come to life to perform their services. The people of Ballana and Qustul, known to archeologists as the X-Group, had acquired a marked overlay of Egyptian-Meroitic culture, but certainly retained features of their own culture. Eventually, they and the peoples of the Sudan as far south as modern Khartoum became Christian under the teachings of the Byzantine Church.

Egypt made little attempt to influence other parts of Africa beyond Kush; rather, it held them at arm's length, concentrating all its effort in its own domain. Whether this was equally true of Kush cannot yet be seen. Except at Axum, where three undoubtedly Meroitic bronze bowls were found, and in the kingdom of Darfur in the western Sudan, where a Meroitic stone thumb ring is thought to have been found, almost nothing of certain Egyptian or Sudanese origin has so far been discovered in any other part of Africa. (A single faience bead in the Coryndon Museum in Nairobi could be Egyptian, but it is of doubtful provenance.)

As yet there is little archeological evidence for the passage of ideas, either for their actual passage or for the direction in which they flowed. The Nile Valley may have sent knowledge of agricultural and metallurgical techniques upstream and out across the deserts and savannas, or they may equally well have been independent inventions elsewhere.

It is not known when agriculture started in West Africa, for example, either in the Sudanic belt or in the forest areas to the south. Agricultural techniques were transmitted slowly—it appears to have taken about a thousand years for the practices in use in the Fayum to reach Shaheinab. Moreover, the crops which grew well in Egypt—wheat and barley—were not suited to climates farther south, so that different grains, mostly sorghum and other millets, had to be cultivated, and these are still the main crops of the Sudanic belt. Farther south in West Africa yam cultivation took the place of grain, calling for different tools and techniques, and there, particularly, agriculture may have been a separate invention; but because it leaves no traces—no grains, no bins, no grinding stones—knowledge of when it started may never be discovered.

Information about events and human development west of the Nile is much more limited, partly because the societies there were illiterate and partly because less investigation has been undertaken. Such cultural traits as are common between the Nile civilizations and those to the west of them may be a product of common African thought, as divine kingship for example, or may have been transmitted by the Saharan peoples over a long period of time. Although it has frequently been suggested that Meroë was the center from which the knowledge of ironworking spread throughout Africa, this skill might more easily have reached West Africa by trans-Saharan routes from Phoenician Carthage, where ironworking was well known, or it could have been independently discovered. The earliest iron-using communities yet discovered in West Africa are those of the Nok culture, named after a village on the Jos Plateau of north Nigeria. In the course of open-cast mining operations at Nok were found some remarkable terra-cotta heads of men and animals, together with iron and stone tools. A second site of the same people, at Taruga, produced an iron-smelting furnace. There is no doubt that iron was smelted and worked there from about 300 B.C., a date obtained by radiocarbon methods.

The working of iron gave to its users improved weapons, more control over their environment, and was instrumental in enabling them to establish the trading centers, which in time developed into an important feature of the western Sudan. The basis of trade was the gold, produced in an area to the southwest of the Sahara and transported by desert caravan to North Africa. The middlemen in this operation—those who met the caravans, brought the gold from the producers to them, and arranged an exchange of goods—were the ones who set up the trading centers that later became the great medieval states of the western Sudan. The earliest of these was Ghana, a state that grew up in southern Mauritania; its connection with the present Republic of Ghana is only indirect. Nothing is known of its beginnings as yet, and it is first mentioned by Arab travelers about A.D. 800; but according to local tradition, which was written down in the sixteenth and seventeenth centuries, it was already flourishing by the seventh century, and its early days may well reach further back into history.

While a great deal is known about ancient Egypt, the history of the civilizations of the rest of Africa is only now emerging. There are many tantalizing threads to follow, though they may never be fitted into the tapestry: the possibly Indian influences in Kush; the stone terracing that transformed the agriculture of Ethiopia and is seen also at Zimbabwe in southern Rhodesia; the bronze casting by the lost-wax process known in ancient Egypt and used again, much later, by the West African artists of Ife and Benin; the facts behind the statement by the medieval Arab geographer Al-Masudi that the sons of Kush, having crossed the Nile, separated, and some "very numerous, marched toward the setting sun," to mention but a few of them. Little is known of the comings and goings of peoples or of the interchange of ideas and techniques across this vast continent. Literate Egypt, with all its achievements, overshadows the rest of Africa; but more research, exploration, and excavation may help to redress the balance.

OF MEN AND MYTHS

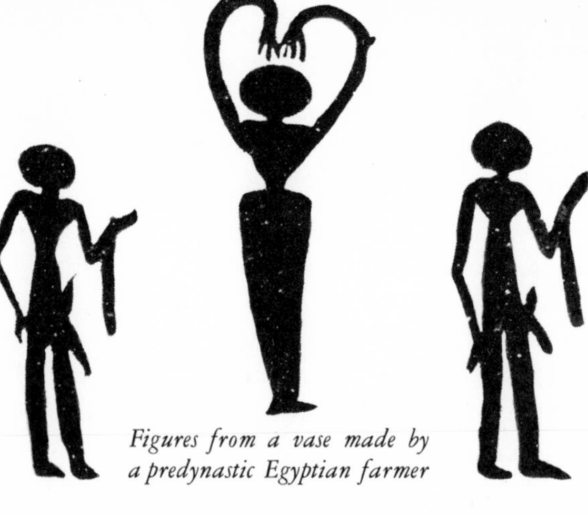
Figures from a vase made by a predynastic Egyptian farmer

METROPOLITAN MUSEUM OF ART, ROGERS FUND, 1912

THE SOURCE

Ancient Europeans' knowledge of the Nile was mostly based on hearsay, and that remarkably inaccurate. It was commonly accepted that the river rose somewhere in Mauretania (Morocco and part of Algeria), and not until the Greek geographer Strabo made a visit to Egypt did these misconceptions begin to be replaced with observed data. The world's longest river actually rises in equatorial Africa, from whence it flows some 4,160 miles to the Delta and the Mediterranean. It is fed by two principal courses: the White Nile and the Blue Nile. The former originates in Lakes Victoria and Albert, and then sweeps briskly into the Sudan, where it becomes choked in the sudd, 50,000 square miles of almost impassable swamp. At Khartoum it is joined by the Blue Nile, which, especially during the monsoon season, comes flooding down from the Ethiopian highlands. Then, after being met by another Ethiopian tributary, the Atbara, the Nile enters a region of six rapids, the last at Aswan. From there to the sea it runs some 750 miles through a narrow valley, never more than twelve miles in width, until it reaches the Delta, whose seven branches run to the sea. Strabo's commentary on his own discoveries, made around A.D. *19, and his professional criticism of earlier geographers' assertions is excerpted in the passage below.*

The Nile flows from the Aethiopian boundaries toward the north in a straight line to the district called "Delta," and then, being "split at the head," as Plato says, the Nile makes this place as it were the vertex of a triangle, the sides of the triangle being formed by the streams that split in either direction and extend to the sea. . . . An island, therefore, has been formed by the sea and the two streams of the river; and it is called Delta on account of the similarity of its shape; and the district at the vertex has been given the same name because it is the beginning of the above-mentioned figure; and the village there is also called Delta. Now these are two mouths of the Nile, of which one is called Pelusiac and the other Canobic or Heracleiotic; but between these there are five other outlets, those at least that are worth mentioning, and several that are smaller; for, beginning with the first parts of the Delta, many branches of the river have been split off throughout the whole island and have formed many streams and islands, so that the whole Delta has become navigable—canals on canals having been cut, which are navigated with such ease that some people even use earthenware ferry-boats. Now the island as a whole is as much as three thousand stadia in perimeter; and they also call it, together with the opposite river-lands of the Delta, Lower Egypt; but at the rising of the Nile the whole country is under water and becomes a lake, except the settlements; and these are situated on natural hills or on artificial mounds, and contain cities of considerable size and villages, which, when viewed from afar, resemble islands. The water stays more than forty days in summer and then goes down gradually just as it rose; and in sixty days the plain is completely bared and begins to dry out; and the sooner the drying takes place, the sooner the ploughing and the sowing; and the drying takes place sooner in those parts where the heat is greater. . . . Aegypt consists of only the river-land, I mean the last stretch of river-land on either side of the Nile, which, beginning at the boundaries of Aethiopia and extending to the vertex of the Delta, scarcely anywhere occupies a continuous habitable space as broad as three hundred stadia. Accordingly, when it is dried, it resembles lengthwise a girdle-band, the greater diversions of the river being excepted. . . .

Now the ancients depended mostly on conjecture, but the men of later times, having become eye-witnesses, perceived that the Nile was filled by summer rains, when Upper Aethiopia was flooded, and particularly in the region of its farthermost mountains, and that when the rains ceased the inundation gradually ceased. This fact was particularly clear to those who navigated the Arabian Gulf as far as the Cinnamon-bearing country [of the Somali], and to those who were sent out to hunt elephants or upon any other business which may have prompted the Ptolemaic kings of Aegypt to dispatch men thither. . . . When Cambyses took possession of Aegypt, he advanced with the Aegyptians even as far as Meroë; and indeed this name was given by him to both the island and the city, it is said, because his sister Meroë—some say his wife—died there. The name, at any rate, he bestowed upon the place in honor of the woman. It is surprising, therefore, that the men of that time, having such knowledge to begin with, did not possess a perfectly clear knowledge of the rains. . . . They should have investigated, if they made any investigations at all, the question, which even to this day is still being investigated, I mean why in the world rains fall in summer but not in winter, and in the southernmost parts but not in Thebais and the country round Syene; but the fact that the rising of the river results from rains should not have been investigated, nor yet should this matter have needed such witnesses as Poseidonius mentions; for instance, he says that it was Callisthenes who states that the summer rains are the cause of the risings, though Callisthenes took the assertion from Aristotle, and Aristotle from Thrasyalces the Thasian [one of the early physicists], and Thrasyalces from someone else, and he from Homer, who calls the Nile "heaven-fed": "And back again to the land of Aegyptus, heaven-fed river."

HYMN TO THE NILE

Adoration of the Nile is as old as Egyptian civilization itself. This paean was probably written around 1600 B.C. for the annual Theban festival marking the river's rise.

Praise to thee, O Nile, that issuest forth from the earth and comest to nourish the dwellers in Egypt. Secret of movement, a darkness in the daytime.
That waterest the meadows which Re hath created to nourish all cattle.
That givest drink to the desert places which are far from water; his dew it is that falleth from heaven.
Beloved of the Earth-God, controller of the Corn-God, that maketh every workshop of Ptah to flourish.
Lord of fish, that maketh the water fowl to go upstream, without a bird falling.
That maketh barley and createth wheat, that maketh the temples to keep festival.
If he is sluggish the nostrils are stopped up, and all men are brought low;
The offerings of the gods are diminished, and millions perish from among mankind.
When he arises earth rejoices and all men are glad; every jaw laughs and every tooth is uncovered.
Bringer of nourishment, plenteous of sustenance, creating all things good.
Lord of reverence, sweet of savor, appeasing evil.
Creating herbage for the cattle, causing sacrifice to be made to every god.
He is in the Underworld, in heaven, and upon earth,
Filling the barns and widening the granaries; giving to the poor.
Causing trees to grow according to the uttermost desire,
So that men go not in lack of them.

MEMPHIS, THE FAIR ONE

This love song, written during the Nineteenth Dynasty (1320–1200 B.C.), is dedicated to Memphis. According to historical tradition, Narmer created the city as part of his plan to unite Upper and Lower Egypt into a single nation. The brilliant capital, built near the apex of the Delta, the ancient division between the Two Lands, remained an economic and religious center throughout Egypt's dynastic history, losing its influence only when Alexandria was established in 332 B.C.

My boat sails downstream
In time to the strokes of the oarsmen.

A bunch of reeds is on my shoulder,
And I am traveling to Memphis, "Life of the Two Lands."
And I shall say to the god Ptah, Lord of Truth:
"Give me my fair one tonight."
The god Ptah is her tuft of reeds,

Riverine paradise as seen by the Egyptians
EGYPTIAN MUSEUM, CAIRO

The goddess Sekhmet is her posy of blossoms,
The goddess Earit is her budding lotus,
The god Nefertum is her blooming flower.
My love will be happy!
The dawn irradiates her beauty.

Memphis is a crop of pomegranates,
Placed before the god with the handsome countenance.

KING ZOSER'S MAGICIAN

Imhotep, a universal genius of pharaonic times, was counselor and architect to King Zoser, constructing for him the famous Step Pyramid of Saqqara around 2650 B.C. In the following modern biography, the English physician and historical writer Jamieson B. Hurry outlines Imhotep's feats in medicine, magic, literature, and building, and also describes his deification as god of medicine.

Imhotep devoted his life to various activities . . . [including] A. Vizier, B. Architect, C. Chief Lector Priest or Ritualist, D. Sage and Scribe, E. Astronomer, F. Magician-Physician.

The office of vizier to the ruling Pharaoh was one of high dignity and responsibility. The occupant of the post . . . [had] jurisdiction . . . over the various departments of state. . . . The following list of titles in itself indicates the multitudinous responsibilities: "chief judge," "overseer of the King's records," "bearer of the royal seal," "chief of all works of the King," "supervisor of that which Heaven brings, the Earth creates and the Nile brings," "supervisor of everything in this entire land." Amongst some of the departments of his office are enumerated the Judiciary, the Treasury, War [Army and Navy], the Interior, Agriculture, and the General Executive. . . .

As architect, Imhotep [was called] "the chief of all the works of the King of Upper and Lower Egypt". . . . [He] doubtless owed some of his architectural knowledge to his father Kanofer, a man of some distinction who was known as the "Architect of South and North Egypt."

In all probability Imhotep designed for his royal master the well-known Step-Pyramid of Sakkarah near Memphis. . . .

Imhotep [was] chief lector priest or ritualist. The Egyptian priesthood included two main classes of priests, the higher class being designated prophets . . . or servants of the gods, and the lower class ordinary priests. . . . Some priests were permanent officials of a temple, others served in rotation and enjoyed an interval of three months' leave between two periods of service. The chief lector priest or ritualist belonged to the higher class and was a permanent functionary entrusted with important duties. One of these was to attend the daily cult of the temple, where he sprinkled the god with water, fumigated him with incense, clothed and anointed him, applied cosmetics to his eyes and arrayed him with various ornaments. He also had to recite prayers from the holy books during the temple liturgy, and since according to the Egyptian faith these religious texts possessed magical powers, the common people regarded this priest as a magician.

The chief lector priest also assisted at the ritual of embalmment and recited spells while the manipulations were in progress. Further, he officiated at the ceremonies connected with the presentation of offerings in the mortuary cult, which has been called the "Liturgy of Funerary Offerings." The formula which was pronounced over each element in that liturgy was intended to impart to the mummy after restoration of its faculties offerings of food and drink to sustain its renewed physical life. . . .

Another series of ceremonies was known as "The Opening the Mouth," the object being to restore to the inert corpse the functions of which it had been deprived by death and embalmment. The mouth was symbolically opened that the mummy might speak, and the eyes touched that they might see. . . .

TRUSTEES OF THE BRITISH MUSEUM

Imhotep

As regards his literary activities, [he] is said to have produced works on medicine and architecture, as well as on more general subjects, and some of his works were extant at the dawn of the Christian era. His proverbs, embodying the philosophy of life which experience had taught, were handed down from generation to generation, and were noted for their grace and poetic diction, their author being described as a "master of poetry."

A remarkable song, or rather dirge, known as the "Song of the Harper," has survived in which the names of Imhotep and Hardedef [another wise man] are linked together and in which these two sages dilate on the uncertainty and brevity of life, and enforce the doctrine that since man is so soon gone and forgotten, he should enjoy his life to the full. . . .

Although Imhotep was a noted magician, it appears that medicine was the mistress he most zealously wooed; it is his eminence as a healer of the sick that has given him imperishable fame, and that led eventually to his deification. For a time he was probably both court physician and vizier to King Zoser; he evidently moved in the highest social circles. . . . Magic and medicine were closely associated in therapeutics. . . . Magical papyri are leavened with medical prescriptions, while medical papyri . . . are constantly interspersed with incantations and invocations. . . . The fact that he later on received divine honors—a most unusual event except in the case of a Pharaoh—proves him to have been a man of rare distinction. . . .

The worship of the demigod Imhotep doubtless originated at his tomb, which was probably not far removed from the Step-Pyramid which had been erected, probably by Imhotep himself, for his royal master Zoser. The mastaba of the famous magician-physician by degrees became a place of pilgrimage, especially for sick and suffering persons, and apparently . . . some temples were erected in his honor. . . . The custom arose amongst Egyptian scribes of pouring a libation out of their water-bowl to Imhotep "that most famous of scribes." This custom . . . doubtless arose from the scribe's desire to prosper his own task, and the words of invocation "Water from the water-bowl of every scribe to thy *Ka*, O Imhotep!" were frequently inscribed on the roll of papyrus which so often lies on the knees of the statuettes of the demigod. . . .

Well-nigh twenty-five centuries elapsed between the time Imhotep held office under the Pharaoh Zoser and the time he was raised to the rank of full deity of medicine. His apotheosis appears to have taken place somewhere about 525 B.C., the year in which Egypt was conquered by Cambyses and became a Persian province.

The preceding period in Egyptian history, lasting from the expulsion of the Assyrians in 654 B.C. to the Persian Conquest in 525 B.C. and corresponding with the XXVIth Dynasty, is known as the Saitic Restoration. . . . With the return of ordered government a great national revival took place resulting in increased economic prosperity. Industry flourished, art revived, a veneration for the glorious history of the Pyramid Age impressed itself on the soul of the nation. The worship of the early Pharaohs who had ruled at Memphis was restored and the ritual of their mortuary services was resuscitated and endowed. Even the pyramids were repaired on an extensive scale.

As further indication of the desire to pay honor to those who in former days had brought glory to the nation, the famous Imhotep . . . was now advanced to the status of full deity of medicine with the title of son of Ptah, one of the oldest of all Egyptian deities, and also god of healing. . . .

An interesting story has survived which illustrates the practice of incubation at Imhotep's temples. . . . The story relates to a man named Satmi Khamuas, the son of the Pharaoh Usermares, who had no man-child by his wife Mahituaskhit; this troubled him greatly in his heart, and his wife Mahituaskhit was greatly afflicted with him. One day, when Satmi was more depressed than usual, his wife Mahituaskhit went to the temple of Imhotep, son of Ptah, and uttered this prayer before him, saying: "Turn thy face towards me, my lord Imhotep, son of Ptah: it is thou who dost work miracles, and who are beneficent in all thy deeds; it is thou who givest a son to her who has none. Listen to my lamentation and give me conception of a man-child."

That same night Mahituaskhit, the wife of Satmi, slept in the temple and dreamed a dream in which one spake with her, "Art thou not Mahituaskhit, the wife of Satmi, who dost sleep in the temple to receive a remedy for thy sterility from the hands of the god? When to-morrow morning comes, go to the bath-room of Satmi thy husband, and thou wilt find a root of colocasia that is growing there. The colocasia that thou meetest with thou shalt gather with its leaves; thou shalt make of it a remedy that thou shalt give to thy husband, then thou shalt lie by his side, and thou shalt conceive by him the same night."

When Mahituaskhit awoke from her dream after seeing the vision, she at once carried out the instructions given her in her dream; then she lay by the side of Satmi, her husband, and conceived by him. . . .

Religious festivals played a prominent part in the life of the Egyptians and were celebrated by vociferous demonstrations of joy. Great processions were organized in which took part the priests with shaven heads, clad in linen of spotless white, as well as throngs of devotees, all eager to do honor to their deities. Music, singing, dancing, floral decorations, banquets all added to the gaiety of the ceremonies, while at night numerous torches illuminated the streets with flickering lights and prolonged the feasting far into the night. Important festivals might extend over several days or even weeks. . . . Under the Ptolemies regular festivals were celebrated at Memphis in honor of the god Imhotep.

METROPOLITAN MUSEUM OF ART, ROGERS FUND, 1946

Thoth

THE SILENT MAN

For the ancient Egyptians, who believed that the universe was essentially static, life was a constant striving to maintain a perfect integration with the established order, or maat. *Anyone who broke the existing equilibrium was a wrongdoer acting out of ignorance or lack of self-control. This prayer to Thoth, god of wisdom and patron of scribes, was written in the thirteenth century* B.C. *and was used as a school text. The supplicant, proclaiming himself a "silent man," hence the master of his impulses and in harmony with the divine order, seeks to gain Thoth's support at the last judgment. Conversely, the "noisy man" could expect no solace in the afterlife.*

O Thoth, take me to Hermopolis, to thy city, where it is pleasant to live.
Thou suppliest what I need in bread and beer and thou keepest watch over my mouth when I speak.

Would that I had Thoth behind me tomorrow (when I shall die)!
Come to me when I enter before the Lords of Maat (the judges in the hereafter)
And so shall I come forth justified.
Thou great dom palm, sixty cubits high, whereon are fruits;
Stones are in the fruits and water is in the stones.
Thou who bringest water to a distant place, come deliver me, the silent man.
Thoth, thou sweet well for one who thirsts in the desert;
It is closed for one who argues but open for him who keeps silence.
The silent one comes and finds the well.
The hot-headed comes and thou art [choked].

THE AMARNA HERESY

The Hymn to Aten, *which follows, is one of ancient Egypt's literary masterpieces. It was written during the reign of Amenhotep* IV (1370–1353 B.C.), *who initiated a religious and artistic revolution, which was short-lived. He discredited Egypt's innumerable deities and substituted a faith based on the worship of the Aten, the "One God," whose symbol was the sun disc. The "Heretic King" even changed his name to Akhenaten, "he who is serviceable to the Aten," and moved his capital from Thebes to Amarna in Middle Egypt. He also encouraged realism in art. Akhenaten's religion never gained followers among the masses of people; after his death Egypt returned to its ancient polytheism.*

Thou appearest beautifully on the horizon of heaven,
Thou living Aten, the beginning of life!
When thou art risen on the eastern horizon,
Thou hast filled every land with thy beauty.
Thou art gracious, great, glistening, and high over every land;
Thy rays encompass the lands to . . . all that thou hast made:
As thou art Re, thou reachest to the end of them;
(Thou) subduest them (for) thy beloved son.
Though thou art far away, thy rays are on earth;
Though thou art in their faces, no one knows thy going.

When thou settest in the western horizon,
The land is in darkness, in the manner of death.
They sleep in a room, with heads wrapped up,
Nor sees one eye the other.
All their goods which are under their heads might be stolen,
(But) they would not perceive (it).
Every lion is come forth from his den;
All creeping things, they sting.
Darkness is a shroud, and the earth is in stillness.
For he who made them rests in his horizon.

At daybreak, when thou arisest on the horizon,
When thou shinest as the Aten by day,
Thou drivest away the darkness and givest thy rays.
The Two Lands are in festivity every day,
Awake and standing upon (their) feet,
For thou hast raised them up.
Washing their bodies, taking (their) clothing,
Their arms are (raised) in praise at thy appearance.
All the world, they do their work.

All beasts are content with their pasturage;
Trees and plants are flourishing.
The birds which fly from their nests,
Their wings are (stretched out) in praise to thy *ka*.
All beasts spring upon (their) feet.
Whatever flies and alights,
They live when thou hast risen (for) them.
The ships are sailing north and south as well,
For every way is open at thy appearance.
The fish in the river dart before thy face;
Thy rays are in the midst of the great green sea.

Creator of seed in woman,
Thou who makest fluid into man,
Who maintainest the son in the womb of his mother,
Who soothest him with that which stills his weeping,
Thou nurse (even) in the womb,
Who givest breath to sustain all that he has made!
When he descends from the womb to breathe
On the day when he is born,
Thou openest his mouth completely,
Thou suppliest his necessities.
When the chick in the egg speaks within the shell,
Thou givest him breath within it to maintain him.
When thou hast made him his fulfillment within the egg, to break it,
He comes forth from the egg to speak at his completed (time);
He walks upon his legs when he comes forth from it.

How manifold it is, what thou has made!
They are hidden from the face (of man).
O sole god, like whom there is no other!
Thou didst create the world according to thy desire,
Whilst thou wert alone.
All men, cattle, and wild beasts,
Whatever is on earth, going upon (its) feet,
And what is on high, flying with its wings.

Thy rays suckle every meadow.
When thou risest, they live, they grow for thee.
Thou makest the seasons in order to rear all that thou hast made,
The winter to cool them,
And the heat that they may taste thee.
Thou has made the distant sky in order to rise therein,
In order to see all that thou dost make.
Whilst thou wert alone,
Rising in thy form as the living Aten,
Appearing, shining, withdrawing, or approaching,
Thou madest millions of forms of thyself alone.
Cities, towns, fields, road, and river—
Every eye beholds thee over against them . . .

Thou art in my heart,
And there is no other that knows thee
Save thy son Neferkheperure Waenre,
For thou hast made him well-versed in thy plans and in thy strength.
The world came into being by thy hand,
According as thou has made them.
When thou hast risen they live,
When thou settest they die.
Thou art lifetime thy own self,
For one lives (only) through thee.
Eyes are (fixed) on beauty until thou settest.
All work is laid aside when thou settest in the west.
(But) when (thou) rises (again),
[Everything is] made to flourish for the king . . .
Since thou didst found the earth
And raise them up for thy son,
Who came forth from thy body:
the King of Upper and Lower Egypt . . . Akhenaten . . .
and the Chief Wife of the King . . . Nefertiti, living and
youthful forever and ever.

EGYPTIAN WAY OF DEATH

The fight for immortality gave rise to two abiding symbols of Egyptian civilization: pyramids and mummies. The Greek historian Herodotus, who visited the Nile Valley in the fifth century B.C., *has left us a fairly accurate account of Egyptian burial customs. The following passage, from his* Histories, *fails to mention the one foe against whom even a pharaoh was not secure: the tomb robber.*

The following is the way in which they conduct their mournings and their funerals:—On the death in any house of a man of consequence, forthwith the women of the family beplaster their heads, and sometimes even their faces, with mud; and then, leaving the body indoors, sally forth and wander through the city, with their dress fastened by a band, and their bosoms bare, beating themselves as they walk. All the female relations join them and do the same. The men, too, similarly begirt, beat their breasts separately. When these ceremonies are over, the body is carried away to be embalmed.

There are a set of men in Egypt who practice the art of embalming, and make it their proper business. These persons, when a body is brought to them, show the bearers various models of corpses, made in wood, and painted so as to resemble nature. The most perfect is said to be after the manner of [Osiris] whom I do not think it religious to name in connection with such a matter; the second sort is inferior to the first, and less costly; the third is the cheapest of all. All this the embalmers explain, and then ask in which way it is wished that the corpse should be prepared. The bearers tell them, and having concluded their bargain, take their departure, while the embalmers, left to themselves, proceed to their task. The mode of embalming, according to the most perfect process, is the following:—They take first a crooked piece of iron, and with it draw out the brain through the nostrils, thus getting rid of a portion, while the skull is cleared of the rest by rinsing with drugs; next they make a cut along the flank with a sharp Ethiopian

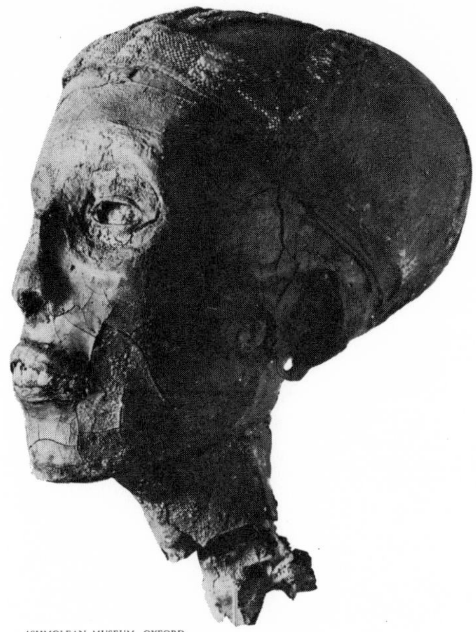

ASHMOLEAN MUSEUM, OXFORD

Mummified head of young king Tutankhamon, discovered in his royal tomb at Thebes

stone, and take out the whole contents of the abdomen, which they then cleanse, washing it thoroughly with palm wine, and again frequently with an infusion of pounded aromatics. After this they fill the cavity with the purest bruised myrrh, with cassia, and every sort of spicery except frankincense, and sew up the opening. Then the body is placed in natron for seventy days, and covered entirely over. After the expiration of that space of time, which must not be exceeded, the body is washed, and wrapped round, from head to foot, with bandages of fine linen cloth, smeared over with gum which is used generally by the Egyptians in the place of glue, and in this state it is given back to the relations, who enclose it in a wooden case which they have made for the purpose, shaped into the figure of a man. Then fastening the case, they place it in a sepulchral chamber upright against the wall. Such is the most costly way of embalming the dead.

If the persons wish to avoid expense, and choose the second process, the following is the method pursued:—Syringes are filled with oil made from the cedar tree, which is then, without any incision or disemboweling, injected into the abdomen. The passage by which it might be likely to return is stopped, and the body laid in natron the prescribed number of days. At the end of the time the cedar oil is allowed to make its escape; and such is its power that it brings with it the whole stomach and intestines in a liquid state. The natron meanwhile has dissolved the flesh, and so nothing is left of the dead body but the skin and the bones. It is returned in this condition to the relatives, without any further trouble being bestowed upon it.

The third method of embalming, which is practiced in the case of the poorer classes, is to clear out the intestines with a clyster, and let the body lie in natron the seventy days, after which it is at once given to those who come to fetch it away.

The wives of men of rank are not given to be embalmed immediately after death, nor indeed are any of the more beautiful and valued women. It is not till they have been dead three or four days that they are carried to the embalmers. This is done to prevent indignities from being offered then. It is said that once a case of this kind occurred; the man was detected by the information of his fellow workman.

SONG OF THE HARPER

During troubled times the ancient Egyptians often cast off their characteristic self-controlled, positive outlook and became hedonistic and agnostic. The poem, whose oldest version dates from either the First or Second Intermediate Periods—two anarchic times—probably stems from a widespread pessimism. It exhorts the living to follow the advice of the renowned sages Imhotep and Hordedef, and to eat, drink and be merry, for man has no certainty that earthly propriety will lead to eternal bliss. The song's great beauty made it popular with the scribes of the Eighteenth and Nineteenth Dynasties, relatively stable times.

All hail to the prince, the good Man,
Whose body must pass away,
While his children remain for aye.

The gods of old rest in their tombs,
And the mummies of men long dead;

LEIDEN MUSEUM—F. L. KENETT

Bas-relief of a harper of the New Kingdom

The Same for both rich and poor.

The words of Imhotep I hear
The words of Hordedef, which say:
"What is prosperity? tell!"

Their fences and walls are destroyed
Their houses exist no more;
And no man cometh again from the tomb
To tell of what passeth below.

Ye go to the place of the mourners,
To the bourne whence none return:
Strengthen your hearts to forget your joys,
Yet fulfill your desires while ye live.

Anoint yourselves, clothe yourselves well,
Use the gifts which the gods bestow,
Fulfill your desires upon earth.

For the days will come to you all
When ye hear not the voice of friends,
When weeping avails you no more;

So feast in tranquillity now,
For none taketh his goods below to the tomb
And none cometh thence back again.

PEPI'S LEGIONS

An Old Kingdom military campaign against an agricultural people, most probably in Palestine, is the subject of the following selection. It is taken from the fragmented cenotaph inscription of a career officer named Uni, who describes his exploits under Pepi I *(around* 2350 B.C.). *Uni derides the enemy as "Sand-Dwellers," in reference to their habitations, and he exaggerates the size of his army.*

When his majesty imposed punishment upon the Asiatics Who-are-Upon-the-Sands, his majesty made an army of many ten-thousands, in the entire Upper Egypt . . . in Lower Egypt . . . among the Nubians . . . and from the land of the Temeh-Libyans. His majesty sent me at the head of this army, while the counts, while the Seal-Bearers of the King of Lower Egypt, while the Sole Companions of the Palace, while the nomarchs and mayors of Upper and Lower Egypt, the companions and chief dragomans, the chief prophets of Upper and Lower Egypt, and the chief bureaucrats were [each] at the head of a troop of Upper or Lower Egypt, or of the villages and towns which they might rule, or of the Nubians of these foreign countries. I was the one who used to make the plan for them, although my office was [only that of] Chief Domain Supervisor of the Palace, because I was [so] fitted for the post that not one of them [so much as] laid a hand upon his fellow, that not one of them appropriated [so much as] a lump of dough or a pair of sandals from a wayfarer, that not one of them carried off [so much as] a loincloth from any town, that not one of them carried off any goat from anybody. . . .

This army returned in safety,
After it had hacked up the land of the [Sand]-Dwellers.
This army returned in safety,
After it had crushed the land of the Sand-Dwellers.
This army returned in safety,
After it had thrown down [the land's] enclosures.
This army returned in safety,
After it had cut down its fig trees and its vines.
This army returned in safety,
After it had cast fire into all its dwellings.
This army returned in safety,
After it had killed troops in it by many ten-thousands.
This army returned in safety,
[After it had taken troops] in it, a great multitude as living captives.

His majesty praised me for it more than anything.

His majesty sent me to lead [this] army five times, in order to repel the land of the Sand-Dwellers each time that they rebelled, with these troops.

THE BROKEN REED

The Hyksos domination of Egypt from 1730 *to* 1570 B.C. *completely shattered Egyptian morale. The following passage is one of the few extant accounts of the invasion. It comes from the writings of Josephus, a Jewish historian of the first century* A.D. *He claims to be quoting the Egyptian historian Manetho, who lived in the third century* B.C. *The record probably exaggerates the savagery of the onslaught and misinterprets the term* hyksos, *which actually comes from the Egyptian words* hikau khasut, *meaning "rulers of foreign countries." Modern scholarship has revealed that the Hyksos were a composite people of preponderantly Semitic origin who were once settled in the uplands of Palestine, Lebanon, Syria, and farther Asia.*

Tutimaios. In his reign, for what cause I know not, a blast of God smote us; and unexpectedly from the regions of the East invaders of obscure race marched in confidence of victory against our land. By main force they easily seized it without striking a blow; and having overpowered the rulers of the land, they then burned our cities ruthlessly, razed to the ground the temples of the gods, and treated all the natives with a cruel hostility, massacring some and leading into slavery the wives and children of others. Finally, they appointed as king one of their number whose name was Salitis. He had his seat at Memphis, levying tribute from Upper and Lower Egypt, and always leaving garrisons behind in the most advantageous places. . . . In the

Sethroite nome [province] he found a city very favorably situated on the east of the Bubastite branch of the Nile [Delta], and called Avaris after an ancient religious tradition. This place he rebuilt and fortified with massive walls. . . . After reigning for 19 years Salitis died; and a second king Bnon succeeded and reigned for 44 years. Next to him came Apachnan, who ruled for 36 years and 7 months; then Apophis for 61, and Iannas for 50 years and 1 month; then finally Assis for 49 years and 2 months. These six kings, their first rulers, were ever more and more eager to extirpate the Egyptian stock. Their race as a whole was called Hyksos, that is "king-shepherds"; for *hyk* in the sacred language means "king" and *sos* in common speech is "shepherd."

THE QUEEN'S PEACE

The Hyksos were finally driven out of Egypt around 1570 B.C. *In an inscription written almost a century later, Queen Hatshepsut expresses her nation's lingering outrage. Her remarks, quoted in part below, are carved on the façade of Istabl Antar temple, Middle Egypt.*

Hear ye, all people and the folk as many as they may be, I have done these things through the counsel of my heart. I have not slept forgetfully, [but] I have restored that which had been ruined. I have raised up that which had gone to pieces formerly, since the Asiatics were in the midst of Avaris of the Northland [the Hyksos capital], and vagabonds were in the midst of them, overthrowing that which had been made. They ruled without Re, and he did not act by divine command down to [the reign of] my majesty. [Now] I am established upon the thrones of Re. I was foretold for the limits of the years as a born conqueror. I am come as the uraeus-serpent of Horus, flaming against my enemies. I have made distant those whom the gods abominate, and earth has carried off their foot[prints]. This is the precept of the father of [my] fathers, who comes at his [appointed] times, Re, and there shall not occur damage to what Amon has commanded. My [own] command endures like the mountains, [while] the sun disc shines forth and spreads rays over the formal titles of my majesty and my falcon is high above [my] name-standard for the duration of eternity.

THE FABLED LAND OF PUNT

Hatshepsut's greatest economic triumph—the revival of trade with the remote regions of Punt—is told in reliefs and hieroglyphs on the walls of her magnificent funerary temple at Deir el Bahri. Scholars differ as to the precise location of Punt, but it was probably on the Somali coast along the Gulf of Aden; "God's Land" was perhaps across the gulf in southwest Arabia. The objective of her mission to the land of myrrh trees was the exchange of Egyptian weapons, beads, rings, and the like for the coveted riches of Punt: apes and incense, ivory and gold, slaves, ebony, greyhounds, leopard skins. In the following account, she exalts herself as the daughter of the god Amon-Re (Thothmes I *was her mortal father) and tells how the god directed her in fulfilling his desires.*

A command was heard from the great throne, an oracle of the god himself [Amon-Re], that the ways to Punt should be searched out, that the highways to the Myrrh-terraces should be penetrated: "I [said the oracle] will lead the army on water and on land, to bring marvels from God's-Land for this god [Hatshepsut], for the fashioner of her beauty." It was done, according to all that the majesty of this revered god commanded, according to the desire of her majesty, in order that she might be given life, stability, and satisfaction, like Re, forever. . . .

"I [Hatshepsut] shine forever in your faces through that which my father hath desired. Truly, it was greatly my desire in doing, that I should make great him that begat me; and in assigning to my father, that I should make splendid for him all his offerings; that which my fathers, the ancestors knew not, I am doing as the Great One [did] to the Lord of Eternity; I am adding increase to that which was formerly done. I will cause it to be said to posterity: 'How beautiful is she, through whom this has happened,' because I have been so very excellent to him, and the heart of my heart has been replete with that which is due to him. I am his splendor [on high, and in the nether world.] I have entered into the qualities of the august god. . . . He hath recognized my excellence. . . . I am the god, the beginning of being, nothing fails that goes out of my mouth. . . . I have given a command of my majesty that the offerings of him who begat me should be made splendid. . . ."

"[I Hatshepsut commanded] to send to the Myrrh-terraces, to explore his ways [for him,] to learn his circuit, to open his highways, according to the command of my father, Amon. . . . Trees were taken up in God's Land, and set in the ground in [Egypt]—— for the king of the gods. They were brought bearing myrrh therein for expressing ointment for the divine limbs, which I owed to the lord of Gods."

Said my majesty. "I will cause you to know that which is commanded me, I have hearkened to my father . . . commanding me to establish for him a Punt in his house, to plant the trees of God's-

Scarabs, used for protective amulets and seals, incised with appropriate hieroglyphs

METROPOLITAN MUSEUM OF ART

Land beside his temple, in his garden, according as he commanded. It was done, in order to endow the offerings which I owed.——I was [not] neglectful of that which he needed. . . . He hath desired me as his favorite; I know all that he loveth. . . . I have made for him a Punt in his garden, just as he commanded me, for Thebes. It is large for him, he walks abroad in it."

IN SEARCH OF PEACE

When Ramses II *became pharaoh, Egypt resumed its war with the Hittites of Asia Minor for possession of Syria and Palestine. By about* 1280 B.C. *both empires, exhausted after eighty years of conflict, were ready to make peace. Portions of the resultant treaty between Ramses and Hattusilis, king of the Hatti, or Hittites, are quoted below. Aside from a mutual nonaggression pact and provisions for a defensive alliance against a third enemy, the agreement also calls for the extradition of political refugees—both great and humble. Elsewhere in the document is included a list of the gods who witnessed it, thus combining the ancient concept of divinity with a sophisticated code of international law. The Egyptian version, used here, was carved on the walls of the Temple of Amon at Karnak and the Ramesseum at Thebes. Predictably, it makes Hattusilis the first to cry for peace; the roles are reversed in the Hittite version. Thus each side preserved its dignity.*

Year 21, 1st month of the second season, day 21 [late November, 1280 B.C.]. . . . On this day, while his majesty was in the town of Per-Ramses Meri-Amon [the capital city of Ramses in the Delta], doing the pleasure of his father Amon-Re [and other gods] . . . there came the Royal Envoy and Deputy . . . and Messenger of Hatti . . . carrying [the tablet of silver which] the Great Prince of Hatti, Hattusilis [caused] to be brought to Pharaoh—life, prosperity, health!—in order to beg [peace from the majesty of (Ramses)], Son of Re . . . bull of rulers, who has made his frontier where he wished. . . .

Behold, Hattusilis, the Great Prince of Hatti, has set himself in regulation with [Ramses], the great ruler of Egypt, beginning from this day, to cause that good peace and brotherhood occur between us forever, while he is in brotherhood with me and he is at peace with me, and I am in brotherhood with him and I am at peace with him forever. . . . [The land of Egypt], with the land of Hatti, [shall be] at peace and in brotherhood like unto us forever. Hostilities shall not occur between them forever. . . .

If another enemy come against the lands of [Ramses II] . . . and he send to the Great Prince of Hatti, saying: "Come with me as reinforcement against him," the Great Prince of Hatti shall [come to him and] the Great Prince of Hatti shall slay his enemy. However, if it is not the desire of the Great Prince of Hatti to go [himself], he shall send his infantry and his chariotry, and he shall slay his enemy. Or, if . . . [the great ruler of Egypt], is enraged against servants belonging to him, and they commit another offense against him, and he go to slay them, the Great Prince of Hatti shall act with him [to slay] everyone [against whom] they shall be enraged.

But [if] another enemy [come] against the Great Prince [of Hatti] . . . [the great ruler of Egypt, shall] come to him as reinforcement to slay his enemy. . . .

If a man flee from the land of Egypt—or two or three—and they come to the Great Prince of Hatti, the Great Prince of Hatti shall lay hold of them, and he shall cause that they be brought back to [Ramses II], the great ruler of Egypt. But, as for the man . . . do not cause that his crime be raised against him; do not cause that his house or his wives or his children be destroyed; [do not cause that] he be [slain]; do not cause that injury be done to his eyes, to his ears, to his mouth, or to his legs; do not let any [crime be raised] against him.

Similarly, if men flee from the land of the Hatti . . . let Ramses . . . lay hold [of them and cause] that they be brought to the Great Prince of Hatti, and the Great Prince of Hatti shall not raise their crime against them. . . .

MISSION TO BYBLOS

By about 1100 B.C. *pharaonic power was illusory and the real rulers of Egypt were Heri-Hor, the high priest of Amon-Re at Thebes, and Ne-su-Ba-neb-Ded, the prince at Tanis in the Delta. Egypt was in a state of chaos, and its prestige in Asia had waned. This sorry state of affairs is elucidated in one of the most famous Egyptian historical papyruses,* The Journey of Wen-Amon to Phoenicia. *It tells of Wen-Amon, an official at Amon-Re's temple at Thebes, who journeys to the Phoenician port of Byblos to buy cedar wood for the god's ceremonial barge. In past generations emissaries of Wen-Amon's position set forth in a grand style befitting their rulers' status and were always courteously received by the princes of Byblos. But Wen-Amon traveled unescorted and could offer only paltry amounts of gold and silver as royal gifts. He is so reduced, in fact, that he does not even have his own vessel, but stops first at Tanis, where Ne-su-Ba-neb-Ded and his wife, Ta-net-Amon, find a passage for him on a Syrian ship. When he finally arrives at Byblos, he is humbled by its prince, as this excerpt indicates. Only after much persuasion does he succeed in his mission.*

I [set myself up in] a tent [on] the shore of the [sea], [in] the harbor of Byblos. And [I hid] Amon-of-the-Road [a portable idol of Amon-Re]. . . .

And the [Prince] of Byblos sent to me, saying: "Get [out of my] harbor!" And I sent to him, saying: "Where should [I go to]? . . . If [you have a ship] to carry me, have me taken to Egypt again!" So I spent twenty-nine days in his [harbor, while] he [spent] the time sending to me every day to say: "Get out [of] my harbor!"

Now while he was making offering to his gods, the god seized one of his youths and made him possessed. And he said to him: "Bring up [the] god! Bring the messenger who is carrying him! Amon is the one who sent him out! . . .

When morning came, [the Prince of Byblos] sent and brought me up, but the god stayed in the tent where he was, [on] the shore of the sea. And I found him sitting [in] his upper room, with his back

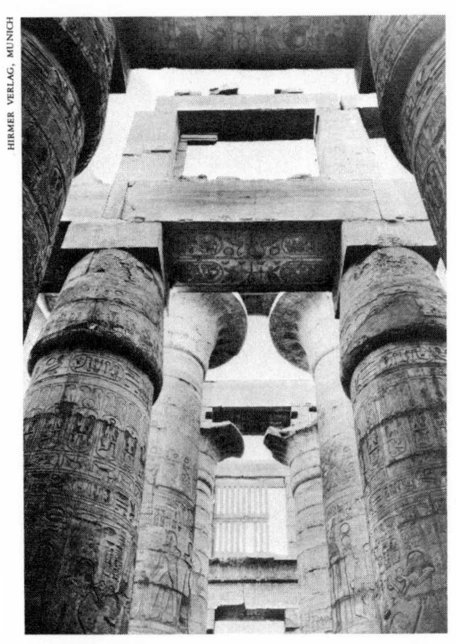

The temple of the god Amon at Karnak

turned to a window, so that the waves of the great Syrian sea broke against the back of his head.

So I said to him: "May Amon favor you!" But he said to me "How long, up to today, since you came from the place where Amon is?" So I said to him: "Five months and one day up to now." And he said to me: "Well, you're truthful! Where is the letter of Amon which [should be] in your hand? Where is the dispatch of the High Priest of Amon which [should be] in your hand?" And I told him: "I gave them to Ne-su-Ba-neb-Ded and Ta-net-Amon." And he was very, very angry, and he said to me: "Now see—neither letters nor dispatches are in your hand! Where is the cedar ship which Ne-su-Ba-neb-Ded gave to you? Where is its Syrian crew? Didn't he turn you over to this foreign ship captain to have him kill you and throw you into the sea? . . . And I was silent in this great time.

And he . . . said to me: "On what business have you come?" So I told him: "I have come after the woodwork for the great and august barque of Amon-Re, King of the Gods. Your father did [it], your grandfather did [it], and you will do it too!" So I spoke to him. But he said to me: "To be sure, they did it! And if you give me [something] for doing it, I will do it! Why, when my people carried out this commission, Pharaoh—life, prosperity, health!—sent six ships loaded with Egyptian goods, and they unloaded them into their storehouses! You—what is it that you're bringing me—me also?" And he had the journal rolls of his fathers brought, and he had them read out in my presence, and they found a thousand *deben* of silver and all kinds of things in his scrolls.

So he said to me: "If the ruler of Egypt were the lord of mine, and I were his servant also, he would not have to send silver and gold, saying: 'Carry out the commission of Amon!' There would be no carrying of a royal-gift, such as they used to do for my father. As for me—me also—I am not your servant! I am not the servant of him who sent you either! . . . What are these silly trips which they have had you make?"

And I said to him: "[That's] not true! What I am on are no 'silly trips' at all! There is no ship upon the River which does not belong to Amon! The sea is his, and the Lebanon is his, of which you say: 'It is mine!' . . . Why, he spoke—Amon-Re, King of the Gods—said to Heri-Hor, my master: 'Send me forth!' So he had me come, carrying this great god [Amon-of-the-Road]. But see, you have made this great god spend these twenty-nine days moored [in] your harbor, although you did not know [it]. Isn't he here? Isn't he the [same] as he was? You are stationed [here] to carry on the commerce of the Lebanon with Amon, its lord. As for your saying that the former kings sent silver and gold—suppose that they had life and health; [then] they would not have had such things sent! [But] they had such things sent to your fathers in place of life and health! Now as for Amon-Re, King of the Gods—he is the lord of this life and health, and he was the lord of your fathers. They spent their lifetimes making offering to Amon. And you also—you are the servant of Amon! If you say to Amon: 'Yes, I will do [it]!' and you carry out his commission, you will live, you will be prosperous, you will be healthy, and you will be good to your entire land and your people! [But] don't wish for yourself anything belonging to Amon-Re, [King of] the Gods. Why, a lion wants his own property! Have your secretary brought to me, so that I may send him to Ne-su-Ba-neb-Ded and Ta-net-Amon, the officers whom Amon put in the north of his land, and they will have all kinds of things sent. . . ."

So he entrusted my letter to his messenger, and he loaded on the keel, the bow-post, the stern-post, along with four other hewn timbers—seven in all—and he had them taken to Egypt. And in the first month of the second season his messenger who had gone to Egypt came back to me in Syria. And Ne-su-Ba-neb-Ded and Ta-net-Amon sent: 4 jars and 1 *kak-men* of gold; 5 jars of silver, 10 pieces of clothing in royal linen; 10 *kherd* of good Upper Egyptian linen; 500 [rolls of] finished papyrus; 500 cowhides; 500 ropes; 20 sacks of lentils; and 30 baskets of fish. And she sent to me [personally]: 5 pieces of clothing in good Upper Egyptian linen; 5 *kherd* of good Upper Egyptian linen; 1 sack of lentils; and 5 baskets of fish.

And the Prince was glad, and he detailed three hundred men and three hundred cattle, and he put supervisors at their head, to have them cut down the timber. So they cut them down, and they spent the second season lying there.

THE KUSHITE TAKEOVER

By the second half of the eighth century B.C. *Egypt was ripe for conquest. The final assault came around 730* B.C. *under the command of Piankhi, king of Kush. His father, Kashta, had invaded Upper Egypt, conquering the temple city of Thebes. Piankhi's military campaign won him control over Egypt; it was so successful that he recorded its progress on a granite stele, which he erected at Jebel Barkal, near his capital of Napata at the Nile's*

Fourth Cataract. The inscription tells of his journey down the river and how he forced all of Egypt's gods and rulers into submission. The selection below opens with Piankhi's swaggering account of himself. Then follows a report on the brilliant strategy that won him Memphis, gateway to the domination of Lower Egypt. Lastly, having laid the foundation for seventy years of Kushite rule, Piankhi loads his ships and sails for home.

"Hear of what I did, more than the ancestors. I am a king, divine emanation, living image of Atum [an aspect of the god of Creation], who came forth from the womb, adorned as a ruler, of whom those greater than he were afraid; whose father knew, and whose mother recognized that he would rule in the egg, the Good God, beloved of the gods, achieving with his hands, Meriamon-Piankhi." . . .

Then [the soldiers] threw themselves upon their bellies before his majesty [saying]: "It is thy name which endues us with might, and thy counsel is the mooring-post of thy army; thy bread is in our bellies on every march, thy beer quenches our thirst. It is thy valor that giveth us might, and there is strength at the remembrance of thy name; [for] no army prevails whose commander is a coward. Who is they equal therein? Thou art a victorious king, achieving with his hands, chief of the work of war." . . .

[His majesty sailed north to] Memphis; then he sent to them, saying: "Shut not up, fight not. . . . As for him that would go in, let him go in; as for him that would come out, let him come out; and let not them that would leave be hindered. . . . [The people] of Memphis [shall be] safe and sound; not [even] a child shall weep. Look ye to the nomes of the South; not a single one has been slain therein, except the enemies who blasphemed against the god, who were dispatched as rebels."

Then they closed their stronghold; they sent forth an army against some of the soldiers of his majesty, being artisans, chief builders and sailors. . . .

Lo, that chief of Sais [Tefnakhte] arrived at Memphis in the night, charging his infantry and his sailors, all the best of his army, a total of 8,000 men, charging them very earnestly: "Behold, Memphis is filled with troops of all the best of the Northland; [with] barley and spelt and all kinds of grain, the granaries are running over; [with] all weapons of [war. It is fortified with] a wall; a great battlement has been built, executed with skillful workmanship. The river flows around the east side, and no [opportunity of] attack is found there. Cattle yards are there, filled with oxen; the treasury is supplied with everything: silver, gold, copper, clothing, incense, honey, oil." . . .

When day broke, at early morning, his majesty [Pianki] reached Memphis. When he had landed on the north of it, he found that the water had approached to the walls, the ships mooring at [the walls of] Memphis. Then his majesty saw that it was strong, and that the wall was raised by a new rampart, and battlements manned with mighty men. There was found no way of attacking it. Every man told his opinion among the army of his majesty, according to every rule of war. Every man said: "Let us besiege [it] —; lo, its troops are numerous." Others said: "Let a causeway be made against it; let us elevate the ground to its walls. Let us bind together a tower; let us erect masts and make the spars into a bridge to it. We will divide it on this [plan] on every side of it, on the high ground and —on the north of it, in order to elevate the ground at its walls, that we may find a way for our feet."

Then his majesty was enraged against [Memphis' defences] like a panther; he said: "I swear, as Re loves me, as my father, Amon [who fashioned me], favors me, this shall befall [the city], according to the command of Amon. . . . I will take it like a flood of water. . . .

Then he sent forth his fleet and his army to assault the harbor of Memphis; they brought him every ferry-boat, every [cargo]-boat, every [transport], and the ships, as many as there were, which had moored in the harbor of Memphis, with the bow-rope fastened among its houses. [There was not] a citizen who wept, among all the soldiers of his majesty. [Either all were considered in the distribution of the spoil, or no man was injured in the assault.]

His majesty himself came to line up the ships, as many as there were. His majesty commanded his army [saying]: "Foward against it! Mount the walls! Penetrate the houses over the river. If one of you gets through upon the wall, let him not halt before it, [so that] the [hostile] troops may not repulse you. . . .

Then Memphis was taken as [by] a flood of water, a multitude of people were slain therein, and brought as living captives to the place where his majesty was. . . .

Then the ships were laden with silver, gold, copper, clothing, and everything of the Northland, every product of Syria, and all sweet woods of God's-Land. His majesty sailed up-stream, with glad heart, the shores on his either side were jubilating. West and east . . . [the people were] jubilating in the presence of his majesty; singing and jubilating as they said: "O mighty, mighty Ruler, Piankhi, O mighty Ruler; thou comest, having gained the dominion of the Northland. Thou makest bulls into women. Happy the heart of the mother who bore thee, and the man who begat thee. Those who are in the valley give to her praise, the cow that hath borne a bull. Thou art unto eternity, thy might endureth, O Ruler, beloved of Thebes."

KING OF PURE MOUNTAIN

Even after they lost control of Egypt around 660 B.C., the kings of Kush (or Cush) styled themselves kings of Upper and Lower Egypt. The Kushites, whose civilization was strongly influenced by Egypt, believed that their rulers, like the pharaohs, were divinely chosen. The following excerpt comes from one of the steles found at the holy site of Jebel Barkal, "Pure Mountain." It describes the nomination, in 593 B.C., of Aspalta as king of

Kush and concludes when Aspalta steps forward to receive the crown and scepter.

Year 1, 2nd month of the second season, day 15, under the majesty of the Horus: Beautiful of Appearances; the Two Goddesses: Beautiful of Appearances; the Horus of Gold: Mighty of Heart; the King of Upper and Lower Egypt, Lord of the Two Lands: [Merka-Re]; the Son of Re, Lord of Diadems: [Aspalta], beloved of Amon-Re, Lord of the Thrones of the Two Lands, Resident in the Pure Mountain.

Now the entire army of his majesty was in the town named Pure Mountain, in which Dedwen, Who Presides over Nubia, is the god—he is [also] the god of Cush—after the death of the Falcon [previous Kushite King] upon his throne. Now then, the trusted commanders from the midst of the army of his majesty were six men, while the trusted commanders and overseers of fortresses were six men. Now then, the trusted chief secretaries were six men, while the officials and chief treasurers of the palace were seven men. Then they said to the entire army: "Come, let us cause our lord to appear, [for we are] like a herd which has no herdsman!" Thereupon this army was very greatly concerned, saying: "Our lord is here with us, [but] we do not know him! Would that we might know him. . . ."

Then the army of his majesty all said with one voice: "Still there is this god Amon-Re, Lord of the Thrones of the Two Lands, Resident in the Pure Mountain. He is [also] a god of Cush. Come, let us go to him. We cannot do a thing without him; nothing is good which is done without him, [but] a good fortune [comes] from the god. He is the god of the kings of Cush since the time of Re. It is he who will guide us. In his hands is the kingship of Cush, which he has given to the son whom he loves. . . ."

So the commanders of his majesty and the courtiers of the palace went to the Temple of Amon. They found the prophets and the major priests waiting. . . .

Then the prophets and the major priests entered into the temple, that they might perform every rite of his purification and his censing. Then the commanders of his majesty and the officials of the palace entered into the temple and put themselves upon their bellies before this god. They said: "We have come to thee, O Amon-Re, Lord of the Thrones of the Two Lands, Resident in the Pure Mountain, that thou might give [to] us a lord, to revive us, to build the temples of the gods of Upper and Lower Egypt, and to present divine offerings. That beneficent office is in thy hands—mayest thou give it to thy son whom thou lovest!"

Then they offered the King's Brothers before this god, [but] he did not take one of them. For a second time there was offered the King's Brother, Son of Amon, and Child of Mut, Lady of Heaven, the Son of Re: [Aspalta], living forever. Then this god, Amon-Re, Lord of the Thrones of the Two Lands, said: "He is your king. It is he who will revive you. It is he who will build every temple of Upper and Lower Egypt. It is he who will present their divine offerings. His father was my son, the Son of Re: [Inle-Amon], the triumphant. His mother is the King's Sister, King's Mother, Mistress of Cush and Daughter of Re: [Nenselsa], living forever. . . ."

THE "ISLAND OF MEROE"

The Kushites most probably shifted their capital from Napata to Meroë after 591 B.C. Meroitic civilization began to bloom about 350 B.C., and by 100 B.C. the city-state had become a large and powerful empire. This first-century A.D. account of Meroë from Pliny the Elder's Natural History *is largely based on the findings of a Roman exploratory expedition—one of the few in ancient times—ordered by Nero to discover the source of the Nile. The river's mystery was not solved, and the naturalist's fantastic description of the peoples of the "extremity" of Ethiopia is a vivid example of how ignorance could spread suspicion among different peoples.*

The persons sent by Nero for the purposes of discovery have reported that . . . from [Napata] to the island of Meroë the distance is three hundred and sixty miles. They also state that the grass in the vicinity of Meroë becomes of a greener and fresher color, and that there is some slight appearance of forests, as also traces of the rhinoceros and elephant. They reported also that the city of Meroë stands at a distance of seventy miles from the first entrance of the island of Meroë, and that close to it is another island, Tadu by name, which forms a harbor facing those who enter the right-hand channel of the river. The buildings in the city, they said, were but few in number, and they stated that a female, whose name was Candace, ruled over the district, that name having passed from queen to queen for many years. They related also that there was a temple of Jupiter Hammon there, held in great veneration, besides smaller shrines erected in honor of him throughout all the country. In addition to these particulars, they were informed that in the days of the Aethiopian dominion, the island of Meroë enjoyed great renown, and that, according to tradition, it was in the habit of maintaining two hundred thousand armed men, and four thousand artisans. The kings of Aethiopia are said even at the present day to be forty-five in number.

The whole of this country has successively had the names of Aetheria, Atlantia, and last of all, Aethiopia, from Aethiops, the son of Vulcan. It is not at all surprising that towards the extremity of this region the men and animals assume a monstrous form, when we consider the changeableness and volubility of fire, the heat of which is the great agent in imparting various forms and shapes to bodies. Indeed, it is reported that in the interior, on the eastern side, there is a people that have no noses, the whole face presenting a plane surface; that others again are destitute of the upper lip, and others are without tongues. Others again, have the mouth grown together, and being destitute of nostrils, breathe through one passage only, imbibing their drink through it by means of the hollow stalk of the oat, which there grows spontaneously and supplies them with its grain for food. Some of these nations have to employ gestures by nodding the head and moving the limbs, instead of speech. Others again were unacquainted with the use of fire before the time of Ptolemy Lathyrus, king of Egypt.

MAKEDA'S EDUCATION

Axum—the forerunner of modern Ethiopia—arose in the fourth century B.C., *at about the same time as Meroë was beginning to develop. Historical tradition and archeological evidence indicate that its appearance was preceded by the migration of peoples from southern Arabia. This merging of Arabians and Africans perhaps forms the basis for one of Christian Ethiopia's most popular traditions, a variation on the biblical story of Solomon and Sheba. The Ethiopian version holds that the Queen of Sheba was an Ethiopian sovereign named Makeda (Magda) and that she returned from her celebrated journey to the court of Solomon in Jerusalem bearing the king's son, David, who became first king of Ethiopia, ruling as Menelik* I.

Ethiopian early miniature of King Solomon
BIBLIOTHEQUE NATIONALE, MS. ETHIOPIEN ABBADIE 105

Makeda's tale is told in an ancient Ethiopian book, the Kebra Negast, *or* Glory of Kings, *from which this romance is taken.*

"Let my voice be heard by all of you, my people. I am going in quest of Wisdom and Learning. My spirit impels me to go and find them out where they are to be had, for I am smitten with the love of Wisdom and I feel myself drawn as tho by a leash toward Learning. Learning is better than treasures of silver and gold, better than all that has been created upon earth. And afterward what can be compared to Learning here below? . . ."

Thereupon the Queen set out with much state and majesty and gladness, for by the will of the Lord, she wished in her heart to make this journey to Jerusalem, to rejoice in the Wisdom of Solomon. They had loaded seven hundred and ninety boats, and mules without number. And the Queen set forth, her trust in God. . . .

After Queen Magda had remained six months in Jerusalem, she desired to return to her own country.

She sent unto Solomon messengers who said to him as follows: "My wish would be to stay with you; but because of those I have brought with me, I must return into my kingdom. God will grant that all I have learned from you may bear fruit in my soul and in the soul of those of my people who, like me, have heard you."

When the King received this message, he meditated in his heart, and he thought: "This woman full of beauty has come to me from the uttermost parts of the earth. Who knows if it be not the will of God that I should have seed of her?"

And so he sent unto the Queen this response: "Since you have done as much as to come hither, will you leave without seeing the glory of my kingdom, the workings of my government, without admiring how my soldiers maneuver, and how I honor the dignitaries of my kingdom? I treat them like saints in Paradise. In each of these things you will find much Wisdom. So I beg of you that you will come and be present at these spectacles. You shall remain behind me, hidden by a curtain. I will show you the things which I tell you of now. You shall become acquainted with all the customs of my kingdom and this Learning which has pleased you shall remain with you until the end of your days."

Magda sent another messenger who brought back this response: "I was ignorant, and through you I have learned Wisdom. . . . That which you now ask of me is only so that my knowledge and my honor may increase. I will come as you desire."

Then was King Solomon satisfied. He bade his dignitaries array themselves in fine apparel. He made his table twice as large as it was. He ordered that the banquet hall and all the palace be got ready in splendor.

The supper of the King was as formal as the Law of the Kingdom. The Queen entered after the King, she was seated behind him with much honor and pomp. She witnessed all that was going on during the repast. She was amazed at what she saw and at what she heard, and in her heart she gave thanks to the God of Israel.

Solomon had raised for her a throne covered with silken carpets bound with fringes of gold, of silver, of pearls, and of brilliants. He had had his servants scatter about the palace all sorts of perfumes. . . . When one entered one was satisfied without eating, because of these perfumes.

Now Solomon caused them to serve unto Magda a repast prepared expressly for her so that she might become very thirsty. . . . She partook of this repast and when Solomon had presided over the banquet until the guests, the stewards, the councilors, the great chiefs, the servitors had been seven times renewed, and had departed, the King rose.

He went in unto the Queen and finding her alone he said: "I beg you to rest here until to-morrow, out of love for me."

She answered: "Swear to me by your God, by the God of Israel, that you will not use of your strength against me? If in any way whatever I transgress from the law of my country, I shall be plunged into sorrow, into sickness and suffering. . . ."

Solomon answered: "I swear to you that my force shall make no attack upon your honor. But now you in turn must swear that you will touch nothing within this palace." . . .

She answered: "Then swear that you will not lay hold with violence upon my honor, and I will promise with all my heart to touch nothing of what belongs to you."

He swore, and he made her swear.

Then he got upon his bed which was made ready in the next room to this one. And she remained where she was.

Immediately he gave orders to the servants in attendance to wash a vase and to fill it with very pure water, and to put it where it might be seen in the room of the Queen. Then the man was to close the doors and the outside windows. The servant did as Solomon had ordered him in a language which the Queen did not understand.

Solomon did not go to sleep but he feigned unconsciousness. As for the Queen, she dozed a little, then she roused herself, got up, and found that her mouth was dry, for the King had with malice given her food which creates a thirst. She was tormented by this thirst. She tried to bring saliva to her lips to moisten them. But she found none. Then she wished to drink the water she had seen before she had fallen asleep. She looked toward Solomon, and she could see him. . . .

The King pretended to sleep heavily but he was awake and he was watching until the Queen should rouse herself to drink the water.

She got down from her bed, she walked stealthily, she lifted with her hands the vase of pure water. But before she could drink he had seized her by the arm.

He said: "Why have you broken your vow? You promised that you would touch nothing in my palace."

She was trembling, she answered: "Is it breaking my vow to drink a little water?"

"And what more precious treasure than water have you known under the sun?"

She said: "I have sinned against myself. But you, you will be faithful to your vow and you will permit me to drink?"

He asked: "Do you free me of the oath which I have given?"

She said: "Be free of it but let me drink. . . ."

He let fall her arm, she drank. And after she had drunk he did as he would with her, and they slept together.

Now as the King was sleeping he had a vision. He saw a dazzling sun which came down from the heavens and shed its rays upon Israel. This brilliancy endured a certain length of time, then the sun moved away. It stopt in its course over Ethiopia and it seemed that it was shining there for centuries. The King waited for the return of this star to Israel, but it did not come back. And again he saw a second sun which came down from the heavens and which shone upon Judaea. It was brighter than the sun which had preceded it, but the Israelites blasphemed it because of its ardor. They raised against it their hands with sticks and with swords. They wished to extinguish it, so that the earth trembled and clouds darkened the world. Those of Israel thought that this star would not rise a second time. They had put out its light. They had buried it. But in spite of their watchfulness the buried sun rose up again. It lighted the world. Its light illuminated the sea, the two rivers of Ethiopia, and the Empire of Rome. Further than ever it withdrew from Israel and it mounted upon its former throne.

While this vision was descending upon King Solomon in his sleep, his soul was troubled and his mind worked like lightning. He awoke trembling. Then he admired the courage, the force, the beauty, the innocence and the virginity of the Queen, for she had governed her country since her earliest youth and during this delightful time she had kept her body in purity.

Then Queen Magda said to King Solomon: "Send me back to my country."

He went within his palace, he opened his treasure, he gave splendid presents for Ethiopia and important riches, dazzling raiment, and everything that is good. Then he got ready the caravan of the Queen: chariots, animals. The chariots numbered six thousand. They were laden with precious things. Some of them rolled upon the ground, others moved by the aid of the wind. The King had built them according to the learning which God had given him.

The Queen went away satisfied. She departed, and set out upon her way. Now Solomon accompanied her with much pomp and majesty.

When they had gone a certain distance he wished to speak alone with Queen Magda. He took from his finger a ring. He gave it to her and said: "Take this ring and keep it as a token of my love. If thou shouldst ever bear a child this ring will be the sign of recognition. If it should be a son send him to me. And in any case may the peace of God be with thee. While I was sleeping by thy side I had a vision. The sun which before my eyes was shining upon Israel, moved away. It went and soared above Ethiopia. It remained there. Who knows but that thy country may be blessed because of thee? Above all keep the truth which I have brought thee. Worship God. . . . May thy journey be a safe one."

SHOPPERS' GUIDE TO AXUM

The Periplus of the Erythrean Sea *was written by an unknown Greek in the second half of the first century* A.D. *The document is a sailors' and commercial travelers' guide to the Indian Ocean, the Aden and Persian gulfs, and the bustling ports along the way. The following selection describes the Axumite city of Adulis, the chief entrepôt for goods from the Ethiopian interior and such far places as India and the Mediterranean world.*

Adulis [is] a port established by law, lying at the inner end of a bay that runs in toward the south. Before the harbor lies the so-called Mountain Island, about two hundred stadia seaward from the very head of the bay, with the shores of the mainland close to it on both sides. Ships bound for this port now anchor here because of attacks from the land. They used formerly to anchor at the very head of the bay, by an island called Diodorus, close to the shore, which could be reached on foot from the land; by which means the barbarous natives attacked the island. Opposite Mountain Island, on the mainland twenty stadia from the shore, lies Adulis, a fair-sized village, from which there is a three days' journey to Coloe, an inland town and the first market for ivory. From that place to [Axum] the city of the people called Auxumites there is a five days' journey more, to that place all the ivory is brought from the country beyond the Nile through the district called Cyeneum [probably modern Sennaar, in the Eastern Sudan], and thence to Adulis. Practically the whole number of elephants and rhinoceros that are killed live in the places inland, although at rare intervals they are hunted on the seacoast even near Adulis.

There are imported into these places, undressed cloth made in Egypt for the Berbers; robes from Arsinoë [modern Suez]; cloaks of poor quality dyed in colors; double-fringed linen mantles; many articles of flint glass, and others of murrhine [probably agate or carnelian], made in Diospolis [probably Thebes]; and brass, which is used for ornament and in cut pieces instead of coin; sheets of soft copper, used for cooking utensils and cut up for bracelets and anklets for the women; iron, which is made into spears used against the elephants and other wild beasts, and in their wars. Besides these, small axes are imported, and adzes and swords; copper drinking-cups, round and large; a little coin for those coming to the market; wine of Laodicea [on the Syrian coast] and Italy, not much; olive oil, not much; for the King, gold and silver plate made after the fashion of the country, and for clothing, military cloaks, and thin coats of skin, of no great value. Likewise from the district of Ariaca [on northwest coast of India around Gulf of Cambay] across this sea, there are imported Indian cloth called *monaché* [fine quality cotton] and that called *sagmotogene* [probably tree cotton], and girdles, and coats of skin and mallow-colored cloth, and a few muslins, and colored lac. There are exported from these places ivory, and tortoise-shell and rhinoceros-horn. The most from Egypt is brought to this market [Adulis] from the month of January to September, that is from Tylei to Thoth; but seasonably they put to sea about the month of September.

KING EZANA'S CRUSADE

Trade between Meroë and Axum flourished until the early centuries of Christianity. Then the Noba, or Nubians, gradually began to infiltrate Meroë, taking over some of its cities, where they built their characteristic straw huts amongst the Meroitic brick buildings. By the early fourth century the Noba had become the dominant power. Around A.D. 350 *Ezana, the first Christian king of Axum, who also claimed sovereignty over Meroë, set out to crush the Noba, who were making frequent attacks on his kingdom and its dependencies. His campaign most probably dealt a death blow to Meroitic Kush, which subsequently vanished from history. Ezana left a lively description of this memorable military expedition on a stele, from which the following is taken. The Noba eventually adopted much of Meroitic culture, and in* 543 *they converted to Christianity, building a literate Nubian civilization that lasted until it was slowly engulfed by the faith of Islam between* 1275 *and the end of the fifteenth century.*

"I, 'Ezana, the son of 'Ella 'Amida, a native of Halen, king of Axum and of Himyar and Raydan and of Saba, and of Salhen, and of Seyamo and of Beja [Blemmyes] and of Kasu [Kush-Meroë], king of kings . . . made war upon Noba, for the peoples had rebelled and had boasted of it . . . "They [the Axumites] will not cross the river Takkaze [the River Atbara]," said the peoples of Noba. And they were in the habit of attacking the peoples of Mangurto and Khasa and Barya and the blacks and of making war upon the red peoples [citizens of Axum]. Twice and thrice they had broken their solemn oaths, and had killed their neighbors without mercy, and they had stripped our deputies and messengers whom I sent to enquire into their raids, and had stolen their weapons and belongings. And as I had warned them, and they would not listen but refused to cease from their evil deeds and betook themselves to flight, I made war on them . . . and fought with them on the Takkaze, at the ford of Kemalke. They fled without making a stand, and I pursued them for 23 days, killing some and capturing others . . . I burnt their towns, both those built of bricks and those built of reeds, and my army carried off their food and copper and iron . . . and destroyed the statues in their temples, their granaries, and cotton trees and cast them into the river Seda [Nile]. And I came to Kasu [Kush, where indigenous Meroitic peoples still lived] and fought a battle and captured prisoners at the junction of the rivers Seda and Takkaze. And the next day I dispatched the army Mahaza, and the army Hara, and Damawa and Falha and Sera up the Seda to raid the country and the cities built of bricks and of reeds. The cities built of brick were 'Alwa [possibly Meroë] and Daro [possibly Kadaro north of Khartoum] . . . and after that I sent the army of Halen and the army of Laken down the Seda against the four towns of the Noba which are made of reeds. . . . The towns built of bricks which the Noba had taken were Tabito and Fertoti. And my peoples reached the frontier of the Red Noba [presumably Napata] and they returned in safety, having defeated the Noba and spoiled them by the might of the Lord of Heaven. And I planted a throne in that country at the place where the rivers Seda and Takkaze join. . . .

The Step Pyramid at Saqqara, near Cairo, constructed around 2650 B.C.

RADIANT DAWN

The joyous season of harvest is celebrated above, in a drawing after a wall painting in an Eighteenth Dynasty Theban tomb. Menna, the pharaoh's "field scribe," oversees activities from his canopied stool, receiving a report from one of his stewards, while another encourages reapers to greater efforts. The detail opposite above, from an Eleventh Dynasty relief, shows a cow being milked.

Canals to drain the land in wet seasons and irrigate crops in the dry are among Egypt's oldest technological achievements. As shown at left, these ancient waterways have helped to support a mixed economy, including cattle, grains, and fruit-bearing trees. Since early times river water has been raised to fill them by a device known as a shadoof, *the counterpoised sweep pictured opposite.*

BLACK STAR—TOR EIGELAND

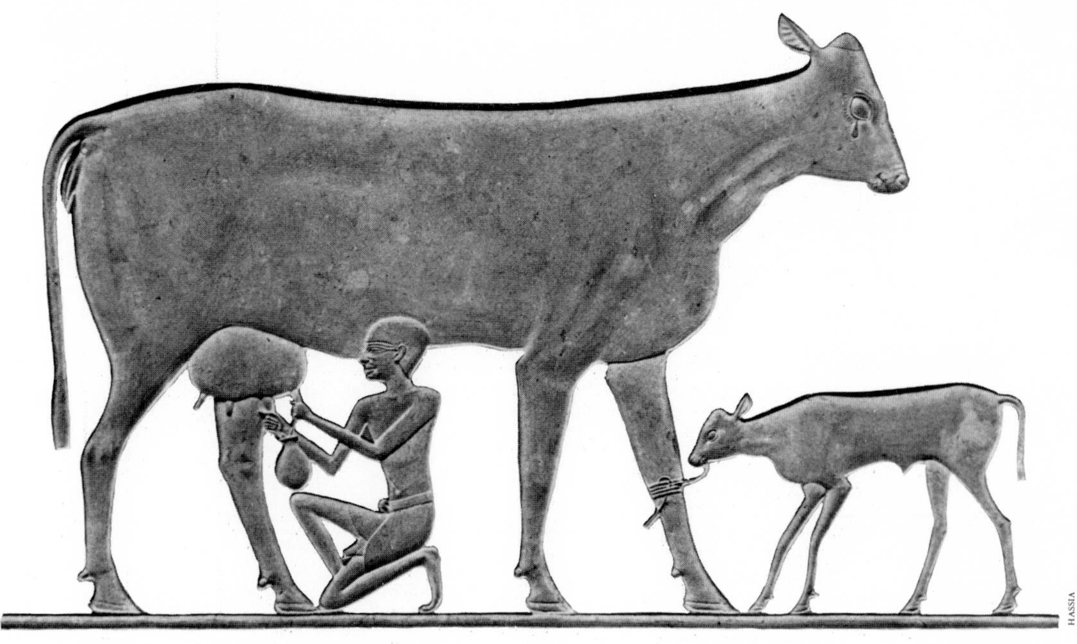

HASSIA

BLACK STAR—TOR EIGELAND

THE GREAT PROVIDER

The agricultural revolution probably came to the hunters and gatherers of the Lower Nile around 5000 B.C. The two basic techniques of food production—plant cultivation and animal husbandry—were introduced most likely from western Asia, but their development in Egypt's arid lands depended upon a highly organized system of water control and conservation. Each year after the harvest season armies of peasants were impressed to repair and extend the kingdom's canals, and through these efforts a belt of some 12,000 square miles was made cultivable along the Nile's banks. Planting began after the annual floods receded, generally in December, and most crops were harvested in late spring. Barley and wheat were cereals essential to the making of bread and beer, and orchards, vegetable gardens, beehives, and vineyards yielded in abundance. It was said of the royal grapes at Luxor that their juice was "more plentiful than the water of the Nile at its highest mark."

The votive Palette of Narmer dates from the Archaic Period. On the front of the slate (left) King Narmer wears the White Crown of Upper Egypt and smites a captive. On the reverse (opposite) he has assumed the Red Crown of conquered Lower Egypt and, in triumph, inspects the headless bodies of his victims; below him, slaves snare two long-necked panthers.

BOTH: EGYPTIAN MUSEUM, CAIRO

BUILDERS OF CIVILIZATION

The political unification of Upper and Lower Egypt, around 3100 B.C., brought to an end centuries of strife between the powerful kings of the Nile Valley and the Delta. Narmer, one of the chieftains of Upper Egypt, is generally credited with the inauguration of the dynastic period, which was to continue, despite foreign invasion and internal disruption, until Egypt fell into the hands of the Romans. As the first of the pharoahs, Narmer seems to have formalized the concept of the divine king, and in recognition of the dual source of his temporal power, he began the building of a new capital, Memphis, near the meeting point of the two ancient kingdoms. Greater political organization followed: a growing corps of ministers was entrusted with overseeing Egypt's agricultural, mining, trade, public works, and military interests, and the state was divided into nomes, or districts, to see that the work was carried out efficiently.

ELIOT ELISOFON

Fluted columns above, in imitation of papyrus reeds, once supported Zoser's temple at Saqqara. The ruins stand adjacent to his Step Pyramid, which in form and construction was the precursor of the pyramids at Giza. Pharoah Menkaure, pictured below with his wife, followed Cheops and Chephren in building these incomparable monuments to immortality.

MUSEUM OF FINE ARTS, BOSTON

ROGER WOOD

THE KING AND HIS PEOPLE

According to the most ancient African concept of kingship, the ruler was not mortal, but a god in the guise of man; he was the bridge between the divine forces of nature and his subjects. The efficacy of his powers maintained his people while he ruled, and also helped to sustain them from his tomb. These attributes were adopted by Egypt's kings at the beginning of the Archaic Period, around 3100 B.C. Specifically Egyptian, however, was the identification of the living king with the falcon-headed god Horus, and in death with the god Osiris, ruler of the underworld. The pharoah stood at the apex of society. He was hailed as "the beautiful silver hawk, who protects Egypt with his wings . . . the castle of strength and of victory." He was responsible for the flooding of the Nile, the bounty of the harvest, and his nation's success in peace and war. Egyptian society, from the highest noble to the lowliest peasant, willingly expedited his commands to gain his blessings in the afterlife and to ensure the nation's well-being.

The pharaoh's majesty is symbolically represented in the massive portrait of Zoser opposite. The realm was run by a multitude of officials. Mitri, a Fifth Dynasty provincial administrator, is shown with his staff and scepter in the wooden statue at lower left. His contemporary, a scribe, is portrayed in the painted limestone statue (detail, below right); also a civil servant, he kept accounts and copied documents. But life was not all work, and reminders of its pleasures, like the Old Kingdom sculpture at right of children playing leapfrog, often accompanied rulers to the next world.

OVERLEAF: *Many different races helped forge the splendid civilization of dynastic Egypt. Some are depicted in this copy of a wall painting that decorates the tomb of Seti* I, *who was buried in the Valley of the Kings at Thebes around* 1300 B.C. *Reading from the top row right, the parade shows white-skinned people of Libya; black-skinned people of Kush, or Nubia; and brown-skinned people of Canaan in the Levant. The four figures at bottom center are Egyptians; they have a reddish skin tone, in keeping with an artistic convention that men be painted red, and women yellow. Horus, symbol of the living king, ends the procession.*

LEPSIUS, *Denkmaler . . .*, 1860

METROPOLITAN MUSEUM OF ART, ROGERS FUND, 1926

EGYPTIAN MUSEUM, CAIRO

d

1. 2. 3. 4. 5. 6. 7. 8. 9.

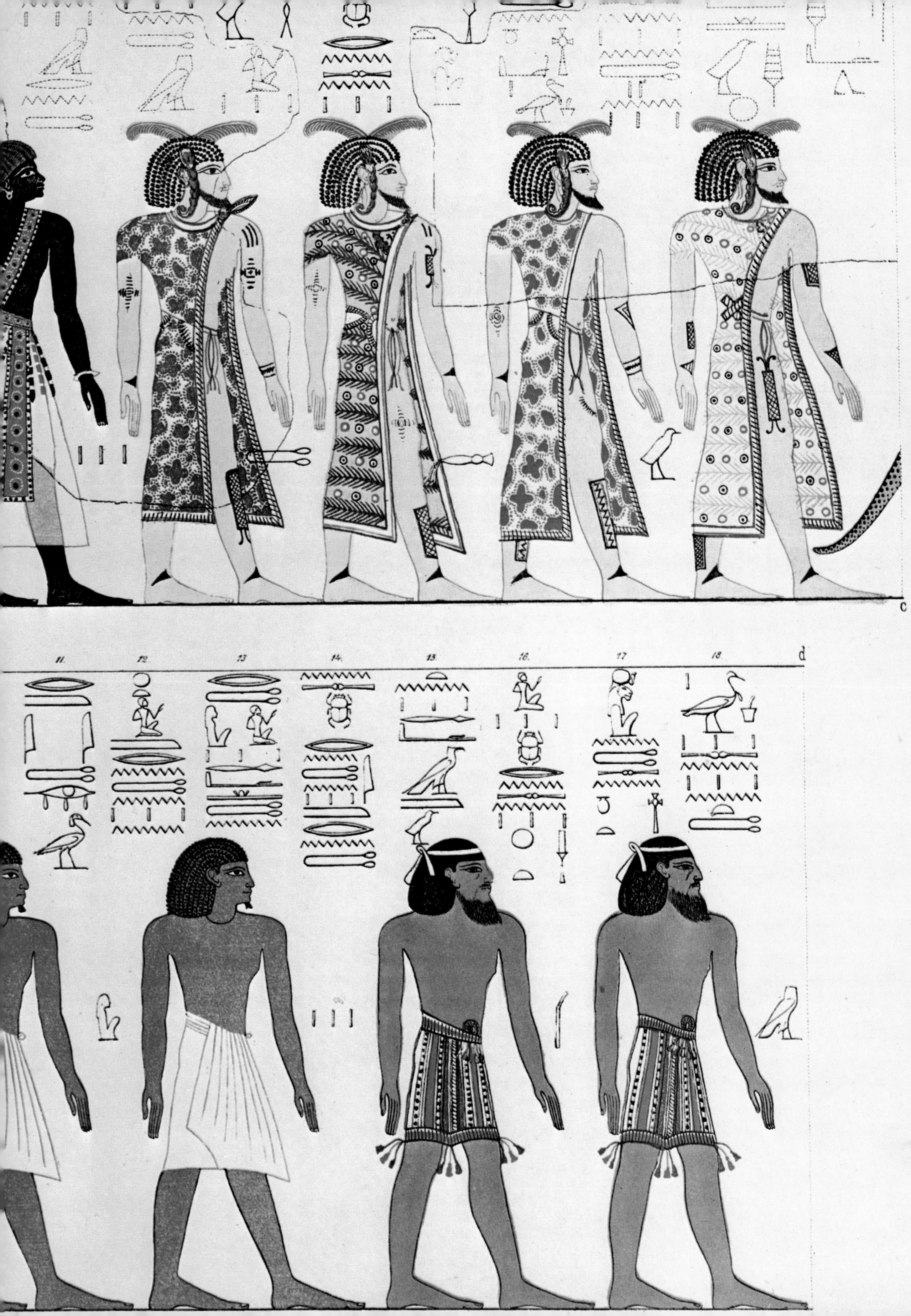

c

d

11. 12. 13 14. 15. 16. 17 18.

The horse-drawn chariot, like the one seen above, was a means of transportation developed chiefly for warfare. It was introduced by the Hyksos, who invaded in the eighteenth century B.C. *Egyptian ships, however, were of indigenous invention. Vessels, such as the one below in the copy of a Sixth Dynasty tomb painting, were constructed of wood and papyrus and propelled by linen sails and a team of rowers. As technology advanced, ships up to one hundred feet in length and able to carry eighty tons of cargo, were put into service on rivers and seas.*

A MERGING OF IDEAS

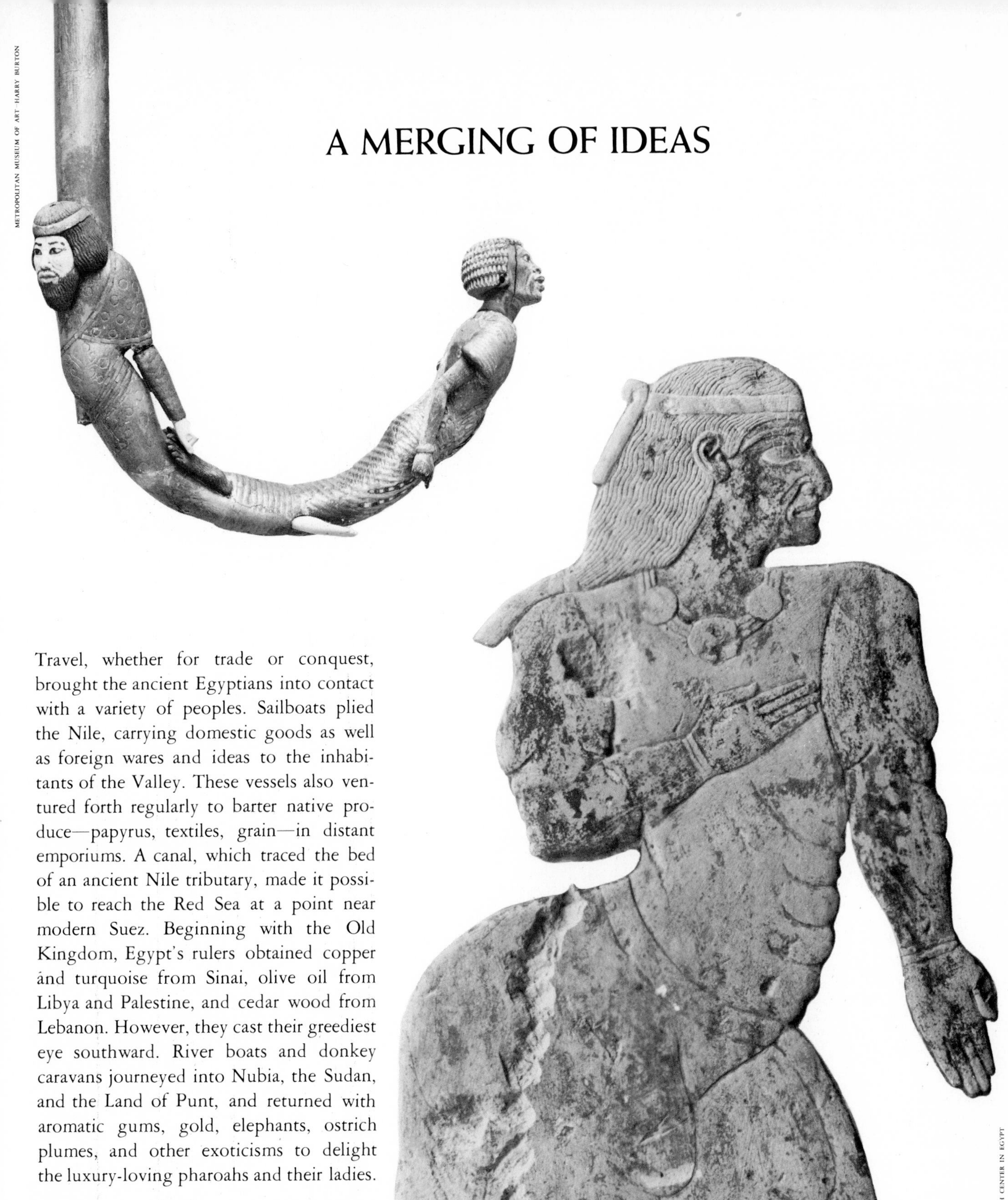

METROPOLITAN MUSEUM OF ART—HARRY BURTON

Travel, whether for trade or conquest, brought the ancient Egyptians into contact with a variety of peoples. Sailboats plied the Nile, carrying domestic goods as well as foreign wares and ideas to the inhabitants of the Valley. These vessels also ventured forth regularly to barter native produce—papyrus, textiles, grain—in distant emporiums. A canal, which traced the bed of an ancient Nile tributary, made it possible to reach the Red Sea at a point near modern Suez. Beginning with the Old Kingdom, Egypt's rulers obtained copper and turquoise from Sinai, olive oil from Libya and Palestine, and cedar wood from Lebanon. However, they cast their greediest eye southward. River boats and donkey caravans journeyed into Nubia, the Sudan, and the Land of Punt, and returned with aromatic gums, gold, elephants, ostrich plumes, and other exoticisms to delight the luxury-loving pharoahs and their ladies.

Hatshepsut's ministers to Punt were met by the formidable queen, who is shown at right in a detail from an Egyptian relief. Her posture is attributed to a hip dislocation. The carvings above of a Syrian and a Nubian grace an ivory ceremonial cane from Tutankhamon's tomb.

EGYPTIAN MUSEUM, CAIRO; AMERICAN RESEARCH CENTER IN EGYPT

W. B. EMERY, LONDON

GATEWAY TO THE SOUTH

METROPOLITAN MUSEUM OF ART, CARNARVON COLLECTION, GIFT OF EDWARD S. HARKNESS, 1926

Nubians, like the one in the relief opposite, swelled the ranks of Egypt's armies and left a strong mark on its culture. Their close ties are also manifest in such objects as the New Kingdom razor handle at right, topped with a Negro lutist. The site above is the north wall of the newly excavated fort at Buhen.

From the third millennium B.C., if not earlier, Nubia and the northern Sudan were a vital crossroads for cultural interchange between the peoples of Egypt and those farther south and west. Various pottery-making techniques and weapons may have come into Egypt from the Sudan. Egypt's kings coveted the land of Kush, rich in gold and copper and the gateway to the south. During the Middle Kingdom they built a series of fortresses, including one at Buhen just below the Second Cataract. These strongholds gave them control of Kush as far as Semna. Then, during the New Kingdom, Egypt advanced its frontiers to the "Horns of the World," probably below the Fourth Cataract. The late tenth and ninth centuries B.C. saw a resurgence of Kushite independence. From 751 to 656 B.C. a line of Kushites ruled Egypt as the Twenty-fifth Dynasty.

The giant steles of Axum, like those pictured here, evoke the city's triumphal past. Hewn from granitelike stone, they rise skyward up to one hundred ten feet. Most likely they were erected between the second century B.C. *and the fourth century* A.D. *Some may have been funerary monuments or religious symbols. Others, carved with windows and doorways to resemble multistoried houses, and having richly decorated sacrificial altars at their bases, were used in pagan rites. However, since the precise purpose of these monuments is still shrouded in mystery, they offer the archeologist an intriguing field for study.*

WERNER FORMAN

Pyramids of the Kushite kings, as depicted in an 1833 engraving
AMERICAN MUSEUM OF NATURAL HISTORY

MEROE AND AXUM

The two greatest African empires to rise in the lands beyond Egypt were Meroë, an outgrowth of Kush, and Axum, parent of modern Ethiopia. After 591 B.C. the Kushites shifted their capital from Napata to Meroë, near the Sixth Cataract. Thenceforth the city-state developed a distinctive style of art and architecture. Meroë also gained renown as an important iron-working center, and was probably instrumental in the spread of iron technology to more southerly parts of Africa. It traded in distant Asia and on the continent, and may have had contacts with peoples as far west as Lake Chad. However, after the first century A.D. Meroë was gradually eclipsed by Axum, its neighbor to the east. Axum became the foremost commercial power of the southern Red Sea area—the center for trade between the Mediterranean, Central and East Africa, Arabia, and the lands of the Indian Ocean. In the fourth century it delivered the final blow to Meroë, adopted Christianity, and began forging the unique, and still existing culture of Christian Ethiopia.

A painted pot from Kush
WERNER FORMAN

Chapter Three

THE BARBARY COAST

(c. 500 B.C.–A.D. 639)

by

Stuart Schaar

TWO DISTINCT GEOGRAPHICAL REGIONS are found in North Africa: in the east Egypt and Cyrenaica (eastern Libya); in the west Tripolitania (western Libya), Tunisia, Algeria, and Morocco. The western region juts out of the Sahara, forming an erratic quadrilateral surrounded by water on three sides. To medieval Arab geographers, who saw the Sahara as a vast sea of sand, the western portion of North Africa, with its many oases, seemed an island of refuge, and so they named the region *jazirat al-maghreb*, "the island of the west." Egypt and its geological appendage Cyrenaica, separated from the Maghreb by one of the most desolate stretches of the Sahara, more often than not shared a common history. Yet, though sand and sea have at times acted as barriers isolating the Maghreb from sub-Saharan Africa, Egypt, and Europe, these same barriers also served as bridges for the diffusion of new ideas and technology and as highways for invaders, traders, and missionaries.

The western Sahara, the massive Atlas Mountains, and the Mediterranean Sea have molded the Maghreb into a unit. The Sahara is more than just sand; it comprises high, arid mountains reaching to ten thousand feet, deep depressions similar in appearance to those on the surface of the moon, salt flats, high steppelands, moving dunes, and fertile oases that support large settlements. Life depends on underground rivers and natural springs scattered throughout the vast desert, and sudden rains, at times followed by flash floods, make even the most arid regions bloom.

To the north of the Sahara the Atlas Mountains, called by different names from west to east, stretch out between Morocco and Tripolitania and keep the desert sands from invading the fertile, densely settled coastal plains. (The Jebel Akhdar range in Cyrenaica, though geologically distinct from the Atlas range, also serves the same protec-

…cchic figures disport on a fragment of linen tapestry, woven in Coptic Egypt in the fifth century A.D.

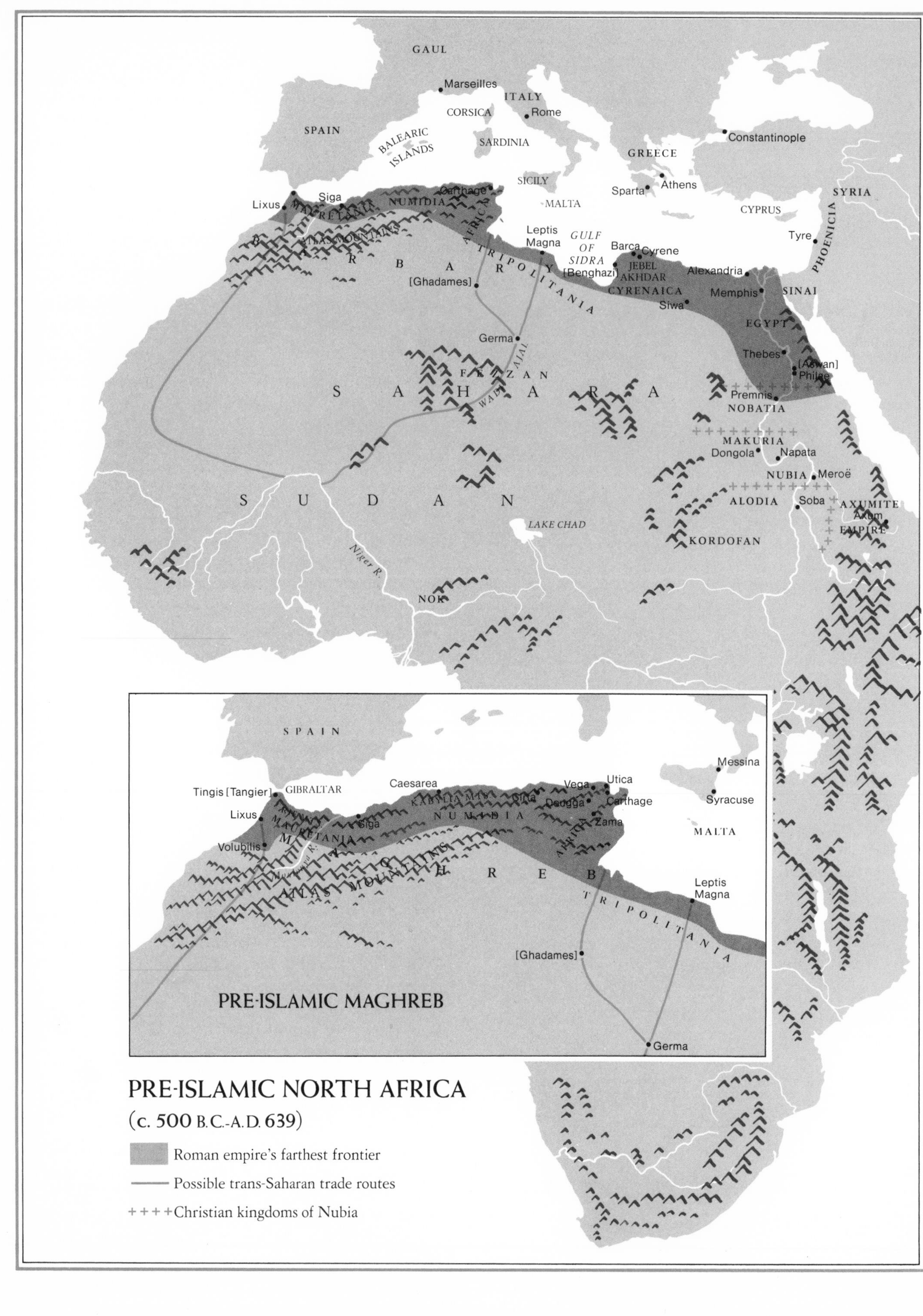

PRE-ISLAMIC NORTH AFRICA
(c. 500 B.C.–A.D. 639)

tive function.) The Atlas peaks are highest in Morocco, reaching 13,600 feet. Their maximum elevation in Algeria is 7,600 feet, less than 4,500 feet in Tunisia, and 2,500 feet in Tripolitania, becoming hills. The coastal plains start out as a very narrow strip in Tripolitania and widen to between fifty and one hundred miles as they extend westward, reaching their widest expanse on the Atlantic coast of Morocco, an area of abundant rainfall.

Rainfall in North Africa becomes irregular and unpredictable in duration and intensity as one moves from west to east, and water sources become less plentiful. Cyrenaica consists of oases surrounded by desert, and other than the Nile Valley, the Suez region, and some scattered oases, Egypt is all desert. Most of the North African population has therefore lived in dispersed plains or oases, separated from one another by gorgelike valleys or inhospitable deserts. Internal communications have been especially difficult in Morocco and Algeria because of the ruggedness of the mountains and the hazards of crossing valleys.

As large portions of the Sahara, Morocco, and Algeria have traditionally been inaccessible, especially the Atlas chain and the more northerly Rif and Kabylia mountains, the Berber peoples of North Africa tended over the centuries to seek safety from foreign conquests in mountainous and desert zones. As they escaped from conquerors, they trekked westward so that, according to one recent estimate, 45 per cent of the Moroccan population speak Berber, 30 per cent do so in Algeria, and less than 2 per cent do in Tunisia. Other Berber-speaking people live in the Siwa oasis in Egypt near the Libyan frontier and throughout the Sahara, and some are located south of the Niger River.

Notable among the desert dwellers are the Tuareg, who are the only modern Berber people known to have an alphabet. When other Berbers wish to write their language, they have on rare occasions in recent centuries composed their works in Arabic script. The language used in antiquity by the ancestors of the Berbers, containing an alphabet of twenty-three consonants, has long been forgotten, and although the Tuareg have partly derived their own dialect and writing system from it, knowledge of the Tuareg alphabet does not help them to decipher hundreds of Berber inscriptions that date from Roman times.

Where the Berbers originated and how they got to North Africa remain mysteries. Ancient inscriptions, which seem to have been written by the ancestors of the modern Berbers, have been discovered in the Sinai peninsula and in the Nile Delta, leading some scholars to conclude that these people migrated into Africa from southwest Asia. Recent analysis of African languages lends some credence to this view. Linguists, notably Joseph Greenberg, have grouped the numerous Berber dialects, which vary from region to region, with the larger Afro-Asiatic family of languages, along with old Egyptian, Somali, Galla, Hebrew, and Arabic.

Whatever the outcome of future research into the problems of when and if these intruders conquered North Africa from other people, it is known that by the fifth century before the Christian era, when written sources were available for the Maghreb, the Berbers had already spread throughout the northern third of the continent. There they had come into contact with a darker-skinned population. According to numerous Greek and Latin texts, these dark-skinned people, known generically as Ethiopians in antiquity, occupied the majority of the oases in the Sahara until the first few centuries of the Christian era. Supposedly they formed nations and moved about as they pleased.

These Negroid people shared a common culture; they traced their earlier history to Neolithic fishing-and-hunting communities located along rivers near marshes and dominating the Sahara. It seems that these people migrated after a wet phase, between approximately 5500 and 3000 B.C., when the Sahara began drying up. Those moving south would have mixed with the Sudanese population. Migrants to the north and those remaining on oases presumably later intermarried with the ancestors of the Berbers and Egyptians of North Africa and the Galla, Somali, and Beja of the East African Horn. Such migrations and communications over once-navigable rivers probably aided in the diffusion into surrounding areas of social and cultural institutions.

The most powerful of the ancient desert dwellers, the Garamantes, whose skin color is still a matter of controversy, lived on the Wadi Ajal, a populous hundred-mile-long chain of oases located south of the Tripolitanian coast in the desert region known as the Fezzan. As Herodotus noted, from at least the fifth century B.C. commercial relations between the Tripolitanian coast and the Fezzan flourished. The intervening routes offered few obstacles to communication; thus the Garamantes were placed at the heart of an important crossroads that connected Egypt, the coast, and the south. Their commercial empire, with its center at the town of Germa, extended westward to the town of Ghadames and possibly reached southward to the central Sudan around Lake Chad. Their forts protected trade routes, and the horses that they bred were used to police the desert. United into a kingdom since at least Roman times, they served as the chief middlemen in the central Saharan trade.

The Sahara, meaning "desert" in Arabic, covers more than 3,000,000 *square miles, much of it windswept, barely passable dunes like these.*

Just as some Saharans mixed with the Berbers, so did other peoples, for in antiquity Phoenicians, Greeks, Egyptians, Persians, Romans, Vandals, and Byzantines controlled parts of the Maghreb. Yet, despite these contacts, the Berbers remained aloof from external controls and influences. Long distances and the difficulty of the terrain limited communications and restricted the number of permanent settlers who came to the Maghreb. Although oxen and horses crossed the Sahara during the first millennium B.C., the desert ceased to be an impenetrable barrier in the Maghreb only after the second century A.D., when the use of camels became widespread.

The stereotyped prejudices that classical writers developed about the North Africans tended to heighten Berber isolation even more. Many authors viewed them scornfully as uncivilized, violent, and passionate people who lacked subtlety. Although some Greek and Latin literary sources at times portrayed them as courageous, sober, and persevering, most writers reproached them for sensuality, apparent cruelty, turbulence, laziness, love of raiding and pillaging, and double standards of truth. Since the Berbers lived outside the pale of classical civilization, the Greeks and Romans considered them barbarians, from which the name "Berber" evolved to designate the light-skinned inhabitants of North Africa. The Arabs later called the area they inhabited Barbary. (Alternatively, the area was known by the Greek name "Libya," after the Lebu Berbers.)

Barbary entered written history about 1100 B.C. The first foreign settlements were made by Phoenicians from the city-state of Tyre in present-day Lebanon, who were drawn west by the prospects of gaining access to silver, copper, tin, and lead in the Iberian Peninsula. In the last quarter of the ninth century B.C. these Middle Easterners founded Carthage (*Kart Hadasht*, or "New City"), and within three centuries this tiny settlement had grown into a city-state, asserted its independence from Tyre, and organized the other Phoenician colonies in the western Mediterranean into a powerful Punic empire under its leadership.

Toward the start of the fifth century B.C. Carthage became the first maritime and commercial power in the western Mediterranean. It had set the limits to the expansion of the Greeks, restricting their activity in southern Spain and sweeping them out of Sardinia and the African coast west of Cyrenaica. Despite gigantic efforts and the establishment of several strongholds in western Sicily, Carthage had failed to destroy Greek colonies in the eastern regions of the island. This enemy presence was a threat to the whole system of Carthaginian dominance: Sicily served as an ideal staging base to launch invasions against North Africa and as a gateway to both Spain, with its metal production, and Sardinia, where African Berbers had settled. The Sicilian and Sardinian colonies also provided Carthage with precious wheat supplies, which they exacted as a tithe on produce, and soldiers. Both were critically needed during African revolts and invasions, when the city-state was deprived of local agricultural resources and manpower. All attempts by Greeks and Romans to drive the Carthaginians from Sicily were therefore resisted fiercely; it became a cornerstone of Punic foreign policy to maintain a foothold there.

Carthage had escaped the westward onslaught of Iranians when the Phoenicians, vassals of Persia between 538 and 332 B.C., refused to join in the invasion of Carthage because, in the words of Herodotus, "of the close bond which connected Phoenicia and Carthage, and the wickedness of making war against their own children." King Cambyses of Persia conquered Egypt in 525 B.C., but failed to conquer both the Nubian country to the south and the site of the oracle of Amon-Re at the Siwa oasis in Egypt's western desert. It fell to Darius I (521–486 B.C.) to pacify the sprawling Persian empire, torn by revolt, and to organize Egypt into one of twenty satrapies ruled from the Middle East. Darius, after extending his realm beyond the Indus River in India, sent his troops as far as Euesperides (Benghazi) on the Cyrenaican coast and annexed Cyrenaica in 515 B.C. The Greek towns of Cyrene and Barca were joined to the Egyptian satrapy and helped pay the seven hundred talents in tribute offered annually. Neighboring Libyans added gifts, and the Nubians were required to bring to the Persians every second year two quarts of gold, two hundred ebony logs, five young boys, and twenty elephant tusks.

The combination of Persian power to the east and Greek hostility in Sicily forced various Phoenician settlements in North Africa to unite with others in southern Spain, western Sicily, Sardinia, the Balearic Islands, and Corsica, all under Carthaginian leadership. Carthage also sought to protect itself through alliance with the Etruscans of Italy in the sixth century B.C., but in 474 the Greeks defeated these allies. Earlier they had repelled an invasion of the Greek mainland by King Xerxes of Persia (485–465 B.C.) and the Carthaginian attempt to conquer Sicily. Also, the Greeks of Marseilles closed ports of Gaul and Spain to Punic ships. Athens even attacked the Phoenician coast in 459 B.C., but its ambitions were soon checked when it supported an unsuccessful rising in Egypt. The Greek historian Thucydides in his *History of the Peloponnesian War* describes the events that followed:

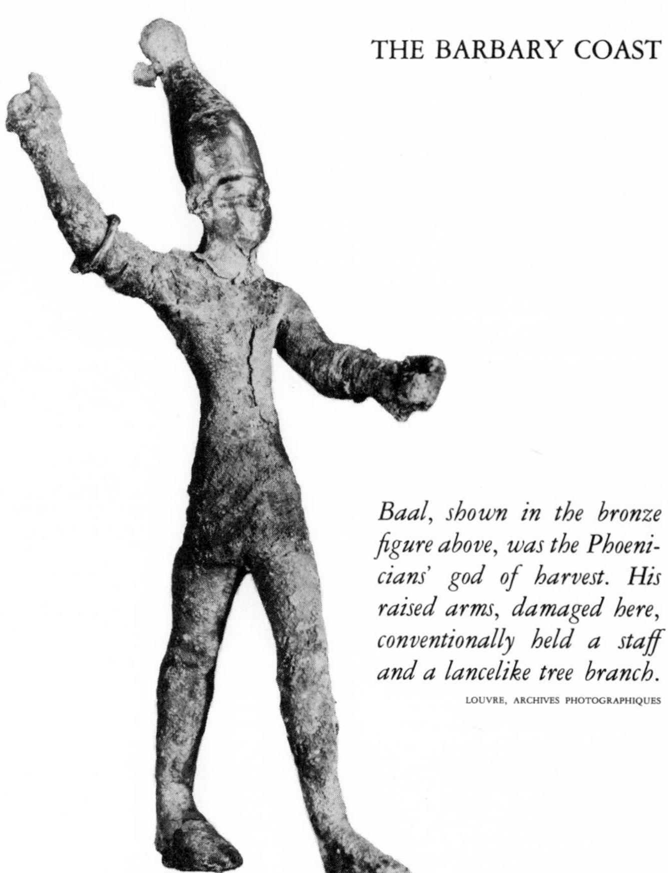

Baal, shown in the bronze figure above, was the Phoenicians' god of harvest. His raised arms, damaged here, conventionally held a staff and a lancelike tree branch.

LOUVRE, ARCHIVES PHOTOGRAPHIQUES

> . . . a Libyan king . . . on the Egyptian border . . . caused a revolt of almost the whole of Egypt from King Artaxerxes [Persian ruler from 465–424 B.C.], and placing himself at its head, invited the Athenians to his assistance. Abandoning a Cyprien expedition upon which they happened to be engaged with two hundred ships . . . they arrived in Egypt and sailed from the sea into the Nile . . . making themselves masters of the river and two-thirds of Memphis . . . and the king sent . . . a Persian to Lacedaemon [Sparta] with money to bribe the Pelopennesians to invade Attica and so draw off the Athenians from Egypt. Finding that the matter made no progress, and that the money was only being wasted, he . . . sent . . . a Persian with a large army to Egypt. Arriving by land he defeated the Egyptians and their allies in a battle, and drove the Hellenes out of Memphis. . . . the Libyan king, the sole author of the Egyptian revolt, was betrayed, taken and crucified.

Thenceforth until 332 B.C., the moment of Alexander the Great's invasion, Egypt remained under nominal Persian control; but periodic revolts broke out, and as early as 404 B.C. rulers of the satrapy asserted their independence.

Throughout the fifth and fourth centuries B.C. Carthage

fought the Greeks for control of Sicily. By 375 Carthage had won control over the western third of the island, which it retained more or less for a century. But continual wars weakened both belligerents, benefiting an expanding Rome.

However, the wars served to accelerate the introduction into Barbary of Hellenic influences—to a slight degree in religion, but significantly in the arts, military science, and weaponry. A large number of rich Carthaginians settled in Syracuse; many members of the Punic aristocracy served in the army or in Sicilian diplomatic posts and came into direct contact with Greek civilization. In the fourth century splendid works of art were brought as booty to Africa from Sicily. An important Hellenic colony settled at Carthage, Greek cults spread, and Greek mercenaries joined the Punic army. Carthage could no longer remain aloof.

During the turbulent first half of the fifth century B.C. Carthage's trade with the Mediterranean world had declined, and outlets for selling raw materials and precious metals dried up. This commercial depression, combined with the necessity to use its silver and gold to pay for mercenary troops and its initial stalemate in Sicily, had also turned Carthage inward to Africa. By the middle of the fifth century it had built a land empire so that fifty years later, despite numerous Berber revolts against Punic expansionism, the new territory (corresponding to northeastern Tunisia) provided the bulk of army recruits; by the early third century, with the assistance of Numidia (corresponding to parts of present-day Algeria and western Tunisia) it raised adequate grain to feed Carthage's population of about 400,000, including slaves and foreigners.

In the century after its founding, Carthage had paid an annual tribute to the neighboring Berbers as a form of rent for the soil it occupied. During a part of the sixth century it had freed itself of this burden and ceased to pay anything for many years. But toward the end of the century it had to submit once again. Sometime around 475 to 450 B.C. Carthage permanently revoked the obligation. This was accompanied or followed by the growth of a sizable settlement beyond the city so that by 400 B.C. Carthage reached its greatest extent. At the same time the Carthaginians settled sites along the Barbary coast between Cyrenaica and the Atlantic and established regular commercial relations with the Berbers.

In the western Mediterranean Carthage sought to reserve for itself the exclusive exploitation of vast markets and supplies of raw materials. From the fourth century its dependencies save Sicily were closed to all but Punic merchants. The Punic fleet even sank ships that navigated toward the Strait of Gibraltar, and to discourage foreign exploration, sailors or merchants invented imaginative tales of the dangers and obstacles in the Atlantic Ocean, including encounters with gigantic sand bars, impassable fields of algae, enormous sea monsters, and thick fogs. Herodotus, taking his information from Carthaginian sources, describes how Punic traders bartered merchandise for gold along the same Atlantic coast:

> The Carthaginians also tell us that they trade with a race of men who live in a part of Libya beyond the Pillars of Heracles. On reaching this country, they unload their goods, arrange them tidily along the beach, and then, returning to their boats, raise a smoke. Seeing the smoke, the natives come down to the beach, place on the ground a certain quantity of gold in exchange for the goods, and go off again to a distance. The Carthaginians then come ashore and take a look at the gold; and if they think it represents a fair price for their wares, they collect it and go away; if, on the other hand, it seems too little, they go back aboard and wait, and the natives come and add to the gold until they are satisfied. There is perfect honesty on both sides; the Carthaginians never touch the gold until it equals in value what they have offered for sale, and the natives never touch the goods until the gold has been taken away.

About 470 B.C. Hanno, a member of the Carthaginian ruling class, supposedly led a group of settlers on a voyage of colonization along Africa's Atlantic coast, ostensibly to consolidate the gold trade, a major Punic enterprise. It now seems well established that Hanno's description of his voyage was not, as has long been thought, a Greek translation of an inscription on a Carthaginian temple; rather, it was the product of pure fantasy mixed with some facts drawn from earlier authors and was composed perhaps as a school exercise in the first century B.C. A Greek geographer of Asia, known as the Pseudo-Scylax, writing about 338 B.C., also reports that Phoenicians exchanged perfume, Egyptian stones, and Athenian pottery for animal skins, hides, and tusks, all of which could have been found in the region corresponding to present-day Morocco. He, like the author of the document describing Hanno's voyage, omitted to mention the gold trade, which the Carthaginians did not readily publicize. Doubtless some Punic colonies beyond the Strait of Gibraltar traded in gold on a small scale until Roman times. According to a source that the Greek geographer Strabo mistrusted, this trade ended prior to the first century A.D., when the Pharusians and the Nigrites attacked. (They were nomadic horsemen and archers about whom we know little more than that they lived south of Morocco.) Strabo relates that they destroyed more than three hundred trading posts on the Atlantic coast.

Punic merchants rarely, if at all, had direct commercial relations with the Sudan. Instead, as previously stated, the Garamantes played the role of middlemen, supplying Carthage with precious stones known as carbuncles and possibly slaves, whom, according to Herodotus, they "hunted" in horse-drawn chariots in the Sahara south of the Tripolitanian coast. One series of rock drawings shows these chariots were in use from the Fezzan to the Niger Bend, but nothing indicates that Carthage received gold from the Fezzan. Rather, the weight of evidence suggests that Carthaginian gold came entirely from the Atlantic coast, and even this source seemingly ceased to be active by Roman times.

Finds of tomb jewelry attest that Carthage had gold objects in quantity during the seventh and sixth centuries B.C. Although they had stopped burying such valuable commodities in their graves by the fifth century, the reliable historian Thucydides informs us that the enemies of Carthage believed that they possessed a great deal of gold and silver. But supplies of these metals did not suffice to underwrite the Sicilian wars of the fourth century B.C. During this period and in the following century Carthage passed through a financial crisis. During the First Punic War against Rome (264–241 B.C.) the North African state lacked money to the point that it had to double taxes on Berber subjects, taking from them fifty per cent of their harvests, and even then could not pay its mercenaries. Only the conquest of the entire Iberian Peninsula, beginning in 237 B.C., provided large amounts of silver to pay off the Roman indemnity and later to fight the Second Punic War (219–201 B.C.).

With commerce as the main source of Carthaginian riches, land never became a major concern of the ruling class, whose members remained basically wholesale merchants and shipping magnates. Commercial needs therefore dictated foreign policy. By force or by treaties or by founding colonies the state opened up new markets for the merchants and, where possible, organized monopolies and negotiated reciprocal trade agreements. It also assured the liberty of navigation against pirate attacks.

By the fifth century B.C. about three hundred of the wealthiest Carthaginians shared in the control of the state through the agency of the senate. Although they were divided into rival clans, they came to terms with each other in order to maintain stability for trade. Short wars increased the senators' fortunes and filled the treasury with booty. Conquests also benefited the ruling families by expanding markets, eliminating competitors, producing new administrative posts, and, in Africa, extending their private property. However, senators disdained long wars. Besides being costly, such drawn-out struggles disrupted trade and fortified the position of ambitious generals.

In addition to two *sufets*, executive officers who held office for a year and presided over the senate and an assembly of citizens, the Carthaginians appointed generals as commanders in chief on extraordinary occasions, usually for the duration of a war. They, too, were traditionally chosen from the upper class. Fearing that popular commanders might usurp their power and establish tyrannies, the senators generally chose mediocre men for these posts. By the middle of the fifth century B.C. a court of one hundred four judges, chosen from the senate, supervised and oversaw the activities of the generals. In the third century a few members out of an executive body of at least thirty senators accompanied officers overseas to exercise control over political decisions. The fear of sentences passed by the high court dissuaded the best men from assuming a command, and more than one incapable or unlucky general was fined, had his property confiscated, lost his life, or faced exile, as a result of senatorial action.

Below the senate was an assembly of citizens composed of retail merchants, manufacturers, administrators, and employees of large firms, who depended on the senatorial aristocracy for their jobs and livelihood. We do not know the exact number of citizens within the capital of Carthage (estimates range in the area of eighty thousand) or how many among them qualified for membership in the assembly. Citizenship could be granted to foreigners whom the state judged worthy of the honor, and Phoenicians from the Middle East and citizens of other Phoenician or Carthaginian colonies also probably enjoyed rights of citizenship in Carthage.

Until the late third century the citizen assembly scarcely affected government. If the senate and the *sufets* agreed on policies, there was no need to submit issues to any other body. At times a popular vote took place in the assembly even when the two executives and the senators agreed in order to obtain general support for hazardous ventures. This procedure gave citizens the illusion of participation. In return for their collaboration, citizens paid no taxes in peacetime, and after the sixth century B.C., did not have to serve in the army. Contingents were then drawn from among Carthage's disfranchised subjects and government-financed mercenaries. It had become cheaper to use precious metals to hire mercenaries than to withdraw a large number of citizens from wealth-producing trade. Moreover, there were far too few citizens in Carthage to provide for the defense of the empire. Two serious army defeats would have wiped out their forces, so that if Carthage had relied on a citizen army, it might have disappeared long before 146 B.C., when Rome ulitmately defeated Carthage because of its greater manpower reserves.

Besides the citizens, the population of Carthage included Libyans, who had migrated to the city from surrounding rural areas to find work, and also slaves, who were imported from all over the Mediterranean, the Sahara, and farther south. Most Libyans and all slaves had no political rights in Carthage. Merchants, commercial agents, and artisans also flocked to the city-state from Sicily, Italy, and Greece. Fusion with the citizenry was not easy, but Carthaginians did intermarry with other peoples. Mixed marriages were especially frequent with Libyans, less perhaps in the capital than in the coastal colonies. No source indicates how many Libyans became Carthaginian citizens.

In urban centers slaves were employed by the Carthaginians as servants in rich families or as workers in artisanal shops, commercial houses, and state arsenals. On the sea they manned merchant and war galleys. A few Negroes served as slaves in the cities or regions of Barbary close to the coasts, but it does not seem that at this time they furnished enough manpower to play an important role in the working of the agrarian estates of the aristocracy. North Africa was well enough populated with poor Berbers to provide a cheap local supply of farm labor, and rich Carthaginians certainly used war prisoners and victims of piracy to cultivate their fields. We do not know, however, if these captives were purchased by their masters or loaned out by the state. The rural Berber population rarely had slaves. They were too poor to buy them, and if any were acquired in warfare, the Berbers were better off selling their captives than feeding them. Besides, women did most of the hard labor among the Berbers. It is possible that Punic merchants sold Negro slaves to Greeks and Italians, but in smaller numbers than those that reached the Mediterranean by way of Egypt.

The slaves who cultivated the suburban estates of the rich had little to lose by revolting against their masters, and there were periodic uprisings in the fourth century B.C. They therefore had to be watched carefully. Also, a part of the free Libyan population that had migrated to the cities joined urban riots in rare periods of crisis, often just for the chance to raid the homes of the rich. To offset rebellious reactions, the ruling class responded with utmost ferocity and cruelty when threatened.

Meanwhile, Rome was regarding Carthage with increasing jealousy. The potential for a clash between the two had become evident in 268 B.C., when Carthage took over the Sicilian seaport of Messina, across the channel from the Italian coast. Between 264 and 241 B.C. the two powers fought the First Punic War, which ended in the destruction of the Carthaginian fleet. Carthage finally had to evacuate Sicily and pay Rome a heavy indemnity. To compensate for the loss of Sicily, Sardinia, and Corsica, the Carthaginian general Hamilcar Barca led a campaign to conquer Spain beginning in 237 B.C. The booty and the precious metals sent back to Carthage from the Iberian Peninsula enriched the treasury, and the conquest opened new Spanish markets to Carthaginian commerce and industry. His son, Hannibal, became the most famous of the Barcids. While in his mid-twenties he provoked the Second Punic War with Rome. With the vast silver mines and manpower of Spain at his disposal, and backed by the popular support of the Carthaginians, he crossed the Alps in 218 B.C., leading his soldiers and elephants into Italy. In order to prevent revolts during these war years, he sent Spanish soldiers to Africa and Berbers to Spain. These men did not get along with the population among whom they lived, but while serving as hostages they kept the peace.

Hannibal's fortunes were reversed in 203 B.C. when, after fifteen years of military campaigns on the Italian peninsula, he was forced to return to Carthage to oppose the Roman legions of Publius Cornelius Scipio, thereafter known as Scipio Africanus. Hannibal was defeated and ultimately forced to flee Carthage when he attempted to reform its government structure. He then served several Hellenistic princes, among them Antiochus III of Syria in his unsuccessful resistance to Rome. Finally, to avoid being handed over to the Romans, he committed suicide in 183 B.C., apparently by taking poison.

His career has been immortalized in the following description by the less than objective Roman satirist Juvenal:

> Put Hannibal in the scales: how many pounds will
> that peerless
> General mark up today? This is the man for whom
> Africa
> Was too small a continent, though it stretched from
> the surf-beaten
> Ocean shores of Morocco east to the steamy Nile,

To Ethiopian tribesmen, and new elephants' habitats.
Now Spain swells his empire, now he surmounts
The Pyrenees. Nature throws in his path
High Alpine passes, blizzards of snow: but he splits
The very rocks asunder, moves mountains with vinegar.
Now Italy is his, yet he still forces on:
"We have accomplished nothing," he cries, "till we have stormed
The gates of Rome, till our Carthaginian standard
Is set in the City's heart." A fine sight it must have been,
Fit subject for caricature, the one-eyed commander
Perched on his monstrous beast! Alas, alas for glory,
What an end was here: the defeat, the ignominious
Flight into exile, everyone crowding to see
The once-mighty Hannibal turned humble hanger-on,
Sitting outside the door of a petty Eastern despot
Till his Majesty deign to awake. No sword, no spear,
No battle-flung stone was to snuff the fiery spirit
That once had wrecked a world: those crushing defeats,
Those rivers of spilt blood were all wiped out by a
Ring, a poisoned ring. Oh, on, you madman, drive
Over your savage Alps, to thrill young schoolboys
And supply a theme for speech-day recitations!

Thus, despite Hannibal's efforts, Carthage lost the war. It gave up Spain and its colonies along the North African coast and had to pay Rome another heavy indemnity. By 200 B.C. Rome had become the center of the Mediterranean world, and Carthage was relegated to the status of a weak dependency of the Latin state. Fifty years later Rome, jealous of Carthage's continued commercial success, provoked the state's leaders into violating the peace treaty and sent its army to enforce stiffer demands. The Carthaginians surrendered, but when the Romans insisted as a condition of future peace that they raze their city and build a new one inland, the Carthaginians locked the city's gates. This was the beginning of the Third Punic War. Legionnaires destroyed Carthage in 146 B.C., and the people who survived, an estimated fifty thousand, were sold into slavery, bringing a once-powerful state to an ignoble end.

Hannibal, as shown on a Punic shekel
TRUSTEES OF THE BRITISH MUSEUM

Like later North African conquerors in antiquity, the Carthaginians had settled in urban clusters located mainly along the Mediterranean. Such cities as Carthage, Utica, and Lebda (Leptis Magna) served as pockets of cosmopolitan influence, but being artificial, albeit glorious, creations, they scarcely affected the way of life in the hinterland. Moreover, as stated earlier, from the fifth to the mid-third century B.C. Carthage prohibited outsiders from sailing into the western Mediterranean, so the chances to renew and enrich the culture through foreign contacts were restricted. Adaptation to external influences took place only gradually; and it was most successful when Berber dynasties molded foreign practices and beliefs to local conditions. Mediterranean civilization reached the Berbers largely through the efforts of Berber kings, who ruled over large, loosely administered states in the shadow of Carthage and Rome.

Since the end of the second millennium B.C. kingship was hereditary among the Lebu, a Berber people living west of Egypt in an area that is now part of modern Libya. In the next millennium iron and the horse were introduced into North Africa, two innovations that enhanced the military and technological strength of those who possessed them. Most probably Berber states were formed by the unification under one authority of diverse lineage groups. Originally, chieftains were necessary only in time of war. When circumstances warranted it, an assembly of family elders met and decided on common action. In case of external threat, they would choose a chief for the duration of the hostilities or for a year. But such a chief might abuse his authority or refuse to give up his office once peace was restored. If a loyal following grouped around him or if he amassed allies, he became a prince, though he would still have to respect the autonomy of the lineages that supported his authority and consult with their representatives. Once he consolidated his personal power through victorious war-

A five-part Berber drinking vessel with ritual ornamentation
MUSEUM FUR VOLKERKUNDE, HAMBURG

fare, a prince could impose himself on others, making his territory and his lineage the center of a rudimentary state. The chief would have then become a king and would, in all likelihood, establish a dynasty.

Kingly rule was constantly challenged in antiquity. Berbers in the mountains, who in their inaccessibility were almost immune to nomadic raids, periodically pillaged the kingdoms of the plains. Also, internal rivalries among ambitious chiefs and pretenders abounded. To limit treason and rebellion, kings held members of powerful families as hostages in their retinues. They also chose wives from among the daughters of the chiefs and kept the sons of rural notables in their bodyguard. When a ruler died or was deposed, crises erupted, and the interregnums were marked by civil wars. Being menaced from all sides, these kings had to work diligently to maintain authority over their subjects. Ultimately, sovereigns sought ways to enhance their legitimacy and celebrated the "divinity" of former kings.

The main wealth of Berber kingdoms came from the agricultural produce of the sedentary population living on the plains. Monarchs therefore favored agriculture in order to increase tax yields, and whenever possible, they forced nomads to settle. A primary function of the kings was to protect farmers against nomadic raids and town dwellers against foreign invasions. They needed at their disposal both mobile forces to police their territory and regular troops to man strategic garrisons and to fight in wars for and against Carthage or Rome. These forces watched over nomadic displacements and helped to collect taxes on transhumant livestock. Even when they could not enter turbulent areas, Berber princes could control dissidents by threatening to close down regional markets, where the population came to buy and sell. The rulers developed commercial relations and guaranteed the flow of goods within their realms. Sales and market taxes as well as custom dues probably helped to fill the treasury. Since rural taxes were paid in kind, kings served as the greatest merchants of their states. They exported wheat, wool, skins, livestock, horses, wild animals, carbuncles, ivory, wood, marble, and some slaves.

In the third century B.C. three large kingdoms dominated the Moroccan, Algerian, and Tunisian hinterland. To the extreme west (corresponding to modern Morocco) were the Moors (*Mauri* in Latin), who lived in the kingdom of Mauretania. Moving eastward from the Moulouya River, there were at least two Numidian kingdoms, that of the Massaesylins, centering on the province of Oran, and that of the Massylins, smaller in size and bordering on Carthage.

The Massaesylin king Syphax, who died in 201 B.C., was the first Berber monarch about whom we have any detailed historical information. According to the Roman historian Titus Livy, he was the "wealthiest of the African princes," and before the Romans defeated him in 203 B.C., he controlled all but the Saharan regions of the country that is now called Algeria. He had two capitals: Siga in the extreme west of Oran province; Cirta (modern Constantine) in the east. Both Rome and Carthage tried to make Syphax an ally, but for a time the king believed that he could play the arbiter between these adversaries. He imitated Hellenistic monarchs by wearing a crown and minting coins engraved with his image. Recognizing his importance, one of the most powerful Carthaginian families gave him a daughter to marry.

Syphax lost his territories to Masinissa, an heir to the Massylin throne and an ally of Rome. Masinissa, who died in 148 B.C., was one of the greatest Berber personalities in history. This intelligent, fearless, and subtle man is shown on contemporary coins as a king in his forties or fifties, with sharp features, wide eyes, thick eyebrows, long hair, and a pointed beard. He led an extraordinarily vigorous life, so that at eighty he still could jump on his horse without aid and ride bareback. At the age of eighty-six one of his wives bore him a son, bringing the total of his male progeny to at least forty-four. Several of them survived him when he died at the age of ninety. His kingdom was divided among three of his sons, and his dynasty ruled Numidia for a century, then transferred to Mauretania to reign for sixty years more.

In Spain Masinissa had seen Roman legions in action, and he predicted that the Latins would reign over all of Libya. He wisely allied his kingdom with Rome against

Carthage and King Syphax, who was at this time aligned with the Punic state. In return Rome allowed Masinissa slowly to absorb the maritime colonies that had once belonged to Carthage, leaving him a free hand to conquer Berber subjects. In this way he extended his kingdom from the frontiers of Cyrenaica to the Moulouya River. Conveniently, this expansion into Carthaginian territory also provided Rome with the pretext to destroy Carthage in the Third Punic War.

Masinissa possessed a palace at Cirta, where in the manner of the Carthaginians he gave lavish banquets complete with silver dishes, gold baskets, and Greek musicians to entertain his guests. Although he was raised in the tradition of the Berbers—indeed, his mother had been a popular Berber prophetess—he knew the refined culture of Carthage, where he perhaps spent some of his early years. He married the daughter of a leading Carthaginian and gave his sons a Greek education. The Carthaginians of high rank so respected kings such as Syphax and Masinissa that they did not believe they were lowering their social status by giving their children as wives or sons-in-law.

Berber kings helped to diffuse Carthaginian religious practices throughout Barbary. From earliest times the Berbers were nature worshipers; they had developed cults venerating the sun, mountains, water, trees, and other natural phenomena. Phoenicians, who worshiped nature gods, probably contributed elements to these cults, and certainly Berber influences entered Punic beliefs when Carthage expanded into North African territory in the fifth century B.C. Even after Rome conquered Barbary, the Carthaginian deities of Baal Hammon, the lord of harvests, and Tanit, goddess of life and fertility, still had a large number of devotees, though their names were Romanized respectively as Saturn and Caelestis. Inscriptions discovered at Constantine and its suburbs, in the heart of Numidia, prove that the Berbers, like the Carthaginians, at times sacrificed their first-born children before the Romans prohibited the practice. Rationale for this custom lay in the belief that the virtue of the gods must be maintained by a continual supply of blood. The practice fit into the general character of the Punic religion, which accepted the premise that man was weak and had to submit to capricious and powerful gods who demanded to be appeased.

A large number of Berbers, especially women, still follow magical rites that apparently have their origins in antiquity. These include ceremonies invoking the gods of fertility and incantations to produce rain. Others accompany birth, marriage, and death. Women still tie rags to trees and gather stones, only to throw them away, thus transferring evil to other objects. From the Stone Age, Berbers have worn amulets, which they believe give protection through a genie, or jinni, who deposited some of his power in the object. The fear of the evil eye, the practice of anthropolatry (the worship of men), the belief in genies, and the ritual sacrifice of animals are also holdovers from pre-Islamic times.

In the maritime colonies and over a large part of Tunisia and eastern Algeria the population spoke Punic. Army veterans and merchants gradually spread the language throughout the Maghreb, beyond the towns and regions under direct Carthaginian control. To Berber princes Punic was the lingua franca, since the people they ruled spoke a multitude of Berber dialects. Under Rome, neo-Punic, a development of the old Carthaginian language, was gradually replaced by Latin in the cities, but in some rural areas it died out very slowly and was not extinguished until the beginning of the third century A.D.

The Berbers adopted new agricultural and stockbreeding techniques from their Carthaginian mentors. However, outside Punic Tunisia olive-tree cultivation, grain farming, and viticulture hardly spread before Roman times; most other North Africans continued to raise livestock. The Phoenicians also taught the Berbers how to use bronze and iron in the manufacture of tools and other objects. Exploitation of a copper mine in Numidia only began under the Phoenicians, and Barbary lacked tin to make bronze.

Carthaginians brought Greek and Italian ceramics and Egyptian glassware into Barbary; however, most of these goods were probably beyond the purchasing power of the Berbers, who manufactured their own pottery. They also produced clothes of wool and leather, and ambulant or local blacksmiths supplied them with their iron weapons, plows, utensils, and tools. It was most likely that Carthage furnished Berber princes and chiefs with luxury goods such as ornamented weapons, fine textiles, jewels, perfume, and rugs. Less expensive merchandise was probably sold to veterans who had served in Carthaginian armies. Goods supplied to the general populace in the interior were handled through the intermediary of Berber princes.

Direct relations were established between Carthage and Egypt after Alexander the Great's conquest of the East and the founding of Alexandria in 332 B.C. Alexandria was made the capital of Egypt by Ptolemy, one of Alexander's Macedonian generals and founder of the Ptolemaic dynasty. From the end of the fourth century Carthage competed with Alexandria as Africa's chief trade center, exporting to the burgeoning Hellenistic centers.

Egypt also challenged Carthage on the political front. In 310 B.C. an independent Ptolemaic governor of the Greek cities of Cyrenaica plotted with a tyrant of Syracuse to annihilate the Punic capital. In return for his aid the governor was promised all of Carthage's North African possessions, but the Syracusan killed his co-plotter and the scheme never materialized. During the first war against Rome (264–241 B.C.) Carthage, lacking money to pay its mercenaries, asked King Ptolemy II of Egypt (285–246 B.C.) for a loan of two thousand talents. Although the monarch refused, the fact that Carthage could approach him for such a large sum attests to the close ties between the Nile Valley and the Maghreb.

Other evidence of these connections can be seen in Egyptian styles of architecture and art, which entered the Maghreb with the Phoenicians, who themselves had borrowed heavily from the older civilization of the Nile Valley. The Phoenicians introduced such Egyptian construction procedures as placing blocks of stone on one another without mortar, baking large bricks in the sun, and making stucco. The Carthaginians also borrowed Egyptian weights and measures, including the cubit—a linear measure based on the length of the arm from the elbow to the fingertip. Phoenician merchants who had commercial establishments on the Nile Delta and formed an important colony at Memphis initially imported Egyptian pottery, statuettes, ritual razors decorated with Egyptian divinities, gold work, seals, scarabs used as amulets, and small pendant masks, many of which later Maghrebin artisans copied locally. The cult of the Egyptian sun god Amon-Re spread from Thebes into the Siwa oasis. The Greeks of Cyrenaica knew him under the name of Zeus, and Berbers accepted him as a great nature god.

The Roman emperors, however, regarded Egypt as their private domain, and except for its trade, attempted to keep the Nile Valley isolated from the rest of the empire. An experienced businessman known for his loyalty to the emperor was usually chosen as the Egyptian prefect and acted as the personal representative of the imperial household. To ensure Egypt's isolation, no member of the Roman senate could enter the province without the permission of the emperor.

Under Roman rule the senate was entrusted with administering a truncated version of the old Carthaginian empire—a political unit known by the Latin name "Africa" and encompassing an area of some five thousand square miles. Initially, the senators showed little interest in "Africa." Masinissa's heirs controlled and policed that part of Barbary bordering on the new possession, and some coastal cities enjoyed for a time autonomy and exemption from taxation. Very few Romans settled in the province; those that did, viewed their sojourn as an opportunity to make a quick fortune, which they hoped to spend in Rome.

After surveying its newly conquered lands, Rome allowed small holders to continue farming, but compelled them to pay taxes. The province barely brought in as much revenue as was needed to pay the cost of administration. Rome confiscated estates belonging to the Carthaginian aristocracy and distributed some of them to Roman war veterans and other deserving citizens, who mostly had to work their plots by themselves or with the aid of a few slaves. Rich absentee landlords employed overseers to supervise slaves or freemen to cultivate their property.

Berber kings were at first allowed considerable independence by the Romans since the central government wanted rulers at their disposal who facilitated commands, organized contingents to fight in wars, and co-operated readily in selling wheat to Latin merchants. These kings policed also frontiers and facilitated the penetration of Roman commerce into their territory. But they were allies who had to be treated well and were not humble or docile vassals.

Masinissa's grandson, Jugurtha, broke with dynastic tradition and opposed Rome in the Jugurthine Wars (111–105 B.C.). In an attempt to wrest all of Numidia from Rome, he bribed a number of Roman senators. When the plot was revealed, Jugurtha was summoned to the capital, where he is quoted as saying, "Rome is a city for sale, and doomed to perish if it can find a purchaser." The Roman historian and politician Sallust provides some clues to Jugurtha's charisma. He writes:

> As soon as Jugurtha grew up, endowed as he was with great strength and handsome looks, but above all with a powerful intellect, he did not let himself be spoiled by luxury or idleness, but took part in the national pursuits of riding and javelin-throwing and competed with other young men in running; and though he outshone them all he was universally beloved. He also devoted much time to hunting; and was always to the fore at the killing of lions and other wild beasts. His energy was equaled by his modesty: he never boasted of his exploits . . . [later, when fighting in Spain] by dint of hard work and careful attention to duty, by unquestioning obedience and the readiness with which he exposed himself to

Cleopatra, shown in this temple relief, was the last of the Ptolemies and Egypt's last native ruler.

H. ROGER VIOLLET

> risk, he won such renown as to become the idol of the Roman soldiers and the terror of the enemy. He was in fact both a tough fighter and a wise counselor—qualities extremely hard to combine. . . .

Another Berber king, Juba II, who died in A.D. 23 or 24, married Cleopatra Silene, the daughter of Antony and Cleopatra. This legendary couple, who really lacked the proper administrative ability to make Egypt a profitable province, had provided Rome with the pretext for annexing Egypt. Juba, although an Algerian, had been raised in Rome and was given the best Greek education possible; he became an art connoisseur, and wrote or compiled at least fifty works in Greek, none of which, unfortunately, has survived. Pliny the Elder wrote that during the forty-eight years Juba was king of Mauretania his "glory as a scholar was greater than his reputation as a sovereign." Indeed, he had great difficulty in maintaining the loyalty of his subjects and was confronted with a series of Berber revolts that ultimately were crushed through Roman intervention. Apparently, he carried his cultural affinities and friendship with Rome to extremes, antagonizing his subjects. Even when he attempted to establish himself as a living god, he failed to enhance his legitimacy adequately enough to prevent rebellions.

It was his wife, Cleopatra Silene, who probably introduced the Egyptian cult of Isis, the mother goddess of fertility, into Mauretania. The same cult also spread to Tripolitania. Latin soldiers introduced the popular Egyptian god Sarapis (the Ptolemaic amalgam of the two male fertility symbols, Osiris and Apis the bull) into the Berber pantheon. The success of these cults stemmed from the vagueness of Egyptian doctrines. Since Egyptians viewed their gods as mere symbols of cosmic or ethical forces, they could be easily syncretized with the most popular local deities. Ornate Egyptian rituals and mysterious ceremonies must have intrigued initiates, but at the same time the Osirin influence injected optimism into their religion and promised the faithful immortality and life after death. The Berbers easily associated Sarapis with Baal Hammon or Saturn, and Isis with the Punic goddess Tanit. Under Christianity, statues of Isis would readily become identified with the Virgin Mary, and some Isiac rituals would find their correlatives in Christian practice.

By A.D. 40 Rome had extended its control over Numidia and Mauretania and extinguished the Berber dynasties. The Roman senatorial aristocracy, sometimes by means of small payments and with the connivance of the state, carved for themselves vast holdings out of former Berber crown lands.

In the majority of cases the new owners lived in Italy and leased their land to companies; these in turn sublet plots to North Africans, who at first became hereditary occupants, and by the fourth century, serfs. The Berbers paid rent to the companies, and both master and farmer paid taxes to the state. The chief exception to this pattern was the domains of the emperor, acquired through bequests, purchases, or confiscations. Those who leased estates from the Crown paid as rent one third of their produce, usually wheat. However, if they were slaves, they worked the imperial domains without compensation. Over the centuries more and more acreage would come under these latter systems.

By A.D. 50 Rome faced the problem of depopulation at home and could not spare settlers for Africa. The emperors therefore had to send experts to teach Africans how to administer their holdings. They had to depend on the local population to run the bureaucracy and serve in the army. To garrison the province of "Africa" after A.D. 150, the Romans recruited the Third Legion from 5,500 locally born sons of legionnaires. In addition, until about the end of the fourth century, they used about 7,500 Berber auxiliaries in Numidia and 15,000 in Mauretania to keep the peace. During revolts locally conscripted irregulars swelled these ranks. Much earlier Rome had fortified its North African cities and allowed the people to arm themselves in case of

Berber or pirate attacks. Large farms also had their citadels.

Under the empire not only did Roman Africa contain several large and beautiful cities, among them Carthage, Leptis Magna, Volubilis, and Dougga, but the Romans created a special municipal spirit. This cosmopolitanism permeated several hundred small towns (numbering more than 450 in the fourth century) each with 3,000 to 10,000 people, who prospered and possessed municipal councils, forums, temples, and baths and other amenities. Town dwellers, including merchants, artisans, and farmers, came to believe that municipal life was the highest and, ultimately, the only form of civilization. This ideology, stemming from the practice of granting citizenship to urbanites, made city dwellers feel superior to that part of the rural population that lived in the remote regions, and set them apart as an elite. Although most townsmen had some Berber ancestry by the fourth century and although the most famous of their countrymen, Septimius Severus of Leptis Magna, reigned over the Roman empire from A.D. 193 to 211, the Romans only had a limited success in incorporating large numbers of Berbers into urban civilization. They succeeded most in those areas where Carthaginian and Numidian cities had previously flourished.

By organizing the imperial cult, Rome won the support of the urban aristocracy and, through their influence, a majority of the subject population. Every town elected delegates from among the upper class, who celebrated the cult at the provincial capital once a year. At that time every province chose a single priest from those delegates who, among other things, presented local grievances to the governor and could, if he had a complaint against this high official, carry his case directly to the emperor.

The closer a peasant lived to a municipal center, the more fully Roman magistrates protected his legal rights. In isolated regions the rural population was forced to submit to local lords, though at times, when their grievances went unanswered, sharecroppers would stage a strike by remaining at home and refusing to work. This put pressure on imperial or private landlords to come to terms, improve conditions, reduce the number of corvées, or lower taxes.

Rome preferred that taxes and rents be paid in kind, and collectors assembled revenues in warehouses throughout Barbary. After the African garrisons received their rations and collectors removed their share as salaries from these stores, the remaining stocks were dispatched to ports and transported to Rome. From 125 B.C. to the time of Julius Caesar, who died in 44 B.C., a sector of the population of Rome received a monthly allotment of five free bushels of wheat per man from the state. Shortly after 63 B.C. about 320,000 citizens were receiving a dole. In 46 B.C. Caesar reduced the number to 150,000, but in the time of Augustus (63 B.C.–A.D. 14) the number had risen to 200,000. In addition to distributing these handouts, the state sold cereals at reduced prices. At the beginning of the empire the Maghreb and Egypt each provided one third of Rome's wheat supplies while other provinces such as Sicily and Sardinia produced the rest. When Sicilian and Italian agricultural yields declined, Barbary's surplus provided enough grain to feed the entire city of Rome, including those receiving free food, for eight months out of a year; the Egyptians contributed enough to cover the remaining four months. After the foundation of Constantinople in A.D. 330 and the takeover of Egypt by eastern emperors, Rome depended on grain from the Maghreb alone.

When oil became scarce in Italy during the second century, the people of the Maghreb increased the acreage devoted to olive trees. Initially, Romans disliked the strong taste of African oil, but as production methods improved, both Romans and Egyptians imported large quantities for cooking, bathing, and fueling their lamps. Although the grain trade, mining, and marble quarrying had all been Roman state monopolies, commerce in oil remained in private hands. Not only did peasants in eastern Barbary become rich from their olive trees, but a large number of middlemen thrived as never before. In the second and third centuries these businessmen invested their wealth in numerous public monuments. By the second century a local ceramic industry had developed in the olive-producing areas so that Roman Africans, instead of importing luxury-quality pottery, as they formerly had done, were able not only to satisfy their own needs but to become exporters of pottery.

As the Romans developed techniques for growing olives in dry country, they extended cultivation into semiarid zones. They planted trees several feet apart, destroyed all weeds near them, kept the ground clean, and painstakingly worked the soil so that it would absorb all available moisture. (At the end of the nineteenth century the French in southern Tunisia, learning from the archeologists, applied these techniques with gratifying results to land that had reverted to scrub over the centuries following Roman occupation.) The Romans also employed engineering specialists called *aquilegi*, whose task was to seek out water sources. Hydraulic devices allowed them to take full advantage of rain and spring water, and to conserve water use. They erected dams, and dug wells and cisterns. Dikes diverted water to the plains, where canals and trenches carried it to

MUSEUM OF ANCIENT ART, HAIFA

Septimus Severus, shown above with his family, was born near Leptis Magna. He rose by military coup to become Rome's emperor in A.D. 193. *His successor, Caracalla, is seen beside the blurred image of his murdered brother. The portrait at left depicts a Romanized citizen of third-century* A.D. *Fayum.*

STATE MUSEUM, BERLIN

fields, while aqueducts supplied the towns.

The Roman expansion of agriculture into southern zones far from the Barbary coast provoked serious clashes with the nomadic population of the Maghrebin steppe and desert. Their constant movement and pillaging brought them into contact with their neighbors to the north and south, and, like the strongest Berber kings before the Christian era, imperial Rome tried unsuccessfully to extend its domination over them.

By the first century A.D. the political situation between the Romans and the Maghrebin nomads had become critical. Forced into restricted areas, somewhat like reservations, they demanded more and better pasturage for their goats and sheep. Between A.D. 17 and 24 the southern part of North Africa from Roman Mauretania to Tripolitania rose up under the leadership of the Numidian Tacfarinas. His defeat signaled the temporary victory of the sedentary population over the nomads.

The Garamantes, too, caused Rome much trouble in the Fezzan. In addition to raiding "Ethiopians" in the south, they attacked coastal settlements along the Gulf of Sidra, aided Tacfarinas, and offered a haven to other fugitives. For these acts the Romans punished them several times. Short of permanently occupying the Fezzan, Roman governors stopped the Garamantes from further pillaging and, to ensure communications in the Sahara, formed a protectorate over them. Evidence of Roman presence on the Fezzan oases has been unearthed: traces of Roman-style irrigation and remains of Roman merchandise. Rome certainly received tusks from the Garamantes by way of the overland Saharan route to compensate for dwindling supplies of ivory in Barbary by the fourth century A.D. Toward the end of the first century a king of the Garamantes had led some Roman officers into a Sudanese region that he dominated. However, this and another expedition were exceptional.

The official limits of Roman occupation in the Maghreb stopped at the northern boundaries of the Sahara. In southern Numidia Romans hardly entered the desert areas, and in Mauretania they stayed away from it completely. From A.D. 24, and for more than two hundred years thereafter, Rome either settled colonies of veterans in the south and the far west or founded military posts on the edge of the desert to control the nomads. Their frontier defenses, or *limes*, which extended through Numidia from Tripolitania, consisted of ditches, walls, camps, forts, lookout towers, and road networks.

Beginning in the second century, Rome also imported as guards Syrian nomads with camels. Known for their speed and their ability to go without water for up to ten days, the *mehari*, or riding camel, made it possible to cover greater distances between wells than horses or oxen could, thereby adding to the mobility of the nomads. Besides rendering the chariot obsolete in the Sahara, these camels facilitated the disruptive raids of nomadic fugitives, whose migrations and conquests would continue into the Islamic period.

For a long time before the Roman conquest, ancestors of the Berbers living in the Libyan region of the Sahara had dominated the habitable oases. From the end of the second millennium B.C., if not earlier, they had attempted to settle in Egypt, but they never presented major threats to the inhabitants of the Nile Valley. In the Roman period, as the following passage from Strabo's *Geography* shows, Egypt lived in peace with its neighbors to the west and south.

> Now Aegypt was generally inclined to peace from the outset, because of the self-sufficiency of the country and the difficulty of invasion by outsiders, being protected on the north by a harborless coast and by the Aegyptian Sea, and on the east and west by the desert mountains of Libya and Arabia . . . and the remaining parts, those towards the south, are inhabited by the Troglodytes, Blemmyes, Nubae [Noba], and Megabari, those Aethiopians who live above Syene. These are nomads, and not numerous, or warlike either, though they were thought to be so by the ancients, because often, like brigands, they would attack defenseless persons. As for those Aethiopians who extend towards the south of Meroë, they are not numerous either, nor do they collect in one mass, inasmuch as they inhabit a long, narrow, and winding stretch of riverland . . . neither are they well equipped either for warfare or for any other kind of life. And now, too, the whole country is similarly disposed to peace.

Strabo, however, refers to incidents following Rome's conquest of Egypt in 30 B.C., when Kushites revolted and raided Syene (Aswan) in a series of attempts to seize lower Nubia. Rome retaliated and sacked Napata near the Fourth Cataract in 23 B.C., but moved no farther south. Instead, a garrison was stationed at Premnis (Qsar Ibrim). According to a papyrus dating from the second half of the first century A.D., Romans and "Ethiopians" clashed somewhere in the eastern desert, but no other sources recorded the specific incident. Was there a connection between this skirmish and the decision of the Roman emperor Nero to send the Praetorian Guard on a mission to Meroë about A.D. 61? Perhaps future archeological finds will provide an answer to this question.

In Hellenistic times, when the Ptolemies established the Nile Delta as the hub of an international commercial network, contacts between Egypt and Nubia had been the rule. The Egyptians received through Nubia gold, ivory, ebony, panther skins, incense, gums, slaves, and wild animals in exchange for manufactured goods, wine, corn, and olive oil.

Under Rome, commerce and travel between Egyptian rule and Meroë continued, but gradually slackened. The Meroites sent some ambassadors to the Romans, and occasional envoys probably returned these visits. Meroite pilgrims mixed with Romanized Egyptians at Philae, the site of the temple to Isis, and Egyptian artisans had a hand in temple building in the south. However, by the third century Meroitic rulers were no longer being buried with imported luxury goods, and pyramid construction had deteriorated—signs of the decline in Meroë's power.

At the end of that century, when Roman control over Egypt weakened, the Blemmyes, mounted on camels, began to infiltrate the Upper Nile Valley. Their raids forced Rome to evacuate Nubia in A.D. 289 and to relocate its southern border at the First Cataract. Seven years later Emperor Diocletian called in a people known as the Nobatae (perhaps the same people as the Noba mentioned by Strabo) to protect the southern frontier from further Blemmye incursions. Early in the fourth century Meroë collapsed as a result of conflicts with the Nobatae, and Axumite raids under King Ezana (about 320–360) would help to extinguish the dying kingdom. During his reign Axum converted to Christianity and established close links with the Alexandrine patriarchate and the Byzantine empire. Meanwhile, Axum also had indirect commercial ties with India and must have competed successfully with Meroë for control of the caravan routes to Central Africa.

Following the destruction of Meroë, Nubia experienced a period of political fragmentation. The former enemies, Blemmyes and Nobatae, united forces and toward A.D. 450 attacked the temple site of Philae. Rome, in turn, defeated them by 453, forcing them to give up Roman prisoners and pay an indemnity for the damage they committed. In return, the nomads were allowed to visit the Isis sanctuary and even carry her statue back periodically to Nubia. When these nomads broke the peace a few years later, another Roman expedition punished them, and Rome agreed to pay them a subsidy for a period of one hundred years to keep the peace.

The Roman territories in North Africa, excluding Egypt and Cyrenaica, covered only about 140,000 square miles during the period of its strength. This relatively small area,

The temple to Isis at Aswan, today submerged in the Nile, was a durable symbol of ancient Egyptian religion. Built to honor the wife of Osiris, it attracted not only Egyptians and Nubians but Roman schismatics who preferred her mysteries to their own militant state creed.
AMERICAN MUSEUM OF NATURAL HISTORY

mainly the fertile, "useful" zone in the north, represented less than ten per cent of the present-day Maghreb, but it contained most of the Maghrebin population of approximately 6,500,000 people. The region was divided into four provinces during the high empire: Africa Proconsularis (Tunisia and coastal Tripolitania), Numidia (eastern Algeria), Mauretania Caesariensis (western Algeria), and Mauretania Tingitana (northern Morocco). But even this proved too large an area to control effectively. At the end of the third century Rome amputated about one third of its territory around Tripolitania and in the west, leaving intact a region relatively safe from the nomads. Rome also regrouped the provinces: it joined Egypt and Cyrenaica with other eastern holdings, and for administrative convenience, attached Mauretania Tingitana to Spain and divided the rest of the Maghreb into seven smaller provinces.

Numerous revolts in the far west taxed the Romans during much of the third and fourth centuries, but the emperors never attempted to restrict the movement of nomads in and out of the Mauretanias. Most mountainous zones also escaped Roman control. By A.D. 253 mountaineers began raiding their lowland neighbors; they continued their attacks on and off until the end of the century. About A.D. 370 the Berber prince Firmus, based in the mountainous region of Kabylia, a perennial stronghold for dissidents, led a destructive revolt that spread through Numidia, and the Romans imported troops from Europe to crush the rebellion in 375. A revolt that lasted from 396 to 398, led by Firmus' brother Gildo, proved to be less serious and was easily put down. Both, however, represented Berber aspirations for autonomy and their desire for revenge against the rich masters. They had the sympathy of North Africa's growing Christian community, especially the Donatist heretics, who themselves led a revolt against official Christianity from their remote rural settlements in Numidia.

Before the end of the first century, Christianity had spread into Egypt, to the Greek-speaking educated urban population, who increasingly were moving toward a monotheistic belief. Important Church fathers, among them Clement and Origen, helped establish this initial Greek predominance, with Alexandria as the most significant theological center of the empire, vying with Rome for pre-eminence. When large numbers of Copts, as the indigenous Egyptians were known, converted in the last years of the third century, Church leaders produced a corpus of Coptic literature written in the Greek alphabet, helping to fuse Greek and Coptic elements of the population into a new unity. Hermits, who withdrew alone or in groups into the Egyptian desert, where the demons of temptation were believed to dwell, helped organize the first monasteries in Christendom. As monks, they spread the faith among most of the rural folk during the fourth century. Attempts were also made to convert the Nubians, but they had little effect before the sixth century, when new Nubian states arose.

Christianity took root in the Maghreb during the second century among slaves, Berber agricultural laborers, and lower-class urbanites. By the third and fourth centuries, when the faith had spread throughout the country, the Maghreb, with its many towns, contained six hundred bishops, more than Gaul and Egypt combined, and produced such great Church fathers as Tertullian, Cyprian, and Augustine. Christian missionaries attempted to convert the Jewish minority, some of whom dated back to the Phoenician settlement and others to the destruction of the Temple in Jerusalem in A.D. 70.

Starting in the third century, North Africa, from Egypt to Morocco, became the scene of furious religious controversies, denunciations, and persecutions, which led to the establishment of local or national Christian churches such as those at the Monophysites in the Nile Valley and of the Donatists and Arians in Barbary. Doctrinal and partisan issues confused the illiterate, who often blindly followed their bishops in or out of the orthodox Church.

The affinity for rebellion or rejection of submission and orthodoxy shielded the technologically weak, and therefore vulnerable, Berbers and other North African peoples from total assimilation and loss of identity despite centuries of alien rule. It eased North African integration into a wider ecumene, for by passing over the heretical road, segments of the population assimilated the basic ideas of their overlords without having to sacrifice their local heritages.

Donatism began as a simple heresy within a puritanical tradition; it emphasized martyrdom, unremitting faith, morality, and poverty. However, Donatism became the vehicle of a great social revolt of agricultural laborers whose situation had deteriorated by the fourth century. The Donatist heresy centered around the issue of whether or not members of the clergy who had yielded to Rome during its persecution of North African Christians should be restored to communion with the Church. Besides making Christianity palatable to the population of the central Maghreb, it acted as a convenient substitute for armed rebellion. It reached extremes by equating martyrdom with suicide and in allying itself with violent bands of migrant workers, the Circumcellions, who refused to be tied to the land. Until the Donatist sect was outlawed in A.D. 412, and even afterward, it won many adherents, especially in Numidia, and split the Church into an orthodox wing loyal to Rome and a puritanical African branch supported by many Berbers.

The Monophysite movement developed out of complicated theological disputes over the nature of God (whether he had one or two natures as the Father and the Son), with the Egyptians, led by the Alexandrine patriarchs, championing a strict unitary position. Until A.D. 451 the Alexandrines prevailed in Church councils, and their views were considered orthodox; but at the Council of Chalcedon the bishops, led by the Constantinople hierarchy, rejected the Monophysite creed and declared that Christ had two natures. Those who supported the council came to be known as Melchites, or royalist followers of Constantinople, whereas the others, the Monophysites, were branded as heretics.

The partisan roots of this controversy dated back to A.D. 381, when Constantinople was declared the second city in Christendom, thereby pre-empting Alexandria's position as a rival to Rome. Alexandrine leaders fought this decision and used the Monophysite doctrine as a vehicle to outmaneuver Constantinople and maintain their dominance in the Church. The issue became an Egyptian cause, and the doctrine served as an ideology of national unity. When the bishops of Alexandria lost their majority at the Council of Chalcedon, the Egyptians broke away from the Roman-Byzantine Church, though Egypt still remained part of the empire until 616, when the Persians conquered the country.

With the doctrinal split between the Orthodox and Coptic sects well defined, the two competed for converts in the region of the Upper Nile. By A.D. 540 there were three separate Nubian kingdoms: the northernmost, Nobatae, or Nobatia, between the First and Third Cataracts; Makuria, with its royal city at Dongola; and farther south, Alodia, with its capital at Soba. After A.D. 640 Nobatia and Makuria were united into a single kingdom, with its capital at Dongola, and Monophysite Christianity became the state religion. Sometime early in the seventh century Alodia also converted to the same sect. Greek became the liturgical language of all Nubia and was later supplemented by Coptic and Nubian, including Greek loan-words and written in the Greek alphabet.

After A.D. 410 the Maghreb was the only part of the western Mediterranean not seriously disrupted by Germanic hordes. The relative prosperity of Barbary, even though in decline, certainly must have attracted their attention. By this time the Roman army in Africa consisted mainly of Goth mercenaries who constantly fought desert marauders. In A.D. 429 cousins of the Goths, the Vandals, crossed over from Spain to North Africa in Roman ships, after their king Genseric received an invitation from Bonifacius, the Roman governor of Africa, to join his mercenary forces. Within the next ten years the Vandals, numbering some 80,000 and including 15,000 soldiers, had become ambitious in their own behalf and in A.D. 439 went on unopposed to conquer Carthage, nominally held by Rome.

All of Morocco and most of Algeria were untouched by the Vandal conquerors, who concentrated their rule on Tunisia and a small part of Algeria. Most of the Tunisian laborers who worked the large Roman domains stood by and watched one landlord replace another. The wealthy fled when they could to the Italian peninsula or Constantinople. Vandal governors won the support of non-Romanized pagan Berbers, and with their aid Genseric formed a powerful fleet, which he used for piracy.

The conquest allowed independent Berber mountain republics to develop, and mountaineers raided Numidia and Mauretania. These desert invasions further hastened the disintegration of urban life. The Vandals respected the Roman civilization that they found there and did not ruin the country through "vandalism"—a term first coined in eighteenth-century France. They returned most of it to nomads and mountaineers, who brought to a standstill the slow assimilation processes that had characterized Carthaginian and Roman rule for a millennium.

The Vandal army, weakened by constant struggles against marauding Berbers and, more significantly, against invading Tripolitanian nomads, crumbled when the Byzantines launched their seaborne invasion in A.D. 533. The eastern Roman army contained trained archers who had perfected their warlike skills in battles with the Persians. The Vandals, accustomed to fighting with swords and spears, were technologically overwhelmed. The conquerors shipped the majority of Vandal male captives to Constantinople, where they were integrated into the imperial army. A small number remained in Barbary as slaves or artisans, and Vandal women married Byzantine soldiers.

The Byzantines conquered Vandal territories with the aid of Berber chiefs, to whom they promised autonomy after victory. Instead, eastern administrators and lawyers attempted to re-establish Barbary as it was prior to the coming of the Vandals. Vandal proprietors were dislodged, and land was returned to descendants of former owners or turned over to the Church, the imperial Crown, or the conquering officers. The Byzantines also disestablished Arianism, the Christian heresy adopted by the Vandals. Because the eastern Romans did not fulfill their part of the bargain, they had to fight off continual revolts. Although the Garamantes converted to Christianity after signing a treaty of alliance with the Byzantines in A.D. 569, such alliances hardly sufficed to prevent nomads from raiding up to the walls of Carthage.

The Vandals had appointed new Arian bishops, who championed yet another heresy to weaken Christianity as a whole in Africa. People became confused even further when the Byzantines attempted to re-establish orthodoxy after ejecting the descendants of Genseric from Barbary and the Persians from Egypt in A.D. 626. In addition to the general corruption of the Eastern empire and Church, the newcomers persecuted Arians, Donatists, Monophysites, pagans, and Jews alike, and succeeded in alienating the population that they had hoped to win over. A general atmosphere of disillusionment prevailed. Social solidarity, already strained by late Roman and Vandal times, was taxed even further, and resistance to foreign conquest crumbled. The way was opened to a syncretic religion like Islam, which in one prodigious sweep would render doctrinal controversies meaningless.

The new followers of Islam, invading from the East, took Egypt and Cyrenaica from A.D. 641 to 642. Tripolitania fell in 643, setting the stage for the first raids to the west, which began in 647. Although the new invaders faced little opposition from the Byzantine army, their initial conquests proved superficial. The real battles of establishing political control over the North Africans and winning them over first to Islam and then to Arabic culture still lay ahead. They accomplished these tasks in the Maghreb over centuries filled with rebellion, mass migrations, new heresies, and much political bargaining, and only, finally, on terms acceptable to the North Africans.

Mythological figure; detail of a frieze
COLLECTION OF MR. AND MRS. JAN MITCHELL

THE COPTIC VISION

Egypt's Coptic art was born of the peasant. It was the plastic expression of a people's adherence to their own folk traditions in the face of major efforts by others to impose foreign—Greek, Roman, Byzantine—traditions upon the land. The art was modest, reflecting the fundamentalist creed that inspired it. Produced in monasteries far from such sophisticated urban centers as Alexandria, its practitioners had neither the means nor the instinct to produce monumentality, and the materials used were commonplace—limestone, wood, linen, wool—rather than the porphyry, granite, gold, and silks, with which others glorified their gods. The Coptic artists also maintained a distinct personality in the subject matter of their work, honoring a galaxy of local saints, many of them martyred by the Romans for their doctrinal intransigence.

Christ presenting a saint, possibly an abbot of the Apollo Monastery at El Bawiti, source of this sixth-century icon
LOUVRE

ART MUSEUM, PRINCETON UNIVERSITY

Above, an obscure personage, perhaps a military hero, being received into Heaven, in a bas-relief of the fourth to sixth centuries

Below, an architectural frieze, combining the cross with such pagan motifs as birds and grapevines, from a Christian site near Thebes

METROPOLITAN MUSEUM OF ART

ANDRE EMMERICH GALLERY—LEE BOLTIN

BIBLIOTHEQUE NATIONALE, ARCHIVES PHOTOGRAPHIQUES, MS. COPTE 13

Above, the three Wise Men and the Virgin, as shown in a twelfth-century manuscript

Left, a rare example of Coptic scultpure-in-the-round, showing Hellenistic influences

BETWEEN SEA AND SAND

PHOTO RESEARCHERS—GEORGE HOLTON

BERBER BELIEFS

North Africa has been host to numerous colonizers—including the Phoenicians, Romans, Vandals, Byzantines, and Arabs. Most have come and gone, but Barbary's indigenous Berber culture has persisted. Edward Westermarck, the author of the next two selections, is a noted expert on Morocco, where the greatest number of Berber-speaking people live today. The passages are from Ritual and Belief in Morocco (1926).

Owing to our very defective knowledge of the early Berbers it is to a large extent impossible to decide what elements in the demonology of Morocco are indigenous and what not, though a more minute comparison between Moorish and Eastern practices and beliefs than could be undertaken at present might throw some new light on the subject. The extreme prevalence of fowl sacrifices in the cult of *jnun* as well as of saints is a North African peculiarity. Al-Bakri speaks of a Berber tribe called Ursifan, who never went to war without previously sacrificing a black cow to the *semarih*, as they named their demons. The idea that butchers and slaughtering-places are haunted seems to have a Berber origin, to judge by the dread which the aborigines of Gran Canaria had of butchers and the present Tuareg have of slaughtering-places; but similar ideas may of course have prevailed among the Arab invaders. The occult "science" which enables the magician to call up *jinn* and make them do his bidding by invoking them by name and by writing down mysteriously arranged letters, figures, words, and numbers, is widespread in the East, but the Maghrebins are reputed the most learned and skillful in it. . . . Both in Arabia and Egypt Maghrebins excell in the art of discovering hidden treasures, and Barbary sends there "whole troops of adventurers, who have no other means of living than the arts of magic." Thus the *jinn-cult* of the West has also influenced that of the East, and not only been influenced by it. Klunzinger observes in his book on Upper Egypt that the names of the *jinn* summoned "generally sound unlike Arabic, and may afford the philologist not uninteresting hints regarding the origin of this 'science'." In Morocco some names of *jnun* are expressly said to be Sudanese; and it is notable that the chief magicians, who practice their art by the instrumentality of the *jnun*, come from Sus, the southernmost part of Morocco, where the negro influence is considerable.

The *jinn* are usually invisible, but they are capable of assuming various shapes. They may appear in the shape of human beings, sometimes of the stature of men and sometimes of a size enormously gigantic. . . . In the *Arabian Nights* they are often represented as appearing, first of all, in a monstrous undefined shape, like an enormous pillar, and as only gradually assuming a human shape.

Even today some Berbers cling to their age-old superstitions. The omnipresent menace of the evil eye is a continual threat to a happy life.

Besides the *jnun* the evil eye is a very frequent cause of misfortune. It is said that "the evil eye owns two-thirds of the graveyards" . . . or that "one half of mankind dies from the evil eye" . . . or that at any rate one-third of all living beings are killed by the same enemy. There is another saying, that "the evil eye empties the castles [or 'houses'] and fills the graves." . . . So firmly is the evil eye believed in, that if some accident happens at a wedding or any other feast where a person reputed to have an evil eye is present, it is attributed to him and he may have to pay damages; and if such a person looks at another's animal and it shortly afterwards dies, he is likewise held responsible for the loss. . . .

The belief in the evil eye is obviously rooted both in the expressiveness and the uncanniness of the look, which makes the eye appear on the one hand as an instrument of transmitting evil wishes, and on the other hand also as an original source of injurious energy emanating from it involuntarily. [Francis] Bacon said, "There seemeth to be acknowledged, in the act of envy, an ejaculation, or irradiation of the eye." In Morocco the danger is considered to be particularly great when the look is accompanied with speech. There is not only an evil eye, but an evil mouth; in many cases, as we shall see, magic influence is attributed to the spoken word. . . . The worst of all persons is he who has a black heart and a joking mouth. But jocular, allegorical, or laudatory speech, when combined with a look, is feared even though there is no feeling of ill-will or envy. As instances of this may be quoted the following stories, which I heard among the Jbala of Andjra.

A party of men were sitting together near a place where black lambs belonging to one of them were playing. A man of the party who had the evil eye said to the others, "Look at those ravens, how they have pounced upon corpses." This was said merely as a joke, without any evil intention. Nevertheless on the following night the lambs began to die, and after some time not one of them was left. Their owner, who also possessed the evil eye, decided to take revenge. One afternoon, when he saw the other man riding on a white mare, he said to the people, "Look, that funeral is coming alone and there is nobody with it." On the same night the mare got stomach-ache, and on the next day she was dead. The owner thought of accusing the man who had caused the death of his mare, but he refrained from doing so because, if he did, the other man might accuse him of killing his lambs.

A man had an enemy in his village, whom he tried to injure by his look, but without success. He then went to a neighboring village to fetch another man, who was known to have very dangerous eyes, so as to achieve his aim with his assistance. When they came near the enemy's village the other man said, "Now I am going to shut my eyes, tell me when we arrive at the house of your enemy." By closing his eyes he wanted to give greater efficacy to his evil look, the first glance always being the most powerful. When they came to the house the man who had fetched him said jokingly, "Now set loose those greyhounds," meaning that he should open his eyes and cast an evil look upon the enemy, just as a greyhound is let loose on its prey. But as the man who uttered these words also possessed an evil eye, the result was that the eyes of the other one fell out. "You are worse than I am," the latter said; "you brought me here and caused my eyes to fall out." There was a man whose eyes were so terrible that he killed all his children by looking at them.

A group of young Berber goatherds

BLACK STAR—YVONNE GRAFIN KANITZ

THE TONGUE

This delightful legend is typical of the morality tales cherished by the Berbers of Morocco.

One day, a man, at the hour of his death, sent for his son and said to him: "Go to the sacrificer and ask him to give you the best part of an animal he has sacrificed."

The son went immediately to a butcher, who gave him a tongue and he took it to his father and said to him "See, this is the best part." The father again said to him, "Go now and find for me the worst part."

And the son returned to the butcher. This time he gave him another tongue, which he took immediately to his father.

Then the father said to him: "It is for you to understand, before I die, that the tongue can be the best and it can be the worst. The reason for this, is because through it comes equally the good and the bad."

HANNIBAL'S OATH

Rome became increasingly jealous of Carthage's wealth, and conflict between the two powers led to the three Punic Wars (264–146 B.C.). One of the chief protagonists was the Carthaginian general Hannibal. Polybius, writing about the Punic Wars, said of this hero: "Of all that befell the Romans and Carthaginians, good or bad, the cause was one man and one mind—Hannibal." Polybius, who lived from about 202 to 120 B.C., was a diligent Greek scholar, whose work is accorded a high degree of credibility. In this excerpt from his Histories, *Hannibal addresses his ally, Antiochus* III, *king of Syria.*

When my father [Hamilcar Barca] was about to go on his Iberian expedition I was nine years old: and as he was offering the sacrifice to Zeus I stood near the altar. The sacrifice successfully performed, my father poured the libation and went through the usual ritual. He then bade all the other worshipers stand a little back, and calling me to him asked me affectionately whether I wished to go with him on his expedition. Upon my eagerly assenting, and begging with boyish enthusiasm to be allowed to go, he took me by the right hand and led me to the altar, and bade me lay my hand upon the victim and swear that I would never be friends with Rome. So long, then, Antiochus, as your policy is one of hostility to Rome, you may feel quite secure of having in me a most thoroughgoing supporter. But if ever you make terms or friendship with her, then you need not wait for any slander to make you distrust me and be on your guard against me; for there is nothing in my power that I would not do against her.

RULE IN CARTHAGE

By the end of the fifth century B.C. the city-state of Carthage had become the dominant power in the western Mediterranean. It was the only non-Greek state whose constitution was admired by Greek political writers. However, the document itself is now lost. All that survives are scattered comments by classical authors, among them this analysis given in the fourth century B.C. in Aristotle's Politics. *Aristotle's chief criticism of the Carthaginian political system was that it was oligarchical, by which he meant a government by a class whose qualification was wealth not virtue. Indeed, the Carthaginians' principal interest was commerce and trade.*

The Carthaginians are also considered to have an excellent form of government, which differs from that of any other state in several respects, though it is in some very like the Lacedaemonian. Indeed, all three states—the Lacedaemonian, the Cretan, and the Carthaginian—nearly resemble one another, and are very different from any others. Many of the Carthaginian institutions are excellent. The superiority of their constitution is proved by the fact that the common people remain loyal to the constitution; the Carthaginians have never had any rebellion worth speaking of, and have never been under the rule of a tyrant.

Among the points in which the Carthaginian constitution resembles the Lacedaemonian are the following:—The common tables of the clubs answer to the Spartan phiditia, and their magistracy of the 104 to the Ephors; but, whereas the Ephors are any chance persons, the magistrates of the Carthaginians are elected according to merit—this is an improvement. They have also their kings and their gerusia, or council of elders, who correspond to the kings and elders of Sparta. Their kings, unlike the Spartan, are not always of the same family, nor that an ordinary one, but if there is some distinguished family they are selected out of it and not appointed by seniority—this is far better. Such officers have great power, and therefore, if they are persons of little worth, do a great deal of harm, and they have already done harm at Lacedaemon.

Most of the defects or deviations from the perfect state, for which the Carthaginian constitution would be censured, apply equally to all the forms of government which we have mentioned. But of the deflections from aristocracy and constitutional government, some incline more to democracy and some to oligarchy. The kings and elders, if unanimous, may determine whether they will or will not bring a matter before the people, but when they are not unanimous, the people decide on such matters as well. And whatever the kings and elders bring before the people is not only heard but also determined by them, and any one who likes may oppose it; now this is not permitted in Sparta and Crete. That the magistracies of five who have under them many important matters should be co-opted, that they should choose the supreme council of 100, and should hold office longer than other magistrates (for they are virtually rulers both before and after they hold office)—these are oligarchical features; their being without salary and not elected by lot, and any similar points, such as the practice of having all suits tried by the magistrates, and not some by one class of judges or jurors and some by another, as at Lacedaemon, are characteristic of aristocracy. The Carthaginian constitution deviates from aristocracy and inclines to oligarchy, chiefly on a point where popular opinion is on their side. For men in general think that magistrates should be chosen not only for their merit, but for their wealth: a man, they say, who is poor cannot rule well—he has not the leisure. If, then, election of magistrates for their wealth be characteristic of oligarchy, and election for merit of aristocracy, there will be a third form under which the constitution of Carthage is comprehended; for the Carthaginians choose their magistrates, and particularly the highest of them—their kings and generals—with an eye both to merit and to wealth.

But we must acknowledge that, in thus deviating from aristocracy, the legislator has committed an error. Nothing is more absolutely necessary than to provide that the highest class, not only when in office, but when out of office, should have leisure and not disgrace themselves in any way; and to this his attention should be first directed. Even if you must have regard to wealth, in order to secure leisure, yet it is surely a bad thing that the greatest offices, such as those of kings and generals, should be bought. The law which allows this abuse makes wealth of more account than virtue, and the whole state becomes avaricious. For, whenever the chiefs of the state deem anything honorable, the other citizens are sure to follow their example; and, where virtue has not the first place, there aristocracy cannot be firmly established. Those who have been at the expense of purchasing their places will be in the habit of repaying themselves; and it is absurd to suppose that a poor and honest man will be wanting to make gains, and that a lower stamp of man who has incurred a great expense will not. Wherefore they should rule who are able to rule best. And even if the legislator does not care to protect the good from poverty, he should at any rate secure leisure for them when in office.

It would seem also to be a bad principle that the same person should hold many offices, which is a favorite practice among the Carthaginians, for one business is better done by one man. The legislator should see to this and should not appoint the same person to be a flute-player and a shoemaker. Hence, where the state is large, it is more in accordance both with constitutional and with democratic principles that the offices of state should be distributed among many persons. For, as I said, this arrangement is fairer to all, and any action familiarized by repetition is better and sooner performed. We have a proof in military and naval matters; the duties of command

A Punic coin honors the steadfast elephants that followed Hannibal to Italy in 218 B.C.

TRUSTEES OF THE BRITISH MUSEUM

Numidian Berbers, influenced by the Romans, built this second-century B.C. *royal tomb.*

and of obedience in both these services extend to all.

The government of the Carthaginians is oligarchical, but they successfully escape the evils of oligarchy by enriching one portion of the people after another by sending them to their colonies. This is their panacea and the means by which they give stability to the state. Accident favors them, but the legislator should be able to provide against revolution without trusting to accidents. As things are, if any misfortune occurred, and the bulk of the subjects revolted, there would be no way of restoring peace by legal methods.

THE WEALTH OF CARTHAGE

One of Carthage's early accessions was the fertile Cape Bon peninsula, which lay east of the great city-state. It is described in the following selection by Diodorus Siculus, a first-century B.C. *Greek historian. His account presents a vivid picture of the region as it was around* 310 B.C., *some years before the Punic Wars, when Carthage was at its zenith.*

It was divided into market gardens and orchards of all sorts of fruit trees, with many streams of water flowing in channels irrigating every part. There were country houses everywhere, lavishly built and covered with stucco which testified to the wealth of their owners. The barns were filled with all that was needed to maintain a luxurious standard of living, as the inhabitants had been able to store up an abundance of everything in a long period of peace. Part of the land was planted with vines, part with olives and other productive trees. Beyond these, cattle and sheep were pastured on the plains, and there were meadows filled with grazing horses. Such were the signs of prosperity of these regions where leading Carthaginians had their estates.

ARBITER OF DESTINY

Masinissa's "divine achievement" is set forth in the following excerpt from the Histories *of Polybius. This monarch became so powerful that the Romans determined to destroy Carthage rather than see him gain the prize.*

Masinissa, king of the Numidians in Africa, was the best man of all the kings of our time, and the most completely fortunate; for he reigned more than sixty years in the soundest health and to extreme old age,—for he was ninety when he died. He was, besides, the most powerful man physically of all his contemporaries; for instance, when it was necessary to stand, he would do so without moving a foot all day long; and again, when he had once sat down to business he remained there the whole day; nor did it distress him the least to remain in the saddle day and night continuously; and at ninety years old, at which age he died, he left a son only four years old, called Sthembanus, who was afterwards adopted by Micipses, and four sons besides. Owing, again, to the affection existing between these sons, he kept his whole life free from any treasonable plot and his kingdom unpolluted by any family tragedy. But his greatest and most divine achievement was this: Numidia had been before his time universally unproductive, and was looked upon as incapable of producing any cultivated fruits. He was the first and only man who showed that it could produce cultivated fruits just as well as any other country whatever. . . .

UNWELCOME MIRACLE

For many Berbers, the Roman conquest of North Africa signified the exchanging of one adversary for another. This Tunisian legend reflects the pride of the indigenous population.

When the Romans undertook the conquest of the country it was governed by a wise Berber monarch. But its armies could not resist the shock of the invaders and our monarch finally had to yield. However this ruler had a daughter who was said to be astonishingly beautiful. As soon as the Roman leader saw her he fell deeply in love and asked for her hand. The Berber princess who had a proud and noble soul refused to become the wife of the man who had enslaved her country. "Ask me for whatever you wish and I shall deposit it at your feet, but consent to share my life," said the Roman leader. And the princess replied, "Let the united waters of the Zaghouan and the Djouggar be brought to Carthage without touching the earth, and I shall then consent." She believed, poor child, that her consent would depend on an impossible condition. But for the Romans nothing was impossible and their leader ordered the construction of the most remarkable aqueduct anyone had ever seen.

One by one the arches, of which the ruins are still visible, rose towards the sky. At last the day came when, through the conduits they supported, flowed the waters of the Zaghouan and the Djouggar conjugated by the forces of men. The Roman leader then led the princess to this wonder of the world built for her. In order to admire fully the Roman masterpiece the princess asked if she could climb to the top of one of the arches. As soon as she reached that height she looked over the country of her birth, flung herself into space and was killed.

TACFARINAS' REVOLT

The nomadic peoples of the interior posed a continuous threat to the governance of Africa

Romana. Attempts by the emperors' armies to occupy the vast desert proved impossible, and periodic shows of force at oases settlements had only short-term effect. This excerpt, from the Annals *of Tacitus, a first-century* A.D. *Roman historian, gives a partisan view of such an uprising. Led by Tacfarinas, these nomads harassed Roman legions for seven years before being defeated.*

In this same year [A.D. 17] a war broke out in Africa, where the enemy was led by Tacfarinas. A Numidian by birth, he had served as an auxiliary in the Roman camp, then becoming a deserter, he at first gathered round him a roving band familiar with robbery, for plunder and for rapine. After a while, he marshaled them like regular soldiers, under standards and in troops, till at last he was regarded as the leader, not of an undisciplined rabble, but of the Musulamian people. This powerful tribe, bordering on the deserts of Africa, and even then with none of the civilization of cities, took up arms and drew their Moorish neighbors into the war. These too had a leader, Mazippa. The army was so divided that Tacfarinas kept the picked men who were armed in Roman fashion within a camp, and familiarized them with a commander's authority, while Mazippa, with light troops, spread around him fire, slaughter, and consternation. They had forced the Ciniphii, a far from contemptible tribe, into their cause, when Furius Camillus, proconsul of Africa, united in one force a legion and all the regularly enlisted allies, and, with an army insignificant indeed compared with the multitude of the Numidians and Moors, marched against the enemy. There was nothing however which he strove so much to avoid as their eluding an engagement out of fear. It was by the hope of victory that they were lured on only to be defeated. The legion was in the army's center; the light cohorts and two cavalry squadrons on its wings. Nor did Tacfarinas refuse battle. The Numidians were routed, and after a number of years the name of Furius won military renown.

A PATERNAL SCOLDING

The tribulations of a citizen of Roman Egypt are reflected in this lively letter. It was written from the Fayum during the first century A.D.

Hermocrates to his son Chaeras greetings. First of all I hope that you are well. [I have often begged you] to write about your health and your needs, and at other times I have written you about the property at Psya, but you never answered nor came. And now, if you do not come, I am likely to abandon the place. My partner did not give any help. The well was not even cleaned out. Besides the irrigation ditch was choked with sand, and the estate is unfit for cultivation. Not a single tenant wanted to take it. I am merely paying taxes without any return. There is hardly water enough for a single garden plot. So come without fail, for the trees are in danger of dying. Your sister sends greetings. Your mother is angry with you because you never answered her letters; besides she is bothered enough with the tax-collectors because you did not send them to yourself. So now send to her [the amount due on taxes?]. Farewell.

CARACALLA'S EDICT

This decree was issued by Emperor Caracalla in A.D. 215, *a census year. However, it is less concerned with ascertaining the population of Alexandria than with forcing the peasants to return to the countryside, from where they had fled to avoid taxation.*

All Egyptians who are in Alexandria, especially peasants, whoever have fled from elsewhere and can easily be found, must in every possible way be driven out, except, however, the traders in pigs, rivermen, and those who bring down reeds for heating the baths. Drive out the rest, whoever by mere numbers and for no good bring the city into an uproar. I learn that at the festival of Sarapis and on certain other feast days, or even on other days, the Egyptians are accustomed to bring down bulls or other beasts for sacrifice. In this matter they are not to be restrained. Those ought to be banned who have fled from their native place to avoid their farm duties, not however those who gather here to see the sights of the most glorious city of Alexandria or who come down for the sake of more urbane life or occasional business. After other matters: In regard to the linen-weavers, the real Egyptians may easily be recognized by their dialect or else their features and built reveal [them to be different] from others. Besides their way of living shows that the peasants are alien to city life.

UP FROM POVERTY

The following selection, a translation of an inscription found at the Roman colony of Mactaris in central Tunisia, recounts a rare instance of peasant success. It is written by a third-century Berber farmer who gained wealth and honor through hard labor.

I was born of poor parents, my father had neither an income nor his own house. From the day of my birth I always cultivated my field; neither my land nor I

Bust of a satyr found off the Tunisian coast

MAGNUM

ever had any rest. When the season of ripened harvests came I was the first to cut my thatch; and in the country when you would see the groups of harvesters who hire themselves out around Cirta, the Numidian capital, or in the plain dominated by the mountain of Jupiter, I was first to harvest my field. Then I left my country and for twelve years I harvested for another under a fiery sun; for eleven years I was head of a harvesting team and mowed the wheat in the Numidian fields. Thanks to my labors and since I was content with little, I finally became owner of a house and land: today I live at ease. I have even obtained honor, I was named to sit in the senate of my city: the modest peasant became censor. I have seen my children and grandchildren grow up; my life had been occupied, peaceful, and honored by all.

SERMONS AT HIPPO REGIUS

Saint Augustine, one of the foremost theologians of all time, was born at Tagaste near Hippo Regius (modern Bone, Algeria) in A.D. 354 *and was in all probability a Berber. He is ranked as one of the original Doctors of the Church—a title given since the Middle Ages to outstanding theologians of acknowledged saintliness. He became coadjutor bishop of Hippo in* 395, *and soon after, its sole bishop, a position he held until his death in August,* 430, *when the Vandals were besieging the town. During his episcopate Augustine was obliged to deal with the many schisms that were dividing the African Church. He was especially avid in combatting the Donatists and in eradicating the remnants of paganism, which still colored the thinking of most North African Christians. The following selection, comprised of excerpts from his sermons, provides a glimpse of the life of rich and poor on the eve of the Vandal conquest.*

Brethren, let us imagine some rich dwelling. What a magnificent display of wealth there is! What luxury! How many gold and silver vases there are! What a great number of slaves, of beasts of burden and other animals! Finally, what delight the house itself gives, with its paintings, its marble, its paneled ceilings, its pillars, its courts and chambers.

Can it be said that these things are good: gold, silver, a beautiful estate, marble walls, and gilded ceilings? God forbid. . . . For the starry skies are more pleasing to the poor man than gilded ceilings are to the rich. . . .

Just as the term *house* is used to signify the inhabitants of a house; so, in this sense, we say that a marble house is bad and a smoky house is good. You find a smoky house in which good people dwell, and you say: "This is a good house." You find a marble house with decorated ceilings, in which the wicked dwell, and you say: "This is a bad house,"—calling the occupants, not the walls and rooms, a house. . . .

When men engage in the most unjust lawsuits for the right of sunshine and light in their buildings so that the rays of the sun may penetrate more fully through their windows, they often strive to demolish the houses of others and, with the most implacable enmity, they attack those who with unquestionable right oppose them. If, for the sake of the enjoyment of sunlight, a powerful person unjustly and wickedly oppresses one who is weaker; if he robs him and forces him into exile, or even death; is this the crime of the sun?

You accuse the miser and he, in turn, accuses God because He made gold. "God should not have made gold," [he says]. It now remains that because you cannot restrain yourselves from evil deeds, you blame the good works of God. The Creator of the universe displeases you. Then He should not have made the sun, because many dispute with regard to the openings for light and they drag one another into court.

You love silver because it is better than iron and copper; you love gold more, because it is better than silver; you love precious stones more, because they surpass even gold in their value; finally, you love that light which everyone who fears death fears to lose; you love that light, I say, with that intense love of the blind man who, following Jesus, cried out: "Have pity on me, Son of David."

For you are not rich, and the angel poor, who has not [as you have] horses and traveling carriages and numerous slaves. . . .

"When shall I bless God?" Is it when he is kind to you? when worldly possessions abound? when there is a great abundance of grain, oil, wine, gold, silver, slaves, and cattle? . . .

Is it not happiness to possess robust sons, well-dressed daughters, well-filled store-houses, numerous cattle; to have no broken wall and not even a broken hedge; to have no tumult nor clamor in the streets, but peace, repose, and an abundance of wealth, in homes and in cities? . . .

And in order that you may know that not money but avarice is condemned in the rich, give attention to what I say. You see this rich man standing next to you: perchance, he has wealth without avarice, whereas you have avarice without wealth.

But perhaps you have been reduced to extreme poverty and indigence because you had some sort of an inheritance or other to support you, and some calumny on the part of a rival took it from you. I hear you groan; you accuse the times; and if you could, you would do that which you deplore. Do we not see it? Are there not many daily examples of this? Yesterday, he was murmuring because he lost his fortune; today, attaching himself to a more powerful man, he robs others.

What is this patrimony? Is it gold, or silver, or precious stones, or estates and beautiful farms?

He is rich either from his parents, or from gifts and inheritances. . . .

As we enter and leave the church, the poor accost us and beg that we exhort you, that they may receive something from you. They have asked us to speak to you, and when they see that they do not receive from you, they think that we are laboring among you in vain. They expect something from us also. We give as much as we have; we give as much as we can; nevertheless, are we not powerless to provide for all their needs? Since, therefore, we are incapable of providing for their needs, we are their ambassadors to you. You have understood; you have applauded. Thanks be to God! . . .

Avarice commands not only "set forth," but also, "cross the seas and seek unknown lands." You must transport your merchandise to India. You do not know the Indic language, but the language of avarice is everywhere understood. You land among a people of whom you have never heard; you give and receive things in exchange; you buy articles which you carry back with you. The dangers which attended you on your oversea voyage to India also attend your return, and you cry to God amidst the tempest which tosses your vessel: "O God deliver me!" But do you not hear Him answer, "Did I send you hither? It is Avarice who bade you acquire that which you did not possess; whereas I have commanded you to give, without any labor on your part, to the poor man at your door. Avarice sent you as far as India to bring back gold. I placed Christ at your door so that you might purchase from Him the kingdom of heaven. You do everything to serve Avarice and nothing to obey Me". . . .

What do not merchants endure to satisfy their avarice? They cross the seas, subject their bodies and souls to winds and storms, forsake their own country and seek unknown lands. . . . And what will be the result when you will have obeyed the orders of Avarice? Your house will overflow with gold and silver.

JUSTINIAN'S AFRICA

In A.D. 533 *the Byzantine army, led by Belisarius, the greatest general of the age, wrested Barbary from the Vandals. One of Byzantium's most vivid historians was Procopius, who accompanied the general and wrote the supportive* Histories *of his campaigns. By contrast, Procopius' vituperative* Secret History, *or* Anecdota, *from which this excerpt is taken, was composed in* 550 *for posthumous publication. "What I shall write," declares Procopius in his introduction, "now follows a different plan, supplementing the previous formal chronicle with a disclosure of what really happened." This account of North Africa under Justinian is highly exaggerated; nevertheless, it gives an idea of the ruin, social upheaval, and general disillusionment that helped to set the stage for the spread of Islam in the seventh century.*

That Justinian was not a man, but a demon, as I have said, in human form, one might prove by considering the enormity of the evils he brought upon mankind. For in the monstrousness of his actions the power of a fiend is manifest. Certainly an accurate reckoning of all those whom he destroyed would be impossible, I think, for anyone but God to make. Sooner could one number, I fancy, the sands of the sea than the men this Emperor murdered. Examining the countries that he made desolate of inhabitants, I would say he slew a trillion people. For Libya [North Africa], vast as it is, he so devastated that you would have to go a long way to find a single man, and he would be remarkable. Yet eighty thousand Vandals capable of bearing arms had dwelt there, and as for their wives and children and servants, who could guess their number? Yet still more numerous than these were the Mauretanians, who with their wives and children were all exterminated. And again, many Roman soldiers and those who followed them to Constantinople, the earth now covers; so that if one should venture to say that five million men perished in Libya alone, he would not, I imagine, be telling the half of it.

The reason for this was that after the Vandals were defeated, Justinian planned, not how he might best strengthen his hold on the country, nor how by safeguarding the interests of those who were loyal to him he might have the goodwill of his subjects: but instead he foolishly recalled Belisarius at once, on the charge that the latter intended to make himself King (an idea of which Belisarius was utterly incapable), and so that he might manage affairs there himself and be able to plunder the whole of Libya. Sending commissioners to value the province, he imposed grievous taxes where before there had been none. Whatever lands were most valuable, he seized, and prohibited the Arians from observing their religious ceremonies. Negligent toward sending necessary supplies to the soldiers, he was overstrict with them in other ways; wherefore mutinies arose resulting in the deaths of many. For he was never able to abide by established customs, but naturally threw everything into confusion and disturbance. . . .

So while he was Emperor, the whole earth ran red with . . . blood. . . .

THE FIRST HERMIT

Christian monasticism originated among the indigenous Coptic population of Upper Egypt. Acting independently, a number of Christians abandoned the world and sought refuge in the desert, where they lived solitary and ascetic lives. According to tradition, the first Christian hermit was Saint Paul of Thebes, whose life reputedly spanned some one hundred thirteen years of the third and fourth centuries A.D. *His story is told by Saint Jerome in a biography, from which the excerpt below is taken. Saint Anthony, another famous anchorite, is discussed in the next selection.*

During the reign of Decius [A.D. 249–251] and Valerian [A.D. 253–260], the persecutors, about the time when Cornelius at Rome, Cyprian at Carthage, spilt their glorious blood, a fierce tempest made havoc of many churches in Egypt and the Thebaid. It was the Christian's prayer in those days that he might, for Christ's sake, die by the sword. But their crafty enemy sought out torments wherein death came slowly: desiring rather to slaughter the soul than the body. And as Cyprian wrote, who was himself to suffer: *They long for death, and dying is denied them.* . . .

Now at this very time, while such deeds as these were being done, the death of both parents left Paul heir to great wealth in the Lower Thebaid: his sister was already married. He was then about fifteen years of age, excellently versed alike in Greek and Egyptian letters, of a gentle spirit, and a strong lover of God. When the storm of persecution began its thunder, he betook himself to a farm in the country, for the sake of its remoteness and secrecy. But

"*What wilt thou not drive mortal hearts*
to do,
O thou dread thirst for gold?"

His. sister's husband began to meditate the betrayal of the lad whom it was his duty to conceal. Neither the tears of his wife, nor the bond of blood, nor God looking down upon it all from on high, could call him back from the crime, spurred on by a cruelty that seemed to ape religion. The boy, far-sighted as he was, had the wit to discern it, and took flight to the mountains, there to wait while the persecution ran its course. What had been his necessity became his free choice. Little by little he made his way, sometimes turning back and again returning, till at length he came upon a rocky mountain, and at its foot, at no great distance, a huge cave, its mouth closed by a stone. There is a thirst in men to pry into the unknown: he moved the stone, and eagerly exploring came within on a spacious courtyard open to the sky, roofed by the wide-spreading branches of an ancient palm, and with a spring of clear shining water. . . .

So then, in this beloved habitation, offered to him as it were by God himself, he lived his life through in prayer and solitude: the palm-tree provided him with food and clothing. [This is] incredible to those who believe not that all things are possible to him that believeth.

Paul, aged one hundred thirteen years, received a visit from Saint Anthony of Egypt.

And as they talked they perceived that a crow had settled on a branch of the tree, and softly flying down, deposited a whole loaf before their wondering eyes. And when he had withdrawn, "Behold," said Paul, "God hath sent us our dinner, God the merciful, God the compassionate. It is now sixty years since I have had each day a half loaf of bread: but at thy coming, Christ hath doubled His soldiers' rations." And when they had given thanks to God, they sat down beside the margin of the crystal spring. . . . Then they drank a little water, holding their mouths to the spring: and offering to God the sacrifice of praise, they passed the night in vigil.

But as day returned to the earth, the Blessed Paul spoke to Antony. "From old time, my brother, I have known that thou wert a dweller in these parts: from old time God had promised that thou, my fellow-servant, wouldst come to me. But since the time has come for sleeping, and (for I have ever desired to be dissolved and to be with Christ) the race is run, there remaineth for me a crown of righteousness; thou hast been sent by God to shelter this poor body in the ground, returning earth to earth."

At this Antony, weeping and groaning, began pleading with him not to leave him but take him with him as a fellow-traveler on that journey. . . .

Paul, knowing that he was about to die, asked Anthony to fetch him a cloak in which he could be buried. Anthony complied, and traversed the desert to procure the garment. He then recrossed the dry terrain and returned to Paul, only to find him dead.

Entering the cave, he saw on its bent knees, the head erect and the hands stretched out to heaven, the lifeless body: yet first, thinking he yet lived, he knelt and prayed beside him. Yet no accustomed sigh of prayer came to him: he kissed him, weeping, and then knew that the dead body of the holy man still knelt and prayed to God, to whom all things live.

So then he wrapped the body round and carried it outside, chanting the hymns and psalms of Christian tradition. But sadness came on Antony, because he had no spade to dig the ground. His mind was shaken, turning this way and that. For if I should go back to the monastery, he said, it is a three days' journey: if I stay here, there is no more that I can do. Let me die, therefore, as is meet: and falling beside thy soldier, Christ, let me draw my last breath.

But even as he pondered, behold two lions came coursing, their manes flying, from the inner desert, and made towards him. At sight of them, he was at first in dread: then, turning his mind to God, he waited undismayed, as though he looked on doves. They came straight to the body of the holy dead, and halted by it wagging their tails, then couched themselves at his feet, roaring mightily; and Antony well knew they were lamenting him, as best they could. Then, going a little way off, they began to scratch up the ground with their paws, vying with one another in throwing up the sand, till they had dug a grave roomy enough for a man: and thereupon, as though to ask the reward of their work, they came up to Antony, with drooping ears and downbent heads, licking his hands and his feet. He saw that they were begging for his blessing; and pouring out his soul in praise to Christ for that even the dumb beasts feel that there is God, "Lord," he said, "without whom no leaf lights from the tree, nor a single sparrow falls upon the ground, give unto these even as Thou knowest."

Then, motioning with his hand, he signed to them to depart. And when they had gone away, he bowed his aged shoulders under the weight of the holy body: and laying it in the grave, he gathered the earth above it, and made the wonted mound. Another day broke: and then, lest the pious heir should receive none of the goods of the intestate, he claimed for himself the tunic which the saint had woven out of palm-leaves as one weaves baskets. And so returning to the monastery, he told the whole story to his disciples in order as it befell: and on the solemn feasts of Easter and Pentecost, he wore the tunic of Paul.

A choir boy pauses before one of the ten monolithic churches built by Ethiopia's King Lalibela.

SAINT ANTHONY OF EGYPT

Saint Anthony, the most famous of the early hermits, was born around A.D. 251 *at Koma in central Egypt. He came from a prosperous family. His biography, a small section of which follows, was written by a contemporary, Saint Athanasius, bishop of Alexandria. Anthony devoted himself to asceticism when he was about eighteen and later became a desert hermit. When he was middle aged he abandoned solitude and organized his disciples into a loosely knit community, whose members shared a minimal common life. This modification of the eremitical life would mark the first significant step toward the development of Christian monastic orders.*

And again as . . . [Anthony] went into the church, hearing the Lord say in the Gospel, "be not anxious for the morrow," he could stay no longer, but went out and gave those things also to the poor. Having committed his sister to known and faithful virgins, and put her into a convent to be brought up, he henceforth devoted himself outside his house to discipline, taking heed to himself and training himself with patience. For there were not yet so many monasteries in Egypt, and no monk at all knew of the distant desert; but all who wished to give heed to themselves practiced the discipline in solitude near their own village. Now there was then in the next village an old man who had lived the life of a hermit from his youth up. Antony, after he had seen this man, imitated him in piety. And at first he began to abide in places outside the village; then if he heard of a good man anywhere, like the prudent bee, he went forth and sought him, nor turned back to his own place until he had seen him; and he returned, having got from the good man as it were supplies for his journey in the way of virtue. So dwelling there at first, he confirmed his purpose not to return to the abode of his fathers nor to the remembrance of his kinsfolk; but to keep all his desire and energy for perfecting his discipline. He worked, however, with his hands, having heard, "he who is idle let him not eat," and part he spent on bread and part he gave to the needy. And he was constant in prayer, knowing that a man ought to pray in secret unceasingly. For he had given such heed to what was read that none of the things that were written fell from him to the ground, but he remembered all, and afterwards his memory served him for books.

GOD'S "SAUCY SERVANTS"

The first code of monastic behavior was drawn up by another venerable Copt, Saint Pachomius (c. A.D. *290–346). Born in Upper Egypt of heathen parents, he served in the imperial army before converting to Christianity. He then lived as a hermit until about* A.D. *320, when he built a monastery north of Luxor, at Tabennisi. There the inmates enjoyed a common life under an abbot. The Rule of Pachomius, now lost, gradually spread all over Christendom. The following passage was written by Palladius (c.* A.D. *365–425), the most illustrious historian of early monasticism. It purports to give an approximate idea of the abbot's original rules.*

There is a place in the Thebaid called Tabenna, in which lived a certain monk Pachomius, one of those men who have attained the highest form of life, so that he was granted predictions of the future and angelic visions. He was a great lover of the poor, and had great love to men. When, therefore, he was sitting in a cave an angel of the Lord came in and appeared to him and said: Pachomius you have done well those things which pertain to your own affairs; therefore sit no longer idle in this cave. Up, therefore, go forth and gather all the younger monks and dwell with them and give them laws according to the form which I give thee. And he gave him a brass tablet on which the following things were written:

1. Give to each to eat and drink according to his strength; and give labors according to the powers of those eating, and forbid neither fasting nor eating. Thus appoint difficult labors to the stronger and those who eat, but the lighter and easy tasks to those who discipline themselves more and are weaker.

2. Make separate cells in the same place; and let three remain in a cell. But let the food of all be prepared in one house.

3. They may not sleep lying down, but having made seats built inclining backward let them place their bedding on them and sleep seated.

4. But by night let them wear linen tunics, being girded about. Let each of them have a shaggy goatskin, made white. Without this let them neither eat nor sleep. When they go in unto the communion of the mysteries of Christ every Sabbath and Lord's Day, let them loose their girdles and put off the goatskin, and enter with only their cuculla. . . . But he made the cuculla for them without any fleece, as for boys; and he commanded to place upon them certain branding marks of a purple cross.

5. He commanded that there be twenty-four groups of the brethren, according to the number of the twenty-four letters. And he prescribed that to

each group should be given as a name a letter of the Greek alphabet, from Alpha and Beta, one after another, to Omega, in order that when the archimandrite [the superior general] asked for any one in so great a company, that one may be asked who is the second in each, how group Alpha is, or how the group Beta; again let him salute the group Rho; the name of the letters following its own proper sign. And upon the simpler and more guileless place the name Iota; and upon those who are more ill-tempered and less righteous the letter Xi. And thus in harmony with the principles and the life and manners of them arrange the names of the letters, only the spiritual understanding the meaning.

6. There was written on the tablet that if there come a stranger of another monastery, having a different form of life, he shall not eat nor drink with them, nor go in with them into the monastery, unless he shall be found in the way outside of the monastery.

7. But do not receive for three years into the contest of proficients him who has entered once for all to remain with them; but when he has performed the more difficult tasks, then let him after a period of three years enter the stadium.

8. When they eat let them veil their faces, that one brother may not see another brother eating. They are not to speak while they eat; nor outside of their dish or off the table shall they turn their eyes toward anything else.

9. And he made it a rule that during the whole day they should offer twelve prayers; and at the time of lighting the lamps, twelve; and in the course of the night, twelve; and at the ninth hour, three; but when it seemed good for the whole company to eat, he directed that each group should first sing a psalm at each prayer.

But when the great Pachomius replied to the angel that the prayers were few, the angel said to him: I have appointed these that the little ones may advance and fulfill the law and not be distressed; but the perfect do not need to have laws given to them. For being by themselves in their cells, they have dedicated their entire life to contemplation on God. But to these, as many as do not have an intelligent mind, I will give a law that as saucy servants out of fear for the Master they may fulfil the whole order of life and direct it properly. When the angel had given these directions and fulfilled his ministry he departed from the great Pachomius. There are monasteries observing this rule, composed of seven thousand men, but the first and great monastery, wherein the blessed Pachomius dwelt, and which gave birth to the other places of asceticism, has one thousand three hundred men.

THE DESERT FATHERS

The following selection is from the History of the Monks in Egypt, *originally written in Latin by Rufinus, the fourth-century presbyter of Aquileia in northern Italy. He visited Egypt about* A.D. 371, *where he observed both cenobitic and eremitical monasticism.*

In the country around about Arsinoë, we saw a certain Serapion, priest and father of many monasteries: under his care he had more than ten thousand monks, in many and diverse congregations, and all of them earned their bread by the work of their hands, and the great part of what they earned, especially at harvest time, they brought to this Father, for the use of the poor. For it was the custom not only among these, but almost all the Egyptian monks, to hire themselves out at harvest time as harvesters, and each one among them would earn eighty measures of corn, more or less, and offer the greater part of it to the poor, so that not only were the hungry folk of that countryside fed, but ships were sent to Alexandria, laden with corn, to be divided among such as were prisoners in gaols, or as were foreigners and in need. For there was not poverty enough in Egypt to consume the fruit of their compassion and their lavishness.

So we came to Nitria [now Wadi el-Natrun]; the place most famous among all the monasteries of Egypt, about thirty-seven miles distant from Alexandria, and named after the neighboring town in which nitre is collected, as though in the providence of God it was foreseen that in these parts the sins of men would be washed and utterly effaced, even as stains by nitre are cleansed. In this place there are about fifty (or not many less) habitations, set near together and under one father, in some of which many brethern live together, in some a few, in some a brother lives alone: but though they be divided in their dwelling, yet do they abide bound and inseparable in spirit and faith and loving-kindness. . . .

Beyond this [Mount Nitria] there is another place in the inner desert, about nine miles distant: and this place, by reason of the multitude of cells dispersed through the desert, they call Cellia, The Cells. To this place those who have had their first initiation and who desire to live a remoter life, stripped of all its trappings, withdraw themselves: for the desert is vast, and the cells are sundered from one another by so wide a space, that none is in sight of his neighbor, nor can any voice be heard.

One by one they abide in their cells, a mighty silence and a great quiet among them: only on the Saturday and the Sunday do they come together to church, and there they see each other face to face as folk restored in heaven. If by chance any one is missing in that gathering, straightway they understand that he has been detained by some unevenness of his body and they all go to visit him, not indeed all of them together but at different times, and each carrying with him whatever he may have by him at home that might seem grateful to the sick. But for no other cause dare any disturb the silence of his neighbor, unless perchance to strengthen by a good word, or as it might be to anoint with the comfort of counsel the athletes set for the struggle. Many of them go three and four miles to church, and the distance dividing one cell from another is no less great: but so great is the love that is in them and by so strong affection are they bound towards one another and towards all brethren that they be an example and a wonder to all. So that if any one by chance should desire to dwell with them, as soon as they perceive it, each man offers his own cell.

BYZANTINE INTRIGUE

The conversion of the peoples of Nubia to Christianity in the sixth century has been picturesquely told by a contemporary Syrian, John, bishop of Ephesus. At that time Nubia was divided into the three kingdoms of Nobatia, Makuria, and Alodia. The following selection is from the bishop's Ecclesiastical History, *which is probably fairly accurate. It describes the court intrigue between the Monophysite empress Theodora and her Melchite husband, Emperor Justinian, over sending a missionary to Nobatia in* A.D. 543.

Among the clergy in attendance upon pope Theodosius, was a presbyter named Julianus, an old man of great worth, who conceived an earnest spiritual desire to christianize the wandering people who dwell on the eastern borders of the Thebais beyond Egypt, and who are not only not subject to the authority of the Roman empire, but even receive a subsidy on condition that they do not enter nor pillage Egypt. The blessed Julianus, therefore, being full of anxiety for his people, went and spoke about them to the late queen Theodora, in the hope of awakening in her a similar desire for their conversion; and as the queen was fervent in zeal for God, she received the proposal with joy, and promised . . . . and anxiously desired to send the blessed Julian thither. But when the king [Justinian] heard that the person she intended to send was opposed to the council of Chalcedon [i.e., a Monophysite], he was not pleased, and determined to write to the bishops of his own [Melchite] side in the Thebais, with orders for them to proceed thither and instruct them, and plant among them the name of the synod. And as he entered upon the matter with great zeal, he sent thither, without a moment's delay, ambassadors with gold and baptismal robes, and gifts of honor for the king of that people, and letters for the duke of the Thebais [the Byzantine governor of Upper Egypt], enjoining him to take every care of the embassy, and escort them to the territories of the Nobadae [Nobatia]. When, however, the queen learnt these things, she quickly, with much cunning, wrote letters to the duke of the Thebais, and sent a mandatory of her court to carry them to him; and which were as follows: "Inasmuch as both his majesty and myself have purposed to send an embassy to the people of the Nobadae, and I am now despatching a blessed man named Julian; and further my will is, that my ambassador should arrive at the aforesaid people before his majesty's; be warned, that if you permit his ambassador to arrive there before mine, and do not hinder him by various pretexts until mine shall have reached you, and have passed through your province, and arrived at his destination, your life shall answer for it; for I will immediately send and take off your head." Soon after the receipt of this letter the king's ambassador also came, and the duke said to him, "You must wait a little, while we look out and procure beasts of burden, and men who know the deserts; and then you will be able to proceed." And thus he delayed him until the arrival of the merciful queen's embassy, who found horses and guides in waiting, and the same day, without loss of time, under a show of doing it by violence, they laid hands upon them, and were the first to proceed. As for the duke, he made his excuses to the king's ambassador, saying, "Lo! when I had made my preparations, and was desirous of sending you onward, ambassadors from the queen arrived, and fell upon me with violence, and took away the beasts of burden I had got ready, and have passed onward. And I am too well acquainted with the fear in which the queen is held, to venture to oppose them. But abide still with me, until I can make fresh preparations for you, and then you also shall go in peace." And when he heard these things, he rent his garments, and threatened him terribly, and reviled him; and after some time he also was able to proceed, and followed the other's track, without being aware of the fraud which had been practiced upon him.

The blessed Julian, meanwhile, and the ambassadors who accompanied him, had arrived at the confines of the Nobadae, whence they sent to the king and his princes, informing him of their coming: upon which an armed escort set out, who received them joyfully, and brought them into their land unto the king. And he too received them with pleasure, and her majesty's letter was presented, and read to him, and the purport of it explained. They accepted also the magnificent honors sent them, and the numerous baptismal robes, and every thing else richly provided for their use. And immediately with joy they yielded themselves up, and utterly abjured the error of their forefathers, and confessed the God of the Christians, saying, "that He is the one true God, and there is no other beside Him." . . . As for the blessed Julian, he remained with them for two years, though suffering greatly from the extreme heat. For he used to say that from nine o'clock until four in the afternoon he was obliged to take refuge in caverns, full of water, where he sat undressed and girt with a linen garment, such as the people of the country wear. And if he left the water his skin, he said, was blistered by the heat. Nevertheless, he endured it patiently, and taught them, and baptized both the king and his nobles, and much people also. He had with him also a bishop from the Thebais, an old man, named Theodore, and after giving them instruction and setting things in order, he delivered them over to his charge and himself departed, and arrived in safety at Constantinople, where he was most honorably received by the queen.

A Roman aqueduct casts its shadow on a road in Tunisia, once part of Africa Proconsularis.

NORTHERN RIM

THE INSIDERS

Since late paleolithic times North Africa and parts of the Sahara have been inhabited by peoples of different skin colors and physical types. The Greeks dubbed them "Libyans," a term derived from the Lebu nomads, a group native to what is now Libya; the Romans called them *barbari*, meaning "foreigners" and thus rude; and in time the name was corrupted to "Berber." Their place of origin and the manner by which they came to Barbary is one of the great mysteries of African history. Possibly they migrated from southwest Asia. Since ancient times the Berbers have called themselves *imazighen*, or "freemen," their distinguishing characteristic being a fierce love of individual and group liberty. They have always been the true overlords of Barbary's mountain regions, their "homeland," and of many Saharan oases, where they were forced to adapt to desert conditions. Wherever they settled, they combined farming and animal husbandry with extensive trading enterprises. None of North Africa's colonizers ever managed to subjugate them completely. With the coming of the Arabs after the seventh century, numerous Berbers migrated or were pushed into the central or southern Sahara and even into the Sudan. A small number in the remoter areas retained their Berber dialects, but eventually most became Arabized, adopting the language, customs, religion, and dress of the Muslim conquerors.

Life MAGAZINE © TIME INC.–JOHN SADOVY

The once-verdant Sahara is now reduced to an arid waste, relieved only by scattered oases, such as the Algerian site below. Cave paintings of horse-drawn war chariots dating from the second millennium B.C., *like the one from the Fezzan shown above, attest to trans-Saharan contacts in ancient times. Similar depictions are distributed across the desert along ancient trade routes. The Berber girls opposite clap to the rhythm of village musicians at a festival in the Atlas Mountains. The distinctively striped wool shawls they wear identify their clan affiliation.*

MAGNUM–GEORGE RODGER

PHOTO RESEARCHERS—GEORGE HOLTON

THE OUTSIDERS

A broad-beamed Phoenician cargo ship, as shown in a tomb relief
GIRAUDON

Throughout antiquity prospects of trade lured outsiders to the northern shores of Africa. The Phoenicians, who arrived about 1200 B.C., founded the maritime-based Punic empire, which dominated the coast for the next millennium. Next, the Latins transformed Barbary, "arid nurse of the lions," into the granary of Rome, supplying the empire's cities with abundant cereals. In addition, galleys returning to Ostia were laden with fruits, ivory, wine, olive oil, horses, and even wild beasts (an estimated 3,500 were killed for sport at one twenty-six-day celebration in the reign of Augustus). Then, in the seventh century A.D., after two centuries of persecution and corruption—first by the Vandals and then the Byzantines—Europe lost control of North Africa.

Cyrenaic exports readied for shipping, from a vase painted about 568 B.C.
BIBLIOTHEQUE NATIONALE, SERVICE PHOTOGRAPHIQUE

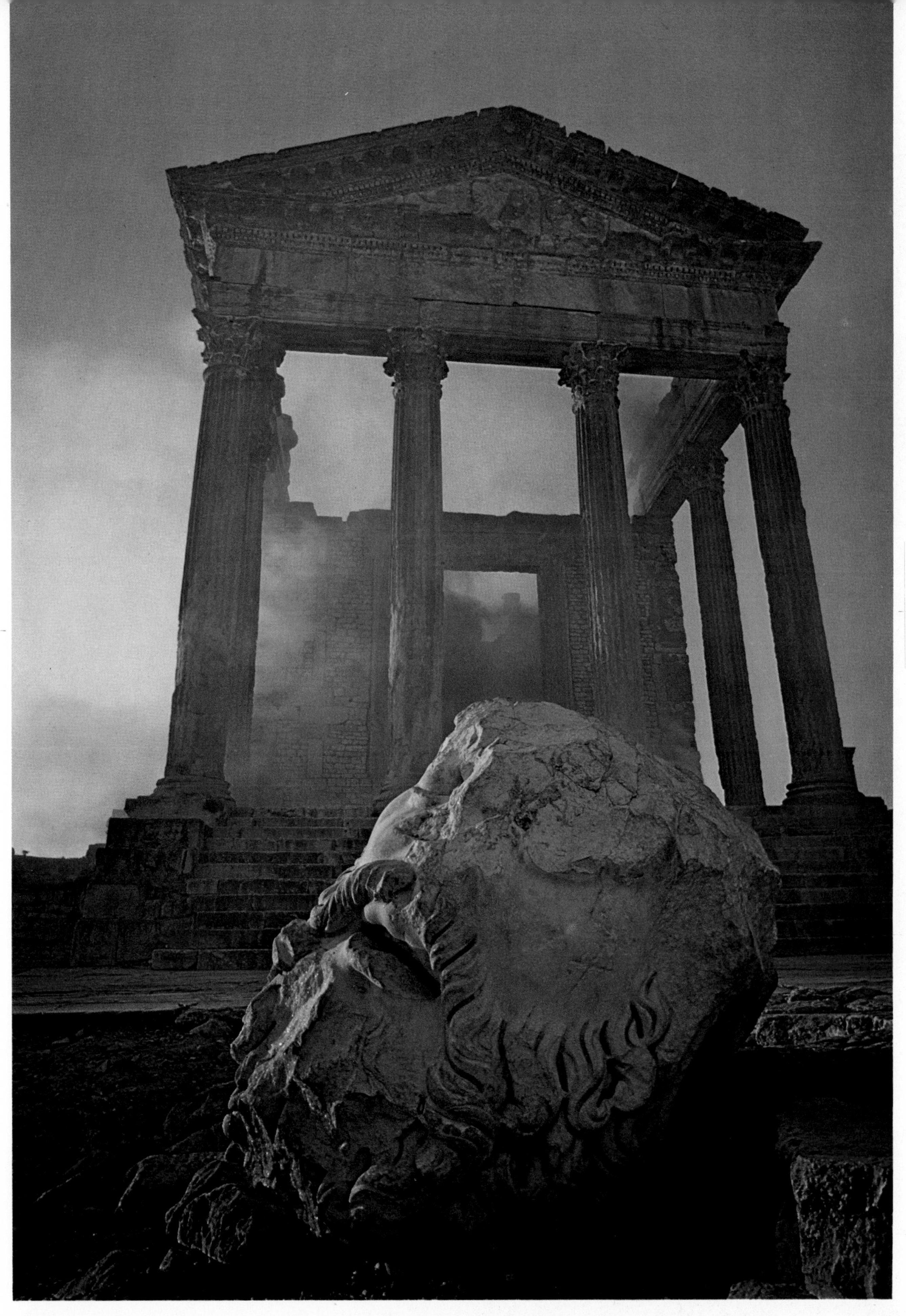

Recalling the glory of Africa Romana, this crumbling head of Jupiter now lies before a temple built to him at Dougga in Tunisia.

RAPHO-GUILLUMETTE—BRIAN BRAKE

A king of Ethiopia, head of Church and state, receives a ceremonial blessing from his bishop before Axum's Cathedral of St. Mary of Zion.

RAPHO-GUILLUMETTE–MARC AND EVELYNE BERNHEIM

"ATHLETES OF GOD"

Aside from various pagan cults, Christianity is Africa's oldest living religion. It spread to Egypt and the Maghreb during the first and second centuries A.D., becoming the official religion of Axumite Ethiopia in the fourth century and reaching Nubia in the sixth. It was accompanied by bitter schisms. Hundreds of martyrs, or "athletes of god," as one theologian called them, died for their faith and inspired myriad conversions. Some Christians sought refuge in the Egyptian desert, where they founded prototypes of eremetical and monastic communities. Doctrinal disputes so weakened Maghrebin Christianity that it eventually lost its following to the militant new creed of Islam. However, the Arabs tolerated Egypt's Monophysite Coptic Church, which survives as a minority faith today. Nubia, having fallen to the Muslims in 1504, also adopted Monophysitism, as did Ethiopia. The Ethiopian Orthodox Church, a blend of Jewish, traditional animist, and Coptic elements, is a truly indigenous Christian institution in the heart of Africa.

WERNER FORMAN

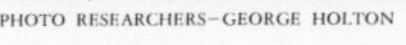

PHOTO RESEARCHERS–GEORGE HOLTON

METROPOLITAN MUSEUM OF ART; *Life* MAGAZINE © TIME INC.–YALE JOEL

The most ambitious of Ethiopia's architectural undertakings was the building in the 1200's of the rock-hewn edifices at Lalibela. Some are dug inside caverns; others, like that above, are carved into the sides of cliffs. Still others are freestanding, cut from a single rock.

Reverence for the Egyptian goddess Isis and her son Horus, shown at left in an Egyptian statuette of the Ptolemaic period, was easily converted to veneration of Mary and Jesus. The fourth-century fresco at far left of the Madonna and Child adorns a Coptic monastery.

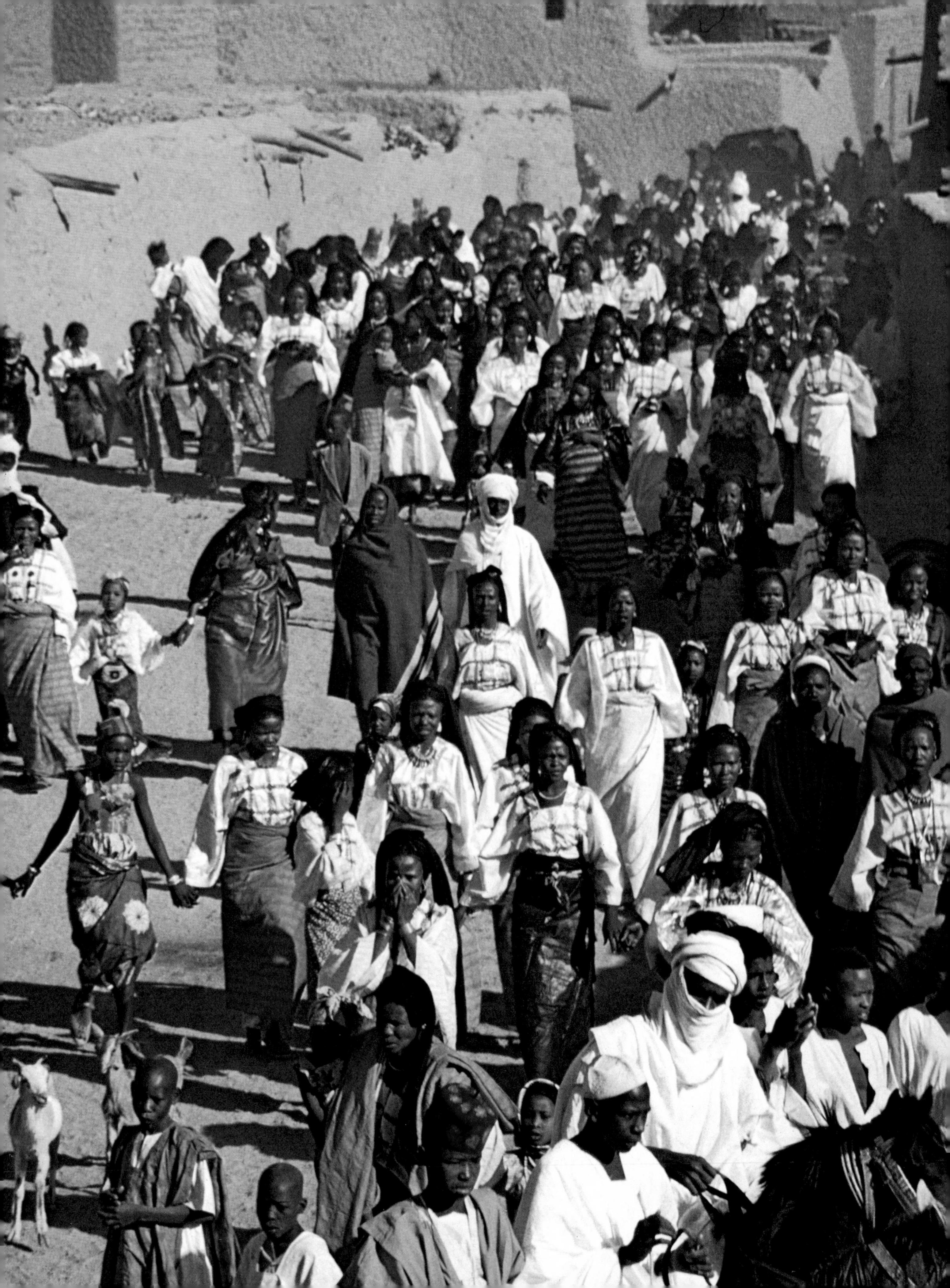

Chapter Four

THE SPREAD OF ISLAM

(c. A.D. 500–1500)

by

John Ralph Willis

THE MILLENNIUM BETWEEN A.D. 500 and 1500 witnessed significant changes in the historical evolution of Abyssinia (Ethiopia), Arabia, and the East African littoral. At the commencement of this epoch the Christian civilization of Axum was at its apogee. In the fourth century, somewhere between A.D. 320 and 350, Axumite warriors had successfully overthrown the power of Kush, invading its once-celebrated capital at Meroë. The final collapse of Meroë, which seems already to have been in decline, shifted the focal point of Nile Valley culture from ancient Kush to its successor states, the Christian kingdoms of Nubia. The prosperity of Axum derived from the strategic location of its chief port, Adulis, a favorite emporium for Greek ships frequenting the Red Sea routes and other vessels participating in the east-west trade between the Yemen and the Nile Valley.

With the rise of Islam and the development of Arab power, however, came the disruption of the lucrative Red Sea trade and the eclipse of Abyssinian influence in this region. Henceforth, until the appearance of the Portuguese toward the end of the millennium, Arab culture and influence became the dominating force in the trading communities that sprang up along the East African coast. The rise of Arab power brought forth a rapid and wide-ranging diffusion of Islam into significant portions of East Africa (including parts of Abyssinia itself), and as far as North and northwest Africa, where it took root among Berber and Sudanic peoples. The chapter begins with a discussion of relations between Abyssinia and Arabia at the dawn of the Islamic period. Later sections trace the development of Arab culture on the East African coast and in the region of northwest and West Africa, where Islam emerged the dominant religion.

The sixth century seems to mark the apogee of Abyssinian

Devout Muslims stream through Agadès in the Niger Republic during the fast month of Ramadan.

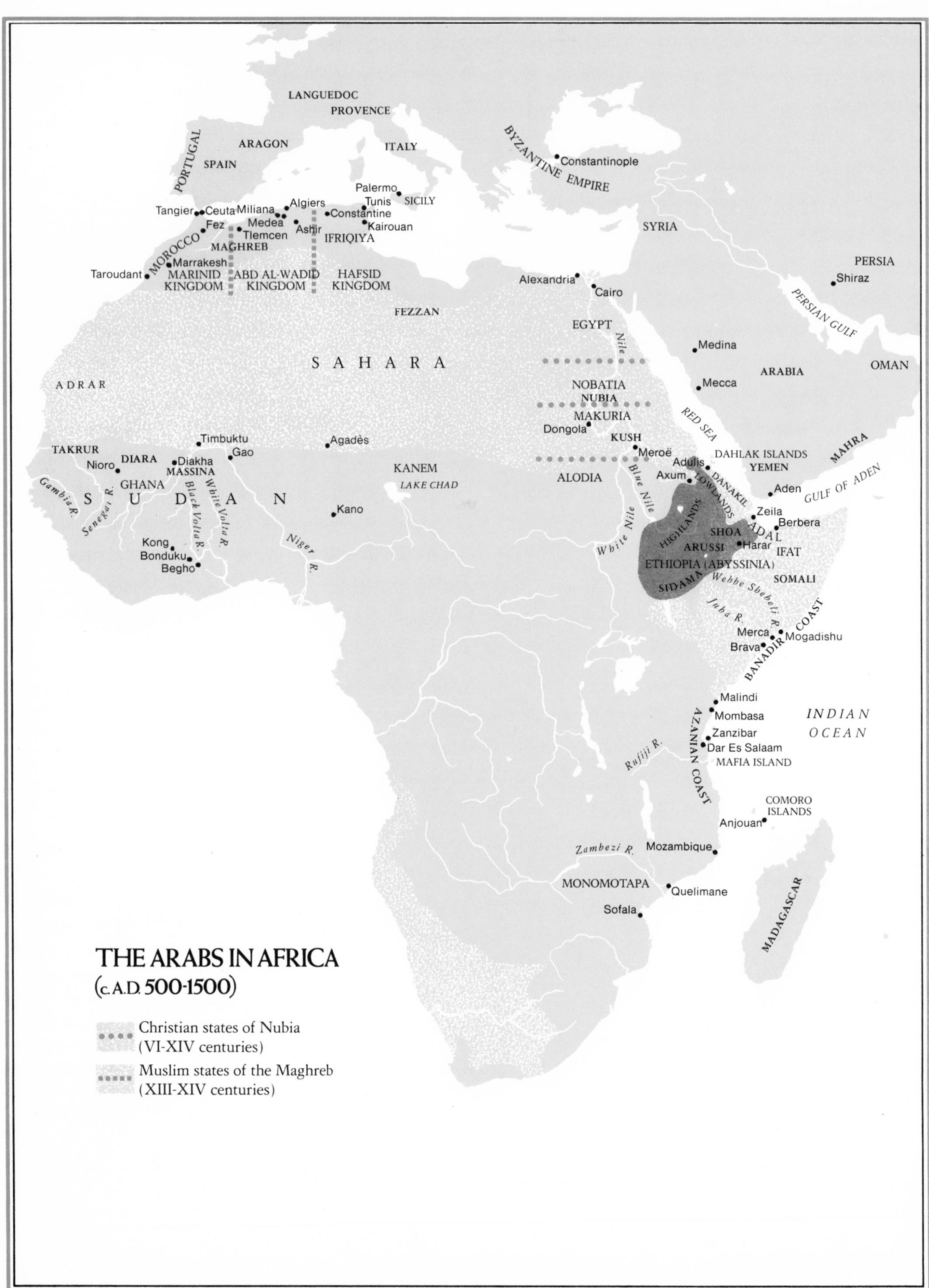

THE ARABS IN AFRICA
(c. A.D. 500-1500)
Christian states of Nubia (VI-XIV centuries)
Muslim states of the Maghreb (XIII-XIV centuries)
LANGUEDOC
PROVENCE
PORTUGAL
ARAGON
SPAIN
ITALY
BYZANTINE EMPIRE
Constantinople
Palermo
SICILY
Tangier
Ceuta
Miliana
Algiers
Tunis
Constantine
Kairouan
Fez
Medea
Ashir
Tlemcen
IFRIQIYA
MOROCCO
MAGHREB
Marrakesh
Taroudant
MARINID KINGDOM
ABD AL-WADID KINGDOM
HAFSID KINGDOM
SYRIA
PERSIA
Shiraz
PERSIAN GULF
Alexandria
Cairo
FEZZAN
EGYPT
Nile
Medina
SAHARA
ARABIA
OMAN
ADRAR
NOBATIA
NUBIA
Mecca
MAKURIA
RED SEA
Dongola
KUSH
MAHRA
TAKRUR
Timbuktu
Agadès
Meroë
DAHLAK ISLANDS
Adulis
YEMEN
DIARA
Diakha
Gao
KANEM
Nioro
MASSINA
ALODIA
Axum
DANAKIL
LOWLANDS
Aden
GULF OF ADEN
GHANA
LAKE CHAD
Gambia R.
Senegal R.
SUDAN
Black Volta R.
White Volta R.
Blue Nile
Kano
HIGHLANDS
Zeila
Berbera
SHOA
ADAL
White Nile
Niger R.
Kong
Bonduku
Begho
ARUSSI
Harar
IFAT
ETHIOPIA (ABYSSINIA)
SIDAMA
Webbe Shebeli R.
SOMALI
Juba R.
COAST
Merca
Mogadishu
Brava
BANADIR
Malindi
Mombasa
INDIAN OCEAN
AZANIAN COAST
Zanzibar
Dar Es Salaam
Rufiji R.
MAFIA ISLAND
COMORO ISLANDS
Anjouan
Zambezi R.
Mozambique
MONOMOTAPA
Quelimane
Sofala
MADAGASCAR

influence in the Red Sea region. In A.D. 531 the Abyssinians succeeded in establishing their authority in southern Arabia. Subsequently, however, Abyssinians who had ruled in south Arabia at the pleasure of the Christian Negus broke away from Abyssinian control and set up an independent regime in the Yemen. The leader of this new state was a Christian Abyssinian called Abraha, formerly the slave of a Byzantine merchant of Adulis. The creation of a government in south Arabia, which fell outside the sphere of Abyssinia, caused difficulties for the latter as well as Byzantium, which together were at that time attempting to counteract Persian influence in the Red Sea zone. It was also in A.D. 530–531 that Justinian entered into negotiations with the Abyssinians, proposing that they attempt to purchase silk from the Indians and resell it to the Romans, thus circumventing their common competitor, the Persians. This scheme proved untenable, however, because Persian merchants had succeeded in taking control of the key harbors frequented by Indian ships and, in addition, had occupied the adjoining areas. By purchasing the entire cargoes of these ships, the Persians were able to monopolize Indian trade in the Red Sea region.

Toward the end of the sixth century the Christian Yemenite leader Abraha is said to have launched an attack on Mecca, which was to result in the unification of the Arabs and the sealing off of their country against Abyssinian influence for all time. This was the beginning of the so-called War of the Elephant, romanticized in Arab history and mentioned in the following verses of the Holy Qur'an (Koran):

> In the name of Allah, the
> Beneficent, the Merciful.
> Hast thou not seen how thy
> Lord dealt with the possessors of the elephant?
> Did He not cause their war
> to end in confusion?
> And send against them birds
> in flocks?
> Casting at them decreed
> stones—
> So he rendered them like
> straw eaten up?

Legend recalls that Abraha wished to undermine the attraction of the Kaaba, the ancient pagan shrine in Mecca to which pilgrims flocked from all over Arabia. According to Muslim tradition, Abraha set out to destroy the Kaaba, accompanied by a large number of troops and one (some sources say more than one) elephant. But upon entering the vicinity of the Meccan territory, the elephant is said to have kneeled down and refused to advance farther toward the city of Mecca, though when his head was turned in any other direction his movement went unrestricted. Flights of birds are said to have dropped stones upon the invading troops, as mentioned in the Qur'an, who all died. A rationalizing explanation of this phenomenon held that the invading troops were in actuality smitten with smallpox. Abraha himself, it is claimed, was afflicted with the loathsome disease and repatriated to the Yemen, where he soon died.

Some authorities contend, however, that the legendary story of Abraha the Christian Yemenite is in reality a conflation of two records of south Arabian attacks on Mecca: that by Abraha and a much earlier one led by the Axumite king Afilas, whom numismatic evidence places at about A.D. 300. It was during this period that the kingdom of Axum exercised a brief hegemony over south Arabia, and it is thought that a military enterprise farther north was not an impossibility. According to these authorities, the word "Afilas," the Abyssinian, and *al-fil*, the "elephant" in Arabic, became confused as the two legends merged into one. A modern interpretation hazards that if Abraha had actually undertaken such an expedition, a more likely explanation of his aims is that the rapprochement between Abraha and his former Abyssinian superiors against Persian intrusions allowed Abraha to adopt a more aggressive policy toward Persia. According to this interpretation, the expedition was the first move in a projected attack on Persian dominions. In Islamic history the main relevance of the episode of the "Elephant" was that tradition ascribes the birth of the Prophet Muhammad to this period, known historically as the Year of the Elephant (about A.D. 570).

In the Muslim view, the Islamic Dispensation constitutes the last in a series of Covenants between Allah and His people. Muslims readily recognize that other peoples, notably Jews and Christians, have entered into Covenants with the Almighty. Indeed, the Islamic revelations continue the Judaic and Christian traditions insofar as Islam accepts the authenticity of previous prophets and messengers through whom Allah communicated His Will. But the Qur'an is seen as the ultimate communication of the Divine Will, and Muhammad is looked upon as the final prophet of Allah. The followers of Muhammad are called Muslims because by embracing the message that Allah revealed to Muhammad, as contained in the Qur'an, they thereby "submit" themselves to the Divine Will. Hence the words "Islam" and "Muslim," derived from

As the Islamic legend of the "Year of the Elephant" indicates, the elephant is regarded by Muslims as a creature of remarkable wisdom and is treated with due respect. A versatile beast, it is able to exist in a variety of climates and consequently has played a major part in the local and trading economy of many African peoples. Unlike the Indian elephant, it is rarely domesticated; rather it is hunted with great ritual for its meat, ivory, bristle, and hide. Even the ear has its use—as the skin of royal drums. This miniature is from The Description of Animals, *an Arab bestiary done before* 1258.

TRUSTEES OF THE BRITISH MUSEUM, MS. OR 2784

the same root, both stress the necessity of "submission" to what Allah commanded Muhammad to "recite" (the meaning of "Qur'an") to his people.

It was the genius of Muhammad that over a remarkably short period he was able to transform the basis of Arab society—to mold out of the anonymity of collective life a place for the individual. The ties of Islam and the community of faith were to supersede the bonds of kinship. The inauguration of the Islamic Dispensation was to herald a new relationship between men. "The white man was not to be above the black nor the black above the yellow," said the tradition, "all men were to be equal before their Maker," and equal before the Law. Among believers, superiority was to be marked only by priority in the faith or by stricter observance of its precepts.

The Islamic religion came to be premised upon five pillars. Believers were required to accept the Muslim faith, professed in the words, "there is no Deity but Allah, and Muhammad is the Prophet of Allah." Belief in the "oneness" of Allah remains a fundamental tenet in Islam. Second, Muslims were required to pray at five prescribed times of the day. A third duty obliged all believers to give alms to the needy, and a collection was taken up for this purpose at certain times of the year. Muslims were further under obligation to endure a thirty-day fast, called Ramadan, during which they could neither eat nor drink between sunrise and sunset. A fifth duty prescribed that all Muslims undertake the pilgrimage to Mecca and Medina, the cherished cities of Islam, at least once in their lifetime, provided they had the means.

When Muhammad died in A.D. 632, he bequeathed a legacy of unity within his religious community. Four successors, who continued his work but did not inherit his gift of prophecy, were elected by the community, though not without opposition. Muhammad had been accepted by his people both as prophet and political leader. The Meccan and Medinan peoples through their *shaykhs*, or leaders, entered into a compact with Muhammad and recognized his authority. It became the task of his successors to maintain those treaties, and often they found it necessary to resort to force in order to secure the unity for which he had strived. Efforts to subdue opposition to the new leaders of Islam generated a movement that reached beyond Arabia and culminated in the expansion of Islam in many lands. The ancient provinces of the Roman empire, including Egypt and Syria, as well as the once-powerful Persian dominions, all fell within the sphere of the rising Crescent.

But the expansion of Islam can be attributed to another factor. Islam spread from the Arabian Peninsula by virtue of the jihad Muhammad's followers declared upon his enemies. Despite its popular conception, the jihad, another fundamental duty in Islam, involves much more than "holy war" waged to expand Islamic frontiers or to defend the faith against foreign intrusion. For the believer, jihad is a form of effort—"a struggle in the path of Allah"—that can be undertaken by peaceful or military means. In short, the diffusion of Islam was viewed by Muslims as a serious effort to be undertaken for Allah's sake, as indeed the Crusades were launched by Christians "for the glory of God" and the protection of His Church.

If the Persian intrusion had served to disrupt the sea and trade routes in the Red Sea to the detriment of Abyssinian interests, the expansion of Islam, which soon enveloped the whole of Arabia, had an equally damaging effect of severing Abyssinia, at least temporarily, from its spiritual source, the patriarchate of Alexandria. This was indeed the beginning of many centuries of isolation for Abyssinia, whose peoples retired within their impregnable mountain fastnesses. Moreover, the penetration of Islam led to the Islamization of the Abyssinian lowlands, as Muslim powers were able to establish sovereignty over the African Red Sea littoral. As the pace of conversion accelerated in Abyssinia, Islam reached as far as eastern Shoa and the Sidama country.

For Abyssinia, the period from the tenth century to the twelfth was a time of great internal weakness, as well as one that witnessed the continued penetration of Islam over a wide area. Early in the tenth century a people called Falasha, Hamitic-speaking peoples who practiced the Jewish religion, were able to dislodge the "Solomonian" dynasty of Abyssinia (so called because of the attempts of Abyssinian rulers to link themselves genealogically with King Solomon of biblical times) and establish their own power. The result of this change of dynasty was that the preservers of "Solomonian" claims took refuge in Shoa to the south, and Axum (the ancient capital) ceased to be the political capital, though it remained the principal religious center and the place where subsequent kings of the "Solomonian" line were installed.

Muslim traders and men of religion were instrumental in the spread of Islam throughout parts of Abyssinia and the adjoining regions. Islam took root in the Dahlak archipelago, the Danakil and Somali coasts, among the Bedja (Beja) in the north, in the Ifat imamate of eastern Shoa, at Harar in the east, and near Lake Zway in the west. The religion also made converts of the Sidama peoples in the south, whose ruling classes, through trading relations, are said to have adopted the new persuasion.

Moreover, the slave trade proved a powerful stimulant to the Islamization of the coastal plains. This was because trading in slaves, largely controlled by Muslim merchants, brought about a link with the Arab world and resulted in the creation and sustenance of such Muslim-controlled centers as Zeila and Mogadishu, which became linked with the Danakil and Somali hinterlands. It is further believed that slave raiding greatly aided in the diffusion of Islam among pagan peoples of the East African coast, as conversion would have been an expedient means of avoiding the difficulties of a slave existence. Islamic law forbade the enslavement of free Muslims, but tolerated the continued enslavement of peoples who converted after their capture. Finally, it is known that the slave-raiding activity itself generated a process of state-building, which culminated in the establishment of Muslim power in Harar, Arussi, and the lake district in the southwest. Powerful slave merchants used their slaves as a source of influence and military power, and ultimately, as a basis for the establishment of independent states.

The beginnings of the Muslim state in eastern Shoa date most probably from the late ninth century A.D. In 1285, however, the Shoan imamate was overthrown and absorbed into that of Ifat, the predominant Muslim state of Abyssinia and the *foyer* of Muslim expansion throughout that region. From the fourteenth until the sixteenth century a war of attrition ensued between the highlands of Christian Abyssinia and the swiftly developing Muslim imamates or communities that became entrenched all along the eastern and southern fringes of the Abyssinian plateau. It was during this period that the walled city of Harar to the south of Zeila became a Muslim city-state and a powerful center of Islamic commerce and cultural propagation.

Shortly after the rise of Islam, Muslim Arabs and Persians created a series of coastal settlements in the region that came to be called Somalia. In these towns Arab and Persian merchants settled as local aristocracies, initiated a process of Islamization, and by intermarrying with local women formed a mixed Somali-Arab culture—the Somali counterpart to the more extensive Swahili society of the East African coast to the south. The Somali traditionally set much store on alleged descent from noble Arab lineages and, indeed, from the family of Muhammad himself. Such claims commemorate the prolonged period of contact between the Somali and the civilization of the Arabian coasts—a contact that has brought Islam and many other elements of Muslim-Arab culture to Somaliland. Such cultural borrowings betray themselves in the Somali language, which contains numerous Arabic loan-words, and again are manifest in the widespread use of Arabic as a second language. Conversely, however, the Somali language retains its unique character as a separate and vigorous tongue possessing an unusually rich oral literature. Poetry among the Somali is not merely the private medium of the author, but frequently the collective tongue of a clan or other group.

The two warriors at left, depicted somewhat fancifully by a nineteenth-century Italian, belonged to Ethiopia's ancient professional army. The empire regularly kept one of the largest forces on the continent; it was estimated by one observer to number more than 200,000 men. But Ethiopia's geographical location, which placed the militant faith of Christianity in uneasy proximity to that of Islam, and the constant challenge of the pastoral Galla peoples of the south, permitted few peaceful years.

FERRARIO, *Costume Antico e Moderno*, 1815

Typical of those centers of Arab influence in northern Somalia were the seaports of Zeila and Berbera. The walled city of Zeila, after the decline of Axum in the sixth century A.D., became the most important port for the coffee trade of the Abyssinian highlands; it was described by Ibn al-Wardi (about 1340) as the "emporium of the Habash," or Abyssinians. It emerged also as one of the largest ports for the slave trade with Arabia. In ancient times goat skins were the chief export that the Yemen market absorbed in great quantities during the course of a rapid development of the leather industry under Persian rule. In the fourteenth century Zeila was visited by the celebrated Arab traveler Ibn Battuta, who died in 1377. While conceding its importance as a commercial center, Ibn Battuta described the town as "vile and evil-smelling." The infamous stench of Zeila rose from the great quantity of fish that was brought there, as well as from the blood of camels customarily slain in the streets. In the fifteenth century Zeila was occupied by the Turks; but in 1516 they gave way to the Portuguese, who burned the town.

Berbera, southeast of Zeila and opposite Aden, was identified by the *Periplus*, Ptolemy, and Cosmas Indicopleustes as the Land of Frankincense—a designation more properly ascribed to the Arabian region of Mahra, the most productive source of aromatic plants. Situated in the state of Ifat, Berbera formed part of the Muslim province of Adal, whose amir, or commander, was apparently strong enough to rule Ifat in the fifteenth century. Founded in the ninth or tenth century, Adal frequently served as a refuge for Muslims farther to the south, who sought to flee Abyssinian jurisdiction. Its rulers belonged to the ruling house of Zeila, and the history of the two areas was often linked. Adal reached its zenith in the fourteenth century, but declined precipitously during the Muslim struggles to conquer Abyssinia in the sixteenth century.

In later times, when the Somali began to expand, their relationship with the Arab cities of the Banadir coast—Mogadishu, Merca, and Brava—developed from that of a trading partnership to one of political domination. The Arab cities of the Banadir were commercial towns largely dependent for their prosperity upon the trade between Abyssinia, Arabia, and the markets of the East.

The foundation of Mogadishu (Maqdishu) as an Arabian colony is ascribed to the tenth century A.D. Evidence from certain inscriptions points as well to a Persian settlement, which took place at about the same time. João de Barros, writing in the sixteenth century, noted that the first people to export gold from Sofala were the merchants of Mogadishu. By the end of the twelfth century, however, the gold trade had passed into the hands of Kilwa traders. The original commercial treaty was made between Mogadishu and Sofala, but later this most favored treatment was acquired by Kilwa, and with it the gold trade of Sofala. The merchants of this Indian Ocean entrepôt were constrained at times to band together against the Somali threat, which seemed to be constant, and against other invaders who came by sea. They organized themselves into a confederation of thirty-nine clans. One of these clans, the *Muqri*, acquired a religious supremacy over the others who agreed that the *qadi*, or jurisconsul, in religious matters should be appointed from within its ranks. In the sixteenth century Mogadishu declined in commercial prosperity due to continued Somali intrusions. Archeological remains uncovered at Mogadishu reveal it as larger than and culturally superior to Kilwa, though the latter was more important as a commercial center.

Brava (Barawa), directly south of Mogadishu, was known to the Arab geographer Yaqut al-Rumi, who died in A.D. 1229, as an amber-exporting area. Tradition holds that it was founded shortly after Mogadishu, and the commercial fate of the two cities was always closely linked. The Bantu language "Chimbelazi" survives in the town of Brava and is probably derived from the common speech of the coastal cities in Somalia.

In the earlier period of its history African traders frequented the coast with slaves and ivory, which were conveniently stored in centers near the mouth of a river or on some offshore island until they could be gathered by dhows, which came south before the beginning of the monsoon season. Gold and ivory were brought from the region of what is today Rhodesia and exchanged at Sofala for Indian beads. The trade route down to Sofala and by sea along the coast of Kilwa was of crucial importance to the economic prosperity of East Africa. Other commodities that drew merchants to the coast were leopard skins, palm oil, copper and iron, tortoise shells, rhinoceros horns, and the more prosaic hides. In addition to beads, foreign traders used spears, knives, axes, and porcelain as items of exchange.

By the tenth century a striking change in the commercial character of the coast had taken place. No longer were the participants traders from the Yemen, as the East African trade was now separated from that of the Aden Gulf coast. In place of the Yemenites we find merchants from the Persian Gulf and Oman. And by this period the trade had extended itself as far as the Comoro Islands, the lands of the Zambezi, and the great island of Madagascar. The trade in ivory was probably the most important at this period. According to al-Masudi, who died in A.D. 956, ivory was seldom employed for indigenous use owing to its value as an export item. Although the slave trade is not specifically mentioned by this author, it doubtless continued to be of considerable importance.

Kilwa served as an entrepôt for gold traded from Mutapa (Mwenemutapa or Monomotapa) through Sofala. Its domains are said to have included the settlements that developed along the coast as far as Kilwa Kivinje, and possibly to the Rufiji River, the island of Mafia, and in the south, to the region of Mozambique and Sofala. It was probably at its apogee in the twelfth and thirteenth centuries, but regained some distinction after the rebuilding of the Great Mosque, the finest surviving monument in East Africa. It struck a copper coinage of a single denomination from the commencement of the thirteenth century, but it is conjectured that this might have been more a matter of prestige than of commercial convenience.

Vasco da Gama, who visited Kilwa (Quiloa) on his second voyage, left a detailed description of the town and its inhabitants (about 1502). He described the city as large, and being of "good buildings of stone and mortar with terraces, and . . . much wood works. The city comes down to the shore, and is entirely surrounded by a wall and towers, within which there may be 12,000 inhabitants. The country all round is very luxuriant with many trees and gardens of all sorts of vegetables, citrons, lemons, and the best sweet oranges that were ever seen, sugarcanes, figs, pomegranates, and a great abundance of flocks, especially sheep, which have fat in the tail, which is almost the size of the body, and very savory. The streets of the city are very narrow as the houses are very high, of three and four stories, and one can run along the tops of them upon the terraces, as the houses are very close together: and in the port there were many ships."

There is some evidence of an Umayyad-Abbasid tradition of architecture at Kilwa. According to the *Kitab al-Zanuj* (the Chronicle of the Zanj) and other late sources, all of which are difficult to assess as to their reliability, immigrants came to East Africa from Arab lands during the chronological period spanned by the Umayyad and Abbasid dynasties (A.D. 661–1258). One is tempted to associate this architectural tradition with these early immigrants, although there is an alternative hypothesis. The Kilwa Chronicle speaks of immigrants arriving from the Persian city of Shiraz and settling at Kilwa in about the tenth century A.D. Some authorities have suggested that these immigrants might have been responsible for the distinctly Umayyad-Abbasid type architecture at Kilwa. Recent archeological

In East Africa slavery remained legal until this century, as this early photograph of a Dar es Salaam master and his obeisant servant records. Swahili society recognized a hierarchy even within the slave class, based on length of ancestral service, type of employment, reputation, and the owner's status.
LIBRARY OF CONGRESS © KEYSTONE VIEW COMPANY

findings in the region, however, point toward a much later immigration of the Shiraz newcomers. These investigations indicate that the Shiraz settlement took place some two hundred years later than the date in the latter part of the tenth century, which has hitherto been accepted. The arrival of the Shirazi, as they are called, is related to the appearance of coins of Ali b. al-Hasan, who is identified with the first ruler of the so-called Shirazi dynasty at Kilwa (about A.D. 1200). From this change of dynasty is interpreted a marked cultural break in the latter part of the thirteenth or early fourteenth century. Subsequent to this event came a fresh settlement of immigrants and the seizure of Sofala and its gold trade. Finally, it is contended that the Shiraz settlement consisted not of a migration of people from the Persian Gulf directly to Kilwa and other places, as was formerly held, but rather a movement of settlers from the Banadir coast.

The legendary Sofala, situated in the southern region of Mozambique, was often called Sofala or Zanj or Golden Sofala in order to differentiate it from another port by the same name near Bombay in India. This medieval emporium was known to al-Masudi as a rich gold-producing area possessing an agreeable climate and a fertile land. It was also al-Masudi who pointed to Sofala as the place wherein the Zanj built their capital—important evidence that may lend support to the contention that the Bantu (if we read "Bantu" for "Zanj") had already inhabited the coast of Africa south of the equator by the tenth century. (A full discussion of the Bantu migrations appears in Chapter Seven.) The Bantu are known to have arrived from the interior, and at their farthest northern extension, they are said to have reached the Webbe Shebeli river, which flows through Somalia, curving southward parallel to Mogadishu and Brava.

Subsequently, however (probably about the eleventh century), these Bantu speakers were driven south by the Somali to the valley of the Juba River in southern Somaliland. Here they remained for another five hundred years. The Bantu, however, cannot be considered a significant factor in molding the culture of the East African coast during the period under discussion. Their impact was farther south and in the interior, though they are known to have forged important trading links with the Arab settlements on the coast. Export to Kilwa from various Bantu-dominated areas can be presumed for an earlier period, while more regular trade developed after the establishment of Sofala by the Arabs in the tenth century.

According to al-Idrisi, who died in A.D. 1166, Sofala was famous for its iron mines as well as its gold. Yaqut perpetuated Sofala's reputation as a land of gold; he mentions that commercial transactions were effected by means of "dumb barter" (that is, the participants made no actual contact with each other during the trade). During the time of the Arab geographer Ibn al-Wardi (about 1340), Sofala gained some distinction for its iron deposits. Iron from Sofala mines was considered purer and more malleable than that found in India. The Indians smelted the iron and made steel, from which tools and weapons with fine cutting edges were fashioned. De Barros spoke of a "tower" at Sofala over twelve stories high, as well as similar erections of stone, all of which the Zanj called *zimbabwe* (literally "stone house") in referring to the official residences of their leaders. Modern archeology has revealed the Zanj as a hunting and fishing people of the Bushman type—at least this designation would apply to those who inhabited the Azanian coast. The implements of these autochthonous inhabitants of the coast have been found in many places, and it is from their discovery that archeologists have been able to reconstruct something of their cultural characteristics.

In the sixteenth century the commerce of Sofala shifted to Quelimane in the region north of the Zambezi, and by the seventeenth century Sofala's exports were insignificant. When the Portuguese upset the balance of power and the pattern of trade in the Indian Ocean, Arab trading settlements such as Sofala were at their zenith. The results of the Portuguese intrusion were manifest in the interruption of the gold trade between the coast and India. The Portuguese sought to redirect this trade to their own advantage, and in the course of doing so, wrought much destruction upon the wealth of Arab trading cities, which had so long monopolized commercial transactions on the coast.

Islam and Arab civilization also took root in many parts of North and West Africa. In East Africa Islam failed to develop significantly in the hinterland, although Arabs were able to evolve a prosperous series of settlements along the coast. In contrast, Islam in North and West Africa was accepted by urban dwellers along the coast and in the interior, as well as by nomadic groups who inhabited the vast Saharan regions. The Islamization of North and West Africa, however, was a very long and uneven process. Although Islam made its first appearance in this area in the seventh century (as early as A.D. 639), the initial Arab venture was more a reconnaissance mission than a settling migration. The first Arabs in North Africa came for the purpose of establishing a foothold. The military contingents used for this purpose were not extensive, and the soldiers were compelled to leave their families behind and bring only that which was necessary to accomplish a limited military objective. Hence it is highly unlikely that substantial conversions to Islam could have taken place much before the beginning of the eighth century on the coast and the tenth century in the interior. The diffusion of Islam before the eighth century would have taken a veritable army of specialized religious teachers to preach Islamic doctrines appropriately. Moreover, these teachers would have had to speak Berber, the language of the dominant group on the coast, and further, would have had to establish the necessary rapport among the people conducive to the spread of a new religion.

In North Africa as in East Africa, Muslim proselytizers achieved the more rapid success along the coast. Urban centers were created or revived by the Arab occupiers, and because of a larger Arab presence, the Islam that developed in metropolitan areas came to differ quite markedly from that which took root in the hinterland. Qairawan (Kairouan), the first Muslim military outpost (established in what is today Tunisia) also became an important religious center, with an important mosque and several places of religious instruction. Other cities, however, were slow to develop, a factor that seriously restricted the intensity of Islamic diffusion. Indeed, until the creation of Fez (A.D. 808), one can hardly speak of cities in Morocco, except for Tangier and Ceuta, which were quite atypical. Between Tlemcen and Constantine was a barren area almost totally devoid of settlement. It would not be until the second half of the tenth century that such cities as Ashir, Medea, Miliana, and Algiers would make their appearance or reappearance. Only Ifriqiya (Tunis) could demonstrate a relatively substantial urban density.

Qairawan, the capital of Ifriqiya, was built by Uqba b. Nafi, the Arab commander who led the initial reconnaissance expedition to North Africa. The city was established in A.D. 670 as a base of operations, supply depot, and a means of keeping in awe the numerous Berber groups that inhabited adjacent areas. "I intend," the historian al-Nuwairi makes him say, "to build a town which can serve as a depot of arms [Qairawan] for Islam to the end of time." The site of the new town, two days' journey from the shore, had been chosen to put the Muslims beyond the danger of an attack from the Byzantines, who still held the towns on the coast. The earlier part of its existence, to the mid-eleventh century, is commonly held to have been one of great economic prosperity, especially remarkable for its agriculture. A political, economic, and cultural metropolis, Qairawan seems also to have been a major commercial and industrial center.

Until very recently it was thought that the prosperity of Qairawan declined sharply as a result of the eleventh-century invasion of Ifriqiya by the nomadic Hilali Arabs. Unlike the first Arab intrusion in this region, described above as a reconnaissance mission, the Hilalian invasion was a veritable settling migration involving nomadic Arabs as well as their women and children. It differed further from the initial mission in that the Hilalians settled in the interior among the Berber peoples, who carried on a similar nomadic existence. The Hilalian appearance in this region was likened to a swarm of locusts swooping down upon the unattended agricultural plains of Ifriqiya and wreaking havoc and destruction in its wake. The Hilalians are further made responsible for a cessation of gold trade from the Sudanic lands of the deep interior to Qairawan on the coast.

Such traditional interpretations, which make the Hilalians the cause of Ifriqiya's woes, have fallen into disfavor. Recent research reasons that the effect of the Hilalis was perhaps more to precipitate a development already well advanced, to wit, the gradual weening away of Qairawan's satellite regions from the metropole. A final and crucial distinction that must be made between the initial reconnaissance mission and the Hilalian settling migration is that the latter was of great quantitative significance. Although figures advanced to reckon Hilalis in the millions are doubtlessly a gross exaggeration, one may conservatively hazard that their numbers must have been in the thousands, whereas the initial wave of the Arab quest numbered no more than a few hundred fighting men. In short, for the first time Arabs arrived in sufficient numbers to make a lasting impact on the culture and civilization of the North African hinterland and beyond.

In the thirteenth and fourteenth centuries Arab nomads arrived in the Maghreb in ever-increasing numbers, settling not so much along the coast, but rather in the interior, among Berber nomads. These series of nomadic Arab settlements culminated in the Arabization and Islamization of Berber peoples throughout the region. Arabic became a principal language among these people, and through its use they began to acquire the basic rudiments of Arab culture. At least initially, Islamic doctrine was poorly understood by those Berbers, as indeed it had been superficially held by their nomadic Arab counterparts. What is important to remember, however, is that despite its unlearned character, rural Islam developed within a decidedly Muslim framework and attained a certain vigor that was to give rise to the two great Islamic revivalist movements of the period under discussion. The Almoravid and Almohad revolutions, as they were called, were generated from the rural hinterland by militant Berber groups seeking to diffuse Islam among unconverted pagan peoples. The Almoravid movement gained numerous adherents among the Sanhaja Berbers of the western Sahara. It began as a movement to implement stricter Islamic practices among various Berber groups that later formed the Sanhaja confederation. Its leader, Abd Allah b. Yasin, attempted to impose a rigid adherence to Islamic law upon those Berbers who were constrained to follow closely classical legal texts that interpreted Qur'anic dictates for the believers. The Almohad movement rose partly as a reaction to such rigidity, and its leader, Ibn Tumart, a Berber of the Masmuda clan, sought to allow a more direct access to Qur'anic teachings without total reliance upon classical Muslim exegetists. The Almoravid movement, begun in the middle of the eleventh century, was carried to Morocco, as far as Algiers, and then to Spain, where the ideology of the Muslim West and a part of Christian Europe merged in a new synthesis. Similarly, however, the Almohad efforts at Muslim revival were not restricted to the Maghreb, as the followers of the Ibn Tumart's teachings subjected much of Spain after A.D. 1145.

In the thirteenth century, after its temporary unification under the Almohads, the Maghreb was divided into three independent states: the Marinid regime prevailing at Fez, the Abd al-Wadid state with its capital at Tilimsan (Tlemcen), and the Hafsid state of Ifriqiya. The last was to become the most formidable of these states, ultimately bringing the others under its control. Hafsid power spread as far as Morocco and Spain, which fell under a token submission. The Hafsids entered into treaties with Provence, Languedoc, and the Italian republics, and from 1239 onward relations with Sicily became more intimate. At about the same time bonds of friendship were forged between the Hafsids and Aragon, and Christian merchant communities (notably Spanish, Provençal, and Italian) settled in the ports of Ifriqiya, each with its own consul. Moreover, during this period many Spanish Muslims, craftsmen, and men of letters emigrated to Hafsid domains, and before long constituted a powerful Andalusian political force. Hafsid rulers continued relations with Christian nations, especially with the kingdom of Aragon, which came to the assistance of the Hafsids during several internal crises.

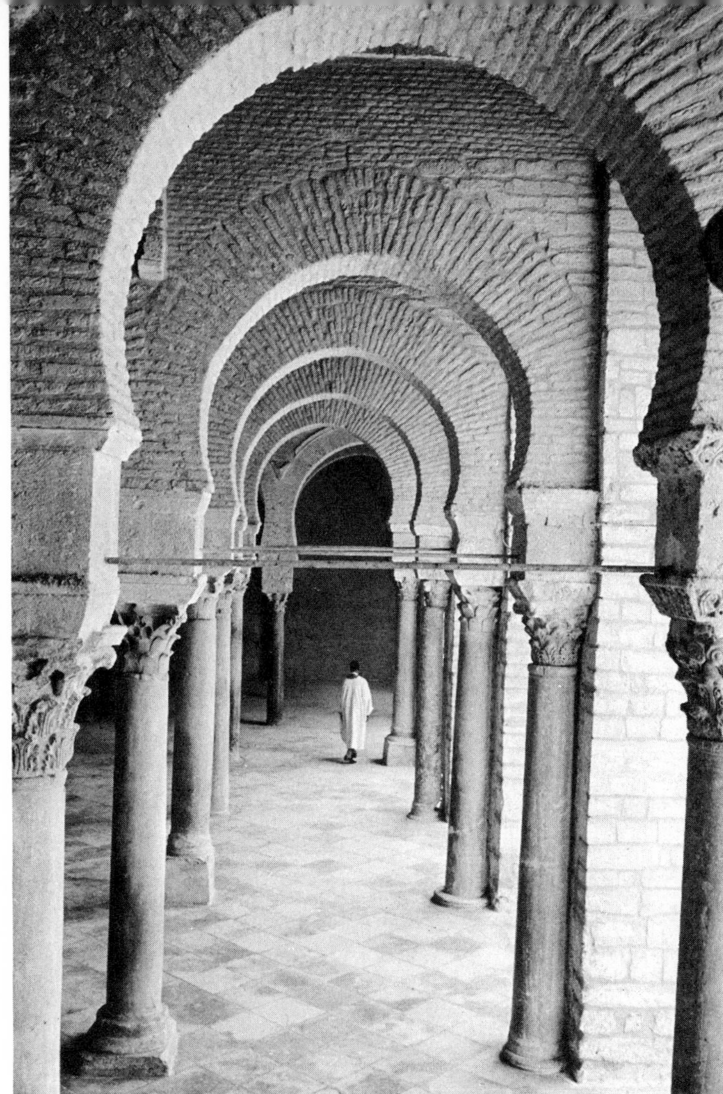

The Great Mosque at Kairouan, Tunisia, is judged by Muslims to be so sublime in conception that the city itself is ranked with Mecca, Medina, and Jerusalem as one of the four gates of Paradise. Work on the mosque was begun around A.D. 836; *it stands on the site of one constructed by Uqba ibn Nafi, who founded Kairouan in* A.D. 670 *as a base of operation against the Berbers. Shown at left is one of the galleries.*
RAPHO-GUILLUMETTE—GEORG GERSTER

Tunis under the Hafsids developed into a thriving commercial state. Many markets were established under the direction of merchants trading in cereals (during times of good harvest), dates, wax, olive oil, salted fish, fabrics, tapestries, coral, armaments, items of leather, and above all, wool. In exchange for these export commodities, the Hafsids imported cereals, wild fowl, items made from wood, armaments, jewels, ironmongery, cotton, silk, flax, hemp, and various metals, perfumes, medicinal plants, and spices.

It was during the period from the thirteenth to the sixteenth centuries that Islamic culture attained maturity in North Africa. By the middle of the thirteenth century the Hafsids had already adopted the madrasa, a kind of religious boarding school, as a center of learning. The institution of the madrasa in Islam grew out of the older form of education associated with the mosque, which was at once a place of worship and religious study. In Muslim education students were encouraged to commit the Qur'an to memory and to master the corpus of Hadith, consisting of all the actions and sayings of Muhammad, which formed the basis of proper conduct for the believer. Within one hundred and fifty years, some ten major madrasas were founded, one of the more famous being al-Zaytuna, which is still extant in Tunis. From the beginning the madrasa was a state institution, enjoying the patronage of the sovereign. One of its functions was to defend Islamic orthodoxy against heretical doctrines, though it emerged also as a principal center for the exposition of legal texts.

Sufism, or Islamic mysticism, developed rapidly in the Maghreb from the thirteenth century onward. Originally, it was the expression of the devotional feeling of the townsmen—grinding a channel of its own that burst the bonds of orthodox discipline and found a new freedom in the ranges of mysticism. As early as the eleventh century Sufism enlisted in its service a large proportion of the vital spiritual energies of the Muslim community and created within Islam a fount of self-renewal, which maintained its spiritual vigor throughout the later period of political and economic decay.

The movement in its early stages was personal and individual, but late in the eleventh century it became organized, and confronted the opposition of the official Islamic clerisy and sometimes the leading political figures of the state. Simultaneously, however, the movement swelled beyond the ranks of the faithful and appealed to the popular imagination, supplying a spiritual satisfaction and vitality that militated against the rigidity of the law and its teachings—in short, it emphasized the inwardly felt spiritual needs of the believer, whereas the law, made somewhat sterile by the strict interpretations that prevailed, stressed the external or formal requirements of Islam. The earliest religious confraternity to rise from North African soil was the Shadhiliyya, based on the teachings of Nur al-Din al-Shadhili (1196–1258). Tunis provided a rich recruiting ground for the new order, but al-Shadhili later encountered hostility from political authorities and was forced to flee to Alexandria, where he was instantly successful in his teaching.

In the Maghreb, Islam had been, down to the end of the fourteenth century, a religion of towns and cities. Late in this century and early in the following this situation radically changed. Islam became primarily a rural phenomenon. The *zawiya*, the Sufi religious center, replaced the mosque and the madrasa as the chief center of learning, and the Sufis displaced the traditional clerisy as guardians and expounders of the faith.

The Islamization of the Sanhaja Berbers, which culminated in the Almoravid movement, meant the ultimate defeat and displacement of the Sarakholle (a Mande-speaking group also known as the Soninke) living in the Adrar in the early part of the ninth century. According to tradition, the desert (before the outbreak of the Almoravid movement) was inhabited by black peoples who led a sedentary existence. It was at the end of the eighth century that the Lamtuna, part of the large Sanhaja confederation, adopted the militant creed of the Almoravids, which espoused a purified version of Islam—to be spread by force if necessary. The result of their efforts was the partial Islamization of the Sarakholle, some of whom went on to take their place among the most avid agents of Islamic diffusion. Sarakholle proselytizing activity took place in Diara (a region of Nioro in the Sahel) and in some of their colonies in Massina (in Mali), notably Dia (Diakha). The cultivation of Islam by the Sarakholle also occurred in Galam (near Bakel in Senegal) and in Takrur (Futa Toro, Senegal)—an area which itself became synonymous in the eyes of Arab geographers and historians with West African Islam. Countless Takruris (or Sudanis, to cite another common term) made pilgrimage to the Muslim holy cities of Mecca and Medina.

Similarly, the Mande-Diula traders (who, according to their traditions, also emanated from Massina and merged

RAPHO-GUILLUMETTE—MARC AND EVELYNE BERNHEIM

with the Sarakholle of Dia) were greatly responsible for the diffusion of Islam around the Niger Bend as far as the limits of the dense forest region at Begho on the Black Volta. It was at this time, near the end of the fourteenth century and the beginning of the fifteenth, that the Muslim cities of Bonduku and Kong in present-day Ivory Coast were founded.

What was the impact of Islam on the western Sudan at this early date? Islam has been made responsible for far more than its implantation in this region would seem to warrant. Many authors have held that Islamic conversion brought with it a "higher culture" and the development of a unique trading system that arose along the trans-Saharan caravan trails. Such vigorous assertions must be regarded with considerable caution. The role of Islam in the development of the so-called Sudanese empires is still a subject of heated debate. (See also Chapter Five.) There is good reason to believe that Islam acted more as a stimulant than a catalyst in the evolution of these states. It is undeniable that the early Sudanese states of Ghana, Mali, and Songhai had already achieved a high degree of development before the adoption of Islam by their ruling aristocracies. What seems also irrefutable, however, is that Islam fertilized anew

PHOTO RESEARCHERS

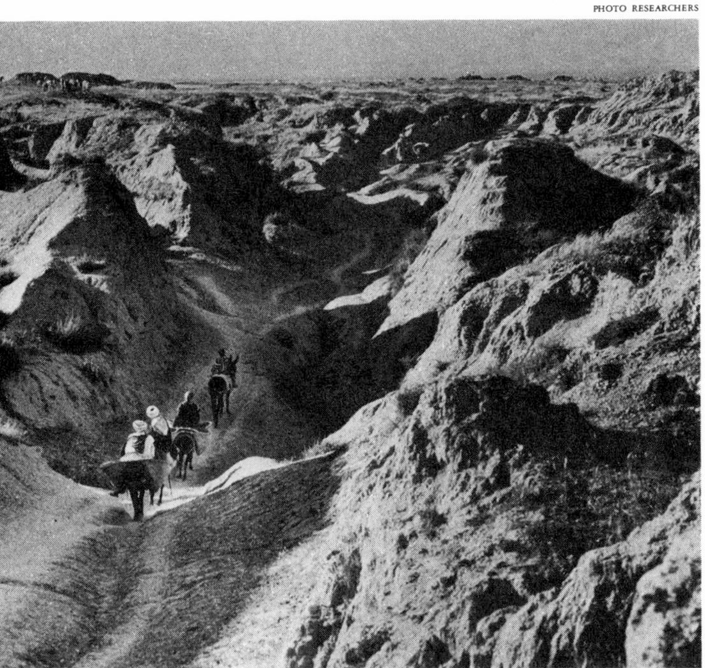

Out of Mauritania's inhospitable Adrar massif (opposite) came the Almoravid zealots, whose jihad was to carry them south of the Sahara and north to the Atlas range. The traders above ride toward one of the towns they took, the Berber oasis of Taroudant.

the more ancient culture of the Sudan and stimulated new growth and new forms of government and institutions. But what is often lost sight of is that the old institutions formed the basis of these developments; that they were rarely completely abolished or overthrown; and that when change did take place, it was more in the guise of syncretistic developments, which owed their origin to the old as well as the new.

There is little basis, for example, for crediting Islam with the creation of a commercial network in the western Sudan. When Muslim merchants first entered the Sudan, they encountered a well-arranged system of commerce established everywhere, and conducted along roads well suited to their purpose. This is not to deprive the Muslims of specific innovations that brought about change within the network—it is simply to emphasize that such creations took place within an ancient framework.

The implantation of Islam among the common people was slow to take effect. To understand the reasons for this slow, albeit steady, development, it is necessary to say something of the nature of African society. To early authorities such as Maurice Delafosse and Jules Brévié, Islam had appeared in Black Africa as a religion of travelers and Berber nomads, whereas the indigenous population (largely composed of sedentary cultivators) remained animist or "naturalist." "Naturalism" was a direct outgrowth of the communal needs and temperament of animist hunters and cultivators, whereas Islam corresponded more closely to the requirements of wandering nomads. The Arab, observed Brévié, condemned to travel eternally in solitude at the head of his flock, would not take easily to a *religion du foyer*—a faith that would attach him to the tomb of his ancestors. The nomad's conception of the deity was one of a "unique, omnipresent God, in whom the believer is immersed at every hour, and in every place, who will not abandon the believer during the course of his errancy, who may be invoked at each hour of the five daily prayers without recourse to priests, nor need of temples, and whose eyes are forever watchful over him." Hence, when the nomad perished in the wilderness, his comrades commended his spirit to Allah and his body to the desert, and departed. The religious life of the "naturalist," however, was seen as a successive link in a sequence of transformations: the "naturalist" was not his own master, he was but an element of the clan. While living, he dwelled beside his ancestors (interred at his bedside) and communed with them constantly for his very sustenance. At death, he entered the familial burial ground, where he awaited the moment of incarnation. As a consequence, neither peasants who pained over the soil nor artisans wedded to ancient methods of exploiting iron—to whom the land was the source of all their requirements—could conceive of a religion in which the earth, the rain, the rivers, and the stones were not the focal point of veneration.

In contrast to this rural majority was a minority of individuals who did not live off the land, either because they had left tillage to inferiors or because they had taken to a commercial existence of an itinerant nature. These town dwellers had lost contact with the land, and they had gained in the interim an important intangible: leisure. And it was precisely this sector among the African populace that emerged the most susceptible to Islamic conversion. Islam seemed to satisfy their pietist sentiments derived from preoccupation with an agrarian cult; it responded to their philistine instincts to differentiate themselves from their rural counterparts; it flattered their urge to instruct themselves and to occupy their leisure with theological and canonical discussions, the reading of sacred texts and famous secular works. They were to constitute the Islamic elite in Black Africa, and there would fall to them the task of convincing their ethnic counterparts of the superiority of this new dispensation.

IN THE NAME OF ALLAH

Allah's messenger to the Prophet Muhammad

N.Y. PUBLIC LIBRARY, SPENCER COLLECTION

GOD'S MESSENGER

Muhammad, Islam's holy prophet, was born at Mecca in A.D. 570. *The first biography of this inspired leader, whose new faith and teachings had a vital impact on Africa as well as on Arabia, was written by Ibn Ishaq, who died at Baghdad about* A.D. 767. *Although the original is lost, the story is preserved in a ninth-century version by Ibn Hisham. This excerpt, from the* Life of Muhammad, *describes the beginning of Muhammad's mission—his call from Allah.*

When Muhammad the apostle of God reached the age of forty God sent him in compassion to mankind, "as an evangelist to all men." . . . God said to Muhammad, "When God made a covenant with the prophets [He said] this is the scripture and wisdom which I have given you, afterwards an apostle will come confirming what you know that you may believe in him and help him." . . .

'Abdu' l-Malik b. 'Ubaydullah b. Abu Sufyan b. al-'Ala' b. Jariya the Thaqafite who had a retentive memory related to me [the author, Ibn Ishaq] from a certain scholar that the apostle at the time when Allah willed to bestow His grace upon him and endow him with prophethood would go forth for his affair and journey far afield until he reached the glens of Mecca and the beds of its valleys where no house was in sight; and not a stone or tree that he passed by but would say, "Peace unto thee, O apostle of Allah." And the apostle would turn to his right and left and look behind him and he would see naught but trees and stones. Thus he stayed seeing and hearing so long as it pleased Allah that he should stay. Then Gabriel came to him with the gift of God's grace whilst he was on Hira' [a hill outside Mecca] in the month of Ramadan. . . . The apostle would pray in seclusion on Hira' every year for a month to practice *tahannuth* as was the custom of Quraysh [Muhammad's tribe] in heathen days. *Tahannuth* is religious devotion. . . .

Wahb b. Kaisan told me that 'Ubayd said to him: Every year during that month the apostle would pray in seclusion and give food to the poor that came to him. And when he completed the month and returned from his seclusion, first of all before entering his house he would go to the Ka'ba [Kaaba shrine] and walk round it seven times or as often as it pleased God; then he would go back to his house until in the year when God sent him, in the month of Ramadan in which God willed concerning him what He willed of His grace, the apostle set forth to Hira' as was his wont, and his family with him. When it was the night on which God honored him with his mission and showed mercy on His servants thereby, Gabriel brought him the command of God. "He came to me," said the apostle of God, "while I was asleep, with a coverlet of brocade whereon was some writing, and said, 'Read!' I said, 'What shall I read?' He pressed me with it so tightly that I thought it was death; then he let me go and said, 'Read!' I said, 'What shall I read?' He pressed me with it again so that I thought it was death; then he let me go and said 'Read!' I said, 'What shall I read?' He pressed me with it the third time so that I thought it was death and said 'Read!' I said, 'What then shall I read?'—and this I said only to deliver myself from him, lest he should do the same to me again. He said:

> 'Read in the name of thy Lord who created,
> Who created man of blood coagulated.
> Read! Thy Lord is the most beneficent,
> Who taught by the pen,
> Taught that which they knew not unto men.'

So I read it, and he departed from me. And I awoke from my sleep, and it was as though these words were written on my heart. . . .

"When I was midway on the mountain, I heard a voice from heaven saying, 'O Muhammad! thou art the apostle of God and I am Gabriel.' I raised my head towards heaven to see [who was speaking], and lo, Gabriel in the form of a man with feet astride the horizon, saying, 'O Muhammad! thou art the apostle of God and I am Gabriel.' I stood gazing at him, moving neither forward nor backward; then I began to turn my face away from him, but towards whatever region of the sky I looked, I saw him as before. And I continued standing there, neither advancing nor turning back, until Khadija [Muhammad's wife] sent her messengers in search of me and they gained the high ground above Mecca and returned to her while I was standing in the same place; then he parted from me and I from him, returning to my family. And I came to Khadija and sat by her thigh and drew close to her. She said, 'O Abu'l-Qasim, where hast thou been? By God, I sent my messengers in search of thee, and they reached the high ground above Mecca and returned. . . .' "

Isma'il b. Abu Hakin, a freedman of the family of al-Zubayr, told me on Khadija's authority that she said to the apostle of God, "O son of my uncle, are you able to tell me about your visitant, when he comes to you?" He replied that he could, and she asked him to tell her when he came. So when Gabriel came to him, as he was wont, the apostle said to Khadija, "This is Gabriel who has just come to me." "Get up, O son of my uncle," she said, "and sit by my left thigh." The apostle did so, and she said, "Can you see him?" "Yes," he said. She said, "Then turn round and sit on my right thigh." He did so, and she said, "Can you see him?" When he said that he could she asked him to move and sit in her lap. When he had done this she again asked if he could see him, and when he said yes, she disclosed her form and cast aside her veil while the apostle was sitting in her lap. Then she said, "Can you see him?" And he replied "No." She said "O son of my uncle, rejoice and be of good heart, by God he is an angel and not a satan."

THE FIRST MUEZZIN

This selection, also from the copy of Ibn Ishaq's Life, *describes the origin of the call to worship—the same one that still resounds throughout the Islamic world five times a day, at daybreak, noon, midafternoon, after sunset, and in the early evening. Bilal, a tall, gaunt Ethiopian who had been brought to Arabia as a slave, became the first muezzin, or caller to prayer. In a stentorian voice he summoned Medina's faithful from a rooftop.*

When the apostle was firmly settled in Medina and his brethren the emigrants were gathered to him and the affairs of the helpers were arranged Islam became firmly established. Prayer was instituted, the alms tax and fasting were prescribed, legal punishments fixed, the forbidden and the permitted prescribed, and Islam took up its abode with them. It was this clan of the helpers who "have taken up their abode [in the city of the prophet] and in the faith." When the apostle first came, the people gathered to him for prayer at the appointed times without being summoned. At first the apostle thought of using a trumpet like that of the Jews who used it to summon to prayer. Afterwards he disliked the idea and ordered a clapper to be made, so it was duly fashioned to be beaten when the Muslims should pray.

Meanwhile [a disciple] heard a voice in a dream, and came to the apostle saying: "A phantom visited me in the night. There passed by me a man wearing two green garments carrying a clapper in his hand, and I asked him to sell it to me. When he asked me what I wanted it for I told him that it was to summon people to prayer, whereupon he offered to show me a better way: it was to say thrice 'Allah Akbar. I bear witness that there is no God but Allah I bear witness that Muhammad is the apostle of God. Come to prayer. Come to prayer. Come to divine service. Come to divine service. Allah Akbar. Allah Akbar. There is no God but Allah.' " When the apostle was told of this he said that it was a true vision if God so willed it, and that he should go with Bilal and communicate it to him so that he might call to prayer thus, for he had a more penetrating voice. When Bilal acted as muezzin 'Umar heard him in his house and came to the apostle dragging his cloak on the ground and saying that he had seen precisely the same vision. The apostle said, "God be praised for that!". . .

Bilal used to give the call . . . at dawn every day. He used to come before daybreak and would sit on the housetop waiting for the dawn. When he saw it he would stretch his arms and say, "O God, I praise thee and ask thy help for Quraysh that they may accept thy religion." I never knew him to omit these words for a single night.

THE WORD OF GOD

To African Muslims, as to all true children of Islam, the Koran is literally the word of God, revealed to Muhammad at various intervals during his lifetime through the angel Gabriel. The text, as we now know it, was fairly well established early in the eighth century, a hundred years after the beginning of the Muslim era. The book is divided into one hundred fourteen suras, or chapters. Ex-

According to Muslim tradition, the decision to use a muezzin to summon worshipers to the mosque was made upon the instruction of the angel Gabriel. That interview is depicted in the sixteenth-century Turkish miniature at right. Belief that portraying Muhammad's face was a sacrilege led the artist to shroud the Prophet in a veil.

N.Y. PUBLIC LIBRARY, SPENCER COLLECTION

cept for the first one, quoted below, the suras are arranged roughly in order of length, beginning with the longest and ending with the shortest. The first sura is recited daily at each of the five fixed times of prayer and before the completion of all solemn contracts and transactions. "The Opening of the Scripture" or "The Essence of the Koran", as it has been variously named, serves the same ritual function as the Lord's Prayer. The following version was translated by Marmaduke Pickthall.

In the name of Allah, the Beneficent, the Merciful.

1. Praise be to Allah, Lord of the Worlds,
2. The Beneficent, the Merciful.
3. Owner of the Day of Judgment,
4. Thee [alone] we worship; Thee [alone] we ask for help.
5. Show us the straight path,
6. The path of those whom Thou hast favored;
7. Not [the path] of those who earn Thine anger nor of those who go astray.

THE FIRST REVELATION

Each sura takes its name from a striking word or phrase contained within it, and all but one begin with the invocation: "In the name of Allah, the Beneficent, the Merciful." Sura XCVI, *which follows in a translation by Marmaduke Pickthall, is entitled "The Clot." According to tradition, it was the first revelation. The prophet is said to have heard it before he received the call. In some English translations the words "blood coagulated" are used in place of "clot."*

In the name of Allah, the Beneficent, the Merciful.

1. Read: In the name of thy Lord who createth,
2. Createth man from a clot.
3. Read: And thy Lord is the Most Bounteous,
4. Who teacheth by the pen,
5. Teacheth man that which he knew not.
6. Nay, but verily man is rebellious
7. That he thinketh himself independent!
8. Lo! unto thy Lord is the return.
9. Hast thou seen him who dissuadeth
10. A slave when he prayeth?
11. Hast thou seen if he [relieth] on the guidance [of Allah]
12. Or enjoineth piety?
13. Hast thou seen if he denieth [Allah's guidance] and is froward?
14. Is he then unaware that Allah seeth?
15. Nay, but if he cease not. We will seize him by the forelock—
16. The lying, sinful forelock—
17. Then let him call upon his henchmen!
18. We will call the guards of hell.
19. Nay! Obey not thou him. But prostrate thyself, and draw near [unto Allah].

"THE CITY"

The most humane portions of the Koran concern the treatment of slaves, orphans, and strangers. Manumission of slaves is deemed extremely pleasing to Allah and worthy expiation of many a sin. Sura XC, *which follows, describes the two highways of life: the arduous path of virtue and the facile one of vice. Those who follow the path of charity and love will become "Companions of the Right Hand" and will attain salvation. "The City" is Mecca, Muhammad's birthplace.*

In the name of Allah, the Beneficent, the Merciful.

1. Nay, I swear by this city—
2. And thou art an indweller of this city—
3. And the begetter and that which he begat,
4. We verily have created man in an atmosphere:
5. Thinketh he that none hath power over him?
6. And he saith: I have destroyed vast wealth:
7. Thinketh he that none beholdeth him?
8. Did We not assign unto him two eyes
9. And a tongue and two lips,
10. And guide him to the parting of the mountain ways?
11. But he hath not attempted the Ascent—
12. Ah, what will convey unto thee what the Ascent is!—
13. [It is] to free a slave,
14. And to feed in the day of hunger
15. An orphan near of kin,
16. Or some poor wretch in misery,
17. And to be of those who believe and exhort one another to perseverance and exhort one another to pity.
18. Their place will be on the right hand.
19. But those who disbelieve Our revelations, their place will be on the left hand.
20. Fire will be an awning over them.

ANTAR THE LION

The paragon of Arab chivalry is the warrior Antar, who was born in Arabia about the middle of the sixth century A.D. *and who died around 615. His mother was a black Ethiopian slave; his father, a Bedouin chieftain. Antar's early youth was spent as a lowly camelkeeper. However, because of his great strength and leonine courage, he was soon promoted from his menial role to a fighting man. Eventually he won his freedom and became the leader of his tribe. His numerous exploits—both military and amorous—are the subject of one of the most popular anonymous works in Africa's Islamic literature,* Sirat Antar, *or* The Romance of Antar, *from which the subsequent selection is taken.*

"What Arab art thou?" said he.

"My Lord," replied Antar, "I am of the tribe of the noble Abs."

"One of its warriors," demanded Monzar, "or one of its slaves?"

"Nobility, my lord," said Antar, "amongst liberal men, is the thrust of the spear, the blow of the sword, the patience beneath the battle dust. I am the physician of the tribe of Abs when they are in sickness, their protector in disgrace, the defender of their wives when they are in trouble, and their horseman when they are in glory, and their sword when they rush to arms."

Monzar was astonished at his fluency of speech, his magnanimity, and his in-

Transcribing the Koran was the supreme artistic challenge for a Muslim calligrapher. The page depicted is from an Andalusian copy executed in 1304 *at a madrasa in Granada.*
BIBLIOTHEQUE NATIONALE, SERVICE PHOTOGRAPHIQUE, MS. ARAB 385

trepidity, for he was then in the dishonorable state of a prisoner, and force had overpowered him. "What urged thee to this violence on my property," added Monzar, "and seizure of my camels?"

"My lord," said Antar, "the tyranny of my uncle obliged me to this act: for I was brought up with his daughter, and I had passed my life in her service. And when he saw me demand her in marriage, he asked of me as a marriage dower, a thousand Asafeer camels. I was ignorant, and knew nothing about them; so I consented to his demand, and set out in quest of them; I have outraged you, and am consequently reduced to this miserable state."

"Hast thou then," said Monzar, "with all this fortitude and eloquence, and propriety of manners, exposed thy life to the sea of death, and endangered thine existence for the sake of an Arab girl?"

"Yes, my lord," said Antar; "it is love that emboldens to encounter dangers and horrors; and no lover is excusable but he who tastes the bitterness of absence after the sweetness of enjoyment; and there is no peril to be apprehended, but from a look from beneath the corner of a veil; and what misfortune can drive man to his destruction, but a woman who is the root and branch of it!"

ANTAR THE POET

Antar was also a highly skilled poet, whose works combine an exaltation of war with sublime sentiments of love. One of his odes received the highest honor possible for a Muslim poet: it was chosen as one of the seven poems, known as the Mu Allakat, *that were written in gold and displayed in the Kaaba shrine at Mecca. His ode, from which the two following passages are excerpted, has moved generations of Arabs with its similes, stirring sensuality, and many dramatic battle scenes.*

'Twas then her beauties first enslaved my heart—
Those glittering pearls and ruby lips, whose kiss
Was sweeter far than honey to the taste.
As when a merchant opes a precious box
Of perfume, such an odor from her breath
Came toward thee, harbinger of her approach;
Or like an untouched meadow, where the rain
Hath fallen freshly on the fragrant herbs
That carpet all its pure untrodden soil:
A meadow where the frequent rain-drops fall
Like coins of silver in the quiet pools,
And irrigate it with perpetual streams;
A meadow where the sportive insects hum
Like listless topers singing o'er their cups.

"As soon as I beheld the legions of our enemies advancing and animating one another to battle, I, too, rushed forward and acted without reproach.

"The troops called out, Antara! while javelins long as the cords of a well were forcibly thrust against the chest of my dark steed.

"I ceased not to charge the foe with the neck and breast of my horse until he was mantled in blood.

"My steed, bent aside with the strokes of the lances in his forehead, complained to me with gushing tears and tender sobbing.

"In the midst of the black dust the horses were impetuously rushing with disfiguring countenance every robust stallion and every strong-limbed mare.

"Then my soul was healed and all my anguish was dispersed by the cry of the warriors: 'Well done, charge again!'"

MUSLIM BATTLE CODE

Ibn Khaldun (1332–1406), *the greatest historical philosopher of the Islamic world, was born in Tunis of a Spanish-Arab family. His* Kitab al-Ibar, *or* Universal History, *deals with the Arabs, the Berbers, and the Muslim dynasties of North Africa. However, it is the* Muqaddimah, *meaning "introduction," that has won the author fame and the title "Father of Sociology." This exceptional work deals with the nature and principles of Islamic life and is the first interpretation of historical events to consider climate and geography as well as moral and spiritual forces. In the subsequent passage Ibn Khaldun prescribes some effective methods of warfare.*

Straighten out your lines like a strongly constructed building.

Place the armed men in front, and those who are not armed in the rear.

Bite on your molars. This makes it harder for sword blows to harm the head.

Keep [something] wrapped around [?] the tips of the spears. This preserves the sharpness of points.

Keep the eyes down. This keeps the soul more concentrated and gives greater peace to the heart.

Kill [all] noises. This drives vacillation away more effectively and is more becoming to dignity.

Do not hold your flags inclined and do not remove them. Place them in the hands only of those among you who are brave.

Call upon truth and endurance for aid, for "after endurance there is victory."

TARIK THE MOOR

Few heroes have been as splendidly immortalized as Tarik, for whom Gibraltar (from

EL ESCORIAL, MS. T-I-1

Moors take Christian captives, as shown in a thirteenth-century miniature from the Cantigas *of Alfonso* X, *a collection of Spanish poems.*

Gebel Tarik, or "Mount of Tarik") is named. The Muslim campaign on the Iberian Peninsula was their most glorious military operation in Europe. The initial reconnaissance was launched in July, 710, *and its success inspired Musa, the Arab governor of the Maghreb, to dispatch his Berber freedman, Tarik ibn Zayyad, across the strait. The story of Tarik's decisive victory over King Roderick is retold below in an excerpt from the* History of the Moors in Spain (1887), *by Stanley Lane-Poole, an Arabic scholar.*

In 711, learning that Roderick was busy in the north of his dominions, where there was a rising of the Basques, Musa despatched one of his generals, the Moor [Berber] Tarik, with 7,000 troops, most of whom were also Moors, to make another raid upon Andalusia. The raid carried him further than he expected. Tarik landed at the lion's rock, which has ever since borne his name. . . , and after capturing Carteya, advanced inland. He had not proceeded far when he perceived the whole force of the Goths under Roderick advancing to encounter him. The two armies met on the banks of a little river. . . . The Prophet himself is said to have appeared to Tarik, and to have bidden him be of good courage, to strike, and to conquer; and many like fables are related. But whatever may have been the dreams and visions of the armies then encamped over against one another near the river Guadelete, the result of the combat was never doubtful. Tarik, indeed, although he had been reinforced with 5,000 Berbers, commanded still but a little army of 12,000 troops, and Roderick had six times as many men to his back. But the invaders were bold and hardy men, used to war, and led by a hero; the Spaniards were a crowd of ill-treated slaves, and among their commanders were treacherous nobles. The kinsmen of Witiza [Roderick's predecessor] were there, obedient to the summons of Roderick; but they intended to desert to the enemy's side in the midst of the battle and win the day for the Saracens. They had no idea that they were betraying Spain. They thought that the invaders were only in search of booty; and that, the raid over and the booty secured, they would go back to Africa, when the line of Witiza would be restored to its ancient seat. And thus they lent a hand to the day's work which placed the fairest provinces of Spain for eight centuries under the Moslem domination.

When the Moors saw the mighty army that Roderick had brought against them, and beheld the king in his splendid armor under a magnificent canopy, their hearts for a moment sank within them. But Tarik cried aloud, "Men, before you is the enemy, and the sea is at your backs. By Allah, there is no escape for you save in valor and resolution." And they plucked up courage and shouted, "We will follow thee, O Tarik," and rushed after their general into the fray. The battle lasted a whole week, and prodigies of valor are recorded on both sides. Roderick rallied his army again and again; but the desertion of the partisans of Witiza turned the fortune of the field and it became the scene of a disastrous rout. . . .

"O Commander of the Faithful, these are not common conquests; they are like the meeting of the nations on the Day of Judgment." Thus wrote Musa, the Governor of Africa, to the Khalif Welid, describing the victory of the Guadalete. There is little wonder that the Saracens stood amazed at the completeness of their triumph. Leaving the regions of myth, with which the Spanish chroniclers have surrounded the fall of Roderick, it is matter of sober history that the victory of the Guadalete gave all Spain into the hands of the Moors. Tarik and his twelve thousand Berbers had by a single action won the whole peninsula, and it needed but ordinary energy and promptness to reduce the feeble resistance which some of the cities still offered. The victor lost no time in following up his success. In defiance of an order from Musa, who was bitterly jealous of the unexpected glory which had come to his Berber lieutenant, and commanded him to advance no further, the fortunate general pushed on without delay. Dividing his forces into three brigades, he spread them over the peninsula, and reduced city after city with little difficulty. Mughith, one of his officers, was despatched with seven hundred horses to seize Cordova. Lying hid till darkness came on, Mughith stealthily approached the city. A storm of hail, which the Moslems regarded as a special favor of Providence, muffled the clatter of their horses' hoofs. A shepherd pointed out a breach in the walls, and here the Moors determined to make the assault. One of them, more active than the rest, climbed a fig-tree which grew beneath the breach, and thence, springing on to the wall, flung the end of a long turban to the others, and pulled them up after him. They instantly surprised the guard, and threw open the gates to the main body of the invaders, and the town was captured with hardly a blow. The governor and garrison took refuge in a convent, where for three months they were closely beleaguered. When at length they surrendered, Cordova was left in the keeping of the Jews, who had proved themselves staunch allies of the Moslems in the campaign, and who ever afterwards enjoyed great consideration at the hands of the conquerors. The Moors admitted them to their intimacy, and, until very late times, never persecuted them as the Gothic priests had done. . . . When the fighting was over, Jew and Moor and Persian joined in that cultivation of learning and philosophy, arts and sciences, which pre-eminently distinguished the rule of the Saracens in the Middle Ages.

HOW TO GET RICH QUICKLY

The following excerpt, from the Muqaddimah, *contains Ibn Khaldun's shrewd guide to success in commerce. By the fourteenth century Morocco and a number of West African kingdoms were partners in an active trans-Saharan trade that enriched not only the principals but a host of desert-dwelling middlemen. Caravans transported such commodities as wheat, dried fruit, brass, clothing, horses, books, and salt southward, and gold, honey, rice, and kola nuts northward.*

The merchant who knows his business will travel only with such goods as are generally needed by rich and poor, rulers and commoners alike. [General need] makes for a large demand for his goods. If he restricts his good to those needed only by a few [people], it may be impossible for him to sell them, since these few may for some reason find it difficult to buy them. Then, his business would slump, and he would make no profit.

Also, a merchant who travels with needed goods should do so only with medium quality goods. The best quality of any type of goods is restricted to wealthy people and the entourage of the ruler. They are very few in number. As is well known, the medium quality of anything is what suits most people. This should by all means be kept in mind by the merchant, because it makes the difference between selling his goods and not selling them.

Likewise, it is more advantageous and more profitable for the merchant's enterprise, and a better guarantee [that he will be able to take advantage of] market fluctuations, if he brings goods from a country that is far away and where there is danger on the road. In such a case, the goods transported will be few and rare, because the place where they come from is far away or because the road over which they come is beset with perils, so that there are few who would bring them, and they are very rare. When goods are few and rare, their prices go up. On the other hand, when the country is near and the road safe for traveling, there will be many to transport the goods. Thus, they will be found in large quantities, and the prices will go down.

Therefore, the merchants who dare to enter the Sudan country are the most prosperous and wealthy of all people. The distance and the difficulty of the road they travel are great. They have to cross a difficult desert which is made [almost] inaccessible by fear [of danger] and beset by [the danger of] thirst. Water is found there only in a few well-known spots to which caravan guides lead the way. The distance of this road is braved only by a very few people. Therefore, the goods of the Sudan country are found only in small quantities among us, and they are particularly expensive. The same applies to our goods among them.

Thus, merchandise becomes more valuable when merchants transport it from one country to another. [Merchants who do so] quickly get rich and wealthy. The same applies to merchants who travel from our country to the East, also because of the great distance to be traversed. On the other hand, those who travel back and forth between the cities and countries of one particular region earn little and make a very small profit, because their goods are available in large quantities and there is a great number of merchants who travel with them.

God "gives sustenance. He is strong and solid."

A POPE'S LETTER

During the Middle Ages relations between Christian Europe and Muslim North Africa were often marred by periods of bitter fighting. Nevertheless, the money-minded entrepreneurs and rulers of both continents often transcended moral and political differences in order to enjoy the profits of trade. Indeed, commercial activities existed between the Maghreb and such cities as Amalfi, Genoa, Pisa, and Venice. The following letter dates from the eleventh century. It was dispatched by Pope Gregory VII *to Al-Nasir (variously known as Anzir), sovereign of Mauretania. Al-Nasir had established diplomatic relations with the Vatican in an attempt to attract Christian merchants to his country.*

Gregory, bishop, servant of servants of god, to Anzir, King of Mauretania, of the province situated in Africa: greetings and papal blessings. Your Highness wrote to us this year to ask to consecrate as bishop, in accordance with the Christian principles, the priest Servand, which we are eager to do because your request is justified. At the same time you sent us presents; you have, in deference for the Blessed Peter, Prince of Apostles, and through love for us, ransomed the Christians who were captives in your land and promised to buy back those who are still to be found there. God, creator of all things, without whom we are nothing, has clearly instilled this goodness in you and has prompted your heart to this generous act. The Almighty God, who wants all men to be saved that no one may perish, sanctions in us the love of

Young North Africans receiving instruction in the tenets of Islamic faith at an outdoor school

fellow man, after love which we owe to him, and the fulfillment of this rule: Do unto others as you would have others do unto you. We in particular, more than other people, must practice this virtue of charity, you and we, who, in different ways, adore the same, one God and each day must praise and worship the Creator of Centuries and the Master of the World. The nobles of the city of Rome, having learned through us of the act God inspired you to do, admire the loftiness of your heart and sing out your praises. Two among them, our habitual companions, Alberic and Ceucius, raised from their childhood with us at the palace of Rome, eagerly desire to make friends and trade favors with you. They will be happy to oblige you in this country. They will send you some of their men, who will tell you how much respect their masters have for your deed and your greatness, and how content they will be to serve you here. We recommend them to Your Magnificence, and we ask for them the same love and devotion that we will always have for you and all that concerns you. God knows that respect for the Almighty God inspires the friendship we have vowed to you, and how much we wish for your well being and your glory in this life and in the life to come. We pray from the bottom of our heart that you will be received after a long life in the breast of the blessedness of the saintly patriarch Abraham.

INSTRUCTION OF CHILDREN

The Arabs conferred great intellectual benefits on the cities and towns that were scattered throughout the Maghreb. The next excerpt, from the Muqaddimah, *describes the manner in which Koranic study was transmitted.*

It should be known that instructing children in the Qur'an [Koran] is a symbol of Islam. Muslims have, and practice, such instruction in all their cities, because it imbues hearts with a firm belief [in Islam] and its articles of faith, which are [derived] from the verses of the Qur'an and certain Prophetic traditions. The Qur'an has become the basis of instruction, the foundation for all habits that may be acquired later on. . . . The methods of instructing children in the Qur'an differ according to differences of opinion as to the habits that are to result from that instruction.

The Maghribi method is to restrict the education of children to instruction in the Qur'an and to practice, during the course [of instruction], in Qur'an orthography and its problems and the differences among Qur'an experts on this score. The [Maghribis] do not bring up any other subjects in their classes, such as traditions, jurisprudence, poetry, or Arabic philology, until the pupil is skilled in [the Qur'an], or drops out before becoming skilled in it. . . .

The Spanish method is instruction in reading and writing as such. That is what they pay attention to in the instruction [of children]. However, since the Qur'an is the basis and foundation of [all] that and the source of Islam and [all] the sciences, they make it the basis of instruction, but they do not restrict their instruction of children exclusively to [the Qur'an]. They also bring in [other subjects], mainly poetry and composition, and they give the children an expert knowledge of Arabic. They do not stress teaching of the Qur'an more than the other subjects. . . .

The people of Ifriqiyah [Tunisia] combine the instruction of children in the Qur'an, usually, with the teaching of traditions. They also teach basic scientific norms and certain scientific problems. However, they stress giving their children a good knowledge of the Qur'an and acquainting them with its various recensions and readings more than anything else. Next they stress handwriting. In general, their method of instruction in the Qur'an is closer to the Spanish method [than to Maghribi or Eastern methods], because their [educational tradition] derives from the Spanish *shaykhs* who crossed over when the Christians conquered Spain. . . .

In his *Rihlah*, Judge Abu Bakr b. al-'Arabi made a remarkable statement about instruction, which retains [the best of] the old, and presents [some good] new features. He placed instruction in Arabic and poetry ahead of all the other sciences, as in the Spanish method, since, he said, "poetry is the archive of the Arabs. Poetry and Arabic philology should be taught first because of the [existing] corruption of the language. From there, the [student] should go on to arithmetic and study it assiduously, until he knows its basic norms. He should then go on to the study of the Qur'an, because with his [previous] preparation, it will be easy for him." [Ibn al-'Arabi] continued: "How thoughtless are our compatriots in that they teach children the Qur'an when they are first starting out. They read things they do not understand and work hard at something that is not as important for them as other matters." He concluded: "The student should study successively the principles of Islam, the principles of jurisprudence, disputation, and then the Prophetic traditions and the sciences connected with them." He also forbade teaching two disciplines at the same time, save to the student with a good mind and sufficient energy. . . .

Severe punishment in the course of instruction does harm to the student, especially to little children, because it belongs among [the things that make for a] bad habit. Students, slaves, and servants who are brought up with injustice and [tyrannical] force are overcome by it. It makes them feel oppressed and causes them to lose their energy. It makes them lazy and induces them to lie and be insincere. That is, their outward behavior differs from what they are thinking, because they are afraid that they will have to suffer tyrannical treatment [if they tell the truth]. Thus, they are taught deceit and trickery. This becomes their custom and character.

WHAT TO WEAR TO MECCA

The Muqaddimah *also contains the following information on the crafts of weaving and tailoring, particularly as they apply to garments to be worn on the hadj, or pilgrimage, to Mecca. This journey is obligatory for all Muslims who have the strength and means to undertake it. It is an incentive to travel and fosters cultural exchanges between Africans and Muslims of many other lands.*

It should be known that people who are temperate in their humanity cannot avoid giving some thought to keeping warm, as they do to shelter. One manages to keep warm by using woven material as protective cover against both heat and cold. This requires the interlacing of yarn, until it turns out to be a complete garment. This is spinning and weaving.

Desert people restrict themselves to this. But people who are inclined toward sedentary culture cut the woven material into pieces of the right size to cover the form of the body and all of its numerous limbs in their various locations. They then put the different pieces together with thread, until they turn out to be a complete garment that fits the body and can be worn by people. The craft that makes things fit is tailoring.

These two crafts are necessary in civilization, because human beings must keep warm.

The purpose of [weaving] is to weave wool and cotton yarn in warp and woof and do it well, so that the texture will be strong. Pieces of cloth of certain measurements are thus produced. Some are garments of wool for covering. Others are garments of cotton and linen for wear.

The purpose of tailoring is to give the woven material a certain form in accordance with the many different shapes and customs [that may occur in this connection]. The material is first cut with scissors into pieces that fit the limbs of the body. The pieces are then joined together with the help of skillful tailoring according to the rules, either by the use of thread, or with bands, or [one] quilts [them], or cuts openings. This [craft] is restricted to sedentary culture, since the inhabitants of the desert can dispense with it. They merely cover themselves with cloth. The tailoring of clothes, the cutting, fitting, and sewing of the material, is one of the various methods and aspects of sedentary culture.

This should be understood, in order to understand the reason why the wearing of sewn garments is forbidden on the pilgrimage. According to the religious law, the pilgrimage requires, among other things, the discarding of all worldly attachments and the return to God as He created us in the beginning. Man should not set his heart upon any of his luxury customs, such as perfume, women, sewn garments, or boots. He should not go hunting or expose himself to any other of the customs with which his soul and character have become colored. When he dies, he will necessarily lose them [anyhow]. He should come [to the pilgrimage] as if he were going to the Last Judgment, humble in his heart, sincerely devoted to his Lord. If he is completely sincere in this respect, his reward will be that he will shed his sins [and be] like he was on the day when his mother gave birth to him. Praised be You! How kind have You been with Your servants and how compassionate have You been with them in their search for guidance toward You!

IBN YASIN'S JIHAD

The powerful Almoravid movement dominated North Africa and Spain from the middle of the eleventh to the middle of the twelfth century. Its fortunes are described in this excerpt from the Encyclopedia of Islam, *a mammoth compilation prepared in England early in this century by a team of leading Orientalists. Ibn Yasin, the founder of the movement, called on his disciples to join the jihad, or holy war, and urged them to "maintain the truth, to repress injustice, and to abolish all taxes not based on law."*

Almoravids is the name of a Muslim dynasty. This word has been derived from the Arabic *al-Murabitun*, a sort of warrior-monks inhabiting a *ribat* or convent more or less fortified. . . .

Under the name of Almoravids we understand especially the royal dynasty founded by several branches of the large Sahara-tribe of the Sanhadja [Sanhaja], which, grouped under the authority of a religious leader, invaded and conquered the Maghrib in the first half of the 5th [by the Christian calendar the middle of the 11th] century, afterwards breaking into Andalusia and mastering that as well.

In the first centuries of Islam the tribes forming the great group of the Sanhadja . . . wearers of the *litham* (a veil covering the face below the eyes; hence also the name *mulaththamun* sometimes given to Almoravids) inhabited the vast wastes of the Sahara as far as the Sudan; they lived there as nomads, as their descendants, the Touaregs [Tuaregs], do to the present time.

Muslim writers, who do not always agree as to the dates of events of which we here give a résumé, are unanimous in tracing the origin of the Almoravid empire as follows:

In the first half of the 5th century of the Hidjra [Muhammad's flight to Medina] a chief of the Sanhadja, Yahya b. Ibrahim, of the branch of the Djaddala (or Gaddala) made the pilgrimage accompanied by men of distinction in his tribe. On his way back he met at Kairawan in Ifrikiya the professor of malikite law 'Abu 'Imiran al-Fasi. Yahya b. Ibrahim desirous of bringing among his uncultured compatriots a man able to direct them in true Muslim doctrine, asked the professor to entrust him with one of his disciples for this purpose. Not being able to find the man of letters he wanted at Kairawan, Yahya b. Ibrahim discovered him, on the recommendation of the professor Abu 'Imran, in the town of Nefis (now belonging to Morocco) among the followers of the professor Waggag, a disciple of Abu 'Imran, in the person of 'Abd Allah b. Yasin.

After having settled among the Sanhadja, Ibn Yasin, followed by seven or eight companions among whom were the two chiefs of the Lamtuna (a branch of the Sanhadja), Yahya b. 'Omar and his brother Abu Bekr b. 'Omar, constructed a hermitage for his companions and himself on an island in the Niger (or in the Senegal). This convent was a *ribat* and Ibn Yasin himself called his followers *Murabitun* (Almoravids). Soon the reputation of the sanctity of this spot and its pious inhabitants spread and a vast number of neophytes came to apply for admittance into this religious brotherhood. Ibn Yasin having gathered to his *ribat* about a thousand monks who were absolutely devoted to him and had all been recruited from among the warriors and the chiefs of the Lamtuna and of the Masufa, now thought of taking up a more active line. He sent forth his partisans, in the name of the true faith, against the different tribes of the Sanhadja, which had to submit one after the other. The victories and the booty soon persuaded those who had hesitated and the number of Almoravid warriors increased rapidly.

Ibn Yasin, keeping for himself the supreme direction of affairs and the political and financial administration of the brotherhood, entrusted his faithful disciple Yahya b. 'Omar with the leadership of the Almoravid army. After having brought the Saharean tribes under their authority Yahya b. 'Omar and Ibn Yasin advanced as far as the Wadi Dar'a where they made important raids. The sovereign of Sidjilmasa, Mas'ud b. Wanudin al-Maghrawi, offering opposition to the conquest of his kingdom, perished in a battle and his capital was taken [447 is 1055–1056 on the Christian calendar].

On the death of Yahya b. 'Omar which took place at about 447 or 448 (1055–1057), his brother Abu Bekr became commander in chief and marching northward continued the conquests begun in the south of the extreme Maghrib. The countries of Sus and their capital Tarudant were subjugated; next Aghmat and its province submitted to the power of the Almoravid conquerors. Abu Bekr married the widow of the king of Aghmat, the beautiful Zainab, of the tribe of the Nafzawa, who was destined to play a certain part in the establishment of the Almoravid empire.

Subsequently Abu Bekr and Ibn Yasin attacked the Berghwata Berbers, whose territories extended as far as the Atlantic Ocean. The Berghwata professed the subversive doctrines of their prophet Salih; it would be a good work to bring them to Islam. But these Berbers energetically resisted the attack of the Almoravids and Ibn Yasin, taking an active part in the military operations, found his death in a battle [in 1059]. Perhaps Ibn Yasin appointed a spiritual leader to take his place at the head of the Almoravids; Ibn Khaldun mentions as such Ibn 'Addu who, if he did exist at all, played a very subordinate part compared with Abu Bekr b. 'Omar. The latter appears as the real chief of the Almoravids and had coins struck in his name; he continued the war against Berghwata and subjugated them [in 1060]. Shortly afterwards he was informed that Bulugin, lord of the Kal'a of the Banu Hammad [who ruled Algeria], was marching with a large force against the countries of the extreme Maghrib, and at the same time that those portions of the Sanhadja who had remained in the desert were carrying on war with one another. He took advantage of the latter fact to leave the Maghrib for the time being and go back to the desert in order to re-establish peace among the Almoravids. Before leaving, Abu Bekr gave the command over the troops in the Maghrib and the direction of affairs to Yusuf b. Tashfin; he also abandoned to him, after divorcing her, his wife Zainab, who thus became the wife of Yusuf b. Tashfin. . . . This woman of remarkable intelligence, rare energy and great beauty acquired considerable ascendancy over her new husband's mind and had a happy influence on the fate of the young empire. Yusuf b. Tashfin continued the conquests in the extreme and in the central Maghrib. Abu Bekr, after having re-established order in the desert and having received the news of his lieutenant's

Travelers in the Algerian Sahara, their faces toward Mecca, kneeling to recite their prayers
LIBRARY OF CONGRESS, CARPENTER COLLECTION

success, returned to the North to take again command over the Almoravids. But following Zainab's advice Yusuf b. Tashfin loaded him with presents and made him understand clearly that he was not at all disposed to give up the supreme authority. Abu Bekr judged it wise not to insist; he retired to the Sahara and to the Sudan where he died in 480 (1087–1088).

In his quality of supreme chief of the Almoravids Yusuf b. Tashfin founded Marrakush which became his capital and that of his successors; then he went on with his conquests in the extreme and in the central Maghrib as far as Algiers. In 475 (1082–1083) he came back to Marrakush after having left Almoravid officers in the conquered countries as governors.

Urged by the Muslim princes of Andalusia (*reyes de Taifas*), and in particular by . . . [the] king of Sevilla, Yusuf decided to cross to Spain with a strong army in order to make war against the Christians under Alfonso VI, king of Leon and Castile; he gained over the Christian armies the great victory of Zallaka [12 Radjab 479, or October 23, 1086] which was for the Almoravides the prelude to the conquest of Spain. Certain authors maintain that from this day Yusuf took the title of *Amir al-Mu'minin*. This assertion is doubtful, at least it does not appear that the great Almoravid conqueror long retained this title denoting temporal and spiritual authority at the same time. We even know as a fact beyond dispute that the Almoravid sovereigns, while reserving for themselves temporal authority with the title of *Amir al-Muslimin*, attributed supreme authority and suzerainty in matters spiritual to the 'Abbasids of the East with the title of *Amir al-Mu'minin*, given to the Caliph.

The petty Muslim kings of Andalusia, al-Mu'tamid included, soon found out that the risks, their authority and their riches ran through the Almoravid chief, were much more formidable than those they feared from the Christians. They were soon robbed of their dignities and banished by Yusuf b. Tashfin, who left in Spain Almoravid troops and governors, chosen from among his relatives.

When Yusuf b. Tashfin died in 500 (1106–1107) he bequeathed to his son 'Ali a vast empire, comprising the countries of the Maghrib, a part of Ifrikiya and Muslim Spain (extending to the north as far as Fraga). His descendants succeeded each other on the throne of Marrakush for less than half a century and the Almoravid dynasty was destroyed in Africa when the Almohades led by 'Abd al-Mu'min conquered Marrakush [in 541, or 1146–1147] and killed the last Almoravid king of the house of Yusuf. . . . Soon after the Almohades conquered Spain . . . and at the death of the Almoravid governor of Spain [in 1148–1149], the authority of the Almoravids in the peninsula was at an end.

THE BOOK OF ROGER

The first Western notice of the East African coast occurs in the writings of Al-Idrisi, a twelfth-century Moroccan Muslim scholar who spent most of his life in Palermo at the court of Roger II, *a Norman ruler of Sicily. There, Al-Idrisi compiled the history of the whole known world, relying entirely on the writings of other historians and on the reports of informants who traveled at Roger's expense. His work, the source of this colorful selection, is known as the* Kitab Rujar, *or* Book of Roger. *Its alternate title,* Nuzhat al Mushtaq fi Ikhtiraq al-Afaq, *has been freely translated as* "The Recreation of Him Who Yearns to Travel the Lands."

The Zanj of the East African coast have no ships to voyage in, but use vessels from Oman and other countries which sail to the islands of Zanj which depend on the Indies. These foreigners sell their goods there, and buy the produce of the country. The people of the Djawaga islands go to Zanzibar in large and small ships, and use them for trading their goods, for they understand each others' language. Opposite the Zanj coasts are the Djawaga islands; they are numerous and vast; their inhabitants are very dark in color, and everything that is cultivated there, fruit, sorghum, sugar-cane and camphor trees, is black in color. Among the number of the islands is Sribuza, which is said to be 1,200 miles round; and pearl fisheries and various kinds of aromatic plants and perfumes are to be found there, which attract the merchants.

Among the islands of Djawaga included in the present section is Andjuba [Anjouan-Johanna], whose principal town is called Unguja in the language of Zanzibar, and whose people, although mixed, are actually mostly Muslims. The distance from it to Banas on the Zanj coast is 100 miles. The island is 400 miles round; bananas are the chief food. There are five kinds, as follows: the bananas called *kundi; fili* whose weight is sometimes twelve ounces; *omani, muriani, sukari.* It is a healthy, sweet, and pleasant food. The island is traversed by a mountain called Wabra. The vagabonds who are expelled from the town flee there, and form a brave and numerous company which frequently infests the surroundings of the town, and which lives at the top of the mountain in a state of defense against the ruler of the island. They are courageous, and feared for their arms and their number. The island is very populous; there are many villages and cattle. They grow rice. There is a great trade in it, and each year various products and goods are brought for exchange and consumption.

From Medouna [on the Somali coast] to Malindi, a town of the Zanj, one follows the coast for three days and three nights by sea. Malindi lies on the shore, at the mouth of a river of sweet water. It is a large town, whose people engage in hunting and fishing. On land they hunt the tiger and other wild beasts. They obtain various kinds of fish from the sea, which they cure and sell.

They own and exploit iron mines; for them iron is an article of trade and the source of their largest profits. They pretend to know how to bewitch the most poisonous snakes so as to make them harmless to everyone except those for whom they wish evil or on whom they wish to take vengeance. They also pretend that by means of these enchantments the tigers and lions cannot hurt them. These wizards are called *al-Musnafu* in the language of the people.

It is two days' journey along the coast to Mombasa. This is a small place and a dependency of the Zanj. Its inhabitants work in the iron mines and hunt tigers. They have red colored dogs which fight every kind of wild beast and even lions. This town lies on the sea shore near a large gulf up which ships travel two days' journey; its banks are uninhabited because of the wild beasts that live in the forests where the Zanj go and hunt, as we have already said. In this town lives the King of Zanzibar. His guards go on foot because they have no mounts: horses cannot live there.

THE LAND OF THE ZANJ

Islam spread to Africa's east coast more as a result of commerce than religious zeal. The first Muslims to establish themselves in the "Land of the Zanj," as the Arabs called the coastal area south of the Horn, were probably lured by gold. The story of the first settlements in this area, at Mogadishu and Brava, is told by the sixteenth-century Portuguese historian João de Barros. His précis of the now lost Chronicle of the Kings of Kilwa, from which this excerpt is taken, is one of the two extant summaries of this important work. However, De Barros appears to have consulted other sources besides the Chronicle. If accurate, these immigrations from Arabia may have occurred as early as the eighth or as late as the eleventh century; scholars disagree.

As the land of Arabia is very close to these lands, the first foreign people who came to settle in the land of Zanzibar were a tribe of Arabs, who had been banished after adopting a sect of Muhammad. As we learn from a Chronicle of the Kings of Kilwa, of which we shall make mention, they were called Zaidites. The cause of the banishment was that they followed the doctrines of a Moor named Zaid, who was the grandson of Husain, the son of 'Ali, who was the nephew of Muhammad, and had married his daughter Axa. This Zaid held some opinions which were contrary to those of the Koran, and the Moors call all who follow his doctrine Zaidites, that is to say followers of Zaid, and consider them heretics. As these were the first to come from outside to dwell in this land, they did not make any notable settlements, but only gathered together in parts where they could live safe from the Kafirs [black Africans who were not Muslims].

After their arrival, they worked their way like a slow plague along the coast, taking possession of fresh settlements, until there arrived three ships with a large number of Arabs in the company of seven brothers. These belonged to a tribe near the city of al-Hasa, which is over forty leagues from the island of Bahrein, which is at the entrance to the Persian Sea, very close to the land of Arabia and its interior. The cause of their coming was that they were very much persecuted by the king of al-Hasa. The first settlement they made in this land of *Ajan* [a form of the word Zanj] was the city of Mogadishu, and the next at Barawa [Brava], which even at the present time is governed by twelve chiefs in the manner of a republic, and they are descendants of these brothers. Mogadishu so excelled in power and statesmanship that it became overlord and capital of all the Moors of this coast. As the first people to come, who were called Zaidites, held different opinions from the Arabs regarding their faith, they were not willing to submit to them, and withdrew to the interior, intermarrying with the Kafirs and adopting their customs so that they became in all respects half breeds. These are the people the Moors who live along the coast called Baduis, a common name, just as among ourselves we call the country folk Alarves.

The first foreign nation to trade by sailing ships with the Sofala mine was this city of Mogadishu; not that they went to explore the coast, but because a ship belonging to it was driven there in a storm and by the force of the currents.

THE GOLD OF SOFALA

João de Barros is our only authority concerning Kilwa's miraculous evolution from a series of unprestigious commercial settlements to the principal trader of gold in the western Indian Ocean. This change probably began in the first quarter of the twelfth century, when the sultan of Kilwa learned of gold-rich Sofala and promptly secured what amounted to a trade monopoly on the precious commodity. The first part of this excerpt comes from the same source as the preceding selection; the second part, from his history, De Asia, *which was first published in* 1552.

This settlement, which the Moors had made in this place called Sofala, was not made by force of arms, nor against the will of the natives of the land, but by their wish and that of the prince who ruled at that time; because, by reason of this intercourse they [the people of Sofala] obtained benefits as well as cloth and other things which they had never had before, and for which they gave gold and ivory, which was of no use to them, and which, until then, had never been exported from Sofala. And, although this barbarous race never left the village in which they were born, and were not given to navigation, nor to travel by land in pursuit of commerce, gold nevertheless has this quality, namely, that wherever it is found on earth, the report of it spreads from one person to another so that they go to find its place of origin.

However it happened, we learn from the Chronicle of the Kings of Kilwa, which we have already mentioned, that the first people on this coast who came to the land of Sofala in search of gold were inhabitants of the city of Mogadishu. How the kings of Kilwa came into possession was in this manner. A man was fishing in a canoe outside the bar of Kilwa near an island called Miza. He caught a fish on the hook of the line he had cast into the sea. Feeling from the struggles of the fish that it was very large and not wishing to lose it, he weighed anchor and left himself at the will of the fish. Sometimes the vessel went where the fish took it and sometimes where the currents, which are very strong there, so that when the fisherman wished to return to the port whence he had come, he could not reach it. At last, more dead than alive from hunger and thirst, he came to the port of Sofala, where he found a ship of Mogadishu, which had come there to trade. In this vessel he returned to Kilwa and related what had occurred and what he had seen of the gold trade.

It was part of the agreement between these Gentiles and the Moors of Mogadishu that every year they should send some young Moors so that there should be some of this race there. When the King of Kilwa learnt this part of the contract and its conditions from the fisherman, he sent a ship there to arrange commerce with the Kafirs. With regard to the young Moors for whom they asked, he offered to give so many cloths a head in lieu of those they asked, or, if they wanted them so as to have a race of them there, he said some of the inhabitants of Kilwa would go and settle there in a factory for merchandise, and that they would be glad to take their daughters as wives, by which means the people would multiply. By means of this entry the Moors of Kilwa got possession of the trade.

In course of time by means of the trade which the Moors had with these Kafirs, the kings of Kilwa became absolute masters of the gold trade. Chief among them was a man named Daut [Daud ibn Sulaiman, c. 1311–1170] . . . who resided there for some time and afterwards went to rule in Kilwa. From that time onwards the kings of Kilwa sent their governors to Sofala, so that everything might be transacted through their factors. . . .

Daut reigned at Kilwa for forty years and was succeeded by his son Soleiman Hacen, who conquered the greater part of the [this?] coast. With his father's support he became master of the trade of Sofala and of the islands of Pemba, Momfia, Zanzibar and a large part of the mainland coast. Besides being a conqueror, he beautified the city of Quiloa [Kilwa], erecting there a fortress of stone and lime, with walls, towers and other houses, whereas up till that time nearly the whole of the dwellings in the city had been made of wood. All these things he accomplished during the eighteen years he reigned.

MOGADISHU IN 1331

The well-organized life style of the peoples of Mogadishu is the subject of this piece by Ibn Battuta, the great fourteenth-century Moroccan traveler. Aside from making four pilgrimages to Mecca, this tireless peregrinator was qadi, *or judge, of Delhi in India and of the Maldive Islands; he also visited all the countries of the Middle East, as well as East and West Africa, Ceylon, and China. He is the only medieval Muslim to have left an eyewitness description of the towns of the East African littoral, which he visited in* 1331.

From [Zeila] we sailed fifteen nights and arrived at Mogadishu, which is a very large town. The people have very many camels, and slaughter many hundreds every day. They have also many sheep. The merchants are wealthy, and manufacture a material which takes its name from the town and which is exported to Egypt and elsewhere.

Among the customs of the people of this town is the following: when a ship comes into port, it is boarded from *sanbuqs*, that is to say, little boats. Each *sanbuq* carries a crowd of young men, each carrying a covered dish, containing food. Each one of them presents his dish to a merchant on board, and calls out: "This man is my guest." And his fellows do the same. Not one of the merchants disembarks except to go to the house of his host among the young men, save frequent visitors to the country. In such a case they go where they like. When a merchant has settled in his host's house, the latter sells for him what he has brought and makes his purchases for him. Buying anything from a merchant below its market price or selling him anything except in his host's presence is disapproved of by the people of Mogadishu. They find it of advantage to keep to this rule.

When the young men came on board the ship on which I was, one of them approached me. My companions said to him: "He is not one of the merchants: he is a lawyer." Then the young man called his companions and said: "This man is a guest of the Qadi." One of the Qadi's friends came among them, and he told him of this. The Qadi came down to the beach with some of his pupils and sent one on board to fetch me. Then I disembarked with my companions, and greeted the Qadi and his followers. He said to me: "In the name of God, let us go and greet the Shaikh." "Who is the Shaikh?" I asked, and he replied: "The Sultan." For it is their custom here to call the Sultan "Shaikh." I answered the Qadi: "I will visit him as soon as I have found lodging." He replied: "It is the custom here, whenever a lawyer, or a Sharif or a holy man comes, that he should not go to his lodging until he has seen the Sultan." So I did what I was asked in accordance with their custom.

As we have said, the Sultan of Mogadishu is called Shaikh by his subjects. His name is Abu Bakr ibn Shaikh Omar, and by race he is a Berber. He talks in the dialect of Mogadishu, but knows Arabic. When a ship arrives, it is the custom for it to be boarded by the Sultan's *sanbuq*, to inquire whence it has come, who are the owners and who its captain is. They also inquire the nature of the cargo and what merchants or other persons are on board. All this is told to the Sultan, who invites as his guest anyone worthy of such honor.

When I arrived at the palace with the Qadi, whose name was Ibn Burhan al-Misri, a eunuch came out and greeted him. The Qadi said: "Go and do your duty, and inform our master the Shaikh that this man has arrived from the Hijaz." He delivered the message and returned with a dish of betel leaves and areca nuts. He gave me six leaves of betel and some nuts, and the same amount to the Qadi: the rest he divided among my companions and the pupils of the Qadi. Then he brought a bottle of Damascus rose-water, and sprinkled some on me and on the Qadi, and said: "Our master orders that he be lodged in the house of the pupils."

This house was built specially for them. The Qadi took me by the hand, and we went to this house, which is near that of the Shaikh. It was decorated with carpets and contained everything needful. Later the same eunuch brought us food from the Shaikh's house. He was accompanied by one of the wazirs, whose particular duty it was to look after guests. He said to us: "Our master greets you and bids you welcome." After this the meal was served and we ate.

The food of these people is rice cooked with butter, served on a large wooden dish. With it they serve side-dishes, stews of chicken, meat, fish, and vegetables. They cook unripe bananas in fresh milk, and serve them as a sauce. They put curdled milk in another vessel with peppercorns, vinegar, and saffron, green ginger and mangoes, which look like apples but have a nut inside. Ripe mangoes are very sweet and are eaten like fruit; but unripe mangoes are as acid as lemons, and are cooked in vinegar. When the Mogadishu people have taken a mouthful of rice, they take some of these pickles. One of them eats as much as several of us: they are very fat and corpulent.

When we had eaten, the Qadi went away. We stayed there for three days, and each day they brought us food three times a day, as is their custom. The fourth day, which was a Friday, the Qadi, his pupils and one of the wazirs of the Shaikh came and brought me a suit of clothes. Their dress consists of a loincloth, which is fastened round the waist, instead of drawers, of which they are ignorant. There was a tunic of Egyptian linen with a border, a cloak of Jerusalem stuff, doubled, and a fringed turban of Egyptian material. They also brought my companions clothes suitable to their rank.

We went to the chief mosque, and prayed behind the *maqsurah*, the enclosure for the Shaikh. When he came out of the *maqsurah*, I greeted him with the Qadi. He replied with his good wishes for us both, and talked to the Qadi in the local language, and then said to me in Arabic: "You are welcome: you have honored our country by coming and have rejoiced us." He went out into the courtyard of the mosque and stopped at the tomb of his son, which is there. He recited a passage from the Koran and prayed. Then came the wazirs, the amirs and military commanders and greeted him. In doing this they observed the same customs as are followed in the Yemen. The man who gives his greeting places his forefinger on the ground, and then on his head, and says: "May God make you glorious!"

After that the Shaikh went out of the door of the mosque and put his sandals on. He ordered the Qadi and myself to do likewise, and set off on foot to his house, which is near the mosque, everyone else following barefoot. Over his head they carried a silk canopy, its four poles topped with a golden bird. He wore a sweeping cloak of green Jerusalem stuff, over clothes of Egyptian linen. He had a silk girdle and a large turban. In front of him they beat drums and played trumpets and oboes. He was preceded by the amirs of the army, and followed by the Qadi, the lawyers and the Sharifs.

With this ceremony he entered his audience hall. The wazirs, amirs and military commanders took their places on a bench set for them. A special carpet was spread for the Qadi on which he sat alone. He was accompanied by the lawyers and Sharifs. There they all remained until the afternoon prayer, which they said together with the Shaikh. Then all the soldiers were drawn up in lines according to their rank, and the drums, oboes, trumpets, and flutes played. While they played, everyone stayed in his place, and anyone, who happened to be moving about, immediately stood still. When the band stopped playing, those present greeted the Shaikh with their fingers in the manner we have described and then went away. This is their custom every Friday.

On Saturday the people come to the door of the Shaikh's house and sit on benches outside. The Qadi, the lawyers, the Sharifs, the holy men, the shaikhs and those who have made the pilgrimage enter an outer room and sit on wooden benches arranged for that purpose. The Qadi sits on his bench alone, and each of these classes of person has its own bench, which is not shared with any other. The Shaikh then takes his place in his hall of audience, and sends for the Qadi. He takes his place on the Shaikh's left, and then the lawyers come in, and the chief of them sit in front of the Shaikh. The others greet the Shaikh and go back again. Then the Sharifs enter, and the chief of them sit before him: the remainder greet him and go back outside. But if they are guests of the Shaikh, they sit on his right hand. The same ceremonial is observed by persons of position and pilgrims, and then by the wazirs, the amirs and the military commanders, each rank by itself.

Then food is brought, and the Qadi, the Sharifs and those who are in the audience chamber eat in the presence of the Shaikh, and he with them. If he wishes to honor one of the chief amirs, he sends for him and has him eat with them. The rest eat in a refectory. There they observe the same precedence as that of their entering the Shaikh's audience chamber.

After this the Shaikh retires to his private apartments, and the Qadi, the wazirs, the private secretary and four of the chief amirs sit to hear causes and complaints. Questions of religious law are decided by the Qadi: other cases are judged by the council, that is, the wazirs and amirs. If a case requires the views of the Sultan, it is put in writing for him. He sends back an immediate reply, written on the back of the paper, as his discretion may decide. This has always been the custom among these people.

A GIRAFFE FOR THE EMPEROR

One of the most alluring chapters of East African history concerns that area's relations with China. Before the Ming dynasty (1368–1644) the regions traded indirectly, and no Chinese ever visited Africa. However, during the early 1400's the Chinese sponsored seven major expeditions to the ports of the Indian Ocean; two sailed all the way to Africa and visited Malindi, Brava, and Mogadishu. The undertakings were part of the Chinese government's effort to invigorate foreign trade and to strengthen its international prestige. The fleets were commanded by Cheng Ho, a court eunuch known as the "Three-jewel Eunuch." The following discussion of China's discovery of Africa is by J. J. L. Duyvendak, professor of Chinese at Leyden University. It is a lecture he gave in London in 1947.

It may be asked what was the motive that took the Chinese . . . as far as the east coast of Africa? This is a very peculiar one. It should be remembered that the expeditions, on their visit to the distant countries, collected as many rare and precious objects as possible. Among these objects strange animals always occupied an important place. . . . There was, in the capital, an Imperial Zoological Garden in which such rarities were kept, and when the expeditions returned they were regularly followed by a string of foreign ambassadors (including, on one occasion, even an ambassador from "Misr," Egypt) with their gifts of lions, tigers, oryxes, nilgaus, zebras, ostriches, etc. Now we learn that in 1414 a present arrived from Bengal (that had been visited by one of the secondary expeditions, detailed from the major fleet), consisting of a giraffe. Bengal, of course, is not a country where the giraffe is native, so it must have come from elsewhere. I think the riddle is solved by the fact that the following year suddenly the African country of Melinda [Malindi], with which China so far never had entertained any relations, came to Court presenting a giraffe. I believe that what happened is this: we know that in Bengal there just was a new king, Saifu'd-Din, who on ascending the throne, naturally received presents from the various Mohammedan, including African, countries. Among these presents must have been giraffes, one of which he passed on to the Chinese Emperor, and the Chinese must have met the Ambassadors from Melinda and given them a hint that such an animal would be a very welcome gift at Court. The result was that the following year Melinda came to present a giraffe. These ambassadors had to be conducted home, and so we see that on the fifth voyage (1417–1419) for the first time the itinerary is extended . . . to Melinda. It was the giraffe, therefore, that caused the Chinese to sail to Africa. . . .

The first giraffe in China, the gift of an African ruler, arrived in 1414. A contemporary artist recorded the remarkable event.

PRIVATE COLLECTION

It happens that in the Somali language the giraffe is called *girin* which, to Chinese ears, would sound like *ki-lin*. Now this sound is very close to that of the word *k'i-lin* (modern pronunciation *ch'i-lin*) the fabulous animal, which we equate generally with our "unicorn."

The appearance of the unicorn was always regarded as a happy portent; it was a sign of Heaven's favor and proof of the virtue of the Emperor. Under a perfect reign the cosmic forces could come to such complete development that from the surplus, as it were, such wonderful beings as dragons and giraffes could develop and exercise their beneficent influence. Now there was a superficial resemblance between the giraffe and the K'i-lin which was supposed to have "the body of a deer and the tail of an ox," to eat only herbs and to harm no living being. For the eunuchs, leaders of the expeditions, professional flatterers as they were, this resemblance of form and sound of the name was enough: the presentation of a K'i-lin would be a supreme flattery of the Emperor. In the previous years several supernatural appearances had already been reported, such as vegetarian tigers, extraordinarily large ears of grain, sweet dew, etc. A K'i-lin would cap this series in masterly fashion. Not knowing whether the giraffe from Bengal would stand the hardships of the transportation, they made sure that . . . the Melinda people would present another sample.

When the giraffe from Bengal arrived at Court on September 20, 1414, under the guise of a K'i-lin or unicorn, it caused quite a stir. The Board of Rites asked to be allowed to present a Memorial of Congratulation. The Emperor declined, saying: "Let the Ministers but early and late exert themselves in assisting the government for the welfare of the world. If the world is at peace, even without K'i-lins there is nothing that hinders good government. Let congratulations be omitted."

When, however, in the following year the giraffe from Melinda arrived, a similar request was made and, although the Emperor again declined, he went out to the Feng-t'ien gate to receive the animal in great state, together with a "celestial horse" (zebra) and a "celestial stag" (oryx?), and all the officials prostrated themselves and offered congratulations. The Emperor said: "This event is due to the abundant virtue of the late Emperor, my father, and also to the assistance rendered me by my Ministers. That is why distant people arrive in uninterrupted succession. From now on it behoves Us even more than in the past to cling to virtue and it behoves you to remonstrate with Us about Our shortcomings."

The members of the Imperial Academy, the Han-lin, as well as the Court painters did not miss the opportunity to immortalize the extraordinary event of the arrival of a K'i-lin at Court. . . . [One courtier wrote:] "Respectfully I consider that Your Majesty succeeded to the Emperor T'ai-tsu's Grand Heritage and that Your virtue transforms [the world] and causes the Three Luminaries to follow their regular course and all living souls to perform their duty. Consequently a Tsou-yü [vegetarian tiger] has appeared, Wonderful Ears are produced, Sweet Dew has descended, the Yellow River has been Clear and Savory Springs have gushed forth. All the creatures that spell good fortune arrive. In the 9th month of the year *chia-wu* of the Yung-lo period [1414] a K'i-lin [giraffe] came from the country of Bengal and was formally presented as tribute to the Court. The ministers and the people all gathered to gaze at it and their joy knows no end. I, Your servant, have heard that, when a Sage possesses the virtue of the utmost benevolence so that he illuminates the darkest places, then a K'i-lin appears. This shows that Your Majesty's virtue equals that of Heaven; its merciful blessings have spread far and wide so that its harmonious vapors have emanated a K'i-lin, as an endless bliss to the state for a myriad myriad years. . . ."

Thus it happened that the giraffe from the African wilderness, as it strode into the Emperor's Court, became the emblem of Perfect Virtue, Perfect Government, and Perfect Harmony in the Empire and in the Universe. Rarely have such extravagant cosmic claims been made in such refined language for any living animal. Surely it is the most sophisticated instance of therolatry in history, the apogee of the lore of the unicorn! This is what the discovery of Africa did for Chinese Confucian ideology.

CHINA LOOKS AT AFRICA

Admiral Cheng Ho's reports on his naval expeditions are not extant. However, Fei Hsin, a scholar who traveled with the fleet as a petty officer, kept the account from which the following description of Djubo, probably present-day Giumbo in Somalia, is taken.

The country of *Djubo:* "They live in solitary and dispersed villages. The country is situated in a remote corner of the west. The walls are made of piled up bricks, and the houses are masoned in high blocks. The customs are very simple. There grow neither herbs nor trees. Men and women wear their hair in rolls; when they go out, they wear a linen hood. The mountains are uncultivated and the land is wide; it rains very rarely. There are deep wells worked by means of cog-wheels. Fish are caught in the sea with nets. The products of the country are lions, gold-spotted leopards, and camel-birds which are six or seven feet tall. There are Dragon Saliva [ambergris], incense and golden amber. As merchandise are used vermilion, colored silks, gold, silver, porcelains, pepper, colored satins, rice, and other cereals."

THE PILLAR OF ZION

Medieval Ethiopia remained stalwartly Christian despite the many attempts made by its Muslim neighbors to conquer it. One of the most "perfect" Christian soldiers was Emperor Amda Seyon, or "Pillar of Zion." When this king came to the throne in 1313, his country was being seriously threatened by Muslim attacks. The first leader to campaign against him was Sabr ad-Din, the ruler of the Muslim principality of Ifat, to the east of Shoa. The Ethiopian monarch defeated Sabr as well as many other Arab leaders, and resolved not to cease fighting as long as the infidels continued to menace him.

He was everywhere victorious, and as related in the following passage from the reconstructed version of Ethiopian Royal Chronicles, many Muslim rulers joined forces against him. The translation is by Sir Wallace Ernest Alfred Budge, an archeologist.

The kings and governors made ready to throw off all allegiance to the king of Abyssinia, and banded themselves together to make war upon him. They were in number 2722 . . . and the number of their soldiers [?], not including those of Zalan and Gabal, was 12,048.

At this juncture Jamal ad-Din, whom 'Amda Seyon had made governor of the country in place of his brother Sabr ad-Din, revolted, and he sent a message to the king of 'Adal to this effect. "The king of Abyssinia is shut up in a mountain defile from which he cannot get out. Now you must do one of two things; either take gifts to him or do not. If you take gifts to him, before you do so sell your wife and children and all that you possess, for if you give him gifts you will make yourself and your posterity his servants for ever. If you wish to act wisely, send him no gifts, and gather together all your men who are able to fight with sword, bow, shield, javelin, lance and club, and I will join you with my cavalry and infantry and we will fall upon the king and his army and kill them with one blow." . . . The king of 'Adal and all the other kings collected their soldiers, and four months had elapsed before they had joined the army of Jamal ad-Din. When the host was ready for war this arrogant Arab began to boast what he would do to the Christians, and with the view of securing all the spoil of the Christians for himself he decided not to wait for the troops from Ifat, because the loot would not be sufficient for their king and himself.

Now at that moment it happened that 'Amda Seyon was alone, and he had none of his picked troups with him. His regiments of "Eyes of needles" and "Wolves" and the Korani horsemen, and the Barya, and the Harab Gonda, and many other great regiments were absent on duty elsewhere. When they fought they struck like eagles, and leaped like rams, their feet were like stone rollers and the noise of their feet was like that of the sea. And 'Amda Seyon lay sick in his tent, and for seven days and seven nights he had eaten and drunk nothing. He had sent out one of his men called Zana Yamanu with the dogs into the desert to hunt game for him, and whilst this man was hunting he came across the Arab army; he returned forthwith to the king and told him what he had seen, adding, "We have come back to die with you." The king sent out horsemen to reconnoitre, and they reported that the enemy were in numbers like a cloud of grasshoppers which had covered the earth. On hearing this he struggled up from his bed and tried to go outside the tent, but when he began to put on his war belt, his legs doubled up under him and he collapsed on his bed. His servants lifted him up and put on his belt, and he managed to go outside the tent, but he swayed from side to side through weakness. His two queens followed him and begged him to give up the idea of fighting, but he replied, "Am I to die like a woman? Certainly not. I know how to die like a soldier." Then he turned and ordered the queens to return to their tents. The elder of them, Djan Mangasha, prayed with tears to God to strengthen her lord, the priests prayed, and the king prayed, committing himself into the hands of God.

Meanwhile the Arab armies were advancing, every man armed, and in number they were as the stars of heaven and the sand of the sea-shore, and the rain clouds of the sky; as they marched the earth shook, and the wild beasts were so terrified that they ran before them and took refuge in the camp of 'Amda Seyon. And the queen sent to 'Amda Seyon a quantity of Jordan water and some dust from Golgotha. The king called the priest Takla Seyon and told him to baptize him with the water, as he stood there in full armor; and as the water fell upon him his weakness departed and the strength of God came upon him. And the king himself sprinkled his horses and his men with the water. The Arab army came on and in its van were a number of women who shrieked out curses. 'Amda Seyon sprinkled some of the water about to annul the effects of the curses, and sent on a detachment of horsemen to open the battle; these turned and fled, and entreated him to fight in his camp. When he refused, his friends kissed him and fled, leaving him alone to meet death as best he might. As they departed he hurled reproaches after them, and then being filled with rage, he sprang up like a tiger and leaped upon his horse . . . and ordered his chief officer of cavalry, called Zanasfare, to ride into the enemy's ranks on the right. Zanasfare, followed by five horsemen among whom was the king's son Saf-Sagad, did as he was bid. The king charged the enemy on the left, looking neither before him nor behind him, and at once became the target for arrows, javelins and spears, and the object of a shower of blows. Nothing stopped him, and when the enemy saw him spearing two men at a time they broke and fled. The soldiers who had forsaken him returned and joined Zanasfare and his men, and drove the fleeing enemy into a deep ditch which God seemed to have prepared for them. Then the king dismounted and attacked the enemy with his sword and smote them down until his strength failed. The enemy were men of huge stature and wore their hair hanging down to their waists like women, and though they tied themselves to each other by means of their clothes so that no man might flee, they were conquered by the king. 'Amda Seyon remounted his horse and set out with his soldiers to cut down those who were fleeing, and meanwhile the Abyssinian women came out and stripped the dead and carried their weapons back to their camp. The battle raged for six hours, until sunset, by which time the Muslims were either scattered or slain, and the king's arm was attached so tightly to his lance by the blood of the slain that force

had to be used to detach it. The dead lay round about in heaps, and the wounded could not be counted.

When the battle was over 'Amda Seyon returned to his camp, and entering his chapel gave thanks to God for the victory He had given him.

THE HILALIAN INVASION

In the middle of the eleventh century the Maghreb was invaded by Bedouin Arabs, the Beni Hilal and Beni Sulaim tribes. They were nomads who had moved from Arabia into Egypt. The Fatimid caliph of Cairo, anxious to rid his country of this troublesome element, urged them to invade Ifriqiya, where his authority had recently been repudiated. Cyrenaica, Tripolitania, the Fezzan, and much of Ifriqiya were overrun, and many of the Beni Hilal ultimately settled in Morocco. Historians are still weighing the degrees of destruction or enrichment the Arabs wrought in North Africa. Their legendary history and military exploits are described in a lengthy epic, Sira Beni Hilal, *that was subsequently set down in Arabic. This work, still part of Arab Africa's oral tradition, is the source of the following selection, which describes the tribe's migration and conquest of Ifriqiya. The hero is Abu Zeid, and his adversary, the sultan of Ilam, is thought to be a Tuareg Berber chieftain.*

Abu Zeid gathered his people together and addressed them saying:—

Make ready for war O! sons of the Beni Hilal.
I shall take you on a journey.
And you must not even ask why.
I shall encamp with you in the vast open spaces,
Fit for the galloping of horses.
I shall encamp with you by Amdizira and by Tiziriya.
By Kimar and Ligiya the Pleasant.
Three ponds, the pools of Abu Riz
Which have made you prosperous.
There will be camels like the mountain Abu Faja.
They march onwards and appear from behind to sway backward and forward,
I shall encamp with you by the lakes of Amseriha which make a chain of pools,
We shall catch the young of the hippopotamus,
And eat the young of the fish "Umm Sharib".

His people said to him, "This is to our own liking." Again he addressed them saying:—

O! sons of the Beni Hilal.
I shall take you on a journey.
Where there are neither gad flies nor sweat flies.
Nor mosquitoes to prevent one from sleeping.
But wave on wave of the seven fingered "Abu Asaba" grass,
And on the ant-hills
Where the hartbeeste is striped
Where you will eat and sleep.

His people were willing and said, "Take us away." He said to them:—

If we migrate on a Tuesday,
People will say that is a peculiar day.
If we start on a Wednesday,
They will say that is the fourth of the days.
If we start on a Thursday
They will say that is an unpropitious day.
If we start on a Friday,
They will say that bad luck will come our way:
Our horses will be captured,
Our leaders will die.
If we start on a Saturday,
They will say that we shall not see the next Saturday.
If we start on a Sunday,
They will say that Sunday is a division between the living and the many dead.
If we start on a Monday,
They will say that this is the day that will be propitious:
Its mornings may be ill-omened, but its afternoons are sweet indeed.

They said, "Thus it is. Let us migrate with him." So we set off with him.

We leave the old women on the highway,
And we let the slave-girl, wearer of

The stone and mud dwellings opposite, near Medenine, were originally used by Tunisian nomads as storage bins. In recent years, as the population has become more settled, the huts have formed the nucleus of a village.
LIBRARY OF CONGRESS

the loin-cloth,
Sleep and awake in her shoes.
We let the slow-marching Bazgi camel
Lie down and rise again with his loads.
We let the mare Umm Dar'an
Lie down and rise again in her bridle
We let the goats, long-eared and long-horned,
Lie down and rise again with binding on their teats.

Abu Zeid went again to his mother and said to her:—

Mother, O! my mother.
We shall journey as the Zerma,
And as a king,
And as the prophets journeyed.
When they set out in search of Mecca.

His mother said to him:—

Go take counsel with your men
And let them tie the food bags on their horses,
Twin son, whose father and grandsire were both twins.
Do not undertake a night journey:
Let your wives travel in the day time,
And let the horses march behind them.
When your army lines up for battle
You take your stand between the lines of horses.
Like a rainbow
That shines from morn till night.
(Setting out on an expedition) is difficult for the man who has not seven young slave-girls,
With their bags of cumin seed,
And whose owner can take his repose near hanging draperies.
The horses of the strong and brave (Abu Zeid) assemble and line up in battle array,
The fat man dies and becomes food for birds.

Again Abu Zeid spoke and said:—

Hard for the man who has not seven newly-calved cows,
Their udders full of milk,
Hard for him who has not seven warriors
To shoulder the hardships of war.
Hard for him who has not seven concubines
To bring him edible fruits.
Hard for him who has not seven slaves
To carry the camel-bags.
We saddle our sleek steeds
Their well-kept bodies all covered with fat,
Our spears in our hands drawn ready for use, the long ones towering above the short ones.
Our followers mounted on barren mares which appeared like geldings,
Old men with beards, and youths the pride of maidens
Chewing the tobacco of prostitutes.
Saddle and mount for now the day of truth has come.

Again he said:—

I went out of my way to water and filled my water-skin,
And watered my steed,
Took up a short coat of mail and donned it,
And took up Al Jaz's coat and with it tied my loins.
The back of my head is as hard as nails,
Away on the outskirts of the town I heard people praising me.

So Abu Zeid went away with his tribesmen and came to Ilam [Tunis]. His men were so numerous that the wild animals came to the Sultan of Ilam's town, and the Sultan's wife said, "The whole of the bush is full of these wild animals." The Sultan of Ilam sent one of his men into the bush to bring them news of what was happening. He went off and found that the crowd was the tribesmen of Abu Zeid. He walked along their ranks for about forty days, and even then he did not get to the end of them. So he went back to the Sultan of Ilam and gave him the news. The Sultan said, "Of what does their wealth consist?" The man said to the Sultan:—

Their wealth is beasts whose backs have humps,
And whose lips are split.
They call them "Bazgi,"
And we call them "Ibl."
I fear them, they will despoil our land.
Let us go out and meet them in the bush.

So they went out towards them, but before they came to them they found a slave-girl belonging to Abu Zeid, who was digging up ant-hills. They said to her, "Whose slave-girl are you?" She answered, "I am Abu Zeid's slave-girl." They said to her, "Where is the place in which Abu Zeid has encamped?" She answered, "Beneath that tree yonder, he and his tribesmen are there." They said to her, "Where is the tree that will seat him and all his tribesmen?" She said to them, "The tree has seven large branches from each of which shoot other seven branches, and beneath each branch there are seven wells, and by each well there are seven troughs, and at each trough there water seventy-seven horses and seventy-seven shield-bearers and seventy-seven herds of camels." Then the Sultan of Ilam said to his tribesmen, "Go back home. We cannot prevail against them. So they went back. Abu Zeid's slave-girl cried out and Abu Zeid heard and came to where the slave-girl was. Now the people of the Sultan of Ilam were carrying water in water-skins, and because they were so much afraid they poured the water on the ground and urinated, and the ground all turned to mud because of the dampness and prevented Abu Zeid from following them.

Now a slave of Abu Zeid was herding cattle, and he fell asleep. His name was Sa'id Zerbul, the son of Sa'idi Jugongot. This slave held his feet in the air [while he slept] and he had long legs. When the people of Ilam in the town saw this, they mounted their horses and came to where the slave was and found him asleep. They thrust him with a spear, and he thought that it was a mosquito which had bitten him. He touched the place where the spear had pierced him and said:—

Here there are neither gad flies,
Nor sweat flies,
Nor mosquitoes to hinder one from sleeping,
What is it then that is biting me in this place?

Then he opened his eyes and saw mounted men completely surrounding him. He said to them, "If you are hunters, away with you and hunt your game: and if you drive guinea-fowl, be off and chase them." They said to him,

Sa'id Zerbul
Son of a woman whose food is chaff,
Her favorite food,
Who will retrieve your herds when the cattle raids come?

Sa'id answered them,

The man who retrieves our cattle when we are harried
Is Abu Zeid, who keeps every one right,
Abu Zeid the left-handed,
Who is like rain that falls from morn till the afternoon,
He and his nephew, with the broad chest and few bad qualities.

At that they frightened away the cattle, and he said to them, "Why have you driven off the cattle in the middle of the day?" He went off home, and Abu Zeid came out with his men against the Sultan of Ilam, and the Sultan, too, came out with his men against Abu Zeid. When they had drawn up in battle array the Sultan of Ilam said to his tribesmen, "To the man who kills Abu Zeid and brings his camel to me, I shall give wife upon wife and town upon town, and I shall give him my daughter Aze in marriage for him to live with her as his wife." Some of Abu Zeid's followers said of him:—

There is not amongst us or in our tribe any one like him,
Whoever meets him [in battle] will not live to rejoin his family.
As to meeting a maiden—
Food, even, he will not eat.
If Abu Zeid should charge at us with his horse
Our mares would drop their foals;
And if he should slash at us with his sword
Our spears would be twisted out of shape.

Abu Zeid's followers said to him, "We are hungry, excuse us and allow us to go and eat and satisfy our hunger and then we shall fight." Abu Zeid excused them, but said to their women folk, "Your men will break faith with me. Laziness has taken hold of them."

Now the son of the Sultan of Ilam's sister was putting on his armor and was mounting his horse to come against Abu Zeid's people, saying, "O! sons of the Beni Hilal, who amongst you is my equal or my uncle's equal?" They said to him "There is no one amongst us like you or like your uncle." Abu Zeid took up his sword, and sharpening it, would go in amongst the people of Ilam: and he turned to the Sultan of Ilam's nephew and killed him. Then he came to the Sultan of Ilam and caught hold of him and said to Diyab "Stab him!" So Diyab stabbed him. When he caught hold of him, Abu Zeid said to him, "Who am I, O! Sultan of Ilam?" The Sultan of Ilam said to him, "You are indeed a jester, a son of mirth." Abu Zeid said to him, "I am not a jester nor one of humor's sons. My mother is a Sherif. My forbears were as the prophets." At that he killed him. When he came to them, his people said to Abu Zeid, "We have brought the white mare whose galloping is like the flapping of a bird's wings, and who can fly as a bird, and [Ilam] was on its back making a great shout." Abu Zeid said to them:—

Since we set out we have drunk only fresh milk
And eaten prime meat.

Again Abu Zeid returned to the people of Ilam, and took prisoner the son of the Sultan of Ilam and said to him:—

We are brothers of yours
And your neighbors
Let us meet, and let a pact of peace
Be made between us and you:
You take our daughters in marriage
And we shall take yours,
And let us become related by marriage.

The Sultan of Ilam's son refused, saying:—

Life did not last for ever for Cana'an
Whose house was of iron and silver and gold and coral.

Abu Zeid's men said to him "Kill him." They said:—

Life did not last for ever for Thamra
Whose mother's children were nine in number,
Whose father's children were eight,
And whose own numbered ten.
They all died. Her eyes came out,
Her legs broke,
She begged water to drink but got not even that and she died.

So Abu Zeid killed him and his men despoiled their land.

FOLK WISDOM

These Moroccan proverbs, a commingling of Berber and Arabic cultures, were collected in this century by Edward Westermarck.

The pumpkin gives birth and the fence has the trouble.

A stone from the hand of a friend is an apple.

The tar of my country is better than the honey of others.

If you are a peg, endure the knocking; if you are a mallet, strike.

Among walnuts only the empty one speaks.

The world has not promised anything to anybody.

An old cat will not learn how to dance.

A pilgrim caravan is shown on its way to Mecca in this thirteenth-century Muslim painting.

OUT OF ARABIA

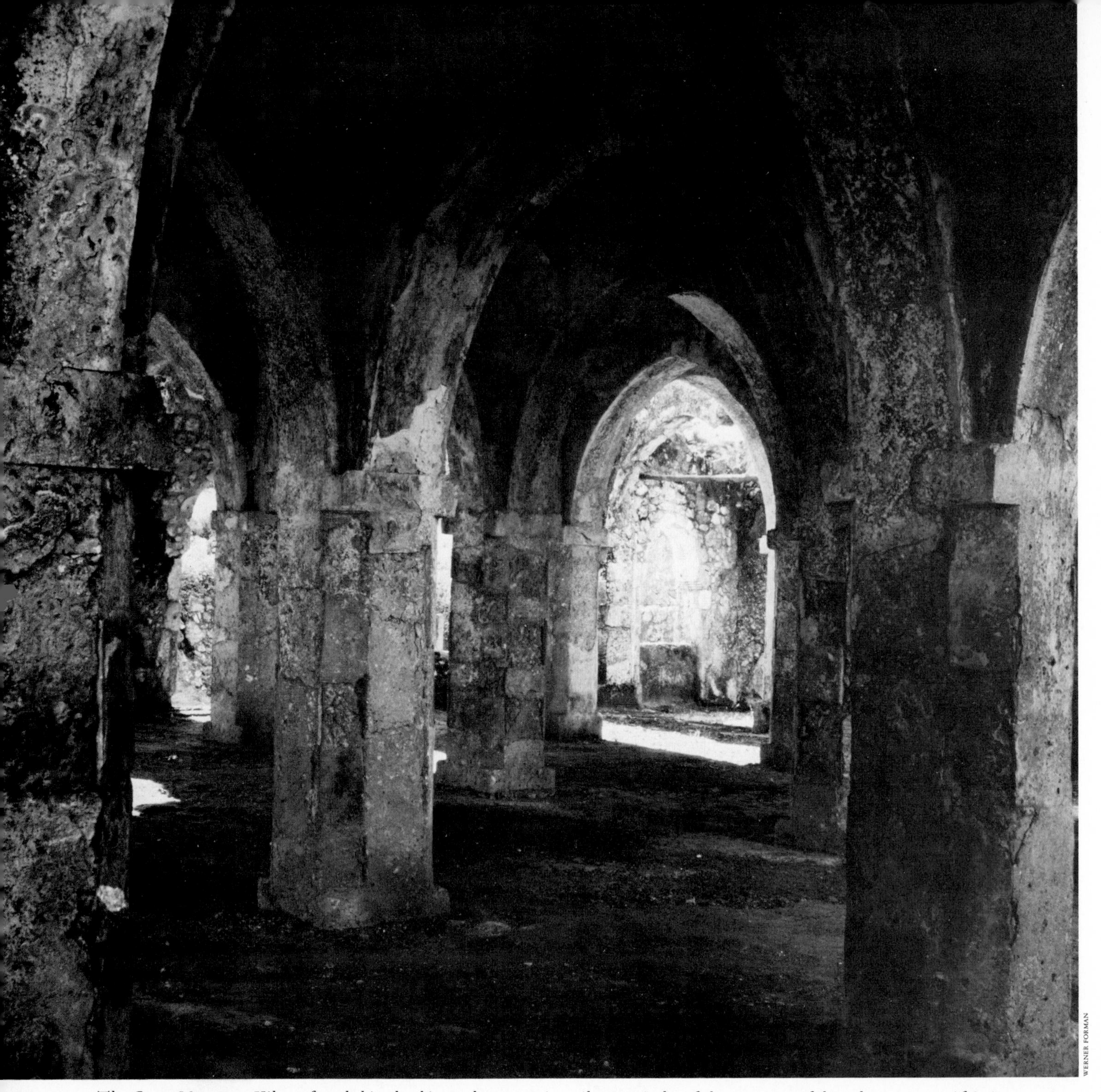

The Great Mosque at Kilwa, founded in the thirteenth century, is a silent reminder of the once-powerful trade center on Africa's east coast.

DOWN THE EAST COAST

Islam's penetration of East Africa was based on the development of maritime trade and was essentially peaceful. Difficult terrain and strong Christian states in Nubia and Ethiopia were obstacles to expansion from the north by land. However, by following sea routes long used by others, Muslims from Arabia and Persia settled along the East African coast, where towns already engaged in a trade that reached to China and Indonesia were discovered. Intermarrying with Africans and implanting Islamic religion and culture from the Red Sea coast to Mozambique, they created a string of city-states and sultanates like Kilwa in present-day Tanzania, whose wealth rested on the export of gold and ivory.

JOHN H.A. JEWELL, MOMBASA, KENYA

Evoking the image of Sinbad the Sailor, the Mombasa seaman at left combines Arab and African strains. Men like him, sailing Arab dhows (below), with their distinctive lateen sails, have conducted the commerce of East African coastal ports for centuries. A Ming Dynasty Chinese plate at right, probably from the fifteenth century, was discovered in an Arab burial ground in Dar es Salaam, evidence of the trade between Africa and far Asia.

WERNER FORMAN

RAPHO-GUILLUMETTE—MARC AND EVELYNE BERNHEIM

Islamic armies of North Africa, like those seen at the left in a twelfth-century view of a naval assault on Spain, included Berbers as well as Muslims from the Sudanese states south of the Sahara. The Muslim standard shown below was carried on an expedition to the Iberian Peninsula and was captured by Christians at the siege of Salado.

EL ESCORIAL, MADRID, MS. T-I-1

TOLEDO CATHEDRAL

RAPHO-GUILLUMETTE—MARC AND EVELYNE BERNHEIM

ACROSS NORTH AFRICA

Unlike its gradual expansion in East Africa, Islam virtually exploded across North Africa. Armies of Bedouins, Arabian Desert dwellers, entered Egypt in A.D. 639 and by 711 were invading the Iberian Peninsula from the Maghreb, far in the west. Despite divisions and almost constant warfare among rival Muslim groups in the following centuries, the Islamic religion became firmly rooted. Everywhere in North Africa, save among a minority in Egypt, Christianity all but died out. Islam gave enduring cultural unity to the region, but competing factions kept it politically divided. As a result, several new capitals were built, including that of Fez below, founded in 808 by the Idrisids in the western Maghreb.

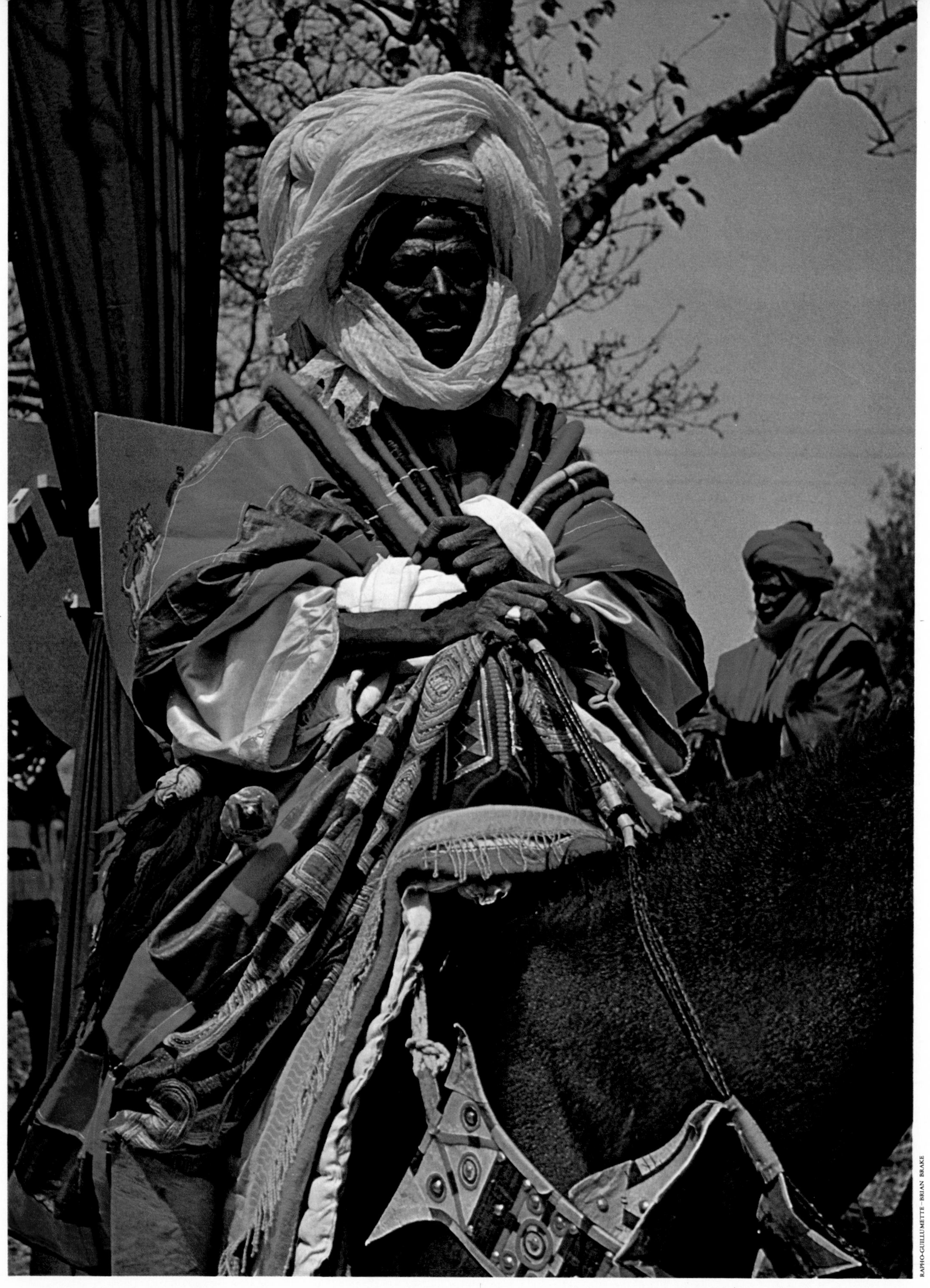

RAPHO-GUILLUMETTE—BRIAN BRAKE

Swathed in a voluminous turban and colorful robes, this horseman of modern Kano in northern Nigeria reflects Arab influences of long ago.

INTO THE DESERT

The map below, the first European depiction of the region of West Africa, was drawn in 1375 by Abraham Cresques. Relying on information from North African Muslim traders, the artist shows the Atlas range as a stone wall; he describes the Muslim ruler of Mali, Mansa Musa, shown lower right, as "the richest and most noble king in all the land."

RAPHO-GUILLUMETTE–MARC AND EVELYNE BERNHEIM

The Arab armies that overran North Africa made little more than occasional raids into the Fezzan and trips of exploration in the desert south of their newly won territories. The trans-Saharan trade with the black peoples of the Sudan was left in the hands of Tuareg and other Berber tribesmen who had been plying the caravan routes across the desert for centuries. Only gradually, as these tribes became converted to Islam, was the Muslims' influence felt in the Sudanese states. But their involvement deepened early in the ninth century when Arabs, lured by the gold trade, established increasing contact with the rulers of Kanem, near Lake Chad, and of Ghana. By the eleventh century the kings of Kanem had converted to Islam, and mosques, like the one at left at Agadès in the present-day Niger Republic, arose across the savanna country of the sub-Sahara. In time all the principal states of the Sudan were Muslim, and Black cities such as Timbuktu and Gao had become centers of Islamic power and learning.

BIBLIOTHEQUE NATIONALE

Chapter Five

KINGDOMS OF WEST AFRICA

(c. A.D. 500–1600)

by

A. Adu Boahen

IN WEST AFRICA, the area bounded to the north by the Sahara desert, to the south by the Atlantic Ocean, and to the east by Lake Chad and modern Cameroon, a number of independent states and empires evolved in the period between A.D. 500 and 1470. Among them were Ghana, Mali, Songhai, Kanem-Bornu, and the Hausa states, which were clustered along the southern frontier of the Sahara. Still farther south, between these states and the forest region, arose the Mole-Dagbane states and the Mossi states. Finally, in the forest and coastal zones of Guinea emerged the states of Takrur and Wolof in the region of the Senegal and Gambia rivers, or Senegambia; the Akan, Fante, and Ga states in the area of modern Ghana; and the states of Ife, Oyo, and Benin in Nigeria.

The questions that we shall attempt to answer here are: When did these states and empires crystallize and when did each attain its peak of greatness? How and why were they formed, and how were they governed? And what cultures and civilizations did they develop before the arrival of the Portuguese?

It is significant that the earliest of these states to grow into large kingdoms and empires were those in the savanna immediately to the south of the Sahara. Of these three, namely Ghana, Mali, and Songhai, the first to reach maturity was Ghana, peopled by the Soninke. It is not known for certain when it took form as a state. However, if there were as many as twenty-two kings before the rise of Islam in A.D. 622, as the oral traditions of Ghana tells, and if by the time the Persian geographer Al-Fazari was writing in A.D. 773–774 Ghana was already well known to North African and Middle Eastern traders as the Land of Gold, it is not unreasonable to suppose that it emerged as a full-fledged state in the fifth or sixth century A.D.

Benin ivory mask, once inlaid with iron, copper, and coral, and topped with a row of Portuguese heads

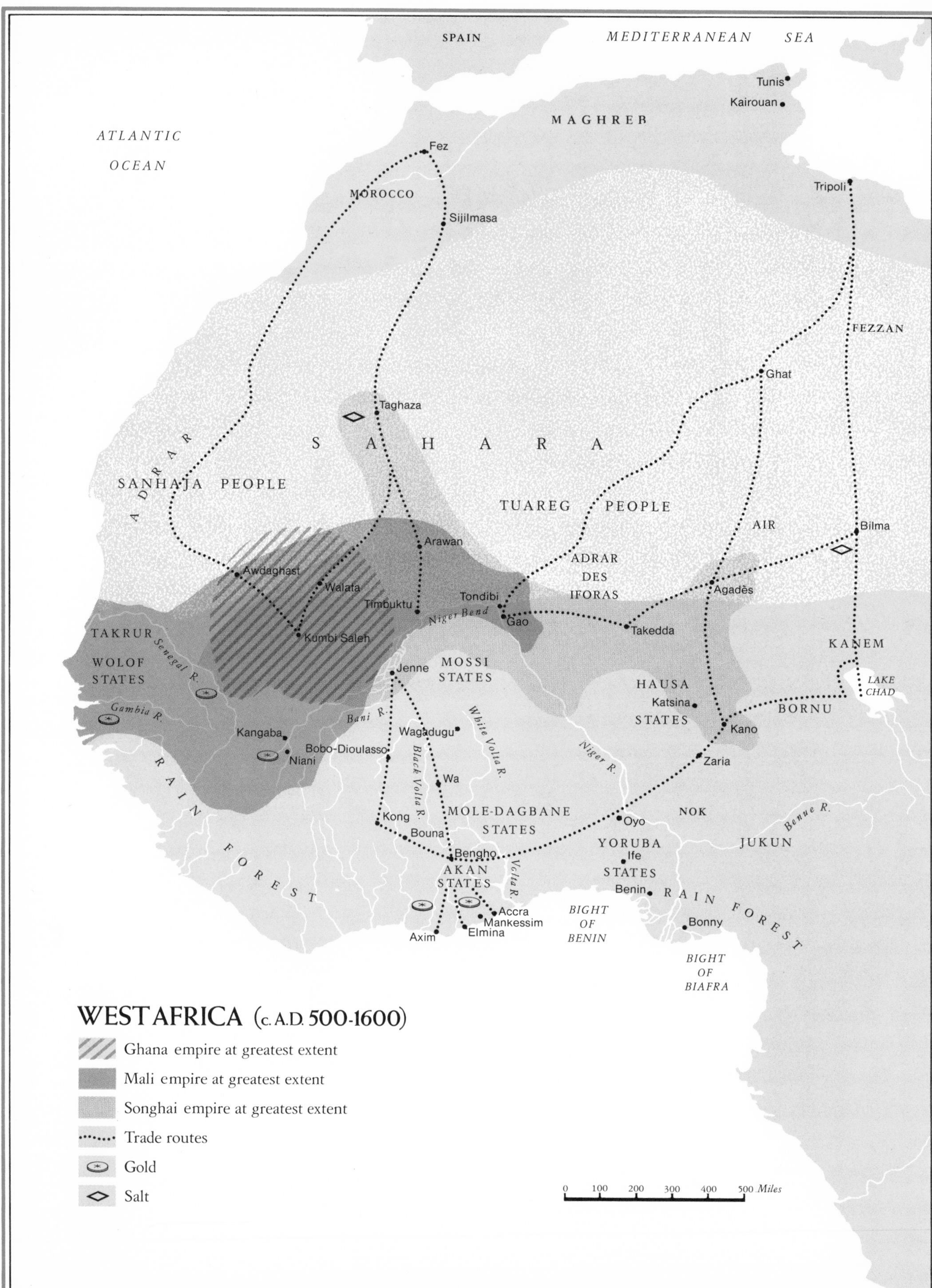
SPAIN
MEDITERRANEAN SEA
Tunis
Kairouan
MAGHREB
ATLANTIC
OCEAN
Fez
MOROCCO
Sijilmasa
Tripoli
FEZZAN
Ghat
Taghaza
S A H A R A
ADRAR
SANHAJA PEOPLE
TUAREG PEOPLE
AIR
Bilma
Arawan
ADRAR
DES
IFORAS
Awdaghast
Walata
Agadès
Tondibi
Timbuktu
Niger Bend
Gao
Takedda
TAKRUR
Senegal R.
Kumbi Saleh
KANEM
WOLOF
STATES
MOSSI
STATES
Jenne
HAUSA
Katsina
STATES
LAKE
CHAD
BORNU
Gambia R.
Bani R.
Kano
Kangaba
Wagadugu
White Volta R.
Niger R.
Niani
Bobo-Dioulasso
Zaria
Black Volta R.
Wa
RAIN FOREST
Kong
MOLE-DAGBANE
STATES
NOK
Oyo
Benue R.
Bouna
YORUBA
JUKUN
Bengho
Ife
AKAN
STATES
Volta R.
STATES
Benin
RAIN FOREST
Accra
Mankessim
Elmina
Axim
BIGHT
OF
BENIN
Bonny
BIGHT
OF
BIAFRA
WEST AFRICA (c. A.D. 500-1600)
Ghana empire at greatest extent
Mali empire at greatest extent
Songhai empire at greatest extent
Trade routes
Gold
Salt
0 100 200 300 400 500 Miles

There is no doubt that by A.D. 1000 Ghana had attained the peak of its power, an empire ruling over a number of smaller tribute-paying states and monopolizing West Africa's enormous and valuable gold trade to North Africa and Europe. This meant that Ghana and its formidable armies also dominated the roads of the Sahara and the savanna. Ibn Hawqal, the first known Arab explorer of the western Sudan, offers in his tenth-century *Book of Ways and Provinces* his impression of the Ghanaian sovereign: "the wealthiest of all kings on the face of the earth on account of the riches he owns and the hoards of gold acquired by him and inherited from his predecessors since ancient times." He based his estimate on the quantity of goods he saw being shipped through the Moroccan entrepôt of Sijilmasa.

Ghana's capital city was then Kumbi Saleh, which the Arab writer Al-Bakri described in 1067 as consisting of "two towns situated on a plain, one principally inhabited by Muslim traders, the other settled by the emperor and the local populace." The Muslim town was "large and possessed twelve mosques; in one of these mosques they assembled for the prayers on Fridays. There were imams and muezzins as well as jurists and scholars."

Ghana, however, began to decline during the second half of the eleventh century. Saharan Berbers, driven by territorial ambitions and inspired by Almoravid zeal, succeeded in disorganizing trade and stirring up rebellion among Ghana's tributaries. The empire was overthrown in 1235 by one of its former vassal states, the Susu kingdom, under its ruler Sumanguru Kante.

Mali, which succeeded Ghana, had emerged as a rather small principality by the end of the ninth century A.D. Between the eleventh and the thirteenth centuries it was dominated first by Ghana and then by the Susu kingdom, and it was not until the reign of Sundiata (1230–1255) that Mali embarked on its career of conquest. Building upon the administrative model of Ghana, it extended its trading empire over large parts of the western Sudan, and through the leadership of Mansa Kankan Musa, who reigned from 1312 to 1337, it absorbed such centers as Timbuktu, Gao, and Walata. Ibn Battuta, visiting Mali two decades after Mansa Musa's death, was astounded by the peace, order, and racial tolerance that prevailed in the empire:

> The Negroes possess some admirable qualities. They are seldom unjust and have a greater abhorrence of injustice than any other people. Their Sultan shows no mercy to any one guilty of the least act of it. There is complete security in their country. Neither traveler nor inhabitant in it has anything to fear from robbers or men of violence. They do not confiscate the property of any white man who dies in their country, even if it be uncounted wealth. On the contrary, they give it into the charge of some trust-worthy person among the whites, until the rightful heir takes possession of it.

Although the Portuguese, when they first came ashore in 1441, found that most of the states on the coast as well as in the immediate hinterland were still under the control of Mali, the state was already in a period of decline and Songhai was on the rise.

The Songhai people, with the city-state of Gao, or Al-Kawkaw, as their political center, had become active in the trans-Saharan trade by the end of the ninth century. Al-Yaqubi described Gao in 871 as "the greatest of the realms of the as-Sudan, the most important and most powerful, and all the other kingdoms obey its rulers." However, until the last quarter of the fourteenth century, it was controlled first by Ghana and then by Mali. Ibn Battuta, visiting Gao during the era of its vassalage to Mali, described it as "one of the finest towns in the Negroland. It is also one of their biggest and best provisioned towns with rice in plenty, milk and fish. . . ."

In 1375, however, Gao broke away from Mali, though it did not grow into an empire until the reign of Sunni Ali, the celebrated politician, soldier, and administrator who reigned from 1464 until 1492. The empire was consolidated and its frontiers further extended by the second of its most famous rulers, Askia Muhammad the Great. It was during his reign, which lasted from 1493 to 1528, that Songhai attained its peak, controlling the entire central region of the western Sudan.

Leo Africanus, a Christianized Arab geographer who visited Songhai in about 1510, has left us some vivid accounts of its intellectual and commercial life. For example, Gao was a town full of "exceeding rich merchants: and hither continually resort great store of Negroes which buy cloth here brought out of Barbarie and Europe. . . . It is a woonder to see what plentie of Merchandize is dayly brought hither, and how costly and sumptuous all things be."

However, during the last decade of that very century, for reasons to be discussed later, this sprawling and famous empire completely disintegrated. Its rulers were forced to retreat south along the Niger into their ancestral home in the region of Dendi.

In conformity with the Hamitic hypothesis, scholars of

the 1930's and 1940's attributed the foundation of these three states, as well as that of Kanem-Bornu and the Hausa states (which will be discussed in greater detail in Chapter Six), simply to some white-skinned invaders from the north. More recently, the introduction of the use of iron has been emphasized as the determining factor. To the present writer, their ascendance was the result of several major developments. The first was the rapid growth of population in the area immediately to the south of the Sahara and especially in the regions of the Niger Bend and the Senegambia. The second was the development of the caravan trade and the subsequent activities of wealthy and therefore powerful and ambitious families. The third was the spread of Islam.

The steady increase of the savanna's population between 1000 B.C. and A.D. 300 or 400 was caused in part by the Neolithic revolution (that is, the change from the hunting of wild animals and the collection of wild fruits to the cultivation of food crops and domestication of animals). Historians and ethnobotanists are still hotly debating whether or not there was an independent Neolithic revolution among the Mande peoples in the region of the Niger Bend in about 5000 B.C. But even if this revolution was introduced into Africa from Asia via Egypt, there is no doubt that the area between the Niger Bend and the middle Senegal River as well as the areas around Lake Chad proved a superior environment for the cereal crops, especially sorghum and millet, which were among the first crops to be cultivated. The Mande and the Kanuri peoples of those areas must, therefore, have obtained an early lead over all the others. Since they could also supplement their diet through fishing, these peoples must have been able to produce food in such quantities that their numbers multiplied. As the contemporary British Africanist J. D. Fage has pointed out, this Neolithic revolution must have also led to "the beginnings of urbanization and of organized government and administration, and, even, perhaps, the flourishing of the idea of a king as a god-like being supreme over all his subjects."

This increase in population must have been further accelerated by the steady desiccation of the Sahara from about 3000 B.C. onward. As the Sahara slowly assumed its barren look, a process that was complete by 1500 B.C., some of its inhabitants began to drift into the savanna belt.

The use of iron tools must also have had its effect on population growth in that it facilitated agriculture, but surely it was not, as some scholars have argued, the principal factor in the rise of the western Sudanese states. If this were so, it would follow that the states would have emerged much earlier—nearer 300 B.C., when iron technology is thought to have reached the Nok culture on the lower Niger—and first in the east rather than in the west as, in fact, happened.

It would seem then to this writer that by about the last century B.C. or the first century A.D. the whole of the savanna in general, and the regions of Lake Chad, the Niger Bend, and Nok in particular, must have been occupied by large populations living in family, lineage, or clan groups, in villages bound together by kinship ties or even in city-states and small kingdoms ruled possibly by "divine" kings. Something else must have been needed to stimulate one or more of these nuclei to develop into larger kingdoms and, eventually, empires, and this stimulus must have been provided by the caravan trade. From rock paintings of two-wheeled horse-drawn war chariots and from other archeological data, it is clear that by 1000 B.C. the caravan trade was well established along two main routes. These were a western route through Morocco to the Niger Bend and a central route through the Fezzan, Ghat, and Adrar des Iforas, possibly to the region of Gao on the Niger. The main beasts of burden were bullocks and, after 1200 B.C., horses. It is equally clear from the fifth-century B.C. accounts of Herodotus and from other ancient Greek and Roman sources that both the Carthaginians and the Romans were trading with the people of the savanna belt through Berber intermediaries settled in the Fezzan and the western Sahara.

However, this trade could not have been very extensive until the introduction of the camel. The use of this singularly endowed beast of burden spread westward and then southward into the Sahara, and as a result, a complicated network of caravan routes across the Sahara was developed between about A.D. 200 and 500. To the Morocco-Niger route and the old Garamantes' route from Tripoli to Chad and to Gao was added a caravan route from Egypt to Gao by way of the Saharan oases, including Ghat and the future site of Agadès.

As trade expanded with the use of the camel, not only did more and more people grow wealthy but handicrafts, mining, and agriculture were stimulated. So, too, urban centers grew in size and influence. Wealth, of course, generates among individuals and families still greater ambition and the desire to control more and more trading activities and trade routes. It is the activities of the talented members of these families (especially of such men as Sundiata and Mansa Musa of Mali and Sunni Ali and Askia Muhammad of Songhai) and not the mere use of iron that bring about

The people of the Nok culture, in northern Nigeria, produced these sublime terra-cotta heads more than two thousand years ago. These and other artifacts offer a glimpse of an emerging agricultural society, which, further research may show, extended over hundreds of square miles. Material remains also indicate that the Nok were versed in ironworking and adept in making stone tools, not unlike those that are in use today.
ALL: F. L. KENETT

the creation of large states and empires.

The people who would be the first beneficiaries of this increasing trade would naturally be those living in the border zone between the Sahara and the savanna, an ideal position from which to play the lucrative role of the middleman. The Soninke of Ghana and the Kanuri of the old state of Kanem were the peoples at the crossroads of the Sahara and the savanna, and they were among the first to develop kingdoms and then empires. The fact that no large kingdoms emerged in Hausaland until the fourteenth century, when the north-south trade began there, provides a further indication of the importance of caravan trade in state-building.

The final factor, which did not cause, but rather accelerated or facilitated to some extent the growth of the empires of Mali and Songhai, as well as Kanem-Bornu and the Hausa states, must have been the introduction of Islâm. This religion penetrated the Sahara via the caravan routes and reached the savanna in the ninth and tenth centuries.

Islam is not just a body of doctrines, but a complete way of life, having its own laws, its own system of taxation and administration of justice, its own statecraft, and its own language and traditions of scholarship. Islam's adoption by the rulers of Gao in the tenth century and of Mali and Kanem in the eleventh century must have given them access to all these sciences as well as the means by which to create an educated bureaucracy. A more intense exposure to Islam was gained by those who took the hadj, or pilgrimage, to the Islamic civilization of the Middle East.

It is known, for instance, that on Mansa Musa's celebrated pilgrimage to Mecca in 1324–1325, he met the Spanish scholar, poet, and architect As-Sahili, whom he successfully persuaded to go with him to Mali. It is also known that not only did As-Sahili insist on a strict observance of Islam, but he revolutionalized architecture of Mali and of the western Sudan in general by introducing brick as the building material for mosques and palaces. Similarly, during his equally famous hadj to Mecca in 1497 Askia Muhammad the Great also met and befriended great scholars such as Abd ar-Rahman as-Suyuti and Muhammad al-Majhili, with whom he began a lifelong correspondence. The latter actually visited him in Songhai and gave him as well as the king of Kano a great deal of advice on religion and politics.

Nevertheless, the governments of all these early Sudanese empires were of the divine-kingship type, a typically African conception, indicating that these states did not derive their political institutions from Islam, but possibly from ancient Ghana or, in any case, from indigenous Mande institutions. At the head of each was a hereditary monarch. He was assisted by a council of ministers, whose members, following the introduction of Islam, were mostly literate Muslims. Al-Bakri, writing in 1067, tells us that even though the king of Ghana held animistic beliefs, the official in charge of his treasury and the majority of his ministers were Muslims. Unfortunately, we do not have the titles of the ministers of Ghana, but they were probably similar to those of Songhai, whose cabinet included the *hi-koy* (the commander of the navy), *dyina-koy* (commander in chief of the army), *hari-farma* (minister in charge of navigation and fishing), *fari-mundyo* (minister of taxation), *waney-farma* (minister in charge of property), *korey-farma* (minister in charge of foreigners), and *sao-koy* (minister in charge of forests).

The divine-kingship nature of the government is further borne out by descriptions that we have of their court protocol and ceremonial. According to Al-Bakri:

A caravan approaching Timbuktu, the intellectual and trading center of the Songhai empire, as depicted in an 1853 German engraving
BARTH, *Travels in Central Africa*, 1857

The king [of Ghana] adorns himself like a woman wearing necklaces round his neck and bracelets on his forearms, and when he sits before the people he puts on a high cap decorated with gold and wrapped in a turban of fine cloth. The court of Appeal is held in a domed pavilion around which stand ten horses covered with gold-embroidered materials. Behind the king stand ten pages holding shields and swords decorated with gold and on his right are the sons of the vassal kings of his country wearing splendid garments and their hair plaited with gold. The governor of the city sits on the ground before the king and around are ministers seated likewise. At the door of the pavilion are dogs of excellent pedigree who hardly ever leave the place where the king is, guarding him. Round their necks, they wear collars of gold and silver studded with a number of balls of the same metal. The audience is announced by the beating of a drum which they call daba, made from a long hollow log. When the people who profess the same religion as the king approach him, they fall on their knees and sprinkle dust on their heads for this is their way of showing respect for him. As for the Muslims, they greet him only by clapping their hands.

Ibn Battuta, who visited and had an audience with Mansa Sulaiman, the brother and successor of Mansa Musa, describes another court ritual:

> On certain days the Sultan holds audience in the palace yard.... The Sultan comes out of a door in a corner of the palace, carrying a bow in his hand and a quiver on his back. On his head he has a golden skull cap... [he] is preceded by his musicians.... As he takes his seat the drums, trumpets and bugles are sounded .... Two saddled and bridled horses are brought, along with two goats which they hold to serve as a protection against the evil eye.... The Negroes are of all people the most submissive to their king and the most abject in their behavior before him. They swear by his name.... If he summons any of them while he is holding an audience in his pavilion, the person summoned takes off his clothes and puts on worn garments, removes his turban and dons a dirty skull-cap, and enters with his garments and trousers raised knee-high. He goes forward in an attitude of humility and dejection, and knocks the ground hard with his elbows, then stands with bowed head and bent back listening to what he says. If any one addresses the king and receives a reply from him, he uncovers his back and throws dust over his head and back for

> all the world like a bather splashing himself with water. I used to wonder how it was they did not blind themselves.

And finally, from Leo Africanus' eyewitness account of the court of Songhai at Timbuktu:

> The rich king of Tombuto hath many plates and scepters of gold, some whereof weigh 1300 poundes . . . and he keepes a magnificent and well furnished court. When he travelleth any whither he rideth upon a camell, which is led by some of his noblemen; and so he doth likewise when hee goeth to warfar, and all his souldiers ride upon horses. Whosoever will speake unto this king must first fall downe before his feete, & then taking up earth must sprinkle it upon his owne head & shoulders: which custom is ordinarily observed by them that never saluted the king before, or come as ambassadors from other princes.

The drums, the linguists, the praise singers, the gold swords and caps, the prostrations and the removal of sandals in the presence of the king are closely observed to this very day in some courts of African kings (for example, among the Akan of modern Ghana). It is true that both Mali and Songhai added such Muslim trappings as banquets and Turkish and Egyptian bodyguards to their courts, while some of their symbols of investiture—the tunic, turban, and sword—were certainly Islamic. But the basic court ceremonial and protocol, and the position of the king in both Mali and Songhai, were definitely pre-Islamic and African in origin, most probably deriving from those of ancient Ghana.

However, some differences appear in the system of royal succession. It is clear from Al-Bakri's account that like the present practice among the Akan people, royal succession in Ghana was matrilineal, whereas in the later Mali and Songhai empires it was patrilineal. Al-Bakri was informed that Tunka Manin succeeded not his father but his maternal uncle. And as if to dispel any doubts, he added: "This is their custom and their habit, that the kingdom is inherited only by the son of the king's sister." He goes on to give an explanation of what appeared to him to be a most odd and non-Muslim practice: "He the king has no doubt that his successor is a son of his sister, while he is not certain that his son is in fact his own, and he does not rely on the genuineness of this relationship."

Although the fourteenth-century Tunisian historian Ibn Khaldun did report that one of the kings of Mali, Abu Bakr, was the son of a daughter of Sundiata, and although it has been inferred from this that royal succession in Mali at times went through the female line, a recent authority has shown that this was an exception to the rule. It would appear then that royal succession in both Mali and Songhai generally followed the patrilineal rather than the matrilineal rule. This difference might well be due to the impact of Islam.

The systems of provincial government in these Sudanese empires show some differences, but in degree rather than in kind. In all three cases the kings were directly responsible for the administration of the core, or metropolitan part, of the empire, which they divided into provinces ruled by governors. In the case of both Mali and Songhai, these governors either were members of the royal family or former generals. The governors in turn appointed district chiefs to administer a number of villages, each of which was ruled by a village chief.

The other parts of the empire, consisting of states conquered and reduced to vassal or tributary status, were governed in a variety of ways. In Ghana it would appear that the states remained under their own rulers and that their main obligations were to pay annual tribute and to supply contingents to the king's army when called upon to do so. Sons of vassal rulers were occasionally kept at the king's court to ensure their fathers' continued allegiance. In Mali the same system prevailed, with some minor improvements: the sovereigns of the conquered states retained their right to rule, but only after being invested by the Mansa and given a Mande title; the swearing of allegiance and the payment of tribute were seen as proofs of loyalty.

The kings of Songhai, especially Askia Muhammad, made still greater improvements toward centralizing the administration of government. Askia Muhammad ruled metropolitan Gao directly, but he reduced the status of the conquered rulers further by placing governors and minor governors over them. As was the case in Mali, these were court favorites or members of the royal family. Above this structure he created four viceroyalties, or regions, each under a viceroy, or commissioner, who was in charge of a cluster of provinces. These viceroyalties were Dendi, Bal, Benga, and Kurmina. Since most of these administrative posts were appointive rather than hereditary, Songhai must have had a much more tightly controlled and more effective system of provincial administration than the other two.

Arabic sources do not throw much light on the system of justice in these states. For the most part, the kings were directly responsible for its administration. We are told by Al-Bakri that the kings of Ghana went out on horses every day to summon those people who had been wronged or had suffered any injustice to come and lodge a complaint. Trial by wood was also practiced in ancient Ghana. According to Al-Bakri, "When a man is accused of denying a debt or having shed blood or some other crime, a headman takes a thin piece of wood, which is sour and bitter to taste, and pours upon it some water which he then gives to the defendant to drink. If the man vomits, his innocence is recognized and he is congratulated. If he does not vomit and the drink remains in his stomach, the accusation is accepted as justified." The kings held what seem to have been courts of appeal in their palaces. Cases were initially heard, especially in the towns, by *qadis*, who obviously administered justice in accordance with the Koran and the Sharia (Muslim law). These judges also wielded great influence at the court of the kings. Ibn Battuta's main contact with the king of Mali was a *qadi*, whom he described as "a negro, a pilgrim, and a man of fine character." The chroniclers of the Timbuktu *Tarikh* indicate that the *qadis* of that town were all from the Aqit family and wielded considerable influence over the Askias. One of them, Al-Aqib, who died in 1583, was noted for his frankness. "He was of stout heart," wrote one of the chroniclers, "bold in the mighty affairs that others hesitate before, courageous in dealing with the ruler and those beneath him. He had many conflicts with them and they used to be submissive and obedient to him in every matter. If he saw something he thought reprehensible, he would suspend his activities as *qadi* and keep himself aloof. Then they would conciliate him until he returned."

These high-ranking officials appear to have been rewarded for their services. Most of them, certainly those of Mali and Songhai, were given fiefs, or serf domains, as well as valuable goods. According to Al-Umari, some of the provincial governors of Mali received as much as "1500 mithqals [a unitary measure equal to one eighth of an ounce] of gold every year besides which he the king keeps them in horses and clothes." To encourage civil servants and military men, the kings of Mali instituted various decorations, such as the award of golden bracelets, collars, and anklets. The highest of all the awards, presumably given to soldiers, was the Honor of the Trousers. An eyewitness told the fourteenth-century writer Al-Umari: "Whenever a hero adds to the list of his exploits, the King gives him a pair of wide trousers, and the greater the number of a knight's exploits the bigger the size of his trousers. These trousers are characterised by narrowness in the leg and ampleness in the seat."

It is interesting to note that the Scottish explorer Alexander Gordon Laing, who visited among the Mandingos of Solimana in 1822, observed: "The width of the trousers is a great mark of distinction." This is true of the Dagomba and Mamprusi of northern Ghana to this day.

For the maintenance of law and order, and for defensive as well as offensive purposes, each of these west Sudanese empires had an army. Mali and Ghana had no standing armies; they, like many African kingdoms, depended on contingents contributed upon demand by vassal states. According to Al-Bakri, the kings of Ghana could raise an army of 200,000, of whom 40,000 were archers; and Mansa Musa of Mali could call up 100,000, a tenth of whom were cavalrymen. Songhai also relied on levies until the reign of Askia Muhammad, who instituted a professional army. It was this new army that enabled him not only to ensure stability and order, but to extend the boundaries of the empire that he had inherited from Sunni Ali. The armies of all these empires used the same weapons and were organized in the same way. They were divided into cavalry and infantry, their main weapons being spears, swords, javelins, and bows and arrows. Firearms were completely unknown until the Moroccan invasion late in the sixteenth century.

It would appear that both Mali and Songhai established diplomatic relations with the Maghreb and Egypt and kept up regular contacts with the sultan of Morocco. Mansa Sulaiman, Mansa Musa's brother and successor as king of the Mali, exchanged deputations with Morocco's Marinid sultans, and on the occasion of a new sultan's enthronement, sent an embassy to do him honor. Sulaiman's successor is also known to have sent gifts to the new sultan of Morocco. Among them was a giraffe, which the Moroccans talked about for a long time "because of the various adornments and markings which it combined in its body and attributes."

The complex administrative machineries of these states must have been expensive to run. Three main sources filled the royal treasury: tribute from vassal states, import and export duties, and imperial domains. Details of the annual levies have not been preserved, but of the duties collected in Ghana, Al-Bakri writes, "for every donkey loaded with salt that enters the country, the king takes a duty of one gold dinar, and two dinars from every one that leaves. From a load of copper the king's due is five mithqals and from a load of other goods ten mithqals." We are also told that in Ghana any gold nugget found by anybody had to be surrendered to the king. Both Mali and Songhai imposed similar duties on goods coming to and fro. In fact, Songhai had a minister solely concerned with taxation.

The third, and probably the greatest, source of revenue was from the royal estates. Ghana's records are quite silent on this; but it is clear from the accounts of Mali and Songhai that the kings had royal domains—some hereditary and some acquired by war—in different parts of the empire. After his victory over Mali, Askia Muhammad is said to have added twenty-four fiefs to his holdings. These were occupied and worked by slaves whose overseers, or *fanfa*, were charged with raising a fixed quantity of produce every year for the kings.

"Some of these *fanfa*," says the chronicler of the Askia dynasty, "had under them 100 slaves employed in cultivation, whilst others had 60, 50, 40, or 20." Each estate had a special function: some had to provide such commodities as yams, grain, or fish; others had to manufacture such goods as bows and arrows. Before the reign of Askia Muhammad the Great, the quantity of articles or provisions to be produced by each fief was not fixed, but Askia the Great set rigid quotas. Thus the Abda estate in the province of Dendi had to produce 1,000 sunhas (6,500 bushels) of rice annually. A chronicler reported: "This was fixed, which could neither be increased nor reduced." The Dyam Tene and Dya Wali estates had to supply 100 iron spears and 100 arrows per family per year. As the personal property of the kings, the estates were often given away as presents to trusted courtiers and friends.

The principal exports of Ghana, Mali, and Songhai were gold, ivory, slaves, and later, from the thirteenth century onward, kola nuts, a stimulant highly prized among Muslims. Most of these commodities, especially gold and kola nuts, came from the forest regions along trade routes controlled mainly by the Diula, a Mande people. The chief imports from the north were salt, horses, textiles, linen, books, writing paper, swords, and knives.

Ghana, situated as it was in the borderlands between the Sahara and the savanna, was most dependent upon the caravan trade; its people played the leading role as middlemen between producers and merchants. Al-Yaqut says of thirteenth-century Ghana: "From here, one enters the arid waste when going to the land of gold, and without the town of Ghana, this journey would be impossible."

Elsewhere Al-Yaqut adds that merchants from the north took with them Ghanaians as interpreters and go-betweens in negotiating with gold miners to the south. (It would appear that only small amounts of gold were mined in Ghana itself.) Ghana was also able to control the crucial and very lucrative trade in salt imported from the Taghaza mines of the western Sahara, "the source of an enormous income," according to Al-Bakri.

Since both Mali and Songhai successively gained direct control over some of the southern gold-producing regions, Wangara in particular, and since they were able to establish peace and order along the caravan routes, they must have derived even more income from trade than had Ghana. It is quite clear from Maghrebin, Egyptian, and Sudanese sources that from the thirteenth to the fifteenth centuries, when Europe and the Muslim world were facing an acute shortage of precious metals, the western Sudan was their chief source of gold. The enormous quantities of gold that both Mansa Musa and Askia Muhammad took with them on their pilgrimages to Mecca, in 1324 and 1497 respectively, leaves no doubt about the wealth their states possessed in gold.

However, other commodities also contributed to the income of Mali and Songhai. Both were favorably situated to practice agriculture, cattle breeding, and fishing. Ibn Battuta and Leo Africanus indicate that a certain amount of rice and millet was exported great distances. Fishing was quite important among the Sorko clans of Songhai, and some of the royal estates had their quota of fish to catch. Numerous craftsmen, tailors, blacksmiths, and cloth weavers attracted traders, too. Leo Africanus reports that Timbuktu had "many shops of artificers and merchants and especially such as weave linen and cotton cloth." Another chronicler wrote that there were as many as twenty-six tailors' workshops in the crossroads city, each with between fifty and one hundred apprentices.

Society in the Sudanese states was highly stratified. At the top was the ruling aristocracy, consisting of the royal families, officials, and Muslim scholars. The second and major part of the population consisted of merchants, farmers, fishermen, and cattle breeders. At the bottom were the slaves, who constituted only a small percentage of the population. It should be emphasized that the status of a slave in these early states, as indeed in almost all African societies, was fundamentally different from that which would prevail in the Americas. Not only was the number relatively small but slaves were treated as human beings rather than as chattel.

Although Islam had remained essentially the religion of foreigners in ancient Ghana, superficial changes reflecting the influence of the new faith began to appear in Mali and Songhai. The administration of justice and the system of taxation in those states were based on the Koran. The architecture of the principal buildings, the mosques, and the palaces was Islamic, as was the attire of the town dwellers. Al-Umari wrote that "they wear turbans with ends tied under their chin like the Arabs, their cloth is white and made of cotton which they cultivate and weave in a most excellent fashion." Ibn Battuta was also impressed by the attention paid to religious worship. "They are careful to observe the hours of prayer," he noted, "and assiduous in attending them in congregations, and in bringing up their children to them."

By the late fifteenth century Timbuktu had developed into the educational and commercial metropolis of the western Sudan, or rather, as one writer called it, the Queen of the Sudan. Its university, in the Sankore district of the city, produced such scholars and historians as Mahmud al-Kati, author of the *Kitab al-Fattash*, a chronicle of Songhai's Askia dynasty, and Abd al-Rahman as-Sadi, author of the *Tarikh as-Sudan*, a chronicle of the Sudan. Even the West African historian J. Spencer Trimingham, who is rather skeptical about Sankore as a university, admits that there were as many as one hundred fifty Koranic schools in Timbuktu alone. Leo Africanus also talks of "the great store of doctors, judges, priests, and other learned men that are bountifully maintained at the King's cost and charges. And hither are brought diverse manuscripts or written books out of Barbarie which are sold for more money than any other merchandise."

Mahmud al-Kati pays tribute in the *Kitab al-Fattash* to his colleagues: "The scholars of this period were the most respected among the believers for their generosity, their force of character, and their discretion." We also have the names of scholars who went on lecture tours and set up schools in different parts of the western Sudan, and especially in Hausaland. Mahmud Ibn Umar, for instance, lectured in Kano in 1485 to large and reverent crowds of people. Indeed, the Timbuktu tradition of learning dominated the cities of the western and central Sudan until the beginning of the nineteenth century.

But if the towns in Mali and Songhai assumed an Islamic hue, it would appear that the rural areas of both empires stuck to their traditional ways. They maintained their animistic beliefs, their traditional cults and indigenous African way of life, their initiation rites, their sorcerers, and their family and clan heads and chiefs, who administered justice in accordance with customary law.

It should be obvious from the above that, in spite of the skepticisms of certain European writers, the early empires of the western Sudan were true states, with all the fundamental attributes of government that statehood implies. They had paid bureaucracies, strong economies based on trade, mining, agriculture, and political machinery capable of ensuring law, order, security, and diplomatic exchange.

Using a hand hoe, the farmer at right prepares soil for cultivation along the banks of the Niger near Timbuktu. Africans of the western Sudan are credited among mankind's leading agricultural innovators, having developed a wide range of cereal grains such as fonio, acha grass, hungry rice, pearl millet, and sorghum. The cone-shaped structures opposite are granaries built by the Dogon people of Mali. Sun-dried bricks and thatch are the traditionally used construction materials.

BLACK STAR—C. TRIESCHMANN

The fall of all these states was due to both internal and external factors. The internal factors were usually the rivalries among members of the royal family. The external factors were for the most part foreign attacks. With the possible exception of Songhai, none of these empires had a really durable provincial administrative structure. As pointed out earlier, the conquered states and kingdoms within each empire were governed by their own rulers and were held to the central authority mainly by military might. Moreover, each empire was composed of different ethnic and linguistic groups, hence it lacked cultural and ethnic homogeneity. Some of the rulers of both Mali and Songhai did attempt to use Islam to provide cohesion, but only with very limited success. Both Ghana's central authority and its army were weakened as a result of the defeats they suffered between 1054 and 1076 by the adherents of the Almoravid movement. As described more fully in Chapter Four, this was an Islamic movement that arose in the eleventh century among the Sanhaja Berbers who occupied the western Sahara. Although Ghana did reconquer its capital from the Almoravids after 1087, it never really recovered from those earlier blows, and its vassal states broke away. The coup de grâce,

WERNER FORMAN

however, was delivered in 1203 by an external force, the rulers of the Susu kingdom to the south.

Mali fell victim principally to the internal breakdown of the central government, as a result of the inordinate ambition and frivolity of its royal family. The trouble began at the end of the reign of Mansa Sulaiman in 1359–1360. The history of the kings of Mali for the next several decades was a sordid record of regicides, civil wars, contested successions, and coups d'état. Indeed, within the brief period from 1360 to 1390 as many as seven people were enthroned, four of them between 1387 and 1390. Central authority collapsed, anarchy and instability came in its wake, and as in Ghana, the vassal states began to break away. The demise of the empire came after Mali had been attacked from three sides: the Tuareg attacked from the north, the Mossi from the south, and the Songhai from the east. By 1433 the Tuareg had captured Arawan, Walata, and Timbuktu, and in the 1460's and the 1470's the Mossi took arms against the southern and even the central regions of Mali. The rulers of Mali appealed to Portugal for assistance in the 1490's and again in the 1530's. The Portuguese could do nothing but send words of encouragement. The Songhai attacks delivered the final blow, and by the fourth decade of the sixteenth century Mali had shrunk again into the tiny Mande principality of Kangaba.

Songhai's glory lasted little more than a century after its victories over Mali. The establishment of the Askia dynasty in Songhai in 1493, a result of the military coup organized and led by Askia Muhammad, was the beginning of the internal division of the country. Being of the Soninke rather than the Songhai people, he tried to replace the animistic beliefs of the Songhai with Islam, as indeed Sunni Ali, his predecessor, had done in an effort to unify the empire. Though Askia Muhammad's attempts only alienated the Songhai people, he was shrewd and strong enough to contain these internal differences. His successors could not. As had been the case in Mali, a series of disputed successions, revolts, and usurpations broke out among members of his family. In the sixty years after his deposition as many as eight people mounted the throne. However, it would appear that at least one of the rulers, Askia Daud, was quite competent, and during his long reign from 1549 to 1582 the fortunes of Songhai improved. Although disputed successions broke out again after Daud, and as many as three rulers came to the throne between 1582 and 1591, the central authority would appear to have remained intact.

It was the decisive defeat inflicted by the forces of Sultan Al-Mansur of Morocco that precipitated the disintegration of the empire. Led by Judar Pasha, a young Spanish eunuch, the sultan's army crushed the Songhai army at the battle of Tondibi in 1591 and marched south in search of Songhai's fabled riches. The Songhai army was estimated by Al-Kati to have been a huge one consisting of 18,000 cavalry and 9,700 infantry, while the Moroccans are said to have numbered only 4,000. The Moroccan victory was in some measure due to the fact that the Songhai fought with spears, swords, and bows and arrows, whereas the Moroccan army was equipped with harquebuses and cannon. When the advisers of Al-Mansur tried to dissuade him from undertaking what they considered to be a crazy enterprise, the sultan is said to have replied:

> You talk of the dangerous desert we have to cross, of the fatal solitudes, barren of water and pasture, but you forget the defenseless and ill-equipped merchants who, mounted or on foot, regularly cross these wastes which caravans have never ceased to traverse. I, who am so much better equipped than they, can surely do the same with an army which inspires terror wherever it goes. . . . Moreover, our predecessors would have found great difficulty if they had tried to do what I now propose, for their armies were composed only of horsemen armed with spears and of bowmen; gunpowder was unknown to them, and so were firearms and their terrifying effect. Today the Sudanese have only spears and swords, weapons which will be useless against modern arms. It will therefore be easy for us to wage a successful war against these people and prevail over them.

Following Al-Mansur's military success, however, anarchy broke out in the area of the Niger Bend, and it would continue intermittently until the late nineteenth century.

And what was happening in the regions to the south of the empires of Ghana, Mali, and Songhai? As has been already pointed out, a simultaneous process of state formation was at work. Arising just to the west in the regions of the Senegambia was the kingdom of Wolof; to the south emerged the Mole-Dagbane states and the Mossi kingdoms. Still farther south arose a number of forest and coastal states: Ife, Oyo, and Benin in Nigeria; the Ga kingdom and Akan states in modern Ghana. Their emergence was due to factors similar to those that gave birth to Ghana, Mali, and Songhai. Of first importance was the extension of the caravan trade routes southward into the savanna, the forest, and the coastal regions; of second was the the development within the region of trade among the coastal peoples; and of third were the activities of the wealthy and ambitious families or clan groups who were stimulated by those commercial activities.

As has already been pointed out, the mainstays of the caravan trade—gold, kola nuts, ivory, and slaves—could all be obtained in the regions of the southern savanna and forest. From evidence rapidly accumulating today, it is certain that by the end of the fourteenth century, at the height of Mali's power, the trade routes from the Sahara, which had earlier stopped at the savanna cities of Walata, Timbuktu, Jenne, and Gao, had now been extended westward and southward.

The people who were responsible for the development of this trade between the forest regions and the states of Mali and Songhai were certainly the Diula group of the Mande people. They founded a number of caravan posts, including Bobo-Dioulasso (in modern Upper Volta), Kong and Bouna (in modern Ivory Coast), and Wa and Begho (in modern Ghana). Begho, the last of them, was established just north of the forest zone in about 1400. From Begho, routes radiated directly south to the coastal regions of Axim (in southwest Ghana) and southeastward through Asante to the coastal region of modern Cape Coast and Elmina.

Proof of the extension of northern trade routes to the coast can be taken from the fact that two items of clothing, *lanbens* (shawls) and *aljaravais* (dressing gowns) that were manufactured in Morocco and Tunis were in great demand on the coast of modern Ghana before the arrival of the Portuguese. Describing that trade in 1500, the Portuguese agent Pacheco Pereira also mentions peoples from the interior: "Boroes, Mandingoes, Cacres, Andeses, or Souzos." Here again, the "Boroes" are obviously the Bono of northern Asante, the "Cacres" are possibly the Kasena-Grusi of northern Ghana, and the "Mandingoes" and "Souzos" are readily identifiable as the Mandingos and the Susu of the larger family of Mande peoples.

The Portuguese and later the Dutch traders found the coastal peoples enjoying very lucrative salt and fish trade with the inland peoples. The Dutchman Pieter de Marees, writing in 1601 about one of the Akan settlements, states that "the inhabitants of the sea-side, come also to the markets with their . . . fish, which their husbands have gotten in the sea, whereof the women buy much and carrie them to other townes within the land, to get some profit by them, so that the fish which is taken in the sea, is carried at least one hundred or two hundred miles up into the land, for a great present." William Bosman, an official of the Dutch West India Company who came to the coast during the second half of the seventeenth century, made a similar observation. There is no reason to think that trade in salt and fish was not going on prior to the arrival of the Portuguese. Salt has always been an indispensable commodity and has generated contact between people who produce it and those who do not, and we know that salt is not found in the forest region and can be produced only in very small quantities in the savanna regions to the north.

It also seems clear that the Mande were responsible for the extension of the routes eastward from Timbuktu and Gao into the Hausa states, probably in the fourteenth century. From these Hausa states, trade routes radiated southwestward across the Niger and through the Mole-Dagbane areas into the gold- and kola-producing areas of Asante in modern Ghana. The Kano Chronicle states that kola nuts reached Hausaland from northern Ghana during the first half of the fifteenth century. Other routes also led southward through the regions surrounding the confluence of the Benue and Niger rivers and into the Yoruba and Benin areas to the southwest. Ibn Battuta talks of copper from the Takedda mines being exported southward into Nigeria, and judging from the bronze works of Ife and Benin (to be discussed later), it is not unlikely, as the British ethnographer Frank Willett has suggested that "some of this Takedda ore eventually found its way even farther south."

Pre-European trade also existed between east and west via the sea, especially between the coasts of modern Ghana and Nigeria. Evidence for this conclusion is found in the oral tradition, very widely held among the Ga and the people of Asebu (one of the Akan states), that they migrated from Benin by sea into the coastal regions of modern Ghana and that the Ga kingdom was in fact a part of the empire of Benin. However, on the basis of linguistic and other ethnological data, it is exceedingly unlikely that the Ga and the Asebu did in fact originate from Benin. Rather, the oral tradition seems to be an echo of the old trading contacts between the people of Benin and those of the coast of modern Ghana. The fifteenth- and early sixteenth-century accounts of the Portuguese traders suggest that they merely exploited a pre-existing pattern of trade to their own advantage. Pacheco Pereira, who was there in the 1500's, says that they bought slaves at the port of Benin for "twelve or fifteen brass bracelets each, or for copper bracelets which they prize more; from there the slaves are brought to the castle of S. Jorze da Mina [the extant fortress of São Jorge at Elmina on the Ghana coast] where they are sold for gold." He also says that they traded on the Niger near the coast of the Bight of Benin, "principally in slaves, in cotton stuff, some leopard skins, palm oil, and blue beads with red stripes which they call 'coris'—and other things which we are accustomed to buy here for brass and copper bracelets. All these commodities have value at the castle of S. Jorze da Mina. The Factor of our prince sells them to Negro traders in exchange for gold."

Pereira goes on to describe the local people's manner of travel: "At the mouth of the River Real [the Bonny River] . . . there is a very large village, consisting of about 2,000 souls. Much salt is made here, and in this country are to be found the largest canoes, made of a single trunk, that are known in the whole of Ethiopia of Guinea; some are so large that they hold 80 men. They travel distances of a hundred leagues and more down the river, and bring many yams, which are very good here and make a tolerable diet, many slaves, cows, goats and sheep."

Writing early in the next century, Pieter de Marees also describes the canoes in use on the coast of Ghana. He notes that the people of Accra had large canoes "to fish or go to sea withall," and that he saw one "cut out of a tree which was five and thirty foot long and five foot broad and three foot high, which was as big as a shallop, so that it would have held thirty men." In the same century Jean Barbot, agent general of the French Royal Africa Company, also saw canoes on the coast of Ghana of sizes ranging from fourteen to forty feet long, and he added that the largest of them could "carry above ten tons of goods with eighteen or twenty blacks to paddle them." He stated further that the best canoe men were the Elmina blacks, who "drive a great trade along the Gold Coast, and at Wida by Sea [Ovidah, a seaport in the area of modern Dahomey], and are the fittest and the most experienc'd men to manage and paddle the canoes over the bars and breakings, which render this coast, and that of Wida so perilous and toilsome to land either men, goods or provisions." One may conclude from these descriptions that going to sea in large canoes was already well established on the eve of the Portuguese arrival. Indeed, it probably dated as far back as the first millennium A.D., when the coastal areas began to be occupied by peoples from the interior, and commercial and cultural contacts were initiated.

As was the case farther north, the West African peoples who were geographically situated to play the role of middlemen would be those who could develop large states and kingdoms. To the south of Ghana and Mali, the first states to become sizable kingdoms were the Wolof kingdom to the west, the Mole-Dagbane and Mossi states to the south in the Volta River Basin, and the Ife, Oyo, and Benin kingdoms to the southeast. All except Benin were situated in the southern savanna belt. The Wolof people could control not only the lucrative salt trade from the sea, but could share in the gold trade with Morocco. The Mole-Dagbane states and the closely related Mossi states—all of which were founded during the first half of the fifteenth century—expanded mainly to establish a firm control over the trade routes linking the Niger Bend and Hausaland with the Akan's gold fields and kola-tree groves.

The oral traditions of the Akan peoples indicate that the first Akan states to emerge early in the fifteenth century were Bono-Manso in the region between the savanna and the forest and Adansi and Assin in the region where gold was obtained. Later on, different groups migrated northward to establish city-states, which were all within a few miles of where the routes that led from the Niger Bend terminated. It was these states that would later form the nucleus of the famous Asante empire.

The other Akan states of Aguafo, Fetu, Asebu, Fante, Agona, and the Ga kingdom—the so-called Gold Coast states—were created mainly in response to the demands of the transoceanic as well as the overland north-south trade. Their failure to develop into powerful kingdoms prior to the arrival of the Portuguese can be explained by the fact that they were one step further removed from the source of gold, trading through the intermediary of their sister Akan states in the interior. The Gold Coast states were also hampered by being crowded into a relatively short stretch of coast—the five Akan states occupied no more than one hundred miles.

Primarily by virtue of its geographical position, Benin became a center of both overland and sea trade, the latter by way of Ghana. Of the Yoruba states that later developed to the northwest of Benin, between 1380 and 1420, the first to develop into a sizable kingdom was Oyo. This northernmost Yoruba state was situated in the savanna region just below the Niger and, by the end of the fifteenth century, was able to claim the dominant share of trade between Hausaland and the Niger Bend and the other Yoruba states to the south. However, since Oyo had as rivals other centralized states to the south and west, its expansion could not be as rapid as that of Benin. Indeed, it was not until the seventeenth and eighteenth centuries that, using guns, Oyo's army extended its frontiers to the Guinea coast.

What then were these kingdoms like when the Portuguese first established contact with them? Pacheco Pereira reported in 1505: "Here at the Senegal you find the first black people. This is the kingdom of Wolof, a hundred leagues long and eight broad. The kingdom of Wolof can put into the field an army of about 10,000 cavalry and 100,000 infantry." It would appear from the early sixteenth-century accounts of Alvise da Cadamosto, a Venetian explorer in the service of Prince Henry of Portugal, that the kingdom consisted of five polities, all under a single ruler. Valentine Fernandes, a Lisbon printer of Moravian origin, writing in the same period, furnishes us with further details. He says the king had many subjects under him and administered his state with the aid of Muslim "dignitaries after the fashion of dukes and counts" and "white bischerigs who are priests and preachers of Mahomet, and can read and write." He adds that some of the ordinary people had embraced Islam, though the majority of them were sticking to their animistic beliefs. It is not surprising that some of the people should be Muslims, since the kingdom was situated to the south of Takrur, into which Islam had penetrated as early as A.D. 1000.

The Portuguese found the fifteen-hundred-mile-long stretch from Gambia to the borders of modern Ghana only sparsely settled; it appears that no state of any size emerged along that coast before the end of the fifteenth century. But in the area of modern Ghana, between the Pra and Volta rivers, the explorers-traders came upon the cluster of Akan states described earlier.

The three contiguous Akan states of Aguafo, Fetu, and Asebu were similar in organization: at the head of each state was a king (he lived in a capital a few miles from the coast), who was assisted by a council of elders. Eustace de la Fosse, writing in 1479, reports taking security from the "Mansa and Caramansa," who, he adds, "are the king and viceroy of Aguafo," and it was with the viceroy that Don Diego de Azambuja negotiated for the plot at Elmina, on which the castle São Jorge was built in 1482. Each of these states had trading villages or outlets, some of which became European settlements.

In contrast, the Fante state seems to have been composed of a series of inland townships, or quarters, within about three to five miles of one another. Collectively, they made up the capital district of Mankessim (alternatively Fantyn), and each quarter was under a chief, or *braffo*, who was advised by the family or clan heads. One *braffo* was recognized as overall leader, though his authority was limited, and he had to consult the others before he could declare war or make peace. It is also evident from the oral traditions and from a shrine that has survived near Mankessim that all the Fante recognized one national god, whom they called Nanaam. Orders emanating from the chief priest of Nanaam were binding on all the Fante. Thus, the government of the Fante was a sort of theocracy with political power being controlled by the chief ruler and the chief priests. Like the other states, the Fante also had some coastal outlets; these were Anomabu, Little Fantyn, and Kormantin. The Fante remained in Mankessim until the last three decades of the seventeenth century when, probably as a result of population pressure, they began to move out of the townships to establish kingdoms within a twenty- or thirty-mile radius of the capital.

No sizable states had emerged in the area between the mouth of the Volta River and Yorubaland by the middle of the fifteenth century, but in the western and midwestern regions of Nigeria, the Portuguese found the Yoruba and Edo peoples living in what were probably the most advanced and certainly the most interesting states of the Guinea coast: Ife, Benin, and Oyo. The oldest of these was Ife. Indeed, the Yoruba-speaking peoples regard Ife as the center of the world and the cradle of their civilization. According to one of their traditional accounts, it was there that God's children landed and set about to create the world. The most senior of these children was Oduduwa, whom they regarded as the first ruler, or *oni*, of Ife. He is said to have had sixteen children, whom he sent out to found the Yoruba states.

From a careful analysis of these oral traditions and the terra-cotta art of Ife, Willett has concluded that these oral traditions represent the arrival of "a small, but influential group of people," probably from the east or northeast. He postulates further that these people found the indigenous Yoruba and Igbo peoples already working in terra cotta, and that they introduced the art of bronze casting and the ideas of divine kingship, and that these new arrivals founded Ife, from which place the other Yoruba kingdoms would be created. Whether founded by the Yoruba or by invaders from the east, Ife never developed into a kingdom, for reasons that are still not apparent. It remained throughout essentially a city-state ruled by a "divine" king, who, as a Portuguese observer put it, was held "in great reveration as is the Supreme Pontiff with us." Nevertheless, Ife is of vital interest because it has remained from its foundation the religious center of all the Yoruba peoples and because it was there that the Yoruba's world-acclaimed sculpture in bronze, wood, and terra cotta was first developed.

From there this unique art spread to the whole of West Africa. The bronze sculptures, their supreme achievement, were made by the lost-wax process. The best of these were created in the classical period of Ife art, which conventionally has been said to have lasted from the beginning of the thirteenth to the middle of the fourteenth century. However, in view of the bronze sculptures recently discovered at Igbo-Ukwu, which have been dated by the radiocarbon process to the ninth century A.D., many scholars are beginning to accept an earlier date for Ife's classical period, probably before our millennium, bringing it closer to the Nok culture.

To the southeast of Ife, in the forest area, Benin emerged. Whereas Ife remained a city-state, Benin had developed into a sizable kingdom by the middle of the fifteenth century. Pereira, who visited Benin four times, wrote in 1505:

> A league up this river on the left two tributaries enter the main stream: if you ascend the second of these for twelve leagues you find a town called Huguatoo [Gwato], of some 2,000 souls: this is the harbor of a great city of Beny [Benin], which lies nine leagues in the interior with a good road between them. Small ships of fifty tons can go as far as Huguatoo. This city is about a league long from gate to gate; it has no wall but is surrounded by a large moat, very wide and deep, which suffices for its defense . . . . Its houses are made of mud walls covered with palm leaves. The Kingdom of Beny is about eighty leagues long and forty wide; it is usually at war with its neighbors. . . .

It seems clear from the traditional accounts of Benin that there are at least two periods of Benin history. All that can be pieced together is that during the first period Benin was a city-state under the rule of the Ogiso dynasty and that this family was replaced by the Oba dynasty sometime before 1300. Establishing themselves among the Edo-speaking peoples, who were organized only into clans, lineages, and village groups, the new Oba kings claimed supernatural powers. They soon succeeded in converting the city-state into the sizable and thriving kingdom that the Portuguese found on their arrival in the 1470's.

The oral traditions of Benin, Ife, and Oyo shed some light on how the Oba dynasty came to power. The histories of all three kingdoms agree that after a period of anarchy, the people of Benin beseeched the *oni* of Ife, Oduduwa himself, for a ruler, and he sent his son Oranmiyan. But believing that it would be better for a native of Benin to rule there, Oranmiyan married a daughter of one of the local chiefs and shortly thereafter had a son, Eweka, to whom he gave the throne. Oranmiyan then returned to Ife and from there went on to establish the kingdom of Oyo. Eweka thus became the first *oba* of Benin, but he had to obtain his insignia of office from the *oni* of Ife. It seems obvious from this account that the founders of the Oba dynasty of Benin, like the founders of Oyo, came from Ife.

To govern this kingdom, it would appear that the Oba kings developed certain political institutions that were an amalgam of Ife traditions and local political and social ideas. At the head of the kingdom was the *oba*, who, like the rulers of the early Sudanese states and those of Ife, was a "divine" king. As the English explorer Thomas Wyndham observed in 1553: "And here to speak of the great reverence they give to their king, it is such, that if we would give as much to our Saviour Christ, we should remove from our heads many plagues which we daily deserve. . . ."

The king was assisted by three ranking classes. The first class was the *uzama*, or king makers, whose position dates from Benin's early dynastic era. They had to perform certain important state rituals, including the installation of the *oba*. The second group was the *eghaevbo n'ogbe*, or palace chiefs, who were responsible not only for the *oba*'s regalia, his wives and children, his personal relations, and his doctors and divine men but also for the administration of the provinces, or fiefs. The third estate was the *eghaevbo n'ore*, or town chiefs, whose leader was the *iyase*, the prime minister and commander in chief of the army, and from whom other war leaders as well as other governors of provinces were chosen. Since most of these officials were appointed by the *oba* himself, he enjoyed considerable powers, though he still had to ensure his position by playing one group against another.

Provincial Benin, that is the conquered territories, was divided into three administrative units. At the base was the village under a village head; at the intermediate level was the chiefdom made up of a number of villages, each administered by a chief appointed by the king; at a higher level were the fiefs, or provinces, each consisting of a number of chiefdoms and directed by either a town or palace chief. This system of administration remained without any fundamental changes until the late nineteenth century.

Regarding Benin's achievements in art, the local oral tradition admits to learning the art of bronze casting from Ife. It is related that Oguola, the fifth *oba* of the second dynasty, who reigned during the end of the fourteenth century, sent to the *oni* of Ife for a bronzesmith to teach his people. The *oni* is said to have agreed and sent Iguegha, who is worshiped to this day in Benin as the patron of bronzesmiths. In fact, the style of the early Benin bronzes is quite similar to that of Ife, but by the sixteenth century, using the same lost-wax process known in Ife, Benin artists had evolved a distinctive style of their own, which was less naturalistic and more formal. As in Ife, the people of Benin also worked in wood, ivory, and raffia.

Despite the widespread tradition that attributes the founding of both Benin and Oyo to Oranmiyan, it is now generally agreed that Oyo's founding occurred nearly a century later, between the last two decades of the fourteenth and the first three decades of the fifteenth centuries. That it had grown into a fairly large kingdom by the end of the fifteenth century through expansion northward must have been due partly to the ability of Oyo's founding kings and partly, as we have seen, to its position in an area best suited for the domination of the trade routes from the north. Their art was derived from Ife, but as Frank Willett has pointed out, it shows "gradually declining naturalism, as if the social pressures which produced the naturalism of Classical Ife have gradually weakened."

Oyo's political institutions were based, as in the other kingdoms of West Africa, upon a "divine" king. The *alafin* ruled the kingdom with the advice of a council composed of seven notables known as the *oyo mesi* under the leadership of the *bashorun*, or prime minister. The *oyo mesi* was not only responsible for the election of the *alafin*, but according to a historian of Yoruba tradition, Samuel Johnson, its members "represent the voice of the nation, on them developed the chief duty of protecting the interests of the kingdom." The *alafin* could not declare war or peace without their consent. Moreover, should the *bashorun* ever declare three times, "the gods reject you, the people reject you, the earth rejects you," the *alafin* was obliged to commit suicide. However, some safeguards were instituted against the abuse of this power. Firstly, one of the members of the *oyo mesi*, known as "the *alafin*'s friend," had to die with the *alafin*. Secondly, both the *alafin* and the council were controlled by the *ogboni*, a secret earth cult consisting of all members of the *oyo mesi*, heads of the other cults, rich traders, and prominent diviners. This society had to ratify certain decisions of the *oyo mesi*, among them the rejection of the *alafin* by the *bashorun*. It seems clear that the people of Oyo devised a system that had checks and balances built into it to eliminate arbitrary or dictatorial exercise of power.

In summation, the people of West Africa, stimulated by trade and ruled and inspired by talented leaders, did form states and develop political institutions that were truly unique and truly African between 500 and 1450. Some of them also developed artistic skills, which in their aesthetic sensitivities were comparable, if not superior, to those of contemporary Europe.

THE ART OF IFE

Long before the Renaissance burst upon Europe, one of the world's great art traditions arose among the Yoruba and Edo peoples of what is now western Nigeria. Beginning perhaps as early as the ninth century (and deriving influences possibly from the earlier Nok culture), artists in the city-state of Ife, the Yoruba's religious center, produced masterpieces in bronze, wood, ivory, and terra cotta, like the life-sized bronze head at right. With artists at Benin and Oyo, to whom they taught their skills, they achieved for several centuries a naturalism and monumentality comparable to the qualities found in classical sculpture.

IFE MUSEUM—F.L. KENETT

NIGERIAN MUSEUM, LAGOS—F.L. KENETT

Details of two sensitively designed bronzes, made by the lost-wax process, reflect the sophisticated cultures of the ancient Yoruban societies. Opposite is a Benin bronze of a mounted warrior in a plumed headdress, possibly a visitor from the north. An oni, *or king, of Ife is seen at right.*

IFE MUSEUM–F.L. KENETT

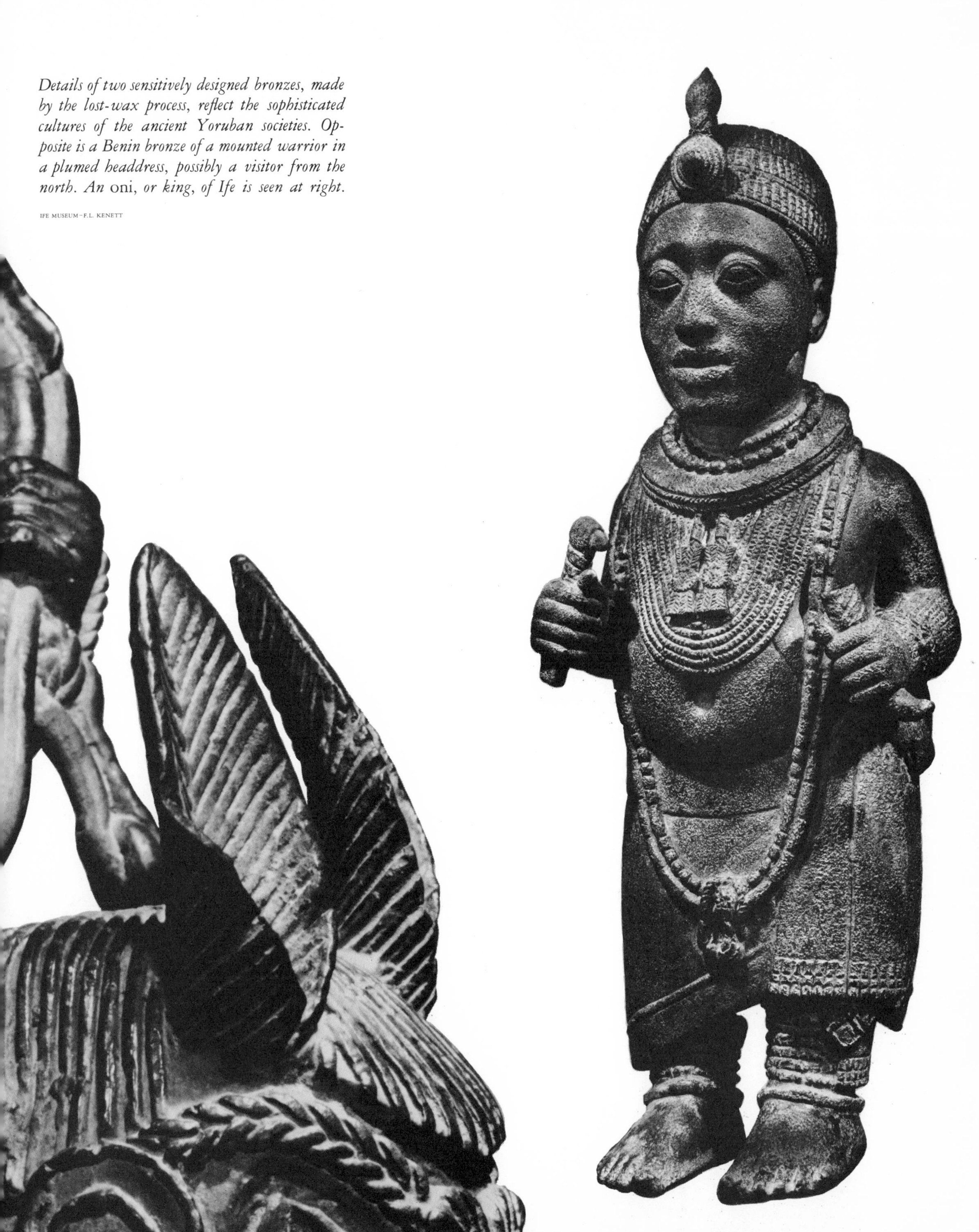

OVERLEAF: *Symbolizing royal authority and power, this pair of leopards, designed as water vessels, was used in the washing of the* oba's *hands before important ceremonies. They are among the finest examples of Benin artists' technical mastery.*
NIGERIAN MUSEUM, LAGOS–F.L. KENETT

In earlier times members of the Ife royal family painted their faces for certain festivals with an extract of blister beetles, which raised welts like those on the almost life-sized head above; the terra cotta may originally have been part of a figure.
IFE MUSEUM–F.L. KENETT

The subject of the handsome terra-cotta head opposite is shrouded in Ife legend. One version says it represents Lajuwa, a usurper who gained power by deceit after the death of an oni. *Eventually the rightful successor had him executed.*
IFE MUSEUM–F.L. KENETT

The majestic figure of a king at right, regarded by many experts as the finest Ife bronze yet discovered, sat for centuries on a bank of the Niger River at Tada. The 21-inch-high work, cast perhaps before A.D. 1000, *was held sacred by the villagers, who believed that the founder of the Nupe kingdom had brought it as a symbol of his rule. Ritual washings wore away its limbs.*
F.L. KENETT

THE GOLDEN IMPERATIVE

Asante gold weights

COLLECTION OF RENEE AND CHAIM GROSS—ELIOT ELISOFON

THE SERPENT OF WAGADU

Ghana, the first empire to rise in West Africa, flourished from the sixth to the thirteenth century, reaping most of its profits from gold-rich lands to the south. This legend recounts Ghana's downfall. Wagadu, which still survives, is a city in Upper Volta.

The prosperity of Ghana was not a human work. The empire owed its wealth to an enormous serpent, which everyone worshiped. The reptile was named Bida and lived in a pit. Tradition dictated that each year he must be given as a propitiatory offering the most beautiful girl of the empire, adorned with all her finery. Each clan, each tribe, fulfilled by turns this sorrowful sacrifice. . . .

Wagadu was a region of miraculous prosperity. Rains of water brought nourishment to the earth and carried it to the cotton, the sorghum, and the fruit trees, which, thanks to this sustenance, produced magnificent harvests; rains of gold bestowed the metal from which were chiseled the heads of walking sticks for men as well as their spurs, and the jewels and rings of women. The dense population was a mosaic in which moved the Bambara, overly eloquent warriors; the Sarakholle, raconteurs and philosophers; the Kasonke, a race of artists; and the Poulho, great lords fiercely attached to the pastoral life. The Poulho women wore heavy amber beads, in necklaces on their bronzed chests and set at the crests of their enormous hairdos, like stars in the firmament. The Mousso had a light and supple stride, accentuated by the slow dance of their arms, which moved in the muslin sleeves of their *boubous*. They wore gold as bracelets, as necklaces, as rings on their feet, and as earrings. . . . All the cities of the empire were protected by a magic invisible barrier that held invaders in check.

Thus one year it happened that the martyr of the serpent of Wagadu was to be a young girl of unparalleled beauty named Sia. She was the fiancée of Amadou Sefedokote, Amadou the Taciturn. Sia, at sixteen, was already a fine young woman. . . . The most beautiful jewels were put to shame by her fine appearance, the sweetness of her voice, the curve of her breasts, and the graceful proportions of her hips. And Amadou the Taciturn loved his fiancée more than his taboo. It was with suffering that he watched approaching the dawn of the day on which Sia was to be swallowed by the sacred serpent of Wagadu.

On the eve Amadou spent a night of torments. An immense sadness seized him and he threw himself on his tara [a bed made of tree stalks joined together with strips of bark], his head boiling with bitter thoughts. . . .

The sun rose slowly in the east; its clear, straight rays encircled it with a halo shaded with purple. With great fright Amadou saw the day filter through a slit made by the door of his room. He left his hut like an automaton. He took his saber from its sheath of mottled leather, which preserved it from rust. And all day, in order to escape his grief, he sharpened his sword on a gritty stone. Toward evening the saber was so sharp that it cut the wind.

When the sun had set, without the knowledge of anyone, Amadou went near the large pit, surrounded with offerings, where Bida lived. In haste he built a straw hut sheltered behind a screen of trees. There, he hid himself.

The ancient ones had formed a procession that was to carry Sia to the ritual sacrifice. Darkness had drowned the huts, deepening around them, and night had swallowed everything in its depths, even the thoughts of men. And suddenly, the deep tones of a tam-tam shattered the night with its arrows, which struck through the shadows, pouring out their significant meaning. It was the signal of the hour of the sacrifice. The tam-tams had tried to say it in the lively rhythms, which on other nights bathed with the moon had carried the long line of girls toward the marriage hut—in the same way their sweet song was beat out. But the tam-tams in their gay motif sent forth this time the lamentations of sorrow. . . . Sia was wrapped with the loincloth, which during her free time she had made under the shade of the yellow fig tree with the blue leaves in the hope of making it her marriage costume. During the night while one could distinguish only the lugubrious echoes of a weeping tam-tam, Sia went forward slowly, pushed toward death by the inexorable escort of the ancient ones. When they were a few steps from the refuge of Bida, they abandoned the young girl after the most ancient of the ancients had pronounced the solemn sentence, full of resignation: "Remain here and forgive us."

Sia no longer had the use of her legs. She knelt down, her hands over her eyes in the naive gesture of the hare, which, head thrust in a thicket, believes it possible to escape danger because he no longer sees it.

Soon the pointed head of Bida emerged from the pit. The serpent then rose through the darkness; with a rapid thrust, it moved toward the inert ball that the young girl had become, shielded in her loincloth.

Bida scented its prey with caution and brusquely dashed back into its home. An instant afterward, the long, flexible body of the serpent spurted out like an arrow, belly glistening; there was a moment of pause, then the hideous animal drenched the young girl with its venom, and with an imperceptible movement, plunged down into its pit again.

The sticky liquid that the serpent had spit, shook Sia Tounkara with repugnance. Screaming, she tried vainly to disentangle herself from her loincloth and her *boubou*, which were enveloped in the same horrible paste that stuck to her and froze her with terror.

But Amadou the Taciturn awaited in the darkness. . . . Although he was very much afraid, his jaws frozen, he maintained his senses. He knew that Bida only struck its victim on the third appearance. He now held himself tensed, and opened his eyes wide, because the moment of combat approached.

From the pit arose a gray arrow, vertical and oblique all at the same time, which threw itself on Sia, circling her with an astonishing precision. But Bida was not as fast as Amadou, and with one stroke of his flawless saber the head of the serpent of Wagadu was cut off! Bida regenerated with the rapidity of drops of rain following one upon another, a second, a third, a fifth, seventh head, all animated by the same intention of swallowing the young girl, but none of them was able to withstand the saber of Amadou, who loved his fiancée more than his fetish.

The last head cut off flew away saying: "For seven years, seven months, and seven days, Ghana will receive neither rains of water nor rains of gold," and Bida fell into the Boure [a river where the Mandingos find gold].

The body of Bida was convulsed in enormous coils of which the successive waves died on the edge of the pit. In a final movement, it left its refuge, with the effect that the tail broke off and flew away. It fell in the valley of the Faleme [where the golden riches of the Senegal are found]. . . .

For seven years, seven months, and seven days, no rain watered Ghana. The rivers dried up, the valleys became barren, famine and thirst decimated men, who fled toward lands where life was possible.

Thus did Ghana end—the most famous empire and the cradle of African civilization. Its splendors became only evocations, the sad dreams of the African guitar under the shrouds of sand.

FATHER OF BRIGHT COUNTRY

The great medieval empire of Mali began as a small Mandingo chieftaincy in the late ninth century. In 1203 it was conquered and annexed by Sumanguru Kante, ruler of the Susu kingdom. As related in the following story, taken from an epic of old Mali, Sundiata returned thirty-two years later to crush Sumanguru (given here in its variant form, Soumaoro) and the Susu (Sosso) at the battle of Kirina (Krina). In the tradition of heroic legends, Sumanguru's legendary ancestors are repeatedly invoked, and he is called the son of the buffalo and the lion, references to the totems of his mother and father. The epic is part of West Africa's oral history and has been preserved since ancient times by the griots, *now mostly a class of professional musicians, but formerly the counselors of kings. The* griots *memorized constitutions, customs, and governmental history, and tutored the children of Mali's princely class.*

Sundiata went and pitched camp at Dayala in the valley of the Niger. Now it was he who was blocking Soumaoro's road to the south. . . .

Soumaoro advanced as far as Krina, near the village of Dayala on the Niger and decided to assert his rights before joining battle. Soumaoro knew that Sundiata also was a sorcerer, so, instead of sending an embassy, he committed his words to one of his owls. The night bird came and perched on the roof of Djata's [Sundiata's] tent and spoke. The son of Sogolon [another epithet for Sundiata] in his turn sent his own to Soumaoro. Here is the dialogue of the sorcerer kings:

"Stop, young man. Henceforth I am the king of Mali. If you want peace, return to where you came from," said Soumaoro.

"I am coming back, Soumaoro, to recapture my kingdom. If you want peace you will make amends to my allies and return to Sosso where you are the king."

"I am king of Mali by force of arms. My rights have been established by conquest."

"Then I will take Mali from you by force of arms and chase you from my kingdom."

"Know, then, that I am the wild yam of the rocks; nothing will make me leave Mali."

"Know, also that I have in my camp seven master smiths who will shatter the rocks. Then, yam, I will eat you."

"I am the poisonous mushroom that makes the fearless vomit."

"As for me, I am the ravenous cock, the poison does not matter to me."

"Behave yourself, little boy, or you will burn your foot, for I am the red-hot cinder."

"But me, I am the rain that extinguishes the cinder; I am the boisterous torrent that will carry you off."

"I am the mighty silk-cotton tree that looks from on high on the tops of other trees."

"And I, I am the strangling creeper that climbs to the top of the forest giant."

"Enough of this argument. You shall not have Mali."

"Know that there is not room for two kings on the same skin, Soumaoro; you will let me have your place."

"Very well, since you want war I will wage war against you, but I would have you know that I have killed nine kings whose heads adorn my room. What a pity that your head should take its place beside those of your fellow madcaps."

Equestrian sculpture by the Dogon of Mali
MUSEUM OF PRIMITIVE ART

"Prepare yourself, Soumaoro, for it will be long before the calamity that is going to crash down upon you and yours comes to an end."

Thus Sundiata and Soumaoro spoke together. After the war of mouths, swords had to decide the issue. . . .

Sundiata wanted to have done with Soumaoro before the rainy season, so he struck camp and marched on Krina where Soumaoro was encamped. . . . The great battle was for the next day.

In the evening, to raise the men's spirits, Djata gave a great feast, for he was anxious that his men should wake up happy in the morning. Several oxen were slaughtered and that evening Balla Fasseke [Sundiata's *griot*], in front of the whole army, called to mind the history of old Mali. He praised Sundiata, seated amidst his lieutenants, in this manner:

"Now I address myself to you, Maghan Sundiata, I speak to you king of Mali, to whom dethroned monarchs flock. The time foretold to you by the jinn is now coming. Sundiata, kingdoms and empires are in the likeness of man; like him they are born, they grow and disappear. Each sovereign embodies one moment of that life. Formerly, the kings of Ghana extended their kingdom over all the lands inhabited by the black man, but the circle has closed and the Cisses of Wagadou are nothing more than petty princes in a desolate land. Today, another kingdom looms up, powerful, the kingdom of Sosso. Humbled kings have borne their tribute to Sosso, Soumaoro's arrogance knows no more bounds and his cruelty is equal to his ambition. . . . The kingship of Sosso is but the growth of yesterday, whereas that of Mali dates from the time of Bilali [Bilal]. Each kingdom has its childhood, but Soumaoro wants to force the pace, and so Sosso will collapse under him like a horse worn out beneath its rider. . . .

"You are the outgrowth of Mali just as the silk-cotton [kapok] tree is the growth of the earth, born of deep and mighty roots. To face the tempest the tree must have long roots and gnarled branches. Maghan Sundiata, has not the tree grown? . . .

"You are the son of Nare Maghan, but you are also the son of your mother Sogolon, the buffalo-woman, before whom powerless sorcerers shrank in fear. You have the strength and majesty of the lion, you have the might of the buffalo. . . .

"Tomorrow allow me to sing the 'Song of the Vultures' over the bodies of the thousands of Sossos whom your sword will have laid low before evening." . . .

At break of day, Fakoli came and woke up Sundiata to tell him that Soumaoro had begun to move his *sofas* [infantry] out of Krina. The son of Sogolon appeared dressed like a hunter king. He wore tight-fitting, ochre-colored trousers. He gave the order to draw up the *sofas* across the plain, and while his chiefs bustled about, [two officers] came into Djata's tent.

"Brother," said Manding Bory, "have you got the bow ready?"

"Yes," replied Sundiata. "Look."

He unhooked his bow from the wall, along with the deadly arrow. It was not an iron arrow at all, but was made of wood and pointed with the spur of a white cock. The cock's spur was the Tana of Soumaoro, the secret which Nana Triban had managed to draw out of the king of Sosso. . . .

The sun had risen on the other side of the river and already lit the whole plain. Sundiata's troops deployed from the edge of the river across the plain, but Soumaoro's army was so big that other *sofas* remaining in Krina had ascended the ramparts to see the battle. Soumaoro was already distinguishable in the distance by his tall headdress, and the wings of his enormous army brushed the river on one side and the hills on the other. . . . Sundiata did not deploy all his forces. The bowmen of Wagadou and the Djallonkes stood at the rear ready to spill out on the left towards the hills as the battle spread. Fakoli Koroma [king of the Koroma tribe and a defector from the army of Soumaoro, his uncle] and Kamandjan were in the front line with Sundiata and his cavalry.

With his powerful voice Sundiata cried, "*An gnewa!* [Forward!]" The order was repeated from tribe to tribe and the army started off. Soumaoro stood on the right with his cavalry.

Djata and his cavalry charged with great dash but they were stopped by the horsemen of Diaghan and a struggle to the death began. Tabon Wana and the archers of Wagadou stretched out their lines towards the hills and the battle spread over the entire plain, while an unrelenting sun climbed in the sky. The horses of Mema were extremely agile, and they reared forward with their fore hooves raised and swooped down on the horsemen of Diaghan, who rolled on the ground trampled under the horses' hooves. Presently the men of Diaghan gave ground and fell back towards the rear. The enemy center was broken.

It was then that Manding Bory galloped up to announce to Sundiata that Soumaoro, having thrown in all his reserve, had swept down on Fakoli and his smiths. . . .

His eyes red with anger, Sundiata pulled his cavalry over to the left in the direction of the hills where Fakoli was valiantly enduring his uncle's blows. But wherever the son of the buffalo passed, death rejoiced. . . . [Sundiata] looked for Soumaoro and caught sight of him in the middle of the fray. Sundiata struck out right and left and the Sossos scrambled out of his way. The king of Sosso, who did not want Sundiata to get near him, retreated far behind his men, but Sundiata followed him with his eyes. He stopped and bent his bow. The arrow flew and grazed Soumaoro on the shoulder. The cock's spur no more than scratched him, but the effect was immediate and Soumaoro felt his powers leave him. His eyes met Sundiata's. Now trembling like a man in the grip of a fever, the vanquished Soumaoro looked up towards the sun. A great black bird flew over above the fray and he understood. It was a bird of misfortune.

"The bird of Krina," he muttered.

The king of Sosso let out a great cry and, turning his horse's head, he took to flight. The Sossos saw the king and fled in their turn. It was a rout. Death hovered over the great plain and blood poured out of a thousand wounds. Who can tell how many Sossos perished at Krina? The rout was complete and Sundiata then dashed off in pursuit of Soumaoro. . . .

When Djata had been joined by all the army he marched on Sosso. Soumaoro's city, Sosso, the impregnable city, the city of smiths skilled in wielding the spear. . . .

Sosso was a magnificent city. In the open plain her triple rampart with awe-inspiring towers reached into the sky. The city comprised a hundred and eighty-eight fortresses and the palace of Soumaoro loomed above the whole city like a gigantic tower. . . .

From the top of a hill, Djata and his general staff gazed upon the fearsome city of the sorcerer-king. The army encamped in the plain opposite the great gate of the city and fires were lit in the camp. Djata resolved to take Sosso in the course of a morning. He fed his men a double ration and the tam-tams beat all night to stir up the victors of Krina.

At daybreak the towers of the ramparts were black with *sofas*. Others were positioned on the ramparts themselves. They were the archers. The Mandingoes were masters in the art of storming a town. In the front line Sundiata placed the *sofas* of Mali, while those who held the ladders were in the second line protected by the shields of the spearmen. The main body of the army was to attack the city gate. When all was ready, Djata gave the order to attack. The drums resounded, the horns blared and like a tide the Mandingo front line moved off, giving mighty shouts. With their shields raised above their heads the Mandingoes advanced up to the foot of the wall, then the Sossos began to rain large stones down on the assailants. From the rear, the bowmen of Wagadou shot arrows at the ramparts. The attack spread and the town was assaulted at all points. Sundiata had a murderous reserve; they were the bowmen whom the king of the Bobos had sent shortly before Krina. The archers of Bobo are the best in the world. On one knee the archers fired flaming arrows over the ramparts. Within the walls the thatched huts took fire and the smoke swirled up. The ladders stood against the curtain wall and the first Mandingo *sofas* were already at the top. Seized by panic through seeing the town on fire, the Sossos hesitated a moment. The huge tower surmounting the gate surrendered, for Fakoli's smiths had made themselves masters of it. . . . They opened the gates to the main body of the army. . . .

Soumaoro's palace was now at Sundiata's mercy. While everywhere the Sossos were begging for quarter, Sundiata, preceded by Balla Fasseke, entered Soumaoro's tower. The *griot* knew every nook and cranny of the palace from his captivity and he led Sundiata to Soumaoro's magic chamber. . . .

The inmates of the chamber had lost their power. The snake in the pitcher was in the throes of death, the owls from the perch were flapping pitifully about on the ground. Everything was dying in the sorcerer's abode. It was all up with the power of Soumaoro. Sundiata had all Soumaoro's fetishes taken down and before the palace were gathered together all Soumaoro's wives, all princesses taken from their families by force. The prisoners, their hands tied behind their backs, were already herded together. Just as he had wished, Sundiata had taken Sosso in the course of a morning. When everything was outside of the town and all that there was to take had been taken out, Sundiata gave the order to complete its destruction. The last houses were set fire to and prisoners were employed in the razing of the walls. . . .

Yes, Sosso was razed to the ground. It has disappeared, the proud city of Soumaoro. A ghastly wilderness extends over the places where kings came and humbled themselves before the sorcerer king. . . .

Sosso vanished from the earth and it was Sundiata, the son of the buffalo, who gave these places over to solitude. After the destruction of Soumaoro's capital the world knew no other master but Sundiata.

THE LAND OF ODUDUWA

The first sizable kingdoms to develop in the area southeast of Ghana and Mali were the Yoruba states of Ife, Oyo, and Benin. Today the Yoruba peoples form the dominant stock in Nigeria's western region; they are also found in its northern region, as well as in Dahomey and northern Togo. They share a common culture, language, and belief in their descent from a common ancestor, Oduduwa, the first ruler of Ife. Although the Yoruba have many different creation myths, all describe Ife as the cradle of their culture and the center of the world. The version excerpted below is told by E. Bolaji Idowu, who teaches at University College in Ibadan, Nigeria.

The King of Ile-Ife is regarded by most of the Yoruba as the Father of the race as well as their spiritual leader. It is generally believed that he derives his status from *Oduduwa* whom the Yoruba believe to be their original ancestor and a priest-king of Ile-Ife. There is traditional evidence that in the ancient days, the priest-king of Ile-Ife was the one in whom resided all authority, religious and secular, and that he held a pontifical sway over all. Even after the scepter had branched off and part-authority went to Oyo and elsewhere, the Yoruba continue to look upon Ile-Ife as "the Home," the unique, sacred spot which was the source and fountain of all . . . .

We shall now proceed to tell the story of the creation of the earth and its fullness. What is now our earth was once a watery, marshy waste. Up above was the skyey heaven which was the abode of Olodumare [the Supreme Being] and the divinities, with some other beings. The watery waste constituted, in a way, the sporting place for those dwellers above. Upon it they used to descend by strands of spider's web which also formed bridges by which they walked over it. Some of them came down from time to time for the purpose of hunting.

What moved Olodumare to think of creating the solid earth, no one knows. However, He conceived the idea and at once carried it into effect. He summoned Orisa-nla, the arch-divinity, to His presence and charged him with the duty: for material, He gave him a leaf packet of loose earth (some say that the loose earth was in a snail's shell), and for tools a five-toed hen and a pigeon.

When Orisa-nla arrived, he threw the loose earth on a suitable spot on the watery waste. Then he let loose the hen and the pigeon; and these immediately began the work of scattering and spreading the loose earth. This they did until a great portion of the waste was covered. When enough of it had been covered, Orisa-nla went back and reported to Olodumare that the work had been accomplished. Whereupon, Olodumare dispatched the chameleon to go down and inspect what had been done. The chameleon, it must be noted, was chosen on the merit of the extraordinary carefulness and delicacy with which it moves about, and the still more extraordinary way in which it can take in any situation immediately. From the first visit, the chameleon took back the report that although the earth was indeed wide enough, it was not yet sufficiently dry for any further operation; from the second visit, however, it returned with the cheering report that it was both "wide enough" and sufficiently dry.

The sacred spot where the work began was named Ife—"That which is wide," from the Yoruba word *fe*, meaning "to be wide." And that, according to the tradition, was how Ife, the Holy City of the Yoruba, got its name. The prefix *Ile-* [meaning "house"] was added much later on to signify that it was the original home of all and to distinguish it from the other towns called Ife which have come into existence as a result of migrations.

The creation of the earth was completed in four days; the fifth day was therefore set apart for the worship of the Deity and for rest. When Olodumare was satisfied that the work had indeed been accomplished, He sent Orisa-nla back to equip and embellish the earth. This time, He sent Orunmila to accompany him and be his counselor. To Orisa-nla, Olodumare handed the primeval *Igi Ope* (Palm Tree). This he was to plant—its juice would give drink, its seed would give oil as well as kernels for food. He gave him also three other trees which were full of sap. These were *Ire* (Silk Rubber Tree), *Awun* (Whitewood), and *Dodo*. These also were to be planted and propagated: their juices would give drink. For as yet, there was no rain upon the earth. The original hen and pigeon which had been used in spreading the loose earth should now increase and multiply and provide meat for the dwellers on earth.

Orisa-nla came down and did as he was told. When all was ready, Oreluere, one of the beings who had been prepared beforehand, was commissioned to lead a party of those beings down to the earth. He brought them down as he was instructed and those became the nucleus of the human occupation of the earth.

When the affairs of the earth had been running for some time and its inhabitants were multiplying, it was discovered that there was not enough water for use. Therefore, Orisa-nla appealed to Olodumare and, as a result, rain began to fall upon the earth.

Orisa-nla was assigned another special job. He was made the "creator" of human physical features for the future. It is not clear from the oral traditions when he first began to do the work. However, he got the job; and his allotted duty was thenceforth to mould man's physical form from the dust of the earth. He thus became the sculptor-divinity. But the right to give life Olodumare reserved to Himself alone for ever. . . .

The word [*olodumare*] is said to be a contraction of the phrase-name Olodu-omo-ere—"Olodu, the offspring of the boa." This suggestion is based upon a myth which derives from the natural phenomenon of the rainbow. The Yoruba believe, generally, that the rainbow is produced by a very large boa: the reptile discharges from its inside the sulfurous matter which sets all its surroundings aglow and causes a reflection, which is the rainbow (*Osumare*), in the sky. The matter which is so discharged is known as *Imi Osumare* ("rainbow-excrement") and is considered very valuable for making people wealthy and prosperous. It is the Yoruba equivalent of the "philosopher's stone"! . . . It is, however, very rarely obtained, in spite of the fact that it is so much earnestly sought after, one reason being that anyone who approached the spot at the moment when it is on the ground would be consumed forthwith; and another that the reptile itself has the miserly habit of swallowing it all up again when the ritual is over! . . .

The myth has it that the name of this personage who is above was originally Olodu. He was the offspring of the large primordial boa, and was a prodigy from birth. Very early he acquired a reputation for prowess and goodness. For some reason, the earth could no longer contain him, and so he went to dwell in heaven. There he exceedingly increased in all good and divine qualities. But before he went up, both he and his parent had entered into a covenant that they would always remember, and from time to time communicate with, each other. The rainbow which occurs in the sky is the sign of that age-long covenant and communion between Olodu and the boa, a sign that the covenant remains for ever. . . .

[There are] two other very important names by which Olodumare is known. These are Olofin-Orun and Olorun. . . . The name Olorun is the one commonly used in popular language.

HOW BRONZES ARE MADE

It was at Ife that the renowned Yoruba sculpture in bronze, wood, and terra cotta first developed. The Ife bronzes, which most probably were made before the beginning of our millennium, were cast by the lost-wax process, which has since been widely used in West Africa. According to oral tradition, the artisans of Benin—a sizable Yoruba-ruled kingdom by the mid-1400's—learned lost-wax bronze casting from their Ife neighbors. However, whereas it is certain that there was artistic contact between the two states, there is now considerable evidence to indicate that the influence was in both directions. Ife bronzes are characterized by a sophisticated naturalism; Benin's, by stylization. The neighboring Hausa people of northern Nigeria give this oral account of the technique.

In the name of Allah the Compassionate, the Merciful. This account will show how the [Benin] figures are made. This work is one to cause wonder. Now this kind of work is done with clay, and wax, and red metal [copper], and solder [zinc], and lead, and fire. The first thing to be done if one of the figures is to be made, is to get clay and work it most thoroughly, and get the little stones which are in it worked out. It is well worked in the hands. Next the shape of the top of a head is constructed [from the clay], and then the jaws on the same piece as the top of the head. Then the nose is shaped, and the eyes and the lips made. Then a certain stick which has been shaped like a knife is put [against the model] and it is smoothed [with this]. A very little water is put on when it is being thus smoothed until it is perfect; then it is set in the sun to dry. Next wax is melted and poured over it [the clay model],

Messenger of Death, a Benin bronze plaque
WERNER FORMAN

[and] then it is gone over [again] with the knife. As it [the wax] hardens it is smoothed over. When it has been well done, then a fire is kindled, [and] a knife put in the fire. When it is slightly warm it is taken up and pressed over the wax in order that it may adhere well [to the clay foundation]. The eyes get the finishing touches, [and] the eyebrows, and mouth and chin and beard. Then this stick like a knife is got out [and] dipped in water [and] pressed against the wax, [and] passed over it—it is well smoothed [and] shines [all over]. If the model is of a woman's head then the hair adornment is put on. How the adornment of the hair is made, is as follows. Wax is rolled out till it is like a string—water is used; it forms a long piece. Then he [the smith] cuts it into pieces [and] fastens them on top of the head. Then he takes a razor [and] cuts [them the required length]. Next he cuts off other short pieces of wax [and] sticks them along the head. Then he rolls out another bit of wax with water, making it long like a rope. He divides it in two [down the middle, not across], lays them side by side, and puts them on the top of the first upright pieces and sticks [the whole] on. The part left over he cuts off [and] casts aside. Then he prepares a certain broad piece of wax and makes ears out of it [and] fixes them on. But whenever he is about to stick any piece on, first he puts the knife in the fire and presses it against the wax. Then he sits down—this [part of the work] is completed. There remains the pouring in of the metal. When he has finished [the part just described] he takes up mud [and] covers the whole head with it; leaving only a small hole. He puts it in the sun to dry—this part is finished. There remains the pouring in of the metal.

This description is of the pouring in of the metal. The way the metal is poured in is [as follows]. When the fire has been brought it is poured into the melting-furnace, [and] the bellows are set to work [and] the fire blown [and] charcoal poured in. Then the model is lifted [and] placed on the fire. Water is poured into a pot or cup. When the model has become heated then the wax inside melts. Then it is taken up, the tongs, or some [take] a stick, are placed across the pot [of water], and the figure put on top, and the wax keeps dropping out. And it is held so till all the wax has melted and dropped into the water. Then a great quantity of charcoal is poured [into the furnace]. The figure [in clay] is set on the fire.

Bars of metal are continually being cut with a hammer; many pieces are broken up in this way, [and] put in the smelting-pot. Then they scrape out a hole in the charcoal and put the smelting-pot in, replace the charcoal again, [and] cover up. The [mud] figure is brought and set. [It is set] on the fire. They keep blowing the bellows, and this clay lump is turned till red hot. Then the metal has melted, then the figure is taken up, a hole is dug, [and] it is placed in it so that it is firmly set. The hole left in the clay is cleared out and the melted metal poured in. If it is filled, that is well; if not, more is added to fill it. If full then [the work] is finished. Next it is set aside to cool, then [the outside covering of clay] is broken off. Then you see a beautiful figure. That is it. The work of Ali is completed.

A CHILD IS . . .

Central to Yoruba philosophy is belief in a cycle of reincarnation. Deceased ancestors are said to be reborn into the same family. Thus, having children carries additional genealogical significance. Three months after the birth of a child, the parents consult an oracle to find out which ancestor the child has brought back to life. This poem was translated by Ulli Beier, a distinguished Africanist who specializes in Yoruba literature.

A child is like a rare bird.
A child is precious like coral.
A child is precious like brass.
You cannot buy a child on the market.
Not for all the money in the world.
The child you can buy for money is
a slave.
We may have twenty slaves,
We may have thirty laborers,
Only a child brings us joy.
One's child is one's child.
The buttocks of our child are not so flat
That we should tie the beads on another
child's hips.
One's child is one's child.
It may have a watery head or a square
head,
One's child is one's child.
It is better to leave behind a child,
Than let the slaves inherit one's house.
A child is the beginning and end of
happiness.
One must not rejoice too soon over
a child.
Only the one who is buried by his child,
Is the one who has truly born a child.
On the day of our death, our hand
cannot hold a single cowrie.
We need a child to inherit our
belongings.

THE ILLUSTRIOUS METAL

The wealth of Ghana and of the subsequent empires that flourished in the western and central Sudan during the Middle Ages was largely dependent on these states' roles as middlemen in the lucrative gold trade. Gold was a basic commodity in trans-Saharan commerce from the eighth to the fifteenth century, during which period the Sudan furnished a major share of the world's gold. One of the best reports on gold production is by William Bosman, a seventeenth-century Dutchman who spent fourteen years on the Guinea coast, where he was an official for the Dutch West India Company. There he observed methods that had been in use for hundreds of years. The following extract on the subject is from his New and Accurate Description of the Coast of Guinea *first published in English in London in 1705.*

This Illustrious Metal is generally found in three sorts of places: First, the best is found in or betwixt particular Hills; and the *Negroes* apprehending where the Gold is, dig Pits; and separate it from the Earth which comes out with it.

The second place is in, at, and about some Rivers and Water-falls; whose violence washeth down great Quantities of Earth, which carry the Gold with it.

The third is on the Sea shore; where (as at *Elmina* and *Axim*) there are little Branches or Rivulets into which the Gold is driven from Mountainous Places, as well as to the Rivers; and after violent Showers of Rain in the Night, next Morning these places are sure to be visited by hundreds of *Negro*-Women naked, except a Cloth wrapped about them to hide what Modesty obligeth. Each of these Women is furnished with large and small Troughs or Tray, which they first fill full of Earth and Sand, which they wash with repeated fresh Water, till they have cleansed it from all its Earth; and if there be any Gold, its Ponderosity forces it to the bottom of the Trough; which if they find, it is thrown into the small Tray, and so they go to washing it again: which Operation generally holds them till Noon: Some of them not getting above the value of Sixpence; some of them find pieces of six or seven Shillings, though not frequently; and often they entirely loose their labor. Thus the digging of Pits, the gathering it, at or about the Rivers, and this last mentioned manner, are all the ways they know to come at Gold.

The Gold thus digged or found, is of two sorts; one is called Dust-Gold, or Gold-Dust, which is almost as fine as Flower, and is the best, bearing also the greatest Price in *Europe:* The other sort is in pieces of different sizes; some being hardly the weight of a Farthing, others weighing as heavy as twenty or thirty Guineas; though of the last sort not many occur. The *Negroes* indeed tell us, that in the Country Pieces as heavy as one or two hundred Guineas, are found. These Lumps or Pieces are called Mountain-Gold; which being melted, touch better than Dust-Gold; but the multitude of small Stones which always adhere

West African craftsmen plying traditional village trades: a goldsmith opposite hammers a fire-heated ingot; and a woman below hand spins yarn upon a spindle.
ALL: SHOBERL, *The World in Miniature*, 1827

to 'em, occasion a great loss in the melting; for which reason Gold-Dust is most esteemed. Thus much of the good and pure Gold; and now to touch upon the false. The first sort is that mixed with Silver or Copper, and cast into *Fetiches* [ingots]. . . . These *Fetiches* are cut into small bits by the *Negroes*. . . . The *Negroe* Women know the exact value of these bits so well at sight, that they never are mistaken; and accordingly they tell them to each other without weighing, as we do coined Money.

YORUBA PROVERBS

Proverbs have been called the national poetry of the Yoruba. They are highly refined contrivances; however, they also embody an ethical code, and most are sententious observations on men, manners, and morals. The sound of the language may be heard in the following example: "Owe li esin oro bi oro ba no owe li afi iwa a, owe on oro ni irin." *It means "a proverb is the horse of conversation; when the conversation [flags], a proverb revives it: proverbs and conversation follow each other." This group was compiled by Richard Burton in the last century.*

Mouth not keeping to mouth, and lip not keeping to lip, bring trouble to the jaws.
(Talk is silver, silence is gold.)

When the day dawns the trader betakes himself to his trade;
The spinner takes her distaff [or spindle], the warrior takes his shield;
The weaver bends over his Asa, or sley [stoops to his batten];
The farmer awakes, he and his hoe-handle;
The hunter awakes with his quiver and bow.
(A correct and picturesque description of the daybreak scene in every Yoruba town. It also instructs that no one should remain idle.)

When the spear sees the battle, it dances; when the lance sees the battle, it joys.

The thread follows the needle.

The calabash having saved them [in time of famine], they said, "Let us cut it for a drinking cup."

He fled from the sword and hid in the scabbard.
("Out of the frying pan into the fire.")

There is no market in which the dove with the prominent breast has not traded.
(The cowry, on account of its circulation as currency, is compared with the dove.)

Peace is the father of friendship.

Wrangling is the father of fighting.

One here, two there, [so gathers] a vast multitude.

The jaw is the house of laughter.
(The jaw is here compared with a happy family.)

The young cannot teach tradition to the old.

I have tied the leopard skin round my waist; you cannot sell me.
(Meaning, I have the protection of powerful friends; you cannot ruin me with law expenses.)

One who does not understand the yellow palm-bird says the yellow palm-bird is noisy.
(Men are prone to despise what they do not understand.)

As a calabash receives the sediment of water, so an elder must exercise forebearance.

"SCUFFLES OFTEN OCCUR"

Ijala *is one of the many types of oral poetry recited by Yoruba-speaking people. Mythically and ritually these chants are associated with the worship of Ogun, the Yoruba god of iron, who is believed to have been a hunter*

An itinerant weaver at a portable loom

during his earthly life, and who, as a god, oversees all iron implements. Ijala *chants are primarily performed at hunters' celebrations, but they also figure at happy occasions not specifically connected with Ogun or the hunt, such as weddings, naming of children, and housewarmings. The subject matter of the chants depends on the type of festivity: there are salutes to animals and birds, praise songs honoring royal lineages, and benedictions for social occasions. There is also a type of* ijala *having no central theme and devoted to random observations on Yoruba life. The next example, compiled by S. A. Babalola, himself a Yoruba, belongs to the last category. The Ata Ari, Apateere, and Ologbongan referred to are villages near Ibadan. At Ikeeku, also near Ibadan, water is deep underground. The "prospective chief is not a fool" because he watches the drummer's beating hand and thereby cannot be tricked into taking a false step. The* sekere *musician rattles a bottle gourd covered with strings of tiny cowry shells.*

Scuffles often occur when people sing at Ata Ari.

Unless you have a bucket with a long strong rope tied to its handle, you cannot have water at Apateere.

Unless you dig a water-hole of your own, you cannot have water to drink at Ikeeku.

Isn't the pond near Ologbongan? Verify this from anyone you see.

Verify this, I say, from anyone you see.

For a dance, the appropriate dress is an *agbada*.

For a social visit, the appropriate dress is a caftan.

The fitting place for a hat is the head, the fitting place for a string of beads is the waist.

The hips of a hiking trader on the move are never at ease.

A hawker's head is usually bald in the middle.

A minstrel's eyes show no signs of any shyness.

The hips of a corn-grinder in action
Never stay erect.

A pepper-grinder's head does not stay motionless.

A drummer drumming trickishly, to catch out his dancer,
Is matched by the dancing prospective chief who is not a fool.

A drummer was one day drumming before another man's wife.

As he drummed, he peered from the edge of the woman's wrapper, to catch a glimpse of her waist beads.

As he drummed, he lifted up the edge of the woman's cloth to look upon the woman's seat.

However, by the time he got back to his house,

A *sekere* music man had abducted his wife, so he clasped his hands together and heaved a long protracted sigh.

A YORUBA PRAISE SONG

The most common type of Yoruba poetry is the oriki, *a poetic word used to describe and extol a person or god. In the course of his life every Yoruban, commoner or prince, acquires a set of* oriki, *or praise names. These are chanted by professional musicians. The most poetic* oriki *are those dedicated to the* orisha, *the Yoruba deities who mediate between Olodumare, the supreme god, and man. The* orisha *are usually hero-kings, or ancestors, or founders of cities. The following* oriki, *translated by Ulli Beier, is that of Oshun, one of the three river wives of Shango, the deity of thunder. Oshun is a beautitul coquette, a healer, and a mother goddess. Here she is also identified with Iyalode, the title of a female chief in Yoruba towns. She is associated with brass, and her color is yellow.*

We call her and she replies with wisdom.
She can cure those whom the doctor has failed.
She cures the sick with cold water.
When she cures the child, she does not charge the father.
We can remain in the world without fear.
Iyalode who cures children—help me to have my own child.
Her medicines are free—she feeds honey to the children.
She is rich and her words are sweet.
Large forest with plenty of food.
Let a child embrace my body.
The touch of a child's hand is sweet.
Owner of brass.
Owner of parrots' feathers.
Owner of money.

My mother, you are beautiful, very beautiful.
Your eyes sparkle like brass.
Your skin is soft and smooth,
You are black like velvet.

Everybody greets you when you descend on the world.
Everybody sings your praises.

YORUBA RIDDLES

Riddles are often used at the beginning of a storytelling session, where they test the acuity of the audience and arouse interest. The following Yoruba riddles and their surprise answers were translated by Ulli Beier.

We call the dead—they answer.
We call the living—they do not answer.
(Dry leaves sound when trodden on. Fresh ones don't.)

We are going to Ife—we face Ife.
We are returning from Ife—we still face Ife.
(Climbing and descending a palm tree one faces the same direction.)

We are pounding yam—
The dog is dancing.
(A woman's breasts dance when she is pounding yams.)

The black one is squatting,
The red one is licking his bottom.
(Cooking pot on the fire is licked by the flame.)

Two tiny birds
Jump over two hundred trees.
(A man's eyes can carry him far.)

The bereaved one has stopped weeping.
The compassionate friend is still crying.
(After the rain stops, the leaves continue to drip.)

The essence of authority: Golden regalia worn by an Asante ruler in modern Ghana

THE LONG HERITAGE

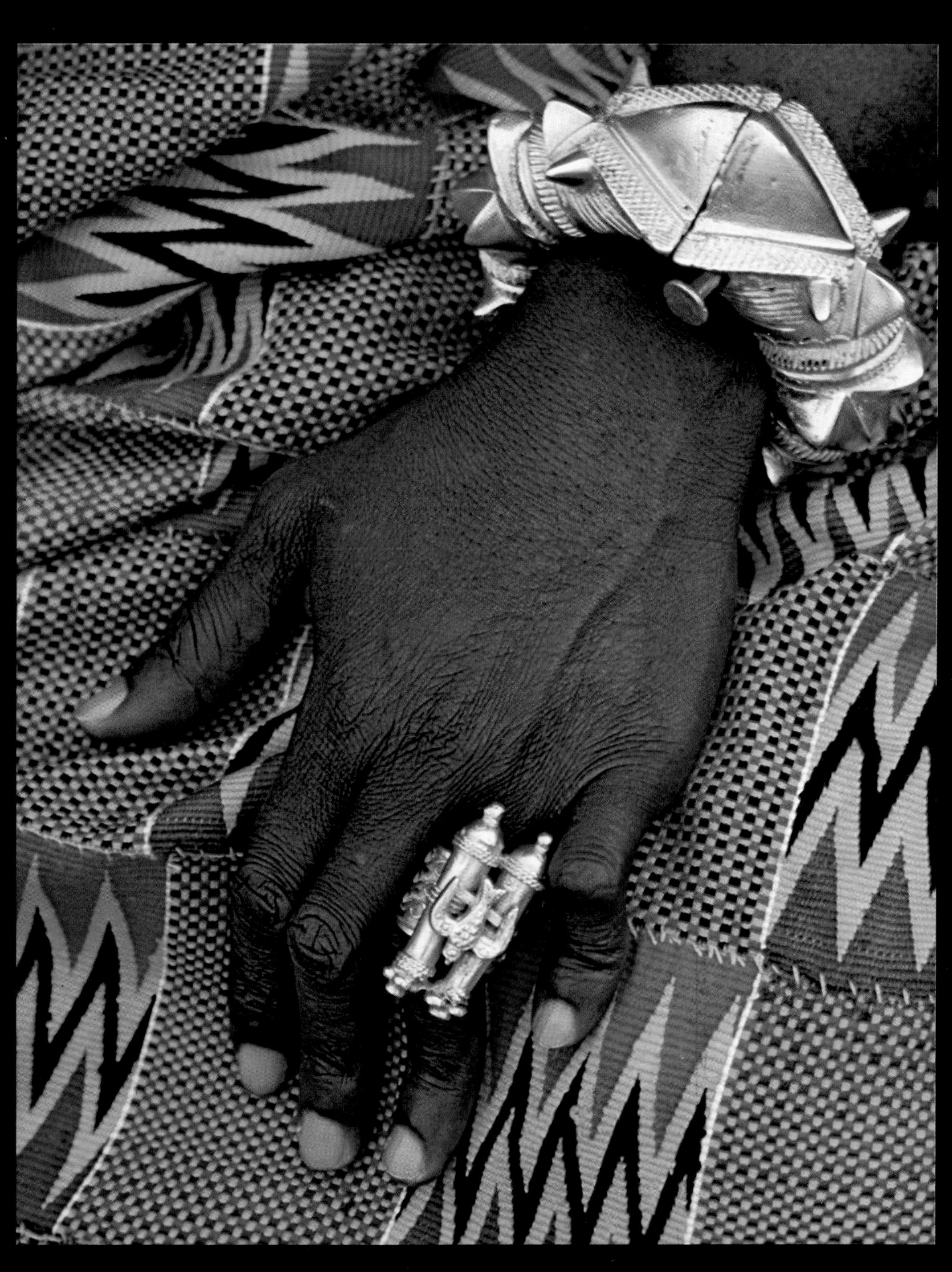

ERA OF EMPIRES

During the one thousand years that Europe was experiencing the Middle Ages and the Renaissance, kingdoms and empires, conquering armies and powerful rulers, rose and fell in the fertile lands of West Africa south of the Sahara. Travelers from North Africa made legendary such names as Ghana, Mali, and Songhai, and told of the glories of busy cities like Kumbi Saleh, Gao, Jenne, and Timbuktu. Among the rulers were some of Africa's greatest: Sundiata, Mansa Musa, Sunni Ali, Askia Muhammad. In 1591 a Moroccan armed force overran the area, and West Africa's great age ended. Even though some of its cities had disappeared by the nineteenth century, memories lived on in oral accounts and Arab travelers' writings.

Wealth from trade financed large armies, and warfare was common. The cavalryman at left, with a shield and wearing chain mail, is from a northern Nigerian area that was once part of the Hausa states.

KEN HEYMAN

BIBLIOTHEQUE NATIONALE, SERVICE PHOTOGRAPHIQUE

Timbuktu, rich trade and cultural center of Mansa Musa's Mali empire, was sacked and razed by many conquerors. The sketch above, drawn by René Caillié in 1828, gives only a hint of its great past.

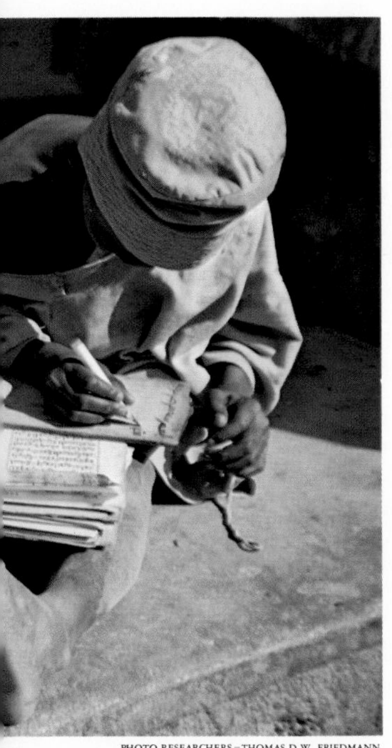

PHOTO RESEARCHERS—THOMAS D.W. FRIEDMANN

The university in the Sankore quarter of Timbuktu was famed throughout the Muslim world. But other cities were also centers of Islamic learning, where youths like the ones seen at left studied the Koran.

The Great Mosque at right, dating from the fourteenth century, is at Jenne on the Niger River. Despite Islam's sway, local religious practices persisted outside the cities and even in court ceremonies.

WERNER FORMAN

A modern-day caravan approaches Timbuktu. Camels, introduced to the Sahara from the Near East in Roman times, permitted the opening of new routes across waterless stretches.
PHOTO TRENDS

THE GOLD TRADE

As far back as history records, there were trade contacts between North Africa and the savanna region south of the Sahara. By 1000 B.C. caravans of bullocks or horses, guided by desert dwellers, were carrying goods from oasis to oasis between the areas. In the south agriculture and iron had created a base for a populous and expanding civilization. The earliest traders to the south might have brought salt, an eagerly sought commodity, and just as early they might have been paid for it with gold. In time the Sudanese trading towns became important suppliers of gold to the Mediterranean area, and Ghana, the first of the West African kingdoms, was known as the Land of Gold. The gold-producing regions, including Wangara near the upper Niger and Senegal rivers, actually lay south of Ghana, and sites were often kept secret from the northern traders. Wangara was later enfolded in the Mali and Songhai empires, and until the discovery of the New World, caravans to North Africa from those Sudanese states brought European kingdoms the major part of their gold.

In addition to trading gold, West Africans themselves also worked the metal into many dazzling objects of splendid artistry. The ornamental pendant mask above was made by the Baule of the Ivory Coast, a people that formerly lived in the Asante kingdom of present-day Ghana.
MUSEUM OF PRIMITIVE ART–LEE BOLTIN

'raditional gold emblems of high office adorn the asantehene, *or paramount chief of Asante.*
OTO RESEARCHERS–THOMAS D.W. FRIEDMANN

WERNER FORMAN

Canoes up to forty feet long plied Nigeria's waters. This nineteenth-century view shows an Ibo craft, its flags decorated with the enemy's emblem, dismembered limbs, and other oddments.

LANDER, *Journal of an Expedition*, 1832

THE GUINEA COAST

When Portuguese navigators first reached the West African coast in the fifteenth century, they called it by the Moroccan Berber phrase *Akal n-Iguinawen*, "Land of the Blacks." For generations thereafter the Guinea coast, a center of gold and slave trade, was the only part of sub-Saharan Africa even vaguely known to most Westerners. Inland, through the great belt of forest and northward to the old empires of the Sudan, was a vast network of trade routes, linking a multitude of kingdoms, city-states, and communities of many different peoples. Only in the last century has the white man, or for that matter other Africans, recognized the variety of sophisticated cultures that flourished in West Africa.

NIGERIAN MUSEUM, LAGOS—F.L. KENETT

The Benin River (left) winds through the Nigerian forest and the heart of the once-powerful kingdom of Benin. Benin's artists excelled in naturalistic sculpture, as shown in this sixteenth-century bronze portrait of a queen mother at right.

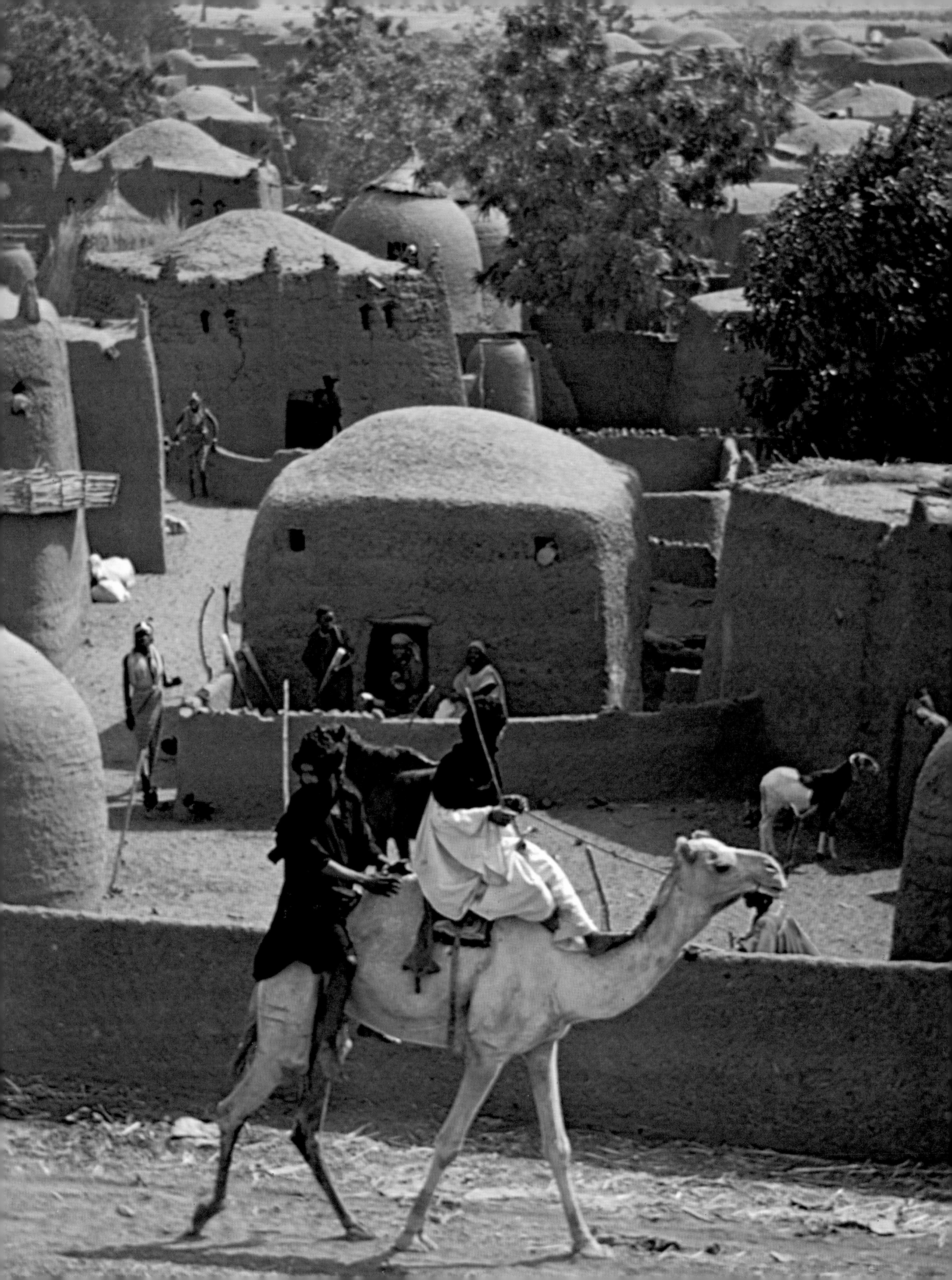

Chapter Six

THE NIGER TO THE NILE

(c. A.D. 500–1600)

by

Basil Davidson

EASTWARD FROM THE WESTERN SUDAN, from the states of the upper and middle Niger, from the lands of ancient Ghana and Mali and Songhai, the same broad plains of grass and sifting soil flow for two thousand miles until they reach and overleap the waters of the Nile. These plains of the central Sudan traverse Hausaland and Bornu, their populous heart and center, encircle the marsh-trimmed mirrors of Lake Chad, and lead on thirstily through the solitudes of Kanem and Zaghawa and Wadai, lands where the world is altogether flat but for the slow deception of long-dry riverbeds.

Then, as though reflecting the drama of this great region's history, the plains confront the sudden glacis of Darfur, where green peaks rise into the mists of Jebel Marra's 10,100-foot summit. But at once the land falls away to plains again. They flow on now into the hard cattle country of little water and infrequent pasture that is Kordofan. Beyond Kordofan they come to the oases lands of Nubia and the White Nile. They cross these and continue to the Blue Nile and the highlands of Ethiopia. And that, at last, is their frontier.

The peoples of the central Sudan, like their neighbors in the western Sudan, have an interrelated history much the same in kind and content. Its dominant themes are those of political adventure and ambition; of swift conquest and defeat among peoples to whom good horsemanship and fine horses have always mattered much; of ceaseless movement and migration brought to rest and stability only where long-distance trade routes crossed and became knit together within the defensive walls of market towns or royal capitals. Its poets and scholars, Muslim but rooted in African tradition, have told similar stories of empires and warriors, of battles and booty, of the joys of home.

n the Sudan corridor, diverse peoples like these Hausa villagers and Tuareg nomads are neighbors.

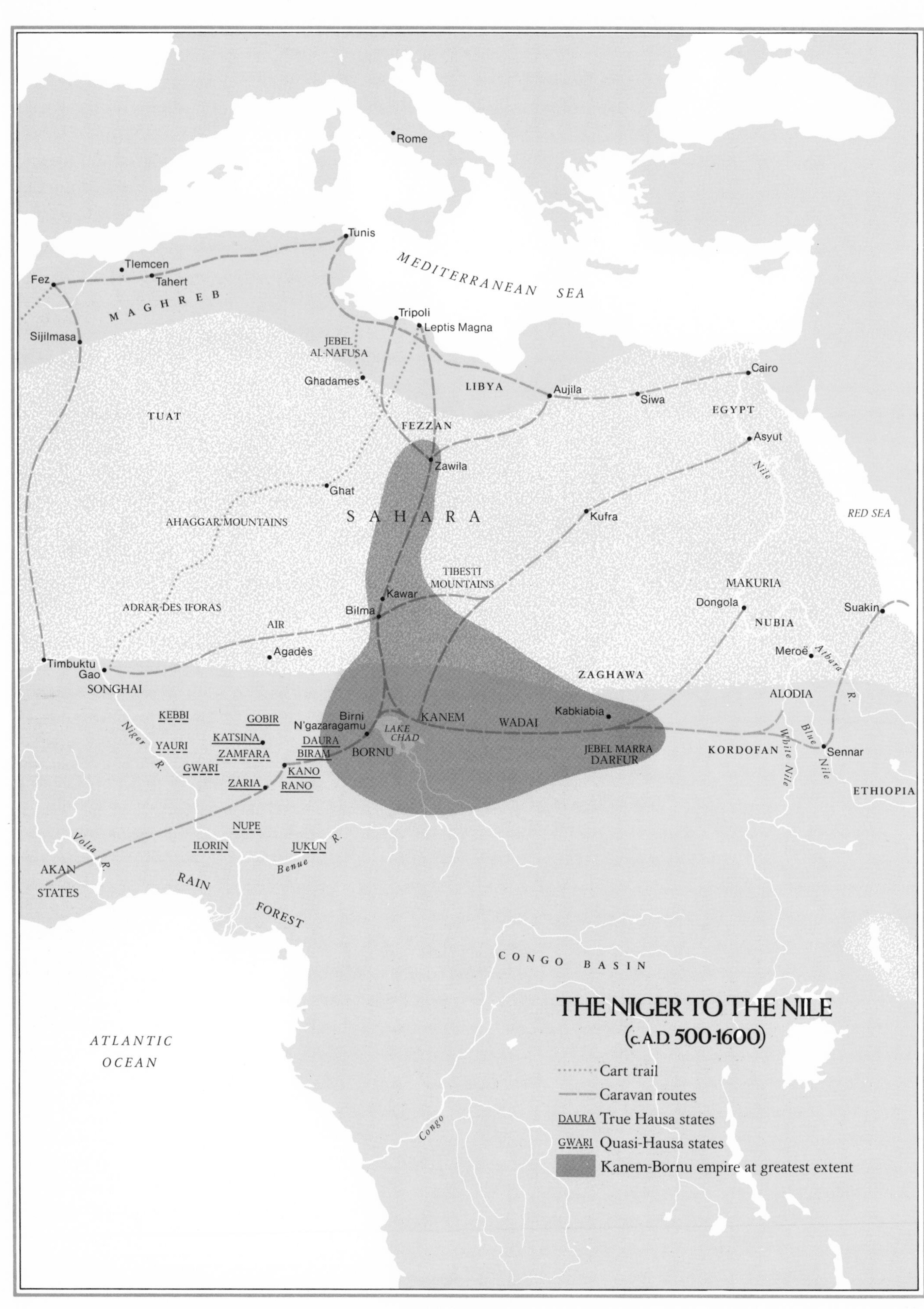
THE NIGER TO THE NILE
(c.A.D. 500-1600)
Cart trail
Caravan routes
DAURA True Hausa states
GWARI Quasi-Hausa states
Kanem-Bornu empire at greatest extent
Rome
MEDITERRANEAN SEA
Tunis
Tlemcen
Tahert
Fez
MAGHREB
Sijilmasa
Tripoli
Leptis Magna
JEBEL AL-NAFUSA
Ghadames
LIBYA
Aujila
Siwa
Cairo
EGYPT
TUAT
FEZZAN
Asyut
Nile
Zawila
Ghat
SAHARA
AHAGGAR MOUNTAINS
Kufra
RED SEA
TIBESTI MOUNTAINS
MAKURIA
Kawar
Bilma
ADRAR DES IFORAS
Dongola
Suakin
NUBIA
AIR
Agadès
Meroë
Atbara R.
Timbuktu
Gao
SONGHAI
ZAGHAWA
ALODIA
KEBBI
GOBIR
Birni N'gazaragamu
KANEM
WADAI
Kabkiabia
KATSINA
DAURA
LAKE CHAD
YAURI
ZAMFARA
BIRAM
BORNU
JEBEL MARRA
DARFUR
KORDOFAN
White Nile
Blue Nile
Sennar
Niger R.
GWARI
KANO
ZARIA
RANO
ETHIOPIA
NUPE
ILORIN
JUKUN
Benue R.
Volta R.
AKAN STATES
RAIN FOREST
CONGO BASIN
ATLANTIC OCEAN
Congo

"The clash of spears had long been doubtful, yet it ended in glory. . . . These were our deeds: they lived in the memory of all. Oh, triumphant expedition! But the greatest joy is still to tell, joy most precious, the recovery of my lost love, a part of myself! Silks from India are less soft than is her skin, her noble form is timid as a fawn. . . ." It was thus that a Bornu ruler returning from a fight set down his praise poem in due and proper verse. The poem is from the nineteenth century, but could have been written any time back to about A.D. 1000.

In contrast with the oral traditions and written records of many parts of Africa, the histories of the central Sudan are for the most part dynastic. They are principally concerned with powerful monarchs and their rise to power, with the enclosure of broad areas of trade and tribute within systems of centralized rule, with the impact of Islam upon methods of government or upon social and moral attitudes and customs. The characteristic note of these chronicles is epic. "On the next day, all the soldiers mounted their horses after equipping themselves and their horses with armor, with breastplates, shields and their best clothing," wrote a courtier of the great Idris Alooma (1570–1602), who was *mai*, or ruler, of Kanem-Bornu at the same time that Queen Elizabeth I was reigning over England. "When we had all ridden a short distance we met the messengers of the lord of Stambul, the Sultan of Turkey. . . . Our troops charged toward them, and they galloped their horses toward us. This continued for a long time until the infantry were tired of standing still. . . ."

Nearly two centuries later, passing far eastward through the Sudanic sultanate of Sennar on the Blue Nile, the Scottish traveler James Bruce described the cavalry of the Funj people as though he were speaking of the same scene. Each lancer possessed a shirt of mail and a helmet of beaten copper, and their horses were "all above sixteen hands high, of the breed of the old Saracen horses, all finely made and as strong as our coach horses, but exceedingly nimble in their motion."

This sort of history may read agreeably, but it has the disadvantage of telling little about everyday life. In countries pestered by royal ambition, whether in Africa or not, peaceful or productive citizens figure little in the records. Yet the deeper truths, revealed by archeological discoveries over the past twenty years or so and by the very recent probing of modern historians, are reasonably clear in their general shape and outline.

From very early times the Niger-Nile region formed a zone of migration and slow settlement, where indigenous Stone Age peoples were joined by groups from the southern Sahara and other neighboring regions. This mingling gave rise in remote antiquity to new peoples, ancestors of the peoples who inhabit the region today. By A.D. 500 they had begun to acquire their characteristic cultures, modes of speech, religious beliefs, political systems, and notions about themselves. By A.D. 1000 they had assumed patterns of community life that would give rise to all subsequent development down to the twentieth century, even now marking these peoples with a distinctive quality.

Central to the history of much of the region is the record of the Kanuri and their thousand-year predominance in the Lake Chad region. The Kanuri played the same role here, in the sense of being the "core" people of a masterful centralizing polity, that the Soninke played in Ghana, the Mandinka (or Mandingo, as they are frequently known) in Mali, and the Songhai in the middle Niger area.

Peripherally, there were many other peoples. There were nomads of the southern Sahara, seminomads of the grasslands, and sedentary farmers in the forest zone to the west and south, some of the last group being culturally linked to the peoples of the northern Congo Basin. Several of these smaller societies early acquired small centralizing polities of their own, opposed the Kanuri in their bid for mastery, and fought them in many wars and raids. Others, somewhat farther away, stayed altogether free of Kanuri overlordship. Even then the Kanuri influence continued.

Prominent among these more distant neighbors were the Hausa-speaking groups to the west; the Nupe and Jukun astride the Benue valley to the south; the Berber raiders and traders of Aïr and Bilma, the little kingships of the central-southern Sahara. And woven into their midst, at least from the middle of the fifteenth century, there were groups of Fulbe, or Fulani, as their Hausa neighbors and subsequent historians have called them; their origins were far in the west. These Fulani were sometimes to play a vigorous role in religion and politics.

All these peoples belong to the "Country of the Blacks," as the region is commonly known; however, there is considerable variation in skin pigmentation of its inhabitants, ranging from the relative pallor of the Fulani to the luminous "black" of the Hausa. Despite these apparent differences, they shared a common pastoralist culture, which continues much the same even today. The people of the central Sudan early took advantage of grasslands, which were largely free of the menace of tsetse flies, to raise sizable herds of cattle, and many were farmers whose skills in growing millet and other crops were developed two thou-

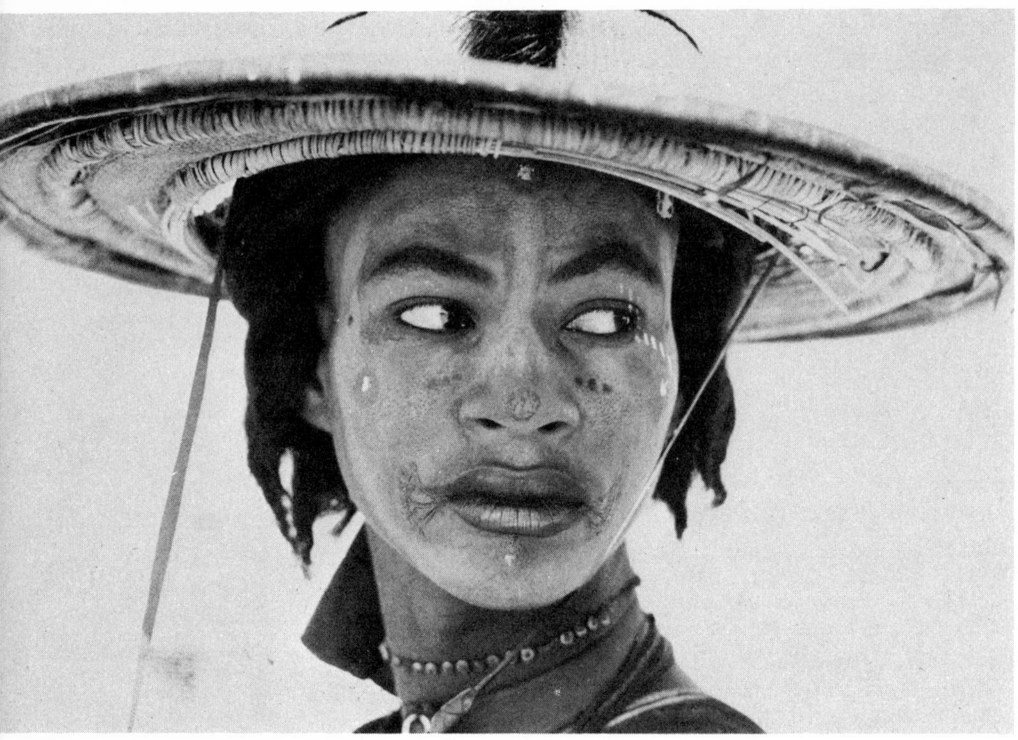

The young nomad at left wears the elaborate facial ornament of the Fulani, a widely dispersed people dwelling in minority enclaves from Senegal to Lake Chad. His copper-colored skin, straight hair, and slender frame are common among his own Bororo group; however, other Fulani often show strongly Negroid characteristics. The diversity reflects a continued racial intermixing that has marked Fulani history. Their social organization, too, follows differing forms: many Fulani live in sedentary villages, and some have become aggressive state builders; the Bororo are pastoralists, basing their wealth and communal life around large herds of cattle, like that pictured opposite.

BOTH: VICTOR ENGLEBERT

sand years ago and more. Some of them acquired the techniques of ironworking not much later than that.

Two factors influenced the development of those among them who formed kingdoms and organized under some type of governmental rule: long-distance trade and Islam. As A. Adu Boahen has argued in his preceding chapter on the western Sudan, these elements are fundamental to West African history as a whole; but the roots of the Niger-Nile region have supported a distinctively different cultural flowering from that in the western Sudan. So far as the first of these shaping factors is concerned, this difference is explained by the fact that the north-south routes of the trans-Saharan commerce were supplemented in the central Sudan by an important system of lateral communications from the region of Wadai through Darfur to such crossroads towns as Sennar, which linked the region with routes running to Egypt, the Red Sea, and the Horn of Africa.

At any rate, since the rise of the post-Meroitic Christian kingdoms of Nubia after A.D. 540, and probably much earlier during Meroitic times, there was trade and travel along well-known routes reaching between Lake Chad and the Nile. Little or nothing is known of those who may have passed that way, if only because detailed histories of Meroë and the Nubian kingdoms are almost entirely lost; today there remains just a scattering of potsherds to indicate the connection. Sherds of probable Meroitic origin have been picked up in long-dry wadis east of Lake Chad, but at present the sole sure fragmentary evidence of a Christian presence (or of links with Christian Nubia) is a single piece of pottery, found in the ruins of one of the old Kanuri capitals east of the lake. According to A.D.H. Bivar, a noted British Africanist, it bears the characteristic cream slip of the pottery from the Nubian state of Makuria, which flourished between about A.D. 600 and 1300. That so little material evidence has survived is disappointing, especially in view of the known trading enterprise of the Nubian kingdoms. Yet the hint of influence from the Nile remains curiously insistent in central Sudanese civilization, not least of all in the old Kanuri skills of building in brick, such as the Meroites and Nubians possessed.

Of early north-south connections there are far more sure indicators, though these, too, are tantalizingly rare and often imprecise. During Carthaginian and Roman times in North Africa, the Garamantes of the central Fezzan seem mainly to have used a trail going southwestward from their country through the Ahaggar massif to the Adrar des

Iforas mountains and probably onward to the middle Niger. But to the east, the central-southern Sahara also offered valuable commodities and oases to lure and sustain the trader (for example, the salt deposits of the Bilma oasis in the modern Niger Republic). The existence of many later links between the Fezzan and the Chad area makes it very probable that the Garamantes had also come this way.

Writing soon after 450 B.C., the Greek historian Herodotus says that the Garamantes "hunt the Ethiopian [among classical writers the generic term for "African"] hole-men, or troglodytes, in four-horse chariots, for these troglodytes are exceedingly swift of foot—more so than any people of whom we have any information. They eat snakes and lizards and other reptiles." These cave dwellers were possibly the Tebu people, between whose homeland in the Tibesti Mountains and the Fezzan there are at least two sites where ancient wall paintings of horse chariots are found. If the Garamantes themselves had left any written records, they would no doubt have revealed much more information on the subject. Roman records are almost as silent. An expedition led by one Julius Maternus of Leptis Magna reached the "land of Agisymba." Judging by the report that they found rhinoceroses in abundance there, the adventurers must have been somewhere in the Sudan; whatever else they may have learned about this land, aside from its being a country where black people lived, remains unknown.

Yet early north-south links seem probable. Though lacking gold, the Lake Chad region could provide elephant ivory, and it probably did. There had once been great numbers of elephants in North Africa as well as in the Sudan, but Mediterranean demand for ivory may well have depleted the local supply. (So honored was the creature in Leptis Magna that the authorities erected a statue of an elephant in one of their streets.) Accordingly, behind the history of the Niger-to-the-Nile region there hangs a shadowy backdrop painted with the symbols of ancient trade and contact with North Africa and the Nile, and possibly, though on this the records are entirely silent, with the Congo Basin and southern Nigeria.

If the central Sudan was a trading crossroads from ancient times, it was little used for a long time, and its indigenous peoples were left to evolve their own early structures of self-rule and development. How and when they did this remains a matter for conjecture. All that can be affirmed is that toward the ninth century, four or five protostates can be

People living along the shores of Lake Chad are farmers, but they supplement their diet with fish and, occasionally, the meat of the hippopotamus, an amphibious beast that once inhabited the shallow waters in great numbers. The engraving at right shows hunters closing in for a kill. The hippo's habitat, which seasonally varies in size from 4,000 to 10,000 square miles, was once an inland ocean.

BARTH, *Travels in Central Africa*, 1857

discerned in the region around Lake Chad. These began to be dominated by the Kanuri people, operating under powerful chiefs of the Saifuwa lineage. The Saifuwa were able to rise to power over their neighbors for reasons far from certain, though a good central position commanding trade routes west and east and a relatively fertile land were no doubt high on the list.

Their manner of organization also played a determining role. Like the early kings of Ghana, and afterward of Mali and Songhai, the Saifuwa must have drawn their initial strength among the Kanuri from a ritual authority. Saifuwa seniority came, in other words, from their standing in the line of divinely sanctioned ancestors, who were in turn the "owners" of the land.

The Saifuwa were thus the intermediaries between the spiritual power and the people, or so they succeeded in presenting themselves; and from that position of strength, evidently reached late in the ninth century, they were able to accumulate the consequential powers of secular rule, both political and military. The traditions are vague or silent on the ways in which they did this. But it may be inferred from later African examples, which are far better known, that they became kings because the Kanuri (or at least their clan leaders) were agreed on the need for stronger, and hence more unified, means of getting tribute and controlling trade: in short, for assuring themselves of all those desiderata that gave rise to regular governments in Africa and elsewhere. The Kanuri chose to achieve these ends by putting government into the hands of kings.

Stronger than their neighbors, the Kanuri under their early Saifuwa kings embarked on conquest and began the building of an empire, at this time mainly in the region of Kanem to the east of Lake Chad. By the eleventh century, however, Islam was beginning to be a major factor in West African history. The expansion of that faith, which had followed the Muslim conquests in North Africa, profoundly influenced all it touched, including the trans-Saharan commerce and, eventually, the rise of the larger Kanem-Bornu empire.

Kharijite Berbers, dissenters from Abbasid religio-political rule, led the way in opening up the Sahara and, ultimately, the Sudan beyond. They gathered in states greatly given to trading enterprise. Sijilmasa and Tahert became crossroad city-states in the western and central Maghreb, while in the Fezzan two small Kharijite states in the neighborhood of Jebel al-Nafusa and Zawila, only a short distance from the ancient but long-since-abandoned homeland of the Garamantes, took shape toward the end of the eighth century.

Closely linked to one another by religious ties and trading interests, these little states rapidly assumed command of the middle Saharan trade routes. In the steps of the Garamantes they revived the old route southwestward to the Niger, and they pioneered a new route, though perhaps following the trace of one far older, south through the oases of Kawar and Bilma to the borders of Chad and the central Sudan.

This Kharijite primacy in trans-Saharan trade—a trade now to become far greater than before—was due in part to Egypt's abandonment of the Nile-to-the-Niger transversal Saharan route. During the late ninth century caravans appear to have ceased making regular use of this road, which had led from the northern Nile through the Kufra oasis and then on to Gao on the middle Niger, mainly because its perils were considerably greater than those of the alternate routes being opened up throughout the Fezzan and the Maghreb. Partly, too, the Kharijite states owed their success to stubborn enterprise, itself the product of their zealot culture.

One scrap of evidence that seems to affirm their central position in the whole great trading system, now in the course of growth, is the fact that a ninth-century governor of Nafusa could speak "the language of Kanem," presumably Kanuri, in addition to Arabic and his native Berber. Another indication of Saharan contacts with the Mediterranean coast is the fact that Cairo's east gate during the high days of that city's prosperity under the Fatimids was called the Bab al-Zawila, the "Gate of Zawila."

Thus Nafusa and Zawila, like Tahert and Sijilmasa, put the peoples of the western and central Sudan in touch with a worldwide system of trade. For Sudanese kings and traders, business partnership with Muslims meant a growing acquaintance with the manners and attitudes of Islam, and they became attuned to techniques of commercial credit and contract, such as were now becoming indispensable to a trade conducted over distances as great as these were and in volume ever larger than before. As with later incursions of Christianity in Africa, early Islam traveled in the trader's knapsack.

There was, of course, much more significance to these outside contacts than that. At least by the tenth century Islam could teach Sudanese potentates a good deal about new techniques of centralizing government, whether in respect to law or administration. Beyond that it could offer them membership into a wider world of power and prestige than any they had known before, thus broadening the horizons of their provincial obscurity. It could bring them the services of scribes and scholars, and it could lend a sometimes dazzling glint to their majesty and pomp. In other words, Islam could provide a new and necessary cultural framework in which to construct a stronger, more centralized system of government and a more autonomous basis for royal rule. This is not to derogate from the spiritual attractions of Islam. Yet, however real these attractions were, they could not have prevailed without their more secular attendants.

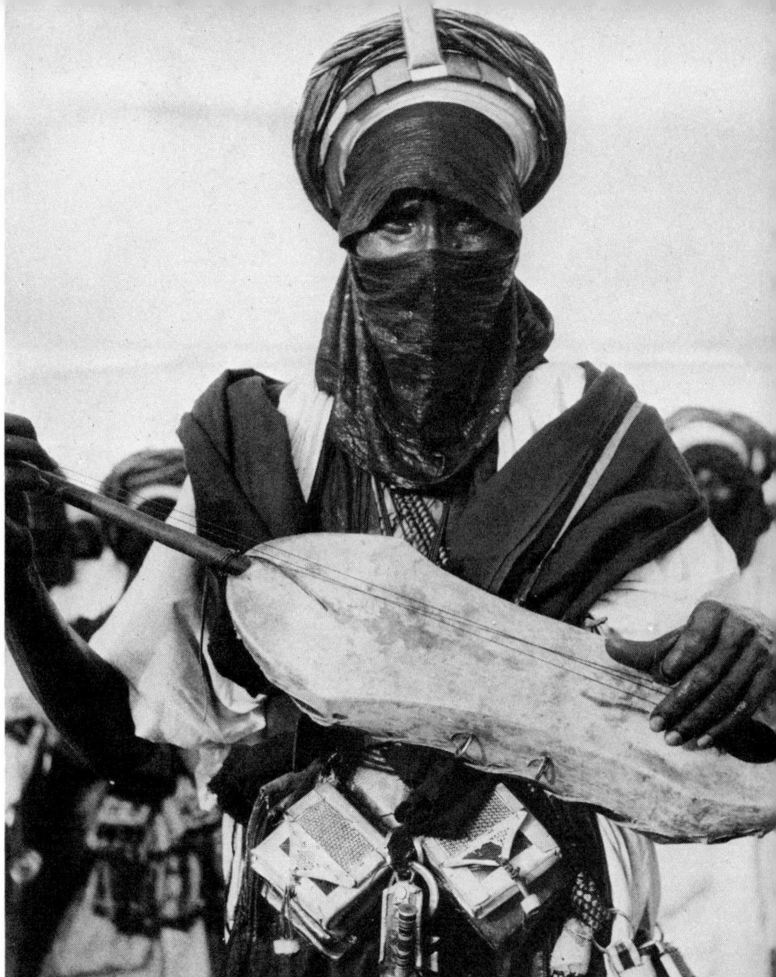

Shrouded in the indigo robes that have given his people the name "blue men," a Tuareg strums a three-stringed lutelike instrument.

PHOTO RESEARCHERS–HECTOR ACEBES

The first Kanuri king to accept Islam for himself and his court was Umme Jilma; Saifuwa traditions award him a reign in the late eleventh century. Thenceforward the Saifuwa kings were all Muslims. They made the pilgrimage to Mecca, some of them more than once. They introduced Muslim laws and customs, being careful (like their contemporaries in the western Sudan) not grossly to offend the sensibilities of their non-Muslim subjects, who would remain a large majority until very recent times. They welcomed scholars from the great schools of Cairo and the Maghreb, and probably from Spain. They encouraged the founding of their own Koranic schools. Gradually, through this cautious spread of Islam in court and market place, they undercut the power of rival nobles who relied upon the religious loyalties of Kanuri tradition. More and more, they gathered to themselves the attributes of supreme monarchs rather than the more limited privileges and powers of leaders of councils of lineage peers. And they tied themselves ever more successfully into the trans-Saharan trade.

At least from the eleventh century these kings had regular contact with the Fatimid rulers of Ifriqiya. Fatimid records tell of presents received from the "Malik al-Sudan," which in this context undoubtedly refers to the *mai*, or king, of the Kanuri. Such presents were mostly *'abid*, a word that may be loosely translated as "slaves," so long as modern implications are not read into the word. These *'abid* were mainly men who had forfeited their civic rights and status for one reason or other, commonly by capture in raiding warfare, and who were used as royal bodyguards. Relatively few in number, they were selected for good health and strength, and were expensive to buy and maintain. Yet Ifriqiya's Fatimid governors, always anxious to re-ensure themselves against uncertain local loyalties, were able to assemble enough *'abid* from the Sudan to maintain a regular company of troops.

These small but successful attempts at diplomacy encouraged the Kanuri kings to extend their hegemony across the northern desert. Late in the twelfth century the Fatimid rulers of Cairo were overthrown by the forces of the Syrian Saladin (Salah al-Din). Not long afterward these voracious, predominately Asian, mercenaries began looting the Kharijite states of the Fezzan. Evidently they continued in this way for a long time. They "set the country ablaze," in the words of a thirteenth-century writer, and greatly disturbed the desert trade. Reacting at last in 1258, the king of Kanem "sent emissaries to kill [one of these mercenaries], and [so] delivered the land from strife. His head was sent to Kanem and exhibited to the people," a detail that suggests that "the people," or least the traders, had by this time lost a lot of sleep over the plundering of their trans-Saharan commerce. After that, Zawila is said to have come under Kanuri control, while the Kanuri kings of this blossoming empire of Kanem-Bornu saw to it that they continued to enjoy fruitful relations with the Hafsid rulers of Tunisia.

Such was the formative framework, so far as external factors were concerned, affecting the Hausa to the west of the Kanuri, as well as many peoples to the east of them. Potent even in early times, the influence of long-distance communications grew in later centuries. Even if the written records are mainly lost, the remaining ones still give strong evidence of these connections. Thus, the earliest attested example of diplomatic correspondence in the central and western Sudan is a letter from a Kanuri king to the Sultan Barquq, of the Mameluk dynasty of Egypt, written sometime around A.D. 1391; it would not have been unique. And when, much later, Mai Idris Alooma's court scribe celebrates a meeting with messengers from the Ottoman sultan in Istambul, he is speaking for a tradition of far-ranging correspondence, which is already very old.

Yet the cultures that took shape in Kanem, as elsewhere in the central Sudan, were far more than copies of their prestigious examples beyond the desert. Although increasingly marked by Islam after the twelfth century, these cultures were no more Arab or Berber than were those of Mali and Songhai. On the contrary, they were the expression of local and indigenous factors of development that have never ceased to mark them with a depth and resonance that is all their own. This was the originality, the power of local beliefs and skills, which explains their long endurance through the years. Islam might show the way to a wider world, whether spiritual or social: all these peoples continued nonetheless to stand, and stand firmly, on their own sense of identity and purpose. Their history shows this very clearly.

Like its neighbors to the east and west, the Kanuri state used Islam to modify and strengthen structures already firmly in place. It was a transformation that took place slowly. King Umme might accept Islam. His successor, Dunama I, might twice make the pilgrimage, and according to tradition, suffer drowning in the Red Sea while on a third trip to Mecca. Those who followed might reinforce their links with the Fezzan and Tunisia or with Libya and Egypt. Yet they continued to owe their power to local concepts of authority and its use. For then and long afterward the king was little more than primus inter pares, or prime minister, of a ruling council of lineage peers. This council numbered twelve, and something is known of its organization. Under the *mai* they formed a government that Ives Urvoy, the first twentieth-century historian to concern himself with these matters, aptly called "the administrative council of the Saifuwa family firm."

As the early empire crystallized, these councilors acquired regular titles and "departments," governorships of provinces, and commands of armed forces. Among such titled offices were the *kaigama*, "lord of the south," who was commander of the kingdom's army; the *galadima*, "governor of the west," who administered the country west of the lake that was later called Bornu; and the *chiroma*, who, in some sense, was the king's deputy and also nominated heir to the throne. Some of these titles have survived to this day. A modern visitor to the palace of the emir of Kano in northern Nigeria will be asked to obtain a pass from the office of the *madaki*, a Hausa corruption of the Bornu title *mai dawaki*, "the lord of the cavalry"; once inside, he may find not only the emir, but also the emir's *chiroma*. In Bornu the survivals are still more numerous.

In early times the Saifuwa made their *main* capital—for they had several, like all such states resting upon a network of tributary power over long distances—at N'jimi, whose exact location is unknown, but was undoubtedly near the eastern borders of Lake Chad. Here they developed a court at which the *magira*, or queen mother, had much authority, as did also the *gumsa*, the king's senior wife, and where the Saifuwa "family council" met. Here, too, as Islam grew in influence, *'ulama*, or learned men, wrestled with the growing problems of juridical and economic development. From time to time the court shifted its residence, following the king to one or other of the regional capitals, whose imposing brick ruins may still be seen by anyone who can take the time to go there—though it seems that the builders of a new Africa are fast making away with the bricks.

This pattern of government expanded greatly in the thirteenth century, when Kanuri power ranged far to the east of Lake Chad, as well as some way to the west, and had its northern outposts as distant as the Fezzan. Kings numbered eighteen to twenty-one in lists established by Ronald Cohen, an American cultural anthropologist, were all entitled *Dunama*, "the Great," and were the leaders of a large imperial enterprise. Their reign dates were probably between about A.D. 1150 and the beginning of the next century. They were succeeded by others—down to about number thirty in Cohen's lists—who enjoyed a similarly wide-ranging power.

But what proved good for the Kanuri proved also good for some of their neighbors. Even before A.D. 1400 there were several vassal peoples, among them the Bulala, who were east of Chad and who had grown strong enough to contest Kanuri overlordship; coupled with dynastic strife, this challenge led to a major shift in the fortunes of the Saifuwa and their dependents. Driven out of that portion of Kanem east of Chad, they took refuge in the territory governed by the *galadima* west of the lake. Here in Bornu they developed a new capital at Birni N'gazaragamu, which is today situated near the border between Nigeria and the Republic of Niger. From this place, surrounded by a tough brick wall, the Kanuri successors were to rule until well into the nineteenth century. Having recuperated their dynastic

Bornu's ablest warriors guarded the royal personage, who by custom never defended himself, it being deemed beneath his dignity.

DENHAM, *Travels and Discoveries in Africa*, 1827

and military strength, their kings were able to embark on fresh imperial adventures not long before A.D. 1500. Again they thrust their armies east of Chad, subduing the Bulala and possibly pushing on as far as Darfur. And once more they mastered the southerly terminals of the Saharan trails to the Fezzan and Libya.

This new Kanuri empire reached its zenith under the sixtieth king in Cohen's lists. This was the memorable Mai Idris Alooma, who reigned in the last quarter of the sixteenth century, and whose power possibly reached as far east as Kordofan. The empire largely remained at this pinnacle of power until about A.D. 1750, when Al-Hajj Ali Dunama saw the outset of a new time of troubles. The last ruler of the Saifuwa dynasty, the seventy-fifth king, died shortly after 1846, ending more than one thousand years of royal succession.

More telling than the events of this dynastic history are the changes in structure that enabled these Bornu kings to reassert the primacy of their forebears in Kanem. From

Bornu foot soldiers, even in the 1800's when this engraving was made, continued to rely on the lance and the bow in waging war.

DENHAM, *Travels and Discoveries in Africa*, 1827

about 1450 there came the same political evolution that, a little later, was to characterize Songhai under Askia Muhammad I. This is the gradual and cautious development of administrative power by appointment rather than by right of birth. In ways that remain to be understood in detail, the grand council of Saifuwa peers begins to lose its authority to a king, who is still a constitutional monarch in that he is bound by law and custom, as well as by the balance of internal power within the structure, but is no longer merely primus inter pares. While continuing to uphold Kanuri religion, if only because it is Kanuri religion that lies at the root of his power, he relies increasingly on Islam for the shaping of new forms of delegated power, which stand outside the customary lineage network.

Adapting Muslim examples in Egypt and elsewhere, commoners and "slaves," who are sometimes eunuchs, begin to form an administrative corps of "king's men," whose loyalty is not to any lineage but to the person of the king himself. The *kaigama*, for example, was almost certainly considered to be of noble lineage in early times. A Kanuri praise song composed shortly before 1700 celebrates him as "the chief slave" of the king: "star of the morning, holder of the principal of the king's offices, less than the king certainly, yet greater than all the prosperous men. . . ."

Having such men at his command, the king can begin to offset the authority of his princely rivals and nobles, and even displace them in their governorships and commands. Building on the same method, he selects captives for a troop of "king's soldiers," and so provides himself with an armed force whose loyalties are likewise outside the lineage structure. Mai Idris Alooma even imported Turkish musketry instructors and formed a little corps of musketeers.

With all this increase in prestige and power, royal expenses multiply. Long-service soldiers prove expensive, and so do their armaments and horses. A growing administration drains the royal purse, while heightened prestige calls for still larger palaces and still higher walls of clay and timber. Royal hospitality has to be lavish if it is not to seem ridiculous. Somehow there has to be ever more revenue from taxation and tributes, and so the imperial process acquires a momentum of its own. Only the corresponding growth and rivalry of neighboring peoples will bring it to a halt. This did not happen to the Kanuri empire until the eighteenth century.

Important among neighboring state systems, which developed by much the same constellation of local and intrusive factors of growth, were those of the Hausa, lying west and southwest of Bornu. Although the early formative factors in Hausaland were similar to those of the Kanuri, the results were markedly different.

Like the Kanuri, the Hausa emerged around or soon after the middle of the first millennium A.D. from a mingling of ancestral stocks; some of their ancestors may have come from Bornu or Kanem or possibly farther east. Like them, the early Hausa were pastoralists and farmers, workers in iron, and traders, who took a lead among other ethnic groups in the localities where they had settled and proved able to dominate large areas. Unlike the Kanuri, however, the Hausa evolved no single unifying system. Their independent cities, each governing lands extending a long way from its walled center, were rivals rather than allies, and this rivalry, thanks to the competition fostered by long-distance trade, grew stronger with time. Enterprising in commerce, skilled in handicrafts, shrewd in their handling of community affairs, these city-states were to become a most notable element in the whole West African scene.

At the very beginning, according to Hausa traditions, there were seven true states: Biram, Gobir, Daura, Kano, Katsina, Rano, and Zaria. Their rulers were all grandsons of a "founding-hero" called Bayagidda, also said to have been the son of a princess of Bornu, an early pointer to the influence of Bornu that recurs throughout their history. Then, at some later time, there likewise appeared seven "illegitimate" Hausa states: Kebbi, Kamfara, Gwari, Jukun, Nupe, Yauri and Ilorin (referring here to Yoruba, north of the forest). Their founders had not been among the progeny of Bayagidda, but had adopted Hausa ideas and institutions. These traditions manifestly point to an early period of population movements and cultural interchange.

From the first, it seems, these emergent Hausa communities acquired their separate identities in stockaded villages, or *birni*, where initially villagers and nearby farmers took shelter in times of trouble. About a thousand years ago these *birni* appear to have grown into towns governed by kings. Here they developed their language and their customs, their beliefs and political structures. This is indicated by detailed Kano traditions, which now begin to be supported by new archeological research. By 1300, in any case, these towns had become the centers of states with frontiers between them. If such frontiers for a long time marked out little more than claims to spheres of interest, they were already well enough defined to set the pattern of possession and rivalry between power systems whose institutions remained closely similar.

Although the legitimate states of Kano, Katsina, and Zaria took the lead sometime before the fifteenth century, all the Hausa city-states manifested a dominant interest in local and long-distance trade, at which their men excelled, and they served both as emporiums and as centers of handicraft manufacture in textiles, leather, metals, and other goods. After 1400, with Islam becoming increasingly more influential, they were also centers of learning, and the level of intellectual discourse there was high enough to attract noted scholars from distant places. Except for a time in the sixteenth century when western Hausaland and even Kano came under the influence and partial control of the Songhai emperor Askia Muhammad I, the Hausa states looked generally to Bornu and its rulers for new ideas about government and for solutions to new problems. Some of the states even came under official Bornu overlordship.

Here, as elsewhere, society was becoming more deeply stratified; kings were acquiring more power; new forms of servitude were beginning to appear. Of King Abdullahi Burja, who ruled in Kano between about 1438 and 1452 and who was probably under strong Bornu influence, the traditions say that he set up "slave settlements" by regularly raiding their non-Muslim enemies for captives who could be put to productive work. This was clearly an innovation that reflected the growth of deeper social divisions, just as it did in Bornu. But it would be wrong to see in this the transformation of Kano's economy to one based on slavery. The actual status of slaves probably differed little in practice from that of neighboring free villagers, and nothing like a plantation economy ever developed.

A few decades later King Muhammad Rumfa of Kano established a nine-man council of state that was possibly modeled on Saifuwa practice. No doubt to emphasize his power, he built himself a new palace, which appeared grand and glorious to his courtiers and was to be the model of other and later palaces in Hausaland. More important in the long run, Rumfa also gave a strong thrust to that process of appointing "king's men"—whether commoners, eunuchs, or other "slaves"—who stood outside the aristocratic establishment and enabled Kano and other Hausa states to evolve the intricate checks and balances of their monarchial systems.

Such innovations, and the socioeconomic reasons that provoked them, called for the introduction of new laws and customs. Learned men were expected to show how this could best be done. Intellectuals at court might have been ornamental, but they were looked to for practical advice as well. According to the Kano Chronicle, soon after 1450 a number of Fulani priests "came to Hausaland from Mali, bringing with them books of divinity and etymology"; they initiated a period of Fulani intellectual leadership that persists to this day.

But the scholar best remembered as an influence on the remodeling of Hausa institutions was, as it happened, neither from the western Sudan nor from Bornu. He was Muhammad al-Majhili, a renowned jurist of Tlemcen in western Algeria, who sojourned in Kano at the end of the fifteenth century; he wrote for Muhammad Rumfa a book whose title is reasonably translated as *The Obligations of Princes*. A little later, as the previous chapter has shown, Al-Majhili went to Gao and gave advice to Askia Muhammad I.

Evolving in this way, the stronger of these states flourished by trade and tribute. They became vital components in the whole long-distance commerce of West Africa. Al-

The establishment of one state's hegemony over another was often accompanied by the taking of slaves to fill the ranks of armies and to perform civilian tasks in the societies of the conquerors. As the centuries passed, slaves also became a major source of revenue for the ruling classes. In this 1891 engraving, rifle-bearing African traders lead off their captives, having decimated the ill-defended village.
Illustrated American, MAY 2, 1891

though they often quarreled with each other, their wars stopped short of large-scale destruction. Menaced from time to time by Songhai or Bornu, they managed for the most part to retain their independence. Much can be guessed from their traditions.

Happily for history, however, there appeared in 1550 the celebrated eyewitness description of Leo Africanus. It is unlikely to have been a very reliable description, as it was written many years after Leo's visit to Hausaland and for a European audience with no means of critical judgment, as Leo must well have known; but it was and is the only one of its kind and therefore the best. Published in Venice nearly a quarter of a century after the writing was finished, this work startled mercantile Europe with a vision of distant power and wealth in much the same way as Columbus' reports on the Americas had done fifty years earlier.

Leo Africanus, whose given name was Al-Hasan ibn Muhammad al-Wazzan az-Zayyati, had visited Timbuktu at the age of seventeen with an uncle who was a Moroccan ambassador. Soon after 1500 (the date remains uncertain) he made another journey to the Sudan, at which time he passed through Hausaland. By now he was about thirty and in the diplomatic service of the king of Fez in Morocco.

While sailing westward from Tripoli in 1518, he was captured by a Christian pirate named Pietro Bovadiglia. Realizing that he had an important prisoner on his hands, Bovadiglia turned the future Leo over to Pope Leo X, who imprisoned him for a year in Rome's Castel Sant' Angelo on the banks of the Tiber. There, the young captive was instructed in Christianity by three bishops; in 1518 he was baptized as Giovanni Leo de' Medici, after the pope. Soon afterward he began making notes for a book about his African travels. This he completed in 1526; the notes are lost, but what appears to be the finished manuscript came to light in 1931. The manuscript had been edited sometime before 1550 by a leading Venetian administrator, Giovanni Ramusio, who brushed up the author's faulty Italian (Ramusio also gave Leo the name by which he is remembered) and published the result.

Ramusio's volume had an instant and widespread success, and was subsequently translated into numerous European languages, including an English version by John Pory, whose 1600 edition is quoted throughout this text. Considering the history of its production, the story is a lively one and may still be read with pleasure. In it the Hausa states of the early sixteenth century are vividly depicted. Gobir, Leo Africanus found, was rich in cattle and people, many of them living in thriving towns. "Heere are also great store of artificers and linnen weavers: and heere are such shooes made . . . the greatest part whereof be carried to Tombuto [Timbuktu] and Gago [Gao]."

Leo described another state later absorbed by Katsina as "very populous, and having a king raigning over it, which maintaineth a garison of seven thousand archers, and five hundred horsemen. . . .", or cavalry, that is, hired as mercenaries from some other state. "The inhabitants are very rich, and have continuall traffique with the nations adjoining. Southward thereof lieth a region greatly abounding with gold," is a reference to Hausa trade with the gold-producing country of the Akan in present-day Ghana.

Kano appeared to Leo as a great capital whose "walles and houses whereof are built for the most part of a kind of chalke [baked clay]." (These structures can be seen today.) "The inhabitants are rich merchants and most civill people," just as the German explorer Heinrich Barth would find them more than three centuries later, and just as they are now. Of Zaria he writes: "The inhabitants are rich and have great traffique unto other nations." Bornu has "a most puissant prince. . . . Horsemen he hath in continuall readines to the number of three thousand, & an huge number of footmen; for all his subjects are so serviceable and obedient unto him, that whensoever he commandeth them, they will . . . follow him. . . ." The Bornu king, Leo, says, engaged in raiding for captives who could be sold as slaves. He invited

> merchants of Barbary, and willed them to bring him great store of horses: for in this countrey they use to exchange horses for slaves, and to give fifteen and sometime twentie. And by this means there were abundance of horses brought: howbeit the merchants were constrained to stay for their slaves till the king returned home conquerour with a great number of captives, and satisfied his creditors for their horses. And often times it falleth out that the merchants must stay three months togither, before the king returneth from the warres, but they are all that while maintained at the kings charges. Sometimes he bringeth not home slaves enough to satisfie the merchants: and otherwhiles they are constrained to awaite there a whole yeere togither; for the king maketh invasions but every yeere once, & that at one set and appointed time of the yeere. Yea I myselfe met with sundree merchants heere, who despairing of the kings paiment, bicause they had trusted him a whole yeere; determined never to come thither with horses againe. And yet the king seemeth marvellous rich; for his spurres, his bridles, platters, dishes, pots, and other vessels wherein his meate and drinke are brought to the table, are all of pure golde; yea, and the chaines of his dogs and hounds are of golde also.

The little that is known of Hausa rule before A.D. 1600 suggests that its cost continued to grow, as pomp and majesty kept pace with military reinforcement. Later evidence supports that analysis. For example, under Muhammad Sharifa, king of Kano from 1703 to 1731, tradition says that taxes and tribute had increased to such a point that "the Arabs left the town and went to Katsina, and most of the poorer people fled the country." No doubt this exaggerates the situation. But the fact that many Hausa freemen did indeed become acutely discontented with their lot is strongly suggested by the relative ease with which the Fulani jihad, launched in 1804, would succeed.

Yet if taxes and tribute continued to grow heavier, such evidence as there is indicates that the constraining power of Hausa checks and balances within the governing system itself did also. These checks and balances turned upon a shrewdly managed structure of offices, whether filled by appointment or inheritance, whereby the king could maneuver in favor of his own decisions, but could seldom or never act as an autocrat. On one side were the leaders of traditional Hausa lineages—the kingmakers of the past—whereas on the other were slave officials, eunuchs, and similar courtiers, whose privileges depended only upon royal power. Thus Dr. Michael G. Smith, a British anthropolo-

The brick ruin below is thought to have been an ancient Christian monastery. It is north of the Jebel Marra massif in Darfur, an area now within the sphere of Islam and under the local rule of the melik *at left.*

BOTH: BASIL DAVIDSON

gist, has concluded from his study of the evidence that, "in the seventeenth and eighteenth century, a Hausa ruler concentrated his attention on rival chiefdoms [within his state], and on his senior kinsmen or free officials. The ruler took such steps as he could to deprive lineage rivals of power and to reduce powerful officials," playing the one off against the other as opportunity might allow.

Much the same was undoubtedly true of Bornu, just as it was of Songhai after the reforms of Askia Muhammad I. Here, as in contemporary Europe, kings might wish to be dictators, but found in practice that they had to maneuver and mollify the ruling oligarchies, whether free or slave, upon whom they always depended. In so far as the term is valid for monarchies of that period, these were of a constitutional type: they depended upon an institutional structure within which the kings, though always having the last word, could act only by a systematized consent.

In other, lesser polities, east of Lake Chad and the old lands of Kanem, it was probably much the same, though very little is as yet known about them. The state of Darfur appears to have emerged in distant times as a relay intermediary in the Nile-Niger trade. Darfur traditions speak of a dynasty called the Daju, identified only in vague and contradictory legend, which was followed by the slightly better-documented Tunjur dynasty, based in the hills to the north of Darfur's Jebel Marra. Some of these early kings were probably in contact, and perhaps in partnership, with the later rulers of Meroë. In addition, a fine brick complex erected on one of the hills in the Jebel Dar Furnung north of Jebel Marra seems to have been built as a Christian monastery, an indication that the Christian kingdom of Makuria had established a far-western mission settlement there.

Islam evidently came to power in Darfur during the sixteenth century, perhaps under one of Mai Idris Alooma's ancestors or under Idris himself; and there emerged at Jebel Marra a new dynasty known as the Keira, which was undoubtedly ruled with a Muslim constitution similar to that of Bornu. The earliest of these Keira kings, to whom tradition gives the name of Sulaiman Solong, appears to have ruled in the middle of the seventeenth century. He or his successors took over an earlier tradition of building in brick that may have started in Meroë, but in any case had long since passed westward to Kanem and Bornu. By the reign of the seventh Keira monarch, Muhammad Teirab, the kingdom had acquired enough centralized power and wealth to erect imposing, fortified stone structures. Some of these, notably to the southwest of Kabkabia on the western flank of Jebel Marra, were still in a fair state of preservation when the present writer saw them in 1957.

The evidence is inconclusive as to whether or not the kings of Bornu were able during the sixteenth century to bring Darfur, even briefly, within their sphere of influence and tribute, but there is no doubt about one major point. From sometime before A.D. 1500 the history of the peoples of the grasslands east of Darfur, and of Darfur itself, belongs to the tragic afterglow of Christian Nubian civilization.

Already seven centuries old when the kingdom of Makuria collapsed at the end of the fourteenth century Nubia's kingdoms stood for a remarkable African achievement. Internal written records have never been recovered, but surviving Arabic memoirs tell a little of what they were like. Writing in A.D. 1208, Abu Salih the Armenian claimed that Alodia, the southernmost of the three kingdoms, had four hundred churches as well as many monasteries, and praised the wealth and comfort of its capital. Archeological finds during the 1960's have added greatly to the list of its noble church buildings and saved at Faras in the north a large number of superb religious frescoes.

Of the final decades of Christian Nubia almost nothing is known. The Ethiopians, barricaded behind high mountain passes, were able to survive the Muslim onslaught and upheaval and, eventually, to turn the tables on their rivals, notably the sultanate of Adel, located in what is northern Somalia today. But the Nubians had no such natural defenses. Invaded by Mameluk armies from the north, infil-

A hunting party of Sudanese men and boys runs through grass bordering the Blue Nile. Their uncompromising environment offers little more than a seminomadic subsistence economy, largely based on the management of cattle and the gathering of durra, millet, and other grains.
BLACK STAR–HOYNINGEN-HUENE

trated by Muslim migrants moving down the Blue Nile in the south, Christian Nubian civilization disappeared during the fifteenth century into a historical mist that no research has yet managed to penetrate. When at last the mist begins to clear late in the fifteenth century, the scene has altogether changed, and the Islamization of Nubia is far advanced. Nomad peoples dominate Makuria. Control southward from the riverain frontier of Alodia is held by the Funj, a people of uncertain but possibly southern Nilotic origins who had also accepted Islam. In 1503–1504 their first listed ruler, Amara Dunqas, founded his capital at Sennar. Here the Funj kings would rule until the nineteenth century.

These disturbances meant little to the western peoples. Although the ancient trading route from the Nile through Darfur to Chad ceased to feed their commerce, they continued to thrive upon the north-south Saharan routes. By 1600 they were just reaching the apogee of cultures formed a thousand years earlier. Beginning in the seventeenth century, they would come slowly to grips with the challenge of a wider western world from which they were still separated by the vast distances of inner Africa. With modern reassessment of written and oral records, and the aids of archeology, historians can now set forth these cultures not only in outline but also in considerable detail. Here, as Ahmad ibn Fartua, Idris Alooma's chronicler, remarked nearly four centuries ago about his own written history of Bornu, "we have mentioned very little, passing over much from fear of being lengthy and verbose. But the thoughtful reader will understand that beyond the river lies the sea."

If one were to embark on that sea, however, there would be interesting things to speculate about as well as to say. King Idris Alooma and England's Queen Elizabeth I certainly talked different languages, but were their basic administrative and political problems so very dissimilar? Both, after all, were much concerned with the overweening power of nobles and the need for loyal servants; both had a great deal of trouble with each.

In a very different direction, southward into the far interior of Africa, other comparisons with Kanem-Bornu's social order might be found. For there, too, south of the Congo forests in geophysical circumstances not markedly different from those of the Sudan, the sixteenth and seventeenth centuries saw the emergence of another cluster of kingdoms much concerned with trade. Undoubtedly, at least two great differences divided them: in the Sudan there was the formative influence of Islam, reaching into every field of organized life, whereas in the south there was the ever-destructive tsetse fly. Yet the basic nature of the problems of centralizing rule might have been much the same, and the solutions—superficialities aside—of the same order.

The story of the kingdoms and lesser polities of the far interior belong rightly to another chapter. Yet that of the Nile-Niger region, as of the remainder of West Africa, can undoubtedly help to illuminate it.

MERCHANTS AND POTENTATES

DESERT CARAVANS

The central Sudan was the hub of an elaborate system of trails that linked the emporiums of North Africa and the Sahara with the whole of the Sudan from the Niger to the Nile. The steady stream of caravans that made the perilous desert crossing is the subject of this selection. It comes from an unpublished study by Dr. Samir Zoghby, assistant director of the African Section, the Library of Congress.

The history of commerce is strewn with trails with exotic connotations. The Silk Road, the Spice Road, the Gold Road, and the Salt Road have always intrigued our imagination, goaded by such romantic figures as Marco Polo and Vasco da Gama, and, in Islam, the Maqarri brothers and Ibn Battuta.

There were basically four types of caravans in the trans-Saharan trade: military, religious, small commercial, and large commercial. The military was essentially of the *ghazw* [raiding] type, which was also considered as a commercial enterprise and was as thoroughly prepared. The religious caravan was mainly composed of pilgrims on their way to Mecca or sometimes to the tomb of a venerated *marabout* [or holy man]. The small commercial caravans consisted usually of five to one hundred camels, while the large annual ones had from five hundred to two thousand camels. The smaller the caravan, the greater the speed. [A Adu] Boahen states that: ". . . the average rate was fifteen to sixteen miles [per eight hour day] for a heavily laden caravan, seventeen to eighteen for a moderately laden, and twenty to twenty-two a day of ten hours for a lightly laden caravan. As a rule the caravans left the Barbary states between September and October, and departed from the Sudan at the commencement of the rainy season in April or May. Barring accidents and undue delays, the journey lasted from seventy to ninety days depending on the size of the caravan and the weight of each camel load."

The commercial caravans and especially the large commercial ones were very elabroate endeavors. Careful arrangements were made, associations were formed for the trip, and some traders delegated their representatives who traditionally kept one third of the benefit. Sometimes the large caravans were made up of smaller caravans traveling together for safety.

Though the trans-Saharan trade did not have to wait for the camel, it was the latter that made the intensive contacts between the two shores of the Sahara possible. There were usually two types of camel in the caravan. One was the white or greyish *mehari*, which is built for speed, with its elegant frame; and the burden camel for carrying goods, which was brown and stocky. Great care was taken to select camel drivers who loaded and unloaded the beasts, as a wounded or ill-loaded camel could delay and even endanger the caravan.

Four factors have been the cause of most deaths during those tremendous trips. The variations in temperature—as high as 110° F. by day to as low as 20° F. at night—claimed many victims. Sandstorms were reported to have buried entire caravans in oblivion, such as the army sent by Al-Mansur to invade the Songhai before the commando raid of Juder (1591). Thirst, however, has been pictured as the most horrible danger in the desert. Since the ratio of a gallon of water a day per man is the minimum safe allowance, water was a vital necessity. The problem was tackled from two angles. Springs were kept in good order and protected by the "Pinkertons" of the desert and ample water supplies were carried along. Goatskins were filled with water, but as Al-Yaqut reported, sandstorms usually dried up the goatskins, so the merchants resorted to killing camels, specially the ones who had just quenched their thirst, and drinking the somewhat greenish water found in their stomachs.

A different type of Saharan danger was the threat of nomadic robbers. To counter this threat, the merchants selected their guides and camel drivers from the areas crossed. They also concluded agreements with the leaders of the predominant tribes for safe-conduct. The nomads, who realized the importance of the trails, requested seasonable "ransoms," fearing to scare away the customers. At Ghadames, each commercial concern had its special protector and catered to his needs.

The livelihood of these tribes hinged on the power of the two foci of power both north and south of the Sahara. When the Maghreb states were strong, they were able to control the nomads by closing the passes leading to the Tell. Similarly, when the Sudanic empires were powerful, they contained and controlled the nomads and even occupied their strongholds when they upset the trade routes, such as when Ghana occupied Awdaghast in 990.

The desert routes were controlled by

the Tuareg. The western Sahara, from Sijilmasa to Ghana, was the preserve of the Bani Masufa, while the central Sahara between Tuat and the Ahaggar Mountains was controlled by the Ahaggar Tuareg, and the Ajjer Tuareg controlled the trails north of Ghat. . . .

Another trail which became important later on, specially after the collapse of Awdaghast [1055], was the route Sijilmasa-Taghaza-Ghana. The stop at Taghaza allowed the traders to load salt slabs to be sold in the Sudan. Farther east, the Fezzan-Kawar trail was less heavily used, but still reflected a pale shadow of its old frame as the Garamantian Road, the more so since it was the easiest and shortest route from the Mediterranean into Central Africa. The trail *Darb al-Arbi'* in linking Kanem with Asyut in Egypt was discontinued, according to Ibn Hawqal, during the tenth century due to sandstorms and raiders, and the route Cairo-Tunis-Fez-Sijilmasa was adopted.

Once the caravans reached the southern termini, the camels were unloaded, and the goods to the south followed two paths: they were either shipped by canoes down the Niger, whenever possible, or loaded on asses and bullocks, as the camels could not resist the tsetse fly. Once the forest was reached, the goods were once more unloaded and carried by headload to their destination in the forest area.

SEARCHING FOR THE SOURCE

In 1447, while staying at the oases of Tuat (which he had reached from Hono, or Honein, on the coast), an Italian named Antonio Malfante wrote this informative letter to a friend in Genoa. Malfante, who was evidently employed as an agent for one of the Italian banking corporations of the day, had ventured into the Sahara primarily to find the source of the gold that was pouring into Europe from the western Sudan. However, neither he nor any other outsider—until the nineteenth century—would discover the precise location of the mines from which the Sudan kingdoms obtained their gold. The letter, originally written in Latin, provides an engaging account of life in the oases and in the "Land of the Blacks" farther south.

After we had come from the sea, that is from Hono, we journeyed on horseback, always southwards, for about twelve days. For seven days we encountered no dwelling—nothing but sandy plains; we proceeded as though at sea, guided by the sun during the day, at night by the stars. At the end of the seventh day, we arrived at a *ksour* [a village], where dwelt very poor people who supported themselves on water and a little sandy ground. They sow little, living upon the numerous date palms. At this *ksour* we had come into Tueto [the Tuat oases]. In this place there are eighteen quarters, enclosed within one wall, and ruled by an oligarchy. Each ruler of a quarter protects his followers, whether they be in the right or no. The quarters closely adjoin each other and are jealous of their privileges. Everyone arriving here places himself under the protection of one of these rulers, who will protect him to the death: thus merchants enjoy very great security, much greater, in my opinion, than in kingdoms such as Themmicenno [Tlemcen] and Thunisie [Tunis].

Though I am a Christian, no one ever addressed an insulting word to me. They said they had never seen a Christian before. It is true that on my first arrival they were scornful of me, because they all wished to see me, saying with wonder "This Christian has a countenance like ours"—for they believed that Christians had disguised faces. Their curiosity was soon satisfied, and now I can go alone anywhere, with no one to say an evil word to me.

There are many Jews, who lead a good life here, for they are under the protection of the several rulers, each of whom defends his own clients. Thus they enjoy very secure social standing. Trade is in their hands, and many of them are to be trusted with the greatest confidence.

This locality is a mart of the country of the Moors, to which merchants come to sell their goods: gold is carried hither, and bought by those who come up from the coast. This place is De Amamento [Tamentit], and there are many rich men here. The generality, however, are very poor, for they do not sow, nor do they harvest anything, save the dates upon which they subsist. They eat no meat but that of castrated camels, which are scarce and very dear.

It is true that the Arabs with whom I came from the coast brought with them corn and barley which they sell throughout the year . . . .

It never rains here: if it did, the houses, being built of salt in the place of reeds, would be destroyed. It is scarcely ever cold here: in summer the heat is extreme, wherefore they are almost all blacks. The children of both sexes go naked up to the age of fifteen. These people observe the religion and law of Muhammad. In the vicinity there are 150 to 200 *ksour*.

In the lands of the blacks, as well as here, dwell the Philistines [the Tuareg], who live, like the Arabs, in tents. They are without number, and hold sway over the land of Gazola [the Sahara] from the borders of Egypt to the shores of the Ocean . . . and over all the neighboring towns of the blacks. They are fair, strong in body and very handsome in appearance. They ride without stirrups, with simple spurs. They are governed by kings, whose heirs are the sons of their sisters—for such is their law. They keep their mouths and noses covered. I have seen many of them here, and have asked them through an interpreter why they cover their mouths and noses thus. They replied: "We have inherited this custom from our ancestors." They are sworn enemies of the Jews, who do not dare to pass hither. Their faith is that of the Blacks. Their sustenance is milk and flesh, no corn or barley, but much rice. Their sheep, cattle, and camels are without number. One breed of camel, white as snow, can cover in one day a distance which would take a horseman four days to travel. Great warriors, these people are continually at war amongst themselves.

The states which are under their rule border upon the land of the Blacks. I shall speak of those known to men here, and which have inhabitants of the faith of Muhammad. In all, the great majority are Blacks, but there are a small number of whites [Berbers].

First, Thegida [Takedda], which comprises one province and three *ksour;* Checoli, which is as large.

Chuchiam [probably Gao], Thambet [Timbuktu], Geni [Jenne], and Meli [Mali], said to have nine towns;

Thora, Oden, Dendi, Sagoto, Bofon, Igdem, Bembo, all these are great cities, capitals of extensive lands and towns under their rule.

These adhere to the law of Muhammad.

To the south of these are innumerable great cities and territories, the inhabitants of which are all blacks and idolaters, continually at war with each other in defense of their law and slaves which the blacks take in their internecine wars are sold at a very low price, the maximum being two *doubles* a head. . . .

"It is not long since I was in Cuchia [Gao], distant fifty days' journey from here, where there are Moors," my patron said to me. "A heathen king, with five hundred thousand men, came from the south to lay siege to the city of Vallo. Upon the hill within the city were fifty Moors, almost all blacks. They saw that they were by day surrounded by a human river, by night by a girdle of flames and looked upon themselves as already defeated and enslaved. But their king, who was in the city, was a great magician and necromancer; he concluded with the besieger a pact by which each was to produce by incantation a black goat. The two goats would engage in battle, and the master of that which was beaten, was likewise to consider himself defeated. The besieger emerged victorious from the contest, and, taking the town, did not allow one soul to escape, but put the entire population to the sword. He found much treasure there. The town to-day is almost completely deserted save for a poverty-stricken few who have come to dwell there."

Tuareg pounding millet, a staple of their diet
VICTOR ENGLEBERT

Of such were the stories which I heard daily in plenty. The wares for which there is a demand here are many: but the principal articles are copper, and salt in slabs, bars, and cakes. The copper of Romania [the Byzantine empire], which is obtained through Alexandria, is always in great demand throughout the land of the Blacks. I frequently inquired what they did with it, but no one could give me a definite answer. I believe it is that there are so many peoples that there is almost nothing but is of use to them.

The Egyptian merchants come to trade in the land of the Blacks with half a million head of cattle and camels—a figure which is not fantastic in this region.

The place where I am is good for trade, as the Egyptians and other merchants come hither from the land of the Blacks bringing gold, which they exchange for copper and other goods. Thus everything sells well; until there is nothing left for sale. The people here will neither sell nor buy unless at a profit of one hundred per cent. For this reason, I have lost, Laus Deo!, on the goods I brought here, two thousand *doubles.*

From what I can understand, these people neighbor on India [probably Ethiopia]. Indian merchants come hither, and converse through interpreters. These Indians are Christians, adorers of the cross. It is said that in the land of the Blacks there are forty dialects, so that they are unable to understand each other.

I often inquired where the gold was found and collected; my patron always replied "I was fourteen years in the land of the Blacks, and I have never heard nor seen anyone who could reply from definite knowledge. That is my experience, as to how it is found and collected. What appears plain is that it comes from a distant land, and, as I believe, from a definite zone." He also said that he had been in places where silver was as valuable as gold.

This land is twenty-eight days' journey from Cambacies [probably Ghadames], and is the city with the best market. It is twenty-five days from Tunis, from Tripoli in Barbary twenty days, from Trimicen [Tlemcen] thirty days, from Fecia [Fez] twenty days, from Zaffi, Zamor and Messa twenty days on horseback. I finish for the present; elsewhere and at another time, God willing, I will recount much more to you orally. I am always at your orders in Christ.

UMME JILMA, "ANGEL OF GOD"

The Kanuri states of Kanem and Bornu and the Hausa states were the dominant powers in the central Sudan. Kanem, which lies to the north of Lake Chad, was at the southern end of a main trans-Saharan trail. Its ruling dynasty, the Saifuwa, converted to Islam during the reign of Umme Jilma (1085–1097), the mai, *or king, who is said to have died in Egypt while on the hadj to Mecca. This Kanuri praise song, honoring Kanem's first Muslim* mai, *is the oldest of its genre.*

O! Sultan, the good, whose sleep is light as that of a hare:
Sultan, truly a Sultan, who stays not in the house of his father's sister:
Of noble birth from both his father and mother:

Of noble birth indeed, of noble birth
from both his parents:
Where you sit costly carpets are spread
for you; above your head is a canopy
of gold:
O! Sultan, who can discomfit one like
pebbles on one's eyelashes:
O! Sultan, Angel of God.
As there is a protector of the camel's
tongue, do you protect us:
The friend of youth:
Whose writing slate is made of "kabwi"
wood;
At night a warrior on a coal-black horse;
but when day dawns he is to be seen
with his Koran in his hand.
We wait upon your blessing:
Babuma Amadu said to Mai Aji Fannami
at the Sugu war,
"Sultan, even if you are mounted on your
bay horse called 'Kite Kiteram,'
Birni Njimi [the capital] is a long way off
if you want to run away."

KANEM AT ITS HEIGHT

By the mid-thirteenth century the mai *of Kanem controlled the entire Fezzan as well as the trade route to Tripoli. His kingdom stretched eastward as far as Wadai in present-day Chad, westward as far as Kano, and included Bornu, southwest of Lake Chad. This territorial expansion furthered the dissemination of the Islamic culture throughout the Sudan. As related in the following passage by Al-Maqrizi (1364–1442), a Cairo-born historian, the Muslim population of Kanem even built a college and hostel in Cairo. It housed Kanuri students of Islamic law and pilgrims on their way to Mecca. The* mai *still retained much pre-Islamic ritual, such as addressing his subjects from behind a screen. Al-Maqrizi's account also contains the first reference to money in Kanem-Bornu.*

All the Sudanese derive their origin from Fut the son of Ham. Their tribes number nineteen. . . . The inhabitants of Kanem are a great people, and for the most part Muslims. Their city is called Njimi. . . . [Their king] is a nomad in mode of life. When he sits on his throne his courtiers prostrate themselves before him, and fall on their faces. His army, horse and foot and transport, numbers 100,000. . . . The King of Kanem has five feudatory kings subject to him. . . .

Their king in the year 700 A.H. [A.D. 1300] was al-Hajj Ibrahim of the sons of Saif ibn Dhi Yazan, who occupied the throne of Kanem, which is the seat of power of Bornu. There reigned after him his son al-Hajj Idris. Then Idris' brother, Daud ibn Ibrahim; then Umar ibn Idris; then the brother of the latter [and so on].

The first seat of this empire on the side which is near to Egypt is called Zuwila [the Zawila oasis in the Libyan Fezzan]. Between this town and the town of Kaukau [probably Gao], which is on the opposite [western] frontier, the distance is three months' march. The inhabitants of Kanem cover the head with a veil. The king does not show himself except at the time of the two religious festivals, in the morning and afternoon; the rest of the year he is not seen and those who talk to him are placed behind a screen. The principal food of this people is rice which grows wild in the country. They have also cheese, guinea corn, figs, limes, melons, pumpkins and fresh dates. As regards money, they use a kind of cloth which they make and which is called "Wendy." Each piece is ten cubits long, but for facility of exchange it is cut up into pieces of a quarter of a cubit or smaller. Other substances such as shells of different kinds and pieces of copper or gold are equally used in commerce and their value is estimated in an equivalent amount of cloth. In this country the pumpkins are so big that they are used as boats to cross the Nile. . . .

They are of the sect of the Imam Malik. They are particular in enforcing justice and extremely severe as regards religion. In the year 640 A.H. [A.D. 1242], they built in the town of Fustat [Cairo], a college for people belonging to the sect if the Imam Malik known as the college of Ibn Rashid. It is in this college that members of this nation reside if they come to Cairo.

SONG OF THE BORNU SLAVES

A new era of Kanuri history was inaugurated in the late 1300's, when the Saifuwa were forced to retreat into Bornu. Kanem was taken over by the Bulala people and was not reconquered by the Kanuri until the early 1500's. During these centuries Bornu became a chief factor in the trans-Saharan trade. Its principal export was slaves; its main import, horses. As the female slaves crossed the desert from their beloved Bornu, they sang of rubee, *or "gold," and of the longed-for* atka, *or freedom document. This song, recorded in the 1840's, was put into verse by John Greenleaf Whittier. It reflects the desperation of generations of Bornuan slaves as they trekked their way to servitude in unknown lands.*

Where are we going? Where are we
going?
Where are we going, Rubee?
Hear us, save us, make us free;
Send our Atka down from thee!
Here the Ghiblee wind is blowing,
Strange and large the world is growing!
Tell us, Rubee, where are we going?
Where are we going, Rubee?

Bornou! Bornou! Where is Bornou?
Where are we going, Rubee?
Bornou-land was rich and good,
Wells of water, fields of food;
Bornou-land we see no longer,
Here we thirst, and here we hunger,
Here the Moor man smites in anger;
Where are we going, Rubee?

Where are we going? Where are we going?
Hear us, save us, Rubee!
Moons of marches from our eyes,
Bornou-land behind us lies;
Hot the desert wind is blowing,
Wild the waves of sand are flowing!
Hear us! tell us, Where are we going?
Where are we going, Rubee?

A MOST EXCELLENT PRINCE

The Bornu empire reached its apogee in the late sixteenth century during the reign of

Idris ibn Ali (1570–1602), *better known as Idris Alooma. The deeds and talents of this black monarch are particularly well known through the chronicles kept by his chief imam, Ahmad ibn Fartua. Many are recorded in the following extract from Fartua's* History of the First Twelve Years of Mai Idris Alooma. *The* mai *was a zealous Muslim, and in the words of his imam, he was "an accomplished diplomat and was conversant with correct procedure and methods of negotiation." Idris Alooma also excelled as a military tactician. He introduced firearms into the Lake Chad area and was the first to employ camels on the plains of Bornu. These innovations helped him subdue such troublesome elements as the So, the indigenous people of Bornu. At Idris Alooma's death, his empire had no equal between the Niger and the Nile.*

At one of the provincial residences of the sultan of Bornu, all regular business stops when the royal procession arrives. The sultan's attendants carry ceremonial umbrellas and feather fans.
BARTH, *Travels in Central Africa*, 1857

Our Sultan Haj Idris ibn 'Ali ibn Idris sought to follow the example of our Lord and Master Muhammad, the chosen (may the blessing of God and peace rest on him and on all the prophets) in regard to the holy wars which the Prophet (upon whom be the blessing of God and peace) undertook; for God has guided and directed him towards making all his acts, and bearing, and endeavor follow the set road and redound to His glory.

Look how God . . . made easy his path, as we heard from our Sheikhs who have passed away, for the accomplishment of wonders and varied exploits such as no former king had wrought onwards from the days of Sultan al Haj Daud ibn Nigale, who fled to the realm of Bornu. So we will recall what we have learnt so far as we can. . . . .

How then about the exemplary punishment he meted out to the tribe of So, in accord with God's command to fight unbelievers, who are close to Muslims and vexatious to them. . . .

Or again his war with the people of Kano, what time they built many "stockades" in their land, seeking to harm the land of Bornu. They kept raiding and carrying off plunder, flying to their stockades and walled towns; and there hiding their gains among their own possessions.

So they did, till our Sultan attacked them with lofty purpose and aim, and destroyed all their defenses except the great "stockade" called "Dala."

So also his exploits when he fought the Barbara, till the earth in its fulness became too narrow for them and the desert too small for them, so that they found no sufficient place in which to pasture their flocks or dwell. . . .

The people of the land of Jawan brought him a horse as a present, in fear and submission. So they were brought before him and departed assured of his protection.

Look too at his journey to the house of God, that he might win a sure glory. Thus leaving the kingdom he loved and an envied pomp, he went East turning his back on delights and paying his debts to God (be He exalted).

So he made the pilgrimage and visited Tayiba [Medina], the Tayiba of the Prophet, the chosen one (upon whom be peace and the blessing of God), the unique, the victorious over the vicissitudes of day and night.

He was enriched by visiting the tomb of the pious Sahabe the chosen [the companions of the prophet Muhammad], the perfect ones (may the Lord be favorable and beneficent to them), and he bought in the noble city a house and date grove, and settled there some slaves, yearning after a plenteous reward from the Great Master. . . .

Among the benefits which God (Most High) of His bounty and beneficence, generosity, and constancy conferred upon the Sultan was the acquisition of Turkish musketeers and numerous household slaves who became skilled in firing muskets.

Hence the Sultan was able to kill the people of Amsaka [south of Lake Chad] with muskets, and there was no need for other weapons, so that God gave him a great victory by reason of his superiority in arms.

Among the most surprising of his acts was the stand he took against obscenity and adultery, so that no such thing took place openly in his time. Formerly the people had been indifferent to such offenses, committed openly or secretly by day or night. In fact he was a power among his people and from him came their strength.

So he wiped away the disgrace, and the face of the age was blank with astonishment. He cleared away and reformed as far as he could the known wrong doing. . . .

Owing to the Mai's noble precepts all the people had recourse to the sacred Sheria [canon law of Islam], putting aside worldly intrigue in their disputes and affairs, big or little.

From all we have heard, formerly most of the disputes were settled by the chiefs, not by the "Ulema" [learned men].

For example, he stopped wrong doing, hatred and treachery, and fighting between Muslims, in the case of the Kuburi and Kayi. They had been fighting bitterly over their respective prestige, but on the Sultan's accession, he sternly forbade them to fight till they became as brothers in God. . . .

He also came to the people of the hills of Zajadu and the hills of N'garasa, called N'guma, who had allied themselves with the sons of Sultan Daud and his grandsons and relatives and made raids on the land of Bornu, killing men and enslaving women and children right down to the time of our Sultan. . . . He scattered their host, and divided them, but of the N'guma he spared all and established them in settlements under his direction as his subjects nor did they resist or became recalcitrant.

The tribe of N'gizim, the people of Mugulum, and the people of Gamazan and others of the N'gizim stock who were neighbors were insolent and rebellious, till our Sultan went out to them with a large host, destroyed their crops, and burnt their houses in the wet season. Thus they felt the pinch of a ruined country, yielded to him obedience, and submitted to his rule.

He introduced units of measure for corn among these people by the power and might of God. The N'gizim who dwelt in the West, known as Binawa, would not desist from enslaving Muslims in their country and doing other evil and base actions. They kept seizing the walled towns of the Yedi as fortresses and places of refuge and hiding, using them as bases treacherously to attack the Muslims by day and night, without ceasing or respite. But when our Sultan ascended the throne, he and his Wazir in chief Kursu took counsel to stem the torrent of their guile and deceit, so that they left off their wickedness, and some followed the Sultan, others the Wazir Kursu, others various leaders who had waged "Holy War" with the Sultan.

To some the Sultan gave orders to settle, and devote their time to agriculture. . . .

Know, my brethren, that in what we have told you, we have failed to tell all. We have but told you a part of the story of the deeds of the early years of our Sultan's reign, with hand and pen. . . .

Thus we have cut short the recital of all his wars, in this brief compilation. . . .

We have ceased to doubt that our Sultan al Haj Idris ibn 'Ali accomplished much more than his grandfather. . . .

We have seen that the deeds of the Sultan (may God on high enrich His bounty with plenteous beneficence and favor) were such that if an account of this era were narrated and set forth, we should never hear the like recorded of the reign of any of our former kings. . . .

Anyone whose claims to greatness in comparison with his sires, were as the claim of our Sultan would have just cause for pride. It is no mere theory that he surpasses them all and has no peer, exalted above them in his wise counsel, and prompt action. . . .

So it is. Our Sultan the Amir ul Muminin and Khalifa of the Lord of the worlds, who visited the two noble sacred cities Sultan Idris ibn 'Ali, ibn Idris (may God enoble him in both worlds), sought to attack his enemies the So N'gafata, and destroy and scatter them. He therefore built the big town near Damasak and put Shetima Biri Getirama in command, together with his son Ajima Gasma ibn Biri. He made four gates in the town and placed a keeper in charge of each gate—and quartered there a detachment of his army. He ordered all his chiefs who were powerful and possessed of a defense force, to build houses, and leave part of their equipment there as for instance, the horses, and quilted-armor for them and coats of mail.

After he had done this he gave the town the name of Sansana ul Kabir. The people who lived in it were strenuous fighters in "Holy War." They went out morning and evening, seeking the enemy, fending them off, until God designed the ruin of their towns.

The Sultan again built another town to the North of Birni near Sansana and South of it. It was a large town. He placed there Chikama Buma, and made two gates only, the Eastern gate and the Western gate and no more.

He handed over to Chikama Buma many slaves of the Kardi so that by reason of their numbers there was little room. . . .

When our Sultan had finished building the two above mentioned towns, he turned his thoughts toward a policy of cutting off root and branch these evil doers. . . .

In regard to the character of our Sultan, the Amir ul Muminin Haj Idris ibn 'Ali (may the Lord enoble him and endow him with excellence), God laid upon him the obligation to wage Holy War and raid, as a special favor from Him (be He exalted), and gave him good hope of heavenly reward. He did not choose this world in preference to the next, when he had any affair in hand and took counsel and thought. If he found a precedent in the Kura'an or Hadiths upon which the four rightly directed Imams who have gone before agreed, he did it following the example of those who had gone before; if he did not find any precedent in the Kura'an or traditions, he would leave off, and turn aside from his course altogether.

Such were his two lines of action. He kept no secrets from those in whom he reposed confidence. As regards this, if he was upon a journey and heard any news of the enemy by night or day, he did not rest but went forth among his people to the source of the news with the army following him; leading himself for fear any misfortune should befall which he was able to avoid, or in his power to save. He relied on his Lord in everything and he was his support, sure that nothing would happen except by the foreknowledge of God (be He exalted). Hence he was a brave warrior who advanced everywhere, appearing promptly without pausing or beating round, until what he proposed was accomplished. Such was his character and his disposition.

Among the gifts with which God had endowed him, was an impressive appearance. All his followers, small or great, never felt contented except in his presence. Even though he sent large armies in one direction and went in some other direction with a small force himself, his captains were not content to go without him, however large the number of the army.

Thus whatever journey he undertook himself with a small force, leaving the large numbers to go by some other route, they would not agree to remain with the people apart from him. Their hearts did not rest being in a dilemma between the two courses, until God joined them again to their king. (May God give him great victory.) We know this by testing it in many different fields. . . .

Sultan Abdul Jelil, the son of Abdul Jelil of the tribe of Bulala, came to Sima to war with a small army. A fierce fight ensued. People's hearts were in their throats. Then the Amir al Muminin Haj Idris ibn 'Ali, came to them at nine o'-clock on a Thursday in their distress. The enemy were broken and fled like donkeys running away from a hyena. Thus were the Bulala terrified at seeing the dust of the king to the East of them going up to the sky. The Sultan (may God exalt his powers and make his victory great) followed them far, till the horses and mounts grew weary. . . .

He returned in the evening. Had God not favored the host of Bornu, He had not helped them by sending to them the king, even as He helped the host of our lord and master and Prophet, Muhammad the chosen, (may God's blessing rest on him and peace), on the day of Sisaban by the hand of his nephew and son-in-law Haidara, our lord and master 'Ali ibn Abi Talib (may God most high be pleased with him). Had it not been for the Sultan misfortune had happened. So he brought joy to the hearts of the men of Bornu and he made their eyes cool. So they congratulated each other and fell on each other's necks on the Thursday, and Friday and Saturday.

The king gave them robes of gladness in accordance with the universal joy. He then returned to Bornu.

Such is the story we have heard about this Thursday and the fight that took place on the third of the month Shawwal. This was one of the remarkable achievements of our Sultan and with this was the fact that the horses which he left behind him when he went to war were much more numerous than those which he took with him. The same was the case with pack animals. The shields were all left at home and were not sent after him.

Such was his policy and his method, with which God had endowed him from birth. . . .

May God increase the Sultan's majesty and the beauty of his renown and greatness; his goodness and his victoriousness; by the grace of our lord and master Muhammad upon whom be the blessing of God and peace, and by the grace of his companions, the chosen ones, who followed, and of those who followed them; and by the grace of Jibrail and Michail and Israfil and all the prophets and messengers of God. May the blessing of God and peace rest on them all Amen! Amen!! Amen!!!

Such is the account we have given of the character of our Sultan and his wars in the time when he was king. We have written it after there has passed of his reign twelve years.

THE YERIMA'S PRAISE SONG

Among the dignitaries attached to the Bornu court were the galadima, *the* mastrema, *the* kaigama, *and the* yerima, *who were, respectively, the wardens of the western, eastern, southern, and northern sectors of the realm. They, as well as other royal officials, were honored with praise songs sung by the* mai'*s balladeers, the most important of whom were the* ngijima. *At the height of Bornu prosperity these singers occupied exalted positions. They walked at the sultan's side during processions and enjoyed the special honor of being allowed to point at him with their official sticks. The* yerima *addressed in this song served under Mai Idris Alooma.*

Yerima Malumi, he is the strength of the Capital:

Yerima who owns the town of Kurkuri of many jujube trees:

You are the Yerima who owns Dal Karia:

Yerima, you are the owner of Sugugu:

Star of the morning, whose light illumines the East and the West:

These are all attributes of Yerima Malumi:

Yerima, if your father is alive, Dal Karia is yours:

And even if he dies, Dal Karia is yours:

Yerima, for whom a he-goat gives milk and a bull gives milk:

That is what it is to be Yerima.

Is the Kaigama the big man? No, no, the Yerima is the big man:

It is said that people argued on this point:

Where is Adam, Fanta's son? Seek him:

And Yusuf, Palmata's son? Seek him:

And Dunama, Fana's son? Seek him:

They got these three witnesses and they gave their evidence.

[They said], Yerima is like the moon at its full.

That is what it is to be the Yerima:

His father and mother are both of noble birth:

The Yerima is a chief who has his stables in the North, that is the Yerima.

Who is the Kaigama? The Kaigama is a slave.

You Yerima the owner of Firi Kimo and of Firi Mayamiram.

And of Yeri Arbasan, and of Mafi Gudu.

And of Barkawal and Belle:

And the owner of Ngilwasu, and Damaya of the Fan Palms.

Zari the Yerima's town is the gateway [to Bornu] defended with many spears:

Zari the Yerima's town where guns are as numerous as the fruit of the fan palms:

Zari the Yerima's town where those who sit in council with him are as numerous as the "Kindil" [Acacia] trees:

Zari the Yerima's town where vendettas are as numerous as the Acacia Verek trees:

Zari the Yerima's town where silks and silver head-ornaments abound:

Zari the Yerima's town full of milch cows and arrow shafts.

STAR OF THE MORNING

In addition to being the warden of the south section of the Bornu empire, the kaigama *was the commander in chief of the army. He was the sultan's chief slave, but as was the case with many other slaves of royal masters, he held a position of high esteem and responsibility. Kaigama Anterashi, celebrated in the following praise song, was in office during the second half of the seventeenth century.*

Kaigama Anterashi,
He is the Star of the morning:

Chief slave, the rallying point of the spearmen:

The hub of war:

His town Chirami, his personality that of a Sultan:

Morning and evening he is in the midst of the noise [of war]:

A chieftain, the glowing embers of the Sultan's Council:

[His friendship] a death-trap: his friend short-lived:

If a hawk snatches up a chicken,

Following its tracks devolves on the Kaigama:

Holder of the principal of the [Sultan's] offices:

Less than the Sultan, certainly, but greater than all the prosperous men:

If the chief slave wages war, he does not do so in vain.

If he does not engage in war, his idleness is not useless:

Chief slave, if I say to you "Slave,"

I mean the slave of the Sultan:

Chief slave, if I say to you "Bush-cow,"

You are a [man with the heart of] a bush-cow among men:

Chief slave, [if I say] your town is Ngumfane, I mean that you are the forehead of

A Bornu ruler in the robes of his high office
DENHAM, *Narrative of an Expedition*, 1826

all the slaves:

Chief slave, patience is your attribute:

Your patience like that of a dromedary:

Chief slave, in your hand is a large-headed spear:

Chief slave, you practice witch-craft but its source is in the palm of your hand:

Chief slave, my master, war is your hobby:

Your play, play with a shining spear:

You owner of the town of Zarara, your attributes those of a Sultan:

You and a Sultan do not eat from one calabash,

Neither do you eat what a Sultan leaves:

Sun [of greatness], seat [of power]:

Embers of the Sultan's assembly:

If the Sultan counts as ten large whole Kola-nuts,

The Kaigama counts as twenty halves:

If he and the Sultan are sitting together
and their horses are fighting:

He will not catch the Sultan's horse:

Nor will the Sultan catch his:

Some other man will catch them:

These are [the privileges of] a chief slave.

You are the father of all the minor chiefs:

And the older brother of all the great
chiefs:

Chief slave, owner of the town of Ala
and of Alari:

Who lives between the Rivers Shari and
Sharwa:

Chief slave, Commander of Bornu's
army:

Should the Sultan come out of an old
woman's dilapidated hut even,

After him will come the holder of the
office of Kaigama:

Should [the link in] the office of Kaigama break, the Fuguma will join it up
anew:

Fuguma of the games that never cease:

His play not that of the women.

Nor of boys:

They are games played with a polished
spear:

You [Fuguma] have lit the fires of war,
and are feeling their heat:

Other men look on at you from behind a
screen:

You [Kaigama] Chief slave, owner of the
town of Fefelo and of Kafe Fello,

Provide a thousand calabashes of food
for your followers:

The Ngijima, Babuma and Zakkama,

All three have sung their song:

For the success of the holder of the office
of Kaigama:

For the success of Anterashi, son of Lima:

And he has given them seventy slaves.

REMAINS OF THE PAST

Archeological findings, such as those described in the following article on the old Kanuri capitals, are invaluable supplements to oral tradition and chronicles. The authors of this study are A.D.H. Bivar, a noted Africanist, and Peter L. Shinnie, professor of archeology at the University of Khartoum, Sudan. In 1959 they visited all the sites mentioned except N'guru in northern Nigeria.

Though the picture of the Kanuri nation forming in Kanem, to the east of Chad, in the early middle ages and its subsequent move west to Bornu is reasonably clear, the origins of the Kanuri remain obscure and much of the early history is a highly dubious myth. . . .

Much remains to be done to elucidate these problems, and archaeology should be able to make its contribution. . . .

The most conspicuous of the remains left by the Kanuri from earlier times are the ruins of red brick buildings. This type of building, rare until modern times in Africa and presumably of alien origin, is known from a number of sites stretching westwards from the Nile. . . .

These sites are, in Nigeria, Birni N'gazargamo, Gambaru, and N'guru, in the Republic of Niger, Garoumele, and in the Republic of Chad, Tie.

Birni N'gazargamo is the best known as it is the largest of the sites and its history—or at least the dates at which it was first occupied and finally abandoned—are certain. . . .

The outline of the history of the site is reasonably clear. It is known to have been founded in about A.D. 1470 by Ali, son of Dunama, and remained the capital of the kings of Bornu until its capture and destruction by the Fulani in 1812.

In its present state it is an impressive sight. It consists of an enormous earth rampart enclosing a rough circle. This rampart still stands about 7 meters high and the distance across the enclosure is about 2 kilometers. There are five entrances. Traces of ditch can be seen in a few places along the outside of the rampart and it is likely that originally it ran the whole way along but is now silted up. Inside this vast enclosure are a number of red brick ruins consisting of a large complex in the center and a number of other smaller buildings scattered throughout the enclosed area. . . .

It can be safely assumed that the main complex was the palace of the Mais [kings] of Bornu, that the other red brick buildings were the residences of other leading persons, and that the majority of the inhabitants of the town lived in the flimsy grass huts typical of the neighborhood, or in houses of sun-dried brick. These have left no surface indications. The plan gives as much information of the nature of the main central building as can be ascertained. Failing excavation, nothing useful can be said about the usage of the various rooms, nor as to details of internal layout or of any features not visible on the surface. The only additional information is that the small building to the south-east of the main complex is known to the local inhabitants as a mosque and, though there is nothing in the layout, as it can now be seen, to support such a view, they may be right. This mosque seems to be an afterthought and the bricks, though of the same size, look to be of different manufacture and perhaps made of clay from another source. Excavation may answer this question. . . .

Gambaru, which is only 3 miles from Birni N'gazargamo and to its east, is clearly a site of a later period. Tradition, for what it is worth, collected by [H.R.]

Palmer describes it as having been built by Queen Amsa, mother of Idris Aloma, in an attempt to separate him from the court and thus to protect his moral character. If this is so it must be a building of the sixteenth century and this date, rather later than that given for the founding of Birni N'gazargamo, corresponds well with what one can deduce from an inspection of the two structures. Gambaru is in a much better state of repair than the older site and there is some suspicion in our minds that the walls have been restored and repaired at some comparatively recent date. . . .

The site of Garoumele is in the Republic of Niger, immediately to the west of the road that runs from Niamey to N'guigmi at the north end of Chad. . . .

[Ives] Urvoy says that this site was the residence of the kings of Kanem before the foundation of Birni N'gazargamo. He recounts that after the flight from Kanem, Omar Said and Kade Alounou (1388-9) wandered on the south and west confines of Bornu; then their successors established themselves at . . . [Garoumele]. If this is so, it makes the site considerably older than those of Bornu and geographical considerations make this highly likely. The story presumably comes from oral tradition and may well be right, but the archaeological evidence is at present too scanty to make a reasoned judgment. There are few Kanuri in the area today, though there are a number of Kanembu villages along the shore of the lake. . . .

During the course of our journey, we had much in mind the question of the location of Njimi, known to have been the capital of the Kanuri before the settlement at Birni N'gazargamo. . . .

Knowledge of the town of Njimi is derived from the Bornu Arabic text known as the *Kanem Wars of Idris Aloma*, where it is implied that it is in Kanem, i.e. east of Lake Chad: from several other Bornu chronicles and king-lists: and from the Arab geographers. The name is also well remembered in Kanuri oral tradition. . . .

Since the countryside [of Kanem] is in many ways different from that of Bornu and is little visited, it is perhaps worth giving some description of it. This may help to explain some aspects of the development and early history of the Kanuri state.

The country falls into two areas; that of the dunes, often as much as 30 meters high and composed of fine sand, covered for the most part with long grass, tamarisk, or patches of acacia scrub; and the flats, which are depressions of black cotton-soil, surrounded by girdles of palm trees, and with water freely available from shallow wells. Settlements are generally situated on the higher dunes to obtain the benefit of the evening breeze. Water for the towns is carried up on camels from below. The flats are humid and oppressive, but they have shade and with good cultivation can produce a remarkable variety of vegetables. They have the appearance of former lakes, and may still hold water in a generous rainy season. The human inhabitants of the dunes are the Goraan, living in conical grass huts and matting shelters, and possessing cattle, goats, and camels. By contrast, along the flats the people are mainly cattle-raising Kanembu.

The archaeological site at Tie . . . is chiefly characterized by its quantity of scattered brick. It is situated at the crest of a large dune formation, and is nearly 2 miles from possible sources of water. The total area is nearly square being some 243 meters by 218 meters. There are no certain traces of a surrounding wall, but to the north and north-east the boundary is more sharply defined. Elsewhere it is vague and irregular. Apart from the two main buildings at the north-east of the site, and four small mounds along its northern edge, there are few signs of substantial buildings. The area to the west seems likely, however, to have been covered by a number of smallish huts. . . .

Local opinion at Mao attributes this site, and indeed all the others which characteristically make use of baked brick, as of the Bulala period (c. A.D. 1300–1600). If this attribution were correct, it would be natural to connect the demolition of Tie with some episode in the Kanem wars of Mai Idris [Aloma], and therefore probably attributable to the 1570's.

SARKI THE SNAKE

The Hausa emerged around A.D. 500, *at about the same time as the Kanuri, their neighbors to the east. They evolved from an intermingling of diverse peoples who possibly came from the Sahara and the Nilotic Sudan and who merged with the autochthons, including people of the So culture. This admixture accounts for the wide variety of physical types found among the Hausa. Their oft-told "Legend of Daura," which follows, recounts the origin of the seven "true" Hausa states and seems to reflect the infiltration and merging of different peoples that occurred early in Hausa history. It comes from the as yet undated* Girgam, *a written record kept by the kings of Daura, traditionally the first Hausa state and now a tiny emirate east of Katsina. The killing of the snake Sarki probably suggests a change in religious beliefs, and the marriage of the queen of Daura to the hero Abuyazidu could represent a shift from matrilineal to patrilineal succession.*

There was once a prince of Bagdad called Abuyazidu [Bayagidda] who quarreled with his father and left his home in the east. After some time his wanderings brought him to Bornu. There he was given a daughter of the Sultan in marriage, Magira by name. He stayed in Bornu and his affairs prospered so much that in the course of time he became rich and powerful. His wealth and authority only excited hatred and envy, however, and the Sultan began to plot against his life. But Magira, being a daughter of the palace, heard was was afoot and warned her husband. Although she was with child, they decided that the only safety lay in flight. So with nothing but a mule to carry their possessions and a slave-girl to wait on them, they took the road to

Bornu descendants of the Hilalian invaders
DENHAM, *Narrative of an Expedition*, 1827

the west. When they reached a place called Garun Gabas Magira's days were fulfilled and she gave birth to a son. Abuyazidu left her there and, taking the concubine with him, continued his journey.

After a time Abuyazidu came to the town of Daura which was then ruled by a woman, and last of a line of nine Queens. He lodged in the house of an old woman called Waira and in the evening he asked her for water. "Young man" said the old woman "in this town there is no water to be had except on Fridays. Only when all the people are assembled can we draw water."

"Nevertheless" he said "I am going to get some now. Give me a bucket."

He took the bucket which she gave him and went to the well. Now a gigantic snake called "Sarki" [the Hausa word for "king"] lived in the well and when it heard the bucket being lowered it lifted its head out of the well and tried to strike Abuyazidu. But he drew his sword and struck off its head which he then hid. After that he drew water for himself and his horse, gave what was left to the old woman, and went to bed.

Next day as soon as it was light the townspeople saw that the snake was dead. They marveled at its size and the news was quickly taken to the Queen. Escorted by all her warriors, she rode down to the place and she too marveled at the size of the snake which was still lying half in and half out of the well. "I swear" she said "that if I find the man who killed this snake I will divide the town into two and give half of it to him."

"It was I" said one of the bystanders at once.

"Where is its head then?" said the Queen. "If you cannot produce the head you are lying." The man remained silent. Others also came forward and said that they had killed the snake but none of them could produce the head and their claims were all rejected.

At length the old woman Waira spoke up. "Yesterday evening" she said "a stranger came and lodged at my house with a strange animal as big as an ox. He took my bucket, went to the well, drew water, drank some himself, watered his animal, and gave the rest to me. Perhaps it was he who killed the snake."

"Let him be found" said the Queen. When Abuyazidu appeared she asked him if he had killed the snake. He said that he had and when she demanded its head he produced it from where it was hidden. "I made a promise" she said "that I would divide my town in two and give half to him who did this deed."

"Do not divide the town" he said "because I for my part will be amply rewarded if you will deign to take me as your consort." And so it came about that Abuyazidu, Prince of Bagdad, married the Queen of Daura.

After the marriage Abuyazidu took up his residence in the palace. He was given the title of Makas-Sarki, the slayer of the snake, but after a time he came to be known simply as Sarki.

The concubine who had come from Bornu with Abuyazidu now gave birth to a boy. As the Queen seemed to be barren, the girl was confident that one day her son would become Chief so she called him Karabgari or Take-the-Town. But a year or two later the Queen also conceived and in due course she too brought forth a boy. Her son she named Bawogarior or Give-back-the-Town.

In the fulness of time Makas-Sarki and the Queen died and they were succeeded by their son. Bawogari thus became the first Chief of Daura and he in turn had six sons. The eldest Gazaura succeeded him in Daura. The second, by the same mother, was Bagaudu and he became the founder of Kano. The third was Gunguma and he became the founder of Zazzau [Zaria]. The fourth was Duma and he became the founder of Gobir. The fifth was Kumayau and he became the founder of Katsina. The youngest was Zuma Kogi and he became the founder of Rano.

Daura, Kano, Zazzau, Gobir, Katsina, and Rano are six of the seven original Hausa States. The seventh is Garun Gabas and that was founded by the son of Abuyazidu's first wife Magira, the daughter of the Sultan of Bornu, whom he had to leave behind when he was on his way from Bornu to Daura.

These are the origins of the *Hausa Bakwai* or seven original states of Hausaland.

BARBUSHE THE HUNTER

Of all the Hausa states, Kano is the one whose history is best known. This is because of the renowned Kano Chronicle, source of the following story. The selection describes the original inhabitants of Kano and the infiltration, around A.D. 1000, *of immigrants from Daura, led by Bagaudu, grandson of Prince Abuyazidu. Like all African folk myths, it mixes fact with fantasy. Barbushe, the hunter-priest of the local god, is portrayed as a giant able to carry several elephants on his head; this suggests his importance in the community. Most likely the legend symbolizes a conflict that arose when aliens tried to become the overlords of the inhabitants.*

This is the history of the lords of this country called Kano. Barbushe, once its chief, was of the stock of Dala, [who was] a black man of great stature and might, a hunter, who slew elephants with his stick and carried them on his head about nine miles. Dala was of unknown race, but came to this land, and built a house on Dala hill [thenceforth a sacred rock also called Dala]. There he lived—he and his wives. He had seven children—four boys and three girls—of whom the eldest was Garageje. This Garageje was the grandfather of Buzame, who was the father of Barbushe. Barbushe succeeded his forefathers in the knowledge of the lore of Dala, for he was skilled in the various pagan rites. By his wonders and sorceries and the power he gained over his brethren he became chief and lord over them. Among the lesser chiefs with him were Gurzago. . . . After him came Gagina who was so strong that he caught elephants with rope. . . . From Toda to Dan Bakoshi and from Doji to Dankwoi all the people flocked to Barbushe on the two nights of Idi—for he was all-powerful at the sacrificial rites.

Now the name of the place sacred to their god was Kakua. The god's name was Tchunburburai. It was a tree called Shamuz. The man who remained near this tree day and night was called Mai-Tchunburburai. The tree was surrounded by a wall, and no man could come within it save Barbushe. Whoever else entered, he entered but to die. Barbushe never descended from Dala except on the two days of Idi. When the days drew near, the people came in from east and west and south and north, men and women alike. Some brought a black dog, some a black fowl, others a black he-goat, when they met together on the day of Jajibere at the foot of Dala hill at eve. When darkness came, Barbushe went forth from his house with his drummers. He cried aloud and said: "Great Father of us all, we have come nigh to thy dwelling in supplication, Tchunburburai," and the people said: "Look on Tchunburburai, ye men of Kano. Look toward Dala." Then Barbushe descended, and the people went with him to the god. And when they drew near, they sacrificed that which they had brought with them. Barbushe entered the sacred place—he alone—and said "I am the heir of Dala, like it or no, follow me ye must, perforce." And all the people said: "Dweller on the rock, our lord Amane, we follow thee perforce." Thus they spoke and marched round the sacred place till the dawn, when they arose, naked as they were, and ate. Then would Barbushe come forth and tell them of all that would befall through the coming year, even concerning the stranger who should come to this land, whether good or ill. And he foretold how their dominion should be wrested from them, and their tree cast down and burnt, and how this mosque should be built. "A man shall come," said he, "to this land with an army, and gain the mastery over us." They answered, "Why do you say this? it is an evil saying." Barbushe held his peace. "In sooth," said he, "you will see him in the sacred place of Tchunburburai; if he comes not in your time, assuredly he will come in the time of your children, and will conquer all in this country, and forget you and yours and exalt himself and his people for years to come." Then were they exceeding cast down. They knew well that he did not lie. So they believed him and said: "What can we do to avert this great calamity?" He replied, "There is no cure but resignation." They resigned themselves. But the people were still grieving over this loss of dominion at some distant time, when Bagoda, a generation later, came with his host to Kano. There is a dispute, however. Some deny this, and say that it was Bagoda's grandson who first reached Kano, and that he and his son died at Sheme. He, at all events, entered Kano territory first. When he came, he found none of Barbushe's men, save Janbere, Hambarau, Gertsangi, Jandamissa, and Kanfatau. These said, "Is this man he of whom Barbushe told us?" Jambere said, "I swear by Tchunburburai if you allow this people within our land, verily they will rule you, till you are of no account." The people refused to hearken to the words of Jambere and allowed the strangers to enter the country, saying: "Where will Bagoda find strength to conquer us?"

So Bagoda and his host settled in Garazawa and built houses there. . . . Now the chiefs whom Bagoda found holding sway over this land acknowledged no supreme lord save Tchunburburai and the grove of Jakara. Jakara was called "Kurmin Bakkin Rua," because its water was black, and it was surrounded by the grove.

The pagans stood in awe of the terrors of their god and this grove, which stretched from Gorondumasa to Dausarà. The branches and limbs of its trees were still—save, if trouble were coming on this land, it would shriek thrice, and smoke would issue forth in Tchunburburai, which was in the midst of the water. Then they would bring a black dog and sacrifice it at the foot of Tchunburburai. They sacrificed a black he-goat in the grove. If the shrieks and smoke continued, the trouble would indeed reach them, but if they ceased, then the trouble was stayed. The name of the grove was Matsama and the name of Tchunburburai was Randaya.

The greatest of the chiefs of the country was Mazauda, the grandfather of Sarkin Makafi. Gijigiji was the blacksmith; Bugazau was the brewer; Hanburki doctored every sickness; Danbuntunia, the watchman of the town at night, was the progenitor of the Kurmawa. Tsoron Maje was "Sarkin Samri," and Jandodo was "Sarkin Makada Gundua da Kuru." Beside these there was Maguji, who begot the Maguzawa, and was the miner and smelter among them. Again there was Asanni the forefather of minstrels and chief of the dancers. Bakonyaki was the archer. Awar, grandfather of the Awrawa, worked salt of Awar. He was Sarkin Rua of this whole country. In all there were eleven of these pagan chiefs, and each was head of a large clan. They were the original stock of Kano.

YAJI'S REVENGE

Most of the Hausa people are settled in northern Nigeria and in the adjacent regions of the Republic of Niger, which is Hausaland proper. Today they are among the world's most fervid Muslims, and Islam figures prominently in their culture. This excerpt, also from the Kano Chronicle, describes the first and ephemeral introduction of Muhammad's teachings in Hausaland. It states that Islam came to Kano during the reign of Sarki Yaji (1349–1385). However, it is also possible that Muslim influences had penetrated from Bornu, which had been Islamized since the reign of Umme Jilma in the eleventh century. This passage ends with the legend of Kano's sizable community of blind.

The eleventh Sarki was Yaji, called Ali. His mother was Maganarku. He was called Yaji because he had a bad temper when he was a boy, and the name stuck to him. He drove the Serikin Rano from Zamma Gaba, went to Rano, and reigned at Bunu two years. Then he removed to Kur together with the Ajawa and Worjawa and Aurawa. He stayed there. In Yaji's time the Wangarawa [Mandingo] came from Melle [Mali], bringing the Muhammmadan religion. The name of their leader was Abdurahaman Zaite. Others were Yakubu, Mandawali, Famori, Bilkasim, Kanaji, Dukere, Sheshe, Kebe, Murtuku, Liman Jibjin Yallabu, the father of Serikin Pawa, Gurdumus, Auta, Laual, Liman Madatai and others —about forty in all. When they came they commanded the Sarki to observe the times of prayer. He complied, and made Gurdamus his Liman [leader of prayer], and Laual his Muezzin. Auta cut the throats of whatever flesh was eaten. Mandawali was Liman of all the Wangarawa and of the chief men of Kano. Zaite was their Alkali [judge]. The Sarki commanded every town in Kano country to observe the times of prayer. So they all did so. A mosque was built [at Kur, the capital] beneath the sacred tree facing east, and prayers were made at the five appointed times in it. The Sarkin Garazawa was opposed to prayer, and when the Moslems after praying had gone home, he would come with his men and defile the whole mosque and cover it with filth. Danbugi was told off to patrol round the mosque with well-armed men from evening until morning. He kept up a constant halloo. For all that the pagans tried to win him and his men over. Some of his men followed the pagans and went away, but he and the rest refused. The defilement continued till Sheshe said to Famori, "There is no cure for this but prayer." The people assented. They gathered together on a Tuesday in the mosque at the evening hour of prayer and prayed against the pagans until sunrise. They only came away when the sun was well up. Allah received graciously the prayers addressed to him. The chief of the pagans was struck blind that day, and afterwards all the pagans who were present at the defilement—they and all their women. After this they were all afraid. Yaji turned the chief of the pagans out of his office and said to him, "Be thou Sarki among the blind."

THE ISLAMIZATION OF KANO

Yaji's progress in encouraging Islam was destroyed by his son, who was a pagan. However, during the reign of the illustrious Sarki Muhammad Rumfa (1465–1499) a new wave of missionaries entered Kano, and Islam became firmly entrenched as the state religion. As related in the subsequent chapter from the Chronicle, Kano's sacred tree—probably that worshiped by Barbushe and his tribe—was finally cut down and replaced by a mosque.

The twentieth Sarki was Mohamma, son of Yakubu, commonly called Rimfa. His mother's name was Fasima Berana. He was a good man, just and learned. He can have no equal in might, from the time of the founding of Kano, until it shall end. In his time the Sherifs came to Kano. They were Abdu Rahaman and his people. There is a story that the Prophet appeared to Abdu Rahaman in a dream and said to him, "Get up and go west and establish Islam." Abdu Rahaman got up

A branched sword, its blade ornamented with markings that seem to have been inspired by Arabic characters, was fashioned in Chad.
GALERIE KAMER, COLLECTION OF MR. AND MRS. JOHN DE MENIL

and took a handful of the soil of Medina, and put it in a cloth, and brought it to Hausaland.

Whenever he came to a town, he took a handful of the soil of the country and put it beside that of Medina. If they did not correspond he passed that town. So he journeyed until he came to Kano. And when he compared the soil of Kano with Medina soil they resembled one another and became as one soil. So he said, "This is the country that I saw in my dream." And he took up his abode at Panisau. Then he sent in to the Sarkin Kano. The Sarkin Kano Rimfa went out together with his men, and escorted Abdu Rahaman back to the city together with his men, of whom the chief were Hanatari, Gemindodo, Gadangami, Fokai and others, ten in all. Abdu Rahaman lived in Kano and established Islam. He brought with him many books. He ordered Rimfa to build a mosque for Friday, and to cut down the sacred tree and build a minaret [or mosque-tower] on the site. And when he had established the

Faith of Islam, and learned men had grown numerous in Kano, and all the country round had accepted the Faith, Abdu Karimi returned to Massar, leaving Sidi Fari as his deputy to carry on his work.

Rimfa was the author of twelve innovations in Kano. He built the Dakin Rimfa. The next year he extended the walls towards the Kofan [gate of] Mata from the Kofan Dagachi and continued the work to Kofan Gertawasa and Kofan Kawayi, and from the Kofan Naissa to the Kofan Kansakali. The next year he entered his house [i.e. he built a new palace, still called the *Gidan Rimfa*]. He established the Kurmi Market. He was the first Sarki who used "Dawakin Zaggi" in the war with Katsina. He was the first Sarki who practiced "Kame." He appointed Durman to go round the dwellings of the Indabawa and take every first-born virgin for him. He was the first Sarki to have a thousand wives. He began the custom of "Kulle" [wife-seclusion]. He began the "Tara-ta-Kano." He was the first to have "Kakaki" [long trumpets] and "Figinni," [ostrich-feather fans] and ostrich-feather sandals. It was in his reign that the Sallam Idi was first celebrated in Kano at Shadakoko. He began the custom of giving to eunuchs the offices of state, among them, Dan Kusuba, Dan Jigawa, Dan Tarbana, Sarkin Gabbas, Sarkin Tudu, Sarkin Rua, Maaji, Sarkin Bai, Sarkin Kofa. There were four eunuchs left without a title. He said to them, "I make you chiefs of the Treasury." The name of one was Turaki, another was Aljira; the names of the other two were Al-Soro and Kashe Kusa.

The Gladima Dabuli built a house at Goda, and the Madawaki Badosa built a house at Hori. Chiroma Bugaya built a house at Dabazaro. Surely there was no Sarki more powerful than Rimfa! He was sung as "The Arab Sarki, of wide sway." In his time occurred the first war with Katsina. It lasted eleven years, without either side winning. He ruled thirty-seven years.

AN EPISTLE ON KINGSHIP

In addition to constructing mosques and encouraging the ritual and belief of Islam, Muhammad Rumfa sought the advice of Muslim scholars concerning the ruling of his kingdom. When Sheikh Muhammad al-Majhili, the famed theologian, preacher, and jurist from Algeria, came to Kano toward the end of Rumfa's reign, the sarki *commissioned him to write a treatise on Islamic government. A passage from the resultant work, whose English title is* The Obligations of Princes, *is quoted below. This North African "Machiavelli" helped Rumfa evolve a monarchical system, with built-in checks and balances, which was to characterize the governmental organization of all Hausa states.*

The sojourn of a prince in the city breeds all manner of trouble and harm. The bird of prey abides in open and wild places. Vigorous is the cock as he struts round his domains. The eagle can only win his realm by firm resolve, and the cock's voice is strong as he masters the hens. Ride, then, the horses of resolution upon the saddles of prudence. Cherish the land from the spoiling drought, from the raging wind, the dust-laden storm, the raucous thunder, the gleaming lightning, the shattering fireball and the beating rain. Kingdoms are held by the sword, not by delays. Can fear be thrust back except by causing fear?

Allow only the nearest of your friends to bring you food and drink and bed and clothes. Do not part with your coat of mail and weapons and let no one approach you save men of trust and virtue. Never sleep in a place of peril. Have near to guard you at all times a band of faithful and gallant men, sentries, bowmen, horse and foot. Times of alarm are not like times of safety. Conceal your secrets from other people until you are master of your undertaking.

THE TWO ROGUES

Islam drew Hausaland into the commercial center of the network linking the Sahara and the western Sudan. Kano, and especially Katsina, prospered through their contacts with the north and the west. The Hausa traders were noted for their shrewdness, a quality shared by Dan-Kano and Dan-Katsina, the protagonists in the following folk tale. Both are bent on acquiring valuable trade goods without paying market value. The chief currency of Hausaland was cowry shells. Since these were not found locally, they had to be imported. For centuries the main source of foreign exchange used to buy cowries was the revenue—often in the form of gold—obtained from the sale of slaves, which were exported to Saharan oases, North Africa, and the Middle East.

There were once two rogues, one of whom came from Kano and the other from Katsina.

One day the rogue from Kano peeled the bark off a boabab tree and took it to the dye-pits and dyed it and beat it to give it a glaze and then wrapped it up in paper to make it look like the best broadcloth.

While the rogue from Kano was doing this, the rogue from Katsina was filling a goatskin with pebbles. Having done that, he covered the pebbles over with a couple of hundred cowries and tied up the mouth of the bag and set off for the market.

On the way to the market the two rogues happened to meet.

"Where are you going to, my friend?" asked the Kano man.

"I'm going to market" said the Katsina man. "Why—what have you got to sell?"

"Best blue broadcloth" said the Kano man.

"Well now, I was going to market to buy broadcloth" said the Katsina man. "I've got my money here" he went on, pointing to his bag "twenty thousand of it."

In this way the two rogues struck a bargain on the road and exchanged their wares before they reached the market. On parting company each thought that that he had got the better of the other and so when they had gone a short distance they turned aside to see what they

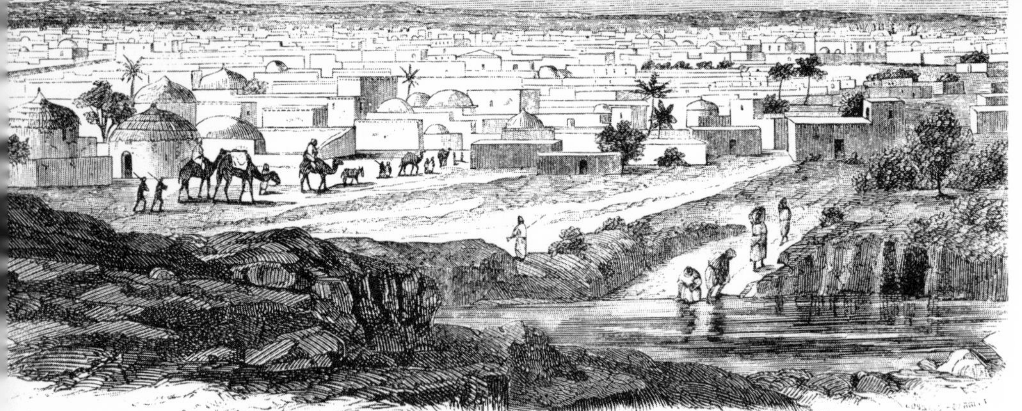

The great trading center of Kano, famed for its brilliantly colored textiles and leather goods
BARTH, *Travels in Central Africa*, 1857

had obtained. The Kano man found that he had got a bag of stones and the Katsina man found that he had got a parcel of bark. . . .

At this they both retraced their steps and when they met again they said: "We are each as crafty as the other and so from now on we had better join forces and seek our fortune together."

So the two rogues joined forces and took the road together. When they came to a town they got themselves water-bottles and staffs and begging-bowls and then, pretending to be blind beggars, they set off again.

They were going along, deep in the bush, when they came to a place where some traders had pitched their camp. They did not show themselves to the traders, however, but hid in the bush near the camp.

When night fell, the two rogues came out of hiding and entered the traders' camp with their eyes closed, pretending that they were blind beggars. The traders let them stay in the camp and in due course went off to sleep. As soon as they were asleep, the two rogues opened their eyes and removed all the traders' goods and carried them over to a dry well into which they threw them.

At daybreak next day the traders got up and found that they had been robbed of all their goods. The blind men also got up and began saying "Where are our water-bottles? Let's hope they haven't been stolen."

This made the traders very angry. "Here we are" they cried "robbed of all we possess and all you miserable beggars can think about is whether your water-bottles have been taken too. It's too much: get out of here before we kick you out." So the two rogues groped their way out of the traders' camp.

Soon afterwards the traders departed, loudly bemoaning the fact they had been robbed. As soon as they had gone, the two rogues opened their eyes again and hurried over to the well into which they had thrown the traders' goods.

"Dan-Katsina" said the Kano man "down you go."

"No Dan-Kano" said Dan-Katsina "you go."

"No you" said Dan-Kano.

So Dan-Katsina went down the well and tied the goods which were at the bottom to a rope which Dan-Kano lowered to him. Dan-Kano thereupon hauled the goods to the top and carried them a little way away from the well and stacked them. After that, each time he went back to the well, he took a large stone with him and these stones he collected in a heap near the head of the well.

When they had been working for some time, Dan-Kano called down the well to his companion. "Dan-Katsina" he said "when the stuff is finished, and you are ready to come up yourself, let me know and I'll haul you up very carefully so that you don't bump yourself against the side."

"Very well" said Dan-Katsina.

They worked away like this until the last bale had been hauled up. But Dan-Katsina did not tell Dan-Kano this. Instead he said: "The next load is going to be a pretty heavy one, Dan-Kano, but after that there are no more." He then crawled into the last of the bales and hid himself inside.

Dan-Kano now hauled up the last bale and carried it over to where he had stacked the others. He did not realize that Dan-Katsina was hiding inside it. Then he went back to where he had collected the pile of stones and started hurling them down into the well where he thought Dan-Katsina still was.

While Dan-Kano was busy throwing all the stones which he had collected down the well, Dan-Katsina crept out of the bale in which he had hidden and quickly started removing the rest of the goods and hiding them in another place. When Dan-Kano came back, therefore, he found that the goods had all vanished.

"Well I'll be blowed!" he said to himself. "While I was dealing with Dan-Katsina, someone else must have come along and taken my things from here."

The thought then occurred to Dan-Kano that as the thief couldn't be far away and would need an animal to move all the stuff he would probably come hurrying back if he heard a donkey braying. So Dan-Kano went into some nearby scrub and started braying like a donkey. Sure enough, Dan-Katsina soon came hurrying up saying: "Steady Neddy! Hold hard there! Come on boy!" When they saw one another, Dan-Kano said: "Dan-Katsina, you're a scoundrel" and Dan-Katsina said: "Dan-Kano, you're another."

The two rogues now collected their goods and took them to Dan-Kano's house. When they got there Dan-Katsina said: "I want to go on and visit my home, Dan-Kano, so we'll leave the stuff here and I'll come back in three months' time and then we'll split it."

"Very well" said Dan-Kano.

When Dan-Katsina had been gone for two months, Dan-Kano had a grave dug in his compound which he covered over with potsherds and old calabashes. When the three months were nearly up he retired into this grave and his family heaped earth over the potsherds and calabashes.

A few days later Dan-Katsina appeared and asked Dan-Kano's family where he was.

"Haven't you heard?" they said. "Dan-Kano is dead. He died four days ago."

"Indeed?" said Dan-Katsina. "Well then take me to his grave so that I can see it for myself."

When he was taken to the grave Dan-Katsina burst into loud lamentations. "So Dan-Kano has gone the way of all flesh!" he cried. "God's will be done. But you know" he went on, addressing Dan-Kano's relations "you ought to cut thorn and cover up the grave because otherwise hyenas will come and dig him up, poor soul."

"We'll do it tomorrow" said the relations.

"Now take me to my lodging" said Dan-Katsina "for tomorrow I must go home."

The relations prepared a lodging for Dan-Katsina in Dan-Kano's house and brought him stew and dumpling and milk gruel. He did not touch the food, however, because he said that, with his friend in his grave, he couldn't bring himself to eat anything.

In the middle of the night, when all the household were asleep, Dan-Katsina got up and crept out of the house and went to Dan-Kano's grave. There he started growling—Grrr, Grrr, Grrr—and went down on all fours and scrabbled at the earth which covered the grave as if he was a hyena trying to get in.

Inside the grave, Dan-Kano heard the noise outside and was filled with terror. "Help!" he cried. "Mercy! I'm going to be eaten by a hyena. Let me out of here."

"All right" said Dan-Katsina. "Out you come."

And so in the end the two rogues, Dan-Kano and Dan-Katsina, had to divide the goods which they had stolen from the traders equally between them.

"WILDE WOODIE HAUSALAND"

Leo Africanus was an energetic Moorish diplomat when he made two journeys through the Sudan in the early sixteenth century. He later produced an informative travelogue entitled The History and Description of Africa, *from which the following accounts of four of the seven "true" Hausa states—namely Guber, or Gobir; Cano, or Kano; Casena, or Katsina; and Zegzeg, or Zaria—are taken. Leo's given name was actually Al-Hasan ibn Muhammad al-Wazzan az-Zayyati, but in 1518 he was captured by a Christian pirate, taken to Rome, and there he was converted to Christianity and baptized Giovanni Leo de' Medici. In 1526 he completed in Italian his account of Africa; it was edited and published in 1550 by Giovanni Ramusio, a prominent Venetian administrator, who was the first to call him Leo Africanus. This translation was made in 1600 by John Pory.*

Of the kingdome of Guber: It standeth eastward of the kingdome of Gago almost three hundred miles; betweene which two kingdomes lieth a vast desert being much destitute of water, for it is about fortie miles distant from Niger. The kingdome of Guber is environed with high mountaines, and containeth many villages inhabited by shepherds, and other herdsmen. Abundance of cattell here are both great and small: but of a lower stature then the cattell in other places. Heere are also great store of artificers and linnen weavers: and heere are such shooes [probably leather sandals] made as the ancient Romans were woont to weare, the greatest part whereof be carried to Tombuto and Gago. Likewise heere is abundance of rice, and of certaine other graine and pulse, the like whereof I never saw in Italie. But I thinke it groweth in some places in Spaine. At the inundation of Niger all the fields of this region are overflowed, and then the inhabitants cast their seede into the water onely. . . .

Of the province of Cano: The great province of Cano standeth eastward of the river Niger almost five hundred miles. The greatest part of the inhabitants dwelling in villages are some of them herdsmen and others husbandmen. Heere groweth abundance of corne, of rice, and of cotton. Also heere are many deserts and wilde woodie mountains containing many springs of water. In these woods growe plentie of wilde citrons and limons, which differ not much in taste from the best of all. In the midst of this province standeth a towne called by the same name, the walles and houses whereof are built for the most part of a kinde of chalke [baked clay]. The inhabitants are rich merchants and most civill people. Their king was in times past of great puissance, and had mighty troupes of horsemen at his command; but he hath since beene constrained to pay tribute unto the kings of Zegzeg and Casena. . . .

Of the kingdome of Casena: Casena bordering eastward upon the kingdome last described, is full of mountaines, and drie fields, which yeeld notwithstanding great store of barlie and millseed. The inhabitants are extremely black [having great noses and blabber lips.] They dwell in most forlorne and base cottages: neither shall you finde any of their villages containing above three hundred families. And besides their base estate they are mightily oppressed with famine. . . .

Of the kingdome of Zegzeg: The southeast part thereof bordereth upon Cano, and it is distant from Casena almost an hundred and fiftie miles. The inhabitants are rich and have great traffique unto other nations. Some part of this kingdome is plaine, and the residue mountainous, but the mountaines are extremely cold, and the plains intolerably hot. And because they can hardly indure the sharpnes of winter, they kindle great fires in the midst of their houses, laying the coles thereof under their high bedsteads, and so betaking themselves to sleepe. Their fields abounding with water, are exceeding fruitful, & their houses are built like the houses of the kingdom of Casena. They had a king of their own. . . .

BORTORIMI AND THE SPIDER

The wily, wiry spider is one of the most popular animals in African folklore. In Hausa legend he is generally depicted as an unscrupulous, vindictive creature, like the insect of this tale. The spider is, however, a Hausa hero, for he embodies such admired gifts of endurance as cunning, a huge capacity for eating, and a genius for satisfying his needs.

There was once a certain Man whose name was Bortorimi, a Giant was he, there was no one like him in all the world, for, when he used to go to the forest, he would kill some twenty Elephants, and bring them home for his meal. One day the Spider sent his Wife—the female Spider—to Bortorimi's house to get fire. So she went, and while she was there, they gave her a great piece of meat, so she took it home with her. Then the Spider said "Who has given you that meat?" And she replied "I got it at Bortorimi's house." Immediately the Spider said "Put out your fire." And when she had done so, she returned to Bortorimi's house, and said that the fire had gone out. So more meat was given to her.

Then the Spider himself went to Bortorimi's house, but when Bortorimi gave him some meat he ate it all up at once, and did not bring any home. When he had eaten it, he said to Bortorimi "Where do you get this meat?" And the other replied "Over there in the forest, a great way off." "I see," said the Spider, "may I accompany you next time?" And Bortorimi said "Very well," but that he would not be going until the next morning, [so the Spider went home].

But the Spider could not wait until the dawn had come, so he pulled the roof off his hut, and set it on fire, and this made the whole place as light as if day had broken, although it was really not even dawn, but midnight. Then the Spider ran to Bortorimi's house, and stood outside, and called out "Hey, Bortorimi, Bortorimi, awake, awake, it is dawn." But Bortorimi replied "Oh! come, Spider, now I was watching you when you took the roof off your house and burned it." So the Spider went home again.

Soon afterwards he mounted a rock and made the first "Call to Prayer," and said that dawn had come. Then he went and roused Bortorimi, saying "everyone is astir, they are calling to prayer, wake up." But Bortorimi said "Oh! dear Spider, can you not have patience?" and he refused to go.

Now Bortorimi's nose was as big as a house, there was a market inside it. At daybreak they started off, and when they had come to a certain great river, Bortorimi said to the Spider "Drink your fill." And when the Spider had drunk all he wanted, Bortorimi pouted his lips and drank up all the water, leaving only the mud. Then they went on, and at last they reached the depths of the forest where the Elephants used to feed.

When they had arrived at the spot, Bortorimi said to the Spider, "Go and spy on the Animals there, and abuse them, and when you have done so, and they chase you, run and get inside my nose." "Very well," said the Spider, and off he went and abused the Elephants, calling out "Hey, you Animals, you are not properly born." Immediately they charged down upon the Spider, but he went off at a run, and jumped into Bortorimi's nose, and Bortorimi captured the whole herd and killed them.

Now as soon as the Spider got inside the nose (where there was a market) he began his tricks, saying that he was a King's Son, and so he ought to have a present of ground-nuts to eat, and the Old Woman selling them gave him some.

Just then Bortorimi finished killing the Elephants, and he began calling out "Spider, Spider, come out." So the Spider emerged, and Bortorimi said to him "Now choose the Elephant that you are going to take." But the Spider said that he could not carry one, so Bortorimi heaped them all together and carried the lot. When they had got home, Bortorimi said "Now Spider, here is yours," and the Spider skinned the Elephant, and roasted it, and ate every bit, he would not give any to his Wife.

As soon as the Spider had eaten it, he returned to Bortorimi's house, and said "O, Bortorimi, are you not going back to the hunting-ground?" But Bortorimi said "Umm, I shall not return, this is enough for me."

HAUSA PROVERBS

Today Hausa is the lingua franca of the central Sudan and as such is one of Black Africa's most important tongues. Proverbs such as abokin sarki sarki ne," *a friend of a chief is a chief,*" *and those that follow, would be readily understood by millions of Africans.*

Each end of the fire has its smoke.
(Everything has its own consequences.)

Even the Niger has an island.
(The mightiest things do not have it all their own way.)

Everything done to a free man he will pay back except digging a grave.
(A free man kicks till death stops him.)

God made beautiful the silk cotton tree, the rubber tree must cease being angry.
(Quarrel not with what God ordains.)

Although a man doesn't own a camel, he knows [the word for] "kneel."
(It is evident to the meanest intelligence.)

Before one comes out of water one does not squeeze [one's] loincloth.
(Wait to finish the work before cleaning up.)

Where the boy picked up a cowry there he goes on digging.
(Exploiting a "pocket.")

It's the squeezing that makes the drum sound sweet.
("I won't," implies ability to choose.)

The road to the Gold Coast, far away and profitable.
(Long journeys make heavy purses.)

The man who looks like going is sent.
(Give your orders to those who are likely to obey them.)

If music changes so does the dance.
(One must move with the times.)

South of the Sahara and Lake Chad, a Musgu horn player summons an audience.

The Tuareg are the undisputed masters of the salt trade. Navigating by the sun, stars, dunes, and rocks, they cross the Sahara to the markets of the Sudan. There they barter their blocks of salt (left) for millet, sugar, tea, and cotton. Caravans like that below once comprised as many as 25,000 camels, or "ships of the desert."

Contrary to the usual Muslim practice, Tuareg men, rather than women, swathe their faces in cloth. Warriors, each in a tagilmust, *or "mouth muffler," are shown in the engravings opposite and at right. Left, traders at the salt-rich oasis of Bilma mend their clothes behind a wind screen of pack saddles, while a servant pounds millet.*

LYONS, *L'Afrique*, 1821

FACES OF THE SUDAN

The "Country of the Blacks" is the home of peoples of different physical types whose economies have long nurtured pastoralists, farmers, traders, and ironworkers. These peoples organized prototypical Sudanese states as early as the ninth century A.D. and recognized "divine" kings as rulers. But it was the spread of Islam in the eleventh century that signaled the Sudan's entry into the mainstream of world commerce. By the thirteenth century most of the region's merchants were Muslims, who also diffused the faith. Many kings espoused Islam, thereby commanding the allegiance of a larger number of subjects than those restricted to local kinship ties. The new religion encouraged the growth of an educated class, which formed the bureaucratic cadres of the Sudan's emerging nations and empires. However, until the nineteenth century, Islam's hold on most Sudanese peoples was superficial; their culture and beliefs remained basically those of their ancestors.

RAPHO-GUILLUMETTE · GEORG GERSTER

Ethiopia, still a "Christian island in a Muslim sea," has about 14,000 churches, served by some 250,000 clerics. The priest above holds a characteristic processional cross, allegedly that of King Lalibela. He wears the turbanlike temtem, *standard garb for married priests and* debteras, *laymen who are experts in the liturgy and traditional wisdom of the Church. At right, Hausa traders confer at the market of Kano in northern Nigeria.*

PHOTO RESEARCHERS · THOMAS D. W. FRIEDMANN

PHOTO RESEARCHERS—DIANE RAWSON

The epitome of feminine pulchritude among the Sara of Chad was the wearing of lip plates, inserted during childhood. The custom may have originated as part of initiation or as a device to discourage enslavement by the Arabs. Their use is waning; they are worn mainly by the aged, as above. At right is a young Tuareg.

PHOTO RESEARCHERS—VICTOR ENGLEBERT

Below left is a Fulani from Niger; at right is a Dangaleat girl from Chad. Both belong to predominantly cattle-owning societies.

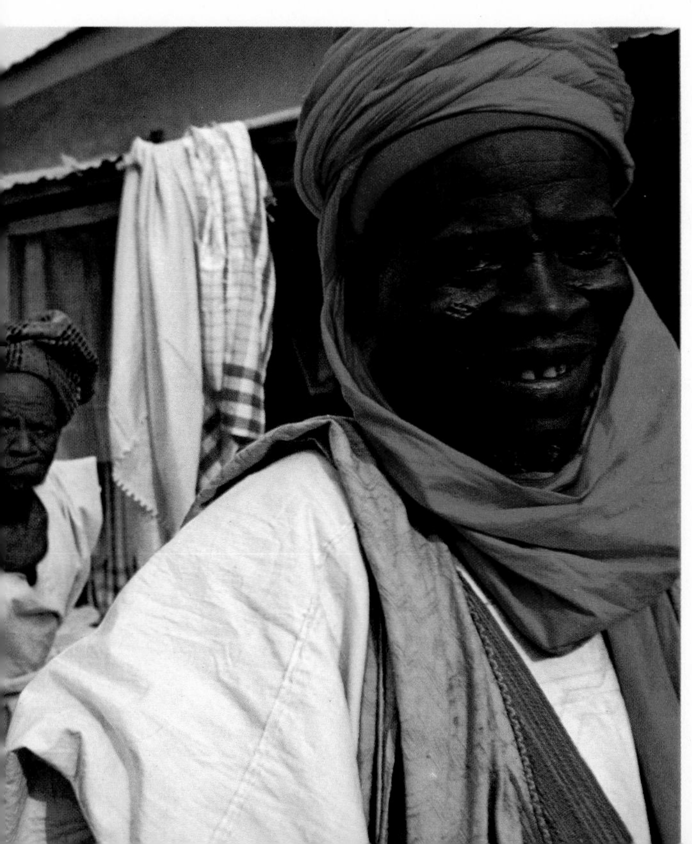

BOTH: RAPHO-GUILLUMETTE—MARC AND EVELYNE BERNHEIM

PETE TURNER

TRADE LINKS

From ancient times Africa's principal routes of trade led to the Sudan and Lake Chad, inland "ocean" of the sub-Sahara. The three greatest of these trails, all much traveled until the nineteenth century, were the Taghaza-Timbuktu road in the west, the Ghadames road to Kano and Katsina in the center, and the Fezzan-Kawar road to Bornu in the east. A lateral system connected the Chad area with Darfur, Kordofan, and Sennar. The proliferation of markets along these highways was accompanied by the development of political units and the rise of dynasties eager to control the emporiums.

The central Sudan is bordered on the east by the Nile, pictured opposite. Most of the region's sparse population lives in round or oval houses built of mud and clay, as in the Chad town above. Thatch is also a common material, as in the Niger hamlet below.

OVERLEAF: *A Hausa rider at Agadès, Niger Republic*

PHOTO RESEARCHERS–VICTOR ENGLEBERT

PHOTO RESEARCHERS–VICTOR ENGLEBERT

Chapter Seven

INNER AFRICA

(c. A.D. 500–1800)

by

Jan Vansina

INNER AFRICA ENTERS HISTORY on the tide of a huge migration that covered a subcontinent—all of Africa south of a line from the Bight of Benin to southern Somalia. This invasion of Bantu-speaking people was one of the great upheavals of all time because of the area affected, the time span covered, and above all, because of the linguistic and cultural tradition it left.

Among the results of the migrations was the formation of four-hundred-odd different languages, all as closely related to each other as are the Romance languages. Just as the peoples speaking Romance languages inherited many features of Rome's civilization, shaping it by their indigenous cultures and their subsequent history, so the Bantu speakers inherited the civilization of their common ancestors and diversified the common inheritance in similar ways.

The original people are called the Bantu, and in recognition of the great cultural and physical mixing that has since occurred, their descendants are most properly known as Bantu speakers. The word *bantu* means "the people," plural of *muntu*, "a person." It is still found in this form in all the Bantu languages and comes from the ancestral speech, the proto-Bantu language. Much of the vocabulary of proto-Bantu has thus survived, and from this as well as from the geographical distribution of languages scholars can tell how the original Bantu lived, where they came from, and how they migrated; but they cannot date with any exactitude their coming.

The original home of the Bantu was territory south of the middle Benue River valley in eastern Nigeria, an area well watered, fertile, rich in fauna and flora because it lay on the fringes of forest and savanna. The people were principally fishermen. They used dug-out canoes, nets, lines, and fishhooks in their business. They also hunted big and

uatorial Africa's rain forest, an insalubrious region where lush flora and the tsetse fly thrive

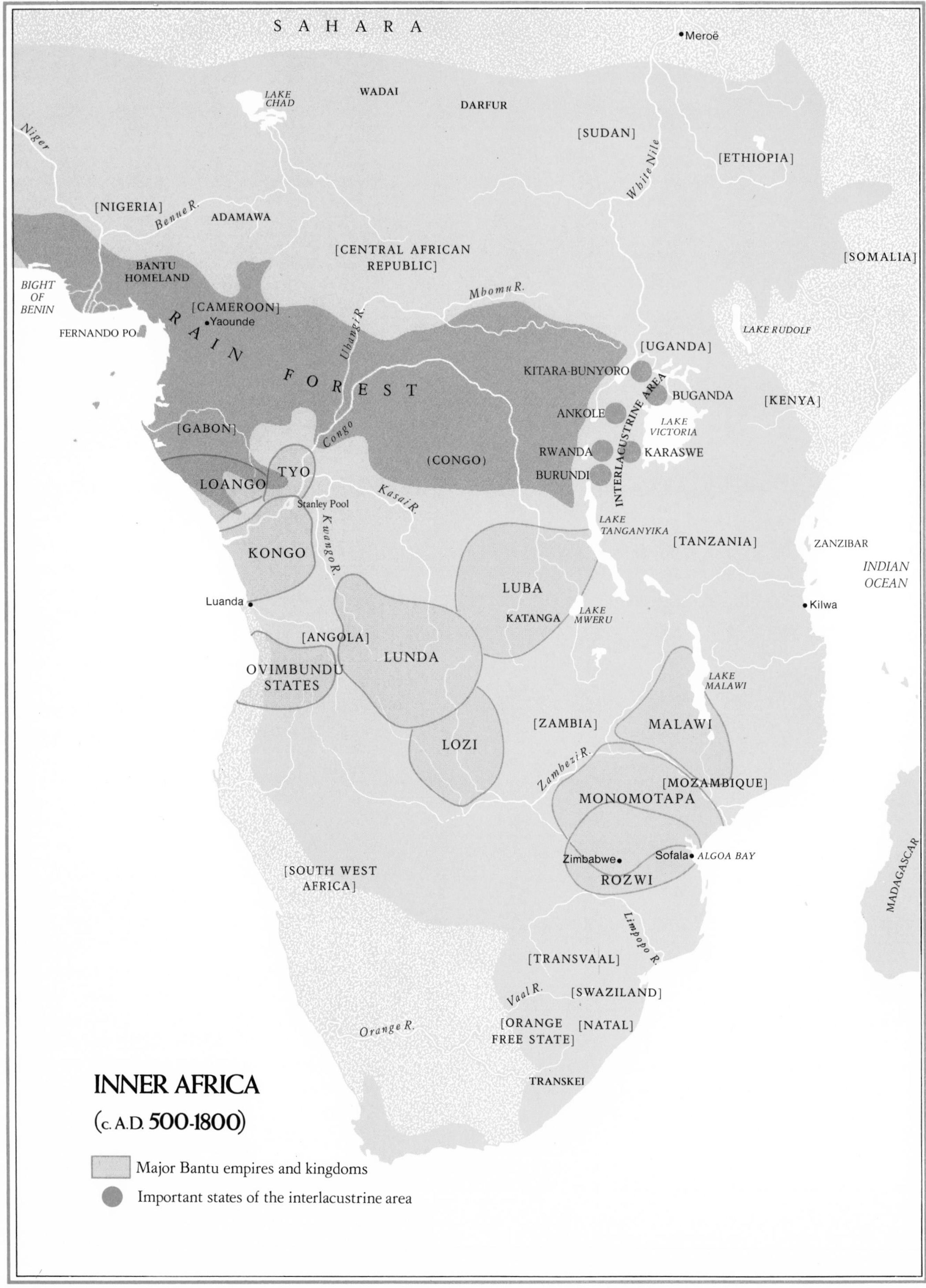

SAHARA
Meroë
LAKE CHAD
WADAI
DARFUR
Niger
[SUDAN]
White Nile
[ETHIOPIA]
[NIGERIA]
Benue R.
ADAMAWA
[CENTRAL AFRICAN REPUBLIC]
[SOMALIA]
BANTU HOMELAND
BIGHT OF BENIN
[CAMEROON]
Yaounde
Mbomu R.
Ubangi R.
FERNANDO PO
RAIN FOREST
LAKE RUDOLF
[UGANDA]
KITARA-BUNYORO
BUGANDA
[KENYA]
ANKOLE
INTERLACUSTRINE AREA
LAKE VICTORIA
[GABON]
Congo
RWANDA
KARASWE
TYO
(CONGO)
BURUNDI
LOANGO
Stanley Pool
Kasai R.
Kwango R.
LAKE TANGANYIKA
KONGO
[TANZANIA]
ZANZIBAR
INDIAN OCEAN
LUBA
Luanda
Kilwa
KATANGA
LAKE MWERU
[ANGOLA]
LUNDA
OVIMBUNDU STATES
LAKE MALAWI
[ZAMBIA]
MALAWI
LOZI
Zambezi R.
[MOZAMBIQUE]
MONOMOTAPA
Zimbabwe
Sofala
ALGOA BAY
ROZWI
[SOUTH WEST AFRICA]
MADAGASCAR
Limpopo R.
[TRANSVAAL]
Vaal R.
[SWAZILAND]
[ORANGE FREE STATE]
[NATAL]
Orange R.
TRANSKEI
INNER AFRICA
(c. A.D. 500-1800)
Major Bantu empires and kingdoms
Important states of the interlacustrine area

small game, and cultivated African yams and palm trees as well as some millet and sorghum. They made pottery, used bark cloth, and perhaps already wove fibers of the raffia tree on wide looms. They bred goats, perhaps sheep, and some cattle. (But the last could not thrive near the forest, so they would leave them behind during the migration.) Iron was not worked; rather, tools were fashioned out of wood or stone.

These fishermen were sedentary and lived in compact villages of unknown size. Their communities were organized in part on a basis of kinship. The leaders were the older men, and all others obeyed them because the elders were their grandfathers, fathers, uncles, and granduncles. The right to exercise authority was legitimized by common ties of blood, and in matters of succession and inheritance, kinship among them was matrilineal. Thus a man's estate went to the son of his sister, not to his own son. Polygyny was common. Because of the nature of the descent system and the fact that women left their villages to follow their husbands, the descent groups, or lineages, were dispersed over different villages. As a result, village organization could not be based entirely on kinship; rather, the settlement may have been governed by a council. Certainly, chiefs were recognized and had territorial power, but we do not know if they ruled over one or several villages.

The Bantu also had religious specialists, acting as both medicine men and diviners, though the roles were often performed by the same person. The Bantu believed that witchcraft was a major cause of misfortune. They may have believed as well in the influence on the lives of men of nature spirits or ancestors. Nothing is known about their arts, and no archeological sites traceable to them have yet been found. They must, however, have been excellent woodcarvers, and they may have produced terra-cotta sculpture.

The Bantu expansion was triggered probably by a great influx of population in Nigeria, which itself was the result of the arrival of many people who had gradually been driven out of the increasingly arid Sahara after 2500 B.C. At first the population pressure found an exit eastward by expanding along the forest fringes as far as the present border of the Republic of Sudan. The invaders were farmers of the savanna; they spoke a language belonging to the Adamawa Eastern group that spoke a Central Sudanese language and had lived in those areas before them. The older inhabitants were scattered north, east, and south until an equilibrium of forces was reached.

Then the pressure in Nigeria built up once again. It was relieved this time by the Bantu southward migrations, which were made easier because of their ability to adapt successfully to life in the forest near the rivers. The forest became their home and it was a good home. It furnished as much timber as was needed for housing and canoes, and the people could fell trees without woodsmen's tools, by burning them at the base of the trunk.

The forest was rich in game, and the marshes and rivers were well stocked with fish. It was more pleasant than the savanna because it was cool, provided a more temperate climate, and was never dusty. It also contained scattered huge patches of savanna called the *esobe*, where flora and fauna typical of the savanna could be found. Within the forest the Bantu could find all the advantages they had known in the mixed environment of the forest fringe.

As for the Bantu's means and manner of migration, being fishermen, they were able to load themselves, their goods, and livestock aboard canoes. The larger boats could take as much as a ton and a half, and the Bantu were carried along rivers and thence along the Atlantic coast, settling the island of Fernando Po early on. They knew where to go because scouting comes naturally to fishermen, whose quests take them many miles from home.

The migration was not a single mass movement, but a gradual process. People packed and went farther on when they felt they had too many neighbors or when there had been quarrels or when they feared witchcraft at work in their village. Because the waterways made travel relatively easy, a village might, in a single move, migrate a substantial distance. Reckoned in centuries, the rate of Bantu dispersion was relatively rapid, and thus at the end of the first phase the people had come to occupy most of the equatorial forest, mixing with the indigenous peoples, including Pygmies and Negroid hunters of a larger stature, about whom nothing more is known.

The movement slowed down for a time when the Bantu encountered new environments on the far sides of the forest and were forced to adapt their economies accordingly. To the east a different sort of forest—more tropical in its vegetation and providing no *esobe*, or clearings—was reached. There the tropical forest covered the great mountain range west of the Great Rift Valley, and the society based on fishing had to transform itself into a hunting and agricultural community. Similarly, where open savanna was reached again in the south, the cultivation of cereals became more important.

Another consequence of these adaptations was a differentiation in the Bantu language as it was spoken among the increasingly dispersed migrants. Thus one can later distinguish between western and eastern subgroups of Bantu speech, the more marked innovations appearing in the east, where other aspects of the Bantu culture would also undergo considerable changes through the influence of a substantial autochthonous population there. But no certain trace of these aborigines has remained to give a clue to their racial identities.

Once the adaptation to the savanna had been made, the southern migrations gained momentum again. The Bantu speakers still stuck to the rivers where possible, not only for the fish found there but also because something approaching the ideal conditions of the savanna-forest fringe could be found in the less dense gallery forests that grew along the river banks. One migratory route seems to have gone downriver on the Congo and then eastward and southward on the Kasai River and other Congo affluents. Following a network of lesser rivers and occasionally traveling overland, this group reached the headwaters of the Zambezi River, from whence they could float downriver to the Indian Ocean and the island of Zanzibar, and then paddle north along the coast as far as Somalia.

At the same time the mass of Bantu migrators that had initially taken a more direct route eastward toward the Great Rift Valley and the interlacustrine area was making much slower headway. The terrain of the Great Lakes area was difficult, and the eastern Bantu had adapted to the social organization of the indigenous population living in relatively dense, well-defined societies. So these Bantu, traveling along their more obstructed route, may have reached Lake Victoria at about the same time the southern wave reached Zanzibar.

During the later part of this second period of expansion some remarkable technological changes percolated throughout the whole Bantu world. First, they learned how to smelt and work iron. The new technology came to them from several sources. This author concludes that the art had spread south from Meroë after 500 B.C., reaching East Africa shortly after the beginning of the Christian era. It reached northern Nigeria around 300 B.C., perhaps from North Africa. So the northwestern Bantu—those who joined the later waves of migrations—acquired the knowledge from Nigeria; the Bantu who moved through the interlacustrine area received it from pre-existing populations in East Africa; and those who moved southeastward and then up the coast were introduced to ironworking by sailors from southern Arabia, perhaps in the first century A.D. or earlier. From all these sources the knowledge spread to other Bantu speakers. In the equatorial forest excellent charcoal could be manufactured, and soon the metal produced there, probably from ore bought in trade for other goods, surpassed what was made anywhere else in inner Africa. It is a sign of the cohesion of the Bantu world that the terminology for working iron developed homogeneously over the whole area occupied by Bantu speakers.

Other innovations at first produced more dramatic results than the knowledge of iron smelting. Banana and taro, crops of southeast Asian origin, had been introduced in East Africa late in the first millennium B.C. By way of the Zambezi valley and the Great Rift regions the new crops spread all over Central Africa, becoming the staples for the forest populations as well as for the peoples of the interlacustrine area. If it was the Bantu peoples who picked up these crops along the coast and transported them inland, they must have migrated there before the birth of Christ.

Lastly, the eastern and southeastern Bantu reacquired cattle. (Their ancestors had lost their incidental herds to the ravages of the tsetse fly when they first entered the forests.) They met with cattle-keeping people in East Africa and perhaps Zambia, and learned the art of husbandry from them. So at the end of this phase the Bantu peoples had acquired a totally new mode of life. They were now farmers and herdsmen rather than fishermen, grew banana and taro as well as cereals, and smelted iron—with consequent changes in social organization. The lapse of time required to change the old way of life must have lasted well over a century and probably much longer.

And then the expansion began once again. Between the first and the fifth century A.D. the Bantu speakers, with their cattle, went from the Zambezi valley all the way to the Transvaal (in the northeastern region of what is now the Republic of South Africa) and continued southward. By the thirteenth century A.D. at the latest they were in the Transkei (a territory within South Africa's Cape Province); but there is evidence that they may have completed their move much earlier. During this last period they also moved into the regions of southern Angola and South West Africa (known to its indigenous inhabitants as Namibia).

In East Africa further gains of territory were slow, even though Bantu speakers advanced from the west, south, and east into the interior of Kenya and Tanzania. Progress was slow because the Eastern Rift of Kenya and Tanzania and large parts of northern Kenya and Uganda were not sufficiently fertile to support sedentary farmers, but were well suited to support pastoral nomads; peoples engaged in herding were already occupying these lands. So the Bantu farmers could not deeply penetrate those areas. Then there were places in the region of Tanzania with a fairly dense population and established cultural patterns, which did not allow for Bantu speech or customs to assert themselves.

However, as a general rule, the Bantu immigrants assimilated the native peoples they encountered, transmitting not only speech but often their whole civilization; the Bantu and successive autochthones often merged, becoming one population. How did this happen?

The Bantu civilization was generally not much more complex or appealing than the civilizations of the local peoples. This was not comparable to the spread of Rome's superior civilization over much of barbaric Europe. Rather, the process of Bantuization seems to have been similar to that of urbanization. The immigrants lived in compact settlements that acted as centers or "towns" for the more dispersed nomadic camps of the non-Bantu peoples around them. The aboriginal hunters and/or farmers came to these centers to exchange produce with the Bantu, married with them, took gradually to their speech, and through it, adopted the Bantu civilization. And, to a lesser extent, the Bantu took on features of the aboriginal peoples as well.

Since the Bantu villages were small, the difference between "town" and "country" was slight, and the process of assimilation went on very slowly. Still slower was the Bantuization of indigenous hunters, whose nomadic life brought only intermittent contacts with the villagers. Examples in Zambia show that Bantu farmers and autochthonous hunters lived side by side without amalgamating until the thirteenth or perhaps even the fifteenth century.

Bantuization, then, did not take just a few centuries, but covered almost two millenniums. The process was completed only in the western and central equatorial forests and in the savanna as far south as southern Angola and Rhodesia. Pockets of hunters surviving in the forest in southern Africa and even in parts of East Africa represent specialized populations that have adopted Bantu speech and live in a symbiotic economic relationship with the Bantu. But among others assimilation never happened (for example, the Pygmy hunters living in the oriental parts of the great equatorial forest).

And so the Bantu civilizations evolved from a mixture of proto-Bantu culture and of features produced after the migrations by internal invention and even more by contact with neighboring groups. The Bantu languages cannot be classified in clearly recognizable genetic subgroups. Languages grow only in relative isolation from each other. A particular language first develops dialects, and these become daughter languages of the ancestral mother language after the passage of some centuries. But if the communities that speak those dialects are not sufficiently isolated, as happened among the English in Great Britain, it then becomes impossible to find out in what way the daughter languages descended from the ancestral tongue. This is obviously what happened with the Bantu languages. One can recognize that the original Bantu divided into two languages called Proto-Bantu A and Proto-Bantu B. One can also see that the four-hundred-odd languages that are spoken now stem from eighty to ninety mother languages. But the relations between them cannot be determined with precision, which proves that at all times since the original expansion Bantu speakers have kept up a great deal of communication with each other all over the huge subcontinent they occupied.

The relatively constant communication between these people must be attributed above all to the development of trade. Everywhere fishing folk exchanged pottery, fish, game, and vegetal and cereal foods. Areas blessed with the required raw materials exported such goods as ironware, copper, salt, basketry, mats, and sometimes even canoes and wooden tools. Trade was fueled not only by the needs of people but by their tastes. Thus a householder in the southern Congo might add imported woven ware to his store of locally made baskets and mats simply because the designs or shapes appealed to him.

If trade was of great importance in opening avenues of contact between near and distant neighbors, the accompanying spread of technological skills was also of major significance in the Bantuization process. The effects are visible both from linguistic evidence and the diffusion of items found. Among the objects and techniques that came into use over wide parts of the Bantu-speaking area, perhaps the most important set of items is the shaft furnace and its associated technology, which between A.D. 700 and 1200 ushered in the later iron age for inner Africa. These had been developed in the forests of the Congo, mainly because the hardwoods growing there produced a charcoal that allowed iron to be treated at much higher temperatures. This area remained foremost in the quality of its iron and steel products well into the twentieth century. Other, lesser centers of metallurgical skills were in Katanga, where evidence of the later iron age is attested as early as the eighth century and somewhat later in central Angola. This new technology allowed men to fashion large iron tools, both for peace and war. These broad-bladed hoes, heavy axes, and large spears enabled people to carry out their tasks much more effectively than did the brittle and clumsy small iron tools they had used before this time.

Also, archeological evidence tells us that by A.D. 1200 the Bantu civilizations had reached the point at which one finds in each region a set of different but related cultures, and no further differentiation occurred. Even though the major proof for this development stems from an examination of pottery, it is sufficiently established that the regional Bantu cultures of 1200 are the direct forerunners of those ethnic cultures that began to be identifiable by 1800. From this time on, the history of the continent is best told by geographical areas: the savanna north of the equatorial forest, the forest itself, the southern savanna, Africa south of the Zambezi River, and East Africa.

The peoples of the northern savanna, both the autochthonous Central Sudanese speakers and the Adamawa Eastern speakers who had invaded the area, never lost touch completely with the culture of the Sahel (between Lake Chad and the Nile), and the Bantu never made any imprint here. The early evolution of this area is still shrouded in mystery. A complicated set of population movements resulted in the present crazy quilt of language groups, but a fairly uniform culture pattern was preserved over most of the area now occupied by the Central African Republic, the northern Congo, southern Sudan, and parts of Cameroon. The people were skilled farmers, living in dispersed homesteads that were organized into tiny kinship groups, and they recognized leaders only in time of war.

On the upper Ubangi River one group of people began to organize a kinship system that included many hundreds of relatives or supposed relatives and brought them under the control of a tribal patriarch. By 1600 the concept of territorial kingship had been introduced, and a fairly small kingdom was born. The first tiny states were led by members of the Bandia clan, whose kinsmen, the Avongara, also developed a microkingdom. By 1750 one of these protostates began a career of conquest, pushing farther eastward with each generation. (This was to become the Zande nation in the nineteenth century.) The result of the expansion was the adoption by the new inhabitants of an incredible range of objects, techniques, behavior, and values, producing in their fusion an extraordinarily complex new civilization. They took over every indigenous crop cultivated by the people they subjugated, adding them to their own repertoire. This could only be accomplished by altering the rotation of crops, and it ultimately produced a wholly new type of agriculture that relied on the growing of perhaps forty crops rather than two or three staples.

Trade between this northern savanna and other areas may have remained negligible before the eighteenth century, though the existence of ancient underground iron mines not far from the Ubangi Bend indicates a brisk trade in iron. Traders from Darfur and even distant Egypt reached the Mbomu by traveling directly south. From then on the relative isolation of the area was completely shattered. The mystery is why influences from the Sahel had not percolated much sooner all over these great grasslands, especially along the fourteen-hundred-mile-long Chari River, whose many tributaries linked parts of Central Africa with the Lake Chad region.

As stated earlier, a major consequence of the Bantu migrations was a change in their way of life as they entered new vegetation zones. Following their arrival in the forest zone, the Bantu began very slowly to specialize. Some groups turned to farming and hunting, while others remained fishermen. In the Congo Bend area, where the specialization was most marked, the fishermen, owing to their greater mobility, took on additional roles as traders. The local trading networks grew bigger and bigger with the passage of time as one group of fishermen made contact with other groups and markets arose among them.

There was no lack of products to trade. People outside the forest needed ironware, red camwood for ornamentation and medicine, copal (a kind of resin obtained from trees), canoes, and later even such particularized items as sugar-cane wine, certain types of knives, and certain kinds of caterpillars to eat. In exchange, people in the forest sought such goods as copper and copperware, coastal salt or salt from Katanga, iron ore (probably from the Ubangi region), and later, raffia cloth, ornaments, and certain types of seashells used in monetary exchange. In a general sense the same situation prevailed all along the coast, from the Niger delta to the mouth of the Congo and up the estuaries of the rivers there. The trade can be attested by such traces as the strong similarities found in polychrome sculpture from Yorubaland to the Congo. Just before 1700 a European trader even claimed that African sailors from the Gold Coast traveled all along the coast southward, reaching as far as Loango, near the mouth of the Congo.

But in the area roughly equivalent to the mountainous parts of southern Cameroon, Gabon, and eastern Congo there was no such specialization between Bantu fishermen-traders and farmers. There, especially in the northeastern Congo, the intermixture with autochthonous hunting bands became very pronounced. By the thirteenth century A.D. new Bantu-speaking immigrants from the area of the Great Lakes arrived in the hospitable country. In some cases their superior social and political structures enabled them to wrest the leadership from the autochthones. In most cases, however, the newcomers lost their own cultural background almost totally and blended with the cultures they found. In the northeastern Congo the process was less complex and happened on a much smaller scale, but still many Bantu groups there began to take on Pygmy physical features. But the effect was rendered less distinct when the mighty nineteenth-century invasion of the Bantu-speaking Fang overran the area, adding still another element to the culture.

In the central portions of the forest, all along the affluents of the Congo, an institution of ritual chieftainship arose between perhaps the thirteenth and the seventeenth centuries. This was an important change in the whole way of life because it replaced the notion of authority by virtue of superior age in the kinship system with the notion of authority based on territory. The new system also led to a great flowering of rituals, all of which are related in their oral tradition.

Thus the spread of ideas, intense trade, and local migrations brought about a remarkable uniformity of civilization over equatorial Africa. The influence of the forest environment is particularly noticeable in the realm of religion. For the Pygmies there was only one god: the forest. The Bantu speakers observed a more complex set of beliefs, wherein the banks of pools and the thickets were the abode of nature spirits whose whims controlled life; but ancestors and forms of magic also had a place in the system.

In other aspects of their cultural life as well, the Bantu speakers achieved a high degree of sophistication. The popular image of tiny settlements lost in the awesome majesty of unending depths of foliage could not be more wrong. The people were neither lost nor barbarous, and some of the most original monuments of African civilization originate with the forest peoples. From the lake regions of the Great Rift Valley to Cameroon, the forest was the home of great epics, literary masterpieces of a scope and length unequaled elsewhere in Africa. In the eastern Congo and Gabon a rich and delicate tradition of sculpture existed, and in the central forest the arts of dancing and polyphonic song achieved great distinction.

By the eighteenth century the increase in trade and the linkage of more and more local networks into large commercial systems led to the fusion of all into one far-reaching system for the purpose of exporting slaves and ivory to the coast. By 1800 the network that fed into Stanley Pool (a lakelike expansion of the Congo some three hundred fifty miles from its mouth), and thence to the Atlantic, spanned a thousand miles, reaching to the Central African Republic, the Adamawa plateau in Cameroon, and to the Stanley Falls in the Democratic Republic of the Congo. Indeed, the northern affluents of the Congo connected with Darfur and Egypt. A systematic study of this far-flung and complex commerce still remains to be done.

In the southern savanna two areas stand out as centers of Bantu evolution: northern Katanga and the lower Congo. Archeological finds from the former area show that by the eighth or ninth century a complex culture existed there. Several earlier cultures had fused together, as evidenced from pottery, and both potters' art and metalwork had reached amazing virtuosity. The distribution of the population was dense; there can be no doubt that a political structure based on the occupation of common territory had evolved and that a form of chieftainship had developed. By the twelfth century long-distance trade in copper was under way, differences in wealth between poor and rich had increased, and chiefs or kings ruled over larger areas than earlier. The territorial structure had expanded so that certain chiefs had authority over headmen of villages, but themselves became subjected to overlords, whom we can call kings. With the development of this type of kingship came an increase in the complexity of the ideology of kingship, the etiquette connected with it, the quality and number of regalia that expressed it.

Descendants of these twelfth-century chiefs arose to lead great kingdoms, perhaps in the sixteenth century, if not somewhat earlier. The renowned Luba kingdom was created by Kalala Ilunga, whose deeds are recorded in Luba oral history. Kalala Ilunga introduced the notion of *bulopwe*, a form of sacred kingship. All the descendants of his line were supposed to have a special sort of blood, and its virtues were such that anyone endowed with this blood had a right to rule. Only people with *bulopwe* could mystically protect the country against harm and promote the fertility of crops and of women or ensure the success of the hunt—the central concerns of all Luba.

Well before 1600, but after the foundation of the Luba kingdom, a prince from that realm introduced the Luba concept of *bulopwe* to the Lunda people to the west. Tradition has it that the Lunda were then governed by a young queen, Rweej. She met the handsome Kibinda Ilunga, a Luba hunter, at a camp near an idyllic brook, married him, and let him rule. Her twin brothers, dissatisfied with the arrangement, left for the interior of Angola to carve out new chiefdoms for themselves.

The Luba kingdom proper did not expand beyond the plains of the upper Lomami River before the eighteenth century, and even then the territories added were lost again by 1850. The kingdom was a collection of hereditary chiefdoms of all sizes, joined by a common allegiance to the sovereign. Despite the theory of *bulopwe*, or rather beyond it, the kings in practice enforced their government by the use of a small bureaucracy of titled officers and the threat of force against recalcitrant chiefs, who were never fully welcomed into the system of Luba kinship.

The Lunda adopted a modified form of this, blending it with a political institution of their own. Their earlier form of government had fused in an original way the idea of ties by blood with territorial authority and structure. Everyone in the family was supposed to obey senior members and also to collaborate with junior members (that is, men of equal status). From this it evolved that chiefs were considered to be members of a family headed by the Lunda king or queen. So chiefs were related to one another as brothers, cousins, nephews, and the like, at least fictionally. To preserve the fiction it became practice that a successor took over the name of the deceased chief and his whole personality so that he, too, now was the brother, nephew, cousin, and so on, of other chiefs. Even the wives of the deceased became his wives; so much did the successor "become" the dead man.

It was easy to adapt this principle to the titled bureaucracy introduced by the Luba. It allowed the whole political system to function, whatever the social structure of a people might be, since it could be adapted to any system of political succession. The Luba system, by contrast, could not. The Luba were patrilineal, and offices were inherited either by the brothers of the deceased or by their male children. This hampered the diffusion of the Luba model of government whenever societies were organized matrilineally (for example, whenever their practice was to have nephews rather than sons as heirs). In addition, the Luba system meant that with the passing of each generation the ties between chiefs weakened, and attempts at breaking away from the realm or wars between chiefdoms in the kingdom became more and more probable as time passed.

The difference between the Lunda and Luba systems explains why large numbers of peoples actually subjected themselves to the rule of Lunda chiefs. These chiefs still remained in touch with the Lunda emperor. By 1750 the Lunda had created an empire stretching from the Kwango River in the west to the Luapula River and Lake Mweru in the east, ruling over a million inhabitants or more.

The net effect of the Luba and Lunda expansion was to establish transcontinental long-distance trading routes from Angola to Mozambique and to leave a powerful imprint upon the civilizations of all the peoples living in the southern savanna east of the Kwango, as will be shown later in this chapter. The commodities traded were mainly slaves, but also included ivory, copper, salt, European goods, as well as items of local produce. Ramifications of the trade routes covered the whole savanna and linked up with the forest peoples' network.

As for the cultural influence, all sorts of institutions were diffused—from initiation rituals for girls to veneration of a special tree in ancestor worship. The most remarkable facet of this was perhaps the extraordinary efflorescence of a system of common symbols. Using these symbols, the southern savanna peoples elaborated a complex philosophy applicable both to an investigation of reality and to the ordering of societal relationships. But the diffusion was not total; in some fields there was none. For instance, the Luba homeland and central Angola were two centers where very distinct styles of sculpture developed before 1600. Not only did these two styles not influence one another, but the Lunda, who lived between the centers, did not take to sculpture at all. The example of sculpture brings home the point that diffusion is not an automatic process. The societies that are exposed to new objects, behavior, or ideas are selective, taking only those things that complement their own traditions well.

North of the lower Congo river chiefdoms began to form primitive states perhaps as early as the twelfth century. Continuing growth led to the establishment of three major kingdoms, Congo, Loango, and Tio—all by the fifteenth century at the latest. Of these, Congo became the most famous. Congo civilization encompassed the kingdoms of Congo and Loango, and stretched from there through northern Angola to the Kwanza River and beyond; east of the Kwango River, Congo influence mingled with Lunda features. The Tio type of civilization asserted itself on all the high and drier plateaus around the Stanley Pool and toward the lower Kasai River.

By 1480 Congo was a flourishing state. Initially, the staple crops were millet and banana, superseded in the sixteenth century by maize and a hundred years later by cassava. A rich and highly accomplished technology flourished. Pottery making, weaving, smithing, and other crafts were fully established, and a brisk trade brought products from all parts of the kingdom and beyond to its major markets. The arts were well developed, especially sculpture.

Stone statues of chiefs, dating to the seventeenth century, have survived.

There was state-controlled currency, based on the exchange of a small seashell found only near the coastal town of Luanda, and it was controlled by the state's treasurer. Government was somewhat more centralized than elsewhere in Central Africa, in part because the king could depose any chief, and hereditary succession was not recognized except for kingship. All lesser officers served at the pleasure of the rulers, at least in theory. In practice the relations between a territorial chief and a king were determined by power politics, and there are many instances in which the sovereign could not oust some of his lesser officers. Despite the fact then that Congo was perhaps the most centralized of the Central African kingdoms, the structure of the state was still unimpressive when compared with the West African states.

Conflicts developed between the aristocracy and the farmers, and the system of royal succession worked poorly. Finally, contact with the Portuguese brought about the state's downfall after 1665. The increased slave trade that followed in the whole area, unhampered by political checks and balances, allowed individual entrepreneurs to become wealthy and powerful men. They invested their profit in guns and armed guards, made up of slaves and poorer kinsmen. Thus the very fact that power could be achieved by anyone who was successful in trade undermined the belief that only the nobility should or could rule and indirectly undermined the basis for any royal authority itself. For the authority of a monarchy was based ultimately on the belief that the king ruled because it was preordained by his birth into a royal lineage, and the royal lineage ruled as if preordained by natural law. The emergence of powerful merchants changed all this. The monarchies survived, but after 1800 the major states had either fallen apart or had become hollow shells, mere shadows of a former structure.

Two other influential Bantu-speaking civilizations were those of the Lozi and the Ovimbundu. Lunda migrants to the upper Zambezi blended with the locals to form the Lozi kingdom, in which a new, unique culture arose. The Ovimbundu civilization grew out of a mixture of Lunda and Congo elements, with some southwestern cattle-keeping Bantu intermingled in the Angolan highlands. Cattle raids by the Ovimbundu chiefdoms kept them perennially at war until their restlessness was turned toward the acquisition of wealth through trade after 1750. The Ovimbundu became, especially in the nineteenth century, the most successful long-distance traders in the interior.

In southern Africa, even before 1200, the development of localized cultures resulted in the establishment of the main distinct civilizations that have since dominated there: the *bantu botatwe*, or "the three-people group" in Zambia; the Malawi, living in what is now the Republic of Malawi; the Shona in Rhodesia; and the Sotho and perhaps the Nguni speakers (including the Xhosa, Zulu, and Swazi) of South Africa. All of these are set apart from the civilizations discussed so far by their emphasis on cattle: possession meant wealth and power. The transfer of cattle regulated all intergroup relations: tribute to the king was paid in cattle; bridewealth was paid in cattle to the father of the prospective bride by the father of the groom; important sacrifices required the slaughtering of cattle.

The great importance cattle assumed in these societies is called the cattle complex. Historically, the complex originated in East Africa. Cattle were not sacred animals as in India, but there was an intimate bond between cattle and people. Men had their favorite single steer or ox and identified with the animal even more than some Western people do with their pets. Cattle were considered the most beautiful creations of nature, and much of the poetry in East Africa and also in southern Africa describes the beauty of the hides, horns, and behavior of herds or individual beasts. Cattle were also the intermediaries between man and the spirits. When an ox was sacrificed, one often told the animal before it was killed what to say to the ancestors in the next world. Cattle produced wealth for their owners by producing offspring or by being hired out. In addition, men could be made vassals of a lord simply because they were entrusted with his herd. There is no aspect of life in which cattle did not figure prominently.

The civilizations south of the Zambezi did not only absorb features from East and Central Africa, they interacted daily and for a full millennium with non-Bantu peoples: the Khoikhoi (Hottentots) and San (Bushmen). The former were nomadic pastoralists; the latter hunters and gatherers. The farther one goes from the Zambezi to the south or to the west, the more one finds the imprint of Khoi or San ways of life on the cultures of the Bantu speakers. Thus in the region of South West Africa the black and Bantu-speaking Herero are culturally pastoralists like the Khoikhoi, whereas the black and Khoi-speaking Bergdama took over a Bushman way of life. Thus one can show that language, culture, and race do not necessarily go together at all. The Herero took over only a Khoi way of life, but kept their language; the Bergdama took over a Khoi language and a San way of life. Both Herero and Bergdama are black, and different from the yellowish Khoi or San.

After 1300 the influence of the Luba civilization began to affect the technology and political organization of the area. Luba emigrants founded a large kingdom in Malawi, while the Shona, new settlers in Rhodesia, founded the states that were to fuse into the empire of Monomotapa by 1450. Even before the Luba's arrival, however, trade had developed with ports along the Indian Ocean. Gold had been mined in Rhodesia perhaps as early as the fifth century A.D. As discussed in Chapter Four, the precious ore became a major export around A.D. 1100, being sought after by Arab and Portuguese traders, and it rapidly turned into the keystone of the prosperity of all the Swahili cities on the east coast. The gold trade brought through the harbor of Sofala such imports as cloth, beads, and porcelain. The presence of foreign traders also stimulated the export of other commodities along the Zambezi, mainly ivory, leading to the creation of a dense network of local exchange in all manner of minerals, household goods, and luxury items. With the arrival of the Portuguese in Mozambique the patterns and volume of trade did not change much, but the routes did. A steady expansion continued until the eighteenth century, when even north Transvaal had become a major trading area. By the end of the eighteenth century the goods, including many slaves now, went from Lake Malawi to the Portuguese coastal settlements at Kilwa, the Zambezi estuary, and Algoa Bay.

The Malawi kingdom did not long outlast the arrival of the Portuguese. It was a loose confederation, and the power of the monarch was linked directly to the control of trade. The state reached its zenith in the seventeenth century with Portuguese help and then fell apart when the Yao, a Bantu-speaking people dwelling in Mozambique and southern Tanzania, managed to wrest the commerce in ivory and slaves.

Meanwhile, the Monomotapa empire had gradually grown from a set of chiefdoms into a very large state. But after fifty-odd years, in about 1475, its southern half broke away and became the kingdom of the Rozwi, a Shona clan. The Shona people are responsible for some spectacular stone ruins in Rhodesia; but these do not include the ruins at Zimbabwe, a site that antedated the empire of Monomotapa. The size of the walls, the wealth in gold, stone sculpture, and oriental porcelain, led to wild speculations as to when the site was founded. Some even held that this was the land of the Queen of Sheba! Now it is evident that the place was occupied over a very long period by Bantu speakers and that it developed along with the growth of local states.

The Rozwi were skilled builders in stone, and their art was passed on to peoples in South Africa, where builders copied the forms in wattle and daub as well as wood. Their empty villages are still found from the Zambezi River to the Orange Free State.

Beyond statecraft and architecture, the Shona were remarkable for their spiritual beliefs and organization. There was an official religion invoking royal and lordly ancestors by oracle, in the person of a chief priest, who transmitted to kings and commoners the wishes of Mwari, the creator-god. The oracle's authority extended throughout the kingdom, and lower priests were linked to him in a loose hierarchy.

Of the peoples living in what is now South Africa, little is yet known of the period before colonial rule was established. The stone ruins probably belonged to the Sotho; traces of Nguni settlement have not yet been found, even though the Nguni were presumed to have reached Natal by the eleventh century and are known to have developed chiefdoms there by the fourteenth. All evidence indicates that there was a slow growth of territorial chiefdoms over a long period of time. These political units were not welded into kingdoms, perhaps because there always was room for further expansion in unoccupied or sparsely settled territory, a situation to which political practice among the Nguni had adapted itself. Whenever a quarrel for the succession to a chieftainship broke out among two contenders, one could always move out of settled territory with his followers and set up a brand-new chiefdom. When no further expansion was possible, however, weaker chiefdoms were incorporated into bigger states, and the process culminated with the creation of the Zulu nation in what is now the South African province of Natal.

Meanwhile, the San and Khoikhoi lived on in western South Africa, where desert conditions made farming impossible. The Bantu who arrived in this environment adapted to it and were unable to Bantuize the original inhabitants, who kept their traditional ways. These civilizations have been remarkable not only for the skills exhibited by Bushmen rock painters and engravers but especially for the mythology and religious beliefs that they developed. The myths are richer, more varied, and infinitely more poetic than those of the agricultural peoples, and the mythology influenced deeply the oral literature of both the southwestern and southeastern Bantu peoples.

In East Africa the evolution of the societies turned out to be more complex than in any other part of inner Africa. The great variety of environments in the area, including the ex-

These Watusi dancers are members of an elite corps of professional entertainers that performs for the Burundi court. Chosen for exceptional height—they average well over six feet—these scions of the aristocracy have been given rigorous training not only in dance but also in military sciences, law, oral history, and the social graces. While performing, they wear leopard skins and headdresses made of fur from the rare colobus monkey. The Watusi people have for centuries been the overlords of Burundi and Rwanda and hold the Bantu-speaking Bahutu and the Pygmy Batwa people in servitude. The Watusi, themselves, are cattle owners who measure wealth in the size of a man's herd.

PHOTO RESEARCHERS—THOMAS D. W. FRIEDMANN

ceptionally arid Great Rift Valley of central Kenya and Tanzania, can be held responsible in part for the complexity. The pattern of immigration further complicated matters.

Sometime before 1500 B.C. the indigenous Khoikhoi and San hunters encountered migrations of peoples of Ethiopian origin, who made pots and owned cattle. These farmers occupied the fringes of the Rift Valley and dispersed over southern Tanzania. Next, there appeared a group of truly nomadic pastoralists, speaking kindred tongues known technically as the Nilotic languages. These people originated in the area between the White Nile and the Ethiopian highlands well over two thousand years ago. By the time of the birth of Christ their languages had split into three branches: Western, Eastern, and Southern Nilotic. The speakers of Western Nilotic migrated toward the White Nile, while the speakers of Eastern Nilotic stayed in the area of their collective origin. Southern Nilotic speakers moved toward the Great Rift Valley of East Africa, where they became the first people to perfect a pastoral economy suitable to the arid environment of the Rift Valley. There they were able to maintain a social organization that allowed nomadic life and yet provided an orderly society on a fairly large scale.

The basis of the specific institutions by which this feat was achieved were systems of age grades, which guided the males of a society as they passed, with other males of their generation, through a succession of duties and roles within the community. Each age set, recognizing leaders within its number, entered the system as boys, when they underwent initiation. After a fixed number of years the young men moved from one grade to the next. The most junior grade was that of the warriors. At the next level the men founded households; at the next they formed councils and directed the group; and at the most senior level the old men were advisers to the leaders. On this pattern each society embroidered its own arabesques to make the system even more effective. Most of the Southern Nilotic speakers remained in Kenya, the exception being the Tatog, who occupied the fertile plains south of Lake Victoria. This, therefore, was the mixture of people the Bantu found on their arrival in the area.

The Bantu first absorbed the Ethiopian farmers of southern Tanzania and chased the Tatog away from the fertile parts of the eastern Tanzanian plateau. Near the Great Rift Valley, however, both the hunters and the Ethiopian farmers stood their ground, and a very complicated interaction with the Bantu followed. Some of the farmers began to take over Bantu speech, as happened perhaps with the Gogo and Iramba, while in other cases the Bantu speakers lost the speech of their ancestors and for a time adopted that of the farmers of Ethiopian origin, as was evidently the case with the Iraqw. The way of life of the incoming Bantu speakers and that of the aboriginal farmers was equally well adapted to the environment and equally complex, which explains this pattern of mutual interaction. By 1500, however, the whole of eastern and southern Tanzania was Bantu speaking, and the highlands of Kenya east of the Great Rift were also occupied by Bantu speakers. On the coast itself, where the Bantu had arrived sometime earlier (as indicated previously), they accepted many features of the Persian and Arab ways of life, and by A.D. 800 Swahili civilization was already formed there. A major influence is evident in the language; nearly half the vocabulary is borrowed from these foreign sources. Such observances as Nauruz, the New Year's festival, are also of Middle Eastern origin.

After Bantu settlement, development in southern and eastern Tanzania came about much more slowly than in the southern Congo, yet on the same lines. Internal trade in salt, pottery, basketry, and iron developed locally. The dominant form of government was the chiefdom; but as in South Africa, chiefdoms did not amalgamate into kingdoms. Whenever they attained a certain size, they split, and by 1750 there were hundreds of these microstates on the plains. True, clusters could be recognized among them wherever people followed the same customs or spoke similar dialects or where their chiefs claimed descent from a common ancestor. But growth into bigger states would not come here until the nineteenth century. Only in parts of northeastern Tanzania do kingdoms form before 1880—near the Kenya-Tanzania border part of the Pare Mountain people were united under one dynasty as early as the sixteenth century, and the neighboring Shambaa were welded into one monarchy around 1700. In eastern Kenya the Bantu adopted age-grade organizations, similar to those recognized by the Southern Nilotic speakers, and thus remained on the whole loosely structured.

All this stands in sharp contrast to the interlacustrine area, where the population was growing fast because of the great fertility of the soil, for which banana and beans as well as millet were very well suited. Around A.D. 1000 pastoralists of unknown cultural affiliation from northern Kenya or southern Ethiopia arrived in the area, occupying the less fertile and consequently almost unpopulated land that they prized for their cattle.

Being more mobile and better able to call up greater numbers of men at a shorter notice than the Bantu-speaking chiefdoms they encountered, they finally became lords over most of the Bantu speakers, adopting Bantu rituals and sacred kingships. In Uganda the large state of Kitara grew and survives in legend. Founded perhaps before 1300, it was overrun around 1450 by Western Nilotic speakers, who moved upstream from the White Nile. The Chwezi, rulers of Kitara, were defeated; they were replaced by invaders, the Kitara Bunyoro, who also gave dynasties to two tiny states in the vicinity, one of which was to become Buganda.

The defeated Chwezi, or at least a group of them, went south and founded a host of smaller states on the western shore of Lake Victoria. Among these, Ankole and Karagwe were to become the biggest. From 1500 to 1800 the two major developments in the area were the unending struggles between Buganda and Bunyoro, in which the former gradually took the lead, and the emergence of Rwanda as the leading state in the south. After 1800 Burundi was to become as powerful as Rwanda, and these two kingdoms are the only ones that survived the colonial period to become independent nations.

Every one of the four major states was organized in a somewhat different manner. For most of the period Bunyoro was the greatest in territory, but its population, principally millet farmers, was small. A significant part of the aristocracy was seminomadic, and consequently, royal control remained limited. In Buganda agriculture was based on the cultivation of bananas, which are land-intensive but labor-extensive crops, thus freeing relatively more men to perform other duties such as warfare. Buganda saw the power of its king grow all during this period, and by the end of the nineteenth century its bureaucracy was the tightest and most centralized of all kingdoms, with its state encompassing about one million inhabitants. The Rwanda monarchy followed the example of Buganda in strengthening the powers of the king. However, the internal caste structure of the country meant that the nobility remained much more dominant than in Buganda, and the bureaucracy was less well developed, even though Rwanda controlled perhaps two million inhabitants. As for Burundi, it was a major power only for a relatively short time, and its kings never succeeded in asserting their power over that of their own relatives in most of the country. It, too, controlled over two million inhabitants.

The contrasting civilizations that existed and the caste systems that have developed out of them are reflections of this history. The three major castes are: Pygmy hunters, Bantu-speaking agriculturalists, and Nilotic or other pastoral rulers. The complicated set of values linked with the cattle complex was the main ingredient brought by the pastoralists, whereas the complex rites of kingship were a Bantu inheritance. A peculiar effect of the downfall of the Chwezi was their transformation in the memory of their former subjects into glorious heroes around whom a religious cult arose. This spread over the whole interlacustrine area and even into eastern Tanzania. Despite a great many local variations, there remains everywhere a common core of myth and ritual as well as an ideology of equality that clashes violently with the fundamental inequality inherent in the caste system. In time each of the civilizations developed further by internal growth. Thus the political structures, especially the particular forms of landholding and rights over cattle, evolved in different ways.

The invaders of Kitara had only been a fraction of the Western Nilotic speakers. The others continued their trek in northern Uganda and then along the eastern shore of Lake Victoria. They settled in all these lands and turned to a mixed economy. In some places Bantu speech ousted Nilotic, whereas in others Nilotic dominated. But the cultures were quite comparable blends of Bantu, Western Nilotic, and some Southern and Eastern Nilotic features. This process of settlement lasted from 1450 to the end of the nineteenth century. The Eastern Nilotic speakers moved southward from the cradle lands of all Nilotic speakers into what is now Kenya and adjacent parts of Uganda, probably before 1000 and certainly before 1450.

Meanwhile, the Nandi, another southern Nilotic group, occupied the whole Rift Valley from 1500 to 1650. Their pastoral way of life was much better adapted to local conditions than any of the other peoples living there. Yet they, too, were swept away from the Great Rift by an Eastern Nilotic group, the Masai. The Masai had improved on the military and the political organization of the Nandi. In less than a full century they occupied the Great Rift. After that, stiff resistance from Bantu groups on the edges of the Rift Valley and the sedentarization of the Kwavi, an offshoot of the Masai, blocked further advances and produced an armed stalemate, which was to last throughout most of the nineteenth century.

Northern Kenya, that part of the Rift Valley and the highlands to the west of the Rift, remained home for different groups of Nilotic nomads. The tragedy of all the nomads in East Africa was to be the very success of their adaptation to the environment in which they lived. For their nomadic ways were to become a major handicap to modernization in our times.

The history of inner Africa is the story of how large numbers of original civilizations grew from Late Stone Age cultures and the common inheritance of the original Bantu civilization. Further growth and development stemmed from internal developments and also from mutual borrowing; these were facilitated by the increase in trade, political growth, conquest, and the more modest practice of intermarriage between groups. These processes led to increasing cultural elaboration, both in the direction of a better adaptation to each particular environment and in the direction of an intellectually more satisfying way of life. Personalities must have played substantial roles in these developments; but the nature of our sources is such that little is known about their impact. Only the fruits of their works are still visible.

As these civilizations emerged, they left a unique legacy for all mankind. Inner Africa has been less affected by the world outside than most of the other civilizations elsewhere on the earth. At the same time the complexity of these ways of life takes them out of the range of the simple societies; there is nothing primitive about them. As Leo Frobenius, the German ethnologist and explorer, said: "They are civilized to the marrow of their bones." Because they grew in relative isolation, the flowering of human ingenuity and creativity that these civilizations and their history represents is a unique thread in the cloth that is the achievement of mankind. And so inner Africa's history teaches man more about himself everywhere.

THE MWINDO EPIC

THE MUSEUM OF PRIMITIVE ART

From the forest peoples of inner Africa have come some of the continent's literary masterpieces, including the Mwindo epic that follows. This work is part of the rich oral tradition of the Nyanga, a Bantu-speaking group that lives in the mountainous rain forest of the former Kivu province in the eastern part of the Democratic Republic of the Congo.

The story was recorded by Professor Daniel Biebuyck, an anthropologist on the faculty at the University of Delaware, who lived and taught in the former Belgian Congo and did field research in its forest zones. He first visited the territory of the Nyanga in 1952, beginning his study among them two years later. In 1956 he spent several weeks in Kisimba, one of the more remote forest areas of the Kivu province, and there was able to transcribe the epic. By that time he had become well acquainted with the Nyanga people and their culture, and had learned that they had a special type of adventure story, known generically as karisi, *or epic text, which he had previously heard only in confused or fragmentary form.*

In the Kisimba region he visited the village of Bese in a dense rain forest known as Ihimbi. At Bese he met She-karisi Candi Rureke (she-karisi *means "maker of an epic text"), a bard who agreed to recite the Mwindo epic for him. For twelve consecutive days the bard narrated, sang, and enacted the many episodes of the tale, while Professor Biebuyck and his aides wrote it down verbatim. However, the narrator stressed to his listeners that the epic was never performed by the Nyanga in immediate sequence within a short span of time, but was told episode by episode at different times. Rureke, who had learned the epic from Kanyangara of Bese, an expert bard, was the only great performer of the epic still alive in 1956.*

The population of the Nyanga is about 27,000. They are predominantly trappers, gatherers of wild foods, and cultivators (the plantain is their main crop), but they also hunt and fish. Nyanga chiefs, however, are traditionally prohibited from hunting and trapping. The people of Nyanga observe two forms of wedlock: that between husband and wife, and ritual union in which a woman marries a spirit. In the latter observance the woman dwells apart from her spiritual husband and may have a human lover.

The action of the Mwindo epic takes place in the distant past and is centered in the village of Tubondo in the Ihimbi forest. According to the Nyanga, the universe is divided into four spheres: butu, *or "sky";* mwanya, *or "atmosphere";* oto, *or "earth"; and* kwirunga, *or "underworld." All are settings for the text.*

The hero is called Mwindo, a traditional Nyanga name for a male child who is born after a series of girls. Other important characters are Mwindo's father, Shemwindo, who is the chief of Tubondo, and Shemwindo's sister, Iyangura, who is Mwindo's paternal aunt and the ritual wife of the mythical water serpent Mukiti. Iyangura, whose marriage to Mukiti is not included in the following abridged version of the epic, lives apart from her spouse and wields great power; she is one of Mwindo's principal helpmates.

The narrative begins before the hero's birth, when Shemwindo declares that any of his seven wives who bears him a son shall be killed along with the infant. Thus when Mwindo appears, the midwives are reluctant to reveal his sex; but it is betrayed by a cricket, who in Nyanga legend often divulges secrets and brings ill fortune. Shemwindo unsuccessfully tries to kill his son, but the infant, who can speak and walk at birth and whose most frequent epithet is "Little-one-just-born-he-walked," outwits him. In a last desperate attempt to kill the hero, Shemwindo throws him into a pool, which is part of Mukiti's realm. Mwindo survives and begins a long aquatic journey in search of his aunt Iyangura. His watery road is blocked by crabs and fish, all of whom are Mukiti's allies or enemies. Along the way the hero encounters the water serpent deity Musoka, sister of Mukiti.

After finding Musoka, who is hostile, but never actually in direct conflict with him, Mwindo returns to Tubondo. With the intervention of Nkuba, the divinity of lightning, Mwindo kills all its inhabitants except his father, who escapes; Mwindo then goes in search of him. He begins a lengthy subterranean journey, which he makes alone because everyone else is accustomed only to earthly foods. Entering the underworld through the kikota-*fern root, Mwindo travels to the enemy territory of Muisa, a Nyanga god who lives in a desolate underground region where there is no fire. In this bleak land Mwindo encounters Kahindo, Muisa's daughter; Ntumba, the aardvark; and Sheburungu, the supreme deity of fire. He eventually locates his father, who accompanies him on a subterranean journey back to Tubondo, their original starting place.*

Finding the village totally destroyed, the hero revives all its inhabitants. A statewide conclave and enthronement rite follow, and Shemwindo acknowledges his errors. Ihimbi is split into two chiefdoms: one ruled by Mwindo, the other by Shemwindo. The final episodes tell of a dragon hunt and a celestial journey. Mwindo overcomes the dreaded dragon Kirimu and is then tested by Nkutu, who takes him on a terrifying journey through extreme heat and cold. During the experience Mwindo become a passive sufferer. He undergoes a catharsis and returns to Tubondo a wiser, better, and more benevolent ruler.

The words in brackets are in the Nyanga text, but add awkwardness to the translation; those in parentheses have been included to help clarify the meaning of the original. The epic was conceived as oral history, and it should be read aloud to gain an appreciation of its original power and beauty.

Long ago there was in a place a chief called Shemwindo. That chief built a village called Tubondo, in the state of Ihimbi. Shemwindo was born with a sister called Iyangura. And in that village of Shemwindo there were seven meeting places of his people. After Shemwindo had married those [his] seven wives, he summoned together all his people. Shemwindo sat down in the middle of them; he made an appeal, saying: "You my wives, the one who will bear a male child among you my seven wives, I will kill him/her; all of you must each time give birth to girls only." Having made this interdiction, he threw himself hurriedly into the houses of the wives, then launched the sperm where his wives were. After a fixed number of days, those [his] seven wives carried pregnancies.

When (many) days had passed, six of his wives pulled through; they gave birth merely to female children. When the preferred-one realized that her companions had already given birth, and that she remained with (her) pregnancy, she kept on complaining: "How terrible this is! It is only I who am persecuted by this pregnancy. What then shall I do?" Where the child was dwelling in the womb of its mother, it meditated to itself in the womb, saying that it could not come out from the underpart of the body of its mother, so that they might not make fun of it saying that it was the child of a woman; neither did it want to come out from the mouth of its mother, so that they might not make fun of it saying that it had been vomited like a bat. When the pregnancy had already begun to be bitter, old midwives, wives of the counselors, arrived there; they arrived there when the preferred-one was already being troubled with (the pains of the) pregnancy. Where the child was dwelling in the womb, it climbed up in the belly, it descended the limb, and it went (and) came out through the medius. The old midwives, seeing him wailing on the ground, were astonished, they pointed at him asking: "What (kind of) child (is it)?" Some among the old midwives answered: "It's a male child." Where the counselors were sitting together with Shemwindo, they shouted, asking: "What child is born there?" The old midwives who were sitting in the house kept silent. After the birth of the child, the midwives gave him the name Mwindo, because he was the (first) male child who followed only female children in [their] order of birth.

In that house where the child had been born (that day), there was a cricket on the wall. The cricket left the house and went to say to Shemwindo: "You, chief, a male child was born there (from where I came); his name is Mwindo; that is why those who are in that hut there have not answered you." When Shemwindo heard that his preferred-one had given birth to a boy, he took up his spear; he went with it where the child had been born. The moment he prepared to throw it into the birth hut, the child shouted from where it was; it said: "May this spear end up (each time it is being thrown) at the bottom of the house pole; may it never end up where these old midwives are seated here; may it neither arrive at the place where my mother is." Shemwindo threw the spear into the house six times, each time reaching nothing but [at] the pole. When Shemwindo had become exhausted from running back and forth with his spear and had completely failed to kill Mwindo, he spoke to his counselors, saying that they should dig a grave in order to throw Mwindo into it, because he did not want to see a male child. When (the grave) was finished, they went to fetch the child Mwindo; they went to bury him in the grave. Mwindo howled within the grave, saying: "Oh, my father, this is (the death) that you will die, (but) first you will suffer many sorrows." Lo! at his birth, Mwindo was born with a *conga*-scepter, holding it in his right hand. He was also born with an adze, holding it in his left hand. He was also born with a little bag of the spirit of Kahombo (female spirit of good fortune), wearing it slung across his back on the left side; in that little bag there was a long rope. Mwindo was born laughing and also speaking.

When the day had ended, those who were sitting outdoors, seeing that where Mwindo had been thrown away [earlier in the day] there was light as though the sun were shining there, went to tell the men (about it) and the (latter) also arrived (there); they saw the place; they could not (bear to) stay a moment "which is long as what?" because the great heat, which was like fire, burned them. When all the people were already asleep, Mwindo got out of the grave; he went to sneak into the house of his mother. As Mwindo was wailing in the house of his mother, Shemwindo began to hear the way in which the child was wailing, he was very much astonished, saying: "This time what was never seen is seen; again a child cries in that house. Has my wife just given birth to another child?" Shemwindo went into the house of his wife, slithering like a snake, without letting his steps be noisy. He questioned his wife, saying: "Where does this child come from again?" His wife replied to him: "This is Mwindo inside here." Where Mwindo was sitting on the ground, he kept silent. Shemwindo, witnessing this marvelous event, left the house without having retorted another word. He went to wake up the counselors. He told them: "What is there (behind me), is what is there; it is astounding." He told them also: "Tomorrow, when the sky will have become day, then you will go to cut a piece from the trunk of a tree; you will carve in it a husk for a drum; you will then put the hide of a *mukaka*-antelope in the river to soften."

When the sky had become day, the people assembled together to see Mwindo in the house of his mother. Mwindo was devoured by the many longing eyes. After they had looked at him, the counselors went to the forest to cut a piece of wood for the husk of the drum. They returned with it to the village. They carved the wood; they hollowed it out so that it became a husk. When the husk was finished, they went again to fetch Mwindo; they carried him; they stuck him into the husk of the drum. Mwindo said: "This time, my father has no mercy; what! a small baby is willingly maltreated!" The Banashemwindo (followers of Shemwindo) went to get the hide for the drum; they glued it on top of the drum; they covered it (the drum) with it. When Shemwindo had seen how his son had been laid in the drum, he declared to all his people that he wanted two expert divers, swimmers, to go [the next day] and throw this drum into the pool where nothing moves. The swimmers with the drum entered the pool, swimming in the river. When they arrived in the middle of the pool, they asked in a loud voice: "Shall we drop him here?" All those who were sitting on the edge of the river answered "Yes," all saying together: "It is there, so that you will not be the cause of his return." That day, when Mwindo was thrown away, earth and heaven joined together because of the heavy rain; it rained for seven days; hailing left the earth no more; that rain brought much famine to Tubondo.

Where the drum was in the water on the sand, it arose all alone to the surface of the water. From Tubondo, from the village where the people dwelt, came a row of maidens; they went to draw water from the river at the wading place. Arriving at the river, they saw the drum on the surface of the water, which was turning around there; they said inquiringly to one another: "Companions, we have dazzling apparitions; lo! the drum that was thrown with Mwindo—there it is!" While the maidens still had their attention fixed there toward the drum, Mwindo threw sweet words into his mouth; he sang:

> I am saying farewell to Shemwindo!
> I am saying farewell to Shemwindo!
> I shall die, oh! Bira!
> My little father threw me into the drum!
> I shall die, Mwindo!
> The counselors abandoned Shemwindo;
> The counselors will become dried leaves. . . .
> The counselors have failed (in their) counseling! . . .
> The little-one is joining Iyangura,
> The little-one is joining Iyangura,
> Iyangura, the sister of Shemwindo.

When the girls heard the way in which Mwindo was singing in the drum, they climbed up to the village, running and rushing, in disarray. The men, seeing them appear at the outskirts running and rushing, took their spears and went, believing that they were being chased by a wild beast. Seeing the spears, the maidens beseeched their fathers: "Hold it! We are going to bring the news to you of how the drum that you threw into the pool has stayed; it is singing: 'The counselors of Shemwindo, the counselors have failed in (their) counseling; the counselors will become dried leaves.'" When Shemwindo heard that, he assembled (again) all his people; everybody deserted (the village) for the river carrying spears, arrows, and fire (torches).

When Mwindo noticed them waiting in a group on the shore (of the river), he threw sweet words into (his) mouth; he sang:

> I am saying farewell to Shemwindo;
> I shall die, oh Bira! . . .
> What will die and what will be safe
> Are going to encounter Iyangura.

When Mwindo had finished singing like that, saying farewell to his father and to all the Banashemwindo, the drum sank into the pool; waves made rings at the surface.

Where Mwindo headed inside the water, he went upstream; he went to the river's source, at Kinkunduri's (crab found at river source), to begin it. When he arrived at Kinkunduri's, he lodged there; he said that he was joining Iyangura, his paternal aunt, there, whither she had gone; the news had been given him by Kahungu (hawk). He joined his aunt Iyangura downstream; he sang:

> Mungai, get out of my way!
> For Ikukuhi shall I go out of the way?
> You are impotent against Mwindo,
> Mwindo is the Little-one just-born-he-walked.
> I am going to meet Iyangura.
> For Kabusa, shall I go out of the way?
> You are helpless against Mwindo,
> For Mwindo is the Little-one-just-born-he-walked.
> Canta, get out of my way!
> Canta, you are impotent against Mwindo.
> I am going to encounter Iyangura, my aunt.
> For Mutaka shall I go out of the way?
> You are helpless against Mwindo!
> I am going to meet Iyangura, my aunt. . . .

Each time Mwindo arrived in a place where an aquatic animal was, he said that it should get out of the way for him. When Mwindo arrived at Cayo's, he spent the night there; in the morning he went right after awakening; he sang:

> For Ntsuka shall I go out of the way?
> You see that I am going to encounter Iyangura.
> You see that you are powerless against Mwindo.
> Mwindo is the Little-one-just-born-he-walked. . . .

Musoka, the junior sister of Mukiti, had gone to live upstream from Mukiti:

> For Musoka shall I go out of the way?
> You are powerless against Mwindo
> Mwindo is the Little-one-just-born-he-has-walked.

When Musoka saw Mwindo arriving at her place, she sent an envoy to Mukiti to say that there was a person there who was in the act of joining Iyangura. Mukiti replied to that envoy that he should tell Musoka that that man should not pass beyond her place; "If not, why would I have placed her there?" That envoy arrived at Musoka's; he announced the news of how he had been spoken to by

Mukiti. Musoka kept on forbidding Mwindo like that, without knowing that he was a child of Mukiti's wife, Iyangura. Musoka replied to Mwindo, saying: "Mukiti refuses to let you pass; I here, Musoka, I am placing barriers here; you will not find a trail to pass on." Mwindo answered her, softening his voice: "I, Mwindo, never am I forbidden (to pass on) a trail; I will thrust through there where you are blocking." Mwindo left the water above (him); he dug inside the sand; and he went to appear in between Musoka and Mukiti. After Mwindo had passed Musoka, having broken through the dam of Musoka, he praised himself: "Here I am, the Little-one-just-born-he-walked; one never points a finger at me."

After Mwindo had passed Musoka, he began a journey to go to Mukiti's; he sang:

> In Mukiti's, in Mariba's dwelling place!
> For Mukiti shall I get out of my way?
> You see I am going to encounter Iyangura,
> Iyangura, sister of Shemwindo.
> Mukiti, you are powerless against Mwindo.
> Mwindo is the Little-one-just-born-he-walked.

When Mukiti in his dwelling place heard (this), he moved, asking who had just mentioned his wife. He shook heaven and earth; the whole pool moved. Mwindo on his side said: "This time we shall (get to) know each other today, we with Mukiti." Mwindo pulled himself together; he went to appear at the knot where Mukiti was coiled up. When Mukiti saw him, he said: "This time it is not the one (whom I expected to see); he surpasses (expectation)!" He asked: "Who are you?" Mwindo referred to himself saying that he was Mwindo, the Little-one-just-born-he-walked, child of Iyangura. Mukiti said to Mwindo: "How then?" Mwindo answered him saying that he was going to encounter his paternal aunt Iyangura. Hearing that, Mukiti said to Mwindo: "You are lying; here never anybody passes, who would have crossed over these logs and dried leaves. While Mukiti and Mwindo were still talking to each other like that, maidens went from Iyangura's place to draw water; at Mukiti's place, there it was that the water hole was. As soon as the maidens witnessed the way in which Mwindo constantly mentioned Iyangura saying (she was his) aunt, they ran to Iyangura; (and) said: "Over there, where your husband Mukiti is, there is a little man saying that Mukiti should release him, that he is Mwindo, that he is going to encounter Iyangura, his paternal aunt." When Iyangura heard that news, she said: "Lo! that is my child, let me first go to where he is." Iyangura climbed up the slope; she went to appear at the water hole. As soon as Mwindo in his drum saw his paternal aunt coming to see him, he sang:

> I am suffering much, Mwindo.
> I will die, Mwindo.

He went on singing looking in the direction from which his aunt was coming.

> Aunt Iyangura,
> Mukiti has forbidden me the road.
> I am going to meet Aunt Iyangura,
> I am going to encounter Iyangura,
> Sister of Shemwindo.
> For Mukiti shall I go out of the way? . . .

Aunt Iyangura howled, then she said: "If the sororal nephew of the Banamitandi is in this drum, let it arrive here so that I can see it before me." When the aunt cited the Banamitandi in this way, the drum refused to move in the direction of Iyangura. His aunt said anew: "If you really are the nephew of the Baniyana, come here before me." When Mwindo heard that, he went singing, in [his] leaving the pool:

> I am going to my Aunt Iyangura,
> Iyangura, sister of Shemwindo.
> Kabarebare and Ntabare-mountain,
> Where the husband of my senior sister sets *byroo*-traps.
> And a girl who is nice is a lady,
> And a nice young man is a *kakoma*-pole (pillar of society). . . .

His aunt seized the drum; her people gave her a knife; she slashed the drum; removing the hide, she saw the multiple rays of the rising sun and the moon. That is the beauty of the child Mwindo. Mwindo got out of the drum, still holding his *conga*-scepter and his axe, together with his little bag in which the rope was. When Kahungu saw Mwindo meeting with his aunt, he went to bring the news to the *mutambo*-elder who had been given to Iyangura to keep watch over her continually. Hearing (the) news, Kasiyembe (guardian of Iyangura) said: "[You] envoy, you go! When you will have arrived at Mwindo's, tell him he should not even try to pass this side; (otherwise) I shall tear out his spinal column; I here am setting up traps, pits and pointed sticks and razors in the ground, so that I shall know where he will step." Seeing that, Katee (the hedgehog) went to appear where Mwindo was (and) told him: "I am going to have a road go by, so that it emerges from the place where you are, and I want to make it come out inside the house of your aunt, at the base of the house pole." Mwindo told his aunt Iyangura: "You, Aunt, you be already on your way home; I shall meet you there; and that Kasiyembe threatening me over there, I shall first meet up with him; if he really has force, I shall deal with him (today)." He also said to his aunt: "Tell him, the one who is threatening me there, that he should prepare himself." Master Spider also emerged from within the pits, (he was) building bridges; he made them come out above the pits; the pits became merely bridges; he said to himself that it was there that Mwindo was going to play. "As far as I, Master Spider, am concerned, Mwindo cannot completely perish, since we are there." Mwindo took the road (made by) Katee; he came out in the house of his aunt. When Kasiyembe saw him, he said: "Mwindo is already over here; now, from where has he emerged?"

When Iyangura saw Mwindo she said to him: "My son, don't eat food yet; come first to this side, so that we may dance (to the rhythm of) the drum." He told his aunt that there he was, that he was going to dance without having eaten food, that he was going to faint with this drum. She replied: "What shall I do then, since the one whom I was given to take care of me is saying you must dance?" Mwindo said: "Oh! Right you are; let me first dance; hunger never kills a man." Mwindo sang; he howled. Mwindo went round about in the middle of the pits; he marched bent over the pits, without even being injured by the razors; he passed and passed everywhere where Kasiyembe had placed traps for him, without injuring himself. He danced; he agitated his *conga*-scepter to and fro, singing:

> It is Katee who is crackling of
> dried leaves . . .

Iyangura told her son to eat some food. Iyangura gave her son a bovine as a token of hospitality; he/she felled it. After Mwindo had eaten the hospitality gift of the bovine, which his aunt had offered to him, together with the maidens, Kasiyembe, the man of hatred, persisted in trying to kill him, saying: "Is this the boy against whom I shall be impotent?" Kasiyembe implored Nkuba, the lightning-hurler, saying: "You, Nkuba, you will have to come down; may you cut Mwindo into two pieces, in the house here where he is together with all these maidens who are with him here." When Mwindo heard the way in which Kasiyembe threatened him, over and over again, he told the maidens sitting with him in the house to sit down on one side with him. Then Mwindo said threateningly to Master Nkuba: "You, Nkuba, since you come down, you must come down on one side of the house; don't come down on the side where Mwindo is." Master Nkuba, on hearing the voice of Kasiyembe, descended onto the house where Mwindo was; Mwindo pointed him out, saying: "You too will die the same (death); you are climbing on a hard tree." Master Nkuba came down seven times; he did not come close to the place where he (Mwindo) was; the fire burned on one side; that side became merely ashes.

Mwindo came out of the house together with the maidens; he presented himself (before) the crowd of people; he declared about himself that there he was, the Little-one-just-born-he-walked. He said to his aunt to come close to where he was so that he could speak to her. He told his aunt that within the twinkling of an eye, the mop of hair of Kasiyembe would already be burning. Where Kasiyembe was, (people) were all of a sudden struck (by the fact that) in the mop of hair of Kasiyembe the fire was already flaring up; the tongues (of flame) rose into the air; all the lice and all the vermin that were nestled on his head, all were entirely consumed. The people of Kasiyembe thought about fetching water in the jars in order to extinguish the fire on the head of Kasiyembe. When they arrived at the jars, in arriving there, there was no water left. They went straight to the herbaceous stalks of the plantains; they were (already) dried up. They said: "What then! Spit some saliva on (his) head!" Saliva was lacking among all the people. When they experienced this, they said: "This Kasiyembe is about to die. Go and look for help for him at his Master's; it is at Mukiti's that there is a pool." Arriving there, they found Mukiti with butterflies and flies flitting about him; for him, too, the water had dried up. When his aunt saw that, she went to beg before her son: "Widen your heart, you my son. Set your heart down; undo my husband together with his *mutambo*-elder, this one Kasiyembe; heal them without harboring further resentment against them." Mwindo woke up Kasiyembe, waving his *conga*-scepter above him; he sang:

> He who went to sleep wakes up.
> You are impotent against Mwindo,
> Mwindo is the Little-one-just-born-
> he-walked.

"Wake up thanks to my *conga* here of *nderema*-fibers."

Suddenly, Kasiyembe was saved. And the jars, water returned again in them; and the herbaceous stalks of all the plantains, in them again was water; and there where Mukiti was, the water came back again for him; the river was full again. When they saw that feat, they were much astonished, saying: "Lo! Mwindo, he too, is a great man." Kasiyembe gave Mwindo a salute, saying: "Hail! hail! oh! Mwindo." And Mwindo answered, "Yes." Mwindo said to his aunt that tomorrow he would be going to Tubondo to fight with his father. The aunt told him: "Oh! my father, you will be impotent at your father's, in Tubondo; you, (just) yesterday's child, born just a while ago, is it you who will be capable of Tubondo, village with seven meeting places? Iyanguara! I had you taken out from within the drum; as far as I am concerned, I say 'No,' strongly; never again try to go alone; the lonely path is never nice." When Mwindo heard the way in which his aunt was speaking, he refused. The aunt told him: "Do not go to fight with your father; if you go, then I also shall go with you to see how your father will be cutting you into pieces." She went to tell the maidens to pack up her household objects, so as to go with Mwindo, because the lonely path is not nice; it never fails to find something that could kill a man. Mwindo went together with his aunt, together with his servants who were chanting the refrain. Mwindo sang:

> I am going over there to Tubondo;
> I shall fight over there in Tubondo,

Even though Tubondo has seven entries.
We are saying, oh Bira!
Aunt, give me advice
To fight with the people downstream;
They carry spears and shields. . . .

During this journey that Mwindo was making, evening went to find him at his maternal uncles, the Baniyana. He slept there after they had killed a goat of hospitality for him. After he had eaten that goat, Mwindo said to his maternal uncles: "I am going to fight Shemwindo in Tubondo; forge me, you [who are] blacksmiths of large light spears, you my uncles. They dressed him in shoes made entirely of iron and pants of iron; they also forged him an iron shirt and a hat of iron. They told him: "Since you are going to fight your father, may the spears that they will unceasingly hurl at you go striking on this iron (covering) that is on (your) body." After the uncles had finished forging him, they said they would be going with him. In the morning, Mwindo began the journey together with his uncles and his aunt Iyangura, and the servants of his aunt. Mwindo went singing; he howled.

When they arrived in the glen, he said: "Let us spend the night in this village." His aunt howled, she said: "Where will we sleep, here there is no house? Lo! Kiruka-nyambura has arrived, bearer of rain that never ceases." Mwindo looked around, he said that he wanted (to have) houses: (and) the houses built themselves. His aunt shouted saying: "Yes, my father Mwindo, hail for (these) [our] houses. Lo! Shemwindo has brought forth a hero." When they were there in the glen, Mwindo's aunt said to him: "Oh! my father Mwindo, let us get away; you are powerless against this mass of people who are in Tubondo." Mwindo said that first he would try. Iyangura said to him: "Oh! my father Mwindo, what shall we eat then?" He lifted his eyes to the sky; he said to himself that he first wanted to have all the food that was over there in Tubondo come; so (the food) having joined him, he would go to fight with them. Mwindo sang while transporting the food that was with his father. Mwindo howled, he sang:

The pastes that are in Tubondo,
May the pastes join Mwindo,
Mwindo, the Little-one-just-born-he-walked.
The animals that are in Tubondo,
May the animals join Mwindo.
The meats that Shemwindo stores,
May the meats join Mwindo Mboru,
Mwindo, the Little-one-just-born-he-walked.
The wood that Shemwindo keeps,
Oh, father, may it join Mwindo Mboru,
For Mwindo is the Little-one-just-born-he walked.
And the fire that Shemwindo possesses,
May the fire also join Mwindo.
And the water that Shemwindo possesses,
May the water also join Mwindo Mboru.
The jars that are at Shemwindo's
May the jars join Mwindo,
Mwindo, the Little-one-just-born-he-walked.
The clothes that are at Shemwindo's,
May the clothes join Mwindo,
Mwindo is going to fight!
The wooden dishes that are in Tubondo,
May the wooden dishes also join Mwindo,
Oh father! the Little-one-just-born-he-has-walked
Hopes to be victorious.
The beds that Shemwindo possesses,
May the beds join Mwindo.
And the wicker plates that Shemwindo possesses,
May the wicker plates also join Mwindo.
And the salt that Shemwindo possesses,
May the salt also join Mwindo,
The Little-one-just-born-he-walked.

It was in this way that Mwindo was speaking!

And the chickens that Shemwindo possesses,
May the chickens also join Mwindo. . . .
That which-will-die and that which-will-be-saved,
May it join Iyangura here,
Iyangura, sister of Shemwindo.
The goats that are at Shemwindo's,
May the goats join Mwindo.
The cattle that are in Tubondo
May the cattle join Mwindo. . . .
The banana groves that are in Tubondo,
May the banana groves join Mwindo.
And the tobacco also that is at Shemwindo's,
May the tobacco also join Mwindo. . . .

Mwindo and his uncles and his aunt and the servants who had arrived with them, the singers and the drummers, when (the latter) opened their eyes—all the things that were in Tubondo at Shemwindo's (had) joined them there where they were. When Mwindo had seen that the things of his father had come to join him, he said that his father (now) remained over there merely as a destitute person. He said to his aunt that he wanted his uncles to go ahead and fight first, and that he, Mwindo, would remain with his aunt for a while here in the vale so that he might first see the way in which his uncles handled their force. They fought on land and in the air, but the people of Tubondo said: "You will not solve the case today."

After a while, Mwindo's uncles were completely wiped out; they died. One of Mwindo's uncles escaped in the middle of the war, being already seriously injured; he fled to Mwindo to report the news to him. Mwindo said to his aunt: "I shall go to find out first the reason why my uncles are all wiped out, and if Shemwindo does not come up face to face with me, then I am not Mwindo. You, aunt, remain with my axe here and my little bag in which there is a rope; and I, Mwindo, am leaving with my *conga* here." When Mwindo arrived in Tubondo, he said to the people of that village that he wanted to dance (to the rhythm of) a drum. The people of that village answered him: "You are helpless against our drums here, you (are a) little fool." The people of that village told him that there was no drum there. To that Mwindo said that the drums would be coming. Mwindo went on speaking in that way with the people of that village, his father being in his compound. Mwindo sang:

He is climbing up here in Tubondo,
He is going to fight with Shemwindo.

While he was singing, he went on enunciating (distinctly): "May what will die and what will be saved join Iyangura."

What will never die but will be saved,
May it, oh father, join Iyangura,
Iyangura, sister of Shemwindo. . . .

Mwindo shouted, saying:

Hatred is in the heart.
My friend, Nkuba, may you be victorious.
I shall fight here in Tubondo,
Even if Tubondo has seven entrances.
Here in Tubondo seven lightning flashes!
I shall fight here in Tubondo.
I want seven lightning flashes right now!
Mwindo reviewed (the causes of) his griefs;
The counselors retreated (before) Shemwindo. . . .

Mwindo raised his eyes into heaven (and) said:

My friend, Nkuba,
Here in Tubondo seven lightning flashes!

While Mwindo was looking up into the sky, he (also) stretched his *conga* toward there. From the sky at Nkuba's things came; there appeared seven lightning flashes; they descended on Tubondo in the village. Tubondo turned into dust, and the dust rose up; all who lived there turned into mere dust. Where Shemwindo was sitting in (his) compound, he exclaimed: "There is no time for lingering here." Where he fled, he went to arrive where there was a *kikoka*-plant. He tore it out; he entered at its root's base. After he had become victorious in Tubondo, Mwindo praised himself in the middle of the village; he said: "This time the one who climbs on me, the one who digs into me while fighting with me, will be wearing himself out in vain." Mwindo went down to where his aunt had remained in the glen. The aunt asked him: "Good news there from where you are coming?" Mwindo answered her that Tubondo was on fire. He also told them: "Now let's go up to Tubondo which is high up; let's get away from here in the glen." They climbed up to Tubondo; they arrived there. Mwindo said that he could not chase his father so long as he had not resuscitated his uncles. He woke them up beating them (with his) *conga* and singing:

He who went to sleep awakes,
My uncle, my mother, wake up.
I have been testing the Baniyana.
My uncle, my mother, forge me!
Shemwindo, you are powerless against Mwindo,
Mwindo is the Little-one-just-born-he-walked. . . .

Where Shemwindo had fled, he went harming himself running into everything; he went to arrive at Musia's, the place where no one ever clusters around the fire. Mwindo said to his aunt: "You, my aunt, you stay here in the village of your birth, in Tubondo; here is the rope; remain with one end, holding it in your hand, whereas I shall follow my father where he fled to Muisa's; if (one day) you feel that this rope has become still, if it does not move anymore, then pay no more attention to where I have gone; lo! the fire has dwindled; I am dead then." After he had spoken like that, Master Sparrow alit where he was, he told him: "Come here for me to show you the path that your father took and where he entered at the base of the root of the *kikoka*-plant. Mwindo in [his] leaving said farewell to his aunt; he held one end of the rope and the aunt remained holding (the other) end of the rope. When he arrived at the *kikoka*-plant, where his father had entered, he too pulled out the *kikoka*-plant; he passed through; he went to appear at the well. Arriving there, he met Kahindo (female spirit of good fortune), daughter of Muisa. Kahindo embraced him, saying: "This is my welcome, Mwindo." Mwindo in reply said "Yes." She said to him: "Where are you going?" Mwindo answered her that he was going to Muisa's to look for his father. She told him again: "Stop first here where I am. Over there in Muisa's village one never goes through; is it you who will (succeed) in getting through there like that, with all (your) pride?" Kahindo said to Mwindo: "Now you are going to Muisa's. When you will have arrived there, having entered the meeting place, if you see a very big man and tall too, curled up in the ashes near the hearth, it is he who is Muisa; and if he greets you, if he says: 'Blessing (be) with you, my father,' you too will answer, 'Yes, my father'; and when he will have left you a stool, then you will refuse it; you will tell him: 'No, my father; will the head of a man's father become a stool?' When he will have handed over to you a little gourd of banana beer for you to drink, you will refuse, answering: 'No, my father, even though a person is one's child, is that a reason why he should drink the urine of his father?' After Muisa will have recognized you in that way, he will say to you: 'Blessing, blessing, Mwindo'; and you will answer him: 'And to you blessing, blessing also, father.' When he will have given you paste to eat, you will answer him: 'Even though a person is one's child, is that a reason why he should eat the excrements of his father?' "

After Mwindo had heard Kahindo speaking these useful words to him, he went and climbed up to Muisa's. Muisa, seeing him, greeted him with "Blessing." Mwindo answered, "Yes, my father." Muisa recollected: "Let them give a chair to Mwindo to sit on it." Mwindo answered him: "Not at all, my father, even though a man is a guest, is that a reason for him to sit down on the head of his father?" Muisa also said that he had left a gourd of beer here: "Let me pour you a bit." Mwindo said: "No, my father, even though a man is a guest, is that a reason for him to drink the urine of his father?" Muisa said: "Blessing, blessing, my father." Muisa again said: "Let them prepare some paste for you, oh Mwindo!" Mwindo answered him: "No, my father, even though a man is a guest, is that a reason for him to eat the excrements of his father?" Hearing that, Muisa said to him: "Blessing, blessing, Mwindo. Go and take a rest in the house there of your sister Kahindo." Mwindo went inside. When she saw that Mwindo had entered into the house, she said to herself: "Lo!, Mwindo has hunger." She got up, she went to make some paste, "a little like that," of ashes. After she had stirred it, she brought it to Mwindo in her sacred hut. When Muisa saw Kahindo bringing (the paste) to Mwindo, he dashed quickly toward the house of his daughter; he said to Mwindo: "Oh, my father Mwindo, tomorrow you will start cultivating a new banana grove for me; may you first cut leaves, then plant the banana trees, then fell the trees; may you then cut the newly grown weeds, then prune the banana trees, then prop them up, then bring ripe bananas. It's after you will have performed all those works that I shall know to give you your father." He also said to him: "When you leave for cultivating, I shall give you a man to observe the way in which you are performing."

When the sky had become daylight, in the morning, Mwindo equipped himself with his billhook; Mwindo went to cultivate. When they arrived in the forest, the man whom Muisa had picked out showed Mwindo a mountain with mango trees on it. Mwindo placed the billhooks on the ground; all by themselves, they laid out the fresh trails. Having finished the trail, they cut the grasses. Having cut the grasses, the banana trees planted themselves; the banana trees having planted themselves, Mwindo sent a bunch of axes down on them; the axes by themselves finished felling the trees. Finishing, he sent a bunch of billhooks down on it (the grove); those billhooks went across the banana grove cutting the newly grown weeds. The companion of Mwindo returned to Muisa. He brought Muisa the news, saying: "This time he there is not (merely) a cultivator; he is fast, a cultivator of marvelous things; he has not touched one iron tool; the iron tools themselves are cultivating—and felling trees and cutting weeds." Having given the news, he returned again where Mwindo was on the fresh banana field. Where Mwindo was, the billhooks having finished cutting their weeds, they now cut gaffs; the gaffs themselves propped up the banana trees. The gaffs having finished sustaining the trees, the banana stems were ripe. The companion ran to bring the news to Muisa. "It is not a man who is there; he has cultivated today; the banana trees already have stems and the bananas already (are) ripe." Having thus been astonished, Muisa sent his *karemba*-belt of cowries over there; he said to it: "You, my *karemba*, you are going to Mwindo; when you will have seen him, you will have to bend him, then you will have to smash his mouth against the ground." *Karemba*, having heard the way in which it had been instructed by its master, went to the banana grove. When it saw Mwindo, it went to where he was; it fell upon him where he was; it made Mwindo scream; it crushed him; it planted his mouth against the ground. Having seen its master missing all means of getting out, Mwindo's *conga* recalled (its duty); it wagged itself above the head of Mwindo; Mwindo succeeded in sneezing; he raised his eyes upward; he opened his eyes; he raised them; he gazed about a little. After Mwindo had been wedged by Muisa's *karemba*, the rope became still, it did not move any more. Where his aunt had remained in Tubondo, where she had held one end of the rope, she threw herself down saying that lo! her son was dead. She uttered a cry, low and high, imploring the divinities, she said: "It is the one who will escape there who is (my) child." Where Mwindo was, when he lifted up (his) eyes, he sang:

> Muisa slaughtered Mwindo,
> I shall die, on Bira!
> Muisa, you are helpless against
> Mwindo,
> Against Mwindo, the Little-one-
> just-born-he-has-walked.

Mwindo, while singing, remembered his aunt: "You there in Tubondo, I had already felt that my rope did not move; but don't suffer from anxiety any more." Mwindo now sent his *conga* to Muisa in the village, saying: "You, my *conga*, when you will have arrived where Muisa is in the village, you will have to smash him with force; you must plant his mouth to the ground; his tongue must penetrate inside the earth; so long as I shall not be back, so long as I shall not have come there into the village, you should not have released him again." The *conga* went whirling around; when it arrived at

Muisa's meeting place, it smashed him; it planted his mouth to the ground; the tongue dug into the earth; breath found no way of coming out. Where Mwindo remained in the banana grove, he prepared a load of green bananas together with ripe bananas. He returned to the village. When he cast his eyes at the meeting place, he saw Muisa—foam had come out of his mouth and nostrils. Kahindo, Muisa's daughter, seeing Mwindo, hurried to the place where he was; she told him: "You are arriving, whereas my father here has already cooled off." Mwindo answered Kahindo that he had come here looking for his father: "Now give me my father here, so that I may go home with him." Kahindo answered him: "Begin first by healing my father, so that I know how to unveil your father. Mwindo sang while awakening Muisa. When Musia had awakened, he said: "You, Mwindo, lo! you also are a man." Muisa also said to Mwindo: "You, child, go as soon as you are awake to extract for me my honey which is in that tree there." Mwindo complained: "This time I am dead once more." When the sky had become day, Mwindo provided himself with his axe; he went ahead into the forest to extract the honey; he also took fire. When he arrived at the base of the tree, he climbed (up into) the tree; he went to arrive at the fascicle where the honey was; he called: "Is this the place?" They answered him: "There it is." Mwindo poked up the fire for it. He struck his axe at the tree.

Where Muisa remained in the village, he said: "Lo! this man will finally extract this honey!" Muisa sent his *karemba*-belt; it went and smashed Mwindo on the tree; it planted his mouth into the trunk of the tree; his breath could not get out; wine and excrements trickled down from him.

Where Mwindo (had) left his *conga* down on the ground, the *conga* realized that lo! its master was dead; it climbed up where he was; it went to beat and beat on the head of Mwindo. Mwindo sneezed; he lifted his eyes and a bit of breath came out. Mwindo said: "Lo! while I was perched, lo! I was on the verge of death."

In climbing down (from the tree), he implored Nkuba (the lightning divinity), he gazed into the sky: "My friend Nkuba, I am suffering." When Nkuba heard the cry of his friend Mwindo, he came down onto the tree; he cleaved it into pieces. His friend Mwindo went down (but) he did not have a single wound. When he was down with the basket of honey, he went up to Muisa's with the honey. Where Mwindo and Muisa remained, Mwindo told him the truth bluntly. "Give me my father on the shot. Make him come out from where you have hidden him so that I may go with him. You (had) said that when I would have cultivated a field for you, when I would have extracted honey for you, you would then give me my father. I want you to take him out right now; don't let the saliva dry up without having taken him out." When Muisa heard how Mwindo was criticizing him, he twitched his eyes; he said: "This time, this boy makes my belly swell here in my own village."

Having seen that Muisa did not bring his father out, Mwindo beat Muisa on top of his head with his *conga*; Muisa tossed his hoofs up into the air; he stiffened like a *mukusa*-viper. Mwindo said: "Stay like that, you dog." Mwindo went in pursuit of his father, where he had gone to Ntumba's (Ntumba, the aardvark). Mwindo went on singing:

> I am searching for Shemwindo
> In the place where Shemwindo went.
> Shemwindo fled into Ntumba's dwelling,
> Into Muisa's dwelling.
> I am searching for Ntumba's dwelling.
> For Mumundu's (Munundu, epithet for Ntumba), dwelling.
> Ntumba, open for me.
> Shemwindo has set a barrier inside Munundu's dwelling;
> Shemwindo is in flight inside Ntumba's dwelling.
> I am searching for my father Shemwindo
> In Ntumba's, in Munundu's dwelling.
> The sun sets down.
> I am searching for Shemwindo;
> Shemwindo is in flight inside Ntumba's dwelling,
> Inside Munundu's.
> My little father threw me into the drum.

Mwindo implored Nkuba, saying:

> My friend Nkuba, may you be victorious.
> Hatred is in the heart.
> My little father, the dearest one,
> I am searching for my father in Ntumba's dwelling,
> In Munundu's. . . .

While Mwindo was still pacing around Ntumba's cave where his father was, and Ntumba from the inside (at first) paid no attention (to him), then Ntumba made a sign to Shemwindo, saying: "You be ready to go; the little male at the door here is strong, and you are witnessing the way in which he is threatening at the entrance of the cave." Shemwindo went to escape to Sheburungu's (creator god Ongo). Where Kahungu dwelt in the sky, he came down; he went to bring the news to Mwindo; he arrived saying: "You know, you Mwindo, that Ntumba has made your father escape; your father had fled to Sheburungu's." Mwindo continued to follow his father, going in search of him all wrapped up in hatred, he went to arrive at the entrance of

Sheburungu's village. He met little children there; they greeted him, saying: "Are you awake, oh Mwindo?" Mwindo answered them: "Yes." They told him: "You, Mwindo don't draw ahead of us; we are hungry; we ask you for food." Mwindo implored his aunt Iyangura to send him food (telling her) that the children of Sheburungu were hungy. Mwindo howled, he said:

> Oh! father, where Iyangura remained,
> Sister of Shemwindo,
> I claim seven portions (of food).
> You see where Mwindo passed,
> I am suffering from hunger.
> Aunt Iyangura,
> I am claiming meat.

Having implored his aunt, saying that he wanted seven pastes with meat to join him in the place where he was with the children of Sheburungu, when Mwindo looked up, the pastes were already there, having come from his aunt Iyangura. After the food had arrived, Mwindo gave it to the youngsters. When the children had finished eating, Mwindo sent back the wicker plates, singing:

> I send back the wicker and wooden plates.
> Oh! Aunt Iyangura,
> I send back the wicker and wooden plates.

He proceeded to climb up to Sheburungu's, and the youngsters followed him. He went up to Sheburungu's, singing:

> Sheburungu, you,
> I am looking for Shemwindo.
> Shemwindo gave birth to a hero
> In giving birth to the Little-one-just-born-he-walked.
> Sheburungu,
> I am looking for Shemwindo,
> My little father, the dearest one.

Sheburungu shouted and said:

> Oh Mwindo, let us play *wiki* (a gambling game) together!

And Mwindo shouted, he said:

> Oh my father, give me Shemwindo!
> My little father threw me into the drum;
> My little father threw me into the river. . . .

After Mwindo had entreated Sheburungu, asking him to give him back his father, Sheburungu said to him: "I cannot give you your father; I am asking that we first play *wiki* together, so that I may deliver your father to you, so that you may go home with him." Mwindo answered him: "Spread them (the *wiki*) out on the ground; I will not flee from you; you know the dangers from which I have escaped." After Sheburungu had heard the way in which he was being answered by Mwindo, he went to fetch a mat; he spread it out on the ground; he also went to get the very old *wiki*-seeds of the *isea*-tree. Sheburungu wagered: "You, Mwindo, if you beat me, you will carry your father off (with you), and here (are) three bunches of *butea*-money; if you beat me, you will carry them off." Mwindo wagered three bunches of *butea*-money. After they had wagered things with each other in that way, Sheburungu was the first to take a handful of *wiki*-seeds; when he picked them up, with the first take-up, he won Mwindo's *butea*-money. Mwindo wagered everything and his aunt; Sheburungu again took the seeds; he won all the goods and the people and his aunt from Mwindo. Mwindo remained all alone with his *conga*, his partner. After Mwindo had been losing all his things and his people, he wagered his *conga*. When Sheburungu tried to take the seeds, he failed. Mwindo took the seeds; he won on eight; all that Sheburungu had wagered, Mwindo won it back. He won all the things of Sheburungu: people, goats, cattle. Mwindo piled up (things); Sheburungu remained all alone by himself.

Where Kantori and Kahungu remained, they arrived where Mwindo was; they warned him: "You, Mwindo, come quickly; your father wants to flee again." Mwindo abandoned the *wiki*-game; he headed very quickly to join his father in the banana grove of Sheburungu. Seeing his father, Mwindo inquired of him: "Oh my father, is it you here?" Shemwindo answered: "Here I am." Mwindo again inquired of his father: "Oh Shemwindo, is it really you?" Shemwindo again answered: "Here I am, you, my son." After Mwindo had seized his father like that, he returned with him; he climbed up with him to Sheburungu's. Mwindo said to Sheburungu: "You, Sheburungu, you have been hiding my father away." Mwindo said further to Sheburungu: "I don't want any of your things that I have won; now keep all your things that I have won; here I am going with my father." Mwindo gave his farewell to Sheburungu and to all his people: "Oh, my father Sheburungu, farewell!" Sheburungu answered: "Yes, you too, Mwindo, go and be strong, along with your father Shemwindo." Mwindo returned singing:

> Listen, Ntumba Munundu,
> He who went (away) comes back.

Mwindo shook the rope, he reminded his aunt; and where his aunt remained, she had bells attached to the rope. Mwindo sang:

> He who went (away) comes back;
> You see I am carrying Shemwindo.

Mwindo rushed headlong to Ntumba's cave. Mwindo said to Ntumba: "Why did you hide my father away? Here I am with my father." Mwindo sang:

> Ntumba, you are powerless against Mwindo,
> For Mwindo is the Little-one-just-born-he-has-walked.
> I am on my way home from this point on in Ntumba's house.
> Look, I am carrying Shemwindo,
> My little father, the dearest-one,
> Shemwindo, senior brother of Iyangura.
> It is Shemwindo, the one who gave birth to a hero.
> Aunt Iyangura, I am on my way back.
> Mwindo is the Little-one-just-born-he-walked.
> I am carrying my little father,
> Shemwindo. . . .

When Mwindo left Ntumba's, together with his father, he went singing, reminding his aunt in Tubondo:

He who has gone away is back.
Muisa!
The sky has become day.
The rooster cock-a-doodle-dooed,
And the sparrow pointed him out.
Mwindo will arrive in the house of
 Muisa,
In the house of Nyarire;
I come from Ntumba's,
From Munundu's.
Muisa, you are helpless against
 Mwindo,
Since Mwindo is the Little-one-
 just-born-he-has-walked.
It is you who are wrong in
 offending me in vain.
Look! I am carrying Shemwindo.
Muisa, you are helpless against
 Mwindo,
Since Mwindo is the Little-one-
 just-born-he-walked.
Look! I am carrying Shemwindo.
I am returning to Tubondo,
Where remained my aunt Iyangura,
Iyangura, sister of Shemwindo,
Aunt, birth-giver, Iyangura.
I shall eat on the wicker and
 wooden plates
Only when I shall arrive in Tubondo.

When Mwindo left Ntumba's village with his father Shemwindo, he went headlong into Muisa's house. Kahindo came to Mwindo saying: "You see my father here, his bones fill a basket; what shall I do then? It is befitting that you heal my father; don't leave him like that; wake him up, because he is the chief of all the people." After Kahindo had spoken to Mwindo in that way, Mwindo woke up Muisa singing. While awakening Muisa, he kept on striking him all the time with his *conga*, telling him: "You have offended me in vain; you have tried to be equal to Mwindo, whereas Mwindo is the Little-one-just-born-he-walked, the little one who does not eat terrestrial foods; and the day he was born, he did not drink at the breasts of his mother." After Muisa had resuscitated, Mwindo told him that he had been forged by his uncles, the Baniyana. "My body is covered with iron only; and you, Muisa, don't you see me?" Muisa asked Mwindo: "You, Mwindo, how were you born? Do you have a medicine that enables your going?" Mwindo unfolded for him the thread of the news of how he was born.

When Mwindo was already as Muisa's, he agitated the rope where his aunt remained in Tubondo; he reminded her. Iyangura said to Mwindo's uncles, the Baniyana, that in the place where Mwindo had gone, he had long ago finished seizing his father, that he was on his way home with him. While returning to Tubondo, Mwindo said farewell to Muisa; he sang:

You, Muisa,
You see me already going,
You, Muisa, taker of others'
 things.
Where Aunt Iyangura remains
In Tubondo,
He who went away is back.

When Muisa saw Mwindo going, he said to him: "Oh, Mwindo, you my son, it's befitting that you marry my Kahindo here." Mwindo answered him: "I cannot marry here; I shall marry (later) in Tubondo of Shemwindo."

In leaving Muisa's village, Mwindo began the trip; he and his father went home. When Mwindo and Shemwindo arrived at the entrance of Tubondo, those who were in the village, Iyangura and the uncles of Mwindo, swarmed in the village like bees; they went to greet Mwindo and his father at the entrance. Iyangura and the uncles of Mwindo lifted him up into the air; they carried him on their fingertips. When they traversed the village of Tubondo, Mwindo told them to let him down. They put him down in the middle of the village place; they went to take a lot of spearheads, and it is on them that Mwindo sat down—they stood for the *utebe*-stool. Mwindo gave his aunt the news from where he had come and the way in which he had fought, searching for his father. Iyangura gave her son the order: "Since you have arrived with your father, bring him first into the *iremeso*-hut to let him rest there." In giving hospitality to his father, Mwindo killed for him the goat that never defecates and never urinates; they cooked it, along with rice, for his father. He said to his father: "It is you who were wrong in vain; you made yourself awkward to Mwindo, the Little-one-just-born-he-walked, when you said that you did not want (any) boys, that you wanted girls; Lo! you did not know the strength of the blessing of Mwindo." After Mwindo had given food to his father, Iyangura said to him: "You, my son, shall we go on living always in this desolate village. I, Iyangura, I want you first to save all the people who lived here in this village; when they have resuscitated, it is then only that I shall know to ask our young man, Shemwindo, to tell me some of the news of the ways in which he acted, all the evil that he did against you." Mwindo listened to the order of his aunt to heal those who had died. His uncles, the Baniyana, beat the drum for him while he, Mwindo, was dancing because of the joys of seeing his father. They sang. Aunt shouted and said:

My father, eternal savior of people.

Mwindo said:

Oh, father, they tell me to save the
 people;
I say: "He who went to sleep
 wakes up."
Little Mwindo is the Little-one-
 just-born-he-walked. . . .

While Mwindo was healing those who died in Tubondo, he continued on in the (following) way: when he arrived at the bone of a man, he beat it with his *conga*

so that the man would then wake up. The resuscitation was as follows:

each one who died in pregnancy resuscitated with her pregnancy;
each one who died in labor resuscitated being in labor;
each one who was preparing paste resuscitated stirring paste;
each one who died defecating resuscitated defecating;
each one who died setting up traps resuscitated trapping;
each one who died copulating resuscitated copulating;
each one who died forging resuscitated forging;
each one who died cultivating resuscitated cultivating;
each one who died while making pots and jars resuscitated shaping;
each one who died carving dishes resuscitated carving;
each one who died quarreling with a partner resuscitated quarreling.

Mwindo stayed in the village for three days resuscitating people; he was dead of weariness. The people and all the houses—each person resuscitated being straight up in his house. Tubondo filled itself again with the people and the goats, the dogs, the cattle, the poultry, the male and the female ewes, the teenage boys and girls, the children and the youngsters, the old males and females; in the middle of all those people (were) the nobles and the counselors and the Pygmies and all the royal initiators; all those also were straight up. All the descent groups that formerly dwelt in Tubondo resuscitated; again they became as they were before, each person who died having things of a certain quantity, resuscitated still having his things. Tubondo again became a big village with seven entrances. When the people were resuscitated, Iyangura began to speak in the middle of the crowd of people, saying: "You, Shemwindo, my brother, in the middle of the whole country of yours, have them prepare much beer and cows and goats; let all the people meet here in Tubondo. Shemwindo uttered a cry, high and low, to all his people, saying that they should bring beer together.

After a week had passed, all groups within his state swarmed into Tubondo, together with beer and meats. All the people of all the villages of Shemwindo's state pressed together in the assembly. Mwindo dressed himself and became like the anus of a snail (very clean). His aunt Iyangura, she too threw on her clothes, those famous ones of Mukiti's. His father Shemwindo, he too dressed himself from top to bottom: *tuhuhuma*-bark cloths on which (were) red color and castor oil, *ndorera*-fringes, *masia*-hair ornaments. He too became something beautiful. Servants stretched mats out on the ground, there where Mwindo and his father and his aunt would pass. There was sacred silence. Those three radiant stars, Mwindo and his father and his aunt, appeared from inside the house. They marched solemnly. Those who were in the gathering of the assembly gave them the gift of their eyes: there where they appeared, that is where their attention was focused. Mwindo beseeched his friend Nkuba, asking him for three copper chairs. Nkuba made them come down. When they were close to the ground, they remained suspended in the air about five meters from the ground. Mwindo and his father and his aunt climbed up onto the chairs; Iyangura sat down in the middle of both, Shemwindo on the right side and Mwindo on the left side.

When all the men had finished grouping themselves together and had finished becoming silent, Mwindo stood up from his chair; he raised his eyes into the air, he implored Nkuba, saying: "Oh, my friend Nkuba, prevent the sky from falling!" Having spoken like that, he lowered his eyes toward the ground, down upon the mass of people; he lauded them, saying: "Be strong, you chiefs." They approved of it. Then he: "You seniors, be strong." They approved. Mwindo praised the council, holding all the things with which he was born: *conga*, axe, the little bag in which the rope was; he also held an ancient stick to praise the council. Mwindo made a proclamation: "Among the seven groups that are here in Tubondo, may each group be seated together in a cluster; and the chiefs and the seniors of the other villages, may they also be seated in their (own) cluster." After he had finished speaking like that, the people grouped themselves in an orderly manner, each group in its own cluster. Mwindo also ordered that all his seven mothers be seated in one group but that Nyamwindo, the mother who gave birth to him, should separate herself somewhat from his little mothers. Mwindo also ordered: "Now you, my father, it is your turn. Explain to the chiefs the reason why you have had a grudge against me; if I have taken a portion larger than yours, if I have borne ill will against you because of your goods, if I have snatched them away from you, tell the chiefs the news so that they may understand." Where Shemwindo was sitting, he was flabbergasted: sweat arose from his big toe, climbed up to his testicles, went to arrive at the hair on his head; in his virile impetus Shemwindo got up. Because of the great shame in the eyes of Shemwindo, he did not even praise the chiefs anymore; he spoke while quivering, and a little spitting cough clung to the centipede of his throat, without warning: (all this) caused by the great evil of destruction.

Shemwindo said:

"All you chiefs who are here, I don't deny all the evil that I have done against this, my offspring, my son; indeed, I had passed an interdiction on my wives in the middle of the group of counselors and nobles, stating that I would kill the one among my wives who would give birth to a son, together with her child. After my beloved-one had given birth to a boy, I despised her; my preferred wife became my despised-one. From then on, I always looked at the soles of her feet. In the middle of all this anger, I armed myself with a spear; I threw it into the birth hut six times; I wanted to kill the child with its mother. When I saw that the child was not dead, I made an agreement with the counselors and the nobles; they threw this child away into a grave. When we woke up in the morning, we saw the child already wailing again in its mother's house. When I noticed that, I asked myself in my heart, I said: 'If I continue to fail to kill this child, then it will oust me from my royal chair.' It's only then that I carried him into the drum and that I threw him into the river. Where this child went, I believed that I was harming him, whereas I was only making him strong(er). From there it is that this child's anger stems. From that moment on, my son set out in search of me; he went to take me away in the abyss of evil in which I was involved; he went to seize me at the country's border. I was at that time withered like dried bananas. And it is like that that I arrive here in the village of Tubondo. So may the male progeny be saved, because it has let me see the way in which the sky becomes daylight and has (given me) the joy of witnessing again the warmth of the people and of all the things [of] here in Tubondo."

Iyangura spoke to the men who were sitting in the assembly, reproaching openly their young man here, Shemwindo:

"Here I am, aunt of Mwindo, you chiefs, in your presence. Our young man here, Shemwindo, has married me out to Mukiti. Thanks to my labor and to getting along with him, my husband placed me high up, so that he loved me above all the wives he had married. Suddenly, this child appeared where I lived; Mukiti was then on the verge of killing him because he did not know that he was my child; but his intelligence and his malice saved him. It is from then on that I followed him and followed him to point out to him the way to Shemwindo's. It's there that Mwindo's fights with his father began, because of the anger (caused by) all the evils that his father perpetrated against him. He subdued this village, Tubondo; his father fled. Mwindo went in search of him, saying that his father should not go to die in the leaves. When he joined him, he seized him; it is that, that Mwindo has made his father return again to this village, Tubondo. So it is that we are in this meeting of the assembly of the chiefs."

After Iyangura had finished speaking, Mwindo also stood up; he praised the assembly, he said:

"As for me, I, Mwindo, man of many feats, the Little-one-just-born-he-walked, I am not holding a grudge against my father; may my father here not be frightened, believing that I am still angry with him; no, I am not angry with my father. What my father did against me and what I did against my father, all that is already over. Now let us examine what is to come, the evil and the good. Now, let us live in harmony in our country, let us care for our people well."

Shemwindo declared that as far as he was concerned, no longer was he chief, that now it was Mwindo who remained in his succession. When Mwindo heard his father's voice, he answered him: "You, father, just sit down on your royal chair; I cannot be chief as long as you are alive." Where the counselors and nobles were seated, they assented to Mwindo; they said to Shemwindo: "Your son did not speak wrongly; divide the country into two parts; let your son take a part and you a part, since, if you were to give away all authority, you would again be immensely jealous of him, and this jealousy could eventually trouble this country." Shemwindo said: "Since you, my counselors and my nobles, come to give this advice, so I am ready to divide the country into two parts: Mwindo a part and I, Shemwindo, a part, because of the fear (you inspire); but in my own name I had wanted to leave the country to Mwindo, and from then on I would always have been eating food after my son Mwindo, because I have felt and do feel much shame in the face of my son and of all the people."

After Shemwindo had spoken like that, he conferred the kingship upon his son: he stripped himself of all the things of kingship which he bore: a dress dyed red and two red belts; he also gave him *butea watukushi* (string rings) to wear on his arms when he would pile up the *bsebse*-meat, and *butea* (to wear) on the legs; he also gave him a *ncambi*-belt; he also gave him a *kembo*-hat; he also gave him the hide of a white goat. Shemwindo dressed Mwindo (in) all those things while Mwindo was standing up, because a chief is always being dressed in (such) things while standing. The counselors went to fetch the chair imbued with *ukaru*-powder and castor oil; they gave it to Shemwindo; Shemwindo made Mwindo sit on it. Shemwindo handed over to Mwindo the scepter of copper on which there were lamels imbued with *ukaru*-powder and castor oil. He (Shemwindo) handed these things over to him when he was already seated on the chair. When he stood up, his father also handed over to him the wrist protector and the bow; he also gave him the quiver in which there were arrows. Shemwindo also handed Pygmies over to his son; he gave him the *bandirabitambo*-initiators: *mwamihesi* (chief blacksmith), *mushonga* (the cook), *mubei* (the barber), *mushumbiya* (the drummer), *muheri* (the sacrificer), *shemumbo*, counselors, nobles. They dressed him (in) all these things in the guesthouse. After Shemwindo had enthroned his son like that, Mwindo shouted that he now had become famous, that he would not want (to act) as his father had so that only one descent group would remain on earth. "May all the descent groups establish themselves in the country; may boys and girls be born; may there be born deaf and cripples, because a country is never without (some) handicapped-ones." After Shemwindo had dressed his son, he distributed beer and meat for the chiefs who were there; each group took a goat and a cow. They also gave Iyangura one cow for returning to her husband Mukiti. The chiefs and the counselors who were there said: "Let Mwindo remain here in Tubondo and let Shemwindo go to dwell on another mountain." Hearing this, Shemwindo clapped his hands; he was very satisfied. During Mwindo's enthronement, his uncles, the Baniyana, gave him a maiden, and Shamwami also gave him a maiden; Mwindo's father, he too, gave him a maiden called Katobororo and the Pygmies gave him one. After Mwindo had been enthroned, the assembly dispersed: all those who came from somewhere returned there; Shemwindo also took possession of his mountain; he left to his son Tubondo. When Iyangura, aunt of Mwindo, returned to her husband, she anointed Mwindo in the middle of the group saying:

Oh, Mwindo, hail!
Blessing, here, hail!
If your father throws you into the grave, hail!
Don't harbor resentment, hail!
May you stand up and make your first step, hail!
May you be safe, may you be blessed, hail!
And your father and your mother, hail!
May you bring forth tall children, boys and girls.
Be strong, my father; as for me, there is nothing ominous left, hail!

When Mwindo took leave of his father, his father also gave him a blessing. Mwindo handed over to his aunt two counselors to accompany her; he also gave her four goats and a return gift of twenty baskets of rice and five little chicken baskets.

While hunting, Mwindo's Pygmies are swallowed by Kirimu the dragon. A sole survivor, Nkurongo, brings Mwindo the news. Mwindo overcomes the Dragon with a song of defiance and with his conga*-scepter. Mwindo's* conga *flies through the air to collect people to carry the monster back to the village. The Dragon is carried to the village, cut up, distributed (with the injunction that every part be eaten); many people are liberated from the monster's belly. Finally, the eyes are roasted and from each, as it bursts in a splatter, come a thousand people. Lightning, who without Mwindo's knowledge had made a blood pact, smells the roasting eyes and decides to put his ally Mwindo to the test.*

Where Nkuba resided in the sky it so happened that he had made a blood pact with Dragon. When he inhaled the odor of his friend Dragon, which was passing with the wind, froth dropped from his nose; tears came out his eyes; he said: "What shall I do with this friend here, Mwindo?" He said that he first wanted to make him suffer in order that he would not begin again. Mwindo sang:

Nkuba has just come to take Mwindo;
Nkuba came to carry Mwindo away
From the heights of Tubondo,
When he inhaled the smell (of roasting).
Mwindo howled, he said:
Eh! Nkuba, you are helpless against Mwindo;
Shemwindo brought forth a hero.
Eh! Nkuba, you are helpless against Mwindo Mboru.

Mwindo said farewell (to the people), one by one.

Nkuba descended on the spot to take Mwindo. He arrived in Mwindo's village. Nkuba said to Mwindo: "I come to take you, you my friend, since you dared to kill Dragon, whereas Dragon was my friend; so know that you are doing wrong." Hearing this, Mwindo was not afraid of going away with his friend; but his people were stricken with anxiety, thinking that their chief was gone forever. Mwindo sang:

Let us go up to Bisherya [sky] over there,
For Nkuba has come to take Mwindo.
I am about to climb up to Bisherya over there,
For Nkuba has come to take Mwindo.
Oh, Nkuba, you are powerless against Mwindo,
For Mwindo is the Little-one-just born-he-has-walked.
Shemwindo gave birth to a hero;
My friends, you are powerless against Mwindo. . . .

Mwindo went on singing like that while Nkuba was climbing up slowly with him into the air, and the people of Mwindo had their attention diverted by (what was happening) above. Nkuba disappeared into the clouds, together with Mwindo; and they arrived at Nkuba's. Nkuba still said to Mwindo: "I have rescued you many times from many dangers, so then you show that you are equal to me." Mwindo arrived there at Nkuba's; he felt there much cold, and the icy wind there was strong. No house! They lived there in mere nomadism, no settling in one spot. Nkuba seized Mwindo; he climbed up with him to Rain. When Rain saw Mwindo, he told him: "You, Mwindo, never accept being criticized; the news about your toughness, your heroism, we surely have heard the news, but over here, there is no room for your heroism." Rain fell upon Mwindo seven and seven times more; he had Hail fall upon him, and he soaked him thoroughly. Mwindo said: "This time I am in trouble in every way." Nkuba lifted Mwindo up again; he had him ramble across Moon's domain. When Moon saw Mwindo, he pointed at him: "This time the news was given us that you were tough, but here in the sky there is no room for your pride." Moon burned Mwindo's hair; Mwindo complained: "Oh, father Shemwindo, bless me, and may my *conga* not get out of my hands." Nkuba lifted Mwindo up again; he went and climbed up with him to the domain of Sun. When Sun saw Mwindo, he harassed him hotly; Mwindo lacked all means (of defense) against Sun; his throat became dry; thirst strangulated him; he asked for water. They said to him: "No, there is never any water; now we advise you to grit your teeth; we advise you to put your heart on your knee." After Sun had made Mwindo sustain these pains, Nkuba lifted Mwindo up; he went and made him arrive in the domain of Star. When Star saw him, he pointed him out; he told him: "The news about you was given us that surely you are very tough; but here there is no room for your heroism." *Kubikubi*-star ordered Rain and Sun (to come). All—Nkuba, Rain, Sun, Star—all those told Mwindo but one single thing: "We have respect for you, just that much; otherwise, you would vanish right here. You, Mwindo, you are ordered to go back; never a day should you kill an animal of the forest or of the village or even an insect like a centipede or like a *ntsine*. If one day we would learn the news that you began again to kill a thing among those that we just forbade, then you will die, then your people would never see you again." They pulled his ears seven times and seven more, saying: "Understand?" And he: "Yes, I have understood." They also said to Mwindo: "It is Nkuba here who is your guardian; if you have done wrong, it is Nkuba who will give the news, and that day he will seize you all at once, without any longer saying farewell to your people.

After Nkuba had made Mwindo ramble everywhere through the sky, they gave him back (the right) of home, saying he was allowed to return. On his return, Mwindo had then finished spending one year in the sky, seeing all the good and all the bad things that are in the sky. Nkuba raised Mwindo up; he returned with him to Tubondo. Mwindo threw sweet words into his mouth; he sang:

Mwindo was already arriving
Where Shemwindo had remained;
Where Shemwindo had remained
Mwindo was already arriving
He who went away returns.
Shemwindo brought forth a hero.
What will die and what will be safe,
Oh my senior sister, may it join Mwindo!
My friend Nkuba, be victorious.
Let me go to Tubondo,
To Tubondo, village of my mothers.
May I see my mother.
I descend here in Tubondo,
In father's village, my dearest one.
And if, Mwindo, you kill a game,
It is I who have a right to the tail,
In which (normally) father's elder brother has a right.

The will says: "Mwindo, if you kill an animal, then you die."

When Nkuba was returning with Mwindo, he went on slowly descending with him; and led him down in the very middle of the village place of Tubondo. When his father Shemwindo saw his son being brought back by Nkuba, he gave Nkuba a reward of a maiden who was dressed with a bracelet of copper of Nkuba; they also gave him the prescribed white fowl. It is there that originated the custom of rendering cult to Nkuba; from then on they always dedicated to him a maiden and her copper ring. After Nkuba had received (his) gift, he returned to his domain in the sky.

After Mwindo had taken rest, he assembled all his people. They arrived. He told them: "I, Mwindo, the Little-one-just-born-he-walked, performer of many wonderful things, I tell you the news from the place from where I have come in the sky. When I arrived in the sky, I met with Rain and Moon and Sun and Kubikubi-Star and Lightning. These five personages forbade me to kill the animals of the forest and of the village, and all the little animals of the forest, of the rivers, and of the village, saying that the day I would dare to touch a thing in order to kill it, that day (the fire) would be extinguished; then Nkuba would come to take me without my saying farewell to my people, that then the return was lost forever." He also told them: "I have seen in the sky things unseen of which I could not divulge." When they had finished listening to Mwindo's words, those who were there dispersed. Shemwindo's and Nyamwindo's many hairs went, say as "high as that" as the long hairs of an *mpaca*-ghost; and in Tubondo the drums had not sounded anymore; the rooster had not crowed any more. On the day that Mwindo appeared there, his father's and his mother's long hairs were shaved, and the roosters crowed, and that day (all) the drums were being beaten all around.

When Mwindo was in his village, his fame grew and stretched widely. He passed laws to all his people, saying to them:

May you grow many foods and many crops.

May you live in good houses; may you moreover live in a beautiful village.

Don't quarrel with one another.

Don't pursue another's spouse.

Don't mock the invalid passing in the village.

And he who seduces another's wife will be killed!

Accept the chief; fear him; may he also fear you.

May you agree with one another, all together; no enmity in the land nor too much hate.

May you bring forth tall and short children; in so doing you will bring them forth for the chief.

After Mwindo had spoken like that, he went from then on to remain always in his village. He had much fame, and his father and his mother, and his wives and his people! His great fame went through his country; it spread into other countries, and other people from other countries came to pay allegiance to him.

Polychrome mask used by the Yaka people of the Congo (Kinshasa) during initiation rites

BANTU LEGACY

THE FIRST MIGRANTS

LAURENCE R. LOWRY

PHOTO RESEARCHERS—THOMAS D. W. FRIEDMANN

The 2900 mile-long Congo river was the principal highway of the Bantu migrations; its marshy, lakelike segment, known as the Stanley Pool, is pictured above. At left, in a village on the thickly forested Ituri tributary, a woman pounds cassava.

The ancestral homeland of the original Bantu was probably in the Benue valley, along the present-day Nigeria-Cameroon border. At an unknown date (perhaps at the dawn of our era or possibly earlier) groups of Bantu-speaking fishermen—probably only several hundred all told—took their few belongings and headed southward. The easily navigable rivers of the Congo drainage system afforded them quick passage through the rain forests of the Congo Basin, and they soon emerged in a lightly wooded area in what is now northern Katanga. This region would become the nucleus from which Bantu speakers would fan out in all directions.

Stool made by the Luba of the central Congo

PAUL AND RUTH TISHMAN COLLECTION, RAPHO-GUILLUMETTE—MARC AND EVELYNE BERNHEIM

High up in the forest-covered Kigezi mountain range on the Congo border of Uganda, girls perform a ritual dance.
MAGNUM—GEORGE RODGER

BROOKLYN MUSEUM–ELIOT ELISOFON

Since the early seventeenth century, the Kuba, Bantu speakers of the Congo (Kinshasa), have been making wooden effigies of their rulers. The one at left portrays Bom Bosh, a great warrior king of the 1650's. Bope Mabinshe, a modern Kuba monarch, is shown opposite at his coronation in 1947. The epitome of Bantu kingship, he, like all Kuba kings, rules by divine right.

The Ituri forest is the home of some 32,000 Mbuti Pygmies, like those pictured at right after a successful hunt.

BLACK STAR–LENNART NILSSON

INTO THE FOREST

From the forest fringes, waves of Bantu-speaking pioneers moved southward across the Zambezi and eastward to the coast, probably reaching Cape Delgado in the fourth century A.D. There they may have learned to cultivate the banana, Asian yam, and taro, which had been introduced into Africa from southeast Asia. These crops flourish in humid climates, and it is plausible that they were disseminated throughout the rain forests by those Bantu speakers who doubled back and settled in the Congo Basin. The migrants had probably learned to work iron before the Christian era. They were technologically and agriculturally superior to the Neolithic hunters and gatherers—notably the Pygmies—they encountered in their peregrinations, and thus could usually assimilate them without armed conflict.

Bantu-speaking forest dwellers have traditionally lived in small communities. Some forged cosmopolitan kingdoms, like Buganda in modern Uganda. The engraving above of Rubaga, capital of Buganda, was drawn by an eyewitness in 1875. The avenue leads to the royal palace.

STANLEY, *Through the Dark Continent*, 1878

MAGNUM—MARC RIBOUD

In southern Rhodesia, near Fort Victoria, stands a group of ruins called Zimbabwe, from a local term denoting royal court. Zimbabwe served as the capital of several Bantu kingdoms, such as that of Monomotapa in the fifteenth century. This thirty-four-foot tower dominated the king's residence. Zimbabwe's earliest builders may or may not have been Bantu speakers, but the fine granite surfacing was probably added by them after A.D. 1000.

THE SOUTHWARD WAVE

Those Bantu speakers who gradually moved southward across the Zambezi valley developed enduring civilizations wherever they settled. By A.D. 1300 the southerly migrations had intensified, and peoples from the Bantu heartland (in the Luba kingdom of northern Katanga) had founded such states as Malawi. The Shona and the Thonga nations were developing in Rhodesia and southern Mozambique, and the Sotho and Nguni spread out all over what is now the Republic of South Africa. By this time Bantu speakers had also occupied southern Angola and southwest Africa, and in the eighteenth century the Tswana branch of the Sotho would migrate westward into what is now Botswana. These southern Bantu societies were pastoral—they probably learned cattle-raising techniques at an early date in East Africa. They would also absorb much from the cultures of southern Africa's indigenous inhabitants: the nomadic San hunters and gatherers, and the Hottentots, with whom they often intermarried.

BURCHELL, *Travels in South Africa*, 1822

PHOTO RESEARCHERS—VAN MEISS

PHOTO RESEARCHERS—CARL FRANK

Both the Hottentots and Bantu speakers of southern Africa are pastoralists who live in kraals, which, as shown in the 1822 print at top, are clusters of huts arranged around a cattle corral. The painting above decorates the mud-walled granary of a Rhodesian Bantu group. The warrior at left is a Bantu-speaking Zulu. His ancestors intermarried with the San.

Ekoi (Nigeria)

Lwalwa (Congo, Kinshasa)

Luba (Congo, Kinshasa)

ALL: PAUL AND RUTH TISHMAN COLLECTION, RAPHO GUILLUMETTE–MARC AND EVELYNE BERNHEIM

In Africa, as in many areas where people are in close touch with the powers of nature, masks are endowed with supernatural properties and are much more than mere disguises. They conjure up magical forces and are often worn with a costume that covers the entire body. When the masquerader dons his attire, he is transformed into the being he represents, and holds his audience in thrall. The wearing of masks is intimately connected with the dance. They are intrinsic accouterments of funerary rites, where they create a link between the living and the dead; at initiations; and at numerous other festivities.

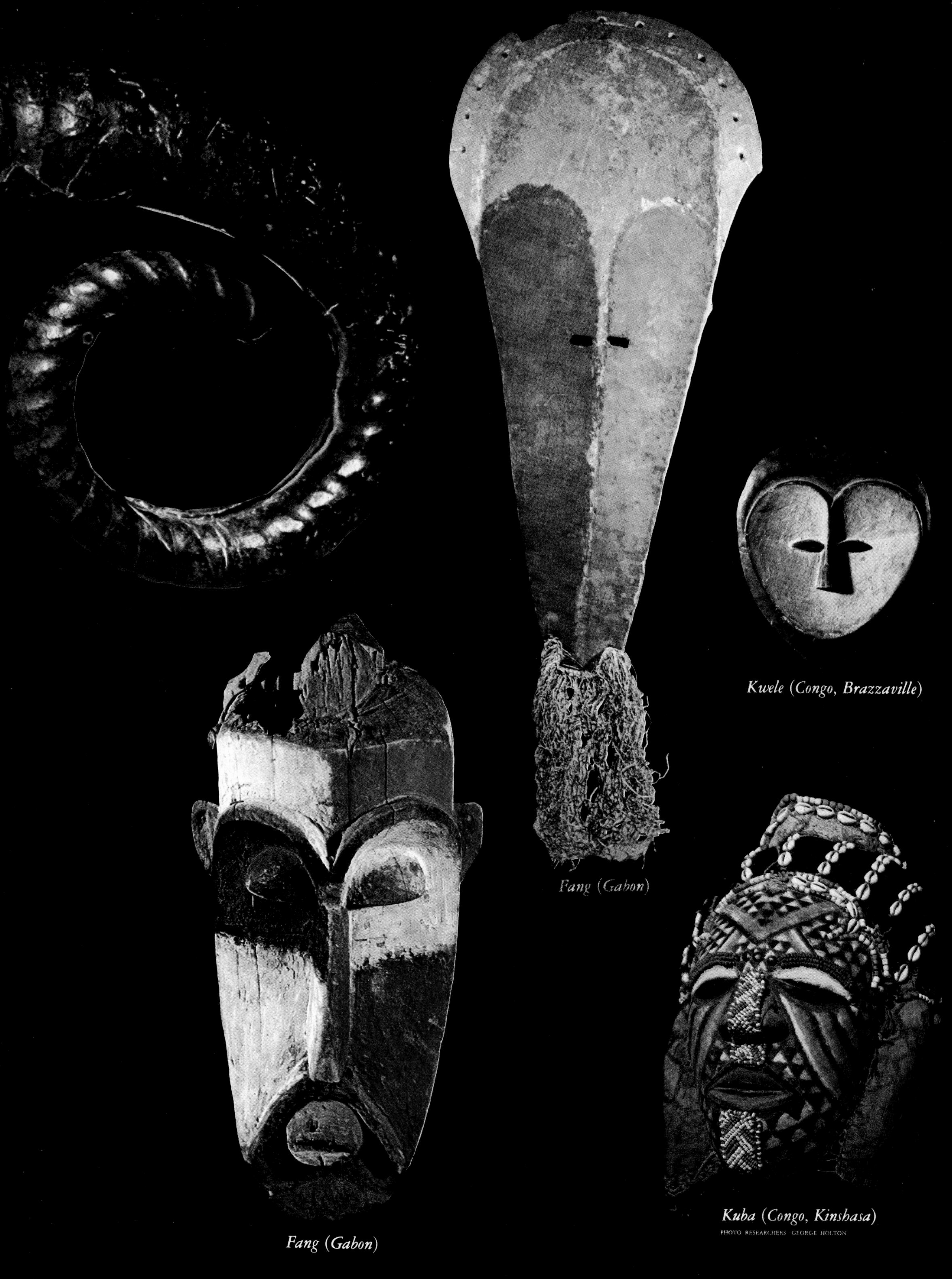

Kwele (Congo, Brazzaville)

Fang (Gabon)

Fang (Gabon)

Kuba (Congo, Kinshasa)

PHOTO RESEARCHERS GEORGE HOLTON

Above, Nilotic Turkana girl of Kenya in everyday clothes

RAPHO-GUILLUMETTE—MARC AND EVELYNE BERNHEIM

Right, Luo woman of northern Kenya bedecked in bridewealth of beads, brass rings

RAPHO-GUILLUMETTE—MARC AND EVELYNE BERNHEIM

Young Masai warrior, with characteristic forelock of hair

ELIOT ELISOFON

A farmwoman of Kenya wearing Kikuyu adornments

RAPHO-GUILLUMETTE—MARC AND EVELYNE BERNHEIM

MAGNUM—GEORGE RODGER

CATTLE COMPLEX

When groups of Bantu speakers reached East Africa during the first millennium A.D., they found a diversity of peoples—the indigenous Hottentots and Bushmen as well as Nilotic and Cushitic speakers and Persian, Arab, and Indian settlers. Many of the predominantly agricultural Bantu speakers learned cattle-raising techniques from Nilotes and Cushites, and later passed these skills to the Bantu speakers of southern Africa. In some areas, such as the Great Lakes region, Bantu speech finally prevailed.

The Masai are a Nilotic people now living in Kenya and northern Tanzania. Most are nomadic pastoralists, wandering throughout the year, but some have become agriculturalists. They subsist on cereals, meat, milk products, and quantities of fresh blood, which they draw from the necks of their cattle with special arrows. Above, Masai men perform this ritual upon a calf. Below is a view of a Masai settlement in a Tanzanian part of the arid Rift Valley.

LAURENCE R. LOWRY

PHOTO RESEARCHERS—GEORGE HOLTON

Bamileke dancers of the central Cameroon highlands are pictured at left in the typical long-nosed, high-hatted, beaded masks of the region.

OVERLEAF: *A procession of girls and women from northern Cameroon winds around a man, as hand-clapping male spectators provide the rhythm.*

MICHEL HUET

THE ART OF THE DANCER

The dance, more than any other art form, reflects the ethos of African life. Like oral literature, dance modes have been handed down, with little change, from one generation to another. Styles differ widely from region to region, but throughout the continent dance is always a direct expression of life—its joys and freedoms, its fears and anxieties. Performers are usually masked and brilliantly costumed, but under this patina of unfettered excitement, ritual dancing is taken very seriously. For many African culture groups the masked dance is the means by which they bring the mysterious, magical forces of nature and the supernatural under control. Through movement, a village thanks its guardian spirits or prays for rain and the fecundity of the soil, a hunter asks for success or gives thanks for his kill, a girl woos her lover, or a group celebrates the circumcision of boys emerging from initiation. Leaping, stooping, scuffling, and stomping, the dancer moves to the throbbing of drums, bells, calabashes, chants, and other rhythm makers. At times he seems as free floating as a will-o'-the-wisp or as frenzied as a whirling dervish. Solo dances are rare, as are those involving couples. Generally, several dancers enter the arena together, single file, and they usually move in circular formation.

RAPHO-GUILLUMETTE—MARC AND EVELYNE BERNHEIM

Costumed as a bird—with a swishing tail and a beak atop his head—a hunter (opposite) from the village of Pia in northern Cameroon joyously springs into the dusty air. At right is a Luo dancer of Kenya in traditional plumed headgear.

Os montes claros em affrica
Serra lioa:
Castello damina

Chapter Eight

THE COMING OF THE EUROPEANS

(c. 1440–1700)

by

A. Adu Boahen

AFRICA SOUTH OF THE SAHARA has been known to Europeans since Greco-Roman times, but it was not until the fourth decade of the fifteenth century that they began to arrive in numbers on its shores. The first to come were the Portuguese. They were followed in the 1450's by the Spaniards, who soon after abandoned Africa to explore the Americas; toward the end of the century some English and French adventurers and traders arrived. However, their governments were not to give official backing to such enterprises until the sixteenth and seventeenth centuries. The Dutch were the next to appear on the African scene, and during the last decade of the sixteenth century they effectively challenged the lead enjoyed by the Portuguese. The Danes dropped anchor in 1642, the Swedes in 1647, and the Brandenburgers in 1682.

The reasons for this sudden surge of interest were partly political, partly economic, partly technological. In the first place, no overseas activities could succeed without the patronage and direction of a strong nation-state enjoying stable and peaceful conditions at home, and no such nation-states emerged in Europe until after the end of the fourteenth century; and these continued to be wracked by foreign and civil wars for another hundred years or more.

Portugal was the first European state where conditions were favorable for overseas expansion. It had expelled the Moors in 1262, and a new dynasty, the house of Aviz, had emerged in 1385. The new ruling family drew its support mainly from the towns, and the first of its rulers, John and his wife Philippa, the daughter of John of Gaunt of England, raised a new aristocracy rooted "not in blood and landed estates, but in commercial enterprise." Therefore, unlike most of their contemporaries, the kings of Portugal could count on the support of the aristocracy in any over-

A Portuguese map of 1502 depicts with considerable accuracy the shape of West Africa's coast.

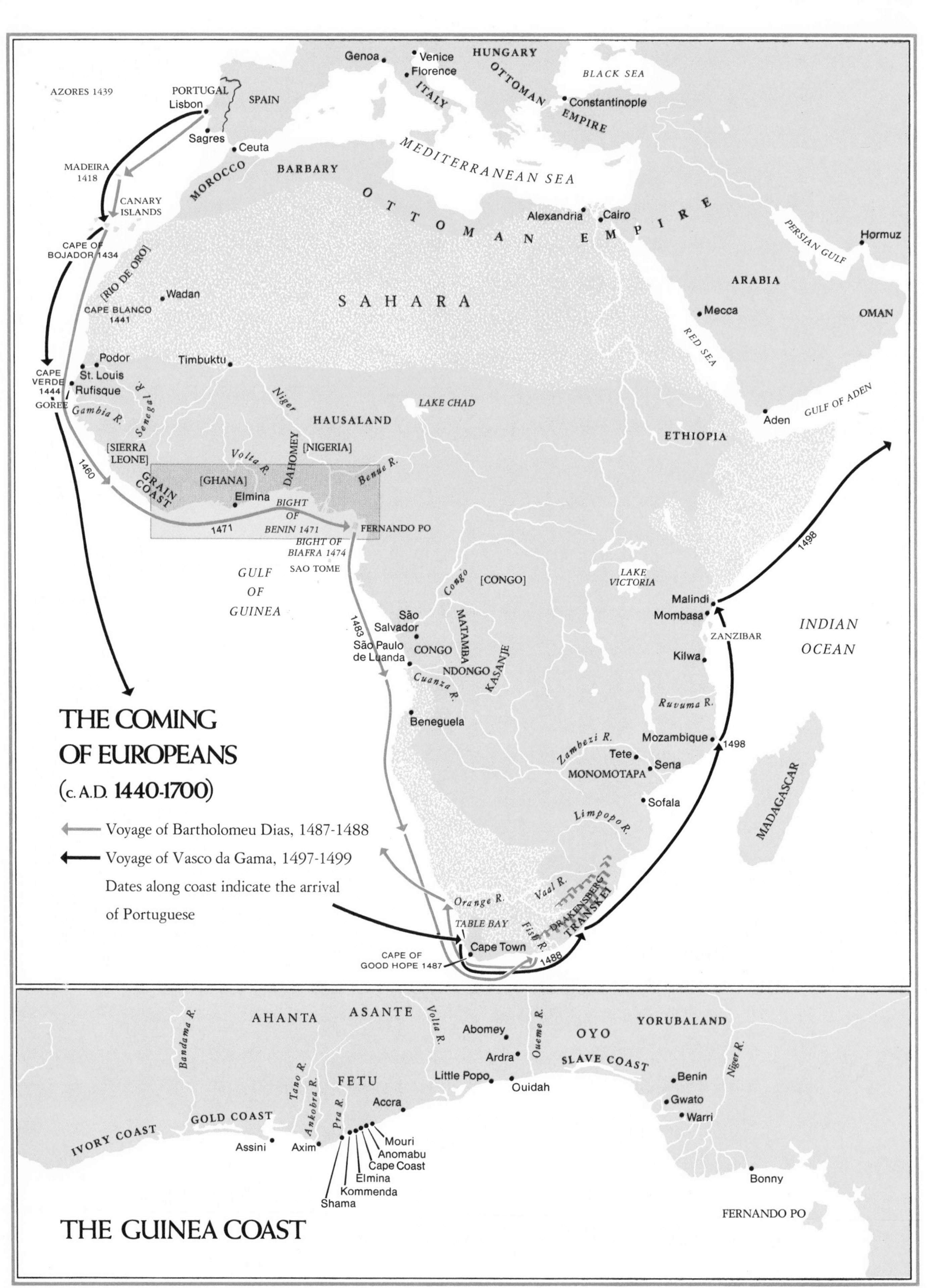

THE COMING OF EUROPEANS (c. A.D. 1440-1700)
Voyage of Bartholomeu Dias, 1487-1488
Voyage of Vasco da Gama, 1497-1499
Dates along coast indicate the arrival of Portuguese
AZORES 1439
PORTUGAL
Lisbon
Sagres
SPAIN
Ceuta
Genoa
Venice
Florence
ITALY
HUNGARY
OTTOMAN EMPIRE
BLACK SEA
Constantinople
MADEIRA 1418
CANARY ISLANDS
MOROCCO
BARBARY
MEDITERRANEAN SEA
OTTOMAN EMPIRE
Alexandria
Cairo
PERSIAN GULF
Hormuz
CAPE OF BOJADOR 1434
[RIO DE ORO]
Wadan
CAPE BLANCO 1441
SAHARA
ARABIA
Mecca
OMAN
RED SEA
CAPE VERDE 1444
GOREE
Podor
St. Louis
Rufisque
Gambia R.
Senegal R.
Timbuktu
Niger
HAUSALAND
LAKE CHAD
Aden
GULF OF ADEN
ETHIOPIA
[SIERRA LEONE]
GRAIN COAST
1460
Volta R.
DAHOMEY
[NIGERIA]
Benue R.
[GHANA]
Elmina
BIGHT OF BENIN 1471
1471
FERNANDO PO
BIGHT OF BIAFRA 1474
SAO TOME
GULF OF GUINEA
Congo
[CONGO]
LAKE VICTORIA
Malindi
Mombasa
1498
ZANZIBAR
INDIAN OCEAN
1483
São Salvador
São Paulo de Luanda
CONGO
MATAMBA
NDONGO
KASANJE
Cuanza R.
Kilwa
Ruvuma R.
Beneguela
Zambezi R.
Mozambique
1498
Tete
Sena
MONOMOTAPA
Sofala
MADAGASCAR
Limpopo R.
Vaal R.
Orange R.
DRAKENSBERG
TRANSKEI
TABLE BAY
Fish R.
Cape Town
CAPE OF GOOD HOPE 1487
1488
THE GUINEA COAST
AHANTA
ASANTE
Bandama R.
Volta R.
Abomey
Oueme R.
OYO
YORUBALAND
Ardra
SLAVE COAST
Niger R.
Little Popo
Ouidah
Benin
Tano R.
Ankobra R.
FETU
Pra R.
Accra
Gwato
Warri
GOLD COAST
IVORY COAST
Assini
Axim
Mouri
Anomabu
Cape Coast
Elmina
Kommenda
Shama
Bonny
FERNANDO PO

seas activities. Furthermore, John had five sons, all of whom were anxious to win laurels on the battlefield. The third of them, Henry, later to be called the Navigator, was ready to provide patronage, inspiration, and direction for overseas exploration, especially after 1415, when the Portuguese conquered Ceuta, a Muslim stronghold on the Moroccan side of the Strait of Gibraltar.

It was during this campaign that Prince Henry is said to have had "a vision and a purpose to which he would remain faithful to his death." According to Gomez Eannes de Azurara, the chronicler of his activities, Henry's vision and purpose were to find out what lay beyond the Canary Islands and Cape Bojador, to capture the trans-Saharan trade, to investigate the extent of Muslim power, to convert people to Christianity, and to form an anti-Muslim alliance with any Christian ruler who might be found, especially with Prester John, the legendary ruler of a Christian kingdom thought to be located in the heart of Africa. With the financial and moral support of the Crown, Prince Henry provided the essential impetus to the commencement of overseas adventures, namely patronage, inspiration, and direction.

On his return from Ceuta, Henry settled at Sagres on the southwestern tip of Portugal. There he founded a school of navigation, gathering around him map makers, astronomers, sailors, and shipbuilders, and began the systematic exploration and study of the coast of Africa. Thenceforth, until the seventeenth century, the young and united kingdom of Portugal—under the rule of a new and energetic dynasty, free from attacks from its neighbors as well as from internal struggles, and full of crusading ardor—held the lead in overseas adventuring.

Besides these political conditions, there were also economic and technological reasons for the sudden interest of Europeans in western and southern Africa. Until the fifteenth century Europe did not have much difficulty in obtaining prized commodities from the Orient. Chinese and Persian silks, Indian cloth and emeralds, rubies from Burma, sapphires from Ceylon, and above all, spices, all came by sea, mostly in Venetian, Genoese, and Florentine ships. However, with the occupation of much of the Middle East by the Ottoman Turks in the fifteenth century, not only did the volume of trade decrease but prices of Oriental goods in Europe soared, owing to the prohibitive duties imposed on them. Therefore European consumers began to look for alternative supplies or alternative routes to the East. According to Azurara, Prince Henry was aware of the commercial possibilities of a sea route to the East, and the Spanish Crown certainly had as one of its cardinal aims the discovery of an overseas route to India and beyond.

Equally strong was the pull exerted by gold. With the steady emergence of nation-states had come the growth of international banking, with many nations beginning to mint gold instead of silver coins. As Europe did not supply any goods to the East in exchange, Europe's reserves of the precious metal were diminishing faster than Hungary and the other continental suppliers could replenish them. It had long been known that the gold that was imported into Europe from Barbary originated in the regions south of the Sahara; but, however strong the economic motivation, Europeans could not have sailed to western and southern Africa until the fifteenth century for the simple reason that it was not technologically feasible.

The types of ships used in western Europe from Roman times until the fourteenth century were the oar-driven galley and the cog. While both were suitable for the calm seas of the Mediterranean, they were helpless in heavy seas and totally unsuitable for long ocean voyages. It was not until the first half of the fifteenth century that, borrowing from the superior technology of Arab sailors, the Portuguese and other western Europeans were able to devise ships capable of undertaking long-distance voyages. The caravel, which had both square sails and fore-and-aft-rigged triangular sails, was able to sail into the wind without the help of oars. This revolutionary development in ship design made possible the great voyages that characterized the fifteenth century.

Furthermore, it was in that same century that most of the problems of navigation were finally solved. By the fifteenth century an experienced navigator could find his latitude and had a good compass and charts to plot his course. It is not surprising that Portugal was the first to begin the systematic exploration of the coast of western and southern Africa, for it was technologically superior and politically more stable than any other European state.

The voyages, under the auspices of the Portuguese kings and Prince Henry the Navigator, began in 1417, and Portuguese explorers reached Madeira in 1418. Cape Bojador was rounded by Gil Eanes in 1434, and in 1441 Nuno Tristão and Antão Gonzalves reached Cape Blanco on the coast of present-day Mauritania; three years later Dinis Dias explored the mouth of the Senegal River and Cape Verde. The mouth of the Gambia River was reached in 1446, and the coast of Sierra Leone was explored in 1460, the year in which the prince died. After a break from 1462 to 1469, due mainly to the fact that King Affonso v of Portugal was engaged in

São Jorge da Mina—Saint George's Mine, as the Portuguese optimistically named their Gold Coast fort—was built in 1482 with labor and materials imported from home. As shown in this engraving, it was a sizable enterprise, housing a garrison of sixty Portuguese soldiers plus African reinforcements. A dozen or more ships, laden with gold and other riches, sailed from this harbor yearly, turning a handsome profit for their owners.
DE BRY, *Small Voyages*, 1604

a crusade against Morocco, the voyages were resumed. The coast of modern Ghana was reached in 1471, the Bights of Benin and Biafra between 1471 and 1474, and the mouth of the Congo in 1483; in December, 1487, Bartholomeu Dias rounded the Cape of Good Hope and sailed as far up the east coast as the Fish River in South Africa. After another pause of ten years an expedition under the command of Vasco da Gama retraced Dias' course, continuing onward along the East African coast as far as Malindi in modern-day Kenya, from which he set sail for India. Thus by the end of the fifteenth century the Portuguese had greatly expanded Europe's geographical knowledge of the world beyond its shores, though it is important to note that with the exception of the interior regions of Angola and Mozambique, this knowledge was to be confined to the coast of Africa until the second half of the eighteenth century.

It is quite evident from the accounts of the Portuguese explorers, particularly those of Alvise da Cadamosto, Pacheco Pereira, Ruy de Pina, and above all, Vasco da Gama, that they were astounded and elated by the complex, even sophisticated, character of the African civilizations they came across, by the extent of political development, and by the wealth and splendor of the courts. They particularly admired the city-states of the East African coast, where a lucrative trade with other Indian Ocean markets had long existed, and the gold and silver mines in the area of modern Ghana, Angola, and Mozambique.

Finally, accounts of the legendary Prester John and his Christian utopia, as related by Vasco da Gama, must also have filled the hearts of the Church fathers with hope. To quote the explorer: "We were told . . . that Prester John . . . held many cities along the coast, and that the inhabitants of those cities were great merchants and owned big ships. . . . This information, and many other things which we heard, rendered us so happy that we cried with joy, and prayed to God to grant us health, so that we might behold what we so much desired."

Up until 1518, a date that marks the end of the first period of European contact with Africa, the Portuguese were the only Europeans effectively operating in Africa south of the Sahara. Politically, the Portuguese showed interest in colonization, though this interest was confined exclusively to the Atlantic islands off the coast of Africa—the Canaries, Madeira, the Azores, the Cape Verde Islands, São Tomé, and Fernando Po—where they established sugar plantations and vineyards.

On the continent of Africa itself, however, the Portuguese did not attempt any extensive settlement, partly for reasons of climate, but mainly because of the opposition of the Africans themselves. Instead, they erected a number of forts and posts to protect themselves against the African kingdoms as well as other European nations and to serve as collecting centers and depots.

The first and the most impressive of these forts was São Jorge, built in 1482 at Elmina on the coast of modern Ghana; on the same coast were erected during this period forts at

Axim, Shama, and Accra. In 1487, farther north of the Senegal River, the Portuguese established an inland post at the caravan center of Wadan to tap the gold trade across the Sahara; it was abandoned in 1513. They also erected a fort (later named Freetown) on the coast of modern Sierra Leone and another at Gwato, the port of Benin, but soon abandoned both, the latter in 1516.

The very limited nature of the Portuguese colonizing activities in West Africa makes the title "Lord of Guinea," which their king John II assumed in 1486, a particularly empty one. They did not at this time rule any Africans, but engaged in commerce with them. During this first period they also acted as proselytizers. In spite of what some historians say, there is absolutely no doubt that during this first period the Portuguese took the work of converting Africans to the Christian religion very seriously indeed and with the full support and blessing of the pope of the Catholic Church.

The effort began in earnest as soon as the first West African islands were explored; indeed, there were some Franciscan monks aboard the Portuguese ships that anchored at Madeira in 1420 and Cape Verde in 1446. In 1441, when the first shipload of black people was brought to Portugal under circumstances to be discussed below, Prince Henry, as grand master of the Order of Christ, had them baptized. He also selected the most talented man among them to be trained as a missionary, but the African died before repatriation. Again, when in 1458 Henry received reports of the favorable disposition of the rulers of the Wolof kingdom toward Christianity, he promptly dispatched the abbot of Soto de Casa; unfortunately, we do not know the outcome of this mission. By the time of Henry's death in 1460 Christianity had been firmly established on the Portuguese-held islands. Interest in evangelical work continued, and in 1462 Father Alphonsus Bolano was appointed as the missionary, or prefect apostolic, for the whole of Guinea.

Subsequently, when the Portuguese built their castle at Elmina, they also dedicated a church to Saint Anthony; according to the Portuguese chronicler João de Barros, some Africans were converted. It is also recorded that when King John II of Portugal received news of the *oba* of Benin's request for missionaries, he was quick to comply. Not only did the *oba* welcome them and grant permission for a church to be built in Benin but he also "gave his own son and some of his noblemen, the greatest in his kingdom—so that they might become Christians."

Even more spectacular and surprisingly successful were the early Portuguese missionary activities that began in 1484 or 1485, a year or more after the first visit of Diogo Cão. During Cão's second visit the king of the Congo (Kongo), Nzinga Nkuwu, accepted the Christian religion and sent some of his people to Portugal to be educated. He also asked King John for assistance, to which the Portuguese king responded in 1490 by sending three ships with a group of priests, masons, carpenters, and other skilled artisans. This mission was successful, and Nzinga Nkuwu, most of the members of the Congolese royal family, and some of the king's subordinate chiefs were baptized. Nzinga Mvemba, one of the royal family to embrace the religion, was baptized as Affonso and succeeded to the Congo throne in 1507. During his long reign, from 1507 to 1543, Affonso remained a sincere Christian and did initially receive assistance from the Portuguese in his effort to convert his kingdom into a Christian and modernized state. He learned to read and write Portuguese, and he gave every encouragement to the missionaries in their work. He himself supervised the building of a cathedral and other state churches in his capital at Mbanzakongo and saw to the building of schools and churches throughout the kingdom. In 1513 two members of Affonso's family, who were educated in Portugal, headed a Portuguese embassy to the pope. One of them had been baptized with the name of Dom Henrique and was later consecrated as bishop of Utica in Tunis. He returned to the Congo in 1521 as vicar apostolic, and with the assistance of several Congolese who had been ordained priests, he continued the evangelical work in progress. Dom Affonso also established a new court modeled on that of Lisbon, bestowing Portuguese titles of marquis, duke, count, et cetera, on his courtiers and ministers. It looked as if Christianity was taking firm root in the Congo, and that all was set for the conversion of the Congo into the first Christian and Westernized kingdom in western Africa.

Besides their colonizing and missionary activities, the Portuguese also paid a great deal of attention to commerce. And in this field, too, their achievements were not inconsiderable. Portuguese traders literally followed the explorers. The first commodity to be shipped was dried fish, which was obtained from the valuable fishing grounds between Cape Bojador and Rio de Oro, and along various parts of the Guinea coast. Sugar produced from cane grown on the Cape Verde Islands as well as on São Tomé and Fernando Po was the next export, and the output steadily increased throughout the fifteenth century. The traffic in pepper from what became known as the Grain Coast as well as from

Portuguese soldier bearing a matchlock, as portrayed by a Benin artist.
TRUSTEES OF THE BRITISH MUSEUM

Benin was also sought. Ivory was another prized commodity obtained along the West African coast—especially in Ghana, the region of Little Popo, and the area that was to become known as the Ivory Coast. Other minor exports were wax, hides, amber, and indigo.

By the end of the fifteenth century, however, gold and slaves had superseded all other exports. The first quantity of Ghana coast gold was brought to Portugal by Gonzalves in 1441, and subsequently, so much gold was found in the area that the Portuguese dubbed it the Gold Coast. (This name was later applied to the whole of the British colony, and it was not changed to Ghana until March, 1957, when that colony won its independence from Britain.) By the sixteenth century the monetary value of this export was about one hundred thousand pounds per year (reckoned by the British historian J. D. Fage to be one tenth of the world's supply of gold at the time).

The first batch of slaves consisted of twelve men, who were captured in raids conducted by the explorers Gonzalves and Tristão and brought to Portugal in 1441. At the time of Prince Henry's death in 1460, five hundred slaves were being exported annually to Portugal and its Atlantic island colonies. By 1500 the slave trade had increased to about six hundred seventy a year, according to Philip Curtin's recent figures. These slaves were obtained mainly from the Senegambia region, the Slave Coast, and the area of the Congo. It was not until 1518 that the first shipment of slaves was sent directly to the New World, an event that can be seen as opening the second phase of Afro-European contact.

At this juncture the Portuguese Crown took complete control of the lucrative commercial contacts that its subjects had developed, making it a capital offense for any Portuguese to go to Guinea without a license. In exchange for gold, fish, sugar, pepper, ivory, and slaves, agents of the king exported to states of western Africa horses, silk items of clothing (imported mainly from the Barbary states and Benin), brassware, beads, handkerchiefs, and wine.

One other accidental but very useful and very lasting by-product of the first phase of the European contact with West Africa was the introduction of a number of food plants from the Americas and the East Indies. From the former the Portuguese brought maize, tobacco, cassava, the sweet potato, the pineapple, and the tomato. From the Indies were introduced oranges, lemons, limes, rice, and sugar cane. The cultivation of these food items, especially maize, the tomato, and rice, spread rapidly throughout western Africa, and there is no doubt that these food crops greatly accelerated the population growth in the coastal regions.

What was the reaction of the Africans to the Europeans during this first phase of their confrontation? Naturally, the Africans found the new arrivals, with their white skin, long hair, and funny-looking ships, profoundly strange. In the beginning trade between the two took the form of dumb barter, or silent trade. However, after a period of fear and distrust, mutual confidence developed, and the Africans began to meet the European ships, and the Europeans to go ashore. It would appear that genuine trouble began only when the Portuguese asked for permission from the African kings to erect permanent fortified posts. João de Barros has left us a detailed account of the negotiations that took place in 1482 between Diego de Azambuja and the representative of the king of Fetu for permission to build a castle on the coast of modern Ghana. Azambuja and his men attended the palaver "smartly dressed but with hidden arms in case of need," while the *caramansa*, the king of Fetu's representative, who was also the chief of that coastal village, turned up with his men in full battle array, "armed after their manner, some with spears and buckles, others with bows and quivers of arrows." After the initial exchange of courtesies, Diego de Azambuja asked for permission to build a storehouse where merchandise could be kept and in which the traders could be housed. He emphasized that that castle could be of advantage to the king "since that same house, and the power of the King [of Portugal] would be there to defend him." Azambuja also expressed the anxiousness of his ruler to convert the chief and his people to Christianity. To this request the *caramansa* replied in words that should be written in letters of gold. Responding courteously to the Portuguese envoy's remark, the *caramansa* is reported to have said:

> During that time nothing had astonished him as much as the captain's arrival; on the other ships he had seen ill-dressed and ragged men only, who were content with whatever he gave them in exchange for their goods. This was the aim of their voyages to those parts; all they asked was to be dealt with immediately, since they preferred to return to their country rather than to live abroad. But with him, the captain, it was otherwise. He came with many people, and with much more gold and jewels than there were in these parts where they were found, and moreover with a new request—that he might establish a residence in that land. From this he conjectured . . . that a man as important as he was surely came on great affairs, such as those of God, who made the day and night, about whom he had heard so much, and whose servant his King was. But considering the nature of so important a man as the captain, and also of the gallant people who accompanied him, he perceived that men of such quality must always require things on a lavish scale; and, because the spirit of such a noble people would scarcely endure the poverty and simplicity of that savage land of Guinea, quarrels and passions might arise between them all; he asked him, therefore, to be pleased to depart, and to allow the ships to come in future as they had come in the past, so that there would always be peace and concord between them. Friends who met occasionally remained better friends than if they were neighbors, on account of the nature of the human heart. . . . He did not speak thus to disobey the commands of the king of Portugal, but for the benefit of peace and the trade he desired to have with those who might come to that port; and also because, with peace between them, his people would be more ready to hear of God, whom he wished them to know. Therefore, since time would reveal these inconveniences, he asked the captain to avoid them by allowing the traffic to continue as it had before.

What words of tact, wisdom, and above all, prophecy! Had the Portuguese listened to them or, alternatively, had they not been allowed to settle or build forts, but carried on their trade from their ships, the course of the European-African confrontation would most probably have been different. However, the *caramansa* and his king allowed themselves to be persuaded by Azambuja to grant permission for the fort on condition that the Portuguese pay rent for the land on which it was built. And as the *caramansa* had predicted, time did reveal the "inconveniences." In fact, shortly after the completion of the fort, Diego de Azambuja burned down the village as punishment for "so many thefts and evil deeds" that the subjects of the *caramansa* were alleged to have committed. However, during this first phase such "reprisals" were very infrequent. The Portuguese by and large remained on good relations with the people of the west coast and treated the African kings as equals and allies rather than subordinates or vassals.

The reception given the first ambassadors from Benin and Wolof, and the early letters exchanged between the kings of Portugal and those of the Congo, bear eloquent testimony of the respect they were accorded. De Barros reported that Prince Bemoym of Wolof, who went to Portugal in 1488, was "treated in every respect as a Sovereign Lord, accustomed to our civilization and not as a barbarous Prince outside the law." In the letters exchanged between the king of the Congo and the king of Portugal between 1512 and 1540, the former referred to the latter as "Most high and powerful prince and king my brother," while the king of Portugal addressed his Congolese counterpart as "Most powerful and excellent king of Manikongo," and as his "friend and brother."

Finally, throughout this period, it was the Africans themselves who dictated the terms of trade, and without their cooperation nothing could be done. It is not surprising that in the 1590's Richard Eden would give the following advice to his English compatriots: "They are a very wary people in their bargaining, and will not lose one sparke of golde of any value. They use weights and measures, and are very circumspect in occupying the same. They that shall have to doe with them, must use them gently; for they will not trafique or bring in any wares, if they be evill used."

There is no doubt that the first phase of European contact with Africa was, from the point of view of the peoples of western Africa and the Congo, both beneficial and promising. Although the trade in slaves had begun, it was relatively small in volume, for the demand was still confined to São Tomé, the Atlantic islands, and the Iberian Peninsula, where it would soon have reached a saturation point. The new food crops that were introduced caught on very rapidly, and two of them, grain and rice, soon became the principal diet of most coastal peoples. The seeds of Christianity were also being sown, and there was every indication that Western education and techniques would soon be firmly established in the Congo and possibly on the coast of Ghana, whence they would spread to other parts of the continent. And throughout, there was an attitude of mutual respect. The first period must have ended, then, on a note of great hope.

Meanwhile, Portuguese policies and activities in Central, South, and East Africa during the first period were quite different from those they pursued in West Africa and the Congo. From the beginning the Portuguese officially ignored the area of western Africa that is modern Angola, though both the Congo kings and the Portuguese living in São Tomé obtained some of their slaves from there. It was not until 1520 that the first official expedition was dispatched to Angola in search of souls and silver. The Portuguese also ignored southern Africa. The reports of the explorers made it clear that there were no prospects there for trade in minerals, spices, and ivory, the commodities then of primary interest to the Portuguese. In fact, it was not until after 1650 that those areas were of any strategic interest to either Portugal or the rest of Europe.

However, along the east coast of central Africa, precisely for strategic considerations—wresting control of the Indian Ocean trade from the Arabs and their Swahili allies—and also because of the great hopes raised by stories of the fabulous gold and silver mines in the African hinterland, the Portuguese Crown did commence activities. As early as 1502 Vasco da Gama returned to East Africa, this time as an invader, compelling the ruler of Kilwa to pay tribute to the Portuguese Crown. He was followed in 1503 by Ruy Ravasco, who sailed along the coast, pillaging and raiding and finally besieging Zanzibar.

Most of the well-established and wealthy states in the region successfully resisted these early attacks, but in 1505 a carefully prepared expedition under the command of Francisco de Almeida was dispatched to subdue the entire East African and Mozambique coast. Sofala yielded after little resistance, and a fort was erected there. Kilwa and Mombasa resisted, but both were captured; a fort was built at Kilwa. Only Malindi, in the north, was friendly to the invaders, and it became one of the two administrative centers from which Portugal controlled the entire coast of Mozambique and East Africa. The other center was the island town of Mozambique in the south, where in 1507 the Portuguese built a fort, a hospital, and administrative buildings. It soon replaced Sofala as the main depot for the Zambezi region and as a revictualing and refitting center for ships bound for India, and the fort at Sofala was abandoned in 1512.

However, apart from isolated journeys, mainly by Antonio Fernandez, the interior parts of the whole of Africa and even some of the coastal areas had still not directly felt the presence of the Europeans. This and every other aspect of the Afro-European confrontation were to undergo revolutionary changes during the second phase from 1518 to 1700, and these changes were by and large to be disastrous to the Africans.

The first and probably the most conspicuous of these changes was the great increase in the number of European nations operating in Africa. The English were the first to encroach on the thitherto exclusive Portuguese preserve. The first English trading voyage to Guinea during this period was undertaken by William Hawkins in 1530. He was followed by Thomas Wyndham in 1553, who traded in Benin late in 1554, and by William Towerson, who made three voyages to West Africa between 1555 and 1557. It is important to note that all these early English traders did not deal in slaves, but in gold, ivory, camwood, wax, and pepper. It was not until 1562 that, with the full support and blessing of the queen of England, John Hawkins (the son of William Hawkins) set off on the first English slave-trading voyage. He made two more voyages: in 1564 and in 1567, selling his captives to planters in the Caribbean.

The French also entered the Guinea trade in 1530, and within a few years their trading and piratic activities had extended as far as the Bight of Benin. It was the Dutch who were the first to successfully challenge the Portuguese monopoly. Entering the Guinea trade for the first time in 1593, soon after their struggle for independence, the Dutch launched systematic attacks on the Portuguese, both in Africa and in the Indian Ocean. Although their attack on Mozambique in 1607 was unsuccessful, by 1610 they had completely destroyed Portuguese naval power in the Indian Ocean. From there they turned their attention to the west

A Dutch legation, sent in 1642 to conclude an alliance with the king of the Congo, discovers that others have preceded it. Here the Congolese Alvaro II, *in European boots and with a Christian gold cross at his elbow, receives the disappointed party beneath an imported chandelier.*
DOPPER, *Description de l'Afrique*, 1686

coast of Africa. There they soon gained a footing on the coveted golden coast of Ghana. They built a fort at Mouri in 1612, and five years later they also built two forts on Gorée island and established a trading post on the opposite mainland at Rufisque. Finally, between 1637 and 1642, they captured the Portuguese strongholds of Elmina and Axim in Ghana as well as São Tomé and the port of Angola, and they even took Brazil. Although the Portuguese were able to reconquer Angola, São Tomé, and Brazil between 1648 and 1654, they never regained their position on the coast of Ghana. Likewise, the Danes, Swedes, and the Brandenburgers, all focused their attention on coastal Ghana.

The appearance of so many European nations on the African coast touched off a cutthroat rivalry among them. The Dutch, having replaced the Portuguese in the interior regions of Ghana and the Gambia, lost to the English and the French. They then concentrated on the coast of Ghana and on South Africa, which, as will be seen presently, they occupied in 1652. Soon after, the Swedes were eliminated altogether from Africa's shores. It was partly because of this rivalry and partly because of the political divisions on the coast of Africa, and especially that of Ghana, that a great number of European-manned forts and castles were built on the west coast of Africa.

On the east coast the position of the Portuguese was first challenged from the hinterland when the Zimba invaders, a Central Bantu people, captured Kilwa in 1587 and attacked Mombasa. In the following century the Portuguese also had to face seaborne challenges from the Dutch, the Turks, and the Arabs of Oman on the Arabian Peninsula. At the invitation of the indigenous peoples of the coast, the Oman Arabs invaded Portuguese enclaves in 1652, 1660, 1667, and 1679, and by 1700 had succeeded in expelling them from the area of the East African coast north of the Ruvuma River.

Despite the intensity with which grabs for trade hegemony were purused, no European showed any interest in inland exploration. Traders remained blatantly ignorant of these regions, as dramatically illustrated by the fact that they did not know the direction of the flow of the Niger River until the 1790's or of the location of its mouth until 1830. Scientific curiosity, which had been one of the motives behind Prince Henry and his countrymen, completely lost its thrust during the second period of expansion. Nor did the Europeans show any interest in colonization—not the British, nor the Dutch, nor the Danes, nor the Brandenburgers. Only the French attempted to establish a colony at the mouth of the Senegal River in 1687, but this failed mainly because of the opposition of the king of Cayor. Thus the record of the Europeans in the field of colonization in the second period was nil.

The attempts to introduce Christianity, Western education, and Western technology were also gradually abandoned. The Portuguese did continue their missionary efforts in the sixteenth century, but very haphazardly and halfheartedly. They gave up all interest in missionary work in Benin after 1538. When evangelical activities were resumed in 1657 by the Capuchin Order, they were under the auspices of the *Sacra Congregazione di Propaganda Fide*, founded by the papacy; but the missionaries were soon expelled from Benin for interfering with religious festivals involving human sacrifice. Although the Capuchins sent missions to Benin and Warri in 1663, 1684, 1687, 1691, and 1695, no success attended their efforts, and in 1713 they, too, finally abandoned the attempt.

Christianization was impressed with a similar lack of fervor in the Congo. Whereas both the Portuguese and Affonso, the king of the Congo, had initially taken the work of converting the kingdom into a Westernized Christian state very seriously, the Portuguese seem later to lose interest in this aspect of their activities. For instance, in 1526 Affonso, in a very moving and sincere letter, appealed for "two physicians and two apothecaries and one surgeon, so that they may come with their drug-stores and all the necessary things to stay in our kingdoms." In the same year he wrote to the king, asking him to send neither "merchants nor wares," only "priests and people to teach in schools, and no other goods but wine and flour for the holy sacrament." The Portuguese paid no heed. In 1540 missionary work was resumed with the arrival of three Jesuit priests and a teacher. About two thousand people were baptized within the first four months, three churches were built at Mbanzakongo, which was now renamed São Salvador, and schools were also established. But these successes were short-lived. In 1552, mainly because of the opposition of the Manikongo people and the resident Portuguese community, but partly because even some of the priests took to slave trading, the mission abandoned the Congo. A second mission followed in 1553, but that also failed for the same reason and withdrew in 1555. It would appear that no serious efforts were made again in this field, and by 1700 there was hardly a trace of western education or Christian life in the Congo, excepting the deserted city of São Salvador with its twelve ruined churches.

The English, the Dutch, and the French also made some efforts in the missionary and educational fields, but these initiatives were sporadic, evanescent, and very unproductive. For instance, chaplains who were supposed to administer to the whites as well as the blacks were attached to Dutch stations on the west coast. In 1634 the Dutch actually opened a school for the education of African children at Mouri, but it was soon abandoned. In 1644 they also mooted the idea of establishing a school at the port of Accra, but the scheme was never carried out. Nothing more was heard of Dutch schooling throughout the second half of the century. In 1694 an English mission set up a school at Ghana's Cape Coast, but it was abandoned two years later when its only teacher died. In 1705 a similar attempt failed. The French also made some efforts in the seventeenth century. In 1637 they sent five Capuchins to Assini, another West African port. Subsequently, two young men of the place, Lewis Aniaba (Hannibal) and a man named Roanga, were selected for further training and sent to France in 1687 to be educated. We do not know what happened to Roanga, but Aniaba returned home in 1701 and, upon his arrival, is reported to have done away with his French clothes, his foreign manners, and his Christian faith. The Capuchins, who like the Jesuits lacked the financial resources and manpower to sustain their efforts and were doubtless ill-adjusted to the coastal climate, soon withdrew from Assini, and with this vanished all traces of missionary activities in that area. Although Christianity was flourishing on the Atlantic islands and São Tomé, it had gained no permanent footing anywhere on the mainland.

However, in spite of the many setbacks in the fields of science, missionary work, colonization, and exploration, in this second phase of Afro-European contact (between 1518 and 1700) the Europeans not only stayed on in West Africa but increased their numbers. This was due to one main activity that occupied their attention: trade. Unfortunately for Africa, in this activity they found increasing profit. Indeed, the goods traded became vital to the growing capitalist and industrial economy of western Europe, and the plantation economy of the New World.

As has previously been pointed out, during the first four or even five decades of this second phase of expansion the principal interest of all the European nations involved was in articles such as pepper, gum, wax, ivory, and above all, gold. Had trade been confined to these natural products, there is absolutely no doubt that all would have been well; but in the coastal areas of the Congo, and in areas included in the modern states of Nigeria, Dahomey, Togo, Ghana,

São Salvador, a Portuguese post on Angola's Luege River, was an early collecting point for goods coming from the Congolese interior.
AMERICAN HERITAGE COLLECTION

the Gambia, and Senegal, human beings constituted the main export commodity by the end of the sixteenth century. From the end of the seventeenth century to the first four decades of the nineteenth century, the slave trade would completely eclipse all other trade on the entire coast of West Africa and the Congo.

Although the overseas slave trade began as early as 1441, it still had not become the principal objective of the Portuguese even a hundred years later. It was the exploration of the Americas and the West Indies between 1492 and 1504, and the subsequent commencement of mining activities and the establishment of tobacco and sugar plantations there, that brought the slave trade to its full growth. The Europeans, confronted with an acute labor shortage in their attempts to exploit the natural resources of the New World, at first tried to use Indians to work the mines and plantations, but they proved unequal to the task. As one Spaniard reported in 1518: "When Hispaniola [modern Haiti and the Dominican Republic] was discovered, it contained 1,130,000 Indians. Today, their number does not exceed 11,000. And judging by what has happened, there will be none left in three or four years' time unless some remedy is applied." The remedy was indeed found in Africa, and the first cargo of black slaves was transported from Spain to the Americas in 1501; the second shipment of seventeen slaves followed in 1505. In 1510 the Spanish Crown legalized the sale of white as well as black slaves in the New World. In 1515 the first slave-grown sugar from the Caribbean entered Spain. It was, however, not until 1518 that the first cargo of slaves was shipped directly to the Americas from the west coast of Africa in a Spanish ship. The Portuguese joined in November, 1532, when the *Santo Antonio* transported 201 slaves from the island of São Tomé to Santo Domingo and San Juan. In 1562 the English, represented by John Hawkins, also sent their first cargo of slaves directly to the West Indies. In 1619 a Dutch frigate landed the first twenty Negro slaves on the mainland of North America at Jamestown in Virginia. The Atlantic slave trade had well and truly been inaugurated.

According to Philip Curtin's calculations, the number of slaves that landed in the New World increased from 125,000 between 1501 and 1600 to 1,280,000 between 1601 and 1700 (greatly accelerated in the last quarter of that century by the stepped-up demand for slaves on the North American mainland), and to 6,265,000 between 1701 and 1810. Assuming that about sixteen per cent of them died during

African slaves work a Barbados refinery, where sugar cane is turned into sugar, molasses, and rum for the trans-Atlantic triangular trade.
DUTERTRE, *Histoire Generale des Antilles*, 1667

the "middle passage," or sea voyage, Curtin reckons that a total of 11,300,000 slaves were exported from Africa to the New World before slavery ended. (Earlier writers such as W. E. B. Du Bois, Robert R. Kucynski, Roland Oliver, J. D. Fage, and Robert Rotberg have offered estimates of as many as fifteen million forcibly removed from Africa.)

Treated with extreme brutality and inhumanity, all these slaves were used in the New World mainly for the extraction of minerals such as silver and copper and for the raising of sugar, cotton, tobacco, and indigo. It was the ready supply of these commodities that, as Eric Williams has shown in his brilliant study *Capitalism and Slavery*, gave birth to the textile, distilling, sugar-refining, metallurgical, and indirectly, the shipbuilding industries—enterprises on which the economies of the countries of western Europe so heavily depended. And it was some of the simple products of these industries that were exchanged at enormous profits in Africa for the slaves who were sold in the New World for even greater profits. With the rise of the Atlantic slave trade then, the European-African contact developed into a wider European-African-American contact, and as the sole producers of the manufactured goods involved, as the sole sellers of the slaves in the New World, and as owners of the plantations in the New World, the European nations were obviously the greatest beneficiaries. It is not surprising therefore that all of Europe's leading traders and financiers had interests in one or more sides of the triangle. As the great nineteenth-century British historian L. B. Namier has concluded: "There were comparatively few big merchants in Great Britain in 1761, who in one connection or another, did not trade with the West Indies, and a considerable number of the gentry families had interests in the Sugar Islands, just as vast numbers of Englishmen now hold shares in Asiatic rubber or tea plantations or oil fields." And this was also true of France and Holland; as the French historian G. Gaston-Martin has written: "The founding of industries, private fortunes, public opulence, the rebuilding of towns, the social glories of a new class: great merchants eager for public office that should reflect their economic importance and impatient to be rid of what they called, with careless exaggeration, 'the shame of servitude'; such were the sum of the essential consequences for eighteenth-century France of the African slave trade."

What was the role of the African in all these activities? In

Under the stern direction of their slave trader, a gang of newly arrived captives is lined up for review before a prospective purchaser.
LIBRARY OF CONGRESS

West Africa and to some extent in the Congo, during this period of expansion as in the former period, the Africans themselves were responsible for the production and the supply of all the commodities as well as the slaves involved in the trade. As the Dutch merchant William Bosman correctly pointed out in a letter to his uncle in 1701: "There is no small number of Men in Europe who believe that the Gold Mines are in our Power; that we, like the Spaniards in the West-Indies, have no more to do but to work them by our Slaves. Though you perfectly know we have no manner of access to these Treasures. . . ." Indeed, attempts made by the Dutch themselves in the 1650's and 1690's to prospect for gold along the Ankolora River and in Kommenda in modern Ghana were met with stout local resistance and had to be abandoned.

In the case of the slaves, early forays made by the Portuguese were soon abandoned as a method of acquisition. From about 1500 onward, apart from a few kidnaping attempts made by unscrupulous captains or an occasional adventurer like John Hawkins, it was the Africans themselves who delivered slaves to the Europeans for sale. These slaves were obtained in four principal ways: criminals sold as punishment by their rulers; domestic slaves who were resold; persons obtained from raids upon neighboring states; and prisoners of full-scale wars. It is evident from a recent study of some one hundred seventy-nine freed slaves in Freetown, Sierra Leone, that the principal sources of the slave trade were raids and wars. Similarly, most of the slaves from Ghana, Ouidah, Yorubaland, and Benin were products of war. However, some coastal areas were also ravaged by slave raiders. Likewise in the Congo, the slaves were obtained either as a result of wars or were brought from the inland regions by the *pombeiros*, Afro-Portuguese subtraders who traveled "a hundred and fifty or two hundred leagues up the country to buy or raid for slaves." But throughout West Africa and the Congo it was the ruling aristocracy—the kings and their nobles—who were ultimately responsible for supplying these slaves, for they waged the wars, organized the raids, tried the criminals and debtors, and passed the judgments. The French factor Jean Barbot was correct when he wrote that "the trade in slaves is the business of kings, rich men, and prime merchants."

Why then did African rulers cooperate with the Europeans in this hideous traffic? Before answering this question, it must be pointed out first that some of these rulers did try to stop the slave trade when they realized its disastrous effects. A typical example was Affonso, the king of the Congo. In one of his letters to the king of Portugal in 1526 he complained bitterly:

> . . . we cannot reckon how great the damage is, since the mentioned merchants are taking everyday our natives, sons of the land and the sons of our noblemen and vassals and our relatives, because the thieves and men of bad conscience grab them wishing to have the things and wares of this Kingdom which they are ambitious of; they grab them and get them sold; and so great, Sir, is the corruption and licentiousness that our country is being completely depopulated, and Your Highness should not agree with this or accept it as in Your service. . . . It is our will that in these kingdoms there should not be any trade of slaves nor outlet for them . . .

But no heed was paid to his appeal, and the trade received increasing support from subsequent Congolese kings and the Portuguese authorities. As the Nigerian historian I. A. Akinjogbin has recently shown, another unsuccessful attempt to put a stop to the trade was made by the kings of Dahomey, who extended their sway from the inland town of Abomey to the coast and conquered Ouidah and Ardra. But they also failed and were compelled to join a devil they could not beat.

Alan Ryder, an authority on Benin's history, has also emphasized the *oba*'s "general indifference to the demands and opportunities of the European slave trade" in the early decades of the sixteenth century. Indeed, until the close of the seventeenth century the kings of Benin enforced a total embargo on the export of male slaves.

As European commerce had become increasingly limited to the acquisition of slaves, and as most of the African kings and the members of the aristocracy had by then become addicted to the European goods, especially to spirits, tobacco, guns, and gunpowder, they had no choice but to sell their fellow men to obtain them. From about the middle of the seventeenth century in most areas of West Africa and the Congo the European traders demanded only slaves. C. B. Wadström, who toured many parts of western Africa in the 1780's and made a special study of the slave trade, told England's Privy Council Committee of 1789 that "the Kings of Africa . . . incited by the merchandise shown them, which consists principally of strong liquors, give orders to their military to attack their own villages in the night. . . ." James Watt, who visited Timbo in Sierra Leone around the same time, reported that he was told by the *almani*'s deputy "with a shocking degree of openness, that the sole object of their wars was to produce slaves, as they could not obtain European goods without slaves, and they could not get slaves without fighting for them."

Cooperation in this shameful business must also, in this author's opinion, have been made easier by the African rulers' ignorance regarding the treatment of slaves on the other side of the Atlantic. Slavery and the slave trade were not European introductions to Africa. Both had existed from time immemorial in many areas in Africa, but a slave in any African society was treated as a human being who could own property, marry, and have children. He lived and was treated as a full member of the household, and very often occupied offices of responsibility. Slavery was a relatively humane institution in Africa and in the Muslim world. It was this humane institution that the African suppliers of slaves must have assumed they were dealing with in the New World. It is this author's feeling that had the kings and chiefs been aware of the enormity of the difference in the status of a slave in their own society and in the society of the New World, they probably would have put up greater and more sustained resistance.

Besides controlling the production and supply of the commodities, the Africans of the coast of West Africa also had a decisive say in the conduct of that trade. Without the permission of the rulers, no European nation could build any fort or trading post, and land rental had to be paid in all cases. In some areas such as Ouidah, Ardra, and later Dahomey, the kings even specified the material that was to be used in the construction of the forts. If the rent was not paid, trade could be stopped. In 1723 the London officials of the Royal African Company wrote to the agent in Sierra Leone: "We are sorry to find there are misunderstandings between you and the Africans. We find it arose from the not paying them the small rent due to them." Furthermore, the Europeans had to pay duties on all imports or give presents before they were allowed to trade. In Ouidah, as Bosman reported: "The first business of one of our Factors . . . is to satisfie the Customs of the King and the great Men, which amount to about 100 Pounds in Guinea value, as the Goods must yield there. After which we have free License to Trade, which is published throughout the whole Land by the Cryer." As the kings and chiefs were traders themselves in many areas, their products and slaves had to be bought first before those of their subjects. Bosman added that "before we can deal with any Person, we are obliged to buy the King's whole stock of Slaves at a set price; which is commonly one third or one fourth higher than ordinary: After which we obtain free leave to deal with all his Subjects of what Rank soever." This was true also in Benin and Bonny. Lastly, the chiefs and leading merchants had a decisive say in fixing the basis of exchange and the prices of commodities, especially of slaves, and this was done after a series of palavers that often dragged on for days, much to the disgust and discomfort of the European traders. Some Africans even set up their own trading concerns and came to gain almost monopolistic control over the trade in their own towns or regions. Typical examples of such merchant-princes of the seventeenth century were John Claesen and John Hennequa of Fetu, John Cabes of Kommenda, John Currantee of Anomabu, and John Konny of Ahanta, all in modern Ghana.

With a view to gaining control of trade, the Europeans encouraged Africans to live around the forts and castles they built. The Europeans furthermore sought treaties giving them exclusive trading rights. However, though many such treaties were exacted, especially by the Dutch and the English, the Africans paid absolutely no heed to their terms and throughout traded with everyone as they chose. Finally, the Europeans resorted to the practice of interfering in local politics, especially in succession disputes, with a view to putting their own nominees on the throne and in other influential positions. The English and the Dutch constantly did this in Kommenda, Aguafo, and Fetu; the Dutch, the French, and the English in Ardra and Ouidah; and the Portuguese in the Congo and Angola. But these methods proved ineffective. Hence, during the second period as in the first, the Africans on the west coast, and to some extent in the Congo, maintained their predominant position and rigidly controlled the trading activities of the Europeans while their states enjoyed complete autonomy.

In Angola, Mozambique, and South Africa, however, the situation was different. Although the people of the Congo and the Portuguese settlers on São Tomé had been unofficially trading for slaves in the region now called Angola in the late fifteenth and the beginning of the sixteenth centuries, it was not until 1520 that the Portuguese dispatched the first official trading mission there. Its leader, Balthasar de Castro, met with failure. Arriving in the kingdom of Ndongo, then a vassal state of the kingdom of the Congo, he was imprisoned by the ruling *ngola*, or king, the title from which the Portuguese formulated the name Angola. Nothing more was done to formalize relations for another forty years, though trade between São Tomé and the Angola region continued, and it was with the assistance of some of these Portuguese traders that the *ngola* was able to defeat a punitive expedition sent against him by the king of Congo in 1556 and to declare himself independent. Four years later the *ngola* appealed for a Portuguese political, religious, and commercial mission, obviously to prove that he was the equal of his former Congo overlord. Under strong pressure from the Jesuits, who were anxious to start missionary work in that region, the Portuguese Crown dispatched Paulo Dias de Novais and four missionaries; they were to convert the king and his people to Christianity. The 1560 mission was a total failure. They arrived to find that the *ngola* who had issued the invitation was dead, and his successor promptly imprisoned Dias de Novais and one of his Jesuit companions, Father Gouveia. Novais was released five years later, but Gouveia was kept prisoner until his death in 1575. Partly because of the continued imprisonment of the missionary and partly because of the hope of exploiting the silver and copper mines rumored to be in existence in the interior, in 1571 the king of Portugal granted Paulo Dias de Novais a charter for the conquest of Angola and its conversion into a Christian Portuguese colony.

The expedition landed in 1575, and the conquest of Angola and the search for the mines began in 1579. In the following one hundred years and through intermittent wars the Portuguese completed the conquest of Ndongo, or Angola, founded the coastal towns of São Paulo de Luanda and Benguela in 1576 and 1617 respectively, and established a number of fortresses and towns inland. An administrative machinery was also established. The colony was divided into military districts, or *presidios*, ruled by captains who were responsible to the governor of the colony. Each *presidio* was made up of a number of chiefdoms under traditional rulers, on whom the administration imposed a head tax, or *Peca da India*, paid in slaves.

Jesuit missionaries operated in Angola from the time of their first appearance with the 1560 mission. But their number was insignificant, and some of the few soon took on so much trading and political activities that very few converts were won. As late as 1694, according to James Duffy, there were only thirty-six priests actively operating in the whole of the interior, and most of the churches and schools had by then fallen into ruins.

The Portuguese also paid some attention initially to locating the reported silver and copper mines of Angola. In 1604, however, Cambambe, the reputed center of silver mining, was finally reached by Manuel Cerveira Pereira, and a blockhouse was built there. However, no fabulous or even productive mines were found, and with this evaporated all the earlier hopes of mineral wealth. Attention thenceforth was focused essentially on the trade in human beings. According to David Birmingham, by the middle of the seventeenth century as many as ten thousand slaves were being exported annually from Angola, mainly to Brazil.

And what was the reaction of the Africans to all this? Probably nowhere in Africa has an African people put up as stout, spirited, and sustained a resistance to European penetration as in the region of Angola. The opposition existed from the very first Portuguese mission of 1520, when the brave king arrested and imprisoned its leader. Nor did a second mission fare better, and when the Portuguese, bent on conquest, began their invasion in 1579, the *ngola* killed all the thirty or forty European traders in his town and confiscated their goods. He then raised an army and routed a huge force estimated at sixty thousand Congolese and fifty European officers sent to assist Dias. So successful was this resistance that by the time of Dias' death in 1589, he had been able to advance only seventy miles up the Cuanza River. His successors continued the wars, and though they captured hundreds of slaves, by 1600 they had not advanced farther inland.

Only when Ngola Mbandi held the throne from 1617 to 1624 did Angola's will appear to fail, and so the Portuguese were able to conquer the kingdom. The invaders devastated whole areas and even burned the capital city of the kingdom. On his death in 1624, however, Ngola Mbandi was succeeded by his sister Nzinga Mbandi, a woman of extraordinary tact and courage. She was born in 1580 and had been baptized in 1620 or 1621 and given the ridiculous name of Dona Ana de Souza. However, despite her attachments to Portugal, no sooner was she on the throne than she resumed the war against the Portuguese, and she continued fighting till 1636. When she failed to regain Ndongo in this protracted war, Queen Nzinga moved northeastward and conquered the state of Matamba, which she soon developed into a very strong trading kingdom. As soon as the Dutch conquered Luanda in 1641, Queen Nzinga established an alliance with them, and it was a joint force of the queen and the Dutch that attacked and took the last stronghold of the Portuguese at Massangano between 1647 and 1648. But just before the final onslaught a powerful Portuguese fleet under the command of Salvador Correia de Sa entered Luanda and expelled the Dutch, reconquered the Mbundu of Angola, and imposed a humiliating treaty on the Congo, which had also joined the anti-Portuguese coalition, Queen Nzinga, however, continued her resistance from her inland headquarters. Anxious to resume the trade, especially in slaves to meet the inexhaustible demand from Brazil and the Spanish colonies, the Portuguese began peace negotiations with the queen. Under the terms of the resulting treaty of friendship between the two in 1656, the Portuguese were compelled to recognize the independence of Matamba, and commercial and friendly relations are said to have been maintained until her death in 1663.

This treaty was not the end of resistance to the Portuguese. In Ndongo itself the new dynasty established by the Portuguese after the withdrawal of Queen Nzinga and her royal household began to kick against the Portuguese. In 1671 the reigning *ngola* actually declared war on the Portuguese in a bid to re-establish Ndongo as a truly independent state. The Portuguese, however, moved in a strong army under Louis Lopes de Sequeira that defeated and killed the dissident ruler. They followed this up by establishing a fort on the site of the royal capital.

Farther inland the successors of Queen Nzinga also revived the struggle against the Portuguese in the 1670's, and in 1680 they attacked and took over the kingdom of Kasanje, an ally of the Portuguese to the east. Once more the Portuguese sent Louis Lopes de Sequeira against them. His first attack was repulsed by Kanini, the king of Matamba, and De Sequeira was killed; only the death of Kanini soon afterward prevented the Africans from following up this victory. Kanini's successor, another queen, reopened peace talks; in her anxiety to resume trade with the Portuguese she signed another, more costly treaty in 1683. In this treaty it was agreed that all slaves that had sought refuge from Portuguese territory were to be sent back, and that the kingdom of Matamba was to pay a war indemnity and was not to trade with any other nation but Portugal.

It is clear then that right from the beginning of the second period almost to its very end the Mbundu people of Angola, led by their rulers, put up stiff and spirited resistance to the Portuguese. Despite the fact that they had lost their Ndongo homeland to the Portuguese, their old dynasty continued to survive under the arrangement, enjoying an antonomous existence in Matamba that would last until the nineteenth century.

Between 1518 and 1700, in the region of Mozambique on the other side of the continent, the same attempts at penetration inland and colonization characterized Portuguese activities. Their drive began in 1530, when they established within the empire of the Shona a trading post, or market, at Sena, about a hundred miles up the Zambezi,

Coastal South Africa's wealth of subtropical flora and fauna was a marvel to visiting Europeans. In this engraving a British amateur naturalist records some of the sights of his travels there in 1746, including a variety of palms, a hyena, tiger, crocodile, and elephant.
CHURCHILL, *Collection of Voyages*, 1746

and a second market at Tete, another one hundred fifty miles farther upriver. But the Portuguese did not make any move to colonize or conquer the reputed gold mines of the interior until 1569, when a huge and well-equipped expedition under the command of Francesco Barreto was sent out. This expedition pushed on to Sena in 1571, and with the approval of the *monomotapa*, as the king of the Shona was known, Barreto launched a series of attacks on one of its rebellious vassal chiefs. (Monomotapa came to be applied to the Shona kingdom as well as its capital.) These attacks failed, and Barreto had to retreat to Sena, where he died shortly thereafter. His successor, Vasco Fernandes Homem, and a small party pushed on to the gold mines, but found them very disappointing. Because of Homem's discouraging report, coupled with the high rate of mortality, no government expeditions were sent inland again until the first decade of the seventeenth century.

However, it would appear that during the second half of the sixteenth century independent Portuguese traders and adventurers pushed inland in search of gold and trade, and by 1600 a number of them had acquired large land and mining concessions from the local chiefs. After the turn of the century the *monomotapa*, who was facing a series of revolts, again invited the Portuguese government to render aid. In return he made generous concessions of land, and trading and mining rights. In 1629, however, the new *monomotapa*,

Kapararidze, embarked on a policy of driving out all the Portuguese from his empire, and by 1630 only five agents were surviving in the Shona territory and only seven in Manicoland to the south. In retaliation, the Portuguese dispatched a huge army under the command of Diogo da Meneses. This army inflicted a decisive defeat on Kapararidze, who was then executed. A new king, reportedly a Christian, was appointed by the Portuguese, and he was forced to sign a humiliating treaty with them on May 24, 1629. Under its terms the *monomotapa* was to consider himself a vassal of the Portuguese; he was to "make his lands free to the Portuguese" and was to allow complete freedom to Portuguese traders, miners, and missionaries; he was to expel the Arabs, and within a year he was expected to recognize a Portuguese envoy as "Captain of the Gates" at Masapa, the principal Shona market. From then on, more and more Portuguese and Indians living on the coast moved inland to acquire estates, or *prazos*. Many trading posts were also established throughout the gold-bearing regions of Mashonaland. The most important of these were Luanze, Ongoe, Dambarare, and the aforementioned Masapa.

By the 1650's it has been estimated that at Tete there were about forty Portuguese residents and about six hundred Christian Africans and half-castes living in the district. The power of the Portuguese representatives at Masapa had also grown with the years, as is evident from the following account of João Dos Santos, who visited that region at the beginning of the seventeenth century: "The Captain at Masapa has jurisdiction . . . over all the Kaffirs who come to Masapa, and those who live on his lands or within his borders. He has power to give verbal sentence in all cases, and can even comdemn the guilty to be hanged. This authority has been given him by Monomotapa. He serves as agent in all matters between the Portuguese and Monomotapa . . . [and receives] all the duties paid to him by the merchant, Christian or Arab, which are one piece of cloth for every twenty brought into these lands to be sold."

It would appear then that by the middle of the seventeenth century the Portuguese had succeeded in establishing their control over the hinterland of Sofala and Mozambique and the territory of the *monomotapa*. They governed the areas directly under their control through the *prazo* system. The colony was made up of *prazos*, or estates, owned by individual Portuguese. Each *prazo*-holder was ultimately responsible for the people, or *colonos* (freemen), living within his district; but local rule was maintained by headmen, or chiefs, known as *fumos*. The *prazo*-holder appointed and dismissed the *fumos*, dispensed justice, collected tribute, and could use his *colonos* as guides, carriers, and even soldiers. The armed might of each *prazo*-holder was based on a private force of his own, consisting usually of slaves. The *prazo* system was not abolished until 1832.

In Mozambique the primary interest of the Portuguese was not in slaves, but in gold and ivory. However, as A. J. Willis has pointed out, "it is doubtful whether the government gained more from the gold trade than sufficed to balance the expenditure on forts and warehouses and on official salaries at Sofala and elsewhere." Some missionary efforts were also made in Mozambique in the sixteenth and seventeenth centuries, especially by the Dominican friars; but as late as 1700, as in other parts of mainland Africa, there was hardly a trace of Christian influence anywhere among the Africans, and it can be said that the Portuguese efforts in Mozambique were almost a total failure.

As was the case in Angola, the rulers and people of the eastern interior did not remain indifferent to the encroachment of the Portuguese. The Shona kings of the sixteenth and early seventeenth centuries welcomed them because they needed their help to suppress the numerous revolts with which they were confronted. But as soon as they felt secure, they took up arms against the Portuguese. A trader who visited the interior in 1634 reported that he found the position of the Europeans rather insecure. "The Portuguese," he noted, "have many forts in the empire of Monomotapa. . . . They have to depend chiefly on their flintlocks, which each person keeps ready; for in Kaffir country where trading goes on, rebellions often break out, and then each one's best defense is his gun. . . . The power of the natives is vastly greater than that of the Portuguese in this country." He also noticed the relatively strong position of the Arabs. "Many Arabs," he wrote, "dwell in the empire of Monomotapa. They are opposed to us always and everywhere." As the years rolled on, and as the Portuguese *prazo*-holders grew more arrogant and oppressive, the *monomotapas* and their subjects became more restive. In their helplessness the *monomotapas* appealed to the Changamire rulers of the Rozwi kingdom for help against the Portuguese. In 1693 the Changamire attacked the Portuguese fair at Dambarare and wiped out its residents. Then, after seizing the other posts, they turned against the ruling *monomotapa* and overthrew his kingdom. Thus by 1700 the Portuguese were confined to the Zambezi valley and the immediate hinterland of the coastal areas, the area more or less of modern Mozambique. Politically, economically, and religiously, their adventure in east Central Africa had brought no gains.

On the southern tip of Africa the Portuguese had shown

Dutch flags fly over Commander Simon van der Stel's camp in Namaqualand, a region of the Cape Colony where his Boer party had trekked in search of copper in 1685. *Their efforts were rewarded, for they found the mountains "colored from top to bottom with verdigris."*
SOUTH AFRICAN MUSEUM, CAPE TOWN

little interest after the late fifteenth-century exploratory visits of Bartholomeu Dias and Vasco da Gama. Meanwhile, by 1610 the Dutch had wrested control of the East Indies from the Portuguese. Failing to capture Mozambique, traditionally the jumping-off point for eastern voyages, they found a more convenient and direct route to the Indies in 1611. This route placed the Cape midway between Europe and the Indies, thus making it of strategic importance in controlling trade. As Dutch, English, and French ships began to stop there, it was obvious that one of these nations would establish a station sooner or later; eventually the Dutch East India Company did so. In April, 1652, it dispatched an expedition of about ninety men under Jan van Riebeeck to the Cape. Van Riebeeck and his men landed at Table Bay in May, 1652, and soon a fort, a hospital, workshops, a mill, houses, and fruit gardens were established. By 1659 the station was flourishing, and each Dutch ship was leaving there victualed with at least a twelve- or fourteen-day supply of carrots, beets, parsnips, turnips, and other sturdy vegetables, plus numbers of live sheep.

The Dutch had no intention of establishing a colony at the Cape. Their decision to found that settlement was precipitated by their need for a refreshment station and by the fear that their deadly enemies, the Portuguese and Spaniards, might otherwise use the Cape as a base for attack. Indeed, Van Riebeeck was given strict instructions to keep the station as small as possible, not to colonize inland, and not to interfere in the affairs of the local people. Lest too much land be acquired, Van Riebeeck ordered planted a hedge enclosing the approximately six thousand acres that he deemed adequate for the task. Less than a decade later the need to raise more cattle as well as crops, and the continued fear of French or English attack, compelled the Dutch East India Company to permit free farmers, or burghers, to migrate there. As a consequence, slaves from Angola and West Africa began to be imported in 1658. By 1679 the number of burghers had increased to two hundred fifty-nine, and by 1680 settlements had been founded as far inland as Stellenbosch. The number of whites at the Cape was further increased after 1688 by the arrival of two hundred Huguenots, who left France following the revocation of the Edict of Nantes. At the close of our second period then, the Dutch revictualing station had developed into a thriving settlement, producing far more grain, cattle, sheep, and provisions than was demanded by Cape Town and passing ships.

Socially, four groups had emerged. The first consisted of black slaves from West Africa and Angola, who by 1700 numbered about seventeen thousand. The second was made up of the company's European employees, who were regarded as temporary residents. The third consisted of the Dutch Boers, or farmers, and Huguenots, who made the

These Hottentot herders, recognizable by their distinctive "peppercorn" hair, high cheekbones, and yellow-brownish complexion, are, with the Bergdama, South Africa's oldest settlers. When this photograph was taken in 1882, the Hottentots were already a disappearing people, many having been decimated by the white man's smallpox, others having been absorbed into the mixed Boer-Malay-Bergdama colored population.
RADIO TIMES HULTON PICTURE LIBRARY

Cape as their permanent home. The fourth was the colored group, who were a product of the miscegenation between the whites and the blacks.

The Boers, numbering about sixteen hundred by 1700, were fanatical adherents of the Calvinist faith. They identified themselves as the chosen people of the Old Testament and regarded the slaves and the blacks as the damned. Thus were formed the racist attitudes that would harden in the eighteenth and nineteenth centuries into the hideous philosophy of apartheid, the philosophy that governs the relations between the Boers and the blacks and colored of South Africa to this very day.

What sort of people did the Europeans find in the region of South Africa on their arrival there in the 1480's and 1490's? Contrary to the contentions of some misguided Boer historians and advocates of apartheid today, South Africa was not unoccupied when the Portuguese and the Dutch arrived there. It is clear from archeological and ethnological evidence as well as from the early accounts of Portuguese sailors that the area was occupied by two principal peoples: the Khoisan-speaking peoples and the Bantu-speaking peoples. The Khoisan group was made up of two principal peoples: the Bushmen and the Hottentots. Both of them had a tawny-yellow skin color, were rather short in stature, and spoke languages with the unique clicking sounds. Although they shared common religious beliefs and practices, they differed in many other respects.

The Bushmen neither practiced agriculture nor kept cattle, but lived in small units of a hundred or so, hunting and gathering wild fruits and tubers. Although they led a wandering life, each unit had a specific territory, which it guarded jealously. The Bushmen had been living in southern and central Africa for thousands of years, though by the time of the Portuguese arrival, they had been forced into the interior part of southern Africa.

Their fellow Khoisan speakers, the Hottentots, were cattle breeders, and though they, too, were nomadic, each group had to have its own home area. They were organized into much larger units than the Bushmen, with each unit made up of a number of related clans under a chief. As cattle owners, the Hottentots recognized wealth and private property. Less widely distributed than the Bushmen, at the time of the Portuguese arrival they occupied southwest Africa, the coastal areas around the Cape of Good Hope, and the eastern coastal strip as far north as Transkei.

The Bantu speakers, consisting of three principal subgroups, were living in the areas mainly to the north of the Orange and Vaal rivers and on the east coast. They were mixed farmers, rearing cattle and cultivating the land. The most numerous of them were the Nguni-speaking peoples—Zulu, Pondo, Tembu, Xhosa—who lived in the fertile and well-watered regions of the east coast. To the west of them were the Central Bantu, or the Sotho-Tswana, peoples, who occupied most of the central plateaus west of the Drakensberg mountains. Farther to the west were the Western Bantu—the Herero and the Ambo. All these Bantu peoples were organized into relatively small kingdoms ruled by chiefs, who were assisted by officials often called *indunas*, or military leaders.

The Bushmen and the Hottentots were the first to come into contact with the Europeans in the 1480's and 1490's; not until 1702 did the Bantu and the Europeans confront each other near the present-day South African town of Somerset East. The Hottentots consistently met the Portuguese with great hostility. They fought with the men of both Bartholomeu Dias and Vasco da Gama. In 1503 the Hottentots attacked and wounded Antonio de Saldanha and his men when they landed at Table Bay. In 1510 they attacked a party led by Francisco de Almeida, the Portuguese viceroy at Gao, and killed sixty of them, including the leader. As a result, the Hottentots earned a reputation as a really fierce and dangerous people, and reports that they were cannibals gained currency in Europe. Indeed, it was not until the favorable reports brought back to Holland by the crew of the *Haarlem*, who lived in Table Bay for a year after having been shipwrecked there in 1647, that the Hottentots' unsavory reputation was perhaps neutralized, thus preparing the way for the establishment of the victualing stations.

It would appear that the Hottentots took more kindly to the Dutch settlers, and they were the main suppliers of meat to the Dutch ships. However, as soon as the Dutch settlers began to expand inland and to occupy the land for farming purposes, both the Hottentots and Bushmen reacted sharply, and the first war between the Hottentots and the Boers broke out in 1658 and lasted two years. Van Riebeeck, having interviewed a Hottentot prisoner, summarized their grievances. They made war on the Dutch, he said, "for no other reason than that they saw that we kept in possession the best lands, and grazed our cattle where they used to do so, and that everywhere with houses and plantations we endeavored to establish ourselves so permanently as if we intended never to leave again, but take permanent possession of this Cape land (which had belonged to them during all the centuries) for our sole use; yea to such an extent that their cattle could not come and drink at this fresh water without going over the corn lands, which we did not like them to do." The Dutch, of course, were not prepared to leave, and a second war broke out in 1673 and continued till 1677. Induced by European commodities, especially tobacco and brandy, and decimated by the white's man's diseases such as smallpox, the remaining Hottentots gave up resistance and began to take on jobs as servants and laborers of the Boers.

The Bushmen, however, proved less susceptible. Unused to the concept of wealth and unattracted by the baubles and liquor introduced by the Europeans, they continued their resistance. They constantly attacked the burghers and killed, maimed, or drove off their cattle, all in defense of their hunting grounds and water holes. With a view to breaking this resistance, the Boers developed the commando system. Organizing themselves into mounted groups and equipped with three days' rations, firearms, and ammunition, which were supplied by the government, they went on periodic hunts for the Bushmen. In this way they steadily exterminated the indigenous population, driving them farther and farther inland to the semidesert areas of the northwest Cape and beyond the Orange River, where they are found to this day. By the middle of the eighteenth century the resistance of the Bushmen had been completely broken.

The Dutch had yet to subdue the third and largest group, the Bantu, and as pointed out already, it was not until the last quarter of the eighteenth century that the Boers, steadily moving eastward, confronted the main body of the Eastern Bantu across the Great Fish River. The result was the Kaffir Wars, which raged throughout the eighteenth and the nineteenth centuries and which in some sense have continued among their descendants to this very day.

By the end of the period under review, there was hardly a coastal region of Africa in which the European nations were not operating. In the case of Angola, South Africa, and Mozambique, they did not confine themselves to trading from their forts and castles as they did in West Africa, but had become colonizers and administrators, thus provoking deadly conflicts with the Africans. It is to the lasting shame of these European nations in general, and to the Portuguese in particular, that they abandoned almost all the activities that would have benefited and improved the lot of the African, at least materially if not spiritually, to concentrate on the most inhuman, the most destructive, sale of man by man.

Politically, Europe's impact on Africa was at best a mixed blessing. In the Congo, Angola, and on the East African coast it led to the weakening and total disintegration of almost all kingdoms that were in existence on their arrival: the kingdom of the Manikongo in the Congo, the Mbundu kingdom in Angola, nearly all the city-states on the east coast of Africa, and above all, the remarkable kingdom of Monomotapa. All these states were the victims of active foreign interference in their internal affairs, coupled with military attack on them by the Portuguese, or by other African invaders, or by both—the Portuguese in Angola, the Rozwi in Monomotapa, the Zimba in Mombasa and Kilwa, and both the Portuguese and the Jaga in the Congo.

The west coast, on the other hand, experienced the rise or rapid expansion of a number of city-states, especially in the Niger delta area, and of no less than four empires—Asante, Dahomey, Oyo, and Benin—which were to dominate West Africa in the eighteenth and the nineteenth centuries. Indeed, many historians are of the opinion that these empires were the product specifically of the Atlantic slave trade, built upon the desire of their rulers to capture slaves for sale. It seems clear to this writer, however, that such an explanation is true only of the states that emerged in the area of the Niger delta, such as Bonny, Opobo, Brass, Cross, and Creek Town, all of which started as trading corporations organized to supply slaves either by war or raids. Significantly, however, not one of them grew into a large kingdom. The empires of Benin, Oyo, Asante, and Dahomey, on the other hand, were not creations of the Atlantic slave trade. As described in Chapter Five, the rise of both Benin and Oyo began long before any European set foot on the coast of Guinea. And though both Asante and Dahomey did commence their development during the second half of the seventeenth century, other motivating factors are indicated. Dahomey's drive toward the coast was initiated with a view to stopping the slave trade. Asante's rise, as is evident from recent research, was inspired first and foremost by a desire to throw off the tyrannical rule of the kingdom of Denkyra to the south and second to gain control of the trade routes running not only southward to the coast but also northward to Hausaland and the Niger Bend.

It is nevertheless true that the presence of Europeans did affect the growth or expansion of all these empires. Most important, the Europeans brought guns and gunpowder to West Africa, especially after 1640, and there is no doubt that the growth of the four inland states of Oyo, Benin, Asante, and Dahomey was greatly accelerated by the use of these weapons. Additionally, the presence of the Europeans on the coast provided these inland states with a motive to extend their sway down to the coast, thereby trading directly with the Europeans and eliminating the middlemen and their sharp practices. Although these states expanded mostly by waging wars against their weaker neighbors and although most of the captives they took were sold as slaves, it is wrong to see these wars as motivated primarily by the desire to profit from the slave trade. Slaves were only accidental by-products.

The economic effects of the impact of Europe on Africa were even more profound. With the exception of the east coast, the centers of wealth and economic opportunity prior to the arrival of the Europeans were inland. Now trade began to be diverted more and more toward the coastal regions, with the inland states extending themselves to meet the challenge, as we have seen. However, West Africa's ancient trade with the north and the Saharan regions continued, though its volume decreased as the greater part of it, especially the trade in gold, was diverted southward.

The second principal economic effect was that in western and west-central Africa agricultural, hence peaceful, pursuits were neglected, and orderly economic development was ruled out as the slave trade became the principal occupation of the area's rulers. Some historians, including J. D. Fage, have argued to the contrary, saying that the slave trade must "have been a considerable stimulus to the internal economic development in Guinea." But this view is untenable. The sale of slaves simply could not have brought about any internal economic development. On the contrary, by taking away Africans mainly between the ages of fifteen and thirty who could have worked and produced wealth at home, by carting away craftsmen and traditional industrialists, by killing local industries such as the textile industry through the importation of cheap wares and copies, by retarding agricultural development, and by giving to Africans in return for their products only baubles and barrels of liquor, the European trade with Africa in general and the Atlantic slave trade in particular definitely delayed economic development in Africa for well over three hundred years.

It was in the social sphere, however, that the European impact was virtually an unmitigated disaster—in fact, a crime against Africa. The first and obvious effect was the depopulation of Africa. As we have seen, historians are still arguing about the number of slaves that were actually taken out of Africa, from 15 million to Curtin's most recent figure of 9.4 million. Of course, neither figure includes the uncounted numbers of Africans who must have been killed during the raids or in the wars or who died during the march from the inland regions to the coast. But it can be asserted that the total loss of population to Africa as a result of the Atlantic slave trade was something close to 20 million. Some European historians have contended that not only did Africa not suffer far-reaching depopulation, but as J. D. Fage argues, "it may have been preferable for some parts of this area to have exported the equivalent of its natural growth of population rather than to have kept it at home." These views are highly objectionable. Firstly, depopulation in the magnitude of 20 million people—people in the prime of manhood—is very serious and very far-reaching. Secondly, it is nonsensical to talk of overpopulation in sub-Saharan Africa even today, let alone two hundred years ago! And, in any case, given a choice between dying in Africa of hunger or being reduced to chattel and being humiliated, flogged, or worked to death in the New World, this writer, as an African, would have chosen the former!

Beyond the matter of decimating the population, the perpetual raids and wars for slaves must have created an atmosphere of social insecurity, fear, and chaos. The English observer John Atkins wrote in 1721 that on the west coast "they never care to walk even a mile from home without fire arms." Such an atmosphere could not help but impede all orderly social development and retard cultural activities. Indeed, by 1700 the great art and sculpture of the people of Ife, Benin, and Oyo had virtually disappeared. Missionary and educational activities were also halted, partly because of the insecurity and anarchy caused by the inhuman traffic and partly because of the fact that even some of the priests, missionaries, and teachers turned to that traffic themselves. Significantly, it was only after the steady suppression of the slave trade that missionary activities began to take root in Africa.

Furthermore, the slave trade brutalized everyone involved, white as well as black, but especially the traditional African rulers. In their anxiety to obtain people for sale, these rulers abused customary law and practice, fabricated charges of adultery, theft, or treason, and even imposed slavery instead of fines as punishment for petty offenses. In his travels in the northern districts of Sierra Leone in 1822 Alexander Gordon Laing noted that following an investigation into the death of a young girl in a village he visited, the authorities were not able to place blame on anyone. "Had the slave trade existed," he commented, "some unfortunate individual might have been accused and sold into captivity." African religious leaders also abused their offices by turning them into instruments of enslavement. For instance, the Aro people of Iboland, in present-day Nigeria, used their famous oracle Chukwu to enslave thousands of Ibo from the inland regions. There is no doubt that the European presence in general and the slave trade in particular brought about the moral degeneration of many members of the ruling aristocracy.

Another deplorable effect of the trade was the change in the attitude of Europeans toward Africans, or the black race. Once the white man began to buy blacks and to treat them as chattel and beasts of burden, he naturally began to develop an attitude of contempt toward his victims. The feeling of equality and mutual respect that had characterized the first period of Afro-European contact was steadily replaced by one of superiority on the part of the Europeans, an attitude that has not entirely disappeared to this day.

The social impact was not confined to Africa alone, but could be seen in the New World. It was in the United States, South America, and the Caribbean islands that the feeling of white superiority and black inferiority reached extreme proportions, becoming the basis of the present, highly explosive confrontation between blacks and whites.

On balance then, politically, economically, and socially, the European presence and activities in Africa during the second period were virtually an unmitigated disaster for the Africans. By 1700 all the great hopes that had been conjured up during the earlier phase of exploration had turned sour. To borrow Basil Davidson's term, Africa had by then been turned into the "Black Mother," producing slaves solely in the interest of the growing capitalist system in Europe and the New World, and it was to do this for another hundred and fifty years. At the beginning of their contact, sub-Saharan Africa was politically, culturally, and artistically comparable to Europe. By 1700 Europe had leaped forward technologically and socially, but Africa and its black peoples had become paralyzed and impoverished, a tragedy from which they still have not recovered.

RAPE OF THE COAST

SHIPWRECK OFF NATAL

To the historian, the era of slavery offers many ironies. What began with numerous instances of courage and moral fortitude was to end in venality and corruption as exploration gave way to slavery. Typical of the growing hostility of most whites is this highly partisan story of the wreck of the São João, *a Portuguese galleon. The vessel and most aboard it came to a pitiful end after they were shipwrecked off Natal on June 24, 1552. The tragedy was one of the most famous maritime disasters of the period. Contemporary historians bemoaned the fate of the gallant captain, Manoel de Sousa Sepúlveda, and his family and crew, who perished at the hands of the "cruel Kaffirs" of Africa. The following is an abridged version of the tale as it was told to an anonymous chronicler by the boatswain, one of the few survivors of the* São João *ordeal.*

On 13th April, Manoel de Sousa came in sight of the coast of the Cape at thirty-two degrees. . . . [He and his crew] no longer had any other sails than those on the yards after the other equipment of sails had been carried away by a storm they had met with on the Line [the equator], and . . . their present ones were so torn that they were not to be trusted. . . . The violence of the wind and sea would not let them make any reparations and not a man of them could keep his footing. . . . Everything foretold greater hardships; for their sins, nothing availed them. They had not seen land since they left the Cape, but they must have been about fifteen to twenty leagues from it. . . .

Thus Manoel de Sousa was very near land, though helpless. So he asked the opinion of his officers. They all said that the best manner of saving their lives from death at sea was to wait until they reached ten fathoms, and, when they sounded that depth, drop anchor, and launch the long-boat for them to disembark. They launched a small boat then and there with some men in it to examine the beach and find out which would be their best place to land in. They agreed that, after all had disembarked and come ashore in the long-boat or the smaller boat, such stores and arms as could be fetched should be. . . . Manoel de Sousa could see his galleon would go to the bottom, and that there was no help for it. So he called the master and pilot and told them that the first thing they were to do was to put him ashore with his wife and children, and twenty men to guard them; then they must go and fetch the arms, provisions, and powder out of the ship, and also some cambric cloth, in case there should be some means of purchasing provisions on land. . . .

While they were still in the place to which they had escaped from the galleon, seven or eight Kaffirs leading a cow appeared on a hill. The Christians made them signs to come down, and the captain went to speak to them. When the negroes were fairly cornered they made signs that they wanted iron. Then the captain sent for half a dozen nails and showed them to them, and they were very pleased to see these, and came nearer our men and began to bargain for the price of the cow. Everything had been settled when five Kaffirs appeared on another hill and began to call out to them in their language not to give the cow in exchange for nails. Immediately the Kaffirs went away, taking the cow with them and not saying a word. And the captain . . . called a council to decide what they should do. And, before they discussed the matter, he spoke to them as follows:

"Gentlemen and friends, you can clearly see the state we are reduced to for our sins. I truly believe that my own alone would have been enough for us to have been submitted to these great privations you see we are undergoing. But Our Lord is pitiful, and He was so merciful to us that He willed that we should not sink to the bottom in that ship, despite the great quantity of water which we had below decks. His will be done, for it is His object to lead us to a Christian country, and may their souls be saved who end their lives in the trials of our quest. . . . I ask one favor of you, not to abandon me or leave me if I cannot travel as fast as the fastest of you because of my wife and children. And may God in His mercy help us all." . . .

They began to move off from the beach (which was at thirty-one degrees) where they had been wrecked, on 7th June [1553]. In the vanguard went André Vaz and his company carrying a banner with a crucifix. Then came Manoel de Sousa with his wife and children, and eighty Portuguese, and slaves; Dona Leonor, the captain's wife, was carried by slaves, in a litter. Immediately behind them followed the master of the galleon with the seamen and the female slaves. Pantaleão de Sá came in the rearguard with the rest of the Portuguese and of the slaves, about two hundred people. Altogether they were about five hundred people, a hundred and eighty of whom were

Portuguese. They proceeded like this for a month, enduring great hardships and great hunger and thirst. All this time they ate nothing but the rice which had been rescued from the galleon and some jungle fruits, for they found no other food in the country, nor any one to sell it to them. So that they went through privations which can neither be believed nor written. . . .

It often happened that these people sold each other a pint pitcher of water for ten crusadoes; and for a cauldron which held two gallons they asked a hundred crusadoes. As this sometimes gave rise to disorders the captain took to sending for a cauldron of it, since the company had no larger vessels, and paying a hundred crusadoes to the man who went to fetch it. The captain then portioned it out with his own hand, and what he took for his wife and children cost him eight and ten crusadoes the pint. . . . For many days they had only had the fruits they found by chance to sustain them, and toasted bones. Often snake-skins were sold in the encampment for fifteen crusadoes. Even when they were dry, they threw them into water and then ate them as they were.

When they went along the beaches they lived on shell-fish or fish thrown up by the sea. In the end they came across a Kaffir, an old man, who was a chief of two villages. He seemed to them a man of merit, and so he was, as can be seen by the welcome he gave them. He told them not to go on any further, but stay with him, and he would supply them as best he could. . . .

They were ready to move on again, but they saw a band of Kaffirs coming. On which they prepared to fight if necessary, thinking the negroes had come to rob them. The band drew near; they began to parley, and the Kaffirs asked our people who they were and what they wanted. Our people replied that they were Christians and that they had been wrecked, and they asked them to guide them to a broad river which lay on ahead. Moreover, if the Kaffirs had provisions, let them bring them and they should be paid for them. The negroes replied, through a negress who came from Sofala, that if they required supplies they should come with them to a place where their king was, and that he would give them a good welcome. . . .

The Kaffirs' treachery had been planned beforehand and, as soon as they saw that the Portuguese had no weapons, they began to separate them and rob them and take them through the jungle in the groups they had been sorted into. When they reached the appointed places they stripped them, and left them with nothing on them and drove them out, beating them severely. Manoel de Sousa did not go in any of these groups. He, and his wife and children, the pilot André Vaz, and about twenty other people, stayed with the king because they had a great quantity of jewels and precious stones and coins. It is said that what that company brought all that way with it was worth more than a hundred thousand crusadoes. As soon as Manoel de Sousa and his wife and those twenty other people had been separated from the rest they were immediately robbed of all they had brought with them, though the king did not strip them. He told him that he might go away at once in search of his company, for he did not wish to do him any more harm, nor hurt his person or that of his wife. When this happened to Manoel de Sousa he must have seen very clearly what a great mistake he had made in giving up the arms. But he had to do what they told him, for it was not in his power to do otherwise.

The other members of the company, ninety in all, including Pantaleão de Sá, and three other gentlemen, though they had all been separated from each other and robbed and stripped by the Kaffirs to whom they had been apportioned by the king, managed to come together again, little by little, because they were not far from each other. So they started out again together, beaten, despondent, without arms, clothes, or money to buy food with, and without their captain. . . .

By now Dona Leonor was very weak, sad, and disconsolate, because she saw how ill her husband was, and because she found the others were so far off that she thought it impossible ever to join them. To think of it is a thing to break one's heart. As they went along thus the Kaffirs again came upon the captain, his wife, and the few people who were in their company and stripped them there without leaving anything on them. When they were both left like that, with two very young children with them, they commended themselves finally to the Lord.

Here they say that Dona Leonor would not let herself be stripped, but defended herself with buffets and blows, for she was of a nature to prefer being killed by the Kaffirs to being left naked before all the people. There is no doubt, even, but that her life would have been over if Manoel de Sousa had not begged her to let herself be stripped, reminding her that all were born naked, and, as it was God's will, she should not now refuse to be so, too. One of their great trials was seeing those two little children of theirs there crying and asking for food whilst they, the parents, were unable to help them.

After Vasco Da Gama's 1497 voyage to India, map makers were able to sketch in Africa's eastern contours, as in this 1508 map.
RADIO TIMES HULTON PICTURE LIBRARY

When Dona Leonor was left without clothes she flung herself on the ground immediately and covered herself completely with her hair, which was very long. She made a hole in the sand in which she buried herself up to the waist and never arose from it again. . . .

Truly I do not know who could consider this without great pity and sadness. Here was a most noble woman, the daughter and the wife of very honorable gentlemen, most cruelly and ignominiously used! When the men who were still in their company saw Manoel de Sousa and his wife naked they moved away a little, being ashamed to see their captain and Dona Leonor so. Then she said to André Vaz the pilot: "You see the state we are in and that we cannot go on any further and that we must end our lives here, for our sins. Go on your way, save yourselves, and commend us to God. If you reach India or Portugal at some future time, tell them how you left Manoel de Sousa and myself and our children."

THE VERDANT CAPE

The travelogue of the Venetian explorer Alvise da Cadamosto remains a major source of information on the early European "discovery" of the coast of West Africa. In 1455, traveling in the service of Prince Henry the Navigator of Portugal, Cadamosto sailed southward along that shore as far as the Gambia River. His description of Cape Verde, on the coast between the Senegal and Gambia rivers, and the nearby islands, follows.

This Capo Verde is so called because the first to discover it (who were Portuguese) about a year before I was in these parts found it all green with great trees [mangrove swamps], which remained in leaf throughout the year. For this reason they gave it the name of Capo Verde: just as Capo Bianco, of which we have already spoken, was found entirely sandy and white and was therefore called "Capo Bianco." This Capo Verde is very beautiful and lofty: on the point there are two hillocks. It runs far into the sea, and on the cape and in its vicinity there are many dwellings of negro peasants, huts of straw, close to the sea, and visible to those who pass. These negroes belong to the said Kingdom of Senega.

[Off the cape there are dry patches which extend about half a mile out to sea.] Off it we found three small islands, not very far from the land, uninhabited and covered with tall green trees. Being in need of water, we anchored off one of them [Gorée], which appeared the largest and most fruitful, to ascertain if any springs were to be found there. On landing we found no water, except in one spot where there was a little water, but which was of no use to us. We found many nests on the island, and eggs of various birds [un]known to us. While we remained here we all fished with lines and large hooks and caught a great number of fish: among them shell fish and very large mature dories, weighing from twelve to fifteen pounds each. This was in the month of June.

Thence, the following day, we continued to sail on our voyage, always within sight of land. Beyond Capo Verde there is a gulf inland. All the coast is low, covered with very fine, tall, green trees, which never shed their leaves throughout the year [that is they never wither, as do ours], for new leaves appear before the old fall. These trees come right down to within a bowshot of the beach, so that it appears as though they flourished in the sea—a very beautiful sight. In my opinion, who have sailed to many places in the Levant and in the west, I have never seen a more beautiful coast than this appeared to me—watered by many rivers, and streams of little account, since large vessels cannot enter them.

Running with the wind along this coast, still voyaging southwards, we discovered the mouth of a river, perhaps a bowshot wide, and of no great depth. To this river we gave the name of Rio di Barbazini [the Joal], and thus it is named on the "carta da navigar" of this country

A griot *retelling the stirring history of his people to the accompaniment of a drummer*
BIBLIOTHEQUE NATIONALE

made by me. It is distant sixty miles from the Capo Verde. We always navigated this coast and beyond by day, anchoring each evening at a deserted spot in ten or twelve *passa* [two *passa* equal roughly one fathom] of water, and four or five miles from the shore. At dawn we made sail, always stationing one man aloft and two men in the bows of the caravel to watch for breakers which would disclose the presence of shoals.

Sailing thus we reached the mouth of another large river, which appeared to be no smaller than the Rio de Senega. When we saw this fine river [the estuary of the Solum and Jumbas rivers], and the beautiful country, we cast anchor, and debated whether we should send ashore one of our interpreters—for each of our ships had negro interpreters on board brought from Portugal, who had been sold by the lords of Senega to the first Portuguese to discover this land of the Blacks.

These slaves had been made Christians in Portugal, and knew Spanish well: we had had them from their owners on the understanding that for the hire and pay of each we would give one slave to be chosen from all our captives. Each interpreter, also, who secured four slaves for his master was to be given his freedom. Lots were drawn to decide whose interpreter was to go ashore, and it fell to the

Genoese. Whereupon having fitted out his boat, he sent off his man, with orders that the boat was not to be run ashore except in as far as was necessary to land the slave. He was instructed to ascertain the condition of the country, to whom it was subject, and whether gold and other objects of use to us were to be obtained there. Accordingly, when he had landed, and the boat had withdrawn a short distance, he suddenly encountered a great number of negroes who, having observed the ships approaching, had lain in wait with bows and arrows and other weapons to accost any of our men who might land. They conversed for a short while; what he said to them we do not know, but they began furiously to strike at him with their short Moorish swords, and quickly put him to death, those in the boat being unable to succor him.

When we were informed by our men of this, we were left stupefied, realizing that they must be very cruel men to do such a thing to a negro of their own race, and that they might reasonably be expected to treat us much worse. On this account, we set sail, still holding our southerly course within sight of the shore, which appeared to us continually more beautiful, more thickly covered with green trees, and always low, until at length we reached the mouth of the river of Gambra [the Gambia]. Perceiving it was very wide, not less than three or four miles in the narrowest reach, so that our ships could enter in safety, we decided to lie there with the intention of ascertaining on the following day whether this was the country of Gambra, which we so greatly desired to find.

THE GUINEA TRADE

In December, 1460, King Affonso V *of Portugal gave one of the Cape Verde Islands, São Tiago, to his brother, Prince Fernando. However, settling it proved difficult, and six years later the king gave his sibling and the Santiagians additional privileges, including trade rights in Guinea. São Tiago soon became the chief center for lucrative commerce with the African mainland. An English translation of the text of Affonso's grant follows.*

To all to whom this letter shall come, we make known that prince dom Fernando, my most dear and beloved brother, has sent to inform us that some four years ago he began to populate his island of Santiago, which is opposite Cabo Verde, and that, because it is so remote from our kingdoms, people are unwilling to go to live there, unless they are given very wide privileges and franchises and go at his expense. He, knowing the great profit it would yield us and him, if the island were thus populated, as he wished, in which cause he was ready to go to much personal expense so as to carry it to perfection, and being hopeful of success with God's help, prayed us to be pleased to grant him some privileges for them. We, having seen his petition and having considered it carefully, believe that we may thereby be very well served. And so that we may graciously reward my said brother, we are pleased to command him to be given the following privileges, namely: first, we give and grant him civil and criminal authority over all Moors, black and white, free and captive, and over all their descendants, who are in the said island, although they be Christians, and this while our favor continues. This civil and criminal authority, which we thus grant him in the manner stated, is additional to the authority which already before this we gave him in the said island, as is contained in the patent of the said grant which he has from us.

A dense cluster of thatch-roofed, mud-walled houses in a southern Senegalese bush village

RAPHO-GUILLUMETTE—MARC AND EVELYNE BERNHEIM

Furthermore, we are pleased to authorize him that henceforward and always the inhabitants of the said island may have and hold license, whenever they wish, to be able to go with ships to trade and to buy in all our trades of the parts of Guiné (save our trade of Arguim [Arguin on the coast of Mauritania], where we do not wish anyone to trade or do anything either in the said trade or in its limits, except him to whom we are pleased to grant license and permission) all the goods, which the said inhabitants of the said island have and desire to carry, except arms and iron tools, ships and their equipment, because our pleasure is that none of these things should be bartered in any manner in the said trades, and we have strictly forbidden this before, under the penalty for such a thing already imposed. . . .

These, our officers, whom we thus appoint there in the said island, shall be ready and diligent to supply clerks to the said shippers, so that each shall carry one, as is required in each ship which goes there, according as is now done in the ships which go from our kingdoms to the said port of Guiné.

The said customs officer or receiver shall thus be ready to collect the said dues, which are to accrue to us from the said ships which are equipped in the said island, as soon as they return from the said ports of Guiné. If the said officers are not ready to collect the said dues and to provide the said clerks, in their absence he may collect and provide who has charge of the government and captaincy of the said island for my said brother, and he shall keep these dues

Nigerian traders, as shown in the Dutch-made Novus Atlas *of 1648, by Willem Blaeu*

NEW YORK PUBLIC LIBRARY, ASTOR LENOX AND TILDEN FOUNDATIONS

himself until we send for them. When this happens, the said governor or captain shall advise us thereof by letter.

These clerks, thus to be supplied, shall be such as are fully competent and suitable for our service, and for their salary they shall receive everything which we have ordered and commanded is to be given to clerks who go from our kingdom to the said parts of Guiné. They shall receive this from the day when the said ship leaves the said island for the said trades till they return to it, and no more.

Furthermore, it is our will and pleasure that, when the amount of our dues has been paid on all the said imported negroes and goods, the said inhabitants of the said island may sell on their own accounts what they have left to all persons, who want and desire them, not only in the said island but in all our kingdoms and abroad; and if they sell in the said island, the buyers shall not have to pay on the said goods, in these kingdoms when they are brought here, either the tenth or any other dues; and if they do not sell them in the said island but wish to bring them to our kingdoms or to carry them to other parts, they may do this, because they are exempt from having to pay us the said dues; and this, provided they carry certificates from our officers, whom we shall thus appoint in the said island, showing that they have already paid our dues. . . .

Furthermore, it is our will and pleasure, in the event hereafter of our farming out the said trades of the parts of Guiné, or a part thereof, that, should we do this, this license, which we thus grant my said brother for the inhabitants of the said island, shall not transgress or stay such a farm, and this shall be thus enacted so that we shall not be reminded of this grant to my said brother.

Furthermore, it is our will and pleasure that henceforward the inhabitants of the said island are always to be freed and exempted from the payment to us in all our kingdoms and lordships of the tenth of all goods which they transport from the said island, not only of goods which are of their own inheritance and gathering, but also of goods which they buy, or secure by exchange, or obtain in any other way.

Likewise, they shall be exempted from the payment to us of the tenth of all goods, which they buy and secure by exchange of other articles of their own in the islands of Canaria, Madeira, Porto Santo and the Açores, and in all the other islands in the ocean sea, and which they bring to our kingdom. This shall be, provided our officers are notified that the said persons are inhabitants of the said island of S. Thiago by report of the captains of the said island.

Therefore, we command all overseers of our exchequer, accountants, treasurers, customs officers and receivers, clerks, magistrates, judges and justices, and other officers and persons whatsoever, to whom this letter shall be shown, and who are cognisant thereof, that henceforward they shall observe and keep it, and cause it to be properly observed and kept, and in the manner stated herein.

Should any desire to disobey this, we command them in no wise to permit it, forasmuch as this is our wish, notwithstanding any doubt or embargo which others may raise or impose. And for its security and our remembrance, we command them to be given this letter, signed by our hand and sealed with our pendent seal. Given in Beja. 12 June 1466. Pedro da Alcaçova made this.

THE CONVERSION OF BEMOYM

In the early years of their involvement in Africa, the Portuguese played the role of ostensibly benevolent outsiders rather than that of oppressors. This excerpt describes the 1488 conversion to Christianity of Bemoym, prince of the Wolof of Guinea, by King John II of Portugal. In contrast to the attitudes that later Europeans would have, no honor was too great for the black king. The account is from the Chronicle of John II, *by Ruy de Pina, a Portuguese historian of the period.*

In this year one thousand four hundred and eighty-eight, while the king [John II] was in Setuvel [Setúbal, near Lisbon], he made a Christian of Bemoym, a negro prince of the kingdom of Gelof [Wolof], which is at the entrance of the Rio de Çanaga [Senegal] in Guinee. . . . Because the said Bemoym was treacherously driven out of his kingdom, he determined to embark on one of the caravels of the trade, which frequent the coast, and to come in person to seek aid, assistance and justice from [John II], who was in Setuvel. Bemoym arrived in Lixboa [Lisbon], accompanied by some negroes of his own royal blood and sons of persons closely related to men of importance. When the king had been informed of their arrival, he commanded that they should come to be entertained at Palmella, where he forthwith commanded his men to make abundant provision for him and to serve him with silver and attendants and every other civility which was proper to his station. Also he commanded all to be given rich and fine clothes to wear, according as the quality and merit of their persons demanded. And when they were in a condition to come to the court, the king sent horses and mules, very well appareled, to them all; and on the day when they were to make their entrance, the king commanded that Bemoym should be received by Dom Francisco Coutinho, the count of Marialva, and with him all the lords and noblemen of the court. . . . Bemoym appeared to be forty years old, and he was a man of great stature, very dark, with a very long beard, limbs all well proportioned and a very gracious presence; and being dressed, he entered the king's rooms, and the king came forward two or three paces from the dais to receive him, raising his cap a little. Then he led him to the dais, where there was a throne; but the king did not sit thereon, and, leaning against it, thus on foot gave ear to him. Then the said Bemoym and all his men threw themselves at his feet to kiss them, and they made a show of taking the earth from under them and, in token of their subjection and his overlordship and of their great respect, threw it over their heads. But the king with much honor and courtesy made him rise, and through negro interpreters, who were already present for this purpose, commanded him to speak. Thereupon, Bemoym with great ease, majesty and considerable gravity made a public speech, which lasted for a long time, and he used such notable words and sentences in support of his case that they did not seem to come from a savage negro but from Prince Grego, educated in Athenas. The substance of his speech was to recount to the king with swift sighs and many tears the tale of his miserable ill-fortune, caused by the treason which had been directed against him in his kingdom. . . . Moreover, he said to him: "Most powerful lord, God knows how, when I heard of thy greatness and thy royal virtues, my spirits were always eager and my eyes desirous to see thee; and I do not know why it was, because the more it pleased me, when I was free and in all my prosperity, the less do my overthrow and exile, by their sad condition, justify my faith and my words; but, it if were thus ordained from above that I should not come and do it so well in other circumstances more favorable to me, since it was ordained for me to see thee, I praise God fervently for my ruin; and this gladness already so satisfies me that I shall not return from this journey discontented." Proceeding further in a word, he said that, if perhaps in reply to his petition for justice and help men should deny that he was a Christian, even as upon other occasions word had been sent to him by way of an excuse for refusing another similar request, there should now be no doubt or contradiction about it, because he and all his men who were present, among whom there were not wanting men of noble and royal birth, advised at other times by His holy warnings, had come in order that in his kingdoms and at his hands they might at once become Christians. He said that the only sorrow and truly grave anxiety, which they had thereby experienced, arose out of the fact that it seemed that the force of his necessity rather than of his faith had caused him to do it. With these he coupled many other sound reasons touching his purpose. Then the king replied to him in a few words, and devoted great care and much wisdom to everything, expressing great pleasure at their meeting and even more pleasure at his final intention to be a Christian. Therefore he gave him hope in this world of assistance in his cause and of restoration to his kingdom, and in the other that of glory and eternal salvation. Thereupon, he dismissed him, and Bemoym went to speak to the queen and to the prince, before whom he made a short speech, in which with shrewd judgment and very natural dignity he asked them for favor and assistance with the king. The queen and the prince dismissed him, showing him much honor and kindness. Then, on another day, Bemoym came to speak with the king, and, alone and apart, with an interpreter, they both conversed for a long time. Here Bemoym again recounted his affairs with great prudence; and he also replied very wisely and exactly to the questions which the king asked him, and the king remained very satisfied with this. In his honor the king ordered bull-fights and tournaments, and he held fancy-dress balls and dances, and in order that he might see them he gave orders for a chair to be placed at the upper end of the state room opposite the king. Moreover, it was the king's wish that Bemoym, before becoming a Christian, should first be instructed in matters of the faith; for Bemoym was of the sect of Mafamede in whom he believed, because of his being a neighbor of, and dealer with, the Azanegues, and he had some knowledge of the contents of the Bible. For this reason, theologians and learned men conversed with him and taught and advised him. Then it was decided that he should see and listen to a mass for the king, and this mass was said in pontifical and with great formality and ceremonial in the church of Santa Maria de Todolos Santos. Bemoym with his men and with learned Christians was in the choir, and, at the elevation of the body of Our Lord, when he saw all on their knees with their hands raised in the act of prayer, his hand went up to the cap which he had on his head; and thus, like everybody, with his knees on the ground and his head uncovered, he prayed. Then he said with many indications of truth that the remorse, which he experienced in his heart in that hour, he took as clear proof that this was the only true God of salvation. Then for two days the king proceeded to banquet publicly, for which purpose he put on his robes and he commanded that the house and the table were to be furnished with plate and tapestries, dishes and service, and there were to be minstrels and dances, all in great perfection; for the king was deliberately very particular and exact about ceremonial above all in matters touching his estate. At the second hour of the night of the third day of the month of November, the said Bemoym, and six of the principal persons who had come with him, became Christians in the chamber of the queen, which was decorated for the occasion with elaborate formality. His godfathers were the king, the queen, the prince, the duke, a commissary of the pope who was at the court, and the bishop of Tanger who at that time was the licentiate Calçadilha. Dom Justo, bishop of Cepta, who in pontifical performed the office, baptized them, and Bemoym received the name Dom Joham for love of the king. Moreover, on the seventh day of November, the king dubbed him a knight; and twenty-four of his men were made Christians in the counting-house of the said town. The king gave him a coat-of-arms consisting of a golden cross on a red field surrounded by the escutcheon of the arms of Portugal. On this same day, in a solemn act and speaking as a great lord he rendered obedience and paid homage to the king. Also he sent another submission, written in Latin, to the pope, wherein he gave an account of his case and of his conversion to the faith in words of deep devotion and high praise to the king. The king determined to give him help and assistance, and gave him twenty armed caravels. . . .

CRY OF ALARM

The Portuguese began evangelizing the peoples of the Congo in 1484 *or* 1485. *During the next few years they converted most of the Congolese royal family. One member, Nzinga Mvemba, who was baptized Affonso, came to the throne in* 1507. *He ruled as* manikongo, *or king, until* 1543, *and was a sincere and diligent Christian. However, by the late* 1400*'s slaves and gold had become Africa's major exports, and King Affonso grew alarmed as he saw his kingdom being depopulated by the Portuguese. He wrote numerous letters of protest to the sovereign of Portugal. The one given here is dated October* 18, 1526.

Moreover, Sir, in our Kingdoms there is another great inconvenience which is of little service to God, and this is that many of our people [*naturaes*], keenly desirous as they are of the wares and things of your Kingdoms, which are brought here by your people, and in order to satisfy their voracious appetite, seize many of our people, freed and exempt men; and very often it happens that they kidnap even noblemen and the sons of noblemen, and our relatives, and take them to be sold to the white men who are in our Kingdoms; and for this purpose they have concealed them; and others are brought during the night so that they might not be recognized.

And as soon as they are taken by the white men they are immediately ironed and branded with fire, and when they are carried to be embarked, if they are caught by our guards' men the whites allege that they have bought them but they cannot say from whom, so that it is our duty to do justice and to restore to the freemen their freedom, but it cannot be done if your subjects feel offended, as they claim to be.

And to avoid such a great evil we passed a law so that any white man living in our Kingdoms and wanting to purchase goods in any way should first inform three of our noblemen and officials of our court whom we rely upon in this matter, and these are Dom Pedro Manipanza and Dom Manuel Manissaba, our chief usher, and Gonçalo Pires our chief freighter, who should investigate if the mentioned goods are captives or free men, and if cleared by them there will be no further doubt nor embargo for them to be taken and embarked. But if the white men do not comply with it they will lose the aforementioned goods. And if we do them this favor and concession it is for the part Your Highness has in it, since we know that it is in your service too that these goods are taken from our Kingdom, otherwise we should not consent to this.

MAKING NEW CHRISTIANS

It did not take the Portuguese long to appreciate the enormous profitability of the slave trade. On the other hand, many individuals and groups, including the Crown, were repelled by commerce in human beings. But, as would be the case elsewhere until the nineteenth century, their repugnance spurred them to justify rather than to cease their evil activities. In 1444 *one of the earliest cargoes of African slaves reached the coast of Algarve, Portugal's southernmost province. Henry the Navigator allegedly ordered one of his chroniclers, Gomes Eannes de Azurara, to whitewash the whole episode. As is apparent in the subsequent description of the slave market from Azurara's* Chronicle of Guinea, *the historian could not disguise the inhumanity of the spectacle. The best he could do was applaud the Infante's pious intentions.*

On the eighth day of August, 1444, very early in the morning on account of the heat, the mariners began to assemble their lighters and to disembark their captives, according to their orders. Which captives were gathered together in a field, and marvelous it was to see among them some of a rosy whiteness, fair and well made; others less white, verging on grey, others again as black as moles, as various in their complexions as in their shapes. . . . And what heart was so hard as not to be moved to pity by the sight of this multitude, some with bowed heads and tearful countenances, others groaning dolorously and with eyes uplifted towards heaven, as if to implore help from the Father of all mankind; while there were others who covered their faces with their hands and flung themselves down upon the ground, and some again who gave vent to their sorrow in a dirge, after the manner of their country; and although we could not understand the words, well we appreciated the depth of their distress. And now, to aggravate their woe, men came to parcel them out into five distinct lots, to do which they tore the son from his father, the wife from the husband, the brother from his brethren. No tie of blood or comradeship was respected; each was thrown into a place by chance. O irresistible fortune, thou which ridest roughshod over the affairs of this world, bring to the knowledge of these most unhappy folk those ultimate truths from which they may receive consolation! And ye that are charged with this division into lots, deplore so great a misery, and observe how these unhappy ones embrace one another so tightly that it needs no little strength to tear them apart. Such a division indeed, was not to be effected without great trouble, since parents and children, finding themselves in different groups, would run back to each other—mothers clutched up their children and ran away with them, caring not about the blows they received so long as their little ones should not be torn from them. After this toilsome fashion was the task of division accomplished, the work being rendered more difficult by the crowds which flocked from the neighboring towns and villages, neglecting their work, to see this novel sight. And some of these spectators moved to tears, others chattering, they made a tumult which hindered those charged with the business. The Infante (Dom Henry), mounted on a powerful horse, disdained to take his own share, some forty-six souls, but threw it back into the common stock, taking pleasure only in the thought of so many souls being redeemed from perdition. And truly, his hope was not vain, since so soon as they learned the language, with very little trouble, these people became Christians; and I who write this history saw afterwards in the town of Lagos, young men and women, the offspring of these, born in the country, as good and genuine Christians as if they had been descended from the generation first baptized under the dispensation of Christ.

NEGOTIATING FOR CHATTEL

William Bosman, who is quoted below, was the Dutch West India Company's chief factor, or European agent, at Elmina in the late seventeenth century. A factor's right to purchase slaves in a given area was granted by the local black chief in return for "coomey," or customs duty. Bosman's description of Guinean slave dealing, which follows, was given in one of twenty letters he wrote to a friend in Holland. In 1705 these were published in London in English under the title A New and Accurate Description of Guinea.

Most of the Slaves that are offered to us are Prisoners of War, which are sold by the Victors as their Booty.

When these slaves come to *Fida* [in present-day Dahomey], they are put in Prison all together, and when we treat concerning buying them, they are all brought out together in a large Plain; where by our Chirurgeons, whose Province it is, they are thoroughly examined, even to the smallest Member, and that naked too both Men and Women, without the least Distinction or Modesty. Those which are approved as good are set on one side; and the lame or faulty are set by as *Invalides*, which are here called *Mackrons*. These are such as are above five and thirty Years old, or are maimed in the Arms, Legs, Hands or Feet, have lost a Tooth, are grey-haired or have Films over their eyes; as well as all those which are affected with any Venereal Distemper, or with several other Diseases.

The *Invalides* and the Maimed being thrown out . . . the remainder are numbred, and it is entered who delivered them. In the meanwhile, a burning Iron with the Arms or Name of the Companies, lyes in the Fire; with which ours are marked on the Breast. . . . but we yet take all possible care that they are not burned too hard, especially the Women who are more tender than the Men.

We are seldom long detained in the buying of these Slaves, because their price is established, the Women being . . . cheaper than the Men. . . .

When we have agreed with the Owners of the Slaves, they are returned to their Prison; where from that time forwards they are kept at our charge, cost us twopence a day a Slave; which serves to subsist them, like our Criminals, on Bread and Water: So that to save Charges we send them on Board our Ships with the very first Opportunity; before which their Masters strip them of all they have on their Backs . . . as well Women as Men: In which condition they are obliged to continue, if the Master of the Ship is not so Charitable (which he commonly is) as to bestow something on them to cover their Nakedness.

THE MIDDLE PASSAGE

The ocean crossing from Africa to the Americas was called the middle passage. It was the most terrifying segment of the slave's journey to bondage; there was no chance of escape, and most of the captives had never before seen the sea. This description of the trans-Atlantic nightmare is from Human Livestock, An Account of the Share of the English-speaking People in the Maintenance and Abolition of Slavery, *published in 1933. The author, British historian Edmund B. d'Auvergne, relied largely on records of testimonies made by slavetraders themselves before parliamentary committees.*

A common type of slaving vessel employed about the middle of the eighteenth century was called a snow, of about 140 tons, square of stern, 57 feet keel, 21 feet beam, 5 feet between decks, 9 feet in the hold. The dimensions of the *Brooks*, a frigate-built ship of 320 tons burthen, without forecastle and pierced for twenty guns were stated by a [British] Government inspector in the year 1786 to be length, 100 feet, beam 25 ft. 4 in., height between decks, 5 feet 8 in. The number of air ports was fourteen. Legally allowed to carry only 450 souls, on leaving the coast of Africa, she carried in addition to her crew of forty-five, 609 slaves (351 men, 127 women, 90 boys, 41 girls). Overcrowding was almost essential to carrying on the slave business. In days of sail, shipmasters could hardly guess the number of trips they might make in a year; and while overcrowding increased the mortality, it might equally result in more survivors to be sold for a profit. In Charles II's time Captain Tallers bought some negroes from another ship which had had them *three months* aboard. They were almost starved and "surfeycatted" [suffocated]. They were fed with little else than musty corn. "There must have been something extraordinary," concludes the letter, "that so many died." The voyage from Guinea to Antigua in the eighteenth century was reckoned at five or six weeks. The longest passage of nine ships reported was fifty days.

Between decks, where it will have been noted a tall man could not stand upright, the human cargo was stowed, males and females in separate compartments. The women were left unfettered. The men were generally kept throughout the voyage chained in pairs, wrist to wrist, ankle to ankle. Those who were left unchained were packed in couples, side by side, like sardines, or spoon-fashion—the head of one against the feet of the other. "They are about as comfortable," one witness told the commission, "as a man might be in his coffin." The slaves, said one captain, often quarreled among themselves—not seldom because one of the pair either could not or would not move when his wretched partner wished to ease himself. One is not surprised to hear that those who went below in the evening apparently in good health were not seldom found dead in the morning; dead and living were often found chained together.

A ship's surgeon says: "Some wet and blowing weather having occasioned the port-holes to be shut and the grating to be covered, fluxes and fevers among the negroes resulted. While they were in this situation, my profession requiring it, I frequently went down among them, till at length their apartments became so extremely hot as to be only sufferable for a very short time. But the excessive heat was not the only thing that rendered their situation intolerable. The deck, that is the floor of their rooms, was so covered with the blood and mucus which had proceeded from them in consequence of the flux, that it resembled a slaughterhouse. It is not in the power of the human imagination to picture a situation more dreadful and disgusting. Numbers of the slaves had fainted, they were carried on deck, where several of them died, and the rest were with difficulty restored. It nearly proved fatal to me also." To these horrors must be added the agonies of sea-sickness, to which most of the wretched creatures must have been subject. Gomer Williams, comparing statistics, finds that out of 7,904 slaves purchased on the Coast, 2,053 died on the Middle Passage. The *Priscilla*, of Liverpool, lost ninety-four out of 350 slaves. On another occasion, during a gale, fifty slaves perished within eighteen hours.

THE RISE OF GUMBO SMART

Occasionally, through sheer wit or cunning, a slave improved his lot. Following is the success story of Gumbo Smart, who made the best of his enslavement on Bance (now Bunce) Island in the Sierra Leone River. The extract is from the journal of Zachary Macaulay, who was a white colonist living in the region.

June 3, 1797. . . . This Smart I have formerly told you had been a slave on Bance Island. He is a native of the Loko Country which lies three days' journey or more beyond Rokelle [Rokel]. He had been intended for a ship bound for the West Indies, but on the day the slaves were being put on board, he had concealed himself. . . . In the meantime he was employed in boats, and showing much acuteness and fidelity he was retained on the island.

He grew in favor and was at length promoted to be a factor and sent to Rokelle with goods to buy slaves. As this was the key to his native country he had an opportunity of buying numbers of his own Countrymen, none of whom he sent to the Island, but either kept them as domestics, or exchanged them with their friends for slaves of other nations. By this policy he has made himself powerful and independent. So that even Bance Island whose slave he is, stands in awe of him and scarce ventures to press him for the Payment of 150 Slaves which he owes them. His adherents amount to several Hundreds, exclusive of his own family, [which] consists of no less than thirty wives and eighty children alive.

THE CONSUMMATE VILLAINS

One of the more outspoken opponents of slavery was the Reverend John Newton (1725–1807), *an Englishman who before entering the Church had been a dealer in human flesh on Sherbro Island off Sierra Leone and had also captained trans-Atlantic slave brigs. In* 1788 *he published in London an anti-slave-trade pamphlet,* Thoughts upon the African Slave Trade, *which contained this description of the mutually deceptive means by which the trade was conducted.*

Not an article that is capable of diminution or adulteration is delivered genuine or entire. The spirits are lowered by water. False heads are put into the kegs that contain the gunpowder; so that, though the keg appears large, there is no more powder in it, than in a much smaller. The linen and cotton cloths are opened, and two or three yards . . . cut off, not from the end, but out of the middle, where it is not so readily noticed.

The Natives are cheated, in the number, weight, measure, or quality of what they purchase in every possible way. And, by habit and emulation, a marvelous dexterity is acquired in these practices. And thus the Natives, in their turn, in proportion to their commerce with the Europeans, and (I am sorry to add) particularly with the English, become jealous, insidious, and revengeful.

They know with whom they have to deal, and are accordingly prepared. . . . Retaliation on their part furnishes a plea for reprisal on ours. Thus, in one place or another, trade is often suspended, all intercourse cut off, and things are in a state of war; till necessity, either on the ship's part, or on theirs, produces overtures of peace, and dictates the price which the offending party must pay. . . . For, with a few exceptions, the English and Africans, reciprocally, consider each other as consummate villains, who are always watching opportunities to do mischief. In short, we have, I fear too deservedly, a very unfavorable character upon the Coast. When I have charged a Black with unfairness and dishonesty, he has answered, if able to clear himself, with an air of disdain, "What! do you think I am a White Man?". . .

A sixteenth-century Nigerian clay sculpture portrays a fierce Portuguese soldier.

THE INTRUDERS

PIERPONT MORGAN LIBRARY, MS. COUSAS RARAS 525

High-pooped Portuguese caravels, like those in the armada above, brought the African coasts within the sphere of European interest. Opposite, a 1493 Portuguese map of Africa locates Prester John's realm along the Upper Nile.

THE EYES OF PORTUGAL

Europeans first touched the sub-Saharan mainland in 1444, when Portuguese explorers under the direction and inspiration of Prince Henry reached the mouth of the Senegal River. What motivated the Navigator were grander designs, among them sheer curiosity to know what his captains would find when they entered southern waters. Technology had made Henry's goal possible: by the early fifteenth century the Portuguese had developed a sailing ship capable of making long ocean voyages. Historic legend abetted the search. Henry sought to discover deep within the uncharted continent the legendary Christian kingdom of Prester John and to enlist his friendly forces in a two-pronged crusade against Islam. Commerical ambitions seem at this stage to have played a relatively minor role. Relations between Europeans and Africans at the start, at least, were auspicious.

N.Y. PUBLIC LIBRARY, MAP DIVISION

magna
Carena
egito
carena
tebais
nubia
pentapolis
babilona
ethiopia

TRUSTEES OF THE BRITISH MUSEUM

An ivory saltcellar at left, from West Africa, combines Portuguese motifs with African craftsmanship. The heavily bearded figure represents a Portuguese official. Below is a French rendering of the huge Portuguese citadel at Mombasa, an Indian Ocean port that the Portuguese seized in 1505. Opposite is a statue of Saint Anthony of Padua made on the Congo coast, where Portugal was most successful in proselytizing.

SECURING A FOOTHOLD

Between the Portuguese and Africans the first formal link was trade, a mutually profitable exchange of European textiles and metalware for African pepper, ivory, and gold. To put the thriving commerce on a permanent basis and secure it from European interlopers, the Portuguese built the fortress-depot of São Jorge in 1482 on the coast of present-day Ghana. It was the first of many such Portuguese stations, which would eventually dot the African coast from Senegal to Zanzibar. Close behind the traders came diplomats and missionaries, for in the early days of contact Portugal looked upon a Christianized Africa as a vital ally in its grand design of humbling the Muslim empire. Missionary success was striking in the kingdom of the Congo, whose ruler, baptized Affonso, became an efficient propagator of the faith. By the early decades of the sixteenth century the Congo seemed well on its way to becoming a Westernized Christian realm in the heart of Africa.

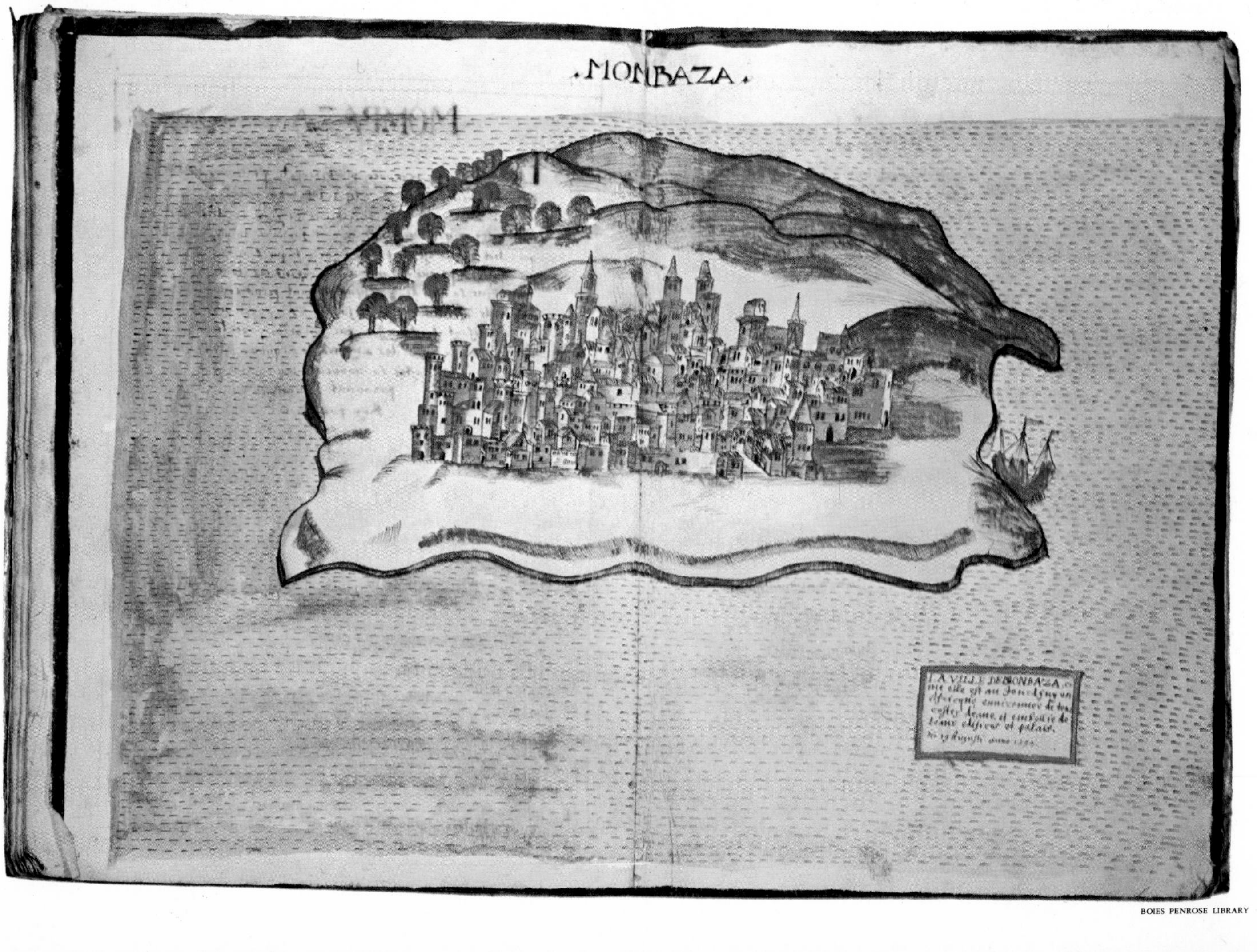

BOIES PENROSE LIBRARY

RIJKSMUSEUM VOOR VOLKENKUNDE, LEIDEN

An enthroned King Affonso of the Congo is depicted here in an audience with the Portuguese envoy. A Christian convert, he asks for missionaries and holy objects.

Upon the advice of the Europeans, Affonso orders his subjects to burn their idols. This and the engraving above are from Théodore de Bry's Petits Voyages, 1598.

BOTH: DE BRY, *Small Voyages*, 1598

WONDERS THAT CEASED

Africa held surprises in abundance for the early European voyagers. First, there were the portents of seemingly unprecedented wealth. "Precious stones were so plentiful," Vasco da Gama was told in Mozambique in 1498, "that there was no need to purchase them as they could be collected in baskets." There were the prospering seaports of East Africa such as Kilwa, "with many fair houses of stones and mortar with many windows after our own fashion, very well arranged in streets." Above all, to Europeans, there was the might and authority of African monarchs. "The King of Wolof can put ten thousand horsemen and one hundred thousand footmen in the field," a Portuguese visitor to Senegal reported in 1505. The great reverence they give to their king filled an English sea captain with awe after he visited the Benin kingdom in 1553. By then, however, the export of slaves to America had begun, and the Africa of wonders would soon cease to exist for Europeans.

THEVET, *Cosmographie Universelle*, 1575

The East African plant opposite was cited in André Thevet's Cosmographie Universelle, 1575, *as the source of a miracle cure for snakebite. At right is the sea monster that, he asserted, ruled the Red Sea. Below is an engraving from a 1686 work by Olfert Dopper purporting to record how the natives of Guinea dive for gold.*

THEVET, *Cosmographie Universelle*, 1575

DOPPER, *Description de l'Afrique*, 1686

THEVET, *Cosmographie Universelle*, 1575

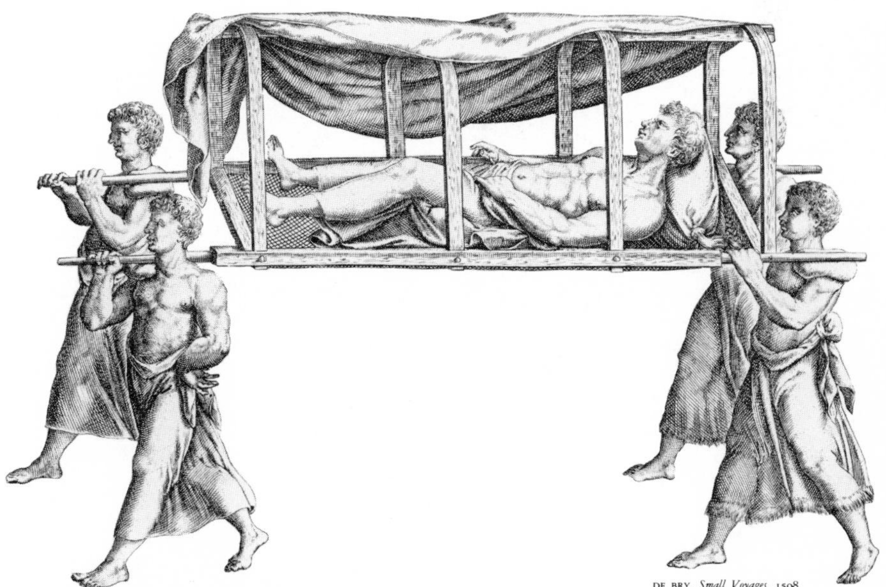

DE BRY, *Small Voyages*, 1598

The Congolese nobility traveled in litters like that above, according to De Bry's hearsay book on Africa. At left, West Africans defend their village against lions, "scourge of the countryside," as shown in the Cosmographie.

OVERLEAF: *The king of Benin sallies from his palace in the company of his retinue in a 1686 French print displaying the pomp of an African ruler.*

DOPPER, DESCRIPTION DE L'AFRIQUE, 1686

NEW YORK PUBLIC LIBRARY

Awaiting shipment to the New World, an African slave sits beneath a heavy forked log, one device used in coffling captives. Below, in a Dahomey appliqué tapestry done in the early eighteenth century, opposing African forces are shown in combat. The work dates from the reign of King Agaja, who, like other inland rulers, was expanding his domain toward the sea in order to deal directly with the Europeans and thus monopolize the local slave trade. At right is a bronze statuette from Benin representing an armed Benin warrior. Regarded with terror by less powerful states, these professionals were the leading procurers of slaves.

RAPHO-GUILLUMETTE–MARC AND EVELYNE BERNHEIM

BALTIMORE MUSEUM OF ART, WURTZBURGER COLLECTION

BIBLIOTHEQUE NATIONALE, SERVICE PHOTOGRAPHIQUE

A Portuguese force deploys in square defensive lines to hold off Angolan attackers in the Portuguese sketch at left. To secure Angola as a supply base for the Brazilian slave trade, the Portuguese in 1575 sharply reversed their former policies. Setting up a colony at Luanda, they not only waged war against local kingdoms but trained local forces to carry out raids for them, bringing strife and decay to the entire Angolan coast. In time the nearby Congo kingdom was sucked into the maelstrom, and when it eventually rose up against its former friends and fellow Christians, the kingdom was torn apart and destroyed.

THE HIDEOUS TRADE

When Europeans decided to use slave labor in the Americas, they set the seal of doom on vast portions of sub-Saharan Africa. Before the opening of the New World the African slave trade with Europe had been a small and circumscribed evil; some five hundred slaves were sold to the Portuguese each year. Fifty years after the discovery of the Americas the yearly figure climbed to ten thousand. A few decades later the annual figure was doubled again. After 1650 slaves were the main West African commodity that European traders would buy. But it was African rulers themselves who were among the chief suppliers, using their power and position to organize slave hunts for the bustling coastal markets. Even European missionaries neglected their religious duties in order to share in the profits of slavery; and by 1700 Christianity had vanished from tropical Africa. Crippled by the slave hunters' reign of terror, African art and sculpture virtually disappeared from such great centers as Ife and Benin. Luxuries for the profiteers were all that the slave trade brought to Africa, and guns to capture yet more slaves in a widening spiral of greed and ruin.

INTERNATIONAL RIVALRY

Other European nations did not stand idle while Portugal reaped the profits of its African trade monopoly. Avid for Portugal's spoils, they eventually took them by force. Simple thievery was the first method: French and British corsairs would pirate Portuguese ships or pillage Portuguese trade centers in daring, one-shot raids. In 1612, however, the Dutch took a bolder step. They built a fort on the Gold Coast; by 1642 they had ousted the Portuguese from that coveted portion of the coast. As Portuguese control crumbled, the French seized the foreign trade of Senegal and that of the Ivory Coast, and the British took the rest of West Africa's commerce. Nothing, however, was settled. The newcomers were as ready to prey on each other as they had been to prey on the Portuguese. Skirmishing perpetually against one another from massive coastal forts, they added by their bitter competition a further infusion of conflict to the chaos inherent in the slave trade. This the intruders accomplished even before they set foot in the interior.

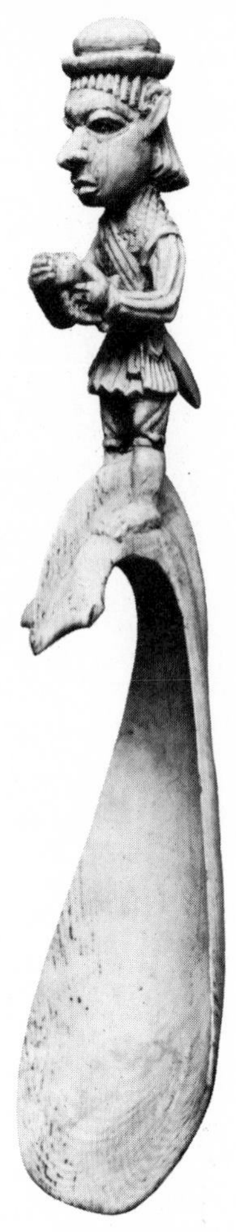

The figure of a plump-cheeked Portuguese at left adorns an ivory spoon carved in Africa around 1525, when the Portuguese were still the only Europeans that West Africans had encountered. Below is Britain's chief Gold Coast installation at Cape Coast Castle as it looked in 1806. The British Crown won control of the Gold Coast trade in the 1700's, succeeding the Dutch and the Portuguese before them.

OVERLEAF: *Troops of Sir Francis Drake put to flight the defenders of São Tiago, largest of the Cape Verde Islands. Drake stopped to pillage this tropical settlement in 1585 on his way to the Caribbean.*

TRUSTEES OF THE BRITISH MUSEUM

PEABODY MUSEUM, SALEM

DE BRY, *Small Voyages*, 1598

The arrival of the Dutch on Gabon's shores, as imagined by De Bry, was largely an occasion for rejoicing. Here, a nearly naked king and queen tender a warm welcome to two officers. Depicted in the water color below is the international market town of Xavier in the Guinea kingdom of Juda. From adjacent walled compounds the Portuguese, French, English, and Dutch vied for shares in a lively foreign trade.

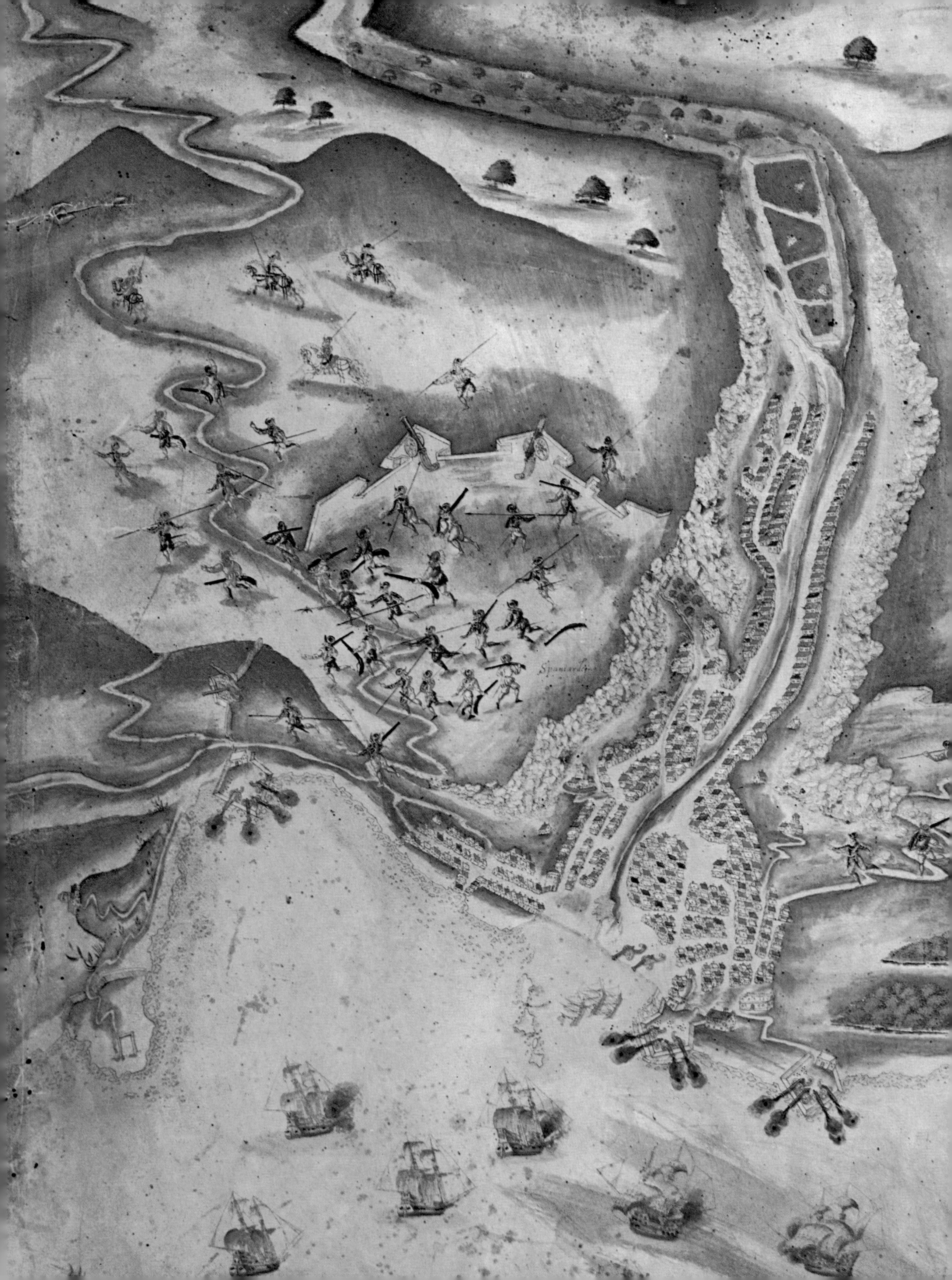
Spaniards

Chapter Nine

TIME OF TROUBLES

(c. 1492–1828)

by

John Henrik Clarke

AFRICA'S TIME OF TRAGEDY AND DECLINE started both in Europe and in Africa itself. For more than a thousand years Africans had been bringing into being empire after empire. But the opening of Europe's era of exploration, Africa's own internal strife, and the slave trade turned what had been Africa's golden age into a time of troubles.

The Crusades may be called the beginning of Europe's reawakening. A religious fervor, not unrelated to politics, had stirred Europeans out of their lethargy and their indifference to the larger world. The First Crusade, begun in 1095, was precipitated by the Seljuk Turks, whose persecution of Christians had placed even Constantinople in jeopardy. The Eastern heads of the Church appealed to Pope Urban II for help. At a great Church council in France the pope pointed out that if Constantinople fell to the Turks, Western Europe would soon be overrun. He made an eloquent plea to the kings and princes gathered, and to all Western European Christendom, to rally to the aid of the Christians in the East and to drive the "infidels" from the Holy Land.

This religious crisis gave Europe a semblance of unity; and although it can be said that the Crusades were military and religious failures, they did provide the opportunity to bring new information to Europe. The religious wars also had a profound effect on the political development of Europe. The Western monarchs were able to strengthen their authority and develop a strong central government while many members of their turbulent aristocracies were fighting in the Holy Land.

Contact with the East had a deep and lasting effect on the Crusaders, who belonged to a civilization where culture and learning had almost vanished during the Dark Ages. The princes in their castles and the peasants in their huts were

low deck on a slaver, as recorded by a member of the British patrol that captured the vessel in 1846

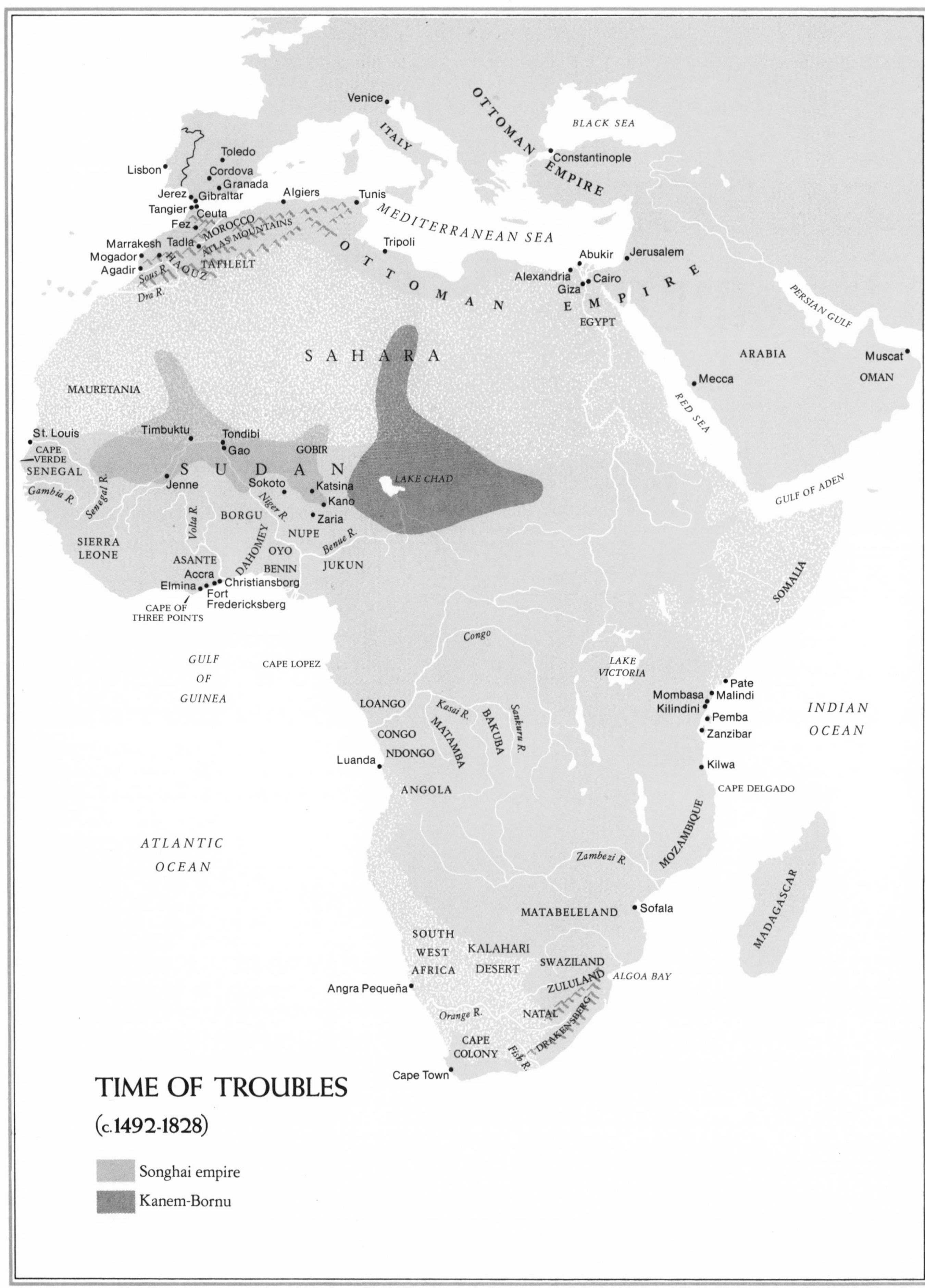

TIME OF TROUBLES
(c.1492-1828)
Songhai empire
Kanem-Bornu
Venice
OTTOMAN EMPIRE
BLACK SEA
ITALY
Constantinople
Toledo
Lisbon
Cordova
Granada
Jerez
Gibraltar
Algiers
Tunis
Tangier
Ceuta
MEDITERRANEAN SEA
Fez
MOROCCO
ATLAS MOUNTAINS
Marrakesh
Tadla
Mogador
HAOUZ
Agadir
TAFILELT
Sous R.
Dra R.
Tripoli
OTTOMAN EMPIRE
Abukir
Jerusalem
Alexandria
Cairo
Giza
EGYPT
PERSIAN GULF
SAHARA
ARABIA
Muscat
OMAN
Mecca
MAURETANIA
RED SEA
St. Louis
Timbuktu
Tondibi
Gao
GOBIR
CAPE VERDE
SENEGAL
SUDAN
Jenne
Sokoto
Katsina
Kano
LAKE CHAD
Gambia R.
Senegal R.
Niger R.
Zaria
GULF OF ADEN
Volta R.
BORGU
NUPE
SIERRA LEONE
DAHOMEY
OYO
Benue R.
ASANTE
Accra
BENIN
JUKUN
Elmina
Christiansborg
Fort Fredericksberg
CAPE OF THREE POINTS
SOMALIA
Congo
GULF OF GUINEA
CAPE LOPEZ
LAKE VICTORIA
Pate
Mombasa
Malindi
Kilindini
Pemba
Zanzibar
LOANGO
Kasai R.
BAKUBA
Sankuru R.
MATAMBA
CONGO
NDONGO
INDIAN OCEAN
Luanda
Kilwa
ANGOLA
CAPE DELGADO
MOZAMBIQUE
ATLANTIC OCEAN
Zambezi R.
MADAGASCAR
MATABELELAND
Sofala
SOUTH WEST AFRICA
KALAHARI DESERT
SWAZILAND
ZULULAND
ALGOA BAY
Angra Pequeña
Orange R.
NATAL
DRAKENSBERG
CAPE COLONY
Fish R.
Cape Town

equally ignorant and uneducated. When they arrived in the East, they soon realized how backward were the people of the West. They marveled at the beautiful cities, the thriving commerce, the busy industries, the art, and the learning. The impetus for exploration was fueled by what the Crusaders met along the way. Ships built to ferry the Crusaders to the Holy Land returned laden with the products of the East. The cargoes of spices, fruits, rich silks, satins, velvets, and other luxury goods had found a ready market. Thus the Crusades brought into being the first attempts to open fresh trade routes to the East. Early in the fifteenth century Europeans, in search of new worlds to conquer and of a food supply to feed the continent's hungry population, began to venture across the seas.

NORTH AFRICA: By 1492 North Africa was confronted with the painful fact of its waning influence in Mediterranean Europe. Spain and Portugal, which had broken the yoke of North African domination, were asserting themselves as powerful, independent nations with colonial aspirations in the lands of their former conquerors. Islam, a great religious and military force in North Africa and the Middle East since the latter part of the seventh century, was now torn apart by internal strife and bickering. The relationship of North Africa to the people of the western Sudan was deteriorating. For hundreds of years this relationship had been good. Africans from the western Sudan had participated in large numbers in the conquest of Spain in the year A.D. 711. These Africans made up the major military force that kept Spain under North African domination, and they participated in that country's intellectual life, as is still reflected in Spain's art, culture, and literature.

In order to understand this neglected aspect of history—the role of Africans in the conquering and ruling of Spain—it is necessary to go back in time to retell, at least briefly, the part that black Africans played in the rise of Islam and in the spread of Islamic influence to Mediterranean Europe.

Hadzrat Bilal ibn Rahab (more often referred to simply as Bilal) was the first high priest of the Islamic empire. After Muhammad himself, it may be said that this great religion began with Bilal, who was an Ethiopian. Bilal is considered to be the Prophet's first African convert. Zayd ibn Harithah, another convert to Muhammad's faith, later became one of the Prophet's foremost generals. Muhammad adopted him as his son and later made him governor of his people, the proud Koreish who lived in what is today Saudi Arabia. Like Bilal, Zayd ibn Harithah was also an Ethiopian. He eventually married into the Prophet's family, the highest honor possible. Zayd ibn Harithah was killed in battle while leading his men against the armies of the Byzantine empire. The authoritative *Encyclopedia of Islam* has hailed him as one of the first great heroes of Islam.

By the early part of the eighth century the followers of Islam had swept across North Africa and were moving into the western Sudan. Among the Africans' military chiefs who converted to the Islamic faith during the Arab invasion of Morocco was a great general known as Tarik ibn Zayyad. Tarik held the rank of general in the Arab-Moorish armies of Musa ibn Nusayr, the governor of North Africa. Tarik entered into friendly relations with Count Julian, the Christian governor of Ceuta, who was on bad terms with his master, Roderick, the king of Spain. Count Julian urged Tarik to invade Spain. In the meantime, Musa ibn Nusayr learned that the Spanish king was busy in the north of his country in a campaign to put down an uprising of the Basques. Musa decided that time was ripe for an invasion of the Visigothic realm. An African army was recruited and placed under the leadership of Tarik. In 711 the army landed on a Spanish promontory just thirteen miles across the Mediterranean from Ceuta. The place was later named Gebel Tarik, meaning the "Hill of Tarik," or as we now call it, Gibraltar.

Tarik's army captured several Spanish towns near Gibraltar, among them Heraclea. Then he advanced toward Andalusia. King Roderick learned of the invasion and raised an army for defense. The two armies met in battle at a place called Jerez, not far from the Guadalete River. In this battle King Roderick was defeated. Tarik sent for reinforcements from Africa, and with them conquered most of the Iberian Peninsula. Thus began the African domination of Spain. The Gothic kingdom of Spain was laid low by Africans who had been converted to the Islamic faith, not by Arabs.

After consolidating their position in Spain, the Muslims began to establish institutions of research and learning, whose brilliance was felt far beyond Spain's borders. This was an achievement not of the Arabs alone. It was brought into being by a combination of Africans and Arabs, collectively referred to by Europeans as Moors. (The word "Moor" entered the vocabulary of the Europeans meaning "blacks," as in "blackamoor.") The Moors built magnificent cities in Spain. Cordova in the ninth century was much like a modern city, with streets paved and illuminated at night, and sidewalks for pedestrians.

The intellectual achievement of the Africans in Spain outweighs all other things that can be credited to them.

These Islamic Africans re-examined the moral foundations supporting Western civilization. They found that it had been the legacy of the Greeks that had enabled the West to make intellectual progress. This answer created a question: What had gone wrong in Europe—spiritually and intellectually—before and after the decline of the Roman empire? The inquiry led in essence to the following conclusion: By the time Europe's Christian foundation was firmly set, the intellectual means and moral fiber of the people were exceedingly weak, and there existed a deep gulf between faith and reason.

These Muslim Africans in Spain came to this conclusion while trying to bridge a similar gap in relation to their own religion and culture. While Europe was largely ignorant of its Greek legacy, these Africans rediscovered and preserved it. Their assimilation and distribution of that treasure forms one of the most fascinating chapters in the history of man's quest for knowledge.

In the course of their labors the African conquerors of Spain did far more than mere translation. They commented upon and explained the Greeks, gradually erecting upon the Greek foundation an intellectual edifice of their own. While the initial work was done in the Near East, it was greatly elaborated upon by other scholars, mainly in Sicily, Spain, and Morocco.

In the meantime Islam had moved deeper into Africa. The Arabs' language and religion brought together a large number of peoples and cultures that had not previously related one to another. When the second wave of North African merchants reached the western Sudan about the year A.D. 1000, they found flourishing kingdoms that had already been influenced by Islam. The commercial relations they established there lasted for more than five hundred years despite continuing conflict. The Africans south of the Sahara made a rallying cry around Islam and in large numbers began to prey on the nations in West Africa and the Niger River area, accusing the people of not properly observing the faith—Islam. Very often the spread of Islam and trade with North Africa came at the same time. Therefore in the western Sudan the defenders of this religion had both a commercial and a religious motive.

This gave rise to the dynasty of the Almoravids, who derived their name from the Arabic *al-Murabitin*, meaning "members of the ribat," a kind of militarized convent. The Almoravids were started by Ibn Yasin, head of a tough, warlike family from Senegal, across the desert. Puritanical in their approach to Islam, they sought to impose their own interpretation of the faith. After establishing a series of ribats where the disciples devoted themselves to strict religious practices and military exercises, the Almoravids swept north across the Mauritanian deserts and gained possession of the mountainous regions of Morocco. Ibn Yasin's successor, Yusuf ibn Tashfin, founded the capital at Marrakesh in 1062 and laid siege to Fez in the following year.

The Almoravids succeeded in reuniting Morocco, parts of West Africa, and Islamic Spain. By 1076 they had conquered the ancient empire of Ghana. After ruling this fallen country for ten years, they pulled most of their armies out of Ghana in order to give more support to their coreligionists in Spain. There they were successful in stemming the Christian tide that threatened to engulf all Islamic Spain after the fall of Toledo in 1085.

In the middle of the thirteenth century (about A.D. 1240) another dynasty rose up within the framework of Islam and challenged the rule of the Almoravids in Spain and in Morocco. Its followers are known by the name "Almohads," a Spanish corruption of an Arab word meaning "unitarians." They, too, were a religious and military movement, offering another puritanical interpretation. The conflicts between the Almoravids and the Almohads weakened the Africans' control over Spain. The eventual decline of both dynasties affected all North Africa, the western Sudan, and Mediterranean Europe.

The Almohads did not yield their power easily. They called upon other followers of Islam for support. A vigorous people from the Sahara, known as the Marinids, came to their assistance and eventually usurped the waning power of the Almohads. This dynasty consisted mainly of soldiers and administrators. Abu Yohya (1248–1258) established the Marinid capital at Fez and prepared the ground for another leader, Yaqub al-Mansur, who extended their religious empire into what is now Algeria. The Marinids left their stamp both on Spain and North Africa, where they proved to be some of the greatest builders and patrons of the arts that Morocco had known.

By the end of the fourteenth century southern Europe had gained enough strength—military and otherwise—to challenge their African masters. The constant pressure from Christians in Spain and from the new waves of Arab immigrants from the East created a situation that the Marinids found difficult to handle. By the end of the fifteenth century the Moors had lost all Spain except the kingdom of Granada. The Christians, although they also had their internal disputes, were finally united. The marriage of Ferdinand and Isabella joined the formerly hostile royal houses of Aragon and Castile, and together their forces blockaded the city of

Granada. After eight months the Moorish governor finally surrendered.

This marked the end of an era. Europe had literally been reborn. The Africans who had planted the seeds of progress in southern Europe had not made the best use of the harvest that followed. The progress and excitement that had inspired Europe during the fifteenth century and had carried medieval Europe over into the modern world had brought no progressive changes to North Africa, now rocked with conflict.

In the countries of North Africa, especially in Morocco, political stagnation seemed to be the general rule, and strong men with selfish intent found their opportunity to seize power. They no longer protected the poets and scholars; they left no monuments to embellish the conquered cities. To North Africans the fifteenth century was a time in which Spain was a lost and hated land, a century in which Portugal robbed North Africa of a large part of its western seacoast.

The news in 1492 of Christopher Columbus' discovery of the New World came swiftly to the courts of Fez, Marrakesh, and Cairo, and was no cause for rejoicing. To the marabouts, who were the interpreters of the Islamic world of that day, this event was grave indeed. The same year Granada fell, and Moorish exiles returned to their homes in Morocco without the customary heroes' welcome.

During the early part of the sixteenth century the forces in North Africa were turning two ways. Attempts were made to settle internal differences, and plans to take over the still-rich nations in the western Sudan were formalized. The nations of the western Sudan were comparatively stable, due in part to their lack of firearms and the conflicts that would have resulted.

Portugal's growing control of the northern coast now began to impede commercial progress. This came at a time when the vassals and allies that the Portuguese had among the North African people began to desert them in favor of reawakened nationalism. Most Muslims regarded the Christian Portuguese with hostility and were determined that they should be driven into the sea. To accomplish this, the Muslims needed a leader. The search led them to Abu Abdullah, sheik of the Beni Saadi, a people of Arabian descent who had established themselves in the Dra River region of southern Morocco. Under the leadership of Abu Abdullah, the people of the Sous valley moved against the Portuguese, who had established a port on the Atlantic coast of Morocco at Agadir. Abdullah's power increased, although not all of his wars were successful. In the coastal strip west of the Atlas Mountains of Morocco he and his two sons established a capital and fought the Portuguese. When Abu Abdullah died in 1518, his sons, as expected, carried on his work. The years of nationalist feeling in North Africa had produced a number of leaders who were able men determined to drive the Portuguese from their land. In 1541 Portuguese power in North Africa began to decline. They lost their stronghold at Agadir, and subsequently, as they became more involved in their Asian colonies, they abandoned other North African territories under their domination.

Meanwhile, in 1549, the Saadian dynasty came to power in Morocco and showed itself to be equal to the job of nation building. The greatest of the Saadian kings was Ahmad al-Mansur, who ruled from 1578 to 1603. He not only defended Morocco from Turkish invasion, strengthening the strategic fortifications of the country and reorganizing it on the Turkish model, but also developed the agriculture of the Sus and Haouz regions and won a favored position for Morocco in the markets of western Europe.

While the reign of Ahmad al-Mansur brought a high degree of security and prosperity to Morocco, it brought tragedy and decline to the nations of the western Sudan, for the Saadians lusted after the gold of the Niger River nations and tried to seize it by force. They were by no means the first Moroccan dynasty to make this national policy; in the eleventh century the Almoravids had financed their northward movement with gold from this region.

After the death of Askia Muhammad in 1528, his great Songhai empire showed signs of having seen its last days of power and glory. Ahmad al-Mansur systematically planned the conquest of the western Sudan, giving his profound attention to this military and administrative heart of West Africa. In the year 1591 an army of some four thousand musketeers under the leadership of a Spanish mercenary officer, Judar Pasha, crossed the Sahara and was on the borders of Songhai before any serious attention was paid to the danger. Songhai's ruler, Askia Ishak II, called up an army that was superior in numbers but armed with traditional weapons. The two armies met on April 12, 1591, at a small town called Tondibi, about fifty miles from the capital city of Gao. In spite of the brave stand made by the army of Songhai, the Moroccan soldiers moved into the country, and the wrack and ruin began.

Ahmad al-Mansur expected great treasures in gold to be sent back to Morocco soon after the conquest. When these treasures were not forthcoming, Ahmad dismissed Judar Pasha and sent another general, Mahmud ibn Zergun, to

Napoleon "the liberator" and local dignitaries observe French soldiers at a Nile reclamation project in a contemporary French print.
BIBLIOTHEQUE NATIONALE, ESTAMPES; BULLOZ

Songhai. His orders were to take charge of the army and press onward until he had driven Askia Ishak out of the Sudan and discovered the place where the people were hiding the gold.

The Moroccan invasion of Songhai and other nations of the western Sudan was made all the more tragic because in most cases it was Muslim against Muslim. The invaders from North Africa and their European mercenary troops did not spare anyone—not man, woman, or child. They pitilessly slew the now demoralized citizens who cried out to them: "We are Muslims; we are your brothers in religion." The war brought no honor to either side, and in the years that followed, an appreciation of their intellectual and material contribution to Spain and the other nations of the Mediterranean sphere was lost from the respectful commentary of human history.

While the drama of Morocco and the western Sudan was unfolding, Egypt and other North African nations were encountering a new force. Like the Mameluks before them, this new force came from Turkey, where its dreams of empire had begun to take shape with the conquest of Constantinople in 1453. By 1516 the eastern Mediterranean from Greece through Asia Minor and Syria was under Ottoman rule. By 1517 the reigning Mameluk sultan of Cairo had been publicly executed and replaced by an Ottoman ruler. Algeria was taken in 1518 by Khayr al-Din Barbarossa, who went on to make his reputation as the admiral of Turkey's dreaded corsair fleet. The Barbary Coast states of Tripolitania and Tunis became semi-independent tributaries of the Ottoman empire in the 1550's.

Cultural ties with the Islamic world of northwest Africa and the Middle East continued as before. The Ottoman Turks were content to rule through military oligarchies and to collect taxes, holding the land under a feudal system that invited a steady decline in the prosperity of the people and the fertility of the land. No fresh ideas came in; all business was operated in the interest of the Turks.

It was not until the end of the eighteenth century that a number of influences were combined to rescue Egypt from the decadence of Ottoman rule. First, in 1798, came Napoleon's abortive expedition immediately designed to cut Great Britain's route to the Indian subcontinent. (The French had been considering the idea of seizing Egypt since 1769, when annexation was proposed as compensation for the loss of its American territories.) Napoleon's invasion fleet arrived off Alexandria on July 1. Three weeks later he met the Ottoman forces at Embaba on the left bank of the Nile, just north of Giza. Winning a dramatic victory in the Battle of the Pyramids, Napoleon seemed to have laid France's claim to Egypt. But ten days later Admiral Horatio Nelson located Napoleon's fleet in Abukir Bay, and in the brief Battle of the Nile that followed, gave Napoleon's Egyptian campaign a major setback. (Napoleon would remain in Egypt for another year, his decimated forces suffering further defeats from a variety of diseases and from the Turkish army.) Napoleon returned to France in 1799, leaving Jean-Baptiste Kléber and his lieutenants to oversee the province. They, too, were forced to leave in 1801 when a British expedition of some seventeen thousand men and a Turkish army combined to deliver the final blow.

The United States, as a newborn maritime nation, was confronted with the costly problem of securing safe passage in the Mediterranean for its merchant ships. European states had swallowed pride and capitulated to the tribute demands of the Barbary Coast pirates, but a bumptious America was ready to meet the challenge with arms. Jefferson dispatched a squadron to the shores of Tripoli in 1801; early defeats were followed by Stephen Decatur's daring entry of Tripoli's harbor, where the American frigate Philadelphia *had been impounded. As shown in the print, right, the Yankees chose to burn the ship rather than leave it to the pirates. Strife continued until peace was signed in 1815.*

PEABODY MUSEUM, SALEM, OLDS COLLECTION

Short-lived though the occupation was, the awakening of European interest in the cultural and scientific achievements of ancient Egypt was to have a permanent effect. Napoleon's occupation had included a scientific commission, the Institute of Egypt, which applied itself to studying zoological and botanical curiosities, surveying the land, and exploring the archeological ruins of the ancient Egyptian kingdoms. (At the Delta town of Rashid, called Rosetta by the French, a French engineer stumbled upon a stone showing the multilingual inscription that would lead to the deciphering of Egyptian hieroglyphs.)

Next, Muhammad Ali, an enlightened Turkish soldier who had come to Egypt to expel the French, initiated the modernization of Egypt. Named the Turkish viceroy in Egypt in 1806, he gradually strengthened his power base until, in 1811, he was able to break with the Ottoman empire. The way to Egypt's renaissance was thus opened. Having observed the technological achievements of the French occupation, Muhammad Ali undertook to revolutionize Egypt's agriculture, industry, and army along Western lines. To supply an ever-growing demand for Egyptian cotton, he invited European hydraulic engineers to work with indigenous specialists to revive and improve the land's use of irrigation, and within a few years the Nile Valley was producing two crops per year where one had been the rule. As a further aid to productivity, he nationalized the land, making the peasants all but owners of their fields so long as they paid taxes. The considerable profits realized from these reforms were invested in the military and economic development of the country, for it was one of the tenets of Muhammad Ali's rule that foreign investment capital should be kept out. His remarkable success proved so troublesome to British interests that outside pressures were eventually brought against him. The last years of Muhammad Ali's life showed a considerable slowing down of the modernization process.

THE WESTERN AND CENTRAL SUDAN: The collapse of the western Sudan after the Moroccan invasion of 1591 is one of the saddest events in African history. Security gave way to fear, and violence succeeded tranquillity.

After the fall of Songhai many of their conquered provinces revolted, pillaging and destroying lands to the south and east. Half the kingdom fell prey to anarchy. By 1595 the Moroccans had brought the main parts of the once great empire of Songhai under control. The administrator of the colony, who was appointed by the king of Morocco and served as his representative, took the title of pasha, or governor.

One result of the Moroccan conquest of the western Sudan was the decline of the once-prosperous trans-Saharan trade. The city of Timbuktu, at one time the pride of the western Sudan, was now a ghost of its former self. The Songhai chronicler Abd al-Rahman as-Sadi had once called Timbuktu "an exquisite city, pure, delicious, blessed with luxury and full of life." He boasted that its people had "never been soiled by the worship of idols." Timbuktu, he went on to say, "gradually developed into a trade center. Its greatest days came during the time it was the meeting place for traders from Egypt, the Libyan Desert, the Oases of Tuat, Fez, and the gold lands."

One of the most shameful and far-reaching tragedies of the Moroccan occupation was the attempted destruction of the intellectual life of the nation. The attack on the university of Sankore at Timbuktu and the exiling of its black scholars was an act of inexcusable arrogance. Moroccan troops and their white mercenary leaders literally declared war on all institutions and intellectuals. In 1594 the great scholar Ahmad Baba was exiled to Morocco. He had been the last chancellor at Sankore. Ahmad Baba was the author of more than forty books in Arabic, ranging from Arabic grammar to astronomy. His life is a brilliant example of the range and depth of West African intellectual activity before the colonial era.

With the loss of all its scholars, businessmen, judges, and men of religion, the light of knowledge and education went out in the western Sudan. Moroccan soldiers robbed the houses of valuables, including maps and manuscripts containing the history of the western Sudan. Revolts against the invaders, and the further suppressions that followed, worsened matters, as did internal revolts among the subject people.

The royal family that the Moroccans found on the throne of Songhai was still trying to save the country from the worst aspects of the invaders' wrath. Ishak II had been banished because of his opposition. His brother, Muhammad Gao, became the next *askia*. He pledged allegiance to the sultan of Morocco, but the Moroccans did not completely trust him. Nevertheless, during the great famine of 1592 they were forced to rely heavily on him for their food supplies. Mahmud ibn Zergun, the governor, asked the new *askia* to prove his loyalty by sending the much-needed food to the Moroccan army. This Muhammad Gao did in good faith. He ordered all crops on the Hausa side of the river to be cut and brought to the Moorish camp. Then Pasha Mahmud ibn Zergun chose to test his loyalty again. He asked Muhammad Gao to call the local kings and men of affairs to swear obedience to the sultan of Morocco. This was done, and the assembled men were murdered without warning. Muhammad Gao now knew that none of the Moroccans could be trusted. He continued to go through the motions of being their puppet while passing information to his rebel brother, Askia Nuh.

Nuh had not accepted Moroccan rule. He was an astute leader and fighter. Some of the fragmented army of Songhai rallied around him and helped to keep up continued harassment of the enemy army. The people of Songhai, in defiance of their Moroccan overlords, declared him *askia* and said that they would obey no other ruler. He was wise enough to avoid giving his enemies a chance to open battle. The hills, swamps, and thick bush of Borgu, a region in northern Nigeria, became his encampment. He attacked the Moroccan outposts at night and withdrew to the forest and the hills. The people of Borgu did not particularly like the army of Songhai, which at a previous time had conquered them; but they united and fought with Askia Nuh because they hated the Moroccans still more, and like the people of Songhai, wanted to drive out the Moroccans.

The pressure and the harassment inflicted by Askia Nuh forced Mahmud ibn Zergun to turn once more to the sultan of Morocco for help. He complained that the tsetse fly was killing his horses and that disease and bad food and water were causing many deaths among his men. The sultan sent more soldiers and supplies and continued to wait for the treasures in gold that he had long expected. At the end of two years Mahmud ibn Zergun had neither large amounts of gold nor news of great success to send to his sultan. He was forced to give up the fight with Askia Nuh for a while, and he returned to Timbuktu.

There he faced more disappointments. The people living in Timbuktu had rebelled against the Moorish guard left to hold the city. The troublesome Tuaregs were raiding the Niger valley again. Ibn Zergun, now an angry and frustrated man, suspected that the educated people were the cause of the rebellions, and he conceived a plan to punish them further.

An announcement was made that all the homes in the town would once again be searched for weapons, except the houses belonging to descendants of a revered local *qadi*, which meant, in effect, the houses of the educated class. Hearing this, the rest of the citizenry took their valuables to the exempted houses for safekeeping. Then the pasha ordered all the holy man's descendants to go to the Great Mosque of Sankore to swear obedience to the sultan of Morocco. Only after the group had gathered at the mosque did they discover the governor's very cunning plan. These men, who had lived in comfort most of their lives, were put in chains and sent together with their wives and children across the desert to Morocco to be sold as slaves. Few of them survived the journey.

Mahmud ibn Zergun derived no benefit from this cruelty. Soon he was once again in trouble with the sultan of Morocco. Out of the vast riches that he had at last obtained from the rape of Timbuktu and other major cities in Songhai, he had sent the sultan only one hundred thousand mithqals of gold. Though this was a large amount, the sultan thought that it should be much larger. In his anger he decided that he could no longer trust Ibn Zergun. After ordering that he be arrested and put to death, the sultan sent another governor.

The news reached Mahmud ibn Zergun before the new governor, Mansur Abdurrahmen, arrived. He left Timbuktu and decided to risk a more honorable fate in the continued fight against his old enemy, Askia Nuh. Mahmud ibn Zergun met his death in the city of Zaria, located in present-day northern Nigeria.

Over the years Moroccan pashas were either poisoned or forced to leave the Sudan after failing to bring the area under control. The first contingent of invaders from Morocco who were still in the Sudan chose to elect their own officers. Some had married into the local population and had local loyalties. Some had fought fiercely among themselves over the control of what was left of Songhai. (In certain ways this condition would still prevail when the French arrived in this area during the latter part of the nineteenth century.)

Intermarriage between the local Africans and the Moroccan invaders produced, in another generation, a large number of Africans bent on the pursuit of power alone. Fights over who would inherit their fathers' land and power lasted for well over a hundred years; they wrecked or retarded the progress of most of the nations in inner West Africa and the central Sudan. Still, old nations were reorganized, and new nations were born in the midst of this recurring conflict. We should look, at least briefly, at some of these nations and how they survived Africa's time of troubles.

A number of states began to emerge in the area that is present-day Nigeria. Some of the former colonies of Songhai began to consolidate their territories and form new states. In parts of the central Sudan a degree of safety and security was re-established by people who moved away from the area of Moroccan domination. Some of the internal trade routes of the sub-Sahara not specifically connected with North Africa were reopened.

Among the new states that emerged before and during the Moroccan occupation of the western Sudan, Kanem-Bornu is outstanding. This state had the strength and leadership that was needed to preserve its independence from the Moroccans. Perhaps the greatest of the Bornu kings was Mai Idris Alooma, who reigned from 1570 to 1602 and was a contemporary of Queen Elizabeth of England. Although the slave trade had already started, the central Sudan would not feel its full effect until much later. The Hausa states had already reached a high level of prosperity and cultural development. The Yoruba, the Ibo, and the people of Nupe, Borgu, and Jukun were also developing powerful state structures.

At the close of the eighteenth century the two most powerful states in Hausaland were Gobir in the northwest and Bornu in the northeast. The Jukun kingdom had ceased to be a menace, but Nupe retained its independence, though much weakend. Some of the Hausa states were nominally independent, but still under some strong influence from Bornu. This was the political situation on the eve of the nineteenth-century Fulani wars, which would resolve some of the old problems and create new ones.

Meanwhile, the effects of the coastal slave trade had reached the states of inner West Africa while the area was still trying to recover from the Moroccan invasions. With the aid of firearms, the Europeans and their corrupted African partners pushed the slave trade farther into the interior. When the conflicts between rival West African states did not produce enough prisoners of war to be sold into slavery, new conflicts were created. As a result, a number of states collapsed. This first occurred along the coast in such once-powerful states as Benin, Dahomey, and Asante; within a hundred years the pressure of the slave trade was felt in the interior, diverting energies from the development of politics, the arts, and culture to a preoccupation with slaving wars and wanton destruction. Africans who had lived in peace with their neighbors for hundreds of years now became suspicious and started wars to capture their neighbors, for fear their neighbors would capture them.

With the opening up of the New World, and the vast plantation systems that followed, very often the slave-hungry Portuguese literally put a gun in an African's hand and pointed another one at his stomach, saying, in effect, "Either you capture a slave for me or you become one." And thus Africans were caught in one of the most tragic binds in history. Other Africans went into the slave trade because they were corrupt, having developed a liking for European liquor, clothes, guns, and other foreign goods.

Apart from the physical destructiveness and social dislocations that the Europeans inflicted on African societies, the absence of political unity exposed some of the small and poorly organized African communities to the ravages of their more powerful neighbors. Entire communities were fragmented and driven from their original homes. Those African people who did not have strong leadership attached themselves to one of the larger and stronger nation-states for protection. Sometimes the attached people were reduced to vassals; sometimes they were sold as slaves; sometimes they were totally integrated into the larger society, enjoying all benefits, responsibilities, and privileges of that society.

The slave trade had projected the Africans into a crossfire the like of which no one had ever before encountered. On the economic side the slave trade had damaged the production of goods and the creation of wealth in Africa. The market towns in many cases went out of existence. The most valuable African resource, human labor, was forced into slavery and sent to the New World. Those African craftsmen who had escaped slavery could not compete economically with European manufacturers. As a result, African art and craftsmanship deteriorated and in some cases had to be abandoned.

The long period of slavery had completely undermined all elements of culture and growth in Africa. In some cases the evidence of the achievements of medieval times had been destroyed. At Timbuktu the once-great university of Sankore was now a fallen heap of bricks, stone, and mud. There was no one alive who could remember Ahmad Baba.

Near the end of the eighteenth century, when the era of slavery was drawing to a close, Islam reasserted itself in the western Sudan, and several jihads, or holy wars, were set in motion. The most noted of these was led by Usman Dan Fodio of northern Nigeria's Fulani. The real nature of Usman Dan Fodio's jihad is still in debate. To understand this war it is necessary that we know more about the Fulani people and their evolving role in the Sudan.

At the time when England and other European powers were attempting to end the slave trade and start the colonial system, the Fulani movement burst upon northern Nigeria like a thunder clap, setting in motion a long chain of events that is still reverberating.

The Fulani were a pastoral people living in scattered clusters from the Atlantic margin of the Sudan in the Senegal valley to the Adamawa plateau in Cameroon. They generally lived without opposition on the fringes of agricultural societies, taking those lands that were relatively poor for crop cultivation. Their origins are usually traced to the Senegal valley, where, it is thought, they long ago mixed with Berber nomads who had been driven south from Morocco in the eleventh century. This theory would account for the remarkable physical diversity found among the Fulani, who range in complexion from the light skin of a large number of North Africans to the darker complexion and more Negroid physical features of most of the people of western Africa. Prospering, the Fulani began to expand eastward from the Senegal basin, marrying with still other peoples along the way, leaving large settled populations in Futa Toro, Futa Jallon, Kita, Macina, Liptako, Sokoto, Bauchi, and Adamawa. Their search for new grazing land for their large herds of cattle was combined with a search for new areas to convert to Islam.

A careful examination of the events leading up to the jihad shows that the movement was purely religious at first, owing much to the inspiration of Islam. It would develop, according to some interpreters, into a national and political movement of the Fulani people seeking domination over peasants and traders. Usman Dan Fodio became the great national leader, taking the title of Sarkin Musulmi (meaning "commander of the faithful"), which is still borne by his descendants. He was born in the Hausa state of Gobir in 1754, and in his youth became known as a strict Muslim teacher, continually traveling to the countries of northern Nigeria to exhort the people to a more conscientious performance in their religious duties. This eventually brought him into conflict with the young *sarkin* of Gobir, one of his former pupils, who was also a leader of a northern Nigerian movement that did not strictly impose Islam upon all his subjects. Disciples and adherents flocked to both men. The younger man hoped to defeat Dan Fodio's movement before it could gain a foothold in the large cities. The *sarkin* of Gobir attacked the town of Degel, where Usman Dan Fodio was living. Not being prepared to fight at this time, Dan Fodio fled to the city of Gudu, where he was joined by others who believed in his cause. The *sarkin* of Gobir, who had pursued him, was defeated on June 21, 1804, at Tabkin Kwotto on the shores of Lake Tobin. This battle began the Fulani wars.

The Lake Tobin outbreak also stirred up other opponents of the Fulani. Some of the Hausa kings attacked the followers of Usman Dan Fodio and were met with a widespread Fulani uprising, led by the trusted generals of Dan Fodio. Each general had a flag personally given to him by his leader. These flag bearers took over most of northern Nigeria and claimed the land for their respective families. (The descendants of these generals are even today considered the rightful bearers of power in northern Nigeria.) Very quickly they swept through Hausaland. In 1804 the city of Zaria was taken, followed in 1805 by Katsina and Kano. Before the *shehu* met any formidable opposition, the great trading cities of northern Nigeria had fallen. Not until Dan Fodio's forces reached Bornu did a national leader, Al-Kanemi, successfully resist Fulani advances. The Fulani army was able to take only the border country. The rest of Bornu maintained its independence. By 1810 the jihad was almost over. Usman Dan Fodio had established his rule over more than one hundred thousand square miles and was recognized as sovereign by five million people. He died in 1817 and was buried in the city of Sokoto.

In many ways the ground had been prepared for Usman Dan Fodio before he was born. The Niger River states had been torn with internal strife since the early part of the eighteenth century. The Oyo empire had long been in decline before the jihad. The warning signs began to appear during the period of Bashorun Gaha (1754–1774). During this time the Egba people revolted and were not brought back into the fold of the empire. As the Oyo army became a mere shadow of its former self, other peoples broke away from Oyo domination. Eight years before the jihad the collapse of the empire was already noticeable; the jihad merely accentuated it.

This jihad was the last flowering of African military prowess in the central Sudan before the British and the French took over. It had its glorious aspect and its tragedy, too. Before the war was over, some Muslims were attacking other Muslims. By attacking Bornu, an ancient Islamic state with its roots in the tenth century, the men of the Fulani jihad made it apparent that political ambition as well as religious zeal drove them. The state of Bornu had scrupulously observed the tenets of Islam, and as its ruler Shaykh al-Amin protested, there was no justification for the Fulani to attack. But, as in all revolutions, separate resentments and grievances found their opportunity. In 1812 Dan Fodio retired in triumph, dividing his huge empire between his brother, Abdullah, who received the lands east of Sokoto, and his son, Muhammad Belo, who was given the capital at Sokoto and the remaining Hausa states. As the nineteenth century progressed, threats to Fulani power developed. Some of the original inspiration of the movement faded away, and no further conquests by the Fulani were attempted. The forest and the tsetse fly were obstacles to the kind of cavalry warfare that had made the Fulani warriors famous and feared. Yet the kings and emirs retained their positions, ruling strongly until they were challenged at the very end of the nineteenth century by another invading power: the British.

THE WEST COAST: During the latter half of the fifteenth century Spanish ships began to interfere with the Portuguese slave trade. This caused the Portuguese to build a cluster of forts along the west coast of Africa to protect their interests. The first and most famous of these forts was at Elmina, in what is present-day Ghana. Gold was the currency of the day, and this naturally attracted the Portuguese. They had landed in this part of Africa early in the year 1482. The leader of the expedition, Diego de Azambuja, wasted no time in asking to see the country's reigning king, Nana Kwamena Ansa. The Portuguese offered friendship; but Nana Kwamena Ansa was slow in accepting their offers and in showing that he believed their promises. However, he still did not gain enough time to rally the support of his people and allies. Azambuja's expeditionary force set to work fortifying the area.

Europe's Reformation and the subsequent conversion of England and Holland to Protestantism in the sixteenth century also had repercussions in Africa. Protestant kings no longer felt bound to obey the authority of the pope. Owners of ships in these countries felt free to enter the slave trade in areas that the pope had assigned to the Portuguese and the Spaniards in 1493. Francis I of France voiced his celebrated protest: "The sun shines for me as for others. I should very much like to see the clause in Adam's will that excludes me from a share of the World." The king of Denmark refused to accept the pope's ruling as far as the East Indies was concerned. Sir William Cecil, the famous Elizabethan statesman, denied the pope's right to "give and take kingdoms to whomsoever he pleased."

The years of rivalry among European nations over their place in the African sun had started. At the close of the sixteenth century France had no colonies. Henry IV wished to develop trade with the new lands in America and Africa, including, of course, the slave trade, but his minister of state, the Duc de Sully, who represented large groups of rural interests, did not share the expansionist desires of his monarch. It was not until after the noted Cardinal Richelieu came to power in 1624 that the French began to trade in slaves. Richelieu and Louis XIII approved of the early plans, and the Saint Christopher Company was founded in 1626 to exploit the tobacco and wood found on the Caribbean island of this name. The French also occupied Tortuga and parts of Saint Domingue. In Africa they took over an area stretching from the mouth of the Senegal River to the Bight of Benin and started trading with peoples living along the Gambia River. By virtue of licenses issued on June 24, 1633, the French traders of Dieppe and Rouen obtained "permission to trade in Senegal, Cape Verde, and other places." In 1640 a stockade was constructed on an island at the mouth of the Senegal River, marking the founding of the settlement of St. Louis. The concession for Cape Lopez was accorded the Maloe Company of Guinea, as it was called. This was the first French challenge to the power and territories of the Portuguese; the effort would soon peter out because of the lack of French resources or interest.

By the beginning of Louis XIV's reign in 1643 only a few private traders sustained the original effort poorly, taking no more than a few hundred slaves a year, as the demand was still small. There was no regular commercial traffic between France, its small West African holdings, and the developing colonies in the Caribbean islands. From Cape Verde to the Congo the whole remaining coast of West Africa was in the hands of governments hostile to France or in competition with it commercially.

Of the European nations competing for a place in Africa, France had shown the least astuteness. This condition changed rapidly when it began to understand the importance of the slave trade in the intensive exploitation of their New World colonies. In 1664 Jean-Baptiste Colbert, Louis XIV's minister of finance, officially organized the trade for France. Soon the French caught up with the other European nations in West Africa, becoming at least their equal in competition.

The British, for their part, came late and furious into the slave trade. Captain John Hawkins and his "good ship Jesus" inaugurated the venture with the approval of Queen Elizabeth, who invested some of her personal fortune in underwriting it. The year of this first English slave-trading expedition was 1562. This was a buccaneering expedition that was meant to challenge the papal decree giving Portugal and Spain exclusive rights in Africa. After the establishment of the British colonies in the West Indies and the introduction of the sugar industry, the British participation in the slave trade became widespread and better organized, with various corporations being formed in England for that purpose. King Charles II and King James II held stock in some of these companies.

After the French and the British entered the slave trade, the Portuguese outposts were threatened. For a hundred years the Portuguese had been moving down the west coast of Africa, looking for new lands to conquer and new slave-trading areas. They made their first appearance in the Congo as early as 1482. The people of the Congo did not oppose the Portuguese at this time. The Congolese were a secure people, with years of well-organized government behind them.

Manikongo Nzinga (also known as a Nkuwu) welcomed them to his domain. Diogo Cão, the captain of this expedition, had broken the long isolation of the Congo, but the significance of this act eluded him. He sailed a little farther before going ashore. Months later, after returning to Lisbon, he told the king of Portugal about the Congo discovery. Thenceforth nothing was spared in the effort to make the Congo a Christian nation.

GALERIE KAMER, COLLECTION OF MR. AND MRS. JOHN DE MENIL

All the converts did not stay in the new religion. After having been converted to Catholicism and baptized in 1491, old King Nzinga gradually returned to the religion of his ancestors; but before his death in 1506 he designated as his successor his son, who had been converted under the name Affonso. Once on the throne, Affonso turned out to be a great king, and the kingdom of the Congo entered active international life. However, this good relationship between the kingdom of the Congo and the Portuguese did not last. By the end of the reign of Dom Affonso, extortion, alcoholism, and the slave trade were rampant in the Congo.

In 1590 another *manikongo* started a campaign to expel the Portuguese from the Congo. He made use of the known rivalry between European powers, pretending to put his country under the tutelage of the Holy See. Then he encouraged the arrival in the Congo of the Dutch, who were beginning at the time to acquire a foothold in Africa. The Portuguese were forced to abandon the Congo, and they turned their attention to the region of Angola, which offered them a more favorable field in which to further their commercial ambitions.

Early in the seventeenth century other areas in the Congo showed new life and new creative efforts in state building. One of the most remarkable of these states was the kingdom of Kuba of the Bantu-speaking Shongo people. Situated between the Kasai and Sankuru rivers, it is perhaps the most ancient of the Congolese kingdoms. Among the kingdoms in Central Africa only the Shongo culture kept its records and transmitted them almost intact to modern researchers. Oral tradition preserves what appears to be an accurate list of more than one hundred and twenty Kuba kings, the earliest of whom lived in the fifth century A.D.

In the Congo, where the technology of iron smelting has ancient origins, weaponry is often as beautiful as it is deadly. The artfully curved device opposite is a Congolese throwing knife, its several flat blades subtly balanced for hurling at quarry as much as fifty yards away. Also shown (below and right) are an execution sabre, two elaborately decorated ceremonial swords, and another throwing knife.

GALERIE KAMER

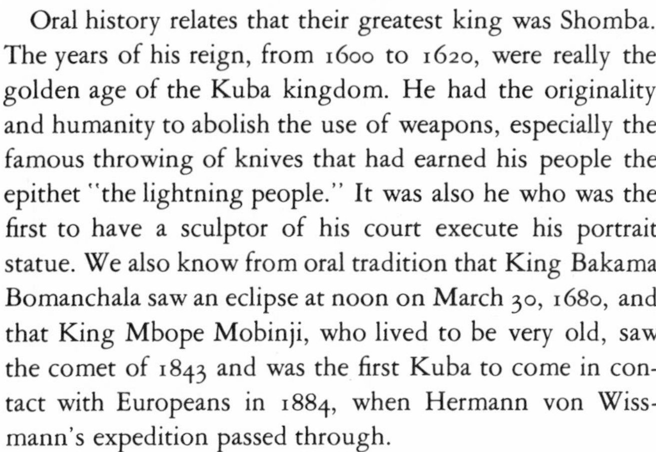

GALERIE KAMER, COLLECTION OF MR. AND MRS. ALLAN GERDAU

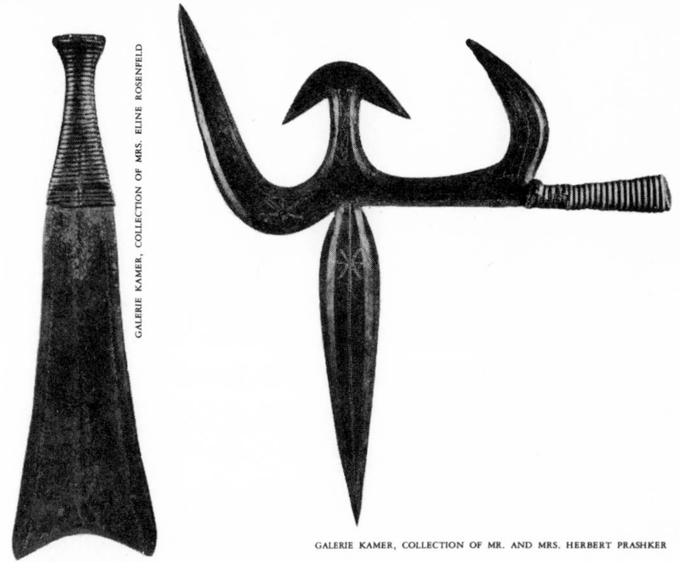

GALERIE KAMER, COLLECTION OF MRS. ELINE ROSENFELD

GALERIE KAMER, COLLECTION OF MR. AND MRS. HERBERT PRASHKER

Oral history relates that their greatest king was Shomba. The years of his reign, from 1600 to 1620, were really the golden age of the Kuba kingdom. He had the originality and humanity to abolish the use of weapons, especially the famous throwing of knives that had earned his people the epithet "the lightning people." It was also he who was the first to have a sculptor of his court execute his portrait statue. We also know from oral tradition that King Bakama Bomanchala saw an eclipse at noon on March 30, 1680, and that King Mbope Mobinji, who lived to be very old, saw the comet of 1843 and was the first Kuba to come in contact with Europeans in 1884, when Hermann von Wissmann's expedition passed through.

In the meantime, while this picture of order and culture was being revealed in one part of the Congo, more troubles were developing wherever the Europeans were involved. The contest between the Netherlands and Portugal for control of the kingdom of the Congo continued throughout the entire seventeenth century. After the Dutch captured Luanda in 1641, thereby briefly supplanting the Portuguese on the western shore of Africa, a new diplomatic current was established between the Dutch and the king of the Congo. The latter sent ambassadors to Brazil and Amsterdam and asked the prince of Orange for help against the Portuguese. On the other hand, a Dutch delegation was received at the Congolese court with ceremonial splendor reportedly equal to anything that the visitors had seen in the courts of Europe.

The Dutch intrusion did not make the Portuguese give up their desire to re-enter the Congo. In a few years the Portuguese recovered their lost positions and some of their military power. In the sixteenth century they had been driven by greed for imaginary gold mines. This greed was now more rampant among them, though they still had no proof of the mines' existence. They embarked on open warfare against the king, Dom Antonio, and defeated him in the battle of Mpila in 1665. A search of the country did not reveal any gold mines. After this they left the Congo and devoted the next one hundred years to completing the conquest of Angola.

In David Birmingham's book, *The Portuguese Conquest of Angola*, we are told: "The first incentive to the Portuguese to conquer a colony in Angola was the hope of acquiring lands suitable for European settlement similar to those which were being settled in Brazil. Another reason was the Portuguese expectation of finding mineral wealth in Angola, which led them to conquer the site of supposed silver mines."

The failure to find the mineral wealth in Angola made the Portuguese double their efforts in the slave trade. Their most stubborn and colorful opposition as they entered the final phase of the conquest of Angola came from a queen who was a great head of state and a military leader. The important facts about her life have been extracted from a biography by the American historian Roy A. Glasgow.

Nzinga's story begins in 1583, when one of the most extraordinary and romantic figures in African history was born. She was the sister of the then-reigning king of Ndongo, Ngola Mbandi. Nzinga was one of a long line of African women freedom-fighters that dates back to the reign of Queen Hatshepsut in Egypt, fifteen hundred years before the birth of Christ. Nzinga belonged to the Jaga people. The Jaga were an extremely militant group and became more so when Queen Nzinga took over their leadership.

Nzinga's ancestry goes back to the end of the fifteenth century when her great-great-grandfather, the king of Matamba, conquered neighboring Ndongo and gave it to his son, Ngola Kiluanju, as an appendage to the other territory held by the Jaga. Nzinga stated that she was descended "from the kings who had reigned over the whole state before it was split into two parts." She based her claim to rule over the entire region upon her ancestral connections.

Queen Nzinga's relations with the Portuguese were from the outset marked with conflict. When she went to Luanda, headquarters of the Portuguese in Angola, to negotiate with the governor, he refused her a chair, a courtesy due one of equal rank. Seemingly undaunted, she is said to have sat down, as shown in this old engraving. Never one to be inhibited by rules, Nzinga circumvented local prohibitions against female sovereigns. She dressed as a male chief and surrounded herself with an entourage of concubines, young men also in disguise.
G. WEIDENFELD AND NICHOLSON

In 1623, at the age of forty-one, Nzinga became queen of Ndongo—even while her right to the throne was being questioned under the law. The supporters of her late brother had not wasted any time before stirring up dissension against her. She began at once to strengthen her position of power. One of her first acts was the strengthening of the traditional laws that ensured the cultural integrity of the Jaga people. She also forbade her subjects to call her queen, preferring to be called king; and when she led her army in battle, she dressed in men's clothing.

Nzinga never accepted the Portuguese conquest of her country and was always on the military offensive. As part of her excellent strategy against the invaders, she formed an alliance with the Dutch, intending to use them to defeat the Portuguese slave trade. At her request she was given a militia of Dutch soldiers. The officer commanding this detachment in 1646 described her as "a cunning and prudent virago so much addicted to the use of arms that she hardly uses other exercise, and withal so generously valiant that she never hurt a Portuguese after quarter was given and commanded all her slaves and soldiers the like."

She believed that after defeating the Portuguese it would be easy to surprise the Dutch and expel them from her country. Consequently, she maintained a good relationship with the Dutch and waited for the appropriate time to move against them. Her ambition extended beyond the task of freeing her country from European control. In addition to being queen of Ndongo, she envisioned commanding a great western empire stretching from Matamba in the east to the Atlantic Ocean in the west. To this end she was an astute agitator-propagandist, easily summoning large groups of her fellow countrymen to hear her. In convincing her people of the evil effects of the Portuguese, she would single out slaves and slave-soldiers who were under Portuguese control and direct intensive political and patriotic messages in their direction, appealing to their pride as Africans. She offered them land and freedom. This resulted in a serious security problem for the Portuguese, with thousands of these slave-soldiers deserting to join her forces. Politically far-sighted, competent, self-sacrificing, and devoted to the resistance movement, she attempted to draw many kings and heads of families to her cause in order that they in turn might recruit their people for her revolution against the Portuguese.

Nzinga's most enduring weapon was her personality. She was astute and successful in consolidating power. She was particularly good at preserving her position by ruthlessly dealing with her foes and graciously rewarding her friends. She possessed both masculine hardness and personal charm, depending on the need and the occasion.

The Portuguese now suspected that they were not going to win her over to their side by peaceful means. The priests were disappointed because they had seemingly lost the battle to convert her to Catholicism. However, in her campaign to drive the Portuguese out of Angola she suffered a series of setbacks in 1645 and 1646. Her sister was taken as a prisoner of war and thrown into the river. Nzinga began to weigh the merits of her own god, Tem-Bon-Dumba, against the god of the Portuguese. Was it possible, she asked, that the Catholic god was stronger? A number of other questions arose for which there was no satisfactory answer. She had heard the Jesuits say that the Christian god was a just person and an enemy of all suffering. Why then did he assist the invaders of her country? Why were the Portuguese building forts in her country without her consent? With these questions still unresolved, she decided to join this religion and test its strength in her favor. For the remainder of her life she used Christianity or put it aside, depending on her needs.

In 1659 she signed a treaty with the Portuguese that brought her no feeling of triumph. However, time would reveal that her part of the treaty had been based upon political and military realities, for she was now faced with overwhelming odds and superior weaponry. She had fought the Portuguese for most of her adult life. She was more than seventy-five years old now, and some of her faithful assistants and followers were dead or had given up the long fight.

On December 17, 1663, this great African woman died, marking the end of one epoch and the beginning of another. With her passing, the planting of the Cross and the occupation of the interior of South West Africa had begun. The massive expansion of the Portuguese slave trade followed.

As stated earlier, the British opened the last phase of the slave trade in West Africa. When Captain John Hawkins organized the manpower and ships for this aspect of England's worldwide expansion, the structure and administration of this inhuman business were permanently changed. Spheres of influence were established among slave traders, guaranteeing one another's rights to conduct business in certain areas of West Africa without interference. In a word, the business was put on a business basis. Because of his success, Captain Hawkins is often referred to as "the man who stole a continent."

It took the British nearly a hundred years to drive the Portuguese and other lesser powers out of West Africa. In 1701 the "Most Christian King of France," Louis XIV, and "His Catholic Majesty," Philip V of Spain, signed an agreement conceding to the Guinea Company a monopoly on the introduction of black slaves into the Spanish West Indies. This agreement lasted ten years, ending in 1712. Its objective was to procure reciprocal profits to both the Catholic king of Spain and the very Christian sovereign of France, who derived considerable revenues from the trade through a head tax levied against the slave merchants for each captive delivered. The Guinea Company pledged to introduce an increased number of slaves from all parts of sub-Saharan Africa, with the exception of Elmina and Cape Verde, the latter still under Portuguese control.

The War of Spanish Succession (1701–1714) radically changed this and other schemes for expansion in Africa. As a consequence of a protracted series of battles on the European continent, French domination of Europe was ended, parts of the Spanish empire were parceled out to a number of claimants, and Britain's supremacy of the seas established. The Peace of Utrecht, which followed, was an attempt to set guidelines for the peaceful expansion of overseas empires, one of several European treaties that decided the destiny of Africa without African participation.

One of its acts, the infamous Asiento Treaty signed on March 26, 1713, granted the British government a monopoly on the importation of slaves to Spain's remaining American empire for a term of thirty years (1713–1743). His British Majesty, no less illustrious than the French and Spanish majesties, pledged through the agency of the South Sea Company to introduce 144,000 slaves of both sexes at

With east coast citadels like Fort Jesus, built at Mombasa in 1593, the Portuguese sought to supplant Arab spiritual and economic influence.

JAMES KIRKMAN

the rate of 4,800 annually. The conditions of the contract, with few exceptions, were the same as those previously made with France. In every possible way the British got the best of the deal. The Anglo-Spanish contract was later altered to permit importation of a still larger number of slaves annually, and at a higher price per head than originally negotiated. For the rest of the eighteenth century, the British would maintain leadership in this hideous business.

By the end of the eighteenth century, however, the slave trade had run its course and was a declining institution. But the Africans had no cause for rejoicing. The British, who led the fight to abolish chattel slavery, became the major architects for the establishment of the colonial system, another form of slavery.

EAST AFRICA: When the Portuguese explorers arrived along the east coast of Africa, they found the shore from Sofala (in present-day Mozambique) to Somalia occupied by a chain of Arab-Swahili settlements, strongly Africanized by centuries of contact with the Bantu-speaking people. They traded with the Africans who brought gold and ivory from the hinterland. They were at first cautious about their interest in slaves. The Portuguese almost at once identified Sofala with the gold-rich biblical Land of Ophir. They built a fortress along this coast in 1505 with the intent of monopolizing trade. In order to accomplish this, the Portuguese first tried to bypass the Arabs and the large number of Swahili-speaking people and deal directly with the Africans. Fortunately for the Portuguese, their arrival in East

Africa occurred during a time when intertribal rivalries prevailed. Some of the great city-states along the coast were in decline. A number of the powerful trading families were torn apart by internal disputes. Later, when the first strategy proved inadequate, the Portuguese took full advantage of this lack of unity to gain a greater measure of control. They supported the sultans of Malindi against the more powerful rulers of Mombasa in the sixteenth century, and in the next century they helped the princes of Faza, another of the coastal city-states, against their Pate (Patta) neighbors.

The main effect of the Portuguese on East Africa was destructive and negative. They built forts, churches, and homes for themselves, while literally declaring war on all local institutions. But they could not govern the coast after the East Africans had turned against them. The traditional rulers still controlled the city-states, and it was largely a matter of political expediency that some of them acknowledged the sovereignty of the Portuguese. The external Muslim powers such as the Turks and the Oman Arabs did not even go that far, as will be shown later.

What can be said of the Portuguese can also be said, with varying degree, of all East Africa's invaders. East Africa, more than any other part of Africa, was preyed upon by one invader after the other for well over one thousand years. All these invaders took more from East Africa than they gave. The modern history of East Africa is the history of a people trying to recover from the aftereffects of invaders and build or rebuild indigenous institutions.

At the beginning of the eighteenth century Portuguese pressure was lessened, but not out of any benevolence. The Portuguese were in serious trouble in other areas of the world, and they did not have the forces that were necessary to maintain their old power connections in East Africa. The divide-and-rule tactics that had worked so well for them in the early years of their expansion were no longer dependable. Some of their puppets now had power ambitions of their own. In Asia their presence was being seriously challenged. In the New World the original settlers of Brazil were questioning the authority of the mother country while still demanding more slaves. To the Portuguese, East Africa was only one part of their global design. They extracted both gold and slaves from the coastal states and did not try to occupy all of them. For a number of years Mombasa Island, off the coast of modern-day Kenya, was their major stronghold in East Africa, along with neighboring Fort Jesus.

The relative security the Portuguese had known along the east coast was first upset in 1649 by the emergence of the Oman leader, Nasir ibn Murshid, who had a navy strong enough to challenge the Portuguese at sea. The Mombasa Chronicle records that the inhabitants of that city made an appeal to Sultan ibn Seif, who became ruler of Oman in 1649. In 1652 vessels from the sultan's fleet raided Zanzibar, one hundred fifty miles south; a number of Portuguese settlers, including several Augustinian Fathers, were killed. As a result of a poorly planned expedition, the following year the queen of Zanzibar was driven off the island by the sultan's forces, who joined with dissident locals. A Portuguese official who was responsible for the defense of the island claimed that he rescued four hundred Christians and saved them from being captured by the Arabs.

For the next forty years the revolts against Portuguese rule continued, mainly in the city-states. The city of Pate was in a state of perpetual revolt. In the punitive expeditions against this city the Portuguese had the assistance of some East African communities that felt threatened by the strength and military prowess of a small and powerful trading city-state like Pate. The king of Faza, who ruled another microkingdom on the island, considered the ruling family of Pate to be his hereditary foe. In 1687 a former king of Pate crossed the Indian Ocean to the Portuguese colony of Goa and offered many concessions in exchange for assistance in his attempt to regain his throne. His most attractive offer was to allow the Portuguese to erect a church at Pate and convert Muslims and pagans without hindrance.

When this king returned to Pate, escorted by a squadron of Portuguese ships, he found that an Arab fleet from the Persian seaport of Muscat had anticipated his action and was ready to forestall him and his allies. The greater damage to the king's pride was in the discovery that his former subjects had turned against him. The Portuguese were not strong enough to fight the Arabs nor could they protect the king. There was no choice for them but to take refuge in Mombasa. For the remainder of the seventeenth century the Portuguese in East Africa would have no rest from conflict; their African allies would fare no better.

On the island of Pemba a state of rebellion kept the Portuguese from making strategic use of the land and the people. In about 1679 a distant faction of the royal family drove out the reigning queen. Like the king of Pate, she took refuge in 1687 in the Portuguese colony of Goa. While there, she became a Christian, an act that destroyed the chance that she would effectively be restored to power in her island kingdom. Nevertheless, the exiled queen continued to speak for the people of Pemba, and the Portuguese listened and indulged themselves. They were slow to realize that the aging queen no longer had power. In an act of desperation, partly in gratitude for refuge she had received, she willed her kingdom to the Portuguese. They were never able to claim this inheritance. In 1694 the island was still in a state of rebellion. The viceroy of India reported the matter to Lisbon, where the decision was made to give up the plan to reduce the Pemba people to submission.

Two years later, in 1696, the Arabs took full advantage of this and other conflicts along the east coast. A fleet from Oman arrived in Kilindini, the chief port of Mombasa, and wasted no time in laying siege to Fort Jesus, where a large number of local inhabitants, including many who were unfriendly to the Arabs, had taken refuge. Among the refugees was Bwana Daud ibn Bwana Shaykh, whose father had been driven from power by the people of Pate in 1686. The struggle lasted nearly three years. The Portuguese sent ships from Goa and Mozambique in support of the Africans, but were not able to lift the siege. Plague and disease reduced the defending forces until they could no longer continue the resistance. Before the Portuguese conceded defeat, the queen of Zanzibar made one last unsuccessful attempt to run the blockade and send supplies to the fort. The garrison became so weak that African women were taking their turn as sentries. With the fall of Mombasa, the Portuguese had lost all of their holding stations north of Cape Delgado. Faza had been abandoned in 1688, when the Arabs of Muscat took possession of Pate Island. Zanzibar had also been taken by the Arabs. Zanzibar's queen, Fatima, who had been loyal to the Portuguese, was deported to Muscat; but she was allowed to return after ten years of exile. Sometime before 1710 the Arabs, in search of materials with which to build a small fort, had partly dismantled the Augustinian church on the island. All evidence of the once-obvious Portuguese presence was destroyed.

The Africans now were trapped in a bind between the Arabs and the Portuguese. They would not extricate themselves for another hundred years. When the Portuguese retreated from Mombasa, some of them went to their Indian colony at Goa, and others went to their southeast African colony at Mozambique. The Arabs at Mombasa acted unwisely, as if the Portuguese threat was over forever. Large numbers of Africans who disliked both Portuguese and Arab rule would attempt to get rid of the Arabs at Mombasa now that the Portuguese had been driven out. The opportunity came quite unexpectedly.

In 1727 Ahmad ibn Said, the Oman governor of Mombasa, set out on a pilgrimage to Mecca and left his deputy, Nasser ibn Abdullah al-Mazrui, in charge. He then began to treat the garrison of soldiers at Mombasa with severity. Grievance over this matter developed into open revolt. The rebels made Ibn Abdullah al-Mazrui a prisoner and took over Fort Jesus. Immediately they began to seek support from the local inhabitants. They, like the mutineers, feared the governor, Ahmad ibn Said, and knew that he could get support from the Arab states. The rebels hoped to organize the local inhabitants in their favor before the governor returned. But a member of the Malindi family persuaded the people not to support this rebellion. They in turn demanded that the rebels surrender the fort. This demand was rejected. The conflict that followed is called a war, but it was really an internal dispute. Without a large supply of arms, the rebels were limited in what they could do. Knowing that Fort Jesus was more or less impregnable, they made no attempt to attack it. They found targets within their limitations and took possession of several walled towns and some outlying forts at Kilindini. The local population had grown accustomed to conflicts and reverses in power struggles, but was somewhat confused over this turn of events. For the rebels, fortune turned temporarily in their favor. The rulers of Oman became involved in civil disorders at home on the Arabian Peninsula and could not send support to the Arabs at Mombasa. The rebels now had the opportunity to set up an independent state, and would have, except for the intervention of the Portuguese, who had partly recovered from their defeat on the island.

The Portuguese found their opportunity when a special emissary was sent by the king of Pate to Goa to obtain Portuguese help in expelling the Oman Arabs from Pate. An agreement was drawn up between the emissary and the Portuguese viceroy at Goa. The main parts of this treaty were: no Portuguese subject, Christian or otherwise, could be compelled to become a Muslim; all previous Christians who had been compelled to become Muslims should have the right to return to the Roman Catholic Church, if they desired to do so. On the other hand, the Inquisition was not to function in the land.

When the Portuguese reached Pate early in 1728, some resistance was offered from one faction, but they eventually surrendered, knowing that they could expect no support from Oman at this time. The Portuguese took full advantage of the unrest at Mombasa and similar dissensions in the island of Pate farther to the north. Both Pate and Mombasa were regained with very little fighting. At Mombasa Shaykh ibn Ahmad al-Malindi at once disclaimed all relations with the rebels. The Arab governor, having little stomach for warfare, quickly surrendered. The Portuguese had promised that he and his men would be given ships to return to Oman.

In celebration of this event the Portuguese entered what was still left of the church of the Augustinian convent and conducted High Mass before a roughly made wooden cross. An Augustinian Father preached on this occasion from the text in Isaiah LXVI: 10: "Rejoice ye with Jerusalem, and be glad with her, all ye that love her: rejoice for joy with her, all ye that mourn for her." Inside the church the Fathers found a chest containing church ornaments; it had been left unharmed for more than thirty years. The chapel of the Misericordia was also found undamaged.

The Portuguese became more confident when the king of Zanzibar came to Mombasa to make submission to the governor. A party of Portuguese soldiers and civil servants was sent to Zanzibar to establish a "factory," or in more precise language, the slave trade.

In their short-lived triumph the Portuguese had overlooked issues relating to their return. They had not been invited back by the populace at large, nor did a large number welcome them. They had been asked back as arbitrators of an internal dispute, mainly involving the rulers of Mombasa, Pate, Zanzibar, and related territories.

In spite of the comparative ease with which the Portuguese seemed to have regained their lost possession, trouble between the Portuguese and the inhabitants was soon to develop. Treaties were barely signed before they were broken. On August 29, 1728, a new treaty was made with Pate. The Portuguese, with unwarranted confidence, made new demands and tried to revise some old ones. They insisted on the payment of tribute and took for themselves a large share of the island's revenue. The African faction that had invited the Portuguese to help them against the Arabs was now having second thoughts. Friction developed between the king of Pate and the Portuguese commander. Eventually, the Portuguese garrison found itself in a state of siege with no local allies. After being reduced to the verge of starvation, the Portuguese were willing to forgo all previous agreements and return to Goa. Also, the Portuguese garrison at Mombasa was expelled and their flag lowered at Fort Jesus for the last time.

Portuguese conduct had destroyed whatever good will had been previously built up among the people in East Africa. The Portuguese were completely intolerant of the Muslims. According to the Mombasa Chronicle: "They flung stones at the people while they were at their prayers; and they used to turn the people out of their houses and take possession of them; and take their wives to themselves."

The loss of Fort Jesus and other Portuguese settlements left the Oman Arabs militarily in charge of the east coast of Africa and the large slave-trading island of Zanzibar. Fort Jesus was handed over to an Oman garrison, and Muhammad ibn Said al-Maamri was installed as governor. After the final withdrawal of the Portuguese from Mombasa, we hear no more of Christianity and Christians in East Africa for a century. An uneasy partnership developed between the Portuguese and the Arabs. The big Portuguese colony of Brazil was calling for more slaves than the Portuguese could furnish, and the Arabs filled the breach as suppliers.

The East African trade, in a formal sense, can trace its roots no further than the first half of the eighteenth century, and the early Portuguese chronicles make only passing mention of the slave trade. Much more important were the gold and ivory traded to Arabia and India. It was in search of these products that the Portuguese invaders had come in the sixteenth and seventeenth centuries. But the Arabs had dealt in human chattel since the twelfth century. Not only along the coast of Kenya and Tanzania but also in Mozambique and Zimbabwe did they deal in slaves. The great trading center at Zanzibar had about one hundred years of active commercial slave trading before the European powers entered the area.

Near the end of the eighteenth century other European powers, principally Great Britain, began to make themselves felt along the east coast of Africa. They would in the next fifty years wage a successful war on the East African slave trade and, subsequently, install the European colonial system.

SOUTH AND SOUTHWEST AFRICA: In the year 1652, when Oliver Cromwell was proclaiming his creed of "liberty and conscience," and American seekers of religious freedom were cautiously penetrating the American continent in search of new lands, a band of thirty white settlers (employees of the powerful Dutch East India Company under the leadership of Jan van Riebeeck) came ashore below the three-thousand-five-hundred-foot shadow of Table Mountain to establish the Cape Colony at the southernmost tip of the horn of Africa. Although this did not mark the first appearance of European people in southern Africa, it was the first sustained attempt to form a permanent white settlement. This was the beginning of South Africa's

BRODE, *Tippoo Tib, The Story of His Career*, 1907

After Europeans and Americans ended the slave trade, Great Britain brought its influence to bear in order to halt the much older traffic in humans along Africa's east coast. The island of Zanzibar, seen below in a view of the 1850's, was the principal center of that trade. In 1840 it had become the capital of Sayyid Said, sultan of the Persian Gulf state of Oman, who ruled the Swahili ports from Somalia to Mozambique and extended Islamic influences inland as far as the Congo. Said built up Zanzibar's famed clove trade, sought Indian investors, and encouraged Arab merchants to venture in search of ivory and slaves to work on the clove plantations. Following those ancient routes by which Africans from the inland had brought goods to the coast, traders like Tippu Tib (left), an Afro-Arab who had been born in Zanzibar, pressed beyond Lake Tanganyika to the central Congo, and with their firearms, established hegemony over large numbers of Bantu-speaking peoples. Said's successors were weaker than he, and his dominions along the coast were gradually divided among Italy, Great Britain, and Germany. In 1890 the British proclaimed a protectorate over Zanzibar and in 1897 officially put an end to slaving activities.

MANSELL COLLECTION

"Troubled Years." Contestants for control of the area would soon be the Dutch, the British, the Hottentots, the Bushmen, and the Bantu-speaking peoples.

Although the Portuguese had landed on the Cape before the arrival of the Dutch, they had not established a trading station. There were many reasons for this. The coast was a stormy one, and there were no settled tribes with whom they could barter for slaves. Almost a hundred and fifty years elapsed before the Dutch decided to set up a station, and only after they had wrested a large part of Europe's Indian Ocean shipping business from the Portuguese.

The stated intent of Van Riebeeck was to start a refueling

station for the ships of the Dutch East India Company on their way to and from the East. His band of settlers absorbed a handful of Huguenot refugees who had arrived ahead of them, and after 1667 started importing slaves from Malaya and other Asian countries. The first African people they encountered were the Hottentots, or more properly, the Khoikhoi people. (The term Khoisan is anthropologists' construct, meant to include both the Khoikhoi and the San, or Bushmen.) A king of the Hottentots, Autshumayo, led them in the first futile attempt in 1659 to stop Van Riebeeck and his company from seizing the best pasture lands in the Cape Peninsula. Thus the nationalist struggle in South Africa had its beginning in this little-known rebellion. King Autshumayo's people were enslaved and deprived of their cattle. The Bushmen were hunted like game. To keep from being destroyed, they retreated into the Kalahari Desert, where they still live. The basic historic conflict in South Africa—the struggle between different national entities to control the land—had been set in motion.

The first European settlers took on some of the habits and traits of the Africans that they had practically destroyed. These Boers, or farmers, acquired large herds of cattle, mainly from Africans whom they had defeated. They became nomadic, land-hungry "white Africans," hunters without human regard for the indigenous people of South Africa.

The settlement grew with infusions of slaves from the east, Mozambique, Angola, and the addition of still more Huguenots and Dutchmen. While the women of the Khoikhoi and the San were sexually used and abused by the white settlers, the Dutch East India Company for a number of years countenanced, and even encouraged, legal marriages between the white settlers and their Asian slaves. They were building the ethnic buffer between themselves and the blacks; this group was to become known as the "Cape Coloreds." In present-day South Africa they number more than a million. The dangerous doctrine of white superiority had already been developed by the Boers (later called Afrikaners), but they did not at this time see that the sanctioned marriages between themselves and their Asian slaves were in contradiction to this concept.

Many of the Boers who made up the first large white settlement in southern Africa were political and religious malcontents before leaving their homes in the Netherlands. Their outlook on life was based on strict Lutheranism and Calvinism, the aftermath of the bitter struggle to preserve the newly established Protestant faith against the powerful attacks of the resurgent Catholic Church.

The Boers had neither security nor peace during their first one hundred years in South Africa. The Khoikhoi people, who were friendly to them when they first arrived, soon began to look upon them as invaders and land grabbers. They saw their land being fenced off and white men with guns protecting the land that the whites had claimed for settlements. The Khoikhoi considered the land to be inalienable and sacred, a part of nature for common use. Continued encroachment on their land caused this friendly and peaceful people to take up arms.

The Khoikhoi fought three major wars to regain the vast grazing lands of South Africa. Between 1786 and 1795 over two thousand five hundred Hottentots were killed and six hundred captured. Those taken prisoner, mainly women and children, were enslaved by the farmers. None of the adult males submitted to the enemy; they fought to the bitter end. Their courage, even in the face of overwhelming odds, was phenomenal. These early wars of resistance have in most cases been lost from the official history of southern Africa.

The lack of labor to tend the vegetables and fruit gardens of the Dutch hampered the work of European settlement. The Khoikhoi could not see the necessity of exchanging their freedom for money when they had the land. The importation of slaves to do the hard work became the next logical step. As for the Boers, the status of being Christian and master was becoming confused in their minds with their being white. Color consciousness helped them to erase the knowledge that all men were human.

The real dynamics of the black-white struggle in South Africa did not reach profound and tragic proportions until after the British occupation of the Cape in 1795. The British pushed the Boers, the Boers pushed the Zulu, and the Zulu pushed back. But this is, of course, an oversimplification. The story of this clashing of powerful forces and the struggle to control South Africa is complicated and protracted. In the meantime, other forces, issues, peoples, and nations were evolving in southern Africa.

South West Africa is a little known, though important, part of southern Africa. This country and its people were late in coming into the mainstream of southern African history. In some ways this was fortunate. During the early period of European expansion South West Africa was not an area desired for large-scale European settlement or slave trade. A number of ethnic groups, but chiefly the Herero, a pastoral people, and the Ambo (Ovamba), an agricultural people, developed small nations within the region.

The Portuguese, led by Diogo Cão, made a brief appearance in South West Africa in 1484, leaving a lonely cross to mark the occasion. John II of Portugal had sent them to explore that area of the coast which until that time had remained for the Europeans a land of fable and mystery. This was eight years before Christopher Columbus and his sailors set foot on the islands of the New World. The landscape that the Portuguese beheld was not encouraging and did not cause them to prolong their stay. There were seemingly endless high sand dunes along the dreary desert coastline, known to later seamen as the Coast of Dead Ships. Two years later Bartholomeu Dias, a Portuguese adventurer, brought an expedition to these shores aboard a little fifty-ton ship. He landed at a narrow southwest bay, which he named Angra Pequeña (today, Lüderitz).

In the next few centuries this part of Africa remained free of any conflict relating to European expansion. The few Europeans who ventured into this large and thinly populated land did not at first make any claim. In 1738 a secret overland expedition was organized by William Van Wyk and other Boer farmers in an attempt to establish trade with the people in this area. The leader of the expedition was surprised to find that another white man, Pieter de Bruyan, had arrived ahead of his party. Bruyan was probably the first white man to set foot in the interior of South West Africa. In 1762 Jacobus Coetsee, an elephant hunter, crossed the Orange River and heard reports of great herds of cattle possessed by the Herero people. Rumors of copper in the interior drew several expeditions to South West Africa during the middle of the eighteenth century. The governor of the Cape, Simon van der Stel, sent an expedition to find the mouth of the Orange River. Men returned from South West Africa with wild stories about long-haired blacks who wore linen clothes. A later expedition, in 1762, also sent out by a Cape governor, found none of these mythical people.

In 1795 the British proclaimed ownership of the South West African coast and declared that only British ships were permitted to hunt whales and seals offshore. This was an empty claim because the British did not have the manpower to patrol this vast area. The full weight and reality of European colonial oppression did not reach South West Africa until the latter part of the nineteenth century. During the period of the partition of Africa in the 1880's, the heavy hand of German colonialism would take over this part of Africa.

Meanwhile, in South Africa the Zulu began to be a force to reckon with. In his book *The Bantu Past and Present* (1920), the South African writer S. M. Molema argues that these Bantu-speaking people have been migrating in and out of southern Africa for more than ten thousand years. South African archeologists discovered in 1970 a mining complex in Swaziland that is reportedly forty-three thousand years old. This opens up still other matters for further investigation (for example, what has been considered to be the youngest part of Africa for human habitation may yet prove to be one of the oldest parts).

In the Nigerian magazine *Tarikh*, November, 1965, J. D. Omer-Cooper presents one of the numerous new appraisals of the Zulu people and the impact of Chaka (Shaka) on South Africa. He tells us, in essence, that the eastern coastland of South Africa, known as Zululand and Natal, is one of the most attractive places for human settlement in all Africa. This is the area where the Zulu people first settled after migrating to southern Africa.

The Zulu were mixed farmers, with cattle as their chief possession. They did not begin to make their mark on the history of South Africa until early in the nineteenth century. Before this time they gave allegiance to the king of the Mtetwa people. Then in 1786 a son was born to the reigning king of the Zulu, Senzangakona. The child's name was Chaka. In his lifetime his impact on southern Africa would be profound, dramatic, and to a degree, tragic. This warrior-nationalist was literally the father of the Zulu nation. He fought to consolidate the blacks of South Africa in order to save them from white enslavement. He was not understood then, and he is not completely understood now. Chaka and his people stood astride the history of South Africa for the entire nineteenth century. For this period the history of this troubled land is essentially the story of the rise and fall of the Zulu people.

Chaka's early years were not easy, and he had to fight for a place among his people. Except for his mother, Nandi, the favorite wife of King Senzangakona, Chaka might have been lost from Zulu history. Nandi was the daughter of the king of the Langeni people and a woman of great influence among the Zulu.

When Chaka was a year old, Nandi took him to her parents' house to be weaned, as was the custom among the Zulu. Chaka was a restless boy who did not get along well with anyone except his mother. It is said that when his father offered him the lion-skin covering that is worn by older Zulu boys to symbolize their future status as warriors, he refused it and behaved disgracefully. This angered his father because he had high hopes for Chaka, his first-born son, and he naturally expected Chaka to grow up and become king after him.

At last Chaka found a friend, probably through the efforts

of his mother. Dingiswayo of the Mtetwa people saw that this troublesome young man had fine qualities. He presented him with the young warrior's lion skin that he had refused to accept from his father years before. Chaka became a soldier in Dingiswayo's army and soon earned the name "Dingiswayo's Hero."

Who was this man whom Chaka was willing to follow? He, too, had had trouble at home with his father. As he grew toward manhood, the Mtetwa prince found that his father, the great King Jobe, suspected him of treachery. The chief thought his elder son was going to rebel and usurp his power. The bitter feud caused the son to be driven into exile, where he remained until his father died. His years of his journeying away from his people earned him the name "Dingiswayo," meaning "The Wanderer."

When the news reached him that Jobe was dead, he sent word that he was coming back to be king. He at once began to teach the Mtetwa to fight a new way. He had lived in the Cape Colony and learned much about European methods of training men for warfare. He had seen firearms and had learned how to use them. Chaka had his first taste of success in battle in Dingiswayo's army.

Chaka had outgrown his brooding and rebellious disposition. In 1816 Senzangakona died, and Dingiswayo helped Chaka become king of the Zulu. The two men—one king of the populous Mtetwa people, the other king of the smaller Zulu people—were friends, and their warriors fought together. But about two years later Dingiswayo was captured by one of his rivals and was put to death. Then the Mtetwa people, who already knew Chaka as one of their leaders in battle, placed themselves and their great army under the Zulu king and took the Zulu name. This was the beginning of the greatness of the Zulu empire, the foundation of their war machine, and the real power of Chaka.

The famous king Moshoeshoe, then trying to build up the Basuto nation, kept Chaka out of his country only by sending the warrior a message declaring that he recognized no other king but Chaka. Mzilikazi, who had been one of Chaka's best commanders, grew sick of the slaughter of other Bantu-speaking people and deserted the Zulu army, taking over fifteen thousand men with him. He went across the Drakensberg mountains and established a new nation called Matabeleland.

Still Chaka's war machine rolled on. He united by conquest the scattered thrones of numerous smaller kingdoms and incorporated their survivors into the Zulu nation. Four years after he started his first campaign, Chaka had conquered a territory larger than France. The loot and indemnities of war had made his people wealthy. He was at the peak of his military prowess, and all his known enemies had been killed or conquered. His magnificent army, one hundred thousand strong, was still ready and restless for more battle, and there were no battles to be fought. Chaka's rigid methods of army training had made the Zulu among the finest soldiers in the world. The whites in South Africa at that time thought it best to be on friendly terms with him.

Chaka's military movement was called the *mfecane*, meaning "the crushing." It was a process of social, political, and military organization and change that was largely internal to African society. In southern Africa this movement was created mainly out of the efforts of several Bantu-speaking peoples who were attempting to establish their status and their salvation. The Zulu were fighting their way up from vassalage. Once this was accomplished, they began to bring other people under their rule. In some respects this movement can be compared to the jihad in northern Nigeria during the early part of the nineteenth century, though it was not a religious movement.

The power of Chaka began to decline in 1827, after the death of his mother. He led the Zulu in mourning for her and seemed not to be able to come out of mourning and lead them again in battle. Chaka became melancholy, constantly pinching his hands in self-reproach. Anyone who did not show grief became repugnant to him. He seemed to have lost all interest in governing his people and his empire. Many self-seekers were quick to take advantage of this. Those Zulu who had silently hated Chaka's terror for years grew openly rebellious.

In 1828, a year after the death of Chaka's mother, his two half brothers, Dingane and Mhlangana, crept into his hut and stabbed him to death. This event shook the Zulu, but the empire did not fall until many years later.

During the last moments of Chaka's life he is reported to have said to Dingane, who was to succeed him: "It is your hope that by killing me you will become kings when I am dead. But you are deluded; it will not be so, for the white man will come and you will be his slave. What have I done to you? Oh, children of my father."

After Chaka's death the Boers began their trek into the hinterland, looking for more land away from the English, who had taxed and restricted them severely. This inland push of the Boers once more set the Zulu in motion. Dingane, now king, led the fight against the encroachment on Zululand. This phase of the struggle for control of South Africa would continue until Dingane was defeated in the Battle of Blood River in December, 1839.

CONTINENT IN TURMOIL

Bakongo maternity figure
THE MUSEUM OF PRIMITIVE ART

"THE UNIQUE PEARL"

The Moroccan invasion and conquest of the Songhai empire in 1591 marks the onset of a tragic epoch in West African history. The northerners made their headquarters at Timbuktu, until then the intellectual center of the entire region. The Moroccans pillaged the city and arrested its leading scholars, sending them and their families across the desert to Marrakesh. Among these learned exiles, all of whom made the trans-Saharan trek in chains, was Ahmad Baba, a distinguished historian attached to the renowned Sankore mosque. The following account of Ahmad Baba's years in Morocco was originally written in French by Félix Du Bois, a scholar who visited the Sudan in the late 1800's.

Among the exiles was a learned doctor, Ahmed Baba by name, born in 1556 at Arawan. . . . In spite of his youth, he enjoyed a considerable reputation in Timbuctoo at the time of the Moorish conquest, and his brethren gave him the title of "The Unique Pearl of his Time." His renown increased in Morocco and became universal, spreading from Marrakesh to Bougie, Tunis, and even to Tripoli. The Arabs of the north called this [African] "very learned and very magnanimous," and his jailers found him "a fount of erudition." At the request of the Moorish scholars the doors of his prison were opened a year after his arrival (1596). All the believers were greatly pleased with his release, and he was conducted in triumph from his prison to the principal mosque of Marrakesh. A great many of the learned men urged him to open a course of instruction. His first thought was to refuse, but overcome by their persistence he accepted a post in the Mosque of the Kerifs and taught rhetoric, law, and theology. An extraordinary number of pupils attended his lectures, and questions of the gravest importance were submitted to him by the magistracy, his decision always being treated as final. With a modesty worthy of his learning, he said concerning these decisions: "I carefully examined from every point of view the questions asked me, and having little confidence in my own judgment I entreated the assistance of God, and the Lord graciously enlightened me."

The ancient histories of Morocco relate many other interesting details, and the author of the *Bedzl el Mouasaha* reports the following utterance of Ahmed Baba: "Of all my friends I had the fewest books, and yet when your soldiers despoiled me they took 1600 volumes." The Nozhel el Hadj gives the following instance of the courage and pride of the [African] sheik: "After he was set at liberty Ahmed Baba presented himself at the palace of El Mansour, and the sultan gave audience to him from behind a curtain. 'God has declared in the Koran,' said the sheik, 'that no human being can communicate with Him hidden behind a veil. If it is your wish to speak to me, come forth from behind that curtain.' When El Mansour raised the curtain and approached him, Ahmed Baba continued, 'What need had you to sack my house, steal my books, and put me into chains to bring me to Morocco? By means of those chains I fell from my camel and broke my leg.' 'We wished to establish unity in the Mussulman world,' replied the sultan, 'and since you were one of the most distinguished representatives of Islam in your country, we expected your submission to be followed by that of your fellow-citizens.' 'If that is so, why did you not seek to establish this unity amongst the Turks of Tlemcen and other places nearer to you?' 'Because the Prophet says, Leave the Turks in peace so long as they do not interfere with thee.' 'That was true at one time,' responded Ahmed Baba, 'but since then Iba Abbas has said, Leave not the Turks in peace even though they should not interfere with thee.' El Mansour, being unable to reply to this, put an end to the audience."

Although apparently free, Ahmed Baba was detained in Morocco for twelve years; the sultan had only released him on that condition, fearing the effect of his influence on his fellow-citizens. It was not until after the death of El Mansour that permission was obtained from his son for the learned man to return to the Sudan. Ahmed Baba then set out for the country to which he had so ardently desired to return, and of which he never spoke without tears in his eyes. The following verses were written by him in his exile:—

"O thou who goest to Gao, turn aside from thy path to breathe my name in Timbuctoo. Bear thither the greeting of an exile who sighs for the soil on which his friends and family reside. Console my near and dear ones for the deaths of their lords, who have been entombed."

The principal marabouts of Marrakesh formed him a guard of honor at his departure, and, at the moment of farewell, one of them seized Ahmed Baba by the hand and saluted him with the following sura from the holy book: "Certainly he who has made the Koran for thee shall lead thee back to thy point of departure"—a customary address to a traveler in wishing him a safe return. On hearing these words, the sheik abruptly withdrew his hand, exclaiming, "May God never bring me back to this meeting, nor make me return to this country!"

He reached Timbuctoo in safety, and died in 1627.

THE RAPE OF GUINEA

British participation in the trans-Atlantic slave trade was inaugurated in the 1560's by John Hawkins, the shrewd, unscrupulous son of William Hawkins. He had already made several trips to the Canary Islands before he embarked on his three triangular voyages (1562, 1564, and 1567) between England, the Guinea coast, and the West Indies. Accounts of these triumphs were included in Richard Hakluyt's Voyages, *which was first published in three volumes in 1598–1600. Hakluyt was a discriminating editor who depended mostly on firsthand information. He reports that while in the Canaries, Hawkins was "assured that Negros were very good Marchandise in Hispaniola and that the store of Negros might easily be had upon the Guinea coast." Below is an extract from Hakluyt's narrative of Hawkins' second Africa-Caribbean voyage, which began at Plymouth on October 18, 1564. The islands from which the raids were made are probably in the Bijagós Islands off Portuguese Guinea.*

Sir John Hawkins, slave trader
NATIONAL MARITIME MUSEUM, GREENWICH, ENGLAND

The 8 of December wee ankered by a small island called Alcatrarsa, wherein at our going a shore, we found nothing but sea-birds, as we call them Ganets, but by the Portugals, called Alcatrarses, who for that cause gave the said Island the same name. Herein halfe of our boates were laden with yong and olde fowle, who not being used to the sight of men, flew so about us that we stroke them down with poles. In this place the two shippes riding, the two Barkes, with their boates, went into an Island of the Sapies, called La Formio, to see if they could take any of them, and there landed to the number of 80 in armour, and espying certaine made to them, but they fled in such order into the woods, that it booted them not to follow: so going on their way forward till they came to a river, which they could not passe over, they espied on the otherside two men, who with their bowes and arrowes shot terribly at them. Whereupon we discharged certaine harquebuzes to them againe, but the ignorant people wayed it not, because they knewe not the danger thereof: but used a marveilous crying in their fight with leaping and turning their tayles, that it was most strange to see, and gave us great pleasure to beholde them. At the last, one being hurt with a harquebuz upon the thigh, looked upon his wound and wist [knew] not howe it came, because hee could not see the pellet. Here Master Hawkins perceiving no good to be done amongst them, because we could not finde their townes, and also not knowing how to goe into Rio grande, for want of a Pilote, which was the very occasion of our comming thither: and finding so many sholes, feared with our great ships to goe in, and therefore departed on our pretended way to the Idols.

The 10 of December, we had a Northeast winde, with raine and storme, which weather continued two dayes together, was the occasion that the Salomon, and Tygre loste our companie; for whereas the Jesus, and pinnesse ankered at one of the Islands called Sambula, the twelfth day, the Salomon and Tygre came not thither till the 14. In this Island we stayed certain daies, going every day on shore, to take the Inhabitants, with burning and spoiling their townes, who before were Sapies, and were conquered by the Samboses, Inhabitants beyond Sierra Leona. These Samboses had inhabited there three yeres before our comming thither, and in so short space have so planted the ground, that they had great plentie of Mil, Rise, Rootes, Pompions, Pullin, goates, of small frye dried, every house full of the Countrey fruite planted by Gods providence, as Palmito trees, fruites like dates, and sundry other in no place in all that Countrey so aboundantly, whereby they lived more deliciously than other. These inhabitants have diverse of the Sapies, which they tooke in the warres as their slaves, whome onely they kept to till the ground, in that they neither have the knowledge thereof, nor yet will worke themselves, of whome wee tooke many in that place, but of the Samboses none at all, for they fled into the maine. All the Samboses have white teeth as we have, farre unlike to the Sapies which doe inhabite about Rio grande, for their teeth are all filed, which they doe for a braverie, to set out themselves, and doe jagge their flesh, both legges, armes, and bodies, as workemanlike, as a Jerkinmaker with us pinketh a jerkin. These Sapies be more civill than the Samboses: for whereas the Samboses live most by the spoile of their enemies, both in taking their victuals, and eating them also. The Sapies do not eate mans flesh, unlesse in the warre they be driven by necessitie thereunto, which they have not used but by the example of the Samboses, but live onely with fruites, and cattell, whereof they have great store.

THE ROYAL ADVENTURERS

The English were anxious to begin their exploitation of Africa, as were all Europeans. In the mid-seventeenth century a group of courtier-adventurers suggested to King

Charles II *that he charter a company "for the purpose of sending an expedition to the Gambia to dig for gold." The result was the Company of the Royal Adventurers into Africa, which thrived from* 1600 *to* 1672 *and which was succeeded by the Royal African Company. The extract below is from a history of the enterprise, written in* 1919 *by George F. Zook, an American educator. This passage points up the organized, commercial aspects of slaving.*

On December 18, 1660, the king, who was pleased with the adventurers for having "undertaken so hopeful an enterprise," granted them a charter under the name of "The Company of the Royal Adventurers into Africa."

By this charter the Royal Adventurers received the land and the adjacent islands on the west coast of Africa from Cape Blanco to the Cape of Good Hope, for a period of one thousand years. . . . The king himself reserved the privilege of becoming an adventurer at any time and to invest an amount of money not exceeding one-sixteenth of the company's stock.

Furthermore, it was provided that the king "shall have, take and receive two third parts of all the gold mines which shall be seized possessed and wrought in the parts and places aforesaid, we . . . paying and bearing two third parts of all the charges incident to the working and transporting of the said gold." The company was to have the other third and bear the remainder of the expense. That this provision was not a matter of mere form, as in so many of the royal charters, is evident from the stimulus which had led to the formation of the company. Indeed in one part of the charter the purpose of the company is presented as "the setting forward and furthering of the trade intended (redwood, hides, elephants' teeth) in the parts aforesaid and the encouragement of the undertakers in discovering the golden mines and setting of plantations there." The trade in slaves was not mentioned in the charter. . . .

The Company of Royal Adventurers . . . received its charter December 18, 1660. In the same month, Captain Robert Holmes sailed from England in command of the five royal ships which composed the first expedition. In March, 1661, he arrived at Cape Verde where he at once informed the Dutch commander that he had orders from Charles II to warn all persons of whatsoever nation that the right of trade and navigation from Cape Verde to the Cape of Good Hope belonged exclusively to the king of England. Holmes ordered the Dutch to vacate their forts and to abandon the coast within six or seven months. Thereupon he seized the island of Boa Vista, one of the Cape Verde group claimed by the Dutch since 1621. Later he sent a frigate into the mouth of the Gambia. . . .

The early trade of the English to the coast of Africa was very largely in exchange for products which could be sold in England. Among these may be mentioned elephants' teeth, wax, malaguetta and gold. . . . The hope of discovering gold mines was the principal cause of the first expedition sent to Africa by the Royal Adventurers in December, 1660. When this scheme to mine gold was abandoned the company's agents traded for gold which was brought down from the interior or washed out by the slow and laborious toil of the natives. The other African products, especially elephants' teeth, were brought to London where they sold quite readily for very good prices.

Although this direct trade between England and Africa was never neglected, the slave trade with the English colonies in the West Indies was destined to absorb the company's attention because the supply of indentured servants was never great enough to meet the needs of the rapidly growing sugar and indigo plantations. From the planters point of view, moreover, slaves had numerous advantages over white servants as plantation laborers. Slaves and their children after them were chattel property for life. The danger of rebellion was very small because often the slaves could not even converse with one another, since they were likely to be from different parts of Africa and therefore to speak a different dialect. Finally, neither the original outlay for slaves nor the cost of feeding and clothing them was great, and therefore slaves were regarded as more economical than indentured servants. Moreover, there was much to be said against encouraging the lower classes of England to come to the plantations, where they often engaged in disturbances of one kind and another. . . . Not only did the company supply the planters with slaves, their greatest necessity, but in exchange for these it took sugar and other plantation products which it carried to England. It was natural that the company should endeavor to make a success of its business. . . .

Sir Thomas Modyford, speaker of the assembly [of Barbadoes], also became the agent for the Royal Adventurers in Barbadoes. Modyford was very enthusiastic about the company's prospects for a profitable trade in Negroes with the Spanish colonies. The people of Barbadoes neither shared Modyford's enthusiasm for this trade nor for the company's monopoly because they believed that thereby the price of slaves was considerably increased. On December 18, 1662, the council and assembly of Barbadoes resolved to ask the king for a free trade to Africa or to be assured that the factors of the Royal Company would sell their slaves for the same price as other merchants. Very shortly, the duke of York, the company's governor, informed Governor Willoughby that the company had made arrangements to provide Barbadoes and the Caribbee Islands with 3,000 slaves per annum and that the needs of the islands would be attended to as conditions changed. Moreover, the company pledged itself to see that all Negroes imported into the island should be sold by lots, as had been the custom, at the average rate of seventeen pounds per head or for commodities of the island rated at that price. The duke of York also requested Governor Willoughby to ascertain if possible how many Negroes were desired by the planters at that rate, and to see that any planters who wished to become members of the company should be given an opportunity to do so. . . .

The monopoly of supplying the colonies with slaves, conferred upon the Company of Royal Adventurers, was most cordially hated on account of the great degree of dependence placed upon slave labor in the plantations. As a result of this conflict of interests the planters early resorted to numerous devices such as the laws for the protection of debtors, to embarrass the company in the exercise of its monopoly. Since the company had received its exclusive privileges by a charter from the crown the English planters in the West Indies soon found that their troubles with the Company of Royal Adventurers brought them also into direct conflict with the king. In this way the planters enjoyed the distinction of being among the first to begin the opposition which later, in the Great Revolution [the Glorious Revolution of 1688], resulted in the overthrow of James II and the royal prerogative.

THE FULANI JIHAD

Historians have long debated the causes and nature of the Fulani jihad, or holy war, that swept across the central Sudan in the early nineteenth century. The war has been viewed as a political revolution in which the Fulani overthrew the tenuous Muslim aristocracy of Hausaland and extended their power over much of the central Sudan, and as a revival movement intent on bringing the region a more austere type of Islam. Certainly both these factors must now be accounted in understanding the jihad, which began in 1804. Its leader was Usman Dan Fodio, a fanatical Muslim who became chief of the Fulani empire. The selection below presents Usman Dan Fodio's personal explanation of the origins of the revolution. It was probably written in 1811, when most of his objectives had been realized and he was about to retire.

I declare, and God the Accomplisher is my witness, that Ahmad Baba ibn Ahmad ibn Al-Hajj laid down in his book, *Exposition and Information about the kinds of Sudanese Captives*, that Bornu, Kano, Katsena, Songhay, and part of Zagzag [Zaria] were Muslim countries, but the whole of the country to the west was a country of the Unbelievers. If someone asks—of what use is this inquiry into the mode of government of the people mentioned in the passage?—I reply, "May God and you, reader, put the information to good use." The people are Muslim except the Afanu [the Hausa]. I do not know from whence these latter come, and never heard. To the west of Hausa all the people are Unbelievers. According to our author, Islam was accepted by some kings and others of these parts in his time. Every learned man judges according to the knowledge of his age. Conditions change with the times, and the cure changes with the disease. It is well known that in our time Islam has become widespread in the land of Hausa among other than kings. The Kings are Unbelievers and nothing else. If they are believers in Islam, why are they idolators, refusing to follow in the way of God, and raising the flag of earthly power above the flag of Islam?

All this is Unbelief, according to the general opinion.

The government of a country is the government of its King without question. If the King is a Muslim, his land is Muslim; if he is an Unbeliever, his land is a land of Unbelievers. In these circumstances it is lawful for anyone to leave it for another country. There is no dispute that the Hausa Kings worshiped many places of idols, and trees, and rocks, and sacrificed to them. This constitutes Unbelief, according to the general opinion.

This view of mine rests on the weight of authority, but does not deny the existence of some Muslims here and there. We cannot judge from exceptions specially chosen:—

> "You should prefer the usual to the unusual; for the usual and common is what we want to elucidate."

The above description was applicable to the condition of the Hausa peoples as we found them, before the *jihad.* Since then we have fought them and put them to flight, and killed some, and driven others from this land by the power of God (Exalted be He).

We have appointed Muslim Governors over the land, and it has become a land of Islam, without doubt. Praise be to God. . . .

To explain our flight from Gobir and the reasons of our holy war with the Hausa Sultans.

I declare, and God the Accomplisher is my witness, that the work of my brother Abdullah on this subject is sufficient. I said to him on a day: "Write for us the reasons for our flight from Gobir and our holy war with the Hausa Sultans, to be our apology to whoever reads the book, if he serve God." He answered that he would write, and wrote:—

. . . Know that our Sheikh, Uthman ibn Muhammad Amir al-Mu'minin (May God prolong his life in his service) came forth to call all persons, wherever they might be, to the Faith, and to expound to all whom he could reach their duty to God, and noble endeavor, trying to clear away their doubts concerning God, to deliver them from the doom to come and to save them, to keep alive the doctrines of Islam and to banish wickedness.

Many people received his teaching, and helped him, till his fame spread abroad. There were learned men, his contemporaries, who disputed and denied his mission.

In the beginning he did not address himself to the kings. After a time his people grew and became famous, till they were known in Hausaland as "*The People.*" Men kept leaving their countries and coming to him. Of the ruling classes some repented, and came to him with all they possessed, leaving their Sultans. Then the Sultans became angry, till there ensued between them and their chiefs the war we remember. Matters did not rest there.

The Sheikh said: "I will not interfere between anyone and his chief; I will not be a cause of parting." He strove to avert a quarrel. But the trouble grew and grew. The Sultans kept sending protests to their people. The rupture became open between the Sheikh and them. They saw the growing numbers of his following and the hold that Islam had gained. Its growing strength made them furious, and devils among Jinns and men urged them on, saying: "If you do not disperse this concourse of people, your power will be gone; they will destroy your country, by causing all the people to leave you and go to them."

The Sultan of Gobir sent to us plotting our destruction, as we discovered. This showed us the true meaning of his words and deeds. But God averted from us his evil design. He told us, what we know, namely, that they only wished to kill us. So we returned to our abode. The Sultan of Gobir attacked the Sheikh's people; they fled, for they were afraid. The Gobir army followed them and captured some and slew others, seizing children and women, and selling them in our midst.

This made us greatly afraid. The Sultan of Gobir ordered the Sheikh to leave the country with his children and wives and relatives, but to take no one else with him, and disperse his people. The Sheikh replied: "I will not disperse my people, but I will go away with any who wish to come with me. Let those who wish to remain, remain."

So we fled from their land in the year 1218 A.H. on the 10th of Dhu'l-qa'da [February 23, 1804] to a place outside Gobir territory.

The Muslims all fled, following us. Many of them joined us with their people and property; some brought nothing but their people; some came with no following at all.

The Sultan of Gobir ordered his Chiefs to seize the goods of all who fled or prevent them leaving.

They seized much property of the Muslims, and killed some of them.

Then he ordered those of the Chiefs nearest to us on the east to keep on killing our people, and plundering, and imprisoning.

The people suffered sorely.

We went to the Sheikh and said: "Truly this matter has become intolerable; recourse must be had to arms. There can be no doubt that the situation demands a prince to manage our affairs, for Muslims should be without order or government."

Then we did homage to the Sheikh, as is directed by the Qur'an and Sunna in such circumstances, and made him the leader of the Holy War.

We rose to ward off attack. Self-defense and defense of dependents and possessions is a righteous act, according to received opinion.

FULANI WISDOM

According to the Fulani, who speak a Nigritic language, "a Fulani will lie but not make a lying proverb." The following collection of adages was compiled by C.E.J. Whitting.

A dark night brings fear but man still more.

However little you think of the elephant, you will not say it will not fill a pot.

The ant-eater's grief is not the monkey's.

Whoever cooks the food of malice, remnants will stick to his pocket.

Alive he was insufficient, dead he is missed.

An enemy slaughters, a friend distributes.

If you want to hear the news of the heart ask the face.

They know the calabash is useful but they make a spoon.

If a knife is lacking, a strip of bark will cut.

It is not his deserts that a man gets but his destiny.

If death encircles the mortar, it wants not the mortar but the pounder.

Fair words, evil deeds.

Hate you your buttocks never so much, you sit on them perforce.

He who rides the horse of greed at a gallop will pull it up at the door of shame.

He who has no authority will not have ceremonial drums.

Six things cannot be trusted, a prince, a river, a knife, a woman, string and darkness.

Concentration brings near the distant camp.

Guile excels strength.

Be the town never so far, there is another beyond it.

A porcupine will not mind needle grass.

KUBA LAW

The kingdom of the Kuba, home of about seventy-five thousand Bantu speakers, is flanked by the Kasai, Sankuru, and Lulua rivers in the former Kasai province of the Congo (Kinshasa). Comprised of several chiefdoms, it is ruled by the centrally located Bushoong chiefdom, whose head is automatically the king of all the Kuba. The king and chiefs hold their offices by divine right and are the only persons who have power over life and death. The Kuba do not use precedents or compare cases to deduce analogies; their legal process is based on equity and the power of Kuba political authorities—the chiefs and the king. The following discussion of Kuba procedural law is by Dr. Jan Vansina, the author of this volume's chapter on inner Africa and professor of history at the University of Wisconsin. The court cere-

monial and formula he describes date back to about A.D. 1650 *and were used until* 1892, *the beginning of the colonial era in Kubaland. Since then there have been some minor changes, but on the local level Kuba law remains as outlined in the following essay.*

A case is introduced by one of the disputing parties. He brings his complaint to any judge in the capital, who directs him to a competent judge. The party deposits a payment of 700 cowries for the formal lodging of the complaint. Through informal consultation the judge then forms a panel. In cases where a public authority has been flouted, the responsible political official, a village headman, for instance, lodges the complaint. When the day of hearing is set, usually a few days after reception of the complaint, the judges send somebody to notify the defendant. The messenger may be the child of one of the judges or *nyim shapdy*, a special messenger. The messengers must be well treated in the villages, for courts can hold villages in contempt. The courts of appeal have their own means of summoning the defendant: baang [the appeals court that oversees marriage cases] sends the *iyol abaang;* kikaam [appeals court for debtors] and the supreme court have the summons announced on the main square of the capital by the town crier. Anybody who meets the accused is under obligation to notify him. When an accused person refuses to answer the summons, he is fined and arrested either by his covillagers or by slaves of the king or the chief, who form the police force. He is then bound and put in the stocks at the jail in the kikaam's compound. The stocks are used only for preventive detention of this sort. Any person may arrest any other *in flagrante delicto*, a fact that often leads to fights. A wise man notifies the two village policemen who exist in every village.

Before the session of the court opens, the accused pays 700 cowries to the panel, and the 1,400 cowries of both parties is divided among the judges. This amount constitutes their salary. Both parties, one after the other, then tell the facts, the plaintiff being the first speaker. At this stage they may be interrupted only by judges or spectators who want to elucidate one or another detail. Eyewitnesses or character witnesses are then called in and are cross-examined by the judges, who also cross-examine the parties. Usually the statements of the parties and the testimony of the witnesses elicit the facts to the satisfaction of the judges. The latter, in any event, have a general knowledge of the facts, having heard about the matter through gossip at the capital or through inquiries made beforehand by the provincial chief. Sometimes, however, the facts are not clear and there are no witnesses. The accused may then propose to swear an oath (*ndokl*). He says that he is innocent, invokes the Creator God as a witness, and steps over a leopard skin, the symbol of political authority. If he lies, he should die on the spot. But the oath is rarely used, for it is believed that the Creator punishes those who swear for trifles. I believe that the judges feel that swearing an oath is taking the matter out of court. A milder oath also exists, but it is considered no more than an emphatic form of speech.

Wooden drum of the Kuba
THE MUSEUM OF PRIMITIVE ART

After the evidence is heard and the facts are elicited to the satisfaction of the judges, they withdraw to deliberate. They must reach a unanimous verdict. After doing so, they emerge and proceed to the announcement of the verdict, which is introduced by the following formula:

The king doesn't walk with a bow the collecting of conflicts, the verdicts of the cases.
The black genette eats the white termites
Be not afraid of the grass the genette carries
The old animal of the councilors of the supreme court
when he proceeds to decide cases, he doesn't like protests.
Above the thieves, the leopard of the witches
the spoon of the porridge
is the instrument which probes the depths of the fire.
It dawns at the chasm which begets the hills
at the world which begets the living.
The river of trade bears the weak ones.
It becomes daylight at Mbeky Butwiim
at Makum maNyaang
at the king who stares intently at the verdicts
at Mboom Kol Mishumn.

The formula means:

The king is in court to
settle the conflicts.
The king destroys the criminals
the innocents must not be afraid.
The king in the supreme court does not stand for protests against the verdicts.
Despite the thieves, the king can find the culprits.
It dawns at the king's who creates the world
who creates all the living beings.
The king protects the weak.
It dawns at the famous capitals
at the king's capital when he holds his court.

The formula is given in full because it is typical of Kuba thought. It emphasizes that the court holds its authority from the king, and that the king has authority by virtue of divine kingship. It reminds the guilty parties that justice will find them out, and the innocent parties that they are protected by the king. It reminds all that verdicts should not be questioned. It expresses the Kuba philosophy of law, and stresses that fundamentally the law has equity. It is guaranteed by the powers of the king, but the equity of the king himself is guaranteed by the supreme court.

SONG OF THE SPIRITS

The divine powers of Kuba kings are emphasized in the "songs of the spirits," which were composed by the women of the king's harem in praise of the souls of deceased rulers. They were sung each month at the appearance of the new moon and have the quality of a dirge. This example, recorded by Jan Vansina, salutes the spirit of Mbope Kyeen, who ruled from 1900 to 1902. Mboong was the name of the first Kuba king, hence it is often used to designate his successors. Mbope Kyeen's death, so soon after his coronation, makes his aged grandmother, Mabiinc, weep.

Mboong has donned the coronation costumes
Come admire him!
And those in the streets will tell the news.
King Mboong, the thread which sews the peoples of the king;
He is the thread who unites the provinces.
Mbope, son of Kyeen speaks:
I am not envious, I am the God who created trees and plains!
The woman Mabiinc of the twin spirits, she who nursed the king's mother speaks:
"I am truly the resident of the royal quarter, I am from that august place.
The dancing mask Mashingady weeps for pity.
The woman of his heart, I come from the village of Mulek, I come from the royal quarter; I Mbaawoot daughter of Pish, daughter of Pash must don the wrapper of mourning, the dress of funeral white."

ANIMAL LYRICS

Ncok *is a lighthearted genre of Kuba poetry recited in song, often to the accompaniment of a dance. Three examples collected by Dr. Vansina in 1953 follow. The first refers to an ancient Kuba myth in which the sun vanishes forever. The hero gives the Bushoong, the Kuba ruling group, a rooster. The cock's cry awakens the sun and chases away the moon, which has been called by the cuckoos.*

The rooster sings during the night
The cuckoos have provoked the rising of the moon
The rooster sang his cry
The rooster the Bushoong have taken.

The crocodile is dying in the water
The crocodile has become deaf
The huge crocodile has become blind.

The land of the goat, we are trampling it
The heaven of God, we touch it with the hand
I will go to the village of the dead, borne on the arms of men.
One day in the future, during the heat
The day of my death, don't bury me
at the foot of the *ngum* tree
I fear its spines;
at the foot of the tree *buncweemy*
I fear the drops of water;
One day in the future, bury me
on the main square near the tree *bushaang*
I want to hear the beat of the drumming
and the rattles of the dancers!

NDABA, A MAN OF AFFAIRS

Praise poems are an integral part of the social life of the Zulu, who belong to the Nguni cluster of Bantu speakers. Today there are over two million Zulu inhabiting Zululand and Natal in the Republic of South Africa. This Zulu praise song is dedicated to Ndaba, an eighteenth-century chief who was probably the grandson or great-grandson of Zulu, legendary founder of the core clan of Zulu people. His name means "man of affairs." Sonani means "What wrong did we do?" The Mababela, Gabela, and Gcabashe are Zulu ancestors. Ndaba lives "with his shield on his knees," as he is always ready to fight.

Ndaba son of Sonani, they say "What wrong did he do?",
Since the people are living with their herds
Belonging to Mababela's people of the Gabela clan.
He who hunted the forests until they murmured,
Until eventually they cried "Enough! Isn't it?",
Today there is so much game
That they snip off a titbit of a duiker for him.
Who when he lay down was the size of rivers,
Who when he got up was the size of mountains.
Precious little amulet of our people, of Gcabashe's people,
That continually lives in a towering rage,
With his shields on his knees,
Watching over the herds of those who meditate evil
Against Mababela's people of the Gabela clan.

CHAKA'S RECEPTION

Henry Francis Fynn, an Englishman, was one of the few white men to be intimately acquainted with Chaka (Shaka), "Father of the Zulu." In 1819 Fynn journeyed to Cape Town, where he became a partner in the Farewell Trading Company. He traveled in the area, and in 1824 went to Natal with the first group of white settlers. He soon learned that Natal was virtually the private property of Chaka and determined to visit the Zulu warrior-king. Negotiations ensued, but Chaka stalled the arrival of Fynn and his party in order to prepare an impressive reception for them. In July, 1824, the coveted invitation finally came. The following account of Fynn's first meeting with Chaka is from his diary, an invaluable source for Africanists.

The distance from the port to Shaka's residence was 200 miles. Our progress was exceedingly slow, each day's journey being arranged by Mbikwana [one of Shaka's aides]. We afterwards found out that he had not taken us by a direct route, but to kraals of minor chiefs and some of the barracks of Shaka's regiments. Cattle-slaughtering occurred sometimes twice and thrice a day. Numbers of Zulu joined our column in order to relieve Mbikwana's people of their burdens. We were struck with astonishment at the order and discipline maintained in the country through which we traveled. The regimental kraals, especially the upper parts thereof, also the kraals of chiefs, showed that cleanliness was a prevailing custom and this not only inside their huts, but outside, for there were considerable spaces where neither dirt nor ashes were to be seen. . . .

Messengers passed three or four times a day between Shaka and Mbikwana, the former enquiring about our progress and doubtless directing how we should proceed so as to fall in with his own preparations for our reception. . . . While encamped that night we saw much commotion going on in our neighborhood. Troops of cattle were being driven in advance; regiments were passing near by and on distant hills, interspersed with regiments of girls, decorated in beads and brass with regimental uniformity, carrying on their heads large pitchers of native beer, milk and cooked food. . . .

The following morning . . . we arrived at a ridge from which we beheld an extensive and very picturesque basin before us, with a river running through it, called the Umfolozi.

We were requested to make a stand under a large euphorbia tree, from whence, about a mile before us, we saw the residence of Shaka, viz: a native kraal nearly two miles in circumference. . . .

On entering the great cattle kraal we found drawn up within it about 80,000 natives in their war attire. Mbikwana requested me to gallop within the circle, and immediately on my starting to do so one general shout broke forth from the whole mass, all pointing at me with their sticks. I was asked to gallop round the circle two or three times in the midst of tremendous shouting of the words, "*UJojo wokhalo!*" (the sharp or active finch of the ridge). Mr. Farewell and I were then led by Mbikwana to the head of the kraal, where the masses of the people were considerably denser than elsewhere. The whole force remained stationary, as, indeed, it had been since the commencement of the reception.

Mbikwana, standing in our midst, addressed some unseen individual in a long speech. . . .

While the speech was being made I caught sight of an individual in the background whom I concluded to be Shaka, and, turning to Farewell, pointed out and said: "Farewell, there is Shaka." This was sufficiently audible for him to hear and perceive that I had recognized him. . . .

Elephant tusks were then brought forward. One was laid before Farewell and another before me. Shaka then raised the stick in his hand and after striking with it right and left, the whole mass broke from their position and formed up into regiments. Portions of each of these rushed to the river and the surrounding hills, while the remainder, forming themselves into a circle, commenced dancing with Shaka in their midst.

It was a most exciting scene, surprising to us, who could not have imagined that a nation termed "savages" could be so disciplined and kept in order.

Regiments of girls, headed by officers of their own sex, then entered the center of the arena to the number of 8,000–10,000, each holding a slight staff in her hand. They joined in the dance, which continued for about two hours. . . .

The King came up to us and told us not to be afraid of his people, who were now coming up to us in small divisions, each division driving cattle before it. The men were singing and dancing and whilst so doing advancing and receding even as one sees the surf do on a seashore. The whole country, as far as our sight could reach, was covered with numbers of people and droves of cattle. The cattle had been assorted according to their color. . . . After exhibiting their cattle for two hours, they drew together in a circle, and sang and danced to their war song. Then the people returned to the cattle, again exhibiting them as before, and, at intervals, dancing and singing. The women now entered the kraal, each having a long thin stick in the right hand, and moving it in time to the song. They had not been dancing many minutes, when they had to make way for the ladies of the seraglio, besides about 150 others, who were called sisters. These danced in parties of eight, arranged in fours, each party wearing different colored beads, which were crossed from the shoulders to the knees. Each wore a head-dress of black feathers, and four brass collars, fitting closely to the neck. When the King joined in the dance, he was accompanied by the men. This dance lasted half an hour. The order observed and the precision of every movement was interpreted to us by his interpreter, Hlambamanzi. He desired to know from us if ever we had seen such order in any other state, assured us that he was the greatest king in existence, that his people were as numerous as the stars, and that his cattle were innumerable. . . . The following morning we were requested to mount our horses and proceed to the King's quarters. We found him sitting under a tree in the upper end of the kraal decorating himself and surrounded by about 200 people. A servant was kneeling by his side holding a shield above him to keep off the glare of the sun. Round his forehead he wore a turban of otter skin with a feather of a crane erect in front, fully two feet long, and a wreath of scarlet feathers, formerly worn, only, by men of high rank. Ear ornaments made from dried sugar cane, carved round the edges, with white ends, and an inch in diameter, were let into the lobes of the ears, which had been cut to admit them. From shoulder to shoulder, he wore bunches, five inches in length, of the skins of monkeys and genets, twisted like the tails of these animals. These hung half down the body. Round the ring on the head, were a dozen tastefully arranged bunches of the loury feathers, neatly tied to thorns which were stuck into the hair. Round his arms were white ox-tail tufts, cut down the middle so as to allow the hair to hang about the arm, to the number of four for each arm. Round the waist, there was a kilt or petticoat, made of skins of monkeys and genets, and twisted as before described, having small tassels round the top. The kilt reached to the knees, below which were white ox-tails fitted to the legs so as to hang down to the ankles. He had a white shield with a single black spot, and one assegai. . . .

Two oxen were slaughtered for us. After dinner we prepared to retire, but messengers from Shaka requested us to go to him, with Jacob the interpreter. I was then led into the seraglio, where I found him seated in a carved wooden chair and surrounded by about 400 girls, two or three chiefs and two servants in attendance.

My name Fynn had been converted into Sofili by the people in general; by this, after desiring me to sit in front of him, he several times accosted me in the course of the following dialogue:

"I hear you have come from umGeorge, is it so? Is he as great a king as I am?"

Fynn: "Yes; King George is one of the greatest kings in the world." . . .

Shaka: "Have you medicine by you?"

Fynn: "Yes."

Shaka: "Then cure me, or I will have you sent to umGeorge to have you killed."

Fynn: "What is the matter with you?"

Shaka: "That is your business to find out."

Fynn: "Stand up and let me see your person."

Shaka: "Why should I stand up?"

Fynn: "That I may see if I can find out what ails you."

Shaka stood up but evidently disliked my approaching him closely. A number of girls held up lighted torches. I looked about his person and, after reflecting on the great activity he had shown during the day, was satisfied he had not much the matter with him. I, however, observed numerous black marks on his loins where native doctors had scarified him, and at once said he had pains in his loins. He held his hand before his mouth in astonishment, upon which my wisdom was applauded by all present. Shaka then strictly charged me not to give medicine to his dogs, and, after a few commonplace questions in which he showed good humor, I was permitted to retire for the night. . . .

He sent the next day requesting me to follow him.

On my arrival he desired me to look at and then to count a large drove of oxen I had not before seen. I did so, making the number 5,654. When I announced the result the crowd that was present burst out laughing asking how it was possible for me to count so many, seeing I had not counted up to ten on my fingers. They at once concluded I had not counted them. . . .

Shaka went on to speak of the gifts of nature, or, as they term it, *uMvelinqangi.* He said that the first forefathers of the Europeans had bestowed on us many gifts by giving us all the knowledge of arts and manufactures, yet they had kept from us the greatest of all gifts, such as a good black skin, for this does not necessitate the wearing of clothes to hide the white skin, which was not pleasant to the eye. He well knew that for a black skin we would give all we were worth in the way of our arts and manufactures. He then asked what use was made of the hides of cattle slaughtered in our country. When I told him they were made into shoes and other articles, which, however, I could not explain so as to make him understand, he exclaimed that that was another proof of the unkindness of our forefathers, for they had obliged us to make use of hides to protect our feet, but as such protection was unnecessary in their case their forefathers revealed to them that hides should be used for making more handsome and serviceable articles, namely shields. This changed the conversation to the superiority of their arms; these he endeavored to show in various ways were more advantageous than our muskets. The shield, he argued, if dipped into water previous to an attack, would be sufficient to ward off the effect of a ball fired when they were at a distance.

THE BRAVE AND MAGIC LAND

The Zulu cultural tradition has been recently enriched by the poems, plays, stories, and essays of the late Herbert Dhlomo, a Zulu poet. His masterpiece which was first published in 1941, *is* Valley of a Thousand Hills, *a poem extolling the heroes and wonders of his Natal homeland. Its prologue follows.*

On your dear fame, proud offspring here
I stand!
Sweet names of a sweet strand!

O charms of my dear fatherland!
Blest spots! I long to see them all!
Where men of yore, great Shaka's band,
Sang wrought and fell! To me they call!

Great scenes of old—like magic wand!—
Of heroes wise and strange feats done,
Where men of might, like ocean sand,
Mocked seas of life . . . and wrought
for fun!

Born sealed with immortality,
Hymned Shaka, god of war-writ fame,
Homeric feats attained, and we
Plumed Trojan Black Bulls, claim a
name!

For Shaka, now our Jove, more than
Sung classic names achieved. His name
More than vain demagogue boasts can,
Or ever will, has brought us fame.

And those whom we in pride adore,
Moshoeshoe, Hintsa, Khama's strain . . .
Hannibal, Aggrey—these and many
more
With gleaming names, deck Shaka's
train.

Out of the living past they haunt me still!
And voices mute forever speak to me!
My eyes with tears, my thoughts with
visions, fill!
I see them all, but see not where they be!

These men and places call to me!
They speak out of Eternity!
I see, I feel, I live it all!
I rise! and yield before the call!

Held captive in a net, a slave sits on the Congo shore waiting to be sold and shipped.

THE RISE OF RACISM

PHOTO RESEARCHERS—BRADLEY SMITH

Emblems of African Spain: above, "stalactite" ceiling embellishing the splendid Granadan citadel of Alhambra, built after 1248 by the last Muslim dynasty in Spain; right, the four-foot-tall "Alhambra Vase," finest extant example of blue pottery made under Moorish patronage.

MUSEUM OF THE ALHAMBRA; DOMINGUEZ

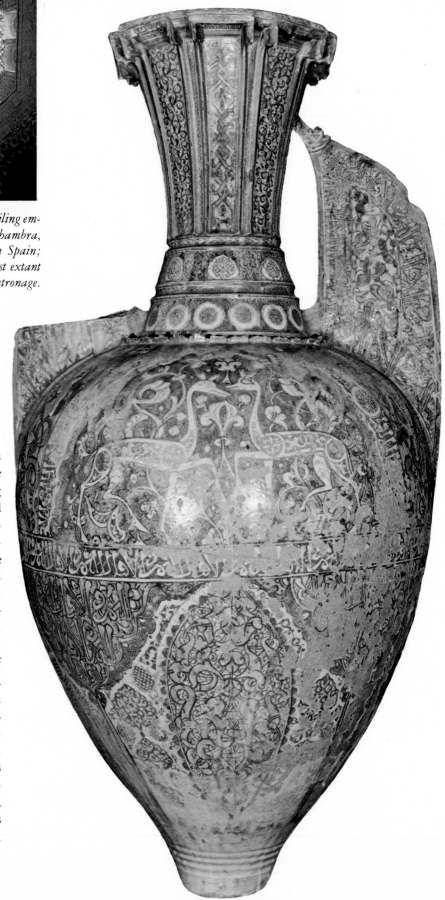

NO TEARS FOR THE MOORS

It is a bitter irony of history that when Europeans first impinged upon Africa, the European spirit was dominated by a surging religious fanaticism. "Reduce to perpetual slavery their persons, domains, and possessions" was the official Church policy toward the "infidels," and no one heeded the call more fiercely than the Catholic rulers of Spain, whose zeal had been tempered in the long struggle against the Moors. The Christian reconquest of Spain did not, however, bring peace between Cross and Crescent; viewing its long struggle as part of a global holy war, Spain soon launched a counteroffensive against the Moors in North Africa. Nor did European religious zeal moderate after the Protestant Reformation in the mid-sixteenth century. Indeed, it intensified. In the continuing conflicts among the aggressive, self-righteous believers—Catholic, Protestant, and Muslim, each wed to a "universal" faith—Africa's diverse animist faiths would be the victims.

The end of Moorish rule is recorded in a Spanish bas-relief retable above. It shows a richly garbed Muhammad XI, *or Boabdil, as the Spanish called him, filing out of the Alhambra en route to surrender to the Catholic monarchs, Ferdinand and Isabella. Muhammad's demise had been brought on by a civil war between him and his uncle, in which it had been Spanish strategy to support Muhammad just long enough to see his rival destroyed. No sooner had Muhammad taken Granada than the Crown demanded he withdraw, and unable to enlist the aid of Muslim rulers in Africa, he retired in* 1492.

YAN-TOULOUSE

The Count of Barcelona, an eleventh-century knight, is shown stabbing a Moor in a medieval manuscript painting.

EL ESCORIAL, MS. Z III 14

PHOTO RESEARCHERS–NORMAN LIGHTFOOT

The girl at left belongs to the Sokoto Fulani of northern Nigeria. The Fulani rose to power in the early nineteenth century in scattered regions of the western Sudan, revolutionizing once again a flagging Muslim culture. Below, the Dogon of Mali hold a funeral. Although Muslim dress is evident, the dance itself is part of the Dogon's animist tradition, in which the vital force of the deceased is passed to a descendant.

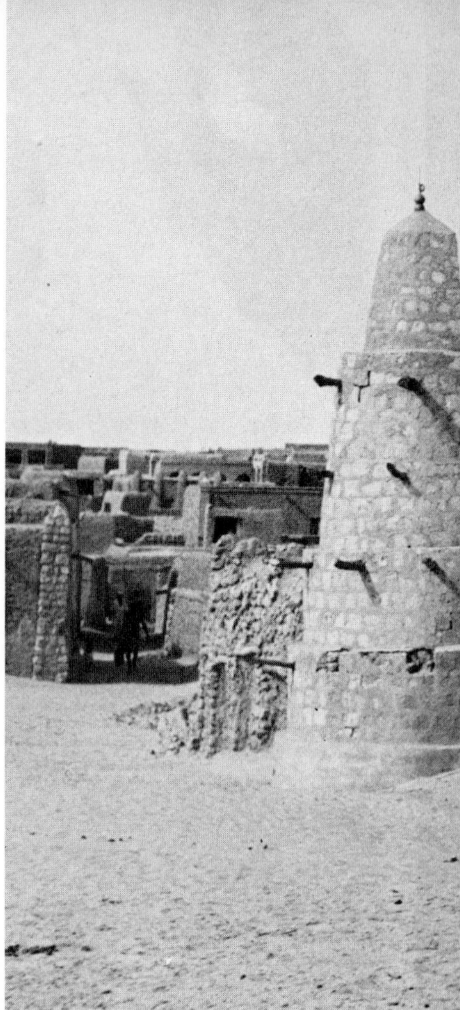

PHOTO RESEARCHERS–DIANE RAWSON

WERNER FORMAN

LOSS OF THE PAST

With Portugal occupying a number of strategic cities in the western Maghreb, Spain holding most of the ports of the central coast, and Turkey pressing from the east, North Africa seemed in the sixteenth century to have surrendered its future to alien rulers. The Turks would long continue to hold their gains as far west as Tunisia, making the southern Mediterranean littoral a haven for Barbary pirates. Morocco, however, met its foreign-borne adversity by spawning the vital Saadian dynasty. One of its sultans, Ahmad al-Mansur, expelled the Portuguese at the battle of Alcazar in 1578. Encouraged by this victory, Morocco's "Victorious One" sent a force across the Sahara, defeated the armies of the Songhai empire, and inaugurated a policy of plunder and destruction there, reducing such centers of learning as Timbuktu to impoverished villages and leaving a commercial civilization in ruins.

Within the shadows of the great brick mosque of Sankore (above) once lived more than a hundred Muslim teaching clerics. The Koranic schools they ran, the extensive libraries they accumulated, went to make up a kind of university quarter for Timbuktu. Below is a reconstruction of the old mosque at Jenne, a rival intellectual center. Said to equal Mecca in architectural magnificence, it was destroyed in 1830 by Seku Ahmadu, Muslim zealot and leader of a Fulani jihad, as punishment for the moral corruption that he judged had infected the citizens.

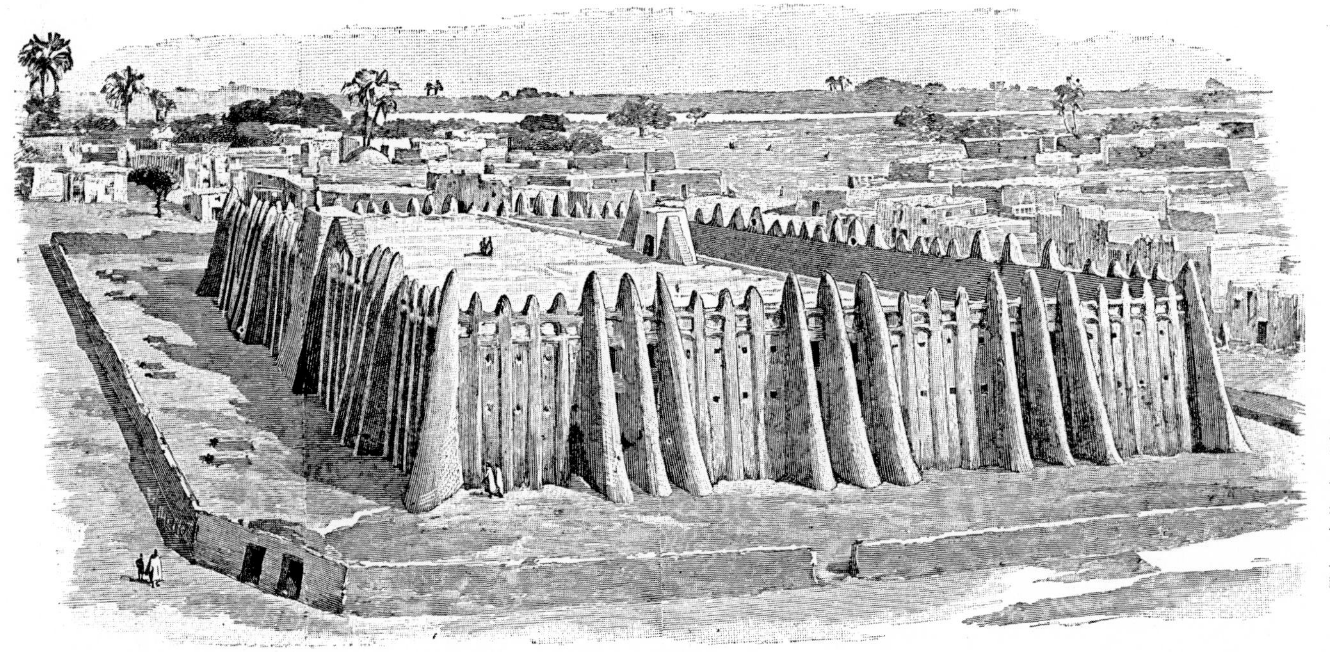

DU BOIS, *Timbuctoo the Mysterious*, 1896

When the kingdom of the Congo sent an emissary to the Vatican at the beginning of the seventeenth century, European attitudes toward their black neighbors were still full of contradictions. Although Rome sanctioned slavery, it still sought to strengthen relations with African monarchs. To this end Antonio (left), "Marquis of Nigritia," as Pope Urban VIII *called him, was cordially received. When Antonio died in the alien city in 1608, he was buried in the Church of Santa Maria Maggiore, where this bust can be seen.*

ALINARI

KOLB, *The Present State of the Cape of Good Hope*, 1731

COLOR AND SLAVERY

The heavier the slave traffic grew and the more dehumanized its victims became in the years after 1650, the more avidly did Europeans search for ways to justify themselves. The theory that the African was an "infidel" could only suffice for a time, for if the chattel became a Christian, where was the justification then? More useful was the premise upon which the Dutch in the Cape Colony defended slavery. Dark-skinned people, it was said, are the sons of Ham. Since Noah had condemned Ham to serve his brothers, clearly the whites were only fulfilling a biblical curse. From deep within such pseudo-Christian rationalizations, certain deadly equations began to emerge (for example, the African stood outside all justice, human and divine). Later these notions would be replaced by equally destructive misapplications of "science." The new ethnological concept of "race" led to classifying peoples as superior and inferior, and even Darwin's theory of the survival of the fittest was bent to prove their argument.

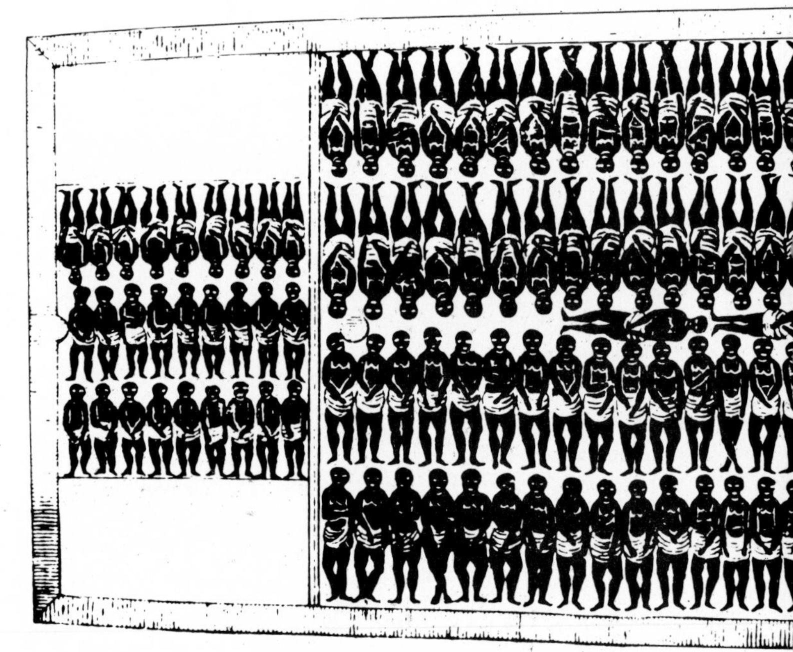

CLARKSON, *History of the Abolition of the African Slave Trade*, 1808

Opposite, a well-dressed Boer imperiously instructs a Hottentot slave in a sketch made by a Dutch scientist who visited the Cape Colony in 1705. Right, the whipping of a bound slave on a plantation near Rio de Janeiro was depicted by a French visitor to Brazil in 1834. Below, a diagram of the hold of a nineteenth-century slave ship showed how to load the maximum number of humans.

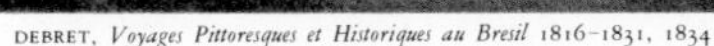

DEBRET, *Voyages Pittoresques et Historiques au Bresil* 1816–1831, 1834

The annual yam harvest festival of the Asante (above) was seen and sketched by Thomas Bowdich, leader of an 1817 British mission to the West African kingdom. The umbrellas belong to the vassals of the Asante king, who is seated beneath the red canopy in the center panel. At the festival, an elaborate affair of state, chiefs and captains accused of some crime were tried and punished. "I never felt so grateful for being born in a civilized country," was Bowdich's smug response to the scene. At right, "messengers of the sacred forest" dance during initiation rites in a Toma village. These Mande people live near the Liberia-Guinea border.

ANDRE PICHTER, PARIS–G. WEIDENFELD AND NICHOLSON, LONDON

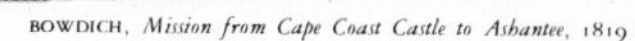

BOWDICH, *Mission from Cape Coast Castle to Ashantee*, 1819

PEOPLES OF "DARKNESS"

Rationalizing the slave trade eventually required Europeans to turn a self-blinded eye toward African life itself. If Africans were accursed and inferior, so the implicit argument ran, then they *could not* have produced anything that was not inherently inferior and accursed. Europeans in general held the view that slavery in the New World was better than "savage barbarism" in Africa. The relatively objective reports of the early explorers now gave way to a kind of perpetual propaganda. Although Europeans had been negotiating with rulers of African states and kingdoms since the earliest days of contact in the fifteenth century, the famed nineteenth-century naturalist Louis Agassiz could declare, with all the authority of "science," that Africans "never originated a regular organization among themselves." Agassiz's logic was the prevailing logic: political organization was a recognized human achievement; therefore Africans had no political organization. To the moralistic, what was different in Africa would appear simply as "repugnant"; to the less censorious, what was different would appear as "colorful" or "quaint" or "childlike." The unfamiliar could not be worthy of respect, of being seen on its own terms.

Wood carvings, once dismissed simply as naive, enliven a door of a palace built for Gezo (1818–1858) *in Abomey, capital of the ancient kingdom of Dahomey.*

MUSEE DE L'HOMME, PARIS–GIRAUDON

British brigantines are careened for repairs at a Guinea river village. The sketch, penciled around 1850, was made by one of the officers.

SOUTH STREET SEAPORT MUSEUM

A German map of West Africa at left, published in 1743, locates numerous coastal trade centers, but leaves the interior largely unpopulated. Its cartographers relied heavily on the recollections of a French missionary, Jean-Baptiste Labat, for data.
SACHSISCHE LANDESBIBLIOTHEK, DRESDEN

A European trader (right), as he appeared to an Angolan woodcarver in 1830; this white man's burden includes a keg of gin, carried atop his hat, a gin bottle in one hand, and a goblet in the other—a sardonic comment on the foreigners' way of life.
TRUSTEES OF THE BRITISH MUSEUM

WHITE MAN'S AFRICA

European outposts on the African coast remained for the most part insecure toeholds until the nineteenth century. They depended entirely on the sufferance of local rulers, whose favors had to be won with gifts and bribes, including that commodity that creates its own demand: alcohol. "You send your boat on Shore," a trader explained in 1789, "to acquaint the Alkaide, or Mayor, of the Town of your arrival; he . . . receives from you Anchorage-money, Ten Gallons of Liquor for the King. . . ." A hundred years earlier a Frenchman already noted the prominence of alcohol in the African trade: "The French commonly compose their cargo . . . of brandy mostly, white and red wine, *ros solis*, firelocks, muskets, flints. . . ." Firearms and firewater, these symbolized European civilization and culture in Africa for three centuries and more.

OVERLEAF: *The capital of the kingdom of Loango on the Congo coast and a slave-trading base when this fanciful view was done in 1732.*
ASTLEY, *Collection of Voyages*, 1732

The *CITY*

from D

REFERENCES.

A. *Kings Palace* . . . .

B. *Womens Palace* . . . .

C. *Cryers Steeple* . . . .

D. *Royal Wine House* . . . .

E. *Royal Banqueting House* . . . . . .

F. *Publick Audience Place* . . . . . .

G. *Kings Garden* . . . .

H. *Queens Garden* . . . .

I. *a Mokisso* . . . .

K. *Another* . . . .

L. *the Broad way Where those found Guilty by the* Imbondo *drink, are dragged and Executed* . . . .

C

G

B

E

A

A

F

I

K

OANGO
D
A
L

BOTH: RADIO TIMES HULTON PICTURE LIBRARY

The Zulu soldiers above perform a pre-battle ceremony in 1879, the year of their last struggle against the British. The kraal at right is the traditional settlement of the cattle-raising Zulu and other Bantu peoples. Below is a portrait of Chaka, the Zulu's military and political hero. He holds the traditional Zulu assagai, which earlier warriors had thrown at their enemies. In line with Chaka's new mode of warfare, the spear would later be shortened for deadly hand-to-hand combat.

OLD HOUSE MUSEUM, DURBAN

STIRRINGS OF PATRIOTISM

His name was Chaka and he was born in the late eighteenth century to a chief of the Zulu, an insignificant clan within a loose grouping of Bantu people living in Natal. By the time he reached manhood, Boers and Bantu farther south had already fought several wars, and Chaka saw with the clarity of genius that the old clan ways were no longer adequate. He set about to forge a new kind of Bantu nation: a nation whose warriors were replaced by a standing army drilled to fight in close formation; a nation in which the tribal chiefs gave way to generals chosen for their ability; a nation centrally organized and ruled by Chaka himself. Before his death in 1828 the little Zulu clan had absorbed through combat a host of smaller states and had raised an aggressive state, which was ready to fight the Boer and the British on equal terms. A cruel nation, it was the product of a cruel time and of one man's extraordinary response to its challenge.

Opposite a woman of Zululand, a segregated territory in Natal, South Afric

BLACK STAR–JOHN MOSS

Chapter Ten

WARS OF RESISTANCE

(c. 1800–1900)

by

Stanlake Samkange

OPPOSITION TO THE SLAVE TRADE had by 1800 gained numerous spokesmen in Africa, Europe, America, and other parts of the world. It will be remembered that in 1526 Affonso, king of the Bakongo along the Congo, told King John III of Portugal: "It is our will that in these kingdoms there should not be any trade in slaves nor market for slaves." In 1724 King Agaja of Dahomey informed the British government that he wanted to stop the export of people from his country. A Swedish traveler visiting Africa in 1789 reported that the *almany*, or ruler, of Futa Toro in northern Senegal, had passed a law forbidding the transportation of slaves through his territories and declared that all the riches in the world would not make him change his mind.

In Europe Frenchmen could cite a royal declaration of 1571, forbidding the importation of slaves into France, and a legal dictum of 1607, not only confirming the freedom of all people in the kingdom but also declaring all slaves to be free as soon as they set foot on French soil and became baptized. In England the reform movement began with Lord Mansfield's judgment of 1772, which declared that common law did not recognize the status of slave; in the United States as many as sixty thousand black men had managed to gain their freedom, and many more had taken up arms for freedom in the Caribbean.

There were several reasons for this attitude. Decent men everywhere had become surfeited with the bestial cruelties perpetrated in the interests of the slave trade. Furthermore, the Industrial Revolution was creating a need for a different kind of labor. Slave traders found themselves less and less influential in political circles because of an organized movement for the abolition of the slave trade.

A strong argument for a new policy was that legitimate

itish efforts to quell the Zulu failed repeatedly, as in this rout, staged at Isandhlwana, Natal, in 1879.

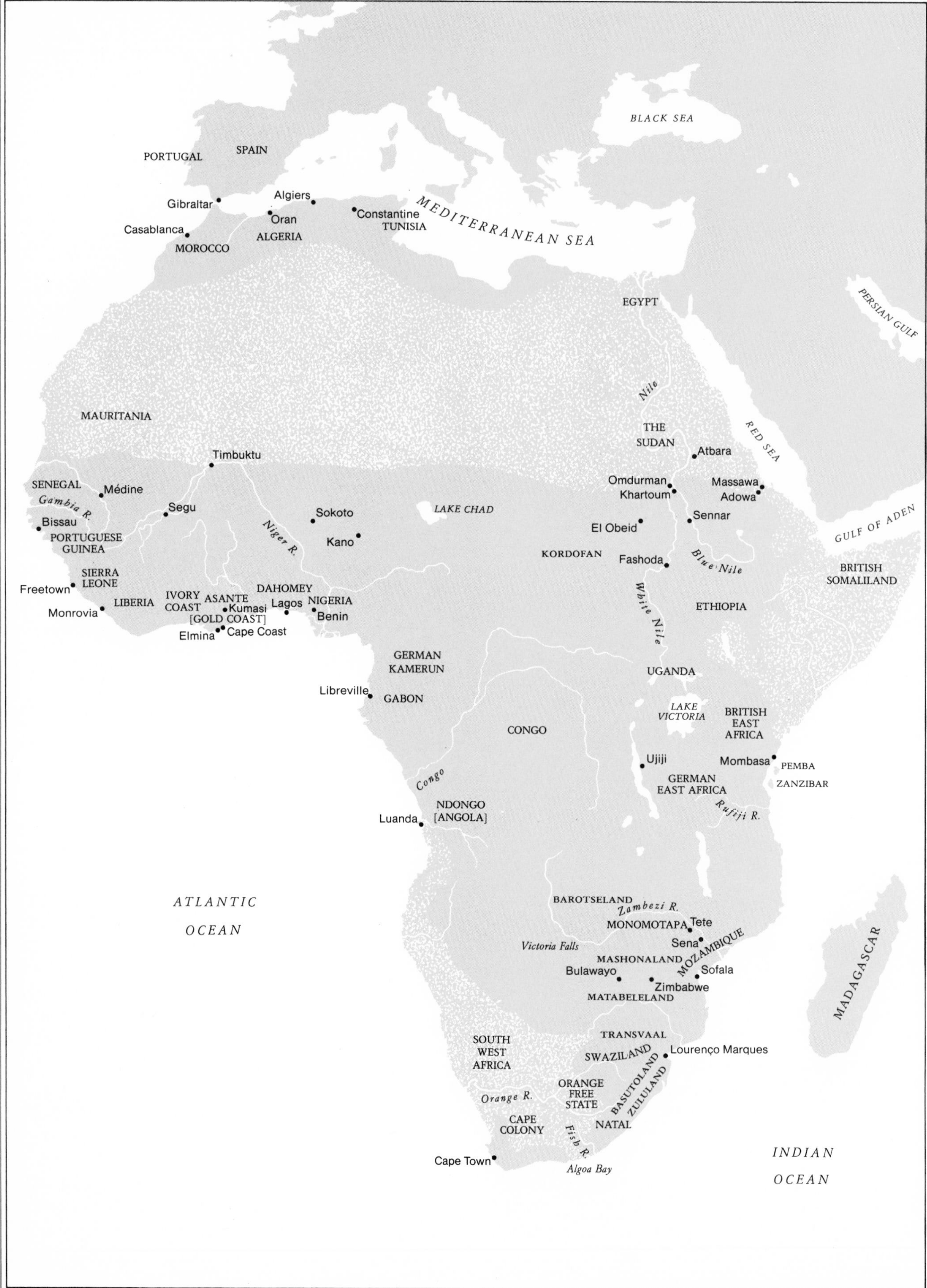
BLACK SEA
PORTUGAL
SPAIN
Gibraltar
Algiers
Oran
Constantine
TUNISIA
MEDITERRANEAN SEA
Casablanca
MOROCCO
ALGERIA
EGYPT
PERSIAN GULF
Nile
MAURITANIA
THE SUDAN
RED SEA
Atbara
Timbuktu
SENEGAL
Médine
Gambia R.
Segu
Bissau
PORTUGUESE GUINEA
Niger R.
Sokoto
Kano
LAKE CHAD
Omdurman
Khartoum
Massawa
Adowa
Sennar
El Obeid
GULF OF ADEN
KORDOFAN
Fashoda
Blue Nile
SIERRA LEONE
Freetown
LIBERIA
Monrovia
IVORY COAST
ASANTE
Kumasi
[GOLD COAST]
Elmina
Cape Coast
DAHOMEY
Lagos
NIGERIA
Benin
BRITISH SOMALILAND
White Nile
ETHIOPIA
GERMAN KAMERUN
UGANDA
Libreville
GABON
CONGO
LAKE VICTORIA
BRITISH EAST AFRICA
Ujiji
Mombasa
PEMBA
ZANZIBAR
GERMAN EAST AFRICA
Rufiji R.
Congo
NDONGO [ANGOLA]
Luanda
ATLANTIC OCEAN
BAROTSELAND
Zambezi R.
MONOMOTAPA
Tete
Sena
Victoria Falls
MASHONALAND
MOZAMBIQUE
Sofala
Bulawayo
Zimbabwe
MATABELELAND
MADAGASCAR
TRANSVAAL
SOUTH WEST AFRICA
SWAZILAND
Lourenço Marques
ORANGE FREE STATE
BASUTOLAND
ZULULAND
Orange R.
CAPE COLONY
NATAL
Fish R.
Cape Town
Algoa Bay
INDIAN OCEAN

trade with Africa in manufactured goods and other merchandise could profitably take the place of slave trade. European industrialists also began to look to Africa for primary products in their own manufacturing enterprises (for example, palm oil used in making soap). Thus Africa became an important potential market and source of raw materials. Before long there was bitter rivalry among European powers for this market and its primary products. So taken were Europeans by this idea that they supported three schemes to repatriate freed slaves to Africa in order that they would become a nucleus for such trade.

Following Justice Mansfield's decision, fifteen thousand destitute black people were set free in England. Abolitionists, among whom was an African and former slave, Olaudah Equiano, later renamed Gustavus Vassa, supported a scheme to repatriate these "Black Poor," as they were called. The Black Poor from England were joined by other black people from Canada, where promises of land made to black soldiers had not been fulfilled, and by blacks—the Maroons—from the West Indies. This movement resulted in the founding of Sierra Leone in 1787.

Another scheme originated in the United States, where the Back-to-Africa movement was supported by wealthy Afro-Americans like Paul Cuffee, who on his own financed voyages of black people returning to Africa. Other prominent white and black Americans sponsored the American Society for Colonizing the Free People of Color (more commonly the American Colonization Society), which led to the founding of Liberia in 1822. A third such settlement was Libreville in Gabon, founded in 1849 under French auspices as a settlement for former slaves.

Europe's contact with Africa through the slave trade resulted in its becoming richer from the wealth generated by the slave labor of the millions upon millions of Africans who crossed the seas in chains. Africa, on the other hand, was impoverished by the loss of its manpower and material wealth. Internecine warfare, engendered by the slave trade, weakened or destroyed its once-proud armies. Its village industries disappeared. Only weakness and disunity remained.

European powers needed to know more about Africa—its geography, natural resources, and people—to trade effectively or stake their claims with any degree of accuracy. So, travelers and explorers, backed by organizations of varied interests and motives, went into the interior of Africa to augment the scanty and sketchy knowledge of the coast that had been provided by sailors and traders. Mungo Park, David Livingstone, Henry M. Stanley, Richard Burton, Heinrich Barth, John Speke, René Caillié, Paul Soleillet, and many others made remarkable journeys and "discoveries." As feats of endurance, these journeys *are* truly remarkable; but perhaps even more remarkable are their inflated claims, for how does one discover, as Livingstone is said to have done, something like the Victoria Falls, which millions and millions of other people have known for generations by the name Mosi Oa Tunya, meaning "smoke that thunders?"

The journeys had another merit to Europeans. They portrayed Africa as virgin land for the planting of Christianity (and some would give the word "planting" the meaning it has in detective stories). So, European missionaries went to Africa to preach the gospel. They wore out soles saving souls and found themselves not only agents of life through death but of peace through war, accord through discord, education through Westernization, civilization through dehumanization, construction through destruction. Europeans were soon persuaded that only by waging ruthless wars of conquest or pacification (as such wars are euphemistically called) could peace reign in Africa. Only through discord—inherent in the injection of Christianity and rejection of traditional African ideas of god—could accord be achieved. Only through keeping Africans ignorant of the good in their culture and of the greatness in their history by teaching them Western values and the superiority of Europeans could they be educated. Only through the abandonment of a culture based on humanistic family and tribal ties, responsibilities, and sanctions, and the imposition of a dehumanizing, individualistic, and materialistic culture, could Africans be civilized. Only through the total destruction of African ideas, values, and mores could a new Africa be built.

The possession of colonies in Africa was regarded by European powers as a means of acquiring national prestige, mollifying wounded national pride, and keeping the balance of power in Europe even. Indeed, it is essential to study European politics of this period in order to understand why certain countries in Africa became colonies of certain powers in Europe and why boundary lines were often drawn in such an arbitrary manner as to put people of identical ethnic backgrounds into different states or lump together people who had no natural political affinity in one state. Some of these boundaries, drawn in the nineteenth century and dictated primarily by events in Europe, are a source of friction even today; indeed, many of Africa's present major problems can be traced to decisions made in Europe at this time.

Actual colonization was, as a rule, undertaken not by

governments but by syndicates and chartered companies because they were better suited for the task. The legal fiction under which such companies operated was that they were not representatives of the governments from whom they derived their charters. Their actions therefore did not necessarily have the agreement and sanction of their governments. This fiction enabled chartered companies to rush in where governments feared to tread. They were financed privately, at no cost to the taxpayer; so, according to the fiction, governments could not scrutinize and control minute details of the companies' operations. In actual fact governments could and did interfere with chartered companies. It suited governments, however, to appear powerless against them because chartered companies were useful tools. They could conveniently be repudiated when they failed to pull off a particularly audacious and reckless plot like the 1895 Jameson Raid, by which British fortune hunters sought to displace the Boer government of the Transvaal in South Africa. On the other hand, territory in which a company operated was invariably taken over by a European power and turned into a protectorate, colony, or overseas province, when convenient.

Often protectorates were proclaimed and colonies carved on the map of Africa on the basis of fraudulent treaties and bogus purchases of land from unsuspecting African rulers. There were also poorly demarcated spheres of influence in which a single European power sought to exercise exclusive trading rights. The cupidity, intrigue, cutthroat competition, and rivalry that characterized the activities of some unscrupulous agents of syndicates and chartered companies generated much friction, hatred, and animosity not only among Africans but also among the nations that licensed them. To bring about some sort of order, the Berlin West African Conference of 1884–1885 was called to lay down ground rules governing the staking of claims and carving of colonies in Africa.

Conferees, which included all the major powers in Europe, plus the USA and the Ottoman empire, decided that any power wishing to claim a colony or protectorate in any part of Africa should formally notify the other signatories and back its claim with demonstrable effective authority in the area concerned. Contrary to British wishes, there was to be freedom of navigation along the Niger and Congo rivers. In spite of the conference's decision requiring the effective occupation of an area before a claim could be recognized, most claims to colonies in Africa continued to be, in fact, based on concessions and treaties of very doubtful and questionable validity. The impressive point, however, is that European powers agreed to base their partition of Africa on a set of rules acceptable to them all, and thus avoided coming to blows.

With this accord in Europe, the age of colonialism began in Africa. Europeans no longer took Africans into slavery in far-off places, but took possession of the land itself. Whereas in 1880 more than ninety per cent of the continent of Africa was ruled by Africans, by 1900, a mere twenty years later, only a tiny fraction—Ethiopia and Liberia—was ruled by Africans.

What was Africa's response to the Berlin conspiracy of 1884–1885? Was there also concerted action to meet the European threat to Africa? It is safe to say that Africans in general knew little about Europe and even less about Berlin. The days when radio, television, and jumbo jets would facilitate the formation of an Organization of African Unity were still far away. Yet, in spite of the social dislocations, in spite of the weakness of African armies, in spite of the inability of African rulers to consult, plan, and agree on a common strategy, the Africans continued to resist. They stood up and fought. Uncoordinated and inadequately armed though they were, Africans took up arms all over the continent. Let us look at these wars more closely. Let us scrutinize, one by one, the attempts of each European power to colonize Africa and see how Africans reacted.

Portugal was the first European power that tried to colonize Africa. It was the first to be resisted. When in 1556 a vassal of the king of the Congo, the *ngola* of Ndongo (or Angola), expected to be attacked by his overlord, he appealed to the Portuguese king for help. The Portuguese king responded by sending an expedition under the command of Paulo Dias de Novais, a grandson of the explorer Bartholomeu Dias. By the time the expedition arrived in Ndongo, however, the people had already fought and defeated the Congo army sent against them and declared their independence. Furthermore, the *ngola* who had requested Portugal's help had died. Succeeding him on the throne was Ngola Mbandi, who received Dias with great politeness, but compelled him to assist the Ndongo army in several local wars in which the Portuguese were not interested.

Paulo Dias was eventually allowed to return to Portugal, after which Sebastião, the king of Portugal, decided to undertake the military conquest of the Ndongo kingdom. Ndongo was divided into two colonies: one part, bounded in the west by the Atlantic, in the north by the Congo, and in the south by the Cuanza River, was to belong to the king; the other area, south of the Cuanza, was to belong to

Portuguese interest in Africa's east coast kept pace with its thriving Indian Ocean spice trade. This engraving, purportedly showing the stylish manner in which the wives of Portuguese traders were carried about in Kilwa, was published in Jan van Linschoten's Itinerario, 1596; *it is hearsay information the author gathered while in the colony of Goa, India. He noted that Kilwa "was inhabited by Mahometans, and they are all most white [reflecting the mixed African-Arab population], apparelled in silk, and clothes of cotton wooll."*
LINSCHOTEN, *Itinerario*, 1596

Paulo Dias and his descendants. Dias was to govern the king's as well as his own portion.

Dias returned to Angola in 1574 with the title "Conqueror, Colonizer, and Governor General of Angola." He took with him seven ships carrying seven hundred men. It was four years before the first skirmish with Africans took place. By that time Africans no doubt knew what the Portuguese were up to. In 1578 they engaged a detachment of eighty Portuguese soldiers, killed twenty, took the rest prisoner, and freed them only after they had been ransomed. Having been warned that Dias was advancing with a strong army to fight him, Ngola Mbandi condemned to death the Portuguese traders at his court, confiscated their goods, and enticed the Portuguese soldiers into combat in the interior. There he massacred five hundred of them and then attacked their fort at Nzele, thirty miles from their principal port at Luanda.

It was not until 1580 that Dias was able to march against Ngola Mbandi once more. This time he first raided several independent African kingdoms, recruiting their men to fight on his side against the army of the *ngola*. Meanwhile, another Congo force was marching against Mbandi. The *ngola* was able to drive off this second threat, but when he met Dias at Massangano, his fatigued army was defeated. However, the Portuguese had not yet won conclusively. One of their detachments, comprising at least a hundred men, was not long after completely routed by another African chief. At his death in 1589, fifteen years after he had set out as "Conquerer, Colonizer, and Governor General of Angola," Paulo Dias had not conquered, colonized, or governed the people of Angola.

Portuguese activity as slavers and would-be colonizers appears to have solidified African resistance, for in 1590 the *ngola* entered into an alliance with his former enemy, the king of the Congo, and with other neighboring kingdoms. That year the African alliance defeated a Portuguese expedition, forcing it to retreat with heavy losses to Massangano. In 1594 another African force, under the command of chief Kafuche Kambara, ambushed and massacred a Portuguese force at Kissama. As long as the alliance held, the Portuguese made no progress toward colonizing Angola. But the alliance broke up about 1600, and the Portuguese gained the advantage.

In 1612 the *ngola* of Ndongo sent his sister Nzinga Mbandi to Luanda to negotiate a peace treaty with the Portuguese. When the Portuguese governor of Luanda would not give her a chair, she called forth one of her attendants, instructed him to get down on his hands and knees, and sat on him. Although the Portuguese agreed to recognize Ndongo as an independent kingdom, they reneged on other agreements. When sometime later the *ngola* died and was succeeded by Nzinga, who immediately renounced Christianity, the Portuguese sought to depose her and install a puppet. War broke out. Nzinga organized another African alliance, and for over thirty years, until her death in 1663, she valiantly warred against the Portuguese.

When the Dutch captured Luanda in 1641, the Portuguese found themselves fighting on two fronts. In 1643 two hundred of their soldiers were captured by an African force, and an army sent to retrieve them was routed. Before his death Ngola Kanini of Matamba defeated a Portuguese army at Katole. Long after, in 1872, another war of resistance to the Portuguese broke out in the Dembo region northwest of Luanda.

Farther south a similar history unfolded. The Mbundu kingdoms of Huambo, Tchiyaka, Bailundo, Ndulu, Bié, and Kakonda resisted Portuguese slavers and colonizers. As early as 1660 Kapango, king of Tchiyaka, prevented the advance of a Portuguese expedition into the interior. In 1718 an African alliance inspired by Kapango's example attacked a Portuguese fortress at Kakonda, forcing them to withdraw from that area. In 1896 Numa, king of Bailundo, died while leading an attack on a Portuguese fort, and in 1902 his successor, Mutu-ya-Kevela, led another attack in an attempt to recover land occupied by Europeans.

In the kingdom of Huíla, Africans launched a series of ten wars, the Nano Wars, resisting Portuguese rule throughout the greater part of the nineteenth century. In the Humbe kingdom there was an uprising against the Portuguese in 1858 that resulted in a temporary withdrawal of the Portuguese from that kingdom. Resistance continued intermittently until the turn of the century, when a Portuguese army was massacred. In 1904 another Portuguese army was ambushed, and three hundred of its soldiers were killed. Resistance in Humbe continued until 1915. Between 1874 and 1916 the Congo region in the north fought eight wars against the Portuguese. In the 1950's resistance to Portuguese colonialism in Angola broke out again and continues to this day.

Along the Atlantic coast of West Africa, in the region now known as Portuguese Guinea, the indigenous peoples also challenged the foreign presence as early as 1679. In that year the African chiefs of Mata and Mompataz unsuccessfully resisted Portuguese domination of the region around the Cacheu estuary. In 1697 the Papel people under Chief Incinhate and the Mandingos again took up arms against Portuguese rule and tried to expel them from the settlement at Farim. These wars persisted throughout the eighteenth century, compelling the Portuguese to maintain a military force for the protection of the European population. In 1753 the Papel people, led by Chief Palance, interfered with Portuguese attempts to rebuild their fort in Bissau, killing nine men.

In 1824, 1842, 1844, and 1846 there were further Papel uprisings against Portuguese rule in Bissau. The last one was supported by the Mandingos, who again attacked Farim. Africans attacked Geba in 1865, assassinated the governor of Bissau in 1871, and massacred a Portuguese military force near Bolor River in 1879.

That same year the Portuguese separated the governance of Guinea from the Cape Verde Islands, creating two colonies. This new policy was aimed at undermining African resistance to its rule through the encouragement of intertribal rivalry. This time-honored colonialist device paid dividends when in 1880 one of the Fulani peoples under Mamadu Paté attacked a Portuguese military post at Buba. Their example was followed a year later by Chief Bacar Guidali of Forrea. One hundred Portuguese soldiers, supported by hundreds of Mandingos, Fula-Preto (another Fulani group), and Beafada marched against the insurgents in 1881. The Portuguese failed to subdue Bacar Guidali, but succeeded in turning Mamadu Paté against him, with the result that Bacar Guidali was defeated by his former ally on behalf of the Portuguese.

In 1882 the Portuguese fought the Beafada at Jabada, and in the following year they attacked the Balanta. In 1884 a Portuguese military force that had been sent to Kakonda was ambushed by Felupe, and its gunboat seized. Two years later another Portuguese army was forced to retreat to Bijante after suffering heavy casualties. The policy of divide and rule stood the Portuguese in good stead, however, when they were challenged in 1886 by Musa Molo. Leading the Fula-Preto, this Fulani chieftain succeeded in taking large areas around Buba and south of the Gambia River. He harassed the Portuguese at Geba and cut communications between that settlement and Bissau by attacking river boats and supply trains. However, the Fula-Preto were forced to desist and retreat when four thousand Fulani and hundreds of Mandingos and Beafada came to Portugal's assistance.

In 1889 the Portuguese were compelled once more to take the field against the Fula-Preto, Mandingos, and Beafada, and the following year they devastated many villages in a four-month campaign against Moli Boia, while Mamadu Paté and Musa Molo resumed their attacks on Buba and Farim. Throughout 1891 and 1892 the Portuguese in Bissau were in a state of siege. In April, 1891, Africans destroyed a Portuguese force at Intim and killed forty-seven Portuguese officers and men near Bissau in May, 1891.

In December, 1893, over three thousand Papel and Balanta tribesmen attacked a Portuguese fortress at Pijiguiti. Later they attacked Bissau. In response, the Portuguese conducted two military operations: one against the Manjaco and the other against the Balanta and Mandingos. The Portuguese had as allies more than three thousand Africans under the combined command of Mamadu Paté and the Beafada chief of Cuor, Infali Sonco. But these allies later turned against the Portuguese, causing them to retreat with heavy casualties.

By 1901 the Portuguese were in a position to resume military operations. In 1904 an expedition against the Manjaco in the Farim district met with disaster when more than four hundred Portuguese soldiers were killed. Infali Sonco, leader of the Beafada, harassed the Portuguese on the Geba River, successfully preventing any commercial intercourse between Bissau on the estuary and Bafatá upriver. The Felupe at Varela, the Balanta at Gole, and the Papel people near Bissau continued their resistance. In 1907 the Portuguese were compelled to mount a major military campaign against African resistance to their rule, plundering and burning many villages. The Papel responded by attacking Bissau. Near the end of the year the Portuguese were ravaging Balanta villages in Gole; the Africans retaliated by attacking the Portuguese military post. The Balanta were driven off after Abdul Injai, a Fulani, joined the Portuguese against them.

In 1912 the Portuguese appointed João Teixeira Pinto commander of forces in Guinea. In March, 1913, with Abdul Injai and several hundred Africans on his side, Pinto was attacked by the Balanta and Mandingos. By June he had occupied Mansoade and Mansaba. From January to April, 1914, Pinto campaigned against the Papel and Manjaco peoples in the Cacheu region. From May to July he marched against the Balanta in Mansoa, and sought revenge against the Papel, who had earlier attacked Bissau, killing eighty-eight Portuguese. Abdul Injai was rewarded for his services to the Portuguese with appointment as chief of Oio, but before long he turned against the Portuguese, who were compelled to mount a campaign against him. The insurgent was exiled from the country.

This was not the end of African resistance to Portuguese colonialism in Guinea. In March, 1917, a state of siege was declared in the Bijajós archipelago, and in July troops were sent to Nhambalam. In 1918 troops were sent to Baiote. There was trouble at Canhabague in 1925; at Bissau in 1931; and again in Canhabague in 1936. Resistance continues to this day.

In Mozambique (or Portuguese East Africa), the colonial government was never without its challengers. In July, 1572, Francesco Barreto set out from Sena to conquer the kingdom of Monomotapa. Barreto commanded an army of eight hundred Europeans and two thousand Africans. Along the Ruwenya River, toward Mount Fura, the Portuguese expedition came across the main village of the Mongaze people. They fired a few rounds and dispossessed the people of their village. For three days they remained in the village, experiencing only minor attempts on the part of the Mongaze to regain their homes.

At dawn on the fourth day, however, Francesco de Sousa reported that there came "like a great dust storm with loud clamor, the Mongaze army: Some sixteen thousand men with great intrepidity and noise of drums." The army was led by a doctor carrying spells in a gourd to assure victory. A cloud of arrows and spears flew toward the Portuguese, who responded with a volley of musketry and a barrage of cannonballs. The doctor and four thousand Mongaze men were killed. The Portuguese lost forty men in the battle.

Although Barreto and his army were decimated by fever before they got to Zimbabwe, Monomotapa's capital, news of their victory over the Mongaze impressed the kingdom's ruler. Chisa Mharu Nogomo, who had problems with his vassals, decided to come to terms with the Portuguese and secure his position on the throne. In 1575 Vasco Fernandes Homem, taking another route, led an expedition of four hundred twelve Portuguese soldiers to Zimbabwe. He met only minor resistance. On the throne of Monomotapa now sat Gatsi Rusere, who honored his predecessor's agreement with the Portuguese. However, Gatsi Rusere was succeeded by Nyambo Kapararidze, who was openly hostile to the Portuguese and forced them to retire. Africans were, once more, resisting foreign domination. His army was defeated by the Portuguese in 1628, and Kapararidze's nephew, Mavura Mhande, who was friendly to the Portuguese, was installed as ruler.

At his death another puppet was appointed; but in 1693 one of his vassals, Changamire, raised an insurrection and routed the *monomotapa*'s army. Changamire then attacked and destroyed a number of Portuguese settlements, including Dambarare. This ended Portuguese political influence beyond the borders of Mozambique.

The Portuguese position in East Africa was once again seriously shaken in the nineteenth century when Nyande, or Joaquin José da Cruz, a half-caste, organized an insurgent force and established inland headquarters at Massangena in the southern region of Mozambique. In 1853 his son Bonga destroyed the colonial post at Tete, and a Portuguese expedition, sent some sixteen years later to regain control of the area, only resulted in Bonga's gaining a still larger territory. When Bonga died in 1885, his brother succeeded him, but was captured three years later.

The Shangana, a Nguni people, also challenged the Portuguese in Mozambique. At the port city of Lourenço Marques near the southern frontier the followers of Soshangana besieged the Portuguese fortress and massacred its garrison. The Shangana also attacked Inhambane in 1834 and Sofala in 1836. They overran Portuguese *prazos*, or estates, south of the Zambezi and occupied Sena. When Soshangana died, however, there were two claimants to his throne. Mahueva, the legitimate successor, was, like his father, opposed to the Portuguese. He lost to Mzila, who maintained official relations with the Portuguese while continuing to demand tribute from them and to raid their settlements. Mzila was succeeded by Gungunyana. He cooperated with both the Portuguese and the British, whose South Africa Company, under the direction of Cecil Rhodes, was eyeing the southern portion of Mozambique.

Wars of resistance also broke out in the eastern Sudan. This ancient land of Kush had in 1805 come under Turko-Egyptian rule. Although the Sudan remained under the official administration of the Egyptian khedive, it came increasingly under the influence and control of the British government.

In 1882 the Anglo-Egyptian consortium suffered a major upset when a Sudanese spiritual leader, Muhammad Ahmad, declared himself the Mahdi, or messiah, and urged his countrymen to rise against the forces of evil. Muhammad Ahmad called for no less than a holy war against the Egyptian government. Before long the holy war became for the Sudanese people a war of liberation from colonialism, injustice, and economic exploitation.

The British government had strived to avoid active involvement. Its efforts were, however, doomed to failure since the Egyptian government was virtually its puppet, obliged to accept British advice on all matters of importance in exchange for British military protection. Thus it was only a matter of time before Queen Victoria's agents were actively involved in suppressing Sudanese resistance. To the Sudanese Africans, however, the issue remained always simple and crystal clear; resistance was seen as a duty inspired and sanctioned by their religion. Its success was believed to be ordained by Allah and assured through the appearance among them of the expected Mahdi.

Soon after Muhammad Ahmad had declared himself the Mahdi, the Egyptian government sent the assistant governor general of the Sudan, Muhammad Bey Abu al-Saud, to talk him into abandoning his claim. When this failed, the government dispatched two companies of regular troops to Aba Island in the Nile, where Muhammed Ahmad and about two hundred of his supporters, including members of the militant dervish sect, were gathered.

Muhammad Ahmad offered his followers the choice of either freely joining him in his holy war or returning to their homes. His followers unanimously swore allegiance to his cause and leadership, whereupon he armed them with swords, spears, and sticks. Then, while awaiting the arrival of the army, he trained them in the rudiments of defense and attack.

One night during the fasting month of Ramadan, while Muhammad Ahmad and his followers were performing their prayers, news reached him that the Nile steamer carrying government troops sent to capture him had arrived in the neighboring city of El Fashashuyah.

The government soldiers disembarked on Aba Island at 3 A.M. and, ignoring instructions to send the local *qadi* to parley with the Mahdi, marched straight to the village. Meeting a villager, they asked him to point out the Mahdi's house. The villager said he did not know. There followed an altercation during which one of the soldiers fired a gun, whereupon the Mahdi's followers, armed only with their primitive weapons, fell upon the soldiers, killing one hundred twenty-six of them, including six officers. The rest of the soldiers ran away and took refuge aboard the steamer that had brought them. The following day, the twelfth of August, 1881, the Mahdi's dervishes completely defeated the government force at the battle of Aba, giving the Mahdi his first great victory.

Emulating the Prophet's flight to Medina, the Mahdi left Aba Island, scene of his first victory, and trekked westward with his followers to Qadir Mountain in the Nuba hills of Kordofan. This was territory inhabited by people who had never completely submitted to government authority.

Hoping that local jealousies and dissension would disintegrate the Mahdi's movement, causing it to collapse of itself, the government decided to take no further military action against the Mahdi. But Rashid, the governor of Fashoda (modern Kodok in southeast Sudan), ignoring instructions, set out against the Mahdi with three hundred fifty soldiers, seventy irregulars, and one thousand Shilluk tribesmen under the leadership of their chief, Kaikun Bey. Rashid's plan was to surprise the Mahdi, so he compelled his men to march long hours; utterly exhausting them. But the Mahdi was not to be taken by surprise. A Qadir chief warned him by lighting large fires on top of a mountain, and a Kinanah woman walked the whole night to report that she had seen the soldiers. It was Rashid who was surprised. The Mahdi laid an ambush for him and completely annihilated Rashid's exhausted force. Only a few Shilluk escaped to tell the tale. The Mahdi had won another great victory, and rumors crediting him with invincibility and the ability to turn bullets into water were related in the Sudan. New adherents flocked to the Mahdi's lair at Qadir.

A new governor general was appointed to the Sudan. While awaiting his arrival, however, the acting governor general, a German known as Geigler Pasha, grossly underrated the Mahdi's strength. He reversed the wait-and-see policy of his predecessor and decided to restore law and order in the Sudan by striking the Mahdi's stronghold with a force of some three thousand five hundred men under the command of Yusuf Pasha al-Shallali.

Geigler Pasha also sent Yusuf Agha al-Malik with fifty soldiers and some officers to the eastern bank of the Blue Nile, where Sherif Ahmad Taha, who claimed to be a descendant of the Prophet, was about to declare his allegiance to the Mahdi. Al-Malik met with disaster. All his officers and most of his soldiers were slain. When he saw that all was lost, rather than be disgraced, Al-Malik calmly sat on his sheepskin and ordered his slave to kill him. On May 4, 1882, Geigler ordered another attack on Sherif Ahmad Taha. Sherif Ahmad Taha was once more victorious, killing two hundred ten officers and men. Reinforced by Awad al-Karim's Shukria tribesmen, Geigler again attacked Sherif Ahmad Taha the following day and completely defeated him.

Meanwhile, the government force sent to Qadir under the command of Al-Shallali traveled via Fashoda, making a long halt at Funqur, where Taifarah, a local chief, reneged on an earlier agreement with the Mahdi and handed over the latter's spies to Al-Shallali. The spies were cruelly and slowly put to death by having their limbs severed, one after another, before a crowd of spectators. But the fortitude with which they met their death, uttering defiance to the executioners and professing a profound conviction in the divine mission of the Mahdi, demoralized the troops. They concluded that the Mahdi must really have supernatural powers if he could make men face death as these spies had done. On June 6, 1882, Al-Shallali's force arrived in the vicinity of the Qadir, fatigued and morally depressed. They hardly had strength to construct a *zaribah* (a thorny enclosure) before falling asleep. At dawn the Mahdi's men attacked and annihilated them in spite of a heroic stand. The wife of one of the slain leaders of the government forces gallantly beat the war drum to rally her husband's troops. The Mahdi had scored another brilliant victory, and again rumor had it that supernatural forces were working in concert with him. It was said that a mysterious fire had consumed the bodies of the soldiers and had left the Mahdi's name clearly written on eggshells and the leaves of trees.

When the new governor general, Abd al-Qadir Pasha, took his appointment, he first made overtures of peace to the Mahdi. Failing in this, he plotted to assassinate the Madhi by sending him a gift of poisoned dates purportedly from an adherent, dispatching a parcel containing dynamite, and hiring two men to murder him. When these attempts failed also, Al-Qadir directed the mufti, Sudan's chief judge of Muslim law, and other learned men to engage in a propaganda war against the Mahdi, while soldiers to fight him were being recruited and trained.

The Mahdi was also changing his course. He decided to abandon the purely defensive policy he had hitherto pursued. In the two months after the annihilation of Al-Shallali's expedition, he sent troops to attack government garrisons in Kordofan. One by one these fell and were occupied by the Mahdi's men; only Kordofan's provincial capital at El Obeid and the nearby city of Bara remained. In August, 1882, the Mahdi's troops began their march against El Obeid, and in September, 1882, the Mahdi sent messengers to the garrison, urging it to surrender. Authorities of El Obeid arrested the messengers and hanged them. As a result, many citizens went over to the Mahdi.

Thirty thousand warriors then rushed El Obeid, as Father Joseph Ohrwalder, who spent ten years as a captive in the Mahdi's camp, described in his memoirs:

> The first ditch was soon crossed, and then the Mahdists spread out and completely encircled the town; masses of wild fanatics rolled like waves through the deserted streets; they did not advance through these alone, but hurrying on from house to house, wall to wall, and yard to yard, they reached the ditch of the Mudirieh, and like a torrent suddenly let loose, regardless of every obstacle, with wild shouts they dashed across it and up the ramparts, from which the din of a thousand rifles and the booming of the guns suddenly burst forth; but these wild hordes, utterly fearless of death, cared neither for the deadly Remington nor the thunder of the guns, and still swept forward in ever-increasing numbers.
>
> The poor garrison, utterly powerless to resist such an assault, ran to the tops of the houses and

> kept up an incessant fire on the masses, which now formed such a crowd that they could scarcely move —indeed the barrels of the rifles from the rapidity of the fire became almost red-hot; and soon the streets and open spaces became literally choked with the bodies of those who had fallen. . . . It was impossible not to admire the reckless bravery of these fanatics who, dancing and shouting, rushed up to the very muzzles of the rifles with nothing but the knotty stick in their hands, only to fall dead one over the other. Numbers of them carried large bundles of Dhurra stalks, which they threw into the ditch, hoping to fill it up and then cross over.

The Mahdi lost about ten thousand men and decided to change his tactics. He surrounded El Obeid and Bara. Before long the besieged inhabitants were short of food and plagued by disease. A government relief expedition under Ali Bey Lufti was attacked and completely destroyed by the Mahdi's men. Over 1,127 of its men were killed. Bara surrendered on the fifth and El Obeid on the seventeenth of January, 1883. Large stores of military equipment, rifles, guns, and ammunition fell into the Mahdi's hands.

A new governor general, Ala al-Din, was appointed, and a new army under the command of William Hicks, a British officer, was sent to reconquer El Obeid. The Mahdi let his army—7,000 infantry, 500 cavalry, 400 *bashbazuks*, or mounted Turkish irregulars, with 10 mounted guns, 100 cuirassiers, 2,000 camp followers, and 5,500 transport camels—wear itself out marching. The insurgents cut its line of retreat, constantly harassed it as it came nearer, and then in November, 1883, attacked and overwhelmed it.

It was at this point that the British government, believing that the Sudan could not be held against the Mahdi, exerted pressure on the Egyptian government to abandon it and evacuate the capital at Khartoum. In response to public demand, the British government also returned General Charles George "Chinese" Gordon, Britain's hero of campaigns in China and Anglo-Egyptian North Africa and former governor of the Sudan. He was instructed to ascertain the best means of evacuating Egyptian forces from the Sudan. Instead, Gordon tried to hold Khartoum against the Mahdi. The Mahdi delayed attacking the city in the hope that it would surrender without bloodshed.

When in the fall of 1884 a British relief column under the command of Sir Herbert Stewart started for Khartoum, the Mahdi was compelled to take action. He dispatched a strong force to meet Stewart's troops and prepared to assault the capital. Near the Abu Tlaih wells, where the relief column had camped for the night, they encountered the Mahdi forces. Early the following morning the Mahdi forces opened fire on the British force as breakfast was being served. Stewart decided to take the offensive and ordered the column to march in square formation. As it marched, the column was subjected to heavy fire and frequently came to a halt in order to enable the rear to catch up. At one such halt Stewart's men were amazed to see a large mounted force of the Mahdi's men emerge from a nearby ravine in which they had been hiding and advance upon them in close formation. In spite of accurate fire from the relief column's Martini-Henry rifles, the Mahdi's army advanced to within eighty yards; then the fire began to take its toll and dead bodies fell one upon another in huge piles. Those still alive veered to the right and attacked the rear of the column, penetrating the square at several points. Sir Charles Wilson, who took over command of the column when Sir Herbert Stewart was wounded, later wrote:

> I remember thinking, by Jove, they will be into the square! and almost the next moment I saw a fine old Shaikh on horse back plant his banner in the center of the square, behind the camels. He was at once shot down falling on his banner. He turned out to be Musa, Amir of Dighaim Arabs, from Kurdufan. I had noticed him in the advance, with his banner in one hand and a book of prayers in the other, and never saw anything finer. The old man never swerved to the right or left, and never ceased chanting his prayers until he had planted his banner in our square. If any man deserved a place in the Moslem paradise he did.

The relief column closed the gaps and killed all who had penetrated the square. The rest of the Mahdi's forces retreated. The British column made it to the river near Metemma, where its wounded and most of its able-bodied men were left in fortified positions while Wilson, with British and African troops, embarked in late January, 1885, on steamers for Khartoum. Khartoum, which had been under siege for over a year by a force of up to one hundred thousand men, was beginning to show the strain. There was famine and disease in the town. The low water level of the Nile at the time of the year made breaching the town's fortifications possible. The Mahdi tried to persuade General Gordon to surrender, even offering him a safe-conduct to the British column. Gordon was defiant and determined to fight.

On January 26 the Mahdi forces launched their attack on Khartoum. The fortifications yielded in the first assault

NATIONAL PORTRAIT GALLERY, LONDON

Mahdist power was finally broken at Omdurman in 1898, when Sir Horatio Herbert Kitchener (right) and his Anglo-Egyptian army devastated the Sudanese army with its ranks of sword-brandishing dervishes (above).

CULVER

and great slaughter followed. General Gordon was killed and Khartoum captured. The fall of Khartoum had a profound effect in England. Queen Victoria told her ministers that earlier action by them might have prevented the catastrophe and saved many precious lives. After this, it became a matter of Britain's national honor to suppress the Mahdiyya, the Mahdi's resistance movement.

However, on June 22, 1895, the Mahdi died. At his death his resistance movement had liberated from foreign rule most of Muslim Sudan. He was succeeded by Abdullahi, Khalifa al-Mahdi. But the new leader's position was shaky, for he could not cope with the military might of England. In 1897 at the battle of Atbara (some two hundred miles downriver from Khartoum) and in 1898 at Omdurman (opposite Khartoum) British and Egyptian regiments under Sir Horatio Herbert Kitchener finally shattered the Khalifa al-Mahdi's power. The Khalifa himself lost his life on the field of battle at Om Dubreikat on November 25, 1899. Despite the Sudan's prolonged bid for independence, the Anglo-Egyptian Sudan had come into existence.

Resistance continued. Among the Dinka people living between the White Nile and the Sobat River there was strong opposition to the new order. In 1904 the British were compelled to send an expedition against the Nyima tribes of the western Bahr-el-Ghazal. In 1908 a Halawi tribesman in Sennar declared himself to be Jesus Christ come to expel Europeans from the Sudan. He was hanged by the British. And during 1911 and 1912 two expeditions were sent against the Annak on the Sobat River.

Between 1899 and 1904, and again between 1908 and 1910, Muhammad ibn Abdallah, sometimes called quite wrongly the Mad Mullah, organized resistance to colonial rule in British Somaliland, that portion of the Horn which Britain had administered as a protectorate since 1884. An army of seven thousand men, raised at a cost of over two million pounds, was sent against him. After more than one disaster had befallen British troops, however, it was decided to leave the interior of British Somaliland alone and to confine British occupation to the coastal towns along the Gulf of Aden.

South of Anglo-Egyptian Sudan, in the territory of modern-day Uganda, Mwanga, the *kabaka*, or king, of Buganda, and Kabarenga, the king of Bunyoro, responded in 1898 to the rivalries of Europe's empire builders by attempting to massacre British officers and missionaries. For over a year the British were kept at bay until Captain John Evatt and a detachment of Sikh soldiers from British India captured the African kings in 1899.

In Zanzibar, where in 1890 the sultanate had been placed under British protection and the administration of the islands of Zanzibar and Pemba conducted by English ministers, a palace revolt occurred in 1896 on the occasion of the death of Sultan Hamid ibn Thwain. It was really a premature outbreak of resistance to British occupation.

Along that part of the East African coast under German "protection"—roughly the area later designated as Tanganyika—between the Tana and Odzi rivers, African resistance to foreign rule resulted in a British naval expedition under Admiral Edmund Fremantle being sent to the area in 1890. Southwest of Mombasa Sir Arthur Hardinge was compelled, on assuming control of British East Africa, to fight a long war of skirmishes, ambushes, and raids of resistance until 1896. Kikuyu warriors attacked British settlers and big game hunters in Kenya.

In southern Africa the earliest resistance to European encroachment on African land rights was in 1659, when Hottentot clans that had always grazed their cattle in the Cape Peninsula were ordered by the Dutch to keep away. Although there was plenty of grazing land to which they could have taken their cattle, they insisted on their right to graze their cattle where they liked. So, the first Hottentot-Dutch war broke out. The Hottentots avoided a pitched battle, and the Europeans were unable to surprise any sizable body of them or inflict large number of casualties.

The second Hottentot-Dutch war was sparked in 1673 by the Europeans' destruction of too much game on land under the Hottentot king Gonnema. Although Hottentot tribes hostile to him joined the Dutch, Gonnema and his people held on in the mountains until both sides desired peace.

In 1779 the Dutch fought their first war against the Bantu-speaking Xhosa, who resisted attempts to remove them from lands west of the Great Fish River. Ten years later the Xhosa reoccupied large areas west of this river. The Dutch tried to expel them, and so the second Xhosa-Dutch war was fought. As the Xhosa proved more than able to hold their own, the Dutch finally agreed to make peace with them.

In 1795 the Cape came under British rule. Four years later Ndlambe, who had been Xhosa regent during the minority of his nephew Gaika, was forced to hand over power to the younger man. Ndlambe escaped, crossed the Great Fish River, and immediately won the allegiance of most clans between the Great Fish and the Kowie rivers. White people in these areas took their cattle and fled. In a few days Ndlambe was master of the entire Zuurveld east of the Sunday River.

Ndlambe's forces attacked a British party on its way to Algoa Bay, under the command of General John Ormsby Vandeleur. The Europeans beat them off and then fell back to form a camp so that an approaching patrol of twenty men could join them. But the Xhosa surrounded the patrol and killed all but four of its members. Then they turned to the camp, rushing it with spear shafts broken so short that they could be used as assagais for stabbing. The charges were met with such a volley of musket balls and grapeshot that the Xhosa were forced to retire. General Vandeleur made it to Algoa Bay, sent some of his soldiers back to Cape Town by sea, and ordered burgher commandos to expel the Xhosa. Some Hottentots joined the Xhosa and overran the area. Twenty-nine white people were killed. Once more Africans had resisted attempts by Europeans to run them off their land.

In 1811 a strong body of European soldiers and a Hottentot regiment was sent to force Ndlambe and his men to abandon the lands they occupied. In a parley with Major Jacob Cuyler, Ndlambe told him, stamping his foot on the ground: "This country is mine; I won it in war, and intend to keep it." Then, shaking an assagai with one hand, he raised a horn to his mouth and signaled his forces, concealed in the thicket, whereupon three hundred men rushed on the British party, which escaped solely because of the fleetness of their horses. Soon after this, the *landdrost*, meaning governor, of Graaff-Reinet, and eight farmers were killed by the Xhosa. In 1812 six Hottentot units, with European soldiers in the rear, attacked the Xhosa and succeeded in forcing them northeast across the Great Fish River.

This was by no means the end of Ndlambe. Several chiefs, including an influential seer named Makana, defected from Gaika and joined him. In the ensuing war between the uncle and nephew, Gaika lost and appealed to the white men for help. Believing Ndlambe to be a much more determined and dangerous enemy, Lord Charles Somerset, governor of the Cape Colony, in 1818 sent European troops to fight side by side with Gaika's men against Ndlambe, who was believed to have eighteen thousand men under arms. Ndlambe's men took shelter in the dense thickets, but their villages were destroyed and twenty-three thousand of their cattle taken.

When the British soldiers withdrew, Ndlambe fell on Gaika and put him to flight. Then he attacked Europeans between the Great Fish and Sunday rivers. A burgher force was called out, but before it could take the field, the British settlement at Grahamstown was attacked on April 22, 1819, by ten thousand warriors led by Ndlambe's ally, Makana.

It was three months later that a strong army of colonists succeeded in driving Ndlambe's warriors northeastward to the Kei River, slaughtering many and burning their kraals, or villages. Makana gave himself up so that his friends could be spared. He was imprisoned on Robben Island off Cape Town, where he died three years later while trying to escape. As a buffer against further trouble, the colonial government placed Gaika's people between the Cape Colony and Ndlambe. Ndlambe died and his sons quarreled for the throne. Gaika also died, leaving Sandile, then a child, as heir; Makoma, his half brother, was named regent. Ndlambe's sons allied themselves with Makoma to win his support.

When in 1834 European soldiers near Fort Beaufort wounded a Xhosa chief and took cattle belonging to Tyali, another of Gaika's sons, the Xhosa regarded this act as a declaration of war. About twenty thousand warriors rushed into the Cape Colony, seized all the cattle east of the Sunday River, burned houses, and killed every white man they found. Knowing that a white commando force would follow, they herded the cattle across the Kei River to the territory of another Xhosa king, Hintsa, before retiring to their mountain strongholds. Hintsa, seeking to avoid further trouble with the Europeans, agreed to give up the cattle, but was treacherously shot dead by a colonist while en route to carry out the terms. Kreli, his son, succeeded him; he undertook to restore the cattle and concluded a peace treaty with the Europeans, but African resistance was by no means over.

In 1846 a Xhosa man accused of stealing an axe at Fort Beaufort was arrested by white constables. While being taken to a magistrate's court for trial, his compatriots swooped down on the police patrol, overpowering it. They killed a Hottentot policeman and released the prisoner. The Europeans applied to Sandile for extradition of the alleged offenders. Sandile ignored the request. Thus began the War of the Axe. A military force was then ordered to occupy Sandile's kraal. A very long wagon train carrying provisions, tents, baggage, and ammunition followed the military force. Xhosa warriors ambushed the wagon train and captured it. The military force was compelled to retreat. Xhosa warriors then took the field and in the area surrounding the town of Vitenhage burned Europeans' houses, killed all Europeans who could not escape, and seized the cattle. The Tembu people joined the Xhosa and devastated European settlements north of Winterberg. Another wagon train, on its way from Grahamstown to a frontier garrison with supplies of food and ammunition, was ambushed, and the supplies fell into Xhosa hands. It was a long time before the colonists could organize themselves and induce Sandile to submit to their rule.

In 1850 war broke out again. Sir Harry Smith, then governor of the Cape, received several reports that the Xhosa were preparing for war. He called a meeting of African chiefs and kings, but the most important figure, Sandile, did not show up. Sir Harry Smith then ordered Sandile, who was known to be in the forests at the headwaters of the Keiskama River, to be arrested. On their way to arrest the Xhosa king, the European troops were attacked by warriors at Boomah. Twenty-three Europeans were killed and many wounded. A few hours later, in another part of the country, a patrol of fifteen European soldiers was completely wiped out by Sandile's warriors, and on Christmas day of that year Xhosa warriors surprised European settlements near Auckland and Woburn, killing forty-six men and burning down houses. European settlements along the frontier districts were devastated once more. Again, the Tembu tribe joined the uprising, and even the Hottentot regiments under colonial arms deserted the Europeans and joined their fellow Africans. This became the longest and, to Europeans, the most costly war in South Africa. The steamship *Birkenhead*, proceeding from Ireland and carrying among its passengers four hundred reinforcements, struck a rock off Danger Point, a few miles beyond the Cape of Good Hope. Women, children, and the sick were put into boats; but the soldiers perished in the shark-infested sea.

Not until their food supplies began to run low did Africans pretend to submit to European rule and hostilities ended, but resistance to European colonialism remained in their hearts and minds. To some of them it became such an obsession that it led to a terrible tragedy. In May, 1856, a girl named Nongqause returned from drawing water at a little stream not far from her village and said she had seen men who differed greatly in appearance from the men she was accustomed to see there. Umhlakaza, her uncle, went to the stream and found the strangers where his niece had indicated. The strangers told Umhlakaza to return home, perform certain rituals, sacrifice an ox to the spirits of the dead, and then return to them on the fourth day.

Since there was in their appearance something that commanded obedience, Umhlakaza did as he had been told and returned to the stream on the fourth day. The strange people were there as before, and to his astonishment he recognized among them his brother, who had been dead for many years. It was then he learned that the strange men were the eternal enemies of white men who had come from battlefields beyond the sea; they would with their invincible power assist the Xhosa in driving the Europeans from the land. He, Umhlakaza, was to be the medium between the kings and chiefs of the land and the strange men. Their first message to the kings, chiefs, and people was to abandon the practice of witchcraft and to kill fat cattle and eat them. One of the kings of the land, Kreli, son of Hintsa, received the message with joy and immediately commanded that the spirits be obeyed throughout his land, and the best cattle be killed and eaten. King Sandile hesitated.

Nongqause again went to the river, and in the presence of a multitude of people, strange unearthly sounds beneath her feet were heard. All averred that they were voices of the spirits holding council over the affairs of men. People were ordered to slay and eat more cattle, and more cattle, and more cattle.

King Sandile joined the believers when his brother told him that he had himself seen and conversed with the spirits of two of his father's dead councilors and that they had commanded Sandile to kill his cattle or perish.

Umhlakaza then communicated the final message of the spirits: when not a single animal out of all their herds was left alive, when not a single grain remained in their granaries, supplications would be complete, and the Xhosa would be worthy of the aid of a spirit host. Then, on a certain day, two blood-red suns would fall and crush to dust the bones of every white man in the land, together with his allies the Fingo, a Zulu subtribe that had consistently supported the white settlers, and every one who opposed the will of the spirits or disobeyed their commands.

Myriad cattle, more beautiful than anyone had ever seen, would issue from the earth and cover pastures far and wide. Large fields of millet, maize, pumpkins, and monkeynuts, ripe and ready for the pot, would appear. The ancient heroes of the Xhosa, the great, brave, and wise ones long since departed, would rise again to feast and dance with the faithful. Trouble, sickness, and old age would disappear, and youth, beauty, peace, and happiness would reign forever. Thus spoke Umhlakaza, spokesman of the spirits.

There were some who thought the real aim of the spirits was to throw the full force and might of all Xhosa, fully armed and desperate for food, on the whites in the Cape Colony. Most, however, took what Umhlakaza said as the literal description of what was to happen. Great kraals were built for the expected cattle, and enormous gourds prepared to contain their milk. Huge granaries were erected to hold the marvelous millet, maize, pumpkins, and monkeynuts.

When the appointed day dawned and there were no blood-red suns over the eastern hills, or the heavens falling to crush white men and their Fingo allies, or myriad beautiful cattle, or large fields of millet, maize, pumpkins, and monkeynuts, or a resurrection of the heroes of the race; misery and death stalked the land. Over thirty thousand Africans died of starvation.

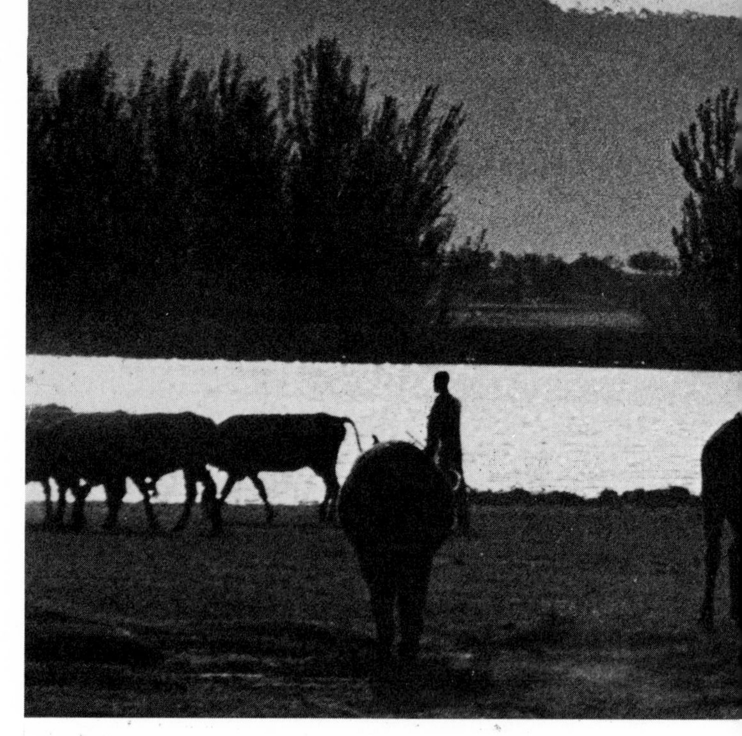

Atop a 5,000-foot plateau of the Drakensberg range, Basuto herdsmen water their cattle. An amalgam of Sotho and Tswana peoples, the Basuto settled in the relative security of these mountains during Chaka's rampages. When the Boers began to move in, King Moshoeshoe was driven to accept British "protectorship"; it lasted until 1966, when the Basuto set up the autonomous kingdom of Lesotho.

MAGNUM—ERNST HAAS

Ironically, the tragic events did much to reduce, for a time, the Xhosa's ability to resist white rule. It was not until February, 1878, twenty-two years later, that five thousand Xhosa, the combined forces of Kreli and Sandile, were able once more to take the field against the white man at Kentani. Several months later Sandile was killed in another action. After his death his people surrendered to the British. Kreli was driven across the Bashee River and spent the rest of his life in a segregated location at Elliotdale. Thus ended, for a time, African wars of resistance in the Cape Colony.

In Basutoland, which is today independent Lesotho entirely surrounded by South Africa, a different course of resistance was followed in the early nineteenth century. The genius behind it was a Sotho king, the great Moshoeshoe (also known as Moshesh). While he was joining together diverse African societies into a single nation of Basuto people, King Moshoeshoe was compelled to resist European encroachment. With his own position among the various tribes far from secure, he could not risk defeat or a prolonged war with the British. Giving in to European demands was, nevertheless, out of the question; so, he resorted to both fighting and diplomacy.

In 1851 Cape governor Sir Harry Smith sent Major Henry Warden with a force of one hundred and sixty-two professional soldiers, one hundred and twenty armed farmers, and fifteen hundred Africans against Chief Molitsane, a vassal of Moshoeshoe. Major Warden's force was drawn into a trap at Viervoet and crushed. Many Boers in the neighboring Orange River Sovereignty saved their skins by promising not to take part in hostilities against the Basuto. Moshoeshoe kept his word not to molest the neutrals, but sought out pro-British farmers and plundered them mercilessly.

It was not until December, 1852, that Sir George Cathcart, who had replaced Sir Harry Smith as governor at the Cape, brought together a well-equipped force of two thousand infantry, five hundred cavalry, and some artillerymen with two field guns, hoping that such a force would intimidate Moshoeshoe into acceding to the demands without fighting. The British governor ordered King Moshoeshoe to comply with certain conditions and deliver, within three days, ten thousand head of cattle and one thousand horses.

Moshoeshoe preferred not to fight, but his people chose to go to war rather than part with so many of their cattle and horses. Moshoeshoe decided to compromise by sending three thousand five hundred head of cattle. He hoped for the best and prepared for the worst by assembling his warriors at a new capital and stronghold at Thaba Bosigo. The compromise was not acceptable to the British, so Sir George Cathcart and his force entered Basutoland.

On Berea Mountain Moshoeshoe left a large herd of cattle, which appeared easy to capture, and with this decoy drew half the British forces into an ambush. Although this deployment seized about four thousand cattle, they suffered heavy losses. The other half of the force, personally led by Sir George, was routed by six thousand Basuto horsemen, some of whom were armed with guns. The British retreated.

Although Moshoeshoe had carried the day, he instructed the Reverend Eugene Casalis, a missionary in his realm, to write what has been called "the most politic document that has ever been penned in South Africa." The communiqué, dated Thaba Bosigo, Midnight, 20th December, 1852, began: "Your Excellency,—This day you have fought against my people, and taken much cattle. As the object for which you have come is to have a compensation for the Boers, I beg you will be satisfied with what you have taken. I entreat peace from you—you have shown your power—you have chastised—let it be enough I pray you; and let me no longer be considered an enemy to the Queen. I will try all I can to keep my people in order for the future. Your humble servant, Moshoeshoe." Sir George Cathcart grasped this opportunity to extricate himself with honor from an awkward situation. He announced he was satisfied with the number of cattle captured and considered his obligations fulfilled. He returned to the Cape.

Burghers in the Orange River Sovereignty elected as president Josias Hoffman, a farmer who was a very close friend of Moshoeshoe. In 1855 the Boers deposed him because they felt by electing a friend of the Basuto king they had conceded more to Moshoeshoe than was consistent with the dignity of an independent state. Jacobus Nicolas Boshof became their next president.

Dingane, who succeeded Chaka as king of the Zulu, showed none of his half brother's political skill. Rather, he devoted his energies to his two passions—eating and dancing. These engravings of the ruler in dancing and ordinary clothes are from Journey to the Zoolu Country, *by Allen Francis Gardiner, a nineteenth-century English missionary who tried to convert Dingane to Christianity.*

OLD HOUSE MUSEUM, DURBAN

Moshoeshoe began harassing them with a view to recovering land lost by some of the tribes who were now his vassals. In 1858 the Boers decided to invade Basutoland and thus carry the war into Moshoeshoe's territory. The Basuto king let the Boers fight their way to the very gates of Thaba Bosigo, where they learned that swarms of Basuto horsemen were at that very moment ravaging their farms back home. Since it was impossible to take Moshoeshoe's mountain stronghold by storm, and they had not the means to lay siege, they abandoned the battle and hurried home, leaving Moshoeshoe master of his land once more. Sir George Grey, who had become Cape governor in 1854, was asked to mediate, and he awarded the Basuto king most of the land he wanted.

Meanwhile, in Zululand in the northern corridor between the Indian Ocean coast of South Africa and the Drakensberg range, political units capable of military resistance to the colonial government were forming. When Chaka, the founder of the Zulu nation, was assassinated in 1828, he predicted the advent of white rule in southern Africa. Dingane, his successor, however, had to deal with the problem. Events were precipitated by the Great Trek, the migration of great numbers of Boer cattlemen into the interior and away from British rule. One such group was led by Pieter Retief. Retief approached Dingane at Umgungundhlovu, his capital, and asked for land to settle his party. Dingane indicated his willingness to consider making a grant of land to Retief if in exchange the Boers would retrieve cattle that had been taken by Sikonyela, one of Dingane's rivals. Retief retrieved the cattle without bloodshed and, accompanied by sixty-five other white men and about thirty Hottentots, waited on Dingane to make the grant of land. Instead, Dingane gave the order, "*Bulalani abathakati!* (Kill the wizards!)" and Retief's party was massacred to a man.

Dingane then sent soldiers to wipe out the rest of Retief's group, temporarily settled at Weenen, the "place of weeping," as the Dutch subsequently named it. Two hundred eighty-two white men, women, and children and fifty African servants perished that day. Fortunately for the white people, one man escaped; he was able to ride and warn other groups so that when the Zulu army arrived, they were already in a laager, their wagons drawn up in a defensive circle for the night.

Pieter Uys, Hendrick Potgieter, Gert Maritz, and some English leaders then assembled an army of three hundred forty-seven men to fight the Zulu. The English were to attack from one side, while Potgieter and Uys attacked from the other. Maritz was to stay and protect the camp. In April, 1838, after a five-day march, the Boers sighted a Zulu army and attacked it impetuously. The Zulu skillfully drew them into a planned ambuscade between two parallel ranges of hills. Retreating into the narrowest part of the gorge, the Boers found themselves surrounded. They were so hemmed in that they could not, as was their usual strategy, fall back rapidly after firing, load again, and charge. The Boers turned back, directed their fire upon a mass of Zulu, cleared a path, rushed through, and escaped, although not without leaving behind many dead and some of their horses, baggage, and spare ammunition. Among the dead were Pieter Uys and his fifteen-year-old son.

The English contingent left the port of Natal with fifteen hundred Africans, four hundred of whom were armed with muskets. On April 17, 1838, some miles south of the Tugela River, they came upon a Zulu regiment. The regiment pretended to take flight; they even left food cooking on fires and a number of assagais and shields lying about. The English contingent pursued with all speed, crossed the Tugela, and took possession of a Zulu kraal on the northern bank before it realized it had been drawn into the horns of a Zulu army, seven thousand strong.

Three times the English contingent beat back the Zulu regiments that furiously charged upon it. Zulu reinforcements arrived. Another rush was made. This time the English contingent was cut in two. One half tried to escape by a path along a steep bank of the Tugela. A Zulu regiment cut off its retreat, but four Englishmen and five hundred Africans escaped.

The other half was completely surrounded. A young Zulu regiment was selected to charge, while the veterans watched from a hill. Whole masses of young Zulu went down before the withering fire, but still they came and came again, until all the Englishmen and over a thousand of their African allies lay dead on the battlefield.

During the winter Dingane sent an army to attack various white groups. The white people, however, were now careful to avoid being lured out of their laagers by any stratagem. In December, 1838, Andries Pretorius assembled a force of four hundred sixty-four men and a sufficient number of wagons to form a laager every night. This army vowed that if God gave it victory, it would build a church and set apart an annual thanksgiving day to commemorate the victory. Pretorious sent word to Dingane, offering to enter into peace negotiations if Dingane restored the property of the white people killed by the Zulu. Dingane's reply was to send an army of ten thousand men. The impi, or army, attacked Pretorius' camp at dawn and for hours sent waves of Zulu warriors charging upon it; thousands were felled by the white man's gunfire. When at length the Zulu withdrew, thousands upon thousands of men lay dead, and a stream that flowed near the field of battle was colored with blood. (From that day this stream has been known as Blood River, and December 16 has been officially celebrated as the Day of the Covenant in South Africa.) Pretorious went on to Umgungundhlovu and found that Dingane had set it on fire and fled. His commando force returned with five thousand cattle.

In September, 1839, Mpande, a half brother of Dingane, conspired to seize the throne. This divided the Zulu nation in two. Mpande's supporters sought white people's support against Dingane. Dingane sent Tambusa, his trusted *induna*, or chief, to negotiate with the white people. But the Boers, bent on avenging Retief's death, arrested Tambusa and executed him and his party.

The combined force of Boers under the command of Pretorius and Mpande's impi under Nongalaza defeated Dingane, who fled north toward the Swazi border, where he was later assassinated. Mpande became king of the Zulu and a vassal of the Boers. With great bravery and loss of life Africans in Zululand had resisted European encroachment, but had succumbed in defeat when internal quarrels divided them in fratricidal strife.

As soon as Mpande was king, he became lethargic both mentally and physically. He grew grossly fat and discipline in his army declined. His two sons, Mbulazi and Cetshwayo, however, were energetic and brilliant men. It became clear that, as no two bulls can remain in one kraal, these two princes could not both live in Zululand. In December, 1856, civil war broke out, and the two princes led opposing forces into battle. The result was a complete victory for the handsome Cetshwayo, who became from that day the real ruler of the Zulu, even though his father lived until 1872. Mbulazi was never heard of again. His followers—men, women, and children—were put to death.

Under Cetshwayo, discipline in the Zulu army was restored, and the Zulu fighting machine became formidable, as it had been in Chaka's time. This was felt by neighboring European settlements, who began to fear for their safety. In 1878 the British governor, Sir Bartle Frere, collected a military force in Natal and sent an ultimatum to Cetshwayo, calling upon the Zulu king to disband his army. Cetshwayo ignored the ultimatum. An army of British soldiers, colonists, and Africans loyal to the colonial government under the command of Lord Frederick Chelmsford entered Zululand in three divisions.

The first division proceeded toward the Buffalo River. One column camped at the foot of Isandlwana Hill. On January 22, 1879, Lord Chelmsford and a small party left camp to attack kraals several miles away. At noon that day the remaining camp suddenly found itself enclosed within the horns of a Zulu impi. Seven hundred British soldiers, over one hundred and thirty colonists, and hundreds of their African allies were killed. Lord Chelmsford's party heard of the disaster in the afternoon, marched back to spend the night among the corpses of their comrades, and the next day returned to Port Natal.

A Zulu impi, under the command of another of Cetshwayo's brothers, Dabulamanzi, attacked a column guarding a depot of provisions at Rock Drift about 5 P.M. on the day of the Zulu victory at Isandhlwana. The one hundred thirty soldiers at the depot had been warned of the attack and formed a laager. Waves of Zulu warriors continued to besiege the depot until dawn, when they retired, leaving seventeen enemy dead and hundreds of their brave comrades killed.

Meanwhile, the division commanded by Colonel Charles Pearson crossed the Tugela River and marched toward Ulundi, where the three divisions intended to unite. A Zulu impi, about five thousand strong, attacked Pearson's column, consisting of two thousand Europeans and an equal force of African allies, at Inyezane and inflicted heavy losses. When he learned of the disaster of Isandhlwana, Colonel Pearson sent most of the remaining cavalry and Africans back to Natal, and with a smaller force fortified a Norwegian mission station near Eshowe, where he remained until reinforcements from England arrived.

The third division, consisting of one thousand seven hundred British soldiers, fifty Boer farmers, and four hundred Africans under Brigadier General Evelyn Wood, fortified a post at Kambula and made frequent sallies on Zulu villages. At Hlobane ninety-six of the column were surrounded by an impi and killed.

When news of the British defeat at Isandhlwana reached England, nine thousand soldiers—cavalry and infantry—with large quantities of munitions and provisions, were sent out. Among the soldiers was Louis Bonaparte, heir to Napoleon III's throne, who lost his life in Zululand while with a reconnoitering party that was surprised by the Zulu. His companions abandoned him and rode away when he was unable to mount his horse. He was stabbed to death.

Cetshwayo's army was eventually defeated by a British force at Ulundi. The Zulu king went into hiding, and for a long time no one could be induced to say where he was. At length one man, threatened with death, revealed the name of a small village where Cetshwayo was found and taken prisoner. In captivity, the Zulu king conducted himself with such dignity that in 1883, after visiting England, he was allowed to return to his throne. In his absence a rival named Sikepu had arisen and won the allegiance of many Zulu. There was civil war. Cetshwayo died and was succeeded by his son, Dinizulu. The war continued, but Dinizulu secured the assistance of Europeans in exchange for land in the Vryheid district in northern Natal. Dinizulu won, but before long fell out with the Europeans and began to resist their rule. In 1889 he was arrested and exiled to the island of St. Helena, and Zululand was put under European rule.

In the area now included in Southern Rhodesia, the Bantu-speaking Mashona also resisted foreign occupation of their country. Europeans entered Mashonaland in 1890. The Mashona, under the impression that the invaders were mere transients interested in trade, were advised by their *midzimu*, or spirit mediums, not to resist, but to trade with them amicably. However, under the auspices of Cecil Rhodes' British South Africa Company, the Europeans began to carve for themselves large farms, and mine gold, eject Africans from what they called their property, impress young men into labor gangs, and abuse African women. When, in short, they gave every indication that they had come to stay, Mashona resistance began to simmer.

In 1893 the British South Africa Company also treacherously invaded Matabeleland, a neighboring kingdom whose capital was near present-day Bulawayo. Six thousand Matabele warriors were on a military expedition across the Zambezi when the white men invaded their land in three columns.

The Matabele king, Lobengula, was informed that the *indunas* he had sent to the Cape at the request of the governor had been murdered by white men at Macloutsie. Lobengula was mad with rage and regarded this act as the most despicable treachery. His *indunas* had been sent on an errand of peace, their safety guaranteed by the high commissioner, yet the white men had turned around and murdered his men. "The white men," he declared, "are the fathers of liars." Ordering his army to take up arms, he appeared before them daubed with paint and carrying an assagai. Before thousands of his warriors Lobengula drove the spear into the earth, signaling war. In response the warriors gave the royal salute, "*Bayete! Bayete! Bayete! Uyi Zulu!*", leaping high and striking their shields, causing such a din as to make the whole earth shake. In the excitement few noticed that the King's assagai broke as it hit the earth—a bad omen.

Although Lobengula's best regiments had been recalled from Barotseland, most of them had contracted smallpox in the north and had been isolated in special kraals so that the disease would not spread. Thus the Matabele army was not at full strength when it went to meet the European invaders.

Several regiments went out to meet the foe. They were prevented by fog from making contact with the enemy in the thick Somabula forests. Consequently, the Matabele met the invaders on the plains of the Shangani, where conditions favored the white men and their guns. Leander Starr Jameson, who was to gain dubious fame as the leader of the Jameson Raid two years later, was with this force. A. J. de Roos, a Hollander who also fought on the side of the invaders, wrote of the Shangani encounter:

> It was full moon, the Matabele had marched all night and were well informed of our movements. Near the laager they waited for the dawn to attack. Their tactics nearly succeeded.
>
> If the Makalangas, who were sleeping outside the laager, had not immediately given the alarm, we would all have gone where the woodbine twineth and the wangdoodtle uttereth its mournful song.
>
> It was still too dark to take in the whole situation, but the surrounding veld was absolutely black with Matabele. On one side the impi was so closely massed that they resembled a stretch of burnt grass in the half light.

However, as dawn approached, the situation changed. De Roos went on to say that the Matabele were so close that it was impossible to miss; he continues: "The maxims and other guns began to speak and within a quarter of an hour one could see that it was all up with them. The sun rose and the surrounding country was strewn with dead and wounded. I estimate that a few thousand Matabele must have taken part in the fight."

Major Forbes pressed on to Bulawayo, the Matabele capital, but on November 18, as the invaders were about to make camp, the Matabele attacked again. De Roos described the battle:

> This was also a surprise attack. Most of the men were occupied in preparing their food, when suddenly shots were heard from the horse pickets. The Matabele nearly captured our horses, and draught animals, and this calamity was averted only by the resolute boldness of few Colonials [Cape Colony Africans] who did not retire nor hesitate, but fired as rapidly as possible at the charging enemy. They, were soon reinforced from the laager. Within half an hour the enemy were in full retreat. Here also the maxims did their deadly work. A thousand Matabele must have fallen before they retreated. A sortie was made to pursue the retreating enemy. A few wounded Matabele were brought into the laager, but they were killed, when the laager broke up and the column trekked on. I say killed. I know what I am saying, for I saw it myself—without trial or hearing. If there is any question of a "blot" anywhere—here is one. No prisoners of war were made at that time. I don't know what the English parson, who taught us to sing: "Onward Christian Soldiers," had to say about it.

Then this Christian army, which slaughtered prisoners of war, marched on to Bulawayo. On November 4, they were met by two traders, who told them that King Lobengula had abandoned his town, after instructing an *induna* to see to the safety of the two white men. When the invaders were close, the *induna* told the traders, "I have carried out my king's instructions and must go now, for your people are not far, and they will kill me. If any harm comes to you, it will be from your own people, not mine." Then he set fire to the royal kraal and disappeared. The imperial force arrived in Bulawayo on November 15.

In Bulawayo, De Roos tells us: "The first thing we did was to hold a thanksgiving service, which was conducted by the English Bishop. The subject of his sermon was that we had been led by the hand of God through all those dangers, to the greater glory of His Name, and His Kingdom and the extension of the glorious Empire. 'Onward, Christian Soldiers,' was sung again, for we had not yet captured Lobengula, with his cattle, diamonds, and gold."

Jameson asked Lobengula to return to Bulawayo, promising him safety and friendly treatment, but threatening pursuit if he refused. The king replied that he was prepared to come, but wanted to know what had happened to the *indunas* he had sent on a peace mission to the white men. Finding no satisfactory answer, Lobengula set off in the direction of the Shangani River, with the British in pursuit.

After he had crossed the Shangani, Lobengula told his men: "Matabele! The white men will never cease following us whilst we have gold in our possession; for gold is what they prize above all things. Collect now my gold, and you, and you [indicating two *indunas*], carry it back to the white men. Tell them they have beaten my regiments, killed my people, burnt my kraals, captured my cattle, and that I want peace." Two *indunas* carried the gold to the white soldiers. The gold was taken by two troopers, and the message ignored.

Matabeleland was placed under white rule, but on March 24, 1896, a white man was killed in the Mzingwane district, and an uprising, very ably described by Terence Ranger in *Revolt in Southern Rhodesia* 1896–7, had begun. From Mzingwane the uprising spread to large parts of Matabeleland and Mashonaland. Prominent among the leaders of the uprising was the Mashona priest Mkwati. His communications network coordinated moves throughout the area as, for once, the Mashona and Ndebele peoples acted in unison. When the uprising in Mashonaland eventually ended, ten per cent of the white population in the country had been killed, "a staggeringly high figure," which, Lewis Gann has noted,

A local chief's version of the Asante kings' Golden Stool.
ELIOT ELISOFON

was "infinitely greater than the proportion of casualties suffered by white colonists in the Algerian national rising or the Mau Mau in Kenya in the twentieth century."

In West Africa the indigenous peoples also struggled to hold their birthright. In the Gambia in 1891 France recognized Britain's claims to both banks of the Gambia River as far as the sea. Soon after this, there was friction between the French and the Mandingos and Fulani. As a result, a chief named Fodi Kabba was exiled to Médine (in present-day Mali), from where he directed a movement against the British. It took a combined British and French military operation in 1901 to destroy Fodi Kabba's movement.

In 1893 another Gambian chief, Fodi Silah, inflicted heavy losses on a British punitive expedition sent against him. He was, however, eventually driven into French-claimed territory, where he died.

In Sierra Leone the indigenous peoples rose against the British in 1898. They massacred white people, including American missionaries, in their opposition to the "hut tax," a tax charged against every dwelling. The British were compelled to mount an expedition, under Sir Francis de Winton, against them.

In the territory of modern Ghana, the Asante in 1807 attacked and destroyed a British fort at Anomabu and the Dutch fort of Kormantin, and besieged the Cape Coast Castle. They held the area until 1824, when the governor of Sierra Leone, Sir Charles Macarthy, landed at Cape Coast Castle while on a tour of inspection. Impetuously he embarked on a war with the Asante. He was defeated and committed suicide. It took the British imperial government three years to contain the Asante.

Between 1871 and 1872 the Dutch turned over their possessions on the Gold Coast to the British in exchange for certain British claims in Sumatra. The transfer of territory involved the latter in another war with the Asante. The Asante king put forty thousand men in the field. The British allied themselves with the Fante, providing the Africans with British weapons. They were badly defeated twice, before the Asante assaulted the British at Elmina. In 1873 Sir Garnet Wolseley, with a strong force of British soldiers, contingents of West Indian regiments, British seamen and marines, joined Sir John Glover, who commanded Hausa levies, in attacking and burning Kumasi, the Asante capital.

In 1895 another war broke out. The British captured Kumasi and demanded an indemnity of 357,000 pounds in gold. When this was not paid the *asantehene*, or king, the queen mother, and important chiefs were exiled to the Seychelles in the Indian Ocean. The British looted the Asante palace and dynamited sacred trees and altars.

To add insult to injury, in 1900 the governor of the Gold Coast, Sir Frederick Hodgson, demanded the surrender of the Golden Stool so that he could sit on it. Not even the *asantehene* himself sits on the Golden Stool, which is believed to hold the soul of the Asante nation; rather, the stool is placed on its side, atop a stool of its own. To defend themselves against this sacrilege the Asante revolted and besieged the governor and his wife in Kumasi from, appropriately, April Fool's Day to June 23, 1900, when, with a force of six hundred Hausa soldiers and British officers, Hodgson fought his way through Asante warriors to the Gold Coast colony. Later, Colonel James Willcocks arrived from Nigeria with several hundred Yoruba and Hausa troops; these were joined by other African and Indian troops from British Central Africa and officers from England. When the British force eventually advanced on Kumasi in July, it numbered three thousand five hundred officers and men and thousands of African allies from regions hostile to the Asante.

In Nigeria the British were compelled in 1851 to mount a naval expedition against Kosoko, the king of Lagos. They expelled the king, putting his cousin on the throne. The British met more resistance, however, from Jaja, who had risen from slavery to become a formidable merchant prince of the Niger delta, capable of putting in the field a large force of fighting men. Jaja jealously guarded his independence, and when threatened, engaged the British with armed forces. He was defeated and removed to the West Indies.

Another Nigerian potentate who resisted the British was the king of Benin. In January, 1897, he massacred an ostensibly peaceful British expedition under the command of J. R. Phillips, the acting consul general. The *oba* was subsequently exiled, and a number of his chiefs executed. Yet another resistance flared up in 1899, when a punitive British expedition was sent to Benin.

Between 1900 and 1910 several wars were fought to subdue the Aro, an Ibo people in the northeastern part of the Niger delta. The Fulani kingdom of Nupe also fought wars of resistance to British rule. Colonel T. L. N. Moreland, with a force of eight hundred African soldiers and British officers, equipped with artillery and maxim guns, was compelled in 1902–1903 to fight not only in Nupe but also in Bornu, Kano, and Sokoto.

French interest in West Africa was stimulated by René Caillié, who in 1827 traveled up the Niger to Timbuktu and across the Sahara to Morocco. At this time the Fulani conqueror, Al Hajj Umar, dominated this area. He blocked Caillié's route and threatened French settlements on the Senegal River. In 1854 General Louis Faidherbe was appointed governor general of Senegal, and he conducted skirmishes against African tribes resisting French rule north of the river. He annexed the Wuli country and built a fort at the river port of Médine. Umar sent an army of twenty thousand men against him.

In 1864 a French expedition under Lieutenant Abdon Mage reached Segu, but was detained for two years by Umar's nephew and successor, Ahmadu ibn Tindani (Ahmadu Seku), who also resisted French forces under General Gustave Borgnis-Desbordes, Colonel Louis Archinard, and other officers.

In 1890 the Tukolor Fulani of Takrur and the Macina Fulani under Ahmadu Abdulei (Ahmadu Cheiku) fought a war of resistance against the French, and the following year a Mandingo king, Samori Touré, also led his people in resisting white rule. In the years 1885 and 1886 the French undertook a campaign against him, but the king's dogged resistance turned it into a seven years' war. In 1894 and 1895 Colonel P. L. Monteil led an unsuccessful military expedition against Samori. Monteil was recalled by the French government; but in 1898 Samori was taken prisoner and exiled to Gabon. Similarly, in Dahomey, King Behanzin fiercely resisted French rule from 1891 to 1893, when he was captured and exiled to the West Indies. Unrest existed as well in other parts of French-held Africa: near Timbuktu in 1894; in the Ivory Coast in 1900; in Mauritania in 1908 and 1909.

In Algeria Abd al-Kader inflicted defeat after defeat on the French between 1835 and 1837. Only after the French had suffered great losses did they send in an army sufficient to rout the guerilla leader. Forced to retire to Morocco, he again attacked the French with a large army. The bey of Constantine, who ruled over much of eastern Algeria, repulsed French assaults for many years until his stronghold finally fell to the enemy in 1847. In 1863 the Kabylia Berbers rose in resistance to French rule, and to the south of Oran there was another uprising under Bu Amama. In Tunisia in 1882 there were uprisings against the French and the bey's government, which had placed the country under French control. A French expedition, led by Paul Flatters, was massacred by the Tuaregs in the Sahara in 1881. In Morocco Europeans were killed, and Casablanca was sacked by Africans in 1907. In response, France sent fifteen thousand troops, who fought sporadically until 1911.

In 1830 the French "swore by their blood" that they seized Algeria only to destroy its piratical oppressors. But by 1845, when this patriotic poster was issued, French colons *were in control of its destiny.*
GIRAUDON

In the Congo the sultan of Bagirmi, who had been induced to accept French protection, was forced to flee, together with the French resident, from the army of Robah Zobeir, sultan of Bornu. It was not until after two years' fighting, in which the French suffered many defeats, that Zobeir was slain. His sons and successors continued the struggle until 1902. To the northeast of Bagirmi, the Wadai ruler attacked French outposts on the Chari River in 1904, thereby opening a war that did not end till 1911.

Relations with the Portuguese, the British, and the French pale before the record left by the Belgians. Few episodes in the history of colonialism in Africa can surpass the

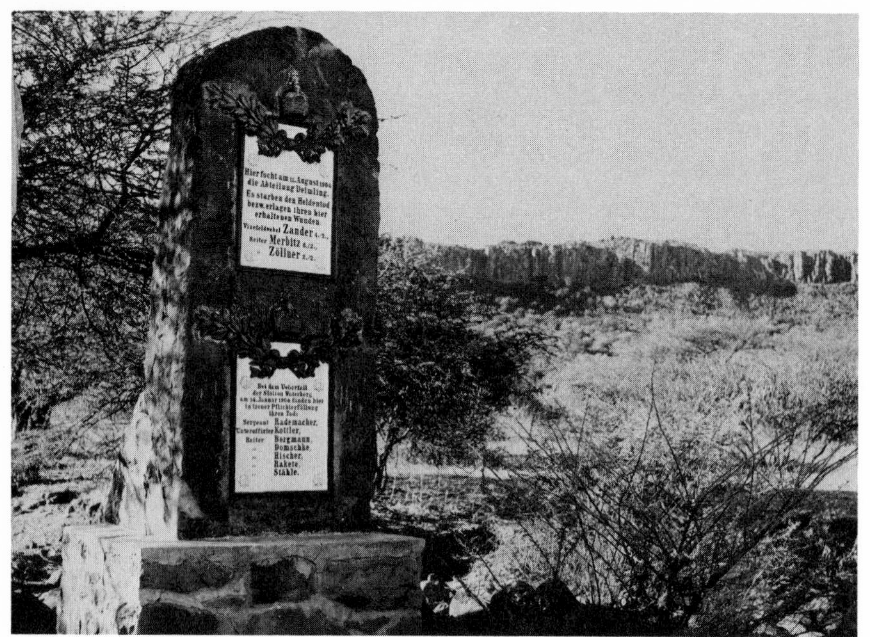

The German encroachment on South West Africa was met with fierce rebellion in the Herero uprising of 1904–1906. Equipped with obsolete rifles and little ammunition, the Herero were no match for the quick-firing Krupp gun used by the Germans. By the end of the war these embattled Africans had been reduced from 80,000 cattle-rich nomads to 15,000 starving fugitives. This memorial, near Waterberg, commemorates ten of the Germans who died in the war.

KEYSTONE PRESS

revolting brutality and sordid crimes committed in the name of Leopold, king of the Belgians, on Africans in the Congo. The imposition of Belgian rule is the most miserable chapter of a miserable story.

In less than twenty years after the first Belgian attack, an African population that had been estimated at between twenty and thirty million was reduced to eight million. Fighting became endemic in the Congo. Belgian officials ordered that recalcitrant villagers be punished by having the hands and sexual organs of males cut off and brought to them for check and tally. In 1892 Belgians were attacked and massacred all over the upper Congo. In 1895, as a result of the murder by the Belgians of Gongo Lutete, chief of the Manyema, there was an uprising at Luluabourg, and another in 1897.

Meanwhile, back on the east coast, the German East Africa Company obtained from the sultan of Zanzibar a fifty-year lease on his mainland territory extending from the Ruvuma River to the Umba River. Over sixty German officials were sent to administer the region. On August 21, 1888, disturbances broke out. A month later the Germans hardly held any post in the interior. Not only Germans but all Europeans suffered. It took a thousand Sudanese troops, two hundred German sailors, and sixty German officers over eighteen months to put down the uprising.

In 1891 the Wahehe, a warlike people on the Rufiji River, rose against German rule and fought a war that lasted until 1893. In 1905, however, other African tribes between northern Nyasaland (present-day Malawi) and the Kilwa coast rose against the Germans. German officials, male and female missionaries, planters, and traders were killed. It took the Germans nearly a year and a half to subdue the Africans, using not only Masai and Sudanese Africans but also New Guinea, Papuan, and Melanesian troops to fight for them.

In German Kamerun (or Cameroon), cruelties committed between 1887 and 1896 resulted in a mutiny of African soldiers. In 1904 and 1905 African groups rose against German rule and were suppressed after much fighting.

In South West Africa the Hottentot leader Hendrik Witbooi led his people in several victories against the Germans, who were eventually persuaded to sign a treaty of peace. In 1903 another group of Hottentots—the Bondelswarts living north of the Orange River—took up arms against the Germans and fought them for four years before being exterminated. While this war was in progress, Bantu-speaking Herero tribes also rose up against Germans. Led by Samuel Maherero, they attacked and killed every white man in sight, burning their houses until they were defeated in the Waterberg Mountains in 1904. Maherero escaped to British territory, where he died while organizing further resistance to the Germans.

Resistance erupted again in the following year, when under Witbooi and his successor Jacob Marengo the Hottentots took up arms. Sixty German settlers in the southeast were killed. By 1908, when the troubles finally came to an end, the Germans in South West Africa had lost five thousand soldiers and settlers, and spent over fifteen million pounds trying to hold on there.

The Italians also entered Africa in the last quarter of the nineteenth century. Italy had for a very long time cast an envious eye over what it called Abyssinia (Ethiopia, as it is known today). In 1873 Italy purchased the small coaling station of Assab on the Red Sea. After the downfall of Egypt, Italy occupied the neighboring port of Massawa and other areas in the region of Eritrea, and so came to loggerheads with Emperor Yohannes IV of Ethiopia.

The Italians had already occupied Sahiti, an inland town formerly under the Egyptians, when the Ethiopian general Ras Alulu moved against them with ten thousand men. An Italian army of four hundred fifty men was completely destroyed. In 1895, when Emperor Menelik sat on the Ethiopian throne, the Italians tried again. First they made secret treaties with one of the vassal kings of Ethiopia—Ras Mangasha of Tigre. Menelik had reason to doubt the loyalty of Ras Mangasha of Tigre, his rival for the emperorship of Ethiopia. In 1891 Ras Mangasha had made a treaty with the Italians: in return for their support, he undertook to detach Tigre from the Ethiopian empire. This the Italians did, though they were still bound by the Treaty of Wichale to support Menelik.

Ras Mangasha, tiring of an alliance that proved to be meaningless, threw in his lot with Menelik in 1895. He ignored Italian general Baratieri's order to disband, and the Italians, being short of men and funds, did nothing about it. Baratieri went to Rome and succeeded in obtaining money and supplies. He, nevertheless, underestimated the strength of Menelik's troops and counted on some vassal kings rising against the emperor. This did not happen. In September, 1895, Menelik had issued a proclamation about the foreign menace, which raised a wave of genuine patriotism among his subjects. All his vassals came to his side.

The Italians staked the reputation of their army on the Ethiopian campaign. Having decided upon a surprise attack on Adowa, the capital of Tigre, Baratieri chose for his attack Sunday, March 1, 1896, a feast day in the Ethiopian Church, with the hope that Ethiopian soldiers would have gone to worship at the holy city of Axum. It never occurred to him that Menelik could move so many troops so quickly from one distant point to another. Nor did he know that Menelik had for some years been importing arms and ammunition. Over and above all, he had faulty and inaccurate maps of Ethiopia.

On the night of February 29 (it was leap year) an Italian force of 14,500 in three columns advanced toward Adowa. Its objective was to occupy three hills commanding the plain. Rain slowed the march. One column, which was to encamp on a hill called Chidan Meret, had far outdistanced the two other Italian detachments. When they encamped at daybreak, there was no sign of the rest of the army, which should have been on its right. Runners, sent to reconnoiter, never returned. The commander's African guides reported that the maps were wrong and that the hill they were on was not Chidan Meret. He seriously considered whether to rely on the map or on his African informants. He decided to rely on his map. The Ethiopians attacked, outmaneuvering and overwhelming the Italian force. A detachment of African troops under Italian command fought well, but could not do anything against a determined Ethiopian attack. Finally, they broke and ran, forcing the Italian officers to surrender. The Ethiopians then cut off the other two Italian columns. Over 8,000 Italians and some 4,000 of their African troops were killed. Fugitives not taken prisoner were harried in the gorges, which were their only way back to Eritrea. Had Menelik not ordered all his troops back into camp on the evening of the battle, his cavalry could have cut off the few passes available to the retreating army and exterminated the entire Italian force. The ignominy of this defeat was never to be forgotten in Italy.

From the evidence presented throughout this chapter, it is abundantly clear that the vast majority of Africans responded bravely to the Berlin conspiracy. The European invader enjoyed the advantage of superior weaponry. In all other aspects of the conflict—in generalship, strategy, and battle tactics—it is clear Africans more than held their own against graduates of the best military academies of Europe. It could be said that in these encounters Africans, armed usually only with spears, displayed greater valor than Europeans firing guns from a safe distance. As a king of the Ndebele once observed: a gun is a weapon that must have been invented by a coward.

What, then, turned the scales in favor of Europeans? It was the assistance they received from a small number of African collaborators, who acted as soldiers, carriers, informants, and food suppliers. Without internal division, then, Europeans would never have been able to win the wars of resistance against them.

Even today in Rhodesia, South West Africa, South Africa, Angola, and Mozambique, where armed opposition to white rule is taking place, the success of the white man in suppressing this resistance is due in no small measure to the extent and manner in which he has been able to use Africans as soldiers, secret agents, and intelligence gatherers. Perhaps this part of our history illustrates the point of the Zulu saying: "*Isitha somunthu nguye uqhobo lwake.* (The enemy of an African is he, himself.)" There can be no doubt, however, that these early wars were a source of great inspiration and spiritual strength to the generation of Africans whose destiny it was to carry on the fight against European colonialism and, from the late 1950's on through the 1960's, eradicate it from most of the soil of Africa.

SPEARS AND MAXIM GUNS

A LOYAL SUBJECT'S PLAINT

For England's "Black Poor," as its African freedmen were called in the late eighteenth century, the idea of returning to Africa and founding a colony in Sierra Leone was extremely appealing. A committee was set up to oversee such a project, and in November, 1786, Olaudah Equiano, an Ibo and a former slave, was appointed Commissary for Stores for the Black Poor Going to Sierra Leone. In 1756, when he was ten or eleven, Equiano had been captured by raiders in eastern Nigeria. He eventually was taken to Virginia, where he was bought by a British naval officer, who renamed him Gustavus Vassa. After adventures in England, the Mediterranean, and Canada, Equiano purchased his freedom in 1766. He returned to England, where he became active as an abolitionist. His description of his role in the settlement of the Black Poor follows. It comes from his autobiography, The Interesting Narrative of the Life of Olaudah, *written following his dismissal from the post of commissary. Equiano spent the rest of his life traveling through Britain, lecturing on abolition and publicizing his best-selling book.*

On my return to London in August I was very agreeably surprised to find that the benevolence of government had adopted the plan of some philanthropic individuals to send the Africans from hence to their native quarter; and that some vessels were then engaged to carry them to Sierra Leone; an act which redounded to the honor of all concerned in its promotion, and filled me with prayers and much rejoicing. There was then in the city a select committee of gentlemen for the black poor, to some of whom I had the honor of being known; and, as soon as they heard of my arrival they sent for me to the committee. When I came there they informed me of the intention of government; and as they seemed to think me qualified to superintend part of the undertaking, they asked me to go with the black poor to Africa. I pointed out to them many objections to my going; and particularly I expressed some difficulties on the account of the slave dealers, as I would certainly oppose their traffic in the human species by every means in my power. However these objections were over-ruled by the gentlemen of the committee, who prevailed on me to go, and recommended me to the honorable Commissioners of his Majesty's Navy as a proper person to act as commissary for government in the intended expedition; and they accordingly appointed me in November 1786 to that office, and gave me sufficient power to act for the government in the capacity of commissary, having received my warrant and the following order.

By the principal Officers and Commissioners of his Majesty's Navy:
Whereas you were directed, by our warrant of the 4th of last month, to receive into your charge from Mr. Irving the surplus provisions remaining of what was provided for the voyage, as well as the provisions for the support of the black poor, after the landing at Sierra Leone, with the clothing, tools, and all other articles provided at government's expense; and as the provisions were laid in at the rate of two months for the voyage, and for four months after the landing, but the number embarked being so much less than was expected, whereby there may be a considerable surplus of provisions, clothing, etc. These are, in addition to former orders, to direct and require you to appropriate or dispose of such surplus to the best advantage you can for the benefit of government, keeping and rendering to us a faithful account of what you do herein. And for your guidance in preventing any white persons going, who are not intended to have the indulgence of being carried thither, we send you herewith a list of those recommended by the Committee for the black poor as proper persons to be permitted to embark, and acquaint you that you are not to suffer any others to go who do not produce a certificate from the committee for the black poor, of their having their permission for it. . . .

I proceeded immediately to the execution of my duty on board the vessels destined for the voyage, where I continued till the March following.

During my continuance in the employment of government, I was struck with the flagrant abuses committed by the agent, and endeavored to remedy them, but without effect. One instance, among many which I could produce, may serve as a specimen. Government had ordered to be provided all necessaries (slops, as they are called, included) for 750 persons; however, not being able to muster more than 426, I was ordered to send the superfluous slops, etc. to the king's stores at Portsmouth; but, when I demanded them for that purpose from the agent, it appeared they had never been bought, though paid for by government. But that was not all, government were not the only objects of peculation; these poor people suffered infinitely more; their accommodations were most wretched; many of them wanted beds, and many more clothing and other necessaries. For the truth of this, and much more, I do not seek credit from my own assertion. I appeal to the testimony of Capt. Thompson, of the *Nautilus*, who convoyed us, to whom I applied in February 1787 for a remedy, when I had remonstrated to the agent in vain, and even brought him to be a witness of the injustice and oppression I complained of. I appeal also to a letter written by these wretched people, so early as the beginning of the preceding January, and published in the *Morning Herald* of the 4th of that month, signed by twenty of their chiefs.

I could not silently suffer government to be thus cheated, and my countrymen plundered and oppressed, and even left destitute of the necessaries for almost their existence. I therefore informed the Commissioners of the Navy of the agent's proceedings; but my dismission was soon after procured, by means of a gentleman in the city, whom the agent, conscious of his peculation, had deceived by letter, and whom, moreover, empowered the same agent to receive on board, at the government's expense, a number of persons as passengers, contrary to the orders I received. By this I suffered a considerable loss in my property: however, the commissioners were satisfied with my conduct, and wrote to Capt. Thompson, expressing their approbation of it.

Thus provided, they proceeded on their voyage; and at last, worn out by treatment, perhaps not the most mild, and wasted by sickness, brought on by want of medicine, clothes, bedding, etc. they reached Sierra Leone just at the commencement of the rains. At that season of the year it is impossible to cultivate the lands; their provisions therefore were exhausted before they could derive any benefit from agriculture; and it is not surprising that many . . . whose constitutions are very tender, and who had been cooped up in ships from October to June, and accommodated in the manner I have mentioned, should be so wasted by their confinement as not long to survive it.

Thus ended my part of the long-talked-of expedition to Sierra Leone; an expedition which, however unfortunate in the event, was humane and politic in its design, nor was its failure owing to government: everything was done on their part; but there was evidently sufficient mismanagement attending the conduct and execution of it to defeat its success.

I should not have been so ample in my account of this transaction, had not the share I bore in it been made the subject of partial animadversion, and even my dismission from my employment thought worthy of being made by some a matter of public triumph. The motives which might influence any person to descend to a petty contest with an obscure African, and to seek gratification by his depression, perhaps it is not proper here to inquire into or relate, even if its detection were necessary to my vindication; but I thank Heaven it is not. I wish to stand by my own integrity, and not to shelter myself under the impropriety of another; and I trust the behavior of the Commissioners of the Navy to me entitle me to make this assertion; for after I had been dismissed, March 24, I drew up a memorial thus:

To the Right Honorable the Lords Commissioners of his Majesty's Treasury: The Memorial and Petition of GUSTAVUS VASSA a black Man, late Commissary to the black Poor going to AFRICA. Humbly Sheweth,

That your Lordships' memorialist was, by the Honorable the Commissioners of his Majesty's Navy, on the 4th of December last, appointed to the above employment by warrant from that board;

That he accordingly proceeded to the execution of his duty on board of the *Vernon*, being one of the ships appointed to proceed to Africa with the above poor;

That your memorialist, to his great grief and astonishment, received a letter of dismission from the Honorable Commissioners of the Navy, by your Lordships' orders;

That, conscious of having acted with the most perfect fidelity and the greatest assiduity in discharging the trust reposed in him, he is altogether at a loss to conceive the reasons of your Lordships' having altered the favorable opinion you were pleased to conceive of him, sensible that your Lordships' would not proceed to so severe a measure without some apparent good cause; he therefore has every reason to believe that his conduct has been grossly misrepresented to your Lordships; and he is the more confirmed in his opinion, because, by opposing measures of others concerned in the same expedition, which tended to defeat your Lordships' humane intentions, and to put the government to a very considerable additional expense, he created a number of enemies, whose misrepresentations, he has too much reason to believe, laid the foundation of his dismission. Unsupported by friends, and unaided by the advantages of a liberal education, he can only hope for redress from the justice of his cause, in addition to the mortification of having been removed from his employment, and the advantage which he reasonably might have expected to have derived therefrom. He has had the misfortune to have sunk a considerable part of his little property in fitting himself out, and in other expenses arising out of his situation, an account of which he here annexes. Your memorialist will not trouble your Lordships with a vindication of any part of his conduct, because he knows not of what crimes he is accused; he, however, earnestly entreats that you will be pleased to direct an inquiry into his behavior during the time he acted in the public service; and, if it be found that his dismission arose from false representations; he is confident that in your Lordships' justice he shall find redress.

Your petitioner therefore humbly

prays that your Lordships will take his case into consideration, and that you will be pleased to order payment of the above referred-to account, amounting to £32 4s. and also the wages intended, which is most humbly submitted.

London, May 12, 1787.

The above petition was delivered into the hands of their Lordships, who were kind enough, in the space of some few months afterwards, without hearing, to order me £50 sterling—that is, £18 wages for the time (upwards of four months) I acted a faithful part in their service. Certainly the sum is more than a free negro would have had in the western colonies!!!

XHOSA FREEDOM FIGHTERS

In the late eighteenth century there appeared among the Xhosa a spiritual leader and warrior named Makana, whose self-proclaimed religious mission was to annihilate all white men and to bring back to life all the Africans and cattle they had killed. In the spring of 1819, provoked by numerous attacks by the whites, he led his army across the Great Fish River into the Cape Colony. The Xhosa were repulsed; by the following summer the British had driven them back across the Fish and as far as the Kei River, slaughtering and burning as they went. Makana went personally to the British camp, hoping that his own surrender would restore peace to the country. He was sentenced to life imprisonment on Robben Island. A few days later a group of his people approached his captors, offering themselves and other prominent Xhosa in exchange for Makana's release. One of them delivered the following speech, recorded by a British officer attending the parley. The British would neither make peace nor free the prophet, who died in 1820 while attempting to escape from the island.

The war, British chiefs, is an unjust one. You are striving to extirpate a people whom you forced to take up arms. When our fathers and the fathers of the Boers first settled in the Suurveld [an area west of the Fish River], they dwelt together in peace. Their flocks grazed on the same hills: there herdsmen smoked together out of the same pipes; they were brothers . . . until the herds of the Xhosas increased so as to make the hearts of the Boers sore. What those covetous men could not get from our fathers for old buttons, they took by force. Our fathers were *men*; they loved their cattle; their wives and children lived upon milk; they fought for their property. They began to hate the colonists who coveted their all, and aimed at their destruction.

Now, their kraals and our fathers' kraals were separate. The Boers made commandos on our fathers. Our fathers drove them out of the Suurveld; and we dwelt there because we had conquered it. There we were circumcised; there we married wives; and there our children were born. The white men hated us, but could not drive us away. When there was war we plundered you. When there was peace some of our bad people stole; but our chiefs forbade it. Your treacherous friend, Gaika [the Xhosa chief who was an ally of the British] always had peace with you; yet, when his people stole, he shared in the plunder. Have your patrols ever found cattle taken in time of peace, runaway slaves or deserters, in the kraals of our chiefs? Have they ever gone into Gaika's country without finding such cattle, such slaves, such deserters, in Gaika's kraals? But he was your friend; and you wished to possess the Suurveld. You came at last like locusts [in attack of 1818]. We stood; we could do no more. You said, "Go over the Fish River . . . that is all we want." We yielded and came here.

We lived in peace. Some of our bad people stole, perhaps; but the nation was quiet . . . the chiefs were quiet. Gaika stole . . . his chiefs stole . . . his people stole. You sent him copper; you sent him beads; you sent him horses, on which he rode to steal more. To us you sent only commandos.

We quarreled with Gaika about grass . . . no business of yours. You sent a commando . . . you took our last cow . . . you left only a few calves, which died for want, along with our children. You gave half of what you took to Gaika; half you kept yourselves. Without milk . . . our corn destroyed . . . we saw our wives and children perish . . . we saw that we must ourselves perish, we followed, therefore, the tracks of our cattle into the Colony. We plundered and we fought for our lives. We found you weak; we destroyed your soldiers. We saw that we were strong; we attacked your headquarters, Grahamstown: . . . and if we had succeeded, our right was good, for you began the war. We failed . . . and you are here.

We wish for peace; we wish to rest in our huts; we wish to get milk for our children; our wives wish to till the land. But your troops cover the plains, and swarm in the thickets, where they cannot distinguish the man from the woman and shoot all.

You want us to submit to Gaika. That man's face is fair to you, but his heart is false. Leave him to himself. Make peace with us. Let him fight for himself. . . . and *we* shall not call on you for help. Set Makana at liberty; and Islambi, Dushani, Kongo and the rest will come to make peace with you at any time we fix. But if you will still make war, you may indeed kill the last man of us . . . but Gaika shall not rule over the followers of those who think him a woman."

THE ZULU ARMY

The following selection is by Colonel G. Hamilton-Browne, a member of Britain's "Noble 24th." It describes the training of the Zulu army. The passage below is from A Lost Legionary in South Africa *(1879).*

As soon as a youth was ten years old he might be inspanned to carry the swag of his father, uncle or elder brother on the war-path; which would consist of a sleeping-mat, water-calabash, cooking-pot, docha-pipe, a few pounds of dried meat or mealies and perhaps a spare assagai and knob-stick. When he reached the age of fourteen or fifteen he would be drafted with other boys of his own age to the nearest military kraal where he would have to do fatigue duties, herd and milk cattle, fetch firewood, etc., at the same time being taught how to use his arms, how to fence with sticks, military drill and dances. During this period of his training, provided he wanted to eat, he had to skirmish around and find or steal the materials for his meal as the only provision for his sustenance, made by the kraal commandant, were a number of the wildest cows, drawn from the royal herd entrusted to the care of the regiment, and these unruly animals the recruit boys had to run down, hold and milk before they dined. This was very rough training and a boy had to be soundly constituted to survive the ordeal of his initiation into military life. As soon as a lad was old enough to be considered fit for active service he might be drafted into a regiment, or if there were enough boys fit for the purpose they might be all formed into a new regiment, each sub-tribe forming its own company, while warriors of repute were selected by the king to officer it. A Zulu regiment numbered from three to six thousand men and had its own kraal at which the men on duty lived, and a newly-formed regiment would have to build its own barracks, break up ground for cultivation, and when this was done it would receive a name from the king and be considered a unit of the royal army. . . .

A warrior's war outfit consisted of a shield made out of dried ox-hide, oval in shape, about 2 feet 6 inches wide and long enough for the owner to look over, when he held it by the middle of the strengthening stick that ran up it lengthways. His offensive arms consisted of from two to three assagais, one of which would be the stabbing assagai (*bogwan*) that had a blade of at least a foot to 18 inches long fixed to a strong shaft of wood about 2 feet in length. This weapon . . . was never thrown but only used in hand-to-hand combat, while the others, if carried, being much lighter might be thrown, though the Zulu warrior was not encouraged to throw his assagai but was taught to rush in, defend himself with his shield and stab home with his bogwan. He also carried a knobkerry and a plain stick both made of hard wood. His food, carried for him by a boy, consisted of a small bag of dried meat and grain, but as all the kraals, on the line of march, had to contribute to the maintenance of the king's troops very little food was carried on an expedition. A force equipped, as above, could easily march 30 miles a day and put up a big fight at the end of their journey or if necessary cover 50 miles a day and continue to do so for weeks at a stretch, so that an army opposed to them must always be on the alert as no cavalry could keep pace with them over rough and broken country. Their favorite time to attack was the early morning, their plan being to surprise and envelop their enemy, when they would rush in and kill everything with the exception of the girls and cattle.

The Zulu discipline was very strict, disobedience or neglect of duty being punished by death; in fact death was the only penalty served out and the guilty one might not only bring death to himself but to all his family and friends; so it behoved a Zulu soldier to obey and obey smartly. He showed no mercy, he expected none, and when ordered on active service he well knew he must conquer or die for certain disgrace and death, probably torture, awaited a beaten army. A Zulu soldier . . . had to put in six months out of the year, under arms, at his military kraal; the balance of the year he might go home but was always liable to be called out at any moment, not only in case of war, for his regiment might be required to do duty at the royal kraal, also at certain feasts the majority of the army would be mobilized, before the king, for the purpose of showing off their capabilities in drill and dancing. At such times petitions might be presented to the sable potentate, who also took the opportunity of rewarding or punishing those brought before him. The most frequent petition was for permission to marry and at times the king would allow aspirants to holy wedlock to prove their right to be considered . . . in the following way: A wild and savage bull would be turned loose into a large enclosed space and a dozen love-lorn young men sent in to kill it with no weapons except their bare hands; should they succeed . . . the king granted their request. . . .

The Zulu march was usually conducted in single file, the companies moving in parallel lines, while each regiment would take its own line for the objective point, and on reaching that point, or rather some given spot a few miles short of it, the leading files of each petty column would halt and the rear close up, until each company formed a dense mass of men in a ring formation, as the Zulu was quite incompetent to form or advance in line.

The regiments having converged together the chief *induna* (General) would give his orders for the attack and the regiments be formed up to carry them out. In case it should be a laager, camp or village to be stormed, the youngest regiments would be placed on the flanks whose first duty was to surround and completely envelop the enemy, thereby preventing the escape of any fugitives and these men were called the horns of the army. The main body, called the chest of the army, never moved until the flankers had taken up their positions. Then a combined attack would be made but always the junior regiments were first engaged.

The Zulu well understood the utility of a flank attack and should the position of the enemy be so extended or their numbers be so great that the Zulus could not surround them they would still try to out-flank them, but all attacks, whether frontal or flanking, were first made by the youngest regiments and should these be beaten back then the more matured and veteran soldiers moved forward to do the work. The oldest veterans formed the reserve which encouraged the fighting line and killed any combatant who turned tail.

The Zulus had no field ambulances, so after a fight the wounded were examined by their *indunas* and if found to be unable to march or to be otherwise seriously hurt were put to death, usually by drowning, provided a river was close at hand, otherwise he was put out of his misery by his nearest relation. . . . The Zulus were very superstitious, being great believers in omens, witchcraft, divinations and bone-throwing and also believed that the moon exercised great power for good and evil and that at certain phases of the luminary it was lucky or most unlucky to undertake any important act especially that of war.

The numerical strength of the Zulu army has always been disputed but I am of the opinion that it must have been near sixty thousand men at the declaration of the war and these men, trained as they were and as mobile as monkeys, were not an enemy to be sneezed at, much less to be treated lightly.

Young Xhosa boys play a stick game, in imitation of traditional methods of warfare.

MAGNUM—ERNST HAAS

ZULU WISDOM

Iqhawe lifel' ebuqhaweni, *or "the hero dies in heroism," was a popular Zulu proverb in the days when warfare was the order of the day and men prayed that they would die in battle fighting valorously for their king. Below is a collection of other Zulu wise sayings.*

A man is not stabbed with one spear.
(A man worthy of the name should not fall down with the first thrust of the spear.)

Even where there is no cock day dawns.
(No one is indispensable.)

He who installs a king never rules with him.
(Kings have short memories, and tend to forget the people who helped them in the days when they were not kings.)

He cries with one eye.
(He pretends to be sorry when he is not.)

The mouth is the shield to protect oneself.
(It is by means of one's mouth that one defends oneself.)

The sheep has killed an elephant.
(The impossible has happened.)

The bite of the black mamba cannot be cured.
(Used to describe a deadly thing for which attempts at cure are almost useless)

There is no frog that does not peep out of its pool.
(Everyone will take a chance in the hope that he will succeed.)

No buffalo was ever beaten by its calf.
(Old people are usually far more experienced than the young.)

Days are things which want to be provided for.
(One has to make proper provision for the bad days.)

One does not follow a snake into its hole.
(It is not wise to take unnecessary risks.)

There is no mountain without a grave.
(Death is everywhere. There is no way of running away from it.)

He holds the spear by the blade.
(A person who has been bragging gives himself away by doing a foolish thing.)

A king is a king because of people.
(A king is no king if he has no followers.)

When the big bird dies, the eggs rot.
(A man's family collapses when he dies.)

AN OFFER OF SAFE CONDUCT

In 1881 Muhammad Ahmad, a Muslim ascetic from the Sudan, declared himself the Mahdi, or messiah, of his country. He proclaimed a jihad and enlisted the support of tens of thousands of followers, who fought brutally and fanatically to free the Sudan from Anglo-Egyptian control. Success followed success as the Mahdists mowed down their enemies. Finally, in January, 1884, England sent out one of its ablest generals, Charles George Gordon, a former governor of the Sudan. Ignoring his instructions to evacuate the Egyptians from the Sudan, Gordon determined to defeat the Mahdi. He stubbornly remained at Khartoum. The following March the Mahdists besieged the city. Wishing to take it without bloodshed, their leader urged the British general to surrender. To this end he wrote Gordon several letters, the last of which appears below. But Gordon stood firm, and on January 26, 1885, the Sudanese breached Khartoum's defenses, taking it amid frightful slaughter. Gordon was pierced with several spears, and his head was sent to the victorious Mahdi.

In the name of God the merciful, the compassionate.

Praise be to God the kind guardian.

May God's blessings and peace be upon our Lord Mohammed and his household.

Greetings.

From: The Servant dependent upon God,

Mohammed el-Mahdi Ibn Abdallahi To: Gordon Pasha, may God protect him from every evil He did not will.

If God wills your happiness and you accept our advice and enter into our security and guarantee—that is what we wish. If, however, you would rather rejoin the English we will send you to them.

Having seen what you have seen, how long are you going to disbelieve us? We have been told by God's Apostle, may God's blessings and peace be upon him, of the imminent destruction of all those in Khartoum, save those who believe and surrender: them God will save. We do not wish you to perish with those doomed to perish because we have frequently heard good of you. Yet often as we have written to you about your regeneration and felicity, you have not returned to us an answer that will lead to your good, as we hear from those who come to us from your place. However, we have not yet despaired of your regeneration and felicity, and because of the virtue we hear is in you we will write you a single text from God's book in the hope that by it God will facilitate your regeneration since he has made us the doorway to his mercy and guidance. For this reason we have repeatedly written to you urging you to return to your own country where your virtue will achieve the highest honor. In order that you should not abandon hope of God's mercy I say to you that God has said "Kill not thyself for God is merciful to thee." Peace be upon you. 25th Rabi' Awwal, 1302 [January 12, 1885].

It was reported to me in the reply you sent us that you had said that the English wished to ransom you alone from us for £20,000. We know that people say many bad things about us which are not in us, in order that those shall be misled whom God has condemned to perdition. The falsehood of these allegations can only be known to those who meet us. As for you, if you accept our advice you will be thereby blessed; but if you wish to rejoin the English we will send you to them without claiming a farthing. Peace be upon you.

ETHIOPIAN RESISTANCE

Another dedicated opponent of European encroachment was Menelik II, *emperor of Ethiopia from* 1889 *to* 1913. *The following letter, from this sovereign to the Khalifa who was the Mahdi's successor, reveals the Ethiopian's determination to strengthen his alliance with the Sudan. Both nations faced the threat of French and British territorial expansion.*

This is to inform you that the Europeans who are present round the White Nile with the English have come out from both the east and the west, and intended to enter between my country and yours and to separate and divide us. And I, when I heard of their plan, dispatched an expedition, sending detachments in five directions. The group [of Europeans] who are near are the English and the French, who are located in the direction from which the Belgians came. And do you remember when I sent to you Kantiba Jiru, you wrote to me by him that you have men in the direction from which the Belgians came?; and I ordered the chiefs of [my] troops that if they met with them, they were to parley with them and explain [my] intention. And now I have ordered my troops to advance towards the White Nile. And perhaps [if] you heard the news from merchants or from others you might misunderstand my action, [so now] I have written to you so that you would understand the object [of this expedition].

And you look to yourself, and do not let the Europeans enter between us. Be strong, lest if the Europeans enter our midst a great disaster befall us and our children have no rest. And if one of the Europeans comes to you as a traveler, do your utmost to send him away in peace; and do not listen to rumors against me. All my intention is to increase my friendship with you, and that our countries may be protected from [their] enemies.

IN PRAISE OF FOLLY

Gabriel Hanotaux (1853–1944), *a French statesman and historian who twice served as his country's foreign minister, wrote this eulogy of French colonialism in* 1896. *His chauvinistic, superior attitude toward Africa is typical of the period and his station in life. Hanotaux earnestly believed, as he wrote in* 1909, *that "the nineteenth century has bequeathed to the twentieth century the colonial achievement. Of its first efforts, we see only the most noble results; the spectacle of mounting progress . . . permits us to hope that the future will surpass our dreams."*

I know of nothing more heartening than the spectacle of the struggle waged for a century by the sons of civilized Europe against the enigmatic sphinx that guards the mystery of Africa. . . .

What . . . is this strange vocation . . . that from early life fixes the destiny of those who are to become heroes of this odyssey?

François Levaillant . . . was seized from infancy with a passionate taste for natural history. . . . He left for the Cape of Good Hope, and in 1780 began his fine explorations of South Africa.

René Caillié, son of a baker of Deux-Sèvres, orphan and apprentice shoemaker, read *The History of Robinson Crusoe* and *l'Histoire des Voyages* when he was twelve. Later, the sight of African maps —broad and blank—awakened a gleam of curiosity in him. . . . In 1816, with sixty francs in his pocket, he embarked at Rochefort for Senegal, . . . and going barefoot through the desert, he plunged himself into the exploration of everything not known on the African continent.

[Heinrich] Barth was a scholar and a professor. . . . After several preliminary archeological excursions, he left for "the places that were Carthage" . . . and then, beginning with the year 1850, he plunged into the Sahara and the Sudan, where he would pass the better years of his life.

[Sir Richard] Burton was an officer in the Indian army, philologist, and expert in oriental languages. . . . On a wager, he disguised himself, joined a Muslim pilgrimage, and visited the holy cities of Arabia. In 1857 he set himself another daring plan: to discover the sources of the Nile. With [John] Speke, another reckless officer, he realized the impossible and the great lakes were discovered.

The best of all, [David] Livingstone, . . . was of a Scottish family in which integrity was heredity. . . . Religious sentiments infused his life. . . . When he had received his doctorate in medicine and had finished his theological studies, he left for Africa and debarked at the Cape in 1840.

Scholar, missionary, army officer, vagabond, adventurer, not one of these men was motivated by a spirit of gain. They were driven to act by a strong and courageous passion, an overflow of life, and a thirst to give of themselves. There is not a businessman among them. . . .

The role of France in the exploration of Africa has been considerable. . . . It is curiosity and the attraction of the strange that sets the French traveler in motion. But in the more recent years, [exploration] has taken on a systematic and practical character owing, in large part, to the intervention of the state. The Department of Scientific Missions plays a preponderant role in these matters. . . .

In the course of one century, three great feats of French initiative have left a decisive mark on the evolution of the African continent: the occupation of Egypt by Bonaparte, the conquest of Algeria, and the construction of the Suez Canal.

The Egyptian campaign was not only a brilliant military operation but it left in the country the seeds of organization and of civilization. . . . Under the influence of the French, who come and go from Marseille to Alexandria, Egypt has developed, enriched, and enlarged itself. . . .

The conquest of Algeria has been the second gash in the border of states that Islam spread out along the coast of the Mediterranean. The country has been occupied and colonized. . . . The question of the Sahara has been approached practically and scientifically. . . .

[Thanks to the Suez Canal] the Mediterranean has recovered all at once the importance that the discovery of the Cape of Good Hope had seized from it. At the same time, the general commerce of the world has again taken up its traditional route. East Africa, from the Red Sea to Madagascar, has suddenly been drawn closer to Europe and placed in immediate contact with civilization. . . . Today the other coast of Africa is a few weeks from Marseille, two steps from Alexandria. . . .

Compared to these considerable undertakings, the works of French exploration seem a small thing, and yet, how extensive and varied they are! . . .

We come now to 1889. . . . The French Committee for Africa was founded; the administration of the colonies was directed by a spirit at once practical and vigorous; diplomats lay hold of their often neglected interests; French traders banded together; the flower of our youth, and above all, of our military youth, offered themselves, a smile on their lips; it was not just the native auxiliaries who contributed their discipline, their endurance, their indefatigable courage. . . . The definitive joining of all our continental colonies by a system of simultaneous exploration was decided upon.

Binger left from Senegal and, crossing the country of the Kong, arrived at the Ivory Coast, after having fallen in with Treich-Laplene. . . . Monteil, leaving from Saint-Louis, penetrated the Niger basin and traversed its entire length, reaching Sokoto, Bornu, and Lake Chad. From there he returned to France by way of Tripoli, accomplishing in the desert the most complete and daring trip that had been achieved up to that time.

Mizon went up the Benue [River] and again plunged deeply into Adamawa. After vicissitudes without number he rejoined Brazza himself, whose brilliant campaign on the Sanga [River] was not only an exploration but a veritable taking of possession. . . .

And ever since then, there has been a constant new assault against the African sphinx, from which daily is wrenched another of its mysteries. . . .

In short, the end is attained. The symbolic event of this combined march was the meeting of Mizon and Brazza on leaving Adamawa, the one coming from the Niger and the other from the Congo; departing from such distant points, they connected with each other without a precise, prearranged meeting place, carried along, so to speak, by the common purpose that drew the one to the other.

Thus a thin ribbon of routes has tied together across the continent, the French colonies that had been separated by chance exploration and occupation. . . .

The merit of our explorers is enhanced still further by the methods employed. They were unusually peaceful, gentle to the natives, tolerant of ignorance, prejudice, and hostile dispositions. . . .

The savage campaigns of the navigators of the sixteenth century, the thirst for gold, the hunting of the Negroes, all the passions and all the violences excited by a cupidity without bridle and without future, have only produced ruin and devastation throughout.

The poor inferior races; do they merit such harsh treatment?

The modern explorers have judged otherwise. In the second half of the nineteenth century their achievement has been ennobled by its peaceful glory. It has at the same time placed the fundamentals of modern African politics on the firm bases of peace, humanity, and unselfishness.

But only useless trails, hastily covered over again with brush, would have been left on the face of the black continent if national expansion and political sanctions had not supported the efforts of the explorers and stamped Africa with the European imprint par excellence—

organization.

"Exploration has prepared the way for the partition of Africa": arms and diplomacy have achieved it.

"NAPOLEON OF THE SUDAN"

Samori Touré, who created the Mandingo empire and opposed French colonialism for many years, was born in the 1830's in what is now southwestern Guinea. At that time the Mandingos were divided into many warring states; some were populated by animists; others had a distinctly Muslim culture. As a youth Samori was probably a pagan and a trader, but he soon gained renown as a warrior. By about 1870 he had become a Muslim and had assumed the title of almami, *or leader of the faithful. He had also begun his conquest of the Mandingo chieftaincies. Within sixteen years his empire became one of the largest political units in the western Sudan, covering 115,000 square miles. It was bounded by the Tukolor empire in the northwest, the state of Futa Jallon in the west, the kingdom of Sikasso in the east, and the forest fringes of Liberia and Sierra Leone to the south. By this time, however, Samori had also begun to clash with French colonial aspirations. Forced to retreat between 1894 and 1898, he moved his empire eastward, but to no avail. The French captured him and overran his state. The following analysis of Samori's achievements is by the French scholar Yves Person, chairman of the history department at Dakar University.*

Without doubt, Samori Turé is one of the most impressive figures of pre-colonial Africa. He is one on whom the young nationalists of post-colonial Africa have placed great stress. To protect his great achievement—the African empire he had built up in the years from 1870 to 1887—Samori fought the French with skill and determination for fifteen years. However, the efforts Samori had to make in seeking to halt French military imperialism were so great that they led to the dissolution of his empire. . . .

Beginning in 1878, Samori organized the conquered territories of the north into military governments. The empire was thus divided into large regions which were occupied and governed by autonomous armies supported by tribute payments. There were never more than five of these autonomous territories and they were all located on the perimeter of the empire. . . .

The entire empire rested on the shoulders of one man who had proved himself by his exceptional ability and who never ceased to reiterate that God had clearly designated him to secure order in the human world. Following the animistic tradition, Samori surrounded himself with a group of friends and relatives. This assembly finally became institutionalized as a council whose decisions Samori always seemed to accept even when he did not completely agree with them. What was remarkable and rather revolutionary was that the council members soon took on specialized tasks resembling ministerial functions—the secretariat, the treasury, justice, religion, and relations with the Europeans. The nonspecialists acted as inspectors and oversaw the various regional governments. . . .

Although Samori's return to the religion of his ancestors has never been questioned, it must be recalled that he started his career by defending his animist "uncles" against the Muslims. But beyond the territorial limits of this loyalty, Samori had fraternized with the Muslim inhabitants of the commercial centers. When he stated that "a woman alone should be able to travel as far as Kempu" (Freetown), he was indicating the kind of order that he intended to establish. Finding this most attractive to their way of life, all the *dyula* [Muslim Mandingo traders] from the traveling salesmen to the big merchants pledged him their loyalty and even served him as spies and propaganda agents.

The empire was thus dependent upon the massive loyalty of the traders to the imperial organization and upon a strong sense of personal loyalty to Samori which was inspired by his exceptional personality. . . . Fearing that the empire would crumble after his death, Samori sought a unifying force capable of cementing together the disparate elements he had assembled through military strength. It was only natural that he would turn toward Islam, because in it he saw the only available culture of any worth and the only available system of universal values. This former trader seems to have been most influenced both by his rivals, the Tukolor, and by his friends of Futa Dyalon, whose frontier he had reached in 1878. . . .

From 1889 on, the ravaged empire was reconstructed on the basis of personal loyalty to Samori, and all efforts were united in the common cause of war against the French. . . .

Until 1881, during the time that his expansion to the north was advancing smoothly, Samori does not seem to have paid much attention to the European menace. He and the dyula tradesmen viewed the Europeans as a not very populous race of educated people who lived on small islands in the middle of the ocean and whose sole business was trade with the African coast. Similarly, the French in Senegal and the British in Sierra Leone, although they had heard vague reports about the conqueror, paid little attention to him.

In 1878 the French began consciously to occupy West Africa. It was their plan to advance from the upper Senegal River to Bamako on the Niger River. Thus they would pass through the Tukolor empire. Samori, who lacked the prestige of al-hajj Omar, the former leader of the Tukolor, and who seemed to be active far to the south of their planned area of penetration, apparently did not worry the new conquerors. . . .

Because the French had to have peace on the Niger, they lost their desired initiative against Samori.

[In March, 1886, Samori signed the treaty of Kényèba-Kura with the French. The agreement] was more concerned with peace and commerce than with the establishment of a French Protectorate. This pleased Samori, especially since he was then able to reopen trade in horses and firearms with the territory under French control. Although he had to forgo all rights to the lands north of the Niger and Tenkiso rivers, the Burè and the Manding in Kangaba were included on the condition that he would station no troops there. Samori showed his confidence in his new allies by entrusting to them his favorite son, Dyaulé-Karamogho. . . .

The treaty had raised a great cry in Paris. . . . [The] terms for peace were considered too lenient by the colonial party. The Ministry of Foreign Affairs demanded nothing less than a Protectorate which would both integrate Samori's lands into the French system and demonstrate to other nations the extent of France's hegemony in Africa. . . .

Samori did not expect any help from new allies, but he did expect the French to observe a benevolent neutrality . . . .

When Samori protested against frontier incidents, he was so sharply rebuffed that he believed he had no choice but to cede all the left bank of the Niger in order to gain time, not realizing that this would cut him off from Sierra Leone. Samori, therefore, signed the Treaty of Nyako on 21 February 1889, and Archinard made arrangements to meet him at Siguiri for formal ratification of the alliance. . . .

Then, in May 1889, Samori denounced the treaty and sent it back to Siguiri. This reversal ruined Archinard's dream of hemming in Sierra Leone and expanding along the Niger. . . .

Colonial historiography has helped to spread the legend that the rupture between Samori and the French began with the rejection of the Treaty of Nyako in 1889. This is not so. The Almami considered that his alliance with the French which dated from the Treaty of Kényèba-Kura in 1886 was still in effect, and a serious study of the events on the frontiers proves that civil, if not cordial, relations reigned until 1891 between the commanders of the French and Samorian forces. . . .

During 1896 Samori showed a strange lack of energy. It is evident that he was looking for a temporary solution and ways to prolong his respite and that he had given up the grand designs of the dyula revolution [by which is meant his Islamization of the Mandingo Empire]. This revolution was of no concern to the Senufo and other Voltaic people who now populated his new domains. Therefore, he was content to exact tribute to support his army. The army had been greatly reduced in size . . . but it had retained its cache of modern arms and the number of soldiers who had been trained in the European style grew every day.

Having been driven back again into the thick forest of the Dan mountains, Samori was surprised, on 29 September [1898] at Géulè (Guelémou) by French reconnaissance troops. These troops had crossed the devasted zone in the west while the Almami had been waiting for an attack from Touba. Thus Samori finally fell into enemy hands. Realizing that his position was hopeless Samori had earlier offered to give himself up on condition that he could live at Sanankoro as a private person. But his actual capture made French concessions unnecessary.

Because he had been deprived of capturing Samori, Trentinian was very harsh toward him. He solemnly notified the Almami at Kayes on 22 December that he would be deported to Gabon. The old man, believing that his earlier negotiations were still valid, felt that he had been tricked and attempted to commit suicide before embarking from Saint-Louis. Samori died of bronchial pneumonia on 2 June 1900, on the small island of Ndjolé in the middle of the Ogooué River in Gabon.

To his adversaries and the writers of colonial history, Samori was, despite his courage and loyalty, a slave merchant and a bloody tyrant—the very personification of evil. To young African leaders, he became one of the great heroes of the anticolonial struggle.

Neither of these two visions of the man is entirely accurate, but the second is closer to reality. Samori was essentially a man of battle and the builder of a state. His work answered the needs of a society in the midst of grave crisis. Events forced him to place himself in the path of the French colonizers. He then wasted most of his ability and strength in the continuous battle against them, even though that had not been his original purpose in assuming power. In fact, from the day on which his struggle against the French absorbed most of his time, the positive aspects of his work began to degenerate.

As a son of the Konyan, his first desire had been to save his own animistic society by regenerating it so that he could undertake the risks of the dyula revolution. But this was possible only through military means, and he soon began to make use of his tactical abilities and strategic genius, both of which were praised by the French. His superiority was manifested in 1885 in his struggle with Combes, and he was only deprived of the ultimate victory by the crushing technical superiority of his adversaries. The same tactical ability is seen in his politics. His policy was to accomplish his objectives through negotiation—not to use force unless all other means failed—but once compelled, he fought with the greatest obstinacy. . . .

It is clear that the action of Samori, in spite of its revolutionary aspect. belonged to the traditions of his society. His conservatism, however, surprises us—for example, his scrupulous respect for the established local chiefs and other notables. It is, therefore, quite difficult to see him as the forerunner of modern nationalism. On the other hand, it is evident that his uprooting and moving of large populations might have been, without his realizing it, the prelude to the upheavals of the colonial era.

His work was condemned to failure because, in spite of all his energy and clairvoyance, he could not make up for his people's technical backwardness.

"Invincible" Algiers falls to the French in 1830, *a prelude to Europe's partition of Africa.*

TIDE OF CONQUEST

A romanticized rendering of English and African partnership, following the Congress of Vienna's condemnation of the slave trade in 1815
BIBLIOTHEQUE NATIONALE

THE END OF SLAVERY

In 1839, *off Cuba, fifty-two African slaves, led by Cinquè (above), mutinied aboard the* Amistad. *The vessel reached the shores of Long Island, where the Africans, who had been illegally captured and sold to Cuban planters, won their freedom.*
NEW HAVEN COLONY HISTORICAL SOCIETY

The eighteenth century—Europe's self-proclaimed age of enlightenment—was also the heyday of the Atlantic slave trade. European nations themselves had little use for slaves, but their Caribbean possessions absorbed all the Africans who had survived the rigors of the middle passage. Under the whip they raised the sugar cane, tobacco, and cotton; these were sold in Europe, providing huge profits for a burgeoning class of colonial tycoons. However, as the new century approached, political and economic interests began to turn slowly but irrevocably toward abolition. The revolutionary egalitarianism emanating from France sparked Negro and mulatto uprisings in the French colony of Saint Domingue, which in 1804 became the independent black-ruled Republic of Haiti. In England, where the first signs of the Industrial Revolution were manifesting themselves, the economy was becoming less dependent on the importation of "king sugar" and more reliant on the exportation of manufactured goods. At the same time, amid a gathering tide of humanitarian liberalism, abolitionists were growing more vocal on both sides of the Atlantic. Sierra Leone and Liberia were founded in 1787 and 1822, respectively, as havens for free Negroes. In 1792 Denmark outlawed the slave trade, the first nation to do so. Britain followed suit in 1807, and for the next half century it maintained a naval force in West African waters to discourage the trade. Parliament banned slavery in 1833, but it would take the United States another thirty years and a civil war before its slaves would be emancipated. In Cuba and Brazil most of the enslaved would not win freedom until the 1880's.

In 1791, having failed to win from the French assembly civil rights and freedom for Haiti's blacks and mulattos, patriot Vincent Ogé returned home, as depicted in the print at right. He led an abortive rebellion and was executed for treason. Resistance leader Toussaint L'Ouverture (below) unified Haiti and improved life on the island before he was imprisoned by the French in 1802.

BIBLIOTHEQUE NATIONALE

The plight of human bondage is shown on the plaque of an English emancipation society.

JOSIAH WEDGWOOD AND SONS

LIBRARY COMPANY OF PHILADELPHIA

Below, American-born black president's mansion in Monrovia, Liberia, about 1840.

LIBRARY OF CONGRESS

Although Africa's white explorers made extravagant claims regarding their exploits, they surmounted many genuine physical dangers, as above.

BOTH: RADIO TIMES HULTON PICTURE LIBRARY

THE EXPLORERS

"The map of the interior regions [of Africa] is still a great white spot on which the geographer . . . has traced out with an uncertain hand a few names of unexplored rivers and doubtful nations." So wrote the founders of the African Association, established by a group of Englishmen in 1788, primarily to open up Africa's uncharted waterways. The main impetus behind the first phase of exploration, which dealt mostly with West Africa, was a well-meaning desire to discourage the slave trade through the introduction of "legitimate commerce" and Christianity. But by the 1850's disinterested probing had given way to exploitation. Most expeditions were now government financed. With the help of African guides, white explorers were "discovering" the natural wonders long known to Africans and were renaming them after European dignitaries and sites. David Livingstone, who went to South Africa in 1841 as a missionary, was blazing a trail across the continent as "Her Majesty's Consul for Inner and Undiscovered Africa." Like many of his fellow discoverers, he was the conscious agent of a government bent on conquest through exploration.

A resolute Henry M. Stanley poses with his solemn, young gunbearer.

John Speke, who "found" the Nile's source, runs from some Somali.
RADIO TIMES HULTON PICTURE LIBRARY

Dixon Denham, explorer of the central Sudan, pursues a giraffe.
SNELLING, *Tales of Travels*, 1831

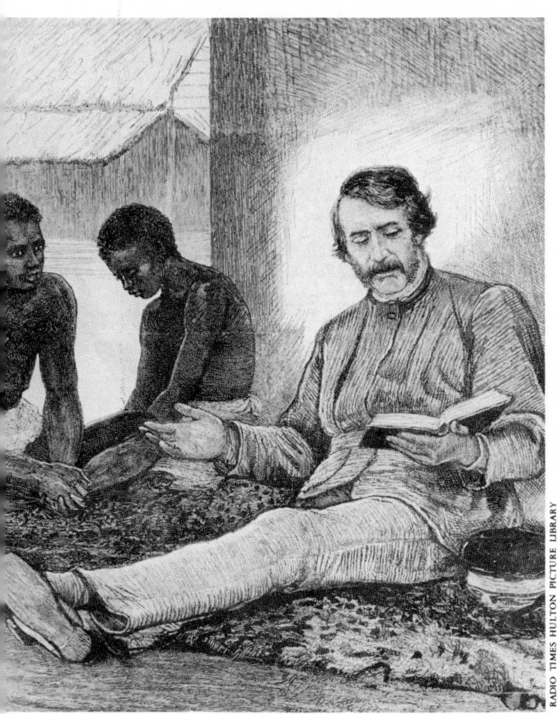

RADIO TIMES HULTON PICTURE LIBRARY

David Livingstone is shown here reading the Bible to his guides. The engraving was done from details given by Stanley, who found the ailing missionary-doctor at Ujiji on Lake Tanganyika in 1871. At Murchison Falls (right), twenty-two miles east of Lake Albert, the Victoria Nile plummets over cleft rocks into a misty gorge. Samuel Baker named them in 1864 for Roderick Murchison, president of the Royal Geographical Society.

BAKER, *The Albert Nyanza*, 1866

NO ROOM FOR THE AFRICANS

During the nineteenth century, when Muslim Africa was torn by jihads, largely against European dominators, the Bantu speakers were waging wars of resistance in southern Africa. For centuries the Bantu had been free to expand, notably in the fertile plains between the Drakensberg range and the Indian Ocean. After the 1770's their movements were impeded by the encroachment of Boers and English settlers. The Bantu fought back under great leaders such as Makana, Chaka, and Moshoeshoe, but in vain. By the mid-nineteenth century the white man was master. The discovery in 1867 of diamond deposits near what is now the city of Kimberley prompted the rise of a new class: a black proletariat, who were the virtual serfs of white industrialists. In 1891 a Lagos editor lamented: "A forcible possession of our land has taken the place of a forcible possession of our persons."

This engraving, from an 1848 issue of the Illustrated London News, *shows a group of Boer Trekkers coaxing their wagon train through the mountain country of the Xhosa.*

Illustrated London News, 1848–MANSELL COLLECTION

Armed only with traditional weapons, Xhosa fighters, like the lance bearer above, were the first Bantu speakers to clash with the Boers and the British of the Cape Colony.

CAPE ARCHIVES

Under the Mahdi, Sudanese warriors, like the hero at right, defeated Anglo-Egyptian forces at Khartoum in 1885; enraged, the British crushed them at Omdurman in 1898.

The Zulu below are descendants of the fierce warriors who under Chaka's leadership forged the Zulu nation and controlled much of southern Africa until the 1880's.

BOTH: LIBRARY OF CONGRESS–CARPENTER COLLECTION

Germany formally entered the Scramble at the Berlin West Africa Conference when Bismarck declared protectorates over four African territories: Togoland, Kamerun, South West Africa, and East Africa. Tanganyika (now Tanzania) was to be a resettlement area for the empire's surplus population, but, as elsewhere, the Germans had first to contend with native opposition. Not until they had defeated the

TANZANIA NATIONAL MUSEUM; RAPHO-GUILLUMETTE—MARC AND EVELYNE BERNHEIM

coastal Swahili did the task of holding this huge area become eased. Thereafter, the urban Swahili were brought into the colonial administration as policemen, clerks, translators, and soldiers, and made to function as the shock troops for Germany's penetration of the hinterland. In the painting above, by a Swahili artist, uniformed African mercenaries under white officers clash with ill-equipped inland people.

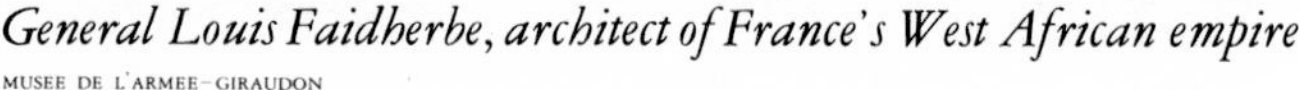

General Louis Faidherbe, architect of France's West African empire

MUSEE DE L'ARMEE–GIRAUDON

H. ROGER VIOLLET

GIRAUDON

African recruits, like the instructor and infantrymen below, swelled the ranks of the French colonial army. The Foreign Legion, several of whose veterans appear at left, was another vital arm of French imperialism.

H. ROGER VIOLLET

Abd al-Kader, bedecked with honorary medals at right, led Algeria's indigenous population in a jihad against the "infidel" French. Proud even in defeat, he hands over his scimitar to the Duc d'Aumale, governor general of Algeria, in the print opposite.

DOCUMENTATION FRANCAISE

THE GALLIC THRUST

France, anxious to restore its waning prestige, attacked Algiers in 1830. The city fell easily, but the Muslim Arabs and Berbers of the mountain fastnesses and desert fringes, who regarded the Christian French with hatred, rose in opposition. Under the leadership of Abd al-Kader, the son of a Muslim holy man, they waged a heroic war of resistance. By 1840 Al-Kader had molded the petty Berber chieftaincies of the Algerian interior into the most substantial polity the region had known for centuries. However, his empire soon conflicted with French dreams of glory. In 1847 he was forced to capitulate and was exiled to Syria. The Arab and Berber masses were a defeated people, whose land would be confiscated by the tens of thousands of European *colons* who flocked there. France tightened its grip on Senegal, which then comprised St. Louis, Gorée island, and several riverine posts. At the conclusion of Louis Faidherbe's governorship in 1865, France controlled most of the Senegal River, a springboard from which to build its West African empire.

AMERICAN MUSEUM OF NATURAL HISTORY

Ethiopian Emperor Menelik II (*left*), *who ruled from* 1889 *to* 1913, *was a reforming monarch, whose* 1896 *victory over the Italians at Adowa won him international respect. The Ethiopian painting opposite depicts scenes of this battle. Menelik's empress, who is popularly believed to have participated, carries a parasol as she rides on horseback into the fray. Saint George intercedes at top; in the center two Italians are emasculated.*

RADIO TIMES HULTON PICTURE LIBRARY

Below, African scouts in English service set fire to an Asante village in the war of 1873–1874.

MANSELL COLLECTION

THE WHITE MAN'S GREED

Throughout the nineteenth century the white man's greed propelled him deeper and deeper into Africa. Much of the continent was deemed climatically unsuitable for European settlement, but the lure of its raw materials proved irresistible. Some nations, such as Italy, were drawn by a thirst for glory. In 1896, on the eve of the battle of Adowa, its premier sent a dispatch to General Baratieri in Ethiopia: "We are ready for any sacrifice in order to save the honor of the army and the prestige of the Monarch." Italy's sacrifice was indeed great, for it lost over 7,500 men, and stalwart Ethiopia retained its cherished independence.

DEFEAT AND SUBMISSION

In 1892, after defining their respective zones of influence on the Gold and Ivory Coasts, France and Britain resumed their subjugation of the hinterland. That year the French finally occupied Abomey, and in 1898, after over sixteen years of guerilla opposition, they conquered Samori Touré's Mandingo empire. Meanwhile, the British were pursuing their drive against the Asante and preventing any alliance between their king, Prempeh, and Samori. In 1896 they occupied Kumasi, Prempeh's capital, humiliating and deporting him. Furthermore, in 1900 they demanded surrender of the Golden Stool, believed to contain the nation's spirit. This sacrilege provoked many months of warfare before England could make Asante a colony.

RADIO TIMES HULTON PICTURE LIBRARY

Above, King Prempeh and the queen mother submit to the British at Kumasi in 1896. Below, French troops prepare to exile Samori Touré, the proud man in the foreground. Opposite, Behanzin of Abomey sits for a royal portrait before his deportation in 1894.

H. ROGER VIOLLET

MUSEE DE L'HOMME, PARIS

Chapter Eleven

UNDER COLONIAL RULE

(c. 1884–1957)

by

George Shepperson

FROM THE WEST AFRICAN CONFERENCE OF BERLIN of 1884–1885 to the independence of Ghana in 1957 the history of Africa is one of terrifying complexity. The former set the stage for the partition of the continent among the powers of Europe in little more than ten years; the latter touched off the emergence of the new, modern Africa of independent states, also largely within a decade. To employ the adjective "terrifying" in this colonial context is not merely to evoke a sensationally journalistic element that was never far from the surface throughout this intricate story; nor is it a confession of the historian's failure to cope with a diverse mass of detail that often defies analysis and generalization.

There was, to be sure, a genuine touch of terror about relations between white and black in Africa during this three quarters of a century. It revealed itself in the obvious horrors of the European presence in Africa, such as Joseph Conrad witnessed during his journey into the Belgian Congo in 1890 and which he was to transmute into the terrifying tale, *Heart of Darkness.* It was to be seen in atrocity and counteratrocity in the many conflicts between European and African, such as the Maji Maji Rising in southern Tanzania against the Germans in 1905, which resulted in the death of some one hundred twenty thousand Africans. But this terror manifested itself, above all, in the harnessing of almost the whole of Africa, through the hectic period of the so-called Scramble for Africa.

Indeed, the leitmotiv of much of the history of Africa in this three quarters of a century is war; not the localized, so-called tribal wars of old Africa, of which Europeans spoke so disparagingly and often inaccurately when they were flush with the confidence of the virtues of their own civilization, but major wars, mainly of European origin. Five such wars provided a challenge and evoked a response from

ench officers survey a captured farmhouse, ruined during their "pacification" of Morocco about 1910.

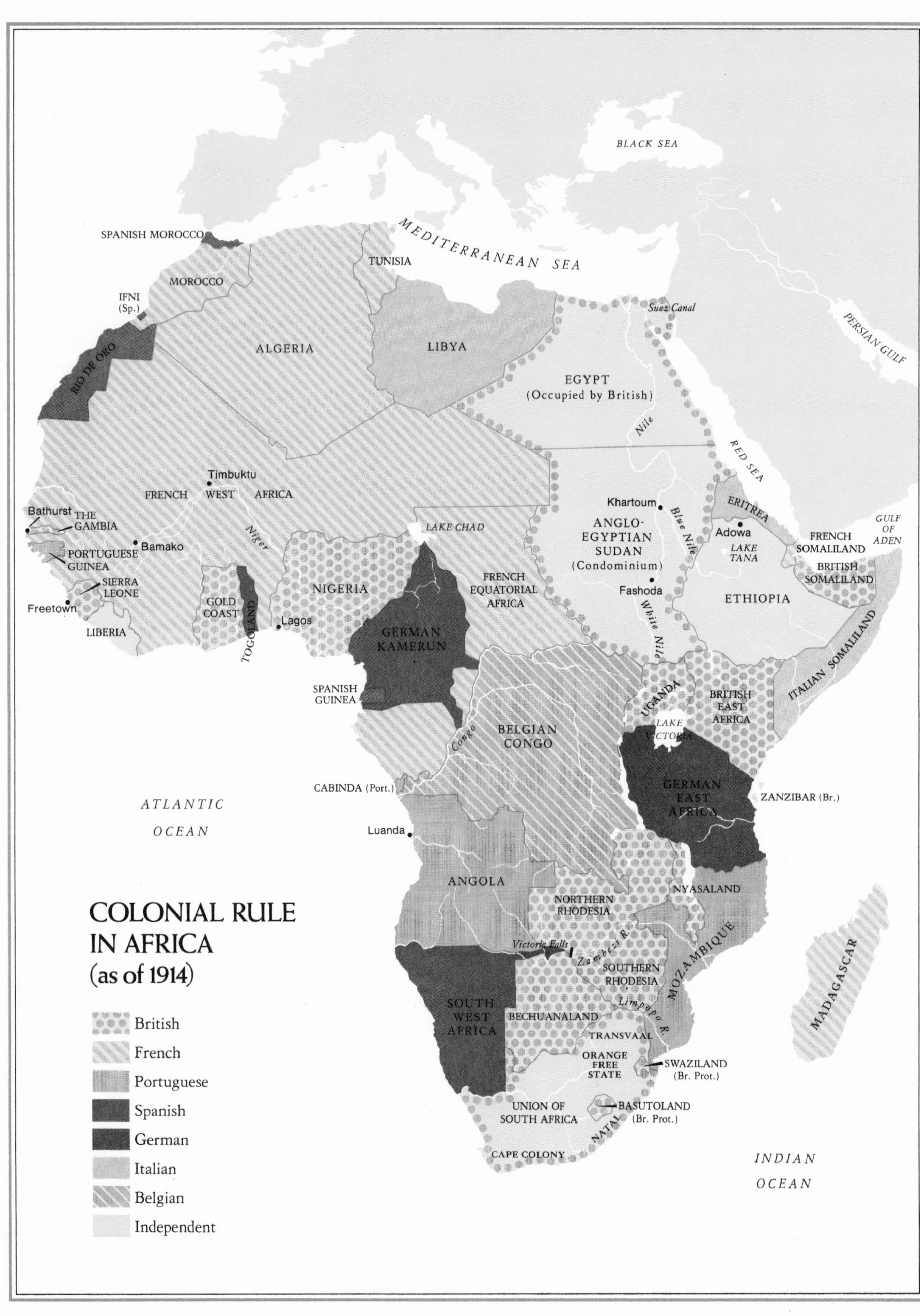
BLACK SEA
MEDITERRANEAN SEA
PERSIAN GULF
SPANISH MOROCCO
TUNISIA
MOROCCO
IFNI (Sp.)
ALGERIA
LIBYA
Suez Canal
RIO DE ORO
EGYPT (Occupied by British)
Nile
RED SEA
Timbuktu
FRENCH WEST AFRICA
Khartoum
Blue Nile
ERITREA
GULF OF ADEN
Bathurst
THE GAMBIA
LAKE CHAD
ANGLO-EGYPTIAN SUDAN (Condominium)
Adowa
LAKE TANA
FRENCH SOMALILAND
PORTUGUESE GUINEA
Bamako
Niger
BRITISH SOMALILAND
SIERRA LEONE
FRENCH EQUATORIAL AFRICA
Fashoda
Freetown
GOLD COAST
NIGERIA
ETHIOPIA
LIBERIA
TOGOLAND
Lagos
White Nile
GERMAN KAMERUN
ITALIAN SOMALILAND
SPANISH GUINEA
UGANDA
BRITISH EAST AFRICA
LAKE VICTORIA
Congo
BELGIAN CONGO
GERMAN EAST AFRICA
CABINDA (Port.)
ZANZIBAR (Br.)
ATLANTIC OCEAN
Luanda
ANGOLA
NYASALAND
NORTHERN RHODESIA
COLONIAL RULE IN AFRICA (as of 1914)
Victoria Falls
Zambezi R.
MOZAMBIQUE
SOUTHERN RHODESIA
MADAGASCAR
SOUTH WEST AFRICA
Limpopo R.
BECHUANALAND
TRANSVAAL
British
French
ORANGE FREE STATE
SWAZILAND (Br. Prot.)
Portuguese
Spanish
UNION OF SOUTH AFRICA
BASUTOLAND (Br. Prot.)
NATAL
German
CAPE COLONY
INDIAN OCEAN
Italian
Belgian
Independent

the people of Africa, whether they came from the sophisticated Islamic societies of the north, from the subsistence economies of central Africa, or from the countries of southern Africa that had experienced European penetration from the fifteenth century onward. These wars were the Franco-Prussian War, 1870–1871 (although it precedes the period discussed in this chapter, it must be noted because its role in the rearrangement of the European state system in the late nineteenth century was an important factor behind the partition of Africa); the war between the British and the Boers in South Africa, 1899–1902; the First World War, 1914–1918; the Italian invasion of Ethiopia, 1935–1936; and the Second World War, 1939–1945. They span the period of the rise and decline of European power in Africa. They pose the perennial questions in an African context: Is war entirely destructive? Is there not also a constructive element in it? They provide a convenient periodization for the complex history of Africa in the age of European colonial rule.

When the architect of the modern German state, Chancellor Otto von Bismarck, declared, "My map of Africa lies in Europe," he indicated, in his circuitous manner, the background to the conference he convened at Berlin from November 15, 1884, to February 25, 1885, to decide the fate of Africa. This West African Conference of Berlin, at which fourteen European countries and the United States of America were represented, is commonly looked upon as the starting point of the Scramble for Africa (*The Times* newspaper of London, indeed, had popularized this phrase in a leading article only two months before the conference began). Yet its roots lay in the previous fifteen years of European history—in particular, in the war between France and Prussia that led to the loss by France of the region of Alsace-Lorraine and to the proclamation of the German empire at Versailles in 1871. A humiliated France faced a new Germany, powerful but not completely convinced of its security. In the decade and a half that followed, Bismarck, the master diplomat, wanted to divert France's ambitions from the recovery of its lost provinces. The best way of doing this was to involve France in rivalries with other European states for overseas territories, especially in Africa.

The old empires of Portugal and Britain and the emerging new empires of Italy and Belgium were, of necessity, involved in the attempt to keep the balance of power in Germany's hands. To political drives were harnessed powerful economic forces: the emergence of industrially based economies throughout Europe, which sought new markets, areas for capital investment, and sources of raw materials overseas. Africa was a convenient field into which this political and economic imbroglio of Europe could extend itself. Although Africa's interior by the 1880's had been charted in considerable outline by European explorers, those parts that were in doubt provided excellent sources of controversy for the powers of Europe, especially Germany, France, and Britain. The extension of European rivalries to another chessboard sometimes had the effect of dissipating them, but more often of exacerbating them. The countries and people of Africa were hardly consulted in the matter, although, as recent historical researches have demonstrated, political and economic forces inside Africa had much to do with deciding where the main thrusts of the powers of Europe into Africa should be directed.

In particular, British and French rivalry in northern Africa converged on Egypt and its hinterland, in the early 1880's under the tenuous rule of the Ottoman empire. The British intervention in and occupation of Egypt in 1881–1882 coincided with the start of the Mahdiyya in the Sudan. The Mahdiyya began with the proclamation by Muhammad Ahmad, son of a boat builder near Khartoum, that he was the Mahdi, the messiah of Islam, who would cast out socioreligious corruption and restore the faith in all its pristine purity. At the same time, but at the other end of Africa, Britain, defeated by rebellious Boers at Majuba Hill on February 27, 1881, was forced to give up its control over the Transvaal. At both ends of Africa, therefore, as well as on the west and east coasts, European rivalries, under the influence of local African problems, were reaching a point of no return.

Bismarck's convening of the Berlin Conference had, no doubt, more than enough of the characteristically Machiavellian motivations of the Iron Chancellor. But his ostensible motive—and that of the powers represented at the conference—was to prevent a European war, and this was serious enough. Much that happened around the conference table at Berlin and in backroom bargaining in those thirteen weeks in 1884–1885 undoubtedly made more certain the Scramble for African territory and concessions by the powers of Europe. It could be argued that it prevented a European war in the mid-1880's, but only at the expense of partitioning and Balkanizing Africa and, ultimately, of ensuring the emergence of a major European war.

It must also not be forgotten that the Berlin Conference indicated a growing American interest in Africa. Some historians would claim that the creation of the so-called conventional basin of the Congo (by which the relatively free sphere of trade was extended beyond the geographical Congo

Meeting at the Berlin residence of Chancellor Otto von Bismarck in 1884, *the foreign ministers of fourteen European powers and the United States established ground rules for the future exploitation of the "dark continent." Africans were not invited or made privy to their decisions.*
CULVER

Basin to include the east coast between the boundaries of what is now southern Somalia and northern Mozambique) owed something to the East African commercial interests of the United States. Its representatives at the conference, by their emphasis on America's interests on the East African coast, ensured that these factors would not be overlooked. But the American Senate, under isolationist influences, did not ratify the General Act, as the resultant treaty was known; and United States' interests in the partition of Africa and the subsequent erection of modern types of colonial administration took the unofficial but nonetheless frequently influential forms of trade and investment, especially in the minerals of southern Africa and the Congo.

It was, indeed, the personal empire of King Leopold II of Belgium that profited most notably from the Berlin Conference. Its General Act led to Leopold's recognition as sovereign head of the Congo Free State, although the checking of British and Portuguese expansion in West and East Africa, French gains in West Africa, and the triumph of Bismarckian diplomacy were also important results. The cunning and avaricious Belgian king took every advantage through his own tortuous brand of diplomacy of the requirements of the conference that claims to colonies and protectorates on any part of the African coast line should be formally notified to the other powers that took part in the Berlin Conference and that such claims must be backed by an effective degree of authority. The calling at Brussels in 1890 of a second international conference on Africa to regularize and humanize the partition was used by Leopold to make a breach in the free-trade provisions of the Berlin Conference to the advantage of his Congo possession. By the mid-1890's the Congo Independent State, a vast area eighty times the size of Belgium, was a reality under the absentee regime of King Leopold.

The Congo Independent State included not only some of the most isolated, culturally traditional peoples of Africa but also the potentially rich rubber territory and wealthy copper country of Katanga. Others besides Leopold had their eyes on this fabulous region where for nearly forty years a Nyamwezi trader, Msiri, had been ruler, presiding from his capital at Bunkeya over a highly profitable commercial network that stretched from Luanda in the west to Zanzibar in the east.

Leopold's most powerful rival for the lordship of Katanga was Cecil Rhodes, the British mining magnate whose British South Africa Company had received a royal charter in 1889. Rhodes wanted Katanga as part of his mining empire in southern and central Africa; and he realized also that the area could be made into a main link in his dream of a "Cape-to-Cairo" corridor of British power, spanning the continent from south to north. Katanga at this time was an element in Rhodes' subsidization of British rule in Nyasa-

BOTH: BROWN BROTHERS

The Congo Free State, conceived as a "neutral" zone to be run by an international association in the interests of bringing science, civilization, and Christianity to the indigens, received the Berlin Conference's blessings. Belgium's King Leopold (left) soon took control, reaping fabulous personal profits through the sale of land and development rights. Scandalously little was reinvested in schools like that shown above.

land (modern Malawi), over which a British protectorate was defined and declared between 1891 and 1893. (It was known as British Central Africa between 1893 and 1907.) The territory, in Rhodes' opinion, could have become a useful link in a trade route from Katanga to the coast of East Africa. But the Belgian king outmaneuvered him; in 1891 one of Leopold's mercenaries shot Msiri, and the modern exploitation of Katanga's riches was started.

Seven years before, Leopold had been about to take into his service in the Congo the mystically minded British soldier of fortune Charles George Gordon, who had served the Ottoman empire between 1874 and 1880 in the Egyptian equatorial provinces and the Sudan. The rise of the Mahdiyya, however, had complicated British policy, particularly as a result of the rapid extension of Mahdist power in the Sudan during the next three years. Gordon was thus persuaded by the British government, which had made itself responsible for the administration of Egypt and its dependencies, to postpone his engagement with Leopold and to go out to Khartoum to evacuate the Turko-Egyptian garrisons that were threatened by Mahdist advances. A year later, on January 26, 1885, while Bismarck and the powers of Europe were attempting to settle the fate of Africa on paper in Berlin, the killing of Gordon by Mahdist forces in Khartoum demonstrated that the people directly involved were determined to have some say in Africa's future.

Shortly after the capture of Khartoum, the Mahdi died. Abdullahi, his general, followed him to power, and was known as the Khalifa, from the Arabic word meaning "successor." He established a strong secular administration that lasted thirteen years. Had the European partition of Africa not taken place, the government of the Mahdiyya in the Sudan, under the Khalifa's rule, might have continued much longer. But British fear of the threat to their strategic interests in Egypt brought an end to the Mahdiyya's rule. In 1896 an Anglo-Egyptian army under Lord Horatio Herbert Kitchener, the British commander, advanced into the Sudan, and in 1898 defeated the Mahdist forces at Omdurman. About twenty thousand Sudanese lost their lives.

Kitchener's services to the British empire in Africa did not end with the defeat of the Mahdiyya. He hastened two hundred miles to the south, with a large army, to the Sudanese city of Fashoda (now Kodok), where Commandant Jean-Baptiste Marchand had taken up a position with a force of French-African soldiers. France and Britain were poised on the brink of a war that seemed likely to be something much larger than a localized conflict in the Sudan. After several months the French gave way; and the so-called Fashoda incident of 1898 was solved in Britain's favor. The détente also signaled the closing of a protracted period of Anglo-French rivalry, especially in Uganda, where English

COMPAGNIE FINANCIERE DE SUEZ, PARIS

RADIO TIMES HULTON PICTURE LIBRARY

Despite steadfast opposition from Britain, the French completed the rebuilding and extension of the pharaonic canal across the hundred-mile Isthmus of Suez in 1869. The genius behind this feat of engineering and financing was Ferdinand de Lesseps (right), who in gaining the Egyptian viceroy's cooperation was insured a huge human labor force. But work went painfully slowly until 1864, when English and American protests against this new slavery embarrassed the French into devising steam-run machinery, including dredgers like those above.

Protestant and French Roman Catholic missionaries had been the chief protagonists, largely in Britain's favor. The British government's fear that the headwaters of the Nile would pass into foreign control and that this, in its turn, would jeopardize Britain's suzerainty over Egypt and the Suez Canal was, if only for a moment, greatly diminished.

The same could not be said at this time for the Italians, who two years earlier had received the most resounding defeat that any European power experienced in Africa during the Scramble. In 1896 Italy had seemed in a strong position vis-à-vis Ethiopia, an ancient Christian state that, in spite of a distinctly centralizing process, from the middle of the nineteenth century onward suffered from the problems of maintaining control over a difficult terrain and from traditional border warfare with its African neighbors. To avenge a border defeat in 1887 by Ethiopian troops, the Mahdists invaded western Ethiopia, and in battle with them in 1889 the Ethiopian emperor Yohannes IV was killed.

Meanwhile, the Italians had been gaining: they held a substantial section of the Red Sea coast bordering on Ethiopia; and from 1886 had shared in the divisions of the sultan of Zanzibar's possessions on the mainland of East Africa by claiming a large portion of the Somali coast adjacent to eastern Ethiopia. Yohannes IV's successor, Menelik II, signed with the Italians on May 2, 1889, the Treaty of Wichale (Ucciali), by which he surrendered some of Ethiopia's northern territory; the area was organized the following year by the Italians as the colony of Eritrea.

Menelik believed that this was the last concession he would have to make to the Italians and that the treaty gave him international recognition. Italy, however, used its interpretation of the treaty to notify the other Berlin Conference participants that it claimed a protectorate over Ethiopia. Protesting to the European governments, Menelik abrogated the whole treaty in 1893. Italy invaded Ethiopia two years later in an attempt to compel Menelik to accept its protectorate. But by this time he had strengthened Ethiopian political unity and had managed to acquire a larger number of firearms. At Adowa, on March 1, 1896, an Ethiopian army of over 80,000 men, outnumbering the Italian forces by about four to one, inflicted a heavy defeat on them: about 6,000 dead, 1,500 wounded, and 3,000 prisoners of war.

Italy was forced to admit that the Treaty of Wichale was void and that Ethiopia was a sovereign and independent state. This gave Menelik the opportunity to return to his mission of extending the boundaries of his kingdom to the south—enlarging them to such an extent that it has been said that he, too, was a participant in the Scramble for Africa. As one of the first occasions in modern times when a non-European army had inflicted a major defeat on a European-led force, the Ethiopian victory also gave heart to Africans all over the continent at a moment when so many of them were losing their ancestral lands and prestige to the might of the white man.

The victory at Adowa in 1896 became an element in what many whites toward the end of the nineteenth century were coming to call "Ethiopianism," by which they meant the Africans' political and religious reaction to European conquest, anticipating pan-Africanism. Many white men at this time, particularly in southern Africa, were fearful that a "Black Peril" would sweep them out of the continent. They believed that this challenge to their supremacy was manifesting itself, to begin with, in the reorganization of African churches, which were breaking away from European tutelage and putting themselves under independent African control. These bodies often called themselves Ethiopian churches, not because they claimed any affiliation with the ancient Coptic Christian Church of Ethiopia but because, in the King James version of the Bible, Black Africa, following the Greek, was called Ethiopia.

The first so-called Ethiopian Church was established in South Africa by black separatist Wesleyans four years before the battle at Adowa. After 1896, therefore, the "Ethiopianism" of the often politically conscious separatist Churches in southern Africa could take pride in the successful militancy of the territorial Ethiopians as well as in their own "Ethiopian" religious self-assertion. The white men, for their part, feared that the day of white domination was coming to an end. Even before the Scramble for Africa drew to a close and Europeans got ready to consolidate and administer their hastily acquired possessions, both the protonationalism of the Ethiopian Church leaders and the real nationalism, bloodied in battle, of Menelik and his followers were forces to be reckoned with. Within little more than half a century they would grow into a movement that would oust Europeans from the political control of the greater part of Africa.

But to this trend there was one great exception, the other nationalism that was growing in southern Africa, the nationalism of the Afrikaners, or as the British and others called them, the Boers. The defeat of the British at Majuba Hill in 1881 did not stop what seemed to the Afrikaners to be a relentless determination on the part of Great Britain to drive on until it had swallowed up the whole of South Africa. The Afrikaners' isolated, agrarian way of life, bolstered by a devout, if often too rigidly inspired, biblical culture, was at odds with the cosmopolitan capitalism that the discovery of gold in the Witwatersrand in 1886 had encouraged in the Boer's South African Republic (as the Transvaal was then called). The British were in an ideal position to profit from these discoveries. Unlike the Boers, they were a people who were accustomed to the intricacies and intrigues of international capitalism; and in the person of Cecil Rhodes they had a financier and a leader who had the capital, knowledge, ruthlessness, and luck to take every advantage of the gold strikes in the southern Transvaal.

Also bolstering the position of British adventurers and speculators in the Transvaal was the establishment, the previous year, of a British protectorate over Bechuanaland (modern Botswana). Lord Salisbury, the British prime minister, had grabbed this arid territory between German South West Africa and the Transvaal in order to gain access not only to the Boer Republic but also to the territories to the north, where many, including Rhodes, believed that a second Witwatersrand, ripe for plundering, was to be found.

Rhodes' British South Africa Company in 1890 pushed its pioneer column of white settlers into the lands north of the Limpopo River. Within six years Rhodesia was created. The great Ndebele chief, Lobengula, died after the defeat of his army in 1893. The Ndebele and the Mashona, angry at the loss of their lands and cattle to the victorious white settlers, made a last effort at resistance in 1896, but gave way to superior fire power.

To many Afrikaners in the Transvaal it must have seemed that Rhodes and his English-speaking followers were all around them, particularly when, from 1890 to 1896, he became the prime minister of the Cape Colony. Rhodes' ideal of a union of all white men south of the Zambezi did not appeal to the majority of the Boers who, although they had ingrained ideas of white supremacy, preferred to live there on their own terms. The Boer president of the South African Republic, Paulus Kruger, and his people angered British immigrants into the Transvaal by taxing them heavily and by making it difficult for them to get the vote.

Rhodes was incensed. With the foreknowledge of the imperialist-minded British Colonial Secretary Joseph Chamberlain and other powerful figures in Britain and South Africa, he supported a sudden invasion of the Transvaal from Bechuanaland in 1895 under the leadership of his lieutenant, Dr. Leander Starr Jameson. The Jameson Raid was a fiasco, easily stopped by the Boers. Rhodes fell from power in the Cape Colony, and while the Fashoda incident was in progress in 1898 far to the north, Britain and the Boers stood at the brink of war.

By 1898, however, the Scramble for the greater part of Africa was largely complete. The French had taken the lion's share of territory, particularly in the north, the Sahara

BROWN BROTHERS

Paulus Kruger (right) devoted his life to the cause of Afrikaner resistance. Elected president of the South African Republic in 1883, he led his state inexorably toward the Boer War, which began in October, 1899. Initial Afrikaner successes were reversed within two months, when British reinforcements landed. Despite the stubborn defense waged by the Boer commandos (at left), Kruger's capital at Pretoria fell the following June. A peace accord was signed in May, 1902.

CULVER

regions, and West Africa. In 1894 Timbuktu fell to them, and in 1896 Say (in the western portion of the modern Niger Republic). And, two years later, their advance down the Niger succeeded in defeating and exiling Samori, the Muslim Mandingo leader whose determined resistance to the French had made him the hero of many African peoples in the huge area between the basin of the Upper Volta and the Niger sources. But Britain was not without compensations in West Africa. Sir George Goldie's Royal Niger Company, which was chartered in 1885, helped to push British power into the Nigerian hinterland; and from its existing coastal possessions, especially in the northward thrust against the Asante of the Gold Coast, Great Britain extended an already sizable empire.

Germany, meanwhile, taking advantage of the bargaining positions obtained by Bismarck, emerged from the Scramble with a sizable empire. It spread-eagled across Africa, from Togo and Kamerun in West Africa, through the extensive possessions of German South West Africa (which, by its closeness to the Transvaal and the obvious sympathy of the Germans to Afrikaner nationalism, was a constant source of worry to the British at this time) to German East Africa. German East Africa's common borders with what later became the British colonies of Kenya and Uganda were defined in a series of agreements in 1890. By this same treaty British claims to Zanzibar were also recognized. A year later Britain and Portugal agreed on their Nyasaland and Rhodesian borders; and Portugal, in spite of evident internal weaknesses, succeeded in maintaining its claim to substantial segments of the vast territories in western and eastern Africa, which, with little effective government in the hinterland, it had insisted on calling its own for three centuries.

It seems hardly accidental, then, that in 1898, at this final stage of the European partition, the Anglo-French writer Hilaire Belloc published *The Modern Traveller*, a satire on the Scramble, a kind of epic poem in reverse, in a sequence of caustic couplets of which the best known are those famous lines that sum up both the confidence and the basic insecurity of the Scramblers:

Whatever happens we have got
The Maxim Gun, and they have not.

The limitations of the Maxim Gun, however, had been demonstrated in the Jameson Raid. A semiautomatic weapon that could create havoc amongst the close formations of Ndebele warriors, and whose praises could be sung by the English officer Frederick Lugard for the "moral effect" of its "long-distance shooting" and its "apparent ubiquity" in the conquest of Uganda, had proved ineffective against the Afrikaners. These skillful sharpshooters did not offer the same kind of target, for they fought a largely guerilla resistance, utilizing every nook and cranny of the land in which they were born. It was this dogged nationalism, harnessed to an almost inborn skill with horse and rifle, that enabled them to stand against the might of the British empire in the Boer War of 1899–1902. The consequences of this war for Africa were profound.

The conflict was precipitated by the deliberate attempts

of Sir Alfred Milner, the British high commissioner in South Africa, to incite the South African Republic to war. The Transvaalers were supported by their fellow Afrikaners in the Orange Free State. Indeed, modern Afrikaner nationalism was consolidated in the fight against Britain. The protracted war led to British reprisals against the Boers, particularly the burning of their farms and the herding of their women and children into concentration camps. The Boers surrendered their independence in the Peace of Vereeniging of May 31, 1902. But, in an attempt to conciliate them, the British bestowed on the Afrikaners in the Transvaal and the Orange Free State the right to decide whether or not the vote should be given to the indigenous Africans. In accordance with their white supremacist traditions, the Boers decided in the negative; and an opportunity was lost to bring about peaceful political change among the nonwhites of South Africa. This British compromise with Boer attitudes continued, helped by former Afrikaner leaders such as Jan Christiaan Smuts and Louis Botha, who were prepared to meet the British more than halfway in order to preserve essential Boer interests. When the four South African provinces united in 1910, it was clear that the block to African political advancement, which had been established at Vereeniging, was to be maintained and, indeed, extended. The Union Act of 1910, while preserving the franchise for qualified Africans at the Cape, ensured that they would have no political rights in the former Boer republics and in Natal. And it also stipulated that not even in the Cape, in spite of all its liberal traditions, should an African be able to stand for Parliament. The Afrikaners may have lost the Boer War on the battlefield, but like the Southerners of the Confederacy in America, they appear to have won it in the council chamber.

A further consequence of the Boer War was that it showed once again how African issues and European diplomacy intertwined and stretched almost to breaking point. This had been seen in an event that was a minor cause of the Boer War and a manifestation of acute tensions in Anglo-German relations: the dispatch of a telegram on June 3, 1896, from Kaiser Wilhelm of Germany to President Kruger congratulating him on his success in suppressing the Jameson Raid. Looking back on the Boer War, behind the scenes as well as at the overt pattern of assistance and sympathy that was given to the combatants, it is possible to see it as a kind of rehearsal for the First World War.

Out of the Boer War came the stimulus to the first important analysis of that imperialism of which the Scramble for Africa had been a leading but not an isolated example.

Jan Smuts, prime minister of South Africa, regarded the racial problem as an "intolerable burden" to be deferred for future solution.

BROWN BROTHERS

In the year of the Treaty of Vereeniging, the English author John A. Hobson produced his seminal work, *Imperialism: A Study*. Nikolai Lenin, the ideologist for many of the responses of today's Third World to European colonialism, acknowledged the importance of Hobson's book for his own influential *Imperialism: The Highest Stage of Capitalism* (1917). Hobson spent the summer and autumn of 1899 in South Africa, and he used his experiences and his meditations on them not only for a book entitled *The War in South Africa* (1900) but also for his masterpiece, *Imperialism*. Recent scholars have been critical of Hobson's economic interpretation of the Anglo-Boer conflict, but no student of the colonial age in Africa can afford to neglect it.

Many Africans could not avoid noticing that the Boer War was a major breach in white unity in Africa; but most of them were in no position to take advantage of this for the advancement of their own emerging nationalist movements. They could, however, draw from it conclusions that were often highly embarrassing for the colonial powers. As one African nationalist could later write: "We reason that if the British Government were so generous with the Dutch, will they not also see to it that we of British Africa have just peace and educational treatment, such as the good missionary pioneers assured us of and which we still confidently look for?"

This was the voice of an African who was prepared to reason with his colonial masters. And, to be sure, this was largely the spirit of the first pan-African conference at which thirty-one delegates, mainly from America and the

The French Foreign Legion, composed largely of European volunteers, was established in 1831 for the purpose of pacifying Algeria. With Saharan forts like that shown, it developed into a fierce instrument for the maintenance of order throughout France's restive African empire.
LIBRARY OF CONGRESS, CARPENTER COLLECTION

West Indies, met in London in July, 1900, to discuss the many problems that confronted men of African descent everywhere as the new century opened. One issue that concerned the delegates was the conflict that had broken out between 1896 and 1898 in Sierra Leone; there, the British, consolidating their rule and imposing relatively heavy taxes on African dwellings, stung many Africans into resistance. Their opposition was stamped out, often with brutality (the systematic razing of African villages was one method). And the delegates to the first pan-African conference protested to Queen Victoria against the treatment of nonwhites in South Africa and Rhodesia. Their feelings were summed up in an "Address to the Nations of the World" that was drafted by the Afro-American scholar W.E.B. Du Bois, in which he first made his famous prophetic statement: "The problem of the twentieth century is the problem of the color line."

Elsewhere in Africa, while the Boer War was being fought, the colonial powers were stamping out much of the old-style resistance to the imposition of their new order. In 1900 the French defeated and killed Rabih, an Arab soldier from the Sudan. He had conquered Bagirmi and much of eastern Bornu, where he had established a slave-raiding state and defied French power in West Africa. By this victory, which came after a long and fierce series of campaigns, the French united their West African and equatorial empires.

From 1898 to 1900, in bitter warfare, the British eradicated the last Asante resistance to their rule in the Gold Coast. And having halted by 1898 Banyoro attempts to stop their expansion in Uganda, they made the Uganda Agreement of 1900. As a not uncommon consequence of European rule in Africa, the settlement favored one group of Africans (in this instance, the Baganda) over another, thereby setting in motion a train of future difficulties for European and African alike. And, although the British had defeated the Mahdiyya in the Sudan, another Mahdi declared himself in British Somaliland in 1899. During the next two decades he would gain virtual control over much of greater Somalia. To the colonialists, he was the Mad Mullah; to his countrymen, he was Said Muhammad and a national hero.

By the end of the period of the Boer War, however, the development of modern communications and economies based on Western models in Europe's colonial possessions —a notable example was the Kenya-Uganda railway—presaged the end of much of the old African order, which had neither the resources nor the communications to match the accomplishments of new conquerors. Although Morocco and Tripolitania were independent at the start of the twentieth century, by the outbreak of World War I in 1914 most of Morocco had been swallowed up by France, with a small portion going to Spain, and Tripolitania passed under Italian domination. Only the Afro-American state of Liberia and proud Ethiopia remained independent.

The characteristic patterns of European colonial administration were established in Africa in the two decades before the First World War: Portuguese "assimilation"; German rational but ruthless "scientific" development; French attempts to create an African elite closely tied to the metro-

Western education, with its potential for stirring discontent, was dispensed sparingly during the colonial era. Students, like those above attending Gordon Memorial College (founded in 1904 and the forerunner of the University of Khartoum), were being trained to serve their various European overlords. But many were also becoming nationalists, members of an elite who sought to borrow Western ideas and technology and apply them to an independent Africa.

LIBRARY OF CONGRESS

politan culture; Belgian barefaced exploitation (at least until an international outcry against Leopold II's methods forced the Belgian nation in 1908 to assume direct responsibility for the Congo); and British pragmatism, drawing upon three centuries of British experience of ruling India, respecting—too often overpaternalistically—the local African cultures and their traditional rulers. The combination, and the conflict, of principle and expediency was best seen in Africa in the British method of indirect rule through traditional chiefs and potentates, of which the outstanding example was the fusion of northern and southern Nigeria in 1914 into a viable but volatile state under the watchful eye of its first governor general, the high priest of indirect rule, Sir Frederick Lugard.

Road, rails, reading, writing, modern medicine, technology, Christianity, and commerce pushed relentlessly into Africa in these years. On both sides of the Sahara many Africans were won over to the charms of the European way of life. It was, to be sure, essential for the colonial powers to win them over because they could not administer their vast territories without the assistance of literate Africans accustomed to the white man's ways and wishes. Nevertheless, many Africans remained unconvinced of the desirability of the new European order. The Maji Maji Rising in German East Africa in 1905 was an outstanding example of this. In German South West Africa the resistance of the Herero and other African peoples from 1904 to 1906 led to the destruction of the Herero in the course of German reprisals. In Angola in 1913 there were extensive risings against Portuguese rule. In the French island of Madagascar the Malagasy people continued their resistance to the rule of the French and their African allies. The last Zulu revolt against the white man in South Africa took place in 1906. A complex web of the resistance of Islamic peoples was spun across North Africa; this embarrassed France, Italy, and Spain. And, in the British-occupied countries of Egypt and the Sudan, the situation was by no means settled, as discontent matured during the First World War, and revolt against the British broke out in Egypt between 1919 and 1920. As if not to be outdone by men of darker skins, a group of pro-German Boers who had still not made their peace with Great Britain revolted in South Africa in 1913.

The First World War rearranged the formal pattern of European colonialism in Africa. Parts of Germany's Togoland and Kamerun were divided between Britain and France, and Germany's East African possessions were split between Britain (receiving Tanganyika) and Belgium (receiving Ruanda-Urundi). World War I also dragged thousands of Africans into a major international conflict against their own choice, dashing the hopes raised by the Berlin Act of 1885. The signatories had then agreed that in time of war among European powers the African territories would be neutralized and African people spared from the kind of modern conflict, of which there had been a foretaste in the Franco-Prussian War.

Although many Germans in East Africa feared that the coming of war into their colony would touch off another African revolt akin to the terrible Maji Maji Rising, the commander of their forces, General Paul von Lettow-Vorbeck, was determined to fight the British in order to embarrass their war effort in Europe. For four years, with remarkable skill, his army resisted combined British and West, East, and South African forces. And Lettow-Vorbeck himself was still fighting when the news of the German capitulation in Europe reached him in 1918. Throughout the East African campaign the armies relied largely on African porters for their communications, as motorized transport was not suited to the difficult terrain. Many of these porters, especially those from Nyasaland and Kenya, went through considerable hardships, and both they, and later their sons, became increasingly critical of the Europeans. The grievances of the African military carriers of the First World War, indeed, were an important factor in the subsequent emergence of African nationalism.

It was curious, however, that the dispersal of the larger part of the West's armies on the European continent between 1914 and 1918 was not made the occasion for a widespread intensification of African resistance to European rule. Certainly, in northern Africa, where an Islamic power, Turkey, was at war with Britain, France, and Italy, the opportunity was taken to embarrass them; particularly troublesome was the Sanusiyya brotherhood, which accepted Turkish support in its own nationalist drive to wrest Libya from the Italian colonial rule. But in tropical Africa resistance was the exception rather than the rule. Many Africans seemed stunned by the sight of fighting among white men, who had come into their countries under the banner of the Prince of Peace. As one Christian missionary witness put it: "They can't understand the war, and ask such questions as: 'Why have the Christian countries gone to war? Have the evil spirits got into the hearts of Kings?' "

In West and East Africa, apart from small disturbances—some of which were more the continuation of traditional grievances than a direct response to the war—the outstanding African militant reaction to it was the rising against the British in Nyasaland led by the pastor of an independent African Baptist Church, John Chilembwe, who had been educated in the United States at Virginia Theological Seminary in Lynchburg, Virginia. Even Chilembwe's rising in 1915 was as much, if not more, the result of grievances against harsh practices by Europeans, particularly planters, in Nyasaland as it was the consequence of the coming of the 1914 war; and it was put down quickly with few casualties on either side. Nevertheless, Chilembwe protested against the war in no uncertain terms: "Let the rich men, bankers, titled men, storekeepers, farmers and landlords go to war and get shot. Instead the poor Africans who have nothing to own in this present world, who in death leave only a long line of widows and orphans in utter want and distress are invited to die for a cause which is not theirs." Chilembwe's movement, moreover, represented something of a break with the traditional, tribal revolts against European rule in Africa; and it stands out not only as an indication of the disturbing effect of the 1914–1918 World War on Africans but also as a foretaste of the new type of African discontent. The point, indeed, was driven home in Norman Leys' *Kenya*, published in 1924. In one of the first important books to emerge from World War I, Leys predicted that nationalist movements would increasingly disturb the continent unless Europeans took the opportunity to reform their colonial rule and to live up to the promises implicit in their Christian and democratic ideologies.

The employment of African troops in European armies, whether as labor battalions, as with South Africa, or as combatants, as in the case of the French Senegalese soldiers, opened the eyes of many Africans to the contradiction between European principle and practice. And many of the two hundred thousand Afro-American soldiers who fought in Europe during the First World War experienced similar disillusion. The ground, indeed, was being prepared for a pan-African approach to the problems of peoples of African descent everywhere.

Leadership was not lacking. There was the fiery Jamaican Marcus Garvey, who had taken his Universal Negro Improvement Association and African Communities League to the United States in 1916; the scholarly Afro-American W.E.B. Du Bois, who had played an important part in the first pan-African conference of 1900; and Blaise Diagne, Senegalese member of the French Chamber of Deputies in Paris, who was given special responsibility by the French during the World War for the recruitment of black soldiers. Diagne's position in France contrasted strikingly with the situation in British Africa, where it was unthinkable that a black man should become a member of a European legislative assembly.

When Du Bois was sent to Europe in 1919 by the National Association for the Advancement of Colored People of the United States to inquire into the grievances of black American troops, it was the influential Blaise Diagne who obtained permission for a second pan-African conference to be held that year in Paris. The congress continued, in the new circumstances of the postwar world, the criticisms of European colonial rule that had been launched by the 1900 conference. And although, like the earlier gathering, it did not ask for African political independence, it insisted that "the natives of Africa must have the right to participate in the Government as fast as their development permits." Du Bois later claimed that the 1919 congress influenced the League of Nations in its mandates system, by which the Allied Powers planned to parcel out the enemy colonial territories among themselves. However, a few other advanced thinkers hoped for a more fundamental approach to the African problem than the League's mandates system: nothing less than a descrambling of Africa. Du Bois favored the establishment of a genuine system of international trusteeships for African underdeveloped countries in which a part would also be played by peoples of African descent settled in other continents.

The following year Garvey's organization arranged in New York a massive thirty-one-day convention at which Marcus Garvey was elected Provisional President of Africa. It was a grandiloquent and unrealistic title; but it indicated his power over many disillusioned blacks in America (some of whom hoped to participate in Garvey's schemes for the settlement of "Negroes" from the New World in Africa). It reveals now, with the insights of recent historical research, that the influence of the Universal Negro Improvement Association, with its defiant assertion of black nationality and its unashamed adherence to black cultural virtues, was greater than has been commonly realized. The 1920 Garveyite convention issued a "Declaration of Rights of the Negro Peoples of the World." It was a moving appeal for a place in the sun for the black man; and it illustrates the attraction of Garveyism, with its perfervid belief in the "African personality," for men of African descent all over the world. It was not accidental that Kwame Nkrumah, the first president of an independent Ghana, declared that during his student period in the United States in the 1930's and 1940's the philosophy and opinions of Marcus Garvey influenced him more than anything else.

Both wings of the pan-African movement, the Garveyite and the Du Bois, suffered not only from factionalism and the feud between their leaders but also from the opposition of Blaise Diagne. In 1921 he refused to condemn French colonial policy, claiming that of all the powers France alone gave constitutional and social equality to its African citizens. With declining support but a nonetheless determined stance, Du Bois and Garvey continued their opposition to European imperialism in Africa in a sequence of Pan-African and Universal Negro Improvement Association conferences and other activities up until the eve of the Second World War.

By 1939, however, a new generation of African politicians indicated that the leadership of nationalism was moving firmly into the hands of native-born organizers and ideologists. But the acceleration of nationalism immediately after the First World War is even more remarkable. To be sure, this indigenous movement started well before the 1914–1918 war, as the life of the talented African bishop of the Niger Delta pastorate, James Johnson, illustrates. Johnson lived from 1836 to 1917, and his pro-African activities and attitudes anticipated much subsequent Africanism, although he was influenced entirely by a West African environment.

Another foretaste of Africanism was provided by the meetings of the National Congress of British West Africa in 1920, 1923, 1925, and 1929 at Accra, Freetown, Bathurst, and Lagos respectively. And, although French colonial administration imposed tight controls on political activities in its overseas possessions, African students in Paris developed a series of militant groups. In this they were often influenced by Marxist thought. The death in 1934 of the paternalist and pro-French Blaise Diagne and the emergence among French-speaking Africans of the pro-black philosophy and poetry of Negritude (a literary movement stressing the importance of black, African values) were also spurs to their growth.

In Kenya opposition to the white settlers' appropriation of land and to their oppressive labor policy led, as early as 1922, to the formation of the East African Association, under Kikuyu leadership. Jomo Kenyatta, who went to Britain in the 1930's to agitate on behalf of East Africans, especially the Kikuyu people, became involved in the association. He wrote that its members were driven underground, where they developed methods of conspiratorial organization: "Forbidden to hold meetings, the members divided into groups of three and four, kept in touch with each other secretly, and continued their work of protest and organization. The Africans of Kenya had their Maquis long before Hitler appeared on the European scene." These words display both the spirit and the techniques that a generation later continued in the so-called Mau Mau insurrection, which erupted in Kenya in 1951.

Similarly, the spirit that was displayed in the Egyptian revolt against the British in 1919 and 1920 forced from the colonial government a measure of independence for Egypt in 1922; and in 1936 the Anglo-Egyptian treaty stipulated that British troops were to be confined to the Suez Canal zone. All over Africa, under the stimulus of the economic depression of the 1930's and the democratic and counter-democratic currents then moving with increasing momentum around the world, organizations demanding social and economic justice and greater autonomy were springing up with a frequency often bewildering to all concerned, rulers and ruled.

In South Africa, despite—and, indeed, because of—the increasing restrictions placed on the movement and freedom of expression of nonwhites, attempts were made at political and economic organization. The South African Native National Congress, founded in 1912, was the first congress movement of its kind in Africa. And in 1919, under the leadership of a migrant worker from Nyasaland, Clements Kadalie, the Industrial and Commercial Workers Union of Africa was started. It grew to a membership of two hundred thousand; and by 1926 it had achieved a degree of militancy rare among African workers at that time. But white men in South Africa sprang to the defense of their own "supremacy" system. In 1934 Generals Jan Christiaan Smuts and James Hertzog formed the United Party, which was to remain in power until 1948. It was then superseded by the still more segregationist Afrikaner National Party, which legislated for outright apartheid. Yet the tendency toward apartheid in South Africa was apparent at least as early as 1936, when the United Party introduced the Natives Representation Act. This legislation swept away the limited multiracial democracy whereby qualified non-Europeans had been able to register as voters on the common roll with whites in the Cape Province. By the mid-1930's, therefore, the leadership of African political movements for greater independence and democracy was clearly passing from South Africa and was moving north. Meanwhile, men such as Nnamdi Azikiwe of Nigeria and Léopold Senghor of Senegal, who were to play leading parts in the securing of independence after the Second World War, were sharpening their wits for the struggle by obtaining an education overseas in Europe and America.

The mid-1930's were for African nationalists, at home and abroad, dark days. Ethiopia, the oldest independent African state, with its ancient history and Christian culture, was invaded and conquered by Italy, then under the brash and brutal Fascist order of Benito Mussolini. Even before the coming of the xenophobic leader, Italy had never been reconciled to its defeat at Adowa in 1896. But it was in no position to take revenge until its war with the Sanusiyya in Libya, which lasted from 1912 to 1931, was at an end. On the eve of the Italian invasion Ethiopia had just received its first modern constitution. The charter anticipated the increasing modernization of the country at the hands of its own people, assisted but not dominated by foreign advisers. Its architect was Haile Selassie (formerly Ras Taffari Makonnen), who had also brought Ethiopia into the League of Nations in 1923. He had shown his independent spirit when he denounced Britain and Italy before the League. Without consulting Ethiopia, the two powers had decided to support each other in plans to construct a dam at Lake Tana and a railway from Eritrea to Italian Somaliland. In 1928 Haile Selassie signed a treaty of friendship with Italy. It proved of no avail.

As early as 1933 the Italians had decided to conquer Ethiopia. An excuse for invasion was found in a border incident at Walwal in December, 1934; and on October 2, 1935, the Italian armies crossed into Ethiopian territory. The Ethiopians experienced the full onslaught of modern weapons, from aerial bombardment to the spraying of poisonous gas over soldiers and civilians alike. Haile Selassie appealed to the League of Nations for action against the Italians; and in a historic speech at its headquarters at Geneva on June 30, 1936, three months after the decisive battle in which the Italians had defeated his army, he asked: "Are the States going to set up a terrible precedent of bowing before force?"

An Italian empire of Eritrea, Somaliland, and, finally, Ethiopia had been created, but nearly forty years after the Scramble for Africa and at a period when most other European powers were reforming their colonial policies and, on paper at least, looking forward to ultimate African independence. Winston S. Churchill, in the first volume of his history of *The Second World War*, commented trenchantly that Mussolini's Ethiopian adventure "belonged to those dark ages when white men felt themselves entitled to conquer yellow, brown, black or red men, and subjugate them by their superior strength and weapons." He went on to describe how Mussolini's show of force had deceived the British government, which might otherwise have stopped him: "Mussolini's bluff succeeded, and an important spectator [Adolph Hitler] drew far-reaching conclusions from the fact." The Second World War, it might be said, really began in Africa.

The Italian conquest of Ethiopia further undermined the confidence of countless Africans in the promises and practices of white men. In London an association called the International African Friends of Abyssinia was formed, the forerunner of the more widely based International African Service Bureau, which began in 1937; this, in turn, prepared the way for the Fifth Pan-African Congress, held in Manchester, England, in 1945. The Italian war on Ethiopia, indeed, brought together black men from many different countries and conditions in a fierce crescendo of criticism of white rule in Africa; it precipitated much of the spirit and some of the structure of the African nationalism that was to triumph after the Second World War. And in the destruction of Mussolini's short-lived empire in East Africa in 1941 not only Ethiopian guerrillas but also other African soldiers played their part.

In the three years before the outbreak of the Second World War, the European powers were recovering from the worst ravages of the economic depression of the 1930's. Their African possessions had suffered with them, especially in those territories in which a start had been made on the export of modern primary products. The mining of the potentially rich copper belt of Northern Rhodesia (now Zambia), which had got off to a splendid start in the early 1920's, and the valuable copper production of the Belgian Congo, were hit almost as drastically as those countries with subsistence economies and little export trade, such as Nyasaland and Tanganyika. Even in the more heavily capitalized white settler areas such as Algeria, Kenya, and Southern Rhodesia (which had voted in 1922 for responsible government under Britain, rather than for incorporation in the Union of South Africa) were hard hit.

The colonial governments could do little to remedy the situation until, on the eve of the Second World War and partly as a consequence of it, prosperity began to return to the metropolitan countries. In the interim, nationalism was sharpened not only among Africans but also among white settlers. Many Southern and Northern Rhodesians at this time were critical of the influence of the British South Africa Company over their economic life. A modest proposal by the French Popular Front government in 1936 to admit Algeria's Muslims to the political rights of French citizens was bitterly opposed by whites. And throughout British-ruled East and Central Africa European settlers fought for closer union between their territories in order to ensure white domination of them. Indeed, the beginnings of the ill-fated Federation of Rhodesia and Nyasaland (1953–1963) may be seen at a 1936 conference at Victoria Falls, when white representatives met to discuss the amalgamation of Southern and Northern Rhodesia.

It was paradoxical, but the outbreak of the Second World War united many black and white nationalists in Africa (if only for the duration of the campaigns) against Fascism, Nazism, and Japanese imperialism. The French in Africa, however, were divided between the supporters of the Vichy government and of General Charles de Gaulle's Free French Forces as France's metropolitan dissensions were exported to its African colonies. The black governor of Chad, Félix Eboué, unlike many white Frenchmen in Africa, supported the Free French Resistance to Germany. He became governor general of the whole of French Equatorial Africa, which by 1943 was in the Gaullist camp. Eventually, French West Africa and Madagascar also went over to the Gaullist side. But the squabbles, intrigues, and dissensions among white Frenchmen during the Second World War reduced their prestige in the eyes of their subjects all over Africa.

A similar process was at work elsewhere in Africa. Although the British had no Vichy-style problems, and many white British fought as comrades-in-arms with Africans in the African and Burmese campaigns, their prestige was also lowered, particularly when their African soldiers witnessed the force of Asian nationalism against their white masters. "General China," as one of the leaders of the insurgents during the Mau Mau emergency in Kenya in the 1950's called himself, is not untypical in dating his political awakening to his war service with the British army in Burma.

Decked out in pith helmet, pince-nez, umbrella, and briefcase, a tourist sets out to "discover" Uganda; Africans tote his valises.

LIBRARY OF CONGRESS

The process of disillusion and political awakening among Africans under colonialism, which the First World War had intensified and the Italian-Ethiopian conflict of 1935–1936 had further increased, was completed during the Second World War.

The generation of Africans who had benefitted from the educational policies of the Europeans, particularly of Britain and France, in the interwar years were anxious for political independence. The five years of the Second World War brought forward the date when this could become possible by weakening the colonial powers and by holding before the eyes of African nationalists and their followers a sequence of democratic promises, from the Atlantic Charter of 1941 to the Charter of the United Nations in 1945.

Unfortunately, the colonial powers had not extended education much beyond the relatively small circles of privileged Africans. Yet this, in its turn, was to sharpen the Africans' appetite for independence all over the continent, whether they had received European-style education or not. The nature of the education given to the subject peoples was different according to the nationality of the colonial power bestowing it. France, by its emphasis on metropolitan-style education, provided exclusively in French, aimed at the creation of an elite of black Frenchmen and produced in them a deep attachment to Parisian norms.

The division between French-speaking and English-

Matadi, typical of centers that grew under the aegis of foreign investments, is the main port of Congo (Kinshasa). Located about one hundred miles upriver from the Atlantic coast, Matadi is also a rail head; it handles a large percentage of the Congo's imports and exports, which are chiefly coffee, cacao, palm products, rice, cotton, copal, and minerals. Good facilities, such as warehouses and cranes, expedite its growing commercial operations.

speaking Africa, which had begun well before 1939, was not diminished during the Second World War. African independence was to come within little more than a decade and a half after the end of the war; but it was to be an independence that was to follow largely the state boundaries the European nations who partitioned Africa had scored across it and the European systems of values and loyalties.

Yet only a month after the surrender of the Japanese at the end of the war, the last pan-African conference to be held outside Africa was convened at Manchester, England, from October 15 to 19, 1945. There were over a hundred delegates, primarily from Africa and the Caribbean. They came predominantly from the English-speaking world; there were, apparently, no representatives from French-speaking Africa, although French translations of the main resolutions were provided. Whether this was the result of poor planning and finances in the immediate postwar situation, or of problems of communication, or of deeper political realities is a matter for research and speculation.

Du Bois, the doyen of pan-Africanism, was present at the 1945 congress; but its control and planning were in the hands of younger men—especially Kwame Nkrumah, Jomo Kenyatta, and George Padmore of Trinidad—most of whom were destined within the next two decades to play leading parts in bringing their countries to independence. The spirit of the conference was one of young men in a hurry, and it matched the mood of the ending of the war. It went further than previous congresses in demanding "for black Africa autonomy and independence"; it spoke out against "a false aristocracy and a discredited Imperialism"; and in its condemnation of "the rule of private wealth and industry for private profit alone," it came close to the concept of African socialism that was to be adopted by many political parties on the achievement of independence.

The 1945 Pan-African Congress was a symbol of the rapid and intense achievement of independence throughout most of colonial Africa. The following year eight hundred delegates from the colonies of French West Africa and French Equatorial Africa met at Bamako (located in what is today Mali) and formed the *Rassemblement Démocratique Africain.* Although it revealed and represented differences between French-speaking African leaders (especially Léopold Senghor of Senegal, Félix Houphouët-Boigny of the Ivory Coast, and Sékou Touré of Guinea) and asserted a characteristic attachment to French ideals, it manifested a growing spirit of impatience at the slow pace of political advancement in French Africa.

In 1946 the first modern political party was founded in Madagascar, with independence as its objective; the island was shaken by a violent rebellion, which, it has been claimed, took forty thousand Malagasy lives. Until the outbreak of the Mau Mau insurrection in Kenya in 1951, however, the course of independence in the British tropical African territories was relatively peaceful. Also in 1951, under social revolutionary pressures, tension mounted in Egypt, whose government abrogated the 1936 treaty with Britain, by which British troops were permitted to remain in the Suez Canal zone. On July 23, 1952, a group of young army officers, led by Colonel Abdel Nasser, seized power; and four years later he nationalized the Suez Canal, forcing Britain to withdraw its troops. Britain and France, assisted by newly formed Israel, attacked Egypt, but were compelled to withdraw under international pressure. The coup represented the destruction of the old imperialist pattern in Egypt and the beginning of the end of the European colonial epoch in northern Africa. In 1956 the Egyptians agreed to British proposals for the independence of the Sudan. It was the first formal break in the chain of British colonial power in Africa; and this was emphasized when the Sudan voted to become a republic and not to remain within the British Commonwealth of Nations.

The achievement of independence by the Gold Coast, together with the British Trust territory of Togoland under the name of the old African state of Ghana, in March, 1957, made a much greater impact on aspiring African nationalisms than did the achievement of self-government in the Sudan. In the leader of its Convention People's Party and its first prime minister, Kwame Nkrumah, it possessed a dramatic and dramatizing leader who passionately believed: "Freedom for the Gold Coast will be the fountain of inspiration from which other African colonial territories can draw when the time comes for them to strike for their freedom." That time was very close at hand. Throughout British, French, and Belgian Africa the ensuing transfer of power took place at a speed that rivaled the partition in the nineteenth century. As was often said at the time, the Scramble for Africa had become the Scram from Africa. Only white South Africa, Rhodesia, and the Portuguese colonies continued to confront the new Africa of the future with little visible change.

At the threshold of independence for the greater part of colonial Africa, the leaders and the led of the emerging new states could look back over three quarters of a century of European political domination and ask what it had all been worth. A similar question had been posed toward the end of the Scramble by the young Winston Churchill after his service with the British forces that defeated the Mahdiyya in the Sudan. Writing in his book *The River War* in 1899, Churchill questioned acutely the relation of means to ends in the imperialist process. Though he was convinced that progress had been made, he observed that it was achieved at great cost to both sides, the dominators and the dominated: "The inevitable gap between conquest and dominion becomes filled with the figures of the greedy trader, the inopportune missionary, the ambitious soldier, and the lying speculator, who disquiet the minds of the conquered and excite the sordid appetites of the conquerors. And as the eye of thought rests on these sinister features, it hardly seems possible for us to believe that any fair prospect is approached by so foul a path." Before he asked this mordant question, however, Churchill had indicated the less negative aims of imperialism, which, as he analyzed it, were: "To give peace to warring tribes, to administer justice where all was violence, to strike the chains off the slave, to draw richness from the soil, to plant the earliest seeds of commerce and learning, to increase in whole peoples their capacities for pleasure and diminish their chances for pain." Churchill undoubtedly exaggerated here the underdevelopment of the complex and differentiated cultures of Africa on the eve of imperialism. Nevertheless, even the harshest critic of its role in Africa between 1885 and 1947 would find it difficult to deny that the European presence in Africa during this period had some advantages for the indigenous inhabitants.

Perhaps the colonialists' greatest service was the extension of scientific medicine in Africa, although this was counterbalanced, as a result of improvement in communications, by the spread of new diseases such as sleeping sickness and influenza, causing thousands of deaths. Europe left Africa Balkanized, with the pan-African dreams of political unity far from realization. It could be argued that Europe had reduced considerably the number of separate sovereignties in Africa, but at the expense of overriding old national boundaries and of splitting up once-complete cultures bound together by intimate ties of language, land, and religion.

Modern industry and the promises of an ever-developing science and technology had been thrust into an increasingly wider area of Africa, but, as in Europe, it was introduced with all the attendant disadvantages of a series of severe cultural shocks. And the colonial powers had introduced into their African possessions, often unconsciously and unintentionally, ideas of democracy, socialism, and nationalism that could be employed not only against Africa's own ancient and variegated ways of life but also against European control of the continent. Discontent was inevitable, whether in the form of the older, "tribal" types of reaction and resistance to the white man's rule or in the newer nationalist movements.

Indeed, as the British imperialist Frederick Lugard put it, speaking of the African peoples whom he and other European conquerors had uprooted from their ancient and well-tried ways of life: "Their very discontent is a measure of their progress." But progress, as in Europe where the concept originated, was purchased in Africa at a steep price. Well might Aimé Césaire, the poet of Negritude, cry out in 1939 when that supreme manifestation of the consequences of European progress, the Second World War, was imminent:

Eia pour ceux qui n'ont jamais rien inventé
pour ceux qui n'ont jamais rien exploré
pour ceux qui n'ont jamais rien dompté . . . .
("Hurrah for those who have never invented anything
for those who have never explored anything
for those who have never conquered anything . . . .")

AFRICA REAFFIRMED

Figures pounding manioc atop a Congo comb
MUSEE ROYAL DE L'AFRIQUE CENTRALE, TERVUREN, BELGIUM

NEGRITUDE DEFINED

It was a group of Paris-exiled poets who in the early nineteen thirties evolved the formal concept of Negritude, by which they sought to affirm the validity of their ancestral culture. These first exponents of Negritude came from many countries, but they shared a commonality of race, colonial experience, and the French language. Léopold Sédar Senghor, a Senegalese poet who was to become his country's president in 1960, was its chief theoretician and most militant communicant. As in the excerpt that immediately follows, he has argued that Negritude is not only a means toward revitalizing the arts but a key to the meaning of the black man's existence (others have defined Negritude in terms of a political instrument against colonial domination). Two of Senghor's poems are also given below. "Black Woman" symbolically relates to his motherland; "For Khalam" is a somber allusion to his strife-torn land. The khalam *mentioned is a stringed instrument, the* tama *a small tam-tam, and the* dyali *a musician.*

Negritude is the whole of the values of civilization—cultural, economic, social, political—which characterize the black peoples, more exactly, the Negro-African world. It is essentially *instinctive reason*, which pervades all these values. It is reason of the impressions, reason that is "seized." It is expressed by the emotions through an abandonment of self and a complete identification with the object; through the myth of the archetype of the collective soul, and the *myth primordial* accorded to the cosmos. In other terms, the sense of communion, the gift of imagination, the gift of rhythm—these are the traits of Negritude, that we find like an indelible seal on all the works and activities of the black man.

BLACK WOMAN

Nude woman, black woman,
Clothed in your color which is life, your form which is beauty!
I grew in your shadow, the sweetness of your hands bandaged my eyes,
And here in the heart of summer and of noon, I discover you, promised land from the height of a burnt mountain,
And your beauty strikes my heart, like the lightning of an eagle.

Nude woman, dark woman,
Ripe fruit of the dark flesh, somber ecstasies of black wine, mouth that causes my mouth to sing;
Savanna of pure horizons, savanna trembling under the fervent caresses of the East wind,
Carved tom-tom, tense tom-tom, grumbling under the fingers of the conqueror,
Your low contralto voice is the song of the lover.

Nude woman, dark woman,
Oil unwrinkled by winds, oil smooth on athletes' thighs, on the thighs of the princes of Mali,
Gazelle with heavenly joints, the pearls are stars on the night of your skin,
Delightful play of the spirit, image of red gold on your flaming skin
In the shadow of your hair, my anguish is relieved by the nearby suns of your eyes.

Nude woman, black woman,
I sing your passing beauty, fixing your form in eternity
Before a jealous fate turns you to ashes to feed the roots of life.

FOR KHALAM

Is it surprising my dear if my melody has become somber
If I have laid aside the smooth reed for the *khalam* and *tama*
And the green smell of the ricefields for the grumbling of the drums?

Listen to the menace of the old men—diviners, cannonade of wrath of God.
Ah! perhaps tomorrow the crimson voice of your *dyali* will cease forever.
That is the reason my rhythm has grown so urgent my fingers bleed on my *khalam*.

Perhaps tomorrow my dear I shall fall on our unappeased soil
Full of regret for your setting eyes, and the drumming of the mortars through the mist, back home.
And in the dusk you will be full of regret for the burning voice that sang once of your dark beauty.

And we shall bathe my dear in an ambience of Africa.
Furniture from Guinea and Congo, heavy and polished, somber and serene.
On the walls, pure primordial masks distant and yet present.
Stools of honor for hereditary guests, for the Princes of the High Lands.
Wild perfumes, thick mats of silence
Cushions of shade and leisure, the noise of a wellspring of peace.
Classic words. In the distance, antiphonal singing like the cloths of the Sudan.

And then, friendly lamp, your kindness to soothe the obsession of this ambience
White black and red, oh red as the soil of Africa.

THE JOY OF BLACKNESS

Aimé Césaire, born on the island of Martinique in 1913, came to Paris as a student in 1928. Eleven years later he published what was to be his most famous poem, "Cahier d'un Retour au Pays Natal (*Memorandum on My Martinique*)." *Césaire is considered the outstanding poet of the Negritude movement.* "Cahier," *from which this excerpt is taken, has been called by the French critic-poet André Breton the greatest lyrical monument of the twentieth century.*

For beauty is Black
and wisdom Black
for endurance is Black
and courage Black
for patience is Black
and irony Black
for charm is Black
and magic Black
for love is Black
and hip swinging Black
for dance is Black
and rhythm Black
for art is Black
and movement Black
for laughter is Black
for joy is Black
for peace is Black
for life is Black

SPACE THAT ONCE WAS MINE

The poet Léon Damas was born in French Guiana in 1912. During a period of study in Paris he became a part of the Negritude movement. The tone of his poetry ranges from irony, directed at his subjection to Western mores, to a deep-seated anger at the results of colonialism. This work, entitled "Limbe," *is taken from a collection of Damas' poems entitled* Pigments, *published in Paris in 1937.*

Will they ever know this rancor in my heart?
From beneath suspicion's eye that opened all too late.
they have robbed me of the space that once was mine
tradition
days
life
song
rhythm
effort
pathway
water
cabin
the gray, fertilized land
wisdom
words
palavers
the aged
cadence
hands
measure
hands
footbeats
soil

SPLENDIDLY ALONE

David Diop's legacy to the literature of Negritude is a slim volume of seventeen poems, Coups de Pilon (Pounding). *Diop was born in Bordeaux in 1927 of African parents and lived for a while in West Africa. He was killed in an air crash over Dakar in 1960; with him went a quantity of unpublished manuscripts. Despite Diop's profound hatred of colonialism, his work is typically tempered with optimism, as in this poem.*

Africa my Africa
Africa of proud warriors on ancestral savannahs
Africa that my grandmother sings
On the bank of her distant river
I have never known you
But my face is full of your blood
Your beautiful black blood which waters the wide fields.
The blood of your sweat
The sweat of your work
The work of your slavery
The slavery of your children
Africa tell me Africa
Is this really you this back which is bent
And breaks under the load of insult
This back trembling with red weals
Which says yes to the whip on the hot roads of noon

Then gravely a voice replies to me
Impetuous son that tree robust and young
That tree over there
Splendidly alone amidst white and faded flowers
That is Africa your Africa which grows
Grows patiently obstinately
And whose fruit little by little learn
The bitter taste of liberty.

AFRICA AT THE CENTER

The young William Edward Burghardt Du Bois wrote in his diary in 1893: "Be the truth what it may, I shall seek it on the pure assumption that it is worth seeking—and Heaven nor Hell, God nor Devil shall turn me from my purpose till I die." Until his death seventy years later, at the age of ninety-five, the man was true to his word. W.E.B. Du Bois was born in Great Barrington, Massachusetts, in 1868. After receiving his doctoral degree from Harvard University in 1895, he taught for several years; but in 1905 he became involved in the Niagara movement, which led to the founding of the National Association for the Advancement of Colored People and to the scholar's emergence as an Afro-American leader. A prolific writer and editor, he is also considered to be the father of the pan-African movement and an outstanding spokesman for African nationalism. Du Bois published more than a dozen books in the black studies area, including Black Reconstruction, *and wrote uncounted speeches and articles in the cause of reawakening African consciousness. The following excerpt is from an essay that appeared in the* Atlantic Monthly *in May, 1915. In it Du Bois cites European rivalries in Africa as the chief cause of World War I.*

Nearly every human empire that has arisen in the world, material and spiritual, has found some of its greatest crises on this continent of Africa, from Greece to

Great Britain. As [the German classical historian Theodor] Mommsen says, "It was through Africa that Christianity became the religion of the world." In Africa the last flood of Germanic invasions spent itself within hearing of the last gasp of Byzantium, and it was again through Africa that Islam came to play its great role of conqueror and civilizer....

So much for the past; and now, today. . . . The methods by which this continent has been stolen have been contemptible and dishonest beyond expression. Lying treaties, rivers of rum, murder, assassination, mutilation, rape and torture have marked the progress of Englishman, German, Frenchman, and Belgian on the Dark Continent. . . .

It all began, singularly enough, like the present war, with Belgium. Many of us remember Stanley's great solution of the puzzle of Central Africa when he traced the mighty Congo sixteen hundred miles from Nyangwe to the sea. Suddenly the world knew that here lay the key to the riches of Central Africa. It stirred uneasily, but Leopold of Belgium was first on his feet, and the result was the Congo Free State—God save the mark! . . .

Thus the world began to invest in color prejudice. The "color line" began to pay dividends. For indeed, while the exploration of the valley of the Congo was the occasion of the scramble for Africa, the cause lay deeper. The Franco-Prussian War turned the eyes of those who sought power and dominion away from Europe. . . .

With the waning of the possibility of the big fortune, gathered by starvation wage and boundless exploitation of one's weaker and poorer fellows at home, arose more magnificently the dream of exploitation abroad. . . .

It is no longer simply the merchant prince, or the aristocratic monopoly, or even the employing class, that is exploiting the world: it is the nation, a new democratic nation composed of united capital and labor. . . .

Such nations it is that rule the modern world. Their national bond is no mere sentimental patriotism, loyalty, or ancestor-worship. It is increased wealth, power, and luxury for all classes on a scale the world never saw before. . . .

Dr. Du Bois at a Paris conference in 1949

UPI

Whence comes this new wealth and on what does its accumulation depend? It comes primarily from the darker nations of the world—Asia and Africa, South and Central America, the West Indies and the islands of the South Seas. . . .

Thus, more and more, the imperialists have concentrated on Africa.

The greater the concentration the more deadly the rivalry. From Fashoda to Agadir, repeatedly the spark has been applied to the European magazine and a general conflagration narrowly averted. We speak of the Balkans as the storm center of Europe and the cause of war, but this is mere habit. The Balkans are convenient for occasions, but the ownership of materials and men in the darker world is the real prize that is setting the nations of Europe at each other's throats today.

The present world war is, then, the result of jealousies engendered by the recent rise of armed national associations of labor and capital whose aim is the exploitation of the wealth of the world mainly outside the European circle of nations. These associations, grown jealous and suspicious at the division of the spoils of trade-empire, are fighting to enlarge their respective shares; they look for expansion, not in Europe but in Asia, and particularly in Africa. "We want no inch of French territory," said Germany to England, but Germany was "unable to give" similar assurances as to France in Africa. . . .

What, then, are we to do, who desire peace and the civilization of all men? . . . How can love of humanity appeal as a motive to nations whose love of luxury is built on the inhuman exploitation of human beings, and who, especially in recent years, have been taught to regard these human beings as inhuman? . . .

What the primitive peoples of Africa and the world need and must have if war is to be abolished is perfectly clear:

First: land. Today Africa is being enslaved by the theft of her land and natural resources. . . .

Secondly: we must train native races in modern civilization. . . .

Lastly, the principle of home rule must extend to groups, nations, and races. . . .

We are calling for European concord today; but at the utmost European concord will mean satisfaction with, or acquiescence in, a given division of the spoils of world dominion. . . . From this will arise three perpetual dangers of war. First, renewed jealousy at any division of colonies or spheres of influence. . . .

Secondly: war will come from the revolutionary revolt of the lowest workers. . . . Finally, the colored peoples will not always submit passively to foreign domination. To some this is a lightly tossed truism. When a people deserve liberty they fight for it and get it, say such philosophers; thus making war a regular, necessary step to liberty. Colored people are familiar with this complacent judgment. They endure the contemptuous treatment meted out by whites to those not "strong" enough to be free. These nations and races, composing as they do a vast majority of humanity, are going to endure this treatment just as long as they must and not a moment longer. Then they are going to fight and the War of the Color Line will outdo in savage inhumanity any war this world has yet seen. For colored folk have much to remember and they will not forget.

But is this inevitable? Must we sit helpless before this awful prospect? . . .

Steadfast faith in humanity must come. The domination of one people by another without the other's consent, be the subject people black or white, must stop. The doctrine of forcible economic expansion over subject peoples must go. . . .

Twenty centuries before Christ a great cloud swept over sea and settled on Africa, darkening and well-nigh blotting out the culture of the land of Egypt. For half a thousand years it rested there until a black woman, Queen Nefertari, "the most venerated figure in Egyptian history," rose to the throne of the Pharaohs and redeemed the world and her people. Twenty centuries after Christ, black Africa, prostrate, raped, and shamed, lies at the feet of the conquering Philistines of Europe. Beyond the awful sea a black woman is weeping and waiting with her sons on her breast. What shall the end be? The world-old and fearful things, war and wealth, murder and luxury? Or shall it be a new thing—a new peace and new democracy of all races: a great humanity of equal men? "*Semper novi quid ex Africa!*"

THE LION OF JUDAH

In 1930 *Ethiopia's regent, Ras Taffari Makonnen, became emperor and assumed the title of Haile Selassie* I *(meaning in Amharic "the power of the Trinity"). Five years later his rule was brutally challenged by Italian invasion. Numerous attempts to arouse the conscience of world leaders were climaxed in* 1938 *by an urgent last plea he placed before the League of Nations, to which Ethiopia belonged. Betrayed by the other members, Haile Selassie was forced into exile until* 1941, *when, with British help, he was restored to power. Since that time numerous internal revolts have shaken, but not unseated, the durable monarch, and small but progressive changes in his administration are discernible. Portions of his speech before the League follow.*

Haile Selassie recording a radio appeal
ACME

Ethiopia, the victim of an inexcusable aggression, had placed her confidence in the signature of the States Members of the League. . . . Since 1935 Ethiopia has with pain noted successive abandonments of signatures that had been appended to the Covenant. Many Powers threatened with aggression and feeling their weakness have abandoned Ethiopia. . . .

Article 10 of the Covenant requires Members to undertake to respect and maintain as against all external aggression the territorial integrity and political independence of each Member. Nevertheless, non-recognition of a conquest by aggression is the least onerous obligation in observing Article 10, since it involves merely a passive attitude. It does not call upon States Members to make any national sacrifice, nor does it lead them to incur any risk of war or reprisals. . . .

To-day, we have the brutal abandonment of this principle, which is contemplated and which even seems to be called for by the powerful British Empire. . . .

I, as legitimate Emperor of Ethiopia, on behalf of my martyred people, address to the nations of the world the most energetic protest. In order to lessen the flagrant violation of the Covenant, the suggestion made to-day to the Council invokes the situation in actual fact in Ethiopia at the present time. But if it were true—and it is not so—that the invader has broken the resistance of my people, even if in fact he occupied and effectively exercised his administration over the territory of my empire—which is not the case—even in those circumstances the proposal submitted to the Council should be set aside without hesitation. Did not the world hail as one of the most important marks of progress in international law . . . the refusal to grant juridical recognition to the effects of aggression?

As legitimate sovereign of the Ethiopian people, I would invoke this principle, for I have incumbent on me the duty to defend the political independence of the Ethiopian people, the territorial integrity of Ethiopia, and at the same time the life, the property and the liberty of each of those individuals and each of those religious or civil institutions which go to make up the Ethiopian people. . . .

Millions of men and women throughout the world are to-day anxiously following the deliberations of the League of Nations. They know that this is the tragic hour in which the destiny of the League is to be determined. Being responsible for ensuring respect for the principles of international justice, is the League of Nations about to end its own existence by tearing up, with its own hands, the Covenant which constitutes its sole reason for existence? The magnificent edifice that has just been reared for the triumph of peace through law, is this henceforth to become an altar reared to the cult of force, a market-place in which the independence of peoples becomes the subject of trafficking, a tomb in which international morality is to be buried? . . .

In order to break down the resistance of my people, its refusal to abandon that independence which it had enjoyed for more than thirty centuries, the Italian authorities are counting upon propaganda with the object of demoralizing the people, and in this they make great play with the abandonment of Ethiopia by the League of Nations. . . .

International law absolutely prohibits the belligerent making any annexation and it prohibits any Power that is foreign to the conflict from recognizing the occupant as the legal sovereign. Thus the *de facto* situation does strengthen and supplement the provisions of the Covenant and of the Pact of Paris, which in the most categorical way prohibit *de jure* recognition of annexation, for that would be recognizing the conquest of territory by force. . . .

The distinguished representative of Great Britain has just put the question very clearly. He said there are at present two ideals in conflict, the ideal of devotion to a lofty aim, and the ideal of ensuring peace as a practical measure. He asserted that it is often difficult to reconcile what is ideally just with what is possible in practice. He asserted that it is the essential mission of the League to maintain peace. Yes, the League has as its essential object the maintenance of peace. But there are different ways to maintain peace; there is the maintenance of peace through right, and there is peace at any cost. Ethiopia firmly believes that the League of Nations has no freedom of choice in this matter. It would be committing suicide if after having been created to maintain peace through right it were to abandon that principle and adopt instead the principle of peace at any price, even the price of the immolation of a State Member at the feet of its aggressor.

THE WEAVER OF DREAMS

Marcus Aurelius Garvey came to the United States from Jamaica about 1916. *According to a re-evaluation of black history, his back-to-Africa movement is a relevant link in the development of Afro-American history and the growing recognition of African kinship. Two million followers joined Garvey's organization, stirred to wild enthusiasm by his infectious exhortations and his dream of an African homeland free from the oppressions of a biased society. Claude McKay, Jamaica-born poet and novelist, product of the Harlem renaissance of literature in the nineteen twenties and thirties, has captured the flamboyant character of the man and the temper of his times in the following excerpt from* Harlem: Negro Metropolis, *published in* 1940.

Garvey en route to a U.N.I.A. rally, 1921
UPI

There has never been a Negro leader like Garvey. None ever enjoyed a fraction of his universal popularity. He winged his way into the firmament of the white world holding aloft a black star and exhorting the Negro people to gaze upon and follow it. His aspiration to reach dizzy heights and dazzle the vision of the Negro world does not remain monumental, like the rugged path of the pioneer or of the hard, calculating, practical builder. But it survives in the memory like the spectacular swath of an unforgettable comet. . . .

In 1917 Garvey organized in Harlem the Universal Negro Improvement Association. He had as a nucleus an intelligent group of men who belonged to a long established History Club, which specialized in the Negro people's ancient past. Auspiciously Garvey started off on a lecture tour, which covered a majority of the States that had a considerable Negro population. He was warmly welcomed and received large contributions of money. . . .

Africa for the Africans! Renaissance of the Negro Race! Back to Africa! A Black Star Line! These were the slogans Garvey broadcast in a thousand different ways to move the mind of the Negro people. There was magic in his method. It worked miraculously. The Negro masses acclaimed the new leader. The black belts clamored to hear his voice and competed with one another for his lectures. Money poured in for subscriptions to the *Negro World*, money that would help establish the Black Star Line and set in motion the Redemption of Africa. Garvey struck African Redemption medals. A bronze cross was bestowed upon subscribers of from $50 to $100, a silver cross for subscribers of from $100 to $500 and a gold cross for donors of $500 to $1000.

Now, after many vicissitudes, Garvey was successfully launched on his career of world leadership of the Negroes. . . .

Girding for a supreme war effort, America had little time to devote to the growing problems of its large Negro minority. Harassed in the South and rebuffed in the North, the southern Negroes eagerly swallowed the sayings and the projects of Garvey.

Marcus Garvey became the mouthpiece of these southern and West Indian migrants to the northern centers of industry. Whether they worked in Jersey or Pennsylvania, Connecticut or Massachusetts, Harlem was their Mecca. They gave Garvey all the money he needed to institute his programme. . . .

Just a few months after the founding of his organization, Garvey was involved in disputes with his most prominent officials. . . . Early in 1919 he was nearly assassinated by one George Tyler, who shot him three times in the arms and leg. He was saved by his secretary, Miss Amy Ashwood, who threw herself between him and his antagonist. . . .

The attempt on Garvey's life, besides his arrest sky-rocketed his stock. He incorporated the Black Star Line, capitalized at ten million dollars. . . . "Up, you mighty race!" cried Garvey. And the race rose up. Garvey spoke and the Negro masses were transformed. "Negro, Black, and Africa," the magic words repeated again and again made Negroes delirious with ecstasy. Wherever Garvey led they were ready to follow. He was the modern Moses, the black savior. His message reached Negroes everywhere. From the plantation of the deep South, they hearkened to his voice, in the islands of the Caribbean they were moved as never before, now that the voice of Marcus Garvey was broadcast from New York. Across the Atlantic, in the heart of the Congo, Negroes talked of the black Messiah. . . .

In the latter part of 1919 . . . Marcus Garvey announced that the Black Star Line had acquired its first boat. . . .

There was a wild invasion of Harlem by Negroes from every black quarter of America. Hordes of disciples came with more dollars to buy more shares. The boat was moored at the pier with its all-Negro crew. And the common people gladly paid half a dollar to go aboard and look over the miracle. . . .

Now, in this first boat of the Black Star Line, owned by the Universal Negro Improvement Association, they saw something different. They saw themselves sailing without making any apology for being passengers. It was their own ship, a Negro ship. It was their money that had bought it. But it had required a black leader to show them how they could do it.

That night Liberty Hall was jammed with Negroes. Hundreds could not get in and the sidewalks overflowed with spectators between Lenox Avenue and Seventh Avenue. Marcus Garvey transformed the great audience into a waving, shouting, frenzied host as he cried: "Up, you mighty race, you can accomplish what you will." . . .

In 1920 Marcus Garvey staged the first Universal Negro Convention in Harlem. . . .

Delegates arrived from Africa, Brazil, Colombia, Panama and other Central American countries, and from the islands of the West Indies. Every State of the Union was represented. Harlem blinked at the dazzling splendor of that wonderful parade. Garvey wore a magnificent uniform of purple, green and black, and a plumed hat. He stood in his car and saluted the cheering crowds. . . .

The following evening, Garvey packed Madison Square Garden with his followers and admirers. In a long speech he exhorted the Negroes to unite and work for the redemption of Africa. . . .

Garvey's invasion of the South, the acclamation of the Black Belts and the attitude of the Southern whites presented a puzzle to northern Negro intellectuals. Garvey had announced previously that he was going South to talk to his own people and that the white man should leave him alone.

Now many Northern blacks and whites had been manhandled and run out of the South for attempting to hold peaceful meetings with colored people! . . .

In Louisiana and Alabama, notably, Garvey succeeded in holding some extremely boisterous and enthusiastic meetings and getting away without a scratch. Of course, he had his way of doing it. He employed a special technique. He thundered, "Africa for the Africans," and shouted at the white South in a semi-religious harangue, "Let my people go!" . . .

Meanwhile, the Federal government had undertaken an investigation of Garvey. In January, 1922, he was arrested on a charge of using the mails to defraud. . . . The charge was that Garvey had used the mails to solicit funds for a Black Star Line which was not established. He was released on bail of $2500. . . .

For the balance of the year he remained unmolested, and organized in Harlem one of his grandest conventions. From every State in the union, from the West Indies, from Central and South America, from Europe and Africa, an inspiring deputation of delegates converged upon Harlem. It was the greatest swarm since Garvey started his movement. They brought gifts to Garvey: special contributions to defend his case, sums for African Redemption and thousands of subscriptions to reorganize the Black Star Line. . . . To the tremendous tributes he responded as befitted a grand potentate. The ribbons and braids of his gleaming satin robe were richer than ever, his plumes were as long as the leaves of the Guinea grass and as white as snow; seated in his car as upon a throne, he received the ovations and salutes of Harlem. . . .

A delegation consisting of three members of the Universal Negro organization was dispatched to Liberia. . . .

The Black Star Line was reorganized as the Black Cross, and the *General Goethals*, a boat of over four thousand tons, was purchased from the government. The first members of the colony were scheduled to sail in 1924. But trouble broke in Liberia. It was said that the Garvey party there was using the world-wide influence of the Universal Negro Organization to overthrow the government. . . .

The August, 1924, convention of the Universal Negro and Black Cross was designed as a monster farewell party to the Negroes who were to leave for Liberia in the fall. . . . Those who were chosen to go were religiously regarded as angels of the New Heaven, Marcus Garvey's promised land, the Negro Zion.

The Archbishop of the African Orthodox Church, the Right Reverend C. A. McGuire, in his robes of state, pronounced a blessing upon the convention, said a special prayer for Marcus Garvey and the Universal Negroes who were the first to have elected to return to Africa. . . .

But in the midst of the thirty-day convention, the Liberian government issued a statement repudiating the Universal Negro organization, and refusing to recognize its advance delegates. . . .

However, if Marcus Garvey felt his movement betrayed by the American-Liberian aristocracy, he and his following were inspirited and uplifted by a significant event. That year the Prince Kogo Honeou Tovalou of Dahomey made his first voyage to America. Prince Kogo, as a royal native potentate, was honored with a picturesque reception at Liberty Hall, where all the colors of God's fertile imagination were assembled in his honor. He made a speech full of praise for the work of the Universal Negro Association and saluted Marcus Garvey as the leader of the Negro people of the world. . . .

And above all there was Garvey's Universal Negro propaganda. Its repercussion in Africa was greater than the American Back-to-Africa devotees realized. In the interior of West Africa legends arose of an African who had been lost in America, but would return to save his people. . . .

Enemies black and white were constantly badgering Garvey and reminding the authorities of his menacing existence. His appeal slowly dragged along its course. . . . Finally, in 1925, the appeal was rejected by the United States Supreme Court. In February, 1925, Marcus Garvey entered Atlanta Federal Penitentiary to serve a five-year term. . . .

But in prison he was perhaps as powerful as he was when free. His message to his followers appeared every week on the front page of the *Negro World.* Often it read like an epistle of one of the Apostles. While he was on trial, the prosecuting attorney referred to him as "The Tiger." . . . The Garvey people delighted in the phrase and . . . they fought hard to free Garvey. His lawyer released a memorandum showing that the chief count upon which Garvey was convicted was untenable. Petitions were sent to the President of the United States. The jury that convicted him came out with a statement in favor of his release. Metropolitan newspapers, such as the *Daily News,* which has a large circulation in Harlem, demanded that Garvey be pardoned. He was turned loose in November, 1927, and deported to Jamaica. . . .

Marcus Garvey's influence over Aframericans, native Africans and people of African descent everywhere was vast. Whether that influence was positive or pervasive and indirect, Negroes of all classes were stirred to a finer feeling of racial consciousness. . . .

The "Black Tiger" and "President-General" of the Negro World, Marcus Garvey, died in London on June 10, 1940. At the time of his death he still was revered as their greatest leader by the American Negro masses.

"STRIKE A BLOW AND DIE"

John Chilembwe, who led an abortive revolt against British coffee and tobacco planters in Nyasaland in 1915, had prepared for his role of African nationalist leader under the aegis of British Protestantism. His mentor, evangelist-egalitarian Joseph Booth, advocated the formation of a separate African Christian Union, which would incorporate local religious practices within its Christian framework. He took Chilembwe to the United States for further training, but encounters there with militant Afro-Americans led the young man to break with Booth. Returning to Nyasaland in 1901, Chilembwe established the Providence Industrial Mission and began to speak against the oppressive colonial system. Just what motivated Chilembwe to take up arms against the British and face almost certain death has been widely debated. It is estimated that a black army, numbering somewhere between two hundred and nine hundred men, was involved. British losses were slight, and Chilembwe was shortly ambushed and killed. However, George Mwase, a Tonga and compatriot of Chilembwe, later wrote A Dialogue of Nyasaland, *in which he gave an account of what he observed.*

When the army gathered on Saturday morning on the 23rd January 1915 [John Chilembwe gave instructions to his army]. After a long debate, he prayed to Almighty God. Then he delivered his speech as follows:

"You are all patriots as you sit. Patriots mean[s] to die for Amor Patria. This very night you are to go and strike the blow and then die. I do not say that you are going to win the war at all. You have no weapons (guns?) with you and you are not at all trained military men even. One great thing you must remember is that Omnia Vincet Amor so for love [of] your own country and country men, I now encourage you to go and strike a blow bravely and die.

"This is only way to show the whiteman, that the treatment they are treating our men and women was most bad and we have determined to strike a first and a last blow, and then all die by the heavy storm of the whitemen's army. The whitemen will then think, after we are dead, that the treatment they are treating our people is almost (most) bad, and they might change to the better for our people. After we are dead and buried. This blows means 'non sibi sed patria.' ['Not for oneself, but for one's country.']

"You must not think that with that blow, you are going to defeat whitemen and then become Kings of your own country, no. If one of you has such an idea in his head, 'God forbid,' he must throw such idea now, before it grows bigger in his head, for it will lead him astray. I am also warning strongly against seizing property from anybody, does not matter what or where. If among you there is a lecher, such a man must not go with you. You are Patriots and not Lechers. Where you are going to find money, goods and other kind of wealth, does not matter what, do not touch such for 'Amor Patria' sake. But where ever your hand is going to lay on any kind of a weapon, take that, for it will help you in your struggle for the 'Amor Patria.' Another order I want you to remember, is about women and young children, do not, in any way, do anything to them, treat them as innocents, what you are to do with them is to bring them over peacefully, and afterwards send them back to the Boma. Women must be carried on Machilla if some will be available. If some of the whitemen will be killed during the assault, one or two of the important men bring the head or heads over, leave the body alone."

He repeated saying "Be of good courage, and strike the blow and die for the 'Amor Patria,' and not with intention to win and become Kings of your own." He bade them "God's speed." At last he prayed again and said "Deusvobiscum." ["God be with you."]

So the army scattered that day for their food. This was the morning of Saturday the 23rd January. The army then gathered themselves, at the evening, and they were divided as I have already said on the front page (earlier). I have also to mention that there were also some members of this army in Zomba Township, but they all shrinked and diminished, and they did not appear for help; although the arrangement was that.

TOWARD POSITIVE ACTION

Gamal Abdel Nasser entered the public political arena in July, 1953, when his Free Officers movement staged a coup d'état, deposing King Farouk and with him Egypt's bankrupt monarchical system. Nasser's cadre was drawn largely from the frustrated lower middle classes; it was committed to a broad reordering of society, including radical agrarian reform. The Free Officers also sought to strengthen Egypt's military establishment and the international Arab League, of which it was the leader. Nasser held a number of posts in the new government, becoming president both of Egypt in 1956 and of the United Arab Republic (Egypt and Syria) from 1958 to 1970. The following excerpt is taken from Nasser's Philosophy of the Revolution *(1953), the manifesto of his master plan for Egypt, Africa, and the Arab world.*

What is it we want to do? And which is the way to it?

There is no doubt we all dream of Egypt free and strong. No Egyptian would ever differ with another about that. As for the way to liberation and strength, that is the most intricate problem in our lives. . . .

Ever since I was at the head of demonstrations in Al Nahda School [Nasser's secondary school], I have clamored for complete independence; others repeated my cries; but these were in vain.

They were blown away by the winds and became faint echoes that do not move mountains or smash rocks. Later "positive action" meant in my opinion that all leaders of Egypt should unite on one thing. Rebellious cheering crowds passed our leaders' homes one by one demanding, in the name of the youth of Egypt, that they should unite on one thing. It was a tragedy to my faith that the one thing they united on was the Treaty of 1936 [an Anglo-Egyptian treaty reducing Britain's military occupation in Egypt to a zone bordering the Suez Canal].

Then came the second World War and the events that preceded it. Both inflamed our youth and spread fire to its innermost feelings. We, the whole generation, began to move towards violence. I confess, and I hope the Attorney-General will not incriminate me on account of this confession, that political assassinations blazed in my inflamed mind during that period as the only positive action from which we could not escape, if we were to save the future of our country. . . .

I thought of assassinating the ex-King and those of his men who tampered with our sacred traditions. In this I was not alone. When I sat with others our thoughts passed from thinking to planning. Many a design did I draw up those days. Many a night did I lie awake preparing the means for the expected positive action. . . .

I remember one night in particular which was decisive in directing my thoughts and my dreams along that channel. We had prepared everything necessary for action. We selected one, whom we found essential to put out of the way. We studied the circumstances of the life of this individual, and made the plot in detail. This plot was to shoot him as he returned home at night. We organized a squad of assault which would shoot him, another to guard this first and a third to organize the plan of getting away to safety after the plot had been fully carried out.

The appointed night came and I went out myself with the squad of execution. Everything went to plan as we imagined.

The scene was empty, as we had expected. The squads lay in the hiding places fixed for them. The person whom we wanted to get out of the way came and bullets were fired at him. The squad of execution withdrew, covered in its retreat by the guards, and the operation of getting away began. I started my motor car and dashed away from the scene of the positive action we planned. Cries, wailings and moans suddenly rang in my ears. The wailing of a woman, the voice of a scared child and the continuous feverish appeals for help assailed my ears. I was steeped in my rebellious set of emotions as my car rushed me along. I then became conscious of something strange; the sounds I heard were still tearing my ears, as well as the cries, wails and moans and the feverish appeals for help. I was then away from the scene, further than sound could reach. Nevertheless I felt all these beginning to haunt and chase me.

I got home, threw myself on the bed, my mind in a fever, my heart and conscience incessantly boiling. The cries, moans and wails and the appeals for help still rang in my ears. All night long I could not sleep. I lay on my bed in darkness, lighting one cigarette after another, wandering away with my rebellious thoughts which were driven away by the sounds that haunted me. "Was I right?" I asked myself. With conviction I answered, "My motives were patriotic." "Was this an unavoidable means?" I again asked myself. In doubt I replied: "What could we have done otherwise? Is it possible that the future of our country could change by getting rid of this one individual or another? Is not the question far deeper than this?" In bewilderment I would say to myself: "I almost feel that the question is deeper. We dream of the glory of a nation. Which is more important? That some one should pass away who should pass away or that someone should come who should come."

As I mention this I see rays of light gradually filtering through these crowded sensations. "What is important," I would say to myself, "is that someone should come who should come. We are dreaming of the glory of a nation: A glory that must be built up." As I tossed on my bed in a room full of smoke and charged with emotions, I found myself asking: "And then?" "And what then?", a mysterious voice called out. . . .

The principal question is to find out the positive action. Since then we began to think of something more deeply rooted, more serious and more far-reaching. We began to draw the preliminary lines of the vision that was realized in the night of July 23rd, namely a revolution springing from the very heart of the people, charged with its aspirations and pursuing completely the steps it had previously taken along its destined path. . . .

Fate has so willed that we should be on the crossroads of the world. Often have we been the road which invaders took and a prey to adventurers. In certain circumstances we found it impossible to explain the factors latent in the soul of our nation without due consideration of these circumstances.

In my opinion we cannot overlook the history of Egypt under the Pharaohs or the reaction between the Greek spirit and ours, the Roman invasion, and Muslim conquest and the waves of Arab migrations that followed.

I believe we should pause for a time and examine the circumstances we went through in the Middle Ages; for it is these that got us up to the stage we are in today.

If the Crusades were the dawn of a renaissance in Europe they were also the commencement of the dark ages in our country. Our nation has borne the brunt of the Crusades. They left it exhausted, poverty-stricken and destitute.

Often, when I go back to turning the pages of our history, I feel sorrow tearing my soul as I consider the period when a tyrannical feudalism was formed, a feudalism which had no other object save sucking the blood of life out of our veins and sapping from these veins the remnants of any feeling of power and of dignity. It left in the depth of our souls an effect that we have to struggle long to overcome.

European society passed through the stages of its evolution in an orderly manner. It crossed the bridge between the Renaissance at the end of the Middle Ages and the Nineteenth Century step by step. . . . In our case everything was sudden. European countries eyed us covetously and regarded us as a crossroad to their colonies in the East and the South.

Torrents of ideas and opinions burst upon us which we were, at that stage of our evolution, incapable of assimilating. Our spirits were still in the Thirteenth Century though the symptoms of the Nineteenth and Twentieth Centuries infiltrated in their various aspects. Our minds were trying to catch up the advancing caravan of humanity. . . .

I believe, without paying any compliment to people's emotions, that our nation has realized a miracle. Any nation, exposed to the same conditions as our country, could be easily lost. It could be swept away by the torrents that fell upon it. But it stood firm in the violent earthquake.

It is true we nearly lost our equilibrium in some circumstances; but generally we did not fall to the ground. As I consider one normal Egyptian family out of the thousands that live in the capital, I find the following: the father, for example, is a turbaned "fellah" from the heart of the country; the mother a lady descended from Turkish stock; the sons of the family are at a school adopting the English system; the daughters the French. All this lies between the Thirteenth century and the outward appearances of the Twentieth.

As I see this I feel within me I can comprehend the bewilderment and the confusion that assail us. Then I say to myself. "This society will crystalize; its component parts will hold together; it will form a homogeneous entity; but this necessitates that we should strain our nerves during the period of transition."

Such are, then, the roots from which sprang our conditions of today. Such are the sources from which our crisis flows. If I add to these social origins the circumstances for which we expelled [King] Farouk and for which we wish to liberate our country from every foreign soldier; if we add all these together, we shall discover the wide sphere in which we labor and which is exposed, from every side, to the winds, to the violent storm that raged in its corners, to flashing lightning and roaring thunder.

Therefore, one may ask, "Which is the way? and what is our role in it?"

The way is that which leads to economic and political freedom.

Many people come to me and exclaim, "You have angered everybody." To which explanation I always reply, "It is not people's anger that influences the situation. The question should be: Was what aroused their anger for the good of the country or for the interest of whom?" I realize we have upset big land-owners; but was it possible not to upset them and yet behold some of us owning thousands of acres, while others do not own the plot of land wherein they are buried after their death?

I realize we have aroused the wrath of old politicians; but was it possible not to do so and yet behold our country a victim to their passions, their corruption and their struggle for the spoils of office?

I realize we have angered many government officials; but without this was it possible to spend more than half the budget on officials' salaries and yet allot, as we have done, forty million pounds for productive projects? What would have happened if we had opened the coffers of the treasury of the state, as they had done, and distributed their contents among officials and let come what may thereafter. The year that ensued would have found the Government unable to pay the salaries of officials.

How easy it would have been to satisfy all those malcontents! But what is the price that our country would pay out of its hopes and its future for that satisfaction? . . .

When I attempt to analyze the components of our power I cannot help but point out three principal forces of power which should be the first to be taken into account.

The first source is that we are a group of neighboring peoples joined together with such spiritual and material bonds as can ever join any group of peoples. Our peoples have traits, components and civilization, in whose atmosphere the three sacred and heavenly creeds have originated. This cannot be altogether ignored in any effort at reconstructing a stable world in which peace prevails.

As for the second source it is our territory itself and the position it has on the map of the world, that important strategic situation which can be rightly considered the meeting-place, the cross-road and the military corridor of the world.

The third source is petroleum which is the vital nerve of civilization, without which all its means cannot possibly exist whether huge works for production, modes of communication by land, sea and air, weapons of war whether they are planes flying above the clouds or submarines submerged under layers of water. All these, without petroleum would become mere pieces of iron, rusty, motionless and lifeless. . . .

Such is the first circle in which we must revolve and attempt to move in as much as we possibly can. It is the Arab circle.

If we direct our attention after that to the second circle, the circle of the continent of Africa, I would say, without exaggeration, that we cannot, in any way, stand aside, even if we wish to, away from the sanguinary and dreadful struggle now raging in the heart of Africa between five million whites and two hundred million Africans.

We cannot do so for one principal and clear reason, namely that we are in Africa. The people of Africa will continue to look up to us, who guard the northern gate of the continent and who are its connecting link with the world outside. We cannot, under any condition, relinquish our responsibility in helping, in every way possible, in diffusing the light and civilization into the farthest parts of that virgin jungle.

There is another important reason. The Nile is the artery of life of our country. It draws its supply of water from the heart of the continent.

There remains the Sudan, our beloved brother, whose boundaries extend deeply into Africa and which is a neighbor to all the sensitive spots in the center of the continent.

It is a certain fact that Africa at present is the scene of an exciting ebullition. White man, who represents several European countries, is trying again to repartition the continent. We cannot stand aside in face of what is taking place in Africa on the assumption that it does not concern or effect us.

The third circle now remains; the circle that goes beyond continents and oceans and to which I referred, as the circle of our brethren in faith who turn with us, whatever part of the world they are in, towards the same Kibla [direction in prayer] in Mecca and whose pious lips whisper reverently the same prayers. . . .

As I stood in front of the Kaaba and felt my sentiments wandering with every part of the world where Islam had extended I found myself exclaiming, "Our idea of the pilgrimage should change. Going to the Kaaba should never be a passport to heaven, after a lengthy life. Neither should it be a simple effort to buy indulgences after an eventful life. The pilgrimage should be a great political power. The press of the world should resort to and follow its news; not as a series of rituals and traditions which are done to amuse and entertain readers, but as a regular political congress wherein the leaders of Muslim states, their public men, their pioneers in every field of knowledge, their writers, their leading industrialists, merchants and youth draw up in this universal Islamic Parliament the main lines of policy for their countries and their cooperation together until they meet again. They should meet reverently, strong, free from greed but active, submissive to the Lord, but powerful against their difficulties and their enemies, dreaming of a new life, firm believers that they have a place under the sun which they should occupy for life."

THE AVENGERS

James T. Ngugi, today a young man in his early thirties, was born in Kenya. While growing up he watched his people, the Kikuyu, struggle to gain a voice in the colonial government. Under men like Jomo Kenyatta, the Kenya Africa Union (K.A.U.) worked for peaceful reform, but in 1952 dissatisfaction over their failure to gain ground exploded into the Mau Mau resistance. Influenced by these events, Ngugi devoted himself to the cause of African justice and African destiny; his writings are a testimony to the valor and hope of his people. Although Weep Not, Child, *excerpted here, was written as a novel, the experiences of Njoroge, the protagonist, closely parallel the author's own life in Kenya.*

Everyone knew that Jomo would win. . . . If he lost, then the black people of Kenya had lost. . . .

At school a little argument ensued. It was begun by Karanja. . . . He said, "Jomo is bound to win. Europeans fear him."

"No. He can't win. My father said so last night."

"Your father is a homeguard," another boy retorted. . . .

"The homeguards with their white masters. They are as bad as Mau Mau."

"No. Mau Mau is not bad. The Freedom boys are fighting against the white settlers. It is bad to fight for one's land? Tell me that."

"But they cut black men's throats."

"Those killed are the traitors! Black white settlers."

"What's Mau Mau?" Njoroge asked. He had never known what it was and his curiosity overcame his fear of being thought ignorant.

Karanja, who had just joined the group, said, "It is a secret Kiama. You 'drink' oath. You become a member. The Kiama has its own soldiers who are fighting for the land. Kimathi is the leader."

"Not Jomo?" a small boy with one bad eye asked.

"I don't know," Karanja continued. "But father says that Kimathi is the leader of the Freedom Army and Jomo is the leader of K.A.U. I like K.A.U. and fear Mau Mau."

"But they are all the same? Fighting for the freedom of the black people." This was said by a tall but weak boy. Then with a distant look in his eyes, "I would like to fight in the forest."

All eyes were turned to him. He seemed to have said a very profound thing. Or

Summarily tried and convicted, a leader of the Mau Mau revolt is led off to execution.
MAGNUM–GEORGE RODGER

seemed to have put in words what most of them felt. . . .

"Hurrah and victory for the black folk!"

"Hurrah and victory for Jomo—" . . .

The bell went, the group dispersed. They rushed back for their evening classes. . . .

Mr. Howlands sat in the office with his left elbow on the table with the palm of the hand supporting his head. . . . He gazed out through the small open glass window with a strained expression. . . .

He stood and walked across the office, wrapped in thought. . . . The present that had made him a D.O. reflected a past from which he had tried to run away. . . . It was no good calling on the name of God for he, Howlands, did not believe in God. There was only one god for him—and that was the farm he had created, the land he had tamed. And who were these Mau Mau who were now claiming that land, his god? Ha, ha! He could have laughed at the whole ludicrous idea, but for the fact that they had forced him into the other life, the life he had tried to avoid. He had been called upon to take up a temporary appointment as a District Officer. . . . If Mau Mau claimed the only thing he believed in, they would see! . . . Who were black men and Mau Mau anyway, he asked for the thousandth time? Mere savages! A nice word—savages. . . . The strike which had made him lose Ngotho and now brought about the emergency had forced him to think, to move out of his shell. But they all would pay for this! . . .

He looked at his watch. . . . He was expecting the Chief. Mr. Howlands despised Jacobo because he was a savage. . . .

There was a knock at the door. Jacobo, gun in hand, came in. He removed his hat and folded it respectfully. There was a big grin which Howlands hated. He had known him for quite a long time. Jacobo had occasionally come to him for advice. . . . In turn Jacobo had helped him to recruit labor and gave him advice on how to get hard work from them. However all this had been a part of the farm. Duty had now thrown them together and he could now see Jacobo in a new light.

"Sit down, Jacobo."

"Thank you, sir."

"What did you want to see me for?"

"Well, sir, it's a long affair."

"Make it short."

"Yes, sir. As I was telling you the other day, I keep an eye on everybody in the village. Now this man Ngotho, as you know, is a bad man. . . . He has taken many oaths." It looked as if Howlands was not attending, so Jacobo paused for a while. Then he beamed. "You know, he is the one who led the strike."

"I know," Howlands cut in. "What has he done?" . . .

You know this man has sons. These sons of his had been away from the village for quite a long time. I think they are bringing trouble in the village. . . . I am very suspicious about Boro, the eldest son. . . .

"Yes! yes! What have they done?"

"I, well, sir, nothing, but you see these people work in secret. I was just thinking that we should sort of remove them from the village . . . send them to one of the detention camps. . . . Their detention would make it easier to keep an eye on this Ngotho because as I was telling you he may be the real leader of Mau Mau."

"All right. Just keep an eye on the sons. Arrest them for anything, curfew, tax, you know what."

"Yes sir." . . .

"All right. You can go." . . .

Ngotho and his family sat in Nyokabi's hut. These days people sat late only in families. Two were missing from the family group. Kamau was in the African market. He preferred staying and even sleeping there. He felt it safer that way. Boro was not in. He would probably be late. They sat in darkness. Lights had to be put out early. And they spoke in whispers, although they did not speak much. . . . They knew the dark night would be long. Boro and Kori kept their beds in Njeri's hut. Her hut was a few yards away from Nyokabi's. Njeri and Kori waited for Boro to turn up but when he failed they rose up to go. Perhaps Boro would come later in the night or he could sleep wherever he was. Who would dare to go home on such a night, and there being curfew order for everyone to be in by six o'clock? They went out. . . .All of a sudden there was a shout that split the night—

"*Halt!*"

Njoroge trembled. He would not go to the door where his father and mother stood looking at whatever was happening outside. . . . His father came back from the door and sat heavily on the stool he had quickly vacated when he had heard the order for Njeri, his wife, and Kori, his son, to stop. Nyokabi later came in. . . .

"They have taken them away," Nyokabi sobbed. Njoroge felt as if there were some invisible dark shapes in the hut. . . .

Mr. Howlands felt a certain gratifying pleasure. The machine he had set in motion was working. The blacks were destroying the blacks. They would destroy themselves to the end. What did it matter with him if the blacks in the forest destroyed a whole village? . . . Let them destroy themselves. Let them fight against each other. The few who remained would be satisfied with the land the white man had preserved for them. . . . He looked up at Chief Jacobo. A wicked smile lit his face. The desire to kick the Chief was uppermost in his mind. The Chief was grinning.

"Are you sure it's Boro who is leading the gang?"

"Well, one can't be quite sure, but—"

"What?"

"This man, as you are aware, is known to be dangerous. I told you so when you and I talked together before he ran away. Well, I think, I mean there are rumors that he probably comes home . . . but even if this is not the case, Ngotho surely knows his son's hiding-place."

"Haven't you planted men to watch Ngotho's movements and report on them?" . . .

"I have, sir, but there's something else. I didn't, you know, want to tell you, but a few days ago I received this note in an envelope dropped at my door." The Chief fumbled in the inner pockets of his coat and took out a hand-written note which he handed to the curious Howlands.

STOP YOUR MURDEROUS ACTIVITIES. OR ELSE WE SHALL COME FOR YOUR HEAD. THIS IS OUR LAST WARNING.

"Why! Have you received more?"

"Yes—two. But—"

"What did you do with them, you fool?" Mr. Howlands was furious. He stood up. Jacobo moved a few steps back to the door. Howlands could never understand such ignorance. To receive two notes of warning and keep quiet! After a time he cooled down. . . .

It was a cold Monday morning. Njoroge had gone through the first two terms and now was in the third. . . . Njoroge woke up as usual, said his prayers and prepared himself for the morning parade. . . .

The first class was English. Njoroge loved English literature.

"Why, you look happy today," a boy teased him.

"But I'm always happy," he said.

"Not when we're doing maths," another boy put in.

They laughed. Njoroge's laughter rang in the class. The first boy who had spoken said, "See, see how he's laughing. He is happy because this is an English class."

"Do you want me to cry?" Njoroge asked. He felt buoyant.

"No. It's only that my mother tells me that a man should not be too happy in the morning. It's an ill-omen. . . ."

Njoroge was in the middle of answering a question when the headmaster came to the door. . . .

His heart beat hard. He did not know what the headmaster could have to say to him. A black car stood outside the office. But it was only when Njoroge entered the office and saw two police officers that he knew that the car outside had something to do with him. Njoroge's heart pounded with fear. . . .

But when Njoroge went to the car he realized that the headmaster had not given him a clue as to what his family had done. His words of comfort had only served to increase Njoroge's torment.

He would never forget his experience in the post. That particular homeguard post was popularly known as the House of Pain. The day following his arrival in the post he was called in to a small room. Two European officers were present. One had a red beard.

"What's your name?" the red beard asked, while the grey eyes looked at him ferociously.

"Njo-ro-ge."

"How old are you?"

"I think 19 or thereabouts."

"Sema affande!" one of the homeguards outside the small room shouted.

"Affande."

"Have you taken the Oath?" . . .

"No affendi."

"How many have you taken?"

"I said none affendi!"

The blow was swift. It blinded him so he saw darkness. . . .

"Have you taken the Oath?"

"I-am-a-school-boy-affendi," he said, automatically lifting his hands to the face.

"How many Oaths have you taken?"

"None, sir."

Another blow. Tears rolled down his cheeks in spite of himself. He remembered the serenity of his school. It was a lost paradise.

"Do you know Boro?"

"He's my—brother—"

"Where is he?"

"I—don't—know—"

Njoroge lay on the dusty floor. The face of the grey eyes had turned red. He never once spoke except to call him Bloody Mau Mau. A few seconds later Njoroge was taken out by the two homeguards at the door. He was senseless. He was covered with blood where the hobnailed shoes of the grey eyes had done their work. . . .

They had not finished with him. He was in the room the next day. . . . His body had swollen all over. But the worst thing for him was the fact he was still in the dark about all this affair.

"You are Njoroge?"

"Yees."

"Have you taken Oath?" All eyes turned to him. Njoroge hesitated for a moment. He noticed that Mr. Howlands was also present. The grey eyes took the momentary hesitation and said, "Mark, you tell us the truth. If you tell the truth, we shall let you go." The pain in his body came and asked him to say *Yes*. But he instinctively said *No* withdrawing a few steps to the door. Nobody touched him.

"Who murdered Jacobo?" Mr. Howlands asked for the first time. For a time, Njoroge was shaken all over. He thought he was going to be sick.

"Murdered?" he hoarsely whispered in utter unbelief. . . .

The white men closely watched him.

"Yes. Murdered."

"By whom?"

"You'll tell us that."

"Me, Sir? But—" . . .

Mr. Howlands rose and came to Njoroge. He was terrible to look at. He said, "I'll show you." He held Njoroge's private parts with a pair of pincers and started to press tentatively.

"You'll be castrated like your father."

Njoroge screamed.

"Tell us. Who really sent you to collect information in Jacobo's house about . . ?"

Njoroge could not hear: the pain was so bad. . . . And whenever he asked a question, he pressed harder.

"You know your father says he murdered Jacobo."

He still screamed. Mr. Howlands watched him. Then he saw the boy raise his eyes and arms as if in supplication before he became limp and collapsed on the ground. Mr. Howlands looked down on the boy and then at the officers and walked out. The red beard and the grey eyes laughed derisively.

Njoroge was not touched again and when he became well a few days later, he and his two mothers were released.

The hut in which he had been put was dark. Ngotho could not tell day or night. For him, darkness and light were the same thing and time was a succession of nothingness. . . .

The awareness that he had failed his children had always shadowed him. Even before this calamity befell him, life for him had become meaningless, divorced as he had been from what he valued.

In spite of his pain, however, he never regretted the death of Jacobo. . . . This was an act of divine justice. For a day or two he had walked upright only later to hear that his son Kamau was arrested in connection with the murder. For a day and a half, he had remained irresolute. . . . But Ngotho could never tell where he had found courage to walk into the D.O.'s office and admit that he had killed Jacobo. It was a confession that had shocked the whole village.

And Ngotho had now for days been tortured in all manner of ways, yet would tell nothing beyond the fact that he had killed Jacobo.

Mr. Howlands had, as was the usual practice with government agents and white men, taken the law into his own hands. He was determined to elicit all the information from the man. So he had Ngotho beaten from day to day. . . .

Ngotho, who had worked for him and had thwarted his will, would not now escape from him. For Ngotho had become for him a symbol of evil that now stood in his path. . . .

But Ngotho had stuck to his story. . . .

Ngotho struggled to one side and for the first time opened his eyes. Nyokabi and Njeri quickly moved nearer the bed. Ngotho's eyes roamed around the hut. They rested on each of the women in turn, Njeri first. He opened his mouth as if to speak. Instead a round tear rolled down his face. He wanted to rub it away. But as he could not lift his hand, he let the tear run down unchecked. . . . Ngotho turned his eyes and rested them on Njoroge. He seemed to struggle with his memory. He then made an effort to speak.

"You are here. . . ."

"Yes, father."

This rekindled hope in Njoroge. He felt a cold security when he saw that his father was still in command.

This was Ngotho's first speech since they moved him from the homeguard post, four days before. Njoroge was long to remember the day. Ngotho had to be supported by a man at either side. His face had been deformed by small wounds and scars. His nose was cleft into two and his legs could only be dragged. For four days now his mouth and eyes had remained shut.

"You come from school—"

"Yes, father."

"To see me—"

"Yes." He lied.

"Did they beat you there?"

"No, father."

"Then—you—come to laugh at me. To laugh at your own father. I'll go home, don't worry."

"Don't say that, father. We owe you everything.". . .

Ngotho went on, "Your brothers are all away?"

"They'll come back, father."

"Ha! At my death. To bury me. Where's Kamau?"

Njoroge hesitated. Ngotho continued, "Perhaps they'll kill him. Didn't they take him to the homeguard post? . . . Now, don't ask, Did I kill Jacobo? Did I shoot him? I don't know. A man doesn't know when he kills. I judged him a long time ago and executed him. Ha! Let him come again. . . ."

Ngotho rambled on. All the time his eyes were fixed on Njoroge.

"I am glad you are acquiring learning. Get all of it. They dare not touch you. . . . Who's knocking at the door? I know. It's Mr. Howlands. He wants to get at my heart. . . ."

Ngotho's laughter was cold. It left something tight and tense in the air. By now darkness had crept into the hut. Nyokabi lit the lantern as if to fight it away. Grotesque shadows mocked her as they flitted on the walls. What was a man's life if he could be reduced to this? And Njoroge thought: Could this be the father he had secretly adored and feared? Njoroge's mind reeled. The world had turned upside down. Ngotho was speaking. Except for his laughter, his words were surprisingly clear.

"Boro went away. He found me out—a useless father. But I always knew that they would change him. He didn't know me when he came. . . . You see. . . ."

Njoroge turned his head. He was aware of another presence in the room. Boro was standing at the door. Nobody has seen him enter. His hair was long and unkempt. Njoroge instinctively shrank from him. Boro went nearer, falteringly, as if he would turn away from the light. The women remained rooted to their place. They saw Boro kneel by the bed where Ngotho lay. And at once, long before Boro began to speak, the truth came to Njoroge. He could only hold his breath.

Ngotho could not at first recognize Boro. He seemed to hesitate. Then his eyes seemed to come alive again.

"Forgive me, father—I didn't know—oh, I thought—" Boro turned his head.

The words came out flatly, falteringly. "It's nothing. Ha, ha, ha! You too have come back—to laugh at me? . . . No. Ha! I meant only good for you all. I didn't want you to go away—"

"I had to fight."

"Oh, there—Now—Don't you ever go away again."

"I can't stay. I can't." Boro cried in a hollow voice. A change came over Ngotho. For a time he looked like the man he had been, firm, commanding—the center of his household.

"You must."

"No, father. Just forgive me."

Ngotho exerted himself and sat up in bed. He lifted his hand with an effort and put it on Boro's head. Boro looked like a child.

"All right. Fight well. Turn your eyes to Murungu and Ruriri. Peace to you all—Ha! What? Njoroge look . . . look—to—your—moth—"

His eyes were still aglow as he sank back into the bed. For a moment there was silence in the hut. Then Boro stood up and whispered, "I should have come earlier. . . ."

He ran quickly out, away from the light into the night. It was only when they turned their eyes to Ngotho that they knew that he too would never return. Nobody cried.

THE WAGES OF JEALOUSY

Birago Diop, born in 1906 in Dakar, Senegal, was trained as a veterinary surgeon and has since served the government of Upper Volta in that capacity. In addition, Diop has achieved distinction as a poet and storyteller, preserving in his work the ancient traditions of the folk tale, though adding his own personal embellishments. The following excerpt is taken from a short story entitled "Mamelles." In it Diop purports to pass on information, given him by an African sage, on the origin of the Mamelles hills, "two humps on the Cape Verde peninsula, the last bits of African soil that the sun contemplates lingeringly each evening before sinking into the big sea."

Where wives are concerned, two is not a good number. Anyone who wants to avoid frequent quarrels, cries, reproaches, and spiteful insinuations, needs either three wives or one, but not two. Two wives in the same home always have with them a third companion who is not only good for nothing but also proves to be the worst of counselors. This companion is Envy with a voice as sharp and bitter as tamarind juice.

Envious, Momar's first wife Khary certainly was. She could have filled ten calabashes with her jealously and thrown them in a well, and still have ten times ten goatskins full in the depths of her evil heart. It is true that Khary probably had no great reason to be too happy about her fate, for she was a hunchback. Oh! hers was an infinitesimal little hump that a well-starched blouse or a wide-pleated boubou could easily hide. But Khary imagined that all eyes were riveted on her hump.

She could still hear ringing in her ears the cries: "Khary-the-hunchback! Khary-the-hunchback!" and the mockery of her playmates when as a little girl she went around, like the others, bare to the waist. Every few minutes her playmates would ask to hold the baby that she carried on her back. Enraged, she would chase them, and woe betide anyone who fell into her clutches! Khary would scratch her, tear out her hair and snatch off her ear-rings. . . .

As she matured, Khary's disposition had not improved, quite the contrary; it had soured like milk stepped over by a genie. And now it was Momar who suffered from the wretched humor of his hunchback wife. When he went to the fields, he had to carry along his own meal. Khary was unwilling to leave the house, for fear of mocking glances, nor would she help her husband with the farming.

Tired of working all day without getting a hot meal until dark, Momar had decided to take a second wife and had wed Koumba. At the sight of her husband's new wife, Khary should have become the best of spouses, the most loving of wives. That was what Momar had naively expected—but nothing of the sort happened.

And yet, Koumba, too, was a hunchback. Her hump really exceeded the bounds of normality. But in spite of her hump, Koumba was gay, sweet, and lovable.

Back in the days when she used to play, bare-breasted, and they poked fun at little Koumba-the-hunchback by asking to hold the baby she had on her back, she would answer, laughing louder than the others: "I hardly think he would go to you. He doesn't even want to come down and nurse."

Later, on meeting adults, Koumba, who knew them to be less mocking, perhaps, but more wicked than children, had not changed her disposition. In her husband's home she remained the same as ever. Considering Khary as a big sister, she tried hard to please her. She did all the heavy housework, sifted the grain, and pounded the millet. Each day she took Momar his meal and helped him with his work in the fields.

Khary was no happier for that, far from it. More than before she was sour and embittered, seeing that Koumba didn't seem to mind being a hunchback. Envy is so gluttonous that it feeds on any food. So Momar lived half-happily between his two wives, both humpbacked, but one, gracious, kind, and amiable, the other mean, grumbling, and ill-disposed.

Often, to help her husband for a long period, Koumba would carry to the fields the meal prepared the evening before or at daybreak. When, after digging and weeding since morning, they saw their shadows crouch beneath them seeking refuge from the sun, Momar and Koumba would stop work. Then Koumba would heat the rice or the stew and share it with her husband. Later they would lie in the shade of the tamarind tree that stood in the middle of the field. Instead of sleeping like Momar, Koumba would stroke his head and perhaps daydream of women with perfect forms.

Of all trees, the tamarind is the one that provides the thickest shade. Through its foliage, which the sun rarely penetrates, one can sometimes catch a glimpse of the stars—in broad daylight. That is why the tamarind is the tree most frequented by spirits, good or bad, calm or dissatisfied.

Many madmen, who were sane on leaving their village or their hut in the morning, scream and sing in the evening. In the middle of the day they have passed beneath a tamarind tree, where they have seen what should not have been seen, beings from another realm, spirits whom they had offended by their words or deeds.

There are women, weeping, laughing, yelling, and singing in the villages, who have gone crazy because they poured on the ground boiling water from a pot and burned spirits who were passing by or resting in the courtyard. These spirits had then waited for them in the shade of a tamarind tree and had touched their brain.

Neither Momar nor Koumba had ever offended or injured the spirits by word or deed. So they could rest in the shade of the tamarind without fearing the visit or vengeance of the wicked spirits.

While Momar was sleeping that day, Koumba, sewing near by, thought she heard a voice in the tamarind tree calling her name. Lifting her head, she saw, on the first branch of the tree, an old, a very old woman whose long hair, whiter than unspun cotton, covered her back.

"Are you at peace, Koumba?" the old woman asked.

"At peace, thank you, Grandmother," Koumba answered.

"Koumba, I know how good-hearted and deserving you have been ever since you were first able to tell right from left. I want to do you a great favor. On Friday under the full moon on N'Guew Hill, the girl-spirits will dance. When the tom-toms are beating furiously, and the dance becomes most animated, and when one dancer hurries to replace another dancer, you will come closer and say to the girl-spirit next to you 'Here, hold the baby I have on my back; it's my turn to dance'." . . .

In the village, those who stayed up latest had already turned over once or twice when Koumba left her hut and started out toward N'Guew Hill.

From afar she heard the irrepressible tom-toms and rhythmic hand-clapping. . . . Koumba drew nearer and clapped her hands to the astounding rhythm of the tom-tom and the frantic whirlwind of dancers as one gave way to another.

One, two, three . . . ten of them had twirled and twirled, with boubous and pagnes flying. Then Koumba, offering her hump to her neighbor on the left, said; "Here, hold my baby; it's my turn to dance."

The girl-spirit took the hump and Koumba ran away. She did not stop running till she was back in her hut, which she entered just as the first cock crowed....

Koumba no longer had her hump. Her finely plaited hair fell down over her long, thin gazelle-like neck. As he left his first wife's hut in the morning, Momar saw Koumba and thought he was still dreaming; he rubbed his eyes several times. Koumba told him what had happened.

Khary's saliva turned to gall in her mouth when she saw Koumba drawing water from the well. Khary's eyes became bloodshot; when she opened her mouth, it was as dry as clay awaiting the first rains. But no sound came forth, and she fell in a faint. Momar and Koumba picked her up and carried her back to the hut. . . .

When Khary recovered from the suffocation of the jealousy rising from her stomach to her throat, Koumba, still friendly, told her how she had lost her hump and indicated how Khary, too, might get rid of hers.

Impatiently Khary awaited the next Friday with a full moon; she thought it would never come. Dragging around all day long, the sun no longer seemed in a hurry to return home, and night lingered long before leaving its hut to lead its herd of stars to pasture.

Finally, the Friday arrived, as everything eventually does. Khary couldn't eat a mouthful that evening. She made Koumba repeat the old woman's advice and instructions. Then she heard all the noises of early nightfall diminish and vanish; she listened as the sounds of later night were born and grew. When the earth was cold she started out toward N'Guew Hill where the girl-spirits were dancing. . . .

Khary approached, clapped her hands as her husband's second wife had advised; then, after one, three, ten girl-spirits had entered the circle twirling and left it gasping for breath, she said to her neighbor; "Here, hold my child; it's my turn to dance."

"Oh! No you don't!" the girl-spirit snapped. "It's my turn. Here, hold this one that was handed to me a whole month ago and that no one has come to claim!"

With this, the girl-spirit stuck on Khary's back the hump that Koumba had entrusted to her. The first cock crowed that very instant, the girl-spirits disappeared, and Khary remained alone on N'Guew Hill, alone with her two humps.

Lifting her skirts, she began to run straight ahead. She ran by night, she ran by day, she ran so far and so fast that she reached the sea and jumped in. But she didn't disappear completely. The sea was unwilling to swallow her whole.

So it's the two humps of Khary-Khougue that overhang the point at Cape Verde. It is them that the last rays of the sun light up on the soil of Africa. It's the two humps of Khary that have become the Mamelles.

Somewhere in western Uganda, a priest hears the confession of a parishioner.

A PLACE IN THE SUN

LOUVRE, CABINET DES DESSINS; AGRACI

Bay of Tangier, a water color from Delacroix's Moroccan sketchbook

THE LURE OF AFRICA

Napoleon's Egyptian campaign of 1798–1801 excited widespread interest in the ancient land of the pharaohs. The French army of invasion was accompanied by a team of scholars whose studies inaugurated the new science of Egyptology. With them also was the artist Baron Dominique Denon, whose sketches and paintings created a mania for pharaonic décor. Suddenly, Egyptian-inspired motifs proliferated in the decorative arts—on turbans and tombstones, as crocodile couches and sphinx sofas. Baudelaire dreamed of a "burning Africa," and affluent Europeans "wintered" in Egypt and the Maghreb. In 1832 Eugène Delacroix sketched his impressions of Morocco and Algiers and wrote that the streets of Tangier "assassinate you with reality." Beyond beckoned even more romantic places like the Gold Coast and Madagascar, known mainly through reports of far-ranging merchants.

A Denon sketch applied to one of the plates in Napoleon's Sèvres service

COLLECTION OF THE DUKE OF WELLINGTON

Former American president Ulysses S. Grant (seated on a rock in the foreground) and party, posing at the Giza pyramids in the late 1870's

LIBRARY OF CONGRESS

BOTH: LIBRARY OF CONGRESS

Above, British troops fight from behind a redoubt at Honey Vest Kloot during the Boer War. Cecil Rhodes (below), "roughing it" in the field while his forces put down one of the last native revolts in Rhodesia, the Matabele Rebellion of 1896.

BROWN BROTHERS

South Africa's industrialization was based on diamonds, first unearthed in 1866. The availability of these gem stones, and of gold, attracted settlers and capital, with which South Africa developed such other enterprises and mineral resources as asbestos, coal, and copper. The Premier Mine near Pretoria (shown at left in a 1927 photograph) is the largest diamond mine in the world. In 1905 it yielded the huge 3,106-carat Cullinan Diamond. At right, gold miners work a vein at Johannesburg's Crown Mine, located in the gold-rich Witwatersrand area.

LIBRARY OF CONGRESS, © KEYSTONE VIEW COMPANY

CECIL RHODES' DREAM

The discovery in the mid-nineteenth century of southern Africa's wealth in diamonds and gold precipitated that region's industrial boom. Railroads and telegraph lines were built to connect the coast with the bountiful resources of the interior. Among the numerous prospectors who went out in the 1870's was Cecil Rhodes, who would eventually control all the diamond mines of southern Africa. Like many other English imperialists, he dreamed of an Africa "all British from the Cape to Cairo." He was prepared to use his millions, ruthlessly if need be, to implement the vision. In 1885 Rhodes persuaded Parliament to annex the land corridor of Bechuanaland as a "Suez Canal to the north." The next year extensive gold deposits were discovered in the Transvaal, spurring his government's determination to add a united South Africa to its expanding empire. Rhodes' British South Africa Company, which received a royal charter in 1889, became the agency for his conquest of what are now Rhodesia and Zambia. Uganda was "protected" by the Crown in 1894, and the Sudan secured by Lord Kitchener in 1898. Britain's victory in the Boer War of 1899–1902 gave it control of all South Africa. Only German-ruled Tanganyika now obstructed its African corridor.

Through the exploitation of labor gangs, like that above, the railway system of southern Africa expanded rapidly. Between 1860 and 1910 tracks were laid from the Cape as far north as Elizabethville in the Congo.

LIBRARY OF CONGRESS

Life MAGAZINE © TIME INC.–ELIOT ELISOFON

Many startling incongruities appeared as white colonialists attempted to impose their manners and life styles on Africans. Left, the black policemen of Natal, South Africa, have borrowed all the trappings of European gendarmes, including whistles, caps, and shining brass buttons, but their feet are bare. The Durban rickshaw boys below have decked themselves in traditional headgear to attract fares. And, in East Africa, a colonial gentleman (opposite below) clears a hurdle on a tamed zebra.

BOTH: LIBRARY OF CONGRESS

The British advocated indirect rule in Africa; the French favored more direct control of their possessions. But both in their behavior sought the affectations of Europe's gentry. The English enjoyed their sports and garden parties. The 1947 photograph (opposite) of a Kenya master of the hunt could have been taken in England were it not for the black estate-hands. And the Moulin Rouge girl and her Foreign Legionnaire "beau" (right) are not in gay Paris, but in Sidi-bel-Abbes, Algeria, long the Legion's headquarters.

H. ROGER VIOLLET

OVERLEAF: *These photographs are from a 1930's album compiled and annotated by a missionary of the United Methodist Church of America. At that time the Methodists had missions in ten African nations—from Tunisia to South Africa, from Angola to Mozambique. Besides their evangelical efforts, they established schools, hospitals, agriculture stations, and community centers. No doubt their medical efforts were invaluable, but it is unlikely that African youths needed to become boy scouts in order to learn camping methods.*

UNITED METHODIST CHURCH BOARD OF MISSIONS

THE COLONIAL SCENE

Aloof, self-satisfied, and patriotic, the English colonialists, who were generally from the upper middle class, took a little bit of England with them wherever they went in their vast empire. Parasoled and pomaded, they always remained unmistakably British—"Just We Our Noble Selves," as Kipling put it. They enjoyed their colonial existence, with its endless round of teas and tennis, but failed to grasp the aspirations of the "natives," whom they considered primitive and uncivilized. However, the Africans would rise up against their exploiters. Charles Domingo, an uneducated black from Nyasaland (now Malawi), expressed the whispers of his continent in 1911: "There is too much failure among all Europeans in Nyasaland. The three combined bodies—Missionaries, Government and Companies or gainers of money—do form the same rule to look upon the native with mockery eyes ... They are altogether too cheaty, too thefty, too mockery. Instead of 'Give,' they say 'Take away from.'"

LIBRARY OF CONGRESS

Wedding of Manuel Kisende, pastor-teacher at Mataba, Quessua District, Angola.

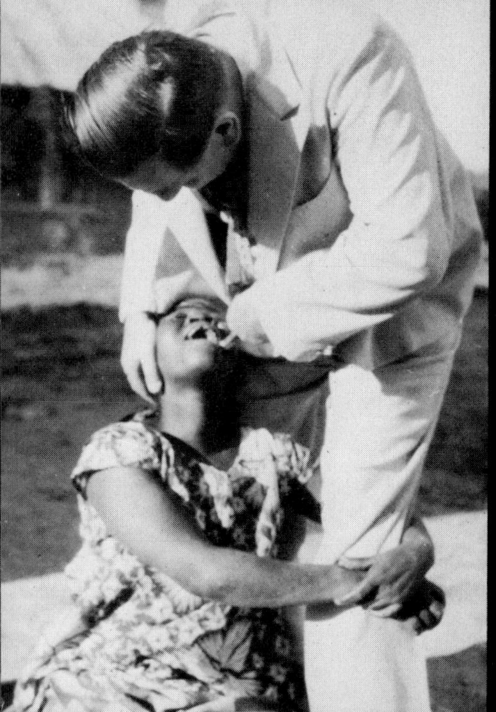

Missionary John Brastrup pulls a tooth, Belgian Congo.

Bishop Moore and native Chiefs Wembo Nyama.

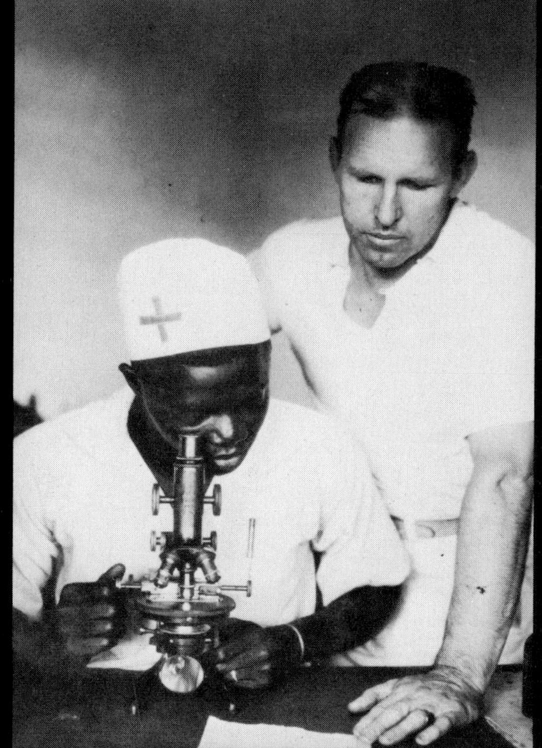

Dr. Sheffey and native assistant in laboratory of Methodist Hospital Wembo Nyama, Belgian Congo.

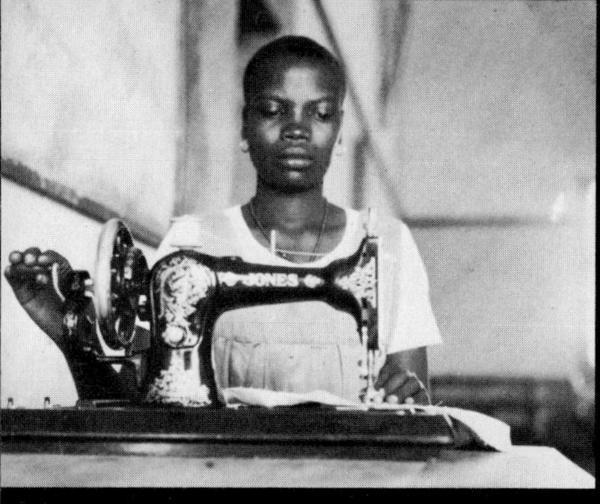

Sewing in the ethodist School Nyadiri, So. Rhodesia.

Group of Pathfinder Scouts, Nyadiri School. So. Rhodesia

Close-up of a witch doctor. Ganta, Liberia

TOWARD A NEW ORDER

Mussolini's conquest of Ethiopia in 1936 enraged Africans all over the continent, adding fuel to the fire of nationalistic sentiments that had been intensifying since World War I. Many Africans had emerged from the Great War yearning for democracy and Wilsonian self-determination. By the 1920's colonial revenues were, for the first time, beginning to show modest profits, and metropolitan governments started to develop medical, educational, agricultural, and veterinary services in their dependencies. Soon a slowly expanding school system was producing Africa's first professionals, a bourgeois class equipped for leadership and participation in government. They watched, horrified, as France stamped out Berber resistance in Morocco and colonial forces subdued local uprisings. They aimed not at the restoration of the precolonial order, but were determined to develop the political and social institutions introduced from Europe. In this spirit they welcomed the establishment of African, or "Ethiopian", churches and launched West Africa's first popular press. European and traditional authorities looked contemptuously at this new elite, calling its members "trousered blacks." But these "handfuls of examination-bred students" would mold Africa's future.

BROWN BROTHERS

The Foreign Legionnaires (opposite) were part of the joint French and Spanish military force that in 1926 finally "pacified" Abd al-Karim and his Berbers in Morocco's Rif mountains. Above, Italian troops prepare to leave for the Ethiopian front in 1935.

H. ROGER VIOLLET

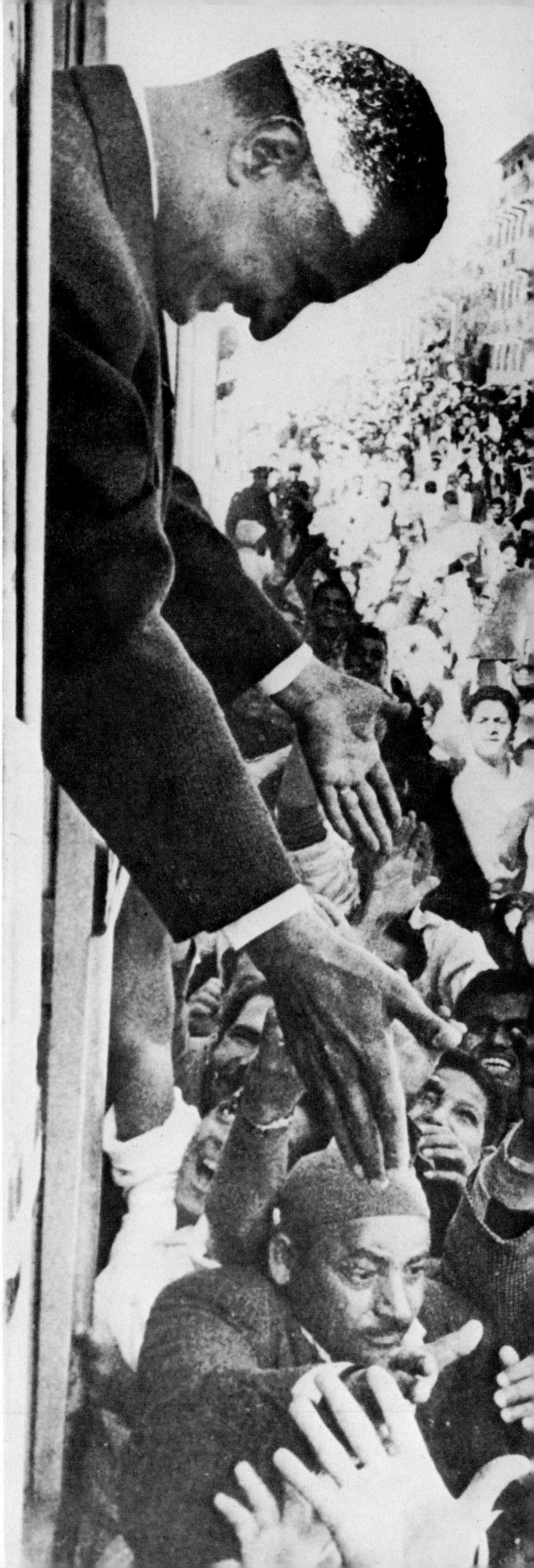

BOTH: UPI

President Gamal Abdel Nasser (right) of the United Arab Republic is greeted by cheering throngs at the Cairo railroad station on his return from a foreign mission. He masterminded the army coup that in 1952 ousted Egypt's King Farouk. Within two years Nasser had established himself as head of state, thus becoming his country's first native-born ruler in over two thousand years. Nasser's seizure of power signaled the beginning of the end of European rule in North Africa. Dashiki-clad Kwame Nkrumah (above) waves to crowds in Accra on Independence Day, March 6, 1957, when the Gold Coast became Ghana. Long a leader of the pan-African movement, Nkrumah, like Nasser, helped create Africa's new order.

FREEDOM NOW

Between the end of World War II and the early 1960's African nationalism intensified. The colonial powers were no longer invincible bastions of strength. Two new super powers, the United States and Soviet Russia, shared the limelight of world domination. Both courted the favor of Africa's emergent states, now part of the nonaligned Third World. For the first time Africans possessed a modicum of political maneuverability. They were also becoming more conscious than ever of the potential of black solidarity in a white world. It was in this atmosphere that Kwame Nkrumah of the Gold Coast agitated for his people's independence, which was won without bloodshed in 1957. In Kenya freedom came in 1963, but only after the violent Mau Mau terror of the 1950's. By this time cries of *uhuru*—Swahili for "freedom"—were reverberating throughout Africa.

KEYSTONE PRESS

Jomo "Burning Spear" Kenyatta, the idolized leader of Kenya's Kikuyu people, is pictured above after his arrest by the British in 1952. Charged with directing the Mau Mau terrorists, he was detained until 1961. Kenyatta then led the fight for independence, becoming prime minister of the new state of Kenya in 1963.
OVERLEAF: *A member of the banned Mau Mau society is captured.*

KEYSTONE PRESS

D
14

Chapter Twelve

AFRICA FOR THE AFRICANS

by

Immanuel Wallerstein

MARCH 6, 1957, was an important, symbolic date in the history of modern Africa. It was the day on which Ghana (formerly the colony of the Gold Coast) became independent, the first Black African state to do so in the twentieth century.

Ghana was not, however, the first autonomous state on the continent. Ethiopia had been independent throughout its history except for a very brief period from 1935 to 1941. Liberia had been founded as a free republic in 1847. Egypt had been independent since 1922. The Union of South Africa had become a self-governing state in 1910 (though under the domination of a white minority).

In addition, a number of states of Arab North Africa had become independent in the six years preceding 1957. Libya had been granted independence in 1951; Tunisia and Morocco in 1956. The Anglo-Egyptian Sudan had become the Republic of the Sudan on January 1, 1956.

Although the Sudan might legitimately be considered by many to be part of Black Africa, it was, nonetheless, Ghana's independence that in the eyes of Africa and of the world represented the dawning of a new era. The countries of the whole world sent representatives to the festivities. Princess Alexandra represented Queen Elizabeth; President Habib Bourguiba of Tunisia came in person. The United States sent its then vice president, Richard M. Nixon.

The independence of Ghana as the "first" independence had a psychological impact on the rest of Africa that far outweighed the importance of this relatively small African state. It meant that for Africans and for others a transfer of power to an all-black independent government was a realizable alternative to the continuance of colonial rule in one guise or another.

The effect could be seen in many places. In nearby Nigeria political leaders of the three regions, into which the

igerian police, in colonial uniforms, salute the new regime during independence day celebrations, 1960.

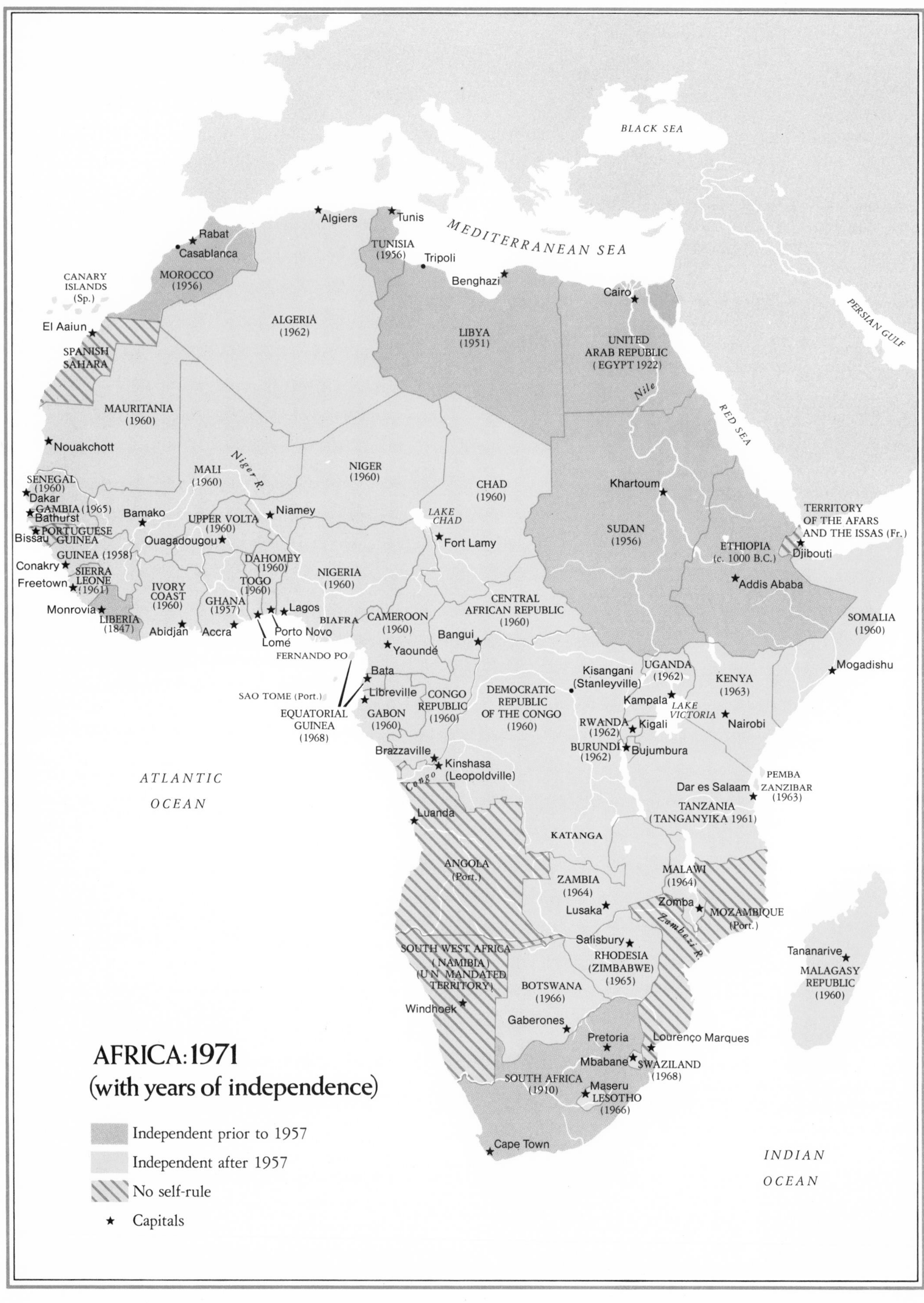

AFRICA: 1971
(with years of independence)
Independent prior to 1957
Independent after 1957
No self-rule
Capitals
BLACK SEA
MEDITERRANEAN SEA
PERSIAN GULF
RED SEA
ATLANTIC OCEAN
INDIAN OCEAN
Algiers
Tunis
Rabat
Casablanca
TUNISIA (1956)
Tripoli
Benghazi
Cairo
MOROCCO (1956)
CANARY ISLANDS (Sp.)
El Aaiun
SPANISH SAHARA
ALGERIA (1962)
LIBYA (1951)
UNITED ARAB REPUBLIC (EGYPT 1922)
Nile
MAURITANIA (1960)
Nouakchott
Niger R.
MALI (1960)
NIGER (1960)
CHAD (1960)
Khartoum
SENEGAL (1960)
Dakar
GAMBIA (1965)
Bathurst
Bamako
Niamey
LAKE CHAD
PORTUGUESE GUINEA
Bissau
UPPER VOLTA (1960)
Ouagadougou
Fort Lamy
SUDAN (1956)
TERRITORY OF THE AFARS AND THE ISSAS (Fr.)
Djibouti
GUINEA (1958)
Conakry
SIERRA LEONE (1961)
Freetown
DAHOMEY (1960)
TOGO (1960)
NIGERIA (1960)
ETHIOPIA (c. 1000 B.C.)
Addis Ababa
IVORY COAST (1960)
GHANA (1957)
Monrovia
LIBERIA (1847)
Abidjan
Accra
Lomé
Porto Novo
Lagos
BIAFRA
CAMEROON (1960)
CENTRAL AFRICAN REPUBLIC (1960)
Bangui
SOMALIA (1960)
Yaoundé
FERNANDO PO
Mogadishu
Bata
Kisangani (Stanleyville)
UGANDA (1962)
KENYA (1963)
SAO TOME (Port.)
Libreville
CONGO REPUBLIC (1960)
DEMOCRATIC REPUBLIC OF THE CONGO (1960)
Kampala
LAKE VICTORIA
Nairobi
EQUATORIAL GUINEA (1968)
GABON (1960)
RWANDA (1962)
Kigali
BURUNDI (1962)
Bujumbura
Brazzaville
Kinshasa (Leopoldville)
Congo
PEMBA
ZANZIBAR (1963)
Dar es Salaam
TANZANIA (TANGANYIKA 1961)
Luanda
KATANGA
ANGOLA (Port.)
ZAMBIA (1964)
MALAWI (1964)
Lusaka
Zomba
MOZAMBIQUE (Port.)
Zambezi R.
Salisbury
SOUTH WEST AFRICA (NAMIBIA) (U.N. MANDATED TERRITORY)
RHODESIA (ZIMBABWE) (1965)
Tananarive
MALAGASY REPUBLIC (1960)
BOTSWANA (1966)
Windhoek
Gaberones
Pretoria
Lourenço Marques
Mbabane
SWAZILAND (1968)
SOUTH AFRICA (1910)
Maseru
LESOTHO (1966)
Cape Town

country was divided, buried their differences the following month and agreed to work together to achieve independence. In French Black Africa the main political movement, the *Rassemblement Démocratique Africain* (RDA), had always eschewed independence as a specific political goal. In October of 1957, however, at the Third Interterritorial Congress of the RDA at Bamako, capital of Mali, the RDA proclaimed that all African states had "the right to independence." In East and Central Africa leaders of nationalist movements rejected "multiracial" formulas—by which the black African, white, and Asian communities were to be separately represented in the legislature—and indicated their intention to strive for independence on the basis of one man, one vote, and majority rule.

Ghana's independence affected the white settler-dominated areas of southern Africa as well. The inconceivable—the governance by blacks of an independent state—had become conceivable. At the conferences of the Commonwealth's British prime ministers, the white prime minister of South Africa found as his peer and colleague the black prime minister of Ghana. The sense of the ongoing revolution was felt throughout the white world—in Africa, in the United States, and in the colonial metropoles of the United Kingdom, France, and Belgium.

Ghana saw its role not merely as a symbol of the new possibilities. The government of Ghana immediately began to pursue an active policy of pan-Africanism, of support for the struggle for independence and majority rule in other African countries. One of the first objectives was to convene a Conference of Independent African States (CIAS), which took place in Accra, Ghana's capital, in April, 1958. *All* independent states on the African continent, even white-dominated South Africa, were invited to the initial preparatory committee meeting. South Africa demanded as a condition of its attendance that an invitation be extended to the various colonial powers. When Ghana rejected this condition, South Africa declined to come. This was the first and last time the white government of South Africa was to be invited to a pan-African conference.

Eight states came to the CIAS meeting in Accra: Ethiopia, Ghana, Liberia, Libya, Morocco, Sudan, Tunisia, and the United Arab Republic. Without the Arab-African states, there would hardly have been a meeting. A crucial turning point in the history of pan-Africanism had been reached; pan-African meetings would thereafter include the whole continent, not just "black" areas. The geopolitical concept that had seemed immutable during the colonial era, that of two Africas—one north of the Sahara and the other south of the Sahara—was all but banished from the vocabulary and the minds of those living on the continent.

Delegates at the first meeting of the CIAS made two decisions of great importance. They decided to give the liberation of still-dependent territories priority in their political efforts. Specifically, they voted to support the Algerian *Front de Libération Nationale* (FLN), leading what was at that time Africa's most significant war of independence. The support was very concrete. The independent African states undertook to send diplomatic missions to potentially sympathetic governments in Scandinavia, Central America, and South America to encourage support for the FLN as the legitimate representative of the Algerian people. Their ultimate goal was to enlist votes for United Nations resolutions, calling on France to negotiate with the FLN and grant independence to Algeria. Indeed, the United Nations was a central focus of African independent states' early politico-diplomatic activity.

The second major decision of the CIAS meeting was to establish permanent consultative machinery in the form of regular meetings in New York of its ambassadors to the United Nations. Thus was formed the so-called African Group, which would play an increasingly important role at the United Nations in the years to come.

Ghana's pan-Africanist thrust did not stop at the convening of the CIAS. Later that same year, in December, 1958, Ghana's Africa Bureau, an agency of Ghana's government to promote pan-African ideas, arranged the first meeting of a new group, the All-African Peoples' Conference (AAPC). The invitees represented were not states but movements—political parties and trade unions—coming not only from independent Africa but also from the states of colonial and white settler-controlled Africa.

The atmosphere of the AAPC was more lively and more militant than that of the CIAS, which had represented governments. Also, from a pan-African point of view, it represented a far larger cross section of the continent's peoples and ideologies. It was at this meeting of the AAPC that the creation of the Commonwealth of Free African States, an all-African governmental structure, was first recognized as an objective of pan-Africanism. It was at this meeting, too, that "tribalism" was denounced as a barrier to African progress.

On colonial issues the AAPC called for the recognition of the Provisional Government of the Algerian Republic (known by its French initials as the GPRA), a structure that had been created by the FLN after the April CIAS meeting. The meeting also called for special efforts to secure

After 1957, *fashionable Ghanaians and other Africans expressed their delight in freedom by wearing Nkrumah-emblazoned clothing.*
KEYSTONE PRESS

UN-supervised elections in French Cameroun *before* independence in order to foil what were considered to be French attempts to install a puppet regime rather than one led by the most militant nationalist organization, the *Union des Populations du Cameroun.* This concern with the Cameroun situation caused the African Group to seek and obtain a special convening of the UN General Assembly in February, 1969, solely to deal with Cameroun. However, in what was to be the first of many frustrations encountered by the African states in attempting to use the UN machinery to achieve difficult political goals, the African Group was unable to secure the UN-supervised elections they sought.

Nonetheless, the years from 1958 to 1960 were years of tremendous forward movement for African nationalism and pan-Africanism. The independence of Ghana, followed by the two Accra conferences of 1958—the CIAS and the AAPC—created a sense of dynamism and optimism that fed upon itself and was to a large degree self-fulfilling.

Events all over the continent reflected this movement. In North Africa the continuing strain of the Algerian war led to a French internal crisis of major proportions in early 1958, which brought Charles de Gaulle back to power. Although many of the forces supporting De Gaulle were motivated by a desire to halt or slow down the decolonization of French Africa, particularly of Algeria, De Gaulle's accession to power nonetheless set in train a series of events that would bring about within four years independence for virtually all of French Africa, even Algeria.

At first, however, the French sought at all costs to keep Algeria. To consolidate his power, De Gaulle submitted a new constitution to a referendum throughout the French Union. The constitution provided for increased powers to the president and increased political rights for French overseas territories, not, however, including Algeria. For voters in France itself, the issue of the referendum was seen to be the structure of the French government. In Algeria a vote in favor of the new constitution was interpreted as a vote to keep Algeria French.

In the rest of French Africa, however, the referendum took on another meaning. This was because, as a concession to growing nationalist sentiment, De Gaulle had written into the proposed laws a new autonomous status for the Black African states. De Gaulle actually went to France's Black African territories to seek support for his referendum. There, egged on by nationalist stirrings, he went one step further. He said he would interpret a "no" vote in any African territory as a rejection of the status of autonomy and a withdrawal from the new French community. "Yes" would mean autonomy; "no" would mean independence.

The states of French Black Africa were faced with an important political choice. Very few political parties decided to seek a "no" vote, and only one of these succeeded in pulling it off: the ruling party of Guinea, affiliated with the RDA, called for a "no" vote and received almost unanimous backing. After the vote the new president of Guinea, Sékou Touré, extended the hand of friendship to France, but President De Gaulle, reacting in pique, abruptly withdrew all French assistance, personnel, and equipment (even some telephone lines) in an attempt to punish and isolate the rebellious state.

As a response to this attempt by France to stifle Guinea's impact on other French African states, Ghana and Guinea announced on November 23, 1958, their union. Although, structurally, the Ghana-Guinea Union amounted to little more than a financial loan by Ghana to Guinea, and the establishment of some joint political committees; psychologically and politically it meant much more. The Ghana-Guinea Union was the first real bridging of the linguistic gap that European colonialism had created in Africa.

Meanwhile, the struggle for independence was escalating throughout Africa. As already noted, Algeria's FLN responded to De Gaulle's return to power by creating the Provisional Government, or GPRA. The determination to gain independence without compromise was reinforced. In East and Central Africa, inspired by the CIAS meeting at which they had been observers, the leaders of the nationalist movements of the various British colonies created the Pan-African Freedom Movement for East Central Africa (PAFMECA) on September 17, 1958. The object of PAFMECA was to coordinate the political efforts of the different parties in order to secure a rapid transfer of power.

In French Black Africa De Gaulle's moves against Guinea were of no avail. Guinea, sustained initially by African and east European assistance, maintained its equilibrium and joined the UN, where it promptly became the most vigorous and radical spokesman of African liberation. Guinea's example spread. By 1960 President De Gaulle was forced to accede by negotiation with the other states within the French community to the very independence that he had been punishing Guinea for achieving. The British agreed to grant Nigeria its independence in 1960. Somalia, an Italian trust territory, had long been scheduled to get independence the same year. In the Belgian Congo, thought to be an impervious stronghold of eternal colonial rule, riots broke out in Leopoldville in January, 1959, a few weeks following the All-African Peoples' Conference, to which Congolese nationalist leaders had gone. Suddenly the dike broke. The Belgians began to talk of decolonization, and one short year later, on June 30, 1960, they agreed to give the Congo its freedom.

Even in the citadel of white-settler ideology—South Africa—events took on a new face. In February, 1960, Prime Minister Harold Macmillan visited South Africa, where he addressed Parliament. This was the famous speech in which he said: "The wind of change is blowing through [Africa], and whether we like it or not this growth of national consciousness is a political fact. We must all accept it as a fact, and our national policies must take account of it."

The very next month was a month of crisis. An African demonstration at Sharpeville was gunned down by the police, and by March 30 a state of emergency had been declared. (By the end of the year South Africa's white electorate had voted to become a republic. The British government deemed that this meant that South Africa had to reapply for membership to the Commonwealth. At first South Africa did so, but in March, 1961, Prime Minister Hendrik Verwoerd withdrew South Africa's application to stay in the Commonwealth as a republic in the face of almost certain refusal.)

Nineteen hundred sixty, often called the Year of Africa, was a year in which much formal political change was occurring on the continent of Africa in the direction of African liberation. Despite this, 1960 was also the year of the first of a series of major setbacks for African liberation. It was the year of the first Congo crisis. On June 30 the Congo became independent. Within one week the Congolese army, the *Force Publique*, had rebelled—largely against the Belgian officers still in command and against the Congolese government, which countenanced this situation. In the confusion that followed, mineral-rich Katanga, under provincial president Moise Tshombe, seceded, and Belgian troops invaded the Congo, ostensibly to protect Belgian lives in areas controlled by the central government. The Belgians, however, actually landed in Katanga. The Congolese government appealed to the UN for troops, which were sent, the contingents coming in part from African countries. The UN troops went to all parts of the Congo except Katanga, where Belgian troops provided a de facto defense shield for the secessionist province. The UN command rather hindered attempts by the Congolese army, partially back under the control of the government, to restore the authority of the central government in Katanga.

Throughout July and August public order continued to be uncertain in the Congo, and the political strains between the two main central government factions—the one led by Prime Minister Patrice Lumumba and the other by President Joseph Kasavubu—worsened steadily. A special meeting of the foreign ministers of the CIAS in Leopoldville in August solved nothing.

In early September Kasavubu dismissed Lumumba in a move of dubious constitutional validity. Lumumba challenged the legality of this action. The army, under Colonel Joseph Mobutu, who had ousted his superior officer, announced neutrality, closed Parliament, and then claimed power itself in conjunction with Kasavubu. The UN command also claimed neutrality, but acted in a way that many observers felt supported Kasavubu.

African independent states, including those with troops in the Congo, split over the question of whether Kasavubu or Lumumba represented the legal central government. Outside Africa, Western powers generally supported Kasa-

SOUTH AFRICAN TOURIST CORPORATION

UPI

Dr. Hendrik Verwoerd (above), South Africa's prime minister from 1958 to 1966, was the chief architect of apartheid. Under this policy the white minority pursues a separate, privileged life, as in the game of bowls at left. Black protest is crushed, as in the scene opposite at Sharpeville in 1960, where the police killed sixty-seven African demonstrators.

vubu. The Soviet Union supported Lumumba. Meanwhile, Katanga's secession continued.

Beneath the welter of detail and the purely legal-constitutional issues of the Congo crisis lay a fundamental political issue that divided Africa, then and ever since. On the one side were those Africans who felt that the achievement of state sovereignty for African states was merely a minor step in a more basic and revolutionary thrust for African liberation. They drew a series of conclusions from this premise. They felt that political independence was not secure as long as other African states were colonized; hence very active support should be given to the remaining anticolonial struggles in southern Africa. They felt that most African states were too small to be politically viable; hence steps toward meaningful African unity had to begin rapidly. They felt that political independence would not bring true independence unless it was coupled with economic independence; hence states should reject "neocolonial" links to their former colonial power and other Western capitalist states. (The third All-African Peoples' Conference, in 1961, denounced as manifestations of neocolonialism: puppet governments; regrouping of states in federations linked to overseas powers; deliberate fragmentation by the creation of artificial political entities; economic interference in a variety of guises, including direct monetary dependence; and the maintenance of foreign military and/or research bases.) They felt, further, that African states should be "nonaligned" internationally, which meant, in their view, cultivation of new diplomatic, political, economic, and cultural ties with the Communist world in order to reduce the primacy of ties with the Western world, and gain a new balance. Finally, they felt that economic development required rapid industrialization and the establishment of socialist modes of organization of the economy.

African political theorists of the opposing view worked on a quite different premise: that Africa, being weak, required assistance from the Western world in order to make economic progress, and that such assistance required a political quid pro quo. They placed less emphasis on the liberation of southern Africa (though they lent verbal support). They thought African political federation to be a utopian goal, and talked of loose forms of economic cooperation. Far from wanting to break economic ties with the West, they wished to reinforce and expand them. Their version of "nonalignment" was limited to a reluctance to form *formal* political alignment with the West. They were

KEYSTONE PRESS

highly suspicious of Communist motives. While sometimes utilizing the term "socialist" to describe their objectives, this group sought to keep African economies open and welcoming to Western capital.

In the immediate Congo crisis the first group supported Lumumba, and the second Kasavubu. In the parallel debate over what kind of action the UN should take on the continuing Algerian war of independence, the first group unequivocally supported the GPRA, the second group sought to be more conciliatory toward France.

This split was soon to take institutional form. In October, 1960, President Félix Houphouët-Boigny of the Ivory Coast invited the states that formerly made up French Black Africa, plus the Malagasy (Malgache) Republic on the Island of Madagascar, to come together in Abidjan to discuss a common position on the Congo and Algerian issues. Soon thereafter this group of states became the *Union Africaine et Malgache* (UAM), otherwise known as the Brazzaville Group. This group supported Joseph Kasavubu. In January, 1961, a countergroup was formed. The so-called Casablanca Group included Ghana, Guinea, Mali, Morocco, the United Arab Republic, and Algeria's GPRA. This group supported Lumumba and, of course, the GPRA.

The states of East and Central Africa were placed in a delicate position by this split among African independent states. The nationalist movements of seven states had created PAFMECA. Three of the PAFMECA states bordered the Congo. All were under British rule, and they were hopeful of achieving independence within the foreseeable future. For the time being they supported Patrice Lumumba.

Lumumba himself fell into the hands of the Kasavubu government and in January, 1961, was turned over to the Katanga authorities, who murdered him. The Lumumbists set up their rival central government in Stanleyville. Lumumba became a martyr to revolutionary Africa.

The Congo turmoil had a direct impact on neighboring Angola, which became the first Portuguese territory to experience armed rebellion. On February 4, 1961, there was an uprising in Luanda, the capital, led by the *Movimento Popular para Libertação da Angola* (MPLA), and on March 15 rural guerrilla warfare started in the northern province adjoining the Congo, led by the *União das Populações da Angola* (UPA). The MPLA-UPA split paralleled the Lumumba-Kasavubu and Casablanca-Brazzaville splits, and alliances were made accordingly.

Some attempts were made to heal this inter-African split.

Some African states belonged neither to the Brazzaville nor the Casablanca groups. In May, 1961, a meeting of all independent states was convened in Monrovia, Liberia. At the last minute the Casablanca powers declined to come. The resulting organization, which called itself the Inter-African and Malagasy Organization (IAMO), or Monrovia Group, was nothing but an enlarged Brazzaville Group.

The attempt to reunify inter-African political structures was premature. In 1962, however, two events occurred that would make such reunification more plausible. One was the Evian Accords, so named because the agreement was reached in the French city of Evian, which led to the independence of Algeria in July, 1962. The second was a temporary internal reconciliation in the Congo. In August, 1961, the two claimants to central power in the Congo—the Kasavubu forces in Leopoldville and the Lumumbists in Stanleyville—agreed to a united government under Cyrille Adoula as prime minister. The UN command strongly supported this new regime and, after two false starts, sent in troops to Katanga in December, 1962, and finally put down the secession. Congolese sovereignty was thus re-established.

The two immediate thorns to African unity being removed—differences concerning the Congo and Algeria—and an international détente between the United States and the Soviet Union seemingly established, the moment was ripe for new attempts at unity.

But just as independent African states were about to shelve their differences and join together in an Organization of African Unity (OAU), the first of a series of coups began when President Sylvanus Olympio of Togo was assassinated by army elements on January 13, 1963. Once again, this "first" was not a real first. Egypt's monarchy had been overthrown by a coup in 1952; in November, 1958, the army overthrew the government of the Sudan and remained in power until October, 1964. However, the Togo coup was the first since the large spate of nations had achieved their separate independences in 1960 and the first marked by an assassination of the top political leader.

Olympio's assassination profoundly shocked the governments of all African states. Many were reluctant to recognize the new regime, and they split anew over the Togo recognition issue. The lines drawn were unexpected. Among the most hostile to recognition were Guinea (of the Casablanca Group) and the Ivory Coast (of the Brazzaville Group). On the other hand, Togo's two neighbors, Ghana (a Casablanca power) and Dahomey (a Brazzaville power), were inclined to work with the new government. Although the Togo recognition issue would not be solved in time for the founding meeting of the Organization of African Unity in May of 1963, and hence Togo was not invited to that meeting, the new government was eventually recognized by all African states, indeed by all states throughout the world. A clear precedent for further coups was set. De facto control would lead to recognition and full participation in inter-African activities.

Frantz Fanon (above), born in Martinique but caught up in Algeria's liberation, became in his brief life a romantic hero of decolonization and a polemicist for the Third World. With Algerian independence achieved, rebel leader and later premier Ahmed Ben Bella (opposite) returns home in 1962.

ALGERIAN MINISTRY OF INFORMATION

MAGNUM—MARC RIBOUD

Between 1963 and 1971 seventeen African states have known successful coups d'état, a few of them several times. In addition, there have been abortive coups in many other states. Although the circumstances vary from case to case, there seem to be two main patterns among the coups, those arising in the Casablanca-type states, sometimes called the revolutionary states, and those in the Monrovia-type states, sometimes called the moderates.

All African states, of whatever bent, have faced some basic dilemmas after independence. The state machinery has been very weak. The bureaucracy has been insufficient in size and effectiveness; nonetheless, government administration has absorbed too large a part of the states' budgets. The budgets of these regimes have steadily expanded under the pressure of demands of the urban middle class and of the workers, both rural and urban. The latter class has

placed particular pressure on expansion of schooling and job-earning opportunities, while the former has pressed for uneconomic expenditures that have provided them with greater facilities and perquisites. These expenditures have been compounded by the "corruption" that has been a widespread feature of the regimes.

However, almost nowhere has governmental income risen to match increased governmental expenditures—partly because of widespread tax evasion, partly because of political resistance to higher taxation by urban wage earners and foreign investors. The only exceptions are some mineral-producing countries, the high demand for whose products has placed them in a relatively better international bargaining position. In any case, the results have been very simple: governments have suffered a steadily increasing budgetary gap.

The Monrovia-type powers have tried to handle this difficulty by maintaining a relatively open economy, and hence continuing close economic involvement in the international economic networks of their former colonial overlords, perhaps supplemented by new links to the United States and West Germany. As unemployment increased because of the swelling numbers of educated individuals who could not be absorbed into a more slowly developing economy, and Western powers became more reluctant to compensate for budget deficits, governments often attempted mild austerity programs. This tended to alienate the cadres against whom they were directed—the new elite in particular—while irritating the unemployed by the mildness of the measures.

In the tight employment situation of such countries, "tribalism" (that is, giving particularistic preference to others coming from the same "tribe" or ethnic group) became a natural corollary of self-protection. This often led to outbreaks of violence, which were increasingly met by political or military repression. Often the outcome was a coup.

To the extent that rivalry among Western powers was important in a particular country, coup leaders may have received the support and encouragement of a power displeased by the former regime. Togo in 1963 is a case in point. The immediate precipitant to the coup was Olympio's austerity program. In furtherance of this program, he refused to employ in the Togo army individual Togolese released from service in the French army. Since many of these persons came from the Kabre people, and many of the noncommissioned officers and privates of the Togo army were also Kabre, the Kabre precipitated a coup. It was not without relevance that France had been very displeased with the Olympio regime because he had opened the country to United States and German economic involvement and had refused to join the Brazzaville Group (despite the fact that Togo was a member of the Monrovia Group). The government that succeeded Olympio's regime developed closer ties with France and joined the Brazzaville Group.

So-called radical regimes were faced with somewhat different dilemmas. (The first of these governments was not to fall until 1965.) These regimes invested more in job opportunities and had tighter monetary and import controls, which meant less luxury expenditures. They had therefore less unemployment and, consequently, less "tribalism." But the bureaucrats, the armies, and the political classes were increasingly unhappy about the constraints on their style of life. There was also growing displeasure among the Western powers, both because of their foreign policy and because of the difficulties caused to Western firms and their employees. In some of these states the accumulation of enemies came to be too much for the regime, and a coup ensued.

In May of 1963, at Addis Ababa, Ethiopia, the division of African states came to an end with the creation of the Organization of African Unity (OAU). It momentarily renewed the optimistic atmosphere so prevalent in early 1960. The divisions of Casablanca and Monrovia seemed surmounted, and the assassination of Olympio was not allowed to undo this new drive for unity. Beneath the euphoria of the founding of the OAU could be discerned the crumbling of internal stability of the independent African states. Yet it was euphoria nonetheless.

Furthermore, unity was based on an unstable compromise between the member states. The Monrovia powers got the kind of loose confederal structure they wanted for the OAU (rather than the United States of Africa some had called for). In addition, they got a promise from the Casablanca states that they would cease giving political support to opposition elements in the Monrovia states. In return, the OAU was officially committed to nonalignment. And most important, all African states were obligated to contribute material aid to the African Liberation Committee (ALC), a body established under the OAU. The function of the ALC was to organize and channel financial, political, and military assistance to liberation movements in the remaining colonies, principally in southern Africa.

Almost immediately the OAU discovered a knotty problem. Most inter-African organizations disbanded in its favor, including the Casablanca and Monrovia groups and PAFMECSA, which consisted of the earlier Pan-African Movement of East and Central Africa, or PAFMECA, begun in 1958 but expanded in 1962 to include southern African parties. But the Brazzaville powers, or UAM, refused to dissolve. They insisted they were a regional organization permitted within the framework of OAU. They did, however, as a gesture, eliminate their office at the UN to indicate they had no political function, and in 1964 they went further and changed the name of the organization so as to emphasize the primarily economic character of the association. It now became the *Union Africaine et Malgache de Coopération Economique* (UAMCE). Some UAM states, notably the Ivory Coast, were unhappy with this shift and declined to participate in the UAMCE. The spirit of OAU primacy appeared to be gaining ground.

TIME INC.–RALPH CRANE

The pace of African liberation also quickened again, and the British timetable for granting independence to its former colonies in East and West Africa was advanced. Kenya, once the great white-settler state of East Africa, became independent under majority rule in 1963. The British broke up the Central African Federation (of the Rhodesias and Nyasaland), which African nationalists had persistently opposed since 1953, and Malawi and Zambia became independent in 1964. There was hope that Southern Rhodesia would follow the path of Kenya.

But the compromise of the OAU was, as stated above, very unstable. By December, 1963, the internal compromise of the Congo had broken down and the ex-Lumumbists established the *Conseil National de Libération* (CNL), with headquarters in neighboring Brazzaville (a more radical

Throughout Africa, modern technology is attacking age-old agricultural problems. The UAR's Soviet-backed Aswan Dam, shown opposite during construction, was completed in 1970. It will control floods and irrigate 1,300,000 acres of previously arid land, but at the same time it prevents silt from reaching the Delta, where farmers are now forced to buy synthetic fertilizers. By the 1960's Rhodesia's tea industry was competing successfully on the world market. As at right, Africans pluck the young tea shoots for processing.

MINISTRY OF INFORMATION, RHODESIA

regime had been installed there after a coup the previous July). Guerrilla warfare broke out in the Congo (Kinshasa). In June, 1964, the last United Nations' troops were scheduled to be withdrawn from the Congo. President Kasavubu, fearing the strength of the CNL forces, appointed the former Katanga secessionist leader Moise Tshombe as prime minister. Tshombe returned to the Congo from exile in Angola with his white, mercenary-led ex-Katanga forces.

Civil war broke out again in the Congo, and the OAU sought to put out the fire. It appointed a special committee under the chairmanship of President Jomo Kenyatta of Kenya. As the situation deteriorated, concern focused on the fact that the CNL forces held hostage a group of whites in Stanleyville, attempting to use these hostages to force central government troops to halt their march on the CNL-held city. In the midst of negotiations under the aegis of the OAU committee, Belgian paratroopers with United States logistical aid (consisting of large US air transport planes) invaded Stanleyville. They liberated most of the hostages, an act that had the effect of militarily ending the civil war in favor of the central government. Half the members of the OAU introduced a resolution calling upon the Security Council at the United Nations to condemn Belgian and United States aggression. In the resultant declaration, much weaker than they had hoped, the UN merely "deplored" the intervention and "encouraged" the OAU to continue its efforts toward resolving the Congo split.

Soon thereafter the Ivory Coast took the lead in recreating the Brazzaville group in a political form. The UAMCE was replaced by the *Organisation Commune Africaine et Malgache* (OCAM). Several members of OCAM began a campaign against the holding of the next OAU meeting in Accra, Ghana, on the grounds that the government of Ghana was involved in active subversion against OAU states, notably Niger. The compromise of the OAU was cracking further.

In the summer of 1965 the OCAM admitted the Congo (Kinshasa) to membership, thus giving moral sanction to Tshombe's government. In Algeria Ahmed Ben Bella was overthrown. Whatever this overthrow involved in terms of internal politics, on the African scene Ben Bella was known as a strong advocate of maximum aid to the liberation movements of southern Africa.

In 1960 the accumulated impact of ten years of struggle in Africa had led to a feeling—both among the African nationalists and the white settlers—that southern Africa was likely to follow the path of the rest of Africa: independence under governments with majority rule. There were small signs in the period from 1960 to 1962 that the Portuguese in their several African colonies and the white regimes of Southern Rhodesia and even South Africa were thinking of making some accommodations to the pressure.

However, the first Congo crisis marked the beginning of the end of what one African leader called "the downward sweep of African liberation," referring to the geographical thrust. The white redoubt of southern Africa stiffened. By the time of the second Congo crisis, there was no longer any doubt that the white rulers would resist to the very end.

When the African Liberation Committee came into existence in 1963, they decided on a strategy of liberation that involved the support of guerrilla warfare in Portuguese Africa. (Fighting had begun in Angola in 1961 and in Portuguese Guinea in 1962. It would break out in Mozambique in 1964.) The eventual use of force was also slated for South Africa. However, the liberation of South West Africa was sought through the International Court of Justice. In 1960 Ethiopia and Liberia, as the only African states then recognized by the World Court, had begun litigation against the Union of South Africa, which, they charged, had violated the League of Nations mandate in South West Africa. The issue was still pending, and the ALC hoped for a favorable decision, which it could use as a political weapon. In the case of Southern Rhodesia the ALC was banking on the assumption that the British would arrange things as they did in Kenya, if only sufficient pressure were put on them by the independent African states who were members of the Commonwealth. This optimism regarding the efficacy of political means for South West Africa and Southern Rhodesia turned out to be seriously misplaced.

The cause of liberation of southern Africa received a series of major blows in 1965 and 1966. The Accra meeting of the OAU was seriously divided, and some members boycotted it. On November 11, 1965, the whites of Southern Rhodesia issued a unilateral declaration of independence of a state they named Rhodesia. The British refused to send troops to put down the rebellion. The OAU was unable to muster any military riposte. Although it voted to respond with a political answer—the breaking of diplomatic ties with Great Britain because of its failure to quell the white revolt—only ten African states actually carried out the resolution.

In January, 1966, Nigeria had a coup, which was at first greeted enthusiastically by the population. However, it led to great internal difficulties in Nigeria, which would force Africa's most populous country to turn inward for several years, unable to devote much attention to the liberation of southern Africa. In February, 1966, Kwame Nkrumah's regime in Ghana was overthrown, thus removing from the OAU one of the dynamic centers of activity on liberation questions. And in July, 1966, the World Court unexpectedly ruled that the complainants against South Africa in the South West Africa case had no legal right to bring suit. The last doorway of peaceful change seemed to have been closed.

The years from 1960 to 1966 can be seen as a shift in Africa from easy optimism to the realization of deep resistance to further change, especially in southern Africa. New tactics were going to have to be developed to meet this new and more difficult struggle. During this very same period there was a parallel shift among black Americans. The optimism of 1960, the period of the great sit-ins that would lead to the Civil Rights Acts of 1964 and 1965, came to be displaced by the realization of great resistance to change. Malcolm X was the prophet of this new awareness, and his address to the OAU meeting in Cairo in 1964 marked the first significant attempt in the postindependence era to link the African and Afro-American struggles.

After a bitter childhood and a prison term, Malcolm X found his course among the American Black Muslims. Expelled in 1964, he formed the more militant Organization of Afro-American Unity.
WIDE WORLD

Nineteen hundred sixty-four also was the year of the Watts riots in Los Angeles, the signal of the great frustration of blacks in urban centers. It was the year that the Mississippi Freedom Democratic Party did not receive recognition at the National Convention of the Democratic Party. In 1965 Malcolm X was assassinated, and in 1966 the Black movement took new directions. A more militant leadership took over the most militant student group, the Student Nonviolent Coordinating Committee (SNCC), and the new leader, Stokely Carmichael, proclaimed the slogan "Black Power." In Lowndes County, Alabama, the Black Panther Party came into existence. This shift in Black America involved the beginning of a new kind of interest in Africa, a directly political interest. The fruits of this new interest, however, were not to be seen immediately.

In the years from 1966 to 1970 the questions of inter-African structures moved to the background of African affairs. In southern Africa it was a time of reorganization and retrenchment for the liberation movements, which sought to find new ways of cracking the strong resistance of the white redoubt. In independent Africa it was a time of considerable instability, in which the case of the Nigerian civil war is especially notable and important.

In October, 1965, nationalist movements from Portuguese Africa met together in Dar es Salaam. It was the third conference of the *Conferência das Organisações Nacionalistas das Colonias Portuguesas* (CONCP), which grouped the radical independence movements of Guinea (PAIGC), Angola (MPLA), and Mozambique (FRELIMO). This loose federation of liberation parties, first formed in 1965, took stock of the situation in Africa and of the setbacks to liberation and African unity. They decided, in the light of what they found, to reinforce their links and plan a coordinated politico-military strategy of the only three areas in colonial Africa then conducting active guerrilla warfare.

Nineteen hundred sixty-six was a year of dilatory activity on Rhodesia. The British, who had refused to use troops against the illegal actions of the white settler government, proposed, instead, a United Nations boycott. Most countries, of course, supported the boycott, but not South Africa or Portugal. Since these two countries controlled the borders of Rhodesia and the outlets for the railway system, their noncooperation made the boycott ineffective. That same year Great Britain made the so-called NIBMAR pledge, NIBMAR standing for "no independence before majority rule." This meant that they would not negotiate any agreement with Rhodesia that would provide for British recognition of Rhodesian independence *before* the majority of the population—that is, the Africans—had the suffrage. White Rhodesians simply held tight, and no agreement was ever negotiated, nor was the white Rhodesian government overthrown. The settlers seemed to have won their gamble for the moment.

In April, 1967, there was an abortive attempt to revive the Casablanca alliance. A so-called Little African Summit was held in Cairo, bringing together the leaders of Algeria, Guinea, the United Arab Republic, and two non-Casablanca powers—Tanzania and Mauritania. The major purpose of the meeting was to discuss ways and means of using force to oust the regime in Rhodesia. Unfortunately, however, the participants did not appear to have uncovered any effective ones.

In May the United Nations General Assembly reacted to the World Court nondecision on South West Africa by ordering that the United Nations assume direct administration of South West Africa, now to be called Namibia. Since, however, no armed force was to be used to oust South Africa from de facto control of the territory of Namibia, the resolution was as politically efficacious as was the UN boycott of Rhodesia.

At this point in time the white southern African governments faced a Black African belt of three countries that spanned the continent: Tanzania, Zambia, and the Congo (Kinshasa). Tanzania was the headquarters of the ALC and offered active support to African liberation movements. Zambia was equally militant in its support, if slightly more prudent. Its prudence derived from a geographical necessity. Zambia is landlocked, and historically its outlet to the sea was largely via Rhodesia and Mozambique. Until it could obtain alternate routes to the sea, it had to cooperate to a limited extent on economic matters with Rhodesia. Zambia was very anxious to get out from under this yoke and had begun the process of constructing a new rail line through Tanzania to the sea.

The Congo (Kinshasa) saw a shift of government in late 1965. Tshombe was removed from power. Soon thereafter Joseph Mobutu staged a military coup and seized control. Although Mobutu represented in pan-African terms a centrist and pro-American position, Tshombe had represented a viewpoint of active cooperation with white settlers. Mobutu's government was willing to give support to anti-Portuguese forces, although they preferred the UPA in Angola (the MPLA was the Angolan group backed by Tanzania and Zambia). Under the circumstances, the governments of Tanzania and Zambia saw Mobutu's regime as a great improvement over Tshombe's, and they moved to create closer links with it.

In 1967 some white mercenary soldiers still in the Congo (Kinshasa), some remaining Belgian settlers, and some remnants of Tshombe's old Katanga forces tried to arrange a pro-Tshombe coup d'état. Thus the third Congo crisis began. This time, however, the fight was between Mobutu and Tshombe, since the United States gave assistance to Mobutu, and the Casablanca-type groups also gave tacit support to Mobutu, who defeated the mercenaries and solidified his control.

The failure of the mercenary-led coup was a rebuff to the South African counteroffensive against the liberation movements. Another setback was the announcement in August by the outlawed African National Congress (ANC) of South Africa and the outlawed Zimbabwe African People's Union (ZAPU) of Rhodesia of a joint military agreement and of their first common guerrilla action in Wankie in Rhodesia.

The riposte of the White government to joint ANC-ZAPU action was the announcement on September 10 by Prime Minister Ian Smith of Rhodesia that he had invited the cooperation of the South African police in "anti-terrorist operations." That very same day the South African government announced a great diplomatic and political achievement. It revealed its first exchange of diplomatic relations with an independent Black African state, Malawi. South Africa offered Malawi economic and technical assistance. In the years to follow, South Africa would seek to enter into more and more such arrangements—with Lesotho, Botswana, Swaziland, Malagasy Republic, and Mauritius—with the intent to both undermine the support of independent African states for the liberation movements and to develop a new economic network of outlets for its own burgeoning industries.

The South African counteroffensive pushed the liberation movements into closer cooperation. In September, 1968, the three members of the federation of liberation parties in Portuguese Africa (CONCP), plus ZAPU and ANC, plus the South West Africa Peoples' Organization (SWAPO), issued a joint statement to the Algiers meeting of the Organization of African Unity. These six organizations were cooperating quite closely. In January, 1969, they met together in Khartoum (Sudan) under the aegis of an International Conference in Support of the Liberation Movements of the Portuguese Colonies and Southern Africa. In February, 1969, the leader of FRELIMO, Dr. Eduardo Mondlane, was assassinated by the Portuguese, which would lead to an internal political crisis in the Mozambique liberation movement.

In April, 1969, the Fifth Summit Conference of East and Central Africa States, meeting in Zambia, issued the so-called Lusaka Manifesto on southern Africa, restating their belief in the equality of men and calling for the reordering of southern Africa to achieve such liberation. It was a moderate statement in view of the events that provoked it, but was given no response by these states except the proclamation in March, 1970, by the white settler regime that Rhodesia would be a republic. In June, 1970, the Sixth Summit Conference of East and Central African States declared that by rejecting the Lusaka Manifesto, Portugal and South Africa had closed the door to the possibility of a peaceful settlement. No progress had been achieved.

This same period (1966 to 1970) saw the acting out of the great Nigerian drama. The first coup in January, 1966, was followed by a second coup in July, 1966, in which army elements coming from northern Nigeria played a large role. In the turmoil that surrounded the second coup, there were riots and murders of persons coming from eastern Nigeria (mainly Ibo) living in northern Nigeria. Nigeria was faced with a typical legacy of the colonial era in which one segment of the population—in this instance the Ibo—had secured greater access to education and hence to bureaucratic positions than many other segments. As typically happens, this more educated sector then began to monopolize bureaucratic and clerical positions in an educationally backward region—in Nigeria's case, the north. As independence came, the educationally backward region began to regard the monopoly of skilled positions in the hands of "outsiders" as oppressive and hateful. In the turmoil of the coup, this resentment led to bloody riots.

The easterners retreated from the hostile north to their own region and began to talk of secession. The issue was complicated by the fact that the Eastern Region was the focus of recently discovered oil, and the Eastern Region came to feel that it in turn was being economically exploited by the rest of Nigeria.

New formulas for governing Nigeria that would reconcile the conflicting interests were sought. In May, 1967, they ended in a breakdown of negotiations. The federal government implemented its twelve-state proposal, eliminating the four existing administrative regions of Nigeria and replacing them by twelve states. From the federal government's point of view this would strengthen the center and eliminate the foci of secession. From eastern Nigeria's point of view this would break up the Eastern Region into three states and weaken them politically. The leaders of the Eastern Region seceded and proclaimed themselves the Republic of Biafra. The central government immediately sought to restore national unity by military means.

At the September, 1967, meeting of the OAU in Kinshasa, the OAU established a consultative commission to help restore peace in Nigeria, carefully refraining from defining the situation as an interstate conflict. This consultative commission functioned throughout the Nigerian civil war with limited effect.

The first nation to recognize Biafra and break the solid African opposition to secession was Tanzania. Tanzania's action, on April 13, 1968, was followed by Zambia's; then came the Ivory Coast and Gabon. Elsewhere in the world no other state was to recognize Biafra, except Haiti. But many outside forces were sympathetic to Biafra. Indeed, the Nigerian civil war was to produce strange bedfellows. Biafra received various kinds of political and economic support, overtly or covertly, from France, Portugal, South Africa, Israel, and Communist China. Some say the American Central Intelligence Agency also gave support. Biafra also received strong support from the Vatican and from various

Nigeria, a polity created under British rule, holds in uneasy union large numbers of Hausa, Yoruba, and Ibo peoples, as well as several smaller societies. The federation was shattered by two coups in 1966, leading to the secession of the Ibo-dominated Eastern Region. The self-proclaimed Republic of Biafra was invaded by federal troops, and in the thirty-month-long civil war that ensued, mass starvation became one of the government's chief weapons. A generation of damaged children, like this refugee, is its tragic legacy.
WIDE WORLD

Protestant relief agencies. The Nigerian federal government received military assistance from Great Britain, the Soviet Union, and the United Arab Republic, and formal support from the US government. Within Africa, Nigeria was supported strongly not only by the majority of states but by the liberation movements of southern Africa.

Ultimately, all initiatives for a peaceful settlement failed. The federal government, however, triumphed on the battlefield, and the secession ended in January, 1970. It was followed by a prompt and reasonably effective policy of reconciliation pursued by the federal government.

Elsewhere in independent Africa there were no civil wars to match that of Nigeria. But political instability remained the norm. In Ghana the overthrow of Kwame Nkrumah's regime led to several years of army rule, which was replaced by a civilian government in 1969, in which the forces historically opposed to the Nkrumah regime assumed the leadership. Ghana's partner in the Casablanca Group, Mali, also saw its regime overthrown by an army coup in November, 1968. The only one of the Casablanca Group regimes in West Africa to survive was Guinea; it was menaced by an abortive Portuguese-led invasion in early 1971, but the commandos were rebuffed.

In the center of Africa we have already described the political evolution of the belt of states opposed to the white domination of South Africa. The most important event in other states in the region occurred in the Congo (Brazzaville), where the radical regime emerging from the 1963 coup survived various attempts to overthrow it or modify its character. In 1968 the regime took a further turn to the left, proclaiming itself a Marxist state. This outlook led to hostile relations with the Congo (Kinshasa), considered an American puppet, and sympathetic ties with the socialist block, especially China and Cuba. The Congo (Brazzaville) nevertheless maintained close links with France and membership in OCAM, the majority of whose member states were former French colonies.

While the OAU was finding itself in great internal difficulties, OCAM was strengthening itself as an organization. Although it lost Mauritania in 1965, it had been able over the years to add to the original Brazzaville Group Togo, Rwanda, the Congo (Kinshasa), and Mauritius, thus embracing most of French-speaking Africa except North Africa.

In 1969 there was a sudden spurt of radicalization in northeast Africa. There were coups in the Sudan (May), Libya (September), and Somalia (October). In all cases military regimes came to power. In all cases the regimes were more anti-Western than their predecessors had been, and they talked of substantive social change at home. The Sudan and Libya moved toward a close alliance with the UAR on the Arab and African scene. About this time Uganda also moved leftward, but this was reversed by a military coup in early 1971. Britain's Conservative government resumed arms shipments to South Africa in defiance of a United Nations ban and over the vigorous protests of the African members of the Commonwealth.

In summary, the years from 1966 to 1971 were years of political uncertainty and relative stagnation for Africa. The liberation movements of southern Africa worked very hard to survive; they succeeded, but did not advance much. Nigeria, Africa's largest country, survived a bloody civil war and was trying to catch its breath. Elsewhere the balance sheet was about even.

The decade from 1960 to 1970 had started high and ended lower. It was the decade to come, 1970–1980, that would probably more clearly indicate how and to what degree Africa would move forward to political liberation and economic development.

THE THIRD WORLD

Cadet corps parading during Ghanaian celebrations
MAGNUM–IAN BERRY

THE MOTION OF DESTINY

The argument for independence for the Gold Coast was eloquently articulated by Kwame Nkrumah, who placed a motion to that purpose before its House of Assembly on July 10, 1953. Four years later the Gold Coast became the first British colony south of the Sahara to achieve independence, with Nkrumah as prime minister of the new republic, renamed Ghana. Following are extracts from that historic speech, since known reverently as "The Motion of Destiny."

The right of a people to decide their own destiny, to make their way in freedom, is not to be measured by the yardstick of color or degree of social development. It is an inalienable right of peoples which they are powerless to exercise when forces, stronger than they themselves, by whatever means, for whatever reasons, take this right away from them. If there is to be a criterion of a people's preparedness for self-government, then I say it is their readiness to assume the responsibilities of ruling themselves. For who but a people themselves can say then they are prepared? . . .

There is no conflict that I can see between our claim and the professed policy of all parties and governments of the United Kingdom. We have here in our country a stable society. Our economy is healthy, as good as any for a country of our size. In many respects, we are very much better off than many Sovereign States. And our potentialities are large. Our people are fundamentally homogeneous, nor are we plagued with religious and tribal problems. And, above all, we have hardly any color bar. In fact, the whole democratic tradition of our society precludes the *herrenvolk* doctrine. The remnants of this doctrine are now an anachronism in our midst, and their days are numbered.

We have traveled long distances from the days when our fathers came under alien subjugation to the present time. We stand now at the threshold of self-government and do not waver. The paths have been tortuous, and fraught with peril, but the positive and tactical action we have adopted is leading us to the New Jerusalem, the golden city of our hearts desire! . . .

Today, more than ever before, Britain needs more "autonomous communities freely associated." For freely associated communities make better friends than those associated by subjugation. We see today how much easier and friendlier are the bonds between Great Britain and her former dependencies of India, Pakistan and Ceylon. So much of the bitterness that poisoned the relations between these former colonies and the Unied Kingdom has been absolved by the healing power of a better feeling so that a new friendship has been cemented in the free association of autonomous communities. . . .

In the very early days of the Christian era, long before England had assumed any importance, long even before her people had united into a nation, our ancestors had attained a great empire, which lasted until the eleventh century, when it fell before the attacks of the Moors of the North. At its height that empire stretched from Timbuktu to Bamako, and even as far as the Atlantic. . . .

Thus may we take pride in the name of Ghana, not out of romanticism, but as an inspiration for the future. It is right and proper that we should know about our past. For just as the future moves from the present, so the present has emerged from the past. Nor need we be ashamed of our past. There was much in it of glory. What our ancestors achieved in the context of their contemporary society gives us confidence that we can create, out of that past, a glorious future, not in terms of war and military pomp, but in terms of social progress and of peace. For we repudiate war and violence. Our battles shall be against the old ideas that keep men trammeled in their own greed; against the crass stupidities that breed hatred, fear and inhumanity. The heroes of our future will be those who can lead our people out of the stifling fog of disintegration through serfdom, into the valley of light where purpose, endeavor and determination will create that brotherhood which Christ proclaimed two thousand years ago, and about which so much is said, but so little done. . . . And so today we recall the birth of the Ashanti [Asante] nation through Okomfo Anokye and Osei Tutu and the symbolism entrenched in the Golden Stool; the valiant wars against the British, the banishment of Nana Prempeh the First to the Seychelles; the temporary disintegration of the nation and its subsequent reunification. And so we come to the Bond of 1844. Following trade with the early merchant adventurers who came to the Gold Coast, the first formal association of Britain with our country was effected by the famous Bond of 1844, which accorded Britain trading rights in the country. But from these humble beginnings of trade and friendship, Britain assumed political control of this country. But our inalienable right remains . . . as my friend, George Padmore, puts it in *The Gold Coast Revolution:* "When the Gold Coast Africans demand self-government today they are, in consequence, merely asserting their birthright which they never really surrendered to the British who, disregarding their treaty obligations of 1844, gradually usurped full sovereignty over the country."

Then the Fanti Confederation: The earliest manifestation of Gold Coast nationalism occurred in 1868 when Fanti Chiefs attempted to form the Fanti Confederation in order to defend themselves against the might of Ashanti and the incipient political encroachments of British merchants. It was also a union of the coastal states for mutual economic and social development. This was declared a dangerous conspiracy with the consequent arrest of its leaders.

Then the Aborigines Rights Protection Society was the next nationalist movement to be formed with its excellent aims and objects, and by putting up their titanic fight for which we cannot be sufficiently grateful, formed an unforgettable bastion for the defense of our God-given land and thus preserved our inherent right to freedom. Such men as Mensah-Sarbah, Atta Ahuma, Sey and Woode have played their role in this great fight.

Next came the National Congress of British West Africa. The end of the first Great War brought its strains and stresses and the echoes of the allied slogan, "We fight for freedom" did not pass unheeded in the ears of Casely-Hayford, Hutton-Mills and other national stalwarts who were some of the moving spirits of the National Congress of British West Africa. But the machinations of imperialism did not take long to smother the dreams of the people concerned, but today their aims and objects are being more than gratified with the appointment of African judges and other improvements in our national life.

As with the case of the National Congress of British West Africa, the United Gold Coast Convention was organized at the end of the Second World War to give expression to the people's desire for better conditions. The British Government, seeing the threat to its security here, arrested six members of the Convention and detained them for several weeks until the Watson Commission came. The stand taken by the Trades Union Congress, the Farmers, Students and Women of the country provides one of the most epic stories in our national struggle.

In June 1949, the Convention People's Party with its uncompromising principles led the awakened masses to effectively demand their long lost heritage. And today the country moves steadily forward to its proud goal. . . .

According to the motto of the valiant *Accra Evening News*—"We prefer self-government with danger to servitude in tranquillity." Doubtless we shall make mistakes as have all other nations. We are human beings and hence fallible. But we can try also to learn from the mistakes of others so that we may avoid the deepest pitfalls into which they have fallen. Moreover, the mistakes we may make will be our own mistakes, and it will be our responsibility to put them right. As long as we are ruled by others we shall lay our mistakes at their door, and our sense of responsibility will remain dulled. Freedom brings responsibilities and our experience can be enriched only by the acceptance of these responsibilities. . . .

Honorable Members, you are called, here and now, as a result of the relentless tide of history, by Nemesis as it were, to a sacred charge, for you hold the destiny of our country in your hands. The eyes and ears of the world are upon you; yea, our oppressed brothers throughout this vast continent of Africa and the New World are looking to you with desperate hope, as an inspiration to continue their grim fight against cruelties which we in this corner of Africa have never known! Cruelties which are a disgrace to humanity and to civilization, which the white man has set himself to teach us. At this time, history is being made; a colonial people in Africa has put forward the first definite claim for independence. An African colonial people proclaim that they are ready to assume the stature of free men and to prove to the world that they are worthy of the trust.

I know that you will not fail those who are listening for the mandate that you will give to your Representative Ministers. For we are ripe for freedom, and our people will not be denied. They are conscious that the right is theirs, and they know that freedom is not something that one people can bestow on another as a gift. They claim it as their own and none can keep it from them.

And while yet we are making our claim for self-government I want to emphasize that self-government is not an end in itself. It is a means to an end, to the building of the good life to the benefit of all, regardless of tribe, creed, color or station in life. Our aim is to make this country a worthy place for all its citizens, a country that will be a shining light throughout the whole continent of Africa, giving inspiration far beyond its frontiers. And this we can do by dedicating ourselves to unselfish service to humanity. We must learn from the mistakes of others so that we may, in so far as we can, avoid a repetition of those tragedies which have overtaken other human societies. . . .

To Britain this is the supreme testing moment in her African relations. When we turn our eyes to the sorry events in South, Central and East Africa, when we hear the dismal news about Kenya and Central African Federation, we are cheered by the more cordial relationship that exists between us and Britain. We are now asking her to allow that relationship to ripen into golden bonds of freedom, equality and fraternity, by complying without delay to our request for self-government. . . .

The self-government which we demand, therefore, is the means by which we shall create the climate in which our people can develop their attributes and express their potentialities to the full. As long as we remain subject to an alien power, too much of our energies is diverted from constructive enterprise. Oppressive forces breed frustration. Imperialism and colonialism are a twofold evil. This theme is expressed in the truism that "no nation which oppresses another can itself be free." Thus we see that this evil not only wounds the people which is subject, but the dominant nations pay the price in a warping of their finer sensibilities through arrogance and greed. Imperialism and colonialism are a barrier to true friendship.

LIBERTY AND FRATERNITY

In the wake of World War II, *among the most influential politicians in French West Africa was Félix Houphouët-Boigny, president of the Ivory Coast since 1960. His is the most prosperous of the former French territories in Africa; his has been the strongest African voice in Paris, where he served as minister in a succession of French cabinets; his has been the most powerful political organization in West Africa (the* Rassemblement Démocratique Africain), *which before independence extended into most French-African territories. Houphouët-Boigny was at one time considered to be a radical and a Communist, but is now regarded as the most conservative of West Africa's leaders, a product of the so-called elite class of Africans whose political and economic prosperity was established during the colonial period. In the following article, Houphouët-Boigny acknowledges his long love affair with France, and argues for maintaining close economic and cultural ties despite political independence.*

I am a man of the African soil, having lived constantly in the midst of our rural Negro masses, sharing their joys and their sorrows, and making their great hope of liberty my own. For ten consecutive years, they have elected me to represent them in the French Parliament. I am the leader of the most powerful African political movement—a movement which continues to this very day to denounce the abuses and errors of colonialism, and to call untiringly for justice

Houphouët-Boigny, president of Ivory Coast
UPI

and equality. For these reasons, I think I have the right to consider myself the authentic spokesman of the millions of African men and women who have chosen, in preference to the type of independence just acquired by the neighboring state of Ghana, a Franco-African community founded on liberty, equality and fraternity.

In considering where the real interests of the colored peoples of the French territories in Africa lie, we do not begin with a blank slate. The relations which prevail between Frenchmen of the mother country and Frenchmen of Africa already exist in an historical complex of events lived in common, in which good and bad memories mingle. . . . I will therefore examine only the present state of relations within the French Union, as they have evolved during the past ten years.

As a preliminary, we must remove the aura which the concept of independence holds in our imaginations. Why do we not demand independence? To answer this question, I can only ask another: What is independence? Industrial and technical revolutions are making peoples more and more dependent on one another. . . . Indeed, who doubts that close and sustained economic relations are essential to a country which wants to raise its standard of living? What countries are self-sufficient? Not even the United States. Indeed, the countries of Europe in the Coal and Steel Community, in Euratom and in the Common Market are prepared to relinquish a part of their sovereignty, that is to say, a part of their national independence. Why, if not to bring about, by association and mutual aid, a more fully elaborated form of civilization which is more advantageous for their peoples and which transcends a nationalism that is too cramped, too dogmatic and by now out of date? . . .

I am a native of a territory whose development has scarcely begun. Between 1939 and 1955 the tonnage handled by the port of Abidjan in the Ivory Coast went from 231,250 tons to 930,000 tons. The population has increased tenfold in the space of a few years and this rate shows no sign of diminishing. The Ivory Coast could not, by itself, find the means of providing the investment monies needed to cope with this heavy and continuing expansion. For many more years —10? 20? 50?—it will require enough capital aid to allow its inhabitants to make up for the heavy handicaps which nature imposes on tropical countries. . . .

The Investment Fund for the Economic and Social Development of the Overseas Territories (F.I.D.E.S.) was created in 1946 to centralize and coordinate, with the cooperation of the Central Fund for France Overseas, a major program of internal development. In the space of ten years, more than 600 billion francs of government funds have been devoted to territories whose area is 9,000,000 square kilometers but whose population does not exceed 30,000,000. . . .

The fact is that the manner in which money is given can be a guarantee of continuity and stability. Perhaps we will on occasion find some creditor, public or private, capable of loaning, if not of giving, the billions necessary for the industrial, technical and social development of the African territories. But what guarantee would we have that this aid would be forthcoming year after year? How could we control the allocation of the loans offered? For what would we be asked in exchange?

We know what France asks of us—to share in her institutions and to share in them as equals. The right of citizenship has been granted without restriction to all the inhabitants of the French Union, and all the electors, whatever their origin, are gathered in a single college. At one stroke universal suffrage has been instituted everywhere—a privilege that not even the state of Ghana nor British Nigeria has yet dared extend to the tribal regions of the interior. No racial or religious discrimination prohibits any activity, public or private. Opportunities are legally the same for all, and if inequalities exist they arise from circumstances or local conditions which the authorities are making every effort to eliminate.

Thus the democratic institutions of republican France have little by little been established in the overseas territories. During the past several months, free elections throughout French Africa have enabled the people to choose those who would direct communal, urban, rural or territorial institutions. As a result, Africans are now in a position to exercise their responsibilities and to assert their political personality. Municipal councils exercise sovereign power over local affairs. Territorial assemblies are endowed with broad deliberative powers allowing them to adopt autonomous laws distinct from legislation which applies to the mother country. They have an executive responsible to them, to whom is entrusted the direction of territorial affairs with the exception of foreign relations, defense and security, which remain in the hands of the central power. It is in some degree self-government, but it maintains essential links with the Republic, and is not without analogy to the federal structure of the United States of America.

What makes it certainly unique, however, among various relationships that have existed in modern times between a mother country and its dependencies is the participation of overseas populations in the central government of the Republic. There are, in the National Assembly and in the Council of the Republic, Negro deputies and senators, elected in the same way as their colleagues of the mother country. The fusion has succeeded so well, mutual courtesy and comprehension have developed so naturally, that no one in France finds it remarkable any longer that the third-ranking dignitary of the Republic, the President of the Senate, is a Negro—Mr. Monnerville. It will seem then just as unremarkable that other colored people have for several years played a part in the Government, and that I myself was able to represent France in the United Nations at the time of the debates on Togo. . . .

Since the French Union is dynamic, our evolution continues on the national level, and other ties are contemplated in a constitutional reform now being prepared and soon to be debated in the French Parliament. We took part in the preparations for this debate, maintaining as our guiding principle the idea of a federal community, freely joining the peoples of French language and culture. The specific terms by which the principle will be expressed must now be decided by French legislators—black and white.

Naturally, we cannot help but compare our own evolution with the experiment which Great Britain has just undertaken in granting independence to the state of Ghana. Actually, the terms of agreement do not differ greatly, although we have not asked for the type of independence which Mr. Nkrumah has just obtained. After much reflection, bearing in mind the highest interest of this Africa which we dearly love, the human relations existing between French and African, and the imperative of this century—the interdependence of nations—from which no power can claim to escape, we have preferred to try a different experiment, more difficult perhaps, but unique of its kind and unknown until now in the long history of nations—that of a community of peoples, equal and fraternal. . . .

Today, no nation, however powerful, can pretend to impose its absolute will on another for long. By doing so, it would irremediably compromise its own future as a great nation. France knows this. Its own best interests no less than its sensitivity to human values and the absence of any racist feelings among its people have led it voluntarily to renounce force as an instrument of policy in Black Africa and to seek new political arrangements with us, actively and sincerely. . . .

The presence of the French in Africa is the result of military conquests or of peaceful penetrations which go back to the end of the last century. France has suppressed slavery wherever it existed and has put an end to the quarrels which set different ethnic groups against one another; it has given its education to the African masses and its culture to an elite; it has instituted sanitary and medical improvements without precedent. In French ranks, in turn, we have poured out our blood on the battlefields for the defense of liberty, and we have won a place in the history of France and of the free world. We do not want to abandon this recent heritage by trying to go back to our origins. . . . It is important that the Franco-African community—egalitarian, humane and fraternal—appear to all nations not only as an example to be emulated but also as an element of international stability on which a sure future can be built.

In our view, that community is an act of faith in this future and also an act of human solidarity. It enables us to bring our stone to the world edifice without losing either our national identity or the French citizenship which we have earned and acquired worthily. And it constitutes a home we wish to keep, as in the definition which Robert Frost gave of it:

"Home is the place where, when
you have to go there,
They have to take you in."

AFRICA'S COMMON MARKET

In response to the urgent need for a radical revision of France's relationship with its overseas territories, Charles de Gaulle dissolved

Guinea's president, Sékou Touré, at the UN
UPI

the Union Française *in* 1958, *"offering" its territories the choice of entering a quasi-federal "community," with France as director of all foreign and economic affairs, or of becoming fully independent. Initially, all the countries agreed to continue their Paris association save Guinea, whose people responded to the French referendum with a "no" vote. In this they were led by Sékou Touré, who has been president, prime minister, and chairman of Guinea's only political party since independence. In the following article, published in* 1962, *Touré presents his program for cooperation within the African community.*

We of course know that the world today is interdependent, and Africa, which cannot live in isolation, does not intend to remain at the margin of this modern world. She thinks she is entitled to benefit from the experience of other nations as well as from the fruits of her own efforts. In turn, she must contribute actively to the creation of a world society in which each nation, while retaining its own personality, will be considered on an equal footing with the others and will, like them, take on its proper share of international responsibilities. . . .

Colonialism's greatest misdeed was to have tried to strip us of our responsibility in conducting our own affairs and convince us that our civilization was nothing less than savagery, thus giving us complexes which led to our being branded as irresponsible and lacking in self-confidence. Our greatest victory, then, will not be the one we are winning over colonialism by securing independence but the victory over ourselves by freeing ourselves from the complexes of colonialism, proudly expressing Africa's authentic values and thoroughly identifying ourselves with them. Thus the African peoples will become fully conscious of their equality with other peoples.

The colonial powers had assimilated each of their colonies into their own economy. . . . We know that we must rebuild Africa. To win and proclaim a nation's independence but keep its old structures is to plow a field but not sow it with grain for a harvest. Africa's political independence is a means which must be used to create and develop the new African economy. Our continent possesses tremendous reserves of raw materials and they, together with its potential sources of power, give it excellent conditions for industrialization. . . .

African unity is no more a goal in itself than was independence. It simply is a means of development, a force of inter-African cooperation. It is indispensable because of the unjust nature of the relationship between the underdeveloped African nations and the economically strong nations. The equality of this relationship must be improved in order to overcome the social inequalities and differentiations in the present levels of development throughout the world. The highly developed nations have economic relations among themselves either of cooperation or of competition. But their relations with the undeveloped nations are those of exploitation, of economic domination. The direct colonial exploitation of former days is being succeeded by exploitation by international monopolies, and this has a tendency to become permanent. Paradoxically, it is the underdeveloped nations, exporting raw materials and crude products, which contribute an important share of the costs and the social improvements from which workers in the fully developed countries benefit. . . .

The mere fact that there are cries of alarm about the production of coffee, cacao or peanuts, while there is silence about the products for which the demand is increasingly active but whose prices remain stable, such as diamonds, gold, oil, radioactive ores, zinc and copper, illustrates the mercantile nature of the economic relations between the highly developed nations and the nations producing raw materials. . . .

Here, as in other realms, the interests of the African peoples are one, and the awareness of this unity is rapidly becoming more and more explicit. The African nations are realizing that in order to solve their urgent social problems they must speed up the transformation of their trade economy; and if this is to be done through industrialization, it cannot be done within the limits of our national micro-economies. But unconditional integration into a multi-national market consisting of highly developed and underdeveloped nations negates the possibility of industrial development in advance; it could only be the association of horse and rider. If they are to complement each other economically, the development of all associated nations must be carried out according to their united needs and common interests. . . . The leaders of the European Economic Community seem not to be aware of all this, at least as far as Africa is concerned, and make no secret of their desire to achieve a political community of Europe which cannot be reconciled with Africa's desire for political independence; Africa remains as grimly hostile as ever to the division of Africa which began with the Congress of Berlin in 1885.

The unity so much desired by all Africans will not be achieved around any one man or any one nation, but around a concrete program, however minimal. The rules of the union must favor and reinforce generally accepted concepts: equality of all nations, large or small; fraternal solidarity in their relationships; the common use of certain resources; and respect for the character and institutions of each state. Not only must there be no interference in the internal affairs of any state by another, but each must help to solve the other's problems. If we do not rapidly achieve such a framework of solidarity, permitting the peaceful evolution of our countries, we risk seeing the cold war enter Africa and divide the African states into antagonistic forces and blocs, jeopardizing their whole future in common.

The evolution of our countries in peace and harmony requires a high degree of cooperation. We have always thought that Africa should be considered like the human body: when a finger is cut off, the whole body suffers. The growing awareness that we all share the same future must make us increase our efforts for this cooperation, for solidarity and active and conscious African participation in world progress. . . .

Some have claimed to see political antagonisms in the formation of various African groupings. Actually these were the first concrete manifestations of unity, and were inspired by human and historical necessity. Skepticism notwithstanding, this tendency toward unity will increase. Political choices which do not correspond to the needs and aspirations of our peoples—and it is important that this be understood—will inevitably fail.

As for what face a united Africa will wear, whatever the choices she makes in her orientation, it will not be turned either against the East or against the West. It will be above all and essentially directed toward the emancipation and progress of Africa and her peoples. In our struggle for freedom there is no room for negative choices, but only for positive thought and constructive action. What will be destroyed or defeated in this struggle are those things that historical necessities, human needs and the forces of progress consign to destruction and oblivion.

To attempt to interpret Africa's behavior in capitalist or Communist terms is to neglect the fundamental fact that Africa's present condition corresponds neither to the given facts of capitalism nor to those . . . of Communism.

Africa's way is the way of peaceful revolution, in which the morality of an action counts much more than its form and conditions. That some believe socialism corresponds best to the aims of the African revolution, while others suppose it is preferable, despite the lack of national capital, to espouse capitalist principles—these considerations will not in the last analysis prevent our peoples from deciding their own fate. It is they who are called on to make the sacrifices and the creative efforts necessary to ensure Africa's development. Their awareness is sufficiently keen to enable them to choose the way they want to go. . . .

African neutralism, then, is not shameful indifference, a sort of political demobilization. On the contrary, it is the expression of a lively faith in a happy future for mankind. It is something active, a participating force, an active agent in the struggle for the achievement of a world society—emancipated, fraternal and united. Let us hope that the highly developed nations and peoples can understand this historical movement in its universal significance, and that they will take full part in it, in the conscious desire to help build a free and prosperous Africa in a world of peace and brotherhood.

FAREWELL WITHOUT TEARS

Patrice Lumumba, once a postal clerk, rose from obscurity to take control of the Mouvement National Congolais *and become first prime minister of the Democratic Republic of the Congo. In a letter to his wife, written in French in January,* 1961, *shortly before his assassination by rival forces, this controversial personage muses on the cruel course of history.*

I am writing these words not knowing whether they will reach you, when they will reach you, and whether I shall still be alive when you read them. All through my struggle for the independence of my country, I have never doubted for a single instant the final triumph of the sacred cause to which my companions and I have devoted all our lives. But what we wished for our country, its right to an honorable life, to unstained dignity, to independence without restrictions, was never desired by the Belgian imperialists and their Western allies, who found direct and indirect support, both deliberate and unintentional, amongst certain high officials of the United Nations, that organization in which we placed all our trust when we called on its assistance.

They have corrupted some of our compatriots and bribed others. They have helped to distort the truth and bring our independence into dishonor. How could I speak otherwise? Dead or alive, free or in prison by order of the imperialists, it is not I myself who count. It is the Congo, it is our poor people for whom independence has been transformed into a cage from beyond whose confines the outside world looks on us, sometimes with kindly sympathy, but at other times with joy and pleasure. But my faith will remain unshakeable. I know and I feel in my heart that sooner or later my people will rid themselves of all their enemies, both internal and external, and that they will rise as one man to say No to the degradation and shame of colonialism, and regain their dignity in the clear light of the sun.

We are not alone. Africa, Asia and the free liberated people from all corners of the world will always be found at the side of the millions of Congolese who will not abandon the struggle until the day when there are no longer any colonialists and their mercenaries in our country. As to my children, whom I leave and whom I may never see again, I should like them to be told that it is for them, as it is for every Congolese, to accomplish the sacred task of reconstructing our independence and our sovereignty: for without dignity there is no liberty, without justice there is no dignity, and without independence there are no free men.

Neither brutality, nor cruelty nor torture will ever bring me to ask for mercy, for I prefer to die with my head unbowed, my faith unshakeable and with profound

Deposed Prime Minister Lumumba in 1960
UPI

trust in the destiny of my country, rather than live under subjection and disregarding sacred principles. History will one day have its say, but it will not be the history that is taught in Brussels, Paris, Washington or in the United Nations, but the history which will be taught in the countries freed from imperialism and its puppets. Africa will write her own history, and to the north and south of the Sahara, it will be a glorious and dignified history.

Do not weep for me, my dear wife. I know that my country, which is suffering so much, will know how to defend its independence and its liberty. Long live the Congo! Long live Africa!

FREEDOM

The political consciousness of the sixties in Africa permeated almost every part of society. Excerpted below is a prize-winning essay submitted in a student competition that was conducted in 1962 by the Uganda-based magazine Transition. *The author, Bertha Lomayani, attended a girls school in Tanganyika, which had become independent in 1961.*

Whenever I see the word "freedom" my mind spreads widely like a flood on a flat land. I begin to think of various things with which it is connected and I have come to conclude that freedom should he given to any creature lacking it. All living creatures need a certain amount of freedom. Even a small child in its first week and unable to talk will cry if it is uncomfortable. I am a Masai by tribe and from my experience I have seen babies who are forbidden to have the automatic freedom: freedom of breathing.

My mothers, the Masai women, carry their children on their backs, covering them all over including the face and head. The material used is animal skins soaked in animal fat which has a distasteful smell. Under this condition the baby can't breath properly, so it suffocates. It feels uncomfortable and begins to cry and dance up and down. If the mother ignores this the baby will start scratching, pinching and beating the mother's back. The mother then becomes angry and releases the baby and carries it in her hands . . . .

Traditionally, Masai women cover their babies because they believe that if a baby is exposed when still young, the sight of men may cause a serious disease and it may die of it, or at least the baby must receive a serious shock. If the older ones who can speak are covered, they will shout: "*Yeyo taboluoki,*" meaning "Mammy—uncover me." The mother may hesitate to uncover the child, thinking she is protecting it, but seeing that the child can bite, scratch and repeat the same words, she uncovers it.

Among the creatures who lack freedom are the people ruled by another country. Under British trusteeship, Tanganyikans still ate food, wore clothes, grew and sold things and performed all other physical functions, but they could not hold responsible jobs or posts because they were thought unable to hold any responsibility. It is clear that the British never beat the natives, but they were still uncomfortable spiritually: there was something torturing their minds, when they thought that they were forbidden to establish ownership over what is theirs—their land. This put a pressure in their minds and the older, thoughtful people in the nation thought so deeply and were so depressed that either they had to take action or, in the extreme cases, they went mad.

Eight years ago a politician appeared: Dr. Julius Nyerere, who started expressing the spiritual discomfort boldly and started TANU, a party which fought for freedom. Just as a Masai woman hesitates to uncover her child, so the governing power hesitates to free the dominated, saying that it is not ready for responsibility. But when will it be ready? The Masai woman says her baby is not ready for exposure yet, but when will it learn to breathe?

CONTINENTAL INTEGRITY

Inter-African political behavior is governed by the Charter of the Organization of African Unity (OAU), founded and agreed upon by thirty-two independent African states at Addis Ababa, Ethiopia, in 1963. The charter and the union represent a practical attempt on the part of African leadership to effect pan-Africanism in matters economical, political, and cultural. Included below are the charter's prologue of purpose and introductory articles.

We, the Heads of African States and Governments assembled in the City of Addis Ababa, Ethiopia;

CONVINCED that it is the inalienable right of all people to control their own destiny;

CONSCIOUS of the fact that freedom, equality, justice and dignity are essential objectives for the achievement of the legitimate aspirations of the African peoples;

CONSCIOUS of our responsibility to harness the natural and human resources of our continent for the total advancement of our peoples in spheres of human endeavor;

INSPIRED by a common determination to promote understanding among our peoples and co-operation among our States in response to the aspirations of our peoples for brotherhood and solidarity, in a larger unity transcending ethnic and national differences;

CONVINCED that, in order to translate this determination into a dynamic force in the cause of human progress, conditions for peace and security must be established and maintained;

DETERMINED to safeguard and consolidate the hard-won independence as well as the sovereignty and territorial integrity of our States, and to fight against neo-colonialism in all its forms;

DEDICATED to the general progress of Africa;

PERSUADED that the Charter of the United Nations and the Universal Declaration of Human Rights, to the principles of which we reaffirm our adherence, provide a solid foundation for peaceful and positive co-operation among States;

DESIROUS that all African States should henceforth unite so that the welfare and well-being of their peoples can be assured;

RESOLVED to reinforce the links between our states by establishing and strengthening common institutions;

HAVE agreed to the present Charter.

ESTABLISHMENT

1. The High Contracting Parties do by the present Charter establish an Organization to be known as the ORGANIZATION OF AFRICAN UNITY.

2. The Organization shall include the Continental African States, Madagascar and other Islands surrounding Africa.

PURPOSES

1. The Organization shall have the following purposes:

    a. to promote the unity and solidarity of the African States;

    b. to co-ordinate and intensify their co-operation and efforts to achieve a better life for the peoples of Africa;

    c. to defend their sovereignty, their territorial integrity and independence;

    d. to eradicate all forms of colonialism from Africa; and

    e. to promote international co-operation, having due regard to the Charter of the United Nations and the Universal Declaration of Human Rights.

2. To these ends, the Member States shall co-ordinate and harmonize their general policies, especially in the following fields:

    a. political and diplomatic co-operation;

    b. economic co-operation, including transport and communications;

    c. educational and cultural co-operation;

    d. health, sanitation, and nutritional co-operation;

    e. scientific and technical co-operation; and

    f. co-operation for defense and security.

PRINCIPLES

The Member States, in pursuit of the purposes stated in Article II, solemnly affirm and declare their adherence to the following principles:

1. the sovereign equality of all Member States;
2. non-interference in the internal affairs of States;
3. respect for the sovereignty and territorial integrity of each State and for its inalienable right to independent existence;
4. peaceful settlement of disputes by negotiation, mediation, conciliation or arbitration;
5. unreserved condemnation, in all its forms, of political assassination as well as of subversive activities on the part of neighboring States or any other State;
6. absolute dedication to the total emancipation of the African territories which are still dependent;
7. affirmation of a policy of non-alignment with regard to all blocs.

PURSUIT OF HAPPINESS

The following lecture, by the late Dunduzu K. Chisiza, former parliamentary secretary to Malawi's ministry of finance, is an assessment of the African personality. His remarks were delivered before the Economic Symposium, held at the town of Blantyre in 1962.

Unlike Easterners who are given to meditation or Westerners who have an inquisitive turn of mind we of Africa, belonging neither to the East nor to the West, are fundamentally observers, penetrating observers, relying more on intuition than on the process of reasoning.

Our field is not that of spiritualism which is the domain of the East nor that of science and technology which is the hobby-horse of the West, but that of human relations. This is where we excel and where we shall set an example for the rest of the world. . . .

With us, life has always meant the pursuit of happiness rather than the pursuit of Beauty or Truth. We pursue happiness by suppressing isolationism, individualism, negative emotions, and tension, on the one hand; and by laying emphasis on a communal way of life, by encouraging positive emotions and habitual relaxation, and by restraining our desires on the other. . . .

Our attitude to religion has more often than not been determined by our habitual desire for change. We adhere to a religious faith only so long as it is the only faith we know. If some other faith comes our way we do not insulate ourselves against its influence. . . . That we behave in this way is no indication that we are fickle; rather it is an indication of the fact that in each one of the religious faiths which we encounter there is an element of divine truth whose fascination we fail to resist. And this is as it should be for religion is one. Iqbal has told us: "There is only one religion but there are many versions of it." . . .

In Africa, we believe in strong family relations. We have been urged by well meaning foreigners to break these ties for one reason or another. No advice could be more dangerous to the fabric of our society. Charity begins at home. So does love of our fellow human beings. . . .

How can a person who has no real affection for his brothers or sisters have any love for a poor Congolese or Chinese peasant? When we talk about international peace, understanding and goodwill, we are actually talking about international love. But universal love does not grow from nothing; its root is family love and unless this root is there it cannot grow. The unification of mankind ultimately depends on the cultivation of family love. . . .

Love for communal activities is another feature of our outlook. Look at any African game or pastime and you notice right away that its performance calls for more than one person. Our dances are *party* dances demanding drummers, singers and dancers. Game hunting is done in *parties*. (Even those Africans who own guns cannot abandon the habit of taking some friends along with them when going out for a hunt!) The telling of fables and stories with us calls for a *group* of boys and girls not just one or two. Draw-net fishing is done by a *group* of people. Fishing with hooks is also done in *canoe parties* of two, three or four; each canoe taking at least two people. The preparation of fields, the weeding, the sowing of seeds, the harvesting, the pounding of grains—all these activities are done in parties of either men or women. . . .

Such an outlook can only emanate from genuine love for each other—an unconscious love which has existed in our society since time immemorial. . . . Foreign missionaries should come to Africa not so much to teach love to the indigenous people but to see living examples of selfless love manifested in the African way of life.

We are also famous for our sense of humor and dislike for melancholy. Gloom on the face of an African is a sure sign that the wearer of that expression has been to a "school" of some kind where he might have got it into his head that joy and melancholy can be bed fellows in his heart. Otherwise our conception of life precludes, as far as possible, the accommodation of dejection. . . .

Even if there are real causes for sorrow somehow our people manage to make molehills of these and mountains of the causes for happiness. . . . Our society stifles malice, revenge and hate with the result that we are free from these cankers. Were we disposed to avenge the wrongs that have been meted out to us by foreigners down through the ages the course of human events would have taken a different turn altogether. . . . But God spared us all that. As a result we tolerate on our soil even neurotic crowds of foreigners who could not be tolerated in their own countries; we waste love on foreign elements which are inveterately selfish, individualistic and ungrateful. Above all, we do not look forward to a day when we shall have nefarious schemes against any race.

Among those who have studied Africa closely we have a reputation for taking delight in generosity, kindness and forgiveness. It has been said, with great truth, by some foreigners that few Africans will ever get rich "for the simple reason that the African tends to be too generous." Well, we do not want to be rich at the cost of being mean! Our society hinges on the practice of "mutual aid and co-operation" whose corrollary is generosity. When our chiefs, kings and emperors gave out acres and acres of land to foreigners they weren't prompted by bribes or stupidity but by this selfsame relishable habit of generosity. . . .

Nor is the scope of our kindness limited to our own race. Many are the days when we have preserved the life of one foreigner or another. Times without number we've gone out of our way to hunt for water, eggs, milk, chicken, fish, meat, fruits, vegetables, etc., for a choosy stranger. We've carried literally thousands of foreigners on our heads and shoulders; we've washed their clothes; we've reared their children; we've looked after their homes; we've stood by their sides in peril; we've defended them in times of war; we've given them land . . . we've given them our all. But all the gratitude we get for all that is ridicule, contempt, ill-treatment and the belief on their part that God created us to be "hewers of wood and drawers of water." No. God knows our kindness does not stem from a feeling of inferiority. God knows we are not kind because we are fools, but because he had it that we should be kindness drunk and not pride drunk.

And yet, in spite of all this ingratitude, we are still capable of forgiving and forgetting. We are in a position to do this because in our society forgiveness is the rule rather than the exception. . . .

Another outstanding characteristic of our outlook is our love for music, dance and rhythm. Our throats are deep with music, our legs full of dance while our bodies tremor with rhythm. The proper sub-title for Africa should have been "Land of music, dance and rhythm." This three pronged phenomenon is indeed the spice of our life. We sing while we hoe. We sing while we paddle our canoes. Our mourning is in the form of dirges. We sing as we pound food grains in mortars. We sing in bereavement just as on festive occasions. Our fables always include a singing part. We sing to while away the monotonous hours of travel. We sing to the strains of our musical instruments. The pulses of our drums evoke in us song responses. We sing under moonlit nights. We sing under the canopy of the blue sky. Gramophone record music entrances us not because it's foreign or something out of the way, but just because it's music. With us music, as also dance and rhythm, is a relishable obsession.

We have war dances, victory dances, stag dances, remedial dances, marriage dances, dances for women only, mixed dances, dances for the initiated only, dances for the youth—but all indulged in with ecstatic abandon. We nod our heads, rock our necks, tilt our heads and pause. We shake our shoulders, throw them back and forth, bounce breasts and halt to intone our thanks to Him who ordained that we be alive. We rhythmically hefty shake our rear ends, our tummies duck and peer, our legs quick march, slow march, tap dribble, quiver and tremble while our feet perform feats. "Dance!" What a world of emotions that word calls forth in us!

But dance and music by themselves are crude art, rough hewn and devoid of sublimity. So to these we unconsciously add rhythm for a blend that possesses both charm and grace. Rhythm is our second nature.

There is rhythm in the winnowing and pounding of grains, there is rhythm in the gait of our women folk; there is highly developed rhythm in coition, there is rhythm in the groan of a sick person, there is complex rhythm in the milking of a cow, there is rhythm in pulling a drawnet to the shore, there is rhythm that beggars description in the beats of our tom-toms, there is rhythm that defies analysis in "marimba," there is rhythm in almost everything we do.

Finally, we have a strong dislike for imposing our beliefs on other people. British people established themselves in their erstwhile and present day dependencies with the self-assuredness of angels. They believed with puritanical fervor—that the British way is the God-vouchsafed way of doing things. Their way of living is what mankind was destined to evolve up to; their ideas the gospel truth; their beliefs the paragons of man's triumph over "superstition." No other way—least of all the colonial people's way—could measure up to it still less be better than it. So they believed there was nothing for them to learn from their colonial subjects while the colonial indigenes had to be recast into the British mould of life, thought and belief.

That mode of thinking was all very well for purposes of empire building. To rule a people successfully you've got to drill it into their heads that you are in every way superior to them and that, therefore, it is the right thing for them to be under you. . . .

If persisted in, this attitude of finality, superiority and self-deception can only promote hate and racial discord. When other peoples do not assert themselves it isn't that they haven't got something to be proud of, something that they believe is unrivaled, but just that they haven't got the same vulgarity of throwing their weight about and imposing themselves and their beliefs on other people. They are willing to live and let live. Further they have the sense of knowing that the part of a listener and an open mind are the "open sesame" to the fortune of knowledge and wisdom. There is a great deal that foreigners, here as well as abroad, have to learn from the colonial peoples.

THE MANIPULATORS

Yambo Ouologuem has described Bound to Violence *as "a fresco, an epic, a legend and a novel." The work, published in France in 1968, chronicles in barely fictional form the brutal sequence of Africa's oppressors—black and white, animist, Muslim, and Christian. In the following excerpt, the Saif of Nakem—symbolizing the state—sets forth his cynical philosophy of men and government.*

"You mustn't imagine," [Saif] went on, clucking softly, "that the sun will never shine again. We are wanderers in disaster, that's a fact; but we fall, we are humble, we gargle with poison from the bloody cup of violence, the chipped glass of values; we are sick, degraded; but that's because the world *is* odd. Steeped in the strangest sediments ever churned by God in His chaotic blessing! I am quite capable of judging Him, and in so loud a voice that Satan would think he was listening to a jubilant angel nearby."

Then in a falsetto:

"You see, my friend, in Nakem we have a tale. Of men and their madness Destiny said: '*I must forgive them, mankind is so young.*' And it waited. And it's still waiting. Like patience on a monument. Isn't that delightful? But suddenly the unforeseen! The rules are thrown headlong: 'What broke down?' The whole human machine, the boiler was ready to burst and it burst. But Destiny is right there, and Destiny always forgives. Its pardon is signed by a cabinet minister: read and approved, place, date, and seal. That's what we call a reprieve; when it expires, mankind in its arch way starts all over again; and Destiny never wearies of forgiving, by proxy. How could it weary? If it did, would it not know Tedium, the empty consciousness of a time without content? The tedious innocence of one who has never sinned! But we are sinners. And God forgives. Out of constraint. Or out of love, perhaps." . . .

"Man is in history, and history is in politics. Politics is cleavage. No solidarity is possible. Nor purity."

"The essential is to despair of purity and to believe one is right to despair. Love is nothing else. Politics does not know the goal but forges a pretext of a goal. Regimes collapse because their politicians don't know how to handle the forge."

"But their awkwardness is unavoidable, because politics is seldom honestly expressed, or rather, politics does not lend itself to honest expression."

A PARADOX

Albert John Luthuli, a Zulu chief, was deposed by the South African government in 1951. He was, nevertheless, deeply committed to an interracial solution to his country's future, and as president-general of the African National Congress, the oldest nonwhite political organization on the continent, he continued to work for reform. Luthuli was placed in detention on his farm in 1959, but when he was awarded the Nobel Peace Prize for his efforts to bring much-needed peace between the races of his homeland, the government reluctantly permitted him to travel to Scandinavia to receive the prize. Following are excerpts from his address, made in Oslo in December, 1961. Luthuli died at his farm in 1967.

It is not necessary for me to speak at length about South Africa. It is a museum piece in our time, a hangover from the dark past of mankind, a relic of an age which everywhere else is dead or dying. Here the cult of race superiority and of white supremacy is worshiped like a god. . . . Thus it is that the golden age of

Africa's independence is also the dark age of South Africa's decline and retrogression. . . .

To remain neutal, in a situation where the laws of the land virtually criticized God for having created men of color, was the sort of thing I could not, as a Christian, tolerate. . . . How great is the paradox and how much greater the honor that an award in support of peace and the brotherhood of man should come to one who is a citizen of a country where the brotherhood of man is an illegal doctrine.

Outlawed, banned, censured, proscribed, and prohibited; where to work, talk, or campaign for the realization in fact and deed of the brotherhood of man, is hazardous, punished with banishment or confinement without trial or imprisonment; where effective democratic channels to peaceful settlement of the race problem have never existed these 300 years, and where white minority power rests on the most heavily armed and equipped military machine in Africa.

JUSTICE FOR NAMIBIA

In 1960, following the Sharpeville massacre in South Africa, all black African parties were banned. Five years later this decree was extended to include South West Africa, which is administered as a protectorate by the Republic of South Africa. (The United Nations charges that the present government operates illegally and that the area should be administered as the UN Trust Territory of Namibia.) Among the blacks caught in the dispute is Herman Toivo Ja Toivo, an Ovambo and an active nationalist. His South West African People's Organization was banned in 1963, and he was imprisoned under the Terrorism Act. Excerpts from his defense before the Pretoria court follow.

We find ourselves here in a foreign country, convicted under laws made by people whom we have always considered as foreigners. We find ourselves tried by a judge who is not our countryman and who has not shared our background. . . .

You, my Lord, decided that you had the right to try us, because your Parliament gave you that right. That ruling has not and could not have changed our feelings. We are Namibians and not South Africans. We do not now, and will not in the future recognize your right to govern us; to make laws for us in which we had no say; to treat our country as if it were your property and us as if you were our masters. We have always regarded South Africa as an intruder in our country. This is how we have always felt and this is how we feel now, and it is on this basis that we have faced this trial. . . .

We are far away from our homes; not a single member of our families has come to visit us, never mind be present at our trial. The Pretoria jail, the police headquarters at Compol, where we were interrogated and where statements were extracted from us, and this Court are all we have seen of Pretoria. We have been cut off from our people and the world. We all wondered whether the head-men would have repeated some of their lies if our people had been present in Court to hear them.

The South African government has again shown its strength by detaining us for as long as it pleased; keeping some of us in solitary confinement for three hundred to four hundred days and bringing us to its capitol to try us. It has shown its strength by passing an act especially for us, and having it made retrospective. It has even chosen an ugly name to call us by. One's own are called patriots, or at least rebels; your opponents are called Terrorists. . . .

It suits the government of South Africa to say that it is ruling South West Africa with the consent of its people. This is not true. Our organization, S.W.A.P.O., is the largest political organization in South West Africa. We consider ourselves a political party. We know that whites do not think of blacks as politicians—only as agitators. Many of our people, through no fault of their own, have had no education at all. This does not mean that they do not know what they want. A man does not have to be formally educated to know that he wants to live with his family where he wants to live, and not where an official chooses to tell him to live; to move about freely and not require a pass; to earn a decent wage; to be free to work for the person of his choice for as long as he wants; and finally, to be ruled by the people that he wants to be ruled by, and not those who rule him because they have more guns than he has. . . .

Those of us who have some education, together with our uneducated brethren, have always struggled to get freedom. The idea of our freedom is not liked by South Africa. . . .

Your government, my Lord, undertook a very special responsibility when it was awarded the mandate over us after the first world war. It assumed a sacred trust to guide us toward independence and to prepare us to take our place among the nations of the world. South Africa has abused that trust because of its belief in racial supremacy (that white people have been chosen by God to rule the world) and apartheid. We believe that for fifty years South Africa has failed to promote the development of our people. Where are our trained men? The wealth of our country has been used to train your people for leadership, and the sacred duty of preparing the indigenous people to take their place among the nations of the world has been ignored. . . .

Nineteen hundred sixty-three for us was to be the year of our freedom. From 1960 it looked as if South Africa could not oppose the world forever. The world is important to us. In the same way as all laughed in Court when they heard that an old man tried to bring down a helicopter with a bow and arrow, we laughed when South Africa said that it would oppose the world. We knew that the world was divided, but as time went on it at least agreed that South Africa had no right to rule us.

I do not claim that it is easy for men of different races to live at peace with one another. I myself had no experience of this in my youth, and at first it surprised me that men of different races could live together in peace. . . . Separation is said to be a natural process. But why, then, is it imposed by force and why then is it that whites have the superiority?

Head-men are used to oppress us. This is not the first time that foreigners have tried to rule indirectly—we know that only those who are prepared to do what their masters tell them become head-men. Most of those who had some feeling for their people and who wanted independence have been intimidated into accepting the policy from above. Their guns and sticks are used to make people say they support them. . . .

Your Lordship emphasized in your judgment the fact that our arms came from communist countries, and also that words commonly used by communists were to be found in our documents. But my Lord, in the documents produced by the State there is another type of language. It appears even more often than the former. Many documents finish up with an appeal to the Almighty to guide us in our struggle for freedom. It is the wish of the South African government that we should be discredited in the Western world. That is why it calls our struggle a communist plot; but this will not be believed by the world. The world knows that we are not interested in ideologies. We feel that the world as a whole has a special responsibility towards us. This is because the land of our fathers was handed over to South Africa by a world body. It is a divided world, but it is a matter of hope for us that it at least agrees about one thing—that we are entitled to freedom and justice. . . .

We are sure that the world's efforts to help us in our plight will continue, whatever South Africans may call us.

That is why we claim independence for South West Africa. We do not expect that independence will end our troubles, but we do believe that our people are entitled—as are all peoples—to rule themselves. It is not really a question of whether South Africa treats us well or badly, but that South West Africa is our country and we wish to be our own masters.

There are some who will say that they are sympathetic with our aims, but that they condemn violence. I would answer that I am not by nature a man of violence and I believe that violence is a sin against God and my fellow men. S.W.A.P.O. itself was a nonviolent organization, but the South African government is not truly interested in whether opposition is violent or nonviolent. It does not wish to hear any opposition to apartheid. Since 1963, S.W.A.P.O. meetings have been banned. It is true that it is the Tribal Authorities who have done so, but they work with the South African government, which has never lifted a finger in favor of political freedom. We have found ourselves voteless in our own country and deprived of the right to meet and state our own political opinions. . . .

I have spent my life working in S.W.A.P.O., which is an ordinary political party like any other. Suddenly we in S.W.A.P.O. found that a war situation had arisen and that our colleagues and South Africa were facing each other on the field of battle. Although I had not been responsible for organizing my people militarily, and although I believed we were unwise to fight the might of South Africa while we were so weak, I could not refuse to help them when the time came. . . .

But some of your countrymen, when called to battle to defend civilization, resorted to sabotage against their own fatherland. I volunteered to face German bullets, and as a guard of military installations, both in South West Africa and the Republic, was prepared to be the victim of their sabotage. Today they are our masters and are considered the heroes, and I am called the coward.

When I consider my country, I am proud that my countrymen have taken up arms for their people and I believe that anyone who calls himself a man would not despise them. . . .

Even though I did not agree that people should go into the bush, I could not refuse to help them when I knew that they were hungry. I even passed on the request for dynamite. It was not an easy decision. Another man might have been able to say "I will have nothing to do with that sort of thing." I was not, and I could not remain a spectator in the struggle of my people for their freedom.

I am a loyal Namibian and I could not betray my people to their enemies. I admit that I decided to assist those who had taken up arms. I know that the struggle will be long and bitter. I also know that my people will wage that struggle, whatever the cost. . . .

We believe that South Africa has a choice—either to live at peace with us or to subdue us by force. If you choose to crush us and impose your will on us then you not only betray your trust, but you will live in security for only so long as your power is greater than ours. No South African will live at peace in South West Africa, for each will know that his security is based on force and that without force he will face rejection by the people of South West Africa.

My co-accused and I have suffered. We are not looking forward to our imprisonment. We do not, however, feel that our efforts and sacrifice have been wasted. We believe that human suffering has its effect even on those who impose it. We hope that what has happened will persuade the whites of South Africa that we and the world may be right and they may be wrong. Only when white South Africans realize this and act on it, will it be possible for us to stop our struggle for freedom and justice in the land of our birth.

THE CHOICE TO COMPETE

Dennis Brutus has been hailed as the poet laureate of South Africa. An ardent campaigner for racial justice, he was shot and wounded by the South African police in 1963 and subsequently jailed for eighteen months for attempting to leave the country to attend the International Olympic Committee at Baden.

Let not this plunder be misconstrued
This is the body's expression of need—
Poor wordless body in its fumbling way
Exposing heart's-hunger by raiding and
 hurt;

Secret recesses of lonely desire
Gnaw at the vitals of spirit and mind
When shards of existence display eager
 blades
To menace and savage the pilgriming
 self:

Bruised through your flesh and all-
 aching my arms
Believe me, my lovely, I too reel from
 our pain—
Plucking from you these agonized gifts
Bares only my tenderness-hungering
 need.

FROM THE GRIM PLACE

Arthur Nortje, a South African poet now a resident in Canada, won the first Mbari Poetry Prize (Nigeria) in 1963. His work conveys the black man's anguish in his land.

The sergeant laughs with strong teeth
 his jackboots nestle under the
 springbok horns
Those bayonets are silent,
the spear of the nation gone to the
 ground.
Warriors prowl in the stars of their
 dungeons.
I've seen the nebulae of a man's eyes
squirm with pain, he sang his life
through cosmic volleys. They call it
genital therapy, the blond bosses.

Why is there no more news?
Bluetits scuffle in the eaves of England,
an easy summer shimmers on the
 water.
Fields of peace, I lie here
in the music of your gaze
so beautiful we seem no strangers.
Curling smoke, a white butt is
brother to my lips and fingers.
You watch the ash on grass blades gently
 crumble.

Your hands are small as roses,
they cancel memory.
Once going down to the sea through the
 mountains
my limbs felt freedom in the glide of air:
over the bridge at the window I found
speech an impossible cry.
Under the fatal shadows spun down the
 chasm
my heart squirmed in the throat of
 snaking water.
I have since forgotten what they call the
 place.

EXIT

Harold Head, a black South African journalist forced into political exile in 1964, relates in this excerpt from a forthcoming autobiography some of his last thoughts as he left his homeland and made his way to freedom.

It was my second day in Pukwane. I had left Cape Town four days ago, and everything so far had gone according to plan. Time was important and had to be measured in terms of the minute hand. My flight had begun with six days between myself and the South Africa-Bechuanaland border and I had, on arrival in Pukwane, already used four days along the route.

The Bechuanaland border was two miles away, but I did not realize it. I had arrived under cover of darkness. Learning, in fact, that I was on the threshold of freedom, I strongly felt that it was not worth the risk after having passed unnoticed across a thousand-mile sea of trepidation, possible apprehension, or death as a result of resisting arrest. Reports were still rife of persons apprehended or shot on the Bechuanaland border.

Time was important. I was required by law to report my presence to the police every Monday morning under the Suppression of Communism Act. (This law has precious little to do with the prevention of Communism in the country, but is merely used to suppress all outspoken opposition to apartheid, whether inspired by socialism, capitalism, religious principles, a sense of justice, or just plain human feeling.) I had acquiesced to this form of repression and human deprivation for two weeks. The third time I reported was my last. Obliquely, but not unobtrusively, I decided to pit black agility against the surveillance of the government's Special Branch and cross the Kalahari Desert.

Just living in South Africa requires guts and the coolness of a call girl. Otherwise, one unconsciously reconciles one's sensibilities to the situation and remains a being without growth. One becomes a still-life victim, forced to apologize or explain his own existence, a subhuman creature, sometimes indifferent or frustrated, always conditioned. And it is this conditioning that gives strength.

I, myself, had forsaken the South African way of life when I reported on the one persistent reality of black humanity, the South African War. As is the case now, I then wrote out of impulse and a sense of duty. I gave up teaching to become a journalist because of my inability to reconcile myself to the structure of life in South Africa. Short-lived was my youth. I was part of the struggle before I was twenty.

Many South Africans have long resigned themselves to accept segregation and the other deformities and infirmities that make up the politics of that guilty land. But there are others: those who will not allow themselves to be governed by the sickness of someone's political aberrations.

When I was served with the banning order, my sword of combat and my shield of protection were taken from me. I was supposed not to write for publication anymore. I was supposed not to speak—or breathe, because the "liberal" Establishment press, which I had tried to use as a vehicle, still obeyed the laws of the land.

Whether these ruminations of life in South Africa were considered during my last hours in apartheidland is uncertain to me now, but in my mind's eye the land I walked through remains crystal clear. The air was tranquil, the women gently going about their tasks of cleaning their modest huts, sweeping the surrounding yards, or making the perpetual trip to the communal fresh-water well to replenish their daily household needs. Viewing this vestige of the old life, I waited for the propitious moment to enter a life of freedom.

The men for their part were involved in a varied number of activities, from working in the fields to tending livestock—mainly for white farmers. They seemed to justify their existence by tinkering on pots or pans or on fences and flat rooftops.

As most sparsely sufficient South African villages must, Pukwane's future balanced on the precipice of frustrating uncertainty, its people wondering whether the illegal activity known as "the government" was really going to declare their tiny homeland a "whites-only" area, as rumored. Consequently, Pukwane had by this time produced a large number of men who measured time and their daily existence in terms only of waiting for the guillotine to cut off the next birthright. They had seen, and some had read, of the power of "the government" elsewhere in the country. And by 1964 the Verwoerd regime had demonstrated quite clearly its invincibility in dealing with the underground resistance movement: this repression had a paralyzing effect on the people who retained only the hope that some day the spirits of Mzilikazi, Cetshewayo, or Chaka would be unleashed to restore them to human dignity. So they waited.

Teko's father was my contact in Pukwane. He was away on a trip to a nearby town when I arrived. Due to South Africa's Sabotage Act, I refrained from letting his wife know the real reason for my sudden presence. As the custom of African women is not to question men, I was accepted and made to feel at home as I waited for the man of the house.

I had told Teko's mother that I was a scoutmaster on my way to meet a patrol in nearby Lichtenberg the following day —*the day*. This story had also been told to a black priest and his daughter in the town where I had spent the night before. I hated myself for not being able to take them into my confidence, but would have hated myself even more had I done so. There are hundreds of innocent persons in South Africa's gaols today who were put away simply because they were taken into the confidence of those entertaining the thought of political freedom.

Four hours later I was greeted by a tall, well-built man nearing fifty, anxious to hear of his student son in one of Cape Town's high schools.

Teko's father had been an activist in the labor movement in the early thirties and forties, but after minor failures of schemes that he had considered important for the liberation of his people, he had ceased being active. His faith was now in what he called the young men of the movement. His time was spent in farming and the operation of one of the local village stores. He was glad that I had not told anyone of my plans. We then made arrangements when I would cross an unmanned fence along the South Africa-Bechuanaland border.

Teko's father and I were still discussing strategy, possible ploys to use to cross the border, when suddenly a light delivery van roared up his driveway. Such vans are common forms of transport used by the South African police. We were together in the guest hut, which had only one door and one window. Instinctively, I jumped up from my bench and dived through the window, managing to catch a glimpse of Teko's father hurriedly trying to hide my knapsack under the bed in the room.

It was pitch dark outside, but for a strong beam of light streaking across the stillness, the van. My immediate reaction on now finding myself in the yard was to climb on top of the hut's downward sloping thatch roof, but it proved too hard and steep to grasp. Without pondering the possibility further, I moved silently into the unknown night on all fours. Thirty yards farther I found myself stumbling into a goat pen! Afraid of the goats being startled and disclosing my whereabouts, I cast my faith to the darkness and lay silently on my stomach. I had made my dash for safety without a coat, and after ten minutes in the goat pen began to feel the cruel frost of the night seeping relentlessly into my skin. It was winter.

Half an hour later the van drove off. I returned to the guest house an hour later, however, even though I could hear Teko's father calling after me as soon as the van was out of hearing distance. I had to be sure.

Thus, this improbable, fateful day dawned. The movement of the minute hand of my pocket watch filled me with intense anxiety. It was Friday—three days away from the morning when I would be expected to keep intact the laws of the land by reporting my presence. I tried not to be engaged in negative thoughts or fear or the knowledge that I was leaving the country forever. But in the forefront of my mind was the very real possibility that I could be ambushed, shot on sight, just as I stood on the threshold of freedom. And so I left my fate in Teko's father's hands. And I concentrated on a show of outward calm, following him as he casually went outside to do his daily chores.

Strangely coming to consciousness, I found myself looking at four boys, aged between five and eight, cheerfully milking some goats. The sight reminded me of a chilly and affectionate memory of an incident the previous night.

Coming out of my reveries, I continued to watch the playfulness of the boys with the goats. It was perhaps the last genuine pleasure I have felt since leaving South Africa.

Soon my silent watching focused only on the goats. I felt a kinship with them and fancied a similarity between their lives and those of the people of South Africa. Of all domesticated animals, goats live on the barest minimum. Still they are expected to produce, contribute —justify their being around.

My romance with the goats was distracted by a gentle tap on my thigh. Looking down I found the youngest of the boys standing in front of me, offering me a drink of goat's milk. There was no longer need for me to check the minute hand of my pocket watch. The time had come. In acknowledgment of our camaraderie and brotherhood we smiled at each other as I took a swig of the hot, sweet milk.

Feeling good, I walked back to the hut where I had spent my last night, oblivious to the shrill iciness in the air.

MY FIRST WEDDING

Amos Tutuola was born in Nigeria in 1920. After six years of elementary education he became a blacksmith, and later a messenger for the Nigerian government's labor department. He published the first of several works of fiction in 1952, The Palm Wine Drinkard. *As in later writings, Tutuola makes Yoruba myth and legend the basis of his whimsical, picaresque tales. The following story is taken from his second novel,* My Life in the Bush of the Ghosts *(1954). It follows the hero from his escape—during a slave raid—to the bush, through which he travels for twenty-four years. In this episode he marries a local ghostess, is baptized, and reluctantly moves on.*

Before the wedding day was reached my friend had chosen one of the most fearful ghosts for me as my "best man" who was always speaking evil words, even he was punished in the fire of hell more than fifty years for these evil talks and cruelties, but was still growing rapidly in bad habits, then he was expelled from hell to the "Bush of Ghosts" to remain there until the judgment day as he was unable to change his evil habits at all. When the wedding day arrived all the ghosts and ghostesses of this town, together with the father of the lady whom I wanted to marry, my friend and his mother, my best man and myself went to the church at about ten o'clock, but it was the ghosts' clock said so. When we reached their church I saw that the Reverend who preached or performed the wedding ceremony was the "Devil." But as he was preaching he reached the point that I should tell them my name which is an earthly person's name and when they heard the name the whole of them in that church exclaimed at the same time . . . "Ah! you will be baptized in this church again before you will marry this lady."

When I heard so from them I agreed, not knowing that Revd. Devil was going to baptize me with fire and hot water as they were baptizing for themselves there. When I was baptized on that day, I was crying loudly so that a person who is at a distance of two miles would not listen before hearing my voice, and within a few minutes every part of my body was scratched by this hot water and fire, but before Revd. Devil could finish the baptism I regretted it. Then I told him to let me go away from their church and I do not want to marry again because I could not bear to be baptized with fire and hot water any longer, but when all of them heard so, they shouted, "Since you have entered this church you are to be baptized with fire and hot water before you will go out of the church, willing or not you ought to wait and complete the baptism." But when I heard so from them again, I exclaimed with a terrible voice that . . . "I will die in their church." So all of them exclaimed again that . . . "you may die if you like, nobody knows you here."

But as ghosts do not know the place or time which is possible to ask questions, so at this stage one of them got up from the seat and asked me . . . "By the way, how did you manage to enter into the 'Bush of Ghosts,' the bush which is on the second side of the world between the heaven and earth and which is strictly banned to every earthly person to be entered, and again you have the privilege to marry in this bush as well?" So as these ghosts have no arrangements for anything at the right time and right place, then I answered that I was too young to know which is "bad" and "good" before I mistakenly entered this bush and since that time or year I am trying my best to find out the right way back to my home town until I reached the town of "burglary-ghosts" from where I came with my friend to this town. After I explained as above, then the questioner stood up again and asked me whether I could show them my friend whom I followed to that town. Of course as my friend was faithful, before I could say anything, he and his mother whom we came to visit got up at the same time and said that I am living with a burglar-ghost in the town of the burglar-ghosts. But when my friend and his mother confirmed all that I said and as all the rest of the ghosts are respecting all the burglar-ghosts most because they were supplying them the earthly properties, so they overlooked my offense, then Revd. Devil continued the baptism with hot water and fire.

After the baptism, then the same Revd. Devil preached again for a few minutes, while "Traitor" read the lesson. All the members of this church were "evildoers." They sang the song of evils with evils' melodious tune, then "Judas" closed the service.

Even "Evil of evils," who was the ruler of all the evils, and who was always seeking evils about, evil-joking, evil-walking, evil-playing, evil-laughing, evil-talking, evil-dressing, evil-moving, worshiping evils in the church of evils and living in the evil-house with his evil family, everything he does is evil, attended the service too, but he was late before he arrived and when he shook hands with me on that day, I was shocked as if I touch a "live electric wire," but my friend was signaling to me with his eyes not to shake hands with him to avoid the shock but I did not understand.

Having finished the marriage service, all of us went to my in-laws' house where everybody was served with a variety of food and all kinds of ghosts' drinks. After that all the ghost and ghostess dancers started to dance. Also all the terrible-creatures sent their representatives as "Skulls," "Long-white creatures," "Invincible and invisible Pawn" or "Give and take" who fought and won the Red people in the Red-town for the "Palm-Wine drinker," "Mountain-creatures," "Spirit of prey" whose eyes flood of light suffocated Palm-Wine Drinker's wife and also the "hungry-creature" who swallowed Palm-Wine Drinker together with his wife when returning from Deads'-town came and saluted my wife's father and they were served immediately they arrived. But at last "Skull" who came from "Skull family's town" reported "Spirit of prey" to my wife's father who was chief secretary to all the terrible and curious creatures in all dangerous bushes, that the spirit of prey stole his meat which the skull put at the edge of the plate in which both were eating as both were served together with one plate, because plates were not sufficient to serve each of them with a plate. But before my wife's father who was their chief secretary could have a chance to come and settle the matter for them, both of them started to fight fiercely so that all the ghosts and all the other representatives came nearer and surrounded them, clapping hands on them in such a way that if one of these fighters surrenders or gives up it would be very shameful to him.

Some of these scene-lookers were clapping, and an old Ape, who was a slave and inherited by my wife's father from his first generation since uncountable years, was beating a big tree under which both these terrible creatures were fighting as a drum which had a very large sound. But as this old slave ape was beating the tree as a drum in such a way that all the scene-lookers who stood round them could not bear the lofty sound of the tree which was beaten as a drum and wait or stand still in one place, so all the ghosts, evils, terrible creatures, my friend, my wife and her father and myself started to dance at the same time. But as I was intoxicated by the strong drinks which I drank on that day, so I mistakenly smashed a small ghost to death who came from the "9th town of ghosts" to enjoy the merriment of the marriage with us as I was staggering about.

At last I was summoned to the court of evil for wilfully killing a small ghost, but as a little mistake is a serious offense as well as big offense in the "Bush of Ghosts," so the "Evil judge" judged the case at one o'clock of the judgment day and luckily I was freed by a kind lawyer whose mother was the native of the "Bottomless Ravine's town," the town which belongs to only "triplet ghosts and ghostesses." But if it was not for this incognito lawyer who was very kind to me without knowing him elsewhere I would be imprisoned for fifty years as this is the shortest years for a slightest offense.

After I freed the case then I returned to my in-laws' town and lived there with my wife for a period of about three months and some days before I remembered my mother and brother again, because I did not remember them again when I married the lady. So one morning, I told the father of my wife that I want to leave this town for another one, but I did not tell him frankly that I want to continue to find the way to my home town which I left since I was seven years old. So I told him that I should leave with his daughter who was my wife, he allowed me to go or to leave, but disallowed his daughter to go with me. Of course, when I thought over within myself that however an earthly person might love ghosts, ghosts could not like him heartily in any respect, then I alone left his town in the evening after I went round the town and bade good-bye to the prominent ghosts.

POLICY TOWARD AFRICA

Dr. Elliott P. Skinner, professor of anthropology at Columbia University, served as United States ambassador to Upper Volta from 1966 to 1969. The following article is excerpted from a policy statement made before a congressional committee in March, 1970.

America can no longer afford an African policy predicated on European primacy in that continent. It can also no longer hide behind a smokescreen of pious words and platitudinous hopes for Africa while doing as little as possible. We must not permit Europeans to provide the guidelines for our policy toward Africa, nor must we continue to protect the short-term interests of racist minorities there. America must develop a realistic policy toward Africa based upon its own ethos, its own national character, its own history and its position in the contemporary world. Failure to do so may have grave implications not only for Africa, but also for the United States during this decade.

America was diplomatically and psychologically unprepared for Africa's entrance upon the world scene in the late 1950's. As a matter of fact, our policy toward Africa during the 1950's was based on the prior consideration that: "All of the so-called colonial powers represented on the continent of Africa are our friends and allies in the worldwide contest between the Free and Communist worlds." Nevertheless, this did not stop Africa's drive for independence and to combat the expected Soviet efforts, President Eisenhower sent Mr. Richard M. Nixon to take part in Ghana's independence celebration as well as to report on the other independent African states.

Mr. Nixon clearly recognized that America needed a new policy toward Africa. He declared: "The leaders and peoples of the countries I visited in Africa have many things in common. They cherish their independence which most of them have only recently acquired, and are determined to protect it against any form of foreign domination. They rightfully expect recognition from us and others of their dignity and equality as individuals and peoples in the family of nations. They want economic progress for their undeveloped economies. . . . There must be a corresponding realization throughout the executive branches of the Government, throughout the Congress and throughout the nation, of the growing importance of Africa to the future of the United States and the Free World and the necessity of assigning higher priority to our relations with that area."

There was the usual cant in this statement, for during the remaining years of the Eisenhower administration the United States followed France's lead with respect to both Algeria and Guinea. The more forward-looking Kennedy administration still recognized Belgium's primacy in the Congo, and did not seriously urge the Portuguese to decolonize Angola, Guinea-Bissau, and Mozambique. We refused to sanction South Africa for its odious policy of apartheid, and followed the British Lion to a stalemate on H.M.S. Tiger, and only reluctantly left Salisbury in order not to embarass the new toothless King of the Beasts. The United States muddled through the Nigerian crisis, faithfully following the lead of Great Britain whose "traditional primacy" in that nation-state we took for granted. And even when the Federal government won the war we insulted its gallant leaders by declaring that we were consulting with France, of all countries, to provide aid to the Biafrans.

Africa's travail during the 1960's was largely due to the difficulties of decolonization, and the trauma of building new institutions to cope with a rapidly changing world. The European-derived political systems have not worked well in Africa, but there is still no evidence that the military regimes in power will persist. Indeed, the political pattern suitable for contemporary African societies has probably not yet emerged, and the process by which it comes into being may well be long and hard. Africa has also not yet decolonized its social systems. Middle-men and stranger groups have come under attack as the societies try to institute freer mobility. There have been grave personal injustices, and this has led to social strife and civil wars. These may well continue until cross-cutting interests in the African societies outweigh parochial ones. Conditions similar to those in the United States, whereby a man from Massachusetts or California could represent New York in this House, may be long in coming. The Africans have also not yet decolonized their economic institutions—normally the most difficult of all institutions to gain control of. Most of their resources are still in expatriate hands, and most African states are still members of foreign-run specie zones. The economic effect is that the Africans cannot freely trade across their borders without contravening trade relations with their ex-Metropoles, nor can they protect their fragile economies from the vicissitudes of the world economies. French Finance Minister, Giscard d'Estaing did not consult nor notify a single African state before devaluating the franc, even though the Africans were to be hurt materially as well as psychologically this action.

America's economic policy toward Africa has always been predicated upon European primacy and has not greatly helped the Africans to deal with their developmental problems. In the 1950's we were willing to play "only a cooperative role with the administering power." Indeed, we primarily wished to "assure the development of mutually advantageous economic relations between Europe and Africa in the interest of contributing to the restoration of a sound European economy and of furthering the aspirations of the African peoples." Our Marshall Aid was expected to help Europe, and the Europeans were left to deal with Africa. In 1957, Mr. Nixon, an economic nationalist, recognized the dilemma of the colonial economic ties between Africa and Europe and recommended that "We should encourage the continuance of these special ties where they are considered mutually advantageous by the states concerned." The difficulty with this recommendation is that the horse and its rider normally have different views about what is mutually beneficial, but only the rider can speak. Nevertheless, we have maintained the naive or perhaps moral position that since the Europeans profitted most from their African colonies, they should bear the burden of African reconstruction. This, indeed, was the thrust of the (General Lucius D.) Clay's report to President Kennedy in 1963, in which he recommended that the African states should seek aid essentially from their former masters to help with their development; that the very limited U.S. grant programs already in Africa be reduced; that new grant projects be discouraged; and that loans be provided only after severe screening. The General felt that America was "trying to do too much for too many too soon" but the fact remains that the Africans were not the ones favored by America's attention.

American economic aid to Africa has always been inferior to that given to the other continents and, as to be expected, designed to be secondary and supplementary to that of the former colonial powers. . . .

Not only has the United States aid to Africa been relatively small, but it has always been distributed to a small group of countries. . . .

Indeed, many Africans and Africanists believe that apart from a few technical assistance programs and Cold-War related loans, U.S. aid to Africa has not been motivated by developmental objectives. . . . The result is that many of our projects failed. . . .

If we are to continue to have diplomatic relations with African states, a well-thought-out aid program is necessary, because at this point in time, African foreign relations are conceived in terms of economic development. Failure to understand this is to jeopardize the other aspects of our relations with the African states. . . .

America is too great a nation to surrender to expediency. Let us develop a realistic policy for Africa during the 1970's.

The sun sets over Tanzania today as at the dawn of history.

RECOMMENDED READING

Arkell, Anthony J., *A History of the Sudan from Earliest Time to 1821,* N.Y., Oxford Univ. Press, 1961.

Boahen A. Adu, *Topics in West African History,* London, Longmans, Green and Co. Ltd., 1966.

Bovill, Edward W. and Robin Hallett, *The Golden Trade of the Moors,* London, Oxford Univ. Press, 1968. Also paperback.

Cartney, Wilfred and Martin Kilson, *The Africa Reader: Colonial Africa; The Africa Reader: Independent Africa,* N.Y., Random House, 1970. Also paperback.

Clark, J. Desmond, *The Prehistory of Africa,* N.Y., Praeger Publishers, Inc., 1970. Also paperback.

Collins, R. O. and R. L. Tignor, *Egypt and the Sudan,* Englewood Cliffs, N.J., Prentice-Hall, Inc., 1967. Also paperback.

Crowder, Michael, *West Africa under Colonial Rule,* Evanston, Northwestern Univ. Press, 1968.

Curtin, Philip D., *The Image of Africa: British Ideas and Action, 1780–1850.* Madison, The Univ. of Wisconsin Press, 1964.

Davidson, Basil, *Africa, History of a Continent,* London, Weidenfeld & Nicolson, 1966.

Black Mother: The Years of the African Slave Trade, Boston, Little, Brown and Company, 1961.

East and Central Africa to the Late Nineteenth Century, London, Longmans, Green and Co. Ltd., 1967. Paperback.

Duffy, James, *Portugal in Africa,* Cambridge, Harvard Univ. Press, 1962.

Fage, J. D., *An Atlas of African History,* N.Y., St. Martin's Press, 1958.

A Geography of Africa, R. Mansell Prothero, ed., N.Y., Frederick A. Praeger, 1969.

Hallett, Robin, *Africa to 1875,* Ann Arbor, The Univ. of Michigan Press, 1970.

Herskovits, Melville J., *The Human Factor in Changing Africa,* N.Y., Random House, 1958. Also paperback, Vintage.

July, Robert W., *A History of the African People,* N.Y., Charles Scribner's Sons, 1970. Also paperback.

Leiris, Michel and Jacqueline Delange, *African Art,* trans. by Michael Ross, N.Y., Western Publishing Co., Inc., 1968.

Marlowe, John, *History of Modern Egypt and Anglo-European Relations, 1800–1956,* 2nd ed., Hamden, Conn., 1966.

The Middle Age of African History, Roland Oliver, ed. London, Oxford Univ. Press, 1967. Also paperback.

Morris, Donald R., *The Washing of the Spears, The Rise and Fall of the Zulu Nation,* N.Y., Simon and Schuster, 1965. Also paperback.

Murdock, George Peter, *Africa: Its People and Their Culture,* N.Y., McGraw Hill Book Company, 1959.

Nickerson, Jane Soames, *A Short History of North Africa,* N.Y., Biblo and Tannen Booksellers and Publishers, Inc., 1968. Copyright © 1961 by the Devin-Adair Company.

Oliver, Roland and J. D. Fage, *A Short History of Africa,* Baltimore, Penguin Books, Inc., 1962. Paperback.

The Oxford History of South Africa, Monica Wilson and Leonard Thompson, eds., N.Y. and Oxford, Oxford Univ. Press, 1969.

Pankhurst, Richard, *An Introduction to the Economic History of Ethiopia, from Early Times to 1800.* Essex, Eng., Lalibela House, 1961.

Protest and Power in Black Africa, Robert I. Rotberg and Ali A. Mazrui, eds., N.Y., Oxford Univ. Press, 1970.

Reuters Guide to the New Africans, London, Paul Hamlyn Ltd., 1967.

Roux, Edward, *Time Longer Than Rope, A History of the Black Man's Struggle for Freedom in South Africa,* Madison, The Univ. of Wisconsin Press, 1964.

Samkange, Stanlake, *On Trial for My Country,* London, Heinemann Education Books Ltd., 1966. Paperback.

Shepperson, George and Thomas Price, *Independent African: John Chilembwe and the Origin, Setting and Significance of the Nyasaland Native Rising of 1915,* Chicago, Aldine Publishing Company, 1958.

Shinnie, Margaret, *Ancient African Kingdoms,* N.Y., St. Martin's Press, 1966.

Shinne, P.L., *Meroe: The Civilization of the Sudan,* N.Y., Praeger Publishers, Inc., 1966.

Skinner, Elliott P., *The Mossi of the Upper Volta: The Political Development of a Sudanese People,* Stanford, Calif., Stanford Univ. Press, 1964.

Snowden, Frank M., Jr., *Blacks in Antiquity: Ethiopians in the Greco-Roman Experience,* Cambridge, Harvard Univ. Press, 1970.

Survey of North Africa, The Magreb, 2nd ed., Nevill Barbour, ed., London, Oxford Univ. Press, 1962.

Tarikh, Journal of African History, Ibadan, Nigeria; N.Y., Humanities Press.

A Thousand Years of West African History, J. Ade Ajayi and Ian Espie, eds., N.Y., Humanities Press, 1969.

Vansina, Jan, *Kingdom of the Savanna,* Madison, The Univ. of Wisconsin Press, 1966. Paperback.

Walker, Eric. A., *A History of Southern Africa,* London, Longmans, Green and Co. Ltd., 1968.

Wallerstein, Immanuel, *Africa: The Politics of Independence,* N.Y., Random House, 1961. Paperback.

Africa: The Politics of Unity, N.Y., Random House, 1967. Paperback.

Webster, J. B. and A. A. Boahen, *History of West Africa: The Revolutionary Years—1815 to Independence,* N.Y., Praeger Publishers, Inc., 1967. Paperback.

West African Kingdoms in the Nineteenth Century, Daryll Fords and P. M. Kaberry, eds., London, Oxford Univ. Press, 1967.

Wilson, John A., *The Culture of Ancient Egypt,* Chicago, The Univ. of Chicago Press, 1951. Paperback.

Zamani: A Survey of East African History, B. A. Ogot and J. A. Kiernan, eds., N.Y., Humanities Press, 1969. Paperback.

ACKNOWLEDGMENTS

The editors gratefully acknowledge the valuable editorial assistance of Douglas Tunstell, Geneva; Urszula Slupik, Paris; Christine Sutherland, London; Audre Proctor. They are also grateful to the following individuals and institutions for providing pictorial material and supplying information:

African American Institute
Harry Stein

African Bibliographic Center
Dan Matthews

I. A. Akinjogbin, University of Ife, Nigeria

Army Museum, London

Marc and Evelyne Bernheim

Bibliothèque Nationale
Estampes
Manuscrits
Service Photographique
Documentation Française

BOAC Library, London

British Museum

William D. Carlebach

Dr. Gwendolyn Carter, Northwestern University

Geoffrey Clement

Columbia University
Graham Irwin
Dr. Hollis Lynch

Eliot Elisofon

Victor Englebert

Dr. Brian Fagan, University of California

Freedomway's Magazine
Ernest Kaiser

André Held, Lausanne

Horniman Museum and Library, London

John H. A. Jewel, Mombasa

Mburumba Kerina, Department of African Studies, Brooklyn College

Library Company of Philadelphia

Library of Congress
Virginia Daiker
Dr. Samie Michel Zoghby

Dr. Richard A. Long, Center for African and African American Studies, Atlanta University

Mansell Collection, London

Mr. and Mrs. Jan Mitchell

Metropolitan Museum of Art
Susan Valenstein
Kent Weeks

Kasimierz Michalowski, Warsaw

Richard Moore

Hon. Joseph Murumbi, Nairobi

Musée d'Ethnographie de Neuchatel

Musée de l'Homme, Paris
Georges Sirot

Musée Royal de l'Afrique Centrale, Tervuren, Belgium

Museum für Volkerkunde, Hamburg
Dr. Wilhelm Seidensticker

Museum of Primitive Art

National Maritime Museum, Greenwich, Eng.

New York Public Library
Miss Elizabeth Roth
Oriental Division
Rare Book Division
Schomberg Collection
Spencer Collection

Pitt Rivers Museum, Oxford, Eng.

Staff College, Cambridge, Eng.

Time Inc.
Vassilia Moore

Constance Turnbull, Nairobi

United Methodist Church Board of Missions
Theodora Cameses

Dr. I. William Zartman, New York University

Maps by Herbert Borst, Francis & Shaw Inc.

Index by Edmée Busch

PERMISSIONS

SEEKING MAN'S ORIGINS: page 36 from *Légendes Africaines,* by Tchicaya U Tam'si. Editions Seghers, Paris. Translation by Kaari Ward. #37 from *The Origin of Life and Death (African Creations Myths),* edited by Ulli Beier. Copyright © 1966. Reprinted by permission of Heinemann Educational Books Ltd., London. #38 "Man's Noble Pedigree" from *The Descent of Man,* by Charles Darwin, in The Modern Library, Random House, Inc./"Emerging Man" from "The Origin of Man," by C. Loring Brace, in *Natural History,* January, 1970. Reprinted by permission of the American Museum of Natural History, New York. #41 from *Finding the Missing Link,* by Robert Broom. Copyright © 1950. Reprinted by permission of C.A. Watts & Co. Ltd., London. #42 from *Adam's Ancestors: The Evolution of Man and His Culture,* by Louis S. Leakey. Reprinted by permission of Harper & Row, New York, Methuen & Co. Ltd., London, and Doctor Louis S. Leakey. #43 from *The Rock Art of South Africa,* by A. R. Willcox. Copyright © 1963. Reprinted by permission of Thomas Nelson & Sons (South Africa) Ltd., Johannesburg. #44 from *Preliminary Report of OvaTjimba Groups,* by H.R. MacCalman and B.J. Grobbelaar. Copyright © 1965. Reprinted by permission of the State Museum, Windhoek, South West Africa. #45 "Bushman's Prayer," from *Ants Will Not Eat Your Fingers: A Selection of Traditional African Poems,* edited by Leonard W. Doob and translated by Viktor Lebzelter. Copyright © 1966. Reprinted by permission of Walker & Co., New York./"Hunters of Modern Africa," from *The Oxford History of South Africa, South Africa to 1870,* vol. I, edited by Monica Wilson and Leonard Thompson. Copyright © 1970. Reprinted by permission of The Clarendon Press, Oxford. #47 "Tracking Father Elephant" "Death of a Hunter" from *Primitive Song,* translated by C.M. Bowra. Copyright © 1962 by C.M. Bowra. Reprinted by permission of The World Publishing Company, New York, and Weidenfeld Ltd., London.

OF MEN AND MYTHS: page 66 from *The Geography of Strabo,* vol. VIII, edited by T.E. Page, E. Capps, and W.H.D. Rouse and translated by Horace Leonard Jones. The Loeb Classical Library. Reprinted by permission of Harvard University Press. #67 "Hymn to the Nile" from *A Comparative Study of the Literature of Egypt, Palestine and Mesopotamia,* edited by T. Eric Peet. Reprinted by permission of The Clarendon Press, Oxford./"Memphis, the Fair One" from "Love Song" in *The Glory of Egypt,* by Samivel and Audrain. Reprinted by permission of Vanguard Press, Inc., New York, and Thames and Hudson, London./"King Zoser's Magician" from *Imhotep, the Vizier and Physician of King Zoser,* by Jamieson B. Hurry. Copyright © 1928. Reprinted by permission of The Clarendon Press, Oxford. #69 "The Silent Man" from *Ancient Egyptian Religion,* by Henri Frankfort. Copyright © 1948. Reprinted by permission of Columbia University Press, New York./"The Amarna Heresy" from *Literature of the Ancient Egyptians,* by Adolph Erman. Reprinted by permission of Methuen & Co. Ltd., London. #71 "Egyptian Way of Death" from *The Great Travelers,* vol. I, edited by Milton Rugoff. Copyright © 1960. Reprinted by permission of Simon and Schuster./"Song of the Harper" from *Egypt: The Home of the Occult Sciences,* edited by T. Gerald Garry. John Bale, Sons & Danielson Ltd., London. #72 "Pepi's Legions" #73 "The Queen's Peace" #74 "In Search of Peace" #76–77 "King of Pure Mountain" from *Ancient Near Eastern Texts Relating to the Old Testament,* 3rd ed., with Supplement, edited by James B. Pritchard. Copyright © 1969. Reprinted by permission of Princeton University Press. #72 "The Broken Reed" from *Egypt of the Pharaohs, and Introduction,* by Sir Alan Gardiner. Copyright © 1961. Reprinted by permission of The Clarendon Press, Oxford. #73 "The Fabled Land of Punt" #75 "The Kushite Takeover" from *Ancient Record of Egypt Historical Documents from the Earliest Times to the Persian Conquest,* vols. II, IV, by James Breasted. The University of Chicago Press. #77 from *The Natural History of Pliny,* translated by John Bostock and H.T. Riley. Henry G. Bohn, Covent Garden, England. #78 from *Kebra Negast (The Glory of Kings),* translated by Mrs. John Van Vorst. Funk & Wagnalls. #79 "Shoppers Guide to Axum" adapted from *Travellers in Ethiopia,* edited by Richard Pankhurst. Copyright © 1965. Reprinted by permission of Oxford University Press in Three Crowns Books. #80 from *A History of the Sudan,* by A.J. Arkell. The Athlone Press of the University of London. (Abstracted from *A Survey of Nubian Origins,* by L.P. Kirwan, from *Sudan Notes and Records,* vol. 20, Khartoum, the Sudan.)

BETWEEN SEA AND SAND: page 118 from *Ritual and Belief in Morocco,* by Edward Westermarck. Copyright © 1926. Reprinted by permission of Macmillan, Basingstoke, England. #119 "The Tongue" from *Contes et légendes populaires du Maroc,* compiled by Doctoress Legey. Editions Ernest Le Roux et de Pine, Paris. Translation by Iris Eaton./"Hannibal's Oath" #121 "Arbiter of Destiny" from *The Histories,* by Polybius, translated by Evelyn S. Shuckburgh. Indiana University Press. #119 "Rule in Carthage" from *Politics,* by Aristotle, in *Oxford Translation of Aristotle,* edited by W.D. Ross. Reprinted by permission of The Clarendon Press, Oxford. #121 "The Wealth of Carthage" from *Carthage,* by B.H. Warmington. Copyright © 1960. Reprinted by permission of Praeger Publishers, Inc., New York, and Robert Hale & Co., London. #121 "Unwelcome Miracle" #122 "Up from Poverty" from *Tunisia,* by Claude Roy and Paul Legab. Published 1961. Reprinted by permission of Delpire Editeur, Paris. Translation by Deirdre Butler. #121 "Tacfarinas' Revolt" from *The Complete Works of Tacitus,* translated by Alfred John Church and William Jackson Brodribb. Copyright © 1942. Reprinted by permission of Random House, Inc. #122 "A Paternal Scolding" "Caracalla's Edict" from *An Economic Survey of Ancient Rome,* vol. II, by Allan Chester Johnson. Copyright © 1936. Reprinted by permission of Johns Hopkins Press. #123 from *The Life of the North Africans as Revealed in the Sermons of Saint Augustine,* by Sister Marie Madeleine Getty, M.A. of the Sisters of the Presentation of Mary, St. Hyacinth, Quebec. Copyright © 1931. Reprinted by permission of The Catholic University of America Press. #124 "Justinian's Africa" from *Secret History,* by Procopius, translated by Richard Atwater. The University of Michigan Press. #124 "The First Hermit" #127 "The Desert Fathers" from *The Desert Fathers,* by Saint Jerome, translated by Helen Waddell. Copyright © 1936. Reprinted by permission of The University of Michigan Press and Constable & Co. Ltd., London. #126 "Saint Anthony of Egypt" from *A History of Christianity: Readings in the History of the Early and Medieval Church,* edited by Ray C. Petry. Copyright © 1962. Reprinted by permission of Prentice-Hall, Inc., Englewood Cliffs, New Jersey./"God's 'Saucy Servants'" from *A Source Book of Ancient Church History,* by Joseph Cullen Ayer. Reprinted by permission of Charles Scribner's Sons. #128 from *Ecclesiastical History of John, Bishop of Ephesus,* translated by Richard Payne Smith. University Press, Oxford.

IN THE NAME OF ALLAH: page 150 "God's Messenger" #151 "The First Muezzin" adapted from "The Life of Muhammad" in *Sirat Rasul Allah,* by Ibn Ishaq, translated by Alfred Guillaume. Copyright © 1955. Reprinted by permission of Oxford University Press, Pakistan. #151 "The Word of God" #152 "The First Revelation" "'The City'" from *The Meaning of the Glorious Koran,* by Mohammed Marmakude Picthall. Reprinted by permission of George Allen & Unwin Ltd., London. #152 "Antar the Lion" from "The Romance of Antar" in *Anthology of Islamic Literature,* selected, edited, and introduced by James Kritzeck. Copyright © 1964. Reprinted by permission of Holt, Rinehart and Winston, Inc. #153 "Antar the Poet" from "Mu Allakt" in *Arabic Literature,* 2nd. ed., by Sir H.A.R. Gibb. Copyright © 1963. Reprinted by permission of The Clarendon Press, Oxford. #153 "Muslim Battle Code" #155 "How to Get Rich Quickly" #156 "Instruction of Children" #157 "What to Wear to Mecca" from *The Muqaddimah, An Introduction to History,* by Ibn Khaldun, translated by Franz Rosenthal. Bollingen Series XLIII. Copyright © 1958 and 1967. Reprinted by permission of Princeton University Press. Footnotes not used. #153 "Tarik the Moor" from *The Moors in Spain,* by Stanley Lane-Poole. #155 "A Pope's Letter" from the unpublished thesis on medieval Africa by Dr. Samir Zoghby, the Library of Congress. Translation by Kaari Ward. #157 "Ibn Yasin's Jihad" from *The Encyclopedia of Islam.* Published by E.J. Brill Ltd., London. #159 from "Book of Roger" #161 "Mogadishu in 1331" from *"Les voyages d'Ibn Batoutah"* both in *East African Coast,* edited by G.S.P. Freeman-Grenville. Copyright © 1962. Reprinted by permission of The Clarendon Press, Oxford. #160 "The Land of the Zanj" "The Gold of Sofala" from *The Medieval History of the Coast of Tanganyika with Special Reference to Recent Archaeological Discoveries.* Copyright © 1962 by G.S.P. Freeman-Grenville. Published by Oxford University Press, London. #163 "A Giraffe for the Emperor" #164 "China Looks at Africa" from lectures given at the University of London by J.J. L Duyvendak, professor of Chinese, Leyden University. Copyright © 1949 Arthur Probsthain, London. #164 "The Pillar of Zion" from *A History of Ethiopia, Nubia, and Abyssinia,* by Sir. W.E.A. Budge. Copyright © 1928. Reprinted by permission of Methuen and Co. Ltd., London. #166 from *The Stories of Abu Zeid the Hilali,* translated by J.R. Patterson. Copyright © 1930. Reprinted by permission of Routledge & Kegan Paul Ltd., London. #168 from *Wit and Wisdom in Morocco,* by Edward Westermarck. Reprinted by permission of Routledge & Kegan Paul Ltd., London.

THE GOLDEN IMPERATIVE: page 200 from *Légendes Africaines,* by Tchicaya U. Tam'si. Editions Seghers, Paris. Translation by Mary Elizabeth Wise. #201 from *Sundiata: An Epic of Old Mali,* by D.T. Niane. Copyright © 1965. Reprinted by permission of Longman Group Ltd., Harlow, England. #203 from *Olodumare, God in Yoruba Belief,* by E. Bolaji Idowu. Copyright © 1963 by E. Bolaji Idowu. Reprinted by permission of Longman Group, Ltd., Harlow, England. #205 from *Hausa Folklore Customs, and Proverbs: Part IV Arts How Benin Figures Are Made,* collected and transliterated, with English translation by R. Sutherland Rattray. Oxford University Press, London. #206 "A Child Is . . ." #208 "Yoruba Praise Song *(Oriki Oshun)*" "Yoruba Riddles" from *Black Orpehus, Yoruba Poetry,* compiled and translated by Ulli Beier. Longmans of Nigeria, Ltd./"The Illustrious Metal" from *West African Explorers,* edited by C. Howard. Copyright © 1955. Reprinted by permission of Oxford University Press, London. #207 "Yoruba Proverbs" from *Wit and Wisdom from West Africa,* compiled by Richard F. Burton. Reprinted by permission of the Negro Universities Press. /"Scuffles Often Occur" from *The Content and Form of Yoruba Ijala,* by S.A. Babalola. Copyright © 1966. Reprinted by permission of The Clarendon Press, Oxford.

MERCHANTS AND POTENTATES: page 232 from the unpublished thesis on medieval Africa, by Dr. Samir Zoghby, the Library of Congress. #233 from *The Voyages of Cadamosta and Other Documents on Western Africa,* second series, no. LXXX, edited and translated by Gerald Crone. Copyright © 1937. Reprinted by permission of Cambridge University Press on behalf of The Hakluyt Society, London. #234 "Umme Jilma" #235 "Kanem at Its Height" from *Nigerian Perspectives,* compiled by Thomas Hodgkin and translated by H.R. Palmer. Copyright © 1960. The Government Printer, Lagos, Nigeria. #235 "Song of the Bornu Slaves" from "Song of the Slaves in the Desert" in *The Languages and Peoples of Bornu Being a Collection of the Writings of P.A. Benton.* Frank Cass & Co. Ltd., London. #235 "A Most Excellent Prince" from *History of the First Twelve Years of the Reign of Mai Idris Alooma of Bornu,* by Ahmed ibn Fartua, translated from the Arabic, with introduction and notes by H.R. Palmer. The Government Printer, Lagos, Nigeria. #238 "The Yerima's Praise Song" #239 "Star of the Morning" from *Kanuri Songs,* translated by J.R. Patterson. The Government Printer, Lagos, Nigeria. #240 from "Old Kanuri Capitals," by A.D. Bivar and P.L. Shinnie, in *Journal of African History,* vol. III, 1962, No. 1. Reprinted by permission of Cambridge University Press, New York. #241 "Sarki the Snake" #245 "The Two Rogues" from *A Selection of Hausa Stories,* compiled and translated by H.A.S. Johnston. Copyright © 1966. Reprinted by permission of The Clarendon Press, Oxford. #242 "Barbushe the Hunter" #244 "Yaji's Revenge" "The Islamization of Kano" from "The Kano Chronicle" in *Sudanese Memoirs,* translated by H.R. Palmer. Frank Cass & Co. Ltd., London. #245 "An Epistle on Kingship" from "The Obligation of Princes," by Sheikh Muhammad al Maghili of Tlemcen, in *The Bornu Sahara and Sudan,* by Sir Richmond Palmer. John Murray, London. #247 "Wilde Woodie Hausaland" from *The Seventh Booke of the Historie of Africa,* by Leo Africanus. The Hakluyt Society, London./"Bortorimi and the Spider" from *Hausa Superstitions and Customs,* by Major A.J.N. Tremearne. John Bale, Sons & Danielson Ltd., London. #248 from *Hausa and Fulani Proverbs,* compiled and edited by C.E.J. Whitting. Copyright © 1940. Reprinted by permission of Gregg International Publishers Ltd., Farnborough, England.

THE MWINDO EPIC: abbreviated from *The Mwindo Epic,* edited and translated by Daniel P. Biebuyck and Kahombo C. Mateene. Copyright © 1969. Originally published by The University of California Press; reprinted by permission of The Regents of the University of California and Daniel P. Biebuyck.

RAPE OF THE COAST: page 328 from Everyman's Library Edition of *Portuguese Voyages, 1498–1663,* edited by Charles David Ley. Copyright © 1947. Reprinted by permission of E.P. Dutton & Co., Inc., New York, and J.M. Dent & Sons Ltd., London. #330 from *The Voyages of Cadamosta and Other Documents on Western Africa,* second series, no. LXXX, edited and translated by Gerald Crone. Copyright © 1937. Reprinted by permission of Cambridge University Press on behalf of The Hakluyt Society, London. #331 "The Guinea Trade" #332 "The Conversion of Bemoym" from *Europeans in West Africa 1450–1560,* translated and edited by John William Blake. Copyright © 1942. Reprinted by permission of Cambridge University Press on behalf of The Hakluyt Society, London. #334 "Cry of Alarm" from *The African Past,* edited by Basil Davidson. Copyright © 1964 by Basil Davidson. Grosset & Dunlap. Reprinted by permission of Basil Davidson. #334 "Making New Christians" #335 "The Middle Passage" from *Human Livestock,* by Edmund B. d'Auvergne. Grayson and Grayson, London. #335 "Negotiating for Chattel" adapted from *West African Explorers,* edited by C. Howard. Copyright © 1955. Reprinted by permission of Oxford University Press, London. #336 "The Rise of Gumbo Smart" "The Consummate Villains" from *Sierra Leone Inheritance,* by Christopher Fyfe, edited by G.S. Graham. West African Graphic Co. Ltd., London.

CONTINENT IN TURMOIL: page 376 from *Timbuctoo the Mysterious,* by Félix du Bois. Longmans Green and Co., London. #377 "The Rape of Guinea" from *The Portable Hakluyt's Voyages,* edited by Irwin R. Blacker. The Viking Press, Inc./"The Royal Adventurers" from "The Company of the Royal Adventurers of England Trading Into Africa, 1660–1672," by George F. Zook, in *Journal of Negro History,* vol. 5, April, 1919. Copyright The Association for the Study of Negro Life and History, Inc. Reprinted by permission of said Journal. #379 from *Nigerian Perspectives,* compiled by Thomas Hodgkin. Copyright © 1960. The Government Printer, Lagos, Nigeria. #380 from "Fulani Wisdom" in *Hausa and Fulani Proverbs,* compiled and edited by C.E.J. Whitting. Copyright © 1940. Reprinted by permission of Gregg International Publishers Ltd., Farnborough, England. #380 "Kuba Law" from *African Law, Adaptation and Development,* edited by Hilda and Leo Kuper. Copyright © 1965. Originally published by The University of California Press; reprinted by permission of The Regents of the University of California. #382 "Songs of the Spirits" "Animal Lyrics," from the unpublished collection of Dr. Jan Vansina. #382 "Ndaba, a Man of Affairs" from *Izibongo: Zulu Praise Poems,* collected by James Stuart, translated by Daniel Malcolm, edited by Trevor Cope. Copyright © 1968. Reprinted by permission of The Clarendon Press, Oxford. #382 "Chaka's Receptions" from *The Diary of Henry Francis Fynn.* Copyright © 1950. Reprinted by permission of Shuter & Shooter (Pty.) Ltd., Pietermaritzburg, Natal, South Africa. #384 from "Prologue" to *Valley of a Thousand Hills,* by H.I.E. Dhlomo. Copyright © 1941. Reprinted by permission of Knox Printing Company (Pty.) Ltd., Durban, Natal, South Africa.

SPEARS AND MAXIM GUNS: page 424 from *Equiano's Travels,* abridged and edited by Paul Edwards. Copyright © 1967 by Paul Edwards. Reprinted by permission of Praeger Publishers, Inc., New York, and Heinemann Educational Books Ltd., London. #26 "Xhosa Freedom Fighter" from *Time Longer Than Rope,* by Edward Roux. Copyright © 1964 by The Regents of The University of Wisconsin. Reprinted by permission of The University of Wisconsin Press./"The Zulu Army" from *A Lost Legionary in South Africa,* by Colonel G. Hamilton-Browne. T. Werner Laurie, London. #428 "Zulu Wisdom" from *Zulu Proverbs,* rev. edition by C.L.S. Nyembezi. (pages 54, 60, 62, 69, 72, 116, 124, 135, 152, 193, 177, 159, 197, 228, 116.) Reprinted by permission of Witwatersrand University Press, 1963, Johannesburg, South Africa. #428 "An Offer of Safe Conduct" from *Sudan Notes and Records,* vol. 24, 1941. Khartoum, the Sudan. #429 "Ethiopian Resistance" from "The Foreign Policy of the Negus Menelik 1896–1898," by G.N. Sanderson, in the *Journal of African History,* vol. 5, 1964. Reprinted by permission of Cambridge University Press./"In Praise of Folly" from *La Partage de l'Afrique: Fachoda,* by Gabriel Hanotaux. Ernest Falmmarion, Editeur, Paris. Translation by Mary Elizabeth Wise. #431 from *Protest and Power in Black Africa,* edited by Robert I. Rotberg and Ali A. Mazuri. Copyright © 1970. Reprinted by permission of Oxford University Press, New York.

AFRICA REAFFIRMED: page 466 "Negritude Defined" from *Léopold Sedar Senghor and the Politics of Negritude,* by Irving Leonard Markovitz. Copyright © 1969 Irving Markovitz. Reprinted by permission of Atheneum Publishers, Inc., New York, and Heinemann Educational Books Ltd., London/"Black Woman" from *African Poetry for Schools and Colleges,* edited by O.R. Dathorne. Copyright © Ulli Beier. Macmillan, London./"For Khalam" from *Selected Poems of Léopold Sedar Senghor,* translated and edited by Clive Wake and John Reed. Copyright © 1964. Reprinted by permission of Atheneum Publishers, Inc., New York, and Oxford University Press, London. #467 "The Joy of Blackness" "Space That Once Was Mine" ("Limbe") from *Whispers from a Continent,* translated by Wilfred Cartey. Copyright © 1969. Reprinted by permission of Vintage Books, Random House, Inc., New York, and Heinemann Educational Books Ltd., London/"Splendidly Alone." The poem "Africa *(Afrique)*" from *Coups de Pilon,* by David Diop. Copyright © 1956. Reprinted by permission of Présence Africaine, Paris. #467 "Africa at the Center" from "The African Roots of War" in *W.E.B. DuBois Speaks: Speeches and Addresses 1891–1919.* Reprinted by permission of Pathfinder Press, Inc. #469 from speech made by Haile Selassie to the League of Nations, 1938. #470 from "Marcus Aurelius Garvey" in *Harlem: Negro Metropolis.* Copyright © 1940 by E.P. Dutton. Reprinted by permission of Harcourt Brace Jovanovich, Inc. #472 from *Strike a Blow and Die,* by George S. Mwase, edited by Robert I. Rotberg. Copyright © 1967 Robert I. Rotberg. Reprinted by permission of Harvard University Press. #473 from *The Philosophy of the Revolution,* by Gamal Abdel Nasser. Copyright © 1959. Reprinted by permission of Smith, Keynes & Marshall, Inc., Buffalo, New York. #475 from *Weep Not, Child,* by James Ngugi. Copyright © 1964 James Ngugi, © 1969 the Macmillan Company. Reprinted by permission of the Macmillan Company, New York, and Heinemann Educational Books Ltd., London. #479 from *Black Orpheus, Yoruba Poetry,* compiled and translated by Ulli Beier. Longmans of Nigeria Ltd.

IN THE THIRD WORLD: page 512 from speech by Dr. Kwame Nkrumah on July 10, 1953, in *Ghana: The Autobiography of Kwame Nkrumah.* Thomas Nelson. #514 "Liberty, Equality, Fraternity" from "Black Africa and the French Union," by Félix Houphouët-Boigny. #515 "Africa's Common Market" from "Africa's Future and the World," by Sékou Touré, in *Africa: A Foreign Affairs Reader,* edited by Philip Quigg. Copyright © 1964 Council on Foreign Relations, Inc. Reprinted by permission of Praeger Publishers, Inc., New York. (Frost quote from "The Death of the Hired Man" from *The Poetry of Robert Frost,* edited by Edward Connery Lathem. Copyright © 1930, 1939, © 1969 by Holt, Rinehart and Winston, Inc. Copyright © 1958 by Robert Frost. Copyright © 1967 by Lesley Frost Ballantine. Reprinted by permission of Holt, Rinehart and Winston, Inc.) #517 from *Congo, My Country,* by Patrice Lumumba. Copyright © 1962 Graham Heath, England. Reprinted by permission of Praeger Publishers, Inc., New York, and Pall Mall Press Ltd., London. #518 essay: "Freedom," by Bertha Lomayani, from *Transition,* October, 1962, Kampala, Uganda./"Continental Integrity" from the Charter of the Organization of African Unity. #519 from speech made before Economic Symposium in Blantyre in 1962, in *The New African,* Columbia University Press. #521 "The Manipulators" from Chapter IV: "Dawn" in *Bound to Violence,* by Yambo Ouologuem, translated by Ralph Manheim. Copyright © 1968 Editions du Seuil, © 1971 Harcourt Brace Jovanovich, Inc., and Martin, Secker & Warburg, Ltd. Reprinted by permission of Harcourt Brace Jovanovich, Inc., New York, and Martin Secker & Warburg Ltd., London. #521 "A Paradox" from the acceptance speech for Nobel Peace Prize made in Oslo, December, 1961, in *The African Nationalist: Luthuli Speaks,* Bantam Books. #522 from the defense of Herman Toivo Ja Toivo before Pretoria court, 1963, in *The African Reader: Independent Africa,* Random House Vintage. #523 "Dennis Brutus" from *Sirens, Knuckles, Boots.* Copyright © 1963 Dennis Brutus. Published by Mbari Publications, Idaban, Nigeria. Reprinted by permission of Dennis Brutus. Also in *African Writings Today,* Penguin Books Ltd., Harmonsworth, England. #524 "From the Grim Place," poem by K.A. Nortje "At Rest from the Grim Place" from *Modern Poetry from Africa,* edited by Gerald Moore and Ulli Beier. Copyright © 1963 Penguin African Library. #524 original, unpublished work by Harold Head, New York. #526 from *My Life in the Bush of Ghosts,* by Amos Tutuola. Reprinted by permission of Grove Press, Inc., New York, and Faber and Faber Ltd., London. All Rights Reserved. #527 from *Policy Toward Africa for 1970,* a speech by Dr. Elliott Skinner before The House Subcommittee on Africa, March, 1970.

TEXT: page 101 Thucydides quote from *History of the Peloponnesian War,* Book I, Chapter IV, Nos. 104 and 109, by Thucydides, translated by Richard Crawley. Everyman's Library Edition. Reprinted by permission of E.P. Dutton & Co., Inc., and J.M. Dent & Sons Ltd., London. #102 Herodotus quote from *The Histories,* by Herodotus, translated by Aubrey de Selincourt. Copyright © 1954 Aubrey de Selincourt. Reprinted by permission of Penguin Classics, Harmondsworth, England. #104 Juvenal quote from *The 16 Satires,* by Juvenal, translated by Peter Greer. Copyright © 1967 Peter Greer. Reprinted by permission of Penguin Classics, Harmondsworth, England. #108 Sallust quote from *Jugurthine War,* by Sallust, translated by S.A. Handford. Copyright © 1953 S.A. Handford. Reprinted by permission of Penguin Classics, Harmondsworth, England. #112 Strabo quote from *The Geography of Strabo,* edited by T.E. Page, E. Capps, and W.H.D. Rouse and translated by Horace Leonard Jones. The Loeb Classical Library. Reprinted by permission of Harvard University Press. #179 #182 Ibn Battuta quotes from *Studies on the Civilization of Islam,* by Hamilton A.R. Gibb. Copyright © 1962 Hamilton A.R. Gibb. Reprinted by permission of Beacon Press, Boston. #183 Leo Africanus quote #188 Sultan Mansur quote both from *The Golden Trade of the Moors,* by E.V. Bovill Copyright © 1968. Reprinted by permission of Oxford University Press, London. #189 #191 Pacheco Pereira quotes from *Arabs,* by E.C. Hodgkin. The Modern World Volume 10. Copyright © 1966. Reprinted by permission of Oxford University Press, London. #310 João de Barros quote from *Pageant of Ghana,* by Freda Wolfson. Copyright © 1958. Reprinted by permission of Cambridge University Press, New York, on behalf of the Hakylut Society. Published by Oxford University Press, London. #318 Affonso letter from *The African Past,* edited by Basil Davidson. Copyright © 1964 Basil Davidson. Published by Grosset & Dunlap. Reprinted by permission of Basil Davidson. #409 Father Ohrwalder quote #410 Sir Charles Wilson quote both from *The Independent Sudan,* by Mekki Shebeika. Copyright © 1959. Reprinted by permission of Robert Speller & Sons, New York. #462 Winston Churchill quote from *The Second World War: The Gathering Storm,* by Winston S. Churchill. Copyright © 1945. Reprinted by permission of Houghton Mifflin Company, Boston, and Cassell & Co., London. #465 Aimé Césaire quote from *Cahier d'un Retour au Pays Natal,* by Aimé Césaire. Copyright © 1956. Published by Présence Africaine, Paris.

INDEX

Page numbers in italics refer to captions.